This is Volume 22 of WEST'S NEW YORK PRACTICE SERIES

West's New York Practice Series

Vol. 1	Walker, et al., New York Limited Liability Companies and Partnerships: A Guide to Law and Practice
Vols. 2-4	Haig, et al., Commercial Litigation in New York State Courts
Vol. 5	Barker and Alexander, Evidence in New York State and Federal Courts
Vol. 6	Greenberg, Marcus, et al., New York Criminal Law
Vol. 7	Marks, et al., New York Pretrial Criminal Procedure
Vol. 8	Davies, Stecich, Gold, et al., New York Civil Appellate Practice
Vol. 9	Ginsberg, Weinberg, et al., Environmental Law and Regulation in New York
Vol. 10	Sobie, et al., New York Family Court Practice
Vols. 11-12	Scheinkman, et al., New York Law of Domestic Relations

Vol. 13	Taber, et al., Employment Litigation in New York
Vols. 14-16	Kreindler, Rodriguez, et al., New York Law of Torts
Vols. 17-19	Field, Moskin, et al., New York and Delaware Business Organizations: Choice, Formation, Operation, Financing and Acquisitions
Vols. 20-25	Ostertag, Benson, et al., General Practice in New York
Vol. 26	Borchers, Markell, et al., New York State Administrative Procedure and Practice
Vol. A	Borges, et al., Enforcing Judgments and Collecting Debts in New York
Vols. B-C	Bensel, Frank, McKeon, et al., Personal Injury Practice in New York
Vols. D-E	Preminger, et al., Trusts and Estates Practice in New York
Vols. F-G	Finkelstein and Ferrara, Landlord and Tenant Practice in New York

COORDINATED RESEARCH IN NEW YORK FROM WEST

New York Practice 2d
David D. Siegel

Handling the DWI Case in New York
Peter Gerstenzang

New York Elder Law Practice
Vincent J. Russo and Marvin Rachlin

WEST'S McKINNEY'S FORMS
Civil Practice Law and Rules

Uniform Commercial Code

Business Corporation Law

Matrimonial and Family Law

Real Property Practice

Estates and Surrogate Practice

Criminal Procedure Law

Not-For-Profit Corporation Law

Tax Practice and Procedure

Local Government Forms

Selected Consolidated Law Forms

McKinney's Consolidated Laws of New York Annotated

West's New York Legal Update

New York Digest

New York Law Finder

PAMPHLETS
New York Civil Practice Law and Rules

New York Sentence Charts

WESTLAW®

COORDINATED RESEARCH FROM WEST

WEST*Check*® and WESTMATE®

West CD–ROM Libraries™

To order any of these New York practice tools, call your West Representative or 1–800–328–9352.

> **NEED RESEARCH HELP?**
>
> **If you have research questions concerning WESTLAW or West Publications, call West's Reference Attorneys at 1–800–733–2889.**

GENERAL PRACTICE IN NEW YORK

By

ROBERT L. OSTERTAG
HON. JAMES D. BENSON

Sections 13.1 to 20.148

ST. PAUL, MINN.
WEST GROUP
1998

GENERAL PRACTICE IN NEW YORK
FORMS ON DISK™

The **Forms on Disk**™ which accompany these volumes provide instant access to WordPerfect 5.1/5.2 versions of the forms included in *General Practice in New York*. These electronic forms will save you hours of time drafting legal documents. The electronic forms can be loaded into your word processing software and formatted to match the document style of your law firm. These electronic forms become templates for you to use over and over without having to retype them each time.

The forms in Volumes 20, 21, 22, 23, 24 and 25 that are included on the accompanying disks are marked with the following disk icon for easy identification.

COPYRIGHT © 1998 By WEST GROUP
610 Opperman Drive
P.O. Box 64526
St. Paul, MN 55164–0526
1–800–328–9352

All rights reserved
Printed in the United States of America
ISBN 0–314–23143–9

TEXT IS PRINTED ON 10% POST CONSUMER RECYCLED PAPER

WESTLAW® ELECTRONIC RESEARCH GUIDE

Coordinating Legal Research with WESTLAW

The *New York Practice Series* is an essential aid to legal research. WESTLAW provides a vast, online library of over 8000 collections of documents and services that can supplement research begun in this publication, encompassing:

- Federal and state primary law (statutes, regulations, rules, and case law), including West's editorial enhancements, such as headnotes, Key Number classifications, annotations

- Secondary law resources (texts and treatises published by West Group and by other publishers, as well as law reviews)

- Legal news

- Directories of attorneys and experts

- Court records and filings

- Citators

Specialized topical subsets of these resources have been created for more than thirty areas of practice.

In addition to legal information, there are general news and reference databases and a broad array of specialized materials frequently useful in connection with legal matters, covering accounting, business, environment, ethics, finance, medicine, social and physical sciences.

This guide will focus on a few aspects of WESTLAW use to supplement research begun in this publication, and will direct you to additional sources of assistance.

Databases

A database is a collection of documents with some features in common. It may contain statutes, court decisions, administrative materials, commentaries, news or other information. Each database has a unique identifier, used in many WESTLAW commands to select a database of interest. For example, the database containing New York cases has the identifier NY-CS.

The WESTLAW Directory is a comprehensive list of databases with information about each database, including the types of documents each

WESTLAW ELECTRONIC RESEARCH GUIDE

contains. The first page of a standard or customized WESTLAW Directory is displayed upon signing on to WESTLAW, except when prior, saved research is resumed. To access the WESTLAW Directory at any time, enter DB.

Databases of potential interest in connection with your research include:

NY-AG	New York Attorney General Opinions
NYETH-EO	New York Ethics Opinions
NYETH-CS	Legal Ethics & Professional Responsibility - New York Cases
WLD-NY	West's Legal Directory - New York
LAWPRAC	The Legal Practice Database

For information as to currentness and search tips regarding any WESTLAW database, enter the SCOPE command SC followed by the database identifier (e.g., SC NY-CS). It is not necessary to include the identifier to obtain scope information about the currently selected database.

WESTLAW Highlights

Use of this publication may be supplemented through the WESTLAW Bulletin (WLB), the WESTLAW New York State Bulletin (WSB-NY) and various Topical Highlights. Highlights databases contain summaries of significant judicial, legislative and administrative developments and are updated daily; they are searchable both from an automatic list of recent documents and using general WESTLAW search methods for documents accumulated over time. The full text of any judicial decision may be retrieved by entering FIND.

Consult the WESTLAW Directory (enter DB) for a complete, current listing of highlights databases.

Retrieving a Specific Case

The FIND command can be used to quickly retrieve a case whose citation is known. For example:

FI 616 A.2d 1336

Updating Case Law Research

There are a variety of citator services on WESTLAW for use in updating research.

Insta-Cite® may be used to verify citations, find parallel citations, ascertain the history of a case, and see whether it remains valid law. References are also provided to secondary sources, such as Corpus Juris Secundum®, that cite the case. To view the Insta-Cite history of a displayed

WESTLAW ELECTRONIC RESEARCH GUIDE

case, simply enter the command IC. To view the Insta-Cite history of a selected case, enter a command in this form:

IC 574 A.2d 502

Shepard's® Citations provides a comprehensive list of cases and publications that have cited a particular case, with explanatory analysis to indicate how the citing cases have treated the case, e.g., "followed," "explained." To view the Shepard's Citations about a displayed case, enter the command SH. Add a case citation, if necessary, as in the prior Insta-Cite example.

For the latest citing references, not yet incorporated in Shepard's Citations, use Shepard's PreView® (SP command) and QuickCite™ (QC command), in the same way.

To see a complete list of publications covered by any of the citator services, enter its service abbreviation (IC, SH, SP or QC) followed by PUBS. To ascertain the scope of coverage for any of the services, enter the SCOPE command (SC) followed by the appropriate service abbreviation. For the complete list of commands available in a citator service, enter its service abbreviation (IC, SH, SP or QC) followed by CMDS.

Retrieving Statutes, Court Rules and Regulations

Annotated and unannotated versions of the New York statutes are searchable on WESTLAW (identifiers NY-ST-ANN and NY-ST), as are New York court rules (NY-RULES) and New York Administrative Code (NY-ADC).

The United States Code and United States Code - Annotated are searchable databases on WESTLAW (identifiers USC and USCA, respectively), as are federal court rules (US-RULES) and regulations (CFR).

In addition, the FIND command may be used to retrieve specific provisions by citation, obviating the need for database selection or search. To FIND a desired document, enter FI, followed by the citation of the desired document, using the full name of the publication, or one of the abbreviated styles recognized by WESTLAW.

If WESTLAW does not recognize the style you enter, you may enter one of the following, using US, NY, or any other state code in place of XX:

FI XX-ST	Displays templates for codified statutes
FI XX-LEGIS	Displays templates for legislation
FI XX-RULES	Displays templates for rules
FI XX-ORDERS	Displays templates for court orders

Alternatively, entering FI followed by the publication's full name or an accepted abbreviation will normally display templates, useful jump possibilities, or helpful information necessary to complete the FIND process. For example:

FI USCA	Displays templates for United States Code - Annotated
FI FRAP	Displays templates for Federal Rules of Appellate Procedure
FI FRCP	Displays templates for Federal Rules of Civil Procedure
FI FRCRP	Displays templates for Federal Rules of Criminal Procedure
FI FRE	Displays templates for Federal Rules of Evidence
FI CFR	Displays templates for Code of Federal Regulations
FI FR	Displays templates for Federal Register

To view the complete list of FINDable documents and associated prescribed forms, enter FI PUBS.

Updating Research in re Statutes, Rules and Regulations

When viewing a statute, rule or regulation on WESTLAW after a search or FIND command, it is easy to update your research. A message will appear on the screen if relevant amendments, repeals or other new material are available through the UPDATE feature. Entering the UPDATE command will display such material.

Documents used to update New York statutes are also searchable in New York Legislative Service (NY-LEGIS). Those used to update rules are searchable in New York Orders (NY-ORDERS).

Documents used to update federal statutes, rules, and regulations are searchable in the United States Public Laws (US-PL), Federal Orders (US-ORDERS) and Federal Register (FR) databases, respectively.

When documents citing a statute, rule or regulation are of interest, Shepard's Citations on WESTLAW may be of assistance. That service covers federal constitutional provisions, statutes and administrative provisions, and corresponding materials from many states. The command SH PUBS displays a directory of publications which may be Shepardized on WESTLAW. Consult the WESTLAW manual for more information about citator services.

Using WESTLAW as a Citator

For research beyond the coverage of any citator service, go directly to the databases (cases, for example) containing citing documents and use standard WESTLAW search techniques to retrieve documents citing specific constitutional provisions, statutes, standard jury instructions or other authorities.

Fortunately, the specific portion of a citation is often reasonably distinctive, such as 22:636.1, 301.65, 401(k), 12-21-5, 12052. When it is, a search on that specific portion alone may retrieve applicable documents without any substantial number of inapplicable ones (unless the number happens to be coincidentally popular in another context).

Similarly, if the citation involves more than one number, such as 42 U.S.C.A. §1201, a search containing both numbers (e.g., 42 +5 1201) is likely to produce mostly desired information, even though the component numbers are common.

If necessary, the search may be limited in several ways:

A. Switch from a general database to one containing mostly cases within the subject area of the cite being researched;

B. Use a connector (&, /S, /P, etc.) to narrow the search to documents including terms which are highly likely to accompany the correct citation in the context of the issue being researched;

C. Include other citation information in the query. Because of the variety of citation formats used in documents, this option should be used primarily where other options prove insufficient. Below are illustrative queries for any database containing New York cases:

> N.Y.Const.! Const.! Constitution /s 6 VI +3 3

will retrieve cases citing the New York State Constitution, Art. 6, §3; and

> "Criminal Procedure Law" CPL /s 30.30

will retrieve cases citing Criminal Procedure Law §30.30.

Alternative Retrieval Methods

WIN® (WESTLAW Is Natural™) allows you to frame your issue in plain English to retrieve documents:

> Does new trial motion extend (toll) the time for filing (taking) appeal?

Alternatively, retrieval may be focused by use of the Terms and Connectors method:

> TO(30) /P DI(NEW +1 TRIAL /P EXTEND!
> EXTENSION TOLL! /P APPEAL)

In databases with Key Numbers, either of the above examples will identify Appeal and Error ⚷345.1 as a Key Number collecting headnotes relevant to this issue if there are pertinent cases.

Since the Key Numbers are affixed to points of law by trained specialists based on conceptual understanding of the case, relevant cases that were not retrieved by either of the language-dependent methods will often be found at a Key Number.

WESTLAW ELECTRONIC RESEARCH GUIDE

Similarly, citations in retrieved documents (to cases, statutes, rules, etc.) may suggest additional, fruitful research using other WESTLAW databases (e.g., annotated statutes, rules) or services (e.g., citator services).

Key Number Search

Frequently, case law research rapidly converges on a few topics, headings and Key Numbers within West's Key Number System that are likely to contain relevant cases. These may be discovered from known, relevant reported cases from any jurisdiction; Library References in West publications; browsing in a digest; or browsing the Key Number System on WESTLAW using the JUMP feature or the KEY command.

Once discovered, topics, subheadings or Key Numbers are useful as search terms (in databases containing reported cases) alone or with other search terms, to focus the search within a narrow range of potentially relevant material.

For example, to retrieve cases with at least one headnote classified to Appeal and Error ⟲345.1, sign on to a caselaw database and enter

30k345.1   [use with other search terms, if desired]

The topic name (Appeal and Error) is replaced by its numerical equivalent (30) and the ⟲ by the letter k. A list of topics and their numerical equivalents is in the WESTLAW Reference Manual and is displayed in WESTLAW when the KEY command is entered.

Using JUMP

WESTLAW's JUMP feature allows you to move from one document to another or from one part of a document to another, then easily return to your original place, without losing your original result. Opportunities to move in this manner are marked in the text with a JUMP symbol (▶). Whenever you see the JUMP symbol, you may move to the place designated by the adjacent reference by using the Tab, arrow keys or mouse click to position the cursor on the JUMP symbol, then pressing Enter or clicking again with the mouse.

Within the text of a court opinion, JUMP arrows are adjacent to case cites and federal statute cites, and adjacent to parenthesized numbers marking discussions corresponding to headnotes.

On a screen containing the text of a headnote, the JUMP arrows allow movement to the corresponding discussion in the text of the opinion,

▶ (3)

and allow browsing West's Key Number System beginning at various heading levels:

- 30 APPEAL AND ERROR
- 30VII Transfer of Cause
- 30VII(A) Time of Taking Proceedings
- 30k343 Commencement of Period of Limitation
- 30k345.1 k. Motion for new trial.

To return from a JUMP, enter GB (except for JUMPs between a headnote and the corresponding discussion in opinion, for which there is a matching number in parenthesis in both headnote and opinion). Returns from successive JUMPs (e.g., from case to cited case to case cited by cited case) without intervening returns may be accomplished by repeated entry of GB or by using the MAP command.

General Information

The information provided above illustrates some of the ways WESTLAW can complement research using this publication. However, this brief overview illustrates only some of the power of WESTLAW. The full range of WESTLAW search techniques is available to support your research.

Please consult the WESTLAW Reference Manual for additional information or assistance or call West's Reference Attorneys at 1-800-REF-ATTY (1-800-733-2889).

For information about subscribing to WESTLAW, please call 1-800-328-9352.

*

WESTLAW REFERENCE RESEARCH GUIDE

Searching WESTLAW's Key Number System begins at various index levels.

W-30	APPEAL AND ERROR
k 70(4)	Transfer of Cause
k 70.80(4)	Time to Taking Transcript
k 90(2)	Commencement of Period of Limit...
k 970.3(4.1)	Reasons for appeal, bid

Subject Key NUMBER's are the TOPIC and KEY Numbers in which most of the information is found. Every number's search starts subject are easier to narrow down. Also, unique and relevant issues can be located in KNIS topic titles. A subject can often be identified by using a key number without determining an analogous continuation to undertaking. This is to say the broad to narrow.

Uses of References

The information given about the realities comes some of the ways WEST-LAW can compliment research using this guideline. However, this brief overview is but one indication of the power of WESTLAW. The full range of WESTLAW search techniques is available to augment your research.

Please consult the WESTLAW Reference Manual for detailed information or see the West's Reference Attorneys at 1-800-REF-ATTY (1-800-733-2889).

For more information about being a WEST ITP, Reference Monitor.

SUMMARY OF CONTENTS

Volume 20

Chapter   Page

1. Business Organizations: Corporations — 2
2. Non-corporate Entities: Limited Liability Companies and Partnerships — 253
3. Municipal Law — 403
4. Administrative Law — 468
5. Commercial Sales Contracts — 594
6. Buying and Selling a Small Business — 670

Volume 21

7. Consumer Law — 2
8. Enforcement of Money Judgments — 181
9. Bankruptcy — 253
10. Mechanic's Liens — 541
11. Mortgage Foreclosure — 683
12. Purchase and Sale of Real Estate — 792

Volume 22

13. Landlord–Tenant Law — 2
14. Eminent Domain — 108
15. Environmental Law — 212
16. New York Land Use Law — 296
17. New York Employment Law — 467
18. Civil Rights Law — 609
19. Immigration and Nationality Law—Permanent Residence Applications — 733
20. Adoptions — 857

Volume 23

21. Domestic Relations — 2
22. Guardianship — 162
23. Elder Law — 329
24. Estate Planning — 448
25. Probate and Estate Administration — 545
26. Personal Injury — 638

SUMMARY OF CONTENTS

Chapter | **Page**
27. Products Liability — 722

Volume 24

28. Legal Malpractice — 2
29. Medical Malpractice — 92
30. Damages — 166
31. Insurance — 251
32. Workers' Compensation — 315
33. Local Criminal Court Practice — 382
34. Social Security Disability Cases — 452
35. Income Tax — 551
36. Alcoholic Beverage Control Law — 653
37. Civil Appellate Practice Before the Appellate Division and Other Intermediate Appellate Courts — 738

Volume 25

38. Criminal Appellate Practice Before the Appellate Division and Other Intermediate Appelllate Courts — 2
39. Civil and Criminal Appeals to the Court of Appeals — 145

Table of Jury Instructions — 235
Table of Forms — 236
Table of Statutes — iii
Table of Rules — iii
Table of Cases — iii
Index — iii

XVI

TABLE OF CONTENTS

Volume 20

CHAPTER 1. BUSINESS ORGANIZATIONS: CORPORATIONS

Sec.
- 1.1 Scope Note.
- 1.2 Strategy.
- 1.3 Strategy Checklist.
- 1.4 Overview.
- 1.5 Definitions.
- 1.6 Formation of Corporations.
- 1.7 ___ Certificates; Notices.
- 1.8 ___ Corporate Seal.
- 1.9 ___ Corporate Purposes.
- 1.10 ___ ___ Upholding and Disregarding the Corporate Entity.
- 1.11 ___ ___ General Powers.
- 1.12 ___ ___ Defense of *Ultra Vires*.
- 1.13 ___ Corporate Name.
- 1.14 ___ ___ Reservation of Name.
- 1.15 ___ Service of Process.
- 1.16 ___ ___ Records and Certificates of Department of State.
- 1.17 ___ ___ Statutory Designation of Secretary of State as Agent for Service of Process.
- 1.18 ___ ___ Registered Agent for Service of Process.
- 1.19 ___ ___ Upon Unauthorized Foreign Corporation.
- 1.20 ___ Incorporators and Promoters.
- 1.21 ___ Certificate of Incorporation.
- 1.22 ___ Bylaws.
- 1.23 ___ Organization Meeting; Biennial Statement; Franchise Tax.
- 1.24 ___ Formation of Corporations Summary.
- 1.25 ___ Formation of Corporations Checklist.
- 1.26 Capital Structure.
- 1.27 ___ Authorized Shares.
- 1.28 ___ Preferred Shares in Series.
- 1.29 ___ Subscription for Shares.
- 1.30 ___ Consideration and Payment for Shares.
- 1.31 ___ Rights to Purchase Shares.
- 1.32 ___ Stated Capital.
- 1.33 ___ Corporate Bonds; Convertible Securities.
- 1.34 ___ Federal Income Taxation Aspects.
- 1.35 ___ Capital Structure Summary.
- 1.36 ___ Capital Structure Checklist.
- 1.37 Distributions.
- 1.38 ___ Dividends; Share Distributions and Changes.
- 1.39 ___ Purchase or Redemption of Shares.

TABLE OF CONTENTS

Sec.
1.40 ____ Federal Income Tax Aspects.
1.41 ____ Distributions Summary.
1.42 ____ Distributions Checklist.
1.43 Shareholders' Meetings and Agreements—Generally.
1.44 ____ Notice Requirements.
1.45 ____ Voting.
1.46 ____ Quorum Requirements.
1.47 ____ Agreements; Voting Trusts.
1.48 ____ Action Without a Meeting.
1.49 Shareholders' Meetings and Agreements Summary.
1.50 Shareholders' Meetings and Agreements Checklist.
1.51 Shareholders' Rights.
1.52 ____ Preemptive Rights.
1.53 ____ Inspection of Books and Records.
1.54 ____ Shareholders' Rights Summary.
1.55 ____ Shareholders' Rights Checklist.
1.56 Shareholders' Liabilities.
1.57 ____ Shareholders' Liabilities Summary.
1.58 ____ Shareholders' Liabilities Checklist.
1.59 Directors.
1.60 ____ Vacancies; New Directorships.
1.61 ____ Removal.
1.62 ____ Meetings.
1.63 ____ ____ Quorum and Voting Requirements.
1.64 ____ Executive Committee; Other Committees.
1.65 ____ Fiduciary Duties.
1.66 ____ Liabilities.
1.67 ____ Directors Summary.
1.68 ____ Directors Checklist.
1.69 Officers.
1.70 ____ Officers Summary.
1.71 ____ Officers Checklist.
1.72 Amendment of Certificate of Incorporation.
1.73 ____ Procedure.
1.74 ____ Class Vote.
1.75 ____ Certificate of Amendment.
1.76 ____ Certificate of Change.
1.77 ____ Restated Certificate of Incorporation.
1.78 ____ Reorganization Under Act of Congress.
1.79 Amendment of Certificate of Incorporation Summary.
1.80 Amendment of Certificate of Incorporation Checklist.
1.81 Business Combinations.
1.82 ____ Mergers and Consolidations.
1.83 ____ ____ Procedures.
1.84 ____ ____ Effect.
1.85 ____ Sale, Lease, Exchange, or Other Disposition of Assets.
1.86 ____ ____ Mortgage or Security Interest in Assets.
1.87 ____ ____ Guarantee Authorized by Shareholders.
1.88 ____ Share Exchanges.
1.89 ____ Takeover Bids.

TABLE OF CONTENTS

Sec.
1.90 ___ Right of Shareholder to Receive Payment for Shares.
1.91 ___ Federal Income Taxation Aspects.
1.92 Business Combinations Summary.
1.93 Business Combinations Checklist.
1.94 Dissolution.
1.95 ___ Non-judicial Dissolution.
1.96 ___ ___ Authorization.
1.97 ___ ___ Certificate of Dissolution.
1.98 ___ ___ Notice to Creditors.
1.99 ___ Judicial Dissolution.
1.100 ___ ___ Attorney General's Action.
1.101 ___ ___ Directors' Petition.
1.102 ___ ___ Shareholders' Petition.
1.103 ___ ___ Petition Upon Deadlock Among Directors or Shareholders and in Other Circumstances.
1.104 ___ ___ Procedures.
1.105 ___ ___ Preservation of Assets; Appointment of Receiver.
1.106 ___ ___ Certain Transfers and Judgments Void; Injunction.
1.107 ___ Liquidation Distributions.
1.108 ___ ___ Federal Income Tax Aspects.
1.109 ___ Dissolution Summary.
1.110 ___ Dissolution Checklist.
1.111 Receivership.
1.112 Receivership—Summary.
1.113 ___ Checklist.
1.114 Foreign Corporations.
1.115 ___ Authorization to Do Business in New York.
1.116 ___ Application for Authority.
1.117 ___ ___ Effect of Filing.
1.118 ___ Surrender of Authority.
1.119 ___ Termination of Existence.
1.120 Foreign Corporations Summary.
1.121 Foreign Corporations Checklist.
1.122 Professional Service Corporations.
1.123 Professional Service Corporations Summary.
1.124 Professional Service Corporations Checklist.
1.125 Foreign Professional Service Corporations.
1.126 Foreign Professional Service Corporations Summary.
1.127 Foreign Professional Service Corporations Checklist.
1.128 Transactional Checklist—Generally.
1.129 ___ Formation ("Birth").
1.130 ___ Operation ("Growth").
1.131 ___ Business Combinations ("Marriage").
1.132 ___ Spin-offs and Split-offs ("Children" and "Divorce").
1.133 ___ Repurchase of Shares ("Redemption").
1.134 ___ Dissolution; Liquidation ("Death").
1.135 Procedural Checklist—Generally.
1.136 ___ Notices.
1.137 ___ Reservation of Corporate Name.
1.138 ___ ___ Foreign Corporations.

TABLE OF CONTENTS

Sec.
1.139 ___ Mandatory and Permissive Provisions in Certificate of Incorporation.
1.140 ___ Incorporation.
1.141 ___ Filing Certificate of Incorporation.
1.142 ___ Bylaws.
1.143 ___ Organization Meetings.
1.144 ___ Share Certificate.
1.145 ___ Shareholder Approval Requirements.
1.146 ___ Shareholder's Right to Receive Payment for Shares.
1.147 ___ Close Corporations.
1.148 ___ Foreign Corporations.
1.149 Drafting Checklist.
1.150 Form—Application to Reserve Corporate Name. 💾
1.151 ___ Certificate of Incorporation. 💾
1.152 ___ Bylaws. 💾
1.153 ___ Subscription Agreement. 💾
1.154 ___ Certificate of Amendment. 💾
1.155 ___ Certificate of Dissolution. 💾

CHAPTER 2. NON-CORPORATE ENTITIES: LIMITED LIABILTY COMPANIES AND PARTNERSHIPS

2.1 Scope Note.
2.2 Strategy—Choice of Entity.
2.3 Tax Classification.
2.4 ___ Eagerly–Awaited Simplification.
2.5 ___ Former Corporate Characteristics Test.
2.6 ___ ___ Limited Liability.
2.7 ___ ___ Continuity of Life.
2.8 ___ ___ Free Transferability of Interests.
2.9 ___ ___ Centralized Management.
2.10 Partnership vs. LLC.
2.11 ___ Tax Implications.
2.12 ___ Liability.
2.13 ___ Flexibility.
2.14 Limited Liability Companies.
2.15 ___ Governing Law.
2.16 ___ Formation.
2.17 ___ ___ Articles of Organization.
2.18 ___ ___ Publication.
2.19 ___ ___ Operating Agreement.
2.20 ___ ___ Other Issues.
2.21 ___ Members.
2.22 ___ ___ Admission of New Members.
2.23 ___ ___ Liability.
2.24 ___ ___ One-member LLCs.
2.25 ___ Management.
2.26 ___ ___ Members vs. Managers.
2.27 ___ ___ Voting: Members.
2.28 ___ ___ Voting: Managers.

TABLE OF CONTENTS

Sec.		
2.29	__ __	Non-waivable Requirements.
2.30	__ __	Delegation of Responsibility.
2.31	__ __	Standard of Care.
2.32	__ __	Agency Authority.
2.33	__	Assignment of Interests.
2.34	__ __	Default Rules.
2.35	__ __	Vote Required to Admit Assignee as Member.
2.36	__	Dissolution.
2.37	__ __	Events.
2.38	__ __	Continuation of Business after Dissolution Event.
2.39	__ __	Winding Up.
2.40	__	Conversions/Mergers.
2.41	__ __	Procedures.
2.42	__ __	Dissenters' Rights.
2.43	__	PLLCs.
2.44		General Partnerships.
2.45	__	Governing Law.
2.46	__	Formation.
2.47	__ __	Agreement.
2.48	__ __	Business Certificate.
2.49	__ __	Publication.
2.50	__ __	Other Issues.
2.51	__	Partners.
2.52	__ __	Admission of New Partners.
2.53	__ __	Liability.
2.54	__ __	Contribution Issues.
2.55	__	Management.
2.56	__ __	Voting.
2.57	__ __	Non-waivable Requirements.
2.58	__ __	Delegation of Responsibility.
2.59	__ __	Standard of Care.
2.60	__ __	Agency Authority.
2.61	__	Assignment of Interests.
2.62	__ __	Default Rules.
2.63	__ __	Vote Required to Admit New Partner.
2.64	__	Dissolution.
2.65	__ __	Events.
2.66	__ __	Continuation of Business after Dissolution Event.
2.67	__ __	Winding Up.
2.68	__	Conversions/Mergers.
2.69	__ __	Procedures.
2.70	__ __	Dissenters' Rights.
2.71	__	Professional Organizations.
2.72		Limited Liability Partnerships.
2.73	__	Governing Law.
2.74	__	Comparison with General Partnerships.
2.75	__	Formation/Registration.
2.76	__	Other Issues.
2.77		Limited Partnerships.
2.78	__	Governing Law.

TABLE OF CONTENTS

Sec.
2.79 ____ Formation.
2.80 ____ ____ Certificate of Limited Partnership.
2.81 ____ ____ Publication.
2.82 ____ ____ Agreement.
2.83 ____ ____ Other Issues.
2.84 ____ Partners.
2.85 ____ ____ Admission of New Partners.
2.86 ____ ____ Liability.
2.87 ____ Contribution Issues.
2.88 ____ Management.
2.89 ____ ____ Voting: General Partners.
2.90 ____ ____ Voting: Limited Partners.
2.91 ____ ____ Delegation of Responsibility.
2.92 ____ ____ Standard of Care.
2.93 ____ ____ Agency Authority.
2.94 ____ Assignment of Interests.
2.95 ____ ____ Default Rules.
2.96 ____ ____ Vote Required to Admit New Partner.
2.97 ____ Dissolution.
2.98 ____ ____ Events.
2.99 ____ ____ Continuation of Business after Dissolution Event.
2.100 ____ ____ Winding Up.
2.101 ____ Conversions/Mergers.
2.102 ____ ____ Procedures.
2.103 ____ ____ Dissenters' Rights.
2.104 ____ Professional Organizations.
2.105 Due Diligence Issues.
2.106 Securities Laws Issues.
2.107 Summary.
2.108 Chart Comparing New York Entities.
2.109 Drafting Checklist.
2.110 Forms.
2.111 ____ LLC Articles of Organization. 💾
2.112 ____ Operating Agreement: Member–Managed LLC. 💾
2.113 ____ Registration as LLP. 💾
2.114 ____ Certificate of Limited Partnership. 💾
2.115 ____ Limited Partnership Agreement. 💾

CHAPTER 3. MUNICIPAL LAW

3.1 Scope Note.
3.2 Strategy.
3.3 Municipal Corporations.
3.4 ____ Creation.
3.5 ____ Consolidation, Annexation and Dissolution.
3.6 ____ ____ Annexation Checklist.
3.7 Powers of Municipal Corporations.
3.8 ____ Governmental v. Proprietary Powers.
3.9 ____ Police Powers.
3.10 Legislative Enactments.

XXII

TABLE OF CONTENTS

Sec.

3.11	____ Resolutions.
3.12	____ Ordinances.
3.13	____ Rules and Regulations.
3.14	____ Local Laws.
3.15	____ Referendum Requirements.
3.16	Acquisition and Disposition of Property.
3.17	Officers and Employees.
3.18	____ Qualifications.
3.19	____ Terms.
3.20	____ Removal.
3.21	____ Collective Bargaining.
3.22	____ Conflicts of Interest.
3.23	____ ____ Checklist.
3.24	Contracts.
3.25	____ Competitive Bidding.
3.26	Municipal Finance.
3.27	____ Municipal Borrowing.
3.28	Public Meetings.
3.29	Access to Records.
3.30	Tort Claims Against Municipalities.
3.31	____ Checklist.
3.32	Challenges to Governmental Determinations.
3.33	Special Purpose Units of Government.
3.34	____ Industrial Development Agencies.
3.35	____ Public Authorities.
3.36	Forms.
3.37	____ Notice of Claim. 💾
3.38	____ Verified Complaint in Tort Action. 💾

CHAPTER 4. ADMINISTRATIVE LAW

4.1	Scope Note.
4.2	Strategy.
4.3	____ Checklist.
4.4	Procedural Due Process.
4.5	____ Individualized State Action.
4.6	____ Protected Interests.
4.7	____ The Process Due.
4.8	____ Summary.
4.9	____ Checklist.
4.10	Adjudicatory Proceedings.
4.11	____ Definition of an Adjudicatory Proceeding.
4.12	____ Notice.
4.13	____ Discovery.
4.14	____ Right to Counsel.
4.15	____ Evidence.
4.16	____ Cross-Examination and Witness Attendance.
4.17	____ Official Notice.
4.18	____ Statement of Decision and Decisional Record.
4.19	____ Burden of Proof.

TABLE OF CONTENTS

Sec.
4.20 ____ Intervention.
4.21 ____ Unreasonable Agency Delay.
4.22 ____ Agency Duty to Decide Consistently.
4.23 ____ Intra-agency Review.
4.24 ____ Checking Agency Bias.
4.25 ____ *Res Judicata* and Collateral Estoppel Effect.
4.26 ____ Special Rules Applicable to Licensing Matters.
4.27 ____ Special Issues in Handling Licensing Matters.
4.28 ____ ____ Basic License Information.
4.29 ____ ____ The Role of SAPA and SEQRA in the Licensing Process.
4.30 ____ ____ Accuracy and Completeness in Applications.
4.31 ____ ____ Opportunities to Expedite the Process.
4.32 ____ ____ Opportunities for Variances from Standard Approaches.
4.33 ____ ____ Renewal, Suspension and Revocation Issues.
4.34 ____ Special Issues in Handling Enforcement Matters.
4.35 ____ ____ Strategies to Minimize Violations.
4.36 ____ ____ Agency Fact–Finding in the Pre-enforcement Phase.
4.37 ____ ____ Agency Enforcement Options.
4.38 ____ ____ The Settlement Process.
4.39 ____ ____ The Hearing Process.
4.40 ____ ____ Post–Hearing Issues.
4.41 ____ Summary.
4.42 ____ Checklist.
4.43 Administrative Rulemaking.
4.44 ____ Rulemaking Compared With Other Agency Action.
4.45 ____ Rulemaking Notice.
4.46 ____ Comments and Agency Assessment of Comments.
4.47 ____ Agency Duty to Reveal Underlying Information.
4.48 ____ Notice of Adoption and Effective Date of Rules.
4.49 ____ Ancillary Documentation and the Role of GORR.
4.50 ____ Rule Filing and Publication.
4.51 ____ Declaratory Rulings Regarding Rules.
4.52 ____ Overlapping State and Federal Rules.
4.53 ____ Special Strategic Considerations in Handling Administrative Rulemaking Matters.
4.54 ____ ____ Basic Sources of Information on Rulemaking.
4.55 ____ ____ Participating in the Rulemaking Process.
4.56 ____ ____ Special Issues in Negotiated Rulemakings.
4.57 ____ ____ Special Issues in Emergency Rulemakings.
4.58 ____ ____ Agency Guidance Documents.
4.59 ____ Summary.
4.60 ____ Checklist.
4.61 Agency Information–Gathering.
4.62 ____ Administrative Searches.
4.63 ____ Administrative Subpoenas.
4.64 ____ Reporting and Recordkeeping Requirements.
4.65 ____ Summary.
4.66 ____ Checklist.
4.67 Judicial Review.
4.68 ____ Delegation of Authority to Agencies.

TABLE OF CONTENTS

Sec.
- 4.69 ___ Standing to Seek Judicial Review.
- 4.70 ___ Ripeness.
- 4.71 ___ Final Order and Relief in the Nature of Prohibition.
- 4.72 ___ Exhaustion of Administrative Remedies.
- 4.73 ___ Primary Jurisdiction.
- 4.74 ___ Statutory Preclusion of Judicial Review.
- 4.75 ___ Article 78 and the Consolidation of the Common Law Prerogative Writs.
- 4.76 ___ Standards of Review.
- 4.77 ___ ___ Review of Agency Determinations of Law.
- 4.78 ___ ___ Review of Agency Determinations of Fact Under the Substantial Evidence Test.
- 4.79 ___ ___ Review of Agency Determinations of Fact Under the Arbitrary and Capricious Test.
- 4.80 ___ ___ Review of Administrative Rules.
- 4.81 ___ ___ Review of Administrative Discretion.
- 4.82 ___ Statutes of Limitation Applicable to Judicial Review of Agency Action.
- 4.83 ___ Venue in Article 78 Proceedings.
- 4.84 ___ Subject Matter Jurisdiction in Article 78 Proceedings.
- 4.85 ___ Summary.
- 4.86 ___ Checklist.
- 4.87 Forms.
- 4.88 ___ Notice of Appearance in Licensing or Permitting Matter.
- 4.89 ___ Notice for Discovery and Inspection in an Administrative Proceeding.
- 4.90 ___ Notice of Deposition in an Administrative Proceeding.
- 4.91 ___ Notice to Permit Entry Upon Real Property.

CHAPTER 5. COMMERCIAL SALES CONTRACTS

- 5.1 Scope Note.
- 5.2 Strategy.
- 5.3 Transactional Checklist—Breach of Contract.
- 5.4 Defining a Contract.
- 5.5 Governing Law.
- 5.6 ___ Freedom to Contract—Generally.
- 5.7 ___ ___ Presumption of Legality.
- 5.8 ___ ___ ___ Burden of Proof.
- 5.9 ___ ___ ___ Determining the Contract's Validity.
- 5.10 ___ ___ ___ Not All Illegal Contracts Are Unenforceable.
- 5.11 ___ Public Policy Issues.
- 5.12 ___ Unconscionability.
- 5.13 ___ ___ Elements.
- 5.14 ___ ___ Codification in UCC.
- 5.15 ___ Duty of Good Faith—Generally.
- 5.16 ___ ___ Codification in UCC.
- 5.17 The Written Contract—Statute of Frauds.
- 5.18 ___ ___ General Rules.
- 5.19 ___ ___ Formal Requirements.

TABLE OF CONTENTS

Sec.	
5.20	___ ___ Nature of the Writing.
5.21	___ Parol or Extrinsic Evidence.
5.22	___ Offer.
5.23	___ Acceptance.
5.24	___ ___ Additional Terms.
5.25	___ Indefiniteness.
5.26	___ Use of Open Terms.
5.27	Warranties.
5.28	___ Warranty of Title Against Infringement.
5.29	___ Express Warranty.
5.30	___ Implied Warranty of Merchantability.
5.31	___ Implied Warranty of Fitness for a Particular Purpose.
5.32	Assumption of the Risk of Loss.
5.33	___ In the Absence of Breach.
5.34	___ In the Event of a Breach.
5.35	Performance.
5.36	___ Buyer's Response to Tender of Delivery.
5.37	___ ___ Acceptance.
5.38	___ ___ Rejection.
5.39	___ ___ Revocation of Acceptance.
5.40	Breach of Contract.
5.41	___ Seller's Remedies.
5.42	___ ___ Action for the Price.
5.43	___ ___ Withholding the Goods and Stopping Delivery.
5.44	___ ___ Recovery of Goods Delivered.
5.45	___ ___ Resale.
5.46	___ ___ Damages for Non-acceptance or Repudiation.
5.47	___ Buyer's Remedies.
5.48	___ ___ Cover.
5.49	___ ___ Damages for Non-delivery.
5.50	___ ___ Damages for Breach Regarding Accepted Goods.
5.51	___ ___ Specific Performance or Replevin.
5.52	___ Liquidated Damages.
5.53	___ Mitigation of Damages.
5.54	Third-Party Interests.
5.55	___ Subsequent Buyers.
5.56	___ Other Creditors.
5.57	Drafting Checklists—Order of Goods for Resale by Buyer.
5.58	___ Verified Complaint On Account Stated for Goods, Services and Wares Delivered.
5.59	___ Plaintiff's Notice of Motion for Summary Judgment in Contract Action.
5.60	___Affidavit of Officer of Plaintiff Company in Support of Summary Judgment Motion in Contract Action.
5.61	___ Notice of Petition for Order Staying Arbitration in Dispute Over Contract for Sale of Goods.
5.62	___ Petition for Order Staying Arbitration in Dispute Over Contract for Sale of Goods.
5.63	___ Affidavit in Opposition to Petition for Order Staying Arbitration in Dispute Over Contract for Sale of Goods.

TABLE OF CONTENTS

Sec.
5.64 ____ Answer to Petition for Order Staying Arbitration in Dispute Over Contract for Sale of Goods.
5.65 Forms—Order of Goods for Resale by Buyer. 💾
5.66 ____ Verified Complaint On Account Stated for Goods, Services and Wares Delivered. 💾
5.67 ____ Plaintiff's Notice of Motion for Summary Judgment in Contract Action. 💾
5.68 ____ Affidavit of Vice President of Plaintiff Purchaser in Support of Summary Judgment Motion in Contract Action. 💾
5.69 ____ Notice of Petition for Order Staying Arbitration in Dispute Over Contract for Sale of Goods. 💾
5.70 ____ Petition for Order Staying Arbitration in Dispute Over Contract for Sale of Goods. 💾
5.71 ____ Affidavit in Opposition to Petition for Order Staying Arbitration in Dispute Over Contract for Sale of Goods. 💾
5.72 ____ Answer to Petition for Order Staying Arbitration in Dispute Over Contract for Sale of Goods. 💾

CHAPTER 6. BUYING AND SELLING A SMALL BUSINESS

6.1 Scope Note.
6.2 Strategy: Representing the Buyer—Introduction.
6.3 ____ The Attorney's Role.
6.4 ____ Different Considerations Depending on the Type of Transaction.
6.5 ____ General Stages of the Transaction.
6.6 Representing the Buyer—Investigating the Business.
6.7 ____ Nature and Operation of Business.
6.8 ____ Geographic Location.
6.9 ____ The Negotiating Team.
6.10 ____ The Letter of Intent.
6.11 ____ Confidentiality Agreements.
6.12 ____ Drafting the Agreement.
6.13 Due Diligence Investigation.
6.14 ____ Legal Issues.
6.15 ____ ____ Organizational Documents.
6.16 ____ ____ Ownership Documents.
6.17 ____ ____ Existing Contracts.
6.18 ____ ____ Liens and Security Interests.
6.19 ____ ____ Corporate and Trade Names.
6.20 ____ ____ Real Estate.
6.21 ____ ____ Compliance With Law.
6.22 ____ ____ Litigation Investigation.
6.23 ____ Financial Issues—General Considerations.
6.24 ____ ____ Seller's Records From the Buyer's Position.
6.25 ____ ____ Buyer's Records From the Seller's Position.
6.26 ____ ____ Public Records.
6.27 ____ ____ Financial Statements.
6.28 ____ ____ The Need for Other Professionals.
6.29 ____ ____ Valuation of the Business.

TABLE OF CONTENTS

Sec.	
6.30	____ ____ Tax Returns.
6.31	Tax Issues for Buyer.
6.32	____ Asset Purchase.
6.33	____ ____ Allocation of Purchase Price.
6.34	____ ____ Depreciation of Assets.
6.35	____ ____ Land.
6.36	____ ____ Good Will and Covenants Not to Compete.
6.37	____ ____ Inventory.
6.38	____ ____ Cash.
6.39	____ ____ Supplies.
6.40	____ ____ Patents, Franchises, Trademarks, Trade Names.
6.41	____ Stock Purchase.
6.42	____ ____ Basis of Stock.
6.43	____ ____ Basis of Corporate Assets.
6.44	____ ____ Election to Treat Stock Purchase as Asset Purchase.
6.45	____ Mergers, Consolidations, and Exchanges.
6.46	Structuring the Buyer's Transaction.
6.47	____ Type of Payment.
6.48	____ Assumption of Seller's Liabilities.
6.49	____ Security to Seller.
6.50	____ Notes.
6.51	____ Escrow Arrangements and Agreements.
6.52	Drafting the Buyer's Asset Purchase Agreement.
6.53	____ Identification of the Parties.
6.54	____ Recitals.
6.55	____ Assets and Property to Be Conveyed.
6.56	____ Retained Assets of Seller.
6.57	____ Purchase Price and Method of Payment.
6.58	____ Closing.
6.59	____ Representations, Warranties and Covenants of Seller.
6.60	____ Representations, Warranties and Covenants of Buyer.
6.61	____ Conduct of Business Prior to Closing.
6.62	____ Indemnifications.
6.63	____ Corporate or Other Name.
6.64	____ ____ Notice to Customers and Suppliers.
6.65	____ ____ UCC Bulk Sale Notices or Escrow Agreement in Lieu of UCC Bulk Sale Notice.
6.66	____ ____ NYS Sales Tax and Bulk Sale Notification.
6.67	____ ____ Covenant Not to Compete.
6.68	____ Matters Respecting Real Property.
6.69	____ Conditions Precedent to Purchaser's Obligations.
6.70	____ Conditions Precedent to Seller's Obligations.
6.71	____ Nature and Survival of Representations and Warranties.
6.72	____ Non-disclosure Provisions.
6.73	____ Miscellaneous Agreements Between Buyer and Seller.
6.74	____ Documents to Be Delivered to Purchaser at Closing.
6.75	____ Documents to Be Delivered to Seller at Closing.
6.76	____ Notices, Severability and Other General Provisions.
6.77	____ Documents to Be Prepared or Reviewed Prior to Closing.
6.78	Drafting the Buyer's Stock Purchase Agreement.

TABLE OF CONTENTS

Sec.	
6.79	____ Identification of the Parties.
6.80	____ Recitals.
6.81	____ Sale of Shares.
6.82	____ Purchase Price and Method of Payment.
6.83	____ Closing.
6.84	____ Representations, Warranties and Covenants of Seller.
6.85	____ Representations, Warranties and Covenants of Buyer.
6.86	____ Conduct of Business Prior to Closing.
6.87	____ Indemnifications.
6.88	____ Covenant Not to Compete.
6.89	____ Matters Respecting Real Property.
6.90	____ Nondisclosure Provisions.
6.91	____ Conditions Precedent to Purchaser's Obligations.
6.92	____ Conditions Precedent to Seller's Obligations.
6.93	____ Nature and Survival of Representations and Warranties.
6.94	____ Documents to Be Delivered to Purchaser at Closing.
6.95	____ Documents to Be Delivered to Seller at Closing.
6.96	____ Notices, Severability and Other General Provisions.
6.97	____ Documents to Be Prepared or Reviewed Prior to Closing.
6.98	Post–Contract and Pre-closing.
6.99	____ Bulk Sales Act—UCC Article 6.
6.100	____ NYS Sales Tax and Bulk Sale Notification.
6.101	____ Plant Closing Notice.
6.102	____ Environmental Searches and Testing.
6.103	____ Certificate of Good Standing.
6.104	____ Real Property Transfer Gains Tax.
6.105	Closing and Post–Closing.
6.106	Strategy: Representing the Seller—Introduction.
6.107	____ The Attorney's Role.
6.108	____ Different Considerations Depending on the Type of Transaction.
6.109	____ General Stages of the Transaction.
6.110	Representing the Seller—General Investigation.
6.111	____ Investigating the Buyer.
6.112	____ The Negotiating Team.
6.113	____ The Letter of Intent.
6.114	____ Confidentiality Agreements.
6.115	____ Drafting the Agreement.
6.116	Tax Issues for the Seller—General Overview.
6.117	____ Asset Sale.
6.118	____ ____ Allocation of Purchase Price.
6.119	____ ____ Depreciation Recapture.
6.120	____ ____ Capital Gains or Losses.
6.121	____ ____ Ordinary Income.
6.122	____ ____ Income to Corporation.
6.123	____ ____ Real Property Transfer Gains Tax.
6.124	____ ____ Covenant Not to Compete and Consulting Agreements.
6.125	____ Stock Sale—General Advantages.
6.126	____ ____ Capital Gain or Loss.
6.127	____ ____ No Concern for Income to a Corporate Entity.

TABLE OF CONTENTS

Sec.	
6.128	__ __ Real Property Transfer Gains Tax.
6.129	__ __ Consulting and Non-compete Agreements.
6.130	__ __ I.R.C. § 1244 Stock and Qualified Small Business Stock.
6.131	__ __ Stock Transfer Tax.
6.132	__ __ Collapsible Corporation.
6.133	__ __ Mergers, Consolidations and Exchanges.
6.134	Structuring the Seller's Transaction—General Overview.
6.135	__ Purchase Price and Payment Terms.
6.136	__ Security to Seller.
6.137	__ Notes.
6.138	__ Escrow Arrangements.
6.139	Drafting the Seller's Asset Sale Agreement.
6.140	__ Identification of the Parties.
6.141	__ Recitals.
6.142	__ Assets and Property to Be Conveyed.
6.143	__ Assets Retained by Seller.
6.144	__ Sale Price and Method of Payment.
6.145	__ Closing.
6.146	__ Representations, Warranties and Covenants of Buyer.
6.147	__ Representations, Warranties and Covenants of Seller.
6.148	__ Conduct of Business Prior to Closing.
6.149	__ Indemnifications.
6.150	__ Matters Respecting Real Property.
6.151	__ Notice to Customers and Suppliers.
6.152	__ Covenant Not to Compete and Consulting Agreements.
6.153	__ UCC Bulk Sale Notices or Escrow Agreements in Lieu of UCC Bulk Sale Notice.
6.154	__ New York State Sales Tax and Bulk Sale Notification.
6.155	__ Nature and Survival of Representations and Warranties.
6.156	__ Non-disclosure Provisions.
6.157	__ Conditions Precedent to Seller's Obligations.
6.158	__ Conditions Precedent to Buyer's Obligations.
6.159	__ Documents to Be Delivered to Seller at Closing.
6.160	__ Documents to Be Delivered to Buyer at Closing.
6.161	__ Notices, Severability and Other General Provisions.
6.162	__ Documents to Be Prepared or Reviewed Prior to Closing.
6.163	Drafting the Seller's Stock Sale Agreement.
6.164	__ Identification of the Parties.
6.165	__ Recitals.
6.166	__ Sale of Shares.
6.167	__ Sale Price and Method of Payment.
6.168	__ Closing.
6.169	__ Representations, Warranties and Covenants of Buyer.
6.170	__ Representations, Warranties and Covenants of Seller.
6.171	__ Conduct of Business Prior to Closing.
6.172	__ Indemnifications.
6.173	__ Matters Respecting Real Property.
6.174	__ Non-disclosure Provisions.
6.175	__ Covenants Not to Compete and Consulting Agreements.
6.176	__ Notice to Customers and Suppliers.

TABLE OF CONTENTS

Sec.
6.177	____ Conditions Precedent to Seller's Obligations.
6.178	____ Conditions Precedent to Buyer's Obligations.
6.179	____ Nature and Survival of Representations and Warranties.
6.180	____ Documents to Be Delivered to Seller at Closing.
6.181	____ Documents to Be Delivered to Buyer at Closing.
6.182	____ Notices, Severability and Other General Provisions.
6.183	____ Documents to Be Prepared or Reviewed Prior to Closing.
6.184	Post–contract and Pre-closing.
6.185	Closing and Post–Closing.
6.186	Forms.
6.187	____ Asset Purchase and Sale Agreement. 💾
6.188	____ Agreement of Purchase and Sale of Stock. 💾

Volume 21

CHAPTER 7. CONSUMER LAW

7.1	Scope Note.
7.2	Strategy—Generally.
7.3	____ Automobile Sales Cases.
7.4	____ Automobile Leasing Cases.
7.5	____ Credit Reporting.
7.6	____ Debt Collection.
7.7	____ Deceptive Business Practices.
7.8	____ Information to Obtain at Outset of Case.
7.9	Lemon Laws.
7.10	____ New Cars.
7.11	____ Used Cars.
7.12	____ Arbitration or Plenary Action?
7.13	____ Arbitration Procedure.
7.14	____ ____ Preparation for the Hearing.
7.15	____ ____ The Hearing.
7.16	____ ____ Appeals and Confirmation Proceedings.
7.17	____ ____ Scope of Review.
7.18	____ Source Materials.
7.19	Automobile Leasing—Overview.
7.20	____ Statutory Protection Overview.
7.21	____ The Consumer Leasing Act.
7.22	____ The Motor Vehicle Retail Leasing Act.
7.23	Motor Vehicle Installment Sales.
7.24	Repossession—Overview.
7.25	____ Prevention and Avoidance.
7.26	____ Defending Deficiency Claims.
7.27	Automobile Repairs.
7.28	Automobile Repair Shop Liens—Overview.
7.29	____ Statutory Challenges.
7.30	Credit Reporting—Overview.
7.31	____ Consumer Rights.
7.32	____ Non-litigation Strategies.
7.33	____ Litigating Credit Reporting Matters.

TABLE OF CONTENTS

Sec.
7.34 Debt Collection—History and Overview.
7.35 ___ Claims for Intentional Infliction of Emotional Distress.
7.36 ___ Statutory Overview.
7.37 ___ FDCPA—Contacts With Third Parties.
7.38 ___ ___Contacts With a Debtor.
7.39 ___ ___ Prohibited Tactics.
7.40 ___ ___ Improper Omissions and Disclosures.
7.41 ___ ___ Harassment or Abuse.
7.42 ___ ___ Improper Demands.
7.43 ___ ___ Judicial Enforcement.
7.44 ___ State Law.
7.45 Deceptive Practices Act—Overview.
7.46 ___ Elements of the Claim.
7.47 ___ Types of Recovery Available.
7.48 Drafting Checklist—List of Essential Allegations.
7.49 Forms—Lemon Law Document Request Pursuant to 13 NYCRR § 300.9(a).
7.50 ___ Notice of Petition to Vacate Lemon Law Arbitration Award Pursuant to CPLR Article 75.
7.51 ___ Petition to Vacate Lemon Law Arbitration Award Pursuant to CPLR Article 75.
7.52 ___ Complaint for Fraud, Breach of Warranties, Deceptive Business Practices, Used Car Lemon Law, Rescission and Revocation of Acceptance for Fraudulent Leasing Practices.
7.53 ___ Answer and Third-party Complaint Alleging Fraud, Deceptive Practices, Breach of Warranty, and Federal Odometer Law Claims in Fraudulent Automobile Lease Case.
7.54 ___ Answer to Complaint by Automobile Leasing Company for Deficiency Following Repossession, Alleging Commercially Unreasonable Resale and Deceptive Business Practices.
7.55 ___ Affirmation in Opposition to Lessor's Motion for Summary Judgment and in Support of Lessee's Cross-motion for Summary Judgment Alleging Commercially Unreasonable Resale.
7.56 ___ Notice of Rescission And/or Revocation of Acceptance and Demand for Restitution Pursuant to UCC 2-601 and 2-608.
7.57 ___ Order to Show Cause in Proceeding under Lien Law § 201-a to Vacate Garageman's Lien.
7.58 ___ Verified Petition in Proceeding under Lien Law § 201-a to Vacate Garageman's Lien.
7.59 ___ Affirmation in Support of Petition in Proceeding under Lien Law § 201-a to Vacate Garageman's Lien.
7.60 ___ Complaint Against Credit Reporting Agency Alleging Violations of the Fair Credit Reporting Act and the New York State Fair Credit Reporting Act and Deceptive Business Practices.
7.61 ___ Stipulation of Settlement of Plaintiff's Lemon Law Claims Providing for Cancellation of Lease and Deletion of Any Derogatory Credit Information.

TABLE OF CONTENTS

Sec.
7.62 ____ Complaint Alleging Violations of the Fair Debt Collection Practices Act and the Deceptive Practices Act. 💾
7.63 ____ Order to Show Cause with Temporary Restraining Order, Seeking Preliminary Injunction in Action Alleging Fraud, Deceptive Business Practices and Breach of Warranties. 💾
7.64 ____ Affirmation in Support of Temporary Restraining Order and Preliminary Injunction in Action Alleging Fraud, Deceptive Business Practices and Breach of Warranties. 💾
7.65 ____ Complaint in Action Alleging Fraud, Deceptive Business Practices and Breach of Warranties. 💾

CHAPTER 8. ENFORCEMENT OF MONEY JUDGMENTS

8.1 Scope Note.
8.2 Strategy.
8.3 Judgments—Generally.
8.4 ____ Methods to Obtain.
8.5 Form of Judgment—Judgment-Roll.
8.6 ____ Interest.
8.7 ____ Fees, Costs and Disbursements.
8.8 ____ Entry.
8.9 ____ Transcript of Judgment.
8.10 Matters Affecting Judgment—Vacatur.
8.11 ____ Satisfaction By Payment or Otherwise.
8.12 ____ Assignment.
8.13 ____ Death of Judgment Debtor.
8.14 ____ Amendment or Correction.
8.15 Actions on Judgments.
8.16 Entry of a Foreign Judgment—Sister-State Judgments.
8.17 ____ Federal Court Judgments.
8.18 ____ Foreign Country Judgments.
8.19 Judgment Enforcement Against Property—Definition of Property.
8.20 ____ Exemptions.
8.21 ____ Property in the Possession of Others.
8.22 ____ Disclosure of Property.
8.23 ____ ____ Subpoenas.
8.24 Article 52 Enforcement Devices—Introduction.
8.25 ____ Restraining Notices—Nature and Use.
8.26 ____ ____ Formal Requirements.
8.27 ____ ____ Service and Punishment for Disobedience.
8.28 ____ Execution.
8.29 ____ ____ Property Execution With Regard to Personal Property.
8.30 ____ ____ ____ Sale, Distribution and Priority In Proceeds.
8.31 ____ ____ Property Execution With Regard to Real Property.
8.32 ____ ____ ____ Notice and Sale of Real Property.
8.33 ____ ____ ____ Distribution of Proceeds of Sale and Conveyance of Title.
8.34 ____ Income Execution.
8.35 ____ Installment Payment Order—Nature and Purpose.
8.36 ____ ____ Form of Application and Service.

TABLE OF CONTENTS

Sec.
8.37	___ Receiver.
8.38	___ ___ Application, Appointment and Extension.
8.39	___ Turnover Orders For Property or Debts.
8.40	___ ___ Turnover Against the Judgment Debtor.
8.41	___ ___ Turnover Against A Garnishee.
8.42	___ Contempt.
8.43	___ Arrest of the Judgment Debtor.
8.44	Protective Orders.
8.45	Proceeding To Determine Adverse Claims.
8.46	Forms.
8.47	___ Statement For Judgment (Default Judgment), Affidavit of Facts Constituting the Claim, the Default and the Amount Due.
8.48	___ Affidavit of Confession of Judgment and Judgment by Confession.
8.49	___ Notice to Judgment Debtor [or Obligor].
8.50	___ Subpoena (*Duces Tecum*) To Take Deposition of Judgment Debtor With Restraining Notice.
8.51	___ Subpoena (*Duces Tecum*) To Take Deposition of Witness With Restraining Notice.
8.52	___ Information Subpoena.
8.53	___ Restraining Notice to Judgment Debtor.
8.54	___ Execution.
8.55	___ Income Execution.
8.56	___ Affirmation and Order To Show Cause To Punish Judgment Debtor—Witness For Contempt.

CHAPTER 9. BANKRUPTCY

9.1	Scope Note.
9.2	Strategy.
9.3	___ Checklist for Representing a Debtor.
9.4	___ Checklist for Representing a Creditor.
9.5	Governing Law.
9.6	Nature of Cases Under Each Chapter of the Bankruptcy Code.
9.7	Eligibility to File.
9.8	Commencement of a Case—Voluntary Cases.
9.9	___ Involuntary Cases.
9.10	___ ___ Procedure.
9.11	___ Additional Requirements.
9.12	___ First–Day Orders.
9.13	Joint Administration.
9.14	Substantive Consolidation.
9.15	Types of Proceedings in Cases Under the Bankruptcy Code.
9.16	___ Adversary Proceedings.
9.17	___ Contested Matters.
9.18	Jurisdiction of the Bankruptcy Court.
9.19	___ Types of Jurisdiction.
9.20	___ Case Ancillary to Foreign Proceedings.
9.21	Venue.
9.22	Withdrawal of Reference.

TABLE OF CONTENTS

Sec.	
9.23	Abstention.
9.24	Removal.
9.25	Appeals—To District Court and Bankruptcy Appellate Panel From Bankruptcy Court.
9.26	___ To Court of Appeals From District Court.
9.27	The Debtor in Possession.
9.28	___ Rights, Powers and Duties.
9.29	Employment of Professionals.
9.30	___ Compensation.
9.31	___ ___ Fee Applications.
9.32	U.S. Trustee.
9.33	___ Duties Owed by Debtors and Trustees.
9.34	Bankruptcy Trustee.
9.35	Mediators.
9.36	Creditors.
9.37	___ Meeting of Creditors.
9.38	___ ___ Scope of Examination.
9.39	Examinations Under Bankruptcy Rule 2004.
9.40	___ Notice Requirements.
9.41	___ Subpoena.
9.42	Right of Parties in Interest to Be Heard.
9.43	Statutory Committees.
9.44	___ Function and Duties.
9.45	___ Right to Bring Litigation.
9.46	___ Fiduciary Duty.
9.47	___ Removal of Members.
9.48	___ Organizational Meeting.
9.49	Property of the Estate.
9.50	Automatic Stay.
9.51	___ Exceptions.
9.52	___ Obtaining Relief.
9.53	___ ___ Strategy.
9.54	___ ___ Hearing.
9.55	___ ___ Single Asset Real Estate Debtor.
9.56	Adequate Protection.
9.57	___ Types.
9.58	___ Strategy.
9.59	___ Objections and Hearing.
9.60	Use, Sale, or Lease of Property.
9.61	___ Ordinary Course of Business.
9.62	___ Outside Ordinary Course of Business.
9.63	___ Sales Free and Clear of Liens.
9.64	___ Appeals from Order Authorizing Sale.
9.65	Cash Collateral.
9.66	___ Strategy.
9.67	___ Hearing.
9.68	___ Postpetition Proceeds.
9.69	___ ___ Security Interests in Rents and Hotel Revenues.
9.70	Abandonment of Property.
9.71	Postpetition Financing.

TABLE OF CONTENTS

Sec.
9.72 ____ Hearing.
9.73 ____ Appeals From Order Authorizing.
9.74 Executory Contracts and Unexpired Leases.
9.75 ____ Strategy.
9.76 ____ Time for Assumption or Rejection.
9.77 ____ Nonresidential Real Property Leases.
9.78 ____ Assumption by the Debtor.
9.79 ____ Assumption and Assignment.
9.80 ____ Exceptions to Assumption and Assignment.
9.81 ____ Rejection by Debtor.
9.82 ____ Damages Arising From Rejection: Debtor as Tenant/Lessee.
9.83 ____ Calculation of Allowed Real Property Lease Rejection Damages.
9.84 ____ Debtor as Landlord/Lessor.
9.85 ____ Unexpired Personal Property Leases.
9.86 Collective Bargaining Agreements.
9.87 Retired Employees' Insurance Benefits.
9.88 ____ Procedure for Modifying.
9.89 Utility Services.
9.90 Claims Procedures.
9.91 ____ Filing Proofs of Claim or Interest.
9.92 ____ ____ Bar Dates.
9.93 ____ Late–Filed Proofs of Claim.
9.94 ____ Amendment of Proofs of Claim or Interest.
9.95 ____ Withdrawal of Claims.
9.96 ____ Allowance of, and Objections to, Claims or Interests.
9.97 ____ Compromise and Settlement of Claims.
9.98 ____ Allowance of Administrative Expense Claims.
9.99 ____ Secured Claims.
9.100 ____ ____ Bifurcation of Claims.
9.101 ____ ____ Avoidance of Liens.
9.102 ____ Interest on Claims and Charges Against Secured Claims.
9.103 ____ Valuation of Collateral.
9.104 ____ ____ Methods of Valuation.
9.105 ____ Reclamation Claims.
9.106 Priorities.
9.107 Subordination.
9.108 ____ Strategy.
9.109 Setoff.
9.110 ____ Strategy.
9.111 ____ Characteristics of Claims.
9.112 Recoupment.
9.113 The Avoiding Powers.
9.114 ____ Strategy.
9.115 ____ Strong Arm Powers.
9.116 ____ Avoidance of Certain Statutory Liens.
9.117 ____ Preferences.
9.118 ____ Exceptions to the Avoidance of Preferential Transfers.
9.119 ____ Fraudulent Conveyances.
9.120 ____ Liability of Transferee of Avoided Transfer.

TABLE OF CONTENTS

Sec.
9.121 ____ Statute of Limitations and Standing.
9.122 ____ Relation–Back Provision.
9.123 ____ Reclamation.
9.124 Return of Goods by Debtor.
9.125 Exemptions.
9.126 ____ Procedure.
9.127 ____ Objections.
9.128 ____ Lien Avoidance.
9.129 ____ Liens on Exempt Property.
9.130 Reaffirmation of Debts.
9.131 ____ Strategy.
9.132 Protection Against Discriminatory Treatment.
9.133 Tax Considerations.
9.134 Conversion and Dismissal of Cases Under Title 11.
9.135 Effect of Conversion.
9.136 Effect of Dismissal.
9.137 Closing and Reopening Cases.
9.138 Chapter 11—Appointment of a Trustee.
9.139 ____ Duties of a Trustee.
9.140 ____ Appointment of an Examiner.
9.141 ____ Duties of an Examiner.
9.142 ____ Exclusivity—Right to File a Plan.
9.143 ____ ____ Small Businesses.
9.144 ____ ____ Strategy: Representing a Debtor.
9.145 ____ ____ Strategy: Representing a Creditor.
9.146 ____ ____ Appealability of Orders.
9.147 ____ Plan.
9.148 ____ ____ Mandatory Provisions.
9.149 ____ ____ Discretionary Provisions.
9.150 ____ ____ Exemption from Securities Registration.
9.151 ____ ____ Retention of Jurisdiction by the Court.
9.152 ____ Classification of Claims.
9.153 ____ ____ Effect on Voting.
9.154 ____ ____ Substantially Similar Claims.
9.155 ____ ____ Convenience Class.
9.156 ____ Recourse and Nonrecourse Claims: The § 1111(b) Election.
9.157 ____ ____ Strategy.
9.158 ____ Impairment of Claims or Interests.
9.159 ____ ____ Rights Are Altered.
9.160 ____ ____ Defaults Are Not Cured.
9.161 ____ Disclosure and Solicitation.
9.162 ____ Acceptance of a Plan.
9.163 ____ Prepackaged and Prenegotiated Plans.
9.164 ____ Modification of a Plan.
9.165 ____ Confirmation.
9.166 ____ Cramdown.
9.167 ____ Effect of Confirmation.
9.168 ____ Discharge.
9.169 ____ ____ Limitations.
9.170 ____ ____ Release of Nondebtor.

TABLE OF CONTENTS

Sec.	
9.171	____ Channelling Injunctions: Asbestos–Related Cases.
9.172	____ Plan Implementation.
9.173	____ Small Business Reorganizations.
9.174	____ Conversion or Dismissal of Cases.
9.175	____ ____ Procedure.
9.176	____ Closing and Reopening Cases.
9.177	Chapter 7—Overview.
9.178	____ Commencement of a Case.
9.179	____ Fees.
9.180	____ Appointment of an Interim Trustee.
9.181	____ Election of a Permanent Trustee.
9.182	____ Duties of a Trustee.
9.183	____ Employment of Professionals.
9.184	____ Creditors' Committee.
9.185	____ Protection Against Discriminatory Treatment.
9.186	____ The Debtor's Statement of Intention.
9.187	____ Exemptions.
9.188	____ Redemption of Property.
9.189	____ ____ Procedure.
9.190	____ Reaffirmation of Debts.
9.191	____ Abandonment of Property.
9.192	____ Debtor's Surrender of Property and Records.
9.193	____ Trustee's Turnover Powers.
9.194	____ Liability of General Partners.
9.195	____ Trustee's Operation of the Business.
9.196	____ Executory Contracts.
9.197	____ Adversary Proceedings to Avoid Liens and Transfers.
9.198	____ ____ Statute of Limitations.
9.199	____ Treatment of Certain Liens.
9.200	____ Trustee's Sale of Assets.
9.201	____ Disposition of Property Subject to the Interest of Another.
9.202	____ Priorities.
9.203	____ Special Tax Provisions.
9.204	____ Discharge.
9.205	____ ____ Exceptions to General Discharge of the Debtor.
9.206	____ ____ Procedure for Objections to General Discharge of the Debtor.
9.207	____ ____ Exceptions to Discharge of Particular Debts.
9.208	____ ____ Procedure for Objections to Discharge of Particular Debts.
9.209	____ Conversion or Dismissal of Cases.
9.210	____ ____ Procedure.
9.211	____ Closing and Reopening Cases.
9.212	Chapter 12—Overview.
9.213	____ Rights and Powers of Debtor.
9.214	____ Appointment of a Trustee.
9.215	____ Duties of a Trustee.
9.216	____ Automatic Stay.
9.217	____ Property of the Estate.
9.218	____ Sales Free of Interests.

TABLE OF CONTENTS

Sec.
9.219	___ Adequate Protection.
9.220	___ Exclusivity—Right to File a Plan.
9.221	___ Plan.
9.222	___ ___ Mandatory Provisions.
9.223	___ ___ Discretionary Provisions.
9.224	___ ___ Modification.
9.225	___ ___ Confirmation.
9.226	___ ___ Confirmation: Objections.
9.227	___ Disbursements.
9.228	___ Effect of Confirmation.
9.229	___ Discharge.
9.230	___ Modification after Confirmation.
9.231	___ Special Tax Provisions.
9.232	___ Revocation of Confirmation Order.
9.233	___ Conversion or Dismissal of Cases.
9.234	___ ___ Procedure.
9.235	___ Closing and Reopening Cases.
9.236	Chapter 13—Overview.
9.237	___ Eligibility.
9.238	___ Rights and Powers of Debtor.
9.239	___ Appointment of a Trustee.
9.240	___ Duties of a Trustee.
9.241	___ Automatic Stay.
9.242	___ ___ Relief.
9.243	___ Property of the Estate.
9.244	___ ___ Use, Sale, or Lease.
9.245	___ Exclusivity—Right to File a Plan.
9.246	___ Plan.
9.247	___ ___ Mandatory Provisions.
9.248	___ ___ Discretionary Provisions.
9.249	___ ___ Discretionary Provisions: Debtor's Principal Residence.
9.250	___ ___ Modification.
9.251	___ ___ Confirmation.
9.252	___ ___ Confirmation: Objections.
9.253	___ ___ Confirmation: Effect.
9.254	___ Payments.
9.255	___ Discharge.
9.256	___ ___ Exceptions.
9.257	___ ___ Objections.
9.258	___ ___ Revocation.
9.259	___ Postconfirmation Modification of a Plan.
9.260	___ Revocation of Confirmation Order.
9.261	___ Conversion or Dismissal of Cases.
9.262	___ ___ Procedure.
9.263	___ Closing and Reopening Cases.
9.264	Procedural Checklist—Commencing a Voluntary Case.
9.265	___ Lists and Schedules to be Filed at the Commencement of a Case Under Chapter 7, 11, 12, or 13.
9.266	___ Commencing an Adversary Proceeding.
9.267	___ Commencing a Contested Matter.

TABLE OF CONTENTS

Sec.

9.268	___ Appeal from an Interlocutory Judgment, Order, or Decree of a Bankruptcy Judge.
9.269	___ Creditor's Motion to Request Relief from the Automatic Stay.
9.270	___ Creditor's Motion to Obtain Adequate Protection.
9.271	___ Debtor's Motion to Use, Sell, or Lease Property of the Estate.
9.272	___ Debtor's Motion to Request Use of Cash Collateral.
9.273	___ Cash Collateral Stipulation.
9.274	___ Debtor's Motion to Obtain Postpetition Financing.
9.275	___ Request to Assume, Reject, or Assign an Executory Contract or Unexpired Nonresidential Real Property Lease.
9.276	___ Debtor's Motion to Reject or Modify a Collective Bargaining Agreement.
9.277	___ Debtor's Motion to Obtain Approval of a Compromise and Settlement of a Claim.
9.278	___ Claiming Exemptions.
9.279	___ Debtor's Motion to Avoid a Judicial Lien or a Nonpossessory, Nonpurchase–Money Security Interest that Impairs Exempt Property.
9.280	___ Debtor's Motion to Obtain Court Approval of a Reaffirmation Agreement.
9.281	___ Debtor's Motion to Request an Extension of Exclusivity.
9.282	___ Filing a Chapter 11 Plan and Disclosure Statement.
9.283	___ Soliciting Acceptance of a Chapter 11 Plan.
9.284	___ Filing a Chapter 12 or 13 Plan of Debt Adjustment.
9.285	___ Objection to a Chapter 12 or 13 Plan.
9.286	___ Debtor's Motion to Request Modification of a Chapter 12 or 13 Plan after Confirmation
9.287	Drafting Checklist—General Rules for all Motions, Applications, and Complaints.
9.288	___ Complaint in an Adversary Proceeding.
9.289	___ Motion for Leave to Appeal From an Interlocutory Judgment, Order, or Decree of a Bankruptcy Judge.
9.290	___ Motion for a Stay of a Bankruptcy Court Judgment or Order Pending Appeal.
9.291	___ Application of Debtor or Statutory Committee to Retain Professionals.
9.292	___ Creditor's Motion to Request Relief From the Automatic Stay.
9.293	___ Creditor's Motion to Obtain Adequate Protection.
9.294	___ Debtor's Motion to Use, Sell, or Lease Property of the Estate.
9.295	___ Debtor's Motion to Request Use of Cash Collateral.
9.296	___ Cash Collateral Stipulation.
9.297	___ Debtor's Motion to Obtain Postpetition Financing.
9.298	___ Motion to Assume or Reject an Executory Contract or Unexpired Non-residential Real Property Lease.
9.299	___ Debtor's Motion to Reject or Modify a Collective Bargaining Agreement (CBA).
9.300	___ Debtor's Motion to Obtain Approval of a Compromise and Settlement of a Claim.

TABLE OF CONTENTS

Sec.
9.301 ____ Debtor's Motion to Avoid a Judicial Lien or a Nonpossessory, Nonpurchase–Money Security Interest that Impairs Exempt Property.
9.302 ____ Reaffirmation Agreement.
9.303 ____ Debtor's Motion for Approval of a Reaffirmation Agreement.
9.304 ____ Debtor's Motion to Request an Extension of Exclusivity.
9.305 Forms—Notice of Appearance and Demand for Service of Documents. 💾
9.306 ____ Contested Matter—Motion. 💾
9.307 ____ ____ Notice of Motion. 💾
9.308 ____ ____ Proposed Order. 💾
9.309 ____ Adversary Proceeding—Complaint. 💾
9.310 ____ Retention of Professionals—Application. 💾
9.311 ____ ____ Affidavit. 💾
9.312 ____ Plan Provision for Retention of Jurisdiction. 💾

CHAPTER 10. MECHANIC'S LIENS

10.1 Scope Note.
10.2 Strategy.
10.3 Nature of Mechanic's Lien.
10.4 Creation of Mechanic's Lien—Elements.
10.5 ____ ____ Protected Class.
10.6 ____ ____ Improvements to Real Property.
10.7 ____ ____ Consent or Request of Owner.
10.8 Extent of Lien—Ownership Interest at Time of Filing.
10.9 ____ Sale of Property.
10.10 ____ Insurance Proceeds.
10.11 ____ Amount.
10.12 ____ Loss of Profits.
10.13 Subcontractors and Materialmen—Derivative Rights.
10.14 ____ ____ Statutory Protections.
10.15 Procedure—Notice of Lien.
10.16 ____ ____ Contents.
10.17 ____ ____ Filing.
10.18 ____ ____ Service.
10.19 Amendment of Notice of Lien.
10.20 Lien for Private Improvements—Checklist.
10.21 Liens Under Contract for Public Improvements—Extent of Lien.
10.22 ____ Notice of Lien.
10.23 ____ Filing of Notice of Lien.
10.24 ____ Notice of Completion and Acceptance.
10.25 ____ Checklist.
10.26 Lien Priorities—Private Improvements—Parity of Mechanic's Liens.
10.27 ____ ____ Assignments of Contract Rights.
10.28 ____ ____ Building Loan Mortgages.
10.29 ____ ____ Contracts of Sale.
10.30 ____ ____ Seller's Mortgage.
10.31 ____ ____ Deeds.

TABLE OF CONTENTS

Sec.
10.32	___ Contracts for Public Improvements.
10.33	Assignment of Liens.
10.34	Assignments of Contracts for Private Improvements and Orders to be Filed—Filing of Notice of Assignment.
10.35	___ Contents of Notice of Assignment.
10.36	___ Extension of Term of Notice of Assignment.
10.37	Assignment of Contracts and Orders for Public Improvements.
10.38	Duration of Lien for Private Improvements—Notice of Pendency.
10.39	___ Extensions.
10.40	Duration of Lien Under Contract for a Public Improvement—Notice of Pendency.
10.41	___ Extension of Lien.
10.42	Discharge of Lien for Private Improvement—Satisfaction of Lien.
10.43	___ Expiration of Term.
10.44	___ Termination of Notice of Pendency.
10.45	___ Failure to Prosecute.
10.46	___ Undertaking.
10.47	___ Judgment.
10.48	___ Defective Lien.
10.49	___ Deposit of Money with County Clerk or Court.
10.50	Discharge of Lien for Public Improvement—Satisfaction of Lien.
10.51	___ Expiration of Lien.
10.52	___ Satisfaction of Judgment.
10.53	___ Deposit of Money.
10.54	___ Undertaking.
10.55	___ Retention of Credit.
10.56	___ Invalidity of Lien.
10.57	___ Failure to Prosecute.
10.58	___ Procedures.
10.59	Building Loan Contracts—Filing Requirements.
10.60	___ Checklist.
10.61	Subordination of Liens—Agreement with Owner.
10.62	___ ___ Postponement of Judgments.
10.63	Subordination of Liens to Subsequent Mortgage.
10.64	Subordination of Notices of *Lis Pendens*.
10.65	Discharge of Liens on Sale of Real Property.
10.66	Limitations on Waiver of Mechanic's Lien.
10.67	Effect of Filing of Notice of Lien on Right of Arbitration.
10.68	Bond to Discharge Liens—Effect of Bond.
10.69	___ Requirements of Bond.
10.70	___ Claim Against Bond.
10.71	___ Notice of Claim.
10.72	___ Action on Bond.
10.73	___ Discharge of Liens and Notices of Claims.
10.74	Protecting the Owner—Itemized Statement.
10.75	___ Lien Wilfully Exaggerated.
10.76	Repossession of Materials Not Used.
10.77	Enforcement of Mechanic's Liens—Courts.
10.78	___ Courts of Record—Procedures.
10.79	___ ___ Necessary Parties.

TABLE OF CONTENTS

Sec.
10.80 ____ Actions in a Court Not of Record—Summons and Complaint.
10.81 ____ ____ Proceedings Upon Return of Summons.
10.82 ____ ____ Judgments and Transcripts.
10.83 ____ Costs and Disbursements.
10.84 ____ Effect of Failure to Establish Lien.
10.85 ____ Deposit of Money or Securities to Discharge Lien—Procedures.
10.86 ____ ____ Effect of Order.
10.87 ____ ____ Preference Over Contractors.
10.88 ____ ____ Delivery of Property in Lieu of Money.
10.89 ____ Deficiency Judgment.
10.90 ____ Vacating of Mechanic's Lien, Cancellation of Bond or Return of Deposit.
10.91 ____ Public Improvements.
10.92 ____ New Parties.
10.93 ____ Service of Answer on State or Public Corporation.
10.94 Trust Funds—Purpose.
10.95 ____ Creation.
10.96 ____ Contractors and Subcontractors.
10.97 ____ Beneficiaries.
10.98 Diversion of Trust Assets.
10.99 Notice of Lending.
10.100 Record Keeping Obligations.
10.101 Right of Beneficiaries to Examine Books or Records.
10.102 Action to Enforce Trust—Standing and Procedure.
10.103 ____ Remedies.
10.104 ____ Preferences.
10.105 Relief After Judgment on Obligation Constituting Trust Claim; Effect on Mechanic's Liens.
10.106 Misappropriation of Trust Funds.
10.107 Procedural Checklist.
10.108 Forms.
10.109 ____ Notice of Mechanic's Lien—General Form.
10.110 ____ Notice of Lien for Public Improvement.
10.111 ____ Form For Demand for Terms of Contract.
10.112 ____ Demand for Notice of Completion and Acceptance of Public Improvement.
10.113 ____ Petition to Amend Notice of Mechanic's Lien—Correct Name of Owner of Property.
10.114 ____ Assignment of Lien for Public Improvement.
10.115 ____ Assignment of Mechanic's Lien.
10.116 ____ Assignment of Moneys Due or to Become Due Under Public Improvement Contract.
10.117 ____ Affidavit for Continuance of Mechanic's Lien.
10.118 ____ Affidavit for Continuance of Lien for Public Improvement.
10.119 ____ Petition to Discharge Mechanic's Lien Where Notice of Lien Defective.
10.120 ____ Petition for Order Discharging Mechanic's Lien Upon Filing of Undertaking.

TABLE OF CONTENTS

Sec.
10.121 ____ Undertaking to Discharge Mechanic's Lien.
10.122 ____ Petition for Order Fixing Amount of Undertaking to Discharge Mechanic's Lien.
10.123 ____ Approval by Lienors of Subordination of Mechanic's Liens to Trust Bond or Note and Mortgage.
10.124 ____ Affidavit for Order Fixing Amount of Bond to Discharge All Mechanic's Liens.
10.125 ____ Petition for Order Requiring Itemized Statement.
10.126 ____ Notice of Application for Order Requiring Itemized Statement.
10.127 ____ Demand for Itemized Statement.
10.128 ____ Affidavit in Support of Application to Cancel Mechanic's Lien for Failure to Furnish Itemized Statement.
10.129 ____ Notice Requiring Lienor to Commence Action to Enforce Mechanic's Lien.
10.130 ____ Affidavit in Support of Application to Cancel Notice of Mechanic's Lien for Failure to Commence Action.
10.131 ____ Notice Requiring Lienor to Commence Action to Enforce Lien for Public Improvement.
10.132 ____ Affidavit in Support of Application to Cancel Notice of Lien for Public Improvement for Failure to Commence Action.
10.133 ____ Complaint for Foreclosure of Lien for Public Improvement.
10.134 ____ Complaint for Foreclosure of Mechanic's Lien—Contractor.
10.135 ____ Defense and Counterclaim Based on Wilful Exaggeration of Mechanic's Lien.
10.136 ____ Affidavit in Support of Motion to Consolidate Actions for Foreclosure of Mechanic's Liens.
10.137 ____ Notice of Motion to Consolidate Actions to Foreclose Mechanic's Liens.
10.138 ____ Acceptance of Offer to Pay Money Into Court in Discharge of Mechanic's Lien.
10.139 ____ Offer to Pay Money Into Court in Discharge of Mechanic's Lien.
10.140 ____ Judgment of Foreclosure and Sale—Mechanic's Lien.
10.141 ____ Judgment of Foreclosure—Lien for Public Improvement—Where Lien Discharged and Fund Retained for Payment.
10.142 ____ Affidavit in Support of Motion for Summary Judgment—Foreclosure of Lien for Public Improvement.
10.143 ____ Demand for Verified Statement from Trustee.
10.144 ____ Petition for Verified Statement from Trustee of Trust Funds.
10.145 ____ Complaint by Subcontractor to Enforce Trust Against Funds Received by Contractor or Assignee of Contractor.
10.146 ____ Complaint by Surety to Have Parties Declared Trustees of Subcontract Moneys and for Accounting.
10.147 ____ Affidavit in Support of Motion to Determine if Class Action Can be Maintained—Action to Impress and Enforce Trust.

TABLE OF CONTENTS

CHAPTER 11. MORTGAGE FORECLOSURE

Sec.
11.1	Scope Note.
11.2	Strategy—Initial Client Interview.
11.3	—— First Review of Loan Documents.
11.4	—— Foreclosure Title Certificate.
11.5	New York Mortgage Foreclosure Law.
11.6	—— Choice of Remedies: Foreclosure Action or Money Action.
11.7	—— Partial Foreclosure Action.
11.8	—— Non–Judicial Foreclosure.
11.9	Representing Subordinate Lienors.
11.10	Pre-commencement Procedure.
11.11	—— Notice of Default.
11.12	—— Notice of Acceleration.
11.13	—— Foreclosure Title Certificate.
11.14	Determining the Necessary Defendants.
11.15	—— The United States As a Necessary Defendant.
11.16	Starting the Foreclosure Action.
11.17	—— Notice of Pendency of Action.
11.18	Summons.
11.19	—— Venue.
11.20	Complaint.
11.21	—— Allegations Regarding Parties.
11.22	—— Allegations Regarding Loan, Note and Mortgage.
11.23	—— References to Pertinent Terms of Note and Mortgage.
11.24	—— Asserting Default(s).
11.25	—— Reserving Right to Add Advances Made by Plaintiff to Indebtedness Secured by Mortgage.
11.26	—— Allegation Regarding Subordinate Interest of Defendant(s).
11.27	—— Whether There Has Been or is Pending Another Action Regarding the Mortgage Debt.
11.28	—— Amendments.
11.29	Receivers.
11.30	—— Considerations in Determining Whether to Seek Appointment of Receiver.
11.31	—— *Ex Parte* Motion for Appointment of Receiver.
11.32	—— Compensation.
11.33	—— Opposing Appointment of Receiver.
11.34	—— Discharging Receiver.
11.35	Defendant's Response.
11.36	—— Motion to Dismiss Complaint.
11.37	—— Answer and Defenses.
11.38	—— Notice of Appearance and Waiver.
11.39	Obtaining Judgment.
11.40	—— Motion for Judgment.
11.41	—— Opposing Motion for Judgment.
11.42	Reference to Compute.
11.43	—— Hearing Before Referee to Compute.
11.44	—— Report of Referee to Compute.
11.45	—— Motion to Confirm Referee's Computation Report and for Judgment of Foreclosure and Sale.

TABLE OF CONTENTS

Sec.
11.46	Judgment of Foreclosure and Sale.
11.47	Foreclosure Sale.
11.48	___ Noticing and Advertising the Sale.
11.49	___ Conducting the Sale.
11.50	___ Vacating the Sale.
11.51	Referee's Deed, Other Closing Documents and Referee's Report of Sale.
11.52	Deficiency Judgment.
11.53	Surplus Money Proceedings.
11.54	Eviction of Tenants and Other Occupants After Foreclosure Sale.
11.55	Drafting Checklists.
11.56	___ Notice of Default.
11.57	___ Notice of Acceleration.
11.58	___ Notice of Pendency of Action.
11.59	___ Summons.
11.60	___ Complaint.
11.61	___ Order Appointing Receiver.
11.62	___ Affidavit in Support of *Ex Parte* Application for Receiver.
11.63	___ Notice of Motion for Summary Judgment and Related Relief.
11.64	___ Affidavit of Regularity and in Support of Plaintiff's Motion for Summary Judgment and Related Relief.
11.65	___ Judgment of Foreclosure and Sale.
11.66	___ Notice of Sale.
11.67	___ Terms and Memorandum of Sale.
11.68	Forms.
11.69	___ Notice of Default. 💾
11.70	___ Notice of Acceleration. 💾
11.71	___ Notice of Pendency of Action. 💾
11.72	___ Summons. 💾
11.73	___ Verified Complaint for Foreclosure of Mortgage Affecting Single Family Residence. 💾
11.74	___ Verified Complaint for Foreclosure of Mortgage Affecting Commercial, Multi–Unit Residential or Mixed Property. 💾
11.75	___ Order Appointing Receiver. 💾
11.76	___ Affidavit in Support of Motion for Appointment of Receiver. 💾
11.77	___ Notice of Motion for Summary Judgment and Related Relief. 💾
11.78	___ Affidavit of Regularity and in Support of Motion for Summary Judgment. 💾
11.79	___ Judgment of Foreclosure and Sale. 💾
11.80	___ Notice of Sale. 💾
11.81	___ Terms and Memorandum of Sale. 💾

CHAPTER 12. PURCHASE AND SALE OF REAL ESTATE

12.1	Scope Note.
12.2	Strategy.
12.3	___ Pre-contract Checklist.
12.4	Contract of Sale.

XLVI

TABLE OF CONTENTS

Sec.
12.5	___ Preparation and Delivery
12.6	___ Recordation.
12.7	Residential Contract of Sale.
12.8	___ Parties.
12.9	___ Premises.
12.10	___ Personal Property.
12.11	___ Purchase Price and Method of Payment.
12.12	___ ___ Down Payment.
12.13	___ ___ Assumption of Existing Mortgage.
12.14	___ ___ Purchase Money Mortgage.
12.15	___ ___ Mortgage Contingency.
12.16	___ ___ Acceptable Funds.
12.17	___ Permitted Exceptions.
12.18	___ Governmental Violations and Orders.
12.19	___ Seller's Representations.
12.20	___ Condition of Property.
12.21	___ Insurable and Marketable Title.
12.22	___ Closing, Deed and Title.
12.23	___ Closing Date and Place.
12.24	___ Conditions to Closing.
12.25	___ Deed Transfer and Recording Taxes.
12.26	___ Apportionments.
12.27	___ Allowance for Unpaid Taxes.
12.28	___ Title Examination; Seller's Inability to Convey; Limitation of Liability.
12.29	___ Defaults and Remedies.
12.30	___ Assignment.
12.31	___ Broker.
12.32	___ Risk of Loss.
12.33	Condominium Contract of Sale.
12.34	___ Comparisons to the Residential Contract of Sale.
12.35	___ Homeowner's Associations.
12.36	Contract of Sale for Office, Commercial and Multi-family Residential Premises.
12.37	Contract of Sale for Cooperative Apartment
12.38	___ Standard Form.
12.39	Contract of Sale for New Construction.
12.40	Title Insurance.
12.41	___ The Buyer's Obligation.
12.42	___ Role of the Title Insurer.
12.43	___ Duration and Cost.
12.44	___ Basic and Extended Coverage.
12.45	Title Insurance Policy.
12.46	___ Loan Policy Coverage.
12.47	___ New York Modifications of Loan Policy.
12.48	___ Owner's Policy Coverage.
12.49	___ New York Modifications of Owner's Policy.
12.50	___ Standard Exceptions.
12.51	___ Endorsements.
12.52	___ Exclusions.

TABLE OF CONTENTS

Sec.
12.53 Title Examination: Recording Title and the Torrens System.
12.54 ____ Objections to Be Disposed of Prior to Closing.
12.55 ____ ____ Checklist.
12.56 The Survey Map.
12.57 ____ What it May Disclose.
12.58 ____ Effect on Marketability of Title.
12.59 ____ ____ Where Contract Is Silent on the Matter of Survey.
12.60 ____ ____ Where Contract Subject to Any State of Facts an Accurate Survey May Show.
12.61 ____ ____ Where Contract Subject to Any State of Facts an Accurate Survey May Show Provided Same Does Not Render Title Unmarketable.
12.62 ____ ____ Where Contract Subject to Specific Encroachments or to Facts Shown on a Specific Survey.
12.63 ____ ____ Suggested Clause.
12.64 Marketability of Title.
12.65 ____ What Renders Title Unmarketable.
12.66 ____ ____ Encroachments Due to Adverse Possession.
12.67 ____ ____ Party Walls.
12.68 ____ Driveway Easements.
12.69 ____ Other Covenants and Restrictions.
12.70 ____ Reservations for Public Utilities.
12.71 ____ Land Abutting Bodies of Water and the Federal Navigational Servitude.
12.72 Closing of Title.
12.73 ____ Checklist.
12.74 ____ Recording Fees and Filings.
12.75 ____ Disclosure and Other Requirements.
12.76 ____ ____ Foreign Investors Real Property Tax.
12.77 ____ ____ Form 1099–S Federal Requirement for One to Four Family Residence.
12.78 ____ ____ Form 1099–S Federal Requirement for One to Four Family Residence—Checklist.
12.79 ____ ____ Cash Payments Received by Businesses in Excess of $10,000.
12.80 ____ ____ Lead Paint Hazards.
12.81 ____ ____ Agricultural Foreign Investment Disclosure Act.
12.82 ____ Payment of Taxes.
12.83 ____ ____ New York State Real Estate Transfer Tax and Mansion Tax.
12.84 ____ ____ Article 31–B—Real Property Transfer Gains Tax.
12.85 ____ ____ New York City Real Property Transfer Tax.
12.86 ____ ____ Cities of Mount Vernon and Yonkers.
12.87 ____ ____ Real Estate Investment Trusts.
12.88 ____ ____ Mortgage Recording Tax Outside New York City.
12.89 ____ ____ Mortgage Recording Tax Rate in New York City.
12.90 ____ Method of Payment.
12.91 ____ Other Required Forms and Information.
12.92 Forms.
12.93 ____ Residential Contract of Sale.

TABLE OF CONTENTS

Sec.
12.94 ___ Contract of Sale—Condominium Unit.
12.95 ___ ___ Office, Commercial and Multi–Family Residential Premises.
12.96 ___ ___ Cooperative Apartment.
12.97 ___ Durable General Power of Attorney. 💾
12.98 ___ Power of Attorney to Take Effect at a Later Time. 💾

Volume 22

CHAPTER 13. LANDLORD–TENANT LAW

13.1 Scope Note.
13.2 Strategy.
13.3 ___ Checklists.
13.4 Summary Proceedings.
13.5 ___ Venue and Jurisdiction.
13.6 ___ Service of Process.
13.7 ___ ___ Personal Delivery.
13.8 ___ ___ Substituted Service.
13.9 ___ ___ Conspicuous Place Service.
13.10 ___ ___ New York City Civil Court "Postcard Requirement."
13.11 Non-payment Proceedings.
13.12 ___ Rent Demands.
13.13 ___ Notice of Petition.
13.14 ___ ___ Form of Notice.
13.15 ___ ___ Content of Notice.
13.16 ___ ___ Defects in the Notice.
13.17 ___ The Petition.
13.18 ___ ___ Defects in the Petition.
13.19 ___ ___ Verification.
13.20 ___ ___ Defects in the Verification.
13.21 Responding to the Non-payment Petition.
13.22 ___ The Answer.
13.23 ___ The Motion to Dismiss.
13.24 ___ The RPAPL § 755 Motion to Stay.
13.25 Tenant Defenses to the Non-payment Proceeding.
13.26 ___ No Landlord Tenant Relationship.
13.27 ___ Tenant Out of Possession.
13.28 ___ Statutory Noncompliance.
13.29 ___ Illegal Rent.
13.30 ___ Actual Eviction.
13.31 ___ Constructive Eviction.
13.32 ___ Warranty of Habitability.
13.33 ___ Laches.
13.34 ___ Payment.
13.35 Holdover Proceedings.
13.36 ___ Predicate Notices.
13.37 ___ ___ Month-to-Month Tenants.
13.38 ___ ___ Illegal Use.
13.39 ___ ___ Rent–Controlled Tenants.

TABLE OF CONTENTS

Sec.
13.40	___ ___ Rent–Stabilized Tenants.
13.41	___ The Notice of Petition.
13.42	___ ___ Defects in the Notice.
13.43	___ Holdover Petition—Form and Content.
13.44	___ ___ Defects in the Petition.
13.45	___ ___ Verification and Verification Defects.
13.46	Responding to the Holdover Petition.
13.47	___ The Answer.
13.48	___ The Motion to Dismiss.
13.49	Tenant Defenses to the Holdover Proceeding.
13.50	___ Acceptance of Rent After Expiration or Termination of Tenancy.
13.51	___ Defective Predicate Notice.
13.52	___ ___ Rent–Regulated Apartments.
13.53	___ Waiver.
13.54	___ Equitable Estoppel.
13.55	___ Succession Rights to Rent–Regulated Apartments.
13.56	Counterclaims.
13.57	Bill of Particulars.
13.58	Discovery.
13.59	___ Notice to Admit.
13.60	___ Freedom of Information Law.
13.61	The Trial—Adjournments.
13.62	___Amending Petition and Burden of Proof.
13.63	Stipulations—Overview.
13.64	___ Non-payment Proceedings.
13.65	___ Holdover Proceedings.
13.66	___ Enforcement and Vacatur.
13.67	The Judgment and Warrant.
13.68	___ Staying the Warrant in Non-payment Proceedings.
13.69	___ Staying the Warrant in New York City Residential Holdover Proceedings.
13.70	Yellowstone Actions.
13.71	___ Obtaining the Injunction.
13.72	Article 7–A Proceedings.
13.73	Rent Regulatory Proceedings.
13.74	___ Rent Overcharge.
13.75	___ Service Reduction.
13.76	___ Major Capital Improvement Rent Increase.
13.77	Checklist of Essential Allegations.
13.78	___ Petition Non-payment.
13.79	___ Holdover Petition.
13.80	___ Stipulation Settling Non-payment Proceeding.
13.81	___ Stipulation Settling Holdover Proceeding.
13.82	Forms.
13.83	___ Petition Non-payment. 💾
13.84	___ Petition Holdover. 💾
13.85	___ Individual Verification. 💾
13.86	___ Corporate Officer Verification. 💾
13.87	___ Partnership Verification. 💾

TABLE OF CONTENTS

Sec.
13.88 ____ Attorney Verification.
13.89 ____ Stipulations.
13.90 ____ ____ Settling Non-payment Proceeding.
13.91 ____ ____ Settling Non-payment Proceeding With Final Judgment in Favor of Petitioner.
13.92 ____ ____ Settling Holdover Proceeding Where Tenant Agrees to Cure Lease Violation.
13.93 ____ ____ Settling Holdover Proceeding Where Tenant–Respondent Agrees to Vacate Premises.

CHAPTER 14. EMINENT DOMAIN

14.1 Scope Note.
14.2 Strategies for Condemnors and Condemnees.
14.3 Exercise of the Power of Eminent Domain.
14.4 ____ The State as Condemnor.
14.5 ____ Other Public Entities as Condemnor.
14.6 ____ Private Entities.
14.7 Property Rights Subject to Acquisition.
14.8 ____ Real Property.
14.9 ____ Easements.
14.10 ____ Leases.
14.11 ____ Personal Property.
14.12 ____ Public Property/Priority of Taking.
14.13 ____ Excess Property.
14.14 *De Facto* Taking.
14.15 Public Use, Benefit or Purpose.
14.16 ____ Particular Uses.
14.17 ____ Incidental Private Benefit.
14.18 Just Compensation.
14.19 Summary.
14.20 The First Stage: The Condemnation Phase.
14.21 Public Hearing.
14.22 Exemptions From the Public Hearing Requirement.
14.23 ____ Overlap with Other Governmental Requirements.
14.24 ____ Overlap with Issuance of a Certificate of Environmental Compatibility and Public Need.
14.25 ____ Alternate Public Hearing.
14.26 ____ *De Minimis* Acquisition or Emergency Situation.
14.27 ____ Section 41.34 of the Mental Hygiene Law.
14.28 Notice.
14.29 Conduct of the Public Hearing and Requirement of a Record.
14.30 Determination and Findings.
14.31 ____ Publication of Synopsis.
14.32 ____ Interplay with SEQRA.
14.33 ____ Amendments for Field Conditions.
14.34 Judicial Review of Determination and Findings.
14.35 ____ Prerequisite Determination.
14.36 ____ Persons Entitled to Review.
14.37 ____ 30–Day Statute of Limitations.

TABLE OF CONTENTS

Sec.
14.38 ──── Scope of Review.
14.39 Summary.
14.40 The Second Stage—The "Offer and Negotiation" Phase.
14.41 ──── Pretaking Appraisals.
14.42 ──── Pretaking Discovery.
14.43 ──── Offer as Payment in Full.
14.44 ──── Advance Payment.
14.45 Use and Occupancy by Condemnee After Taking.
14.46 Summary.
14.47 The Third Stage—The Acquisition Phase.
14.48 ──── Court of Claims v. Supreme Court Jurisdiction.
14.49 ──── Statute of Limitations for Bringing an Acquisition Proceeding.
14.50 ──── ──── Acquisition in Stages.
14.51 ──── Acquisition Map.
14.52 Acquisition of Property—Court of Claims Jurisdiction.
14.53 ──── Condemnors Subject to Court of Claims Jurisdiction.
14.54 ──── Filing and Notice Requirements.
14.55 ──── Vesting of Title.
14.56 Acquisition of Property—Supreme Court Jurisdiction.
14.57 ──── Notice of Pendency.
14.58 ──── Petition in Condemnation.
14.59 ──── ──── Content.
14.60 ──── ──── Additional Content Rules for Certain Non-governmental Condemnors.
14.61 ──── Notice.
14.62 ──── ──── Certification of Names of Reputed Condemnees.
14.63 ──── Answer by Condemnee.
14.64 ──── ──── Defenses.
14.65 ──── Vesting of Title and Order of Condemnation.
14.66 Notice of Acquisition.
14.67 Immediate Entry.
14.68 Summary.
14.69 The Fourth Stage—The Compensation Phase.
14.70 ──── Court of Claims.
14.71 ──── ──── Time to File Claim.
14.72 ──── ──── Service.
14.73 ──── Supreme Court.
14.74 ──── ──── Time to File Claim.
14.75 ──── ──── Service.
14.76 Content of Claim.
14.77 Scope of Just Compensation.
14.78 ──── "Highest and Best Use."
14.79 ──── Total Taking.
14.80 ──── ──── Direct Damages.
14.81 ──── ──── Improvements.
14.82 ──── Partial Taking.
14.83 ──── Temporary Taking.
14.84 ──── ──── Easements.
14.85 Methods of Valuation to Determine Compensation.

TABLE OF CONTENTS

Sec.
14.86 ____ Market Approach to Value.
14.87 ____ Income Approach to Value.
14.88 ____ Cost Approach to Value.
14.89 Specialty Property.
14.90 Effect of Environmental Contamination on Property Value.
14.91 Fixtures.
14.92 ____ Compensable Fixtures.
14.93 ____ Valuation of Fixtures.
14.94 Leasehold Interests.
14.95 ____ Valuation and Compensation.
14.96 Loss of Business and Goodwill.
14.97 Going Concern Value.
14.98 Moving and Relocation Expenses.
14.99 Conflicting Claims by Condemnees.
14.100 ____ Conflicting Claims to the Condemnor's Offer.
14.101 ____ Conflicting Claims to the Award.
14.102 The Trial on Compensation.
14.103 ____ Preference.
14.104 ____ Filing and Exchange of Appraisals.
14.105 ____ Expert Testimony.
14.106 ____ Viewing of the Property.
14.107 ____ Joint or Consolidated Trials.
14.108 ____ Interest.
14.109 Setoff for Indirect Benefit.
14.110 Incidental Expenses and Proration of Taxes.
14.111 Abandonment of Procedure by Condemnor.
14.112 Finding that Condemnor is Not Legally Authorized to Acquire the Property.
14.113 Finding Contrary to Claim by Condemnor That it Did Not Take Property.
14.114 Decision By the Court and Entry of Judgment.
14.115 Additional Allowances for Costs and Expenses.
14.116 Payment Pending Appeal.
14.117 Small Claims Proceedings.
14.118 Summary.
14.119 Procedural Checklist.
14.120 Forms—Demand on Condemnor to File Copy of Proceedings to Determine Need and Location of Public Project with Appellate Division for Purpose of Judicial Review.
14.121 ____ Petition for Review of Determination and Finding that Public Use, Benefit or Purpose Will be Served by Proposed Acquisition.
14.122 ____ Judgment of Appellate Division Rejecting the Determination and Finding that Public Use, Benefit or Purpose Will be Served by Proposed Acquisition.
14.123 ____ Complaint by Condemnee to Establish Fair and Reasonable Value for Temporary Use and Occupancy After Acquisition by Eminent Domain.

TABLE OF CONTENTS

Sec.
14.124 ____ Notice of Pendency of Proceeding in Supreme Court to Acquire Property by Eminent Domain and File Acquisition Map.
14.125 ____ Notice of Petition in Proceeding in Supreme Court to Acquire Property by Eminent Domain and File Acquisition Map.
14.126 ____ Petition in Proceeding in Supreme Court to Acquire Property by Eminent Domain and File Acquisition Map.
14.127 ____ Petition in Proceeding in Supreme Court to Acquire Property by Eminent Domain and File Acquisition Map—Petitioner Exempt from Compliance with Eminent Domain Procedure Law Article 2.
14.128 ____ Answer to Petition in Proceeding in Supreme Court to Acquire Property by Eminent Domain and File Acquisition Map.
14.129 ____ Order to Show Cause Why Condemnor Should Not be Permitted to Enter Immediately upon Real Property and Devote It Temporarily to Public Use Specified in Petition Upon Deposit of a Fixed Sum with the Court.
14.130 ____ Order to Show Cause Why Condemnor Should Not be Permitted to File Acquisition Maps or Enter upon Real Property.
14.131 ____ Order in Proceeding in Supreme Court to Acquire Property by Eminent Domain and File Acquisition Map.
14.132 ____ Notice of Acquisition by Eminent Domain Where Supreme Court Has Jurisdiction.
14.133 ____ Claim for Damages Arising from Acquisition by Eminent Domain—General Form.
14.134 ____ Judgment Awarding Compensation in Claim for Acquisition of Property by Eminent Domain.
14.135 ____ Notice of Motion for Additional Allowance to Condemnee for Expert Witnesses.
14.136 ____ Affidavit in Support of Motion for Additional Allowance to Condemnee for Expert Witnesses.
14.137 ____ Order Granting Additional Allowance to Condemnee for Expert Witnesses.

CHAPTER 15. ENVIRONMENTAL LAW

15.1 Scope Note.
15.2 Strategy.
15.3 State Environmental Quality Review Act.
15.4 ____ Determination of Significance.
15.5 ____ The Environmental Impact Statement and Findings Statement.
15.6 ____ Judicial Review.
15.7 ____ Checklist.
15.8 Water Pollution Control.
15.9 ____ SPDES Permit Program.
15.10 ____ Stormwater Discharges and Oil Spills.
15.11 ____ Enforcement.

TABLE OF CONTENTS

Sec.
15.12 ___ Strategy: Clean Water Act Citizen Suit Checklist.
15.13 Wetlands Protection.
15.14 ___ Strategy: Checklist.
15.15 ___ The Federal Scheme.
15.16 ___ New York Tidal and Freshwater Wetlands Law.
15.17 ___ Permit Procedure and Criteria.
15.18 ___ Penalties.
15.19 Air Pollution Control.
15.20 ___ The 1990 CAA Amendments.
15.21 ___ New York State Requirements.
15.22 ___ Enforcement.
15.23 Regulation of Solid and Hazardous Waste.
15.24 ___ New York Hazardous Waste Regulation.
15.25 ___ Enforcement.
15.26 Regulation of Underground Storage Tanks and Petroleum Storage Tanks—Federal Law.
15.27 ___ New York Law.
15.28 Regulation of Inactive Hazardous Waste Sites—CERCLA.
15.29 ___ CERCLA Section 107(a).
15.30 ___ Lender Liability, Contribution and Indemnification Under CERCLA.
15.31 ___ New York Law.
15.32 Relevant Common Law Doctrines—Nuisance.
15.33 Common Law Doctrines—Trespass.
15.34 Regulatory Takings.
15.35 Drafting Checklist—Clean Water Act Citizen Suit Notice Letter.
15.36 ___ Clean Water Act and Resource Conservation and Recovery Act Citizen Suit Notice Letter.
15.37 ___ Clean Water Act Complaint.
15.38 ___ Nuisance and Trespass Complaint.
15.39 ___ Oil Spill Complaint.
15.40 Forms—Clean Water Act Citizen Suit Notice Letter. 💾
15.41 ___ Clean Water Act and Resource Conservation and Recovery Act Citizen Suit Notice Letter. 💾
15.42 ___ Clean Water Act Complaint. 💾
15.43 ___ Nuisance and Trespass Complaint. 💾
15.44 ___ Oil Spill Complaint. 💾

CHAPTER 16. LAND USE LAW

16.1 Scope Note.
16.2 Strategy.
16.3 Local Land Use Law.
16.4 ___ Delegated Authority.
16.5 ___ Enabling Acts.
16.6 ___ ___ New York City.
16.7 ___ Home Rule Authority.
16.8 ___ ___ Flexibility.
16.9 ___ ___ Floating Zone.
16.10 ___ Summary.

LV

TABLE OF CONTENTS

Sec.
16.11 Comprehensive Plan.
16.12 ____ Judicial Definition.
16.13 ____ Statutory Definition.
16.14 ____ Preparation and Adoption.
16.15 ____ Protects Zoning Against Challenge.
16.16 ____ Summary.
16.17 Substantive Limits—Illustrative Case.
16.18 ____ Substantive Due Process.
16.19 ____ Procedural Due Process.
16.20 ____ Equal Protection.
16.21 ____ *Ultra Vires.*
16.22 ____ Regulatory Takings.
16.23 ____ Vested Rights.
16.24 ____ Preemption.
16.25 ____ First Amendment.
16.26 ____ Summary.
16.27 Local Process.
16.28 ____ Structure of Local Regulations.
16.29 ____ Adoption.
16.30 ____ Amendment.
16.31 ____ Other Regulations/Official Map.
16.32 ____ Building Regulations and Permits.
16.33 ____ Summary.
16.34 Local Boards and Practices.
16.35 ____ Local Legislature.
16.36 ____ Planning Board.
16.37 ____ Zoning Board of Appeals.
16.38 ____ Freedom of Information.
16.39 ____ Open Meetings.
16.40 ____ Conflict of Interests.
16.41 ____ Summary.
16.42 Judicial Review.
16.43 ____ Procedures.
16.44 ____ Standards.
16.45 ____ ____ Local Legislature.
16.46 ____ ____ Zoning Board of Appeals.
16.47 ____ ____ Planning Board.
16.48 ____ Standing.
16.49 ____ Exhaustion.
16.50 ____ Remedies.
16.51 ____ Summary.
16.52 Local Environmental Review.
16.53 ____ Actions Subject to SEQRA.
16.54 ____ ____ Building Permits.
16.55 ____ ____ Variances.
16.56 ____ ____ Subdivisions.
16.57 ____ ____ Site Plans.
16.58 ____ ____ Rezoning.
16.59 ____ Summary.
16.60 Zoning Law—In General.

TABLE OF CONTENTS

Sec.
16.61	As of Right Use.
16.62	Nonconforming Use—Definition and Application.
16.63	___ Changes.
16.64	___ Reconstruction and Restoration.
16.65	___ Enlargement, Alteration or Extension.
16.66	___ Changes to Another Nonconforming Use.
16.67	___ Termination.
16.68	___ Abandonment.
16.69	___ Amortization.
16.70	___ Transfer of Ownership.
16.71	___ Procedures.
16.72	___ Summary.
16.73	Use Variance.
16.74	___ Statutory Standard.
16.75	___ ___ Reasonable Return.
16.76	___ ___ Unique Hardship.
16.77	___ ___ Protect Essential Neighborhood Character.
16.78	___ ___ Self-Created Hardship.
16.79	___ Minimum Variance Needed.
16.80	___ Procedure.
16.81	___ Summary.
16.82	Area Variance.
16.83	___ Statutory Balancing Test.
16.84	___ ___ Guiding Principles from Case Law.
16.85	___ ___ Balancing Factors.
16.86	___ Minimum Variance Needed.
16.87	___ Procedure.
16.88	___ Summary.
16.89	Conditions Imposed on Use and Area Variances.
16.90	Special Use Permits.
16.91	___ Imposition and Use of Standards.
16.92	___ Findings and Determination of Board.
16.93	___ Limitation on Imposition of Conditions.
16.94	___ Procedure.
16.95	___ Summary.
16.96	Subdivision Approval.
16.97	___ Procedure.
16.98	___ ___ How Affected By SEQRA.
16.99	___ Provision of Essential Services.
16.100	___ Parkland.
16.101	___ Decisions and Conditions.
16.102	___ Summary.
16.103	Site Plans.
16.104	___ Responsible Agency.
16.105	___ ___ Procedure.
16.106	___ ___ Standards for Review.
16.107	___ ___ Conditions Imposed.
16.108	___ Summary.
16.109	Particularized Actions.
16.110	___ Spot Zoning.

TABLE OF CONTENTS

Sec.
16.111 ___ ___ Challenge Dismissed.
16.112 ___ ___ Challenge Successful.
16.113 ___ Rezoning.
16.114 ___ ___ Conditions.
16.115 ___ ___ Contract Zoning.
16.116 ___ ___ Development Agreements.
16.117 ___ Summary.
16.118 Special Regulations.
16.119 ___ Accessory Uses.
16.120 ___ Accessory Apartments.
16.121 ___ Home Offices.
16.122 ___ Definition of Family.
16.123 ___ Affordable Housing.
16.124 ___ Mobile Homes.
16.125 ___ Aesthetics.
16.126 ___ ___ Architectural Review.
16.127 ___ ___ Historic Preservation.
16.128 ___ Public Uses.
16.129 ___ ___ Public Utilities.
16.130 ___ ___ Cellular Transmission Facilities.
16.131 ___ ___ Religious Uses.
16.132 ___ Summary.
16.133 Forms—Environmental Assessment—Short Form. 💾
16.134 ___ Environmental Assessment—Long Form. 💾

CHAPTER 17. EMPLOYMENT LAW

17.1 Scope Note.
17.2 Strategy.
17.3 ___ Plaintiff's Counsel's Investigation.
17.4 ___ Defendant's Counsel's Investigation.
17.5 ___ Pre-litigation Settlement Process.
17.6 ___ Negotiating With Opposing Counsel.
17.7 ___ Alternative Dispute Resolution ("ADR").
17.8 ___ ___ Mediation.
17.9 ___ ___ Arbitration.
17.10 ___ Settlement and Severance Agreements.
17.11 ___ ___ Older Workers Benefit Protection Act ("OWBPA").
17.12 ___ ___ COBRA.
17.13 ___ ___ Pay.
17.14 ___ ___ Income Taxes.
17.15 ___ ___ Benefits.
17.16 ___ Other Severance Issues.
17.17 ___ Independent Contractor vs. Employee.
17.18 ___ Checklist: Initial Considerations for Plaintiff.
17.19 ___ Checklist: Terminating an Employee.
17.20 Causes of Action.
17.21 ___ Tort–Assault.
17.22 ___ ___ Battery.
17.23 ___ ___ Conspiracy.

TABLE OF CONTENTS

Sec.
- 17.24 __ __ Conversion.
- 17.25 __ __ Defamation.
- 17.26 __ __ False Imprisonment; Malicious Prosecution.
- 17.27 __ __ Fraud, Negligent Misrepresentation and Fraudulent Inducement.
- 17.28 __ __ Intentional Infliction of Emotional Distress.
- 17.29 __ __ Interference with Business Relations.
- 17.30 __ __ Negligence.
- 17.31 __ __ *Prima Facie* Tort.
- 17.32 __ __ Wrongful Discharge.
- 17.33 __ Contract.
- 17.34 __ __ Express Promises.
- 17.35 __ __ Implied Promises.
- 17.36 __ __ Estoppel.
- 17.37 Statutory Causes of Action—Age Discrimination.
- 17.38 __ Anti-reprisal Provisions of Various Statutes.
- 17.39 __ Arrest Records.
- 17.40 __ Bankruptcy.
- 17.41 __ Convictions.
- 17.42 __ Credit Information.
- 17.43 __ Disability.
- 17.44 __ Equal Pay.
- 17.45 __ Family and Medical Leave Act (FMLA).
- 17.46 __ Health Plan Coverage (COBRA).
- 17.47 __ Legal Off Duty Activities.
- 17.48 __ Marital Status Discrimination.
- 17.49 __ Discrimination on the Basis of Race, Color or National Origin.
- 17.50 __ Pension Plans.
- 17.51 __ Plant Closing, Mass Layoffs.
- 17.52 __ Polygraphs.
- 17.53 __ Public Employees.
- 17.54 __ Pregnancy.
- 17.55 __ Privacy.
- 17.56 __ Religious Discrimination.
- 17.57 __ Sex Discrimination, Harassment.
- 17.58 __ Sexual Orientation Discrimination.
- 17.59 __ Title VII, Burdens of Proof.
- 17.60 __ Unemployment Insurance.
- 17.61 __ Unionization, Rights Within Unions.
- 17.62 __ Unsafe Workplace.
- 17.63 __ Wages; Unpaid Compensation; Overtime.
- 17.64 __ Whistleblowing/*Qui Tam*.
- 17.65 __ Workers' Compensation.
- 17.66 Procedure—Anti-discrimination Agency Practice.
- 17.67 __ Filing and Responding to Administrative Charges.
- 17.68 __ Election of Remedies.
- 17.69 __ Statutes of Limitations and Prerequisites to Private Lawsuits.
- 17.70 Private Lawsuits.

TABLE OF CONTENTS

Sec.
17.71 ____ Discovery—General Considerations.
17.72 ____ ____ Plaintiff's Strategy.
17.73 ____ Summary Judgment.
17.74 ____ Trial.
17.75 ____ Fee Application.
17.76 ____ Post–Trial Motions and Appeal.
17.77 ____ Checklist: Statutes of Limitations.
17.78 ____ Checklist: Commencement of New York State Actions.
17.79 ____ Checklist: Commencement of Federal Court Actions.
17.80 Miscellaneous Practice Issues—OFCCP/Glass Ceiling Audits.
17.81 ____ Employment Policies and Handbooks.
17.82 Drafting the Complaint.
17.83 Drafting Checklist—Complaint.
17.84 Drafting the Answer.
17.85 Drafting Checklist—Answer
17.86 Forms—Client (Plaintiff) Intake Questionnaire.
17.87 ____ Severance/Release Agreement.
17.88 ____ Letter to EEOC Requesting "Mohasco" Waiver of State Processing.
17.89 ____ Charge of Discrimination—New York State Division of Human Rights (Official Form).
17.90 ____ Information Sheet—New York State Division of Human Rights (Official Form).
17.91 ____ SDHR Information Sheet.
17.92 ____ Charge of Discrimination—Equal Employment Opportunity Commission (Official Form).
17.93 ____ Affidavit for a Charge of Discrimination—Equal Employment Opportunity Commission (Official Form).
17.94 ____ EEOC Filing Cover Letter Requesting EEOC Processing of Dual–filed Charge.
17.95 ____ Letter Requesting Administrative Convenience Dismissal from State or City Administrative Agency.
17.96 ____ Pleadings—New York State Complaint.
17.97 ____ ____ New York State Answer.
17.98 ____ ____ Federal Complaint.
17.99 ____ ____ Federal Answer.

CHAPTER 18. CIVIL RIGHTS

18.1 Scope Note.
18.2 Strategy.
18.3 ____ Checklist.
18.4 Overview of New York and Federal Civil Rights Provisions.
18.5 Jurisdiction over Civil Rights Actions.
18.6 New York Bill of Rights.
18.7 ____ Overview.
18.8 ____ Comparison With Federal Bill of Rights.
18.9 ____ Search and Seizure.
18.10 ____ ____ Civil Liability.
18.11 ____ ____ Return of Seized Property.

TABLE OF CONTENTS

Sec.	
18.12	—— Rights of Persons Accused of Crimes.
18.13	—— —— Public Trial/Closure of Courtroom.
18.14	—— —— Exclusion of Public or Press.
18.15	—— Rights of Jurors.
18.16	General Federal Civil Rights Provisions.
18.17	—— 42 U.S.C.A. § 1981.
18.18	—— 42 U.S.C.A. § 1983.
18.19	—— Other Federal Civil Rights Provisions.
18.20	Police and Prosecutorial Misconduct.
18.21	—— Excessive Force.
18.22	—— False Arrest.
18.23	—— False Imprisonment.
18.24	—— Search and Seizure.
18.25	—— Malicious Prosecution.
18.26	First Amendment.
18.27	—— Freedom of Speech.
18.28	—— Freedom of Religion.
18.29	Rights of Prisoners.
18.30	Defenses to Federal Actions.
18.31	—— Absolute Immunity.
18.32	—— Qualified Immunity.
18.33	—— Eleventh Amendment.
18.34	—— *Monell* and Its Progeny.
18.35	—— *Respondeat Superior*.
18.36	—— Abstention.
18.37	—— *Res Judicata* and Collateral Estoppel.
18.38	—— Statute of Limitations.
18.39	Housing.
18.40	—— Prohibition Against Discrimination in Publicly Assisted Housing.
18.41	—— —— Owners and Lessors.
18.42	—— —— Real Estate Agents and Brokers.
18.43	—— —— Remedies for Discrimination.
18.44	—— Prohibition Against Discrimination in Private Housing.
18.45	—— —— Owners and Lessors.
18.46	—— —— Real Estate Agents and Brokers.
18.47	—— —— Cooperatives.
18.48	—— —— Remedies for Discrimination.
18.49	—— —— —— Administrative Proceedings.
18.50	—— —— —— Actions in State and Federal Court.
18.51	—— *Prima Facie* Case and Burden of Proof.
18.52	—— Summary of Procedure for Filing an Administrative Claim and Challenging an SDHR Order.
18.53	Education.
18.54	Equal Rights in Places of Public Accommodation and Amusement.
18.55	—— General Provisions.
18.56	—— Private Clubs.
18.57	—— Persons With Disabilities Accompanied by a Guide Dog, Hearing Dog or Service Dog.
18.58	—— Remedies for Discrimination.

TABLE OF CONTENTS

Sec.
18.59 Employment Discrimination Provisions Exclusive to the New York Civil Rights Law.
18.60 ____ In General.
18.61 ____ Persons With Disabilities.
18.62 ____ Persons With Genetic Disorders.
18.63 Right of Privacy.
18.64 ____ Generally.
18.65 ____ Police Officers, Corrections Officers and Firefighters.
18.66 ____ Victims of Sex Offenses.
18.67 Changing One's Name.
18.68 ____ Procedure for Petition to Change Name.
18.69 ____ ____ Contents of Petition.
18.70 ____ ____ Special Procedures for Infants.
18.71 ____ Factors to Be Considered by the Court.
18.72 ____ Publication Requirement.
18.73 ____ Checklist.
18.74 Heart Balm Statute.
18.75 ____ Penalty for Bringing Action.
18.76 ____ Action for Return of Gifts Made in Contemplation of Marriage.
18.77 ____ ____ Procedure.
18.78 Miscellaneous Rights and Immunities.
18.79 ____ Frivolous Litigation.
18.80 ____ ____ Protection from SLAPP Suits.
18.81 ____ Libel and Slander.
18.82 ____ ____ Defenses.
18.83 ____ Breast Feeding.
18.84 ____ Suspension of Rights Due to Imprisonment.
18.85 ____ Shield Law.
18.86 ____ Performing Abortion.
18.87 ____ "Good Samaritan" Law Provisions.
18.88 Drafting Checklists.
18.89 ____ Framing the Federal Court § 1983 Complaint.
18.90 ____ Petition to Change One's Name.
18.91 Forms.
18.92 ____ Complaint for False Arrest, False Imprisonment and Malicious Prosecution.
18.93 ____ Complaint for Excessive Force.
18.94 ____ Complaint for Return of Seized Property.
18.95 ____ Complaint Against Landlord for Housing Discrimination.
18.96 ____ Complaint Against Cooperative for Discrimination.
18.97 ____ Notice of Commencement of Action for Discrimination.
18.98 ____ Complaint for Discrimination in Place of Public Accommodation.
18.99 ____ Petition to Change Name.

CHAPTER 19. IMMIGRATION AND NATIONALITY LAW—PERMANENT RESIDENCE APPLICATIONS

19.1 Scope Note.

TABLE OF CONTENTS

Sec.	
19.2	Strategy.
19.3	—— Flowchart.
19.4	Overview of the U.S. Immigration System.
19.5	—— Numerical Limitations on Immigrant Selection.
19.6	—— Implementation: Foreign State Chargeability and Quota Allocation.
19.7	Family–Based Immigration.
19.8	—— Immediate Relative Categories.
19.9	—— Family Preference Categories.
19.10	—— Qualifying as a Relation.
19.11	—— —— "Child" and "Parent" Issues.
19.12	—— —— "Marriage" Issues.
19.13	—— Petitioning Procedures and Documentation.
19.14	—— —— I–130 Petition.
19.15	—— Orphans and Amerasians.
19.16	—— Abused Spouse and Children.
19.17	Employment–Based Immigration.
19.18	—— First Employment Preference Applicants (Priority Workers).
19.19	—— —— Extraordinary Ability Aliens.
19.20	—— —— Outstanding Professors and Researchers.
19.21	—— —— Managerial or Executive Intracompany Transferees.
19.22	—— Second Employment Preference Applicants.
19.23	—— —— Exceptional Ability Aliens.
19.24	—— —— Advanced Degree Professionals.
19.25	—— —— The Role of "National Interest."
19.26	—— Third Employment Preference Applicants.
19.27	—— —— Professional and Skilled Workers.
19.28	—— —— Unskilled Workers.
19.29	—— I–140 Petition, Procedures and Documentation.
19.30	—— —— Checklist.
19.31	—— Labor Certification.
19.32	—— —— Procedures.
19.33	—— —— Legal Issues.
19.34	—— —— Job Description.
19.35	—— —— Business Necessity.
19.36	—— —— Recruitment.
19.37	—— —— Approvals.
19.38	—— —— Notices of Findings.
19.39	—— —— Denials and Administrative Appeal.
19.40	—— Fourth Employment Preference Applicants.
19.41	—— —— Religious Workers and Ministers.
19.42	—— Fifth Employment Preference Applicants (Immigrant Investors).
19.43	—— Petition Procedures and Requirements.
19.44	—— —— Special Immigrant Investor Programs.
19.45	Special Categories.
19.46	—— The Diversity (Lottery) Program.
19.47	—— Registry.
19.48	—— Cancellation of Removal.
19.49	—— Legislatively Created Programs.

TABLE OF CONTENTS

Sec.
19.50 ____ Asylum and Refugee Status.
19.51 Applying for Permanent Residence.
19.52 ____ Exclusionary Grounds.
19.53 ____ Immigrant Visa Processing.
19.54 ____ ____ Framework of the Immigrant Visa Processing System.
19.55 ____ ____ Special Requirements, Public Law No. 103–317.
19.56 ____ ____ Checklist of Required Documents.
19.57 ____ Adjustment of Status.
19.58 ____ ____ General Requirements.
19.59 ____ ____ Special Provisions of Section 245(i).
19.60 ____ ____ Discretionary Factors.
19.61 ____ ____ Application Process.
19.62 ____ ____ Concurrent Filing of Petition and Adjustment of Status.
19.63 ____ ____ Completion of the Process.
19.64 ____ ____ Administrative and Judicial Review.
19.65 ____ ____ Checklist.
19.66 ____ Tactical Considerations.
19.67 ____ ____ Nonimmigrant Status as a Factor.
19.68 ____ ____ Immigrant Visa Processing Versus Adjustment of Status.
19.69 ____ ____ Flowchart.
19.70 The Green Card and its Limitations.
19.71 ____ Conditional Residence.
19.72 ____ ____ Marriage Cases, Removal of Condition.
19.73 ____ ____ Immigrant Investors, Removal of Condition.
19.74 ____ Unconditional Permanent Residence.
19.75 Forms.
19.76 ____ Form I–130.
19.77 ____ Form I–140.
19.78 ____ Form I–485.
19.79 ____ Form OF–230.

CHAPTER 20. ADOPTIONS

20.1 Scope Note.
20.2 Strategy.
20.3 ____ Checklist: Pre-adoption—Counsel for Parents.
20.4 ____ Checklist: Interview With Birth Mother.
20.5 Adoptions—Generally.
20.6 ____ Defined.
20.7 ____ Rationale.
20.8 ____ Judicial Construction of Statutes.
20.9 ____ Concurrent Jurisdiction.
20.10 ____ ____ Where to File Adoption Proceedings.
20.11 ____ Choice of Venue.
20.12 ____ Types.
20.13 ____ Effect of Adoption.
20.14 ____ Who May Adopt—Statutory Mandates.
20.15 ____ ____ Separated Persons.

TABLE OF CONTENTS

Sec.
20.16	__ __ Foster Parents: Preference to Adopt.
20.17	__ __ Second Parent Adoptions.
20.18	__ __ Unwed Putative Fathers.
20.19	__ __ Citizens and Aliens.
20.20	__ __ Age as a Factor.
20.21	__ __ Extended Family as Factor.
20.22	__ __ Adult Unmarried Person.
20.23	__ Who May Be Adopted—In General.
20.24	__ __ Adult Adoptions.
20.25	__ __ Aliens.
20.26	__ __ Non-marital Children.
20.27	__ __ Interracial Adoptions.
20.28	__ __ Religion as a Factor.
20.29	__ Consents Required—Statutory Mandate.
20.30	__ __ Rights of Unwed Fathers.
20.31	__ __ When Consent Not Required.
20.32	__ __ Notice of a Proposed Adoption.
20.33	__ __ Checklist of Fathers to Receive Notice of Adoption.
20.34	__ Persons Excluded from Notice.
20.35	__ Purpose of Notice.
20.36	__ Procedure.
20.37	Private Placement Adoptions—In General.
20.38	__ Terminating Parental Rights Based Upon Abandonment.
20.39	__ Terminating Parental Rights Based Upon Mental Retardation.
20.40	__ Dual Representation Prohibited.
20.41	__ Independent Counsel.
20.42	__ Permissible Dual Representation.
20.43	__ Independent Representation of the Child.
20.44	__ The Attorney's Fee.
20.45	__ Locating an Infant for Adoption—The Attorney's Responsibility.
20.46	__ Illegal Sale of Babies.
20.47	__ Advertisement.
20.48	__ Foreign Infants.
20.49	__ Readoption of Foreign Infants.
20.50	__ Native American Children.
20.51	__ Residency Requirements.
20.52	__ Permissible Payments by Adoptive Parents.
20.53	__ Interstate Compact on the Placement of Children.
20.54	__ Pre-certification of Adoptive Parents—In General.
20.55	__ __ Requirement of Pre-certification.
20.56	__ __ Procedure.
20.57	__ __ Checklist of Documents Needed for Certification.
20.58	__ Hospital Procedures—Physical Transfer of Custody of the Infant to the Adoptive Parents.
20.59	__ __ Certification Procedures.
20.60	__ Petition for Temporary Guardianship—Legislative Background.
20.61	__ __ Impact of Pre–placement Certification.

TABLE OF CONTENTS

Sec.
20.62	___ ___ Procedure Upon Filing Petition for Temporary Guardianship.
20.63	___ Consent of Birth Parents.
20.64	___ ___ Extra-Judicial Consent.
20.65	___ ___ Judicial Consents.
20.66	___ ___ Personal Appearances Required.
20.67	___ ___ Step-Parent Adoptions.
20.68	___ Foreign Born Children.
20.69	___ Petition for Adoption.
20.70	___ The Agreement of Adoption.
20.71	___ Affidavit of Attorney Representing Adoptive Parents.
20.72	___ Confidential Affidavit.
20.73	___ Attorney's Affidavit of Financial Disclosure.
20.74	___ Notification of Order of Adoption; Report of Adoption.
20.75	___ Order of Adoption.
20.76	___ Birth Mother's Affidavit Regarding Putative Father.
20.77	___ Affidavit of Intermediary.
20.78	___ Attorney's Affidavit Regarding Legal Fees.
20.79	___ Affidavit of Explanation of Criminal Activity.
20.80	___ Investigation by Disinterested Person.
20.81	___ The Hearing.
20.82	___ Certificate of Adoption.
20.83	___ The New Birth Certificate.
20.84	___ Checklist of Documents Required for Private Placement Adoption.
20.85	Agency Adoptions—Defined.
20.86	___ Definition of "Authorized Agency."
20.87	___ Venue.
20.88	___ Child's Entry into the System.
20.89	___ ___ Voluntary Transfer of Legal Custody of Children to the Authorized Agency.
20.90	___ ___ Judicial Surrender.
20.91	___ ___ Extra-Judicial Surrender.
20.92	___ ___ Court Approval of Extra-Judicial Surrender.
20.93	___ ___ Assigned Counsel.
20.94	___ ___ Required Notice of Application.
20.95	___ ___ Notification to Court.
20.96	___ ___ Court Order.
20.97	___ ___ Conditional Surrender.
20.98	___ ___ Recording a Surrender.
20.99	___ ___ Revocation of Surrender.
20.100	___ ___ Proceedings Subsequent to Execution of Extra-Judicial Surrender.
20.101	___ ___ Court Ordered Transfer of Children to Authorized Agency.
20.102	___ Procedures.
20.103	___ The Petition.
20.104	___ The Agreement of Adoption.
20.105	___ Verified Schedule.
20.106	___ Affidavit of Financial Disclosure.
20.107	___ Confidential Affidavit.

TABLE OF CONTENTS

Sec.
20.108 ____ Marital Affidavit.
20.109 ____ Child's Medical History.
20.110 ____ Supplemental Affidavit.
20.111 ____ Notification of Order of Adoption; Report of Adoption.
20.112 ____ Doctor's Certificate of Health.
20.113 ____ Authorization and Approval for Subsidized Adoption.
20.114 ____ Adoption Homestudy.
20.115 ____ Affidavit Identifying Party.
20.116 ____ Order of Adoption.
20.117 ____ Certificate of Adoption.
20.118 ____ Abuse Clearance Form.
20.119 ____ Unavailability of Abuse Clearance Form and Criminal Conviction Check.
20.120 ____ Attorney's Affidavit of Legal Fees.
20.121 ____ Checklist of Other Required Supporting Documentation.
20.122 ____ The Adoption Hearing.
20.123 Post-adoption Issues—The Open Adoption.
20.124 ____ Visitation With Siblings.
20.125 ____ Sealing Adoption Records.
20.126 ____ ____ Constitutionality of Laws Relating to Sealing Records.
20.127 ____ ____ Good Cause for Unsealing Records.
20.128 ____ ____ ____ Criminal Investigation and Probation Department.
20.129 ____ ____ ____ Requirement of Medical Information.
20.130 ____ ____ ____ Religion.
20.131 ____ Abrogation of Order.
20.132 Checklist of Facts and Allegations to be Included in the Petition for a Private Placement Adoption.
20.133 Forms—Private Placement Adoptions—Petition for Certification as a Qualified Adoptive Parent.
20.134 ____ ____ Petition for Temporary Guardianship.
20.135 ____ ____ Judicial Consent of Natural Parent.
20.136 ____ ____ Extra-Judicial Consent of Natural Parent.
20.137 ____ ____ Petition for Adoption.
20.138 ____ ____ Order of Adoption (Private Placement).
20.139 ____ Agency Adoptions—Petition for Adoption.
20.140 ____ ____ Verified Schedule.
20.141 ____ ____ Marital Affidavit.
20.142 ____ ____ Marital Affidavit Dispensing With Consent of Spouse After Three Year Separation.
20.143 ____ ____ Confidential Affidavit.
20.144 ____ ____ Affidavit Pursuant to Section 111–a of the Domestic Relations Law.
20.145 ____ ____ Agreement of Adoption and Consent.
20.146 ____ ____ Affidavit Identifying Party.
20.147 ____ ____ Affidavit of Financial Disclosure by Parents.
20.148 ____ ____ Order of Adoption.

Volume 23

CHAPTER 21. DOMESTIC RELATIONS

21.1 Scope Note.

LXVII

TABLE OF CONTENTS

Sec.	
21.2	Strategy.
21.3	Jurisdiction.
21.4	⎯⎯ Residence Requirements.
21.5	⎯⎯ Uniform Child Custody Jurisdiction Act.
21.6	Competency of the Court to Grant Relief.
21.7	⎯⎯ Equitable Distribution.
21.8	⎯⎯ Support.
21.9	⎯⎯ Custody and Visitation.
21.10	Jurisdiction Over the Defendant's Person or Property.
21.11	⎯⎯ Personal Jurisdiction.
21.12	⎯⎯ Long Arm Jurisdiction.
21.13	⎯⎯ *In Rem* Jurisdiction.
21.14	*Quasi in Rem* Jurisdiction.
21.15	Venue.
21.16	⎯⎯ Changing Venue.
21.17	Joinder, Consolidation and Joint Trials.
21.18	Grounds for Divorce.
21.19	⎯⎯ No Official No–Fault Ground.
21.20	⎯⎯ Cruel and Inhuman Treatment.
21.21	⎯⎯ ⎯⎯ Defenses.
21.22	⎯⎯ Abandonment.
21.23	⎯⎯ ⎯⎯ Defenses.
21.24	⎯⎯ ⎯⎯ Effect of Separation Agreement.
21.25	⎯⎯ Imprisonment.
21.26	⎯⎯ Adultery.
21.27	⎯⎯ ⎯⎯ Defenses.
21.28	⎯⎯ ⎯⎯ Effect of Separation Agreement.
21.29	⎯⎯ Divorce Action Based Upon Living Apart Pursuant to Separation Decree or Judgment.
21.30	⎯⎯ Divorce Action Based Upon Living Apart Pursuant to Separation Agreement.
21.31	⎯⎯ Dual Divorce.
21.32	Effect of Sister State Divorce Judgment.
21.33	Equitable Distribution.
21.34	⎯⎯ When Available.
21.35	⎯⎯ Identification of Property.
21.36	⎯⎯ Characterization of Property.
21.37	⎯⎯ ⎯⎯ Marital Property.
21.38	⎯⎯ ⎯⎯ ⎯⎯ Pensions.
21.39	⎯⎯ ⎯⎯ ⎯⎯ Professional Practices, Licenses, Degrees and Careers.
21.40	⎯⎯ ⎯⎯ Separate Property.
21.41	⎯⎯ ⎯⎯ Increase in Value of Separate Property.
21.42	⎯⎯ Valuation Dates.
21.43	⎯⎯ Valuation Methods.
21.44	⎯⎯ Distribution Factors.
21.45	⎯⎯ Tax Considerations.
21.46	Maintenance.
21.47	⎯⎯ Legislative Factors.
21.48	⎯⎯ Effect of Fault.

TABLE OF CONTENTS

Sec.
21.49	___ Current Trends.
21.50	___ Payments Fixed by Agreement.
21.51	___ Tax Consequences.
21.52	Child Support.
21.53	___ Child Support Standards Act.
21.54	___ ___ Where Statutory Percentages Are Unfair or Inappropriate.
21.55	___ ___ Recent Trends.
21.56	___ Effect of Agreement or Stipulation.
21.57	Health and Life Insurance.
21.58	Custody.
21.59	___ Visitation.
21.60	___ Relocation of Custodial Parent With the Child.
21.61	___ Joint Custody.
21.62	___ Proceedings in Which Custody Dispositions Are Available.
21.63	Financial Disclosure.
21.64	Disclosure on Matters Going to the Merits of the Case.
21.65	Net Worth Statement.
21.66	Statement of Proposed Disposition.
21.67	Findings of Fact and Conclusions of Law; Judgments.
21.68	Modification.
21.69	___ Maintenance.
21.70	___ Child Support.
21.71	___ Custody.
21.72	Enforcement.
21.73	___ Plenary Action to Enforce Agreement.
21.74	___ Defenses.
21.75	Practice Considerations.
21.76	___ Procedure for Attorneys in Domestic Relations Matters.
21.77	___ Disciplinary Rules.
21.78	___ Fee Arbitration Rules.
21.79	___ Rules Regarding Case Management.
21.80	Procedural Checklist—Calendar Control.
21.81	Drafting Checklist—Retainer Agreements.
21.82	___ Complaint in Action for Divorce.
21.83	___ Statement of Proposed Disposition.
21.84	Forms.
21.85	___ Retainer Agreement.
21.86	___ Complaint for Divorce.
21.87	___ Statement of Net Worth.
21.88	___ Statement of Proposed Disposition.
21.89	___ Findings of Fact and Conclusions of Law.
21.90	___ Matrimonial Judgments.
21.91	___ Referee's Report on Findings of Fact and Conclusions of Law.
21.92	___ Matrimonial Judgment Entered Upon Referee's Report.

CHAPTER 22. GUARDIANSHIP

22.1	Scope Note.

TABLE OF CONTENTS

Sec.
- 22.2 Strategy.
- 22.3 Checklists.
- 22.4 Prior Law—Generally.
- 22.5 ——— Role of Committees and Conservators.
- 22.6 ——— Problems Encountered.
- 22.7 ——— Impact of *Matter of Grinker (Rose)*.
- 22.8 Legislative Purpose of Mental Hygiene Law Article 81.
- 22.9 Definitions.
- 22.10 Summary.
- 22.11 Power to Appoint Guardian—Generally.
- 22.12 ——— Elements.
- 22.13 ——— Incapacity.
- 22.14 ——— Primary Considerations.
- 22.15 ——— Jurisdiction.
- 22.16 ——— Venue.
- 22.17 ——— Standing to Commence Proceeding.
- 22.18 ——— Summary.
- 22.19 Proceeding to Appoint Guardian.
- 22.20 ——— Time and Method of Service of Notice.
- 22.21 ——— Persons Entitled to Notice.
- 22.22 ——— Notice Requirements.
- 22.23 ——— Petition.
- 22.24 ——— Summary.
- 22.25 Court Evaluator—Persons Eligible for Appointment.
- 22.26 ——— Duties.
- 22.27 ——— Compensation.
- 22.28 ——— Appointment of Counsel for the Alleged Incapacitated Person.
- 22.29 ——— Summary.
- 22.30 Hearing and Order—An Overview.
- 22.31 ——— Procedure.
- 22.32 ——— Presence of Person Alleged to be Incapacitated.
- 22.33 ——— Evidence.
- 22.34 ——— Findings of the Court.
- 22.35 ——— ——— Voluntary Appointment.
- 22.36 ——— ——— Personal Needs.
- 22.37 ——— ——— Property Management.
- 22.38 ——— Dispositional Alternatives.
- 22.39 ——— Award of Counsel Fees to Petitioner.
- 22.40 ——— Person to be Appointed Guardian.
- 22.41 ——— Priority and Criteria for Appointment.
- 22.42 ——— Requirement of Bond.
- 22.43 ——— Designation of Clerk and Issuance of Commission.
- 22.44 ——— Summary.
- 22.45 Role of Guardian—Overview.
- 22.46 ——— Duties.
- 22.47 ——— Powers; Property Management.
- 22.48 ——— Substituted Judgment.
- 22.49 ——— Petition for Authorization to Transfer Property.
- 22.50 ——— ——— Notice of Application.

TABLE OF CONTENTS

Sec.
22.51 ____ ____ Considerations of Court.
22.52 ____ ____ Granting Petition.
22.53 ____ Powers; Personal Needs.
22.54 ____ Effect of Appointment on Incapacitated Person.
22.55 ____ Summary.
22.56 Provisional Remedies.
22.57 ____ Temporary Guardian.
22.58 ____ Injunction and Temporary Restraining Orders.
22.59 ____ Notice of Pendency.
22.60 ____ Summary.
22.61 Compensation of Guardian.
22.62 Reports by Guardian.
22.63 ____ Initial Report.
22.64 ____ Annual Report.
22.65 ____ Examination; Court Examiners.
22.66 ____ Intermediate and Final Reports.
22.67 ____ Decree Upon Approving Accounts.
22.68 ____ Summary.
22.69 Removal, Discharge and Resignation of Guardian—Removal.
22.70 ____ Discharge or Modification of Powers.
22.71 ____ Resignation or Suspension of Powers.
22.72 ____ Vacancy in Office; Appointment of Interim and Successor Guardians.
22.73 ____ Standby Guardian.
22.74 ____ Summary.
22.75 Education Requirements—Generally.
22.76 ____ Guardian Training.
22.77 ____ Court Evaluator Training.
22.78 ____ Court Examiner Training.
22.79 ____ Compliance.
22.80 ____ Summary.
22.81 Proceedings to Discover Property Withheld.
22.82 ____ Petition and Supporting Papers.
22.83 ____ Grounds For Inquiry.
22.84 ____ Answer.
22.85 ____ Trial.
22.86 ____ Decree.
22.87 ____ Summary.
22.88 Drafting Checklists.
22.89 ____ Order to Show Cause.
22.90 ____ Petition.
22.91 ____ Court Evaluator's Report.
22.92 ____ Order and Judgment.
22.93 ____ Initial Report of the Guardian.
22.94 ____ Annual Report.
22.95 ____ Decree Approving Accounts.
22.96 ____ Petition on Proceeding to Discover Property Withheld.
22.97 Forms.
22.98 ____ Order to Show Cause.
22.99 ____ Petition.

TABLE OF CONTENTS

Sec.
22.100 ____ Court Evaluator's Report. 💾
22.101 ____ Order and Judgment Appointing Guardian of the Person and Property. 💾
22.102 ____ Oath and Designation of Guardian. 💾
22.103 ____ Commission of Guardian. 💾
22.104 ____ Initial Report of Guardian. 💾
22.105 ____ Annual Report and Inventory of Guardian. 💾
22.106 ____ Decree Upon Approving Accounts. 💾
22.107 ____ Petition on Proceeding to Discover Property Withheld. 💾

CHAPTER 23. ELDER LAW

23.1 Scope Note.
23.2 Strategy.
23.3 Ethical Considerations.
23.4 ____ Identifying the Client.
23.5 ____ Confidentiality.
23.6 ____ Diminished Capacity.
23.7 Social Security Benefits.
23.8 ____ Quarters of Coverage.
23.9 ____ Insured Status.
23.10 ____ Calculation of Benefits.
23.11 ____ Retirement Benefits.
23.12 ____ Benefits for Spouses, Survivors and Dependents.
23.13 ____ Reduction in Benefits Due to Earned Income.
23.14 ____ Overpayments and Underpayments.
23.15 ____ Administrative and Judicial Appeals.
23.16 ____ Representation by Attorneys.
23.17 Supplemental Security Income for the Elderly.
23.18 ____ Categorical Eligibility.
23.19 ____ Financial Eligibility.
23.20 ____ Benefit Calculation.
23.21 ____ Underpayments and Overpayments.
23.22 ____ Administrative and Judicial Appeals.
23.23 ____ Representation by Attorneys.
23.24 Retirement Income from Qualified Plans.
23.25 ____ Eligibility, Vesting and Accrual.
23.26 ____ Contribution Limitations.
23.27 ____ Payment of Benefits.
23.28 ____ Alienation and Assignment.
23.29 ____ Spousal Rights.
23.30 ____ Qualified Domestic Relations Orders.
23.31 ____ Waiver of Spousal Rights.
23.32 ____ Taxation of Contributions.
23.33 ____ Distributions.
23.34 ____ Termination or Merger.
23.35 ____ Appeals.
23.36 Railroad Retirement Benefits.
23.37 Benefits for Federal Employees.
23.38 ____ Federal Employees Retirement System ("FERS").

TABLE OF CONTENTS

Sec.	
23.39	—— Civil Service Retirement Act ("CSRA").
23.40	—— Appeals.
23.41	Veterans' Benefits.
23.42	Medicare.
23.43	—— Eligibility and Enrollment.
23.44	—— Part A Benefits.
23.45	—— —— Hospital Services.
23.46	—— —— Skilled Nursing Facilities.
23.47	—— —— Home Health Care.
23.48	—— —— Hospice Care.
23.49	—— Part B Supplementary Medical Insurance.
23.50	—— —— Deductibles and Coinsurance.
23.51	—— —— Assignment of Claims/Participating Physicians.
23.52	—— —— Limitations on Balance Billing.
23.53	—— Administrative and Judicial Appeals.
23.54	—— —— Eligibility for Benefits.
23.55	—— —— Part A Fiscal Intermediary Decisions.
23.56	—— —— Part A Peer Review Organization Decisions.
23.57	—— —— Part B Determinations.
23.58	Supplemental Medical Insurance (Medigap Plans).
23.59	—— Gaps in Medicare Coverage.
23.60	—— Federal and State Regulation of the Industry.
23.61	—— Ten Standard Plans.
23.62	—— Criteria for Choosing the Right Plan.
23.63	Long Term Care Insurance.
23.64	—— Regulation Under New York Law.
23.65	—— Relationship to Medicaid Eligibility.
23.66	—— The Partnership For Long Term Care/Robert Wood Johnson Program.
23.67	—— Choosing a Policy.
23.68	—— Tax Issues.
23.69	Medicaid.
23.70	—— Covered Services.
23.71	—— Basic Eligibility Requirements.
23.72	—— Surplus Income Program for the "Medically Needy."
23.73	—— Income.
23.74	—— Resources.
23.75	—— Exempt Resources.
23.76	—— Transfer of Resources.
23.77	—— Treatment of Trusts.
23.78	—— —— Self Settled Trusts.
23.79	—— —— Third Party Trusts.
23.80	—— Spousal Budgeting: Protection of Resources and Income for the Community Spouse.
23.81	—— Recoveries Against Estates.
23.82	—— Liens.
23.83	—— Administrative and Judicial Appeals.
23.84	Home Care Coverage.
23.85	—— Medicare.
23.86	—— Medicaid.

TABLE OF CONTENTS

Sec.
23.87 ____ Expanded In–Home Services for the Elderly Program ("EISEP").
23.88 ____ Private Insurance.
23.89 Hospital Patients Rights.
23.90 ____ Bill of Rights.
23.91 ____ Discharge Planning.
23.92 Nursing Home Resident Rights.
23.93 ____ Admission to a Facility.
23.94 ____ Bill of Rights.
23.95 ____ Financial Rights.
23.96 ____ Transfer and Discharge.
23.97 ____ Bed Hold Policy.
23.98 ____ Remedies for Violation of Rights or Improper Treatment.
23.99 Housing Issues.
23.100 ____ Real Property Tax Exemption.
23.101 ____ Real Property Tax Credit.
23.102 ____ Tax Assistance Loans.
23.103 ____ Home Repair Assistance.
23.104 ____ Reverse Mortgages and Home Equity Loans.
23.105 ____ Home Energy Assistance Program ("HEAP").
23.106 ____ Tenant Protections.
23.107 ____ Life Care Retirement Communities.
23.108 ____ Community Based Services.
23.109 Health Care Decision Making.
23.110 ____ Health Care Proxy.
23.111 ____ The Living Will.
23.112 ____ Do Not Resuscitate Orders.
23.113 ____ Physician Assisted Suicide.
23.114 Tax Issues.
23.115 ____ Additional Standard Deduction for the Aged and Blind.
23.116 ____ Incapacity.
23.117 ____ Sale of a Principal Residence.
23.118 ____ Medical Deductions.
23.119 Miscellaneous Programs.
23.120 ____ Elderly Pharmaceutical Insurance Coverage ("EPIC").
23.121 ____ Life Line Telephone Service.
23.122 Forms.
23.123 ____ Documentation Letter. 💾
23.124 ____ Consultation Letter. 💾
23.125 ____ Health Care Proxy Statutory Form. 💾
23.126 ____ Sample Living Will. 💾

CHAPTER 24. ESTATE PLANNING

24.1 Scope Note.
24.2 Strategy.
24.3 Wills.
24.4 ____ Execution Requirements.
24.5 ____ ____ Signature.
24.6 ____ ____ Publication.

TABLE OF CONTENTS

Sec.
- 24.7 ___ ___ Witnesses.
- 24.8 ___ ___ Self Proving Affidavit.
- 24.9 ___ Provisions—Personal Property Dispositions.
- 24.10 ___ ___ Debts and Taxes.
- 24.11 ___ ___ Real Property.
- 24.12 ___ ___ Residuary Estate.
- 24.13 ___ ___ Dispositions in Trust.
- 24.14 ___ ___ Guardianships.
- 24.15 ___ ___ Appointment of Executors and Trustees.
- 24.16 ___ ___ Fiduciary Powers.
- 24.17 ___ ___ Miscellaneous.
- 24.18 Federal Estate and Gift Taxes.
- 24.19 ___ Rates.
- 24.20 New York State Estate and Gift Tax.
- 24.21 Estate Tax Planning—Utilizing the Unified Credit.
- 24.22 ___ Utilizing the Marital Deduction.
- 24.23 ___ Formula Clauses.
- 24.24 Generation Skipping Transfer Tax.
- 24.25 ___ Taxable Termination.
- 24.26 ___ Direct Skip.
- 24.27 ___ Taxable Distribution.
- 24.28 ___ Generation Assignment.
- 24.29 ___ Multiple Skips.
- 24.30 ___ Exemption.
- 24.31 ___ "Reverse QTIP."
- 24.32 Charitable Bequests.
- 24.33 Planning With Certain Assets.
- 24.34 ___ Life Insurance.
- 24.35 ___ ___ Life Insurance Trusts.
- 24.36 ___ ___ ___ "Crummey Powers."
- 24.37 ___ Retirement Benefits.
- 24.38 ___ Closely Held Business Interests.
- 24.39 ___ ___ Buy-Sell Agreements.
- 24.40 ___ ___ Liquidity Issues.
- 24.41 ___ ___ Minority Discounts.
- 24.42 ___ Farms and Business Real Property.
- 24.43 ___ Installment Obligations.
- 24.44 Lifetime Planning.
- 24.45 ___ Valuation of Gifts.
- 24.46 ___ ___ Grantor Retained Trusts.
- 24.47 ___ ___ Residence Trusts.
- 24.48 ___ ___ ___ Income Tax Considerations.
- 24.49 ___ Annual Gift Tax Exclusion.
- 24.50 ___ ___ Section 2503(c) Trusts.
- 24.51 ___ ___ Uniform Transfers to Minor's Act Accounts.
- 24.52 ___ ___ Crummey Trusts.
- 24.53 ___ ___ Family Limited Partnerships.
- 24.54 ___ Charitable Remainder Trusts.
- 24.55 ___ Charitable Lead Trusts.
- 24.56 Planning in Special Situations—Terminally Ill.

TABLE OF CONTENTS

Sec.
- 24.57 ____ ____ Self-Canceling Installment Notes.
- 24.58 ____ Non-citizen Spouses.
- 24.59 ____ Multiple Marriages.
- 24.60 ____ ____ Spousal Rights.
- 24.61 ____ ____ ____ Joint Wills and Contracts to Make Wills.
- 24.62 ____ ____ Long Term Care.
- 24.63 ____ Separation.
- 24.64 ____ Divorce.
- 24.65 ____ ____ Death During Divorce Proceeding.
- 24.66 ____ Unmarried Couples.
- 24.67 Postmortem Planning.
- 24.68 ____ Disclaimers.
- 24.69 ____ ____ Disclaimer Trusts.
- 24.70 ____ ____ Creditor Avoidance.
- 24.71 ____ ____ New York Statutory Requirements.
- 24.72 ____ Partial QTIP Election.
- 24.73 ____ Electing Alternate Valuation Date.
- 24.74 ____ Allocation of Income and Expenses.
- 24.75 ____ ____ U.S. Savings Bonds.
- 24.76 ____ ____ Expenses.
- 24.77 ____ Choosing the Fiscal Year of the Estate.
- 24.78 ____ Electing to File Joint Return with Decedent's Spouse.
- 24.79 ____ Waiving Commissions.
- 24.80 Probate Avoidance.
- 24.81 ____ Revocable Trusts.
- 24.82 ____ Totten Trusts.
- 24.83 ____ Jointly Held Assets.
- 24.84 Asset Protection.
- 24.85 ____ Statutory Exemptions.
- 24.86 ____ Family Partnerships.
- 24.87 ____ Domestic Trusts.
- 24.88 ____ Foreign Trusts.
- 24.89 Powers of Attorney.
- 24.90 Advance Directives.
- 24.91 ____ Health Care Proxy.
- 24.92 ____ Living Will.
- 24.93 Ethical Considerations in Estate Planning.
- 24.94 ____ Multiple Clients.
- 24.95 ____ Attorney/Draftsman as Fiduciary or Beneficiary.
- 24.96 Forms
- 24.97 ____ Estate Planner's Checklist.
- 24.98 ____ Sample Information Request Letter.
- 24.99 ____ Client Questionnaire.
- 24.100 ____ "Durable" Power of Attorney Form.
- 24.101 ____ Crummey Notice.
- 24.102 ____ Spousal Conflicts Letter.

CHAPTER 25. PROBATE AND ESTATE ADMINISTRATION

- 25.1 Scope Note.

TABLE OF CONTENTS

Sec.
25.2   Explanation of Basic Legal Terms in Estate Practice.
25.3   Strategy.
25.4   Who May Commence the Estate of a Person Who Dies Without a Will.
25.5   Who Is Entitled to Letters of Administration.
25.6   Who May Commence the Estate of a Person Who Dies With a Will.
25.7   Documents Required on Application for Letters of Administration.
25.8   Who Must Be Cited on an Application for Letters of Administration.
25.9   When a Guardian *Ad Litem* Must be Appointed.
25.10 Denial or Revocation of Letters of Administration.
25.11 Letters of Temporary Administration.
25.12 Venue.
25.13 Duty of the Fiduciary to Expeditiously Seek Probate.
25.14 When a Beneficiary Should Petition for Probate.
25.15 When a Creditor Should Petition for Probate.
25.16 When a Person in Litigation with an Estate Should Petition for Probate.
25.17 Information to Be Gathered by Attorney.
25.18 Contents of Petition for Probate.
25.19 Documents Required to Accompany Probate Petition.
25.20 What to Do If Your Client Cannot Produce the Original Will.
25.21 Requirements and Procedure for Proving a Will Where the Original Is Lost.
25.22 How to Get a Will Admitted to Probate If None of the Witnesses to the Will are Available.
25.23 When a Court Must Appoint a Guardian *Ad Litem* in a Probate Proceeding.
25.24 Who May Oppose the Admission to Probate of a Will By Filing Objections.
25.25 When Objections Must Be Filed.
25.26 How to Start an Estate Administration Where There Will Be a Delay in Getting a Will Admitted to Probate.
25.27 Form of Objections to Probate.
25.28 Burden of Proof
25.29 Requirement of a Notice of Objections to Complete Jurisdiction in a Contested Probate.
25.30 Right to a Trial by Jury.
25.31 Right to Discovery in a Probate, Administration or Accounting Proceeding.
25.32 Who Is Entitled to Letters of Administration When a Person Dies Without a Will.
25.33 Procedures to Follow in Administering the Estate.
25.34 How to Force an Estate Administration to Be Completed—Compelling an Accounting.
25.35 Concluding an Estate Administration Without an Accounting Proceeding.
25.36 Obtaining a Decree Concluding the Estate Based on Filed Receipts and Releases.
25.37 Concluding an Estate by a Formal Judicial Accounting.

TABLE OF CONTENTS

Sec.
25.38 Objections to an Account.
25.39 Prosecuting Objections to an Account.
25.40 Claims Against an Estate by a Creditor.
25.41 Representing a Claimant Against an Estate.
25.42 Obtaining Information About Estate Assets and Recovering Estate Property.
25.43 How to Proceed When Your Client Has a Claim Against an Estate.
25.44 A Special Provision for an Estate Beneficiary Obtaining Funds for Education.
25.45 Who Is Entitled to Assets When Two or More Fiduciaries Are in Dispute.
25.46 Compensation of Executor and Administrator, When Payable.
25.47 Attorney's Fees.
25.48 Declining to Serve as an Executor or Trustee.
25.49 Renouncing an Inheritance.
25.50 Construction of a Will.
25.51 Forms.
25.52 ____ Probate Petition.
25.53 ____ Affidavit Proving Correct Copy of Will.
25.54 ____ Citation in Probate.
25.55 ____ Affidavit of Service of Citation.
25.56 ____ Affidavit of Mailing Notice of Application for Letters of Administration.
25.57 ____ Waiver and Consent.
25.58 ____ Notice of Probate.
25.59 ____ Deposition Affidavit of Subscribing Witness.
25.60 ____ Objections to Probate.
25.61 ____ Decree Granting Probate.
25.62 ____ Receipt and Release Agreement Concluding an Estate Without an Accounting Proceeding.
25.63 ____ Receipt and Release (Legacy).
25.64 ____ Petition to Judicially Settle Executor's Account.
25.65 ____ Citation to Executor to Show Cause Why Judicially Executor Should Not Account.
25.66 ____ Accounting Form.
25.67 ____ Petition for Letters of Administration or Limited Letters of Administration or Temporary Administration.
25.68 ____ Decree Appointing Administrator.
25.69 ____ Affidavit Asking Court to Fix Amount of Administrator's Bond.
25.70 ____ Waiver of Citation, Renunciation of Signer's Claim to Letters and Consent to Appointment of Administrator.
25.71 ____ Notice of Application for Letters of Administration.
25.72 ____ Citation That Can Be Adopted for Use in Any Proceeding.

CHAPTER 26. PERSONAL INJURY

26.1 Scope Note.
26.2 Strategy.

TABLE OF CONTENTS

Sec.
26.3 ____ Client Interview.
26.4 ____ Valuing the Case.
26.5 ____ Skills and Ethics.
26.6 ____ Retainer.
26.7 ____ ____ Retainer Statement.
26.8 ____ Expenses.
26.9 Investigation.
26.10 ____ Premises Liability.
26.11 ____ Medical Malpractice.
26.12 ____ ____ Hospital.
26.13 ____ ____ Dental and Podiatric Malpractice.
26.14 ____ Products Liability.
26.15 ____ Dog Bites.
26.16 ____ Chemical Exposure.
26.17 ____ Automobile Accidents.
26.18 ____ ____ Police Report.
26.19 ____ ____ Witness Statements.
26.20 ____ ____ MV104.
26.21 ____ ____ Application of No–Fault.
26.22 ____ ____ Medical Records.
26.23 ____ ____ Photographs.
26.24 ____ ____ Insurance Policies and Coverage.
26.25 Claims Procedure for Automobile Accidents.
26.26 ____ Filing Notice of Claim With the Motor Vehicle Accident Indemnity Corporation.
26.27 ____ ____ Procedure for Cases in Which There Is No Insurance.
26.28 ____ ____ Procedure for Cases in Which There Is No Insurance and the Identity of the Wrongdoer Is Not Ascertainable (Hit and Run).
26.29 ____ ____ Procedure for Cases in Which Insurance Initially Is Believed to Exist, But There Is No Insurance After Later Disclaimer.
26.30 ____ ____ Late Claims.
26.31 Theories of Liability.
26.32 Filing the Action.
26.33 ____ When.
26.34 ____ Where.
26.35 ____ Potential Defendants.
26.36 The Summons and the Complaint.
26.37 The Answer.
26.38 Actions Against Municipal Corporations.
26.39 ____ Notice of Claim.
26.40 ____ ____ Content.
26.41 Actions Against the State.
26.42 Discovery—Generally.
26.43 ____ Depositions.
26.44 ____ Interrogatories.
26.45 ____ Document Discovery and Inspection.
26.46 ____ Bills of Particulars.
26.47 ____ Demand for a Bill of Particulars.

TABLE OF CONTENTS

Sec.
- 26.48 Settlement.
- 26.49 Liens.
- 26.50 Alternative Dispute Resolution.
- 26.51 Trial Preparation: Introductory Note.
- 26.52 Trial.
- 26.53 ____ Subpoenas.
- 26.54 ____ Exhibits.
- 26.55 ____ *Voir Dire.*
- 26.56 Disbursement of Proceeds of Settlement or Recovery.
- 26.57 Drafting Checklists.
- 26.58 ____ Complaint.
- 26.59 ____ Answer.
- 26.60 ____ Demand for Bill of Particulars.
- 26.61 ____ Responses to Demand for Bill of Particulars.
- 26.62 Forms—Client's Retainer Agreement. 💾
- 26.63 ____ Retainer Statement. 💾
- 26.64 ____ Department of Motor Vehicles MV104 Form.
- 26.65 ____ Summons and Complaint. 💾
- 26.66 ____ Amended Answer, Counterclaim and Cross Claim. 💾
- 26.67 ____ Defendant's Demand for a Verified Bill of Particulars. 💾
- 26.68 ____ Defendant's CPLR 3101 Demands. 💾
- 26.69 ____ Plaintiff's Demand for a Verified Bill of Particulars. 💾
- 26.70 ____ Plaintiff's CPLR 3101 Demands. 💾
- 26.71 ____ Closing Statement. 💾

CHAPTER 27. PRODUCTS LIABILITY

- 27.1 Scope Note.
- 27.2 Strategy.
- 27.3 Historical Overview.
- 27.4 Bases of a Products Liability Claim.
- 27.5 Theories of Liability.
- 27.6 ____ Manufacturing Defect or Mistake in the Manufacturing Process.
- 27.7 ____ Defective Design.
- 27.8 ____ ____ Burden of Proof.
- 27.9 ____ ____ Defense.
- 27.10 ____ Failure to Warn or Inadequate Warnings.
- 27.11 ____ ____ Burden of Proof.
- 27.12 ____ ____ Duty to Warn.
- 27.13 ____ ____ Adequacy of Warning.
- 27.14 ____ ____ Jury Question.
- 27.15 ____ ____ Informed Intermediary Defense.
- 27.16 ____ ____ Duty to Warn the Unusually Sensitive.
- 27.17 ____ ____ Non-Commercial Cases.
- 27.18 ____ Failure to Test.
- 27.19 ____ ____ FDA Approval.
- 27.20 ____ ____ Jury Question.
- 27.21 ____ ____ Preemption Defense.
- 27.22 Distributors' or Sellers' Liability.

TABLE OF CONTENTS

Sec.
- 27.23 ____ Sale Must Be Part of Ordinary Business.
- 27.24 ____ Service v. Sales.
- 27.25 ____ Medical Care Providers.
- 27.26 Successor Liability.
- 27.27 ____ Burden of Proof.
- 27.28 ____ Punitive Damages.
- 27.29 Liability of the Manufacturer of Component Parts.
- 27.30 Liability of the Manufacturer of the Complete Product.
- 27.31 Introducing Evidence of Post Accident Modification or Repairs.
- 27.32 Introducing Evidence of Other Incidents.
- 27.33 Effect of Destruction of the Product Upon Plaintiff's Ability to Prove a Defect.
- 27.34 Proof of Causation.
- 27.35 ____ Question for the Jury or Question for the Judge.
- 27.36 Foreseeability of Harm.
- 27.37 Discovery Issues.
- 27.38 ____ Confidentiality Orders or Stipulations.
- 27.39 Statute of Limitations.
- 27.40 Intervening Acts of Negligence—Plaintiff's Misuse of the Product.
- 27.41 ____ Alteration of the Product After it Has Left the Hands of the Manufacturer.
- 27.42 Preemption of Private Claims.
- 27.43 ____ Old Rule.
- 27.44 ____ New Rule.
- 27.45 ____ National Traffic & Motor Vehicle Safety Act and Its Savings Clause.
- 27.46 ____ Public Health Cigarette Labeling & Advertising Act of 1965 and the Public Health Cigarette Smoking Act of 1969—The *Cipollone* Decision.
- 27.47 ____ Federal Insecticide, Fungicide and Rodenticide Act (FIFRA) and Its Impact on Labeling Requirements.
- 27.48 ____ Medical Device Amendments to FDA Regulations.
- 27.49 ____ Limits on Preemption and Statutory Defenses.
- 27.50 ____ Validity of the Safety Standard or Regulatory Statute.
- 27.51 ____ Checklist.
- 27.52 Imposing Liability when the Manufacturer of a Fungible or Generic Product Is Unknown (Concert of Action/Market Share Liability).
- 27.53 Collateral Estoppel in Products Liability Cases.
- 27.54 Proof of Allegations Checklist.
- 27.55 Drafting Checklist—Complaint.
- 27.56 ____ Answer.
- 27.57 Forms—Products Liability Complaint.
- 27.58 ____ Products Liability Answer.

Volume 24

CHAPTER 28. LEGAL MALPRACTICE

- 28.1 Scope Note.

TABLE OF CONTENTS

Sec.
28.2 Strategy.
28.3 The Duty of Care.
28.4 ___ Specific Acts—Erroneous Advice.
28.5 ___ ___ Incompetent Tax Advice.
28.6 ___ ___ Proper Withdrawal.
28.7 ___ ___ Detecting Fraud.
28.8 ___ Causation.
28.9 ___ ___ The Doctrine of Compelled Settlement.
28.10 ___ Damages.
28.11 ___ Defenses—The Privity Rule.
28.12 ___ ___ Lawyer's Judgment Rule.
28.13 ___ ___ Statute of Limitations.
28.14 ___ ___ Continuous Representation Tolling Doctrine.
28.15 ___ ___ Extension by Estoppel.
28.16 ___ ___ Standard Negligence Defenses of Lack of Foreseeability and Supervening Act.
28.17 ___ ___ Concealment of Malpractice Not a Separate Cause of Action.
28.18 ___ ___ Need for Consistent Positions.
28.19 The Duty of Loyalty.
28.20 ___ Conflict of Interest.
28.21 ___ Disqualification.
28.22 ___ Misappropriation of Client Funds.
28.23 Liability for Negligence of Independent Contractors.
28.24 Statutory Liability Under Judiciary Law § 487.
28.25 Vicarious Liability for Partner's Misdeeds.
28.26 Liability for Indemnity and Contribution.
28.27 Fee Disputes.
28.28 ___ Alternative Dispute Resolution.
28.29 ___ ___ Retainer Agreements Given Strict Scrutiny.
28.30 ___ ___ Arbitration Clause in Retainer Agreement May Waive Other Client Rights.
28.31 ___ Statutory Limitations.
28.32 ___ Account Stated.
28.33 ___ A Standard of Reasonableness.
28.34 Limited Liability Companies and Limited Liability Partnerships.
28.35 Lawyers Professional Liability Insurance.
28.36 ___ Extended Reporting Period.
28.37 ___ What Is a "Claim" and When Is It "Made"?
28.38 ___ Professional Capacity and Typical Exclusions.
28.39 ___ Limits, Deductibles and Defense.
28.40 ___ Notice of Claim and Notice of Occurrence.
28.41 ___ Cancellation.
28.42 ___ Innocent Partner Coverage.
28.43 ___ Application for Coverage and Rescission of Policy.
28.44 ___ Bad Faith.
28.45 ___ Cautions for Dissolving Law Firms.
28.46 Conclusion.
28.47 Drafting Checklist—Retainer Agreement.
28.48 ___ Malpractice Complaint Against Attorney.

TABLE OF CONTENTS

Sec.
28.49 ____ Answer to Malpractice Complaint on Behalf of Attorney.
28.50 Forms—Retainer Agreement With ADR Clause. 💾
28.51 ____ Retainer Agreement Without ADR Clause. 💾
28.52 ____ Complaint for Malpractice: Commercial Transaction. 💾
28.53 ____ Complaint for Malpractice: Personal Injury Action. 💾
28.54 ____ Answer: Commercial Transaction. 💾
28.55 ____ Answer: Personal Injury Action. 💾

CHAPTER 29. MEDICAL MALPRACTICE

29.1 Scope Note.
29.2 Strategy.
29.3 ____ Determining the Presence or Absence of Medical Malpractice.
29.4 ____ The Nature and Degree of Damages.
29.5 ____ Interviewing the Client.
29.6 ____ ____ History of the Current Condition.
29.7 ____ ____ Past Medical Conditions.
29.8 ____ ____ Current Medical Condition.
29.9 ____ ____ Miscellaneous Issues.
29.10 The Common Law Standards.
29.11 ____ The Standard of Care.
29.12 ____ ____ Hospitals' *Respondeat-Superior* Liability.
29.13 ____ ____ Hospitals' Direct Liability.
29.14 ____ Informed Consent.
29.15 ____ Health Maintenance Organizations.
29.16 ____ Expert Witnesses.
29.17 ____ Defenses in Medical Malpractice Cases.
29.18 Regulatory Standards.
29.19 ____ Qualifications of Nurse Midwives.
29.20 ____ Clinical Laboratories.
29.21 ____ Blood Banks.
29.22 ____ Testing for Phenylketonuria and Other Diseases and Conditions/Early Intervention Program.
29.23 ____ Hospitals.
29.24 Damages.
29.25 Procedure.
29.26 ____ Statutes of Limitation.
29.27 ____ Steps for Filing an Action.
29.28 ____ ____ Certificate of Merit.
29.29 ____ ____ Notice of Medical Malpractice Action.
29.30 ____ ____ Pre-calendar Conferences.
29.31 ____ Periodic Payment of Large Verdicts.
29.32 Hospital Operations and Medical Negligence—Credentialling of Physicians.
29.33 ____ Quality Assurance and Risk Management.
29.34 ____ Departmentalization of Services—Departmental Chairs.
29.35 Training and Education of Physicians.
29.36 ____ Medical School.
29.37 ____ PGY–1 (Internship).
29.38 ____ Residency.

TABLE OF CONTENTS

Sec.
29.39	___ Fellowships.
29.40	___ Board Certification & Re-certification.
29.41	___ Associations, Societies, and Continuing Medical Education.
29.42	___ National Practitioner Data Bank.
29.43	Medical Literature.
29.44	___ Obtaining Medical Literature.
29.45	___ Sources.
29.46	___ Using Medical Literature to Evaluate a Case.
29.47	___ Preparing for Depositions.
29.48	___ Preparing for Trial.
29.49	___ Use of Treatises in State Court.
29.50	___ Use of Treatises in Federal Court.
29.51	Evaluating and Understanding Medical Records—Physician's Records.
29.52	___ Hospital Records.
29.53	___ ___ Informed Consent Forms.
29.54	___ ___ Progress Notes.
29.55	___ ___ Order Sheets.
29.56	___ ___ Consultation Records.
29.57	___ ___ Operative Records.
29.58	___ ___ Medication Records.
29.59	___ ___ Intake and Output Records.
29.60	___ ___ Radiographic Records.
29.61	___ ___ Obstetrical Records.
29.62	___ ___ ICU/CCU Records.
29.63	___ ___ Nurses' Notes.
29.64	Discovery.
29.65	___ Obtaining and Identifying Relevant Records.
29.66	___ ___ Physician's Records.
29.67	___ ___ Hospital Records.
29.68	___ ___ Billing Records.
29.69	___ ___ Pharmacy Records.
29.70	___ ___ Allied Health Provider Records.
29.71	___ ___ Workers' Compensation Claims File.
29.72	___ ___ Autopsy Report.
29.73	___ ___ Workers' Compensation Actions.
29.74	___ ___ Medical Malpractice Actions.
29.75	Trial Preparation.
29.76	Drafting Checklists.
29.77	___ Order to Show Cause to Obtain Medical Records.
29.78	___ Affirmation in Support of Order to Show Cause.
29.79	___ Certificate of Merit.
29.80	Forms
29.81	___ Order to Show Cause to Obtain Medical Records. 💾
29.82	___ Affirmation in Support of Order to Show Cause. 💾
29.83	___ Certificate of Merit. 💾

CHAPTER 30. DAMAGES

30.1　　Scope Note.

TABLE OF CONTENTS

Sec.	
30.2	Strategy.
30.3	____ Pretrial Stage.
30.4	____ Trial Stage.
30.5	The Nature of Damages.
30.6	Compensatory Damages.
30.7	____ Personal Injury.
30.8	____ ____ Physical Pain and Suffering.
30.9	____ ____ Mental or Emotional Pain and Suffering.
30.10	____ ____ Loss of Earnings and Impairment of Future Earning Ability.
30.11	____ ____ Aggravation of Pre-existing Injuries.
30.12	____ Wrongful Death.
30.13	____ ____ Damages Sustained Before Death.
30.14	____ ____ Damages Sustained After Death.
30.15	____ Loss of Consortium.
30.16	____ Property Damage.
30.17	____ ____ Real Property.
30.18	____ Personal Property.
30.19	____ Breach of Contract.
30.20	____ ____ Contract Price and Actual Loss.
30.21	____ ____ Delay in Performance.
30.22	____ ____ Defective Performance.
30.23	____ ____ Anticipatory Breach.
30.24	____ ____ Damages Within the Contemplation of the Parties, and Loss of Profits.
30.25	____ ____ Building and Construction.
30.26	____ Minimizing and Mitigating Damages.
30.27	____ ____ Contracts.
30.28	____ ____ Personal Injury.
30.29	____ Excessive or Inadequate Damages.
30.30	____ ____ Specific Awards.
30.31	Punitive Damages.
30.32	____ Intentional Torts.
30.33	____ Negligence.
30.34	____ Contract.
30.35	____ Awards.
30.36	____ Mitigation.
30.37	Nominal Damages.
30.38	Statutory Damages.
30.39	Liquidated Damages and Penalties.
30.40	Interest.
30.41	Attorney Fees.
30.42	____ Statutory.
30.43	____ Agreements and Miscellaneous.
30.44	Periodic Payment of Judgments.
30.45	Forms.
30.46	____ *Ad Damnum* Clause in Ordinary Complaint.
30.47	____ *Ad Damnum* Clause in Complaint in Medical or Dental Malpractice Action or in Action Against Municipal Government (Supreme Court).

TABLE OF CONTENTS

Sec.

30.48 ____ Clauses in Complaint in Action Involving Automobile Accident. 💾

30.49 ____ Request for Supplemental Demand for Relief in Medical or Dental Malpractice Action or Action Against Municipal Corporation. 💾

30.50 ____ Defense of Culpable Conduct in Answer. 💾

30.51 ____ Defense of Failure to Use Seat Belt Contained in Answer. 💾

30.52 ____ Defense of Indemnification From Collateral Sources. 💾

30.53 ____ Partial Defense; Mitigation of Damages. 💾

30.54 ____ Partial Defense; Mitigation of Damages in Libel Action. 💾

30.55 ____ Partial Defense; Inability to Convey Property. 💾

30.56 ____ Notice of Motion to Amend Verdict (or Judgment) to Add Interest. 💾

30.57 ____ Affidavit in Support of Motion to Amend Verdict (or Judgment) to Add Interest. 💾

30.58 ____ Notice of Motion to Fix Date From Which Interest is to Be Computed. 💾

30.59 ____ Affidavit in Support of Motion to Fix Date From Which Interest is to Be Computed. 💾

30.60 Pattern Jury Instructions.

30.61 ____ Personal Injury—Subsequent Injury, Accident.

30.62 ____ ____ Loss of Earnings.

30.63 ____ Damages—Personal Injury—Shock and Fright and Physical Consequences.

30.64 ____ ____ Aggravation of Injury.

30.65 ____ Payment of Income Taxes on Damages for Personal Injury.

30.66 ____ Reduction to Present Value.

30.67 ____ Wrongful Death—Conscious Pain and Suffering.

30.68 ____ Personal Injury—Collateral Sources—Itemized Verdict (CPLR 4111).

30.69 ____ Damages—Property Without Market Value.

30.70 ____ Damages—Property With Market Value.

30.71 ____ Contracts—Damages—Generally.

30.72 ____ ____ Damages—Employment Contract.

CHAPTER 31. INSURANCE

31.1 Scope Note.
31.2 Strategy.
31.3 ____ Checklist.
31.4 Sources of New York Insurance Law.
31.5 Third Parties Involved in the Placement and Administration of the Insurance Contract.
31.6 ____ Insurance Brokers.
31.7 ____ Insurance Agents.
31.8 Nature of Insurance.
31.9 Interpreting an Insurance Policy.
31.10 Notice.
31.11 The Cooperation Clause.

TABLE OF CONTENTS

Sec.
- 31.12 The Insurer's Duty to Defend.
- 31.13 ____ Responding to a Request for a Defense.
- 31.14 ____ Damages for Breach of the Duty.
- 31.15 Reservations of Rights By an Insurer.
- 31.16 Disclaiming/Denying Coverage.
- 31.17 The Insurer's Duty of Good Faith and Fair Dealing.
- 31.18 Rescission of Insurance Policies.
- 31.19 Reformation.
- 31.20 Lost Policies.
- 31.21 Nature of Relief.
- 31.22 Service of Process.
- 31.23 Pre-answer Security.
- 31.24 Arbitration Clauses.
- 31.25 Choice of Law.
- 31.26 Statutes of Limitation.
- 31.27 Burden of Proof.
- 31.28 Insolvent Insurers.
- 31.29 Subrogation.
- 31.30 Allocation of Losses Between Co-insurers.
- 31.31 Checklist of Essential Allegations.
- 31.32 Forms—Complaint By Policyholder for Declaratory Relief and Breach of Contract.
- 31.33 ____ Complaint By Insurer for Declaratory Relief.
- 31.34 ____ Complaint By Insurer for Rescission.
- 31.35 ____ Affirmative Defenses Asserted By Insurer in a Coverage Action.

CHAPTER 32. WORKERS' COMPENSATION

- 32.1 Scope Note.
- 32.2 Strategy.
- 32.3 ____ Employer's Counsel's Checklist.
- 32.4 ____ Employee's Counsel's Checklist.
- 32.5 Introduction to The Workers' Compensation Law.
- 32.6 ____ History and Theory.
- 32.7 ____ ____ Workmen's Compensation Law of 1910.
- 32.8 ____ ____ Constitutional Amendment.
- 32.9 ____ ____ Workmen's Compensation Law of 1914.
- 32.10 ____ ____ Statutory Changes.
- 32.11 Workers' Compensation Board.
- 32.12 Employer's Obligations and Methods of Coverage.
- 32.13 Compensable Injury.
- 32.14 Exclusive Remedy Doctrine.
- 32.15 ____ Exceptions.
- 32.16 Pre-hearing Conference.
- 32.17 Hearings.
- 32.18 ____ Statute of Limitations.
- 32.19 ____ Burden of Proof, Presumptions and Defenses.
- 32.20 ____ Conciliation Process.
- 32.21 Benefits.

TABLE OF CONTENTS

Sec.
32.22	___ Classification of Disability.
32.23	___ Wage Replacement.
32.24	___ ___ Schedule vs. Non-schedule Awards.
32.25	___ ___ Rehabilitation.
32.26	___ ___ Industrially Disabled.
32.27	___ ___ Special Disability Fund.
32.28	___ Medical Benefits.
32.29	___ Facial Disfigurement.
32.30	___ Death Awards.
32.31	___ ___ Funeral Expenses.
32.32	___ Assignments, Liens and Lump-sum Settlements.
32.33	Board Review of Decisions, Orders and Awards.
32.34	Appeal to Court.
32.35	Reopening Closed Claims.
32.36	Discrimination.
32.37	Licensed Representative.
32.38	Attorney's Fees.
32.39	Posted Notice of Coverage.
32.40	Uninsured Employers' Fund.
32.41	Insurance Policy for Workers' Compensation.
32.42	State Insurance Fund.
32.43	Federal Workers' Compensation Laws and Benefits.
32.44	Disability Benefits Law.
32.45	___ Employer's Obligations.
32.46	___ Exempt Employees.
32.47	___ Benefits and Employee Contribution.
32.48	___ Special Fund.
32.49	___ Employee Eligibility.
32.50	___ Claim Filing.
32.51	___ Pregnancy.
32.52	___ End Note.
32.53	Forms.
32.54	___ Workers' Compensation Board Employee's Claim For Compensation. (C–3 7–97)
32.55	___ Workers' Compensation Board Employer's Report of Work-Related Accident/Occupational Disease. (C–2 10–97)
32.56	___ Workers' Compensation Board Attending Doctor's Report and Carrier/Employer Billing. (C–4 3–97)
32.57	___ Workers' Compensation Board Notice that Right to Compensation is Controverted. (C–7 2–97)
32.58	___ Workers' Compensation Board Notice that Payment of Compensation for Disability has Been Stopped or Modified. (C–8/8.6 4–97)
32.59	___ Notice and Proof of Claim for Disability Benefits. (DB–450 3–97)
32.60	___ Notice of Total or Partial Rejection of Claim for Disability Benefits. (DB–451 3–97)

CHAPTER 33. LOCAL CRIMINAL COURT PRACTICE

33.1	Scope Note.

TABLE OF CONTENTS

Sec.

33.2	Strategy.
33.3	Overview of Local Criminal Court Process.
33.4	Police/Citizen Encounters.
33.5	___ Vehicle Stops.
33.6	___ The Parked Car.
33.7	___ Arrest Without Warrant.
33.8	Accusatory Instruments.
33.9	___ Information.
33.10	___ Simplified Information.
33.11	___ Prosecutor's Information.
33.12	___ Misdemeanor and Felony Complaints.
33.13	___ Supporting Depositions.
33.14	___ ___ Procedure.
33.15	___ ___ When Must They Be Provided?
33.16	___ ___ Who Must Be Served?
33.17	___ ___ Service of Request Must be Timely.
33.18	___ ___ Request By Attorney Requires Service on Counsel.
33.19	___ ___ Dismissal For Failure to Serve.
33.20	___ ___ Motion Must Be In Writing.
33.21	___ ___ Motion to Dismiss Must Be Timely.
33.22	___ ___ Factual Insufficiency Not Jurisdictional: Plea Waives Defect.
33.23	___ ___ Superseding Information Disallowed.
33.24	___ ___ People May File New Information Upon Dismissal of Supporting Deposition.
33.25	___ ___ Failure to Serve Not An Amendable Defect.
33.26	___ ___ Verification.
33.27	Probable Cause Hearing.
33.28	Plea Bargaining.
33.29	___ Plea Bargain Can Be Conditioned Upon Waiver of Right to Appeal.
33.30	___ Plea Bargaining—No Penalty for Asserting Right to Trial.
33.31	Pretrial Discovery.
33.32	___ Applicable to Simplified Informations.
33.33	___ Applicable to Traffic Infractions.
33.34	___ Subpoenas.
33.35	___ Demands to Produce/Bills of Particulars.
33.36	___ ___ Must Be Filed Within 30 Days.
33.37	___ ___ Response Within 15 Days.
33.38	___ ___ People's Failure to Comply With Time Limits.
33.39	___ *Brady* Material.
33.40	___ ___ Prosecutor Need Not Be Aware of Evidence.
33.41	___ ___ Timely Disclosure.
33.42	Evidence.
33.43	___ Motions to Suppress.
33.44	___ *Sandoval* Issues—Prior Convictions.
33.45	___ ___ Procedure.
33.46	___ ___ *Sandoval* Criteria.
33.47	___ ___ Defendant's Presence at *Sandoval* Hearing.
33.48	___ *Miranda*.

TABLE OF CONTENTS

Sec.
33.49 ___ ___ Applicable to Misdemeanor Traffic Offenses.
33.50 ___ ___ Stop and Frisk Does Not Constitute Custodial Interrogation.
33.51 ___ ___ Sobriety Checkpoint Stops Are Non-custodial.
33.52 ___ ___ Interrogation Defined.
33.53 ___ ___ Public Safety Exception.
33.54 ___ ___ Pedigree Exception.
33.55 ___ ___ Waiver Following Assertion of Right to Remain Silent.
33.56 ___ ___ Waiver Following Request for Counsel.
33.57 ___ Involuntary Statements.
33.58 ___ ___ May Not Be Used to Impeach.
33.59 ___ ___ Applicability of Harmless Error Doctrine.
33.60 ___ The Use of Defendant's Pre-arrest Silence.
33.61 ___ Corroboration of Admission or Confession Required.
33.62 Trial.
33.63 ___ Modes of Trial.
33.64 ___ Order of Jury Trial Proceedings.
33.65 ___ Order of Bench Trial Proceedings.
33.66 ___ Trial of Speeding Tickets.
33.67 ___ ___ Discovery.
33.68 ___ ___ People's *Prima Facie* Case.
33.69 ___ ___ When Not to Request a Supporting Deposition.
33.70 ___ ___ Speeding Trial Summary.
33.71 Speedy Trial Pursuant to CPL § 30.20.
33.72 ___ Application to Traffic Infractions.
33.73 ___ Criteria.
33.74 CPL § 30.30.
33.75 ___ Vehicle and Traffic Law Violations Generally Excluded.
33.76 ___ ___ Unless Combined With Felony, Misdemeanor or Violation.
33.77 ___ People's Readiness Rule.
33.78 ___ Requirements for An Assertion of Readiness.
33.79 ___ ___ Actual Readiness for Trial.
33.80 ___ Guilty Plea Waives CPL § 30.30 Motion.
33.81 ___ Burden of Proof.
33.82 ___ Commencement of Criminal Action—Appearance Tickets.
33.83 ___ Uniform Traffic Tickets.
33.84 ___ Excludable Time.
33.85 ___ ___ Motions.
33.86 ___ ___ Defective Accusatory Instrument.
33.87 ___ ___ Adjournments.
33.88 ___ ___ Delays by the Court.
33.89 ___ ___ Effect of Defendant's Unavailability.
33.90 ___ Post Readiness Delay.
33.91 Procedural Checklists.
33.92 ___ Notice of Motion to Dismiss For Failure to Serve a Timely Supporting Deposition/Attorney Affirmation in Support of Motion.
33.93 ___ Demand to Produce: Speeding Ticket.
33.94 Drafting Checklists.

TABLE OF CONTENTS

Sec.
33.95 ____ Notice of Motion to Dismiss For Failure to Serve a Timely Supporting Deposition.
33.96 ____ Attorney Affirmation in Support of Motion to Dismiss For Failure to Serve a Timely Supporting Deposition.
33.97 ____ Demand to Produce: Speeding Ticket.
33.98 Forms.
33.99 ____ Notice of Motion to Dismiss For Failure to Serve a Timely Supporting Deposition. 💾
33.100 ____ Attorney Affirmation in Support of Motion to Dismiss For Failure to Serve a Timely Supporting Deposition. 💾
33.101 ____ Demand to Produce: Speeding Ticket. 💾

CHAPTER 34. SOCIAL SECURITY DISABILITY CASES

34.1 Scope Note.
34.2 Strategy.
34.3 The Law of Disability.
34.4 ____ Statutory Definition of Disability.
34.5 ____ Judicial Definitions.
34.6 ____ Durational Requirements.
34.7 ____ Comparison to Workers' Compensation.
34.8 ____ Assessing Disability: The Sequential Evaluation.
34.9 ____ ____ Substantial Gainful Activity.
34.10 ____ ____ Severity.
34.11 ____ ____ Listings of Impairments.
34.12 ____ ____ Ability to Do Past Relevant Work.
34.13 ____ ____ Ability to Do Other Work.
34.14 ____ ____ Dispensing With Individualized Assessment.
34.15 Financial Consideration of The Two Federal Programs: Social Security Disability Insurance Benefits and Supplemental Security Income.
34.16 ____ Income.
34.17 ____ Assets.
34.18 ____ Amount of Benefits.
34.19 ____ SSI: Based on Financial Need.
34.20 ____ SSDIB: Based on FICA Withholding.
34.21 ____ Eligibility for Both SSI and SSDIB.
34.22 ____ Retroactivity of Benefits.
34.23 Administrative Procedure.
34.24 ____ Application.
34.25 ____ Reconsideration.
34.26 ____ Termination of Benefits.
34.27 ____ Administrative Hearing.
34.28 ____ Appeals Council.
34.29 ____ Federal District Court.
34.30 ____ Court of Appeals, Second Circuit.
34.31 Handling the Case—Generally.
34.32 ____ Initial Interview.
34.33 ____ Retainer Agreements.
34.34 ____ Social Security Administration's Records.

TABLE OF CONTENTS

Sec.
- 34.35 ____ Medical Evidence.
- 34.36 ____ ____ Hospital Records.
- 34.37 ____ ____ Reports from Treating Physicians.
- 34.38 ____ Other Evidence.
- 34.39 ____ ____ Former Co-workers and Employers.
- 34.40 ____ ____ Family Members.
- 34.41 ____ Preparing for the Hearing.
- 34.42 ____ ____ Preparing the Claimant.
- 34.43 ____ ____ Other Witnesses or Documents.
- 34.44 ____ Conducting the Hearing.
- 34.45 ____ ____ Testimony of the Claimant.
- 34.46 ____ ____ Medical Advisors.
- 34.47 ____ ____ Vocational Experts.
- 34.48 ____ Post-hearing Evidence and Memoranda.
- 34.49 Implementing Favorable Decisions.
- 34.50 ____ Collecting SSDIB Benefits.
- 34.51 ____ Collecting SSI Benefits.
- 34.52 ____ Collecting Fees.
- 34.53 ____ ____ Fee Applications.
- 34.54 ____ ____ Fee Agreements.
- 34.55 Appealing Unfavorable Decisions.
- 34.56 ____ Strategic Considerations Regarding Unfavorable Decisions.
- 34.57 ____ Strategic Considerations Regarding Partially Favorable Decisions.
- 34.58 Reopening Prior Applications.
- 34.59 ____ Reopening SSDIB.
- 34.60 ____ Reopening SSI.
- 34.61 ____ Review of Grants of Reopening.
- 34.62 ____ Review of Denials of Reopening.
- 34.63 ____ Court Decisions Requiring Reopening.
- 34.64 ____ Statutes and Regulations Requiring Reopening.
- 34.65 Procedural Checklist.
- 34.66 Checklists of Allegations—Medical Claims.
- 34.67 ____ Psychiatric Claims.
- 34.68 Forms—Claimant Questionnaire.
- 34.69 ____ Retainer Agreement.
- 34.70 ____ Retainer Agreement: Concurrent Benefits.
- 34.71 ____ Fee Agreement: Maximum Fee.
- 34.72 ____ Request for Medical Records.
- 34.73 ____ Medical Release.
- 34.74 ____ Medical Questionnaire for Treating Physician.
- 34.75 ____ Psychiatric Questionnaire.
- 34.76 ____ Cover Letter to Treating Physician.
- 34.77 ____ Thank-you Letter to Treating Physician.
- 34.78 ____ Request for Appeals Council Review.

CHAPTER 35. INCOME TAX

- 35.1 Scope Note.
- 35.2 Strategy.

TABLE OF CONTENTS

Sec.
35.3 ____ Checklist.
35.4 Personal Income Tax.
35.5 ____ Computing Federal Adjusted Gross Income.
35.6 ____ Computing Federal Taxable Income.
35.7 ____ Definition of New York Taxable Income.
35.8 ____ Computing New York Adjusted Gross Income.
35.9 ____ Computing New York Taxable Income.
35.10 ____ New York Personal Exemptions.
35.11 ____ Itemized Deductions for Married Couple.
35.12 ____ Exclusion of Pension and Disability Distributions From New York Income.
35.13 ____ New York Minimum Tax.
35.14 ____ Definition of Residency.
35.15 ____ Burden of Proving Non-residency.
35.16 ____ Domicile and Change of Domicile.
35.17 ____ New York Income Tax on Non-resident Individuals.
35.18 ____ Checklist.
35.19 New York Corporate Franchise Tax.
35.20 ____ Comparison With Federal Taxation.
35.21 ____ Initial Tax on Corporate Capital Structure.
35.22 ____ Foreign Corporations.
35.23 ____ Corporations Subject to Tax.
35.24 ____ Corporations Exempt From Tax.
35.25 ____ Necessary Level of Activity.
35.26 ____ Calculation.
35.27 ____ Tax on Net Income Base.
35.28 ____ ____ Subtractions From Federal Taxable Income.
35.29 ____ Items From Subsidiaries.
35.30 ____ Tax on Capital Base.
35.31 ____ ____ Definition of Capital Base.
35.32 ____ ____ Exemption for Small Businesses.
35.33 ____ Minimum Taxable Income Base.
35.34 ____ Fixed Dollar Minimum Tax.
35.35 ____ Apportionment of Tax Bases to New York.
35.36 ____ ____ Business Allocation Percentage.
35.37 ____ ____ Investment Allocation Percentage.
35.38 ____ Definition of Subsidiary Capital.
35.39 ____ Franchise Tax Checklist.
35.40 Department of Taxation and Finance.
35.41 ____ Role of Office of the Counsel.
35.42 ____ Taxpayer Services Division.
35.43 ____ Office of Revenue and Information Management.
35.44 ____ Office of Tax Operations.
35.45 ____ ____ Audit Division.
35.46 ____ ____ Tax Compliance Division.
35.47 ____ ____ Revenue Opportunity Division.
35.48 ____ ____ Office of Tax Enforcement.
35.49 ____ ____ Division of Tax Appeals.
35.50 ____ Summary.
35.51 Filing Returns.

TABLE OF CONTENTS

Sec.
35.52	——	Where to File.
35.53	——	Keeping Records of Returns.
35.54	——	Extensions of Time for Filing.
35.55	——	Obtaining New York Tax Forms.
35.56	——	Filing Claims for Refund.
35.57	——	Time Limitations.
35.58	——	Where to File.
35.59	——	Special Refund Authority.
35.60	——	Claim Based on Federal Changes.
35.61	——	Petitions for Refund.
35.62	——	Judicial Review of Denied Refund Claims.
35.63	——	Checklist.
35.64		Statutes of Limitation.
35.65	——	General Statutes for Income Tax Assessment.
35.66	——	Effect.
35.67	——	Exceptions.
35.68	——	Request for Prompt Assessment.
35.69	——	Waiver.
35.70		Penalties.
35.71	——	Late Filing.
35.72	——	Late Payment.
35.73	——	Reasonable Cause.
35.74	——	Negligence.
35.75	——	Substantial Understatement.
35.76	——	Underpayment of Estimated Taxes.
35.77	—— ——	Exceptions.
35.78	——	Fraud.
35.79	—— ——	Elements.
35.80	—— ——	Specific Determination Methods.
35.81	—— ——	Common Cases.
35.82	—— ——	Creative Methods of Proof.
35.83	——	Interest on Underpayment or Overpayment.
35.84	——	Checklist.
35.85		Audits and Appeals.
35.86	——	Audit Methods.
35.87	——	Taxpayer Bill of Rights.
35.88	——	Representation of Taxpayer.
35.89	——	Audit Results.
35.90	——	Bureau of Conciliation and Mediation Services.
35.91	—— ——	Requesting a Conciliation Conference.
35.92	—— ——	Conferences.
35.93	—— ——	Conference Orders.
35.94	——	Petition to Division of Tax Appeals.
35.95	—— ——	Referral to Bureau of Conciliation and Mediation Services.
35.96	—— ——	Small Claims Hearings.
35.97	——	Summary.
35.98	——	Checklist.
35.99		Judicial Actions.
35.100	——	Appeal by Article 78 Proceeding.

TABLE OF CONTENTS

Sec.
- 35.101 ____ ____ Payment of Taxes.
- 35.102 ____ ____ Initiation.
- 35.103 ____ ____ Burden of Proof.
- 35.104 ____ Declaratory Judgment Actions.
- 35.105 ____ Appeal to New York Court of Appeals.
- 35.106 ____ Summary.
- 35.107 ____ Checklist.
- 35.108 Assessment and Collection of Tax.
- 35.109 ____ Summary Assessment.
- 35.110 ____ Deficiency Assessment.
- 35.111 ____ Statute of Limitations.
- 35.112 ____ Jeopardy Assessment.
- 35.113 ____ Collection of Tax.
- 35.114 ____ ____ Lien.
- 35.115 ____ ____ Duration of Lien.
- 35.116 ____ Collection by Levy or Warrant.
- 35.117 ____ Installment Payment Agreements.
- 35.118 ____ Offer in Compromise.
- 35.119 ____ Bankruptcy as an Option.
- 35.120 ____ Checklist.
- 35.121 Criminal Tax Provisions.
- 35.122 ____ Failure to File Return.
- 35.123 ____ False or Fraudulent Return.
- 35.124 ____ Aiding or Assisting in False Return or Statement.
- 35.125 ____ Failure to Pay Tax.
- 35.126 ____ Failure to Properly Withhold Taxes.
- 35.127 Forms.
- 35.128 ____ Power of Attorney to Represent an Individual.
- 35.129 ____ Application for Automatic Extension of Time for Filing Return.
- 35.130 ____ Application For Additional Extension of Time to File for Individuals.
- 35.131 ____ Notice of Exception to Tax Tribunal.
- 35.132 ____ Petition to Division of Tax Appeals.
- 35.133 ____ Petition for Advisory Opinion.
- 35.134 ____ Statement of Financial Condition.
- 35.135 ____ Petition for Declaratory Ruling.
- 35.136 ____ Request for Conciliation Conference.
- 35.137 ____ Offer in Compromise.

CHAPTER 36. ALCOHOLIC BEVERAGE CONTROL LAW

- 36.1 Scope Note.
- 36.2 Strategy.
- 36.3 ____ Checklist.
- 36.4 Historical Background of State and Federal Regulations.
- 36.5 Jurisdiction.
- 36.6 New York State Liquor Authority.
- 36.7 Licenses.
- 36.8 ____ Retail Licenses.

TABLE OF CONTENTS

Sec.	
36.9	___ ___ On-Premises Licenses.
36.10	___ ___ Off-Premises Licenses.
36.11	___ Wholesale Licenses.
36.12	___ Manufacturing Licenses.
36.13	___ General Application Requirements.
36.14	___ Special Qualifications for Licensees.
36.15	Permits.
36.16	___ Temporary Permits.
36.17	___ Other Permits.
36.18	Brand and/or Label Registration.
36.19	Penal and Tax Bonds.
36.20	Application Form (Retail) Reviewed.
36.21	___ Lease Information.
36.22	___ Applicant Information.
36.23	___ Information Regarding Premises.
36.24	___ Financial Information and Criminal Background.
36.25	___ Community Notification.
36.26	___ Landlord Information.
36.27	___ Additional Requirements for On–Premises Consumption Licenses.
36.28	___ ___ Neighborhood.
36.29	___ ___ Premises Exterior.
36.30	___ ___ Premises Interior.
36.31	___ ___ Bars.
36.32	___ ___ Kitchen.
36.33	___ ___ Permits.
36.34	___ ___ Hotel.
36.35	___ Proposed Method of Operation.
36.36	___ Additional Requirements for Off–Premises Liquor Store Applicants.
36.37	___ Additional Requirements for Grocery Store Applicants.
36.38	___ Liquidators Permit.
36.39	___ Affidavit Requirements.
36.40	___ Personal Questionnaire.
36.41	___ On–Premises Liquor Applications 500 Foot Verification.
36.42	___ Miscellaneous Requirements.
36.43	___ Checklist.
36.44	Record–Keeping Requirements.
36.45	Reporting Changes.
36.46	___ Application for Endorsement Certificate.
36.47	___ Application for Approval of Corporate Change.
36.48	___ Alteration of Premises.
36.49	___ Removal of Premises.
36.50	___ Financing and Method of Operation.
36.51	Renewals.
36.52	Trade Practices.
36.53	Enforcement.
36.54	Penalties.
36.55	___ Revocation Order.
36.56	___ Cancellation Order.

TABLE OF CONTENTS

Sec.
36.57 ___ Suspension Order.
36.58 ___ ___ Forthwith.
36.59 ___ ___ Deferred.
36.60 ___ ___ Combined Forthwith and Deferred Suspension.
36.61 ___ Letters of Warning.
36.62 ___ Suspension Proceedings.
36.63 ___ Revocation Notice of Pleading.
36.64 Pleadings and Procedure.
36.65 ___ Hearings.
36.66 ___ Judicial Review.
36.67 Forms.
36.68 ___ Application for Alcoholic Beverage Control Retail License.
36.69 ___ Application for Endorsement Certificate.
36.70 ___ Application for Approval of Corporate Change.
36.71 ___ Application for Permission to Make Alterations.
36.72 ___ Application for Wholesale License.
36.73 ___ Retail License and Filing Fee Schedule.

CHAPTER 37. CIVIL APPELLATE PRACTICE BEFORE THE APPELLATE DIVISION AND OTHER INTERMEDIATE APPELLATE COURTS

37.1 Scope Note.
37.2 Strategy.
37.3 Judiciary Structure.
37.4 Administration of the Appellate Division.
37.5 Administrative Powers of the Appellate Division.
37.6 ___ Admission, Removal and Disciplinary Jurisdiction.
37.7 ___ Administration of the Courts.
37.8 ___ Law Guardian Program.
37.9 ___ Mental Hygiene Legal Service Oversight.
37.10 ___ Assigned Counsel.
37.11 ___ Powers Relating to Appellate Term.
37.12 ___ Marshals.
37.13 An Overview of the Statutory Framework of the Appellate System and the Rules of the Court.
37.14 Appeals to the Appellate Division.
37.15 ___ Courts of Original Jurisdiction From Which Appeals Lie.
37.16 ___ ___ Supreme Court and County Court.
37.17 ___ ___ Court of Claims.
37.18 ___ ___ Surrogate's Court.
37.19 ___ ___ Family Court.
37.20 ___ Appeals From Other Appellate Courts.
37.21 ___ Who May Appeal.
37.22 ___ ___ Aggrieved Parties.
37.23 ___ ___ ___ Defaulters; Orders or Judgments on Consent.
37.24 ___ ___ ___ Intervenors.
37.25 ___ ___ ___ Substitution of Parties.
37.26 ___ ___ ___ Third Party Defendants.
37.27 ___ Scope of Review.

TABLE OF CONTENTS

Sec.
37.28	____ ____	Questions of Law.
37.29	____ ____	Questions of Fact and the Exercise of Discretion.
37.30	____ ____	Limitations in Notice of Appeal or Brief.
37.31	____ ____	Mootness.
37.32	____ ____	Change in Law While Case Is Pending.
37.33	____	Appeals as of Right.
37.34	____ ____	Appeals From Final and Interlocutory Judgments.
37.35	____ ____	Appeals From Orders.
37.36	____	Appeals by Permission.
37.37	____	Non-appealable Matters.
37.38	____	Appealable Paper.
37.39	____	Time for Taking the Appeal.
37.40	____ ____	Appeal as of Right.
37.41	____ ____	Appeal by Permission.
37.42	____ ____	Cross-Appeal.
37.43	____ ____	Extensions; Omissions.
37.44	____ ____	Other Statutory Provisions.
37.45	____	Notice of Appeal—Form and Content.
37.46	____ ____	Service and Filing Requirements.
37.47	____	Reargument; Subsequent Orders.
37.48	____	Assignment of Counsel.
37.49	____	Perfecting the Appeal.
37.50	____ ____	Time.
37.51	____ ____	Methods of Perfection.
37.52	____ ____	Briefs.
37.53	____ ____	Consolidation.
37.54	____	What to File; Number of Copies.
37.55	____ ____	First Department.
37.56	____ ____	Second Department.
37.57	____ ____	Third Department.
37.58	____ ____	Fourth Department.
37.59	____	Location; Transfer Plan.
37.60	____	Calendars.
37.61	____	Preferences.
37.62	____	Oral Arguments.
37.63	____	Disposition of the Appeal.
37.64	____ ____	Affirmance.
37.65	____ ____	Reversal or Modification.
37.66	____ ____	Dismissal.
37.67	____ ____	Costs and Disbursements; Attorneys' Fees.
37.68	____	Post-disposition Proceedings.
37.69	____ ____	Reargument.
37.70	____ ____	Leave to Appeal to the Court of Appeals.
37.71	____ ____	Enforcement.
37.72	____ ____	Resettlement or Clarification.
37.73	____ ____	*Certiorari* to the U.S. Supreme Court.
37.74	____	Motion Practice—Generally.
37.75	____ ____	First Department.
37.76	____ ____	Second Department.
37.77	____ ____	Third Department.

TABLE OF CONTENTS

Sec.
37.78 ____ ____ Fourth Department.
37.79 ____ ____ Interim Relief.
37.80 ____ ____ Stays.
37.81 ____ ____ *Amicus Curiae*.
37.82 ____ ____ Miscellaneous Motions.
37.83 ____ Sanctions.
37.84 ____ Preargument Conferences.
37.85 ____ Unperfected Appeals.
37.86 Other Proceedings in the Appellate Division.
37.87 ____ CPLR Article 78 Proceedings.
37.88 ____ Writs of *Habeas Corpus*.
37.89 ____ CPLR 5704 *Ex Parte* Order Review.
37.90 ____ Miscellaneous Proceedings.
37.91 Appeals to Other Intermediate Courts.
37.92 ____ Appeals from Justice Courts.
37.93 ____ ____ Courts to Which Appeals Are Taken.
37.94 ____ ____ Applicability of CPLR Article 55.
37.95 ____ ____ Appeals as of Right and by Permission.
37.96 ____ ____ Taking the Appeal: Settlement of Case and Return on Appeal.
37.97 ____ ____ Perfection of Appeal.
37.98 ____ ____ Costs on Appeal.
37.99 ____ ____ Small Claims Review.
37.100 ____ ____ Rule Governance by Administrative Board.
37.101 ____ Appeals From City Courts.
37.102 ____ ____ Courts to Which Appeals Are Taken.
37.103 ____ ____ Applicability of CPLR Article 55.
37.104 ____ ____ Appeals as of Right and by Permission.
37.105 ____ ____ Taking the Appeal: Settlement of Case and Return on Appeal; Variations from CPLR.
37.106 ____ ____ Perfection of Appeal.
37.107 ____ ____ Costs on Appeal.
37.108 ____ ____ Small Claims Review.
37.109 ____ Appeals From District Courts.
37.110 ____ ____ Court to Which Appeals Are Taken.
37.111 ____ ____ Applicability of CPLR Article 55.
37.112 ____ ____ Appeals as of Right and by Permission.
37.113 ____ ____ Taking the Appeal: Settlement of Case and Return on Appeal.
37.114 ____ ____ Perfecting the Appeal.
37.115 ____ ____ Costs on Appeal.
37.116 ____ ____ Small Claims Review.
37.117 ____ Appeals from the Civil Court of the City of New York.
37.118 ____ ____ Courts to Which Appeals Are Taken.
37.119 ____ ____ Applicability of CPLR Article 55.
37.120 ____ ____ Appeals as of Right and by Permission.
37.121 ____ ____ Appeals to the Court of Appeals.
37.122 ____ ____ Taking the Appeal: Settlement of Case and Return on Appeal; Variations From CPLR.
37.123 ____ ____ Perfecting the Appeal.

TABLE OF CONTENTS

Sec.
37.124 ____ ____ Costs on Appeal.
37.125 ____ ____ Small Claims Review.
37.126 ____ Appeals from County Courts.
37.127 Procedural Checklist.
37.128 Forms.
37.129 ____ Notice of Appeal. 💾
37.130 ____ Notice of Motion for a Stay of Proceedings. 💾
37.131 ____ Order to Show Cause for a Stay of Proceedings. 💾
37.132 ____ Affirmation in Support of Motion or Order To Show Cause for a Stay of Proceedings. 💾
37.133 ____ Notice of Motion for a Preference to Expedite the Appeal. 💾
37.134 ____ Affirmation in Support of Motion for a Preference to Expedite the Appeal. 💾
37.135 ____ Notice of Motion to Enlarge Time for (Appellant to Perfect Appeal)(Respondent To File Brief). 💾
37.136 ____ Affirmation in Support of Motion to Enlarge Time for (Appellant to Perfect Appeal) (Respondent to File Brief). 💾
37.137 ____ Notice of Motion to Strike Matter *Dehors* the Record (Appendix)(Brief). 💾
37.138 ____ Affirmation in Support of Motion to Strike Matter *Dehors* the Record(Appendix)(Brief). 💾
37.139 ____ Notice of Motion for Reargument or Leave to Appeal to the Court of Appeals. 💾
37.140 ____ Affirmation in Support of Motion for Reargument or Leave to Appeal to the Court of Appeals. 💾

Volume 25

CHAPTER 38. CRIMINAL APPELLATE PRACTICE BEFORE THE APPELLATE DIVISION AND OTHER INTERMEDIATE APPELLATE COURTS

38.1 Scope Note.
38.2 Strategy.
38.3 Appeals to the Appellate Division—General Principles.
38.4 ____ Courts of Original Jurisdiction From Which Appeals Lie.
38.5 ____ Who May Appeal.
38.6 ____ ____ Status as Aggrieved by "Adverse" Determination.
38.7 ____ ____ Appeals by the Defendant From Superior Courts.
38.8 ____ ____ ____ As of Right.
38.9 ____ ____ ____ Appeals by Permission.
38.10 ____ ____ Appeals by the People.
38.11 ____ ____ Appeals from Orders Accepting or Sealing Grand Jury Reports; Appeals by Prosecutors; Appeals by Public Servants.
38.12 ____ Appeal Process—Appeals as of Right.
38.13 ____ ____ Appeals by Permission: Certificate Granting Leave.
38.14 ____ ____ Extensions of Time.
38.15 ____ ____ Stay of Judgment or Order.
38.16 ____ ____ Poor Person Relief and Assignment of Counsel.

TABLE OF CONTENTS

Sec.
- 38.17 _____ _____ Perfecting and Calendaring the Appeal.
- 38.18 _____ Scope of Review.
- 38.19 _____ _____ Questions of Law.
- 38.20 _____ _____ Questions of Fact; Weight of Evidence.
- 38.21 _____ _____ Interest of Justice/Discretion.
- 38.22 _____ _____ Change in Law While Case Pending.
- 38.23 _____ Disposition of Appeal.
- 38.24 _____ _____ Affirmance.
- 38.25 _____ _____ Modification.
- 38.26 _____ _____ Reversal.
- 38.27 _____ _____ Character of Order of Reversal or Modification: On the Law, On the Facts, in the Interest of Justice.
- 38.28 _____ _____ Corrective Action.
- 38.29 _____ Post-disposition Proceedings.
- 38.30 _____ _____ Responsibilities of Counsel.
- 38.31 _____ _____ Reargument.
- 38.32 _____ _____ Leave to Appeal.
- 38.33 _____ _____ *Certiorari* to U.S. Supreme Court.
- 38.34 _____ _____ *Coram Nobis*—Ineffective Assistance of Appellate Counsel.
- 38.35 _____ _____ Clarification/Resettlement.
- 38.36 _____ Motions in Connection With Appeals—Generally.
- 38.37 _____ _____ *Pro Se* Supplemental Brief.
- 38.38 _____ _____ *Anders* Brief.
- 38.39 _____ _____ Dismissal.
- 38.40 _____ _____ Reconstruction Hearing; Summary Reversal.
- 38.41 _____ _____ Death or Absence of a Defendant.
- 38.42 _____ _____ Assignment of New Counsel.
- 38.43 _____ _____ Expanding the Judgment Roll.
- 38.44 _____ _____ Briefs.
- 38.45 _____ _____ Withdrawal of Appeal.
- 38.46 Appeals to Intermediate Appellate Courts Other Than the Appellate Division.
- 38.47 _____ Appeals From Village Courts, Town Courts, City Courts and District Courts.
- 38.48 _____ Appeals From Criminal Court of the City of New York.
- 38.49 _____ _____ New York and Bronx County Branches.
- 38.50 _____ _____ Kings, Queens, Richmond County Branches.
- 38.51 _____ Orders, Sentences and Judgments Appealable.
- 38.52 _____ Taking the Appeal—Appeal as of Right.
- 38.53 _____ _____ Appeals by Permission.
- 38.54 _____ Stays Pending Appeal.
- 38.55 _____ Perfecting the Appeal.
- 38.56 _____ Determination of the Appeal.
- 38.57 Governance of the Appellate Term.
- 38.58 Original Application to County Court for Change of Venue.
- 38.59 Procedural Checklist for Appeals to Appellate Division.
- 38.60 Forms—Notice of Motion for a Stay of Execution of Judgment.

CI

TABLE OF CONTENTS

Sec.
38.61 ____ Affirmation in Support of Motion for a Stay of Execution of Judgment. 💾
38.62 ____ Notice of Motion for an Extension of Time to Take an Appeal. 💾
38.63 ____ Affirmation in Support of Motion for an Extension of Time to Take an Appeal. 💾
38.64 Chart.

CHAPTER 39. CIVIL AND CRIMINAL APPEALS TO THE COURT OF APPEALS

39.1 Scope Note.
39.2 Strategy.
39.3 Civil Appeals.
39.4 ____ Finality.
39.5 ____ Non-appealable Orders.
39.6 ____ Appealable Paper.
39.7 ____ Scope of Review.
39.8 ____ Appeal as of Right.
39.9 ____ ____ Appellate Division Orders or Judgments.
39.10 ____ ____ Final Judgment of Court of Original Instance.
39.11 ____ ____ Judgment of Court of Original Instance to Review Prior Non-final Determination of the Appellate Division.
39.12 ____ Appeals by Permission of the Appellate Division or the Court of Appeals.
39.13 ____ ____ Judgment of Court of Original Instance to Review Prior Non-final Determination of the Appellate Division.
39.14 ____ ____ Final Order of the Appellate Division Determining the Action.
39.15 ____ ____ Non-final Appellate Division Orders in Proceedings by or Against Public Officers or Others.
39.16 ____ Appeals by Permission of the Appellate Division.
39.17 ____ Form, Content and Service of Motions for Leave to Appeal.
39.18 ____ ____ Motions Filed in the Appellate Division.
39.19 ____ ____ Motions Filed in the Court of Appeals.
39.20 ____ Time for Taking the Appeal or Moving for Leave to Appeal—Appeals as of Right.
39.21 ____ ____ Motions for Leave to Appeal.
39.22 ____ ____ Cross Appeals.
39.23 ____ ____ Extensions of Time.
39.24 ____ ____ Omissions.
39.25 ____ Notice of Appeal—Form and Content.
39.26 ____ The Jurisdictional Statement.
39.27 ____ Jurisdictional Inquiry.
39.28 ____ Perfecting and Readying the Appeal.
39.29 ____ ____ Full Briefing and Oral Argument.
39.30 ____ ____ *Sua Sponte* Merits Consideration ("SSM").
39.31 ____ Determination of the Appeal—*Remittitur*.
39.32 ____ Motion Practice.
39.33 ____ ____ Motion for a Stay.

TABLE OF CONTENTS

Sec.
39.34 ____ ____ Motion to File an *Amicus* Brief.
39.35 ____ ____ Motion for Poor Person Relief.
39.36 ____ ____ Motion for Reconsideration.
39.37 Criminal Appeals.
39.38 ____ Definition of Criminal Case.
39.39 ____ Orders and Judgments From Which Appeals May Be Taken.
39.40 ____ By the Defendant in Death Penalty Cases.
39.41 ____ By the Prosecution in Death Penalty Cases.
39.42 ____ Intermediate Appellate Courts.
39.43 ____ Additional Limitations on Appealability.
39.44 ____ Appeals by Permission.
39.45 ____ ____ Obligation of Intermediate Appellate Court Counsel.
39.46 ____ ____ Who May Grant Leave to Appeal.
39.47 ____ ____ Criminal Leave Application ("CLA") Practice.
39.48 ____ ____ Stays and Continuation of Bail.
39.49 ____ Appeals Practice.
39.50 ____ Scope of Review.
39.51 ____ Disposition of Appeal.
39.52 ____ Motion Practice.
39.53 ____ ____ Poor Person Relief and Assignment of Counsel.
39.54 ____ ____ Extension of Time to Seek Leave to Appeal.
39.55 ____ ____ Dismissal of Appeal.
39.56 ____ ____ Withdrawal of Appeal.
39.57 ____ ____ Reargument.
39.58 Other Proceedings in the Court of Appeals.
39.59 ____ Review of Determinations of the Commission on Judicial Conduct.
39.60 ____ Certified Questions From Other Courts.
39.61 ____ Matters Regarding Admission of Attorneys and Licensing of Foreign Legal Consultants.
39.62 *Certiorari* to the Supreme Court of the United States.
39.63 Procedural Checklists.
39.64 ____ Civil Appeals as of Right.
39.65 ____ Civil Appeals by Permission of Court of Appeals.
39.66 ____ Criminal Appeals by Leave of a Court of Appeals Judge.
39.67 ____ Civil Appeals by Leave of the Appellate Division and Criminal Appeals by Leave of an Appellate Division Justice.
39.68 ____ Appeals Selected for Expedited Review Pursuant to Rule 500.4
39.69 ____ Appeals Tracked to Full Briefing and Oral Argument.
39.70 Drafting Checklists.
39.71 ____ Notice of Appeal.
39.72 ____ Rule 500.2 Jurisdictional Statement.
39.73 ____ Motion for Leave to Appeal to Court of Appeals Filed in Court of Appeals.
39.74 ____ Application for Leave to Appeal in Criminal Case Filed in Court of Appeals.
39.75 ____ Appellant's Brief on the Merits.
39.76 ____ Respondent's Brief on the Merits.

TABLE OF CONTENTS

Sec.
39.77 Forms—Notice of Appeal to Court of Appeals From Order of Appellate Division Finally Determining Action With Two Dissents on Question of Law. 💾
39.78 ____ Notice of Appeal to Court of Appeals From Order of Appellate Division Finally Determining Action Where Construction of Constitution is Directly Involved. 💾
39.79 ____ Notice of Appeal to Court of Appeals From Judgment of Supreme Court Where Constitutionality of Statute is Directly Involved. 💾
39.80 ____ Notice of Appeal to Court of Appeals From Appellate Division Order of Reversal Granting New Trial With Stipulation for Judgment Absolute. 💾
39.81 ____ Notice of Appeal to Court of Appeals From Judgment of Supreme Court to Review Prior Non-final Determination of Appellate Division. 💾
39.82 ____ Rule 500.2 Jurisdictional Statement. 💾
39.83 ____ Notice of Motion in Court of Appeals for Leave to Appeal to Court of Appeals From Order of Appellate Division. 💾
39.84 ____ Affidavit in Support of Motion in Court of Appeals for Leave to Appeal to Court of Appeals From Order of Appellate Division. 💾
39.85 ____ Notice of Motion in Court of Appeals for Reargument of Motion for Leave to Appeal. 💾
39.86 ____ Notice of Motion in Court of Appeals for Leave to Appear *Amicus Curiae*. 💾
39.87 ____ Notice of Motion to Dismiss Appeal as Untimely Taken. 💾
39.88 ____ Affidavit in Support of Motion to Dismiss Appeal as Untimely Taken. 💾
39.89 ____ CPLR 5531 Statement. 💾
39.90 ____ Letter Seeking Leave to Appeal in Criminal Case. 💾

	Page
Table of Jury Instructions	235
Table of Forms	236
Table of Statutes	iii
Table of Rules	iii
Table of Cases	iii
Index	iii

WEST'S NEW YORK PRACTICE SERIES

GENERAL PRACTICE IN NEW YORK

Volume 22

Chapter 13

LANDLORD–TENANT LAW

by
Warren A. Estis
and
William J. Robbins*

Table of Sections

13.1	Scope Note.
13.2	Strategy.
13.3	___ Checklists.
13.4	Summary Proceedings.
13.5	___ Venue and Jurisdiction.
13.6	___ Service of Process.
13.7	___ ___ Personal Delivery.
13.8	___ ___ Substituted Service.
13.9	___ ___ Conspicuous Place Service.
13.10	___ ___ New York City Civil Court "Postcard Requirement."
13.11	Non-payment Proceedings.
13.12	___ Rent Demands.
13.13	___ Notice of Petition.
13.14	___ ___ Form of Notice.
13.15	___ ___ Content of Notice.
13.16	___ ___ Defects in the Notice.
13.17	___ The Petition.
13.18	___ ___ Defects in the Petition.
13.19	___ ___ Verification.
13.20	___ ___ Defects in the Verification.
13.21	Responding to the Non-payment Petition.
13.22	___ The Answer.
13.23	___ The Motion to Dismiss.
13.24	___ The RPAPL § 755 Motion to Stay.
13.25	Tenant Defenses to the Non-payment Proceeding.
13.26	___ No Landlord Tenant Relationship.
13.27	___ Tenant Out of Possession.
13.28	___ Statutory Noncompliance.
13.29	___ Illegal Rent.
13.30	___ Actual Eviction.
13.31	___ Constructive Eviction.

*The authors thank Mary Ann Hallenborg, Esq. for her invaluable effort in the preparation of this chapter. Without her extensive work, this chapter could never have come to fruition.

Ch. 13　　　　　　　　LANDLORD–TENANT LAW

13.32　＿＿ Warranty of Habitability.
13.33　＿＿ Laches.
13.34　＿＿ Payment.
13.35　Holdover Proceedings.
13.36　＿＿ Predicate Notices.
13.37　＿＿ ＿＿ Month-to-Month Tenants.
13.38　＿＿ ＿＿ Illegal Use.
13.39　＿＿ ＿＿ Rent–Controlled Tenants.
13.40　＿＿ ＿＿ Rent–Stabilized Tenants.
13.41　＿＿ The Notice of Petition.
13.42　＿＿ ＿＿ Defects in the Notice.
13.43　＿＿ Holdover Petition—Form and Content.
13.44　＿＿ ＿＿ Defects in the Petition.
13.45　＿＿ ＿＿ Verification and Verification Defects.
13.46　Responding to the Holdover Petition.
13.47　＿＿ The Answer.
13.48　＿＿ The Motion to Dismiss.
13.49　Tenant Defenses to the Holdover Proceeding.
13.50　＿＿ Acceptance of Rent After Expiration or Termination of Tenancy.
13.51　＿＿ Defective Predicate Notice.
13.52　＿＿ ＿＿ Rent–Regulated Apartments.
13.53　＿＿ Waiver.
13.54　＿＿ Equitable Estoppel.
13.55　＿＿ Succession Rights to Rent–Regulated Apartments.
13.56　Counterclaims.
13.57　Bill of Particulars.
13.58　Discovery.
13.59　＿＿ Notice to Admit.
13.60　＿＿ Freedom of Information Law.
13.61　The Trial—Adjournments.
13.62　＿＿Amending Petition and Burden of Proof.
13.63　Stipulations—Overview.
13.64　＿＿ Non-payment Proceedings.
13.65　＿＿ Holdover Proceedings.
13.66　＿＿ Enforcement and Vacatur.
13.67　The Judgment and Warrant.
13.68　＿＿ Staying the Warrant in Non-payment Proceedings.
13.69　＿＿ Staying the Warrant in New York City Residential Holdover Proceedings.
13.70　Yellowstone Actions.
13.71　＿＿ Obtaining the Injunction.
13.72　Article 7–A Proceedings.
13.73　Rent Regulatory Proceedings.
13.74　＿＿ Rent Overcharge.
13.75　＿＿ Service Reduction.
13.76　＿＿ Major Capital Improvement Rent Increase.
13.77　Checklist of Essential Allegations.
13.78　＿＿ Petition Non-payment.
13.79　＿＿ Holdover Petition.
13.80　＿＿ Stipulation Settling Non-payment Proceeding.
13.81　＿＿ Stipulation Settling Holdover Proceeding.

§ 13.1 LANDLORD–TENANT LAW Ch. 13

13.82 Forms.
13.83 ____ Petition Non-payment. 💾
13.84 ____ Petition Holdover. 💾
13.85 ____ Individual Verification. 💾
13.86 ____ Corporate Officer Verification. 💾
13.87 ____ Partnership Verification. 💾
13.88 ____ Attorney Verification. 💾
13.89 ____ Stipulations. 💾
13.90 ____ ____ Settling Non-payment Proceeding. 💾
13.91 ____ ____ Settling Non-payment Proceeding With Final Judgment in Favor of Petitioner. 💾
13.92 ____ ____ Settling Holdover Proceeding Where Tenant Agrees to Cure Lease Violation. 💾
13.93 ____ ____ Settling Holdover Proceeding Where Tenant–Respondent Agrees to Vacate Premises. 💾

WESTLAW Electronic Research

See WESTLAW Electronic Research Guide preceding the Summary of Contents.

---

§ 13.1 Scope Note

This chapter is intended to guide the practitioner through the summary proceeding, a judicial process commonly used for litigating landlord-tenant disputes. For ease of understanding, the terms "landlord" and "tenant" are used throughout this chapter. Practitioners are advised, however, and we make clear in the text that there are summary proceedings in which the petitioner is a party other than a landlord and the respondent is a party other than a tenant. Such proceedings are intended to give the landlord an expeditious way of adjudicating disputes concerning unpaid rent and possession of real property. Since the summary proceeding is a creature of statute in derogation of the common law action in ejectment, courts require strict adherence to statutory requirements and procedures. As a result, summary proceedings are rife with procedural traps and pitfalls for the unwary practitioner.

The chapter begins with an introductory overview (Sections 13.2 to 13.4) and then a discussion of jurisdiction, venue and service of process in a summary proceeding in Sections 13.6 through 13.10. Sections 13.11 through 13.20 explain the mechanics of bringing the summary nonpayment proceeding, which permits the landlord to sue a tenant to recover unpaid rent and/or possession of the premises. The form and content of the rent demand, the notice of petition, and nonpayment petition, as well as applicable filing requirements are discussed in these Sections. The answer and several tenant defenses to the non-payment proceeding are discussed in Sections 13.21 through 13.34.

The chapter then goes on to discuss the summary holdover proceeding. Such a proceeding may be brought to remove a tenant or occupant who fails to vacate the premises after the tenancy or right of occupancy expires or is otherwise terminated. Sections 13.36 through 13.40 discuss the various default and termination notices which serve as a predicate for holdover proceedings. The mechanics of bringing the proceeding, including the form and content of the notice of petition and the petition, are covered in Sections 13.41 through 13.45. The answer and several common tenant defenses to the holdover proceeding are discussed at Sections 13.46 through 13.55.

Procedural matters including asserting counterclaims, bill of particulars, discovery, the hearing and trial are covered in Sections 13.56 through 13.62.

Rather than proceed to trial, the landlord and tenant frequently elect to settle their case by means of a written agreement, or stipulation. Many commercial and residential summary proceedings are concluded in this manner. Sections 13.63 through 13.66 present key points to consider when drafting stipulations to settle non-payment and holdover summary proceedings. Issues related to the execution and enforcement of stipulations are also addressed.

The chapter in Sections 13.67 through 13.69 goes on to discuss entry of the judgment and the issuing and staying of a warrant to restore the landlord to possession of the premises. Yellowstone injunctions, which allow a tenant who has been served with a notice to cure a lease default to litigate in supreme court whether or not there has been a default, are covered in Sections 13.70 through 13.71. The Article 7–A proceeding brought by tenants of a multiple dwelling for the appointment of an administrator to remedy building conditions dangerous to life and safety is addressed in Section 13.72.

Also included in the chapter is a brief review of proceedings before the State Division of Housing and Community Renewal ("DHCR"), the state agency charged with the enforcement of rent laws and regulations. Sections 13.73 through 13.76 discuss three common rent-adjustment proceedings: the rent overcharge proceeding; the service reduction proceeding; and the major capital improvement rent increase proceeding.

The chapter concludes with checklists of essential allegations to be included in non-payment and holdover petitions and in stipulations settling such proceedings in Sections 13.77 through 13.81. Forms of petitions and stipulations are provided in Sections 13.82 through 13.93.

§ 13.2 Strategy

An initial consideration in handling a residential landlord-tenant matter is to determine whether any rent regulatory (*i.e.*, rent control or rent stabilization) statutes and regulations are involved. It should also be determined whether any subsidized housing programs that operate in New York State are applicable to the client's case. Close attention must be paid to these factors because if such specialized statutes and regulations are applicable, they will govern the relationship between the landlord and tenant. In addition, specific allegations regarding rent regulatory status must be included in the petition in a summary proceeding.

Although a substantive discussion of these various statutes and regulations is beyond the scope of this chapter, the impact of these statutes and regulations on the mechanics of bringing a summary proceeding are discussed throughout the chapter. Rent regulatory statutes and regulations include, (i) as to rent stabilization in New York City, the Rent Stabilization Law of 1969[1] and the Rent Stabilization Code[2]; (ii) as to rent stabilization outside New York City, the Emergency Tenant Protection Act[3] and the Emergency Tenant Protection Regulations;[4] (iii) as to rent control in New York City, the City Rent and Rehabilitation Law[5] and the New York City Rent and Eviction Regulations;[6] and (iv) as to rent control outside New York City, the Emergency Housing Rent Control Law[7] and the State Rent and Eviction Regulations.[8] The most recent rent regulatory statute, which extended and/or amended these various statutes, is the Rent Regulation Reform Act of 1997, chapter 116 of the Laws of 1997.

Subsidized housing programs include the New York State Mitchell-Lama Program for middle income housing and subsidized Public Housing for low income tenants. In addition to the New York State Division of Housing and Community Renewal, other agencies which a practitioner handling a landlord-tenant matter might need to contact regarding applicable regulations and statutes include the New York City Housing Authority and the United States Department of Housing and Urban Development.

Although it has been the topic of discussion, commercial rent regulation has not been implemented. Thus, the statutes mentioned above are not applicable in the context of a commercial landlord-tenant matter. A practitioner involved in such a matter, however, must make sure that there are no local statutes or regulations (*e.g.*, involving a Business Improvement District or otherwise) that could impact on a commercial landlord-tenant dispute.

Another important factor that counsel must review carefully at the outset with the client is the advantages and disadvantages of litigation versus attempting to settle the matter without litigation, or soon after a case is brought. While this should be part of any client representation

---

§ 13.2

1. Administrative Code of the City of New York §§ 26–501 *et seq.* ("N.Y.C. Admin. Code")

2. 9 NYCRR Parts 2520–2530.

3. L. 1974, ch. 576, § 4; McKinney's Unconsol. Laws §§ 8621 *et seq.*

4. 9 NYCRR Parts 2500–2510.

5. N.Y.C. Admin. Code §§ 26–401 et seq.

6. 9 NYCRR Parts 2200–2210.

7. L. 1946, ch. 274 § 1, McKinney's Unconsol. Laws §§ 8581 *et seq.*

8. 9 NYCRR Parts 2100–2109.

whatever the subject matter of the dispute, it is particularly compelling given the context of a landlord-tenant dispute. From the tenant's perspective, the stakes are very high as the possession of one's home or place of business are at stake. Particularly in the setting of a small cooperative or a rental situation where the landlord lives on the premises, there is the psychological factor that such disputes are between neighbors. The parties involved in the litigation will have to see each other in the elevator every day. This type of litigation is anything but impersonal. It cannot easily be compartmentalized into a lawyer's office or a downtown courtroom. As such, the stress level of these disputes may be very high.

As in any lawsuit, costs must also be considered. Under New York law, attorneys' fees cannot be collected by a prevailing party unless they are authorized by an agreement between the parties or by statute. Thus, in most lawsuits in New York State, each side will bear its own legal costs. However, residential leases, invariably drafted by the landlord, and commercial leases frequently contain a provision requiring the tenant to pay the landlord's attorneys' fees if the landlord prevails in a lawsuit based on the tenant's breach of the lease. Needless to say, a corollary provision allowing the tenant to collect attorneys' fees from the landlord is not a part of most residential leases and is also often absent from commercial leases. To achieve parity for residential tenants, the Legislature in 1966 enacted Real Property Law § 234, which provides that in a residential lease containing a provision for the landlord's recovery of attorneys' fees, the law will imply a reciprocal provision that the landlord will pay attorneys' fees incurred by the tenant (1) as the result of the landlord's failure to perform lease covenants, or (2) "in the successful defense" of any lawsuit commenced by the landlord arising out of the lease.

Thus, in residential landlord-tenant litigation, as a result of lease language and statute, the losing party will frequently be responsible not only for his own legal costs, but also for the legal costs of the prevailing opponent. In a commercial context, it is presumed that there will be more equality as to the bargaining power of the parties and thus a greater likelihood that reciprocity as to attorneys' fees will be written into the lease. If a commercial tenant, however, is unable to negotiate such a result, and there is only a provision in the lease for the commercial tenant to pay the prevailing landlord's attorneys' fees, then there is no statutory reciprocity for the prevailing commercial tenant.

From the landlord's perspective, another important consideration is whether to accept rent from the tenant after summary proceedings have been initiated as there are circumstances where the landlord's acceptance of rent may be fatal to a holdover proceeding.[9] Therefore, an attorney representing a landlord should immediately review with the

---

9. *See infra,* § 13.50.

client the issue of whether to accept rent from the tenant. To avoid errors that might be fatal to the landlord's case, counsel should advise the landlord-client not to deposit any rent payment without first consulting with counsel.

If the tenant defaults in appearing, a money judgment for arrears will routinely be granted only if process has been personally delivered to the tenant. Therefore, landlords would be advised to effectuate service in that manner, if possible.

§ 13.3 Strategy—Checklists

Tenant Checklist. If the determination is made to pursue litigation aggressively, and assuming that a summary proceeding is commenced, an attorney representing a tenant should consider the following:

1. Is there a procedural basis for dismissal of the proceeding:
   - Was there improper service? (*See* §§ 13.6—13.10)
   - Are there improper parties? (*See* §§ 13.14, 13.26, 13.35)
   - Was there a failure to comply with the requirements for the notice of petition? (*See* §§ 13.13—13.16 and 13.41—13.42)
   - Was there a failure to comply with the requirements for the content of the petition? (*See* §§ 13.17—13.20 and 13.43—13.45)
   - If the proceeding is a non-payment proceeding, was a rent demand made or the requisite 3-day notice given? (*See* § 13.12)
   - If the proceeding is a holdover proceeding based on a termination of the lease by operation of a conditional limitation, was notice of default and termination served as required by the lease? (*See* §§ 13.36—13.40)
   - If the premises are rent-regulated, was predicate notice to vacate or surrender served as required by statute? (*See* § 13.52)

2. If there is a basis for a dismissal:
   - Is the client better served by a pre-answer motion to dismiss or by pleading the defenses in an answer and pressing ahead with a trial? (*See* §§ 13.22—13.23 and 13.47—13.48)
   - This will involve weighing if a pre-answer motion will significantly delay the case and whether delay is in the tenant's interest. Normally, delay benefits a tenant-respondent in a non-payment or holdover proceeding as long as the tenant, during the period of any delay, remains in possession. However, there may be situations (*e.g.*, because of circumstances

involving availability of witnesses) where the calculus of delay will be different.

3. Should a motion be made for discovery, which in a summary proceeding requires leave of court? (*See* §§ 13.58—13.59)

4. Is there a basis for removing the dispute to supreme court, for example, where full relief cannot be granted in the court of limited jurisdiction where the summary proceeding will be heard or because there is an existing supreme court litigation with which it should be consolidated?

5. Should a RPAPL § 755 motion to stay be made? (*See* § 13.24)

6. What are the possible defenses that can be raised? Be sure to include any affirmative defenses in the answer. In a non-payment proceeding consider the following:

    - Is there a landlord—tenant relationship? (*See* § 13.26)
    - Is the tenant in possession of the premises? (*See* § 13.27)
    - Has there been a violation of a health or safety statute that has a rent-forfeiture penalty for non-compliance? (*See* § 13.28)
    - Is the amount of rent illegal under the lease? (*See* § 13.29)
    - Has there been an actual or constructive eviction? (*See* §§ 13.30—13.31)
    - Has there been a breach of the warranty of habitability? (*See* § 13.32)
    - Is the landlord's claim stale and therefore subject to the equitable defense of laches? (*See* § 13.33)
    - Was the rent in fact paid? (*See* § 13.34)

    In a holdover proceeding consider the following:

    - Did the landlord accept rent after the expiration or termination of the tenancy? (*See* § 13.50)
    - Was the predicate notice defective? (*See* §§ 13.51—13.52)
    - Did the landlord waive the alleged default? (*See* § 13.53)
    - Did the landlord induce the tenant to act to his detriment and is thus estopped from asserting his right against the tenant? (*See* § 13.54)
    - Is the apartment rent regulated? If so, is the respondent either a family member or an unrelated occupant who had a long-standing family-type relationship with the tenant and who has lived with the tenant? (*See* § 13.55)

An attorney representing a tenant, where a notice to cure has been served, should consider commencing a supreme court lawsuit and obtain-

§ 13.3   LANDLORD–TENANT LAW   Ch. 13

ing a Yellowstone injunction. The effect of such an injunction is to toll the running of the cure period and prevent the landlord from terminating the lease and commencing a holdover proceeding. (*See* § 13.70–13.71)

Landlord Checklist. If a determination is made to pursue litigation aggressively, and assuming that a summary proceeding is commenced, counsel representing the landlord should consider the following:

1. Begin to assemble as early as possible the proof necessary to establish the landlord's *prima facie* case. Since the landlord in a nonpayment or holdover proceeding has the burden of going forward first, such early preparation will minimize the risk of having the case dismissed because the landlord is not ready for trial and the court concludes on a given date that the trial should begin. Documents necessary to prove the *prima facie* case could, depending on the type of case include :

   - Proof of right of possession (*e.g.*, certified deed, original net lease, a certified copy of memorandum of net lease, original proprietary lease with assignment and assumption of rent).

   - Certified copies of partnership agreement or certified articles of incorporation

   - Originals of leases and renewals. If originals are not available, a copy of notice to produce served on the other party.

   - Original pre-trial notices, with proofs of service.

   - Where the landlord is claiming that the residence is a non-primary residence proof such as telephone records, utility records, and tax returns.

   - If the premises are rent regulated, proof of rent registration status of apartment (*e.g.*, certified or subpoenaed copies of DHCR apartment registration, certified or subpoenaed records of the Office of Rent Control). (*See* §§ 13.17, 13.43)

   - If the premises are a multiple dwelling, a certified copy of the Multiple Dwelling Registration Card. (*See* §§ 13.17, 13.43)

2. Make sure the notice of petition and the petition are properly served. (*See* §§ 13.6—13.10)

3. If the proceeding is a non-payment proceeding, a rent demand must be made orally or by serving a written "3-day notice." (*See* § 13.12)

4. If the apartment is rent-regulated make sure predicate notice to vacate or surrender is served as required by statute and/or regulation. (*See* §§ 13.39—13.40)

5. If the proceeding is a holdover proceeding based on termination by operation of a conditional limitation in the lease, predicate notice

must be given pursuant to the terms of the lease. (*See* §§ 13.36—13.40)

6. If the proceeding is a holdover proceeding not based on a lease, make sure that any necessary predicate statutory notices have been properly served.

7. Do everything to keep the tenant from "getting a free ride" during the pendency of the summary proceeding.

    - In a holdover proceeding, press at every opportunity for an order of the court requiring the tenant to pay use and occupancy to the landlord or, at a minimum, into escrow with the court or with one of the attorneys.

    - In a non-payment proceeding, press to have the rent paid into court.

    - If the summary proceeding is in New York City, RPAPL § 745(2)(a), as amended by the Rent Regulatory Reform Act of 1997, is relevant. (The amendment to the statutory section is scheduled to take effect 120 days after the June 19, 1997 effective date of the Act.) That statutory section, as amended, mandates the court to direct the deposit of rent or use and occupancy under the circumstances specified therein. (*See* § 13.62.)

8. Be careful about accepting rent from the tenant. Remember, acceptance of rent from the tenant *after* the expiration or termination of the tenant's term and before summary proceedings have been initiated may be fatal to a holdover proceeding. (*See* § 13.50)

§ 13.4 Summary Proceedings

The summary proceeding to recover possession of real property permits the landlord to sue a tenant for non-payment of rent, or for holding-over in the premises after the expiration or termination of the tenancy. The goal of the summary proceeding is the swift determination of disputes between a landlord and tenant. To accomplish that goal, the courts will frequently sever (for resolution in a plenary action) claims that are unrelated to the landlord's claim for rent or possession of the premises.

The summary proceeding is commenced by petition and notice of petition. The pleadings must be served on the tenant and any other named respondents in accordance with the mandates of the Real Property Actions and Proceedings Law ("RPAPL"). A summary proceeding may also be commenced by an order to show cause (in lieu of a notice of petition), provided that some exigency exists to justify the use of the procedure. The tenant must respond to the petition and can answer the petition with any available defenses or allowable counterclaims. Alterna-

§ 13.4   LANDLORD–TENANT LAW   Ch. 13

tively, the tenant can serve a pre-answer motion, pursuant to Civil Practice Law and Rules ("CPLR") 3211, for dismissal of the petition.

To keep the proceeding "summary," the use of disclosure devices is available only upon leave of court. The only exception is the notice to admit. To obtain discovery, the party seeking discovery must demonstrate "ample need" for the information sought from the other party.

The trial in a summary proceeding is generally by the court without a jury. However, when a party has made a proper and timely jury demand, and the right to a jury trial has not been waived by the lease between the parties, there can be a jury trial.

The successful landlord is awarded a judgment of possession of the premises. After a final judgment, the court issues a warrant directed to the sheriff, marshal, or constable to remove the respondent(s) and put the landlord in possession. Before executing the warrant, the officer must give at least 72-hours' notice of eviction to the tenant. A money judgment for rent and/or use and occupancy may also be awarded if the landlord demanded a money judgment in the notice of petition and petition, and personal jurisdiction over the tenant was secured.

If the summary proceeding was for non-payment of rent, the tenant may obtain a stay of the issuance of the warrant by depositing all rent due, plus costs, into court. In actions where the judgment was issued in a New York City residential holdover proceeding based on a claim that the tenant breached the lease, the court will grant a ten-day stay of the issuance of the warrant in order to give the tenant a right to cure and, in effect, reinstate the tenancy. A court may also stay the issuance or execution of the warrant to afford a New York City residential tenant additional time to secure housing.

Library References:
West's Key No. Digests, Landlord and Tenant ⚖︎293.

§ 13.5   Summary Proceedings—Jurisdiction and Venue

Jurisdiction for summary proceedings is governed by RPAPL § 701(1). It permits summary proceedings to recover real property to be maintained in a county court; the court of a village police justice; justice court; city civil court; or district court. Where such a proceeding to recover real property is concerned, these courts can adjudicate monetary claims (*e.g.*, for rent or use and occupancy) even in excess of their jurisdictional limit.

Venue is proper in the jurisdictional area of the court in which all or a portion of the real property is located.[1] If the property is located in an incorporated village which includes parts of two or more towns, the proceedings may be brought before a town justice of any town. If the

---

§ 13.5
1. RPAPL § 701(2).

premises sought to be recovered are in New York City, the summary proceeding must be commenced in the New York City Civil Court for the county in which the premises are located.[2] Residential proceedings must be brought in the civil court's housing part.

Outside of New York City, there may be more than one court in a given municipality which has jurisdiction to hear summary proceedings. For example, if the premises are located in a city, the proceeding may be commenced in that municipality's city court.[3] In addition, if the subject premises are located in a town or village, the proceeding may be commenced in the justice court for that particular town or village.[4] Or, if the premises are located in Nassau County or the western part of Suffolk County, the proceeding may be commenced in the district court for the district in which the premises are located.[5] In such cases, the summary proceeding is usually brought in the lowest court of civil jurisdiction locally available, regardless of the amount of rent sought. Practitioners are urged to consult the court clerk to ascertain where the summary proceeding should be brought.

Library References:

West's Key No. Digests, Landlord and Tenant ⚖302.

§ 13.6 Summary Proceedings—Service of Process

Section 735(1) of the RPAPL governs service of the notice of petition and petition on the tenant. The statutory requirements governing service of process, place of service, or other manner of notice may not be limited by lease provisions.[1] Any conflicts that exist between the requirements of RPAPL § 735 and the terms of a lease must be resolved in favor of the statutory requirements.[2]

The statute permits the notice of petition and petition to be served on the tenant by any one of three methods: personal delivery, substituted service to a person of suitable age and discretion who lives or is employed at the premises sought to be recovered, or conspicuous place, "nail and mail" service.

Library References:

West's Key No. Digests, Landlord and Tenant ⚖304(2).

---

2. New York City Civil Court Act § 204.
3. Uniform City Court Act § 204.
4. Uniform Justice Court Act § 204. While both the town and village courts have jurisdiction to hear summary proceedings, only one court may routinely invoke it. The practitioner should contact the court clerk to ascertain any local rules or customs on where the summary proceeding should be brought.
5. Uniform District Court Act § 204.

§ 13.6

1. Lana Estates, Inc. v. National Energy Reduction Corp., 123 Misc.2d 324, 326, 473 N.Y.S.2d 912, 914 (Civ.Ct., Queens County, 1984) (citing 150 East 73rd Street Corp. v. Wehringer, N.Y.L.J. , 4/17/75, p.2, col.4 (App. Term, 1st Dep't 1975)).

2. Id.

§ 13.7 Summary Proceedings—Service of Process—Personal Delivery

Personal delivery means that the notice of petition and petition must be hand-delivered to the named respondent. If the respondent is a corporation, personal delivery must be made to an officer, director, managing or general agent, cashier or assistant cashier, or any other agent authorized by appointment or law to receive service.[1] If the respondent is a partnership, personal delivery must be made to any partner of the partnership, or to the managing or general agent of the partnership within the state, or the person in charge of the office of the partnership within the state at such office.[2] When the papers are delivered to a partnership agent, or to the person in charge of the partnership office, a copy of the papers must also be sent by first-class mail to the partner intended to be served at his or her last known address, or at the partnership's place of business.[3]

Service is complete upon the personal delivery of the papers.[4] The notice of petition or order to show cause, and petition must be filed with the court or its clerk along with proof of service within three days after the delivery of the papers.[5]

This method of service is optimal because it permits the petitioner to obtain a money judgment in the event of the respondent's default, if a money judgment is demanded in the petition.[6]

Library References:

West's Key No. Digests, Landlord and Tenant ⚖304(2).

§ 13.8 Summary Proceedings—Service of Process—Substituted Service

If personal delivery cannot be made to the named respondent, substituted service may be made by delivering and personally leaving the notice of petition and petition with a person who is of suitable age and discretion and who resides or is employed at the premises sought to be recovered.[1] It has been held that delivery of process to a business tenant's employee at the premises sought to be recovered is sufficient to

---

§ 13.7

1. CPLR 311(a)(1). Subdivisions (a)(2) through (8) of the statute identify the persons upon whom service may be made when service is on a governmental subdivision.
2. CPLR 310(a), (b).
3. CPLR 310(b).
4. RPAPL § 735(2)(a).
5. RPAPL § 735(2).
6. Default judgments are frequent in summary proceedings. In holdover proceedings inquests are held before a default judgment is entered. That is not so in non-payment proceedings. Interpreting RPAPL § 732(3), the Court of Appeals in Brusco v. Braun, 84 N.Y.2d 674, 621 N.Y.S.2d 291, 293, 645 N.E.2d 724 (1994), concluded that the "RPAPL does not provide for fact finding in the case of a defaulting tenant in a non-payment proceeding...."

§ 13.8

1. RPAPL § 735(1).

establish personal jurisdiction over the tenant, regardless of the employee's status in the business organization.[2] For example, a parking garage attendant working at a parking garage premises was found to be a person of suitable age and discretion who could accept service on behalf of the tenant-corporation which operated the garage.[3] Similarly, an office manager of a law firm partnership was found to be a person of suitable age and discretion who could accept service on behalf of the tenant-partnership and its individual partners.[4]

Substituted service carries an additional requirement: a copy of the papers must be mailed to the respondent both by registered or certified mail, and by regular first-class mail, addressed to the respondent at the property sought to be recovered. If that is not the respondent's residence and if the petitioner has written information of the respondent's residence address, then additional mailings in the same manner must also be made to the respondent at the last residence address as to which the petitioner has such information. If the petitioner has no such information, but does have written information of the person's place of business or employment, then additional mailings in the same manner must also be made to the last business or employment address of which petitioner has such information. Failure to comply with the statutory requirements for mailing renders the proceeding jurisdictionally defective.[5]

Where the respondent is a corporation, joint-stock, or other unincorporated association, a copy of the notice of petition and petition must be mailed both by registered or certified mail and by regular first class mail to the respondent at the premises sought to be recovered. If the principal office or principal place of business is not located on the property sought to be recovered, and if the petitioner has written information of the principal office or principal place of business within the state, then additional mailings in the same manner must be made to the respondent at the last place as to which petitioner has such information. If the petitioner has no such information, but has written information of any

---

2. City of New York v. Wall Street Racquet Club, Inc., 136 Misc.2d 405, 518 N.Y.S.2d 737 (Civ.Ct., N.Y. County, 1987).

3. Manhattan Embassy Co. v. Embassy Parking Corp., 164 Misc.2d 977, 980, 627 N.Y.S.2d 245, 247 (Civ.Ct., N.Y. County, 1995) (the delivery of service of process to the parking garage attendant who refused to accept the papers, "when objectively viewed, [was] calculated to adequately and fairly apprise the respondent of an impending lawsuit."). *But see* Broadway 48th–49th St. Associates v. Jacco Garage Corp., Civ. Ct., N.Y. County, Index No. 096465/93, where the court (Fisher-Brandreen, J.) stated that "RPAPL § 735 requires that the individual of suitable age and discretion express a willingness to accept papers."

4. 50 Court Street Assoc. v. Mendelson and Mendelson, 151 Misc.2d 87, 572 N.Y.S.2d 997 (Civ.Ct., Kings County, 1991).

5. *See* Schwartz v. Certified Management Corp., 117 A.D.2d 521, 498 N.Y.S.2d 135 (1st Dep't 1986), appeal dismissed 68 N.Y.2d 806, 506 N.Y.S.2d 1036, 498 N.E.2d 436 (1986) (landlord's failure to mail copy of notice of petition and petition to subletting tenant's known alternate address within one day of affixing papers to apartment door rendered proceeding jurisdictionally defective); *see also* 417 East Realty Assoc. v. Ryan, 110 Misc.2d 607, 442 N.Y.S.2d 880 (Civ.Ct., N.Y. County, 1981) (landlord's failure to mail copy of papers to tenant's temporary medical treatment facility in Minnesota required dismissal of the proceeding).

office or place of business within the state, then additional mailings in the same manner must be made to any such place as to which the petitioner has such information. Allegations as to such information as may affect the mailing address shall be set forth in the petition (*see, e.g.,* § 13.83 at par. 9) or in a separate affidavit and filed as part of the proof of service.[6]

All mailings must be made within one day of the delivery of the petition and notice of petition. Proof of service must be filed with the clerk of the court within three days after completion of the mailings. Service is complete upon filing of the petition, notice of petition, and proof of service with the court or clerk.[7]

Library References:

West's Key No. Digests, Landlord and Tenant ⚖304(2).

§ 13.9 Summary Proceedings—Service of Process—Conspicuous Place Service

If upon "reasonable application," service cannot be effectuated by personal delivery or by substituted service, the notice of petition and petition may be served by "affixing" a copy of the papers to a conspicuous part of the premises—usually at the front door, or by "placing" (that means slipping) the papers under the entry door of the premises sought to be recovered. Affixing requires some sort of attachment—usually scotch tape. Affixing is not squeezing the papers between door and door jamb, or between door knob and door.[1]

The "reasonable application" standard applies to commercial as well as residential summary proceedings.[2] The "reasonable application" standard of RPAPL § 735 does not require an effort as stringent as under the "due diligence" standard of CPLR 308(4).[3] It means making more than one attempt at personal delivery or suitable age and discretion service before resorting to conspicuous place service.[4] In residential

---

6. RPAPL § 735(1)(b).

PRACTICE POINTER: Prudent landlords' attorneys, where their client has written information about multiple addresses for the respondent will mail to all such addresses when relying on suitable age and discretion and nail and mail service.

7. RPAPL § 735(2)(b).

§ 13.9

1. Arkansas Leasing Co. v. Furag, N.Y.L.J., 6/16/93, p.29, col.5 (Civ.Ct., Queens County, 1993).

2. Ancott Realty, Inc. v. Gramercy Stuyvesant Independent Democrats, 127 Misc.2d 490, 486 N.Y.S.2d 672 (Civ.Ct., N.Y. County, 1985).

3. Maspeth Bowl Inc. v. P.M.P. Partnership, N.Y.L.J., 9/16/88, p.22, col.2, 16 HCR 335 (Civ.Ct., Queens County, 1988).

4. *See, e.g.,* Eight Associates v. Hynes, 65 N.Y.2d 739, 492 N.Y.S.2d 15, 481 N.E.2d 555 (1985).

PRACTICE POINTER: Caution dictates that in all proceedings, the landlord's process server should make two attempts at personal delivery or substituted service at different times, when the process server could reasonably expect to find the tenant

summary proceedings, the attempts at personal delivery or suitable age and discretion service must be once during traditional working hours (8 A.M. to 6 P.M.) and once outside traditional working hours. The objective is to make reasonable attempts and therefore the guidelines should not be mechanically applied and the court should view the totality of the circumstances.

A copy of the papers must also be mailed to the respondent both by registered or certified mail, and by regular first-class mail, addressed to the respondent at the property sought to be recovered. If that is not the respondent's residence and if the petitioner has written information of the respondent's residence address, then additional mailings in the same manner must also be made to the respondent at the last residence address as to which the petitioner has such information. If the petitioner has no such information, but does have written information of the person's place of business or employment, then additional mailings in the same manner must also be made to the last business or employment address of which petitioner has such information.[5] Failure to comply with the statutory requirements for mailing renders the proceeding jurisdictionally defective.[6]

A copy of the notice of petition and petition must be mailed both by registered or certified mail and by regular first class mail to the respondent at the premises sought to be recovered where the respondent is a corporation, joint-stock, or other unincorporated association. If the principal office or principal place of business is not located on the property sought to be recovered, and if the petitioner has written information of the principal office or principal place of business within the state, then additional mailings in the same manner must be made to the respondent at the last place as to which petitioner has such information. If the petitioner has no such information, but has written information of any office or place of business within the state, then additional mailings in the same manner must be made to any such place as to which the petitioner has such information. Allegations as to such information as may affect the mailing address shall be set forth in the petition (*see, e.g.,* § 13.83 at par. 9) or in a separate affidavit and filed as part of the proof of service.[7]

All mailings must be made within one day of the delivery of the petition and notice of petition. Proof of service must be filed with the

at the premises, before resorting to conspicuous place service.

5. RPAPL § 735(1)(a).

6. Schwartz v. Certified Management Corp., 117 A.D.2d 521, 498 N.Y.S.2d 135 (1st Dep't 1986), appeal dismissed, 68 N.Y.2d 806, 506 N.Y.S.2d 1036, 498 N.E.2d 436 (1986) (landlord's failure to mail copy of notice of petition and petition to subletting tenant's known alternate address within one day of affixing papers to apartment door rendered proceeding jurisdictionally defective); *see also* 417 East Realty Assoc. v. Ryan, 110 Misc.2d 607, 442 N.Y.S.2d 880 (Civ.Ct., N.Y. County, 1981) (landlord's failure to mail copy of papers to tenant's temporary medical treatment facility in Minnesota required dismissal of the proceeding).

7. RPAPL § 735(1)(b). *See* **PRACTICE POINTER** § 13.9 note 4 *supra*.

clerk of the court within three days after completion of the mailings. Service is complete upon filing of the petition, notice of petition, and proof of service with the court or clerk.[8]

Library References:

West's Key No. Digests, Landlord and Tenant ⛇304(2).

§ 13.10 Summary Proceedings—Service of Process—New York City Civil Court "Postcard" Requirement

When filing a notice of petition, petition, and proof of service in a residential proceeding brought in the New York City Civil Court, the landlord must submit to the clerk a stamped postcard addressed to the respondent at the premises sought to be recovered and any other address at which process was served.[1] A default judgment for failure to answer may not be entered against the tenant unless the landlord has complied with this rule.

The face of the postcard must also contain the address of the clerk's office in the form of a return address. The reverse side of the postcard must contain a written notice to the tenant of the summary proceeding in both English and Spanish. Practitioners should consult Section 208.42(i) of the Uniform Rules for New York State Trial Courts for the exact language which must be used in the postcard notice.

Library References:

West's Key No. Digests, Landlord and Tenant ⛇304(2).

§ 13.11 Non-payment Proceedings

When a tenant defaults in the payment of rent, the landlord may demand the rent from the tenant, and then commence a non-payment proceeding if the rent goes unpaid. In this situation, the tenant has the opportunity—even after trial—to pay any rent found to be due to save its tenancy.[1]

With a commercial tenant, there is a second, more aggressive approach to a rent default which a landlord can take, if allowed by the terms of the lease. A landlord can serve a notice to cure specifying the rent default and, if it is not cured within the period of time stated in the notice, can terminate the lease. If the tenant fails to timely cure the rent

---

8. RPAPL § 735(2)(b).

§ 13.10

1. 22 NYCRR § 208.42(i).

§ 13.11

1. RPAPL § 751(1) provides that at any time before a warrant is issued, a tenant may effect a stay of issuance of the warrant by depositing with the court "the amount of the rent due ... and interest and penalty, if any thereon due, and the cost of the special proceeding...." This statute applies to non-payment, but not to holdover proceedings.

default, or to get a Yellowstone injunction[2], then the landlord may bring a holdover proceeding. The theory of such a proceeding is that the tenant is holding over after the termination of its lease. The lease terminated because of the tenant's failure to cure the rent default within the period specified in the notice to cure. If the court trying the holdover proceeding finds that there has been a rent default and there is no defense to it, then the tenant loses its lease. In these circumstances there is no post-trial opportunity for the commercial tenant to cure and revive the terminated lease.

This second approach is sometimes referred to as exercising a conditional limitation for a rent default. Whether a landlord may exercise a conditional limitation for a rent default depends on the terms of the lease. Most leases contain a conditional limitation provision, *i.e.*, a provision for the early termination of the lease after a notice to cure an alleged default if the tenant fails to cure within the period of time specified in the notice. However, that provision is often limited to non-rent defaults.[3] While conditional limitations for rent defaults in commercial leases are generally enforced,[4] they have been considered violative of public policy in the residential context.[5]

Library References:

West's Key No. Digests, Landlord and Tenant ⚖=293.

§ 13.12 Non-payment Proceedings—Rent Demands

Section 711(2) of the RPAPL requires a pre-petition "rent demand" as a predicate to the non-payment proceeding. This requirement may not be waived by lease provision.[1] The goal of the rent demand is to afford the tenant notice of a rent default, so that the tenant may remedy the default and avoid litigation.[2]

The statute gives the landlord the option of demanding the rent either orally or by written notice. Written demands must be served on the tenant in the same manner as a notice of petition. If the lease precludes the making of an oral demand and requires written notice of

---

2. *See infra*, § 13.70.
3. In the Real Estate Board of New York Inc., standard form of office lease, for example, the default provision authorizing service of a notice to cure applies only to non-rent defaults: "If tenant defaults in fulfilling any of the covenants of this lease other than the covenant for the payment of rent or additional rent.... "
4. *See* Grand Liberte Cooperative, Inc. v. Bilhaud, 126 Misc.2d 961, 487 N.Y.S.2d 250 (App. Term, 1st Dep't 1984).
5. Park Summit Realty Corp. v. Frank, 107 Misc.2d 318, 434 N.Y.S.2d 73 (App. Term, 1st Dep't 1980), aff'd 84 A.D.2d 700, 448 N.Y.S.2d 414 (1st Dep't 1981), aff'd 56 N.Y.2d 1025, 453 N.Y.S.2d 643, 439 N.E.2d 358 (1982).

§ 13.12

1. PAK Realty Assoc. v. RE/MAX Universal, Inc., 157 Misc.2d 985, 599 N.Y.S.2d 399 (Civ.Ct., Queens County, 1993) (public policy requires rent demand before resort to summary proceedings, even when lease states that no demand is necessary).
2. Zenila Realty Corp. v. Masterandrea, 123 Misc.2d 1, 472 N.Y.S.2d 980 (Civ.Ct., N.Y. County, 1984).

rent defaults, the specific lease provision supersedes the statute.[3] If there is any question as to whether a particular lease provision bars oral rent demands, the landlord should err on the side of caution and make a written rent demand. While oral rent demands are quickly and easily made, they are more difficult to prove at trial.

The statute does not specify the content of the rent demand. The following guidance comes from case law. The oral rent demand should be made by the landlord or an authorized agent.[4] The demand may be made to the tenant in person or by telephone.[5] At a minimum, the landlord or his agent should clearly inform the tenant of the particular period for which a rent payment is in default, and of the amount of rent owed for the period.[6]

A written rent demand is sometimes referred to as a "three-day notice" since that is the minimum period for written notices provided for by RPAPL § 711(2). A lease provision requiring a period of written notice longer than three days will prevail over the statutory period.[7] The written notice must require in the alternative, either payment of the rent or the possession of the premises. The statute does not require that the written demand be signed by the landlord. However, where a lease between the parties requires that the demand be signed by the landlord, a rent demand signed by the landlord's attorney or agent is not legally sufficient, unless accompanied by proof of the signer's authority to bind the landlord.[8] Where there is no written lease, such as in the case of a statutory tenant, a "three-day notice" signed by the landlord's attorney is legally sufficient.[9]

---

3. Four Star Holding Co. v. Alex Furs, Inc., 153 Misc.2d 447, 590 N.Y.S.2d 667 (App. Term, 1st Dep't 1992). This case demonstrates the issue which can arise in determining whether the lease is sufficiently specific to supersede the statute. The court was faced with a printed "Bills and Notices" provision in the standard form lease that required bills, statements, notices or communications given from the landlord to the tenant to be in writing. The court "declined to hold" that this provision manifested the adoption of a notice requirement different from the "otherwise controlling statutory procedure." *Id.* at 668. The appellate term also noted that under a different paragraph of the lease, presumably the default provision, "no written notice of default need be served where there has been a default in payment of rent." *Id.* In the context of that particular lease, the court found that an oral demand was adequate.

4. *See* Kwong v. Eng, 147 Misc.2d 750, 557 N.Y.S.2d 1019 (Civ.Ct., N.Y. County, 1990), opinion aff'd as modified 153 Misc.2d 118, 589 N.Y.S.2d 138 (Sup.Ct., N.Y. County, 1991), aff'd 183 A.D.2d 558, 583 N.Y.S.2d 457 (1st Dep't 1992) (three day notice signed by attorney unknown to tenant, and unaccompanied by proof of authorization, is jurisdictionally defective).

5. Schwartz v. Weiss–Newell, 87 Misc.2d 558, 386 N.Y.S.2d 191 (Civ.Ct., N.Y. County, 1976).

6. *See* Solack Estates, Inc. v. Goodman, 102 Misc.2d 504, 425 N.Y.S.2d 906 (App. Term, 1st Dep't 1979), aff'd 78 A.D.2d 512, 432 N.Y.S.2d 3 (1st Dep't 1980); Severin v. Rouse, 134 Misc.2d 940, 513 N.Y.S.2d 928 (Civ.Ct., N.Y. County, 1987).

7. *See* Adamo Properties Inc. v. Almanzar, N.Y.L.J., 1/11/95, p.31, col.6, 23 HCR 27 (Civ.Ct., Kings County, 1995).

8. *See* Siegel v. Kentucky Fried Chicken of Long Island, Inc., 108 A.D.2d 218, 488 N.Y.S.2d 744 (2d Dep't 1985), aff'd 67 N.Y.2d 792, 492 N.E.2d 390, 501 N.Y.S.2d 317 (1986).

9. Kwong v. Eng, 183 A.D.2d 558, 583 N.Y.S.2d 457 (1st Dep't 1992).

A rent demand remains effective as a predicate for a summary proceeding only so long as the amount of rent and the period of default for which the demand is made bears a reasonable relationship to those claimed in the subsequent proceeding. Otherwise, it is "stale." In a leading case on stale demands, *Zenila Realty Corp. v. Masterandrea*,[10] the rent demand on the tenant was made for that month's rent. However, the landlord didn't commence a non-payment proceeding against the tenant until 29 months later. The initial demand for one month's rent no longer bore a reasonable relationship either to the default period or the sum of rent involved in the proceeding. Therefore, the court ruled that it was not a viable predicate notice upon which the non-payment summary proceeding could be based. The proceeding was dismissed with prejudice to the landlord's ability to re-sue in a summary proceeding, but without prejudice for the landlord to commence a proper plenary lawsuit regarding any claims for the 29–month period.

A rent demand may include a demand for payment of legal fees and late charges in addition to rent, if the lease authorizes such charges.[11] In the case of rent-regulated tenants, though, the issue is less clear. Some lower courts have ruled that legal fees, late charges and collection costs are not amounts comprising the legal regulated rent, so they may not be included in the rent demand.[12] The Appellate Term, First Department, rejected that view, however, and allowed a rent demand served on a rent-stabilized tenant to demand legal fees and collection costs.[13]

Library References:

West's Key No. Digests, Landlord and Tenant ⚖297.

§ 13.13 Non-payment Proceedings—Notice of Petition

The non-payment proceeding is commenced by petition and notice of petition.[1] The notice of petition, which is akin to a summons in an

---

10. 123 Misc.2d 1, 472 N.Y.S.2d 980 (Civ.Ct., N.Y. County, 1984).

11. *Commercial proceedings:* Clemons Management Corp. v. Quick Quality Copies, Inc., 164 Misc.2d 144, 623 N.Y.S.2d 498 (Civ.Ct., N.Y. County, 1995) (permitting demand for legal fees in addition to rent); *Residential proceedings*: Brusco v. Miller, 167 Misc.2d 54, 639 N.Y.S.2d 246 (App. Term, 1st Dep't 1995) (permitting demand for legal fees and late charges in addition to rent).

12. *See, e.g.,* London Terrace Gardens v. Stevens, 159 Misc.2d 542, 605 N.Y.S.2d 814, 816 (Civ.Ct., N.Y. County, 1993) (relying on Sections 2525.1 of the Rent Stabilization Code and 2205.1 of the New York City Rent and Eviction Regulations which forbid any person to demand or receive rent in excess of the legal regulated rent or maximum rent). Following London Terrace, at least one court ruled that legal fees may not be included in rent demands to tenants who reside in cooperative apartments, on equal protection grounds. *See* 200 East 74 Corporation v. Dallas, N.Y.L.J., 3/15/95, p.26, col.5 (Civ.Ct., N.Y. County, 1995). The decision of the Appellate Term, First Department, in Brusco, *supra* note 11, puts that result in question.

13. Brusco, *supra* note 11. However, unpaid late charges and legal fees may not be the basis for a possessory judgment. With a regulated tenancy, they may only be the source of a money judgment. *Id.*

§ 13.13

1. RPAPL § 731(1).

§ 13.13 LANDLORD–TENANT LAW Ch. 13

action, informs the tenant of the proceeding. It may be issued by an attorney, a judge, or the court clerk.[2] It may not be issued by a party prosecuting the proceeding.[3] In New York City Civil Court, however, an attorney may not issue the notice of petition. It must be issued by a clerk of the court or by a judge.[4]

Library References:

West's Key No. Digests, Landlord and Tenant ⚖297.

§ 13.14 Non-payment Proceedings—Notice of Petition—Form of Notice

The form of the notice of petition must comply with the form requirements for civil pleadings in New York.[1] The caption must set forth: the name of the court; the venue; the names of the parties to the proceeding; that it is a notice of petition; and the index number of the proceeding.[2] It should also include the address of the premises which are the subject of the proceeding. The party commencing the proceeding, usually the landlord or the lessor of the premises sought to be recovered, is designated the petitioner.[3] Any adverse parties are designated the respondents.[4] The respondents are usually the tenants, subtenants or other occupants of the subject premises. The notice must state the name, address and telephone number for the landlord's attorneys, or if the party does not appear by attorneys, the name, address and phone number of the landlord.[5]

The landlord may not proceed against a subtenant without also naming the tenant in the notice of petition and petition. Where a subtenant's identity is known, the notice of petition must list the subtenant by name as a party.[6] If all or part of the name of anyone occupying the premises is unknown, a fictitious name may be used (*e.g.*, "John Doe" or "Jane Doe"). An attorney must make reasonable efforts to learn the name of an occupant designated by a fictitious name and if all or part of the actual name later becomes known, all subsequent pleadings must state the person's true name and the prior pleadings may be deemed amended.[7]

2. RPAPL § 731(1).
3. Id.
4. New York City Civil Court Act § 401(c).

§ 13.14
1. CPLR 402, 2101(a), (b).
2. CPLR 2101(c).
3. CPLR 401.
4. Id.

5. CPLR 2101(d).

6. Triborough Bridge and Tunnel Authority v. Wimpfheimer, 163 Misc.2d 412, 620 N.Y.S.2d 914 (Civ.Ct., N.Y. County, 1994), modified on other grounds and remanded 165 Misc.2d 584, 633 N.Y.S.2d 695 (App. Term, 1st Dep't 1995).

7. CPLR 1024; Chavez v. Nevell Mgmt. Co., 69 Misc.2d 718, 330 N.Y.S.2d 890 (Civ. Ct., N.Y. County, 1972).

Under the United States and New York Soldiers' and Sailors' Civil Relief Act,[8] a court may not enter a default judgment where the respondent fails to appear unless the petitioner provides an affidavit stating that the respondent is not in the armed services. Under both the federal and state statutes, a dependent of a person in the active military may be not be evicted from a dwelling except by court order, and even then only in certain circumstances.[9]

Library References:

West's Key No. Digests, Landlord and Tenant ⚖=297(2).

§ 13.15 Non-payment Proceedings—Notice of Petition—Content of Notice

Before drafting the notice of petition, the practitioner must ascertain whether the provisions of RPAPL § 732 are applicable in the court where the non-payment proceeding is being brought. In jurisdictions where RPAPL § 732 is applicable, as in the New York City Civil Court,[1] a hearing of the proceeding is scheduled only if an answer is interposed, or if the court finds that an inquest is required.[2] The statute directs entry of judgment for the petitioner if the tenant fails to answer.[3] If RPAPL § 732 is not applicable, the notice must specify the time and place of the hearing of the petition, and the petitioner must appear at the hearing.[4]

Where the provisions of RPAPL § 732 are applicable in the local court, the notice must direct the respondent to answer before the court clerk within five days, and specify the clerk's address. The notice must also state that a date will be fixed for trial or hearing not less than three or more than eight days after joinder of issue.[5] The notice must warn the tenant that if he or she fails to answer within five days, that judgment will be entered in favor of the landlord, and may stay the warrant of eviction no more than ten days from the date of service.[6]

Where the provisions of RPAPL § 732 are not applicable in the local court, the notice of petition must specify where the petition will be heard, including the courthouse part, if any.[7] The notice of petition must

---

8. 50 U.S.C.A. § 520(1); Military Law §§ 300 *et seq.*

9. PRACTICE POINTER: On the bottom of the form notice of petition, add an advisory to tenants who are dependent on persons in the military to advise the clerk of their status. **Example:** "IMPORTANT TO TENANT: If you are dependent upon a person in the military service of the United States or the State of New York, advise the clerk immediately, in order to protect your rights."

§ 13.15
1. 22 NYCRR § 208.42(d).
2. RPAPL § 732(2), (3).
3. RPAPL § 732(3).
4. RPAPL § 731(2).
5. RPAPL § 732 (1), (2).
6. RPAPL § 732(3), (4).
7. RPAPL § 731(2).

PRACTICE POINTER: When preparing the notice, check with the court clerk for the special part of the court where sum-

also specify the time and date of the hearing.[8] When setting the date for the hearing, keep in mind the date on which service of the notice of petition is expected to be completed. The notice of petition must be served on the respondent "at least five and not more than twelve days before the time at which the petition is noticed to the heard."[9] When preparing the notice, pick a return day for the hearing that falls between the fifth and the twelfth day after the date service is expected to be completed. By giving at least eight days' notice, the petitioner may require the respondent to serve an answer at least three days before the return day. (See RPAPL § 743.) If less than eight days' notice is given, the respondent may answer in court on the return day.

All notices of petition must also warn that if the tenant fails to interpose and establish any available defense, then he or she may be precluded from doing so in any other action or proceeding.[10] A description of the relief sought by the landlord should also be included in the notice. The petition may only seek a money judgment for rent if the notice of petition contains a notice that a demand for such a judgment has been made.[11] The Uniform Rules for New York State Trial Courts provide examples of the form of notice of petition for use in the New York City Civil Court,[12] the city courts,[13] and the district courts.[14] The forms comply with the statutory requirements for notice of petition and thus are not subject to attack as jurisdictionally defective, *provided the forms are properly completed*. The official forms are intended as examples. Use of the exact language contained in the official forms is not mandatory.[15]

Library References:
West's Key No. Digests, Landlord and Tenant ⚖=297(2).

§ 13.16 Non-payment Proceedings—Notice of Petition—Defects in the Notice

Errors and omissions in the notice of petition may rise to the level of a jurisdictional defect requiring the petition's dismissal.[1] Such dismissals

---

mary proceedings should be made returnable.

8. RPAPL § 731(2).
9. RPAPL § 733(1).
10. RPAPL § 731(2).
11. RPAPL § 741(5). **Example**: "PLEASE TAKE NOTICE that the annexed petition requests a final judgment of eviction, awarding to the petitioner possession of the premises described as follows [*insert description of premises sought to be recovered*], and that demand is made in the petition for judgment against you for rent in arrears in the sum of $[*insert amount of rent due*], with interest from [*insert date from which interest is to be paid*], together with a judgment for attorneys' fees, costs and disbursements."

12. 22 NYCRR § 208.42(d).
13. 22 NYCRR § 210.42(b), (c).
14. 22 NYCRR § 212.42(b), (c).
15. Chalfonte Realty Corp. v. Streator, Inc., 142 Misc.2d 501, 537 N.Y.S.2d 980 (Civ.Ct., N.Y. County, 1989).

§ 13.16

1. Chalfonte Realty Corp. v. Streator, Inc., 142 Misc.2d 501, 537 N.Y.S.2d 980 (Civ.Ct., N.Y. County, 1989) (defects in notice of petition not amendable since no ac-

are usually without prejudice to the petitioner's right to begin the proceeding anew by service of a new notice. While historically the procedural requirements of summary proceedings were strictly construed in favor of the respondent, the modern trend is to allow defects in the pleadings to be amended, unless the mistake or omission is prejudicial to the respondent.[2]

Notices of petition issued by the wrong person may lead to a dismissal. For example, one city court ruled that a notice signed by the president of petitioner-landlord was jurisdictionally defective.[3] Dismissing the petition, the court noted that the person who signs the notice "issues" it.[4] However, in another case, a notice signed by the petitioner-landlord was allowed to stand where it contained petitioner's attorney's indorsement, and was thus "issued" by an attorney.[5]

Where a notice of petition is drafted to look more like a court order directing the tenant to vacate the premises than a notice of a future hearing, the notice is defective and the proceeding should be dismissed.[6]

If the caption in the notice of petition and petition misstates the petitioner's first name, the defect is ministerial and may be corrected by amendment, so long as there is no confusion on respondent's part as to the identity of the petitioner.[7]

Library References:

West's Key No. Digests, Landlord and Tenant ⬗297(2).

§ 13.17 Non-payment Proceedings—The Petition

RPAPL § 741 governs the contents of the petition. It requires the petition to contain the following information and allegations:

- The petition must state the petitioner's interest in the premises from which removal is sought.[1] Proper petitioners include the

tion is commenced when papers fail to comply with statutory mandate as to substance and content).

2. *See* Birchwood Towers No. 2 Assocs. v. Schwartz, 98 A.D.2d 699, 469 N.Y.S.2d 94 (2d Dep't 1983); Brusco v. Miller, 167 Misc.2d 54, 639 N.Y.S.2d 246 (App. Term, 1st Dep't 1995) (citing Jackson v. New York City Housing Authority, 88 Misc.2d 121, 387 N.Y.S.2d 38 (Sup.Ct., N.Y. County, 1976)). *But see* MSG Pomp Corp. v. Doe, 185 A.D.2d 798, 586 N.Y.S.2d 965 (1st Dep't 1992) (holding that the petition must be dismissed where the petition stated that the premises were "owned by the City" when they were not, and that they were not subject to rent regulations when they were, and thus failed to comply with RPAPL § 741 as to the contents of a petition).

3. Grove St. Realty, Inc. v. Testa, 100 Misc.2d 278, 418 N.Y.S.2d 858 (City Ct., Peekskill, 1979).

4. *Id.*

5. Parker v. Paton Associates, Inc. of Amsterdam, 128 Misc.2d 871, 491 N.Y.S.2d 550 (City Ct., Johnstown, 1985).

6. Chalfonte Realty Corp. v. Streator, Inc. 142 Misc.2d 501, 537 N.Y.S.2d 980 (Civ.Ct., N.Y. County, 1989).

7. Zirinsky v. Violet Mills, Inc., 152 Misc.2d 538, 578 N.Y.S.2d 88 (Civ.Ct., Queens County, 1991).

§ 13.17

1. RPAPL § 741(1). *See infra*, § 13.83 for a petition non-payment form.

§ 13.17   LANDLORD–TENANT LAW   Ch. 13

landlord or lessor.[2] Where the petitioner is a corporation, the petition should state whether it is domestic or foreign, and if a foreign corporation, the state, country or government by or under whose laws it was created and that it was authorized to do business in New York.[3]

- The petition must "state the respondent's interest in the premises, and his relationship to petitioner with regard thereto."[4] If all or part of a fictitious name is used to identify an unknown respondent, an allegation should be made to that effect.[5] If any respondent is a corporation, the petition should state whether it is domestic or foreign, and if foreign, specify the state, country or government by or under whose laws it was created, if it is known or believed by the petitioner.[6]

- The petition "must describe the premises from which removal is sought."[7] The description must be clear and specific enough to allow an officer executing an eviction warrant to locate the premises without additional information.[8]

- The petition must "state the facts upon which the special proceeding is based."[9] The petition must allege that a demand for payment of rent had been made prior to the commencement of the proceeding.[10] A petition which contains no allegation of default in the payment of rent, of oral demand for payment, or the giving of three days' written notice requiring payment of rent or delivery of possession, is insufficient on its face.[11] Where a written rent demand is made, the petition must either describe the notice served upon the respondent, or have a copy of the notice annexed.[12] In addition, the petition must state the manner of service in which the demand was served upon the respondent. This requirement may be satisfied by attaching to the petition a copy of

2. RPAPL § 721(1).
3. CPLR 3015(b).
4. RPAPL § 741(2). **Example:** "Respondent–Tenant Mary Smith is the Tenant of the subject premises pursuant to a rental agreement made October 1, 1994 between the respondent and the petitioner-landlord and ending September 30, 1996."
5. CPLR 1024. **Example:** "The name of the subtenant is fictitious and unknown to the petitioner. The person intended is whomever is in possession of the premises herein described."
6. CPLR 3015(b).
7. RPAPL § 741(3).
8. City of New York v. Mortel, 156 Misc.2d 305, 592 N.Y.S.2d 912 (Civ.Ct., Kings County, 1992), aff'd 161 Misc.2d 681, 616 N.Y.S.2d 683 (App. Term, 2d Dep't 1994).

9. RPAPL § 741(4).

10. RPAPL § 711(2). Material noncompliance with this statute requires dismissal of the petition. Pepe v. Miller & Miller Consulting Actuaries, Inc., 221 A.D.2d 545, 634 N.Y.S.2d 490 (2d Dep't 1995).

11. Stier v. President Hotel, Inc., 28 A.D.2d 795, 281 N.Y.S.2d 140 (3d Dep't 1967).

12. West v. Masso, N.Y.L.J., 2/28/90, p.23, col.1, 18 HCR 101 (Civ.Ct., N.Y. County, 1990); Margolies v. Lawrence, 67 Misc.2d 468, 324 N.Y.S.2d 418, (Civ.Ct., N.Y. County, 1971).

the demand served upon the respondent along with a copy of the affidavit of service.[13]

- For real property located within the City of New York, the petition must also allege whether or not the premises are a multiple dwelling. If the premises are a multiple dwelling, the petition must further state that a currently effective registration statement is on file with the office of code enforcement which designates a managing agent.[14] The petition must also state the multiple dwelling registration number for the premises, its registered managing agent's name, and either the managing agent's residence or business address. It may optionally include the agent's 24-hour telephone number. In addition, the Housing Maintenance Code requires that a copy of the multiple dwelling registration statement receipt be attached to the petition.[15]

- In jurisdictions where rent laws and regulations are in effect, such as in New York City, the petition must describe the rent regulatory status of the premises sought. Specifically, the petition must state whether the premises are subject to rent control or rent stabilization and the compliance by the landlord with applicable rent laws and regulations or the reasons why the premises are exempt from those laws and regulations.[16]

- The petition must state the relief sought, *i.e.*, a possessory judgment in favor of the petitioner and a money judgment for unpaid

---

13. Lorenzo v. Rivera, 132 Misc.2d 591, 504 N.Y.S.2d 955 (Civ.Ct., Kings County, 1986).

14. 22 NYCRR § 208.42g. *See also* Multiple Dwelling Law § 325. A multiple dwelling has three or more dwelling units. Multiple Dwelling Law § 4(7). The designated managing agent must be a natural person over 21 years of age who is in control and responsible for the maintenance and operation of the building.

15. N.Y.C.Admin. Code § 27–2107(b); Oceana Apts. v. Spielman, 164 Misc.2d 98, 623 N.Y.S.2d 724 (Civ.Ct., Kings County, 1995) (holding that annexing the registration receipt is required under the law, but failure to do so was minor, nonprejudicial and correctable error under circumstances there).

16. *See* 251 East 119th Street Tenants Assoc. v. Torres, 125 Misc.2d 279, 479 N.Y.S.2d 466 (Civ.Ct., N.Y. County, 1984); Papacostopulos v. Morrelli, 122 Misc.2d 938, 472 N.Y.S.2d 284 (Civ.Ct., Kings County, 1984); Post v. Reynolds, 101 Misc.2d 504, 421 N.Y.S.2d 320 (Civ.Ct., N.Y. County, 1979) (failure to adequately state facts supporting exemption from rent regulatory laws requires dismissal). **Example**: The following allegations are proper where the premises are located within New York City: *Where the premises are rent-controlled*: "The dwelling is subject to the City Rent and Rehabilitation Law (rent control) and the rent demanded herein does not exceed the maximum rent prescribed by the New York State Division of Housing and Community Renewal." *Where the premises are rent-stabilized*: "The dwelling is presently subject to the Rent Stabilization Law of 1969, and the Premises are registered with the New York State Division of Housing and Community Renewal, and the owner is in compliance with the Rent Stabilization Law and Code; and the rent demanded herein does not exceed the lawful stabilized rent permitted the owner under said Law, Code and appropriate Rent Guidelines Board Order as registered with said agency." *Where the premises are commercial*: "The premises are not subject to the City Rent and Rehabilitation Law (rent control) or the Rent Stabilization Law of 1969, as amended, because the subject premises were leased as and are used for solely business purposes."

rent.[17]

A residential non-payment petition need not allege compliance with the implied warranty of habitability.[18]

Library References:

West's Key No. Digests, Landlord and Tenant ⚖303.

§ 13.18 Non-payment Proceedings—The Petition—Defects in the Petition

Some mistakes and omissions in the petition are treated as jurisdictional defects requiring dismissal of the proceeding. Others, however, are deemed inconsequential irregularities which can either be corrected by subsequent amendment to the petition, or disregarded. While historically the procedural requirements of summary proceedings were strictly construed in favor of the respondent, the modern trend is to treat defects in the petition as amendable unless the mistake or omission is prejudicial to the respondent.[1]

A petition that fails to designate the name of the court and the county where the proceeding is brought has been held jurisdictionally defective.[2] Failure to identify the landlord as a corporation in the body of the caption has been held amendable and is not a jurisdictional defect if the landlord is identified in the body of the petition.[3] Where a landlord is named in the caption, but the body of the petition states that the proceeding is brought by the agent, and is verified by the agent, the petition has been held defective.[4] However, if the landlord is named in the caption as the owner of the premises, but is in fact the net-lessee, the petition has been held amendable.[5]

A caption which misstates the petitioner's first name is a ministerial

---

17. RPAPL § 741(5).

18. See Atlantic Westerly Co. v. DeAlmeida, 117 Misc.2d 1047, 461 N.Y.S.2d 143 (App. Term, 1st Dep't 1982); Presidential Fairfield, Inc. v. Holman, 98 Misc.2d 1095, 415 N.Y.S.2d 348 (Civ.Ct., Kings County, 1979).

§ 13.18

1. Birchwood Towers No. 2 v. Schwartz, 98 A.D.2d 699, 469 N.Y.S.2d 94 (2d Dep't 1983); Brusco v. Miller, 167 Misc.2d 54, 639 N.Y.S.2d 246 (App. Term, 1st Dep't 1995) (citing Jackson v. New York City Housing Authority, 88 Misc.2d 121, 387 N.Y.S.2d 38 (Sup.Ct., N.Y. County, 1976)).

2. CPLR 2101(c); Remanco, Inc. v. Wexler, 98 Misc.2d 955, 415 N.Y.S.2d 179 (City Ct., Yonkers, 1979).

3. Teachers College v. Wolterding, 77 Misc.2d 81, 351 N.Y.S.2d 587 (App.Term, 1st Dep't 1974).

4. Consumers Distributing Co., Ltd. v. Pelham Gourmet Deli, N.Y.L.J., 10/3/88, p.25, col.3, 16 HCR 363 (App. Term, 2d Dep't 1988); 300 West Realty Co. v. Wood, 69 Misc.2d 580, 330 N.Y.S.2d 524 (Civ.Ct., N.Y. County, 1971), aff'd 69 Misc.2d 582, 330 N.Y.S.2d 527 (App. Term, 1st Dep't 1972) (petition which named realty company in caption as petitioner but which was actually submitted by agent was a nullity).

5. Century Realty v. Grass, 117 Misc.2d 224, 457 N.Y.S.2d 731 (Civ.Ct., N.Y. County, 1982).

defect capable of correction by amendment.[6] Likewise, where a caption uses a fictitious name to identify a known subtenant, but the subtenant appears before the court and is not prejudiced by the misidentification, the defect has been held amendable *nunc pro tunc*.[7]

The failure to state the petitioner's interest in the premises has been held a jurisdictional defect requiring dismissal,[8] whereas mistakes in the description of the petitioner's interest are usually amendable. For example, where a petition described the petitioner as an owner, when the petitioner was actually one of four joint-owners with a right of survivorship, the court permitted an amendment to the petition.[9] Likewise, a petition that described a petitioner-net-lessee as the owner of the premises, has been held amendable provided the net lessee had standing to bring the summary proceeding.[10]

Errors and omissions in the description of the premises sought to be recovered have been held to deprive the court of jurisdiction.[11]

In New York City, a petition which omits a statement as to whether or not the premises are a multiple dwelling makes the petition insufficient.[12] The failure to annex a copy of the premises' multiple dwelling registration statement receipt to the petition, however, has been held a minor, non-prejudicial error where the petition states that there is a currently effective the registration statement on file and supplies the registration number.[13] Mistakes in the multiple dwelling recital are generally not fatal as long as the landlord can demonstrate at trial that there was a currently effective registration statement on file at the commencement of the proceeding and that the information contained

---

6. Zirinsky v. Violet Mills, Inc., 152 Misc.2d 538, 578 N.Y.S.2d 88 (Civ.Ct., Queens County, 1991). The Zirinsky court noted that there was long-standing litigation between the parties, that the petitioner's name was correctly stated in the predicate notice for the proceeding, and that the tenant was not confused as to the identity of the petitioner. *Id.*

7. *See* Teachers College v. Wolterding, 77 Misc.2d 81, 351 N.Y.S.2d 587 (App. Term, 1st Dep't 1974); *but see* Capital Resources Corp. v. Doe, 154 Misc.2d 864, 586 N.Y.S.2d 706 (Civ.Ct., Kings County, 1992).

8. Index Const. Corp. v. City of New York, 103 Misc.2d 16, 425 N.Y.S.2d 249 (Civ.Ct., N.Y. County, 1980) (description of petitioner as "landlord and owner" omitted important element of petitioner's interest in premises and was insufficient where petitioner had assigned many of its rights under the lease and only retained limited license to collect rents on behalf of assignee).

9. Singh v. Morales, N.Y.L.J., 9/29/94, p.31, col.2, 22 HCR 555 (App. Term, 2d Dep't 1994).

10. ISJ Management v. Delancy Clothing Inc., N.Y.L.J., 1/4/91, p.22, col.4 (Civ. Ct., N.Y. County, 1991).

11. Papacostopulos v. Morrelli, 122 Misc.2d 938, 472 N.Y.S.2d 284 (Civ.Ct., Kings County, 1984) (description defect may not be waived even when tenant fails to object on that ground and proceeds to trial on merits).

12. Jocar Realty Co., Inc. v. Rukavina, 130 Misc.2d 1009, 498 N.Y.S.2d 244 (Civ.Ct. N.Y. County, 1985), aff'd 137 Misc.2d 1045, 526 N.Y.S.2d 49 (App. Term, 1st Dep't 1987).

13. Oceana Apts. v. Spielman, 164 Misc.2d 98, 623 N.Y.S.2d 724 (Civ.Ct., Kings County, 1995).

§ 13.18 LANDLORD–TENANT LAW Ch. 13

therein was correct.[14] For example, a petition listing the premises' agent's post office box number instead of the agent's actual address in New York City has been held an amendable defect.[15] However, a landlord's failure to prove valid registration before the conclusion of the trial or hearing requires the proceeding to be dismissed.[16]

Early decisions held that the failure to include allegations as to the rent regulatory status of the premises was a jurisdictional defect which required dismissal.[17] The modern trend is to allow the petition to be amended to correct mistakes and omissions as to the rent regulatory status of the premises, provided there was no intentional misrepresentation.[18] A petition that states that the premises are rent stabilized, but fails to state the precise basis for coverage has been held not jurisdictionally defective.[19] However, where a petition claims that the premises are exempt from rent regulation, without stating the basis for the exemption and coverage is at issue, the petition has been held defective and the proceeding should be dismissed.[20] Likewise, a petition that states that the premises are exempt from rent stabilization pursuant to the Emergency Tenant Protection Act of 1974 by reason of "substantial rehabilitation," but does not refer to the building's status under the 1969 Rent Stabilization Law, has been held jurisdictionally defective.[21] A petition which states that the premises are not rent regulated because they are city-owned, when the premises are actually owned by petitioner and subject to rent regulation, has been held also jurisdictionally defective.[22] A petition which alleges a month-to-month tenancy where the premises are in fact rent-stabilized has been dismissed.[23] In addition, misrepresentations as to the rent regulatory status of the subject premises may lead

14. See Jocar Realty Co., Inc. v. Rukavina, 130 Misc.2d 1009, 498 N.Y.S.2d 244 (Civ.Ct., N.Y. County, 1985), aff'd 137 Misc.2d 1045, 526 N.Y.S.2d 49 (App. Term, 1st Dep't 1987); Redmond v. Scaduto, N.Y.L.J. 2/18/83, p.26, col.4 (Civ.Ct., Kings County, 1983)(citing Carjef Realty Corp. v. Straker, N.Y.L.J., 2/18/83, p.13, col.5, 11 HCR 10 (App. Term, 2d Dep't 1983)).

15. Goldstein v. Perez, 133 Misc.2d 303, 506 N.Y.S.2d 999 (Civ.Ct., Kings County, 1986).

16. Normal Realty Co. v. Rios, 109 Misc.2d 555, 440 N.Y.S.2d 442 (Civ.Ct., Bronx County, 1981).

17. 353 Realty Corp. v. Disla, 81 Misc.2d 68, 364 N.Y.S.2d 676 (Civ.Ct., N.Y. County, 1974).

18. See Villas of Forest Hills Co. v. Lumberger, 128 A.D.2d 701, 513 N.Y.S.2d 116 (2d Dep't 1987); Mintz v. Banks, N.Y.L.J., 6/2/76, p.13, col.6 (App. Term, 2d Dep't 1976); Rosgro Realty Co. v. Braynen, 70 Misc.2d 808, 334 N.Y.S.2d 962 (App.

Term, 1st Dep't 1972), aff'd Grosfeld v. Braynen, 41 A.D.2d 605, 339 N.Y.S.2d 1000 (1st Dep't 1973); 251 East 119th Street Tenants Assoc. v. Torres, 125 Misc.2d 279, 479 N.Y.S.2d 466 (Civ.Ct., N.Y. County, 1984).

19. Southcroft Co. v. Konopko, 128 Misc.2d 179, 488 N.Y.S.2d 1011 (Civ.Ct., N.Y. County, 1985).

20. Giannini v. Stuart, 6 A.D.2d 418, 178 N.Y.S.2d 709 (1st Dep't 1958); see also, Papacostopulos v. Morrelli, 122 Misc.2d 938, 472 N.Y.S.2d 284 (Civ.Ct., Kings County, 1984).

21. Disenhouse Assocs. v. Mazzaferro, 135 Misc.2d 1135, 519 N.Y.S.2d 119 (Civ. Ct., N.Y. County, 1987).

22. MSG Pomp Corp. v. Doe, 185 A.D.2d 798, 586 N.Y.S.2d 965 (1st Dep't 1992).

23. 840 West End Avenue Assocs. v. Zurkowski, N.Y.L.J., 2/28/91, p.24, col.4 (App. Term, 1st Dep't 1991).

Ch. 13 PETITION—VERIFICATION **§ 13.19**

to sanctions against the petitioner's attorneys, even if the misrepresentation is inadvertent.[24]

The failure to set forth the facts on which the proceeding is based also renders the petition insufficient.[25] Thus, a petition alleging a right to possession without any statement of the facts upon which the allegation is based, is a bare conclusion making the petition jurisdictionally defective.[26] Similarly, a petition which contains no allegation of a default in the payment of rent, of a demand for payment, or of the giving of three days' notice demanding payment of rent or delivery of possession, is insufficient on its face.[27] Where a written rent demand is made, the petition must either describe the notice served upon the respondent, or have a copy of the notice annexed.[28] In addition, the petition must state the manner of service in which the demand was served upon the respondent. This requirement may be satisfied by attaching to the petition a copy of the demand served upon the respondent along with a copy of the affidavit of service.[29]

Library References:

West's Key No. Digests, Landlord and Tenant ⇌303.

§ 13.19 Non-payment Proceedings—Petition—Verification

The petition must contain a verification, which is a statement under oath that the allegations in the petition are true or believed to be true to the knowledge of the deponent.[1] Generally, the verification is made by the petitioner. Corporate verifications must be made by a corporate officer and partnership verifications should be made by a partner in the partnership.[2] If the petitioner is a state, governmental subdivision,

---

24. Bell v. Duncan, N.Y.L.J., 1/4/95, p.31, col.2, 23 HCR 2 (Civ.Ct., N.Y. County, 1995) (attorney sanctioned for serving computer-generated petition stating premises were not subject to rent-regulation when premises were in fact regulated).

25. Schreier v. Albrecht, 126 Misc.2d 336, 482 N.Y.S.2d 674 (Civ.Ct., Queens County, 1984).

26. Stier v. President Hotel, Inc., 28 A.D.2d 795, 281 N.Y.S.2d 140 (3d Dep't 1967).

27. Id.; Lana Estates, Inc. v. National Energy Reduction Corp., 123 Misc.2d 324, 473 N.Y.S.2d 912 (Civ.Ct., Queens County, 1984).

28. Margolies v. Lawrence, 67 Misc.2d 468, 324 N.Y.S.2d 418 (Civ.Ct., N.Y. County, 1971); West v. Masso, N.Y.L.J., 2/28/90, p.23, col.1, 18 HCR 101 (Civ.Ct., N.Y. County, 1990).

29. Lorenzo v. Rivera, 132 Misc.2d 591, 504 N.Y.S.2d 955 (Civ.Ct., Kings County, 1986).

§ 13.19

1. RPAPL § 741; CPLR 3020(a). The purpose behind the verification requirement is to foster honesty and reliability in the allegations of the petition. See Fisch v. Chason, 99 Misc.2d 1089, 418 N.Y.S.2d 495 (Civ.Ct., N.Y. County, 1979).

2. CPLR 3020(d)(1); Katonah Realties, Inc. v. Wasserman, 98 Misc.2d 630, 414 N.Y.S.2d 234 (Civ.Ct., Bronx County, 1978) (verification of petition by corporate secretary of corporate landlord proper).

§ 13.19

board, commission or agency, or a public officer on behalf of any of them, the verification may be made by any person acquainted with the facts.[3]

RPAPL § 741 permits an attorney to verify a petition "on information and belief notwithstanding the fact that [the petitioner] is in the county where the attorney has his office." The form of the affidavit is specified in CPLR 3021. It requires that the affidavit of verification must, *inter alia*, state "the reason why it is not made by the party."

Library References:

West's Key No. Digests, Landlord and Tenant ⚖303(4).

§ 13.20 Non-payment Proceedings—Petition—Defects in the Verification

Courts differ as to whether defectively verified petitions may be amended. Some courts view petitions with verification defects as unverified petitions, and allow the respondent to treat them as a nullity, provided prompt notice is given to the petitioner's attorney of the respondent's election to reject the petition on that ground.[1] Other courts, however, allow unverified petitions to be amended *nunc pro tunc*.[2] The rationale is that dismissal of the petition would be too harsh a penalty for a minor, inconsequential, non-prejudicial error which should be correctable at any stage of the proceeding.

A verification defect in the petition is deemed waived unless the respondent promptly rejects the verification or gives prompt and specific notice of the respondent's intention to treat the petition as a nullity.[3] An inadvertent omission of the officer's signature to the Jurat, if in fact the affidavit is sworn to before an officer, is an irregularity which is correctable by amendment.[4]

---

3. CPLR 3020(d)(2). See *infra*, §§ 13.85—§ 13.88 for verification forms for individual, corporate, and partnership petitioners and for attorneys.

§ 13.20

1. CPLR 3022; see Ft. Holding Corp. v. Otero, 157 Misc.2d 834, 598 N.Y.S.2d 908 (Civ.Ct., N.Y. County, 1993); Hirent Realty Corp. v. Mosley, 64 Misc.2d 1011, 317 N.Y.S.2d 592 (Civ.Ct., N.Y. County, 1970) (where verification defect raised by respondent in answer, court may treat petition as unverified and dismiss proceeding).

2. See Hablin Realty Corp. v. McCain, 123 Misc.2d 777, 478 N.Y.S.2d 224 (App. Term, 1st Dep't 1984); City of New York v. Brown, 119 Misc.2d 1054, 465 N.Y.S.2d 388 (Civ.Ct., N.Y. County, 1982).

3. Ft. Holding Corp. v. Otero, 157 Misc.2d 834, 598 N.Y.S.2d 908 (Civ.Ct., N.Y. County, 1993) (nine-day period between the date holdover respondent received petition and date tenant's attorney sent notice of rejection of verification was sufficiently prompt notice); KFJ Realty Co. v. Second Ave. Boutique, N.Y.L.J., 6/5/91, p.23, col.4, 19 HCR 348 (Civ.Ct., N.Y. County, 1991) (respondent may not put in general lack of jurisdiction defense and then move at end of case for dismissal based on defective verification).

4. Halpern v. State Furniture Co., 186 Misc. 551, 61 N.Y.S.2d 618 (App. Term, 1st Dep't 1946).

A petition which is not actually signed by the petitioner, but instead contains the verification of the petitioner's attorney, is valid.[5] The absence of a statement as to why the verification is made by an attorney instead of by the petitioner is a technical omission which may be corrected by amendment.[6]

Library References:

West's Key No. Digests, Landlord and Tenant ⇔303(4).

§ 13.21 Responding to the Non-payment Petition

To avoid a default, the tenant must respond to the non-payment petition. The response may take one of three forms.

The tenant may answer the petition with any legal or equitable defense or counterclaim, provided that the tenant did not waive the right to assert counterclaims in the lease.[1] The answer may be oral or written.[2]

Alternatively, the tenant may file a pre-answer motion to dismiss the petition. The motion can be made on short notice provided it is made returnable at the same time as the petition.[3]

The tenant may also answer and move for summary judgment if there are no genuine issues of facts that require a trial. The motion must be returnable on the hearing date. In *Metropolitan Life Ins. Co. v. Carroll*,[4] the Appellate Term, First Department made clear that summary judgment is available in summary proceedings. The court reasoned that since the purpose of a summary proceeding is to provide a means for an expeditious determination, a procedural device which will afford even speedier justice is consistent with the philosophy of a summary proceeding.

A residential tenant sued for non-payment may also seek a stay of the proceeding under RPAPL § 755 on the grounds that a condition persists in the dwelling which has constructively evicted the tenant from

---

5. Suderov v. Robyn Industries, Inc., 130 Misc.2d 339, 496 N.Y.S.2d 618 (City Ct., Mt. Vernon, 1985).

6. Hablin Realty Corp. v. McCain, 123 Misc.2d 777, 478 N.Y.S.2d 224 (App. Term, 1st Dep't 1984); Zirinsky v. Violet Mills, Inc., 152 Misc.2d 538, 578 N.Y.S.2d 88 (Civ. Ct., Queens County, 1991).

§ 13.21

1. See infra, § 13.56.

2. See infra, § 13.22 for a discussion of requirements as to the form and content of the answer. Common defenses raised by tenants in response to the petition are discussed *infra* at §§ 13.25—13.34.

3. CPLR 406; Goldman v. McCord, 120 Misc.2d 754, 466 N.Y.S.2d 584 (Civ.Ct., N.Y. County, 1983) (motion by respondent made returnable the day after service of the notice of motion permitted). It is fair and reasonable for the court to provide an adequate adjournment to allow for a response to those motions which cannot be disposed of summarily on their return date. *Id.* See *infra*, §§ 13.25—13.34 for a discussion of common grounds raised by tenants to dismiss the non-payment proceeding.

4. 43 Misc.2d 639, 251 N.Y.S.2d 693 (App. Term, 1st Dep't 1964).

§ 13.21 LANDLORD–TENANT LAW Ch. 13

a portion of the premises, or is likely to become dangerous.[5] The facts justifying the stay may be brought to the court's attention by way of a defense in the answer or by pre-trial motion.

Library References:
West's Key No. Digests, Landlord and Tenant ⟐305.

§ 13.22 Responding to the Non-payment Petition—The Answer

To avoid a default, the tenant may answer the petition orally, or in writing.[1] Any other person claiming possession of the premises may also answer.[2] A tenant's right to interpose an answer in a summary proceeding may not be waived by lease provision or other agreement.[3]

If the special provisions of RPAPL § 732 are applicable in the court in which the proceeding is brought (such as in the New York City Civil Court),[4] the answer must be made before the clerk of the court within five days after service of the petition. The notice of petition must advise the respondent of this deadline. When the answer is made orally, the clerk will note the substance of the respondent's answer on the petition. If the answer is written, the respondent must serve a copy of the answer on the petitioner's attorney and file the original with the clerk with proof of service.

Where the respondent answers, the clerk schedules a hearing date and notifies the parties by mail.[5] If the respondent fails to answer, the statute directs the entry of a default judgment for the landlord.[6]

If the special provisions of RPAPL § 732 are not applicable in the court in which the proceeding is brought, the requirements of RPAPL § 743 apply and the answer must be made at least three days before the hearing date if the notice of petition was served at least eight days before the hearing date, and the notice so demanded. Otherwise, the respondent may answer on the hearing date.

The answer may raise an objection in point of law[7] to the service of the notice of petition and petition if the facts reveal that service was not made in accordance with RPAPL § 735. It may also raise an objection in point of law that the court lacks subject matter jurisdiction in the proceeding based on defects in the rent demand or service thereof, the notice of petition, the petition or the verification. In addition, the

---

5. RPAPL § 755. See infra, § 13.24 for the requirements of the stay.

§ 13.22
1. RPAPL §§ 743, 732.
2. RPAPL § 743.
3. Lipkis v. Gilmour, 158 Misc.2d 609, 606 N.Y.S.2d 503 (App. Term, 1st Dep't 1993).
4. 22 NYCRR § 208.42(d).
5. RPAPL § 732(2).
6. RPAPL § 732(3).
7. CPLR 404(a).

tenant's answer may contain any other legal or equitable defenses or allowable counterclaims.[8]

The answer may also demand a trial by jury,[9] provided this right has not been waived by the lease between the parties.[10] A respondent may also waive its right to a jury trial by raising only equitable defenses and counterclaims which must be tried by the court.[11] In New York City Civil Court, the tenant is required to file a written jury demand when answering the petition, whereas the landlord can make a demand for a jury any time before the day of trial.[12] However, the court may allow a late demand by the tenant, absent a showing of undue prejudice to the landlord.[13]

Library References:

West's Key No. Digests, Landlord and Tenant ⚖︎305.

§ 13.23 Responding to the Non-payment Petition—The Motion to Dismiss

A motion to dismiss the petition may be filed in lieu of an answer. If RPAPL § 732 applies, the motion must be served within the same time allowed for the answer, and the tenant selects a return date for the motion. (If the landlord believes that the return date selected by the tenant is too far distant, considering that a summary proceeding is involved, the landlord can make a motion to accelerate the return date.) If RPAPL § 732 does not apply, the motion must be made returnable on the hearing date set forth for the proceeding in the notice of petition.[1]

The motion to dismiss may be based on any of the grounds set forth in CPLR 3211(a). Alternatively, any of the grounds listed in CPLR 3211(a) may instead be used as defenses in the answer. For example, the motion to dismiss may raise an objection in point of law[2] to the service of the notice of petition and petition if the facts reveal that service was not made in accordance with RPAPL § 735. This objection is deemed waived if the tenant makes a CPLR 3211(a) motion to dismiss based on other

---

8. RPAPL § 743. *See infra*, §§ 13.25—13.34 for defenses commonly raised by tenants in non-payment proceedings and § 13.56 for counterclaims.

9. RPAPL § 745.

10. *Residential proceeding*: 1202 Realty Assoc. v. Evans, 126 Misc.2d 99, 481 N.Y.S.2d 208 (Civ.Ct., Kings County, 1984); *commercial proceeding*: Lana Estates Inc. v. National Energy Reduction Corp., 123 Misc.2d 324, 473 N.Y.S.2d 912 (Civ.Ct., Queens County, 1984).

11. Lewis v. Levick, 99 A.D.2d 659, 472 N.Y.S.2d 235 (4th Dep't 1984) (respondents waived their right to a jury trial by raising equitable defenses and counterclaims which must be tried by the court); Crossroads Apartments Assocs. v. LeBoo, 152 Misc.2d 830, 578 N.Y.S.2d 1004 (City Ct., Rochester, 1991) (tenant waived right to jury trial by asking court to permanently enjoin landlord from enforcing no-pet lease clause).

12. New York City Civil Court Act § 1303(a).

13. New York City Civil Court Act § 1303(c); 319 West 48 St. Realty Corp. v. Slenis, 117 Misc.2d 259, 458 N.Y.S.2d 153 (Civ.Ct., N.Y. County, 1982).

§ 13.23

1. CPLR 406.

2. CPLR 404(a).

grounds, but fails to raise the improper service objection.[3] To take another example, the motion may also raise an objection in point of law that the court lacks jurisdiction in the proceeding based on improper service of the demand for rent, or on alleged defects in the demand for rent, petition, notice of petition.

If the tenant's motion is denied, the tenant must serve and file an answer within five days after service of the order with notice of entry, unless the order specifies a different length of time to answer.[4]

§ 13.24 Responding to the Non-payment Proceeding—The RPAPL § 755 Motion to Stay

A residential tenant may seek a stay of the non-payment proceeding under RPAPL § 755 on the ground that a condition persists in the dwelling which has constructively evicted the tenant from a portion of the dwelling, or is likely to become dangerous.[1] The facts justifying the stay should be brought to the court's attention in the tenant's answer as a defense or by pre-trial motion. If the condition complained of by the tenant is described in a municipal violation notice or repair order, the landlord has the burden of disproving the condition of the dwelling as described in the notice or order.[2] Otherwise, the tenant must submit proof of the condition.[3] The court may not grant a stay if the condition which triggered the notice or order was created by the willful or negligent act of the tenant or his agent.

To be entitled to the stay, the tenant must deposit all rent due with the clerk of the court. The stay may be vacated upon three days' notice if the respondent fails to deposit the rent with the clerk within five days after it is due.[4] During the continuance of the stay, the court may release some or all of the rents to a vendor or contractor for maintenance or necessary repairs to the building (*e.g.*, payments for fuel, electricity, gas, janitorial services and repairs necessary to remove violations).

Upon the entry of an order vacating the stay, the remaining rent money deposited is paid to the landlord.[5]

Library References:

West's Key No. Digests, Landlord and Tenant ⚖═279.

§ 13.25 Tenant Defenses to the Non-payment Proceeding

The following sections present some common defenses frequently raised by tenants in the non-payment proceeding. Some of the defenses,

3. CPLR 3211(e).
4. CPLR 404(a).

§ 13.24
1. RPAPL § 755(1)(a), (b).
2. RPAPL § 755(1)(a).
3. RPAPL § 755(1)(b).
4. RPAPL § 755(2).
5. RPAPL § 755(3).

such as the warranty of habitability, are based on statutes designed to protect residential tenants from unsafe housing conditions. While commercial tenants are not protected by the warranty of habitability or other statutes designed to protect residential tenants, certain common law doctrines such as constructive eviction are applicable to both commercial and residential tenancies.

Library References:

West's Key No. Digests, Landlord and Tenant ⚖=298(1).

§ 13.26 Tenant Defenses to the Non-payment Proceeding—No Landlord Tenant Relationship

The proceeding must be brought by a person entitled to rent from the tenant and entitled to possession. Generally, this means there must be a landlord-tenant relationship between the petitioner and the respondent for the non-payment proceeding to be maintained.[1]

If the proceeding is brought by a person not entitled to bring the proceeding, the respondent can move to dismiss the petition on that ground, or include that fact as a defense in the answer. For example, it has been held that a cotenant who fails to pay rent to his cotenant, in breach of an agreement to do so, does not thereby subject himself to removal from the premises by summary proceeding.[2] Similarly, in a case where the court described the relationship between two occupants of commercial space as being that of "commercial roommates", the court held that the occupant which had signed the lease with the landlord could not bring a summary proceeding against the other occupant for the latter's share of the rent.[3]

As for contracts of sale of real estate between a landlord and a tenant, upon the passing of the deed to the purchaser, the seller no longer has the right to maintain a summary proceeding because he is no longer entitled to possession of the subject premises.[4] A debtor-creditor

---

§ 13.26

1. RPAPL § 711(2); Cammarota v. Bella Vista Development Corp., 88 A.D.2d 703, 451 N.Y.S.2d 309 (3d Dep't 1982). *But see* statutory exceptions permitting such a proceeding to be brought, for example, by a receiver, when authorized by the court (RPAPL § 721(9)); by an Article 7–A administrator (RPAPL § 778); and by an estate executor or administrator. *See also* RPAPL § 711(2), which provides that "[a]ny person succeeding to the landlord's interest in the premises may proceed under this subdivision for rent due his predecessor in interest if he has a right thereto." Broadly speaking, the statutory exceptions are for persons or entities who in essence step into the shoes of the landlord (even though they technically may not become the landlord).

2. Henry v. Green, 126 Misc.2d 360, 481 N.Y.S.2d 940 (Mt. Vernon City Ct., Westchester County, 1984).

3. Hispano Americano Advertising, Inc. v. Dryer, 112 Misc.2d 936, 448 N.Y.S.2d 128 (Civ.Ct., N.Y. County, 1982).

4. *See generally* on the issue of contracts of sale and summary proceedings, Lind v. Lind, 203 A.D.2d 696, 610 N.Y.S.2d 347 (3d Dep't 1994), appeal denied, 84 N.Y.2d 803, 617 N.Y.S.2d 137, 641 N.E.2d 158 (1994); Raguso v. Ferreira, 60 N.Y.S.2d 418 (Civ.Ct., Queens County, 1946); Babcock v. Dean, 140 Misc. 800, 252 N.Y.S. 419 (County Ct., Livingston County, 1931).

§ 13.26   LANDLORD–TENANT LAW   Ch. 13

relationship is insufficient to support a summary proceeding.[5] An assignee of rents, where the assignee is not entitled to possession of the premises, cannot maintain a summary proceeding.[6]

A party claiming monies due and owing, but not able to bring a summary non-payment proceeding, can pursue a plenary action.

Library References:

West's Key No. Digests, Landlord and Tenant ⚖︎298(1).

§ 13.27   Tenant Defenses to the Non-payment Proceeding—Tenant Out of Possession

A landlord may not maintain a summary proceeding to remove a tenant who is not in actual or constructive possession of the premises sought to be recovered, or who is not claiming the right to possession at the time the proceedings are commenced.[1] A tenant's removal prior to the commencement of proceedings deprives the court of jurisdiction to hear the non-payment proceeding.[2] An out of possession tenant may move to dismiss the petition on that ground, or assert that fact as a defense in the answer.

The issue of whether the tenant is in possession of the premises is a factual determination for the court.[3] Relevant factors include: whether the tenant has surrendered possession of the premises; has wholly vacated the premises; claims any legal right to the premises; or has returned the keys to the landlord.[4] When a tenant is found to have been out of possession at the time the proceeding was commenced, the landlord loses the right to a speedy summary determination, and must proceed by way of a plenary action based on contract instead.[5]

A tenant's surrender of possession after the proceeding has commenced, however, does not divest the court of jurisdiction, provided the tenant was in possession of the premises when the proceeding was

---

5. Matter of Bentley, 12 B.R. 528 (Bkrtcy.S.D.N.Y.1981).

6. Key Bank v. Becker, 88 N.Y.2d 899, 646 N.Y.S.2d 656, 669 N.E.2d 814 (1996); Suderov v. Ogle, 149 Misc.2d 906, 574 N.Y.S.2d 249 (App. Term, 2d Dep't 1991).

§ 13.27

1. South Ferry Building Co. v. The 44 Wall Street Fund, Inc., 142 Misc.2d 54, 535 N.Y.S.2d 685 (Civ.Ct., N.Y. County, 1988) (citing Warrin v. Haverty, 149 App.Div. 564, 567, 133 N.Y.S. 959, 962 (1st Dep't 1912)); see Bank of Nova Scotia v. Cartwright & Goodwin, Inc., 160 Misc.2d 856, 611 N.Y.S.2d 770 (Civ.Ct., N.Y. County, 1994) (to maintain summary proceeding, tenant must be in possession at time of commencement or at time of trial).

2. Darob Holding Co. v. House of Pile Fabrics, Inc., 62 Misc.2d 899, 310 N.Y.S.2d 418 (Civ.Ct., N.Y. County, 1970). See generally Finkelstein and Ferrara, *Landlord and Tenant Practice in New York* (West 1997) Ch. 14 "Nonpayment Proceedings."

3. First National City Bank v. Wall St. Leasing Corp., 80 Misc.2d 707, 363 N.Y.S.2d 699 (Civ.Ct., N.Y. County, 1974).

4. South Ferry Building Co., *supra* note 1 at 142 Misc.2d at 56, 535 N.Y.S.2d at 687 (the "critical question" is whether the tenant has dominion and control over the premises).

5. Id.

commenced.[6] The landlord is permitted to continue the proceeding to establish its right of possession, and for the determination of its demand for a money judgment for rent in arrears.[7]

Library References:

West's Key No. Digests, Landlord and Tenant ⚖=298(1).

§ 13.28 Tenant Defenses to the Non-payment Proceeding—Statutory Noncompliance

A variety of statutes designed to protect the health and safety of tenants carry strict rent-forfeiture penalties for non-compliance.

Multiple Dwelling Law § 302–a, rent-impairing violations. In a multiple dwelling, a "rent-impairing" violation in a residential tenant's unit, or in a common area of the building, will result in a complete rent abatement for any period of time beyond six months after the owner was given notice of the violation where the violation remains uncorrected. The statute applies in all cities within the state with a population of 400,000 or more. A rent-impairing violation is a condition which constitutes, or if not promptly corrected will constitute, a fire hazard or a serious threat to the life, health, or safety of the occupants of the unit or building. The statute requires local municipal departments charged with the enforcement of the Multiple Dwelling Law to promulgate and make public a list of conditions which constitute rent-impairing violations.[1]

To assert the defense, the tenant must plead and prove that a rent-impairing violation was issued and has remained uncorrected for at least six months. The tenant must also deposit with the court clerk the amount of rent sought in the petition. The clerk will release the rent to the prevailing party after determination of the proceeding.[2]

Multiple Dwelling Law § 325, no multiple dwelling registration. Where a landlord is required to register a building as a multiple dwelling, and fails to comply with the requirements for building registration and registration of a managing agent, no rent can be recovered until there is compliance with the registration requirement. Section 325 of the Multiple Dwelling Law applies in any city with a population over one million, and which by local law requires the registration of owners of multiple dwellings.[3]

---

6. Green v. Gray, 237 N.Y.S.2d 788 (App. Term, 1st Dep't 1963) (citing Sheldon Terrace, Inc. v. Schneider, 18 Misc.2d 456, 193 N.Y.S.2d 484 (App. Term, 2d Dep't 1959)) (where tenant is in possession at time of institution of proceeding by landlord, tenant's later voluntary surrender or removal during pendency of proceeding did not deprive court of jurisdiction).

7. *Id.*; *see also* Lex–56th Corp. v. Morgan, 24 Misc.2d 48, 203 N.Y.S.2d 59 (N.Y.C.Mun.Ct., 4th Dist., 1960), appeal denied 13 A.D.2d 912, 217 N.Y.S.2d 1020 (1st Dep't 1961).

§ 13.28

1. Multiple Dwelling Law § 302–a(1), (2).

2. Multiple Dwelling Law § 302–a(3)(c).

3. Multiple Dwelling Law § 325(2).

§ 13.28　LANDLORD–TENANT LAW　Ch. 13

In localities where the statute applies, such as in New York City, the landlord must plead and prove compliance with the statute to maintain the summary proceeding.[4] The failure to do so requires dismissal of the proceeding.[5]

Multiple Dwelling Law § 301, no certificate of occupancy. Section 301 of the Multiple Dwelling Law provides that occupancy of a multiple dwelling is unlawful unless and until a certificate of occupancy ("CO") is issued. Multiple Dwelling Law § 302(1)(b) imposes a rent forfeiture penalty on landlords when they fail to comply with Section 301. The statute has long been applied in such situations.[6] The courts, however, have refused to enforce Multiple Dwelling Law § 302 literally where the health, safety and welfare of the rent-withholding tenant is not endangered by the CO problem or where it would be inequitable to permit the tenant to avoid paying rent.

The absence of a CO will not necessarily trigger the rent forfeiture provisions of Section 302. The courts have refused to apply literally Multiple Dwelling Law § 302 where any of the following circumstances are present: (1) the failure to obtain the CO was caused by the tenant;[7] (2) despite the absence of a CO, there is no showing of unsafe conditions at the premises;[8] or (3) the tenant was aware that no CO existed, but took occupancy anyway.[9]

Tenants have also sought to rely on Section 302 of the Multiple Dwelling Law when there is a non-conforming use, *i.e.*, where the building has a CO, but part of the building is used in a manner that is not in compliance with the CO. Here, the significant factor is whether the non-compliance is in the premises of the tenant withholding rent, or is in another part of the building. Where the non-compliance is not in the tenant's own premises, and neither adversely affects the structural integrity of the building nor renders the rent-withholding tenant's

---

4. Jocar Realty Co., Inc. v. Rukavina, 130 Misc.2d 1009, 498 N.Y.S.2d 244 (Civ. Ct., N.Y. County, 1985), aff'd 137 Misc.2d 1045, 526 N.Y.S.2d 49 (App. Term, 1st Dep't 1987).

5. *See, e.g.*, Blackgold Realty Corp. v. Milne, 69 N.Y.2d 719, 512 N.Y.S.2d 25, 504 N.E.2d 392 (1987).

6. *See e.g.*, 40 Clinton St. Assocs. v. Dolgin, 126 Misc.2d 373, 481 N.Y.S.2d 960 (Civ.Ct., N.Y. County, 1984); *see also* Mathurin v. Jackson, N.Y.L.J., 12/12/90, p.23, col.2, 18 HCR 592 (Civ.Ct., N.Y. County, 1990) (Multiple Dwelling Law § 302 sanctions warranted where CO was absent and building was grossly substandard).

7. *Id.*

8. Renaissance I Assoc. v. Alexander, N.Y.C. Civ.Ct., No. 109428 (Civ.Ct., N.Y. County, Jan. 29, 1993, 21 HCR 131A) (lack of CO stemmed from non-conforming soffit, a condition that did not endanger the tenant's occupancy or render it illegal).

9. Lipkis v. Pikus, 96 Misc.2d 581, 409 N.Y.S.2d 598 (Civ.Ct., N.Y. County, 1978), aff'd 99 Misc.2d 518, 416 N.Y.S.2d 694 (App. Term, 1st Dep't 1979), aff'd 72 A.D.2d 697, 421 N.Y.S.2d 825 (1st Dep't 1979), appeal dismissed 51 N.Y.2d 874, 433 N.Y.S.2d 1019, 414 N.E.2d 399 (1980) (loft tenants well aware that they were occupying the building illegally).

occupancy unlawful, the courts have not applied the rent forfeiture provisions of Multiple Dwelling Law § 302.[10] By contrast, where the illegality specifically relates to the non-rent paying tenant's apartment, the courts have held that rent forfeiture under Section 302 was warranted.[11]

Commercial premises located in a multiple dwelling are subject to Multiple Dwelling Law § 302. For example, in *Ying Lung Corp. v. Medrano*,[12] a landlord could not recover rent from the tenant of a store located in a multiple dwelling prior to the issuance of a CO for the building. In *Elizabeth Broome Realty Corp. v. China Printing Co., Inc.*,[13] the court applied Section 302 of the Multiple Dwelling Law with respect to a commercial tenant in a multiple dwelling, even though the court recognized that the result, the forfeiture of nearly eight months' rent, seemed "disproportionately harsh."

By contrast, the case of *Boyar's Realty Corp. v. Queens–Nassau Auto Sales Corp.*[14] involved leased premises consisting of a used car lot and an adjoining office structure. The civil court held that the tenant's reliance on Multiple Dwelling Law § 302 as a defense to a non-payment proceeding where the landlord did not have a current CO was misplaced because the premises were not a multiple dwelling. Similarly, in *Silver v. Moe's Pizza, Inc.*,[15] the absence of a CO for shopping center space was not fatal to the landlord's entitlement to rent. The court noted that the landlord made no covenant to obtain a certificate of occupancy in the commercial lease, and the tenant's right to possession was wholly undisturbed.

Library References:

West's Key No. Digests, Landlord and Tenant ⚖298(1).

10. *See, e.g.*, 50 E. 78th Corp. v. Jire, N.Y.L.J., 12/2/91, p.25, col.1, 19 HCR 695 (App. Term, 1st Dep't 1991) (illegality did not adversely affect structural integrity of building and did not render unlawful the occupancy of tenants who were not paying rent). In circumstances of additional occupancy of legal one and two family buildings, some courts have allowed final judgments for the landlord in non-payment proceedings where the subject apartment is not the illegal unit, whereas others have dismissed the proceedings.

11. *See, e.g.*, Hornfeld v. Gaare, 130 A.D.2d 398, 515 N.Y.S.2d 258 (1st Dep't 1987); Brownstone School and Daycare Center v. Lenihan, N.Y.L.J., 5/5/92, p.23, col.3, 20 HCR 255 (Civ.Ct., N.Y. County, 1992).

12. 123 Misc.2d 1074, 475 N.Y.S.2d 772 (Civ.Ct., N.Y. County, 1984).

13. 157 Misc.2d 572, 598 N.Y.S.2d 138 (Civ.Ct., N.Y. County, 1993). In this case the CO lapsed for eight months, during which time the landlord's application for a new CO was pending. Without finding that the commercial tenant had been adversely affected (indeed, the court specifically observed that the tenant remained in business the whole time), a Multiple Dwelling Law § 302 rent forfeiture was imposed. The court noted that the statute forbade the collection of rent while no valid CO existed, and that the statute's language was "clear and unambiguous, obviating the need for judicial interpretation." 157 Misc.2d at 575, 598 N.Y.S.2d at 140.

14. N.Y.L.J., 4/17/91, p.25, col.4, 19 HCR 228A (Civ.Ct., Kings County, 1991).

15. 121 A.D.2d 376, 503 N.Y.S.2d 86 (2d Dep't 1986).

§ 13.29 Tenant Defenses to Non-payment Proceedings—Illegal Rent

In a non-payment proceeding, the landlord must plead and prove that the amount of rent demanded in the petition is permitted under the lease agreement, or in the case of rent-regulated premises, that the rent demanded is the legal regulated rent for the premises. Another tenant defense which may be raised in the answer or motion to dismiss is that the rent demanded in the petition exceeds the legal rent for the premises.

The tenant may offer the following documentary evidence to support an illegal rent defense in a CPLR 3211(a)(1) motion to dismiss or at trial: proof of payment of a lower monthly rent where there is no written lease; a lease or evidence of another agreement showing a lower amount of rent than that demanded in the petition; a DHCR registration statement for a rent-regulated apartment showing a rent at a lower amount; a DHCR Rent Reduction Order affecting a rent-stabilized or rent-controlled apartment, or a rent overcharge determination fixing a lower rent than set forth in the lease or registration statement.

Library References:

West's Key No. Digests, Landlord and Tenant ⚖298(1).

§ 13.30 Tenant Defenses to Non-payment Proceedings—Actual Eviction

Another defense to a non-payment proceeding is actual eviction. An actual eviction occurs only when the landlord wrongfully ousts the tenant from physical possession of the leased premises.[1] There must be a physical expulsion or exclusion.[2]

The physical ouster can be total or partial. A total actual eviction occurs where, for example, a landlord bars the tenant from entering the premises, changes the lock, or padlocks the door. A partial actual eviction occurs where the tenant is physically excluded from using part of its premises. For example, a tenant who lost part of its parking lot to another tenant was found to have been partially evicted.[3] In some cases, a partial actual eviction may result when a landlord interferes with a tenant's appurtenant rights, such as the use of a hallway lavatory, access to a freight elevator, or changing or limiting the means of ingress and

---

§ 13.30

1. Barash v. Pennsylvania Terminal Real Estate Corp., 26 N.Y.2d 77, 82, 308 N.Y.S.2d 649, 652, 256 N.E.2d 707 (1970).

2. Id. at 26 N.Y.2d at 82, 308 N.Y.S.2d at 653. See Finkelstein and Ferrara, Landlord and Tenant Practice in New York (West 1997) Ch. 14 "Nonpayment Proceedings."

3. 487 Elmwood, Inc. v. Hassett, 107 A.D.2d 285, 486 N.Y.S.2d 113 (4th Dep't

egress, but not completely denying access to the leased premises.[4]

Total and partial actual eviction are complete defenses to a summary non-payment proceeding. Where they are established, the obligation to pay rent is entirely suspended.[5]

Library References:

West's Key No. Digests, Landlord and Tenant ⚖298(1).

§ 13.31 Tenant Defenses to the Non-payment Proceeding—Constructive Eviction

A tenant may assert the doctrine of constructive eviction as a defense to a non-payment proceeding even if the tenant has only abandoned a portion of the premises.[1] A constructive eviction does not involve a physical expulsion or exclusion, but rather concerns wrongful acts of the landlord which deprive the tenant of use of all or a portion of the premises, resulting in the tenant's abandonment of all or a portion of the premises. If the abandonment is of a portion of the premises, the constructive eviction is partial.

The tenant must allege in the answer or affidavit in support of a motion that he or she has actually abandoned part of the premises.[2]

In the leading New York case on constructive eviction, *Barash v. Pennsylvania Terminal Real Estate Corp.*,[3] the Court of Appeals differentiated an actual eviction from a constructive eviction as follows:

> [A] constructive eviction exists where, although there has been no physical expulsion or exclusion of the tenant, the landlord's wrongful acts substantially and materially deprive the tenant of the beneficial use and enjoyment of the premises ... The tenant, however, must abandon possession in order to claim that there was a constructive eviction.... [4]

Although *Barash* only recognized the doctrine of a partial actual eviction, various courts have now concluded that a constructive eviction may be partial. In the residential context, *East Haven Assoc. Inc. v. Gurian*,[5] examined whether the doctrine of constructive eviction was

---

1985), appeal after remand 161 A.2d 1170, 556 N.Y.S.2d 424 (1990).

4. 524 West End Ave. v. Rawak, 125 Misc. 862, 212 N.Y.S. 287 (App. Term, 1st Dep't 1925); Broadway–Spring St. Corp. v. Jack Berens Export Corp., 12 Misc.2d 460, 171 N.Y.S.2d 342 (N.Y.C.Mun.Ct., 2d Dist., 1958); Seigel v. Neary, 38 Misc. 297, 77 N.Y.S. 854 (Sup.Ct., N.Y. County, 1902).

5. 81 Franklin Co. v. Ginaccini, 160 A.D.2d 558, 554 N.Y.S.2d 207 (1st Dep't 1990).

§ 13.31

1. Minjak Co. v. Randolph, 140 A.D.2d 245, 528 N.Y.S.2d 554 (1st Dep't 1988).

2. Zamzok v. 650 Park Avenue Corp., 167 A.D.2d 252, 561 N.Y.S.2d 752 (1st Dep't 1990).

3. 26 N.Y.2d 77, 82, 308 N.Y.S.2d 649, 652, 256 N.E.2d 707 (1970).

4. *Id.* at 83, 308 N.Y.S.2d at 653.

5. 64 Misc.2d 276, 313 N.Y.S.2d 927 (Civ.Ct., N.Y. County, 1970).

§ 13.31   LANDLORD–TENANT LAW   Ch. 13

available to a tenant who abandoned an uninhabitable portion of the premises, but continued to reside in the rest. There, a central air conditioner steadily emitted green fluid, and the incinerator spewed particles of ash onto the tenant's terrace. As a result, the terrace was rendered unusable for its intended purposes. The tenant abandoned the terrace, although it had been a prime factor in inducing him to enter the lease. The court held that under such circumstances, a partial constructive eviction had occurred.

In *Minjak v. Randolph*,[6] residential tenants used two-thirds of a loft for a music studio and the remainder as their residence. The tenants couldn't use the music studio portion of the loft because it was plagued by repeated water leaks, and huge clouds of dust from shoddy repair work performed by the landlord. The court found that because the tenants were compelled to abandon the music studio portion of the loft, and that the abandonment was due to the landlord's wrongful conduct, that there had been a partial constructive eviction.

The concept of partial constructive eviction also applies to commercial tenancies. For example, a pizza and coffee shop tenant suffered repeated water leaks around its grill from an upstairs apartment. Each time there was a leak, the tenant was forced to close its shop until the water could be cleaned up. The court held that there had been a partial constructive eviction. The leak prevented the tenant from preparing or serving food, and the tenant's repeated need to close the shop was, in essence, a partial abandonment of the premises.[7]

In *Parkchester Apartments Co. v. Metropolitan Retail Recovery, Inc.*,[8] water leaked into an office tenant's premises over a period of nine months. As a result, the tenant rearranged its office furniture, filing cabinets and personnel so that garbage cans and buckets could be placed to "collect seeping and cascading water." The tenant claimed that the leaks disrupted business, caused its staff to operate less efficiently, required it to send its staff home on four occasions, and adversely affected business solicitation. The tenant claimed a functional loss of the beneficial use of 50 percent of its space. The court, however, rejected the tenant's claim of partial constructive eviction because the tenant "did not physically abandon the whole or a clear segregated and distinct part of the whole." Rather, the tenant "continued its business operations, albeit with disruptions, discomfort and delays." The court did not view the tenant's closing for business on four occasions as sufficiently frequent to be considered a partial abandonment.[9]

6. 140 A.D.2d 245, 528 N.Y.S.2d 554 (1st Dep't 1988).

7. Manhattan Mansions v. Moe's Pizza, Inc., 149 Misc.2d 43, 561 N.Y.S.2d 331 (Civ. Ct., N.Y. County, 1990).

8. N.Y.L.J., 11/23/94, p.27, col.4, 22 HCR 666 (Civ.Ct., Bronx County, 1994).

9. The court in Parkchester, nevertheless, found a theory other than partial constructive eviction on which to grant relief to the tenant. It relied on a lease clause captioned, "Destruction, Fire and Other Casualty," which provided that if the premises were "rendered partially unusable by fire or

§ 13.32 Tenant Defenses to the Non-payment Proceeding—Warranty of Habitability

Library References:

West's Key No. Digests, Landlord and Tenant ⚖298(1).

The warranty of habitability, codified in Real Property Law ("RPL") § 235–b, provides that in every residential lease, the landlord is deemed to covenant and warrant that the premises and common areas "are fit for human habitation and for the uses reasonably intended by the parties and that the occupants of such premises shall not be subjected to any conditions which would be dangerous, hazardous or detrimental to their life, health or safety." Courts have interpreted RPL § 235–b as making the tenant's obligation to pay rent "dependent on the landlord's satisfactory maintenance of the premises in habitable condition."[1]

The statute makes any agreement by residential tenants that waives or modifies the warranty of habitability void as contrary to public policy.[2] Courts have interpreted this to allow counterclaims based on an alleged breach of the warranty of habitability to be raised by residential tenants in non-payment proceedings even when the lease contains a waiver of counterclaim clause.[3]

The warranty of habitability has been found to be violated by a variety of conditions, including: a lack of heat and hot water;[4] water leaks;[5] defective paint and plaster;[6] noise disturbances;[7] poor elevator service;[8] a lack of building security;[9] and roach and vermin infestation.[10]

---

other casualty," then the landlord had to repair the premises and, until such repair was substantially completed, the rent "shall be apportioned from the day following the casualty according to the part of the premises which is usable." The court in Parkchester emphasized that this lease provision did "not require the tenant to abandon the premises to receive the benefit of a rent apportionment." The court found that the tenant had 80 percent of the beneficial use of the premises during the nine-month period when there was continuous water leakage, and, accordingly, awarded a 20 percent apportionment in favor of the tenant. *Id.*

§ 13.32

1. *See, e.g.*, Park West Management Corp. v. Mitchell, 47 N.Y.2d 316, 327, 418 N.Y.S.2d 310, 316, 391 N.E.2d 1288 (1979).

2. RPL § 235–b(2).

3. *See, e.g.*, Century Apartments, Inc. v. Yalkowsky, 106 Misc.2d 762, 435 N.Y.S.2d 627 (Civ.Ct., N.Y. County, 1980). *See infra*, § 13.56 for a discussion of counterclaims.

4. Salvan v. 127 Management Corp., 101 A.D.2d 721, 475 N.Y.S.2d 30 (1st Dep't 1984).

5. Ocean Rock Assocs. v. Cruz, 66 A.D.2d 878, 411 N.Y.S.2d 663 (2d Dep't 1978), aff'd 51 N.Y.2d 1001, 435 N.Y.S.2d 981, 417 N.E.2d 93 (1980).

6. Century Apartments v. Yalkowsky, 106 Misc.2d 762, 435 N.Y.S.2d 627 (Civ.Ct., N.Y. County, 1980).

7. Kalikow Properties v. Modny, N.Y.L.J., 5/2/78, p.5, col.1, (App. Term, 1st Dep't 1978) (tenant received 30% rent abatement because landlord, after notice of noisy neighbors, failed to curb problem).

8. Levine v. Ehrenberg, N.Y.L.J., 6/11/73, p.18, col.2 (App. Term, 1st Dep't 1973).

9. Carp v. Marcus, 112 A.D.2d 546, 491 N.Y.S.2d 484 (3d Dep't 1985).

10. Pleasant East Assocs. v. Cabrera, 125 Misc.2d 877, 480 N.Y.S.2d 693 (Civ.Ct., N.Y. County, 1984) (rent abated 35% be-

When a breach of the warranty of habitability is established, the tenant is usually awarded a rent abatement. In determining the abatement amount, the court is not required to rely on expert testimony.[11] In some cases, the tenant may also be awarded legal fees[12] and punitive damages.[13]

Conditions caused by a tenant's misconduct do not constitute a breach of the warranty. If the conditions complained of are caused by a strike or other labor dispute which is not caused primarily by the landlord, the court may deny any abatement, except to the landlord's net savings if any, by reason of the strike or labor dispute allocable to the tenant's premises, provided the landlord has made a good faith attempt, where practicable, to cure the breach.[14]

Library References:

West's Key No. Digests, Landlord and Tenant ⊱298(1).

§ 13.33 Tenant Defenses to the Non–payment Proceeding—Laches

The doctrine of laches may be raised as an equitable defense where the landlord's excessive delay in suing for unpaid rent prejudices the tenant's ability to pay.[1] The rationale is that where a landlord fails for a substantial period of time to avail himself of summary proceedings to the detriment of the tenant, he is no longer entitled to summary relief as to stale claims.

When established, the defense of laches is a bar to a possessory judgment on that portion of the rent claim which is deemed stale.[2] The landlord can obtain a money judgment for the stale rent, but may not be awarded a possessory judgment for non-payment of that money judgment. The landlord's possessory judgment is limited to that portion of the rent claim which is deemed not stale.

In *Gramford Realty Corp. v. Valentin*,[3] one of the first cases to recognize the defense in a summary proceeding, the landlord waited a year before demanding unpaid rent from three rent-controlled tenants. The court dismissed the petitions on the ground that the landlord, by its excessive delay, forfeited its right to resort to summary proceedings.

cause infestation, broken windows, leaky faucets, leaky radiator and inoperable air vent breached warranty of habitability).

11. RPL § 235–b(3)(a).

12. Concord Village Management Co. v. Rubin, 101 Misc.2d 625, 421 N.Y.S.2d 811 (Dist.Ct., Suffolk County, 1979).

13. Smithline v. Monica, 1987 WL 14296 (City Ct., Watertown, 1987) ($10,000 in punitive damages awarded for apartment with severe cockroach problem).

14. RPL § 235–b(3)(b).

§ 13.33

1. Dante v. 310 Assocs., 121 A.D.2d 332, 503 N.Y.S.2d 786 (1st Dep't 1986).

2. City of New York v. Betancourt, 79 Misc.2d 146, 359 N.Y.S.2d 707 (Civ.Ct., N.Y. County, 1974), aff'd 79 Misc.2d 907, 362 N.Y.S.2d 728 (App. Term, 1st Dep't 1974).

3. 71 Misc.2d 784, 337 N.Y.S.2d 160 (Civ.Ct., N.Y. County, 1972).

After *Gramford,* the courts followed a rigid rule that any delay of at least three months in bringing a non-payment proceeding was excessive, and required the dismissal of the petition.[4] Other courts applied the "three-month rule" to establish a presumption of unreasonable delay, which shifted the burden to the landlord to show diligence in bringing the proceeding.[5] Later appellate courts, however, have held that a finding of staleness may not be based on delay of a fixed time period alone. The tenant must show entitlement to relief under the doctrine of laches.[6]

To show entitlement to relief, the tenant must show excessive delay by the landlord and prejudice to the tenant. Excessive delay has been held satisfied by a delay of more than three months in bringing the proceeding.[7] Prejudice to the tenant has been held satisfied by evidence that the tenant is poor and no longer has the resources to pay the large rental arrears.[8] The burden then shifts to the landlord to show a reasonable excuse for the delay. "If the landlord fails to meet this burden, the equitable defense of laches will bar the equitable remedy of possession in a summary proceeding as it relates to the stale rentals."[9] If a landlord proves that timely demands have been made for rent, or can prove some other sufficient demonstration of a continued and active interest in collecting rents from the tenant, then the rent claim will be deemed current, despite the fact that the commencement of summary proceedings was delayed.[10]

When a rent claim is found to be stale, the petition need not be dismissed. Any portion of unpaid rent which is not stale can be the basis for the issuance of a final judgment of possession.[11] The litigation is deemed an action at law for the portion of the claim that has been deemed stale.[12]

Library References:

West's Key No. Digests, Landlord and Tenant ⚖296(3).

4. *See, e.g.,* Maxwell v. Simons, 77 Misc.2d 184, 185, 353 N.Y.S.2d 589, 591 (Civ.Ct., Kings County, 1973)

5. *See, e.g.,* Antillean Holding Co., Inc. v. Lindley, 76 Misc.2d 1044, 352 N.Y.S.2d 557 (Civ.Ct., N.Y. County, 1973).

6. *See, e.g.,* Schwartz v. Abt, N.Y.L.J., 5/4/78, p.5, col.4 (App. Term, 1st Dep't 1978); Trustees of C.I. Mtge. Group v. NY-ILR Ltd., N.Y.L.J., 12/8/78, p.6, col.3 (App. Term, 1st Dep't 1986); Mt. Nebo Baptist Church of NY v. Myers, N.Y.L.J., 4/10/79, p.10, col.5 (App. Term, 1st Dep't 1979); C.H.L.C. Realty Corp. v. Gottlieb, N.Y.L.J., 10/19/88, p.28, col.4, 16 HCR 376 (App. Term, 2d Dep't 1988).

7. Marriott v. Shaw, 151 Misc.2d 938, 574 N.Y.S.2d 477 (Civ.Ct., Kings County, 1991); Dedvukaj v. Madonado, 115 Misc.2d 211, 214, 453 N.Y.S.2d 965, 968 (Civ.Ct., Bronx County, 1982).

8. Dedvukaj, *supra* note 7, 115 Misc.2d at 215, 453 N.Y.S.2d at 968.

9. *Id.* at 215, 453 N.Y.S.2d at 968; 269 Assocs. v. Yerkes, 113 Misc.2d 450, 449 N.Y.S.2d 593 (Civ.Ct., N.Y. County, 1982).

10. *Id.*

11. 352 West 15th St. Assoc. v. Tietz, N.Y.L.J., 9/21/89, p.22, col.3, 17 HCR 353 (App. Term, 1st Dep't 1989); Moskowitz v. Simms, N.Y.L.J., 4/28/75, p.18, col. (App. Term, 2d Dep't 1975); City of New York v. Betancourt, 79 Misc.2d 907, 362 N.Y.S.2d 728 (App. Term, 1st Dep't 1974).

12. Mariott, *supra* note 7.

§ 13.34 Tenant Defense to the Non-payment Proceeding—Payment

Payment of the rent sued for is a ground for a motion to dismiss, or a defense which may be asserted in the tenant's answer.

Documentary evidence, such as canceled checks, traced and cashed money orders, rent receipts,[1] or proof of payment to a utility company pursuant to RPL § 235–a may be submitted as proof of payment.

Library References:

West's Key No. Digests, Landlord and Tenant ⚖298(1).

§ 13.35 Holdover Proceedings

A landlord or new lessee entitled to possession may bring a summary holdover proceeding against a tenant who continues in possession of any portion of the subject premises after the expiration of the term, without permission.[1] Other persons entitled to bring holdover proceedings are set forth in RPAPL § 721. Generally, legal proceedings are required to remove or evict tenants.[2] Tenants who are unlawfully evicted, kept out by force, or put in fear of personal violence in such situations are entitled to treble damages against the wrongdoer.[3]

The term of the tenancy may expire by mere lapse of time, or may be terminated by operation of a conditional limitation. A conditional limitation is a lease provision calling for the automatic termination of the tenancy upon the occurrence of a specified event. Usually, the specified event is the tenant's failure to cure a default of a substantial obligation of the tenancy within a prescribed period of time after notice.

If the tenant fails to vacate the premises after the tenancy expires or is terminated, a holdover proceeding may be commenced by notice of petition and petition. The successful petitioner is awarded a judgment of possession and a warrant of eviction against the tenant and any other named respondents occupying the premises. In addition to the judgment

---

§ 13.34

1. RPL § 235–e requires landlords to give a rent receipt for rent payments made in any form except by personal check.

§ 13.35

1. RPAPL § 711(1).

2. Pursuant to RPAPL § 711, a tenant includes an occupant of one or more rooms in a rooming house or a resident, not including a transient occupant, of one or more rooms in a hotel who has been in possession for 30 consecutive days or longer.

3. RPAPL § 853. Non-tenants, such as licensees and squatters, are not so protected and may be ousted without resort to legal process so long as there is no breach of the peace. See P & A Bros., Inc. v. City of New York Dep't of Parks and Recreation, 184 A.D.2d 267, 585 N.Y.S.2d 335 (1st Dep't 1992). City could oust newsstand operator whose license had expired without legal process in exercise of its rights as landowner. While RPAPL § 713 permits a special proceeding as a means of removing non-tenants, an owner maintains its common-law right to oust interlopers without legal process. Id. See also W. Estis and W. Robbins, Self-Help Evictions, N.Y.L.J., 6/4/97, p.5.

of possession, the petitioner may also be awarded a money judgment for any unpaid rent under the expired rental agreement. The fair market value of the tenant's use and occupancy of the premises during the tenant's holding over may also be awarded provided they were demanded in the notice of petition and petition.

For judgments issued in a New York City residential holdover proceeding "based upon a claim that the tenant or lessee has breached a provision of the lease", the court must grant a ten-day stay of the issuance of the warrant of eviction, in order to give the respondent an opportunity to cure, and in effect, reinstate the tenancy.[4] As to residential holdover proceedings in New York City, the court may also stay the issuance of the warrant for up to six months to afford a tenant additional time to secure alternative housing.[5] For such proceedings outside New York City, per RPAPL § 751(4), a similar stay for up to four months is potentially available.

RPAPL § 713 makes clear that a holdover proceeding can also be brought to remove occupants where no landlord-tenant relationship exists. These include proceedings to remove squatters; to remove licensees no longer entitled to possession; and proceedings to evict employees (such as superintendents) of the petitioner.

Library References:
West's Key No. Digests, Landlord and Tenant ⬄293.

§ 13.36 Holdover Proceedings—Predicate Notices

Generally, if a tenancy of a definite term expires by lapse of time, the landlord may bring a holdover proceeding against the tenant immediately after the expiration of the term without issuing a pre-petition, predicate notice.

Where the tenancy is terminated before the expiration of the lease for a violation of a substantial obligation of the lease, the landlord is usually required under the lease to serve a notice to cure specifying the nature of the default, and providing for termination in the event that the default goes uncured within the time period stated in the notice. If the tenant does not cure the default in the time provided, and does not obtain a Yellowstone injunction,[1] then the landlord may commence a holdover proceeding. The theory of such a proceeding is that the tenant is holding over after the termination of the lease. The lease terminated because of the tenant's failure to cure the default within the period specified in the notice to cure. If the court trying the holdover proceeding finds that there has been a default and there is no defense to it, then the tenant loses its lease.

---

4. RPAPL § 753(4); Finley v. Park Ten Assocs., 83 A.D.2d 537, 441 N.Y.S.2d 475 (1st Dep't 1981).

5. RPAPL § 753.

1. See infra, § 13.70.

§ 13.36   LANDLORD–TENANT LAW

This approach is sometimes referred to as exercising a conditional limitation. A conditional limitation is a provision calling for the automatic termination of a lease upon the occurrence of specified event. The specified event is the passage of time (*i.e.*, the passage of the cure period) without the tenant curing the default.[2]

Before commencing a holdover proceeding, the landlord's counsel must ascertain that all required notices of default and termination have been served in accordance with the provisions of the tenant's lease, and are definite, factually sufficient, and unequivocal.

As to holdover proceedings not involving a landlord-tenant relationship, authorized by RPAPL § 713, generally a ten-day notice to quit must be served as a predicate to such a proceeding. Such a predicate notice, however, is not required to maintain a proceeding under RPAPL § 713(11) to remove an employee of the petitioner from premises provided to him incident to his employment.

The predicate notices to holdover proceedings, where required, must be written, except that the notice to terminate a monthly tenancy or tenancy from month to month outside New York City can be oral (which we view as less desirable).

Library References:

West's Key No. Digests, Landlord and Tenant ⟐297.

§ 13.37   Holdover Proceedings—Predicate Notices— Month-to-Month Tenants

In New York City, RPL § 232–a prohibits landlords from bringing holdover proceedings to remove a monthly or month-to-month tenant unless a written 30–day notice of termination is served upon the tenant.[1] The notice must: (1) state the date the landlord elects to terminate the tenancy and (2) give notification that unless the tenant vacates the premises on the day the term expires, that the landlord will commence summary proceedings to remove the tenant.[2]

---

§ 13.36

2. Whether exercising a conditional limitation for a rent default is available to the landlord depends on the lease. Most leases contain a conditional limitation provision, *i.e.*, a provision for the early termination of the lease after a notice to cure an alleged default if the tenant fails to cure within the period of time specified in the notice. However, that provision is often limited to non-rent defaults. Conditional limitations for rent defaults in commercial leases are generally enforced. See Grand Liberte Cooperative, Inc. v. Bilhaud, 126 Misc.2d 961, 487 N.Y.S.2d 250 (App. Term, 1st Dep't 1984). However, they have been found violative of public policy in the residential context. See Park Summit Realty Corp. v. Frank, 107 Misc.2d 318, 434 N.Y.S.2d 73 (App. Term, 1st Dep't 1980), aff'd 84 A.D.2d 700, 448 N.Y.S.2d 414 (1st Dep't 1981), aff'd 56 N.Y.2d 1025, 453 N.Y.S.2d 643, 439 N.E.2d 358 (1982).

§ 13.37

1. RPL § 232–a. See Finkelstein and Ferrara, *Landlord and Tenant Practice in New York* (West 1997) Ch. 15 "Holdover Proceedings."

2. RPL § 232–a.

Ch. 13   PREDICATE NOTICES—ILLEGAL USE   § 13.38

To terminate the tenancy, the notice mandated by RPL § 232–a must be clear, definite and unequivocal. Any language which could mislead the tenant or place the tenant in an equivocal position is insufficient notice.[3]

The notice of termination must be served upon the tenant at least 30 days before the termination date in the same manner as a notice of petition is required to be served.[4] Where the tenant is a month-to-month tenant for a calendar month, the termination notice must be served at least 30 days prior to the last day of the month.[5] For example, a 30–day notice to terminate a month-to-month tenant served on October 1 and terminating the tenancy on October 31 was found to be timely served under RPL § 232–a.[6]

Outside New York City, RPL § 232–b prohibits landlords from bringing holdover proceedings to remove a monthly or month-to-month tenant unless a one-month notice of termination is given to the tenant. RPL § 232–b also permits tenants outside of New York City to terminate their monthly or month-to-month tenancy by giving the landlord at least one-month's notice of their election to terminate the tenancy.

The notice must state the date that the tenancy will terminate. The notification must be given at least one month before the termination date either orally, or in writing. If written, the notice may be served personally or by mail, provided it is timely, definite, and unequivocal.[7]

Library References:

West's Key No. Digests, Landlord and Tenant ⚭297.

§ 13.38   Holdover Proceeding—Predicate Notices—Illegal Use

The landlord need not serve a notice of default or termination before bringing a holdover proceeding based upon illegal use against a non-rent regulated tenant. Section 711(5) of the RPAPL permits the landlord to remove a tenant using or occupying the premises as a "bawdy house," place of prostitution, or for any illegal trade, manufacture or business without notice.[1]

3. Spencer v. Faulkner, 65 Misc.2d 298, 317 N.Y.S.2d 374 (Civ.Ct., Kings County, 1971).

4. See supra, § 13.6.

5. Clarke v. Shepard, 188 Misc. 588, 68 N.Y.S.2d 707 (App. Term, 1st Dep't 1947).

6. Seminole Housing Corp. v. M & M Garages, Inc., 78 Misc.2d 755, 359 N.Y.S.2d 711 (Civ.Ct., Queens County, 1974), modified on other grounds 78 Misc.2d 762, 359 N.Y.S.2d 710 (App. Term, 2d Dep't 1974), aff'd 47 A.D.2d 651, 364 N.Y.S.2d 26 (2d Dep't 1975).

7. McGloine v. Dominy, 233 N.Y.S.2d 161 (City Ct., Albany, 1962). See also, Finkelstein and Ferrara, *Landlord and Tenant Practice in New York* (West 1997) Ch. 13 "Terminating the Tenancy."

§ 13.38

1. Murphy v. Relaxation Plus Commodore, Ltd., 83 Misc.2d 838, 373 N.Y.S.2d 793 (App. Term, 1st Dep't 1975); 2312–2316 Realty Corp. v. Font, 140 Misc.2d 901, 531 N.Y.S.2d 727 (Civ.Ct., Bronx County, 1988). See also, RPL § 231(1) which provides that when the lessee or occupant other than the

Rent regulated tenants, however, must be served with a termination notice before the holdover proceeding is commenced on the ground of illegal use.[2]

Library References:

West's Key No. Digests, Landlord and Tenant ⚖297.

§ 13.39 Holdover Proceedings—Predicate Notices—Rent-Controlled Tenants

The regulations pertaining to eviction of rent controlled tenants in New York City are found in Part 2204 of the New York City Rent and Eviction Regulations. When eviction is sought on the grounds of occupancy by the landlord or his immediate family, substantial alteration or remodeling, demolition, and withdrawal from the rental market, the regulations detail a procedure whereby the landlord applies to the New York State Division of Housing and Community Renewal ("DHCR") for a certificate of eviction.[1] If such a certificate is obtained, the landlord can then, after a specified waiting period, commence a court proceeding to evict the tenant.

As to holdover proceedings without a certificate of eviction, Section 2204.2 of the New York City Rent and Eviction Regulations specifies and limits the grounds on which such a proceeding can be brought (*e.g.,* violation of a substantial obligation of the tenancy, nuisance, illegal occupancy, illegal or immoral use, refusal of access). Before any such proceeding is commenced, a predicate notice "to vacate or surrender possession"(the statutory term for a termination notice) must be served on the tenant. The termination notice must state the statutory ground upon which the termination is based, the facts necessary to establish the existence of such ground, and the date when the tenant is required to surrender possession (the "termination date").[2]

The length of the termination notice period depends on which ground the landlord relies on to terminate the tenancy, for example:

- Where the ground stated in the notice is nuisance, objectionable conduct,[3] illegal occupancy,[4] or illegal or immoral use,[5] a notice to

owner uses or occupies the premises "for any illegal trade, manufacture or other business," the lease or occupancy agreement "shall thereupon become void ....."

2. *See infra,* §§ 13.39, 13.40.

§ 13.39

1. *See, e.g.,* 9 NYCRR §§ 2204.4 to 2204.9. See also City Rent and Rehabilitation Law, N.Y.C. Admin. Code § 26–408. A discussion of the specifics of the procedure is beyond the scope of this chapter. The practitioner should be aware, however, that the recently enacted Rent Regulation Reform Act of 1997 contains a provision (Section 38 thereof, amending N.Y.C. Admin. Code § 26–408(b)(4) and (5)) which sets forth exemptions to certain stringent requirements pertaining to the demolition of buildings with rent control tenants.

2. 9 NYCRR §§ 2204.2, 2204.3(a), (b).

3. 9 NYCRR § 2204.2(a)(2).

4. 9 NYCRR § 2204.2(a)(3).

5. 9 NYCRR § 2204.2(a)(4).

vacate or surrender must be served on the tenant not less than ten days before the termination date. If the tenant is a weekly tenant, the notice must be served on the tenant at least two days before the termination date.[6]

- Where the ground stated in the notice is the violation of a substantial obligation of the tenancy,[7] the landlord must first serve a notice on the tenant demanding that the violation cease within ten days (*i.e.*, a notice to cure). No such notice is needed if the allegation is that within three months prior to the commencement of the proceeding, the tenant has willfully violated such an obligation, inflicting serious and substantial injury on the landlord. If the tenant fails to cure the violation within the time provided in the notice, the landlord must then serve a notice to vacate or surrender on the tenant not less than one month before the termination date. If the tenant is a weekly tenant, the notice must be served on the tenant not less than seven days before the termination date.[8]

- Where the ground stated in the notice is the unreasonable refusal to permit the landlord access to the unit to make necessary repairs,[9] a notice to vacate or surrender must be served on the tenant not less than one month before the termination date stated in the notice, unless the tenant is a weekly tenant in which case the notice must be served on the tenant not less than seven days before the termination date.

Rent control does not extend to tenants who do not occupy their apartment as their primary residence. Accordingly, a landlord may seek to evict the tenant on this ground by serving a thirty-day notice of termination (terminating the month-to-month tenancy) and notice of intention to commence a proceeding for non-primary residence.[10]

Within 48 hours after a notice to vacate or surrender is served upon a rent controlled tenant, an exact copy of the notice, together with an affidavit of service, must be filed with the New York State Division of Housing and Community Renewal district rent office for the district in which the premises are located. Saturdays, Sundays and legal holidays extend the 48-hour requirement.[11]

For the regulations pertaining to eviction of rent controlled tenants outside New York City, Part 2104 of the State Rent and Eviction Regulations (9 NYCRR §§ 2104.1 to 2104.9) must be consulted. They are substantially similar to, but not exactly the same as, the regulations

---

6. 9 NYCRR § 2204.3(d)(1).
7. 9 NYCRR § 2204.2(a)(1).
8. 9 NYCRR § 2204.3(d)(2).
9. 9 NYCRR § 2204.2(a)(6).
10. *See, e.g.*, City Rent and Rehabilitation Law, N.Y.C. Admin. Code § 26-403(e)(2), (10); First Sterling Corp. v. Zurkowski, 142 Misc.2d 978, 542 N.Y.S.2d 899 (App. Term., 1st Dep't 1989).
11. 9 NYCRR § 2204.3(a), (c).

§ 13.39

pertaining to rent-controlled tenants in New York City. (*See also* Section 5 of the Emergency Housing Rent Control Law, McKinney's Unconsol Laws § 8585.)

Library References:
West's Key No. Digests, Landlord and Tenant ⚖︎297.

§ 13.40 Holdover Proceeding—Predicate Notices—Rent–Stabilized Tenants

The regulations pertaining to eviction of rent stabilized tenants in New York City are found in Part 2524 of the Rent Stabilization Code (9 NYCRR §§ 2524.1 to 2524.5). Section 2524.3, captioned "Proceedings for Eviction—Wrongful Acts of Tenant", specifies grounds for termination of a lease and eviction without agency approval. They include violation of a substantial obligation of the tenancy, nuisance, illegal occupancy, immoral or illegal use, refusal of access, and the tenant's refusal to renew an expiring rent stabilized lease when the renewal is offered by the landlord in accordance with law.

A predicate termination notice must be served before commencing a holdover proceeding based upon the grounds specified in Rent Stabilization Code § 2524.3. The termination notice must state the statutory ground upon which the termination is based, the facts necessary to establish the existence of such ground, and the date when the tenant is required to surrender possession of the premises to the landlord (the "termination date").[1]

Rent stabilized tenants have a right to a renewal lease. Section 2524.4 specifies grounds for refusal to renew a lease, without order of DHCR, and, upon expiration of the existing lease, to commence a proceeding to evict the tenant. These grounds are occupancy by the owner or a member of the owner's immediate family, recovery by a not-for-profit institution and non-primary residence. A predicate termination notice, as described above, is also required before commencing a holdover proceeding based upon the grounds specified in Rent Stabilization Code § 2524.4.

Pursuant to § 2524.5, the owner can seek authorization from DHCR not to renew the lease, and upon expiration of the existing lease term, to commence an action or proceeding to recover possession based on the following additional grounds: withdrawal of the apartment from the rental market, demolition and substantial rehabilitation. A predicate notice of the election not to renew must be given to the tenant at least 120 and not more than 150 days prior to the expiration of the lease term. Specifics concerning the procedures for refusing to renew rent-stabilized leases on the grounds of demolition are set forth in DHCR Operational Bulletin 96–1.

§ 13.40
1. 9 NYCRR § 2524.2(b).

The length of the termination notice period for grounds specified in Rent Stabilization Code §§ 2524.3 and 2524.4 depends on which statutory ground the landlord relies on to terminate the tenancy, for example:

- Where the ground for termination is the tenant's violation of a substantial obligation of the tenancy, the owner must first serve the tenant with written notice to cure the violations within ten days.[2] No such notice to cure is needed if the allegation is that within three months prior to the commencement of the proceeding the tenant has willfully violated such an obligation, inflicting serious and substantial injury on the landlord. If the violation goes uncured within the time set forth in the notice, the landlord must then serve a notice of termination at least seven calendar days before the date set forth therein for surrender of possession.[3]

- Where the ground for termination is the tenant's refusal to renew the lease,[4] the termination notice must be served on the tenant at least 15 days before the termination date in the notice.[5]

- Where the ground for termination is nuisance or objectionable conduct,[6] illegal occupancy,[7] illegal or immoral use,[8] or illegal subletting,[9] the termination notice must be served at least seven days before the termination date set forth in the notice.[10]

- Where the ground for termination is that the tenant is not occupying the premises as a primary residence;[11] that the owner or the owner's immediate family intend to occupy the tenant's premises;[12] or for the recovery of the premises by a not-for-profit institution,[13] the landlord must serve a notice of intention not to renew the lease on the tenant not less than 120 days and not more than 150 days before the date the tenant's lease is set to expire.[14] This notice is commonly known as a notice of non-renewal or "Golub" notice. Additionally, where non-primary residence is involved, the landlord must give 30 days' notice to the tenant of his intention to commence an eviction proceeding based on that ground. That notice can be combined with the "Golub" notice.[15]

2. 9 NYCRR § 2524.3(a).
3. 9 NYCRR § 2524.2(c)(2).
4. 9 NYCRR § 2524.3(f).
5. 9 NYCRR § 2524.2(c)(1).
6. 9 NYCRR § 2524.3(b).
7. 9 NYCRR § 2524.3(c).
8. 9 NYCRR § 2524.3(d).
9. 9 NYCRR § 2524.3(h).
10. 9 NYCRR § 2524.2(c)(2).
11. 9 NYCRR § 2524.4(c).
12. 9 NYCRR § 2524.4(a).

13. 9 NYCRR § 2524.4(b). To recover the premises, the owner must be a hospital, convent, monastery, asylum, public institution, college, school dormitory, or other institution operated exclusively for charitable or educational purposes on a non-profit basis. *Id.*

14. 9 NYCRR § 2524.2(c)(2),(3).

15. *See* Golub v. Frank, 65 N.Y.2d 900, 493 N.Y.S.2d 451, 483 N.E.2d 126 (1985). 9 NYCRR § 2524.4(c).

§ 13.40 LANDLORD–TENANT LAW Ch. 13

The statutory notice periods may not be waived by shorter notice periods in a lease agreement,[16] but a lease may call for more notice than is required by the statute. The Rent Stabilization Code does not specify a method of service for these notices. The practitioner must look to the lease agreement between the parties to determine how the notice should be given.

For the regulations pertaining to eviction of rent stabilized tenants outside New York City, the provisions of Part 2504 of the Emergency Tenant Protection Regulations (9 NYCRR §§ 2504.1 to 2504.4) must be consulted. They are substantially similar to, but not exactly the same as, the regulations pertaining to rent stabilized tenants in New York City.

Library References:

West's Key No. Digests, Landlord and Tenant ⟶297.

§ 13.41 Holdover Proceedings—The Notice of Petition

The holdover proceeding is commenced by petition and notice of petition.[1] The notice informs the tenant of the time and place of the proceeding. The notice may be issued by an attorney, a judge, or the court clerk.[2] It may not be issued by a party prosecuting the proceeding.[3] In New York City Civil Court however, an attorney may not issue the notice of petition. It must be issued by a clerk of the court or by a judge.[4]

In addition to specifying the date and time of the hearing of the petition, the notice must give the name and address of the courthouse where the hearing of the petition will be heard, and the courthouse part, if any.[5] The notice must also warn that if the tenant fails to interpose and establish any available defense, he or she may be precluded from doing so in any other action or proceeding.[6] A notice of the relief sought in the petition should also be included in the notice. The petition may not seek a money judgment for rent or for use and occupancy unless the notice of petition contains a notice that demand for such judgment has been made.[7] After the expiration or termination of the lease, when there is no landlord-tenant relationship, the money due for occupying the premises is referred to as use and occupancy, not rent. A judgment for rent should be demanded if any rent for the period prior to the lease expiration or termination is due. For such rent sought in a holdover proceeding, there is no requirement of a predicate rent demand. When a holdover proceeding is brought where no landlord-tenant relationship

---

16. 9 NYCRR § 2524.2(d).

§ 13.41
1. RPAPL § 731(1)
2. Id.
3. Id.
4. New York City Civil Court Act § 401(c).

5. RPAPL § 731(2).

PRACTICE POINTER: When preparing the notice, check with the court clerk for the special part of the court where summary proceedings should be made returnable.

6. RPAPL § 731(2).
7. RPAPL § 741(5).

ever existed (*e.g.*, a squatter proceeding or a licensee proceeding), the monies sought are use and occupancy, not rent.

When setting the time for the hearing, keep in mind the date on which service of the notice of petition and petition on the respondents is expected to be completed. The notice of petition and petition must be served on the respondents "at least five and not more than twelve days before the time at which the petition is noticed to the heard."[8] When drafting the notice, pick a return day for the hearing that falls between the fifth and the twelfth day after the date you expect service to be completed. By giving at least 8 days' notice of the petition, the petitioner may require the respondent to serve an answer at least 3 days before the return day.[9] If less than 8 days' notice is given, the respondent may answer in court on the return day.

The form of the notice of petition must comply with the requirements for civil pleadings in New York.[10] The Uniform Rules for Trial Courts provide examples of the form of notice of holdover petition for use in the New York City Civil Court,[11] the city courts,[12] and the district courts.[13] The official forms are intended as examples; use of the exact language contained in the official forms is not mandatory.[14]

Library References:

West's Key No. Digests, Landlord and Tenant ⚖297.

§ 13.42 Holdover Proceedings—Notice of Petition—Defects in the Notice

As previously discussed, drafting errors in the notice of petition may lead to a dismissal of the petition.[1]

Library References:

West's Key No. Digests, Landlord and Tenant ⚖297(2).

§ 13.43 Holdover Proceedings—Holdover Petition—Form and Content

The petition sets forth the facts upon which the proceeding is based, and the legal grounds on which recovery of the premises is sought. The

---

8. RPAPL § 733(1).

PRACTICE POINTER: Use care to avoid setting the hearing date on a weekend or holiday. Also consider which days of the week the court hears summary proceedings. While the New York City Civil Court housing part sits every weekday, courts outside New York City may only hear special proceedings on certain days.

9. RPAPL § 743.

10. *See supra*, § 13.14 for a detailed discussion on the form of the notice of petition.

11. 22 NYCRR § 208.42(b), (c).

12. 22 NYCRR § 210.42(b), (c).

13. 22 NYCRR § 212.42(b), (c).

14. Chalfonte Realty Corp. v. Streator, Inc., 142 Misc.2d 501, 537 N.Y.S.2d 980 (Civ.Ct., N.Y. County, 1989).

§ 13.42

1. *See supra*, § 13.16 for a detailed discussion of case law on defects in the notice of petition.

§ 13.43   LANDLORD–TENANT LAW   Ch. 13

petition accompanies the notice of petition when served upon the tenant. The petition must contain the following information and allegations.[1]

- The petition must "state the interest of the petitioner in the premises from which removal is sought."[2] Proper petitioners include lessors and landlords.[3] If the petitioner is a corporation, the petition should state whether it is domestic or foreign, and if foreign, the state, country or government by or under whose laws it was created and that it is authorized to do business in New York State.[4]

- The petition "must state the respondent's interest in the premises, and his relationship to petitioner...."[5] If any respondent is a corporation, the petition should state whether it is domestic or foreign, and if foreign, the state, country or government by or under whose laws it was created, if it is known or believed by the petitioner.[6] If all or part of a fictitious name is used to identify an unknown respondent, an allegation should be made to that effect.[7]

- The petition "must describe the premises from which removal is sought."[8] The description must be clear and specific enough to allow an officer executing an eviction warrant to locate the dwelling without additional information.[9]

- The petition must "state the facts upon which the special proceeding is based."[10] Thus, as to a holdover proceeding based on termination of a tenancy, the petition should allege the lease under which the tenant was in possession; any facts justifying the landlord's termination of the tenancy where applicable; and the manner in which and the date when the lease was terminated.[11] If termination is based on a specific statutory or regulatory provision, the pleadings should show the elements of the cause of action as defined by the statute or regulation. For example, an owner occupancy proceeding is a proceeding where the landlord

§ 13.43

1. See infra, § 13.84 for a holdover petition form.

2. RPAPL § 741(1).

3. A complete list of proper petitioners is listed in RPAPL § 721.

4. CPLR 3015(b).

5. RPAPL § 741(2). **Example:** "Respondent–Tenant Mary Smith is the Tenant of the subject premises pursuant to a rental agreement made Oct. 1, 19 .. between respondent and petitioner and ending September 30, 19 ..."

6. CPLR 3015(b).

7. CPLR 1024. **Example**: "The name of the subtenant is fictitious and unknown to the petitioner. The person intended is whomever is in possession of the premises herein described."

8. RPAPL § 741(3).

9. City of New York v. Mortel, 156 Misc.2d 305, 592 N.Y.S.2d 912 (Civ.Ct., Kings County, 1992), aff'd 161 Misc.2d 681, 616 N.Y.S.2d 683 (App. Term, 2d Dep't 1994).

10. RPAPL § 741(4).

11. See, e.g., Gould v. Pollack, 68 Misc.2d 670, 327 N.Y.S.2d 808, 812 (Civ.Ct., N.Y. County, 1971), aff'd 71 Misc.2d 344, 335 N.Y.S.2d 840 (App. Term, 1st Dep't 1972) (the intent of RPAPL § 741(4) "is to require that the petitioners inform the respondent of the basis for the petitioners' suit").

seeks eviction to use the apartment for himself or his immediate family. (*See* Sections 13.39 and 13.40 above.) Such a proceeding may not be maintained against a New York City rent-stabilized tenant if the tenant or the tenant's spouse is a senior citizen (defined as 62 or older) or a disabled person, unless the landlord offers to provide and, if requested, provides an equivalent or superior housing accommodation at the same or lower regulated rent in a closely proximate area. It has been held that such an offer must be alleged in the petition as a necessary element of stating a cause of action in an owner occupancy proceeding.[12]

- Where a notice of non-renewal, notice of default, notice of termination, or other notice is a predicate to the summary proceeding, the petition must either describe the notice served upon the respondent, or refer to a copy of the notice which is annexed to the petition.[13] In addition, the petition must state the manner in which the relevant notice was served upon the respondent. This requirement may be satisfied by attaching to the petition a copy of the notice or notices served upon the respondent along with a copy of the affidavit of service.[14]

- For real property located within the City of New York, the petition must allege either that the premises are not a multiple dwelling, or that the premises are a multiple dwelling and there is a currently effective registration statement on file with the office of code enforcement designating a managing agent.[15] The petition must also allege the premises' multiple dwelling registration number; the registered managing agent's name; and either the residence or business address of the managing agent. It may optionally include the managing agent's 24–hour telephone number. In addition, the New York City Housing Maintenance Code requires that a copy of the multiple dwelling registration statement receipt be attached to the petition.[16]

- Specifically, the petition must state whether the premises are subject to rent control or rent stabilization and compliance by the landlord with applicable rent laws and regulations or the reasons

---

12. *See, e.g.*, 9 NYCRR §§ 2520.6(p), (q), 2524.4(a)(2) (New York City rent stabilization); Schreier v. Albrecht, 126 Misc.2d 336, 482 N.Y.S.2d 674 (Civ.Ct., Queens County, 1984).

13. Margolies v. Lawrence, 67 Misc.2d 468, 324 N.Y.S.2d 418, (Civ.Ct., N.Y. County, 1971); West v. Masso, N.Y.L.J., 2/28/90, p.23, col.1 (Civ.Ct., N.Y. County, 1990).

14. Lorenzo v. Rivera, 132 Misc.2d 591, 504 N.Y.S.2d 955 (Civ.Ct., Kings County, 1986).

15. Multiple Dwelling Law § 325; 22 NYCRR § 208.42g. A multiple dwelling has three or more dwelling units. *See* Multiple Dwelling Law § 4(7)

16. N.Y.C.Admin. Code § 27–2107(b); Oceana Apts. v. Spielman, 164 Misc.2d 98, 623 N.Y.S.2d 724 (Civ.Ct., Kings County, 1995).

why the dwelling is exempt those laws and regulations.[17]

- The petition must state the relief sought, *i.e.*, a possessory judgment in favor of the petitioner.[18] The relief may include a judgment for unpaid rent, and/or for use and occupancy, provided the notice of petition contains a notice that a demand for such a judgment has been made.[19]

Library References:

West's Key No. Digests, Landlord and Tenant ⇔303.

§ 13.44 Holdover Proceedings—Holdover Petition—Defects in the Petition

Errors and omissions in the allegations of the petition are subject to attack by the tenant as jurisdictional defects, and may result in the dismissal of the proceeding.

The failure to set forth the facts upon which the holdover proceeding is based renders the petition insufficient.[1] A petition which alleges a right to possession without any statement of the facts as to how the tenancy expired or was terminated is a bare conclusion rendering the petition jurisdictionally defective.[2] For example, in a holdover proceeding based on termination of a tenancy, a petition which fails to allege a landlord-tenant relationship, the terms of the lease under which the tenant entered into possession, any facts justifying the landlord's termination of the tenancy, or the date and manner in which the lease expired or terminated, may also be found jurisdictionally defective.

---

17. 251 East 119th Street Tenants Assoc. v. Torres, 125 Misc.2d 279, 479 N.Y.S.2d 466 (Civ.Ct., N.Y. County, 1984); Papacostopulos v. Morrelli, 122 Misc.2d 938, 472 N.Y.S.2d 284 (Civ.Ct., Kings County, 1984); Post v. Reynolds, 101 Misc.2d 504, 421 N.Y.S.2d 320 (Civ.Ct., N.Y. County, 1979) (failure to adequately state facts supporting exemption from rent regulatory laws requires dismissal). **Example:** the following allegations are proper where the premises are located within New York City: *Where the premises are rent controlled:* "The dwelling is subject to the City Rent and Rehabilitation Law (rent control) and the rent demanded herein does not exceed the maximum rent prescribed by the New York State Division of Housing and Community Renewal. *Where the premises are rent-stabilized:* "The dwelling is presently subject to the Rent Stabilization Law of 1969, and the Premises are registered with the New York State Division of Housing and Community Renewal, and the owner is in compliance with the Rent Stabilization Law and Code; and the rent demanded herein does not exceed the lawful stabilized rent permitted the owner under said Law, Code and appropriate Rent Guidelines Board Order as registered with said agency. *Where the premises are commercial:* "The premises are not subject to the City Rent and Rehabilitation Law (rent control) or the Rent Stabilization Law of 1969, as amended, because the subject premises were leased as and are used for solely business purposes."

18. RPAPL § 741(5).

19. RPAPL § 741(5); Barzack Realty Co. v. Joseph Legatti & Son, Inc., 114 Misc.2d 245, 450 N.Y.S.2d 983 (Civ.Ct., N.Y. County, 1982).

§ 13.44

1. Schreier v. Albrecht, 126 Misc.2d 336, 482 N.Y.S.2d 674 (Civ.Ct., Queens County, 1984).

2. Stier v. President Hotel, Inc., 28 A.D.2d 795, 281 N.Y.S.2d 140 (3d Dep't 1967).

A holdover proceeding based on a termination notice incorporated in the petition was held to fail to state sufficient facts when the notice only made vague and general statements about the sale and storage of crack in and around the building.[3] In a holdover proceeding based on termination of a month-to-month tenancy on the grounds of a Department of Housing Preservation and Development vacate order, the failure of the termination notice to specifically identify the conditions which gave rise to the vacate order rendered the petition based on the termination notice jurisdictionally defective.[4]

An allegation of how the predicate notice was served upon the respondent (or annexing a copy of the notice, and an affidavit of service thereof) is a necessary element in any petition in a holdover proceeding. The lack of any such allegation or proof of service of the requisite notice is a jurisdictional defect.[5]

A holdover petition is not required to assert compliance with the implied warranty of habitability, even if the premises sought are residential.[6]

The effect of a defect in the petition's caption, premises description, statement of the parties' interest in the premises, multiple dwelling statement, and rent regulatory status of the premises sought are discussed above. [7]

Library References:

West's Key No. Digests, Landlord and Tenant ⚖303.

§ 13.45 Holdover Proceedings—Holdover Petition—Verification and Verification Defects

To foster honesty and reliability in the pleadings, RPAPL § 741 requires that the holdover petition must be verified by the petitioner, or by the petitioner's legal representative, attorney, or agent. Verification requirements and the effect that a defective verification may have on the proceeding are discussed above.[1]

---

3. City of New York v. Rogers, 165 Misc.2d 240, 629 N.Y.S.2d 628 (Civ. Ct., Kings County 1995).

4. City of New York v. Torres, 164 Misc.2d 1037, 631 N.Y.S.2d 208 (App. Term, 1st Dep't 1995), citing Giannini v. Stuart, 6 A.D.2d 418, 178 N.Y.S.2d 709 (1st Dep't 1958), and MSG Pomp Corp. v. Doe, 185 A.D.2d 798, 586 N.Y.S.2d 965 (1st Dep't 1992).

5. *See, e.g.*, Levesque v. Sharpe, 106 Misc.2d 432, 430 N.Y.S.2d 482 (City Ct., Westchester County, 1980).

6. Atlantic Westerly Co. v. DeAlmeida, 117 Misc.2d 1047, 461 N.Y.S.2d 143 (App. Term, 1st Dep't 1982); Presidential Fairfield, Inc. v. Holman, 98 Misc.2d 1095, 415 N.Y.S.2d 348 (Civ.Ct., Kings County, 1979).

7. *See supra*, § 13.18.

§ 13.45

1. *See supra*, §§ 13.19, 13.20. *See also*, Finkelstein and Ferrara, *Landlord and Tenant Practice in New York* (West 1997) Ch. 15 "Holdover Proceedings."

§ 13.46 Responding to the Holdover Petition

To avoid eviction, the tenant must respond to the holdover petition. The response may take one of three forms.

The tenant may answer the petition with any allowable defense or counterclaim, provided that the tenant did not waive the right to assert counterclaims in the lease.[1] The answer may be oral or written.[2]

Alternatively, the tenant may file a pre-answer motion to dismiss the petition. The motion can be made on short notice provided it is made returnable at the same time as the petition.[3]

The tenant may also answer and move for summary judgment if there are no genuine issues of facts that require a trial. The motion must be returnable on the hearing date. In *Metropolitan Life Ins. Co. v. Carroll*,[4] the Appellate Term, First Department made clear that summary judgment is available in summary proceedings. The court reasoned that since the purpose of a summary proceeding is to provide a means for an expeditious determination, a procedural device which will afford even speedier justice is consistent with the philosophy of a summary proceeding.

§ 13.47 Responding to the Holdover Petition—The Answer

The answer is governed by RPAPL § 743. It permits the tenant to answer the petition orally or in writing.[1] Any other person claiming possession of the premises may also answer.[2] A tenant's right to interpose an answer in a summary proceeding may not be waived or forfeited by lease provision or other agreement.[3] The answer must be made at least three days before the hearing date if the notice of petition was served at least eight days before the hearing date, and the notice so demanded.[4] Otherwise, the respondent may answer on the hearing date.[5]

---

§ 13.46

1. *See infra*, § 13.56.

2. *See infra*, § 13.47 for requirement as to the form and content of the answer, and §§ 13.49–13.56 for defenses and counterclaims.

3. CPLR 406; Goldman v. McCord, 120 Misc.2d 754, 466 N.Y.S.2d 584 (Civ.Ct., N.Y. County, 1983) (motion by respondent made returnable the day after service of the notice of motion permitted). It is fair and reasonable for the court to provide an adequate adjournment to allow for a response to those motions which cannot be disposed of summarily on their return date. *Id.*

4. 43 Misc.2d 639, 251 N.Y.S.2d 693 (App. Term, 1st Dep't 1964).

§ 13.47

1. RPAPL §§ 743, 732.

2. RPAPL § 743.

3. Lipkis v. Gilmour, 158 Misc.2d 609, 606 N.Y.S.2d 503 (App. Term, 1st Dep't 1993).

4. RPAPL § 743.

5. *Id.*

The answer may raise an objection in point of law[6] to the service of the notice of petition and petition if the facts reveal that service was not made in accordance with RPAPL § 735. The answer may also raise an objection in point of law that the court lacks subject matter jurisdiction in the proceeding based on defects in a predicate notice or service thereof, the notice of petition, the petition or the verification. In addition, the tenant's answer may contain any other legal or equitable defenses or allowable counterclaims.[7]

The answer may demand a trial by jury,[8] provided this right has not been waived by the lease between the parties.[9] A respondent may also waive its right to a jury trial by raising only equitable defenses and counterclaims which must be tried by the court.[10] In New York City Civil Court, the tenant is required to file a written jury demand when answering the petition, whereas the landlord has until the day of trial to demand a jury.[11] However, the court may allow a late demand by the tenant, absent a showing of undue prejudice to the landlord.[12]

Library References:

West's Key No. Digests, Landlord and Tenant ⇌305.

§ 13.48 Responding to the Holdover Petition—The Motion to Dismiss

A motion to dismiss the petition may be filed in lieu of an answer. The motion must be made returnable on the hearing date set forth in the notice of petition.[1] The motion to dismiss may be based on any of the grounds set forth in CPLR 3211(a). Alternatively, any of the grounds listed in CPLR 3211(a) may instead be used as defenses in the answer.

For example, the motion to dismiss may raise an objection in point of law[2] to the service of the notice of petition and petition if the facts reveal that service was not made in accordance with RPAPL § 735. This objection is deemed waived if the tenant makes a CPLR 3211(a) motion

---

6. CPLR 404(a).

7. RPAPL § 743 *See infra*, §§ 13.49–13.56 for a discussion of defenses and counterclaims.

8. RPAPL § 745.

9. *Residential proceeding*: 1202 Realty Assoc. v. Evans, 126 Misc.2d 99, 481 N.Y.S.2d 208 (Civ.Ct., Kings County, 1984); *Commercial proceeding*: Lana Estates, Inc. v. National Energy Reduction Corp., 123 Misc.2d 324, 473 N.Y.S.2d 912 (Civ.Ct., Queens County, 1984).

10. Lewis v. Levick, 99 A.D.2d 659, 472 N.Y.S.2d 235 (4th Dep't 1984) (respondents waived their right to a jury trial by raising equitable defenses and counterclaims which must be tried by the court); Crossroads Apartments Assocs. v. LeBoo, 152 Misc.2d 830, 578 N.Y.S.2d 1004 (City Ct., Rochester, 1991) (tenant waived right to jury trial by asking court to permanently enjoin landlord from enforcing no-pet lease clause).

11. New York City Civil Court Act § 1303(a).

12. New York City Civil Court Act § 1303(c); 319 West 48th St. Realty Corp. v. Slenis, 117 Misc.2d 259, 458 N.Y.S.2d 153 (Civ.Ct., N.Y. County, 1982).

§ 13.48

1. CPLR 406.

2. CPLR 404(a).

to dismiss based on other grounds, but fails to raise the improper service objection.[3] To take another example, the motion may also raise an objection in point of law that the court lacks jurisdiction in the proceeding based on improper service of the predicate notices, or on alleged defects in the predicate notices, petition, or notice of petition.

If the tenant's motion is denied, the tenant must serve and file an answer within five days after service of the order with notice of entry, unless the order specifies a different length of time to answer.[4]

Library References:

West's Key No. Digests, Landlord and Tenant ⚖303(1).

§ 13.49 Tenant Defenses to the Holdover Proceeding

The following Sections discuss defenses that are commonly raised by tenants in holdover proceedings.

Library References:

West's Key No. Digests, Landlord and Tenant ⚖298(1).

§ 13.50 Tenant Defenses to the Holdover Proceeding—Acceptance of Rent After Expiration or Termination of Tenancy

If the landlord accepts rent for a period *after* the expiration or termination of the tenant's term, and before the commencement of the proceeding, the expiration or termination of the term is deemed waived. The acceptance of rent by the landlord before the holdover proceeding is brought with knowledge of violations of substantial obligations of the tenancy indicates a waiver of those breaches which is fatal to the later proceeding.[1] For example, in *Melroy Realty Corp. v. Siegel*, where a landlord accepted rent prior to the commencement of the summary proceeding and with full knowledge of an unauthorized subletting, the court found a waiver of the provision of the lease against subletting without the landlord's consent and dismissed the petition.[2]

A landlord who accepts rent after the termination date set forth in a notice of termination and before the commencement of the holdover proceeding waives the right to evict the tenant based on the grounds set forth in the notice of termination.[3]

---

3. CPLR 3211(d).
4. CPLR 404(a).

§ 13.50

1. Oppenheim v. Spike, 107 Misc.2d 55, 56, 437 N.Y.S.2d 826, 828 (App. Term, 1st Dep't 1980).
2. 60 Misc.2d 383, 303 N.Y.S.2d 198 (Civ.Ct., N.Y. County, 1969).

3. 2657 East 68th Street Corp., v. Bergen Beach Yacht Club, 161 Misc.2d 1031, 615 N.Y.S.2d 858 (Civ.Ct., Kings County, 1994).

The acceptance of rent by the landlord after a holdover proceeding is commenced, however, does not terminate the proceeding or affect any award of possession to the landlord.[4] Section 711(1) of the RPAPL authorizes the landlord to accept rent and/or use and occupancy without prejudice during the pendency of the holdover proceeding.

The acceptance of rent after the expiration of a lease creates a month-to-month tenancy.[5] The acceptance of rent after the expiration of a rent stabilized lease will not will not vitiate a notice of non-renewal if properly served, but will create a month-to-month tenancy.[6]

Library References:
West's Key No. Digests, Landlord and Tenant ⚖=298(1).

§ 13.51 Tenant Defenses to the Holdover Proceeding—Defective Predicate Notice

Any notice in whatever form which terminates a tenancy must be timely, definite and unequivocal.[1] The tenant may challenge a predicate notice on the ground that it was insufficient to apprise the tenant of the alleged default, or to terminate the tenancy. A defective notice of default or termination may not be amended after the proceeding has commenced.[2] Nor can the petition be amended to remedy a defective notice.[3] If the notice is deemed insufficient, the court lacks subject matter jurisdiction and must dismiss the proceeding.[4]

A tenant may challenge the notice if it is vague or equivocal. The alleged default must be stated with particularity, so that the tenant knows what to defend against and how to interpose a valid legal defense.[5] The notice should be fact-specific, for example stating the dates of occurrence when discrete wrongful acts of the tenant are at issue.[6] Where a violation of a substantial obligation of the tenancy is alleged, the notice should cite the specific lease provisions or prohibitions which were violated.[7] This requirement of being clear, unambiguous and unequivocal applies to notices of termination as well as notices of default.[8]

---

4. RPAPL § 711(1).
5. RPL § 232–c.
6. Baginski v. Lysiak, 154 Misc.2d 275, 594 N.Y.S.2d 99 (App. Term, 2d Dep't, 1992).

§ 13.51
1. Wolfe v. Frankel, N.Y.L.J., 10/3/79, p.6, col.1 (App. Term, 1st Dep't 1979).
2. 185 East 85th St. v. Gravanis, N.Y.L.J., 1/21/81, p.6, col.2 (App. Term, 1st Dep't 1981).
3. Chinatown Apts., Inc. v. Chu Cho Lam, 51 N.Y.2d 786, 788, 433 N.Y.S.2d 86, 88, 412 N.E.2d 1312 (1980).

4. Stribula v. Wien, 107 Misc.2d 114, 438 N.Y.S.2d 52 (App. Term, 1st Dep't 1980).
5. Carriage Court Inn, Inc. v. Rains, 138 Misc.2d 444, 524 N.Y.S.2d 647 (Civ.Ct., N.Y. County, 1988).
6. Caiado v. Bischoff, 140 Misc.2d 1014, 532 N.Y.S.2d 213 (City Ct., Yonkers, 1988).
7. Chinatown Apts., *supra* note 3.
8. City of Buffalo Urban Renewal Agency v. Lane Bryant Queens, Inc., 90 A.D.2d 976, 456 N.Y.S.2d 568 (4th Dep't 1982), aff'd 59 N.Y.2d 825, 464 N.Y.S.2d 754, 451 N.E.2d 501 (1983).

A notice terminating a tenancy must clearly by its terms provide for the automatic termination of the leasehold and convey this to the tenant. A notice to cure which enables the landlord to thereafter determine whether to deem the default remedied and accept rent, or alternatively, to refuse rent and claim default and termination, cannot be deemed a valid, unambiguous, and unequivocal notice of termination or limitation.[9] Such a notice provides the tenant with no clear course of action. It puts the tenant in a position where even if an effort is made to cure the alleged default, the landlord may nevertheless attempt to retain the benefits of the cure while simultaneously claiming termination of the lease by asserting that the notice to cure was a notice to terminate.[10]

A notice may also be challenged as insufficient if it is issued by the wrong person. Whenever possible, predicate notices should be issued by the landlord. However, a notice issued by the landlord's agent is effective if the tenant has notice of the agent's authority to act on the landlord's behalf. For example, in *Siegel v. Kentucky Fried Chicken of Long Island, Inc.*,[11] an attorney signed and sent a notice of default and notice of termination to a commercial tenant. The tenant's lease required the service of such notices by "the Landlord." Another lawyer was named in the lease as the landlord's escrow agent, and the letter purporting to terminate the tenancy was not authenticated or accompanied by any proof of the writer's authority to bind the landlord in the giving of such notice. The court held that the letter was legally insufficient to terminate the existing tenancy.

In a later case, a notice to cure signed by the landlord's agent was served on a commercial tenant. The tenant contended that the notice was ineffective because it was signed by a person who was neither the landlord or agent under the lease, and was not accompanied by any authorization from the landlord. The appellate division ruled that the notice was valid and effective because the tenant had received prior written notification from the landlord that the agent was authorized to act on its behalf.[12]

A notice may also be challenged if it was improperly served. All default and termination notices must be served in strict accordance with the lease and with any applicable statutes.[13] If the lease does not prescribe any particular method for service of notices, then a notice will not be held improperly served unless there is an applicable statute with

---

9. Kirschenbaum v. M–T–S Franchise Corp., 77 Misc.2d 1012, 355 N.Y.S.2d 256 (Civ.Ct., N.Y. County, 1974).

10. Id.

11. 108 A.D.2d 218, 488 N.Y.S.2d 744 (2d Dep't 1985), aff'd 67 N.Y.2d 792, 501 N.Y.S.2d 317, 492 N.E.2d 390 (1986).

12. Owego Properties v. Campfield, 182 A.D.2d 1058, 583 N.Y.S.2d 37 (3d Dep't 1992).

13. *See, e.g.*, RPL § 232–a which requires notices terminating monthly tenancies in New York City to be served in accordance with RPAPL § 735.

which the landlord did not comply.[14] Practitioners should be aware that even defects relating to predicate notices may be deemed waived, based on inaction in the litigation. For example, in *Metropolitan Transportation Authority v. Cosmopolitan Aviation Corp.*,[15] a commercial tenant waived a defect in service of the notice of default under the lease when it accepted the notice without objection and did not raise any claim of defect until the eighteenth day of trial, 2 ½ years after it received the notice, more than one year after serving its answer and more than six months after the trial began.

Library References:

West's Key No. Digests, Landlord and Tenant ⚖297.

§ 13.52 Tenant Defenses in the Holdover Proceeding—Defective Predicate Notice—Rent-Regulated Apartments

The Rent Stabilization Code,[1] the Emergency Tenant Protection Act,[2] and the New York City Rent and Eviction Regulations[3] require that notices of non-renewal, notices to cure, and notices of termination state "the facts necessary to establish the existence of the ground on which the landlord relies" to terminate the tenancy.[4] A landlord who serves a notice of non-renewal on the ground that the tenant does not occupy the apartment as a primary residence, for example, must state facts supporting the claim. Such factual allegations might include the address of a property, other than the premises sought to be recovered, which the tenant owns or leases, or which is listed on the tenant's driver's license, motor vehicle registration, voter registration, or tax returns.

Rent-regulated tenants frequently challenge predicate notices as lacking the necessary factual allegations to establish the existence of the statutory ground for termination. Where a landlord's notice simply recites the legal ground for termination or non-renewal,[5] or tracks the statutory language, the notice is legally insufficient.[6] For example, a termination notice based on nuisance which alleged "many occasions" of "abusive" dealings and "unreasonable levels of noise and disturbances"

---

14. 61 West 62nd Owners Corp. v. Harkness Apartment Owners Corp., 173 A.D.2d 372, 570 N.Y.S.2d 8 (1st Dep't 1991).

15. 99 A.D.2d 767, 471 N.Y.S.2d 872 (2d Dep't 1984), aff'd 64 N.Y.2d 623, 485 N.Y.S.2d 37, 474 N.E.2d 245 (1984) (The Court of Appeals stated that the waiver issue was "a factual question beyond this Court's power of review.").

§ 13.52

1. 9 NYCRR § 2524.2(b).

2. Unconsolidated Laws § 8621 *et seq.*

3. 9 NYCRR §§ 2200 *et seq.*

4. *See* Finkelstein and Ferrara, *Landlord and Tenant Practice in New York* (West 1997) ¶¶ 15:74, 15:99.

5. The Berkeley Assocs. Co. v. Camlakides, 173 A.D.2d 193, 569 N.Y.S.2d 629 (1st Dep't 1991), aff'd 78 N.Y.2d 1098, 578 N.Y.S.2d 872, 586 N.E.2d 55 (1991).

6. Numano v. Vicario, 165 Misc.2d 457, 632 N.Y.S.2d 926 (App. Term, 1st Dep't 1995).

was deemed insufficient because it stated conclusions rather than required facts.[7]

Another tenant challenge is that the notice was not timely served.[8] Notices of default and termination must be served in accordance with statutory guidelines.[9] For example, notices of non-renewal which inform New York City rent-stabilized tenants of the landlord's intention not to renew on the grounds of non-primary residence, occupancy for the owner or the owner's immediate family, or demolition, may be challenged if not served within the narrow time period before the expiration of the lease known as the "window period".[10] The window period is no less than 120 days and no more than 150 days before the expiration of the tenant's existing lease.[11] Notices served outside the window period, that is, too early or too late, are ineffective, and usually result in the dismissal of the holdover proceeding.

Library References:

West's Key No. Digests, Landlord and Tenant ⚖=297.

§ 13.53 Tenant Defenses to the Holdover Proceeding—Waiver

Under certain circumstances, a tenant may assert the defense that the landlord waived the lease default upon which the holdover proceeding is based. A waiver is the voluntary relinquishment or abandonment of a known right.[1] Though the intent to waive is usually a question of fact, a landlord's acceptance of rent with knowledge of a lease default, and without an effort to terminate the lease, justifies the inference that the landlord has elected to waive the default and hold the tenant to the lease.[2]

However, some leases contain non-waiver clauses which provide that the landlord's acceptance of rent with knowledge of a breach will not be deemed a waiver. Such clauses are generally enforced, since a waiver may not be inferred from the acceptance of rent when the parties have expressly agreed otherwise.[3] If, however, the non-waiver clause does not

---

7. Carriage Court Inn, Inc. v. Rains, 138 Misc.2d 444, 445, 524 N.Y.S.2d 647, 648 (Civ.Ct., N.Y. County, 1988).

8. *See* Finkelstein and Ferrara, *Landlord and Tenant Practice in New York* (West 1997) ¶¶ 15:100ff.

9. *See supra*, § 13.6.

10. Case law refers to this notice as the "Golub Notice." *See*, Golub v. Frank, 65 N.Y.2d 900, 493 N.Y.S.2d 451, 483 N.E.2d 126 (1985). *See* Finkelstein and Ferrara, *Landlord and Tenant Practice in New York* (West 1997) ¶¶ 15:100ff.

11. 9 NYCRR § 2524.2(c)(2).

§ 13.53

1. P & D Cards & Gifts, Inc. v. Matejka, 150 A.D.2d 660, 541 N.Y.S.2d 533 (2d Dep't 1989).

2. Jefpaul Garage Corp. v. Presbyterian Hosp. in City of New York, 61 N.Y.2d 442, 447, 474 N.Y.S.2d 458, 460, 462 N.E.2d 1176, 1178 (1984); Lee v. Wright, 108 A.D.2d 678, 680, 485 N.Y.S.2d 543, 545 (1st Dep't 1985).

3. Jefpaul Garage Corp., *supra* note 2, 61 N.Y.2d at 446, 474 N.Y.S.2d at 458 (clause in lease specifically providing that acceptance of rent would not be a waiver should be enforced).

expressly refer to the acceptance of rent, a waiver may be inferred from the acceptance of rent by a landlord without a prior effort to terminate the lease.[4] In such cases, the landlord's act of accepting rent is said to "waive a no-waiver clause."[5]

A waiver may also be created by statute. For example, under a New York City ordinance, lease provisions prohibiting pets are deemed waived if a landlord knows of the pet and fails to take action for three months.[6] Tenants whose leases are terminated for harboring a pet in violation of a no-pet clause may rely on the statute, if they can demonstrate that the landlord "knew" about the tenant's pet more than three months prior to taking action against the tenant.

Library References:
West's Key No. Digests, Landlord and Tenant ⚖298(1).

§ 13.54 Tenant Defenses to the Holdover Proceeding—Equitable Estoppel

In the landlord-tenant context, equitable estoppel arises when a landlord's words or intentional conduct induces the tenant to act to his detriment in a particular manner.[1] To establish equitable estoppel, there must be proof of: (1) conduct which amounts to a knowing misrepresentation or concealment of material facts; (2) an expectation that such conduct will be acted upon by the tenant; (3) reliance on the conduct by the tenant; and (4) action taken to the detriment or prejudice of the tenant.[2] When established, equitable estoppel prevents the landlord from asserting a right against the tenant he otherwise would have had.

One rent-stabilized tenant raised the doctrine of equitable estoppel in an attempt to prevent the landlord from refusing to renew his lease and maintaining a holdover proceeding based on non-primary residence. The court ruled that the landlord, despite having permitted the tenant to perform $14,000 in apartment renovations, was not estopped from asserting the tenant's non-primary residence as grounds for refusing to renew. The court found that, at the time the improvements were made, the landlord was not aware that the tenant did not intend to maintain the apartment as a primary residence.[3]

---

4. P & D Cards, *supra* note 1, 541 N.Y.S.2d at 535 (landlord's acceptance of rent for over 40 months constituted a waiver of the right to terminate lease based on the alleged failure to pay the security).

5. Lee v. Wright, 108 A.D.2d 678, 679, 485 N.Y.S.2d 543 (1st Dep't 1985).

6. N.Y.C.Admin. Code § 27–2009.1.

§ 13.54

1. Otis Elevator Co. v. Heggie Realty Co., Inc., 107 Misc.2d 67, 437 N.Y.S.2d 832 (App. Term, 1st Dep't 1980).

2. 269 Associates v. Yerkes, 113 Misc.2d 450, 449 N.Y.S.2d 593 (Civ.Ct, N.Y. County, 1982).

3. G. Warhit Real Estate, Inc. v. Krauss, 127 Misc.2d 845, 851 487 N.Y.S.2d 484, 489 (Dist.Ct., Nassau County, 1985), aff'd 131 Misc.2d 429, 502 N.Y.S.2d 899 (App. Term, 2d Dep't, 1985).

§ 13.54   LANDLORD–TENANT LAW

Library References:

West's Key No. Digests, Landlord and Tenant ⚿298(1).

§ 13.55 Tenant Defenses to the Holdover Proceeding— Succession Rights to Rent–Regulated Apartments

Certain occupants have succession rights to rent-stabilized or rent-controlled tenants who have died or vacated the premises. "Family members" are entitled to continued possession of a rent-controlled or rent-stabilized unit.[1]

Prior to passage of the Rent Regulation Reform Act of 1997, DHCR regulations were in existence defining "family member" for purposes of succession rights. Thus, Rent Stabilization Code § 2523.5(b) and New York City Rent and Eviction Regulations § 2204.6(d), applicable in New York City, define a "family member" as a spouse, child, step-child, parent, step-parent, sibling, nephew, niece, uncle, aunt, grandparent, grandchild, father-in-law, mother-in-law, son-in-law or daughter-in-law of the tenant. The pre-existing regulations applicable outside of New York City were State Rent and Eviction Regulations, § 2104.6(d) (rent control) and Emergency Tenant Protection Regulations, § 2500.2(n), 2503.5(d) and (e) (rent stabilization). (All the various DHCR regulations referred to are found at the specified sections of 9 NYCRR.)

Section 21 of the Rent Regulation Reform Act of 1997 adds a new § 14(4) of the Public Housing Law which directs DHCR to promulgate regulations regarding succession for rent stabilized and rent controlled apartment both in and out of New York City. Section 21 specifies precisely what the succession rules should say, which is essentially equivalent to the pre-existing succession regulations. The primary change is that nieces, nephews, aunts and uncles no longer qualify as "family member[s]" eligible for succession. Such persons, however, can still obtain succession rights under the standards applicable to unrelated occupants discussed below.

Family members are protected from eviction if they can show that before the tenant vacated or died they lived with the tenant in the premises: for at least two years; at least one year if the family member is over 62 years old or is disabled; from the beginning of their relationship; or from the beginning of the tenancy. In addition, the family member must show that during that time, the premises was the occupant's primary residence. The occupant-family member must plead and prove

---

§ 13.55

[1] *See* Finkelstein and Ferrara, *Landlord and Tenant Practice in New York*

kinship and primary residence.[2]

Unrelated occupants who had a long-standing family-type relationship with the tenant also qualify as family members. In particular, the unrelated occupant must be able to show that the occupant and tenant had an emotional and financial commitment to each other and interdependence like that of family members. To help determine if an emotional and financial commitment and interdependence existed between the occupant and the family member, the regulations focus on eight issues:

1. Did the occupant have a long relationship with the tenant?
2. Did the occupant and tenant share or rely upon each other for paying household or family expenses?
3. For instance, did they share joint bank accounts, credit cards, and loans, and own personal and real property together?
4. Did they engage in family-type activities, such as attending social and recreational activities, family events, and holiday celebrations together?
5. Did they formalize their legal obligations and intentions toward each other? For example, did they sign wills naming each other as executor and/or beneficiary, grant each other a power of attorney, and/or give each other authority to make health-care decisions? Did they enter into a personal relationship contract or make a domestic partnership declaration together?
6. Did they hold themselves out as family members to others through their words or actions?
7. Did they regularly perform family tasks, such as looking after each other and each other's extended family members, or rely on each other for daily family services?
8. Did the parties engage in any other behavior or action evidencing a "long-term emotionally committed relationship?"[3]

For example, an occupant who claimed succession rights because she and the tenant had been like husband and wife was defeated because she and the tenant never commingled their finances or took care of each other, nor did they entertain together or hold themselves out in public as husband and wife.[4] Another occupant shared an apartment with a rent-stabilized tenant for 17 years before the tenant's death. The court ruled that the owner could evict the occupant because there was no proof that

(West 1997) ¶¶ 15:1462*ff.*

2. Brown v. Halperin, N.Y.L.J., 7/6/94, p.31, col.6 (Sup.Ct., Queens County, 1994) (grandson lost the right to succeed to grandmother's apartment because apartment address wasn't on the grandson's tax returns, driver's license, bank accounts, or other permanent documents).

3. *See* Finkelstein and Ferrara, *Landlord and Tenant Practice in New York* (West 1997) ¶¶ 15:465*ff.*

4. ANF Company v. Cruz, L & T, No. 117631/89 (Civ.Ct., N.Y. County, Jan. 8, 1993).

§ 13.55 LANDLORD–TENANT LAW Ch. 13

the occupant and tenant held themselves out to society as a family, they had no joint bank accounts, and the occupant was not one of the tenant's heirs. Although the tenant and occupant shared expenses, they did not support one another.[5]

A family-type relationship may be found based on financial and emotional interdependence. For example, a court found a family-type relationship where an occupant and tenant shared financial accounts, the tenant showed a familial and financial commitment to the occupant's children, the occupant was a beneficiary in the tenant's will, and the tenant and occupant had lived together in the apartment sought to be recovered for ten years.[6]

Library References:

West's Key No. Digests, Landlord and Tenant ⚖=298(1).

§ 13.56 Counterclaims

The tenant's answer may contain any counterclaim against the landlord.[1] Tenant counterclaims which are unrelated to the landlord's claim, such as claims for personal injuries, are frequently severed as they would inordinately delay disposition of the main claim, and defeat the primary purpose of the summary proceeding.[2]

Many leases contain counterclaim waiver clauses which prohibit the tenant from asserting counterclaims against the landlord in a summary proceeding. Counterclaim waiver clauses are generally enforced by courts,[3] unless the counterclaim is "inextricably intertwined" to the landlord's entitlement to rent or possession.[4] For example, a rent-stabilized tenant's counterclaim against the landlord for rent overcharges was allowed despite contrary lease language because it was "inextricably intertwined" with the landlord's claim against the tenant for possession and rent.[5] However, a commercial tenant's counterclaim seeking lost business damages resulting from a landlord's negligent

---

5. 144 West Corp. v. Pucci, L & T, No. 79419/90 (Civ.Ct., N.Y. County, Dec. 12, 1990).

6. RSP Realty Assocs. v. Paege, N.Y.L.J., 8/14/92, p.21, col.4, 20 HCR 491 (App. Term, 1st Dep't 1992).

§ 13.56

1. RPAPL § 743.

2. Tankoos–Yarmon Hotels, Inc. v. Smith, 58 Misc.2d 1072, 299 N.Y.S.2d 937 (App. Term, 1st Dep't 1968).

3. Bomze v. Jaybee Photo Suppliers, Inc., 117 Misc.2d 957, 460 N.Y.S.2d 862 (App. Term, 1st Dep't 1983); Lana Estates, Inc., v. National Energy Reduction Corp., 123 Misc.2d 324, 473 N.Y.S.2d 912 (Civ.Ct., Queens County, 1984).

4. *Residential proceedings:* Randall Co. v. Alan Lobel Photography, Inc., 120 Misc.2d 112, 465 N.Y.S.2d 489 (Civ.Ct., N.Y. County, 1983); *Commercial proceedings:* Ultrashmere House, Ltd. v. 38 Town Assocs., 123 Misc.2d 102, 473 N.Y.S.2d 120 (Sup.Ct., N.Y. County, 1984).

5. Yanni v. Bruce Brandwen Prods., Inc., 160 Misc.2d 109, 609 N.Y.S.2d 759 (Civ.Ct., N.Y. County, 1994).

elevator maintenance and breach of contract was severed because it was not "inextricably related" to the landlord's claim for rent.[6]

Library References:

West's Key No. Digests, Landlord and Tenant ⬩305.1.

§ 13.57 Bill of Particulars

A bill of particulars is a request for the amplification of the pleadings, and not a disclosure device. Therefore, a bill of particulars should be permitted upon request of either party and without leave of court.[1] Indeed, a motion to preclude has been granted in a summary proceeding where particulars were not provided in response to a proper demand for a bill of particulars.[2] If the demand for a bill of particulars improperly seeks evidentiary material, though, it is in the nature of a disguised disclosure device, and may be stricken or treated as a nullity.[3]

Library References:

West's Key No. Digests, Landlord and Tenant ⬩303(1).

§ 13.58 Discovery

Except for a notice to admit, leave of court is required for disclosure in a summary proceeding.[1] The party seeking discovery must do so by notice of motion or by order to show cause returnable on the return date of the petition.[2] To obtain discovery, there must be a showing of "ample need."[3]

In *New York University v. Farkas,*[4] the court listed six factors which should be considered in deciding whether ample need exists:

1. Whether the landlord has asserted facts to establish a cause of action. A "fishing expedition" utilized by the landlord to formu-

---

6. Amdar Co. v. Hahalis, 145 Misc.2d 987, 554 N.Y.S.2d 759 (App. Term, 1st Dep't 1990).

§ 13.57

1. CPLR 3041, 3042. *See* Finkelstein and Ferrara, *Landlord and Tenant Practice in New York* (West 1997) ¶¶ 15:482*ff.*

2. Ft. Greene Assets v. Fields, N.Y.L.J. 10/26/94, p. 32, col. 6, 22 HCR 615 (Civ. Ct. Kings County). Under a recent amendment to the CPLR, preclusion at trial can be granted without advance notice of motion to preclude.

3. Brocros Realty Corp. v. David Perry Photography, N.Y.L.J. 4/19/95, p.27, col. 1, 23 HCR 210 (Civ. Ct. N.Y. County); 221 E. 10th St., Inc. v. Walker, N.Y.L.J. 6/30/93, p. 21, col. 5, 21 HCR 348 (App. Term 1st Dep't).

§ 13.58

1. CPLR 408.

2. Atkinson v. Trehan, 70 Misc.2d 612, 334 N.Y.S.2d 291 (Civ.Ct., N.Y. County, 1972).

3. *See* Steer Inn Realty Corp. v. Bowen, 52 Misc.2d 963, 277 N.Y.S.2d 231 (Dist.Ct., Suffolk County, 1967); Antillean Holding Co., Inc. v. Lindley, 76 Misc.2d 1044, 352 N.Y.S.2d 557 (Civ.Ct., N.Y. County, 1973) (nature and purpose of summary proceedings are such that disclosure should be granted only when ample need is shown) (citing Dubowsky v. Goldsmith, 202 App. Div. 818, 195 N.Y.S. 67 (2d Dep't 1922)).

4. 121 Misc.2d 643, 468 N.Y.S.2d 808 (Civ.Ct., N.Y. County, 1983).

late a cause of action, or by the tenant to establish a defense, should never be permitted.

2. Whether there is a need to determine information directly related to the cause of action.

3. Whether the requested disclosure is carefully tailored and is likely to clarify the disputed facts.

4. Whether prejudice will result from the granting of an application for disclosure.

5. Whether the prejudice can be diminished or alleviated by an order fashioned by the court for this purpose, *e.g.*, conditioning a grant of a motion for discovery upon the payment of use and occupancy; ordering that all discovery must be done, if at all, within a relatively short time period.

6. Whether the court, in its supervisory role can structure discovery so that *pro se* tenants, in particular, will be protected and not adversely affected by a landlord's discovery requests.

Ample need has been demonstrated in both non-payment proceedings and holdover proceedings. For example, in *Pamela Equities Corp. v. Louis Frey Co., Inc.*,[5] the court ruled that where the rent is variable from year to year, involves the interpretation of a complex lease agreement and the application of complex computations, a presumption in favor of disclosure should be entertained by the court. There is a presumption in favor of disclosure in holdover proceedings based on non-primary residence[6] because often, in such cases, "the information material to the resolution of the issue is within the exclusive knowledge and control of the tenant."[7] As a result, applications in such cases should be liberally reviewed.[8]

§ 13.59 Discovery—Notice to Admit

A CPLR 3123 notice to admit may be served at any time not later than three days before the petition is noticed to be heard. The response to the notice to admit must be served not later than one day before the petition is noticed to be heard, unless the court orders otherwise on a motion made without notice. The notice to admit is the only disclosure device permitted in a summary proceeding without leave of the court.[1]

---

5. 120 Misc.2d 281, 465 N.Y.S.2d 659 (Civ.Ct., N.Y. County, 1983).

6. New York University v. Farkas, 121 Misc.2d 643, 468 N.Y.S.2d 808 (Civ.Ct., N.Y. County, 1983).

7. Century Apartments Assocs. v. Merritt, N.Y.L.J., 6/24/85, p.6, col.1 (App. Term, 1st Dep't 1985).

8. Filali v. Gronowicz, N.Y.L.J., 11/19/85, p.7, col.1, 13 HCR 375 (App. Term, 1st Dep't 1985).

§ 13.59

1. CPLR 408. *See* Finkelstein and Ferrara, *Landlord and Tenant Practice in New York* (West 1997) ¶ ¶ 15:480*ff*.

Library References:

West's Key No. Digests, Pretrial Procedure ⚙➔474.

§ 13.60 Freedom of Information Law

Records of government agencies are often extremely relevant to landlord-tenant proceedings. The practitioner should not overlook the New York State Freedom of Information Law,[1] and the rules promulgated by various agencies in conformity with the statute, as a vehicle for obtaining records from government agencies.

§ 13.61 The Trial—Adjournments

Once issue is joined, at the request of either party, the court may adjourn the trial when time is needed to procure necessary witnesses or when all parties who appear consent to an adjournment. The granting of an adjournment is strictly discretionary, but RPAPL § 745(1) provides that the adjournment may not be longer than ten days unless all parties consent to a longer adjournment.[1]

Special rules apply to adjournments in the New York City Civil Court.[2] Prior to enactment of the Rent Regulation Reform Act of 1997 (L. 1997, ch. 116,§ 1), a provision existed applicable to summary proceedings in New York City—RPAPL § 745(2)—which provided for the court to direct a tenant to post future rent and use and occupancy upon the tenant's second request for an adjournment. This statute was largely discretionary and its provisions were not enforced consistently.

Section 36 of the Rent Regulation Reform Act of 1997 amended RPAPL § 745(2), with the intent of increasing the frequency of deposit of rent or use and occupancy during the pendency of a summary proceeding in New York City. The full scope of the changes effected in that statutory section and in other statutory provisions in conjunction therewith (all scheduled to take effect in October, 1997) are beyond the scope of this chapter. Certain highlights of the new version of RPAPL § 745(2) are that the application for deposit of rent or use and occupancy can now be made upon the tenant's request for a second adjournment or 30 days after the parties' first appearance in court, whichever is sooner.

There are two elements to the amount to be deposited, namely "sums of rent or use and occupancy accrued from the date the petition and notice of petition are served upon the respondent, and all sums as they become due for rent and use and occupancy, which may be established without the use of expert testimony.... " The statute as amended expressly provides that its provisions "requiring the deposit of rent or

---

§ 13.60
1. Public Officers Law §§ 84–90.

§ 13.61
1. RPAPL § 745(1).
2. RPAPL § 745(2).

use and occupancy as it becomes due shall not be waived by the court." The provision of the former statute allowing the court to waive the posting of rent and use and occupancy "for good cause shown" has now been deleted.

The statute expressly defines certain limited circumstances when a deposit will not be required, *i.e.*, if the "respondent can establish, at an immediate hearing, to the satisfaction of the court, that respondent has properly interposed" one of the following defenses or established the following grounds: (i) the petitioner is not a proper party pursuant to RPAPL § 721, (ii) actual eviction, actual partial eviction or constructive eviction and the tenant has quit the premises, (iii) a defense pursuant to § 143–b of the Social Service Law (involving the public welfare department withholding rent because of building violations for hazardous conditions), and (iv) lack of jurisdiction. The deposit requirement does not apply to any portion of rent that is paid as a government subsidy.

The court may dismiss any summary proceeding without prejudice and with costs to the tenant by reason of excessive adjournments requested by the landlord. However, in *Bankers Trust v. Jackson*,[3] a landlord obtained several adjournments over the tenant's opposition and finally secured an adjournment on condition that the tenant be awarded $25 in costs and that the landlord start repairs immediately. However, on the adjourned date the landlord neither appeared nor had begun repairs. The court held that the landlord's conduct constituted "exceptional circumstances" which warranted dismissal with prejudice.

Library References:
West's Key No. Digests, Landlord and Tenant ⚖︎304.

§ 13.62 The Trial—Amending Petition and Burden of Proof

If triable issues of fact are raised by the pleadings, papers, and admissions, they may be tried by the court, or by a jury if one has been timely demanded and there has been no waiver.[1]

A preliminary motion may be made to amend the petition to include all past due rent and/or use and occupancy up to and including the date of trial, thereby incorporating sums that were not included in the petition. In the non-payment proceeding, that amendment is ordinarily made and granted without the landlord making a new rent demand, and the amended rental amount becomes the basis of a possessory judgment.[2]

---

3. 99 Misc.2d 225, 415 N.Y.S.2d 731 (Civ.Ct., N.Y. County, 1979).

§ 13.62
1. CPLR 410; RPAPL 745(1).
2. *But see* Walsam Fifth Ave. Development Co. v. Lions Gate Capital Corp., 163 Misc.2d 1071, 623 N.Y.S.2d 94 (Civ.Ct., N.Y. County, 1995) (denying without prejudice to renewal upon proper papers or at trial a request to amend the petition to add rents that became due after the petition was served on the grounds that "such a

The burden of proof in the trial is on the petitioner-landlord. For its *prima facie* case, the landlord must prove each of the allegations of the petition through documentary evidence or testimony. A corporate landlord may testify through any officer, agent, or employee having sufficient knowledge of the facts.[3]

The respondent has the burden of proving any affirmative defenses and counterclaims raised in the answer which have not been severed.

Library References:

West's Key No. Digests, Landlord and Tenant ⚞307.

§ 13.63 Stipulations—Overview

Rather than proceed to trial, the landlord and tenant may elect to settle their case by means of a written agreement, or stipulation. Most commercial and residential summary proceedings are concluded in this manner. The following Sections present key points to consider when drafting stipulations to settle non-payment and holdover summary proceedings. Issues related to the execution and enforcement of stipulations are also addressed.[1]

The purpose of a stipulation is to document the agreement entered into by the parties to settle the underlying action. A stipulation serves as a binding contract and is subject to all relevant contract laws and rules.[2] Stipulations are enforceable as contracts.[3] The interpretation of a contract must give effect to the intentions of the parties and is limited by the express and unequivocal language stated therein.[4] Similarly, the stipulation must clearly reflect and express the parties' intentions.

Negotiation is essential to the successful creation of a settlement stipulation. The parties to the summary proceeding may negotiate the terms of the stipulation either in or out of court. Settlement conferences which are conducted in court may require the assistance of the judge as a mediator in the negotiation process. The court may volunteer suggestions in furtherance of an agreement, but ultimately the parties themselves must voluntarily agree to settle the proceeding by stipulation. After conferencing, the final stipulation may be drafted and typed in an

request must be predicated upon an additional demand for the subsequently accruing rent.").

3. Emray Realty Corp. v. Edwards, 11 Misc.2d 889, 172 N.Y.S.2d 609 (App. Term, 1st Dep't 1958).

§ 13.63

1. *See also*, Finkelstein and Ferrara, *Landlord and Tenant Practice in New York* (West 1997) ¶¶ 15:484–15:505.

2. Caruso v. Ward, 146 A.D.2d 22, 29, 539 N.Y.S.2d 313, 317 (1st Dep't 1989); Davis v. Sapa, 107 A.D.2d 1005, 484 N.Y.S.2d 568 (3d Dep't 1985). *See* Chapter 5 "Commercial Sales Contracts," *supra*.

3. Teitelbaum Holdings, Ltd. v. Gold, 48 N.Y.2d 51, 421 N.Y.S.2d 556, 396 N.E.2d 1029 (1979); City of Poughkeepsie v. Black, 130 A.D.2d 541, 515 N.Y.S.2d 275 (2d Dep't 1987).

4. Caruso, *supra* note 2; Fiore v. Fiore, 46 N.Y.2d 971, 973, 415 N.Y.S.2d 826, 826, 389 N.E.2d 138, 139 (1979).

§ 13.63 LANDLORD–TENANT LAW Ch. 13

attorney's office, or may be handwritten on stipulation forms available in most courts.

To be enforceable, the stipulation must either be in writing, or be entered into between two attorneys on the record and in open court.[5] As in a contract, a court may not unilaterally create or alter the terms of the stipulation for any purpose, including conceptions of justice or morality.[6] Changes or modifications to the stipulation must be in writing and executed by both parties.

§ 13.64 Stipulations—Non-payment Proceedings

The stipulation settling a non-payment summary proceeding[1] should at a bare minimum cover the following points:

1. **Statement of rent due.** The stipulation should contain a provision which amends the petition to include all rent due through the date of the stipulation. It should specify the total amount of rent and other charges due to the petitioner, identify the time period covered by the arrears, and state the monthly rental rate under the lease. The provision should also state whether the landlord is agreeing to a rent reduction or abatement to settle the proceeding, and the amount of the rent adjustment.

2. **Rental arrears payment schedule.** The stipulation should contain a provision for the payment of rental arrears owed by the tenant identifying the dates when payments are due, the amount of each payment, and the method of payment.

3. **Repair obligations.** If the landlord agrees to perform repairs to settle the proceeding, the stipulation should contain a repair provision detailing the conditions in the premises which require attention. The provision should fix inspection and repair dates, and obligate the tenant to grant access to the premises on those dates. If the tenant claims that repairs are unnecessary or does not wish to have them included in the terms of the agreement, the phrase "Repairs are not an issue." may be inserted into the stipulation.

4. **Remedy for default.** The stipulation should describe the remedies available if, for example, the tenant defaults in the payment of rental arrears, or the landlord defaults in a repair obligation. Generally, one of the following remedies is provided. The stipulation may provide that in the event of a default by either party,

---

5. CPLR 2104; Shanahan v. Shanahan, 92 A.D.2d 566, 459 N.Y.S.2d 319 (2d Dep't 1983); Manning v. Manning, 97 A.D.2d 910, 470 N.Y.S.2d 744 (3d Dep't 1983); Golden Arrow Films, Inc. v. Standard Club of California, Inc., 38 A.D.2d 813, 328 N.Y.S.2d 901 (1st Dep't 1972).

6. Breed v. Insurance Company of North America, 46 N.Y.2d 351, 355, 413 N.Y.S.2d 352, 355, 385 N.E.2d 1280 (1978).

§ 13.64

1. See infra, §§ 13.90, 13.91 for forms of stipulations settling non-payment proceedings.

the proceeding will be restored to the court's calendar for further proceedings. Instead of restoring the proceeding to the calendar, the stipulation may instead provide for a final judgment of possession in favor of the landlord, with the issuance of a warrant of eviction "forthwith" with execution stayed pending the tenant's default, or for the issuance of the warrant upon the tenant's default. This remedy is generally seen when the tenant is afforded a lengthy pay-out schedule, or has already been given an opportunity to pay arrears in a prior stipulation. If the warrant has already been issued and is stayed, the stipulation may provide for the warrant to be executed in the event of the tenant's default, upon service of a 72-hour notice by the city marshal or sheriff.

5. **Legal Fees.** Generally, when there is a stipulated settlement, each party pays its own attorneys' fees. Often, however, a stipulation provides for indemnification for costs, including attorneys' fees, incurred by one party due to the other party's failure to abide by any of the terms and conditions of the stipulation.[2] Stipulations which are silent as to attorneys' fees are usually interpreted as a waiver of attorneys' fees.[3]

Stipulations waiving certain statutory rights of residential tenants are unenforceable:

1. **Warranty of habitability.** In accordance with public policy, any agreement by a residential tenant waiving or modifying his or her warranty of habitability claims is void.[4] However, a stipulation may properly include language that addresses the satisfaction of the tenant's warranty of habitability claims.

2. **Rent overcharges or illegal rents.** Stipulations in which unrepresented or *pro se* tenants obligate themselves to pay a

---

2. In a landlord-tenant proceeding, as in lawsuits generally, a party must pay its own attorneys' fees and disbursements unless an award is authorized by agreement between the parties or by statute or by court rule. *See* Matter of A.G. Ship Maintenance Corp. v. Lezak, 69 N.Y.2d 1, 511 N.Y.S.2d 216, 503 N.E.2d 681 (1986); Paroff v. Muss, 171 A.D.2d 782, 567 N.Y.S.2d 502 (2d Dep't 1991).

A statute that is extremely relevant to the issue of attorneys' fees in landlord-tenant cases that are not settled is RPL § 234. It provides that in a residential lease containing a provision for the landlord's recovery of attorneys' fees, the law will imply a reciprocal provision that the landlord will pay attorneys' fees incurred by the tenant (1) as the result of the landlord's failure to perform lease covenants, or (2) "in the successful defense" of any suit commenced by the landlord arising out of the lease. In practice, the awarding of attorneys' fees in landlord-tenant litigation usually depends on who is deemed the "prevailing party". Because there are frequently no clear cut winners in landlord-tenant litigation, the issue of which party has prevailed has been the subject of considerable controversy in the case law. For a general discussion of the subject, *see* W. Estis and W. Robbins, *Prevailing Party*, N.Y.L.J., 6/5/96, p.5; W. Estis and W. Robbins, *Prevailing Party*, N.Y.L.J., 6/7/95, p.5; W. Estis and W. Robbins, *Section 234 Revisited*, N.Y.L.J., 10/5/94, p.5; W. Estis, W. Robbins and J. Turkel, *Who is the Prevailing Party?*, N.Y.L.J., 8/11/93, p.5.

3. Lewis v. Garber, N.Y.L.J., 2/11/92, p.21,col.2 (App. Term, 1st Dep't 1992).

4. RPL § 235-b(2).

§ 13.64   LANDLORD–TENANT LAW   Ch. 13

rental amount in excess of the legal maximum registered rent are generally not enforced by courts.[5]

§ 13.65   Stipulations—Holdover Proceedings

Generally, stipulations settling holdover proceedings provide for either additional time for the tenant to cure the lease default alleged in the petition, or for additional time for the tenant to vacate the premises.

Where tenant agrees to cure, the stipulation should specify the nature of the lease violation, and describe the action or conduct the tenant agrees to take (or refrain from taking) to cure the lease violation.[1]

Where respondent agrees to vacate, a vacatur provision should set forth the date that the tenant will surrender possession of the premises and return the keys to the petitioner. It should also obligate the respondent to deliver the premises vacant, in broom-clean condition, and provide for abandoned property.[2]

Remedy for default may be provided in the stipulation. The stipulation should state the remedy to the landlord in the event that the tenant fails to either cure the lease violation or to vacate the premises on the date provided in the stipulation. There are three common remedies negotiated in a stipulation: (1) in the event of the tenant's default, the proceeding will be restored to the court's calendar for further proceedings; (2) a final judgment of possession in favor of the landlord, with the issuance of a warrant of eviction "forthwith" with execution stayed pending the tenant's default, or for the issuance of the warrant upon the tenant's default, or (3) if a warrant of eviction has already been issued, the stipulation may provide for the warrant to be executed in the event of the tenant's default, upon service of a 72-hour notice by the city marshal or sheriff. The stipulation may also provide for a money judgment against the tenant for rental arrears and/or use and occupancy of the premises while the tenant holds over.

Generally, when there is a stipulated settlement, each party pays its own attorneys' fees. Often, however, a stipulation provides for indemnification for costs, including attorneys' fees, incurred by one party due to the other party's failure to abide by any of the terms and conditions of the stipulation.[3] Stipulations which are silent as to attorneys' fees are

---

5. 1460 Grand Concourse Assoc. v. Martinez, N.Y.L.J., 5/6/94, p.29, col.1, 22 HCR 269 (App. Term, 1st Dep't 1994).

§ 13.65

1. Example: "Respondent acknowledges that he has illegally altered the subject apartment by installing a partition-wall in the bedroom of the subject apartment without the permission or consent of the petitioner-landlord. Respondent agrees to remove said petition by or before December 1, 19__, and to restore the walls and floors of the subject bedroom to their original condition." *See infra,* § 13.92 for a form of stipulation settling a holdover proceeding where respondent agrees to cure lease violation.

2. *See infra,* § 13.93 for a form of stipulation settling a holdover proceeding where the tenant agrees to vacate.

3. *See supra,* § 13.64 note 2.

usually interpreted as a waiver of attorneys' fees.[4]

The above discussion focuses on points which, at a minimum, should be included in stipulations settling holdover proceedings. Depending on the circumstances, such stipulations can be much more detailed, and include additional areas.

§ 13.66 Stipulations—Enforcement and Vacatur

A court may stay the execution of a warrant of eviction to allow the tenant to effect a late cure. In *TKU-Queens Corp., Inc. v. Mabel Food Corp.*,[1] the parties had stipulated to a schedule of back rents due the landlord. A warrant of eviction obtained by the landlord as a result of the tenant's failure to make a final stipulated payment was stayed in the interests of justice for two months. This allowed the tenant to complete a loan transaction which would provide sufficient funds to make the final back rent payment. If such stay were not granted, eviction would have resulted in the tenant's financial ruin and would have allowed the landlord to take possession of premises with improvements worth more than $100,000, four times the amount of back rent due.

Generally, fraud, collusion or mistake must be shown to vacate a stipulation. However, where a tenant seeking to vacate a stipulation lacked legal representation at the critical time the stipulation was drafted and executed, the court may be more lenient in its analysis of whether the stipulation may be enforced.[2] However, fraud, collusion, or mistake must still be demonstrated. A court will not automatically grant vacatur of a stipulation solely on the basis that a party did not have legal representation at the time of negotiation and execution of a stipulation.[3]

A court may relieve a party from a "so ordered" stipulation that is found to be unjust or harsh even where that stipulation was completely understood and duly authorized by the parties.[4]

---

4. Lewis v. Garber, N.Y.L.J., 2/11/92, p.21,col.2 (App. Term, 1st Dep't 1992).

§ 13.66

1. 90 Misc.2d 48, 393 N.Y.S.2d 272 (Civ. Ct., Queens County, 1977).

2. Cabbad v. Melendez, 81 A.D.2d 626, 438 N.Y.S.2d 120 (2d Dep't 1981) (court vacated judgment for possession where non-English speaking tenant entered into consent judgment without counsel, mistakenly believing that stipulation provided that upon paying all rent owing the proceeding would be resolved and she would retain possession of apartment).

3. Simkowitz v. Stewart, N.Y.L.J. 1/30/90, p.21, col.5, 18 HCR 41 (App. Term, 1st Dep't 1990) (stipulation entered into by pro se tenant enforced because tenant stated in open court that stipulation was fully understood prior to its execution); 121 Realty v. Gonzalez, N.Y.L.J., 11/11/91, p.26, col.5 (App. Term, 1st Dep't 1990) (*pro se* tenant with "change of heart" failed to demonstrate the requisite good cause to vacate stipulation).

4. Solack Estates, Inc. v. Goodman, 102 Misc.2d 504, 506, 425 N.Y.S.2d 906, 907 (App. Term, 1st Dep't 1979), aff'd 78 A.D.2d 512, 432 N.Y.S.2d 3 (1st Dep't 1980) (elderly tenant demonstrated necessary showing of harsh and unjust stipulation by being upset, crying and confused when she signed, and court below observed that tenant was under emotional stress and considerable pressure when stipulation was executed).

§ 13.67 The Judgment and Warrant

If the proceeding is not settled, the court must enter a final judgment determining the rights of the parties.[1] The judgment may include a money judgment, without regard to the dollar jurisdictional limit of the court, against the tenant for rent and/or use and occupancy, and/or against the landlord for such counterclaims as the court may have adjudicated in favor of the tenant.

When a final judgment of possession is awarded to the landlord, the court issues a warrant directing the marshal or sheriff to restore the landlord to possession of the premises.[2] Before executing the warrant, the marshal or sheriff must serve a 72-hour notice of eviction to the respondent, which must be served in the same manner as a notice of petition and petition.[3] The warrant may only be executed during daylight hours.[4]

§ 13.68 Judgment and Warrant—Staying the Warrant in Non-payment Proceedings

All tenants have the opportunity—even after trial of the non-payment proceeding—to pay any rent and other charges found to be due and to save the leasehold. Section 751(1) of the RPAPL provides that at any time before a warrant is issued, a tenant may effect a stay of issuance of the warrant by depositing the amount of rent or additional rent due, with interest plus statutory costs with the court or court clerk, or by delivering to the clerk or court an undertaking in a sum approved by the court that the amounts due will be paid to the petitioner within ten days, at the expiration of which a warrant may issue, unless satisfactory evidence of payment is produced to the court.[1]

A rent tender made after issuance of the warrant will not automatically stay its execution. In *New York City Housing Authority v. Torres*[2] the court stressed that the tenant must show "good cause" to vacate the warrant. There, the tenant had shown only that the rent money was unavailable, which was not good cause for vacatur.

Library References:

West's Key No. Digests, Landlord and Tenant ⚖═313.

§ 13.67
1. RPAPL § 747(1).
2. RPAPL § 749(1).
3. *See* RPAPL § 735 as to the manner of service.
4. RPAPL § 749(2).

§ 13.68
1. RPAPL § 751(1).
2. 61 A.D.2d 681, 403 N.Y.S.2d 527 (1st Dep't 1978).

§ 13.69 Judgment and Warrant—Staying the Warrant in New York City Residential Holdover Proceedings

Under Section 753 of the RPAPL, applicable only in residential holdover proceedings in New York City, there are two circumstances in which a stay of the issuance of the warrant of eviction may be granted. Section 753(4) of the RPAPL, provides for a mandatory ten-day stay of the issuance of the warrant of eviction when the proceeding is based upon a claim that the tenant has violated a provision of the lease. The stay gives the tenant an opportunity to cure the lease violation and in effect reinstate the tenancy. The Court of Appeals has interpreted the statute as permitting the Civil Court to impose a permanent injunction barring the forfeiture of the tenant's lease for the violation alleged if the tenant cures within ten days.[1] The Civil Court may not enlarge the ten-day cure period.[2] It is unclear whether the tenant must complete the cure during the ten-day period, or just begin to cure the default within that time.[3]

In addition, Section 753(1) of the RPAPL provides a discretionary stay of the issuance of the warrant for up to six months where the tenant cannot get suitable similar premises in the same neighborhood after due and reasonable efforts, or extreme hardship to the tenant or the tenant's family would result if the stay is not granted. To be entitled to the stay, the tenant must deposit use and occupancy with the court for the duration of the stay.

A Section 753(1) stay cannot be granted where the landlord makes a good faith showing that the premises are sought in order to demolish them to construct a new building, and plans for the new building have been filed and approved by the proper authority, or where the landlord has pleaded and proved that the tenant holding over is objectionable.[4]

A tenant cannot waive any provisions of RPAPL § 753 in the lease or any other agreement.[5]

§ 13.69

1. Post v. 120 East End Ave. Corp., 62 N.Y.2d 19, 475 N.Y.S.2d 821, 464 N.E.2d 125 (1984).

2. Wilen v. Harridge House Assocs., 94 A.D.2d 123, 463 N.Y.S.2d 453 (1st Dep't 1983) (nothing in the statute empowers the civil court to extend the ten-day period); Belmont Owners Corp. v. Murphy, 153 Misc.2d 444, 590 N.Y.S.2d 659 (App. Term, 2d Dep't, 1992) (Civil Court lacks authority to extend the ten-day stay).

3. The First Department ruled that where it is was not feasible to legalize extensive alterations within the ten-day statutory stay period, all that is required is that the tenant commence to cure within ten days and to diligently and in good faith pursue such cure until the default is remedied. See Wilen v. Harridge House Assocs., 94 A.D.2d 123, 463 N.Y.S.2d 453 (1st Dep't 1983). But see Belmont Owners Corp. v. Murphy, 153 Misc.2d 444, 590 N.Y.S.2d 659 (App. Term, 2d Dep't, 1992) (the court declined to follow this rule).

4. RPAPL § 753(3).

5. RPAPL § 753(5).

§ 13.70 Yellowstone Actions

The Yellowstone injunction allows a tenant who has been served with a notice to cure a lease default to litigate in supreme court whether or not there has been a default, without the risk of losing the lease if the court finds a default.[1] The Yellowstone injunction operates to toll the running of the period of time the tenant has to cure the alleged default. If there is an adverse determination at the end of the lawsuit, the tenant still has time to cure the default and save the lease.

Most leases provide for the early termination of the lease after a notice to cure an alleged default in the event that the tenant fails to cure within the period of time specified in the notice. Often, a tenant served with such a notice to cure disputes that there has been a default. For example, the landlord may serve a notice to cure an alleged default consisting of violation of the use clause of the lease. The tenant may believe that its use of the premises is perfectly appropriate. Such a tenant faces a dilemma. If the tenant cures, it effectively gives up a use of the premises it considers to be in compliance with the lease. If the tenant does not cure, however, and the landlord's allegation of default is found to be correct, then the tenant will be evicted. It will not have an opportunity to cure. The Yellowstone injunction is the answer to the tenant's dilemma. If the proper elements are satisfied, then the tenant gets an opportunity to litigate with the landlord the issue of whether there has been a default, without being in jeopardy of losing its lease if the court finds that there has been a default.

The case which spawned the "Yellowstone" doctrine was the Court of Appeals decision in *First National Stores Inc. v. Yellowstone Shopping Center Inc.*[2] In *Yellowstone*, the landlord and tenant disputed who was responsible for paying for a sprinkler system the Fire Department had ordered to be installed. The landlord demanded that the tenant comply with the Fire Department order. The tenant did not and the landlord, in accordance with the lease, sent a 10–day notice to cure the alleged default. The tenant took no action to cure, nor did it get the court to toll or stay the 10–day period to cure. Instead, the tenant commenced a lawsuit for a declaratory judgment. However, the tenant did not obtain a temporary restraining order. Before the return date of its motion for a preliminary injunction, the cure period had run and the landlord had sent a notice terminating the lease.

---

§ 13.70

1. *See* Finkelstein and Ferrara, *Landlord and Tenant Practice in New York* (West 1997) ¶ 16:299*ff.*

2. 21 N.Y.2d 630, 290 N.Y.S.2d 721, 237 N.E.2d 868 (1968).

The Court of Appeals held that the lease had been terminated in strict accordance with its terms and, having so expired, could not be revived by the Court. Noting that the lease gave the landlord the right to terminate after a 10-day notice of default, the Court of Appeals stated: "Stability of contract obligations must not be undermined by judicial sympathy."[3] As a result of this decision, "tenants developed the practice of obtaining a stay of the cure period before it expired to preserve the lease until the merits of the dispute could be settled in court."[4] The injunction providing such a stay, obtained in supreme court in conjunction with the commencement of an action for declaratory judgment, became known as a "Yellowstone" injunction. This mechanism protects the tenant because the lease cannot be terminated until the cure period expires without the claimed default being cured.

Library References:

West's Key No. Digests, Landlord and Tenant ⚙=299.

§ 13.71 Yellowstone Actions—Obtaining the Injunction

What must the tenant show to obtain "Yellowstone" relief? Courts have generally accepted far less than the showing normally required for a preliminary injunction. As stated by the court in *Stuart v. D & D Associates*, a tenant is entitled to a Yellowstone injunction where it demonstrates that:

> (1) it holds a commercial lease, (2) it has received a notice of default, notice to cure or concrete threat of termination of the lease from the landlord, (3) the application for a temporary restraining order was made and granted prior to the termination of the lease, and (4) it has the desire and ability to cure the alleged default by any means short of vacating the premises.[1]

There are various examples where courts have denied Yellowstone relief because the tenant lacked proof of a desire and ability to cure the alleged default. In *American Airlines, Inc. v. Rolex Realty Co., Inc.*,[2] the landlord served a notice advising the tenant that certain conduct by an undertenant violated the tenant's lease with the landlord. The tenant sent a letter to the under tenant demanding that it cease such conduct. The tenant, however, never itself attempted to terminate the sublease or otherwise remedy the defaults. The undertenant continued the conduct

---

3. *Id.* 21 N.Y.2d at 638, 290 N.Y.S.2d at 725.

4. Post v. 120 East End Ave. Corp., 62 N.Y.2d 19, 25, 475 N.Y.S.2d 821, 823, 464 N.E.2d 125, 127 (1984). The Appellate Division, First Department, in Garland v. Titan West Assocs., 147 A.D.2d 304, 543 N.Y.S.2d 56, 58 (1st Dep't 1989) described the purpose of a Yellowstone injunction as follows: "... to maintain the status quo so that the tenant served with a notice to cure an alleged lease violation may challenge the propriety of the landlord's notice while protecting a valuable leasehold interest."

§ 13.71

1. 160 A.D.2d 547, 548, 554 N.Y.S.2d 197, 198 (1st Dep't 1990).

2. 165 A.D.2d 701, 560 N.Y.S.2d 146 (1st Dep't 1990).

complained of in the default notice. Affirming the denial of a Yellowstone injunction, the First Department held that a willingness and ability to cure the lease defaults had not been demonstrated.

In *Pergament Home Centers, Inc. v. Net Realty Holding Trust*,[3] the Second Department focused on the language of the lease itself in holding that the tenant lacked the ability to cure and therefore was not entitled to Yellowstone relief. The default alleged was the tenant's assigning the lease without the landlord's consent. The court noted that there was no provision in the lease permitting the tenant to cure once it had assigned the lease. Rather, the lease entitled the landlord, upon 30 days notice, "to terminate the lease at any time if Pergament assigned without its consent."[4] Since the lease on its face did not give the tenant the right to cure, the court reasoned that the tenant lacked the ability to cure.

Yellowstone relief must be sought before the cure period expires. Many practitioners make the mistake of believing that as long as a termination notice is not served, Yellowstone relief can be obtained even if the cure period has expired. The prevalent case law appears to be that once the cure period expires, the court cannot grant a Yellowstone injunction.[5]

Library References:

West's Key No. Digests, Landlord and Tenant ⬥299.

§ 13.72 Article 7–A Proceedings

A special proceeding under Article 7–A of the RPAPL may be brought by the tenants of a multiple dwelling for the appointment of an administrator to remedy conditions which are dangerous to the life and safety of the building's occupants.[1] At least one-third of the building's tenants must join in the proceeding.[2]

An Article 7–A proceeding may be brought in the Civil Court of the City of New York, the District Court of Nassau and Suffolk counties, and the County or City Courts in Rockland and Westchester.[3] If the multiple dwelling is in New York City, the proceeding may be brought by the Commissioner of the City's Department of Housing Preservation and Development.[4] Thereafter, one-third or more of the tenants may petition to substitute themselves in place of the commissioner.

---

3. 171 A.D.2d 736, 567 N.Y.S.2d 292 (2d Dep't 1991).

4. 567 N.Y.S.2d at 293.

5. *See, e.g.*, S.E. Nichols, Inc. v. American Shopping Centers, Inc., 115 A.D.2d 856, 495 N.Y.S.2d 810, 812 (3d Dep't 1985) (the "injunction must be sought before the end of the cure period"); *accord* Saada v. Master Apts., Inc., 152 Misc.2d 861, 579 N.Y.S.2d 536, 540 (Sup.Ct., N.Y. County, 1991).

§ 13.72

1. RPAPL § 769 *et seq*. See also, Finkelstein and Ferrara, *Landlord and Tenant Practice in New York* (West 1997) ¶ 16:49*ff*.

2. RPAPL § 770(1).

3. RPAPL § 769(1).

4. RPAPL § 770(2).

§ 13.73 Rent Regulatory Proceedings

The New York State Division of Housing and Community Renewal ("DHCR") has jurisdiction to enforce the state's rent laws and regulations, including those applicable only in New York City. A landlord or tenant whose premises are under the DHCR's jurisdiction may institute a proceeding by filing an application or complaint for a rent adjustment or other lawful relief on forms prescribed by the DHCR. In addition, the DHCR may institute its own proceeding as it deems necessary.

When the DHCR receives an application or complaint, it is required to serve copies on all affected parties.[1] A landlord or tenant who receives notice of a proceeding from DHCR, accompanied by a landlord's application or a tenant's complaint, has 20 days from the date the notice was mailed to answer or reply.[2] Extensions of time may be requested in writing from the agency. Every answer and reply must be verified or affirmed, and an original, plus one copy, must be filed with the DHCR.[3]

The DHCR is authorized to reject applications, conduct investigations, issue subpoenas, and grant or order a hearing at any stage of the proceeding.[4] A DHCR District Rent Administrator ("DRA") determines the proceeding by dismissing or granting the application, or issuing an appropriate order.[5] A DRA's order may be challenged by filing a Petition for Administrative Review within 35 days of the date the order was issued.[6]

§ 13.74 Rent Regulatory Proceedings—Rent Overcharge

Rent-controlled and rent-stabilized tenants may initiate a rent overcharge proceeding by filing a complaint with the DHCR alleging a rent overcharge, and applying for a rent adjustment and refund. A form can be obtained from DHCR for a rent overcharge complaint. The form directs the tenant, *inter alia*, to give information about the rental history, and to state the "legal regulated rent", the basis for the tenant's calculations and the date(s) of the alleged overcharges. The complaint must be filed with the DHCR within four years of the first overcharge alleged.[1]

The landlord must answer the tenant's complaint of overcharge within 20 days by providing a rent history for the apartment, together with copies of leases and registration statements for the unit.

---

§ 13.73
1. *See, e.g.*, Rent Stabilization Code, 9 NYCRR § 2527.3(a).
2. *See, e.g.*, 9 NYCRR § 2527.4.
3. *Id.*
4. *See, e.g.*, 9 NYCRR § 2527.5.
5. *See, e.g.*, 9 NYCRR § 2527.6.
6. *See, e.g.*, 9 NYCRR § 2529.1 *et seq.*

§ 13.74
1. *See* Finkelstein and Ferrara, *Landlord and Tenant Practice in New York* (West 1997) ¶¶ 16:162–16:163.

Any landlord who is found to have collected a rent overcharge from a rent-regulated tenant is potentially liable to the tenant for a penalty equal to three times the amount of the overcharge.[2] If the landlord establishes by a preponderance of the evidence that the overcharge was not willful, then the penalty is limited to the amount of the overcharge plus interest.[3] The treble damages penalty is limited to overcharges collected no more than two years before the filing of the complaint of overcharge.[4]

The Rent Regulation Reform Act of 1997 (L. 1997, ch. 116), at Sections 31 to 34, includes amendments relating to the processing and calculation of overcharge claims. The four-year Statute of Limitations on rent overcharge awards was strengthened and clarified. Thus, if there is no challenge within four years to the rent specified in a rent registration statement, that rent and service of that registration statement can no longer be challenged. Also, the amendments make clear that no determination of an overcharge or calculation of an overcharge award can be based on rental information which goes back further than four years before the filing of the overcharge complaint.

Library References:

West's Key No. Digests, Landlord and Tenant ⚷200.70.

§ 13.75 Rent Regulatory Proceedings—Service Reduction

Rent-controlled and rent-stabilized tenants may initiate a service reduction proceeding by filing a complaint with the DHCR alleging the landlord's failure to maintain required services and applying for a rent reduction.[1] (The term used with respect to rent control is "essential services".) A complaint may be filed by an individual tenant for conditions which affect only the tenant's apartment or, a building-wide service complaint may be filed by tenant representatives on behalf of other tenants. A "required service" is one that was furnished, or was obligated to be furnished, on or after the date the tenant's unit became subject to rent regulation, or which is required under housing laws, ordinances or

---

2. *See, e.g.*, Rent Stabilization Code, 9 NYCRR § 2526.1; Emergency Tenant Protection Act, Unconsolidated Laws § 8632; City Rent and Rehabilitation Law, N.Y.C.Admin. Code § 26–413.

3. *See, e.g.*, Rent Stabilization Law of 1969, N.Y.C.Admin. Code § 26–516(a); Rent Stabilization Code, 9 NYCRR § 2526.1.

4. *See, e.g.*, N.Y.C.Admin. Code § 26–516(a)(2)(i).

§ 13.75

1. *See, e.g.*, Rent Stabilization Code Law of 1969, N.Y.C.Admin. Code § 26–514. A substantially similar provision is contained in § 2523.4 of the Rent Stabilization Code and it applies to all rent stabilized units including stabilized hotels. (See also Emergency Tenant Protection Regulations, 9 NYCRR § 2503.4.) Finkelstein and Ferrara, *Landlord and Tenant Practice in New York* (West 1997) Ch. 17 "Administrative Proceedings."

regulations. Required services may include items such as repairs, painting and maintenance, heating, lighting, and refuse removal.

The landlord has 20 days to file an answer on forms provided by the agency. The owner's answer may raise any relevant legal or factual argument. In prior determinations,[2] the DHCR has ruled that it is inappropriate to order a rent reduction where the service was restored before the complaint was filed where: the tenant refused access to the owner to make repairs;[3] the tenant was unaffected by the decrease in services;[4] or the tenant's complaint is a minor routine maintenance item or preventive maintenance problem which does not constitute a decrease in services.[5]

If the landlord's answer disputes the tenant's allegation, the DHCR conducts an inspection of the premises to determine whether the landlord has failed to maintain services. Where the DHCR finds after an inspection that required services have not been maintained or are absent, the DRA will issue an order listing the specific services the owner failed to maintain, and, as to rent stabilized tenants, reducing the rent retroactive to the first of the month following the date of service on the landlord of the tenant's complaint, and directing the owner to restore the services.

For rent-controlled tenants, if a service reduction is found, the rent reduction is prospective only. The rent is reduced by a specific dollar amount until the date specified in a subsequent rent restoration order. For rent-stabilized tenants, the rent is reduced to the level in effect prior to its most recent guideline adjustment. In addition, the owner may not apply to DHCR for any rent increases or to collect subsequent guideline increases for the rent-stabilized unit until the date specified in a subsequent rent restoration order.

To obtain a rent restoration order, the landlord must file a rent restoration application to the DHCR affirming that the required services have been restored. If the tenant confirms the landlord's statement, then the rent is restored. Otherwise, an inspection is made to determine the

---

2. New York State Division of Housing and Community Renewal (DHCR) Policy Statement 90–2, p.2 ("... if prior to an inspection the owner has restored the service(s) alleged in the complaint, there is generally no rent reduction ordered.")

3. *Id.* ("... the rent will not be reduced ... where there is a finding that a tenant failed to provide reasonable access and such access was necessary to make the repair").

4. The DHCR has previously ruled that it is inappropriate to order a rent reduction for the tenants of an entire building based on a service reduction that affects only one or a few units. *See, e.g.*, Bay Parkway Realty Assocs., DHCR No. AL 220349–RO (8/3/89); Savco Realty Co., DHCR No. CA 130284–RO (7/25/90).

5. In previous rulings, the DHCR has denied rent reductions for *de minimus* routine maintenance problems such as worn out rugs (Hall, DHCR No. CB 1300008) or a dirty basement (Frey Realty, DHCR No. ARL–06767–L). The DHCR has also denied rent reductions for preventive maintenance items such as unpolished mailboxes and dirty window panes (Various Tenants and Albert, DCHR No. BB–130149–RT (12/13/89)); (Maloney, Dock No. CL–110346–RT (11/16/89) and peeling paint on fire escapes.)

§ 13.75 LANDLORD–TENANT LAW Ch. 13

issue. If the tenant denies access for the DHCR inspection, then the rent is restored. A rent restoration order is retroactive to the first of the month following the date of service on the tenant of the owner's application to restore rent.

The Rent Regulation Reform Act of 1997 amends various rent regulation statutes (*e.g.*, § 26–514 of the Administrative Code of the City of New York) and Real Property Law § 235–b to foreclose tenants from obtaining, based upon the same condition, rent reductions from the DHCR (as a service reduction) and from the court (as a breach of the warranty of habitability).

Library References:
West's Key No. Digests, Landlord and Tenant ⟼200.63.

§ 13.76 Rent Regulatory Proceedings—Major Capital Improvement Rent Increase

The landlord may initiate a major capital improvement ("MCI") rent increase proceeding by filing an application for an MCI rent hike. For rent-stabilized units in New York City, the application must be made within two years of the completion of an MCI item. An MCI is a building-wide improvement that is necessary for the operation, preservation, and maintenance of the property, and which benefits all tenants. Examples include new windows, a roof, a new electrical or plumbing system, or a new boiler.[1] Replacements are limited to items which have exceeded their "useful life."[2] Improvements made to individual apartments do not qualify as MCIs, nor do building-wide repairs.

Landlords of properties containing rent-controlled and rent-stabilized units are entitled to recoup the cost of the MCI in seven years by applying to the DHCR for an MCI rent increase. The owner's application is made by filing DHCR Form RA–79, "Owner's Application for a Rent Increase Based on a Major Capital Improvements." There is no requirement that the tenants consent to the MCI. However, tenants are entitled to notification of the landlord's application, and have the right to challenge the rent increase at the time the application is filed, and again at the time the DRA grants the application.

The rents may not be increased until DHCR grants the owner's application and issues an order authorizing the rent increases. The monthly MCI rent hike for each tenant is calculated by taking the total cost of the MCI and dividing it by 84 (representing the number of months in seven years). That sum is then divided by the number of rooms in the building. The result is the cost of the MCI that the owner may collect per room per month.

§ 13.76
1. Rent Stabilization Code § 2422.4 contains a partial list of 30 qualifying MCIs.
2. *See* DHCR Operational Bulletin 90–2.

If an MCI item benefits professional/commercial space, as well as residential space, the cost of the MCI will be reduced by the percentage of the building's income from the professional/commercial space. For example, assume that a building's income is 90% residential and 10% commercial, and a new roof is installed at a cost of $50,000. Since the roof benefits the commercial space, the MCI will be reduced by $5,000. The regulations also provide for a reduction of any MCI rent increase if an owner receives both a rent increase and a J–51 tax benefit for the same MCI item.

There are restrictions on annual MCI rent increases. The owner may not adjust a rent-stabilized tenant's rent for an MCI unless the tenant's lease contains a clause authorizing the owner to do so. A rent-controlled tenant's rent may not increase more than 15 percent annually, and a rent-stabilized tenant's rent may not be increased more than six percent per year.[3]

Library References:

West's Key No. Digests, Landlord and Tenant ⚖︎200.63.

§ 13.77 Checklist of Essential Allegations

The following checklists provide the essential elements that must be alleged in a petition in a non-payment or holdover summary proceeding and in a stipulation settling a non-payment or holdover summary proceeding.

§ 13.78 Checklist of Essential Allegations—Petition Non-payment

1. State the petitioner's interest in the premises from which removal is sought. (*See* § 13.17)

2. State the respondent's interest in the premises, and his relationship to petitioner with regard thereto. (*See id.*)

3. Describe the premises from which removal is sought. (*See id.*)

4. State the facts upon which the non-payment proceeding is based.

5. Allege that a demand for payment of rent had been made prior to the commencement of the proceeding. (*See id.*)

6. Is the property located within the City of New York? If so, allege whether or not the premises are a multiple dwelling. If the premises are a multiple dwelling state that:

---

3. See Bryant Avenue Tenants Assoc. v. Koch, 84 N.Y.2d 960, 620 N.Y.S.2d 825, 644 N.E.2d 1381 (1994).

§ 13.78

- A currently effective registration statement is on file with the office of code enforcement which designates a managing agent. (*See* § 13.17)
- The multiple dwelling registration number for the premises, its registered managing agent's name, and either the managing agent's residence or business address.
- Optionally include the agent's 24–hour telephone number. (*See id.*)

7. Is the action being brought in a jurisdiction where rent laws and regulations are in effect? If so, describe the rent regulatory status of the premises sought. Specifically state:

- Whether the premises are subject to rent control or rent stabilization.
- Compliance by the landlord with applicable rent laws and regulations; or the reasons why the premises are exempt those laws and regulations. (*See* § 13.17)

8. State the relief sought. (*See* § 13.17)

- Possessory judgment.
- Money judgment.

Library References:

West's Key No. Digests, Landlord and Tenant ⚖=303.

§ 13.79 Checklist of Essential Allegations—Holdover Petition

1. State the petitioner's interest in the premises from which removal is sought. (*See* § 13.43)

2. State the respondent's interest in the premises, and his relationship to petitioner with regard thereto. (*See id.*)

3. Describe the premises from which removal is sought. (*See id.*)

4. State the facts upon which the holdover proceeding is based, including, for example:

- As to a holdover proceeding based on termination or expiration of a tenancy, allege the lease under which the tenant was in possession.
- Allege that respondent continues in possession of the premises after the expiration or termination of the tenancy or right of occupancy, without permission. (*See* §§ 13.43, 13.36–13.40)

5. Was the tenancy or right of occupancy terminated? If so, state the manner in which the tenancy or right of occupancy was terminated and the date of termination. (*See* § 13.43.)

Ch. 13   CHECKLIST OF ESSENTIAL ALLEGATIONS   § 13.80

6. Where predicate notice is required, describe the notice served upon the respondent, and the manner of service, or reference an annexed copy of notice of non-renewal, notice of default, notice of termination or other notice, and copy of affidavit of service. (*See id.*)

7. If termination is based on a specific statutory or regulatory provision, allege the elements of the cause of action as defined by the statute or regulation. (*See id.*)

8. Is the real property located within the City of New York? If so, allege whether or not the premises are a multiple dwelling. If the premises are a multiple dwelling, state:

- That a currently effective registration statement is on file with the office of code enforcement which designates a managing agent.
- The multiple dwelling registration number for the premises, its registered managing agent's name, and either the managing agent's residence or business address.
- Optionally include the agent's 24–hour telephone number. (*See id.*)

9. Is the action being brought in a jurisdiction where rent laws and regulations are in effect? If so, describe the rent regulatory status of the premises sought. Specifically, state:

- Whether the premises are subject to rent control or rent stabilization.
- Compliance by the landlord with applicable rent laws and regulations; or the reasons why the premises are exempt those laws and regulations. (*See* §§ 13.43, 13.17)

10. State the relief sought. (*See* § 13.43)

- Possessory judgment.
- Unpaid rent.
- Use and occupancy.

Library References:

West's Key No. Digests, Landlord and Tenant ⚖=303.

§ 13.80 Checklist of Essential Allegations—Stipulation Settling Non-payment Proceeding

1. A statement amending the petition to include all rent due through the date of the stipulation. (*See* §§ 13.63, 13.64)

2. Rental arrears payment schedule. (*See* §§ 13.63, 13.64)

3. Does the landlord have an obligation to make repairs? If so, state repair obligations of the landlord. If there is no obligation or the repairs are not applicable state that "repairs are not at issue." (*See* §§ 13.63, 13.64)

§ 13.80   LANDLORD–TENANT LAW   Ch. 13

4. State remedy for default. Generally, one of the following remedies is provided:

- Restoration of the proceeding to the court's calendar for further proceedings.
- Final judgment of possession in favor of the landlord, with the issuance of a warrant of eviction "forthwith" with execution stayed pending the tenant's default.
- Issuance of the warrant upon the tenant's default. If the warrant has already been issued and is stayed, the stipulation may provide for the warrant to be executed in the event of the tenant's default, upon service of a 72–hour notice by the city marshal or sheriff. (See §§ 13.63, 13.64, 13.66)

5. Legal fees in the event of a default by the opposing party. (See §§ 13.62, 13.65)

§ 13.81   Checklist of Essential Allegations—Stipulation Settling Holdover Proceeding

1. Does the tenant-respondent agree to cure alleged lease default? If so, specify the nature of the lease violation, and describe the action or conduct the tenant agrees to take (or refrain from taking) to cure the lease violation. (See § 13.65)

2. Does the tenant-respondent agree to vacate? If so, set forth the date that respondent will surrender possession of the premises and return the keys to the petitioner. (See § 13.65)

3. State the remedy to the landlord in the event that respondent fails to either cure the lease violation or to vacate the premises on the date provided in the stipulation. The stipulation may provide for:

- The proceedings to be restored to the court's calendar for further proceedings.
- A final judgment of possession in favor of the landlord, with the issuance of a warrant of eviction "forthwith" with execution stayed pending the tenant's default, or for the issuance of the warrant upon the tenant's default.
- Where a warrant of eviction has already been issued, the warrant to be executed in the event of the tenant's default, upon service of a 72–hour notice by the city marshal or sheriff.
- A money judgment against the tenant for rental arrears and/or use and occupancy of the premises while the tenant holds over.(See id.)

4. Attorney's fees in the event of a default in the terms of the stipulation. (See id.)

94

Ch. 13 PETITION NON–PAYMENT § 13.83

§ 13.82 Forms

The following generic forms are designed to be adapted and used by the practitioner in a summary proceeding.

§ 13.83 Forms—Petition Non–payment

COURT _____

[Insert Petitioner's name],

    Petitioner–Landlord,

    -against-

[Insert names of Tenant–Respondents] NON–PAYMENT PETITION
[Insert address of subject premises], [DWELLING/BUSINESS]

    Respondents–Tenants Index No. _____

[Insert names of any sub-tenants or other occupants,]
"John Doe" and "Jane Doe"[1]

    Respondents–Undertenants.

The petition of _____ ("Petitioner" or "Landlord") shows that:

1. Petitioner is the [insert petitioner's relation to the premises, i.e., owner, net lessee, proprietary lessee] and landlord of the premises described below (the "Premises"). [If petitioner is a corporation add: Petitioner is a New York corporation or Petitioner is a (insert state of incorporation) corporation authorized to do business in New York.]

2. Respondent-tenant ("Tenant") is the Tenant of the Premises pursuant to a rental agreement made _____, 19__ between respondent and the Petitioner [or the Landlord's predecessor] ending _____, 19__, [and most recently extended by a renewal agreement dated _____, 19__,] wherein Tenant agreed to pay to Landlord rent [and additional rent] each month in advance on the first day of each month.

3. Respondents–Undertenants _____, "JOHN DOE" and "JANE DOE" are the undertenants of the Tenant.

4. Tenant and respondents-undertenants are now in possession of the premises.

---

§ 13.83
1. Name of undertenant is fictitious and unknown to petitioner. The person intended is whomever is in possession of the premises described in the petition.

§ 13.83   LANDLORD–TENANT LAW   Ch. 13

5. The premises from which removal is sought were rented for [*dwelling/commercial purposes*] and are described as follows:

All rooms, _____ floor, [Apartment No. _____,] in the building known as and located at _____, New York

which is situated in the territorial jurisdiction of the [*Civil or City*] Court of the City of _____ [*or City of New York, County of* _____].

6. Pursuant to the rental agreement there was due to the Landlord from Tenant rent as follows: [*fill in chart below*]

Month/Year   Description   Amount

Tenant has defaulted in the payments thereof and the total rent in arrears is $_____.

7. The rent has been demanded [orally/ by service of a written three day demand (a copy of which is annexed hereto with proof of service)] from Tenant since the same became due.

8. Respondents hold over and continue in possession of the Premises without Landlord's permission after said default.

9. Petitioner lacks written information or notice of any address where the Tenant resides, is employed, has a place of business in New York State, other than the Premises [*insert any other known address for the Tenant*].

10. [In jurisdictions where rent-regulations are in effect, the petition must describe the rent regulatory status of the Premises, the compliance by the landlord with applicable rent laws and/or regulations, or the reasons why the Premises are exempt from those laws or regulations. For example, the following allegations are proper where the premises are located within New York City.]

[*Where the premises are rent controlled add the following allegations*: The dwelling is subject to the City Rent and Rehabilitation Law (rent control) and the premises are registered with the New York State Division of Housing and Community Renewal. The rent demanded herein does not exceed the maximum rent prescribed by the New York State Division of Housing and Community Renewal.

[*Where the premises are rent-stabilized add the following allegations*:] The dwelling is presently subject to the Rent Stabilization Law of 1969, and the Premises are registered with the New York State Division of Housing and Community Renewal. The owner is in compliance with the Rent Stabilization Law and Code and the rent demanded herein does not exceed the lawful stabilized rent permitted the owner under said

Law, Code and appropriate Rent Guidelines Board Order as registered with said agency.

[*Where the premises are residential but not subject to rent regulations*:] The dwelling is not subject to the City Rent and Rehabilitation Law (rent control) and the Rent Stabilization Law of 1969 because [*give reason*].

[*Where the premises are commercial add the following allegation*:] The premises are not subject to the City Rent and Rehabilitation Law (rent control) or the Rent Stabilization Law of 1969, as amended, because the subject premises were leased as and are used for solely business purposes.

11. [*In New York City, the petition must state the multiple dwelling registration status of the premises, as follows*]:

The premises are not a multiple dwelling.

[OR]

The premises are a multiple dwelling and pursuant to the Housing Maintenance Code. Article 41, there is a currently effective registration statement on file with the office of Code Enforcement in which the owner has designated the managing agent named below, a natural person over twenty-one years of age, to be in control of and responsible for the maintenance and operation of the dwelling:

(1) Multiple Dwelling Registration Number:_____

(2) Registered Managing Agent:_____

(3) Business Address:_____

(4) Telephone Number:_____

12. Under the terms of the rental agreement, Petitioner is entitled to recover from Tenant the costs and attorneys fees incurred by the Petitioner. Petitioner has and will incur such costs and fees. The total amount of such costs and fees will be determined by the Court.

WHEREFORE, Petitioner requests a final judgment awarding Petitioner (a) possession of the Premises with the issuance of a warrant to remove respondents from possession of the premises; and (b) a money judgment against Tenant for rent in arrears for $_____ with interest from _____, 19__, attorney's fees in an amount to be determined by the Court but believed to be no less than $_____ and for the costs and disbursements of this proceeding.

Dated: _____, New York

Petitioner

Attorney(s) for Petitioner

§ 13.83   LANDLORD–TENANT LAW   Ch. 13

Office and Post Office Address
Telephone Number

Library References:
West's Key No. Digests, Landlord and Tenant ⚖︎303.

§ 13.84 Forms—Petition Holdover

COURT _____

```
─────────────────────────────────────
                                    )
[Insert Petitioner's name],         )
                                    )
        Petitioner–Landlord,        )
                                    )
           -against-                )
                                    )
[Insert names of Tenant–Respondents] )  HOLDOVER PETITION
[Insert address of subject premises],)  [DWELLING/BUSINESS]
                                    )
        Respondents–Tenants         )  Index No. _____
                                    )
[Insert names of any sub-tenants or )
other occupants,]                   )
"John Doe" and "Jane Doe" [1]       )
                                    )
        Respondents–Undertenants.   )
─────────────────────────────────────
```

The petition of _____ ("Petitioner" or "Landlord") shows that:

1. Petitioner is the [insert petitioner's relation to the premises, i.e., owner, net lessee, proprietary lessee] and landlord of the premises described below (the "Premises"). [If petitioner is a corporation, add: Petitioner is a New York corporation [or] Petitioner is a (insert state of incorporation) corporation authorized to do business in New York.]

2. Respondent-tenant ("Tenant") is the Tenant of the Premises pursuant to a rental agreement made _____, 19__ between respondent and the Petitioner [or the Landlord's predecessor] ending _____, 19__, [and most recently extended by a renewal agreement dated _____, 19__]

[Where the tenant remained in possession as month to month tenant add the following allegation:] Tenant remained in possession as a month-to-month tenant subsequent to the expiration of said agreement.

3. Respondents–Undertenants _____, "JOHN DOE" and "JANE DOE" are the undertenants of the Tenant.

---

§ 13.84
1. Name of undertenant is fictitious and unknown to petitioner. The person intended is whomever is in possession of the premises described in the petition.

Ch. 13 PETITION HOLDOVER § 13.84

4. Tenant and respondents-undertenants are now in possession of the premises.

5. The premises from which removal is sought were rented for dwelling/ commercial purposes and are described as follows:

All rooms, _____floor, [Apartment No. _____,]
in the building known as and located
at _____, New York

which is situated in the territorial jurisdiction of the [*Civil or City*] Court of the City of _____ [*or City of New York, County of* _____].

6. The term for which the Premises were rented by the Tenant expired on _____, 19__.

[*Where tenant was served with, for example, a 30 day notice of termination of tenancy add the following allegation*:] At least 30 days before the expiration of the term, Tenant was served in the manner provided by law with a notice in writing, a copy of which with proof of service is hereby annexed and made a part of this petition that (a) the landlord elected to terminate the tenancy, and (b) unless Tenant removed from the premises on the day on which said term expired, Landlord would commence summary proceedings under the statute to remove the Tenant therefrom.

[*Where tenancy is terminated by operation of a conditional limitation add the following allegation*]: Tenant's term expired for the reasons set forth in the notice to cure and notice of termination, a copy of each of which is annexed hereto with proof of service and made a part hereof, as if fully set forth below.

7. Tenant and respondent-undertenants continue in possession of the Premises without permission of the Landlord after the expiration of said term.

8. Petitioner lacks written information or notice of any address where the Tenant resides, is employed, has a place of business in New York State, other than the Premises and [*insert any other known address for the Tenant*].

9. [*In jurisdictions where rent-regulations are in effect, the petition must describe the rent regulatory status of the Premises, the compliance by the landlord with applicable rent law and/or regulations, or the reasons why the Premises are exempt from those laws or regulations. For example, the following allegations are proper where the premises are located within New York City.*]

[*Where the premises are rent controlled and the following allegations*:] The dwelling is subject to the City Rent and Rehabilitation Law (rent control). [*Where rent is owed add the following clause*:] The rent demanded herein does not exceed the maximum rent prescribed by the New York State Division of Housing and Community Renewal.

§ 13.84   LANDLORD–TENANT LAW

[*Where the premises are rent-stabilized add the following allegations:*] The dwelling is presently subject to the Rent Stabilization Law of 1969, and the Premises are registered with the New York State Division of Housing and Community Renewal. The owner is in compliance with the Rent Stabilization Law and Code. [*Where rent is owed add the following clause:*] The rent demanded herein does not exceed the lawful stabilized rent permitted the owner under said Law, Code and appropriate Rent Guidelines Board Order as registered with said agency.

[*Where the premises are residential but not subject to rent regulations:*] The dwelling is not subject to the City Rent and Rehabilitation Law (rent control) and the Rent Stabilization Law of 1969 because [*give reason*].

[*Where the premises are commercial add the following allegation:*] The premises are not subject to the City Rent and Rehabilitation Law (rent control) or the Rent Stabilization Law of 1969, as amended, because the subject premises were leased as and are used for solely business purposes.

10.   [*In New York City, the petition must state the multiple dwelling registration status of the premises, as follows:*]

The Premises are not a multiple dwelling.

[*OR*]

The Premises are a multiple dwelling and pursuant to the Housing Maintenance Code. Article 41, there is a currently effective registration statement on file with the office of Code Enforcement in which the owner has designated the managing agent named below, a natural person over twenty-one years of age, to be in control of and responsible for the maintenance and operation of the dwelling:

(1) Multiple Dwelling Registration Number:_____

(2) Registered Managing Agent:_____

(3) Business Address:_____

(4) Telephone Number:_____

11.   Under the terms of the rental agreement, Tenant agreed to pay rent for the Premises at the rate of $_____, plus the costs and disbursements, including attorneys' fees, which might be incurred by Petitioner in any action to enforce the Petitioner's rights under the rental agreement. No monies for rent and/or "use and occupancy" have been received and/or accepted for the period after _____, 19__, and Petitioner has or will incur reasonable attorneys' fees. The total amount of such costs and fees will be determined by the Court at or after trial. In addition the fair and reasonable value of respondents' use and occupancy of the Premises is at the rate of at least $_____ per month.

WHEREFORE, Petitioner requests a final judgment awarding Petitioner (a) possession of the Premises with the issuance of a warrant to remove respondents from possession of the premises; (b) a money judgment against Tenant for rent in arrears for $_____$ with interest from _____, 19__, for Tenant's use and occupancy of the Premises in an amount to be determined by the Court, for attorney's fees in an amount to be determined by the Court but believed to be no less than $_____ and for the costs and disbursements of this proceeding; and (c) a money judgment against the remaining respondents for their use and occupancy of the Premises in an amount to be determined by the Court.

Dated: _____, New York

_____
Petitioner

Attorney(s) for Petitioner
Office and Post Office Address
Telephone Number

Library References:
West's Key No. Digests, Landlord and Tenant ☞303.

§ 13.85 Forms—Individual Verification

STATE OF NEW YORK)
)
COUNTY OF   )

[*Insert name of deponent*], being duly sworn deposes and says:

1. I am the petitioner.

2. I have read the foregoing petition and know the contents thereof; and the same is true to my own knowledge, except as to those matters therein stated to be alleged upon information and belief, and as to those matters I believe them to be true.

_____
[*Type deponent's name beneath signature*]

[*Insert Jurat*]

Library References:
West's Key No. Digests, Landlord and Tenant ☞303(4).

§ 13.86 Forms—Corporate Officer Verification

STATE OF NEW YORK)
)
COUNTY OF   )

§ 13.86   LANDLORD–TENANT LAW   Ch. 13

[Insert name of corporate officer], being duly sworn deposes and says:

1. I am the *[insert title of corporate officer]* of petitioner, a New York corporation.

2. I have read the petition and know the content thereof; and the same is true to my own knowledge, except as to those matters therein stated to be alleged upon information and belief, and as to those matters I believe them to be true. The source of my information and belief is the books and records of petitioner.

3. This verification is made by deponent because petitioner is a corporation and I am an officer thereof.

                              [Type deponent's name and title beneath signature]

[Insert Jurat]

   Library References:

      West's Key No. Digests, Landlord and Tenant ⇔303(4).

§ 13.87   Forms—Partnership Verification

STATE OF NEW YORK)
)
COUNTY OF   )

[Insert name of partner], being duly sworn deposes and says:

1. I am a partner in petitioner.

2 I have read the foregoing petition and know the contents thereof; and the same is true to my own knowledge, except as to those matters therein stated to be alleged upon information and belief, and as to those matters I believe them to be true. The source of my information and belief is the books and records of petitioner.

3. This Verification is made by me because petitioner is a partnership and I am a partner thereof.

                              [Type deponent's name beneath signature, Partner]

[Insert Jurat]

   Library References:

      West's Key No. Digests, Landlord and Tenant ⇔303(4).

§ 13.88 Forms—Attorney Verification

STATE OF NEW YORK)
)
COUNTY OF   )

[*Insert name of attorney*], being duly sworn deposes and says:

1. I am a member of the law firm of [*insert name of attorney's firm*], attorney for petitioner.

2. I have read the foregoing petition and know the contents thereof; and the same is verified upon information and belief. The grounds for my belief are statements and records provided by the petitioner, its agents and/or employees.

3. This verification is made pursuant to the provisions of RPAPL § 741.

4. The reason why this verification is not made by the party is that [*insert reason*].

                            [*Type deponent's name beneath signature*]

[*Insert Jurat*]

Library References:
West's Key No. Digests, Landlord and Tenant ⟲303(4).

§ 13.89 Forms—Stipulations

The following stipulations contain only those generic provisions which are essential to a settlement of the non-payment or holdover proceeding. Stipulations may include many other provisions. The provisions here are intended to be adapted and expanded by the practitioner.

§ 13.90 Forms—Stipulations—Settling Non-payment Proceeding

COURT _____

_____

[*Insert Petitioner's name*],   )
)
    Petitioner–Landlord,   )
)
        -against-   )
)
[*Insert names of Tenant–Respondents*],) STIPULATION
[*Insert address of subject premises*],)

§ 13.90 LANDLORD–TENANT LAW Ch. 13

```
                                    ) Index No. _____
       Respondents–Tenants          )
                                    )
[Insert names of any sub-tenants or )
other occupants,]                   )
"John Doe" and "Jane Doe"           )
                                    )
       Respondents–Undertenants.    )
_____)
```

It is hereby stipulated and agreed to between the parties that the underlying action is settled in accordance with the following:

1. The petition is hereby amended to include all rent due through _____.

2. Respondent acknowledges that $_____ is owed in arrears representing rent for the months of _____ at a rate of $_____ per month.

3. Respondent agrees to pay the arrears by _____.

4. In the event of default by Respondent, Petitioner may restore the proceeding to calendar on eight (8) days notice to Respondent.

[*The necessity or lack thereof to repair certain conditions may be addressed at this juncture in the stipulation. If repairs are not needed or requested by Respondent within the stipulation, the terms "repairs are not an issue" may be utilized. If Respondent states that repairs are needed, the following optional paragraph may be inserted:*]

5. Petitioner agrees to inspect and repair as required by law the following conditions alleged by Respondent:_____. Respondent agrees to grant Petitioner access to the subject premises for completion of repairs on _____ 19__. In the event of Petitioner's default, Respondent may restore the case to calendar on eight (8) days written notice to Petitioner.

Dated:_____

_____

_____

[*Signatures*]

Ch. 13 FINAL JUDGMENT IN FAVOR OF PETITIONER § 13.91

§ 13.91 Forms—Stipulations—Settling Non-payment Proceeding With Final Judgment in Favor of Petitioner

COURT _____

[Insert Petitioner's name],	)
Petitioner–Landlord,	)
-against-	)
[Insert names of Tenant–Respondents] [Insert address of subject premises],	) STIPULATION) Index No. _____
Respondents–Tenants	)
[Insert names of any sub-tenants or other occupants,] "John Doe" and "Jane Doe"	)
Respondents–Undertenants.	)

It is hereby stipulated and agreed to between the parties that the underlying action is settled in accordance with the following:

1. The Petition is amended to include all rent owed through _____.

2. Respondent agrees to a Final Judgment in the amount of $_____, representing arrears for the months of _____ at a rate of $_____ per month.

3. In the event Respondent defaults in payment of the arrears, a warrant of eviction shall issue and execute [or] the warrant shall execute (in the case where Petitioner has already obtained the warrant) upon service of 72 hour notice by the [Marshall/Sheriff/Constable].

[*The necessity or lack thereof to repair certain conditions may be addressed at this juncture in the stipulation. If repairs are not needed or requested by Respondent within the stipulation, the terms "repairs are not an issue" may be utilized. If Respondent states that repairs are needed, the following optional paragraph may be used*:]

4. Petitioner agrees to inspect and repair as required by law the following conditions alleged by Respondent: _____. Respondent agrees to grant Petitioner access to the subject premises for completion of repairs on _____ 19__. In the event of Petitioner's default, Respondent may restore the case to calendar on eight (8) days written notice to Petitioner.

105

§ 13.91　　　　LANDLORD–TENANT LAW　　　　Ch. 13

Dated: _____

_____

_____

[Signatures]

§ 13.92　Forms—Stipulations—Settling Holdover Proceeding Where Tenant Agrees to Cure Lease Violation

COURT _____

[*Insert Petitioner's name*],)	
Petitioner–Landlord,)	
-against-)	
[*Insert names of Tenant–Respondents*])	STIPULATION
[*Insert address of subject premises*],)	
)	Index No. _____
Respondents–Tenants)	
[*Insert names of any sub-tenants or other occupants,*])	
"John Doe" and "Jane Doe")	
Respondents–Undertenants.)	

It is hereby stipulated and agreed to between the parties that:

1. Without admitting or denying the actions specified by Petitioner in the underlying Holdover Petition, Respondent agrees to [*specify actions which must be taken or refrained from in order to cure lease violation alleged in the petition*], and agrees to comply with all the terms and conditions of the lease forthwith.

2. In the event that Respondent fails to comply with the terms of this stipulation by or before _____, 19__, Petitioner may restore the case to calendar for appropriate relief.

[Rather than restoring the case to the court calendar, the stipulation may provide for a Final Judgment of Possession in favor of the petitioner. In such a case, the warrant of eviction must additionally be addressed and notice must be served upon respondent prior to the warrant's execution].[1]

Dated: _____

§ 13.92
1. *See infra*, § 13.93.

_____

_____

[*Signatures*]

§ 13.93 Forms—Stipulations—Settling Holdover Proceeding Where Tenant–Respondent Agrees to Vacate Premises

COURT _____

[*Insert Petitioner's name*],	)
Petitioner–Landlord,	)
-against-	)
[*Insert names of Tenant–Respondents*] [*Insert address of subject premises*],	) STIPULATION) Index No. _____
Respondents–Tenants	)
[*Insert names of any sub-tenants or other occupants,*] "John Doe" and "Jane Doe"	)
Respondents–Undertenants.	)

It is hereby stipulated and agreed between the parties that:

1. Respondent agrees to vacate the subject premises on or before _____, 19__, and on such date agrees to return the keys to Petitioner and leave the premises in a broom clean condition, vacant of all persons and property. Any personal property left by Respondent after such date will be deemed abandoned by Respondent.

2. Respondent agrees to a Final Judgment of Possession in Petitioner's favor.

3. In the event of Respondent's default, warrant shall issue [*or*] execute (where warrant is issued forthwith or has already been issued) on __ days notice to Respondent.

Dated: _____

_____

_____

[*Signatures*]

Chapter 14

EMINENT DOMAIN

by
Patricia Youngblood Reyhan

Table of Sections

14.1	Scope Note.
14.2	Strategies for Condemnors and Condemnees.
14.3	Exercise of the Power of Eminent Domain.
14.4	____ The State as Condemnor.
14.5	____ Other Public Entities as Condemnor.
14.6	____ Private Entities.
14.7	Property Rights Subject to Acquisition.
14.8	____ Real Property.
14.9	____ Easements.
14.10	____ Leases.
14.11	____ Personal Property.
14.12	____ Public Property/Priority of Taking.
14.13	____ Excess Property.
14.14	*De Facto* Taking.
14.15	Public Use, Benefit or Purpose.
14.16	____ Particular Uses.
14.17	____ Incidental Private Benefit.
14.18	Just Compensation.
14.19	Summary.
14.20	The First Stage: The Condemnation Phase.
14.21	Public Hearing.
14.22	Exemptions From the Public Hearing Requirement.
14.23	____ Overlap with Other Governmental Requirements.
14.24	____ Overlap with Issuance of a Certificate of Environmental Compatibility and Public Need.
14.25	____ Alternate Public Hearing.
14.26	____ *De Minimis* Acquisition or Emergency Situation.
14.27	____ Section 41.34 of the Mental Hygiene Law.
14.28	Notice.
14.29	Conduct of the Public Hearing and Requirement of a Record.
14.30	Determination and Findings.
14.31	____ Publication of Synopsis.
14.32	____ Interplay with SEQRA.
14.33	____ Amendments for Field Conditions.
14.34	Judicial Review of Determination and Findings.
14.35	____ Prerequisite Determination.

Ch. 14 EMINENT DOMAIN

14.36	___ Persons Entitled to Review.
14.37	___ 30–Day Statute of Limitations.
14.38	___ Scope of Review.
14.39	Summary.
14.40	The Second Stage—The "Offer and Negotiation" Phase.
14.41	___ Pretaking Appraisals.
14.42	___ Pretaking Discovery.
14.43	___ Offer as Payment in Full.
14.44	___ Advance Payment.
14.45	Use and Occupancy by Condemnee After Taking.
14.46	Summary.
14.47	The Third Stage—The Acquisition Phase.
14.48	___ Court of Claims v. Supreme Court Jurisdiction.
14.49	___ Statute of Limitations for Bringing an Acquisition Proceeding.
14.50	___ ___ Acquisition in Stages.
14.51	___ Acquisition Map.
14.52	Acquisition of Property—Court of Claims Jurisdiction.
14.53	___ Condemnors Subject to Court of Claims Jurisdiction.
14.54	___ Filing and Notice Requirements.
14.55	___ Vesting of Title.
14.56	Acquisition of Property—Supreme Court Jurisdiction.
14.57	___ Notice of Pendency.
14.58	___ Petition in Condemnation.
14.59	___ ___ Content.
14.60	___ ___ Additional Content Rules for Certain Non-governmental Condemnors.
14.61	___ Notice.
14.62	___ ___ Certification of Names of Reputed Condemnees.
14.63	___ Answer by Condemnee.
14.64	___ ___ Defenses.
14.65	___ Vesting of Title and Order of Condemnation.
14.66	Notice of Acquisition.
14.67	Immediate Entry.
14.68	Summary.
14.69	The Fourth Stage—The Compensation Phase.
14.70	___ Court of Claims.
14.71	___ ___ Time to File Claim.
14.72	___ ___ Service.
14.73	___ Supreme Court.
14.74	___ ___ Time to File Claim.
14.75	___ ___ Service.
14.76	Content of Claim.
14.77	Scope of Just Compensation.
14.78	___ "Highest and Best Use."
14.79	___ Total Taking.
14.80	___ ___ Direct Damages.
14.81	___ ___ Improvements.
14.82	___ Partial Taking.
14.83	___ Temporary Taking.
14.84	___ ___ Easements.
14.85	Methods of Valuation to Determine Compensation.

14.86	____ Market Approach to Value.
14.87	____ Income Approach to Value.
14.88	____ Cost Approach to Value.
14.89	Specialty Property.
14.90	Effect of Environmental Contamination on Property Value.
14.91	Fixtures.
14.92	____ Compensable Fixtures.
14.93	____ Valuation of Fixtures.
14.94	Leasehold Interests.
14.95	____ Valuation and Compensation.
14.96	Loss of Business and Goodwill.
14.97	Going Concern Value.
14.98	Moving and Relocation Expenses.
14.99	Conflicting Claims by Condemnees.
14.100	____ Conflicting Claims to the Condemnor's Offer.
14.101	____ Conflicting Claims to the Award.
14.102	The Trial on Compensation.
14.103	____ Preference.
14.104	____ Filing and Exchange of Appraisals.
14.105	____ Expert Testimony.
14.106	____ Viewing of the Property.
14.107	____ Joint or Consolidated Trials.
14.108	____ Interest.
14.109	Setoff for Indirect Benefit.
14.110	Incidental Expenses and Proration of Taxes.
14.111	Abandonment of Procedure by Condemnor.
14.112	Finding that Condemnor is Not Legally Authorized to Acquire the Property.
14.113	Finding Contrary to Claim by Condemnor That it Did Not Take Property.
14.114	Decision By the Court and Entry of Judgment.
14.115	Additional Allowances for Costs and Expenses.
14.116	Payment Pending Appeal.
14.117	Small Claims Proceedings.
14.118	Summary.
14.119	Procedural Checklist.
14.120	Forms—Demand on Condemnor to File Copy of Proceedings to Determine Need and Location of Public Project with Appellate Division for Purpose of Judicial Review.
14.121	____ Petition for Review of Determination and Finding that Public Use, Benefit or Purpose Will be Served by Proposed Acquisition.
14.122	____ Judgment of Appellate Division Rejecting the Determination and Finding that Public Use, Benefit or Purpose Will be Served by Proposed Acquisition.
14.123	____ Complaint by Condemnee to Establish Fair and Reasonable Value for Temporary Use and Occupancy After Acquisition by Eminent Domain.
14.124	____ Notice of Pendency of Proceeding in Supreme Court to Acquire Property by Eminent Domain and File Acquisition Map.
14.125	____ Notice of Petition in Proceeding in Supreme Court to Acquire Property by Eminent Domain and File Acquisition Map.

14.126	____ Petition in Proceeding in Supreme Court to Acquire Property by Eminent Domain and File Acquisition Map.
14.127	____ Petition in Proceeding in Supreme Court to Acquire Property by Eminent Domain and File Acquisition Map—Petitioner Exempt from Compliance with Eminent Domain Procedure Law Article 2.
14.128	____ Answer to Petition in Proceeding in Supreme Court to Acquire Property by Eminent Domain and File Acquisition Map.
14.129	____ Order to Show Cause Why Condemnor Should Not be Permitted to Enter Immediately upon Real Property and Devote It Temporarily to Public Use Specified in Petition Upon Deposit of a Fixed Sum with the Court.
14.130	____ Order to Show Cause Why Condemnor Should Not be Permitted to File Acquisition Maps or Enter upon Real Property.
14.131	____ Order in Proceeding in Supreme Court to Acquire Property by Eminent Domain and File Acquisition Map.
14.132	____ Notice of Acquisition by Eminent Domain Where Supreme Court Has Jurisdiction.
14.133	____ Claim for Damages Arising from Acquisition by Eminent Domain—General Form.
14.134	____ Judgment Awarding Compensation in Claim for Acquisition of Property by Eminent Domain.
14.135	____ Notice of Motion for Additional Allowance to Condemnee for Expert Witnesses.
14.136	____ Affidavit in Support of Motion for Additional Allowance to Condemnee for Expert Witnesses.
14.137	____ Order Granting Additional Allowance to Condemnee for Expert Witnesses.

WESTLAW Electronic Research

See WESTLAW Electronic Research Guide preceding the Summary of Contents.

§ 14.1 Scope Note

The current statutory scheme governing takings by eminent domain in New York is the Eminent Domain Procedure Law.[1] It took effect on July 1, 1978, replacing the former Condemnation Law. The Eminent Domain Procedure Law creates procedures more onerous to the condemnor than those required by the earlier statute.[2] Comprehensive amendments to the Eminent Domain Procedure Law were enacted in 1988.

Without question, one of the motivations for enactment of the Eminent Domain Procedure Law was the creation of uniform procedures for the exercise of the power of eminent domain throughout the State of

---

§ 14.1

1. Eminent Domain Procedure Law §§ 101 et seq.

2. New York State Urban Development Corp. v. Vanderlex Merchandise Co., Inc., 98 Misc.2d 264, 413 N.Y.S.2d 982 (Sup.Ct., N.Y. County, 1979).

§ 14.1   EMINENT DOMAIN   Ch. 14

New York. As a result, the Eminent Domain Procedure Law provides that it "shall be uniformly applied to any and all acquisitions by eminent domain of real property within the State of New York."[3]

The Eminent Domain Procedure Law provides that the Civil Practice Law and Rules ("CPLR") apply to eminent domain proceedings mandated by the Eminent Domain Procedure Law, except where the Eminent Domain Procedure Law or appropriate court rules provide otherwise.[4] Further, each condemnor is given the authority to promulgate its own rules "to effectuate the object, intent and provisions" of the Eminent Domain Procedure Law, so long as those rules are consistent with the Eminent Domain Procedure Law.[5]

Reduced to its basics, the Eminent Domain Procedure Law addresses four separate stages in the eminent domain process. These stages correspond roughly to the articulated purposes of the Eminent Domain Procedure Law.[6]

The first stage is the condemnation phase. It focuses on a required public hearing and all pre-and post-hearing requirements that attend it. This stage is governed by Article 2 of the Eminent Domain Procedure Law. As discussed in detail below,[7] the primary focus of the public hearing is on the public project that necessitates the taking rather than on the taking itself. The hearing requirement is designed to further the Eminent Domain Procedure Law's purpose of "establish[ing] opportunity for public participation in the planning of public projects."[8] After the hearing, the condemnor must make findings and a determination with respect to the need for the project, the proper location for it and any potential environmental impacts.[9] This stage is a completely self-contained one and is generally a prerequisite to the other stages.

The Eminent Domain Procedure Law establishes strict rules for appeal of any legal issues arising out of this stage and makes those rules

3. Eminent Domain Procedure Law § 104. In fact, the Eminent Domain Procedure Law is not absolutely exclusive. While it governs the vast majority of takings, a few special statutory provisions govern special types of takings. For example, there are separate rules allowing the Commission on Cable Television to determine the amount of compensation to be paid property owners when cable lines are run across their property against their wishes. Executive Law § 828(1)(b); Loretto v. Teleprompter Manhattan CATV Corp., 58 N.Y.2d 143, 459 N.Y.S.2d 743, 446 N.E.2d 428, reargument denied 59 N.Y.2d 761, 450 N.E.2d 254, 463 N.Y.S.2d 1030 (1983). Additionally, it has been held that Section 18 of the Transportation Law trumps the Eminent Domain Procedure Law in allowing the Commissioner of the Department of Transportation to acquire abandoned railway rights of way without complying with the Eminent Domain Procedure Law. Carparelli Bros., Inc. v. State, 150 Misc.2d 720, 570 N.Y.S.2d 266 (Sup.Ct., Oneida County, 1991).

4. Eminent Domain Procedure Law § 703.

5. Eminent Domain Procedure Law § 707.

6. See Eminent Domain Procedure Law § 101.

7. See infra, §§ 14.21–14.29.

8. Eminent Domain Procedure Law § 101.

9. See infra, § 14.30.

exclusive. As a result, challenges to the wisdom, propriety or legality of the project and its general location must normally be raised at this stage and, whether or not raised, will be foreclosed at later stages. When this stage is complete, identified private properties will have been "condemned." Condemnation means that the property is *going* to be "taken." It has not been taken by the mere act of condemnation; the actual taking occurs in a later stage of the process.

The second stage, the negotiation and offer phase, is one in which the condemnor endeavors either to negotiate the purchase of the property targeted for taking or makes an offer of just compensation to persons whose property is targeted. This stage, the subject of Article 3 of the Eminent Domain Procedure Law, is intended to meet the statute's purpose of "encourag[ing] settlement of claims for just compensation and expedit[ing] payments to property owners...."[10] The condemnor may make its offer in an individual case even before the public hearing, and if the offer is accepted as payment in full by the condemnee, no further proceedings need take place.

If the second stage does not result in a purchase of the property, the condemnor proceeds to the third stage, governed by Article 4 of the Eminent Domain Procedure Law. This stage, the acquisition phase, involves the formal filing of an "acquisition map" by the condemnor.[11] This stage is either relatively simple or relatively complicated, depending on who the condemnor is. When the State is the condemnor, it is required simply to meet the content and filing requirements of Eminent Domain Procedure Law Article 3, and then it acquires title automatically without intervention of a court.[12] All other condemnors must obtain court permission prior to filing the map and thereby acquiring title.[13]

The fourth and final stage, the compensation phase, is covered by Article 5 of the Eminent Domain Procedure Law, which has been the subject, by far, of the most litigation. This stage resolves claims brought by condemnees for just compensation for property taken.[14]

One of the interesting things about eminent domain proceedings, especially as defined by the Eminent Domain Procedure Law in New York, is that the private citizen whose property is taken, and the courts themselves, play a remarkably passive legal role in all but the final stage. This is due in part to the fact that eminent domain is not simply a *power* of the State and its political subdivisions; it is their *right*. The fact that the State must compensate private owners whose land is acquired arises "not from any element of wrongfulness or illegality but, rather, from the notion of according fair compensation to those whose private property

---

10. Eminent Domain Procedure Law § 101; *see infra*, §§ 14.40–14.44.
11. *See infra*, § 14.51.
12. *See infra*, §§ 14.52–14.55.
13. *See infra*, §§ 14.56–14.65.
14. *See infra*, §§ 14.69–14.116.

rights have been subordinated to overriding public policy."[15]

§ 14.2 Strategies for Condemnors and Condemnees

Eminent domain proceedings may involve multiple parties and, thus, multiple attorneys. Because of the unique nature of the power of eminent domain, involving, as it does, very little room for litigation of issues related to the merits, the strategies of the parties will largely focus on procedures in all but the compensation phase of the project.

A condemnor is authorized to take private property only when, and to the extent that, there is constitutional and statutory authorization to do so.[1] A state agency, for example, that desires to take private property to serve the public interest must have legislative authorization, either of a general nature or specifically addressed to a proposed taking, in order to undertake an exercise of the eminent domain power. It is, therefore, incumbent upon counsel for the condemnor to make certain that that authority exists and that the condemnor acts pursuant to any conditions or restrictions on that authority before the condemnor begins the taking process.

As noted in Section 14.1, the first step in the condemnation process is normally the holding of a public hearing.[2] The Eminent Domain Procedure Law provides enumerated exemptions to the public hearing requirement.[3] An obvious question for the condemnor's attorney is whether such an exemption is available and whether the grounds for the exemption are sufficiently firm that the attorney is comfortable recommending that the condemnor forego holding the hearing. This is an important decision. If the hearing is not necessary because an exemption exists, and the hearing is held regardless, unnecessary expense and delay result. If, however, the hearing is not held, and it is later determined that an exemption was not available, the condemnor must begin the process again and may be obligated to pay the condemnee damages as a result. When there is doubt, it is normally advisable to err on the side of holding the public hearing, inasmuch as the condemnor's legal position will thereby be much stronger as the proceeding enters the next stages.

When the condemnor determines that a public hearing will be held, great care must be taken to ensure that all procedural requirements are met. This includes not only notice and publication requirements,[4] but also requirements related to how the hearing is conducted.[5] The attorney for the condemnor should, at the least, oversee both of these aspects of the hearing stage. The Eminent Domain Procedure Law is clear, simple and straightforward on these procedural requirements. If they are met,

---

15. Williamsburg Candy & Tobacco, Inc. v. State, 106 Misc.2d 728, 435 N.Y.S.2d 252 (Ct.Cl.1981).

§ 14.2
1. *See infra*, §§ 14.3–14.6.
2. *See infra*, § 14.21.
3. *See infra*, §§ 14.22–14.27.
4. *See infra*, § 14.28.
5. *See infra*, § 14.29.

there are *no* grounds upon which a condemnee or other affected person can challenge the hearing itself.

After the hearing, the condemnor, assuming it desires to continue the process, must make a formal declaration and findings, must prepare a synopsis of its declaration and findings, and must properly publish and distribute this synopsis.[6] Again, the Eminent Domain Procedure Law thoroughly details the substantive requirements of the determination and findings and the synopsis, as well as the procedural requirements for publication. The condemnor's attorney should oversee the preparation of, if not actually prepare, these documents.

Until this point in the proceeding, a potential condemnee's attorney has played absolutely no role and most likely will not yet have been retained by the condemnee. If retained prior to the hearing, the potential condemnee's attorney certainly should attend the hearing. The attorney will carry no legal status at the hearing, as, for purposes of this hearing, the attorney is simply a member of the public entitled to be present and to offer oral and written testimony. The attorney, and anyone else present, may challenge the proffered public use, benefit or purpose, the selected location, the size of the property considered for condemnation or any other appropriate matter.[7] The primary purpose for the attorney being present at the public hearing, however, is to observe whether the statutory requirements for the conduct of the hearing have been met.

After publication of the synopsis of the determination and findings, the condemnee's attorney truly begins his or her representational role. When a public hearing has been held, there is one avenue for challenging the hearing and the determination and findings following it—immediate appeal to the appellate division.[8] Any other review, in any other forum, is completely foreclosed. Condemnees or other aggrieved persons have only thirty days from the condemnor's fulfillment of the requirement to publish the synopsis to file an appeal. The scope of the appeal will be narrow, however, focusing primarily on proper compliance with the procedural requirements of the Eminent Domain Procedure Law.[9] The condemnee's attorney will want to confirm that each requirement was met, as counsel must raise on this appeal, if it is to be raised, any alleged procedural flaw. In addition, the condemnee will have only two grounds on the merits that may be asserted to invalidate the condemnation. First, the condemnee may challenge the determination that there is a valid public use, purpose or benefit compelling the taking.[10] Second, the condemnee may challenge the scope or size of the condemned land as being greater than is reasonably necessary to accomplish the public

6. *See infra*, §§ 14.30, 14.31.
7. *See infra*, § 14.29.
8. *See infra*, §§ 14.34–14.38.
9. *See infra*, § 14.38.
10. *See infra*, § 14.38.

§ 14.2   EMINENT DOMAIN   Ch. 14

purpose, use or benefit. Again, this is the only opportunity the condemnee will have to raise these issues after the public hearing.[11]

If there is any appeal, or if the appellate division sustains the determinations and findings of the condemnor, the designated property is condemned, and all issues regarding the propriety and legality of the condemnation are foreclosed.[12] The focus of attorneys for both sides will then shift accordingly.

The next stage, the negotiation and offer phase, during which the condemnor endeavors to accomplish a fair purchase of the condemnee's property,[13] does not normally involve a major role for counsel. The condemnor's attorney will want to ensure that the condemnor acts in good faith in making the offer and that the condemnor understands that a "low ball" offer may result in the payment of substantial sums to the condemnee, in addition to compensation for the land, including reasonable attorney's and appraiser's fees. The condemnee's attorney will want to ensure that the condemnee understands the statutory choices available and the consequences of those choices. In particular, the condemnee's attorney must inform the client that rejection of the offer as inadequate compensation may result in a later judicial award less than the amount offered.[14] Put simply, "going for more may leave you with less."

The third stage, the acquisition phase,[15] which is reached only if a purchase is not agreed upon at the second stage, again involves the condemnor's attorney as the active player and the condemnee's attorney as essentially an interested observer. First, it should be noted that this stage is the first time that the identity of the condemnor plays a role, indeed an enormous one. If the condemnor is the State of New York, or a State agency or instrumentality, the acquisition takes place without any court involvement. The State simply meets the filing requirements and notifies the condemnee. The taking or acquisition is then complete.[16] The condemnor's attorney plays the same role as performed earlier, that of ensuring compliance with the procedural requirements. The condemnee, and consequently the condemnee's attorney, plays no role whatsoever. Once this process is complete, the condemnee may make a claim in the Court of Claims for compensation beyond that offered by the condemnor. The role of the attorneys in this process is described later in this section.

Attorneys for the condemnor and the condemnee play a far more active role in the acquisition stage when a non-State entity (e.g., a city, county, town or village) is the condemnor.[17] Property can be acquired by

11. See infra, § 14.38 regarding opportunities to raise these issues when the condemnor has claimed an exemption and has not held the hearing.
12. See infra, § 14.34.
13. See infra, §§ 14.40–14.44.
14. See infra, § 14.44.
15. See infra, §§ 14.47–14.68.
16. See infra, §§ 14.52–14.55.
17. See Chapter 3 "Municipal Law," supra.

such a condemnor only by order of the supreme court within the county in which the property is located.[18] The condemnor must file, *inter alia*, a petition with the court, which includes substantial statutorily-mandated detail. Because private property is to be taken, potential condemnees must be carefully identified, and strict notice and publication requirements must be met. The condemnor's attorney, at this stage, if not before, is likely to have full responsibility for the conduct of the eminent domain proceeding.

The condemnee's attorney will have a role in this scenario as well, unlike the situation in which the State is the condemnor and no judicial process is yet involved. The condemnee is entitled to file an answer to the condemnor's petition, setting forth any defenses the condemnee may have to the taking.[19] But, as was true on appeal to the appellate division after the public hearing and publication of the determination and findings synopsis, the grounds upon which the taking can be challenged are limited almost entirely to alleged non-compliance with statutory procedures.[20] What is clear is that the condemnee's attorney must be well-versed, as the condemnor's attorney should be, in the precise procedural rules that must be followed in the exercise of eminent domain.

One type of challenge to the merits of the taking can be made by condemnee's attorney at this stage. If the condemnor determines that it is exempt from the hearing and synopsis requirements described above, and the hearing is not held, the condemnee, in addition to arguing that a public hearing should have been held, may challenge the proposed taking on the basis that it is not in furtherance of a public use, purpose or benefit, or that the scope or size of the property is excessive in light of the public need.[21]

Assuming that the court finds that the condemnor has met the requirements of the Eminent Domain Procedure Law, the court will grant the petition, and, after certain defined filing requirements have been met, title will vest in the condemnor.

The final step in this third stage, one that must be taken whether the State or a non-State entity is the condemnor, is the serving and recording of a formal notice of acquisition.[22] The notice requirement, which is entirely the responsibility of the condemnor, serves to notify the condemnee of the taking and of the condemnee's rights as a result of the taking. The recording requirement creates constructive notice of termination of the condemnee's ownership.

The fourth and final stage is the compensation phase of the eminent domain proceeding.[23] It is only in this phase that the roles of the condemnee's attorney and the condemnor's attorney are relatively equal.

18. *See infra*, § 14.65.
19. *See infra*, § 14.63.
20. *See infra*, § 14.64.
21. *See infra*, §§ 14.38, 14.64.
22. *See infra*, § 14.66.
23. *See infra*, §§ 14.69–14.115.

This stage is essentially akin to the damages phase of a trial. Whether the claim is brought against a State condemnor in the Court of Claims or against a non-State condemnor in supreme court, the judicial function is the same—to determine what constitutes just compensation for the condemnee.[24] The role of the attorneys is to present the best evidence on behalf of their clients, almost exclusively through the use of expert written appraisals and expert testimony. The condemnee's attorney, in particular, must be familiar with the myriad valuation methods that can properly be considered and numerous elements of damage, other than the strict value of the land taken, that may properly be claimed.[25]

§ 14.3 Exercise of the Power of Eminent Domain

It is often said that the power of eminent domain is inherent in the State, resting on the State's sovereignty and grounded in political necessity.[1] The power of eminent domain is viewed as essential to the State's effective existence, as is its police and taxation power.[2]

Library References:

West's Key No. Digests, Eminent Domain ⟐1–68.

§ 14.4 Exercise of the Power of Eminent Domain—The State as Condemnor

Throughout the procedures set out in the Eminent Domain Procedure Law, a distinction is drawn between the power of eminent domain when exercised "by or in the name of the people of the State of New York"[1] and the power when exercised by any other condemnor.[2] The distinctions are sometimes minimal, but are more often significant, involving the jurisdiction of courts[3] and the entire nature of the actual

---

24. See infra, § 14.77.

25. PRACTICE POINTER: It is highly likely that a targeted condemnee will believe he or she has far greater power to stop the acquisition than in fact the condemnee has. It is also highly likely that the condemnee will seek legal counsel in the belief that counsel can represent the condemnee in the assertion of this perceived power. It is essential that when counsel is approached by a targeted condemnee on this basis, he or she explain how *very* limited the opportunities are for stopping or even slowing what the client will often perceive as a governmental juggernaut. With regard to the question of who will own the land at the end of the process, the winner is essentially decided before the process starts. The condemnee, and thus the condemnee's lawyer, can do little more than make sure that the game is played by the rules. The primary stage at which the condemnee's attorney can make a substantive difference is at the award stage, particularly if the condemnor's offer falls short of what is just. The condemnee will lose his or her land, but the legal system can ensure that the condemnee is fully compensated, in a financial sense, for that loss.

§ 14.3

1. *See, e.g.*, First Broadcasting Corp. v. City of Syracuse, 78 A.D.2d 490, 435 N.Y.S.2d 194 (4th Dep't 1981).

2. *Id.*

§ 14.4

1. Eminent Domain Procedure Law § 501(A).

2. Eminent Domain Procedure Law § 502(B).

3. *See infra*, § 14.48.

appropriation itself.[4] Thus, condemnees seeking to assert rights provided to them by the Eminent Domain Procedure Law must first determine whether the condemnor falls into the category of the "State" for purposes of the Eminent Domain Procedure Law, or whether the condemnor is an entity other than the "State."

The Eminent Domain Procedure Law does not itself provide a definition of those condemnors who act "by or for the people of the State of New York." By necessary inference, however, it is clear that the Eminent Domain Procedure Law intends to include in the notion of "State condemnor" all of those governmental entities that fall within the scope of the Court of Claims' jurisdiction.[5] Thus, a State condemnor includes the State itself, as well as any agency or agent of the State exercising governmental powers. However, it is possible for an entity to be created by the State and yet not be the State or an agency of the State for purposes of eminent domain.[6] As the Court of Appeals has stated, "a particularized inquiry into the nature of the instrumentality and the statute claimed to be applicable to it is required."[7]

Thus, for example, the issue of whether a particular entity was the "State" for purposes of eminent domain arose in *Long Island R. Co. v. Long Island Lighting Co.*[8] The entity at issue was the Long Island Railroad, which is a New York State public benefit corporation. Applying the "particularized inquiry" required by the Court of Appeals,[9] the court found it "clear" that the Railroad was "neither identical with the State nor one of its political subdivisions."[10] As the court noted, "it can hardly be said that the [Railroad] is engaged in operations which are fundamentally governmental in nature."[11] Also significant to the court, in addition to whether governmental functions were being performed, was whether the entity independently transacted its business and whether it hired and compensated its personnel outside the State's civil service system.[12]

The eminent domain power of the State lies with the Legislature, and no agency of the State may exercise the power of eminent domain except with legislative approval.[13] There are no restraints on the right of the Legislature to delegate its power of eminent domain, although a

---

4. *See infra*, §§ 14.52–14.55.

5. New York State Constitution, Art. VI § 9.

6. John Grace & Co., Inc. v. State University Const. Fund, 44 N.Y.2d 84, 404 N.Y.S.2d 316, 375 N.E.2d 377 (1978) (holding, in a different context, that the State University Construction Fund is not a state agency).

7. 44 N.Y.2d at 88, 404 N.Y.S.2d at 318.

8. 103 A.D.2d 156, 479 N.Y.S.2d 355 (2d Dep't 1984), aff'd 64 N.Y.2d 1088, 489 N.Y.S.2d 881, 479 N.E.2d 226 (1985). The precise issue in the case was whether the Long Island Railroad was a political subdivision of the State, whose property was thus exempt from condemnation. *See infra*, § 14.12.

9. *Id.*

10. *Id.* at 164, 479 N.Y.S.2d at 361.

11. *Id.*

12. *Id.* at 165, 479 N.Y.S.2d at 361. *See also* John Grace & Co., Inc., *supra* note 6, 44 N.Y.2d at 89–90, 404 N.Y.S.2d at 322, 375 N.E.2d at 383.

13. Society of New York Hospital v. Johnson, 5 N.Y.2d 102, 180 N.Y.S.2d 287, 154 N.E.2d 550 (1958).

delegatee must be required to comply with state and federal constitutional requirements.[14]

Not only does the Legislature possess the power to delegate, but it may, and does, prescribe the conditions upon which the power can be exercised. If the existence of a statutory delegation is challenged, the statute will be strictly construed, as the power of eminent domain is exercised in derogation of the property rights of private citizens.[15] An agency exercising the power of eminent domain thus has the burden of establishing the statutory delegation and compliance with any conditions attached to it. Particularly where conditions or limitations are attached to the legislative delegation, counsel for the condemnor should ensure that the condemnor acts within its authority. Should the condemnor act outside its authority, the condemnee will have grounds for voiding the condemnation and taking and may recover damages.[16]

Library References:

West's Key No. Digests, Eminent Domain ⚖4, 53.

§ 14.5 Exercise of the Power of Eminent Domain—Other Public Entities as Condemnor

The power of a political subdivision in the State of New York to exercise eminent domain may flow from one of two sources: the State Constitution or the State Legislature. Article IX, § 1(e) of the New York State Constitution provides that "local governments shall have power to take by eminent domain private property within their boundaries for public use...." When a political subdivision wants to take property outside of its boundaries, such taking requires the authorization of the State Legislature.[1]

Whether authorized by the Constitution or the Legislature, all such takings are governed by the Eminent Domain Procedure Law and are subject to the jurisdiction of the state supreme court.[2]

Library References:

West's Key No. Digests, Eminent Domain ⚖6–9, 54–59.

§ 14.6 Exercise of the Power of Eminent Domain—Private Entities

The power of eminent domain that resides with the State may be delegated to a private entity, as long as the power is exercised for a

---

14. See infra, § 14.18.
15. Society of New York Hospital, supra note 13.
16. See infra, § 14.113.

§ 14.5
1. New York State Constitution, Art. IX, § 1(e) ("The legislature may authorize and regulate the exercise of the power of eminent domain ... by a local government outside its boundaries.").

2. See infra, § 14.48.

public purpose. As early as 1870, the Court of Appeals said that it was well settled that the State could take property through agents, whether individuals or corporations.[1] Title can, in fact, vest in private condemnors, as long as the purpose for which the condemnation takes place is a public one.[2] Private recipients of legislatively-delegated eminent domain power include telephone companies, electric companies, pipeline companies, housing companies, urban redevelopment or renewal corporations and railroads. Although it would be highly unusual, the Legislature may also delegate the power of eminent domain to an individual, again, so long as the power is exercised for the required public benefit.

Library References:

West's Key No. Digests, Eminent Domain ⚖10, 60–62.

§ 14.7 Property Rights Subject to Acquisition

The Eminent Domain Procedure Law, case law interpreting it, and predecessor statutes, permit nearly every possible type of property right to be subjected to the State's eminent domain power. Whatever the nature of the property right taken, however, the State is under a duty not to take more property than is necessary or to do greater damage than is required for the intended public use.[1]

Library References:

West's Key No. Digests, Eminent Domain ⚖44–52.

§ 14.8 Property Rights Subject to Acquisition—Real Property

Although the Eminent Domain Procedure Law governs interests in personal property as well as real property,[1] its primary concern is clearly with the exercise of the power of eminent domain over real property. Eminent Domain Procedure Law § 103 defines real property to include:

> all land and improvements, lands under water, waterfront property, the water of any lake, pond or stream, all easements and hereditaments, corporeal or incorporeal, and every estate, interest and right, legal or equitable, in lands or water, and right, interest, privilege, easement and franchise relating to the same, including terms for years and liens by way of mortgage or otherwise.

§ 14.6

1. Rensselaer, etc. R. Co. v. Davis, 43 N.Y. 137 (1870).
2. Id.

§ 14.7

1. Onondaga County v. Sargent, 92 A.D.2d 743, 461 N.Y.S.2d 84 (4th Dep't 1983). The condemnor may negotiate and acquire additional property, however, with the owner's consent. Kohl Indus. Park Co. v. Rockland County, 710 F.2d 895 (2d Cir. 1983).

§ 14.8

1. See infra, § 14.11.

§ 14.8   EMINENT DOMAIN   Ch. 14

It is hard to imagine an interest in real property that would escape such an inclusive definition. Moreover, it is clear that the power of eminent domain extends not only to the land, but to buildings and fixtures[2] located on condemned land.

Library References:

West's Key No. Digests, Eminent Domain ⇌44–47, 52.

§ 14.9 Property Rights Subject to Acquisition—Easements

The power of eminent domain can be, and often is, exercised to acquire an easement on privately-owned land. In fact, in light of the general rule that the condemnor may not take more land than is necessary for public use,[1] the condemnor may be restricted to taking an easement rather than title in fee if an easement is all that is required to meet the public need. The owner of the fee normally remains free to use the land in any manner that does not interfere with the easement.[2]

Library References:

West's Key No. Digests, Eminent Domain ⇌50.

§ 14.10 Property Rights Subject to Acquisition—Leases

The power of eminent domain may be exercised through the taking of a leasehold rather than a fee interest. Again, this may be required if the public need requires only a temporary acquisition. Acquisition of a leasehold interest is still a taking and is fully subject to the requirements of the Eminent Domain Procedure Law.

Library References:

West's Key No. Digests, Eminent Domain ⇌50.

§ 14.11 Property Rights Subject to Acquisition—Personal Property

Although nearly all sections of the Eminent Domain Procedure Law address themselves to public acquisition of privately-owned real property, Section 708 provides, "[w]henever any condemnor is authorized to acquire for public use, title to property other than real property, the acquisition of such property shall be in the manner and procedure prescribed for the acquisition of real property." Although takings of privately-owned personal property by eminent domain are not common,

---

2. See infra, §§ 14.81, 14.91–14.93.

§ 14.9

1. See supra, § 14.7.

2. Onondaga County v. Sargent, 92 A.D.2d 743, 461 N.Y.S.2d 84 (4th Dep't 1983).

they occur occasionally with respect to contract rights, franchises and charters.[1]

Library References:

West's Key No. Digests, Eminent Domain ⚷45.

§ 14.12 Property Rights Subject to Acquisition—Public Property/Priority of Taking

Unique problems arise when a condemnor seeks to acquire property that is already devoted to another public use through an earlier condemnation or purchase authorized as an exercise of the power of eminent domain. The problem is not presented when the State (or its agencies) is the condemnor. If the State is the condemnor, it prevails.[1] The issue is raised, instead, when the condemnor is a corporation, a county, a city or a town. The basic rule, long recognized in this State,[2] is that property already acquired for a public use is presumed protected from subsequent acquisition. This presumption is overcome only by legislative direction clearly authorizing the taking of such property. In *New York Cent. & H.R.R. Co. v. City of Buffalo*,[3] the Court of Appeals stated the principle that a subsequent public use should trump a prior one only when there are "special, unusual or peculiar" reasons to favor the subsequent use.

When the Legislature clearly authorizes the acquisition of land already devoted to public use, that acquisition is permitted even if it completely extinguishes the prior public use. If the two uses may compatibly co-exist, there is no bar to the taking for a second public purpose under this rule.[4]

Occasionally a dispute may arise as to the priority between two simultaneously competing condemnors. In such a case, priority is generally determined by the competitors' relative positions in the condemnation process. For example, if one condemnor purchased the property pursuant to statutory procedures[5] and another corporation subsequently commenced proceedings to acquire the property, the prior purchasing condemnor would prevail, even if it had not yet commenced its public use.[6]

§ 14.11

1. Eighth Ave. Coach Corp. v. New York, 286 N.Y. 84, 35 N.E.2d 907 (1941); New York C. & H.R.R. Co. v. Metropolitan Gas-Light Co., 63 N.Y. 326 (1875).

§ 14.12

1. Long Island R. Co. v. Long Island Lighting Co., 103 A.D.2d 156, 479 N.Y.S.2d 355 (2d Dep't 1984), aff'd 64 N.Y.2d 1088, 489 N.Y.S.2d 881, 479 N.E.2d 226 (1985).

2. People v. Adirondack R. Co., 160 N.Y. 225, 54 N.E. 689 (1899), aff'd Adirondack R. Co. v. People of State of New York, 176 U.S. 335, 20 S.Ct. 460, 44 L.Ed. 492 (1900); Long Island R. Co., *supra* note 1.

3. 200 N.Y. 113, 93 N.E. 520 (1910).

4. Long Island R. Co., *supra* note 1.

5. *See infra*, §§ 14.40–14.44.

6. *See, e.g.*, Pocantico Water-Works Co. v. Bird, 130 N.Y. 249, 29 N.E. 246 (1891).

§ 14.12   EMINENT DOMAIN   Ch. 14

Library References:

West's Key No. Digests, Eminent Domain ⟪46, 47.

§ 14.13   Property Rights Subject to Acquisition—Excess Property

The rule that a condemnor may take only that property that is necessary for the public project, while intended to protect private property rights, may, in certain cases, result in the unacquired parcels being insignificant or inappropriate in size and shape. As a result, condemnors may, if authorized,[1] take such excess land. When such excess land is taken, the condemnee must be appropriately compensated.[2] The condemnor may then sell or lease the excess property.

Library References:

West's Key No. Digests, Eminent Domain ⟪45.

§ 14.14   *De Facto* Taking

It is absolutely clear, as a matter of constitutional and statutory law, that an exercise of the power of eminent domain requires the payment of just compensation.[1] It is equally true that the State and its political subdivisions may enact zoning laws and regulations that restrict a private owner's use of his or her property and will not be required to compensate the owner for the value of prohibited uses.[2] Along the spectrum between the formal act of eminent domain and the enactment and enforcement of zoning laws[3] and regulations lie complicated questions concerning "*de facto* takings."[4]

A "*de facto* taking" has been defined as "a permanent ouster of the owner or a permanent physical or legal interference with the owner's physical use, possession, and enjoyment of the property by one having condemnation powers...."[5] In either instance, a "taking" in the consti-

---

§ 14.13

1. New York State Constitution, Art. IX, §1(e).

2. *See infra*, § 14.18.

§ 14.14

1. *See infra*, § 14.18.

2. Cities Service Oil Co. v. City of New York, 5 N.Y.2d 110, 180 N.Y.S.2d 769, 154 N.E.2d 814 (1958), reh'g denied 5 N.Y.2d 1041, 185 N.Y.S.2d 1025, 158 N.E.2d 131, cert. denied 360 U.S. 934, 79 S.Ct. 1453, 3 L.Ed.2d 1546 (1959); CJOGS Assoc. v. Harris, 151 A.D.2d 571, 542 N.Y.S.2d 679 (2d Dep't 1989).

3. *See* Chapter 16 "Land Use," *infra*.

4. Spears v. Berle, 48 N.Y.2d 254, 422 N.Y.S.2d 636, 397 N.E.2d 1304 (1979) ("[C]ourts have encountered difficulty in formulating a bright-line standard for differentiating permissible police power measures from overly vigorous and hence unconstitutional impositions.").

5. Matter of Ward v. Bennett, 214 A.D.2d 741, 625 N.Y.S.2d 609 (2d Dep't 1995); *see also*, Borntrager v. Delaware County, 76 A.D.2d 969, 428 N.Y.S.2d 766 (3d Dep't 1980), app. after remand 99 A.D.2d 627, 472 N.Y.S.2d 182 (3d Dep't 1984).

tutional sense may occur, and the "taker" will be obliged to pay just compensation.[6]

A direct limitation on an owner's use of property can constitute a taking if the remaining permitted use is so restrictive that there remains no reasonable use.[7] The burden to make this showing is on the landowner, and it is a heavy one.[8] The Court of Appeals has said that to overcome the presumption of constitutionality that attaches to regulations, the landowner must prove every element of his claim beyond a reasonable doubt.[9]

When the "taker" actually physically comes upon an owner's property, whether compensation is due as a result of a *de facto* taking turns on the length of time of the occupation, possession, control or use of the property. As an example, when a county came upon land to change the course of a stream to divert the water to a course along, rather than under, a highway bed, the change in course thereby deprived the property owner of access to 35 acres of his land, and a cause of action for *de facto* appropriation was stated.[10] However, a temporary or intermittent use of property without destruction or appropriation of any right of the owner is a trespass rather than a taking,[11] and the owner may seek damages for the former rather than compensation for the latter.[12] On the other hand, if the presence of the taker, even though temporary, is sufficiently extensive in scope or long in duration, a compensable taking may be found.[13]

Occasionally, a landowner will argue that a "taking" has occurred, requiring just compensation, where the public projects or uses on adja-

---

6. Matter of Ward, *supra* note 4; Onondaga Co. v. Sargent, 92 A.D.2d 743, 461 N.Y.S.2d 84 (4th Dep't 1983).

7. Matter of Ward, *supra* note 4; Waldorf v. Coffey, 5 Misc.2d 80, 159 N.Y.S.2d 852 (Sup.Ct., Sp.Tm., Nassau County, 1957) (a taking of private property for public use occurs when a village decides the owner's lot is too small for his desired use, forbids that use, and there is no other reasonable use of the property). *Compare* Gordon v. Huntington, 230 N.Y.S.2d 619 (Sup.Ct., Sp. Tm., Suffolk County, 1962) (a taking did not occur where the owner was barred by ordinance from constructing a gas station but there was no showing that property could not be otherwise profitably employed).

8. CJOGS Assoc., *supra* note 2.

9. de St. Aubin v. Flacke, 68 N.Y.2d 66, 505 N.Y.S.2d 859, 496 N.E.2d 879 (1986); Spears, *supra* note 3.

10. Borntrager, *supra* note 4.

11. O'Brien v. Syracuse, 54 A.D.2d 186, 388 N.Y.S.2d 866 (4th Dep't 1976), appeal denied 40 N.Y.2d 809, 392 N.Y.S.2d 1027, 360 N.E.2d 1109 (1977), app. dismissed 41 N.Y.2d 1008, 395 N.Y.S.2d 1028, 363 N.E.2d 1195, cert. denied 434 U.S. 807, 98 S.Ct. 37, 54 L.Ed.2d 65 (1977) (characterizing *de facto* takings as an "aggravated" form of trespass). An example of a temporary, intermittent use not amounting to a taking may be found in Mickel v. State, 77 A.D.2d 794, 430 N.Y.S.2d 741 (4th Dep't 1980), aff'd 54 N.Y.2d 858, 444 N.Y.S.2d 916, 429 N.E.2d 423 (1981) (claimant based her claim on the State's mistaken temporary posting of a "Public Fishing" sign on her property and consequent traversing of the property by some members of the public; the State promptly corrected the mistake after being informed of it; claimant was denied recovery for a *de facto* taking).

12. *But see* O'Brien, *supra* note 10, holding that an unsuccessful claimant for compensation for a *de facto* taking is barred by *res judicata* principles from bringing a later action in trespass on the same essential facts.

13. *Id.*

cent land interfere with the owner's use and enjoyment of his or her land. Case law clearly establishes that compensation in such a case is required only if the interference amounts to a virtual destruction of the beneficial use of the claimant's land.[14] Less severe interference will not support a claim for such compensation.[15]

Library References:

West's Key No. Digests, Eminent Domain ⟐2, 266–316.

§ 14.15 Public Use, Benefit or Purpose

Private property can be taken by eminent domain only for a public purpose, use or benefit.[1] As will be seen in later sections,[2] this requirement gives a condemnee who opposes the condemnation one of the few grounds on the merits for challenging the condemnation.[3] It is rare that a condemnee prevails on this ground, however, inasmuch as the definition of a public use, benefit or purpose is quite broad. Any use that contributes to the health, safety, general welfare, convenience or prosperity of the community is a public one.[4] As long as this definition is met, it does not matter if the condemnor realizes a financial gain[5] or other private interest.[6] The Eminent Domain Procedure Law incorporates the notion of a public use, benefit or purpose in the term "public project."[7]

Library References:

West's Key No. Digests, Eminent Domain ⟐12–42.

14. Garvey v. Long Island R. Co., 159 N.Y. 323, 54 N.E. 57 (1899); Cunliffe v. Monroe County, 63 Misc.2d 62, 312 N.Y.S.2d 879 (Sup.Ct., Monroe County, 1970).

15. Lucas v. State, 44 A.D.2d 633, 353 N.Y.S.2d 831 (3d Dep't 1974); Organek v. State, 151 Misc.2d 78, 573 N.Y.S.2d 116 (Ct.Cl.1991).

§ 14.15

1. Byrne on behalf of Pine Grove Beach Ass'n v. New York State Office of Parks, Recreation & Historic Preservation, 101 A.D.2d 701, 476 N.Y.S.2d 42 (4th Dep't 1984).

2. See infra, §§ 14.34, 14.64.

3. **PRACTICE POINTER:** Here again, the condemnee's attorney must counsel the client with regard to the fact that such a challenge is a long shot. Unless there are other grounds upon which to challenge the condemnor's actions, an appeal on this ground alone is not to be advised without due consideration.

4. Byrne on behalf of Pine Grove Beach Ass'n, *supra* note 1.

5. First Broadcasting Corp. v. City of Syracuse, 78 A.D.2d 490, 435 N.Y.S.2d 194 (4th Dep't 1981).

6. *See, e.g.,* Northeast Parent & Child Soc., Inc. v. City of Schenectady Indus. Dev. Agency, 114 A.D.2d 741, 494 N.Y.S.2d 503 (3d Dep't 1985) (incidental private benefit conferred on private party did not vitiate public purpose); New York State Urban Development Corp. v. Vanderlex Merchandise Co., Inc., 98 Misc.2d 264, 413 N.Y.S.2d 982 (Sup.Ct., N.Y.County, 1979) (fact that condemnation served condemnor's own interest did not undermine public purpose).

7. Eminent Domain Procedure Law § 103(G) ("'Public project' means any program or project for which acquisition of property may be required for a public use, benefit or purpose.").

§ 14.16 Public Use, Benefit or Purpose—Particular Uses

Neither the public nor the condemnee is ever required to speculate as to what is the public use, benefit or purpose of a proposed public project. First, the delegating statute authorizing the specific exercise of the eminent domain power often specifies the public use for which the power is delegated. Second, early in the process of accomplishing a taking by eminent domain, the condemnor, in most condemnations, must make formal findings with respect to the purpose, use or benefit of the proposed project, and such findings must be disclosed to the public.[1]

It would not be particularly useful to the reader to detail every public purpose supporting, or capable of supporting, the proper exercise of the power of eminent domain. A brief list of recognized public uses is illustrative of the scope of the concept, however. Such uses include: highways, bridges, tunnels, parking, airports, ferries, cemeteries, housing, slum cleanup, urban renewal, health, hospitals, environmental conservation,[2] historical sites, parks, playgrounds, water supply, flood control, sewage disposal, electric services, cable services, heat and power supplies, agricultural services and prisons.

Library References:

West's Key No. Digests, Eminent Domain ⚖16–42.

§ 14.17 Public Use, Benefit or Purpose—Incidental Private Benefit

The fact that private benefits accrue as a result of a condemnation will not undermine the legality of the action, as long as the private benefit is incidental to the public one.[1] In fact, at least one court has upheld the validity of a condemnation intended for public use, even though the motive for the acquisition was private gain.[2]

Library References:

West's Key No. Digests, Eminent Domain ⚖12–42.

§ 14.16

1. See infra, § 14.30.

2. The Environmental Conservation Law provides an excellent example of the potential breadth of statutory delegation of the power of eminent domain by the Legislature. As long as the Department of Environmental Conservation complies with the Eminent Domain Procedure Law, it may acquire land as the Commissioner of the Department "deems necessary for any of the purposes of the Department." ECL § 3–0305(1). See generally, Chapter 15 "New York Environmental Law," infra.

§ 14.17

1. Sunrise Props. Inc. v. Jamestown Urban Renewal Agency, 206 A.D.2d 913, 614 N.Y.S.2d 841 (4th Dep't 1994); Waldo's Inc. v. Village of Johnson City, 141 A.D.2d 194, 534 N.Y.S.2d 723 (3d Dep't 1988), aff'd 74 N.Y.2d 718, 544 N.Y.S.2d 809, 543 N.E.2d 74 (1989) (construction of 4-way intersection benefitted adjoining landowners, who contributed money for the project, in addition to relieving traffic congestion for the public as a whole).

2. Fremont–Rockland Sewage Corp. v. Bock, 79 A.D.2d 768, 435 N.Y.S.2d 61 (3d Dep't 1980).

§ 14.18 Just Compensation

Both the United States and New York State Constitutions require payment of just compensation to persons whose private property is taken for public use.[1] "Just compensation" means that the condemnee should be indemnified in an amount that would leave him or her as well off, in value if not in kind, as he or she would have been had the taking not occurred.[2] While it is true that decisions regarding exercise of the power of eminent domain lie with the Legislature and local government decision-makers,[3] resolution of issues regarding just compensation lies with the judiciary. Most of the case law, by far, involving eminent domain concerns just compensation.

As will be discussed in Sections 14.69–14.115, the Eminent Domain Procedure Law sets out procedures governing litigation of compensation issues in the courts. The Eminent Domain Procedure Law does not, however, give substantive direction, or even guidance, to the courts with regard to what methods should be used to value the condemnee's property, and thus no guidance is given as to what compensation must be paid by the condemnor. Proper methods of valuation, therefore, must be gleaned from the case law.[4]

Library References:

West's Key No. Digests, Eminent Domain ⬌122–150.

§ 14.19 Summary

As the foregoing discussion indicates, the power of eminent domain is extraordinarily broad. From the standpoint of counsel for both the condemnor and the condemnee, the only legal concern that arises prior to the beginning of the eminent domain proceedings is whether the proper constitutional or legislative authority exists for the taking.[1]

§ 14.20 The First Stage: The Condemnation Phase

The first stage of the process in which the power of eminent domain is exercised under the Eminent Domain Procedure Law may be thought of as the condemnation phase, as the final act of this stage is a declaration that the subject property is condemned, that is, that it is to be acquired for public use. The act of condemnation does not actually accomplish the acquisition, it simply sets the legal stage for the acquisition.[1]

§ 14.18

1. U.S. Constitution, Amend. V; New York State Constitution, Art. I, § 7(a).
2. Wilmot v. State, 32 N.Y.2d 164, 344 N.Y.S.2d 350, 297 N.E.2d 90 (1973).
3. See supra, §§ 14.4, 14.5.
4. See infra, § 14.85–14.88.

§ 14.19

1. See supra, §§ 14.3–14.6.

§ 14.20

1. See infra, §§ 14.47–14.67.

Ch. 14　　EXEMPTIONS FROM PUBLIC HEARING　　§ 14.22

Library References:

West's Key No. Digests, Eminent Domain ⚖=54–68, 166–198.

§ 14.21　Public Hearing

One of the stated purposes of the Eminent Domain Procedure Law is "to establish opportunity for public participation in the planning of public projects necessitating the exercise of eminent domain," thus giving due regard not only to the need to acquire property for public use but also to "the legitimate interests of private property owners, local communities and the quality of the environment...."[1] To this end, except as otherwise provided in the Eminent Domain Procedure Law, the condemnor is required to conduct a public hearing, *prior* to condemnation and acquisition of the condemned property.[2] This requirement, imposed by the Eminent Domain Procedure Law, is not constitutionally mandated.[3]

The pre-acquisition public hearing must be held at a location "reasonably proximate" to the property sought to be acquired.[4] Interestingly, the purpose of the hearing is not so much to "hear" the public as to "inform the public and to review the public use to be served by a proposed public project and the impact on the environment and residents of the locality...."[5] The focus of the hearing is the nature of the public project itself, not the precise location of it. The Court of Appeals has highlighted the link between the requirement that a public hearing be held and the requirement that the taking be for a public purpose by noting that the "principal purpose of article 2 of the EDPL ... is to insure that an agency does not acquire property without having made a reasoned determination that the condemnation will serve a valid public purpose."[6]

Library References:

West's Key No. Digests, Eminent Domain ⚖=198(1).

§ 14.22　Exemptions From the Public Hearing Requirement

Section 206 of the Eminent Domain Procedure Law lists five situations in which a public hearing is not required. These five exemptions from the public hearing requirement are discussed below.

§ 14.21

1. Eminent Domain Procedure Law § 101.
2. Eminent Domain Procedure Law § 201.
3. Brent v. Hoch, 25 Misc.2d 1062, 205 N.Y.S.2d 66 (Sup.Ct., Suffolk County, 1960), aff'd 13 A.D.2d 505, 211 N.Y.S.2d 853 (2d Dep't), app. denied 13 A.D.2d 774, 217 N.Y.S.2d 505 (2d Dep't 1961), app. denied 10 N.Y.2d 706, 221 N.Y.S.2d 1025, 178 N.E.2d 189 (1961).
4. Eminent Domain Procedure Law § 201.
5. *Id.*
6. Jackson v. New York State Urban Development Corp., 67 N.Y.2d 400, 419, 503 N.Y.S.2d 298, 306, 494 N.E.2d 429 (1986).

§ 14.23 Exemptions From the Public Hearing Requirement—Overlap With Other Governmental Requirements

As was noted in Section 14.21, above, the Eminent Domain Procedure Law contemplates the primary function of the public hearing as a means of "notifying" the public, although the public is given the right to be heard. The primacy of this function is made clear by Eminent Domain Procedure Law § 206(A), which exempts condemnors from the public hearing, notice[1] and synopsis requirements[2] of the Eminent Domain Procedure Law if 1) the same information to be decided and communicated by these sections has been considered and submitted to a state, federal or local government agency, board or commission, *and* 2) a license, permit or certificate of public convenience or necessity or other form of approval has been issued by such a state, federal or local government agency, board or commission.[3] In other words, if the condemnor has already received government approval for the proposed project after providing the approving body with the same information that normally would be communicated at, and summarized after, the public hearing, the public hearing requirement[4] and the other requirements of Article 2 are waived.[5]

Library References:

West's Key No. Digests, Eminent Domain ⇔198(1).

§ 14.24 Exemptions From the Public Hearing Requirement—Overlap With Issuance of a Certificate of Environmental Compatibility and Public Need

Eminent Domain Procedure Law § 206(B) provides that a condemnor that has obtained a certificate of environmental compatibility and public need pursuant to Articles VII or VIII of New York's Public Service Law[1] need not hold a public hearing under the Eminent Domain Proce-

---

§ 14.23

1. See infra, § 14.28.
2. Eminent Domain Procedure Law 206(A); see infra, § 14.31.
3. See, e.g., Monroe County v. Morgan, 83 A.D.2d 777, 443 N.Y.S.2d 467 (4th Dep't 1981).
4. See, e.g., Rockland County Sewer Dist. No. 1 v. J & J Dodge, Inc., 213 A.D.2d 409, 635 N.Y.S.2d 233 (2d Dep't 1995); Aswad v. City School Dist. of City of Binghamton, 74 A.D.2d 972, 425 N.Y.S.2d 896 (3d Dep't 1980).
5. See infra, §§ 14.30, 14.31.

§ 14.24

1. Public Service Law § 121.

dure Law.[2]

Library References:

West's Key No. Digests, Eminent Domain ⚖=198(1).

§ 14.25 Exemptions From the Public Hearing Requirement—Alternate Public Hearing

If, pursuant to any other law or regulation, the condemnor conducts, or offers to conduct, a public hearing with notice to the public and to the owners of the property proposed to be acquired, and if the same factors to be included in an Eminent Domain Procedure Law synopsis[1] are considered at that hearing, an Eminent Domain Procedure Law public hearing is not required.[2]

Library References:

West's Key No. Digests, Eminent Domain ⚖=198(1).

§ 14.26 Exemptions From the Public Hearing Requirement—*De Minimis* Acquisition or Emergency Situation

If the condemnor is of the opinion that the proposed acquisition is sufficiently *de minimis* in nature that the public interest will not be prejudiced by the project, a public hearing need not be held.[1] What constitutes a *de minimis* taking has been the subject of a number of legal challenges, although the condemnor's determination is usually upheld. *De minimis* takings have been upheld when the property taken was not being used by the owner, the owner had no immediate plan for its use, and no structures had to be removed as a result of condemnation of an easement.[2] For example, acquisition of a permanent easement for expansion and improvement of a city sanitary sewage system has been upheld as *de minimis*,[3] as has acquisition of a large underground natural gas storage facility.[4]

---

2. Matter of Acquisition of Real Property by Fulton County, 136 A.D.2d 115, 525 N.Y.S.2d 948 (3d Dep't 1988).

§ 14.25

1. See infra, § 14.30.

2. Eminent Domain Procedure Law § 206(C); City of Buffalo Urban Renewal Agency v. Moreton, 100 A.D.2d 20, 473 N.Y.S.2d 278 (4th Dep't 1984).

§ 14.26

1. Eminent Domain Procedure Law 206(D).

2. Rockland County Sewer Dist. No. 1 v. J & J Dodge, Inc., 213 A.D.2d 409, 635 N.Y.S.2d 233 (2d Dep't 1995); Matteson v. Herkimer County, 94 A.D.2d 950, 464 N.Y.S.2d 75 (4th Dep't 1983).

3. Town of Coxsackie v. Dernier, 105 A.D.2d 966, 482 N.Y.S.2d 106 (3d Dep't 1984).

4. Anderson v. National Fuel Gas Supply Corp., 105 A.D.2d 1097, 482 N.Y.S.2d 644 (4th Dep't 1984).

§ 14.26 EMINENT DOMAIN Ch. 14

However, in a case in which the amount of property to be acquired from numerous owners' residential lots in order to build sidewalks was nearly 2600 square feet, and there was considerable public controversy about the location of the proposed sidewalk, the condemnor's conclusion that the taking was *de minimis* was overruled, and an Eminent Domain Procedure Law public hearing was required.[5]

Additionally, if the condemnor believes a public interest or health emergency exists so that the public interest would be endangered by delays caused by compliance with the public hearing requirement, the acquisition may proceed without a public hearing.[6] Endangerment of the public health has most often been found when the acquisition was made to prevent imminent flooding.[7]

Library References:

West's Key No. Digests, Eminent Domain ⟸198(1).

§ 14.27 Exemptions From the Public Hearing Requirement—Section 41.34 of the Mental Hygiene Law

If the condemnor complies with Section 41.34 of the Mental Hygiene Law, it need not hold a public hearing.[1] This statute governs condemnations relating to the establishment of community residences for mentally disabled persons.

Library References:

West's Key No. Digests, Eminent Domain ⟸198(1).

§ 14.28 Notice

Section 202 of the Eminent Domain Procedure Law sets out the formal requirements for notice of the public hearing. First, as to content, the notice must identify the location of the proposed acquisition (and any alternative locations) and must indicate the purpose, time and location of the hearing. The notice is not required to detail all aspects of the acquisition.[1]

---

5. Marshall v. Town of Pittsford, 105 A.D.2d 1140, 482 N.Y.S.2d 619, (4th Dep't 1984), app. denied 64 N.Y.2d 606, 487 N.Y.S.2d 1026, 476 N.E.2d 653 (1985).

6. Eminent Domain Procedure Law § 206(D).

7. City of Yonkers By Green v. Hvizd, 93 A.D.2d 887, 461 N.Y.S.2d 408 (2d Dep't 1983); Matter of Village of Malverne, 70 A.D.2d 920, 418 N.Y.S.2d 93 (2d Dep't 1979).

§ 14.27

1. Eminent Domain Procedure Law § 206(E).

§ 14.28

1. Greenwich Associates v. Metropolitan Transp. Authority, 152 A.D.2d 216, 548 N.Y.S.2d 190 (1st Dep't 1989), appeal dismissed sub. nom. Regency–Lexington Partners v. Metropolitan Transp. Authority, 75 N.Y.2d 865, 552 N.Y.S.2d 930, 552 N.E.2d 178 (1990) (notice was not required to contain reference to the demolition of existing structures on site).

The statute requires that notice be published in a minimum of five successive issues of an "official daily newspaper," if there is one in the locality of the proposed acquisition. If this official newspaper is one of general circulation in that locality, there is no further publication requirement. If the official newspaper is not one of general circulation, then the notice must be published in that newspaper *as well* as in at least five successive issues of a daily newspaper of general circulation in the locality. If there is no official newspaper, the notice must be published in at least five successive issues of a daily newspaper of general circulation in the locality. If the only newspaper in the locality is a weekly one, Section 202 requires publication in at least two successive issues.

This notice must appear within a window of time thirty to ten days before the hearing. It has been held that the required notice must *commence* during this window, it is not required to be completed in the window.[2]

Eminent Domain Procedure Law § 202(C) concerns the consequences of inadvertent failure to provide notice to individual persons. It provides that such failure is not jurisdictional and does not alone invalidate the later condemnation. Failure to meet the requirements of *public* notice in Section 202, however, is jurisdictional and, unless cured by proper publication, invalidates any later proceeding.[3]

Library References:

West's Key No. Digests, Eminent Domain ⚖️179–184.

§ 14.29 Conduct of the Public Hearing and Requirement of a Record

Section 203 of the Eminent Domain Procedure Law addresses the substantive requirements governing the holding of the public hearing. First, a representative of the condemnor must outline 1) the purpose of the public project for which the property is to be acquired; 2) the location (or alternative locations) selected for the project; and 3) any other information the condemnor deems pertinent, including maps of the subject property.

After this report is made, all persons present must be given a reasonable opportunity to make a statement, orally or in writing, and to

---

2. Legal Aid Soc. of Schenectady County, Inc. v. City of Schenectady, 78 A.D.2d 933, 433 N.Y.S.2d 234 (3d Dep't 1980) (notice in five successive issues begun ten days before the hearing met the statutory requirement and survived the due process challenge).

3. New Life Fellowship, Inc. v. City of Cortland, 175 A.D.2d 343, 572 N.Y.S.2d 421 (3d Dep't 1991) (the city had published

§ 14.29   EMINENT DOMAIN   Ch. 14

submit documents relevant to the proposed project.[1] Case law makes clear that these are not to be trial-type hearings subject to the rules of evidence.[2] If required, Section 203 expressly provides for further adjourned hearings. Additionally, the record may be kept open for further written comment.[3]

A record of the hearing is to be kept and is to be available for public viewing in the county clerk's office *and* in the principal office of the condemnor.[4]

Library References:
West's Key No. Digests, Eminent Domain ⚖198(1).

§ 14.30   Determination and Findings

Within ninety days of the conclusion of the public hearing mandated by Eminent Domain Procedure Law § 201, the condemnor must make its findings and determination regarding the proposed project.[1] The condemnor also must prepare a brief synopsis of its findings and determination, specifying:

1) the public use, benefit or purpose of the project;

2) the approximate location of the project and the reason for selection of that site;

3) the project's general effect on the environment and residents of the locality; and

4) other factors it deems relevant.[2]

The synopsis must also state that copies of the findings and determination will be forwarded, without cost, upon written request.[3]

Library References:
West's Key No. Digests, Eminent Domain ⚖198.

§ 14.31   Determination and Findings—Publication of Synopsis

Within ninety days of completion of the public hearing, the condemnor must also publish this synopsis in at least two successive issues of an

---

notice on only three dates in the local daily paper instead of the required five).

§ 14.29

1. Eminent Domain Procedure Law § 203.

2. Jackson v. New York State Urban Development Corp., 67 N.Y.2d 400, 503 N.Y.S.2d 298, 494 N.E.2d 429 (1986).

3. East Thirteenth Street Community Ass'n v. New York State Development Corp., 84 N.Y.2d 287, 617 N.Y.S.2d 706, 641 N.E.2d 1368, motion to amend denied 84 N.Y.2d 974, 622 N.Y.S.2d 903, 647 N.E.2d 108 (1994).

4. Eminent Domain Procedure Law § 203.

§ 14.30

1. Eminent Domain Procedure Law § 204(A).

2. Eminent Domain Procedure Law § 204(B).

3. Eminent Domain Procedure Law § 204(A).

official newspaper, if there is one in the locality.[1] If that newspaper is one of general circulation in the locality, no other publication is required. If the paper is not one of general circulation in the locality, then the synopsis must also appear in two successive issues of a newspaper of general circulation in the locality. Although the number of publications differs, the type of publication in which the synopsis must occur is identical to that required for public notice of the hearing.[2] It has been held that an owner whose property is to be taken is not statutorily or constitutionally entitled to personal service of the synopsis.[3]

Library References:

West's Key No. Digests, Eminent Domain ⟐198(1).

§ 14.32 Determination and Findings—Interplay With SEQRA

The State Environmental Quality Review Act, known as SEQRA, requires all state and local agencies to prepare environmental impact statements, consider alternative courses of action and mitigate environmental harm[1] before making decisions on projects. Since a valid exercise of the power of eminent domain under the Eminent Domain Procedure Law requires that the exercise be in furtherance of a public project, any taking under the Eminent Domain Procedure Law will be separately subject to SEQRA. Thus, the determination and findings must be made in accordance not only with the Eminent Domain Procedure Law but also with SEQRA.[2]

§ 14.33 Determination and Findings—Amendments for Field Conditions

If, after publishing its findings and determination, the condemnor concludes, solely on the basis of further study of field conditions, that the field conditions can only be accommodated by an amendment or alteration of the proposed project, the condemnor may make such an amendment or alteration without holding further public hearings.[1]

Library References:

West's Key No. Digests, Eminent Domain ⟐198(1).

§ 14.31

1. Eminent Domain Procedure Law § 204(A).
2. *See supra*, § 14.28.
3. DeVito v. City of Troy, 72 A.D.2d 866, 421 N.Y.S.2d 719 (3d Dep't 1979).

§ 14.32

1. ECL §§ 8–0101 *et seq.*
2. Matter of Hubbard v. Town of Sand Lake, 211 A.D.2d 1005, 622 N.Y.S.2d 126 (3d Dep't 1995) (determination and findings rejected on appeal on the ground that they were not made in accordance with SEQRA). On appealability issues regarding SEQRA compliance in the context of Article 2 hearings under the Eminent Domain Procedure Law, *see infra*, § 14.38.

§ 14.33

1. Eminent Domain Procedure Law § 205.

§ 14.34 Judicial Review of Determination and Findings

Judicial review of the determinations and findings required by Sections 204(A) & (B)[1] is governed by Sections 207 and 208 of the Eminent Domain Procedure Law. Section 207(A) gives the appellate division of the supreme court *exclusive* jurisdiction over requested judicial reviews of condemnors' determinations and findings under Article 2.[2] The appropriate department is that which embraces the county in which the property to be acquired, or any part of it, is located.[3] Section 207(B) further states that the review by the appellate division, and any subsequent review by the Court of Appeals, must be carried out as expeditiously as possible and with lawful preference over other matters before those courts.

Condemnees should be aware, however, that judicial review by the appellate division at this stage is exclusive *only* when the public hearing required by Section 204 has been held. If the condemnor determines that it is exempt from the public hearing requirement of Section 204, such a determination is not reviewable under Section 207.[4] Review of a claimed exemption under Section 206, when the State is the condemnor, may be sought in an Article 78 proceeding or by seeking injunctive relief in the supreme court.[5] When a non-State entity is the condemnor, review may be sought in an Article 78 proceeding[6] or in later proceedings in the eminent domain process.[7]

Library References:

West's Key No. Digests, Eminent Domain ⚖64–68.

§ 14.35 Judicial Review of Determination and Findings—Prerequisite Determination

The statutory right of judicial review granted by the Eminent Domain Procedure Law accrues only *after* the condemnor has completed

---

§ 14.34

1. Eminent Domain Procedure Law § 204; *see supra*, § 14.30.

2. Eminent Domain Procedure Law § 207(B). Incorporated Village of Patchogue v. Simon, 112 A.D.2d 374, 491 N.Y.S.2d 827 (2d Dep't), appeal denied 66 N.Y.2d 605, 499 N.Y.S.2d 1025, 489 N.E.2d 1302 (1985) (except for the Court of Appeals, no other court possesses jurisdiction in any controversy arising out of Eminent Domain Procedure Law Article 2 that was or could have been decided by appellate division under the Eminent Domain Procedure Law).

3. Eminent Domain Procedure Law § 207(A).

4. Piotrowski v. Town of Glenville, 101 A.D.2d 654, 475 N.Y.S.2d 511 (3d Dep't 1984); *see also*, City of Buffalo Urban Renewal Agency v. Moreton, 100 A.D.2d 20, 26, note 5, 473 N.Y.S.2d 278, 283 note 5 (4th Dep't 1984).

5. Because there is no acquisition proceeding necessary when the State is the condemnor (*see infra*, §§ 14.52–14.55), the condemnee must begin an action against the State in order to challenge the acquisition.

6. *Id. See also*, City of Schenectady v. Flacke, 100 A.D.2d 349, 475 N.Y.S.2d 506 (3d Dep't), app. denied 63 N.Y.2d 603, 480 N.Y.S.2d 1025, 469 N.E.2d 103 (1984).

7. *See, e.g.*, Rockland County Sewer Dist. No. 1 v. J & J Dodge, Inc., 213 A.D.2d 409, 635 N.Y.S.2d 233 (2d Dep't 1995).

the proceedings generally required by the earlier sections of Article 2 of the Eminent Domain Procedure Law, specifically, where required, the holding of a public hearing,[1] the making of findings and a determination[2] and the preparation and publication of a synopsis of the determination and findings.[3] Any challenge made prior to the completion of these requirements is premature.[4]

Library References:

West's Key No. Digests, Eminent Domain ⚖65–68.

§ 14.36 Judicial Review of Determination and Findings—Persons Entitled to Review

Section 207(A) entitles any person or persons, jointly or severally, to seek judicial review of a condemnor's determination and findings *if* that person (or persons) is aggrieved thereby. However, there are few cases in which the term "aggrieved" party is defined.[1]

The Court of Appeals addressed the question of whether non-condemnees, that is, persons whose properties are not to be taken, may be "aggrieved" persons in *East Thirteenth Street Community Ass'n v. New York State Urban Development Corp.*[2] In that case, condominium boards, tenants and residents of buildings near the property targeted for development of public housing sought review of the condemnation under Eminent Domain Procedure Law § 207. First, the court acknowledged that the Eminent Domain Procedure Law arguably changed the historical rule that only persons whose rights would actually be extinguished could challenge the taking, as Section 207 refers to "aggrieved parties" rather than "condemnees." Further, the court acknowledged that only in Article 2 are the interests of non-condemnees noted. Significant to the court, however, was the fact that the Legislature was concerned about creating an opportunity for litigation and delay through introduction of a public hearing component in eminent domain proceedings. Thus, the court, interpreting Article 2 and Section 207 as accomplishing the dual goals of public participation and expeditious exercise of eminent domain, held that "all that [non-condemnees] are entitled to under EDPL is a

---

§ 14.35

1. *See supra*, § 14.21.
2. *See supra*, § 14.30.
3. *See supra*, § 14.31.
4. Sun Co., Inc. (R & M) v. City of Syracuse Indus. Development Agency, 197 A.D.2d 912, 602 N.Y.S.2d 456 (4th Dep't 1993).

§ 14.36

1. *See, e.g.*, Vaccaro v. Jorling, 151 A.D.2d 34, 546 N.Y.S.2d 470 (3d Dep't), app. dismissed 75 N.Y.2d 946, 555 N.Y.S.2d 692, 554 N.E.2d 1280 (1990), app. denied 76 N.Y.2d 704, 559 N.Y.S.2d 983, 559 N.E.2d 677, cert. denied 498 U.S. 963, 111 S.Ct. 397, 112 L.Ed.2d 407 (1990) (life tenants with nonexclusive rights to hunt and fish were held not to be aggrieved by the State's proposed condemnation of a public access way where it would not deprive life tenants of any right or unreasonably interfere with their interests in that access).

2. 84 N.Y.2d 287, 617 N.Y.S.2d 706, 641 N.E.2d 1368, motion to amend denied 84 N.Y.2d 974, 622 N.Y.S.2d 903, 647 N.E.2d 108 (1994).

properly conducted hearing held on proper notice."[3] The right to seek judicial review of the condemnor's determination and findings was limited to those persons actually suffering an injury as a result of the exercise of the eminent domain power.

Library References:

West's Key No. Digests, Eminent Domain ⚖64.

§ 14.37 Judicial Review of Determination and Findings—30–Day Statute of Limitations

The aggrieved person or persons must file the petition seeking judicial review within thirty days after the condemnor's completion of the publication requirements discussed in Section 14.31.[1] This petition must be accompanied by proof of service of a demand upon the condemnor to file with the court a written transcript of the public hearing and a copy of its determination and findings.[2] Upon receipt of this demand, the condemnor must deliver to the court copies of the requested documents. The New York courts have regularly held that aggrieved parties who do not file the petition in a timely fashion may not resort to other procedural avenues to challenge the condemnor's determination and findings.[3] Thus, once the 30–day limitations period has passed, the issue of whether the use is a valid public one cannot be raised.

Library References:

West's Key No. Digests, Eminent Domain ⚖65.1, 174.

§ 14.38 Judicial Review of Determination and Findings—Scope of Review

Section 207(C) of the Eminent Domain Procedure Law mandates that the court either confirm or reject the condemnor's determination and findings.[1] In what is essentially a summary proceeding, the scope of review is limited to the following determinations: whether the proceed-

3. *Id.* at 295, 641 N.E.2d at 1375, 617 N.Y.S.2d at 711.

§ 14.37

1. Eminent Domain Procedure Law § 207(A).

2. *See infra*, §§ 14.121, for a form Demand on Condemnor to File Copy of Proceedings to Determine Need and Location of Public Project with Appellate Division for Purpose of Judicial Review and 14.122, for a form Petition for Review of Determination and Finding that Public Use, Benefit or Purpose Will be Served by Proposed Acquisition.

3. *See, e.g.*, City of New Rochelle v. O. Mueller, Inc., 191 A.D.2d 435, 594 N.Y.S.2d 301 (2d Dep't 1993) (condemnee barred from challenging determination and findings in a vesting procedure under Eminent Domain Procedure Law Article 4 (*see infra*, §§ 14.47–14.66)); Matter of Land for Farmington Access Road of the Town of Farmington, Ontario Co., 156 A.D.2d 936, 549 N.Y.S.2d 236 (4th Dep't 1989).

§ 14.38

1. *See infra*, § 14.123, for a form Judgment of Appellate Division Rejecting the Determination and Finding that Public Use, Benefit or Purpose Will be Served by Proposed Acquisition.

ings were constitutional; whether the proposed acquisition is within the condemnor's authority; whether the determination and findings were made pursuant to the procedure described in Article 2 of the Eminent Domain Procedure Law and in Article 8 of the Environmental Conservation Law;[2] and whether a public use, benefit or purpose will be served by the acquisition.[3] Only the final issue permits the court to inquire into the merits of the proposed acquisition. When this issue is raised, the condemnor must present to the court an "adequate basis" for its finding.[4] If a rational factual basis exists[5] for the condemnor's determination and findings on public use, benefit or purpose,[6] the condemnor's decision is to be confirmed, assuming the procedural requirements were followed.[7]

An example of a case in which a court reversed for failure to satisfy the procedural requirements of Article 2 is *Estate of Birnbaum v. White*.[8] In the *White* case, the condemnor, the Department of Transportation, held a public hearing with respect to one project that did *not* include a second project. The Department condemned property for the latter project without a public hearing thereon. The court held this taking to be improper and ordered that the Department discontinue the use until it had complied with Article 2.

Matters other than those listed in Section 207(C), such as the site of the acquisition,[9] are beyond review of a court unless there is evidence of bad faith or unreasonable arbitrariness in the condemnor's selection.[10] A mere allegation of bad faith, however, is insufficient.[11] The condemnee has the burden of proof on all of the above challenges.[12]

Section 207 was amended in 1991 to permit judicial review of compliance not only with requirements of the Eminent Domain Proce-

2. ECL Art. 8. The requirement of compliance with article 8 of the ECL was added in 1991.

3. Eminent Domain Procedure Law § 207(C). On the issue of what constitutes public use, benefit or purpose, *see supra*, § 14.15.

4. Jackson v. New York State Urban Development Corp., 67 N.Y.2d 400, 503 N.Y.S.2d 298, 494 N.E.2d 429 (1986).

5. Greenwich Associates v. Metropolitan Transp. Authority, 152 A.D.2d 216, 548 N.Y.S.2d 190 (1st Dep't 1989), appeal dismissed sub. nom. Regency–Lexington Partners v. Metropolitan Transp. Authority, 75 N.Y.2d 865, 552 N.Y.S.2d 930, 552 N.E.2d 178 (1990).

6. *See supra*, § 14.30.

7. Sunrise Properties, Inc. v. Jamestown Urban Renewal Agency, 206 A.D.2d 913, 614 N.Y.S.2d 841 (4th Dep't 1994), leave to app. denied 84 N.Y.2d 809, 621 N.Y.S.2d 518, 645 N.E.2d 1218 (1994); Long Island R. Co. v. Long Island Lighting Co., 103 A.D.2d 156, 479 N.Y.S.2d 355 (2d Dep't 1984), aff'd 64 N.Y.2d 1088, 489 N.Y.S.2d 881, 479 N.E.2d 226 (1985).

8. 136 A.D.2d 965, 525 N.Y.S.2d 82 (4th Dep't 1988).

9. Neptune Assoc. Inc. v. Consolidated Edison Co. of New York, Inc., 125 A.D.2d 473, 509 N.Y.S.2d 574 (2d Dep't 1986) ([t]he selection of a particular site is properly a matter for the condemning authority rather than the court).

10. Town of Coxsackie v. Dernier, 105 A.D.2d 966, 482 N.Y.S.2d 106 (3d Dep't 1984).

11. Waldo's Inc. v. Village of Johnson City, 74 N.Y.2d 718, 544 N.Y.S.2d 809, 543 N.E.2d 74 (1989).

12. Spears v. Berle, 48 N.Y.2d 254, 422 N.Y.S.2d 636, 397 N.E.2d 1304 (1979).

§ 14.38   EMINENT DOMAIN   Ch. 14

dure Law but also with those of SEQRA.[13] The reason for this amendment has been described by the Court of Appeals as follows:

> The purpose of incorporating SEQRA review into EDPL was to promote judicial efficiency in proceedings to acquire real property. Under the prior law ... a condemnee seeking review of SEQRA issues and eminent domain issues had to bring two separate proceedings ... and the Appellate Division could conceivably have been forced to review the same case twice, once on direct appeal from the condemnation determination and again upon appeal from article 78 review of the SEQRA challenge.[14]

The 1991 amendment permits both to be brought in the Eminent Domain Procedure Law proceeding. Potential litigants that want to challenge SEQRA findings must be aware that the Eminent Domain Procedure Law expedited review may not be available to them, however. Eminent Domain Procedure Law review under Section 207 can be sought only by "aggrieved" persons.[15] Only those with standing under the Eminent Domain Procedure Law may seek Section 207 review, and they are thus the only persons who can raise the SEQRA challenge through that avenue.[16] The merits of all other challenges to SEQRA must be brought in article 78 or other appropriate proceedings.[17]

Library References:

West's Key No. Digests, Eminent Domain ⚖︎67, 68.

§ 14.39   Summary

As noted in the preceding sections, Article 2's public hearing and synopsis requirements essentially keep condemnees' attorneys on the sidelines until they are completed. Condemnors' attorneys must be actively involved in making certain that all procedural requirements are met, as failure to meet these requirements will give condemnees their only meaningful opportunity for success at the appellate division. For the same reason, condemnees' attorneys must carefully review the condemnor's procedural compliance with the Eminent Domain Procedure Law. The procedural checklist in Section 14.119 should assist counsel on both sides in evaluating procedural compliance.

If the condemnor decides to take advantage of an available exception to Eminent Domain Procedure Law's Article 2 procedures, the condemnee may bring an Article 78 proceeding or prayer for injunctive relief to challenge the condemnor's decision or, if the condemnor is a non-State

---

13. *See supra,* § 14.32.
14. East Thirteenth Street Community Ass'n v. New York State Urban Development Corp., 84 N.Y.2d 287, 297, 617 N.Y.S.2d 706, 710, 641 N.E.2d 1368, 1372, motion to amend denied 84 N.Y.2d 974, 622 N.Y.S.2d 903, 647 N.E.2d 108 (1994).
15. *See supra,* § 14.36.
16. East Thirteenth Street Community Ass'n, *supra* note 14.
17. *Id.*

entity, the condemnee may wait until the acquisition stage of the condemnation process to raise the issue.[1]

§ 14.40 The Second Stage—The "Offer and Negotiation" Phase

The second stage of the eminent domain process ideally is the final one. The Eminent Domain Procedure Law establishes a general policy requiring that the condemnor at all stages of acquisition by eminent domain "make every reasonable and expeditious effort to justly compensate" persons for their real property by means of negotiation and agreement.[1] This requirement is in furtherance of one of the Eminent Domain Procedure Law's purposes, "to encourage settlement of claims for just compensation and expedite payments to property owners...."[2]

Library References:

West's Key No. Digests, Eminent Domain ⚖︎170.

§ 14.41 The Second Stage—The "Offer and Negotiation" Phase—Pretaking Appraisals

As part of Eminent Domain Procedure Law § 301's general obligation to provide just compensation, the condemnor is required to have an appraisal made of the property to be acquired.[1]

Library References:

West's Key No. Digests, Eminent Domain ⚖︎170.

§ 14.42 The Second Stage—The "Offer and Negotiation" Phase—Pretaking Discovery

In order to prepare this appraisal adequately, the condemnor is given the statutory right to inspect the property and, upon reasonable written notice, the owner and those in occupation of the land may be required to provide pertinent information to aid in preparation of the appraisal. If the recipient of a request for such information believes the request to be unreasonable or burdensome, a petition for relief may be made to a court of competent jurisdiction.[1] If the owner fails to comply with such a request, the condemnor's obligation to make an offer is suspended until compliance.

§ 14.39
1. See infra, §§ 14.56–14.65.

§ 14.40
1. Eminent Domain Procedure Law § 301.
2. Eminent Domain Procedure Law § 101.

§ 14.41
1. Eminent Domain Procedure Law § 302.

§ 14.42
1. Eminent Domain Procedure Law § 302.

Library References:

West's Key No. Digests, Eminent Domain ⊜170.

§ 14.43 The Second Stage—The "Offer and Negotiation" Phase—Offer as Payment in Full

Eminent Domain Procedure Law § 302 requires the condemnor to establish a monetary amount that it believes to be just compensation for the property targeted for taking. This amount must be no less than the condemnor's highest approved appraisal. The condemnor must then make a written offer to acquire the property for 100% of such highest appraised value. The offer is to include, if practicable, an itemization of the total direct cost and the total severance or consequential damages and benefits. Failure of the condemnor to make this offer prior to the beginning of the condemnation proceeding may result in an award of costs to the condemnees.[1] Additionally, if an offer is not accepted as full payment by the condemnee, and such amount later proves to be significantly lower than the court's compensation award, the condemnor may be subject to liability for part or all of the condemnee's costs.[2]

Eminent Domain Procedure Law § 304(A) governs the condemnee's options with respect to the written offer, and it requires these options to be disclosed, as follows. First, the offer must state that it constitutes the condemnor's highest approved appraisal and that payment will be made with appropriate interest.[3] Second, the offer must state that the condemnee may accept the offer as payment in full.[4] Third, the offer must state that the condemnee may reject the offer as payment in full and elect to treat the offered amount as an advance payment.[5]

§ 14.44 The Second Stage—The "Offer and Negotiation" Phase—Advance Payment

As noted above, the condemnee has the option to reject the condemnor's offer and treat it as an advance payment. Thus, exercising this option does not affect the condemnee's right to seek further compensation. However, in making this election, the condemnee must comply with Eminent Domain Procedure Law § 503(A)[1] by filing the claim for further

---

§ 14.43

1. Roseton Hills Sewage–Works Corp. v. Leitman, 69 A.D.2d 834, 414 N.Y.S.2d 928 (2d Dep't 1979).

2. Eminent Domain Procedure Law § 701; *see infra*, § 14.115.

PRACTICE POINTER: The condemnor's attorney should stress the possibility of an award of costs at this stage of the proceedings. Courts have shown no reluctance to award very high reasonable attorney's and appraiser's fees when the court's award is significantly higher than the condemnor's offer. *See infra*, § 14.115.

3. Eminent Domain Procedure Law § 304(A)(1).

4. Eminent Domain Procedure Law § 304(A)(2).

5. Eminent Domain Procedure Law § 304(A)(3).

§ 14.44

1. *See supra*, §§ 14.71, 14.74.

compensation in a timely manner, or the advance payment will be treated as full payment.

If, in the subsequent proceeding, the court awards the condemnee *less* than the amount of the advance payment, the condemnor may move for judgment in the amount of the excess plus interest.[2] This possibility, of course, operates as an incentive to the condemnee to accept the offer as full payment. If, however, the condemnee is successful in winning a significantly *higher* amount in the judicial award than that offered by the condemnor, the condemnee may be entitled to an award of costs, including attorney's fees.[3]

If the condemnee accepts the condemnor's offer, either as full or advance payment, the two parties will then enter into an agreement providing for such payment.[4] However, even if such an agreement is reached, the State may withhold payment to the extent it claims a set-off based on monies owed by the condemnee to the State.[5] This is true even where, as will usually be the case, the debt owed bears no relationship to the property taken. The claimed set-off, however, must be a fixed debt owed to the State, not one that is "contingent, possible or *in futuro*."[6]

Eminent Domain Procedure Law § 304, Subpart B, sets out the consequences should the condemnee fail to respond to the offer within ninety days. Such a failure to respond will result in the offer being treated as rejected. Whether rejection of the offer is express or inferred, however, the condemnor will not be required to pay interest on the amount of the offer until such time as the condemnee accepts the offer, either in full or as an advance payment.[7]

Subparts D & E of Eminent Domain Procedure Law § 304 set forth detailed procedures for the deposit of a payment when there is some question as to who is entitled to it.[8]

Where there is a lien against the property acquired, the liens are extinguished on the property, but preserved as liens against the sum to be paid.[9]

Library References;

West's Key No. Digests, Eminent Domain ⬄ 159–165.

2. Eminent Domain Procedure Law § 304(H); Johnson v. State, 72 A.D.2d 487, 426 N.Y.S.2d 98 (3d Dep't 1980).

3. *See infra*, § 14.110.

4. Eminent Domain Procedure Law § 304(A)(4).

5. 3 Lafayette Ave. Corp. v. Comptroller of State of N.Y., 186 A.D.2d 301, 587 N.Y.S.2d 456 (3d Dep't 1992), leave to app. denied 81 N.Y.2d 705, 595 N.Y.S.2d 400, 611 N.E.2d 301, rearg. denied 82 N.Y.2d 706, 601 N.Y.S.2d 586, 619 N.E.2d 664 (1993).

6. Fehlhaber Corp. v. O'Hara, 53 A.D.2d 746, 747, 384 N.Y.S.2d 270, 272 (3d Dep't 1976).

7. Eminent Domain Procedure Law § 304(C).

PRACTICE POINTER: The condemnee's attorney should therefore explain that the condemnee does not gain anything, and in fact loses the value of interest by failing to respond to the offer.

8. Eminent Domain Procedure Law § 304(D), (E); *see infra*, § 14.100.

9. City of Syracuse v. State, 121 Misc.2d 8, 467 N.Y.S.2d 159 (Ct.Cl.1983).

§ 14.45 Use and Occupancy by Condemnee After Taking

If the condemnee or other occupant of the acquired property stays in possession after the date of acquisition by the condemnor, whether the acquisition is by purchase or by Eminent Domain Procedure Law processes later described,[1] he or she is statutorily liable to the condemnor for the fair and reasonable value of such possession.[2] This amount must be paid at reasonable intervals, and, if not paid, it may be set off against any amount owed by the condemnor.[3] If the condemnee objects to the rental value set by the condemnor, the condemnee can bring an action before a court of competent jurisdiction to set a proper value.[4]

The preceding rule does not apply to a condemnee who is in possession of his or her *residence* that is condemned. A condemnee in possession of a residence has ninety days before such liability accrues.[5]

Library References:

West's Key No. Digests, Eminent Domain ⚖187.

§ 14.46 Summary

There is very little law that governs this stage of condemnation proceedings, but as failure to meet the few governing rules may result in a financial price being paid by the violator, whether condemnor or condemnee, counsel must clearly explain the legal duties and practical options that will occur in this part of the process. For a condemnor's attorney, this essentially means that the condemnor must understand that what is required is a good faith offer.[1] Failure to offer a price that is later deemed to be insufficient may result in liability of the condemnor for major expenses incurred by the condemnee.[2]

The major role of the condemnee's attorney is to explain the condemnee's statutory options and their consequences, as follows:

1) The client may accept the condemnor's offer as full payment for the condemned property.[3] If the offer is accepted, the eminent domain process will be over aside from the execution of documents.

---

§ 14.45

1. *See infra*, §§ 14.47–14.68.
2. Eminent Domain Procedure Law § 305(A), (C).
3. Eminent Domain Procedure Law § 305(B).
4. *See infra*, § 14.123, for a form Complaint by Condemnee to Establish Fair and Reasonable Value for Temporary Use and Occupancy After Acquisition by Eminent Domain.
5. *Id.* If the condemnee ceases to use the property for residential purposes, but is otherwise in possession, liability commences with the cessation of residential use, even if it occurs before the 90-day grace period has expired.

§ 14.46

1. *See supra*, § 14.43.
2. *Id.*
3. *Id.*

2) The client may accept the offer as an advance payment.[4] The client will then remain free to seek further compensation in a later stage of the proceeding, but if the client does so and the court awards less than the advance payment, the client may have to return the difference. If the award is significantly higher than the offer, the client will recover the higher value and may also recover the cost of litigation.

3) The client may reject the offer,[5] which will not prevent acquisition of the client's property. If a compensation award is significantly higher than the offer, the client may recover the cost of litigation in addition to the award. Unlike option #2, however, the condemnor will not be required to pay interest on the amount offered between the time of the offer and the payment of the award.

§ 14.47 The Third Stage—The Acquisition Phase

The third stage of the eminent domain process is reached only if the second stage—offer and negotiation[1]—does not result in a purchase of the property by the condemnor. If a voluntary purchase cannot be negotiated, the condemnor must then acquire title from the condemnee through the processes set forth in Article 4 of the Eminent Domain Procedure Law. The nature of the process and procedures that must be followed by the condemnor depend on whether the condemnor is the State or another entity entitled to exercise the power of eminent domain.[2]

Library References:

West's Key No. Digests, Eminent Domain ⟶166–198.

§ 14.48 The Third Stage—The Acquisition Phase—Court of Claims v. Supreme Court Jurisdiction

Whether the Court of Claims or supreme court has jurisdiction over the acquisition phase of an eminent domain proceeding turns on the identity of the *condemnor*. Any issue regarding acquisition of property by the State of New York or one of its agencies is within the exclusive jurisdiction of the Court of Claims.[1] All other acquisition proceedings are within the exclusive jurisdiction of the supreme court in the judicial district where the real property is located. All such proceedings, whether

4. *See supra*, § 14.44.
5. *Id.*

§ 14.47
1. *See supra*, §§ 14.40–14.44.
2. *See infra*, § 14.48.

§ 14.48
1. Eminent Domain Procedure Law § 401(A).

§ 14.48   EMINENT DOMAIN   Ch. 14

in supreme court or the Court of Claims, are held without a jury and without referral to a referee or commissioner.[2]

Library References:

West's Key No. Digests, Eminent Domain ⬅172.

§ 14.49   The Third Stage—The Acquisition Phase—Statute of Limitations for Bringing an Acquisition Proceeding

Section 401(A) of the Eminent Domain Procedure Law provides the time period within which a condemnor must commence proceedings to acquire property for a proposed public project—three years from the conclusion of the latest of three events: publication of the condemnor's determination and findings;[1] if the condemnor relies on one of the exemptions from the Eminent Domain Procedure Law's hearing requirements,[2] the date of completion of the substituted procedure; or, if judicial review is sought, the date of entry of the final order or judgment.[3]

The proposed project is deemed abandoned if the relevant deadline is not met. The condemnor must begin the condemnation process, from stage one as described earlier,[4] again. There is one exception to this bar, however, as described in Section 14.50.

If a timely acquisition proceeding is commenced, and field conditions require the acquisition of additional property after the three-year period has expired, such additional property must be acquired "as soon as practicable."[5]

Library References:

West's Key No. Digests, Eminent Domain ⬅174.

§ 14.50   The Third Stage—The Acquisition Phase—Statute of Limitations for Bringing an Acquisition Proceeding—Acquisition in Stages

The rule governing the time within which the condemnation proceeding must be commenced when the acquisition is to be done in stages is straightforward. If the entire project either requires a public hearing or is properly exempt from it,[1] the rules outlined in Section 14.49 apply to the *first* stage of the acquisition only. The acquisition proceedings for

---

2. Eminent Domain Procedure Law § 402(B).

§ 14.49
1. See supra, § 14.31.
2. See supra, §§ 14.22–14.27.
3. See supra, § 14.34.

4. See supra, §§ 14.20–14.39.
5. Eminent Domain Procedure Law § 401(D).

§ 14.50
1. See supra, § 14.21–14.27.

all later stages must be brought within *ten* years of the latest of the events outlined in Section 14.49.[2]

Library References:

West's Key No. Digests, Eminent Domain ⚖︎166.

§ 14.51 The Third Stage—The Acquisition Phase—Acquisition Map

As described in detail in Sections 14.55 and 14.65 below, whether the State itself is the condemnor, or some other entity is the condemnor, the ultimate vesting of title in the condemnor under Article 4 of the Eminent Domain Procedure Law is coincident with the proper filing of an acquisition map. The map must cover all of the real property deemed necessary for the proposed project, indicating *and* describing the particular easement, interest and right to be taken, and including metes and bounds descriptions or section, block and lot numbers.[1]

Library References:

West's Key No. Digests, Eminent Domain ⚖︎186.

§ 14.52 Acquisition of Property—Court of Claims Jurisdiction

Section 402(A) of the Eminent Domain Procedure Law sets forth the procedure for acquiring property that is subject to the jurisdiction of the Court of Claims. This procedure, especially when compared with the acquisition procedure in supreme court,[1] is relatively simple, imposing only filing and notice requirements.

Library References:

West's Key No. Digests, Eminent Domain ⚖︎172.

§ 14.53 Acquisition of Property—Court of Claims Jurisdiction—Condemnors Subject to Court of Claims Jurisdiction

As noted in Section 14.55, the Court of Claims has exclusive jurisdiction when the condemnor is the State of New York or one of its agencies or departments.[1]

2. Eminent Domain Procedure Law § 402(C).

§ 14.51

1. Eminent Domain Procedure Law § 402(A)(1).

§ 14.52

1. *See infra*, §§ 14.56–14.68.

§ 14.53

1. Eminent Domain Procedure Law § 402(A).

§ 14.54 Acquisition of Property—Court of Claims Jurisdiction—Filing and Notice Requirement

When the State or one of its agencies or departments is the condemnor, the acquisition map is required to be filed in three separate sites. Section 402(A)(1) requires that the original tracing of the map, or a microfilm copy thereof, be filed in the main office of the condemning agency. Eminent Domain Procedure Law § 402(A)(2) requires that a certified copy be filed with the Department of State. When this filing is made, the State must notify condemnees by first-class mail that the condemnor is taking steps to acquire their property.[1] After this notice has been issued, the State, through its officer and agents, may enter the described premises and take possession thereof for any purpose connected with the proposed project.

The third filing must be made in the office of the county clerk of the county in which the property is located.[2]

Library References:

West's Key No. Digests, Eminent Domain ⚖174–194.

§ 14.55 Acquisition of Property—Court of Claims Jurisdiction—Vesting of Title

When the filings and notice requirements described in Section 14.54 have been satisfied, the State's acquisition is deemed complete. Title is then fully vested in the State.[1] The State, as condemnor, cannot then change its mind with respect to the acquisition and the obligation to pay just compensation that flows from it.[2]

It should be noted that this process occurs without court involvement of any kind. No court is required to approve the acquisition, and the State is not required to inform a court of the actions. The Court of Claims enters the picture only when a condemnee challenges the State or makes a monetary claim against it.[3]

§ 14.54

1. If the State fails to give this notice, the condemnee may recover additional money damages for the appropriation. Patten v. State, 99 A.D.2d 922, 473 N.Y.S.2d 47 (3d Dep't 1984), app. denied 63 N.Y.2d 605, 480 N.Y.S.2d 1027, 469 N.E.2d 532 (1984).

2. Eminent Domain Procedure Law § 402(A)(3). This filing is required to be a certified copy of the acquisition map.

§ 14.55

1. Eminent Domain Procedure Law § 402(3).

2. Voorhis v. State, 107 Misc.2d 956, 436 N.Y.S.2d 187 (Ct.Cl.1981).

3. *See infra*, § 14.70.

§ 14.56 Acquisition of Property—Supreme Court Jurisdiction

Eminent Domain Procedure Law § 402(B) governs acquisition proceedings by condemnors other than the State of New York. Unlike exercises of eminent domain by the State, in which the court is not initially involved,[1] all other acquisitions are accomplished only through court proceedings. The first step in the acquisition proceeding when the condemnor is an entity other than the State is the filing of a verified petition in the supreme court in the district in which the property, or any part thereof, is located, requesting an order to acquire the property and for permission to file a map.[2]

Library References:

West's Key No. Digests, Eminent Domain ⚖︎172.

§ 14.57 Acquisition of Property—Supreme Court Jurisdiction—Notice of Pendency

The condemnor must file a notice of the pendency of the acquisition proceeding in the office of the county clerk of the county where the property is located.[1] This notice of pendency should be filed at the same time the petition and notice of petition are filed.[2] The notice of pendency must 1) briefly state the object of the proceeding; 2) include a description either by metes and bounds or by section, block and lot number of the real property to be acquired; and 3) state the names of the reputed condemnees, as may be known.[3] If condemnees are unknown, the notice must so state.

Library References:

West's Key No. Digests, Eminent Domain ⚖︎1–26.

§ 14.58 Acquisition of Property—Supreme Court Jurisdiction—Petition in Condemnation

Eminent Domain Procedure Law § 402(B)(3) requires the condemnor to present to the court a petition verified by an authorized official of the condemnor.

---

§ 14.56

1. See supra, § 14.52–14.55.
2. Eminent Domain Procedure Law § 402(B).

§ 14.57

1. Eminent Domain Procedure Law § 402(B)(1).
2. Op. Atty Gen. (Inf.) (June 25, 1981).
3. See infra, § 14.124, for a form Notice of Pendency of Proceeding in Supreme Court to Acquire Property by Eminent Domain and File Acquisition Map.

Library References:

West's Key No. Digests, Eminent Domain ⚖︎191.

§ 14.59 Acquisition of Property—Supreme Court Jurisdiction—Petition in Condemnation—Content

The petition required to be filed by the condemnor must set forth:

1) a statement that Article 2's public hearing[1] and synopsis publication requirements[2] have been met, complete with a copy of the condemnor's determination and findings.[3] (If the condemnor claims an exemption from Article 2,[4] the basis for that exemption must be set forth);

2) a copy of the proposed acquisition map;

3) the names and places of residence of the condemnees;

4) a description[5] of the real property to be acquired;

5) the public use, benefit or purpose for which the property is being acquired;

6) a request that the court authorize by order the filing of the acquisition map and that, after such filing, the title vest in the condemnor.[6]

Library References:

West's Key No. Digests, Eminent Domain ⚖︎191.

§ 14.60 Acquisition of Property—Supreme Court Jurisdiction—Petition in Condemnation—Additional Content Rules for Certain Non-governmental Condemnors

Non-governmental condemnors subject to the jurisdiction of the Public Service Commission or the Department of Transportation must meet additional requirements with respect to the contents of the petition. Such a condemnor must include in the petition a statement that it

§ 14.59

1. See supra, § 14.21.
2. See supra, § 14.31.
3. See supra, § 14.30.
4. See supra, §§ 14.22–14.27.
5. This description must be by metes and bounds or by section, block and lot number, and it must be referenced to the acquisition map and notice of pendency. Eminent Domain Procedure Law § 402(B)(3)(c). It has been held that the description in the petition must be precise, and the property must be ascertainable from the petition itself without recourse to extrinsic evidence. Town of Webb v. Sisters Realty North Corp., 168 A.D.2d 896, 566 N.Y.S.2d 109 (4th Dep't 1990).

6. See infra, §§ 14.126, for a form Petition in Proceeding in Supreme Court to Acquire Property by Eminent Domain and File Acquisition Map and 14.127, for a form Petition in Proceeding in Supreme Court to Acquire Property by Eminent Domain and File Acquisition Map—Petitioner Exempt from Compliance with Eminent Domain Procedure Law Article 2.

will deposit a bond or undertaking with the clerk, prior to the acquisition, in an amount to be fixed by the court. This bond or undertaking will be applied, as necessary, to pay all or part of damages determined in the acquisition proceeding, if the condemnor should default in payment of these damages.[1] This bond or undertaking is not, however, an "advance payment" to which the condemnee has an automatic right.[2] The parties may, by stipulation, waive this requirement.

If the amount of the bond or undertaking is insufficient to pay the damages, costs, and expenses awarded to a condemnee, judgment will be entered against the condemnor for the deficiency.[3]

Library References:

West's Key No. Digests, Eminent Domain ⚖=191.

§ 14.61 Acquisition of Property—Supreme Court Jurisdiction—Notice

At least twenty days before the return date of the petition, the condemnor must serve a notice of the time, place and object of the proceeding upon the owner of record of the property to be acquired.[1] Service may be accomplished through methods authorized by the CPLR or by registered or certified mail, return receipt requested. If the condemnor chooses to serve by mail, it must send the notice to the last known address of the owner *and* meet the complicated publication requirements of Eminent Domain Procedure Law § 402(B)(2).

These requirements parallel those imposed at the pre-acquisition public hearing stage.[2] Thus, what must be published is a copy of a diagram or representation of the acquisition map, showing the perimeters of the property to be acquired and a proper description.[3]

This information must be published in at least ten successive issues of an official newspaper, if one is designated in the locality, and at least ten successive issues of a newspaper of general circulation.[4] If the only newspaper in the locality is a weekly one, publication must appear in a minimum of three successive issues.

§ 14.60

1. Eminent Domain Procedure Law § 402(B)(3)(f).

2. New York State Elec. & Gas Corp. v. Karas, 119 Misc.2d 373, 463 N.Y.S.2d 138 (Sup.Ct., Sullivan County, 1983).

3. *Id.* This judgment is to be enforced and collected in the same manner as an ordinary judgment of the supreme court.

§ 14.61

1. Eminent Domain Procedure Law § 402(B)(2); *see infra*, § 14.125, for a form Notice of Petition in Proceeding in Supreme Court to Acquire Property by Eminent Domain and File Acquisition Map.

2. *See supra*, § 14.28.

3. This description is to be by metes and bounds or by section, block and lot number.

4. If the official newspaper is one of general circulation, this will suffice without publication in any other newspaper of general circulation. Eminent Domain Procedure Law § 402(B)(2)(a).

§ 14.61 EMINENT DOMAIN Ch. 14

If practicable, the condemnor must also post copies of such notice, in the form of handbills, for the same period of time in at least three conspicuous places on or near the property.[5]

Library References:

West's Key No. Digests, Eminent Domain ⚖︎179–184.

§ 14.62 Acquisition of Property—Supreme Court Jurisdiction—Notice—Certification of Names of Reputed Condemnees

Eminent Domain Procedure Law § 403 requires the condemnor to deliver to its appropriate legal officer and attorney[1] a copy of the acquisition map. The officer or attorney is then required to certify to the condemnor the names of the reputed condemnees of the property to be acquired.

Library References:

West's Key No. Digests, Eminent Domain ⚖︎181.

§ 14.63 Acquisition of Property—Supreme Court Jurisdiction—Answer by Condemnee

A condemnee is entitled to appear in the supreme court and interpose a verified answer.[1] The answer must contain specific denials of each material allegation in the petition controverted by the condemnee, or any knowledge or information of the condemnee sufficient to form a belief with respect to a material allegation, or a statement of a new matter that would constitute a defense to the proceeding.

Library References:

West's Key No. Digests, Eminent Domain ⚖︎192.

§ 14.64 Acquisition of Property—Supreme Court Jurisdiction—Answer by Condemnee—Defenses

It is easiest to begin a discussion of defenses available to a condemnee challenging an acquisition with the one issue that cannot be raised. As previously noted in Sections 14.35 and 14.38, the sole venue for appeal of issues arising out of the public hearing on the proposed

---

5. Eminent Domain Procedure Law § 402(B)(2)(b).

§ 14.62

1. If the State itself is the condemnor, that officer is the State Attorney General.

§ 14.63

1. Eminent Domain Procedure Law § 402(B)(4); see infra, § 14.128, for a form Answer to Petition in Proceeding in Supreme Court to Acquire Property by Eminent Domain and File Acquisition Map.

project, and the findings and determinations made under Article 2,[1] is the appellate division. A condemnee cannot raise challenges to the public project itself or to the findings and determination of the condemnor as a defense to the condemnation.[2] Significantly, however, if the condemnor did not hold a public hearing, claiming instead to be exempt from this requirement,[3] that fact must be set forth by the condemnor in its petition, and the condemnee may challenge the availability of the exemption.[4]

For the most part, the defenses available to condemnees are challenges to the procedures followed by the condemnor. Thus, the condemnee may challenge the adequacy of notice, the sufficiency of the petition, or the failure of the condemnor to negotiate or offer a fair price for the property.[5] One substantive defense that *is* available, focusing on what the condemnor is trying to do as opposed to how the condemnor is going about doing it, is a challenge to the *amount* of property being taken, with the condemnee alleging that the proposed taking is in excess of that necessitated by the public project.[6]

Library References:

West's Key No. Digests, Eminent Domain ⚖171, 192.

§ 14.65 Acquisition of Property—Supreme Court Jurisdiction—Vesting of Title and Order of Condemnation

Eminent Domain Procedure Law § 402(B)(5) governs the vesting of title in condemnation proceedings in the supreme court. Vesting occurs, as a matter of law, after the condemnor has:

- provided due proof of service of notice;
- filed the petition; and
- proved to the court's satisfaction that the procedural requirements of the Eminent Domain Procedure Law have been met.

§ 14.64

1. *See supra*, § 14.30; Metropolitan Transp. Authority v. Pinelawn Cemetery, 135 A.D.2d 686, 522 N.Y.S.2d 586 (2d Dep't 1987).

2. City of New Rochelle v. O. Mueller, Inc., 191 A.D.2d 435, 594 N.Y.S.2d 301 (2d Dep't 1993).

3. *See supra*, §§ 14.22–14.27.

4. Town of Coxsackie v. Dernier, 105 A.D.2d 966, 482 N.Y.S.2d 106 (3d Dep't 1984); City of Buffalo Urban Renewal Agency v. Moreton, 100 A.D.2d 20, 473 N.Y.S.2d 278 (4th Dep't 1984).

5. These challenges often fail. *See e.g.*, In re Consolidated Edison of New York, Inc., 143 A.D.2d 1012, 533 N.Y.S.2d 591 (2d Dep't 1988), resettlement denied 538 N.Y.S.2d 491 (2d Dep't 1989) (the court denied the condemnee's application to amend its answer to interpose the defense that the condemnor failed to bargain in good faith prior to the public hearing, since Eminent Domain Procedure Law does not require bargaining before the hearing).

6. Uah–Braendly Hydro Assocs. v. RKDK Assoc., 138 A.D.2d 493, 526 N.Y.S.2d 122 (2d Dep't 1988) (the trial court erred in dismissing the condemnee's affirmative defense that the property proposed to be acquired was greater than the project area described in the condemnor's license).

§ 14.65 EMINENT DOMAIN Ch. 14

When the condemnor has done so, the court must direct the immediate filing and entry of the order granting the petition.[1] The condemnor then must file and enter the order, together with the acquisition map (and bond if required),[2] in the county clerk's office in the county in which the real property is located. When this filing is completed, title to the property vests in the condemnor.

Library References:

West's Key No. Digests, Eminent Domain ⚬⇒320.

§ 14.66 Notice of Acquisition

The Eminent Domain Procedure Law mandates that, upon vesting of title in the condemnor, a "notice of acquisition" must be given to all condemnees, certified as required by Section 403.[1]

When the State is the condemnor, it is required to serve the notice of acquisition and a copy of the portion of the acquisition map relevant to the recipient upon each condemnee within ninety days of filing of the acquisition map.[2] Proof of service of the notice must then be filed in the office of the county clerk. The clerk then will record the notice in the book of deeds, with the condemnees listed as grantors in the appropriate index. This creates record title in the State. If a condemnee cannot, through reasonable effort, be served in the State, the condemnor will file the acquisition map and notice of acquisition in the county clerk's office,[3] along with a certificate stating that personal service could not be made after a reasonable effort to do so. The clerk then will record the notice and certificate and will index them under the condemnees' names in the grantor index.[4] This recording is presumptive evidence of service.

When the condemnor is not the State, the condemnor must serve the notice of acquisition on each condemnee or attorney of record within thirty days of the entry of the order granting the condemnor's petition to vest title. Alternatively, the condemnor may publish the notice of acquisition[5] and mail a copy to each condemnee or attorney of record.

§ 14.65

1. See infra, §§ 14.130, for a form Order to Show Cause Why Condemnor Should Not be Permitted to File Acquisition Maps or Enter upon Real Property and 14.131, for a form Order in Proceeding in Supreme Court to Acquire Property by Eminent Domain and File Acquisition Map; City of Buffalo Urban Renewal Agency v. Moreton, 100 A.D.2d 20, 473 N.Y.S.2d 278 (4th Dep't 1984) (the trial court must grant the petition if it finds that all procedural rules have been met).

2. See supra, § 14.60.

§ 14.66

1. See supra, § 14.62 and infra, § 14.132, for a form Notice of Acquisition by Eminent Domain Where Supreme Court Has Jurisdiction.

2. Eminent Domain Procedure Law § 502(A)(1).

3. Eminent Domain Procedure Law § 502(A)(2).

4. Eminent Domain Procedure Law § 502(A)(3).

5. Eminent Domain Procedure Law § 502(B). The publication requirements parallel those described in § 14.28, supra.

The notice of acquisition must contain:

- a general description of the acquired property;
- the date of entry of the vesting order;
- a statement that the acquisition map has been filed; and
- identification of the office where the order and map are filed.

The notice must also direct condemnees to file, before a date therein specified,[6] a claim or notice of appearance with the clerk of the court where the property is located and with the condemnor.

Library References:

West's Key No. Digests, Eminent Domain ⚖ 179–184.

§ 14.67 Immediate Entry

Eminent Domain Procedure Law § 402(B)(6) provides an expedited procedure to permit a condemnor to have almost immediate entry onto the property sought to be acquired. The statute provides that, at any stage in the acquisition proceeding, the judge may, if satisfied that the public interest will be prejudiced by delay, direct that the condemnor be permitted to enter the property immediately in order to devote it temporarily to the public use specified in the petition.[1] This right may be exercised, however, only after the condemnor has deposited with the court a sum fixed by the court and has given not less than eight days notice of the action to the parties.

The money deposited with the court will be applied as necessary to the payment of any award to the condemnee, including interest from the date of entry by the condemnor, and costs and expenses of the proceeding. Any remaining funds will be returned to the condemnor. If the acquisition proceeding is abandoned by the condemnor, or the petition is later dismissed, or it is determined that the condemnee is entitled to no award for the taking, the court may nonetheless award the condemnee damages, to be paid from the deposited sum, for entry upon and use of his or her property, as well as costs and expenses. If the sum is insufficient to cover such damages and costs and expenses, a judgment for the deficiency will be entered against the condemnor, with such judgment having the same force and effect as other supreme court judgments.

In addition to the right of entry authorized by Section 402(B)(6), the Eminent Domain Procedure Law gives condemnors and their agents and contractors the right to enter upon property to make surveys, to test

---

6. See infra, §§ 14.71, 14.74.

§ 14.67

1. See infra, § 14.130, for a form Order to Show Cause Why Condemnor Should Not be Permitted to Enter Immediately upon Real Property and Devote It Temporarily to Public Use Specified in Petition Upon Deposit of a Fixed Sum with the Court.

§ 14.67 EMINENT DOMAIN Ch. 14

wells and borings, and to make other investigations, as well as for temporary occupancy during construction.[2] Reasonable advance notice must be given to the property owner, explaining the need for the entry. The condemnor will be held liable for any damage caused as a result of the entry. The court may require the condemnor to post a bond to cover any such damages.[3]

Library References:

West's Key No. Digests, Eminent Domain ⚖︎187.

§ 14.68 Summary

If the condemnor's attorney represents the State, this stage is remarkably easy. First, the attorney must keep an eye on the three-year statute of limitations.[1] Since a public project ordinarily will be on a quicker timetable, this will rarely be a problem. Second, the attorney should review the acquisition map to ensure that it properly identifies and describes the property to be taken.[2] Third, the attorney should oversee compliance with the three filing requirements (main office of condemnor, Department of State, county clerk's office) and the notice requirement (first-class mail to condemnees).[3] Finally, "notice of acquisition" requirements must be met.[4] This notice and the acquisition map must be served upon each condemnee within ninety days and must be duly recorded. With that, the State condemnor's attorney's role in this stage is complete.

The non-State condemnor's attorney has many more procedural rules with which to comply. Again, the three-year statute of limitations must be watched. The attorney must prepare and file a notice of pendency,[5] a petition, and a notice of petition,[6] making sure that the substantive requirements for these documents are satisfied. Notice, and, if relevant, publication requirements must be met.[7] Assuming that the condemnor has complied with all of the Eminent Domain Procedure Law's procedural requirements, the condemnor will receive an order granting the petition and vesting title.[8] The condemnor must also prepare and properly serve the "notice of acquisition."[9]

The condemnee's attorney may ask one simple question in order to define his or her role at this stage of the proceedings: who is the condemnor? If the answer is the State or one of its agencies or depart-

2. Eminent Domain Procedure Law § 404.
3. Sun Co. Inc. (R & M) v. City of Syracuse Indus. Development Agency, 197 A.D.2d 912, 602 N.Y.S.2d 456 (4th Dep't 1993).

§ 14.68
1. See supra, § 14.49.
2. See supra, § 14.51.
3. See supra, § 14.54.
4. See supra, § 14.66.
5. See supra, § 14.57.
6. See supra, §§ 14.58, 14.59.
7. See supra, § 14.61.
8. See supra, § 14.65.
9. See supra, § 14.66.

ments, the attorney will play no role whatsoever at this stage.[10] Any defense the condemnee may wish to interpose will have to be raised in an Article 78 proceeding after title has vested in the condemnor.

When a non-State entity is the condemnor, the condemnee's attorney's role will be slightly more active than in the earlier stages of the proceedings. The condemnee is entitled to appear and interpose an answer, containing specific denials to the condemnor's petition,[11] although the defenses available are severely limited. The relevant question for the condemnee's attorney at this stage of the proceedings is this: did the condemnor hold a public hearing and make determinations and findings under Article 2? If it did, all issues relevant to that process, including whether the "taking" was supported by a proper public purpose, will be foreclosed at this stage.[12] Only challenges to procedural compliance with the Eminent Domain Procedure Law will be able to be raised. However, if an exemption to Article 2 was relied upon by the condemnor, the condemnee will have two important additional grounds upon which to challenge the acquisition.[13] First, the attorney may argue that reliance on the exemption was unwarranted and that the condemnor should be required to hold the hearing. If the condemnee prevails on this point, the acquisition action will be dismissed or stayed until the condemnor has carried out the public hearing and determination and finding requirements of Article 2.[14] If the condemnee does not prevail on this point, or chooses not to raise it, a second defense will be available. In the same manner that a condemnee may challenge a determination, made after a public hearing, that the condemnation serves a "public use or purpose" (through immediate appeal to the appellate division), a condemnee who did not have that avenue because an exemption was claimed may challenge the public use or purpose for the first time at this stage. It should be emphasized that it is exceedingly rare for a condemnee to prevail on this basis.

§ 14.69 The Fourth Stage—The Compensation Phase

As has been noted,[1] the power of eminent domain is broad. As long as there is legislative or constitutional authority for the acquisition, there is a proper public purpose for the acquisition, and the required procedures have been satisfied, a condemnee will not be able to prevent the taking of his or her property. The one additional requirement imposed upon the condemnor is the obligation to pay just compensation for what has been taken from the condemnee.

The fourth and final stage of eminent domain proceedings is the compensation stage. As will be discussed, this stage may involve compli-

10. *See supra,* §§ 14.52–14.55.
11. *See supra,* § 14.63.
12. *See supra,* § 14.64.
13. *Id.*
14. *See supra,* §§ 14.21, 14.30.

§ 14.69

1. *See supra,* §§ 14.3–14.6.

§ 14.69 EMINENT DOMAIN Ch. 14

cated issues, not only with regard to the extent of the injury to the condemnee for which compensation must be paid but also with regard to the proper method of valuing the compensable injuries.

§ 14.70 The Fourth Stage—The Compensation Phase—Court of Claims

It should be remembered that, when the State is the condemnor, the property of the condemnee will have been acquired without petitioning the court.[1] Thus, when the condemnee seeks compensation or damages from the State, it does so by filing a claim with the clerk of the Court of Claims.[2]

§ 14.71 The Fourth Stage—The Compensation Phase—Court of Claims—Time to File Claim

Unless the court establishes a different time period,[1] a condemnee has three years from the later of two dates within which to file a claim for damages: the date of service of a notice of acquisition or the date of vesting. The former more commonly is the relevant date. The claim must be filed with the clerk of the court. If, at any time subsequent to the running of this limitation period, a person files a claim, he or she may receive the amount of the condemnor's offer[2] on proof of entitlement to it. If the condemnee fails to make a claim within the limitations period, this failure will be deemed an acceptance of the condemnor's offer as full settlement of the claim.[3]

§ 14.72 The Fourth Stage—The Compensation Phase—Court of Claims—Service

A condemnee filing such a claim must serve a copy of the claim upon the state attorney general.[1]

§ 14.73 The Fourth Stage—The Compensation Phase—Supreme Court

Claims for damages arising out of acquisition by eminent domain by a condemnor other than the State of New York must be brought in the supreme court, which has exclusive jurisdiction over acquisitions by such

§ 14.70

1. See supra, §§ 14.52–14.55.
2. Eminent Domain Procedure Law § 503(A).

§ 14.71

1. Courts have discretion to permit an untimely claim for compensation to proceed, but the condemnee must offer some reasonable excuse for the delay. Metropolitan Transp. Auth. v. Pizzuti, 156 A.D.2d 546, 549 N.Y.S.2d 52 (2d Dep't 1989).

2. See supra, §§ 14.40–14.44.
3. Eminent Domain Procedure Law § 503(A).

§ 14.72

1. Eminent Domain Procedure Law § 503(A).

condemnors.[1] In such a case, the condemnee must file a written claim or notice of appearance with the clerk of the supreme court.[2]

§ 14.74 The Fourth Stage—The Compensation Phase—Supreme Court—Time to File Claim

When the acquisition proceeding is before the supreme court, and the condemnor must satisfy considerably more prerequisites to acquire title,[1] the court will specify the time within which the condemnee must file a written claim or notice of appearance.[2] This filing must be made with the clerk of the court that has jurisdiction over the matter.

§ 14.75 The Fourth Stage—The Compensation Phase—Supreme Court—Service

The claim or notice of appearance must be served upon either the condemnor's chief legal officer or upon the official designated in the notice of acquisition.[1]

§ 14.76 Content of Claim

Eminent Domain Procedure Law § 504 governs the content of the condemnee's claim; it requires that the claim or notice of appearance include: the name and post office address of the condemnee, a reasonable identification of the property[1] and interest upon which the claim is made, and a general statement of the nature and type of damages claimed, including a schedule of fixture items if they comprise part or all of the damages. If the condemnee is represented by an attorney, the name, office address and telephone number of the attorney must be subscribed at the end of the claim.[2]

§ 14.77 Scope of Just Compensation

The process of valuing property that has been taken by eminent domain can be a complicated one. The goal, simply stated, is to establish an amount of compensation that can be properly characterized as "just." In the sections that follow, many valuation methods are described. It should be remembered by both parties that these methods are a means to an end, not the end itself. A valuation that leads to a just result in one

§ 14.73

1. *See supra*, § 14.48.
2. Eminent Domain Procedure Law § 503(B).

§ 14.74

1. *See supra*, §§ 14.56–14.65.
2. Eminent Domain Procedure Law § 503(B).

§ 14.75

1. Eminent Domain Procedure Law § 503(B).

§ 14.76

1. This may, but need not, be by reference to the acquisition map.
2. *See infra*, § 14.133, for a form Claim for Damage Arising from Acquisition by Eminent Domain—General Form.

§ 14.77   EMINENT DOMAIN   Ch. 14

case may be abandoned in the next case if a more appropriate and adequate method is offered.

The determination of just compensation is guided by principles of equity. Thus, while the court may not disregard the evidence or reach a decision unsupported by it, it has wide discretion among alternative valuation methods.

Library References:

West's Key No. Digests, Eminent Domain ⟸122–150.

§ 14.78 Scope of Just Compensation—"Highest and Best Use"

As a general rule, the determination of what constitutes just compensation does not turn on the use for which the property is employed by its owner at the time of taking, but rather on what is the fair market value of the condemned property in its "highest and best" use.[1] Thus, the condemnee will want to identify all possible available uses and pinpoint the most economically advantageous one. Neither its present use nor the condemnor's planned use are favored as the best uses, unless no other use is put forward by the parties.[2] In arguing the issue of what is the highest and best use, however, assuming that that use is different than the present use, the condemnee must show that the alleged highest and best use could or would have been made in the near future.[3] The asserted use cannot be simply speculative or hypothetical.[4]

Although this test for determining just compensation permits consideration of uses not currently being made of the property, the monetary value of the potential use must be calculated on the basis of present market value, not future value. Thus, the court may assume a possible, non-existent use, but it must value that use as it would be valued if it existed on the date of the taking. This valuation is based on what a reasonable purchaser would pay for the property, being used in its highest and best use, if the offer were made on the date of the condemnor's taking.[5] If the property would have to be altered to permit the highest and best use, the cost of such alterations should be deducted from the value.[6]

§ 14.78

1. Matter of City of New York (Franklin Record Center, Inc.), 59 N.Y.2d 57, 463 N.Y.S.2d 168, 449 N.E.2d 1246 (1983).

2. In re Park Street (Lido Boulevard) Vicinity of Bay Lane, Town of Hempstead, 67 Misc.2d 1065, 325 N.Y.S.2d 555 (Sup.Ct., Nassau County, 1971) (present use held to be the appropriate measure of market value where the parties offered no evidence of highest and best use).

3. Rochester Urban Renewal Agency v. Lee, 83 A.D.2d 770, 443 N.Y.S.2d 479 (4th Dep't 1981).

4. *Id.*; Consolidated Edison Co. of New York, Inc. v. Neptune Associates, 190 A.D.2d 669, 593 N.Y.S.2d 259 (2d Dep't 1993).

5. Freiberger v. State, 33 A.D.2d 619, 304 N.Y.S.2d 782 (3d Dep't 1969).

6. In re Park St., *supra* note 2.

§ 14.79 Scope of Just Compensation—Total Taking

The exercise of the power of eminent domain is constrained not only by the requirement that the power be exercised only in pursuance of a valid public use, benefit or purpose[1] but also by the requirement that the condemnor take no more property than is reasonably necessary for the public project.[2] In some instances this results in a "total" taking, that is, in the total condemnation of the owner's interest in the parcel of land. In other instances, only a "partial" taking will occur.[3] The compensation issues with respect to the former are somewhat more straightforward than those governing the latter.

Library References:

West's Key No. Digests, Eminent Domain ⇐129–134, 139–150.

§ 14.80 Scope of Just Compensation—Total Taking—Direct Damages

By definition, when there is a total taking the damages suffered by the condemnee will be limited to direct damages, that is, damages directly arising out of the taking of the land. Valuation questions in the determination of just compensation will focus solely on the value of the taken parcel.[1] Because there is no remaining portion of the condemnee's parcel or tract subjected to "injury," no questions arise as to indirect damages[2] or benefits[3] that will increase or offset the condemnee's award.

Library References:

West's Key No. Digests, Eminent Domain ⇐129–134.

§ 14.81 Scope of Just Compensation—Total Taking—Improvements

Without question, when private property is taken for public use, the private owner must be compensated not only for the land, but also for buildings and other improvements taken along with the land.[1] As a general rule, when land with improvements is taken, the land and the

---

§ 14.79
1. See supra, § 14.15.
2. See supra, § 14.7.
3. See infra, § 14.82.

§ 14.80
1. For a discussion of the different methods employed to properly identify this value, see infra, §§ 14.85–14.89.

2. See infra, § 14.82.
3. See infra, § 14.109.

§ 14.81
1. Jackson v. State, 213 N.Y. 34, 106 N.E. 758 (1914).

improvements are treated as one unit, rather than separately valued.[2] Improvements thus are considered component parts of the sum value of the property. If the value of the improvements is calculated into the award, because the improvements will continue to be used, the valuation process must also take into account that the land is burdened by the existing use. That is, the condemnee cannot "have his cake and eat it too" by arguing a highest and best use of the land that can only be made *without* use of the improvement and also arguing that the improvements *enhance* the value of the land.[3]

A court has discretion not to follow this general rule and to establish separate values for the land and improvements.[4] When separate valuations are made, however, care must be taken not to double value the improvements. The value of the land pursuant to this method must be computed as if the improvement were not on it.

In certain situations, improvements do not in fact enhance the value of the land, and in such situations, the value of the improvements should not be included in the calculation of just compensation.[5] As noted previously, this is particularly true when the improvements are inconsistent with the highest and best use of the property.

When the condemnor and condemnee agree that the latter may remove an improvement, the condemnor is not required to compensate the condemnee for the improvement.[6] The condemnee may recover the cost of the removal, however.[7]

Occasionally, compensation disputes arise when the condemnee has improved the property immediately before it was taken and, arguably, in anticipation of its being taken. Recovery for the value of such improvements seems to turn on whether the improvement was made in good faith[8] or whether it was made with the primary motive of increasing a compensation award.[9]

Library References:

West's Key No. Digests, Eminent Domain ⚖133.

2. Loucks v. State, 83 A.D.2d 761, 444 N.Y.S.2d 784 (4th Dep't 1981).

3. Matter of Town of Hempstead (Malibu Associates, Inc.), 56 N.Y.2d 1020, 453 N.Y.S.2d 642, 439 N.E.2d 357 (1982); Kaufman v. State, 57 A.D.2d 1025, 395 N.Y.S.2d 513 (3d Dep't 1977).

4. Kaufman v. State, *supra* note 1. An example of a scenario in which separate rather than unit valuation is appropriate is where there is a residence on the property but the land is likely to be rezoned for commercial use. Passaretti v. State, 37 A.D.2d 1021, 325 N.Y.S.2d 707 (3d Dep't 1971).

5. City of Rochester v. S.C. Toth, Inc., 59 A.D.2d 1020, 399 N.Y.S.2d 755 (4th Dep't 1977), aff'd 45 N.Y.2d 984, 413 N.Y.S.2d 146, 385 N.E.2d 1073 (1978).

6. United States v. Bobinski, 244 F.2d 299 (2d Cir.1957) (interpreting New York law).

7. *Id.*

8. MHG Enterprises, Inc. v. City of New York, 91 Misc.2d 842, 399 N.Y.S.2d 837 (Sup.Ct., N.Y.County, 1977).

9. *Id.*

§ 14.82 Scope of Just Compensation—Partial Taking

Unique valuation problems arise when a condemnor takes only a portion of a tract of land. Generally, New York courts apply what is called the "before and after" rule to such partial takings.[1] The measure of damages pursuant to this rule is the difference between the value of the whole tract before the taking and the value of what remains after the taking.[2] The appraisals of the property before and after the taking must be made by use of the same methods.[3]

Courts are not required to apply the "before and after" rule in all cases. Particularly when the condemnee seeks to recover consequential damages to the remainder, the court may simply value the portion taken and separately value the consequential damages to the remainder. The condemnee will have the burden of proof with regard to the damages to the remaining parcel.[4] The court will make separate findings as to the amount directly attributable to the land taken and the amount assessed as consequential damages to the remaining land.[5]

Consequential damages are usually incurred on the retained land as a result of the nature of the use of the taken land by the condemnor. Courts have made clear, however, that temporary inconvenience or discomfort as a result of the condemnor's use will not support an award of damages.[6] Examples of cases in which consequential damages were awarded include those in which there was: a diminution in the highest and best use of the remaining land,[7] loss of view or light,[8] exposure to extensive noise or odor,[9] unsuitable access[10] and even, under limited circumstances, "cancerphobia."[11]

§ 14.82

1. Kaszubowski v. State, 112 A.D.2d 742, 492 N.Y.S.2d 237 (4th Dep't 1985); Donaloio v. State, 99 A.D.2d 335, 472 N.Y.S.2d 946 (3d Dep't 1984), aff'd 64 N.Y.2d 811, 486 N.Y.S.2d 924, 476 N.E.2d 323 (1985).

2. McDonald v. State, 42 N.Y.2d 900, 397 N.Y.S.2d 990, 366 N.E.2d 1344 (1977); City of Batavia v. Bolas, 174 A.D.2d 993, 573 N.Y.S.2d 8 (4th Dep't 1991).

3. Bronxville Palmer, Ltd. v. State, 36 A.D.2d 10, 318 N.Y.S.2d 57 (3d Dep't 1971), app. dismissed 28 N.Y.2d 817, 321 N.Y.S.2d 917, 270 N.E.2d 733, app. denied 28 N.Y.2d 487, 322 N.Y.S.2d 1026, 270 N.E.2d 903 (1971), order modified 30 N.Y.2d 760, 333 N.Y.S.2d 422, 284 N.E.2d 577 (1972).

4. Matter of County of Nassau, 144 A.D.2d 364, 533 N.Y.S.2d 781 (2d Dep't 1988); Niagara Mohawk Power Corp. v. Olin, 138 A.D.2d 940, 526 N.Y.S.2d 278 (4th Dep't 1988).

5. Wineburgh v. State, 20 A.D.2d 961, 249 N.Y.S.2d 763 (4th Dep't 1964).

6. Rymkevitch v. State, 42 Misc.2d 1021, 249 N.Y.S.2d 514 (Ct.Cl.1964).

7. Rider v. State, 192 A.D.2d 983, 596 N.Y.S.2d 900 (3d Dep't 1993); Ingber v. State, 187 A.D.2d 826, 590 N.Y.S.2d 145 (3d Dep't 1992); Wollaber v. State, 80 A.D.2d 706, 437 N.Y.S.2d 748 (3d Dep't 1981).

8. Williams v. State, 90 A.D.2d 882, 456 N.Y.S.2d 528 (3d Dep't 1982).

9. Monser v. State, 96 A.D.2d 702, 466 N.Y.S.2d 780 (3d Dep't 1983).

10. Schreiber v. State, 56 N.Y.2d 760, 452 N.Y.S.2d 16, 437 N.E.2d 275 (1982); Matter of County of Rockland (Kohl Indus. Park Co.), 147 A.D.2d 478, 537 N.Y.S.2d 309 (2d Dep't 1989), app. denied 74 N.Y.2d 607, 545 N.Y.S.2d 103, 543 N.E.2d 746 (1989).

11. Criscuola v. Power Auth. of State of N.Y., 81 N.Y.2d 649, 602 N.Y.S.2d 588, 621 N.E.2d 1195 (1993).

§ 14.82   EMINENT DOMAIN   Ch. 14

The consequences of a partial taking may be complicated if there is a dispute concerning what constitutes the retained land. Certainly, any retained land in a single parcel with a single owner qualifies under the previously described rules governing a partial taking. There is also authority to permit treatment of multiple parcels as one tract when they are contiguous or unified in use and are owned by the condemnee.[12]

Library References:

West's Key No. Digests, Eminent Domain ⟐135–138.

§ 14.83 Scope of Just Compensation—Temporary Taking

Occasionally, a public project will not require a permanent taking, and a temporary taking will be authorized.[1] As a general rule, the condemnee whose property is taken temporarily will be entitled to compensation, as measured by the reasonable rental value during the temporary taking and related losses.[2] The rental value should be determined as of the time of the taking.[3] The condemnee is not limited to the value of the current use of the property but may offer evidence of the best reasonable use.[4]

Library References:

West's Key No. Digests, Eminent Domain ⟐143.

§ 14.84 Scope of Just Compensation—Temporary Taking—Easements

When an easement is temporarily condemned, the condemnee generally is entitled to recover the reasonable rental value of the easement plus any damages caused by the condemnor's use of the easement.[1] It has been held, however, that no compensation is due when there is no interference with the condemnee's use of the property, and no damage is otherwise done.[2]

---

12. Brookhaven v. Gold, 89 A.D.2d 963, 454 N.Y.S.2d 111 (2d Dep't 1982).

§ 14.83

1. *See supra*, § 14.3.
2. City School Dist. of City of Kingston v. Vasilevich, 61 A.D.2d 276, 402 N.Y.S.2d 865 (3d Dep't 1978).
3. In re Castle Hill Houses, Borough of Bronx, City of New York, 113 N.Y.S.2d 417 (Sup.Ct., Bronx County, 1950).
4. City of Yonkers by Kelly v. A. & J. Cianciulli, Inc., 117 N.Y.S.2d 792 (Sup.Ct., Westchester County, 1952).

§ 14.84

1. Town of Pittsford v. Sweeney, 34 Misc.2d 436, 228 N.Y.S.2d 518 (Sup.Ct., Monroe County, 1962).
2. Matter of County of Nassau, 148 A.D.2d 533, 538 N.Y.S.2d 865 (2d Dep't 1989); Kauffman v. State, 43 A.D.2d 1004, 353 N.Y.S.2d 61 (3d Dep't 1974), aff'd 36 N.Y.2d 745, 368 N.Y.S.2d 164, 328 N.E.2d 792 (1975).

§ 14.85 Methods of Valuation to Determine Compensation

Three primary methods are used to value land taken by eminent domain. What must be determined is fair market value, but there is no fixed method to determine that value. As the Court of Appeals has noted, "[t]he ultimate purpose of valuation, ... in eminent domain ..., is to arrive at a fair and realistic value of the property involved...."[1] The primary methods of valuation are the market approach,[2] the income approach,[3] and the cost approach.[4] Which approach is appropriate in a particular case will turn on the nature and use of the condemned property. "Any fair and nondiscriminating method that will achieve that result is acceptable."[5]

It should be noted that the valuation of property taken by eminent domain is essentially a question of fact. A valuation, once decided by the lower court, must be upheld unless the trial judge has made an error of law by using an erroneous theory of valuation or unless the record does not contain evidence to support the valuation.[6] The trial court must make its factual findings and underlying mathematical calculations as explicit as possible to facilitate this review.[7]

The court is not required to value the property within the range set by the expert opinion of appraisers presented at trial. If it does not do so, however, it must adequately explain the basis for its valuation.[8]

Library References:

West's Key No. Digests, Eminent Domain ⚖122–150.

§ 14.85

1. Allied Corp. v. Town of Camillus, 80 N.Y.2d 351, 356, 590 N.Y.S.2d 417, 419, 604 N.E.2d 1348, 1350 (1992).
2. See infra, § 14.86.
3. See infra, § 14.87.
4. See infra, § 14.88.
5. Allied Corp., supra note 1, 80 N.Y.2d at 356, 590 N.Y.S.2d at 419, 604 N.E.2d at 1350.
6. B. Altman & Co. v. City of White Plains, 57 N.Y.2d 904, 456 N.Y.S.2d 755, 442 N.E.2d 1266 (1982); City of New York, College Point Indus. Park, Urban Renewal Project II v. Reiss, 55 N.Y.2d 885, 449 N.Y.S.2d 18, 433 N.E.2d 1266 (1982), on remand 89 A.D.2d 894, 453 N.Y.S.2d 602 (2d Dep't 1982), aff'd 58 N.Y.2d 817, 459 N.Y.S.2d 268, 445 N.E.2d 651 (1983) (findings must either be within the range of expert testimony or be supported by other evidence and adequately explained by the court).
7. Matter of Acquisition of Real Property by Niagara Mohawk Power Corp., 114 A.D.2d 542, 494 N.Y.S.2d 157, app. decided, 118 A.D.2d 891, 499 N.Y.S.2d 809 (3d Dep't 1986); Application of City of New York, South Bronx Neighborhood Development Plan (Bronxchester–Third Taking), 88 A.D.2d 537, 450 N.Y.S.2d 197 (1st Dep't 1982).
8. Denniston's Crossing, Inc. v. State, 76 A.D.2d 988, 429 N.Y.S.2d 304 (3d Dep't 1980).

§ 14.86 Methods of Valuation to Determine Compensation—Market Approach to Value

The market approach to valuation focuses on sales of comparable properties.[1] This comparable sales approach is the preferred method for assessing damages and determining compensation in condemnation cases.[2] Therefore, the burden is on the party who seeks to use a different measure, normally the condemnee, to show that the property cannot reasonably be measured by the market approach.[3]

The clearest way to show the inappropriateness of the market approach is to show that there are too few comparable sales, due to dissimilarities in the compared properties, to provide an accurate valuation.[4] The degree of comparability is a question of fact for the trial court.[5] The court may properly use comparables despite dissimilarities, however, by making adjustments in price based on those dissimilarities.[6]

In arguing that the award should be higher than the present market value, the condemnee may show the likelihood of a "higher or better use," based upon the reasonable probability of rezoning (or judicial invalidation of zoning) to allow that use. When such a showing is made, the market value should be increased by the premium that a knowledgeable buyer would pay for the potential change in the most valuable use.[7] The inverse—a case in which rezoning is likely to diminish value—should result in a lowering of the award.[8]

Library References:

West's Key No. Digests, Eminent Domain ⚖︎122–150.

§ 14.86

1. This approach is not limited to sales of *other* property, however. In a case in which the condemned property itself was recently sold, and there was no evidence that the sale was abnormal, the sales price of the condemned property was directly reflective of its value. Matter of City of New York, 98 A.D.2d 166, 471 N.Y.S.2d 105 (2d Dep't 1983).

2. Allied Corp. v. Town of Camillus, 80 N.Y.2d 351, 356, 590 N.Y.S.2d 417, 419–20, 604 N.E.2d 1348, 1350–51 (1992); Rochester Urban Renewal Agency v. Willsea Works, 48 N.Y.2d 694, 422 N.Y.S.2d 59, 397 N.E.2d 749 (1979).

3. *Id.*

4. Hardele Realty Corp. v. State, 125 A.D.2d 543, 509 N.Y.S.2d 621 (2d Dep't 1986) (earlier sales prices were properly rejected where conditions of the general area were deteriorating).

5. Matter of Village of Johnson City, 215 A.D.2d 917, 626 N.Y.S.2d 869 (3d Dep't 1995) (sales consummated after condemnation were not proper comparables in light of the fact that a highway improvement subsequent to condemnation had a beneficial effect on values); Chase Manhattan Bank, N.A. v. State, 103 A.D.2d 211, 479 N.Y.S.2d 983 (2d Dep't 1984); Matter of City of New York, 98 A.D.2d 166, 471 N.Y.S.2d 105 (2d Dep't 1983).

6. Matter of Broome County, 133 A.D.2d 984, 521 N.Y.S.2d 134 (3d Dep't 1987); Chase Manhattan Bank, N.A., *supra* note 5.

7. Chase Manhattan Bank, N.A., *supra* note 5; *see also* Rodman v. State, 109 A.D.2d 737, 485 N.Y.S.2d 842 (2d Dep't 1985) (claimant failed to establish reasonable evidence of rezoning).

8. Matter of Town of Islip, 49 N.Y.2d 354, 426 N.Y.S.2d 220, 402 N.E.2d 1123 (1980).

§ 14.87 Methods of Valuation to Determine Compensation—Income Approach to Value

The income approach is employed as a valuation method when the property at issue produces an income stream. Thus, this approach would be used for such properties as apartment buildings, office buildings, and shopping malls.[1] The income approach "assumes an investor would pay a certain value in order to obtain the benefits of a future income stream which will generate a necessary rate of return on the investment."[2] This method is often expressed as V = I/R where V represents value, I represents income and R represents the discount or capitalization rate.[3] The capitalization rate is calculated by use of four factors: "1) the 'riskless' rate of return available from interest on long-term government bonds; 2) a compensation factor for lack of liquidity; 3) compensation for 'investment management'; and 4) compensation for risk."[4] The proper capitalization rate to be employed is a fact question for the trial court, on which expert appraisal opinion will be competent evidence.[5]

Library References:

West's Key No. Digests, Eminent Domain ⇒122–150.

§ 14.88 Methods of Valuation to Determine Compensation—Cost Approach to Value

The cost approach typically utilizes three steps to establish the value of land. First, the underlying land is valued. Second, buildings and improvements are valued by subtracting an obsolescence and depreciation factor from the current cost of making the improvement (also known as the "Replacement Cost Less Depreciation" method). Third, the two are added together.

Cost valuation is usually employed when the condemned property does not produce income and does not yield to comparable valuations.[1] Specialty property[2] is often valued by use of the cost method.[3] Generally, however, this valuation method is not favored, because it is the most likely to overvalue the property.[4]

---

§ 14.87

1. Mil-Pine Plaza, Inc. v. State, 72 A.D.2d 460, 424 N.Y.S.2d 937 (4th Dep't 1980); Star Plaza, Inc. v. State, 79 A.D.2d 746, 434 N.Y.S.2d 804 (3d Dep't 1980).

2. L. Lewandrowski, *Toxic Blackacre: Appraisal Techniques & Current Trends in Valuation*, 5 Alb.L.J. of Sci. & Tech. 55, 60 (1994).

3. *Id.*

4. *Id.* at 60–61.

5. Star Plaza Inc., *supra* note 1.

§ 14.88

1. Matter of Suffolk County, 47 N.Y.2d 507, 419 N.Y.S.2d 52, 392 N.E.2d 1236 (1979).

2. *See infra*, § 14.89.

3. Club St. Agnello Abate of Amsterdam, New York, Inc. v. State, 68 A.D.2d 264, 417 N.Y.S.2d 21 (3d Dep't 1979).

4. Allied Corp. v. Town of Camillus, 80 N.Y.2d 351, 357, 590 N.Y.S.2d 417, 420, 604 N.E.2d 1348, 1351 (1992).

§ 14.89 Specialty Property

A condemned parcel of property that is deemed to be sufficiently unique is characterized as "specialty property."[1] Such property is valued by the cost approach[2] and will result in a higher damage award for the condemnee.[3]

The Court of Appeals has identified four criteria to determine whether property is "specialty" property:

(a) [T]he improvement must be unique and must be specially built for the specific purpose for which it is designed; (b) there must be a special use for which the improvement is designed and the improvement must be so specially used; (c) there must be no market for the type of property and no sales of property for such use; and (d) the improvement must be an appropriate improvement at the time of the taking or assessment and its use must be economically feasible and reasonably expected to be replaced.... [4]

In order for the property in question to constitute specialty property, the specialized use of the property must be current. Thus, if the condemnee has abandoned the specialized use, any claim that the property is specialized will have been lost.[5]

The burden of proving that the condemned property is speciality property is on the condemnee.[6]

Library References:

West's Key No. Digests, Eminent Domain ⚖134.

§ 14.90 Effect of Environmental Contamination on Property Value

Valuation problems are hugely exacerbated when the property to be valued has been contaminated, as contamination clearly affects market value. Although still being developed, valuation methods that take into account environmental contamination are available[1] and should be considered when contaminated land is condemned.

---

§ 14.89

1. Matter of Suffolk County, 47 N.Y.2d 507, 419 N.Y.S.2d 52, 392 N.E.2d 1236 (1979).

2. *See supra*, § 14.88.

3. *See id.*, note 4.

4. Allied Corp. v. Town of Camillus, 80 N.Y.2d 351, 357, 590 N.Y.S.2d 417, 420, 604 N.E.2d 1348, 1351 (1992).

5. Matter of Suffolk County, *supra* note 1.

6. Rochester Urban Renewal Agency v. Willsea Works, 48 N.Y.2d 694, 422 N.Y.S.2d 59, 397 N.E.2d 749 (1979).

§ 14.90

1. New York courts have not yet employed these methods. For an excellent discussion of developing methods, nationally, for valuing environmentally contaminated

The problem in fashioning an appropriate valuation method for contaminated properties is the difficulty quantifying three "value-depressing" factors: "clean-up costs, liability, and the stigma which remains after cleanup."[2] These factors have been recognized by the Court of Appeals as making the valuation problem difficult, rendering the normal approach to valuation, market value, inappropriate.[3] The answer in many cases will be to characterize the property as "specialty property," applying valuation techniques appropriate to that kind of property.[4]

One of the reasons there are few litigated cases involving valuation methods specifically tailored to environmentally contaminated land is that expert and appraisal expenses involved in such cases are prohibitively high.[5] In the eminent domain context, this economic fact may inure to the benefit of the condemnee, since it will be the condemnor that seeks to reduce damages based upon the arguably lower market value resulting from such contamination.

Library References:

West's Key No. Digests, Eminent Domain ⚖︎122–150.

§ 14.91 Fixtures

When land is taken, fixtures upon the land are taken as well. Not only is this the general practice, it is required, unless the condemnor and condemnee agree otherwise.[1] Put another way, the condemnor cannot avoid paying compensation for fixtures by arguing that it did not "take" them.[2]

Library References:

West's Key No. Digests, Eminent Domain ⚖︎87, 133.

§ 14.92 Fixtures—Compensable Fixtures

A fixture is an item of personal property so affixed to real property as to become part of it. Whether something is a fixture or not largely turns on whether the person who affixed it intended it to be a permanent addition to the land. In cases in which the owner, or someone at the owner's direction, affixed the chattel to the property, a presumption arises that it was intended to be permanently annexed to and to pass

land in the context of eminent domain, see R. McMurry & D. Pierce, *Environmental Redemption and Eminent Domain* in *Eminent Domain and Land Value Litigation*, ALI–ABA Symposium, Ft. Lauderdale, FL at 105–48 (Jan. 9–11, 1991).

2. L. Lewandrowski, *Toxic Blackacre: Appraisal Techniques & Current Trends in Valuation*, 5 Alb. L.J. of Sci. & Tech. 55, 66 (1994), citing P. Patchin, Valuation of Contaminated Properties, Appraisal J., Jan. 1988 at 11.

3. Allied Corp. v. Town of Camillus, 80 N.Y.2d 351, 356, 590 N.Y.S.2d 417, 420, 604 N.E.2d 1348, 1350–51 (1992).

4. *Id.*; See supra, § 14.89.

5. Lewandrowski, *supra* note 2 at 70.

§ 14.91

1. Jackson v. State, 213 N.Y. 34, 106 N.E. 758 (1914).

2. *Id.*

§ 14.92 EMINENT DOMAIN Ch. 14

with the land.[1] This presumption arises not only with a voluntary sale of the land but also with an involuntary taking.

It should be noted that, in the eminent domain context, the test to determine whether something is a fixture is not whether it is removable from the property. All that is necessary to properly characterize an item as a compensable fixture is that the owner *intended* a permanent annexation of the chattel.[2]

Library References:

West's Key No. Digests, Eminent Domain ⚖︎87.

§ 14.93 Fixtures—Valuation of Fixtures

Fixtures are not normally separately valued as an item of damages but rather are calculated into the value of the land.[1] As a general rule, the calculation of the value of the fixture is based upon the reproduction cost of the fixture less depreciation, what is known as the "sound value."[2] This valuation method may result in a conclusion that the fixture adds no value to the land.[3]

Even though a chattel is properly characterized as a fixture, because the annexor intended it to be permanent, the condemnee may desire to remove it, and the condemnor may be willing to have the condemnee do so.[4] In such a case, the fixture will be valued at the lesser of the cost of removal or the sound value subtracted by the salvage value.[5]

Library References:

West's Key No. Digests, Eminent Domain ⚖︎133.

§ 14.94 Leasehold Interests

Leasehold interests, like any other property interests, may be taken by eminent domain and must be compensated, along with the reversionary fee that is taken. The typical method of valuation when a leasehold

§ 14.92

1. Matter of Suffolk County, 47 N.Y.2d 507, 419 N.Y.S.2d 52, 392 N.E.2d 1236 (1979).

2. Bullis v. State, 51 Misc.2d 448, 273 N.Y.S.2d 392 (Ct.Cl.1966).

§ 14.93

1. Buffalo v. J.W. Cement Co., 28 N.Y.2d 241, 321 N.Y.S.2d 345, 269 N.E.2d 895 (1971); Matter of County of Nassau, 149 A.D.2d 701, 540 N.Y.S.2d 496 (2d Dep't 1989).

2. *Id.*; *But see* Universal Empire Industries, Inc. v. State, 149 Misc.2d 773, 566 N.Y.S.2d 442 (Ct.Cl.1990) (sound value may not be appropriate when a fixture is obsolete because overvaluation will result; the better measure is to ascertain the original cost and trend that value to the date of appraisal by an appropriate inflation figure).

3. In re Harlem River Houses II, Borough of Manhattan, City of N.Y., 22 A.D.2d 882, 254 N.Y.S.2d 647 (1st Dep't 1964), aff'd 17 N.Y.2d 769, 270 N.Y.S.2d 623, 217 N.E.2d 672 (1966).

4. Rose v. State, 24 N.Y.2d 81, 298 N.Y.S.2d 968, 246 N.E.2d 735 (1969).

5. Buffalo, *supra* note 1; In re West Ave., New York City, 27 A.D.2d 539, 275 N.Y.S.2d 119 (2d Dep't 1966); William J. Kline & Son, Inc. v. State, 35 A.D.2d 465, 317 N.Y.S.2d 401 (3d Dep't 1971).

interest is taken is to first value the land in fee and then value the leasehold. The lessee's interest is then subtracted from the value of the fee; the leasehold interest is given to the lessee and the remainder of the sum goes to the feeholder. If the lease addresses the issue of how to allocate an award resulting from the exercise of the power of eminent domain, the lease will control.[1]

Library References:

West's Key No. Digests, Eminent Domain ⚖85, 147.

§ 14.95 Leasehold Interests—Valuation and Compensation

The normal valuation method employed when a leasehold interest is taken is first to determine the reasonable rental value of the leased interest, as well as the rent actually provided in the lease.[1] The value of the leasehold is then deemed to be the excess of rental value over actual rent.[2] This amount is then discounted to present value.[3]

In many, if not most cases, this valuation method will result in the conclusion that the leasehold itself is without value inasmuch as rent is often a reflection of reasonable value.[4] In fact, in the absence of an assertion that the rent is aberrational, the actual rent will be a factor used to calculate the reasonable rental value.[5]

The court retains discretion, however, to determine that the lease has some value beyond that calculated by the above method. The lessee has the burden to show such value, and this showing must be something more than mere speculation by the lessee.[6]

If the lessee has made substantial improvements to the leased premises, knotty valuation problems may be presented. To a large extent, the lessee's award will be a function more of the terms of the lease than of eminent domain law. The requirement to pay "just compensation" that flows from an exercise of the power of eminent domain mandates that the condemnor pay for the value of buildings, improvements and fixtures, but it is the lease and the law governing the

§ 14.94

1. Matter of Albany Community Dev. Agency v. Abdelgader, 205 A.D.2d 905, 613 N.Y.S.2d 473 (3d Dep't 1994) (where the lease provides for termination if property is taken by eminent domain, the tenant should get no share of the condemnation award).

§ 14.95

1. Arlen of Nanuet, Inc. v. State, 26 N.Y.2d 346, 310 N.Y.S.2d 465, 258 N.E.2d 890, on remand Siegel v. State, 64 Misc.2d 179, 313 N.Y.S.2d 923 (Ct.Cl.1970).

2. Application of Bronx River Expressway in City of New York, 278 App.Div. 813, 104 N.Y.S.2d 554 (1st Dep't 1951).

3. Getty Oil Co. v. State, 33 A.D.2d 705, 304 N.Y.S.2d 701 (3d Dep't 1969).

4. Irv-Ceil Realty Corp. v. State, 43 A.D.2d 775, 350 N.Y.S.2d 784 (3d Dep't 1973).

5. Motsiff v. State, 32 A.D.2d 729, 301 N.Y.S.2d 786 (4th Dep't 1969), aff'd 26 N.Y.2d 692, 257 N.E.2d 42, 308 N.Y.S.2d 860 (1970).

6. Irv-Ceil Realty, *supra* note 5.

landlord-tenant relationship that ordinarily will determine the relative rights of the lessor and lessee. With regard to fixtures, the tenant will be entitled to compensation for those taken by eminent domain if the tenant would have had the right to remove them at the end of the lease.[7] If, however, pursuant to the lease, the value of all improvements made and fixtures installed by the lessee would inure to the benefit of the lessor, the lessee would not be compensated for their value as a result of the condemnation.[8]

Assuming that the lessee *is* entitled to be compensated for the value of improvements and fixtures, that value must be quantified. The ordinary measure of this value is the increase in the value of the leasehold as a result of the particular improvement or fixture, rather than its cost.[9]

Library References:

West's Key No. Digests, Eminent Domain ⚍85, 147.

§ 14.96 Loss of Business and Goodwill

The rules governing a condemnee's right to compensation for loss of business and goodwill are relatively straightforward. If the legislative act that authorizes the taking authorizes compensation for this type of loss, the condemnee may be compensated.[1] If there is no such authorization, the condemnee is not entitled to compensation, regardless of the fact that the taking was directly responsible for the loss.[2]

Library References:

West's Key No. Digests, Eminent Domain ⚍107, 147.

§ 14.97 Going Concern Value

The going concern value of a business that is lost through an exercise of eminent domain is not recoverable by the condemnee.[1] However, if the *business* itself is taken for a public use, rather than destroyed by the taking of the land upon which it is operated, the condemnor must pay the going concern value.

---

7. City of New York, College Point Indus. Park Urban Renewal Project II v. G & C Amusements, Inc., 55 N.Y.2d 353, 449 N.Y.S.2d 671, 434 N.E.2d 1038 (1982).

8. Id.

9. Bodnar Industries, Inc. v. State, 19 Misc.2d 720, 187 N.Y.S.2d 359 (Ct.Cl.), app. dismissed 9 A.D.2d 850, 194 N.Y.S.2d 446 (3d Dep't 1959).

§ 14.96

1. *See e.g.*, Agriculture and Markets Law § 27(10), Correction Law § 21(10), ECL § 3–0305(10), Highway Law § 29(8).

2. St. Agnes Cemetery v. State, 3 N.Y.2d 37, 163 N.Y.S.2d 655, 143 N.E.2d 377 (1957).

§ 14.97

1. Humbert v. State, 278 App.Div. 1041, 107 N.Y.S.2d 507 (4th Dep't 1951), aff'd 303 N.Y. 929, 105 N.E.2d 504 (1952).

Ch. 14   CONFLICTING CLAIMS TO CONDEMNOR'S § 14.100

Library References:

West's Key No. Digests, Eminent Domain ⚖︎107.

§ 14.98 Moving and Relocation Expenses

As is the rule with respect to compensation for loss of business and goodwill,[1] moving and relocation expenses are generally recoverable only when authorized by statute. Although there are a limited number of cases permitting such recovery,[2] it is generally the rule that moving and relocation costs are not recoverable in the absence of such authorization.

Library References:

West's Key No. Digests, Eminent Domain ⚖︎95.

§ 14.99 Conflicting Claims by Condemnees

It is not unusual when more than one person or entity claims an interest in condemned land. The Eminent Domain Procedure Law defines a "condemnee" as "the holder of any right, title, interest, lien, charge or encumbrance in real property subject to an acquisition or proposed acquisition."[1] One person may claim title over another, and thus claim the award in the place of the other, as, for example, when a claimant, through adverse possession, challenges the title of the record owner. Other claimants may acknowledge the record owner's title, yet claim an interest arising out of that title, as, for example, a lessee or mortgagee might.

Library References:

West's Key No. Digests, Eminent Domain ⚖︎151–158.

§ 14.100 Conflicting Claims by Condemnees—Conflicting Claims to the Condemnor's Offer

Conflicting claims may present practical problems during two stages of the eminent domain process. First, during the offer and negotiation stage[1] that precedes any acquisition proceeding, the owner has the option to accept the condemnor's offer as either full or advance payment. Problems will arise if a conflicting claim is presented, posing the question, *who* is entitled to the payment in whole or in part.

If the state is the condemnor when such a conflict arises, the Comptroller, if requested, must deposit the payment into a special

§ 14.98

1. *See supra*, § 14.96.
2. Sinclair Refining Co. v. State, 279 App.Div. 692, 107 N.Y.S.2d 934 (3d Dep't 1951).

§ 14.99

1. Eminent Domain Procedure Law § 103(C).

§ 14.100

1. *See supra*, §§ 14.40–14.44.

interest-bearing bank account.[2] The Attorney General must then notify all claimants that the fund has been so deposited and that it may be the subject of a distribution proceeding. This proceeding is the functional equivalent of the proceeding that is held when such a dispute arises at the compensation stage.

Notwithstanding the deposit requirement described above, if a condemnee provides the condemnor with the necessary documents to effect a valid transfer of title to the condemnor, the Comptroller must redeposit the fund, plus interest, into the fund from which it was taken so that the condemnor may effect payment to the condemnee providing such documents. Any further issues with respect to conflicting claims to this money will be left to be resolved among the claimants.

When the condemnor is *not* the State, the process is slightly different. The condemnor deposits the payment with the clerk of the supreme court of the district in which the property is located.[3] The money is then placed into an interest-bearing account until the court directs payment. The condemnor must notify all claimants that the payment has been deposited and that it is subject to a distribution proceeding.

Library References:

West's Key No. Digests, Eminent Domain ⚖151–158.

§ 14.101 Conflicting Claims by Condemnees—Conflicting Claims to the Award

The second stage in the eminent domain process where conflicts among claimants may arise is at the compensation stage. Eminent Domain Procedure Law § 505(A) requires that the condemnor receive, prior to trial, proof of the condemnee's title to the property acquired and, where relevant, proof of liens or encumbrances on that property. If the condemnor disputes the title, lien or encumbrance, or if there is uncertainty as to how an award should be apportioned, the court must interplead anyone who claims to have a conflicting claim or interest.[1] When conflicting claims are presented, the court must determine the condemnees' respective interests and rights as well as the compensation due.[2]

Library References:

West's Key No. Digests, Eminent Domain ⚖151–158.

2. Eminent Domain Procedure Law § 304(E)(1).
3. Eminent Domain Procedure Law § 304(D).

§ 14.101
1. Eminent Domain Procedure Law § 505(B); Owasco River Ry., Inc. v. State, 181 A.D.2d 665, 580 N.Y.S.2d 466 (2d Dep't 1992) (the Court of Claims should have impleaded the contract vendee who had an equitable interest in the property).

2. Eminent Domain Procedure Law § 505(C).

Ch. 14 FILING AND EXCHANGE OF APPRAISALS § 14.104

§ 14.102 The Trial on Compensation

Although the CPLR generally governs eminent domain proceedings, at least when courts are involved, it is supplemented by fairly strict regulations governing compensation trials.[1] These supplemental rules reflect the difficult valuation issues at play and the need to put the parties on a level playing field with regard to these issues. As will be discussed in the succeeding sections,[2] the trial stage of the compensation phase is completely dominated by the preparation and presentation of expert testimony.

Library References:

West's Key No. Digests, Eminent Domain ⚖166–265(5).

§ 14.103 The Trial on Compensation—Preference

Because of the possibility that there will be financial or physical hardship incurred by an owner whose property has been taken by eminent domain, both the Court of Claims and the supreme court, upon a showing of such hardship, may grant the claimant preference on the trial calendar.

§ 14.104 The Trial on Compensation—Filing and Exchange of Appraisals

The Eminent Domain Procedure Law requires the Court of Claims and judicial departments of the supreme court to promulgate rules for the filing and exchange of written appraisals,[1] which these courts have done.[2] Depending on the applicable rule, the appraisal[3] is filed, and the clerk distributes copies to the other parties (this is the case in the Court of Claims) or the attorneys themselves serve the other parties. The key purpose of the rules governing the obligation to exchange appraisals is to provide sufficient advance opportunity to the parties to evaluate the appraisals prior to trial. Most of the rules require simultaneous distribution of all appraisal reports, so that one party does not have the advantage of reviewing an opponent's appraisal prior to submitting his or her own appraisal.[4] For much the same reason, amendments to

---

§ 14.102

1. PRACTICE POINTER: Counsel should carefully review 22 NYCRR § 206.21 to determine the precise rules governing compensation claims in the Court of Claims, and 22 NYCRR §§ 202.59–202.61 with respect to proceedings in supreme court.

2. See infra, §§ 14.104, 14.105.

§ 14.104

1. Eminent Domain Procedure Law § 508.

2. 22 NYCRR § 206.21 (Court of Claims); 22 NYCRR §§ 202.59–202.61 (supreme court).

3. The parties are generally entitled to file appraisal reports of each appraiser whose testimony is intended to be relied upon at trial. 22 NYCRR § 206.21(b).

4. 22 NYCRR § 206.21(d); 22 NYCRR § 202.59(g)(ii).

§ 14.104

appraisals after their circulation are rarely permitted. In general, appraisal reports may not be filed after the trial has begun. An appraisal report that has not been exchanged may not be admitted into evidence.[5]

Both the Court of Claims and the departments of the supreme court have adopted rules governing the content of appraisal reports. These reports must include:

- the appraisal methods used;
- the figures and calculations upon which the conclusion as to value was based;
- the conclusion as to value, including the "highest and best" use of the land;
- comparable sales, leases or other transactions; and
- a statement of the appraiser's qualifications.[6]

The rules governing actions in the Court of Claims are more detailed, requiring the "before and after" value of the property; direct, consequential, and total damages; the details of the appropriation; the details of comparable sales; and all other factors to be relied upon at the trial.[7]

An appraisal report may not be admitted into evidence in the trial unless the expert who prepared it is called to testify. In fact, when the appraisal is brought in as evidence, it is generally treated as supplemental to the expert's testimony, and therefore, the expert should be prepared to testify as to the details of the report.[8]

In the same manner that an appraisal report will not be admitted without the expert being called, an expert cannot be called to testify unless the expert prepared an appraisal report that was properly filed and exchanged.

§ 14.105 The Trial on Compensation—Expert Testimony

The key issue at this stage of the eminent domain proceeding is the proper valuation of the damages suffered by the condemnee and, thus, the determination of what compensation is "just." In the normal proceeding, whether before the Court of Claims or supreme court, proof of proper valuation will be offered by experts called by each side. It should be emphasized that only those experts whose appraisal reports have been properly filed and exchanged[1] will be permitted to testify.

---

5. Cook v. State, 105 Misc.2d 1040, 430 N.Y.S.2d 507 (Ct.Cl.1980); Cronk v. State, 100 Misc.2d 680, 420 N.Y.S.2d 113 (Ct.Cl. 1979).

6. 22 NYCRR §§ 202.59(g)(2), 202.60(g)(3).

7. 22 NYCRR § 206.21(b).

8. Homer v. State, 36 A.D.2d 333, 320 N.Y.S.2d 349 (3d Dep't 1971), aff'd 30 N.Y.2d 723, 332 N.Y.S.2d 895, 283 N.E.2d 767 (1972).

§ 14.105

1. See supra, § 14.104.

Because the courts have held that personal opinion testimony unsupported by facts is entitled to little weight, even if supplied by an expert,[2] the expert should testify in detail concerning the factual support for his or her conclusions. Again, however, an expert will not generally be permitted to testify about matters not contained in the expert's appraisal report.[3]

In the Court of Claims, experts may be used to rebut an opponent's appraisal report. An expert cannot offer rebuttal testimony, unless "an expert report shall be filed within one month after receipt of the document sought to be rebutted."[4] In supreme court, the same rule applies, except that the filing must be within sixty days of the receipt of the document sought to be rebutted.[5] In either court, the judge is permitted to extend these deadlines for good cause shown.

Library References:

West's Key No. Digests, Eminent Domain ⚖196, 199–205; Evidence ⚖ 470–574.

§ 14.106 The Trial on Compensation—Viewing of the Property

The trial judge is required to view the property at issue.[1] This viewing must be made before judgment is rendered.[2] The parties may stipulate to a waiver of this requirement. If the viewing is held, the parties are entitled to attend the viewing.

Library References:

West's Key No. Digests, Eminent Domain ⚖220, 232, 240.

§ 14.107 The Trial on Compensation—Joint or Consolidated Trials

The rules governing joint or consolidated trials differ somewhat if the State is the condemnor and the proceeding is in the Court of Claims, or the condemnor is not the State and the proceeding is in the supreme court.

In the former, two or more acquisition claims arising from the same project may, in the court's discretion, be heard and determined in the same proceeding.[1]

---

2. *See e.g.,* Katz v. State, 10 A.D.2d 164, 198 N.Y.S.2d 463 (3d Dep't 1960).

3. 22 NYCRR § 206.21(h); 22 NYCRR § 202.59(h); 22 NYCRR § 202.60(h); Salesian Soc. v. Ellenville, 121 A.D.2d 823, 505 N.Y.S.2d 197 (3d Dep't 1986).

4. 22 NYCRR § 206.21(f).

5. 22 NYCRR § 202.61.

§ 14.106

1. Eminent Domain Procedure Law § 510.

2. International Salt Co. v. State, 125 Misc.2d 939, 480 N.Y.S.2d 983 (Ct.Cl.1984).

§ 14.107

1. Eminent Domain Procedure Law § 511(A).

Occasionally, some, but not all, claims arising from a single project will have been filed. When this is the case, the judge, upon motion of any party, may make a determination that a joint or consolidated trial is desirable and may order a condemnee who has not filed a claim to do so.[2] This condemnee will be given one-hundred-twenty days after service of the order within which to file a claim. If the condemnee fails to do so, his or her claim will be tried upon presented proof.

In proceedings before the supreme court, the court may consolidate all trials related to a project into a single proceeding in one or more parts, or it may order a joint trial of the claims of any party filing separate notices of appearance.[3]

Library References:

West's Key No. Digests, Eminent Domain ⚖︎166.

§ 14.108 The Trial on Compensation—Interest

As a general rule, a condemnee is entitled to recover lawful interest from the date of the condemnor's acquisition or the date of a *de facto* taking to the date of payment.[1] This obligation does not attach, however, when the condemnor has made an advance payment or has deposited all or part of the compensation in an interest-bearing account.[2] In such a case, the obligation terminates as of the date of payment or deposit.[3]

In proceedings before the Court of Claims,[4] if the condemnee does not file and serve his claim within six months after it has accrued[5] or the condemnee has received service of the notice of acquisition,[6] whichever is later, interest is suspended from that date until the date upon which the claim is filed.[7]

The interest mandated by Eminent Domain Procedure Law § 514 is essentially prejudgment interest in the sense that it is an element of just compensation. As the Court of Appeals has noted, "just compensation requires not only payment of the value of the property at the time of the taking but also interest on that sum to account for delay between the taking and the judgment."[8]

2. Eminent Domain Procedure Law § 511(A).

3. Eminent Domain Procedure Law § 511(B).

§ 14.108

1. Eminent Domain Procedure Law § 514(A).

2. *See supra*, § 14.44.

3. Eminent Domain Procedure Law § 514(A).

4. Eminent Domain Procedure Law § 501(A).

5. *See supra*, § 14.71.

6. *See supra*, § 14.66.

7. Eminent Domain Procedure Law § 514(B).

8. Adventurers Whitestone Corp. v. City of New York, 65 N.Y.2d 83, 87, 489 N.Y.S.2d 896, 899, 479 N.E.2d 241, 244, app. dismissed 474 U.S. 935, 106 S.Ct. 299, 88 L.Ed.2d 276 (1985).

The rate of interest utilized is to be the statutory rate, unless the claimant establishes that that rate is unreasonable when compared with the prevailing market rate.[9]

Library References:

West's Key No. Digests, Eminent Domain ⚖148, 247.

§ 14.109 Setoff for Indirect Benefits

The applicable rule with regard to whether the court may set off the value of benefits received by the condemnee against the condemnee's compensation award turns on whether the setoff is sought to be made against an award of direct damages or an award of consequential damages. Courts in New York have long held that setoffs for benefits may not be made from the award of direct damages, that is, damages for land actually taken by the condemnor.[1]

A setoff may be made against an award of consequential damages, however. Consequential benefits to the remainder of the condemnee's property are to be offset against consequential damages to that property.[2] The condemnor has the burden of proving the existence and value of consequential benefits to the condemnee.[3] A condemnee is never required to pay the condemnor for consequential benefits, however; those benefits can only be used as a setoff.

A benefit need not be limited or special to the condemnee in order to be set off. If all neighboring land is benefitted, as where a new or widened street gives greater or more convenient access to land, that benefit, to the extent it increases the value of the condemnee's remaining parcel, is to be set off. It is important to note that this rule applies only to the portion of the *retained parcel*, not to other land owned by the condemnee.[4] A setoff is generally not permitted where the condemnee is already paying for the benefit, as, for example, when an assessment has been levied on the condemnee's property to fund the public project.

Library References:

West's Key No. Digests, Eminent Domain ⚖144–146.

§ 14.110 Incidental Expenses and Proration of Taxes

Eminent Domain Procedure Law § 702 requires the condemnor to reimburse the condemnee for three categories of expenses: 1) recording

---

9. *Id.*

§ 14.109

1. *See e.g.*, Done Holding Co. v. State, 144 A.D.2d 528, 534 N.Y.S.2d 406 (2d Dep't 1988).

2. Besen v. State, 17 Misc.2d 119, 185 N.Y.S.2d 495 (Ct.Cl.1959) (condemnee benefitted from improved drainage provided by the condemnor).

3. Hogan v. State, 41 A.D.2d 428, 343 N.Y.S.2d 884 (3d Dep't 1973).

4. Brooklyn El. R. Co. v. Flynn, 87 Hun. 104, 33 N.Y.S. 974, app. dismissed 147 N.Y. 344, 41 N.E. 704 (1895).

fees, transfer taxes, and similar expenses associated with the transfer to the condemnor; 2) penalties incurred for prepayment of mortgages encumbering the property; and 3) a pro-rata share of "real property taxes, water rents, sewer rents, special ad valorem taxes and other charges paid or payable to a taxing entity" that were pre-paid by the condemnee.[1] Capital gains taxes are not "transfer taxes" under this section, and, as a result, the condemnor is not required to reimburse the condemnee for them.[2]

§ 14.111 Abandonment of Procedure by Condemnor

If the condemnor abandons the acquisition process prior to acquisition, the condemnor must reimburse the targeted condemnee for costs, disbursements, and expenses, including reasonable fees for attorney representation, appraisers and engineers, as well as other actual damages suffered by reason of the acquisition process.[1]

Library References:

West's Key No. Digests, Eminent Domain ⚖246.

§ 14.112 Finding That Condemnor Is Not Legally Authorized to Acquire the Property

If a court of competent jurisdiction determines that the condemnor was not legally authorized to acquire all or part of the property purportedly acquired,[1] the condemnor must reimburse the condemnee for costs, disbursements and expenses, including reasonable fees for attorney representation, appraisers and engineers, as well as other actual damages suffered by reason of the acquisition process.[2]

Library References:

West's Key No. Digests, Eminent Domain ⚖198(1).

§ 14.113 Finding Contrary to Claim by Condemnor That It Did Not Take Property

When a condemnor denies that it is engaged in a "taking," and therefore denies that it must compensate the condemnee, it is highly unlikely that it would make the offer to settle the condemnee's claim as

§ 14.110
1. Eminent Domain Procedure Law § 702(A)(3).
2. Heller v. State, 180 A.D.2d 299, 585 N.Y.S.2d 579 (3d Dep't 1992), aff'd 81 N.Y.2d 60, 595 N.Y.S.2d 731, 611 N.E.2d 770 (1993).

§ 14.111
1. Eminent Domain Procedure Law § 702(B).

§ 14.112
1. See supra, §§ 14.4, 14.5.
2. Eminent Domain Procedure Law § 702(B).

would otherwise be required by Eminent Domain Procedure Law § 301.[1] If a court of competent jurisdiction determines that the condemnor did in fact take the property, the condemnor must reimburse the condemnee for costs, disbursements and expenses, including reasonable attorney, appraiser and engineer fees that the condemnee incurred in establishing the *de facto* taking.[2]

§ 14.114 Decision by the Court and Entry of Judgment

Eminent Domain Procedure Law § 512 directs the court, upon hearing the testimony and weighing the evidence, to determine the compensation due the condemnees for damages resulting from the condemnor's acquisition. The court's decision, whether oral or in writing, must state the facts deemed by the court to be essential.[1] This decision must be rendered within sixty days after final submission of the matter.[2]

Eminent Domain Procedure Law § 513 mandates that the decision of the court direct preparation and entry of an appropriate judgment.[3] The normal rules with respect to entry of judgments apply, whether in the Court of Claims or supreme court, except that the rules of the former require that the judgment include a description of the acquired land.[4]

Library References:

West's Key No. Digests, Eminent Domain ⚖=240, 241.

§ 14.115 Additional Allowance for Costs and Expenses

When the condemnee brings a claim for compensation under Article 5 of the Eminent Domain Procedure Law,[1] it is usually because the condemnee believes the condemnor's offer pursuant to Article 3 of the Eminent Domain Procedure Law[2] is unacceptably low. Thus, the condemnee is put to the time and expense of bringing a claim that he or she might not have brought had the offer been higher. Eminent Domain Procedure Law § 701 permits the court to award an additional allowance to the condemnee when the condemnee's evaluation of the offer as being

§ 14.113

1. *See supra*, §§ 14.40–14.44.

2. Eminent Domain Procedure Law § 702(C). On *de facto* takings, *see supra*, § 14.14.

§ 14.114

1. Estate of Whitehall v. State, 174 A.D.2d 707, 573 N.Y.S.2d 871 (2d Dep't 1991) (cause remitted to the Court of Claims for a more detailed explanation of the method used to calculate damage award).

2. Eminent Domain Procedure Law § 512, incorporated by reference in CPLR 4213.

3. *See infra*, § 14.134, for a form Judgment Awarding Compensation in Claim for Acquisition of Property by Eminent Domain.

4. 22 NYCRR § 206.18.

§ 14.115

1. *See supra*, §§ 14.69 *et seq*.

2. *See supra*, §§ 14.40–14.44.

§ 14.115   EMINENT DOMAIN   Ch. 14

unacceptably low turns out to be correct.[3] The purpose of Section 701 is to "assure that property owners whose properties have been substantially undervalued will not have to bear costly litigation expenses for proving the inadequacy of the condemnor's offer" and thus to insure that the financial burden of litigation will not require them to forego their right to just compensation.[4] Therefore, when the court's award of compensation to the condemnee is "substantially in excess of the amount of the condemnor's proof," and when "deemed necessary by the court for the condemnee to receive just and adequate compensation," the court, upon application, notice[5] and an opportunity to be heard, may award an additional sum to the condemnee. This sum is for actual and necessary costs plus reasonable actual expenses for attorneys, appraisers and an engineer. In its application for this additional allowance, the condemnee must include affidavits not only of the condemnee,[6] but of all parties that have incurred expenses on the condemnee's behalf. These affidavits must set forth the amount of the incurred expenses. The condemnee may sign a satisfaction of judgment with the condemnor and still seek this additional allowance.[7]

Section 701 has generated a fair amount of litigation, some of which has clarified some ambiguity in the section. In *First Bank & Trust Co. of Corning v. State*,[8] the appellate division read Section 701 to require not only that the award be substantially in excess of the condemnor's offer but that the expenses incurred by the condemnee for which Section 701 compensation is sought must have been necessarily incurred to achieve the higher award. In *First Bank*, the award represented a 294% increase over the offer. The appellate division, nonetheless, upheld the Court of Claims' denial of additional compensation on the grounds that the large expenses incurred by the condemnee had not been required to achieve that award. Other cases have emphasized that the amount of costs awarded under Eminent Domain Procedure Law § 701 must be reasonable in relation to the monetary amount obtained by bringing the compensation claim.[9]

The discretionary nature of the trial court's power to award an additional allowance under Section 701 was emphasized by the Court of

---

3. See infra, § 14.137, for a form Order Granting Additional Allowance to Condemnee for Expert Witnesses.

4. Matter of N.Y. City Transit Authority, 160 A.D.2d 705, 709, 553 N.Y.S.2d 785, 789 (2d Dep't 1990).

5. See infra, § 14.135, for a form Notice of Motion for Additional Allowance to Condemnee for Expert Witnesses.

6. See infra, § 14.136, for a form Affidavit in Support of Motion for Additional Allowance to Condemnee for Expert Witnesses.

7. Taylor v. State, 200 A.D.2d 273, 613 N.Y.S.2d 743 (3d Dep't 1994).

8. 184 A.D.2d 1034, 585 N.Y.S.2d 261 (4th Dep't 1992), aff'd sub nom. Hakes v. State, 81 N.Y.2d 392, 599 N.Y.S.2d 498, 615 N.E.2d 982 (1993).

9. National Fuel Gas Supply Corp. v. Cunningham Natural Gas Corp., 191 A.D.2d 1003, 595 N.Y.S.2d 275 (4th Dep't 1993).

Appeals in an affirmance of the appellate division in *Hakes v. State*,[10] which also affirmed *First Bank*. The court noted that while the right of just compensation was constitutionally based, Section 701 allowances were not. Rather, such allowances are mere incidents of litigation and are not entitlements. "The reason courts are vested with discretion is to limit both the incentive for frivolous litigation and the cost of acquiring land through eminent domain."[11]

Library References:

West's Key No. Digests, Eminent Domain ⚖︎265.

§ 14.116 Payment Pending Appeal

An appeal of an eminent domain proceeding is governed by the same rules that govern civil appeals generally. The Eminent Domain Procedure Law does, however, contain specific rules with respect to payment pending appeal. Whether an appeal is taken by the condemnor or the condemnee, "the condemnor shall pay such portion of the award of the court from which appeal has not been taken upon proof of a condemnee's entitlement thereto."[1]

Library References:

West's Key No. Digests, Eminent Domain ⚖︎258.

§ 14.117 Small Claims Proceedings

Article 6 of the Eminent Domain Procedure Law sets forth special procedures for claims brought by condemnees seeking total compensation under $25,000, exclusive of interest.[1] Under such circumstances, a condemnee may file a claim with the clerk of the appropriate court[2] and a copy on the appropriate legal officer of the condemnor. The claim so filed must include a request to proceed under Section 6, and it must describe briefly the property and set forth the amount demanded in compensation and a concise statement of the basis for that amount.

The court must then view the property and meet with the parties to hear, in an informal manner, the parties' proof as to the amount of compensation due the condemnee.[3] A stenographic record is to be made

---

10. 81 N.Y.2d 392, 599 N.Y.S.2d 498, 615 N.E.2d 982 (1993).

11. *Id.*, 81 N.Y.2d at 397, 599 N.Y.S.2d at 502, 615 N.E.2d at 986.

§ 14.116

1. Eminent Domain Procedure Law § 514(C).

§ 14.117

1. Eminent Domain Procedure Law § 601(A). The monetary total was raised in 1993 from $5,000 for one condemnee to $25,000 from all condemnees.

2. *See supra*, § 14.48.

3. Eminent Domain Procedure Law § 601(B).

of this hearing. After considering the proof offered, the court is to render a decision, direct entry of a judgment, and serve the judgment on the parties.[4] The only ground for appeal of the judgment is that "substantial justice has not been accomplished between the parties according to the rules and principles of substantive law."[5]

The key difference between the procedures of Article 5 and the small claims procedures in Article 6 lies in the presentation of evidence on the issue of appropriate compensation. When the claim for compensation is relatively small, the parties could easily generate costs well in excess of the claim if they were required to prepare appraisal reports and offer expert testimony. Article 6 expressly states that parties need not have legal representation and need not present expert testimony in small claim proceedings.[6]

Library References:

West's Key No. Digests, Eminent Domain ⚖166–265(5).

§ 14.118 Summary

It is in the compensation stage that many lawyers find themselves in more familiar territory, at least in the sense of their representational role. Unlike many other trial settings, the advocates are in pursuit of the same goal—just compensation for the condemnee. But from the standpoint of the law, what is "just" is not what is best for the condemnee, but what is fair, taking into consideration not only the interests of the condemnee but also the interest of the public in not having condemned land overvalued. "There is a constitutional mandate upon the court to give just and fair compensation for any property taken. This means 'just' to the claimant and 'just' to the people who are required to pay for it."[1]

Although counsel for both condemnors and condemnees must be familiar with 1) the kinds of interests that are compensable and 2) the methods available to value those interests, the main task will be to retain qualified appraisers[2] and engineers to prepare and present information relevant to, and ultimate conclusions about, those valuations. The persons retained must be advised that the appraisal reports they

---

4. Eminent Domain Procedure Law § 603.
5. Eminent Domain Procedure Law § 604.
6. Eminent Domain Procedure Law § 602.

§ 14.118
1. Yaphank Dev. Co. v. County of Suffolk, 203 A.D.2d 280, 609 N.Y.S.2d 346 (2d Dep't 1994).

2. **PRACTICE POINTER:** The "Real Estate Appraisers" section of the Yellow Pages in the phone books for larger cities will contain a listing of New York-certified real estate appraisers.

prepare will be the blueprint for their testimony. As a result, these reports must be extraordinarily thorough.

§ 14.119 Procedural Checklist

1. Who is the condemnor?
    - The State of New York or one of its agencies (*See* § 14.4)
    - Another public entity (*See* § 14.5)
    - A private entity (*See* § 14.6)

2. Does the condemnor have express authority to condemn in this instance? (*See* §§ 14.4–14.6)
    - If no, grounds for challenge by condemnee on appeal. (*See* §§ 14.34–14.38)

3. Has the condemnor acted within the scope of its authority? (*See* §§ 14.4–14.6)
    - If no, grounds for challenge by condemnee on appeal. (*See* §§ 14.34–14.38)

4. Has the condemnor indicated the public use, benefit or purpose for which the land is to be taken? (*See* § 14.15)
    - Whether yes or no, grounds for challenge by condemnee on appeal. (*See* §§ 14.34–14.38)

The First Stage—the Condemnation Phase (§§ 14.20–14.39)

5. Has the condemnor held a public hearing? (*See* § 14.21)
    - If no, go to question 10.

6. If yes to #5, did the condemnor meet the pre-hearing public notice requirements? (*See* § 14.28)
    - If no, grounds for challenge by condemnee on appeal. (*See* §§ 14.34–14.38)

7. If yes to #5, did the condemnor properly conduct the public hearing? (*See* § 14.29)
    - If no, grounds for challenge by condemnee on appeal. (*See* §§ 14.34–14.38)

8. If yes to #5, did the condemnor make the required findings and determination and properly publish its synopsis? (*See* §§ 14.30, 14.31)
    - If no, grounds for challenge by condemnee on appeal. (*See* §§ 14.34–14.38)

9. If yes to #5, did the condemnee seek immediate appeal to the appellate division? (*See* § 14.34)

§ 14.119   EMINENT DOMAIN   Ch. 14

- If no, the condemnee is barred from raising any of the challenges arising out of questions 2, 3, 4, 6, 7 and 8.

10. If the condemnor did not hold a public hearing, what is the asserted ground for the exemption? (*See* § 14.22)

    - Overlap. (*See* §§ 14.23–14.24)
    - Alternate hearing. (*See* § 14.25)
    - *De minimis.* (*See* § 14.26)
    - Emergency. (*See* § 14.26)
    - Mental Hygiene Law. (*See* § 14.27)

11. If the condemnor did not hold a public hearing, did the condemnee bring an Article 78 proceeding to challenge the exemption? (*See* § 14.34)

    - If yes, the condemnee may not raise the issue again in a later proceeding nor allege defects related to questions 2, 3 and 4. If no, the condemnee may raise these issues against a non-State condemnor (*see* question 1) in the acquisition proceeding. (*See* §§ 14.56–14.65)

The Second Stage—the Offer and Negotiations Phase

12. Did the condemnor make a good faith offer to purchase the condemned property? (*See* § 14.43)

    - If no, the condemnor may be liable for damages to the condemnee. (*See* §§ 14.43 and 14.115)

13. Which option did the condemnee choose with respect to that offer?

    - Payment in full. (*See* § 14.43)

        (i) If the condemnee chose this option, the process is over, unless there is a conflicting claim. See question 18.

    - Advance payment. (*See* § 14.44)
    - Offer rejected. (*See* § 14.44)

The Third Stage—the Acquisition Phase

14. If the condemnor is the State, has it:

    - Prepared a valid acquisition map? (*See* § 14.51)
    - Met the filing and notice requirements? (*See* § 14.54)
    - Sent the notice of acquisition? (*See* 14.66)
    - If the answer to all three inquiries is yes, title is properly vested in the State. If the answer is no to any of the

questions, the taking can be challenged in an Article 78 proceeding.

15. If the condemnor is not the State, has it:
    - Filed a notice of pendency? (*See* § 14.57)
    - Filed a proper petition? (*See* §§ 14.58–14.60)
    - Given appropriate notice? (*See* § 14.61)
    - If the court granted the petition, has it sent or published the notice of acquisition? (*See* § 14.66)
        (i) If the answer to the above questions is yes, the condemnee will not have a basis to challenge the acquisition unless a ground discussed earlier has not been barred.

The Fourth Stage—the Compensation Phase

16. Did the condemnee file a timely claim? (*See* §§ 14.71 and 14.74)
    - If no, the condemnor's earlier offer will be treated as full payment.

17. Has a total taking (all of the condemnee's parcel) occurred? (*See* § 14.79)
    - If yes, the condemnee is entitled to the value of the land plus improvements. (*See* §§ 14.80, 14.81, 14.85–14.89)
    - If no, a partial taking has occurred, and in addition to compensation for the land taken, the condemnee will be compensated for damages to the remainder of the parcel. (*See* § 14.82)

18. Is there more than one claimed condemnee for the parcel or portion of the parcel?
    - Fee owner. (*See* § 14.99–14.101)
    - Lessee. (*See* § 14.94)
    - Lien holder. (*See* § 14.99)
        (i) If yes, the condemnee will be required to prove the extent of his or her right or interest in the land.

19. Have all appraisal reports intended to be used at trial been properly filed and exchanged? (*See* § 14.104)
    - If no, the appraisal may not be admitted into evidence, and the expert who prepared it will not be allowed to testify with regard to matters in the report. (*See* §§ 14.104, 14.105)

20. Is the award substantially in excess of the condemnor's earlier offer? (See § 14.115)
- If yes, the condemnee may be able to recover costs and fees from the condemnor. (See § 14.115)

§ 14.120 Forms—Demand on Condemnor to File Copy of Proceedings to Determine Need and Location of Public Project With Appellate Division for Purpose of Judicial Review[1]

SUPREME COURT OF THE STATE OF NEW YORK
APPELLATE DIVISION, _____ DEPARTMENT

_____,
          Petitioner
     against
_____,
          Respondent.

DEMAND

Index No. _____

To: [Name of Condemnor]

Demand is hereby made upon you, pursuant to Section 207 of the Eminent Domain Procedure Law, to forthwith file with the Appellate Division of the Supreme Court of the State of New York, _____ Department, a copy of a written transcript of the record of proceedings before you under Article 2 of the Eminent Domain Procedure Law to determine the need and location of a certain public project, namely _____, prior to the acquisition of property therefor, as well as a copy of your determination and findings in said proceeding.

Dated: _____, N.Y.
       _____, 19__.

                              Attorney for Petitioner
                              P.O. Address
                              Tel. No.

§ 14.120
1. Eminent Domain Procedure Law

§ 14.121 Forms—Petition for Review of Determination and Finding That Public Use, Benefit or Purpose Will Be Served by Proposed Acquisition[1]

SUPREME COURT OF THE STATE OF NEW YORK
APPELLATE DIVISION, _____ DEPARTMENT

```
_____ )
                       )
_____,     )
                       )
              Petitioner )
                       )  PETITION
          against      )
                       )  Index No. _____
_____,     )
                       )
              Respondent )
_____ )
```

The petition of _____, respectfully alleges and shows:

1. The petitioner, _____, is a resident of the State of New York.

2. The respondent, _____ Urban Renewal Agency, is a body corporate and politic organized and existing pursuant to Section _____ of the General Municipal Law of the State of New York.

3. The petitioner is the owner of certain real property located in the City of _____, State of New York, described as follows: [*insert description*].

4. The respondent, _____ Urban Renewal Agency, proposes to acquire the above described property, as well as other property by eminent domain for the purpose of constructing a public project thereon, to wit: [*set forth description of proposed project*].

5. Notice of a public hearing on the proposed acquisition and project was duly published between _____, 19__ and _____, 19__, in accordance with Section 202 of the Eminent Domain Procedure Law.

6. On _____, 19__, and pursuant to the aforesaid notice, a public hearing was held on the question of the proposed acquisition and project at the office of the respondent, located at _____ Street, _____, New

---

§ 207(A). *See* § 14.37.   § 207(A). *See* § 14.37.

§ 14.121
1. Eminent Domain Procedure Law

York, in accordance with Section 201 of the Eminent Domain Procedure Law.

7. Subsequently, on _____, 19__ and _____, 19__, the respondent, in accordance with Section 204 of the Eminent Domain Procedure Law, published a brief synopsis of its determination and findings in this matter.

8. Among other things, the respondent determined and found that the public use, benefit or purpose to be served by the proposed project is as follows: [*specify*]; that the approximate location for the proposed project and the reasons for the selection of such location are as follows: [*specify*], and that the general effect of the proposed project on the environment and residents of such locality will be as follows: [*specify*].

9. The petitioner, whose property is proposed to be acquired by eminent domain for the purposes of said project, is aggrieved by said determination and findings.

10. The petitioner contends that no public use, benefit or purpose will be served by the proposed acquisition for the following reasons: [*set forth reasons why no public use, benefit or purpose will be served, e.g., project is not needed because other projects serving same purpose are already located in area, project is too costly in relation to benefits to be derived therefrom, etc.*].

11. On _____, 19__, the petitioner served a demand on respondent to file with this court a copy of a written transcript of the record of the proceeding before it and a copy of its determination and findings. Annexed hereto is the affidavit of service of _____, sworn to _____, 19__.

12. No previous application has been made for the relief sought herein.

WHEREFORE, petitioner prays for a judgment of this court rejecting the determination and findings of the respondent regarding the aforesaid proposed acquisition and granting such other and further relief as the court deems just and proper.

Dated: _____, N.Y.

_____, 19__.

_____
Petitioner

[*Verification*]

§ 14.122 Forms—Judgment of Appellate Division Rejecting the Determination and Finding That Public Use, Benefit or Purpose Will Be Served by Proposed Acquisition[1]

> At a Term of the Appellate Division of the Supreme Court of the State of New York, _____ Judicial Department, held in _____ County on _____, 19__.

HON. _____,
HON. _____,
HON. _____,
HON. _____,
HON. _____,

Acting Presiduing Justice,

Associate Justices.

_____,

         Petitioner

against

_____,

         Respondent

JUDGMENT

Index No. _____

The above named petitioner having commenced a proceeding under Section 207 of the Eminent Domain Procedure Law, in the Appellate Division of the Supreme Court in the _____ Judicial Department by a petition dated _____, 19__, for a judgment rejecting the determination and findings of the respondent, _____ Urban Renewal Agency, dated _____, 19__, that the proposed acquisition by eminent domain of certain property located in the City of _____, New York, for the purpose of constructing the following described public project thereon will serve a public use, benefit or purpose: [_describe public project_], and the proceeding having come on to be heard before this court on _____, 19__, and the issues therein having been argued by _____, 19__, Esq. for petitioner and _____, Esq. for respondent, and due deliberation having been had thereon, and upon this court's opinion and decision heretofore filed, it is

§ 14.122
1. Eminent Domain Procedure Law § 207(C). See § 14.38.

§ 14.122   EMINENT DOMAIN   Ch. 14

ORDERED, ADJUDGED AND DECREED that the petition be and the same hereby is granted, and it is further

ORDERED, ADJUDGED AND DECREED that the determination and findings of the respondent, _____ Urban Renewal Agency, dated _____, 19__, that the proposed acquisition by eminent domain for the public project hereinabove described will serve a public use, benefit or purpose, be and the same hereby are rejected.

Enter,

_____
Clerk of Appellate Division

§ 14.123   Forms—Complaint by Condemnee to Establish Fair and Reasonable Value for Temporary Use and Occupancy After Acquisition by Eminent Domain[1]

[Add title of court and cause]

COMPLAINT
Index No. _____

The plaintiff, by his attorney _____, alleges:

1. That plaintiff is a resident of the County of _____, State of New York.

2. That, upon information and belief, defendant, _____ Urban Renewal Agency, is a body corporate and politic organized and existing pursuant to Section _____ of the General Municipal Law of the State of New York.

3. That defendant is the owner of the following described premises, having acquired the same by eminent domain on _____, 19__ :

[insert description of premises]

4. That prior to said acquisition by the defendant, the plaintiff had been the owner in fee of said premises and had conducted a business thereon since _____, 19__, to wit: *[set forth nature of business]*.

5. That from _____, 19__, the aforesaid date of acquisition of said premises by the defendant, until the present time, the plaintiff has continued to occupy said premises and conduct his business thereon.

---

§ 14.123   § 305(B). *See* § 14.45.
1. Eminent Domain Procedure Law

Ch. 14 NOTICE OF PENDENCY OF PROCEEDING § 14.124

6. That plaintiff intends to continue occupation of said premises until approximately _____, 19__, when he will move his business to a new location, unless forced by the defendant to vacate at an earlier date.

7. That, subsequent to the acquisition of the subject premises by the defendant and on _____, 19__, the defendant notified the plaintiff by letter that it had established the sum of _____ ($_____) Dollars per week as the fair and reasonable value for the temporary use and occupancy of the premises.

8. That by letter dated _____, 19__, the plaintiff informed the defendant that said amount was too high and that he would not pay the same.

9. That subsequently, the defendant has made a number of demands for payment of the amount established by it, and the plaintiff has refused to make such payment.

10. That plaintiff contends that the fair and reasonable amount for the temporary use and occupancy of the subject premises is _____ ($_____) Dollars per week; in that [here set forth facts supporting such contention].

WHEREFORE, plaintiff demands judgment establishing the fair and reasonable value for the temporary use of and occupancy by the plaintiff of the subject premises from _____, 19__, until the property is vacated, and for such other and further relief as the court deems proper.

                                  _____
                                  Attorney for Petitioner
                                  P.O. Address
                                  Tel. No.

[Verification]

§ 14.124 Forms—Notice of Pendency of Proceeding in Supreme Court to Acquire Property by Eminent Domain and File Acquisition Map[1]

[Add title of court and cause]

                                  NOTICE OF PENDENCY
                                  Index No. ____

NOTICE IS HEREBY GIVEN that a proceeding has been commenced and is now pending in this court upon the petition of _____ for the acquisi-

---

§ 14.124
1. Eminent Domain Procedure Law § 402(B)(1). See § 14.57.

§ 14.124   EMINENT DOMAIN   Ch. 14

tion by eminent domain of the real property hereinafter described, situated in the county of _____:

> [insert general description by metes and bounds or by section, block and lot number]

The names of the condemnees of the real property described above, all of whom are known, are as follows: [list condemnees].

Dated: _____, 19__.

            Attorney for Petitioner
            P.O. Address
            Tel. No.

To the Clerk of the County of _____:

You are hereby directed to index the foregoing Notice of Pendency against the names of the condemnees listed therein.

Dated: _____, 19__.

            Attorney for Petitioner
            P.O. Address
            Tel. No.

§ 14.125   Forms—Notice of Petition in Proceeding in Supreme Court to Acquire Property by Eminent Domain and File Acquisition Map[1]

[Add title of court and cause]

            NOTICE OF PETITION
            Index No. ___

PLEASE TAKE NOTICE, that upon the annexed petition of [name of condemnor], verified on the _____ day of _____, 19__, and [specify other supporting papers], an application will be made to a Term, Part _____, of this court to be held at the courthouse thereof, located at _____, on the _____ day of _____, 19__, at _____ o'clock in the forenoon of that day, or as soon thereafter as counsel can be heard, for an order to acquire by eminent domain the real property described in the petition therein and for permission to file the acquisition map thereof in

---

§ 14.125   § 402(B)(2). See § 14.61.
1. Eminent Domain Procedure Law

the office of the County Clerk [or Register] of _____ County, and for such other and further relief as may be just and proper.

PLEASE TAKE FURTHER NOTICE that annexed hereto is a copy of that portion of the proposed acquisition map affecting your property.

Dated: _____, New York
_____, 19__

                                            Attorney for Petitioner
                                            P.O. Address
                                            Tel. No.

To: _____

[*Last known owner or owners of record of property to be acquired, as same appears from record of tax assessor of district wherein parcel or parcels are located*]

§ 14.126 Forms—Petition in Proceeding in Supreme Court to Acquire Property by Eminent Domain and File Acquisition Map[1]

[*Add title of court and cause*]

                                      PETITION
                                      Index No. _____

TO THE SUPREME COURT OF THE STATE OF NEW YORK:

    1. Petitioner is a [*characterize petitioner, e.g., municipal corporation*] created and existing under the laws of the State of New York.

    2. Petitioner seeks to acquire by eminent domain the real property hereinafter described for the purpose of constructing a certain public project thereon, to wit: [*describe proposed project*].

    3. Petitioner has complied with all of the requirements of Article 2 of the Eminent Domain Procedure Law.

or

    3. Petitioner is exempt from compliance with Article 2 of the Eminent Domain Procedure Law in relation to the proposed acquisition in that: [*show basis for exemption*].

---

§ 14.126
1. Eminent Domain Procedure Law § 402(B). *See* § 14.59.

§ 14.126   EMINENT DOMAIN   Ch. 14

[If not exempt from compliance with Article 2, show compliance as in the succeeding 3 paragraphs.]

4. Notice of a public hearing on the proposed acquisition and project was duly published by the petitioner between _____, 19__ and _____, 19__, in accordance with Section 202 of the Eminent Domain Procedure Law.

5. On _____, 19__, and pursuant to the aforesaid notice, a public hearing was held on the question of the proposed acquisition and project at the office of the petitioner located at _____ Street, _____, New York, in accordance with Section 201 of the Eminent Domain Procedure Law.

6. Subsequently, on _____, 19__ and _____, 19__, the respondent, in accordance with Section 204 of the Eminent Domain Procedure Law, published a brief synopsis of its determination and findings in this matter. A copy of the complete determination and findings of the petitioner is annexed hereto.

7. Annexed hereto are copies of the proposed acquisition and notice of pendency of this proceeding.

8. The names and places of residence of the owners of the real property to be acquired are as follows:

Names of Owners	Residence

9. The description and location of the real property to be acquired are as follows:

[set forth description and location, either by metes and bounds of each individual parcel, or section, block and lot number, and by reference to the acquisition map and notice of pendency]

10. The public use, benefit or purpose for which the property is required is: *[set forth public use, benefit or purpose, e.g., the construction of a facility for the care of runaway children]*.

11. *[If petitioner is a non-governmental condemnor subject to the jurisdiction, supervision and regulation of the public service commission or commissioner of transportation, add the following:]* The petitioner shall deposit a bond or undertaking with the clerk of this court prior to the vesting of title to the real property described above in an amount to be fixed by the court on the return date of the petition.

12. *[If the property is to be used for the construction of a major utility transmission facility, as defined in Public Service Law § 120 with respect to which a certificate of environmental compatibility and public need has been issued under such law, add the following:]* On _____,

Ch. 14   PETITIONER EXEMPT FROM COMPLIANCE § 14.127

19__, a certificate of environmental compatibility and public need was issued to the petitioner and is in force.

WHEREFORE, petitioner requests that the court direct entry of an order authorizing the filing of the acquisition map herein in the office of the County Clerk [or Register] of the County of _____, and that upon such filing title to the property described above shall vest in the petitioner.

   Dated: _____, N.Y.
          _____, 19__

                              _____
                              Petitioner

                              By _____
                              [Title]

                              _____
                              Attorney for Petitioner
                              P.O. Address
                              Tel. No.

[Verification]

§ 14.127 Forms—Petition in Proceeding in Supreme Court to Acquire Property by Eminent Domain and File Acquisition Map—Petitioner Exempt From Compliance With Eminent Domain Procedure Law Article 2[1]

[Add title of court and cause]

                       PETITION
                       Index No. __

TO THE SUPREME COURT OF THE STATE OF NEW YORK

   Petitioner, _____ ELECTRIC & GAS CORPORATION, respectfully represents:

   1. Petitioner is an electric and gas corporation organized under the Transportation Corporations Law of the State of New York and is vested by that law with the power of eminent domain.

   2. Petitioner is exempt from the requirements of Article 2 of the EDPL under EDPL Section 206 because petitioner has heretofore ob-

§ 14.127   §§ 206, 402(B). See supra § 14.59.
1. Eminent Domain Procedure Law

§ 14.127 EMINENT DOMAIN Ch. 14

tained a Certificate of Environmental Compatibility and Public Need under Article VII of the Public Service Law of the State of New York, which Certificate is in force.

3. Attached hereto as EXHIBIT B is a copy of the proposed acquisition map to be filed. A copy of the Notice of Pendency of this action is attached hereto as SCHEDULE I.

4. Upon information and belief, the owner of the property to be acquired is _____, and further upon information and belief the following persons have or may have a lien or claim against the said property: _____ and _____.

5. Attached hereto as EXHIBIT A is a metes and bounds description of the easement to be acquired and its location. Said description describes the land shown on the acquisition map and is the same description as that contained in the Notice of Pendency of the proceeding, which is attached hereto as SCHEDULE I.

6. The public use, benefit or purpose for which the property is required is the construction, operation and maintenance of an electric transmission facility, which will be used in providing service to petitioner's customers in _____ County.

7. Prior to the vesting of title, petitioner will deposit a bond or undertaking with the clerk of this court in an amount to be fixed by the court on the return date of the petition, which bond or undertaking Petitioner believes should be set at no more than $_____, the amount of Petitioner's highest approved appraisal.

WHEREFORE, petitioner requests that this court grant an Order (1) authorizing the filing of the acquisition map; (2) authorizing the filing of a bond or undertaking in an amount specified by the court; (3) directing that upon the filing of the Order, the acquisition map, and the bond or undertaking, title shall vest in petitioner; (4) specifying a time for the filing of claims as required by EDPL Section 503; and (5) granting Petitioner such other relief as the court deems just and proper.[2]

Dated: _____, 19__

_____, New York

                                      Attorney for Petitioner
                                      P.O. Address
                                      Tel. No.

[Verification]

2. The above form was adapted from the record in New York State Electric & Gas Corp. v. Karas, 85 A.D.2d 758, 445 N.Y.S.2d 279 (3d Dep't 1981).

§ 14.128 Forms—Answer to Petition in Proceeding in Supreme Court to Acquire Property by Eminent Domain and File Acquisition Map[1]

[Add title of court and cause]

ANSWER
Index No. ___

The undersigned, _____ EW in answer to the petition herein, states as follows:

1. OWNERSHIP. That she is the owner of the real property located at _____ _____ Road, _____, New York which property is the subject of an eminent domain proceeding commenced by the Town of _____, New York to acquire an easement for the construction of a sidewalk; respondent-condemnee is not "_____ CW", the respondent named in the above petition.

2. Respondent-condemnee admits the allegations of the condemnor-petitioner's Petition For Acquisition of Real Property by Eminent Domain, set forth at paragraphs numbered "1", "2", "3", "5" and "7".

3. NEGOTIATIONS. That there have been no negotiations relative to the sidewalk, as to location, price to be paid or anything else.

4. That respondent-condemnee (hereinafter respondent) denies the allegations of condemnor's petition numbered "4", "6", "8", "11" and "12".

5. That respondent has no information as to the allegations in condemnor's petition contained in paragraphs numbered "10", "13", "14", "15" and "16", and therefore, denies same.

FOR AN AFFIRMATIVE AND ALTERNATIVE DEFENSE

6. That petitioner has reviewed the taking map served with the papers herein and states the following:

(1) That a number of years ago, when State Route _____ was improved, the old road which was at grade level with the properties alongside, was raised 4 or 5 feet.

(2) The sidewalks in the Town of _____ are all rather close to the roads they run along, i.e. 2–4 feet from the road. Along _____ Avenue, the sidewalks run alongside of, and are a part of, the pavement.

---

§ 14.128

1. Eminent Domain Procedure Law § 402(B)(4). See § 14.63.

§ 14.128   EMINENT DOMAIN   Ch. 14

(3) The sidewalk to the east of respondent's property, and alongside _____ Road, is about 2 feet from the shoulder of _____. Now when condemnor wishes to extend this sidewalk westerly, first of all to save money, the Town has designed the proposed sidewalk on top of a bank of earth in front of the _____ property and then, runs the sidewalk well into the frontage of this respondent's property, making for an unnecessary and excessive taking. The remaining property between the sidewalk and the road will be rendered valueless to this respondent. The walk, if it has to be, should be placed nearer to _____ Road, and at an elevation equal to the present southerly shoulder of _____ Road. To do otherwise is an unwarranted and excessive invasion of respondent's property and amounts to an improvident exercise of the responsibility and discretion of the officials of the condemnor, Town of _____.

WHEREFORE, _____, (_____ CW being deceased) respectfully asks for an Order:

1. Dismissing the petition herein on the above stated grounds or directing the condemnor to modify or alter the location (a) nearer to the road and at an elevation equal or nearly equal to the shoulder of said road.

2. Granting a hearing to respondent, unless the court shall determine that this Petition is without merit as to the named deceased respondent, "_____ CW".[2]

Dated: _____, 19__

                                    Attorneys for _____
                                    P.O. Address
                                    Tel. No.

[Verification]

§ 14.129 Forms—Order to Show Cause Why Condemnor Should Not Be Permitted to Enter Immediately Upon Real Property and Devote It Temporarily to Public Use Specified in Petition Upon Deposit of a Fixed Sum With the Court[1]

                                  At a Term, Part ___, of the
                                  Supreme Court of the State of

---

2. The above form was adapted from the record in Whiting v. Town of Pittsford, 105 A.D.2d 1141, 482 N.Y.S.2d 1015 (4th Dep't 1984).

§ 14.129
1. Eminent Domain Procedure Law § 402(B)(6). See § 14.67.

Ch. 14 ORDER TO SHOW CAUSE § 14.129

New York, held in and for the County of _____ at the Court House, _____, New York, on the ___ day of ___, 19__.

Present: Hon. _____, Justice.

[*Add title of cause*]

ORDER TO SHOW CAUSE

Index No. ___

Upon the verified petition, the notice of petition and Notice of Pendency, and upon proof of service thereof in accordance with the requirements of the Eminent Domain Procedure Law, the Affidavit of _____, sworn to on the _____ day of _____, 19__, and of _____, sworn to on the ___ day of _____, 19__,

LET any opposing party Show Cause at a Term, Part I, of this Court to be held at the Court House thereof, at _____, New York, on the ___ day of _____, 19__, at ___ o'clock in the ___ noon of that day or as soon thereafter as counsel can be heard,

WHY an Order should not be entered herein pursuant to § 402(B)(6) of the Eminent Domain Procedure Law directing that petitioner be permitted to enter immediately upon the real property to be taken as described in said Petition and devote it temporarily to the public use specified therein upon deposit with the Court of a sum to be fixed by the Court, and

Restraining any party claiming under or through the _____ Society from interfering with or molesting the petitioner, its agents, servants and employees from maintaining the facilities now upon such premises until the further Order of this Court, and for such other and further relief as may be sufficient, proper and equitable; and it is further ordered

Sufficient reason appearing therefor, let service of a copy of this Order, together with the papers upon which it is granted, if served upon the _____ Society, Inc. and The Village of _____, on or before _____ P.M. on the _____ day of _____, 19__, be deemed sufficient service; and it is further

ORDERED that in the meantime, and until further order of this Court, _____ Society, Inc., and all persons acting on its behalf, be and are hereby stayed from interfering with the petitioner, its agents, servants and contractors in maintaining the facilities presently on the said premises and from bringing any action, suit or proceeding arising from the continued maintenance of such facilities, all until further order of this Court.[2]

---

2. The above form was adapted from the record in American Telephone and Telegraph Co. v. Salesian Society, Inc., 77 A.D.2d 706, 430 N.Y.S.2d 408 (3d Dep't),

§ 14.129   EMINENT DOMAIN   Ch. 14

Enter,

_____

J.S.C.

§ 14.130 Forms—Order to Show Cause Why Condemnor Should Not Be Permitted to File Acquisition Maps or Enter Upon Real Property[1]

> At a Term, Part _____, of the Supreme Court of the State of New York, held in and for the County of _____, at _____, on the _____ day of _____, 19__.

Present: Hon. _____, Justice.

[*Add title of cause*]

ORDER TO SHOW CAUSE
Index No. _____

Upon reading and filing the annexed affidavit of _____ dated and sworn to the _____ day of _____, 19__, it is

ORDERED that respondents, _____ SQUARE, INC. and _____ ASSOCIATES, INC., show cause before this Court at a Term, Part _____ thereof, to be held at the County Courthouse, _____ Street, _____, New York, on _____, 19__, at __ a.m., or as soon thereafter as counsel may be heard, why an Order should not be entered pursuant to Section 402(B)(5) of the Eminent Domain Procedure Law (EDPL) granting the petition and directing the immediate filing and entry of the acquisition maps or, alternatively, and pursuant to Section 402(6) of the EDPL, granting _____ immediate entry upon and temporary possession of the lots described in the petition filed herein on _____, 19__ upon the ground that the public interest will be prejudiced by further delays in this proceeding, and granting to _____ such other and further relief as the Court may deem just and proper, and it is further

ORDERED, that service of a copy of this Order to Show Cause and the papers upon which it is based upon _____, Esq., attorney for respondent _____ SQUARE, INC., and _____, _____, _____ & _____, attorneys for respondent _____ ASSOCIATES, INC., by personal delivery to their offices located respectively at _____ Ave.,

---

app. dismissed 51 N.Y.2d 877, 433 N.Y.S.2d 1030, 414 N.E.2d 405, app. denied 52 N.Y.2d 701, 436 N.Y.S.2d 1025, 417 N.E.2d 1013 (1980).

§ 14.130
1. Eminent Domain Procedure Law § 402(B)(5). *See* § 14.65.

Ch. 14   ORDER IN SUPREME COURT   § 14.131

_____, New York and at _____ Street, _____, New York, on _____, 19__, shall be deemed good and sufficient service thereof; and it is further

ORDERED, that answering papers on behalf of respondent are to be served upon the attorney for petitioner by delivering a copy thereof to his office no later than two (2) days before the return date of this motion.[2]

Enter,

_____
J.S.C.

§ 14.131   Forms—Order in Proceeding in Supreme Court to Acquire Property by Eminent Domain and File Acquisition Map[1]

At a Term, Part _____, of the Supreme Court of the State of New York, held in and for the County of _____, at _____, on _____, 19__.

Present: Hon. _____ Justice.

[Add title of cause]

ORDER
Index No. ___

Petitioner _____, having commenced a proceeding to obtain an order to acquire by eminent domain certain real property described in the petition herein and for permission to file the acquisition map pertaining thereto in the office of the County Clerk [or Register] of _____ County,

NOW, upon reading the notice of petition dated, _____, 19__, and the petition verified _____, 19__, and the exhibits thereto with due proof of service thereof, and the answer of _____, verified _____, 19__, and the court having found to its satisfaction that the procedural requirements of the Eminent Domain Procedure Law have been met, it is

ORDERED, that the petition be and the same hereby is granted, and it is further

---

2. The above form was adapted from the record of In the Matter of Consolidated Edison Company of New York, Inc., 143 A.D.2d 1012, 533 N.Y.S.2d 591 (2d Dep't 1988).

§ 14.131

1. Eminent Domain Procedure Law § 402(B)(5). See supra § 14.65.

§ 14.131 EMINENT DOMAIN Ch. 14

ORDERED, that this order shall immediately be filed and entered, and it is further

ORDERED, that the petitioner shall file and enter this order, together with the acquisition map herein, in the office of the County Clerk [or Register] of _____ County, and it is further

ORDERED, that upon the filing of this order and the acquisition map in the office of the County Clerk [or Register] of _____ County, acquisition of the property in such map shall be complete and title thereto shall then be vested in the petitioner, and it is further

[*if petitioner is a nongovernmental condemnor subject to the jurisdiction, supervision and regulation of the public service commission or the commissioner of transportation, add the following:*]

ORDERED, that the bond [or *undertaking*] deposited by the petitioner herein shall be applied, in the amount necessary, for any default by the petitioner in the payment of all or part of the damages determined in the acquisition herein or the abandonment thereof.

Enter,

_____

J.S.C.

§ 14.132 Forms—Notice of Acquisition by Eminent Domain Where Supreme Court Has Jurisdiction[1]

[*Add title of court and cause*]

NOTICE OF ACQUISITION BY
EMINENT DOMAIN
Index No. ___

NOTICE IS HEREBY GIVEN that on _____, 19__, an order of this Court, dated _____, 19__, vesting title in [*name of condemnor*] to the real property hereinafter described pursuant to the Eminent Domain Procedure Law, and the acquisition map pertaining thereto, were entered and filed in the office of the County Clerk [or *Register*] of the County of _____.

The real property so acquired is described as follows: [*insert general description of property*].

NOTICE IS FURTHER GIVEN that any written claim for damages or notice of appearance that you wish to file pursuant to Section 503 of the Eminent Domain Procedure Law must be filed with the clerk of this

---

§ 14.132   § 502(B). *See supra* § 14.66.
1. Eminent Domain Procedure Law

Ch. 14 CLAIM FOR DAMAGES § 14.133

court on or before _____, 19__, and a copy of the same shall be served on _____ [*condemnor's chief legal officer or other official designated*].

[*Name of Condemnor*]

By _____

[*Title*]
P.O. Address
Tel. No.

§ 14.133 Forms—Claim for Damages Arising From Acquisition by Eminent Domain—General Form[1]

[*Add title of court and cause*]

Claim

Claim No. ___ [*if Court of Claims*]

or

Index No. ___ [*if Supreme Court*]

Claimant, _____, for its claim against [*State of New York or other condemnor*], respectfully shows to this court:

1. The post office address of the claimant herein is _____ Street, _____, New York.

2. This claim is for the permanent acquisition by [*name of condemnor*] through the power of eminent domain of the following real property: [*set forth reasonable identification of property by reference to the acquisition map or otherwise*]. Annexed hereto is a copy of the acquisition map filed by [*name of condemnor*].

3. Notice of acquisition was served upon the claimant on _____, 19__,

4. At the time of said acquisition the claimant was the sole owner in fee of said real property.

5. The particulars of claimant's damages are as follows:

Land appropriated .... [$_____]
Improvements appropriated .... [_____]

§ 14.133
1. Eminent Domain Procedure Law

§ 504. *See supra* § 14.76.

205

§ 14.133   EMINENT DOMAIN   Ch. 14

Damages to remaining land and improvements .... [_____]
Total .... [$_____]

Annexed hereto is a schedule of fixture items which comprise part [*or all*] of the damages claimed.

6. This claim has not been assigned in whole or in part.

[*In Court of Claims, add following:*]

7. This claim is filed within three (3) years after [*service of notice of acquisition or date of vesting, whichever is later*] (*or*)

This claim is filed on or before _____, 19__, the time fixed by order of this court.

[*In supreme court, add the following:*]

7. This claim is filed on or before _____, 19__, the time specified by this court.

WHEREFORE, claimant demands judgment against [*State of New York or other condemnor*] in the sum of _____ ($_____) Dollars, together with interest thereon as allowed by law.

Dated: _____, 19__.

                              Attorney for Claimant
                              P.O. Address
                              Tel. No.

[*Verification*]

§ 14.134 Forms—Judgment Awarding Compensation in Claim for Acquisition of Property by Eminent Domain[1]

STATE OF NEW YORK: COURT OF CLAIMS

_____,	)
Claimant	)
against	) JUDGMENT
_____,	) Claim No. _____
Defendant	)

§ 14.134
1. Eminent Domain Procedure Law

§ 513. *See supra* § 14.114.

Ch. 14 JUDGMENT AWARDING COMPENSATION § 14.134

APPEARANCES: For the Claimant:

———, ———, ———,
———, ———, ———,
Esqs.
by: ———, Esq.
of counsel

For the State:

Hon. ————————
Attorney General
by: ————————
Assistant Attorney General of counsel

This claim for the sum of [$———] for damages resulting from the permanent acquisition on ———, 19— of premises situated in the Town of ———, County of ———, described on Acquisition Map No. ———, Parcel Nos. ———, ———, ———, ———, ———, for highway purposes described as the ——— Expressway, Section ———, ——— Road, ——— County, filed ———, 19—, and numbered ———, came on to be heard before this Court at a session thereof held in the City of ———, New York, on ———, 19—, before the Hon. ———, a Judge of the Court of Claims.

The Court having heard proofs and allegations of the parties and having duly made and filed its decision on ———, 19—, the parties having waived the submission of proposed Findings of Fact, it is

ORDERED AND ADJUDGED that ———, the above-named claimant, recover herein against the State of New York the sum of ——— ($———) Dollars, with interest thereon at the rate of ——— percent per annum from ———, 19—, the date of acquisition, to the date of payment thereof, for all damages resulting from the acquisition of said property for:

Proceeding ———
——— EXPRESSWAY
SECTION ———
——— ROAD
——— COUNTY

Acquisition Map ———, Parcels ———, ———, ———, ———, ——— and in full settlement of said claim.

Dated: ———, New York
———, 19—

§ 14.134 EMINENT DOMAIN Ch. 14

Chief Clerk of the Court of Claims

§ 14.135 Forms—Notice of Motion for Additional Allowance to Condemnee for Expert Witnesses[1]

[Add title of court and cause]

NOTICE OF MOTION
Index No. ___

[Name of Assigned Judge]
Oral argument is requested
(check box if applicable) ☐

PLEASE TAKE NOTICE, that upon the annexed affidavit of _____, sworn to on the _____ day of _____, 19_, and upon all of the papers and proceedings heretofore filed and had herein, a motion will be made in this Court at a Term thereof, to be held at the County Courthouse (Room _____), City of _____, New York, on the _____ day of _____, 19 _, at _____ o'clock in the _____ noon of that day or as soon thereafter as counsel can be heard, for an Order pursuant to Section 701 of the Eminent Domain Procedure Law granting to the claimant, _____, an additional allowance for extraordinary expenses incurred for expert witnesses, and for such other and further relief as the court deems proper.

Pursuant to CPLR 2214(b), answering affidavits, if any, are required to be served upon the undersigned at least seven days before the return date of this motion. ☐

(check box if applicable)

Dated: _____, New York
_____, 19_

[Specify name of individual attorney in charge of motion]

_____, _____ & _____
Attorney for Claimant
P.O. Address
Tel. No.

§ 14.135
1. Eminent Domain Procedure Law § 701. See supra § 14.115.

TO: _____

Attorney for Defendant
P.O. Address
Tel. No.

§ 14.136 Forms—Affidavit in Support of Motion for Additional Allowance to Condemnee for Expert Witnesses[1]

[*Add title of court and cause*]

AFFIDAVIT
Index No. _____
[*Name of Assigned Judge*]

STATE OF NEW YORK)
) ss.:
COUNTY OF _____)

_____, being duly sworn, deposes and says:

1. I am the claimant in the above entitled proceeding.

2. This affidavit is submitted in support of claimant's application under Section 701 of the Eminent Domain Procedure Law for an additional allowance for extraordinary expenses for expert witnesses.

3. On _____, 19__, the judgment of this court awarded the claimant the sum of _____ ($_____) Dollars as just compensation for the acquisition by [*condemnor*] of the real property involved herein. This award was substantially in excess of the amount of the condemnor's proof.

4. The issues presented for decision in this matter were both complex and difficult, involving the question of whether the subject property was to be valued on a basis of reproduction costs less depreciation, rather than through the utilization of market or income capitalization approaches.

5. As a result thereof, the claimant was forced to expend substantial sums of money and has borne extraordinary expenses for expert witness fees beyond the expense for the preparation of an expert witness appraisal report for the real property and fixtures. These expenditures were as follows:

Name of Expert Witness	Address	Field of Expertise	Fee

---

§ 14.136
1. Eminent Domain Procedure Law

§ 701. *See supra* § 14.115.

§ 14.136   EMINENT DOMAIN   Ch. 14

Name of Expert Witness	Address	Field of Expertise	Fee

Annexed hereto are the affidavits of the aforesaid expert witnesses setting forth the amount of the expenses incurred.

WHEREFORE, claimant respectfully requests that this court grant an additional allowance in the sum of $_____ to the claimant for extraordinary expenses incurred for expert witnesses, pursuant to Section 701 of the Eminent Domain Procedure Law, and for such other and further relief as the court deems proper.

[Type Name]

[Signature]

§ 14.137 Forms—Order Granting Additional Allowance To Condemnee for Expert Witnesses[1]

At a Term, Part _____, of the Supreme Court of the State of New York, held in and for the County of _____, at _____, on _____, 19__.

Present: Hon. _____ Justice.
[Add title of cause]

ORDER
Index No. __

The claimant, _____, having duly moved for an order, pursuant to Section 701 of the Eminent Domain Procedure Law, granting an additional allowance to him for extraordinary expenses incurred for expert witnesses in connection with his claim for just compensation herein, and said motion having regularly come on to be heard,

Now, upon reading and filing the notice of motion dated _____, 19__, the affidavits of _____, _____, _____, _____ and _____, all sworn to on _____, 19__, and [specify other supporting papers], in support of the motion, and the affidavit of _____, Esq., sworn to on _____, 19__, in opposition thereto, and after hearing _____, Esq. for the claimant in support of the motion, and _____, Esq., of counsel, for the defendant, in opposition thereto, and due deliberation having been held thereon,

§ 14.137
1. Eminent Domain Procedure Law

§ 701. See supra § 14.115.

Now, on motion of _____, Esq., attorney for claimant, it is

ORDERED, that the claimant's application for an additional allowance be and the same hereby is granted and the claimant is awarded the sum of $_____ as an additional allowance pursuant to Section 701 of the Eminent Domain Procedure Law.

                                              Enter,

                                              _____

                                              J.S.C.

Chapter 15

ENVIRONMENTAL LAW

by
Steven Russo

Table of Sections

15.1	Scope Note.
15.2	Strategy.
15.3	State Environmental Quality Review Act.
15.4	____ Determination of Significance.
15.5	____ The Environmental Impact Statement and Findings Statement.
15.6	____ Judicial Review.
15.7	____ Checklist.
15.8	Water Pollution Control.
15.9	____ SPDES Permit Program.
15.10	____ Stormwater Discharges and Oil Spills.
15.11	____ Enforcement.
15.12	____ Strategy: Clean Water Act Citizen Suit Checklist.
15.13	Wetlands Protection.
15.14	____ Strategy: Checklist.
15.15	____ The Federal Scheme.
15.16	____ New York Tidal and Freshwater Wetlands Law.
15.17	____ Permit Procedure and Criteria.
15.18	____ Penalties.
15.19	Air Pollution Control.
15.20	____ The 1990 CAA Amendments.
15.21	____ New York State Requirements.
15.22	____ Enforcement.
15.23	Regulation of Solid and Hazardous Waste.
15.24	____ New York Hazardous Waste Regulation.
15.25	____ Enforcement.
15.26	Regulation of Underground Storage Tanks and Petroleum Storage Tanks—Federal Law.
15.27	____ New York Law.
15.28	Regulation of Inactive Hazardous Waste Sites—CERCLA.
15.29	____ CERCLA Section 107(a).
15.30	____ Lender Liability, Contribution and Indemnification Under CERCLA.
15.31	____ New York Law.
15.32	Relevant Common Law Doctrines—Nuisance.
15.33	Common Law Doctrines—Trespass.
15.34	Regulatory Takings.
15.35	Drafting Checklist—Clean Water Act Citizen Suit Notice Letter.

Ch. 15   **SCOPE NOTE**   **§ 15.1**

15.36 ___ Clean Water Act and Resource Conservation and Recovery Act Citizen Suit Notice Letter.
15.37 ___ Clean Water Act Complaint.
15.38 ___ Nuisance and Trespass Complaint.
15.39 ___ Oil Spill Complaint.
15.40 Forms—Clean Water Act Citizen Suit Notice Letter.
15.41 ___ Clean Water Act and Resource Conservation and Recovery Act Citizen Suit Notice Letter.
15.42 ___ Clean Water Act Complaint.
15.43 ___ Nuisance and Trespass Complaint.
15.44 ___ Oil Spill Complaint.

WESTLAW Electronic Research

See WESTLAW Electronic Research Guide preceding the Summary of Contents.

§ 15.1 Scope Note

This chapter discusses environmental law topics that are most commonly faced by lawyers practicing in New York. The purpose of this chapter is to give the non-specialist an introduction to this highly specialized practice area. Almost every one of the sections within this chapter could be the subject of an entire book. The purpose here is merely to give the reader a basic understanding of the statutes, regulations and important case law that govern these topics.

This chapter addresses both federal and state law requirements because most of the topics discussed herein are subject to concurrent federal and state regulatory schemes. Often New York's laws and regulations implement, reference, derive from or overlap with federal environmental law. Therefore, while the focus of this chapter will be on New York's environmental regulations, federal law is explained when necessary to get an accurate view of a practice area. In many instances there are local, county, town and/or village regulations that are also of concern. Therefore, a practitioner should always investigate whether there are also local rules that govern the topic.

This chapter begins with a discussion of the federal and state environmental impact review statutes, which are designed to inject the consideration of environmental impacts into the governmental decision making process.[1] The remainder of this chapter will follow the structure of the federal and state environmental regulatory schemes. It will focus on the regulatory schemes that are designed to protect a part of the

---

§ 15.1

1. *See infra,* §§ 15.3–15.7. *See also,* Chapter 4, "Administrative Law," *supra.*

environment—such as air,[2] or water[3] or wetlands[4]—and the statutes that govern activities that can have a major impact on our environmental resources—such as regulations governing the generation, transport, handling and disposal of solid and hazardous waste or bulk storage of petroleum.[5] This chapter will also discuss the relevant common law doctrines, such as nuisance and trespass, as well as the constitutional law doctrine limiting regulatory takings of private property, that are often invoked in litigation over the protection and preservation of our environment.[6] The chapter will conclude with drafting checklists and forms that are designed to guide the practitioner in preparing some of the more common documents filed in connection with environmental litigation.[7]

§ 15.2 Strategy

The first—as well as the most important—step in counseling a client about environmental law issues is identifying that a matter raises environmental law issues. Even lawyers who do not practice environmental law must explore whether the issue for which their client seeks assistance is affected by an environmental statute or regulation. Then these statutes or regulations must be identified.

For example, land use matters often have environmental law components. If the land use matter requires some form of discretionary governmental "action," such as a wetlands permit, a change in applicable zoning, or a zoning variance, then federal and/or state environmental review statutes will be implicated and the attorney must assist the client in determining whether an environmental impact statement must be prepared.[1] In addition, a real estate or industrial development project may require permits pursuant to air pollution, water pollution, wetlands and other environmental laws at the federal, state and local levels. Identifying whether and which statutes apply is often one of the most difficult tasks. Asking the correct questions and identifying the key issues is essential.

Environmental liability is also a key legal issue that is raised in connection with a wide variety of business transactions. For example, attorneys negotiating and drafting documents in connection with real estate and other commercial transactions must consider potential liability of their client for clean up of hazardous substances under the Federal Superfund Law. In addition, the attorney should consider the responsibility of their client for underground storage tanks located on properties that are subject of the transaction and are regulated pursuant to federal

---

2. *See infra*, §§ 15.19–15.22.
3. *See infra*, §§ 15.8–15.12.
4. *See infra*, §§ 15.17–15.18.
5. *See infra*, §§ 15.23–15.31.
6. *See infra*, §§ 15.32–15.34.

7. *See* Ginsberg, Weinberg, et al., *Environmental Law and Regulation in New York* (West 1996).

§ 15.2

1. *See infra*, §§ 15.3–15.6.

and state regulations.[2] Before real property is acquired, some type of an environmental assessment should be conducted to determine whether any contamination exists or is likely to exist on the property.[3] In addition, a practitioner must keep liability pursuant to environmental laws in mind when drafting indemnifications and releases in connections with these types of commercial transactions.

Counsel should also keep in mind that there are environmental regulations at the federal, state and local levels and, therefore, always consider compliance with all the various statutes that may be implicated. Sometimes, as in the case of air and water pollution rules, the state regulatory structure derives from, and interrelates with, federal law mandates. In such instances, legal counsel cannot completely understand one regulatory scheme without reference to the other. However, the federal and state mandates, though related, may not be identical because often federal statutes permit states to include controls that go beyond federal law requirements.

For clients seeking to commence litigation under environmental statutes, several threshold issues must be explored. For example, counsel should consider whether the client will have a problem establishing standing to bring the environmental challenge and must draft the complaint to sufficiently establish standing.[4] Counsel also should consider whether the challenge can be brought pursuant to federal law, state law, or both in determining what will be the most advantageous judicial forum for the challenge. In addition, if the action seeks judicial review of an administrative determination, counsel should be aware of the short Statutes of Limitation applicable to such challenges, and that these statutes may differ depending on the type of governmental action challenged.[5]

In sum, a practitioner should be aware of the scope and breadth of the matters subject to, and affected by, environmental laws and regulations. An environmental law issue could be lurking behind what appears to be an otherwise routine legal transaction. The potential applicability of environmental laws must always be considered when counseling your client, even when your client has not sought assistance for an "environmental" problem.

§ 15.3 State Environmental Quality Review Act

The New York State Environmental Quality Review Act, or SEQRA,[1] requires state and local government agencies who propose to directly undertake, fund or approve any activity that "may have a significant effect on the environment" to prepare an environmental

---

2. *See infra*, §§ 15.26–15.31.
3. *See* Chapter 12 "Purchase and Sale of Real Estate," *supra*.
4. *See infra*, § 15.5.
5. *See id.*

§ 15.3
1. ECL §§ 8–0101 *et seq.*

§ 15.3 ENVIRONMENTAL LAW Ch. 15

impact statement ("EIS") to evaluate the environmental impacts of such activity.[2] SEQRA's purpose is to ensure that all state or local agencies undertake actions that affect the quality of the environment only after giving "due consideration ... to preventing environmental damage."[3]

SEQRA is based on the National Environmental Policy Act, or NEPA,[4] and much of SEQRA's legislative findings and declaration parallel the Congressional declaration of national environmental policy set forth in NEPA.[5] NEPA applies to all federal agencies and requires that an EIS be prepared for "every recommendation or report on proposals for legislation and other major federal actions significantly affecting the quality of the human environment."[6]

However, SEQRA and NEPA are not identical and have been interpreted differently in some very important respects. Specifically, the United States Supreme Court has found that, although NEPA sets forth environmental goals for the nation, its mandate is "essentially procedural."[7] Thus, courts have found federal agencies to have complied with NEPA even if they do not choose the alternative that is most consistent with national environmental policy set forth in the Act, as long as they take a "hard look" at the environmental consequences of their actions.[8]

Like NEPA, SEQRA provides for procedural mandates requiring that "social, economic and environmental factors be considered together in reaching decisions on proposed activities."[9] However, SEQRA goes beyond that to provide substantive mandates that require agencies to "use all practicable means to realize the policies and goals set forth ... [in the Act]" and "act and choose alternatives which, consistent with social economic and other essential considerations, to the maximum extent practicable, minimize or avoid adverse environmental effects...."[10] The Court of Appeals has made clear that, unlike NEPA, SEQRA is not merely a disclosure statute, but "imposes far more 'action-forcing' or 'substantive' requirements on state and local decisionmakers than NEPA imposes on their federal counterparts."[11]

---

2. ECL § 8–0109(2).

3. ECL § 8–0103(9).

4. 42 U.S.C.A. § 4321.

5. *Compare* 42 U.S.C.A. §§ 4331, 4332 with ECL §§ 8–0101, 8–0103.

6. 42 U.S.C.A. § 4332(2).

7. Vermont Yankee Nuclear Power Corp. v. Natural Resources Defense Council, Inc., 435 U.S. 519, 558, 98 S.Ct. 1197, 1219, 55 L.Ed.2d 460 (1978); *see also*, Baltimore Gas & Electric Co. v. Natural Resources Defense Council, 462 U.S. 87, 103 S.Ct. 2246, 76 L.Ed.2d 437 (1983).

8. *See e.g.*, Kleppe v. Sierra Club, 427 U.S. 390, 410 note 21, 96 S.Ct. 2718, 2730, 49 L.Ed.2d 576 (1976); Britt v. United States Army Corps. of Engineers, 769 F.2d 84, 90 (2d Cir.1985).

9. ECL § 8–0103(7); Matter of Jackson v. New York State Urban Dev. Corp., 67 N.Y.2d 400, 415, 503 N.Y.S.2d 298, 304, 494 N.E.2d 429, 435 (1986).

10. ECL § 8–0109(1).

11. Jackson, 67 N.Y.2d at 414–15, 503 N.Y.S.2d at 303, 494 N.E.2d at 434; Town of Henrietta v. Department of Environmental Conservation, 76 A.D.2d 215, 221, 430 N.Y.S.2d 440, 446 (4th Dep't 1980) (SEQRA "cannot be construed as merely procedural or informational since it states that all approving agencies involved in an action must actually consider the EIS and formulate its decision on the basis of all the adverse

SEQRA has an extremely broad reach and is implicated when any state or local governmental entity undertakes an "action." "Agency" is defined very broadly to include any "state department, agency, board, public benefit corporation, public authority or commission" and any "local agency, board, district, commission or governing body, including any city, county and other political subdivision of the state."[12] "Actions" covered by SEQRA's disclosure provisions include "projects or activities directly undertaken by any agency, activities supported in whole or part through funding assistance, projects or activities involving the issuance to a person of a "lease, permit, license, certificate or other entitlement for use or permission to act by one or more agencies," or policy, regulations and procedure making of such agencies.[13] Non-discretionary ministerial acts, decisions to initiate or not initiate enforcement proceedings, and ordinary repairs and maintenance of an existing structure or facility are exempted from SEQRA's definition of action.[14]

Library References:

West's Key No. Digests, Health and Environment ⬯25.10(1)–25.10(8).

§ 15.4 State Environmental Quality Review Act—Determination of Significance

SEQRA requires that an agency undertake an initial determination of whether an action is subject to SEQRA "[a]s early as possible in an agency's formulation of an action it proposes to undertake, or as soon as an agency receives an application for a funding or approval action."[1] In order to determine what environmental review, if any, must be undertaken in connection with a proposed agency action, SEQRA must be read in conjunction with the regulations promulgated by the New York State Department of Environmental Conservation ("DEC") pursuant to the Act and located at Title 6 of the New York Code of Rules and Regulations ("NYCRR") Part 617.[2] These regulations restate SEQRA's defini-

environmental impacts disclosed therein (ECL § 8–0109(2))").

12. ECL §§ 8–0105(1), (2), (3).
13. ECL § 8–0105(4).
14. ECL § 8–0105(5).

§ 15.4

1. ECL § 8–0109(4); 6 NYCRR § 617.6. *See supra*, § 4.29; *see generally,* Borchers and Markell, *New York State Administrative Procedure and Practice* (West 1995) § 9.6.

2. **PRACTICE POINTER:** These regulations include the nuts and bolts of the SEQRA process and are an invaluable reference tool for navigating through SEQRA. In September 1995, the DEC issued revised SEQRA regulations that became effective on January 1, 1996 and apply to all actions where a determination of significance was not issued prior to that date. The revised regulations clarify and reorganize the structure of the existing regulations in a more logical manner, but make very few substantive changes in existing environmental review procedures. The principal changes are additions to the list of Type II actions; providing guidance on scoping EISs; modifying provisions relating to critical environmental areas; revising the format for EISs; and providing for the amendment of negative declarations and findings statements. The DEC also has written a SEQRA Handbook that is a "how to" guide for preparing SEQRA documents such as environmental assessments and Draft Environmental Impact Statements ("DEISs").

tion of actions as "projects or physical activities that may affect the environment" that are directly undertaken by an agency, funded by an agency, or require a new or modified approval from an agency.[3] The regulations further classify agency actions as Type I, Type II, or Unlisted actions.[4]

Type I actions are actions listed in the regulations "that are more likely to require the preparation of an EIS."[5] If an action is classified as Type I, it is presumed to be "likely [to] have a significant impact on the environment and require the preparation of an EIS."[6] Type II actions are actions the DEC has determined "not to have a significant effect on the environment," or are "otherwise precluded from environmental review" under SEQRA.[7] They do not require an EIS or any other determination or procedure under SEQRA. If an action is not found on either the Type I or Type II list, it is classified as an Unlisted action and, as with a Type I action, the "lead agency" must determine the environmental significance of the action.[8]

The initial determination of significance must be made by the "lead agency."[9] The lead agency is defined as the governmental entity "principally responsible for carrying out, funding or approving" the proposed action.[10] The SEQRA regulations also set forth the procedures for establishing a lead agency where more than one agency is involved in a proposed action.[11] These regulations require that a lead agency be established before the environmental significance of a proposed action is determined for all Type I actions and Unlisted actions where the agencies are involved in a coordinated review.[12]

In order to determine whether an action "may have a significant effect on the environment,"[13] the lead agency must complete an Environmental Assessment Form ("EAF"). A full EAF[14] is required for Type I

3. 6 NYCRR § 617.2(b).

4. 6 NYCRR § 617.2(ai), (aj) and (ak).

5. 6 NYCRR § 617.4.

6. 6 NYCRR § 617.4(a)(1).

7. 6 NYCRR §§ 617.5(a), 617.6(a)(1)(i).

8. 6 NYCRR §§ 617.2(ak), 617.7(a).

9. ECL § 8–0109(2); 6 NYCRR § 617.2(u); Coca–Cola Bottling Co. v. New York City Board of Estimate, 72 N.Y.2d 674, 681, 536 N.Y.S.2d 33, 36, 532 N.E.2d 1261, 1264 (1988).

CAVEAT: It is critical that the decision-making agency be involved in the environmental assessment. Although private applicants can and do assist in compiling data supporting determinations of significance, the actual assessment of these factors must be done by the lead agency.

10. 6 NYCRR § 617.2(u) (based on ECL § 8–0111(6)); Coca-Cola, 72 N.Y.2d at 680, 536 N.Y.S.2d at 35, 532 N.E.2d at 1263.

11. 6 NYCRR § 617.6(b)(2).

12. 6 NYCRR § 617.6(b)(2)(i). Subsection 617.6(b)(1) provides that, for uncoordinated review of Unlisted actions, an agency shall make a determination of significance as early as possible in the formulation of plans for such Unlisted action and before such agency commits itself to a particular action, or within twenty days of its receipt of an application, EAF and other necessary information.

13. ECL § 8–0109(2). The threshold for when an EIS is required is lower than in NEPA, which requires federal agencies to prepare an EIS for any "major federal actions significantly affecting the quality of the human environment." 42 U.S.C.A. § 4332(2)(c).

14. 6 NYCRR § 617.20, Appendix A.

actions, and a short EAF[15] is required for Unlisted actions, though an agency may use a full EAF for Unlisted actions "if the short EAF would not provide the lead agency with sufficient information to base its determination of significance."[16] The agency then must review the EAF, the criteria set forth in the regulations and any other supporting information in order to identify the relevant areas of environmental concern. The criteria identified in the SEQRA regulations are indicators of significant effects on the environment. These criteria go beyond effects on the physical environment, such as whether the proposed action will create a substantial *adverse* change in air or water quality, to take into account socioeconomic effects and effects on public resources, such as whether the proposed action will increase traffic or solid waste production, or impair the character or quality of an existing community or neighborhood.[17] The agency must thoroughly analyze these relevant areas of environmental concern and determine whether the proposed action may have a significant effect on the environment and set forth, in writing, a "reasoned elaboration" for its determination with reference to any supporting documentation.[18]

If the lead agency determines that the proposed action may include the potential for at least one environmental effect, it issues, in writing, a positive declaration of environmental significance and an EIS will be required. If the lead agency determines that the proposed action will have no environmental effect, or that any effects will not be significant, it issues a written Notice of Negative Declaration of Environmental Significance and the SEQRA process is concluded. For Unlisted actions not directly undertaken by an agency where coordinated review has taken place, the lead agency may also issue a "conditioned negative declaration."[19] A conditioned negative declaration imposes certain conditions that the lead agency determines have eliminated or adequately mitigated all significant environmental effects. Except for certain notice

---

15. 6 NYCRR § 617.20, Appendix C.

16. 6 NYCRR § 617.6(a)(2), (3).

PRACTICE POINTER: DEC publishes both long and short EAFs that are part of the Appendices to the SEQRA regulations. In addition, for actions taken by New York City agencies, the City of New York has promulgated its own EAF pursuant to the City Environmental Quality Review Act ("CEQR"). CEQR, first established in the Mayor's Executive Order No. 91 of 1977, implements SEQRA requirements for actions by New York City agencies. CEQR's current procedures are published in the Rules of the City of New York, Title 62, Chapter 5. A draft Technical Manual for City agencies conducting environmental review under CEQR also has been published by the City of New York. CEQR Draft Technical Manual (May 1993). A copy of this manual can be requested through the Department of City Planning or the Mayor's Office of Environmental Coordination.

17. *See* 6 NYCRR § 617.7(c). The regulations contain a caveat that the criteria set forth are illustrative and thus do not include all the criteria that should be looked at for any particular proposed action.

18. 6 NYCRR § 617.7(b).

PRACTICE POINTER: Often a lead agency and/or project sponsor will retain environmental counsel when a determination of non-significance is likely to be challenged. A project sponsor will often find it advantageous to complete supplemental studies as support for the determination, which should be appended to an EAF.

19. 6 NYCRR § 617.7(d). These regulations also require that the lead agency prepare a full EAF. 6 NYCRR § 617.7(d)(1)(i).

§ 15.4 ENVIRONMENTAL LAW Ch. 15

and public comment requirements following its issuance, a conditioned negative declaration also concludes review under SEQRA.[20]

Library References:
West's Key No. Digests, Health and Environment ⚙︎25.10(3).

§ 15.5 State Environmental Quality Review Act—The Environmental Impact Statement and Findings Statement

An EIS's purpose is to provide "detailed information about the effect which a proposed action is likely to have on the environment, to list ways in which any adverse effects of such an action might be minimized, and to suggest alternatives to such an action so as to form the basis for a decision whether or not to undertake or approve such action."[1] It must include, among other things, a description of the proposed action, the environmental impact of the proposed action, including short-term and long-term effects, adverse environmental impacts which cannot be avoided, alternatives to the proposed action, mitigation measures proposed to minimize the environmental impact and other information required by SEQRA and its regulations.[2] The EIS must include a summary of substantive comments received by the agency from the public and interested agencies and the agency's response to such comments.[3]

An EIS, along with supporting data, can be, and often is, a voluminous and detailed document. SEQRA explicitly permits an agency to allow an applicant, at its option, to prepare or cause to be prepared a draft EIS or DEIS.[4]

The lead agency or a project applicant may initiate a "scoping procedure prior to preparation of an EIS.[5]" The primary goals of scoping are to focus the EIS on potentially significant adverse impacts and to

20. 6 NYCRR § 617.6(d)(2). The revised SEQRA regulations now also provide for the amendment of negative declarations by the lead agency prior to its decision to undertake, fund or approve an action if the lead agency, in its discretion, determines that substantive changes are proposed, new information is discovered, or circumstances have changed. 6 NYCRR § 617.7(e).

§ 15.5

1. ECL § 8–0109(2).

2. ECL § 8–0109(2) (a)-(i); 6 NYCRR § 617.9(b).

3. ECL § 8–0109(2); 6 NYCRR § 617.7(b)(8).

4. ECL § 8–0109(4).

PRACTICE POINTER: For a major public works project like a highway or sewage treatment plant, the lead agency obviously undertakes the primary role in facilitating the preparation of an EIS. In the context of a private development, such as a shopping center or a subdivision requiring zoning approvals triggering SEQRA, a private applicant usually retains an environmental consultant to prepare the EIS. However, the private applicant and its consultant must be careful not to supplant the role of the lead agency in reviewing the DEIS and FEIS and ensuring its completeness. That role must remain with the lead agency. *See e.g.*, City of Rye v. Branca, N.Y.L.J., 4/28/94 (Sup.Ct., Westchester County).

5. 6 NYCRR § 617.8(a).

eliminate consideration of those impacts that are irrelevant or nonsignificant.[6]

After a DEIS is completed, the agency must certify it as complete and file a written notice of completion.[7] The agency may, in its discretion, conduct a public hearing on the DEIS within sixty days of its filing of the notice of completion.[8] After a DEIS has been filed and public comments received, the agency may then prepare a final EIS ("FEIS") and must issue a Notice of Completion of the FEIS.[9] Once the FEIS is filed, other agencies and the public have at least ten days from the date of publication of the Notice of Completion of the FEIS to consider it prior to making the decision on the action.[10]

Once an agency decides to carry out or approve an action which has been the subject of an EIS, it must make and file a written "findings statement" setting forth the facts and conclusions contained in the DEIS and FEIS that were relied on to support the decision.[11] The findings statement must also state that the requirements of SEQRA have been met and "that consistent with social economic and other essential considerations, to the maximum extent practicable, adverse environmental effects revealed in the environmental impact statement process will be minimized or avoided."[12]

Library References:

West's Key No. Digests, Health and Environment ⟐25.10(5, 6.1).

§ 15.6 State Environmental Quality Review Act—Judicial Review

Challenges based on an agency's failure to comply with the dictates of SEQRA are brought pursuant to CPLR Article 78. Because SEQRA does not have its own Statute of Limitations, the four-month limitations period applicable to Article 78 proceedings generally applies to SEQRA challenges. However, if a different limitations period specifically applies to the agency action being reviewed, which is not uncommon, that limitations period will apply.[1]

Calculating when the limitations period begins to run has been a particularly difficult issue for courts to resolve. Generally, the limitations

---

6. *Id.*

PRACTICE POINTER: Although not required, formal scoping is often implemented to involve the public and demonstrate that the agency has reached out to consider all potential impacts. If done properly, scoping can help improve an EIS and make it better able to stand up to judicial scrutiny in a court challenge.

7. ECL § 8–0109(4); 6 NYCRR §§ 617.9(a)(3), 617.12(c), (d).

8. ECL § 8–0109(5); 6 NYCRR § 617.9(a)(4).

9. 6 NYCRR § 617.9(a)(6).

10. 6 NYCRR § 617.11(a).

11. 6 NYCRR § 617.2(p).

12. ECL § 8–0109(8); 6 NYCRR § 617.11(d).

§ 15.6

1. *See e.g.*, Long Island Pine Barrens Soc., Inc. v. Planning Bd. of Town of Brookhaven, 78 N.Y.2d 608, 578 N.Y.S.2d 466, 585 N.E.2d 778 (1991).

period begins to run when the agency commits itself to a definite course of future action, causing an impact on the aggrieved petitioners.[2] This rule equally applies to the review of agency actions taken after it has prepared a Final Environmental Impact Statement ("FEIS"), and to the review of agency actions where it has issued a negative declaration determining that a proposed action is not likely to significantly affect the environment. Thus, when an agency issues a negative declaration, the limitations period is triggered by the agency action impacting the petitioner and not the agency's issuance of the negative declaration.[3] Similarly, if an FEIS has been prepared, the limitations period begins to run from when the agency commits itself to the action triggering the environmental review, not when the FEIS is approved.[4]

When the action being undertaken or considered by the agency requires multiple approvals it can be difficult to determine what action triggers the Statute of Limitations. The last action or approval undertaken by the agency is not necessarily the action which is final for SEQRA purposes—it is the action that commits the agency to a future course of conduct.[5] For example, in *Long Island Pine Barrens Soc., Inc. v. Planning Bd. of Town of Brookhaven*, petitioners challenged a town planning board's final approval of a proposed subdivision. The Court of Appeals found that the challenge was time-barred because the applicable limitations period began to run from the town planning board's "preliminary" plat approval of a subdivision, rather than its final approval, because the preliminary approval was undertaken after the SEQRA process was completed and therefore "was final regarding SEQRA issues."[6]

Standing to review a SEQRA determination is limited to parties asserting particularized environmental injury. Mere allegations of economic injury are not sufficient.[7] For example, in *Mobil Oil Corp v. Syracuse Ind. Dev. Agency*, the Court of Appeals found that Mobil lacked standing to challenge compliance with SEQRA by a local industrial development agency because the harm alleged—that the project would require Mobil to take actions which would cause it to raise fuel prices

---

2. Douglaston and Little Neck Coalition v. Sexton, 145 A.D.2d 480, 481, 535 N.Y.S.2d 634, 635 (2d Dep't 1988); Wing v. Coyne, 129 A.D.2d 213, 517 N.Y.S.2d 576, 578–79 (3d Dep't 1987) ("an administrative determination becomes final and binding within the meaning of CPLR 217 when it has an impact on the aggrieved petitioners").

3. Matter of Town of Yorktown v. New York State Dept. of Mental Hygiene, 92 A.D.2d 897, 459 N.Y.S.2d 891 (2d Dep't 1983), aff'd without op. 59 N.Y.2d 999, 466 N.Y.S.2d 965, 453 N.E.2d 1254 (1983) (challenge to negative declaration timely because brought within four months after issuance of permit by agency).

4. *See* Long Island Pine Barrens Society v. Planning Bd. of Town of Brookhaven, 78 N.Y.2d 608, 578 N.Y.S.2d 466, 585 N.E.2d 778 (1991). *See supra*, § 15.5.

5. *See e.g.*, Matter of Save the Pine Bush v. City of Albany, 70 N.Y.2d 193, 203, 518 N.Y.S.2d 943, 946, 512 N.E.2d 526, 529 (1987).

6. 78 N.Y.2d at 614, 578 N.Y.S.2d at 470, 585 N.E.2d at 781.

7. Mobil Oil Corp. v. Syracuse Ind. Dev. Agency, 76 N.Y.2d 428, 559 N.Y.S.2d 947, 559 N.E.2d 641 (1990).

and thus cause a loss of employment in the region—was merely economic to Mobil and thus did not provide standing under SEQRA.[8]

SEQRA contains no provision regarding judicial review. Thus, courts apply standards generally applicable to judicial review of administrative determinations: whether a determination was made in violation of lawful procedure, was affected by an error of law or was arbitrary and capricious or an abuse of discretion.[9] The Court of Appeals has also emphasized that "it is not the role of the courts to weigh the desirability of any action or choose among alternatives, but to assure that the agency itself has satisfied SEQRA, procedurally and substantively."[10]

Thus courts will review agency procedures to determine whether the review has complied with procedural dictates of SEQRA, such as whether a negative declaration was issued before an action was taken or whether an agency issued SEQRA findings before undertaking an action. Although the case law is not uniform, courts have often held that literal compliance with the procedural dictates of SEQRA is mandatory and have not hesitated to enjoin projects for failure to comply with the procedural or substantive dictates of SEQRA.[11] For example, in *Matter of Rye Town/King Civic Assoc. v. Town of Rye*,[12] petitioners challenged a town's grant of a permit for construction of an office building before making a threshold determination of whether the project would have a significant impact on the environment. The town conceded that it had not made the formal determination, but argued that the town complied with the "spirit" of SEQRA because it fully examined many environmental factors in connection with its consideration of the permit application. The court rejected the town's argument, holding that "literal compliance" with the procedures mandated by SEQRA is required.[13] Nevertheless, other courts have, occasionally, applied a harmless error standard

8. 76 N.Y.2d at 433, 559 N.Y.S.2d at 950, 559 N.E.2d at 644. *See also*, Society of Plastics Ind., Inc. v. County of Suffolk, 77 N.Y.2d 761, 570 N.Y.S.2d 778, 573 N.E.2d 1034 (1991) (industry group and one of its members had no standing to challenge county's adoption of law restricting use of plastic products by retail food establishments without considering SEQRA because plaintiffs did not allege any special injury within the zone of interest of SEQRA different in kind or degree from the public at large). *But cf.*, Matter of Har Enterprises v. Town of Brookhaven, 74 N.Y.2d 524, 549 N.Y.S.2d 638, 548 N.E.2d 1289 (1989) (owner of property rezoned from commercial to residential is "presumptively adversely affected" by county's failure to comply with SEQRA).

9. CPLR 7803(3); Jackson v. New York State Urban Dev. Corp., 67 N.Y.2d 400, 416, 503 N.Y.S.2d 298, 304, 494 N.E.2d 429, 435 (1986).

10. Jackson, 67 N.Y.2d at 416, 503 N.Y.S.2d at 305, 494 N.E.2d at 436.

11. *See e.g.*, Matter of Rye Town/King Civic Assoc. v. Town of Rye, 82 A.D.2d 474, 442 N.Y.S.2d 67, (2d Dep't 1981); Matter of Tri–County Taxpayers Assn., Inc. v. Town Bd. of Queensbury, 55 N.Y.2d 41, 447 N.Y.S.2d 699, 432 N.E.2d 592, (1982) (Court of Appeals annulled special election for creation of a sewer district and building a sewage treatment plant because EIS (*see supra*, § 15.5) was not completed before town adopted resolution placing the issue on the ballot).

12. *Id.*

13. Town of Rye, 82 A.D.2d at 480–81, 442 N.Y.S.2d at 71; *see also*, Glen Head–Glenwood Landing Civic Council v. Town of Oyster Bay, 88 A.D.2d 484, 490–91, 453 N.Y.S.2d 732, 736–37 (2d Dep't 1982).

when certain minor procedural defects have occurred in a SEQRA process.[14]

When determining whether the substantive requirements of SEQRA have been complied with, courts review the record to determine whether the agency identified the relevant areas of environmental concern, took a "hard look" at them, and made a "reasoned elaboration" of the basis for its determination.[15] This standard, which was first applied in cases challenging the sufficiency of negative declarations issued by agencies,[16] has also been applied to cases reviewing the sufficiency of an FEIS.[17]

What particular environmental factors must be examined in connection with any specific agency action or project and whether such factors have been adequately considered is often fact specific. The Court of Appeals has stated that substantive review under SEQRA is governed by a "rule of reason" and the extent to which particular environmental factors are to be considered varies in accordance with the circumstances and nature of particular proposals.[18] Moreover, if an EIS or negative determination demonstrates that the agency has undertaken a thorough analysis and identified likely areas of concern, courts will usually defer to the substantive decision of the agency.[19] "Not every conceivable environmental impact, mitigating measure or alternative must be identified and addressed before a FEIS will satisfy the substantive requirements of SEQRA."[20]

A court will determine that an agency has failed to comply with the substantive requirements of SEQRA when the record is clear that the agency failed to consider impacts of the project or mitigate impacts identified. For example, courts have found that an agency's failure to consider "cumulative impacts" of related actions, where the action

---

14. See Business and Community Coalition to Save Brownsville v. New York City Dept. of Environmental Protection, 173 A.D.2d 586, 570 N.Y.S.2d 169 (2d Dep't 1991) (the court found that although a notice of completion of the DEIS (see supra, § 15.5) failed to expressly state where public comments should be sent, such error was harmless because plaintiff had fully participated in the SEQRA process and had been allowed to submit comments); Golden Triangle Associates v. Town Bd. of Town of Amherst, 185 A.D.2d 617, 585 N.Y.S.2d 895 (4th Dep't 1992) (court upheld the town board's rezoning of a parcel even though the rezoning was approved before the negative declaration was issued; court found this "procedural defect" was cured by the board's subsequent approval of the rezoning).

15. Jackson, 67 N.Y.2d at 417, 503 N.Y.S.2d at 305, 494 N.E.2d at 436; see also, Akpan v. Koch, 75 N.Y.2d 561, 570, 555 N.Y.S.2d 16, 20, 554 N.E.2d 53, 57 (1990); Coalition Against Lincoln West v. City of New York, 94 A.D.2d 483, 491, 465 N.Y.S.2d 170, 176 (1st Dep't), aff'd 60 N.Y.2d 805, 469 N.Y.S.2d 689, 457 N.E.2d 795 (1983); H.O.M.E.S. v. New York State Urban Dev. Corp., 69 A.D.2d 222, 232, 418 N.Y.S.2d 827, 832 (4th Dep't 1979).

16. H.O.M.E.S v. New York State Urban Dev. Corp., 69 A.D.2d 222, 418 N.Y.S.2d 827 (4th Dep't 1979).

17. Jackson, 67 N.Y.2d at 416, 503 N.Y.S.2d at 304, 494 N.E.2d at 435.

18. Akpan, 75 N.Y.2d at 56, 555 N.Y.S.2d at 20, 554 N.E.2d at 57.

19. See Jackson, 67 N.Y.2d at 417, 503 N.Y.S.2d at 305, 494 N.E.2d at 436.

20. Id. (quoting Aldrich v. Pattison, 107 A.D.2d 258, 266, 486 N.Y.S.2d 23, 29 (2d Dep't 1985)).

triggering the EIS is part of a larger municipal development plan, violates SEQRA's substantive requirements.[21] For example, in *Save the Pine Bush, Inc. v. City of Albany*[22] the petitioners claimed that the city did not comply with SEQRA because the EIS prepared in connection with a change in zoning to develop a certain portion of undeveloped pine barrens failed to consider the cumulative impacts of ten similar proposals in other parts of the pine barrens. The Court of Appeals agreed, finding that these other projects, though not commonly owned or dependant on the rezoning at issue, were related, because the approved project affected a "larger plan designed to resolve conflicting specific environmental concerns in a subsection of a municipality with special environmental significance."[23] In subsequent cases, however, the Court of Appeals has emphasized that a specifically enacted municipal development plan must exist before cumulative impact of otherwise unrelated projects will be required.[24] The Court of Appeals has found that a common geographical base, or existence of a generally stated governmental policy to protect a region from unbridled development, is insufficient to require cumulative impact review of otherwise unrelated projects.[25]

A related, but slightly different problem exists when an agency improperly "segments" its environmental review, by splitting a larger project into a two or more smaller projects for the purposes of its analysis of the environmental impacts. In one case, the Court of Appeals found that review by the New York State Department of Transportation ("DOT") of a planned reconstruction of a highway interchange, that was part of a larger project to widen the highway east of the interchange, was improper because DOT only considered the impacts of the interchange construction in determining whether an EIS would be required.[26] The Court found that the two projects were interrelated because the interchange had no utility without the subsequent widening of the highway; thus, the court required DOT to analyze both aspects of the project.[27] The SEQRA regulations promulgated by the DEC provide additional guidance on when cumulative review of related projects will be required.[28]

Library References:

West's Key No. Digests, Health and Environment ⚖=25.10(8).

21. Chinese Staff & Workers Assoc. v. City of New York, 68 N.Y.2d 359, 509 N.Y.S.2d 499, 502 N.E.2d 176 (1986); Save the Pine Bush, Inc. v. City of Albany, 70 N.Y.2d 193, 518 N.Y.S.2d 943, 512 N.E.2d 526 (1987).

22. 70 N.Y.2d 193, 518 N.Y.S.2d 943, 512 N.E.2d 526 (1987).

23. Id.

24. Long Island Pine Barrens Soc., Inc. v. Planning Bd. of Town of Brookhaven, 80 N.Y.2d 500, 514, 591 N.Y.S.2d 982, 988, 606 N.E.2d 1373, 1379 (1992). *See also*, Chapter 3 "Municipal Law," *supra*.

25. Id.

26. Village of Westbury v. Department of Transportation, 75 N.Y.2d 62, 69, 550 N.Y.S.2d 604, 607, 549 N.E.2d 1175, 1178 (1989).

27. Id.

28. 6 NYCRR § 617.3(g).

§ 15.7 State Environmental Quality Review Act—Checklist

1. Is the proposed activity an "action" subject to review under SEQRA? If unsure, examine the following:

    - Does the action fall within SEQRA's broad definition of action.[1]

    - If the answer to the above is yes, then you must determine whether the action is classified as Type II?[2] If yes, then no further SEQRA review is required. If no, an environmental assessment of the action's potential impacts must be completed. (*See* Number 3 below)

2. Has the "lead agency" for the purposes of SEQRA review been identified? If not, examine the following:

    - Relevant regulations.[3]

    - Is more than one agency involved in the action? If so, "coordinated review" will be required.[4]

3. Does the action require the preparation of an Environmental Impact Statement ("EIS")? (*See* § 15.5) If unsure, examine the following:

    - Is the action a Type I action or Unlisted action?[5] If yes, then an Environmental Assessment Form (EAF) examining potential impacts of proposed action must be prepared.[6] (*See* § 15.4)

    - Is the action the type that may have a significant impact on the environment?[7] If yes, then a positive declaration must be issued and an EIS prepared. If no, then a negative declaration setting forth "reasoned elaboration" for the determination must be issued.[8] For Unlisted actions, consider utility of a conditioned negative declaration.[9]

4. Has the EIS examined all the relevant environmental impacts? (*See* § 15.5) If unsure, check the following:

    - The requirements for an EIS, including a description of the proposed action, the impacts of the proposed action, adverse impacts that cannot be avoided, alternative to the proposed action and mitigation measures proposed to minimize the environmental impact.[10]

§ 15.7
1. 6 NYCRR § 617.2(b).
2. *See id.*
3. 6 NYCRR § 617.6.
4. 6 NYCRR § 617.6.
5. 6 NYCRR §§ 617.4, 617.7.
6. 6 NYCRR § 617.7(a).
7. ECL § 8–0109(2).
8. 6 NYCRR § 617.7(b).
9. 6 NYCRR § 617.7(d)(1).
10. 6 NYCRR § 617.9(b).

- Consider scoping to focus EIS on potentially significant adverse impacts (optional).[11]

- After Draft EIS ("DEIS") (*see* § 15.5) is completed, Notice of Completion must be issued and filed, along with the DEIS. Minimum 30–day public comment period after Notice of Completion is filed.[12]

- Consider whether public hearing (optional) on the DEIS will be held.[13] After public comments received and responded to, Notice of Completion issued by lead agency and Final EIS ("FEIS") (*see* § 15.6) filed.[14]

5. If the agency determines to undertake action, Findings Statement must be issued.[15]

   Elements of Findings Statement include:

   - Facts and conclusions contained in the DEIS and FEIS that were relied upon to support the decision.

   - Statement that requirements of SEQRA have been met and that consistent with social economic and other essential considerations, to the maximum extent practicable, adverse environmental effects revealed in the EIS process will be minimized or avoided.[16]

§ 15.8 Water Pollution Control

The discharges of "pollutants" into surface waters within the state is governed by the Federal Water Pollution Control Act, more commonly referred to as the Clean Water Act ("CWA").[1] The CWA sets itself an ambitious goal—"to restore and maintain the chemical, physical, and biological integrity of the Nation's waters." The centerpiece of the CWA is its prohibition on the discharge of "pollutants" from any "point source" into waters of the United States, unless such discharge is made pursuant to a permit issued under the National Pollutant Discharge Elimination System ("NPDES") permitting system established by Section 402 of the Act.[2]

The CWA allows individual states to take over the NPDES permitting program administered by the United States Environmental Protection Agency ("EPA").[3] New York has taken advantage of this program and enacted the State Pollutant Elimination Discharge Elimination System, or SPDES permitting program, that was approved by the EPA

---

11. 6 NYCRR § 617.8.
12. 6 NYCRR § 617.9(a)(3).
13. 6 NYCRR § 617.9(a)(4).
14. 6 NYCRR § 617.9(a)(6).
15. *See id.*
16. 6 NYCRR § 617.11.

§ 15.8
1. 33 U.S.C.A. §§ 1251 *et seq.*
2. 33 U.S.C.A. § 1342.
3. 33 U.S.C.A. § 1342(b).

in 1975.[4] Thus, in New York the DEC has assumed authority for issuing SPDES permits and enforcing the discharge restrictions set forth in the CWA.[5]

Like the CWA, New York's Environmental Conservation Law provides that it "shall be unlawful to discharge pollutants to the waters of the state from any outlet or point source without a SPDES permit ... or in a manner other than prescribed by such permit."[6] The term "pollutant" is broadly defined under federal and state law to encompass a wide variety of solid and liquid wastes, as well as chemical and biological wastes, munitions and construction and demolition material.[7] "Point source" is similarly broadly defined to include "any discernible, confined and discrete conveyance" from which pollutants are or may be discharged.[8] Such conveyances include human-constructed conveyances, such as pipes and tunnels, as well as naturally created, or less permanent conveyances such as ditches or culverts that can collect and direct pollutants into waters.[9] The determining factor for whether a source of the discharge falls within the definition of point source often appears to be whether such pollutants are discharged into the water body by a "discernible, discrete conveyance." Thus, if a discharge is somehow channeled into a water body, that channelling function will likely cause such conveyance to fall within the CWA's definition of point source.[10] However, in a criminal enforcement case under the CWA, the Second Circuit Court of Appeals held that a human being disposing of contaminated blood vials directly into the Hudson River was not a discharge from a point source as defined under the Act.[11]

Point source discharges of pollutants are illegal under New York's

4. ECL §§ 17–0801 et seq. Weinberg, Practice Commentary, ECL § 17–0801.

5. EPA retains authority to enforce these limitations and may oppose the DEC's issuance of a SPDES permit. See 33 U.S.C.A. § 1342(d)(2).

6. ECL § 17–0803.

CAVEAT: A discharge of a pollutant without a permit, or in contravention of a permit, constitute separate violations of the CWA and the ECL.

7. ECL § 17–0105(17); 33 U.S.C.A. § 1362(6). Heat is also considered a pollutant under both of these definitions.

8. ECL § 17–0105(16); 33 U.S.C.A. § 1362(14).

9. Dague v. City of Burlington, 935 F.2d 1343, 1354–55 (2d Cir.1991), rev'd in part on other grounds 505 U.S. 557, 112 S.Ct. 2638, 120 L.Ed.2d 449 (1992) (discharge of landfill leachate into culvert leading to navigable waters was a point source); Avoyelles Sportsmen's League v. Marsh, 715 F.2d 897, 922 (5th Cir.1983) ("point source" includes bulldozing equipment that discharged dredged materials into wetland).

10. Concerned Area Residents for the Environment v. Southview Farm, 34 F.3d 114, 118 (2d Cir.1994), cert. denied __ U.S. __, 115 S.Ct. 1793, 131 L.Ed.2d 721 (1995).

11. United States v. Plaza Health Laboratories, Inc., 3 F.3d 643, 649 (2d Cir.1993), cert. denied 512 U.S. 1245, 114 S.Ct. 2764, 129 L.Ed.2d 878 (1994). The court's analysis may have been affected by the criminal context in which it was interpreting the definition of point source. Although the CWA's definitions are the same regardless of whether it is being enforced civilly or criminally, in Plaza Health the Rule of Lenity required that the court resolve all ambiguities in the definition of point source in the defendant's favor; the court found that interpreting point source to include a human being was at best ambiguous. 3 F.3d at 649.

regulatory scheme when discharged into "waters of the state."[12] "Waters of the state" is defined to include "all ... bodies of surface or underground water." This definition is broader than the definition of "navigable waters" contained in the CWA, which covers "waters of the United States, including territorial seas," but unlike the New York definition, does not cover groundwater.[13]

Library References:

West's Key No. Digests, Health and Environment ⚖=25.7(1)–25.7(25).

§ 15.9 Water Pollution Control—SPDES Permit Program

If the discharge of a pollutant is from a point source to waters of the state, then such discharge is illegal unless a SPDES permit is obtained.[1] State law provides—as it must to enable New York to be delegated permitting authority under the CWA[2]—that SPDES permits issued by the DEC contain all applicable effluent limits contained in the CWA.[3] The CWA regulates point source discharges by imposing "technology-based" and "water quality-based" limitations.[4] Comprehensive, detailed federal regulations relating to various sources of pollutants have been promulgated by the EPA and have been incorporated into the DEC's regulations governing standards, limitations and other requirements in SPDES permits.[5]

The CWA—and therefore New York's SPDES program—also provide for extensive public participation in the permitting process. New York's permitting scheme requires for public notice of every completed SPDES permit application, significant modification or renewal thereof, and disclosure of such applications and supporting data, except to the extent that trade secrets would be disclosed.[6] The public also has a right to submit written comments on the SPDES submission and the DEC may, in its discretion, provide an opportunity for the public to request a public hearing concerning the permit application or submission.[7] A SPDES

12. ECL § 17–0803.

13. Compare ECL § 17–0105(2) with 33 U.S.C.A. § 1362(7). See Kelley for and Behalf of People of State of Michigan v. United States, 618 F.Supp. 1103 (W.D.Mich. 1985). The discharge of groundwater is regulated under federal law pursuant to the Safe Drinking Water Act, 42 U.S.C.A. §§ 300f to 300j.

§ 15.9

1. ECL § 17–0803; 33 U.S.C.A. § 1311.

2. See supra, § 15.8.

3. ECL § 17–0809.

4. 33 U.S.C.A. §§ 1311 (authorizes EPA to issue technology-based standards for existing sources), 1312 (authorizes EPA to issue water quality-based effluent limitations). In addition, Section 306 of the CWA (33 U.S.C.A. § 1316) authorizes EPA to issue technology-based effluent limits for new sources and Section 307 (33 U.S.C.A. § 1317) mandates toxic effluent standards and pretreatment limits for discharges into government-owned waste water treatment systems, referred to in the Act as publicly owned treatment works ("POTWs").

5. 6 NYCRR Pt. 754.

6. ECL § 17–0805(1), (2). See also, 33 U.S.C.A. § 1318(b).

7. ECL § 17–0805(1)(b).

permit hearing is governed by the uniform procedures for permit hearings set forth in the ECL and the DEC regulations promulgated thereto.[8] These procedures require, among other things, that the DEC hold a public hearing whenever "substantive and significant" issues exist as to whether such permit complies with applicable laws and regulations.[9]

SPDES permits (except those issued in lieu of NPDES[10] permits) may be issued for a term not to exceed ten years, but the DEC must review all existing permits for compliance with new federal technology standards and new state water quality standards.[11] In accordance with the CWA, New York's SPDES program also provides an "anti-backsliding" provision that bars the DEC from allowing a reissued permit to be more lenient that its previous permit.[12] A significant change to the DEC's permitting procedures, enacted by the New York State Legislature in 1994, requires the DEC to rank SPDES permits in order of priority and to review them in that order, regardless of the date of permit expiration.[13] Thus, the DEC now need not focus on permits merely because their term has expired and may concentrate on significant discharge permits, or permits that have been affected by changes in federal or state standards or regulations.

Holders of SPDES permits are required to regularly monitor the contents of their discharges to ensure that effluent limits are being complied with.[14] The results of these analyses are set forth in a permittee's Discharge Monitoring Reports, or DMRs. Permittees may also be required to monitor the presence of other pollutants not specifically limited in their permit. The DEC—as well as citizen-plaintiffs—use these DMRs to monitor a permittee's compliance with its permit and to commence enforcement actions for reported violations.

A discharge of a pollutant not limited in a discharger's SPDES permit does not violate Section 301 of the CWA. The Second Circuit Court of Appeals, in *Atlantic States Legal Foundation, Inc. v. Eastman Kodak Co., Inc.*, rejected a plaintiff's argument that Section 301 barred the discharge of any pollutants not expressly provided for in a defendant's SPDES permit and held that "[o]nce within the NPDES or SPDES scheme ... polluters may discharge pollutants not specifically listed in their permits so long as they comply with the appropriate reporting requirements and abide by any new limitations when imposed on such pollutants."[15]

8. ECL § 70–0119; 6 NYCRR § 621.14.

9. ECL § 70–0119.

10. *See supra*, § 15.8.

11. ECL § 17–0817(1), (3).

12. ECL § 17–0809(3). This provision derives from the 1987 amendments to the CWA, *see* 33 U.S.C.A. §§ 1313(d), 1342(o).

13. ECL §§ 17–0805(1)(b), 17–0817(4).

14. 6 NYCRR § 754.5(k); 40 C.F.R. § 122.48.

15. 12 F.3d 353, 357–58 (2d Cir.1993), cert. denied 513 U.S. 811, 115 S.Ct. 62, 130 L.Ed.2d 19 (1994). The plaintiffs in Eastman Kodak also argued that the permit itself provided independent grounds for prohibiting the discharge of unlisted pollutants under New York's SPDES regulations, which are permitted by the CWA to be more

Library References:

West's Key No. Digests, Health and Environment ⚖25.7(13)–25.7(15).

§ 15.10 Water Pollution Control—Stormwater Discharges and Oil Spills

The 1987 Amendments to the CWA also provided for regulation of certain storm water discharges.[1] In accordance with the CWA, New York has adopted provisions regulating discharges from municipal separate storm sewer systems and "discharges associated with industrial activities directly related to manufacturing, processing, or raw materials storage areas at an industrial plant."[2] The EPA has issued detailed regulations outlining what types of "industrial activities," if associated with discharges to surface waters, fall within the scope of the CWA's storm water regulations.[3] The EPA's regulations cover a variety of industrial activities, such as hazardous waste treatment, storage and disposal facilities, landfills, mining facilities, coal handling facilities, transportation facilities and many others.[4] One of the most commonly regulated activities requiring a CWA storm water permit is construction activity, including clearing, grading and excavation, that results in the disturbance of more than five acres of total land area.[5]

In 1993, the DEC issued two general SPDES permits in connection with storm water discharges associated with industrial activity. One general permit covers storm water discharges from construction activities, and the other covers storm water discharges from other industrial activities covered by the EPA's storm water regulations.[6] Dischargers subject to the storm water regulations may be eligible to obtain coverage under the DEC's General Permits. However, in order to obtain coverage,

stringent than effluent limits mandated under federal law. *Id.* (citing 33 U.S.C.A. § 1342(b)). Although the court expressed doubt that New York law prohibited these discharges, it did not reach this issue because it held that, even if New York regulations provided more stringent requirements than mandated under the CWA, plaintiff could not enforce such requirement in a CWA citizen suit. 12 F.3d at 359–60. New York law does not provide for citizen enforcement of the ECL.

§ 15.10
1. 33 U.S.C.A. § 1342(p).
2. ECL § 17–0808.
3. 40 C.F.R. § 122.26(b)(14).
4. **PRACTICE POINTER:** These regulations are extremely detailed and, in many instances, refer to industrial activities by their Standard Industrial Classification ("SIC") Code. Thus, often it is impossible to determine whether a certain industrial activity falls within EPA's regulations without reference to these SIC Codes. Executive Office of the President, Office of Management and Budget, Standard Industrial Classification Manual.

5. 40 C.F.R. § 122.26(b)(14)(x).

6. The DEC, SPDES General Permit For Storm Water Discharges Associated with Industrial Activity *except Construction Activity*, Permit No. GP-93-05 (July 14, 1993); SPDES General Permit For Storm Water Discharges From Construction Activities That Are Classified as "Associated with Construction Activity," Permit No. GP-93-06 (July 14, 1993). These general permits have a five-year term that expires on August 1, 1998.

§ 15.10   ENVIRONMENTAL LAW   Ch. 15

the applicant must submit a Notice of Intent ("NOI") to the DEC requesting coverage under the General Permit.[7] Unless notified by the DEC, the applicant is permitted to discharge pursuant to the General Permit two days after the date that the NOI is postmarked.

Unpermitted discharges of petroleum into waters of the state, or onto lands from which it might flow into these waters, is also prohibited under the New York State Navigation Law.[8] The Navigation Law requires persons responsible for causing a discharge to immediately notify the DEC and requires the discharger to contain and remove such discharges.[9]

Library References:

West's Key No. Digests, Health and Environment ⇔25.5(5.5), 25.7(6.1).

§ 15.11   Water Pollution Control—Enforcement

A person who discharges in waters of the state without a permit, or in violation of a permit, is subject to a civil penalty of up to $25,000 *per day per violation*.[1] The DEC has the power to impose such penalties in administrative enforcement actions, with such assessment reviewable in an Article 78 proceeding.[2] The DEC also has the power to have the Attorney General institute an enforcement proceeding for violations of Article 17 in state court.[3] The DEC also has the power to revoke a discharger's permit and to request that the Attorney General commence

---

[7]. The DEC has issued a standard NOI form for these General Permits that are available upon request. Under either General Permit, the NOI must be submitted at least two days prior to commencement of the activity and, for construction activity, the NOI must be posted at the construction site in a similar fashion to a building permit.

[8]. Navigation Law §§ 173, 172(8).

[9]. Navigation Law §§ 175, 176. For a complete discussion of the requirements of the Navigation Law with regard to petroleum discharges, *see infra*, § 15.27.

§ 15.11

[1]. ECL § 71–1929(1) (emphasis added).

[2]. *See e.g.*, Deutsch Relays, Inc. v. New York State Department of Environmental Conservation, 179 A.D.2d 756, 579 N.Y.S.2d 128 (2d Dep't 1992) (DEC-imposed penalty of $635,000 on a company that violated its SPDES permit effluent limits 874 times and failed to submit monthly non-compliance reports required in its permit was not unreasonable and in accord with the DEC's internal penalty assessment guidelines.)

PRACTICE POINTER: In any enforcement action where the DEC is likely to seek a civil penalty, familiarity with the DEC's penalty assessment policy is essential. This policy can be used to support a lesser penalty due to a discharger's cooperation, or based on other factors that warrant a downward adjustment to the DEC's penalty assessment. The DEC often attempts to use the astronomical maximum penalties that it could potentially seek under Article 71 when negotiating over penalties in DEC consent orders; however, the penalty assessment policy, as well as information regarding what penalty DEC-imposed in similar situations, can be successfully used to argue for a lower penalty than initially proposed by the Department. A defendant is entitled, pursuant to the Freedom of Information Law ("FOIL"), to the DEC consent orders entered to resolve similar violations, and a defendant should request such orders when negotiating or litigating a penalty assessment. *See* Chapter 4 "New York Administrative Law," *supra* for a discussion of FOIL.

[3]. ECL § 71–1927.

an action seeking injunctive relief.[4] The ECL also provides for criminal liability for knowing, intentional and criminally negligent violations of Article 17.[5]

New York law does not provide for citizen enforcement of New York's water pollution control laws, including its SPDES permitting program. However, the CWA[6] does give citizens the right to bring a civil action against any person

> who is alleged to be in violation of (A) an effluent standard or limitation ... or (B) an order issued by the Administrator or a State with respect to such standard of limitation ...[7]

Therefore, in New York a citizen may bring an action against any person alleged to be in violation of an effluent standard or limit under the CWA, including actions alleging that a person is discharging without a SPDES permit or in violation of its SPDES permit.[8] However, only provisions contained in SPDES permits that are based on the CWA may support a citizen suit. "State regulations, including provisions of SPDES permits, which mandate a greater scope of coverage than that required by the Federal CWA and its implementing regulations, are not enforceable through a citizen suit."[9]

In order to maintain a citizen suit, the complaint must allege an ongoing violation of the CWA. In *Gwaltney of Smithfield, Ltd. v. Chesapeake Bay Foundation*,[10] the United States Supreme Court held that, because Section 505 of the CWA requires that any action be against a person "alleged to be in violation" of a standard or limit under the CWA, a citizen suit seeking civil penalties for wholly past violations may not be maintained.[11] Courts have also found that citizen enforcement actions are moot when government enforcement has caused the violations al-

---

4. ECL § 17–1931 empowers the Attorney General to commence an action for injunctive relief at the DEC's request.

5. ECL § 71–1933.

6. See supra, § 15.8.

7. 33 U.S.C.A. § 1365(a)(1). Section 1365(a)(2) enables citizens to commence a civil action against the EPA for failure to perform any non-discretionary act or duty under the CWA.

8. The structure of the CWA provides for very effective enforcement of the Act by citizens and government regulators. Because the CWA requires permittees to monitor discharges and file discharge monitoring reports, or DMRs, these DMRs can and have been effectively used to demonstrate clear violations of the effluent limitations contained in a SPDES permit. If there is no permit, than all that must be established, subject to any defenses, is that there was a discharge of a "pollutant" from a "point source" into "waters of the United States." See supra, § 15.5.

9. Atlantic States Legal Foundation v. Eastman Kodak, Inc. ("Kodak II"), 12 F.3d 353, 359 (2d Cir.1993), cert. denied 513 U.S. 811, 115 S.Ct. 62, 130 L.Ed.2d 19 (1994).

10. 484 U.S. 49, 108 S.Ct. 376, 98 L.Ed.2d 306 (1987).

11. 484 U.S. at 64, 108 S.Ct. at 385. The Supreme Court in Gwaltney made clear that Section 505 "confers jurisdiction over citizen suits when the citizen-plaintiffs make a good faith allegation of continuous or intermittent violations" of the CWA. Id. Proof of ongoing violations is not required, but merely a good faith allegation of such violations. On remand the District Court in Gwaltney found sufficient basis to support an allegation of continuing violations and imposed a civil penalty against the defendant. 688 F.Supp. 1078 (E.D.Va.1988).

leged in the citizen suit to cease without any likelihood of recurrence, even if the violations were ongoing when the citizen action was commenced and thus properly commenced under *Gwaltney*.[12]

Section 505 of the CWA also provides that no citizen suit may be commenced unless a plaintiff has provided sixty days notice of the alleged violation to the EPA, to the state in which the alleged violation occurs, and to the alleged violator.[13] In addition, no citizen suit may be commenced if the EPA or the state "has commenced and is diligently prosecuting a civil or criminal action in a court of the United States, or a state to require compliance with the standard, limitation or order."[14] Although one other circuit has held that this "diligent prosecution" bar may also apply to certain administrative enforcement actions where the regulator has the authority to impose the type of relief imposed by a court, the Second Circuit has ruled that the statute only applies to enforcement actions brought in "a court of the United States or a State."[15]

The 1987 CWA Amendments added additional protection against citizen suits when the EPA has commenced and is diligently prosecuting a civil penalty action pursuant to Section 309(g) of the CWA, or when a State has commenced and is diligently prosecuting an action under a State law "comparable" to Section 309(g).[16] However, this section is of questionable utility in avoiding citizen suits because some courts have held that it only bars citizen suits to the extent such suits seek civil penalties, but does not bar a citizen suit that seeks injunctive relief.[17] Moreover, it is unclear what constitutes a "comparable state law" for the purpose of this provision.[18]

---

12. Atlantic States Legal Foundation, Inc. v. Eastman Kodak, Inc. ("Kodak I"), 933 F.2d 124, 127 (2d Cir.1991); *see also*, EPA v. City of Green Forest, 921 F.2d 1394, 1403–04 (8th Cir.), cert. denied 502 U.S. 956, 112 S.Ct. 414, 116 L.Ed.2d 435 (1991).

13. 33 U.S.C.A. § 1365(b)(1)(A). This notice requirement is jurisdictional. Thus, failure to provide the requisite notice will result in the court's dismissal of the citizen suit. Hallstrom v. Tillamook County, 493 U.S. 20, 31, 110 S.Ct. 304, 311, 107 L.Ed.2d 237 (1989), rehearing denied 493 U.S. 1037, 110 S.Ct. 761, 107 L.Ed.2d 777 (1990).

PRACTICE POINTER: EPA has promulgated regulations governing the contents and service of such notice. 40 C.F.R. Pt. 135, Subpt. A.

14. 33 U.S.C.A. § 1365(b)(1)(B).

15. Friends of the Earth v. Consolidated Rail Corp., 768 F.2d 57, 62 (2d Cir.1985). *But see* Baughman v. Bradford Coal Co., 592 F.2d 215, 219 (3d Cir.), cert. denied 441 U.S. 961, 99 S.Ct. 2406, 60 L.Ed.2d 1066 (1979).

16. 33 U.S.C.A. § 1319(g)(6)(A).

17. Coalition For a Liveable West Side v. New York City Department of Environmental Protection, 830 F.Supp. 194, 196 (S.D.N.Y.1993); Orange Environment, Inc. v. County of Orange, 860 F.Supp. 1003, 1018 (S.D.N.Y.1994). *But see* North & South Rivers Watershed Ass'n v. Town of Scituate, 949 F.2d 552, 558 (1st Cir.1991).

18. Coastal Fishermen's Assn. v. New York City Department of Sanitation, 772 F.Supp. 162, 165 (S.D.N.Y.1991) (without analysis, court assumes New York scheme is comparable to federal law). *But see* Public Interest Research Group of New Jersey v. GAF Corp., 770 F.Supp. 943, 950 (D.N.J. 1991) (New Jersey Water Pollution Control Act did not provide for public notice and participation before assessment of a civil penalty order and thus was not sufficiently comparable to an action by EPA pursuant to Section 309(g)).

The uncertainty surrounding the scope of the CWA's administrative diligent prosecution bar makes it extremely unclear as to the extent that a DEC administrative enforcement action (or consent order) would preclude a subsequent CWA enforcement action. Defendants should thus be cautious in relying upon this provision to preclude additional citizen enforcement actions.[19]

Library References:

West's Key No. Digests, Health and Environment ⚖︎25.7(17)–25.7(20).

§ 15.12 Water Pollution Control—Strategy: Clean Water Act Citizen Suit Checklist

1. May a federal CWA Citizen Suit be maintained? (*See* § 15.8)

    - Does the Complaint allege in good faith an ongoing violation of the CWA? If not, an action may not be maintained.

    - Does the Complaint allege that the defendant is in violation of an "effluent standard or limitation" under the CWA or an order issued by the EPA or a state with respect to such standard or limitation, or, alternatively, does it allege a failure by the EPA to perform a non-discretionary act or duty?[1] If not, no citizen suit may be maintained.

    - Has the plaintiff provided sixty days prior notice to the alleged violation to the EPA, to the state where the alleged violation occurs and to the alleged violator? If not, the citizen suit cannot be maintained until such notice is provided.[2]

    - Has the government regulator already commenced and continued to "diligently prosecute" a civil or criminal action in a court of the United States or a state to require compliance with the standard, limitation or order that is the subject of the citizen suit?[3] If yes, then the citizen suit cannot be maintained.

    - Has the government regulator commenced a civil penalty action pursuant to 33 U.S.C.A. § 1319(g), or a state under a

---

19. PRACTICE POINTER: If a defendant is contemplating settling a DEC enforcement action by entering into an administrative order on consent, the defendant may wish to consider getting more bang for his or her buck by convincing the DEC to commence a judicial enforcement action and enter into a judicially approved consent decree. Such a decree then may be used to preclude a citizen suit based on prior State diligent prosecution. *See* Hudson River Sloop Clearwater, Inc. v. Consolidated Rail Corp., 591 F.Supp. 345, 350 (N.D.N.Y.1984), aff'd in relevant part and rev'd in part sub nom. Friends of the Earth v. Consolidated Rail Corp., 768 F.2d 57 (2d Cir.1985) (" '[o]rdinarily, a consent order should be viewed as sufficient in itself to satisfy the requirement of diligent prosecution' " (quoting Sierra Club v. SCM Corp., 572 F.Supp. 828, 831 note 3 (W.D.N.Y.1983), appeal dismissed 747 F.2d 99 (2d Cir.1984))).

§ 15.12

1. 33 U.S.C.A. § 1365.
2. 40 C.F.R. § 135.2.
3. 33 U.S.C.A. § 1365(b)(1)(B).

law "comparable" to Section 1319(g), for the violations at issue in the citizen suit. If yes, a citizen suit *may* be precluded, or a citizen suit for only civil penalties, but not injunctive relief, *may* be precluded.

§ 15.13 Wetlands Protection

Activities in wetlands located within New York State are potentially subject to regulation under federal, state and sometimes even local laws.[1] Thus, an environmental practitioner must consider the applicability and requirements of federal, state and local schemes when undertaking activities within wetlands, and sometimes in areas adjacent to wetlands. These various regulatory schemes overlap to some extent, but the uses and types of wetlands covered and activities regulated differ in significant ways. In some instances an activity may not be covered under one regulatory scheme, but covered under another, while in other instances permits may be required from several levels of government. This section will briefly focus on regulation of wetlands under Section 404 of the CWA,[2] and under the state regulations governing activities in tidal and freshwater wetlands.[3]

Library References:

West's Key No. Digests, Navigable Waters ⚭38.

§ 15.14 Wetlands Protection—Strategy: Checklist

1. Is the site covered by federal wetlands law? (*See* § 15.12) If unsure, examine the following:

    • Does wetland fall within definition of "waters of the United States"?

    • Check regulatory definition of wetland.[1]

    • Check the EPA's 1987 Wetlands delineation manual. Survey property to see if site meets criteria outlined in manual (expert probably needed).

    • Request jurisdictional determination from the ACE.

§ 15.13

1. The U.S. Army Corps of Engineers ("ACE") has been given primary jurisdiction to administer the federal permitting program, although the EPA has concurrent enforcement with ACE and also has a veto power over ACE permits if there will be an "unacceptable" adverse impact to important aquatic areas. 33 U.S.C.A. § 1344(c). ACE has issued regulations governing the federal wetland process at 33 C.F.R. Pts. 620, *et seq.* The New York State program is administered by the DEC; state wetlands law provides for the delegation of this program to local governments, though few local governments have assumed jurisdiction for the state regulatory scheme. *See* Chapter 16 "Land Use Law," §§ 16.52–16.59, *infra*.

2. *See supra*, § 15.8.

3. 33 U.S.C.A. § 1344(a); ECL §§ 24-0101 *et seq.*, 25-0101 *et seq.*

§ 15.14

1. 33 C.F.R. § 328.3.

2. If site is federally-regulated wetland, is proposed activity to be undertaken within wetlands regulated? (*See* § 15.12) If unsure, examine the following:

   • Does the proposed activity constitute "dredging or filling" under Section 404?

   • Does activity fall with Section 404's exceptions?[2]

   • Check applicable case law interpreting Section 404.

3. If the activity is regulated, does a general permit apply? If unsure, examine the following:

   • Examine the ACE general and nationwide permits.[3]

   • Has the state issued water quality certification for the applicable ACE general or nationwide permit and/or imposed conditions on use of such permit?

   • If the proposed activity is to be undertaken within coastal zone, has the state issued a coastal zone consistency determination?

4. Does general or nationwide permit require prior notification to the ACE before commencing regulated activity?[4]

5. Is an individual permit required? If unsure, examine the following:

   • Does general or nationwide permit apply? (*See* Number 3 above)

   • If required, ensure that a coastal zone consistency determination received from the state if proposed activity is to be undertaken within the coastal zone.

   • If required, ensure that a state water quality certification is received.

6. Is the wetland regulated as a State Freshwater Wetland ("FWW")? If unsure, examine the following:

   • Check the DEC FWW map for county where wetland is located.

   • Is FWW larger than 12.4 acres or of "unusual local importance"?[5]

   • Even if not on wetland map, does wetland meet criteria to be considered FWW?[6]

   • Check the DEC FWW Delineation manual.

2. 33 U.S.C.A. § 1344(f)(1).
3. *See e.g.,* 33 C.F.R. § 330.1(e).
4. *See* 33 C.F.R. § 330.1.
5. 6 NYCRR § 662.1(k).
6. ECL § 24-0107(1).

7. If the wetland is regulated as a FWW, is a permit or letter of permission required to undertake the proposed activity? If unsure, examine the following:
    - Does activity take place within FWW or its adjacent area?
    - Is the activity exempt?[7]
    - What is the classification of the FWW?[8]
    - What is the classification of the proposed use?[9]
8. Is the wetland regulated as a State Tidal Wetland? If unsure, examine the following:
    - Check the DEC Tidal wetlands map for county where wetland is located.
    - Even if not on wetland map, does wetland meet criteria to be considered Tidal wetland?[10]
9. If the wetland is regulated as a State Tidal Wetland, is a permit required to undertake the proposed activity? If unsure, examine the following:
    - Does the proposed activity take place within the Tidal Wetland or its adjacent area?
    - Is the activity exempt?[11]
    - What is the classification of the Tidal Wetland?[12]
    - What is the classification of the proposed use?[13]

§ 15.15 Wetlands Protection—The Federal Scheme

The federal wetlands law—governed by Section 404 of the Federal Clean Water Act—requires a person who desires to "discharge dredged or fill material" into "navigable waters," which include wetlands, to obtain a permit from the ACE before doing so.[1] "Navigable waters" is defined quite broadly in the ACE's regulations as "waters of the United States;" it includes more than waters traditionally considered "navigable" under other federal legislation and also encompasses most wetland areas within the United States, including wetlands that are adjacent to interstate lakes, rivers and streams that are considered navigable waters of the United States.[2] Even local, "isolated" wetlands may be covered if the ACE determines that the wetlands use, degradation or destruction could affect interstate commerce.[3]

---

7. 6 NYCRR § 663.4.
8. 6 NYCRR § 663.5.
9. 6 NYCRR § 663.4.
10. ECL § 25–0103(1); 6 NYCRR § 661.4(h).
11. 6 NYCRR § 661.5.
12. 6 NYCRR § 661.4.
13. 6 NYCRR § 661.5.

§ 15.15
1. 33 U.S.C.A. § 1344(a).
2. 33 C.F.R. § 328.3.
3. Id.

Wetland delineation under the CWA[4] is undertaken by the ACE as part of its administration of the federal wetland permitting program. Wetlands are defined as "those areas that are inundated or saturated by surface or ground water at a frequency and duration sufficient to support, and that under normal circumstances do support, a prevalence of vegetation typically adapted for life in saturated soil conditions."[5] The ACE will look at hydrology, soil matrix and the prevalent type of vegetation in determining whether a site contains wetlands. The technical standards and directions are contained in the federal wetlands manual, that was published by the EPA and the ACE in 1987 to assist in delineating federal wetlands. A property owner is responsible for identifying wetlands that are subject to regulation under Section 404 of the Federal Clean Water Act.[6]

Section 404 of the CWA prohibits the discharge of dredged and fill material into wetlands without a federal permit. This prohibition has been broadly interpreted to encompass any activity where filling—even if inadvertent—is associated with the activity, including placement of piles if used in a manner equivalent to fill, mechanized land clearing activities, and possibly the draining of a wetland, even though the wetland is not technically "filled."[7] Section 404 also provides for certain limited exemption for activities such as construction of irrigation ditches, for farm and forest roads and other similar activities.[8]

If the site of a proposed discharge activity is a wetland, and the activity is not specifically exempted from regulation, a permit for the activity is required from the ACE. There are two types of federal wetlands permits—individual permits and general permits. General permits include nationwide permits, which are often relied upon by regulated parties and are set forth in regulations promulgated by the ACE.[9] If

---

4. *See supra*, § 15.8.

5. 33 C.F.R. § 328.3(b). This definition has been upheld by the United States Supreme Court. United States v. Riverside Bayview Homes, Inc., 474 U.S. 121, 106 S.Ct. 455, 88 L.Ed.2d 419 (1985).

6. Use of the a newer wetlands manual, published in 1989, was prohibited by Congress.

PRACTICE POINTER: A property owner may also request from the ACE a jurisdictional determination of whether the wetlands are subject to regulation. However, a private party proposing an activity on federally regulated wetlands may find it advantageous to submit its own expert preliminary wetlands determination as part of a wetlands permit application. If feasible, this approach is advantageous because it provides the ACE with a proposed delineation that can be the starting point for an application to the ACE concerning proposed activities to be undertaken in federally regulated wetlands.

7. 33 C.F.R. § 323.2(d). In August 1993, the ACE issued regulations that required a Section 404 permit for excavation of wetlands (including mechanized land clearing) that results in the redeposit or fallback of dredged or excavated material. 33 C.F.R. § 323.2(d)(1)(iii). This regulation, known as "Tulloch Rule," was invalidated by the United States District Court for the District of Columbia on the ground that it exceeded the authority of the ACE and the EPA under the CWA. American Mining Congress v. U.S. Army Corps of Engineers, 951 F.Supp. 267 (D.D.C.1997).

8. 33 U.S.C.A. § 1344(f)(1).

9. 33 C.F.R. Pt. 330. The ACE reissued and revised its nationwide permits, effective February 11, 1997. Individual states may refuse to certify a nationwide permit and/or

an activity falls within a nationwide permit, it can be undertaken without the filing of an individual permit application with the ACE. Some nationwide permits require prior notification of the activity by the applicant to the ACE, while others require no notification or other action by the applicant before undertaking the activity. One major nationwide permit—number 26—allows an application, after *prior* notification to the ACE by the applicant, to fill a non-tidal wetland above the headwaters as long as the entire project will not cause the loss or substantial adverse modification of more than one-third of an acre of wetlands, provided that the wetlands are not part of a surface tributary system to interstate waters and not adjacent to such waters.[10]

No federal permit may be issued in New York until a water quality certification is obtained from the DEC.[11] To obtain this certificate, the discharger must demonstrate that the proposed discharge will be within the applicable effluent limits and will not violate state water quality standards and all other applicable state standards and regulations.[12] If the proposed activity will take place within a coastal zone, the permittee also must obtain a determination from the New York Department of State that the project is consistent with New York's Coastal Zone Management Program.[13] If the Department of State fails to act within six months of receiving an applicant's proposed certification of consistency, the state consistency determination is presumed and the activity can be undertaken without any further action taking place.[14]

Both the EPA and the ACE may enforce the requirements of Section 404 of the CWA through the use of administrative orders, administrative penalties, or through the commencement of civil and criminal judicial

impose conditions upon the availability of such permits. 33 C.F.R. § 330.4(c). In addition, EPA may veto ACE's issuance of a discharge permit based on "unacceptable adverse impacts" on certain environmental concerns. 33 U.S.C.A. § 1344(c).

10. 33 C.F.R. § 330.1(e). Nationwide permit 26 also applies to discharges that would cause the loss of less than three acres of wetlands, however, there must be prior notification to the ACE before undertaking the action and the ACE must determine that the proposed discharge would not have more than a minimal effect on the aquatic environment. 33 C.F.R. § 330.1(e). New York, however, has denied water quality certification for filling that would cause the loss of one or more acres of wetlands. Thus, an individual water quality certification from the DEC is required to qualify for a nationwide permit in such circumstances. The ACE has announced its intention to replace nationwide permit 26 with an activity-based nationwide permit by approximately 1999.

11. 33 U.S.C.A. § 1341.

12. 6 NYCRR § 608.7.

13. The New York Department of State also must issue coastal zone consistency determinations for individual and general wetlands permits taking place within a coastal zone. The New York Department of State has not issued a consistency determination for nationwide permit number 26; therefore, an applicant must obtain an individual consistency determination to invoke this nationwide permit for proposed activities within the coastal zone. The Coastal Zone Management Program policies are listed at 6 NYCRR § 600.5. If a locality has adopted its own waterfront development plan that has been approved by the Department of State, then the Department must also find that the proposed activity is consistent with that local plan. *See generally,* 15 C.F.R. § 325.2(b)(2)(ii).

14. 33 C.F.R. § 325.2(b)(2)(ii).

§ 15.16 Wetlands Protection—New York Tidal and Freshwater Wetlands Law

The DEC is responsible for the administration and enforcement of New York's wetlands laws.[1] The DEC regulates activities within both tidal wetlands[2] and freshwater wetlands.[3] Wetlands within the state are primarily delineated based upon the type of vegetation found on the parcel,[4] and also, in the case of tidal wetlands, on the presence of tidal waters. Both freshwater and tidal wetlands are delineated by the DEC, and set forth on detailed wetlands maps that have been promulgated by the DEC.[5] Although there is some conflicting case law on the question, a wetland is likely within the DEC's jurisdiction, and thus protected, even before it has been placed on a DEC wetlands map.[6]

The DEC's regulations set forth the procedure and requirements for obtaining a freshwater wetlands permit.[7] Freshwater wetlands are further defined in these regulations and, unlike the federal regulations, only

---

15. 33 U.S.C.A. § 1319. Administrative penalties for violating Section 404 can be as high as $10,000 per violation, up to $25,000. 33 U.S.C.A. § 1319(g)(2). See Ginsberg, Weinberg, et al., *Environmental Law and Regulation in New York* (West 1996 and 1997 Pocket Part) Ch. 18 "Criminal Enforcement of Environmental Law."

16. 33 U.S.C.A. § 1365.

§ 15.16

1. The Freshwater Wetlands Act permits local governments, after the issuance of a final wetlands map for that area, to assume authority for implementing the statute. ECL § 24–0501(1). However, no local freshwater wetlands law adopted to implement the state act may be less protective of wetlands than what is required under state law. The DEC has promulgated regulations defining the procedural requirements for local governments to assume regulatory authority and the standards that must be attained for such program to be considered as protective of wetlands as state law. 6 NYCRR Pt. 665.

2. ECL §§ 25–0101 et seq.; 6 NYCRR Pt. 661.

3. ECL §§ 24–0101 et seq.; 6 NYCRR Pts. 662, 663.

4. ECL §§ 24–0107(1) (freshwater wetlands), 25–0103(1) (tidal wetlands).

5. CAVEAT: The DEC wetlands maps have a very large scale and are thus of limited utility in determining precise wetland boundaries for a specific parcel. The DEC has, however, promulgated a technical manual providing guidance on precise mapping of freshwater wetlands boundaries that can be obtained from the DEC. DEC, Freshwater Delineation Manual (March 1995).

6. Matter of Tri Cities Industrial Park v. DEC, 76 A.D.2d 232, 430 N.Y.S.2d 411 (3d Dep't 1980), app. den. 51 N.Y.2d 706, 433 N.Y.S.2d 1026, 413 N.E.2d 369 (1980). *But see* People v. Bondi, 104 Misc.2d 627, 429 N.Y.S.2d 146 (Town Ct. of Webster 1980). The Bondi decision has been criticized in the Practice Commentaries to ECL Article 24 as contrary to the legislative policy to protect wetlands set forth in these laws. Weinberg, *Practice Commentary*, ECL § 24–0107.

7. 6 NYCRR Pts. 662, 663. Part 662 contains interim permit procedures that govern the DEC's issuance of permits in areas prior to the DEC's filing of a final freshwater wetlands map for that area. Once a final map is filed, the act will be implemented, either by the appropriate local government, if it has been authorized to issue permits by the DEC, or pursuant to the DEC's uniform permit procedures contained at 6 NYCRR Pts. 621, 624. 6 NYCRR § 662.2(a).

those freshwater wetlands that have an area of 12.4 acres or more, or are smaller but determined by the DEC to be "of unusual local importance," are subject to regulation.[8] A person may ask the DEC whether or not a parcel of land includes "all or part of a freshwater wetland that is 12.4 acres in size and therefore is subject to regulation."[9] If a wetland falls within the DEC's jurisdiction, a permit to conduct any regulated activity within that wetland or its "adjacent area" (that area within 100 feet of a wetland) is required.[10] Mapped freshwater wetlands are classified according to the DEC's assessment of their value and the wetlands functions performed.[11] These classifications are relevant to the burden on the applicant seeking to obtain a permit for an activity within such wetland.[12]

§ 15.17 Wetlands Protection—Permit Procedure and Criteria

Once a final wetland map has been issued, the criteria for obtaining a permit or "letter of permission," which may be issued in lieu of a permit for minor activities within a freshwater wetland, are governed by the criteria set forth in the DEC's freshwater wetlands regulations contained at 6 NYCRR Part 663.[1] These provisions regulate activities in freshwater wetlands and adjacent areas depending on the type of wetland affected, whether the area is wetland or adjacent area, and the type of activity proposed. Proposed uses are classified into three categories—(1) Usually Compatible; (2) Usually Incompatible; and (3) Incompatible.[2] In addition, certain activities, such as the continuance of lawfully existing uses or other uses where no significant impairment of wetlands are involved, are exempt from regulation and thus do not require a permit or letter of permission.[3]

---

8. 6 NYCRR § 662.1(k).

9. 6 NYCRR § 662.4(a).

10. **CAVEAT:** Note that the federal scheme does not have a concept of a wetland "adjacent area"; thus, only activities within federal wetlands are subject to the federal regulatory requirements. In addition, unlike state wetlands, federal wetlands are not generally pre-mapped.

11. Freshwater wetlands are divided into four classes, with Class I wetlands performing the most critical wetlands benefit and the Classes II–IV performing less critical functions in declining order of priority. 6 NYCRR § 663.5(e).

12. 6 NYCRR § 663.4.

§ 15.17

1. If a local government has assumed regulatory authority for this permitting program, Part 663 will not apply. Instead, rules adopted pursuant to 6 NYCRR Part 665 would apply in that locality.

2. 6 NYCRR § 663.4.

PRACTICE POINTER: The DEC has issued a general guidance to the DEC staff on the framework for mitigation measures that may be required in connection with a project affecting regulated freshwater wetlands. The DEC, Freshwater Wetlands Regulation, Guidelines on Compensatory Mitigation (October 1993) (a copy can be requested from the DEC's Division of Fish & Wildlife).

3. 6 NYCRR § 663.4.

Tidal wetlands are also delineated on inventory maps that classify these wetlands into various categories that are important in determining what type of activity is permitted to be undertaken in that type of wetland.[4] The DEC may amend these maps (as well as its freshwater wetlands maps), but it must provide public notice, specific notice to any affected landowner (if a wetland is to be newly mapped or its boundary is expanded), hold a legislative hearing and issue a written determination.[5] Unlike freshwater wetlands, there is no minimum size for designation of an area as tidal wetland. The tidal wetlands law also regulates uses in areas adjacent to tidal wetlands.[6]

As with freshwater wetlands permits, tidal wetlands permits are granted based on the type of activity, or use contemplated, and the category of wetland or adjacent area affected. The use guidelines set forth in the regulations designate each proposed use are the following: (1) a use not requiring a permit; (2) a generally compatible use—permit required; (3) a presumptively incompatible use—permit required; (4) an incompatible use; and (5) not applicable, for each wetland category and adjacent area.[7] There are very few uses that are exempted and thus almost all activities in a wetland or adjacent area will require a DEC letter of permission or permit.[8] The DEC's uniform permit procedures, promulgated pursuant to Article 70 of the Environmental Conservation Law and the regulations promulgated thereto, govern the permit application process for tidal and freshwater wetlands permits.[9]

§ 15.18 Wetlands Protection—Penalties

The ECL provides for penalties of up to $3,000 per violation for conducting regulated activities in a freshwater wetland without a permit or for violating the terms of a DEC-issued freshwater wetlands permit.[1] Penalties for conducting regulated activities in a tidal wetland or adjacent area or violating the terms of a DEC-issued permit can be as high as 10,000 per violation.[2]

---

4. 6 NYCRR § 661.4(h). These categories are coastal fresh marsh, intertidal marsh, coastal shoals, bars and flats, littoral zone, high marsh or salt meadow, and formerly connected tidal wetlands.

5. 6 NYCRR §§ 661.15(b) (tidal), 664.7(a)(2) (freshwater).

6. Adjacent areas for tidal wetlands are defined as the area either (1) 300 feet landward of the most landward boundary of a tidal wetland (150 feet within New York City); (2) to the seaward edge of the closest lawfully, presently existing (as of August 1977) man-made structure; (3) the seaward edge of ten foot elevation mark; or (4) the top of a coastal bluff or dune. 6 NYCRR § 661.4(b).

7. 6 NYCRR § 661.5.

8. In addition, all regulated activities that require a permit are subject to development restrictions. These standards include specific setbacks for structures and septic systems, limits on extent of impervious areas, minimum lot sizes and runoff restrictions. 6 NYCRR § 661.6.

9. 6 NYCRR Pts. 621, 624.

§ 15.18

1. ECL § 71–2303.
2. ECL § 71–2503.

§ 15.19 Air Pollution Control

The Federal Clean Air Act ("CAA") contemplates a federal-state partnership for the regulation of air pollutants. Except for areas that require national uniformity, such as the regulation of emissions from automobiles, the CAA leaves the implementation and enforcement of air quality regulation to the states, in accordance with federal air quality standards—and deadlines for states to achieve these standards—that are set by Congress and the EPA.

The basic structure of the present CAA traces back to the Clean Air Act Amendments of 1970.[1] The CAA was significantly amended and expanded in 1977 and 1990 and is, without a doubt, one of the most complex federal statutes in existence. The 1970 CAA Amendments were the first to require the EPA to promulgate primary and secondary National Ambient Air Quality Standards ("NAAQS"), for criteria pollutants.[2] Presently the EPA has issued NAAQS for six criteria pollutants.[3] Once listed, the CAA provides that the EPA must establish primary emissions standards—standards necessary to protect public health—and secondary standards—standards necessary to protect the public from any known or anticipated adverse effects.[4]

In the CAA, Congress recognized the interstate effects of air pollution and directed the EPA to designate, in consultation with state and local authorities, air quality control regions that were to include "any interstate or major intrastate area" necessary or appropriate for the attainment and maintenance of NAAQS.[5] These regions are further categorized as attainment, nonattainment or unclassifiable, depending on the air quality levels for the six criteria pollutants.[6]

Although NAAQS are issued by the EPA, the actual concrete measures to be implemented to achieve these standards are left to the states. The CAA requires states to develop and submit to the EPA State Implementation Plans ("SIPs") that "provide for implementation, maintenance and enforcement" of the primary NAAQS issued by the EPA.[7] A

---

§ 15.19

1. Congress had made prior attempts to regulate air pollution; however, it was not until 1970 that these efforts resulted in a comprehensive and workable regulatory scheme to curb air pollution.

2. 42 U.S.C.A. § 7408. The basis for listing an air pollutant as a criteria pollutant under the CAA is health-based. EPA is to issue criteria for each air pollutant the "emissions of which . . . cause or contribute to air pollution which may reasonably be anticipated to endanger public health or welfare." 42 U.S.C.A. § 7408(a)(1).

3. These criteria pollutants are particulates, sulfur, carbon monoxide, nitrogen oxide, ozone (a major component of smog) and lead. 40 C.F.R. Pt. 50.

4. 42 U.S.C.A. § 7409(b).

5. 42 U.S.C.A. § 7407(a)-(c). There are well over 200 air quality control regions presently designated by EPA; most of the regions came into being under the authority of the 1967 Air Quality Act. W. H. Rogers, Jr., *Environmental Law*, (2d ed. West 1994) 131.

6. The air quality regions that include parts of New York State and their classifications for the six criteria pollutants are set forth at 40 C.F.R. § 52.1682.

7. 42 U.S.C.A. § 7410(a)(1).

SIP must contain enforceable emission limits and other control measures, including economic incentives, as well as schedules for compliance and devices to monitor and analyze data on air quality.[8] SIPs are subject to EPA-approval and the EPA may issue partial or conditional approval of a SIP.[9]

The CAA also mandates that the EPA promulgate specific emissions standards for categories of any new air pollution source which, in the EPA's judgment, "causes, or contributes significantly to, air pollution which may reasonably be anticipated to endanger public health or welfare."[10] These emissions standards—known as New Source Performance Standards ("NSPS")—must reflect "the degree of emission reduction achievable through application of the best system of emission reduction," taking into account the cost of achieving the reduction and any non-air quality health and environmental impact and energy requirements.[11]

After numerous parts of the country failed to achieve the ambitious deadlines for attainment of NAAQS set forth in the 1970 CAA, Congress enacted significant amendments in 1977. These amendments created Part D of the CAA, which provided for stringent new SIP requirements for "nonattainment" areas and, in exchange, extended the deadline for achievement of these standards.[12]

The new SIP provisions required by the 1977 Amendments required, for the first time, that permits be obtained for the construction and operation of "new or modified major stationary sources anywhere in the nonattainment area."[13] These permits require that new or modified sources achieve the "lowest achievable emission rate," or ("LAER").[14] Moreover, these sources must comply with certain "offset" requirements that mandate that total potential emissions from new sources in the nonattainment area be sufficiently less than the total emissions from existing sources, so as to represent reasonable further progress in achieving NAAQS.[15]

---

8. 42 U.S.C.A. § 7410(a)(2).

9. 42 U.S.C.A. § 7410(k). Pursuant to the CAA, the EPA has promulgated detailed regulations setting forth the requirements for preparation, adoption and submittal of SIPs. 40 C.F.R. Pt. 51.

10. 42 U.S.C.A. § 7411(b)(1)(A).

11. 42 U.S.C.A. § 7411(a)(1). The EPA regulations setting forth NSPS for over seventy source categories are set forth at 40 C.F.R. Part 60.

12. 42 U.S.C.A. §§ 7501–7515. An area is designated "nonattainment" for each specific criteria pollutant NAAQS not achieved. For example, the New York/Northern New Jersey/Long Island air quality control region, which includes all of New York City and its surrounding suburban counties, is currently classified as severe nonattainment for ozone. A large part of this region is also classified as moderate nonattainment for carbon monoxide and New York County (Manhattan) is classified as nonattainment for PM–10 (particulates). A complete list of the status of all air quality regions within New York State can be found at 40 C.F.R. § 81.333.

13. 42 U.S.C.A. § 7502(c)(5).

14. 42 U.S.C.A. § 7503(a)(2).

15. 42 U.S.C.A. § 7503(a)(1).

§ 15.19　ENVIRONMENTAL LAW　Ch. 15

The 1977 Amendments also added Part C to the CAA to maintain air quality in areas of the country that have attained NAAQS.[16] This Part requires that every SIP contain emission limitations and other measures to prevent significant deterioration of air quality in any air region designated by the EPA as "attainment" or "unclassifiable".[17]

Library References:

West's Key No. Digests, Health and Environment ⊙=25.6(1)–25.6(9).

§ 15.20　Air Pollution Control—The 1990 CAA Amendments

Although great strides had been made in improving air quality throughout the nation since 1970, when the CAA was first significantly expanded, many air quality regions were still unable to meet the deadlines for achieving NAAQS[1] (as extended by the 1977 CAA Amendments), especially for carbon monoxide and ozone.[2] The 1990 CAA Amendments represent the latest effort to bring these areas into compliance, as well as meet other significant health threats posed by toxic air pollutants and mobile sources (automobiles). The amended CAA continues to give the states primary responsibility to develop SIPs to achieve NAAQS, but provides additional requirements that these SIPs must meet and requires states to submit SIP revisions to meet these requirements. In exchange, new deadlines are set for attainment of NAAQS, with these new deadlines categorized depending on the severity of the nonattainment area.[3]

The 1990 Amendments also greatly strengthened the air toxics provisions of the CAA, moving regulation of air pollution more towards technology-based standards, rather than health-based standards.[4] In response to the EPA's reluctance to list hazardous air pollutants subject

---

16. 42 U.S.C.A. §§ 7470–7479.

17. 42 U.S.C.A. § 7471. The EPA's Federal Prevention of Significant Deterioration ("PSD") regulations are set forth at 40 C.F.R. Part 51 and include requirements that new and modified stationary sources obtain permits and implement Best Available Control Technology, or BACT, to reduce emissions of air pollutants.

§ 15.20

1. See supra, § 15.19.

2. In the 1977 CAA Amendments, Congress gave nonattainment areas until December 31, 1987 to achieve the NAAQS for ozone and carbon monoxide. That deadline came and went and the New York metropolitan region, as well as many other populous areas of the country, was unable to achieve the NAAQS for these pollutants.

3. 42 U.S.C.A. §§ 7511 (ozone), 7512 (carbon monoxide). The New York metropolitan area, including New York City, Nassau, Suffolk, Westchester and Orange County (part) have been classified as a severe nonattainment area for ozone and thus must achieve the ozone NAAQS no later than November 15, 2005. 40 C.F.R. § 81.333. New York City, Westchester and Nassau Counties have been classified as a moderate nonattainment area for carbon monoxide and were to achieve NAAQS no later than December 31, 1995. EPA extended this deadline to December 1996. As of November 1997, EPA has not determined whether the region has met this deadline. If NAAQS for carbon monoxide is not achieved by that date, then the area will be reclassified as a serious nonattainment area and New York State will be required to implement additional measures in its SIP for the area. 42 U.S.C.A. § 7512(b).

4. 42 U.S.C.A. § 7412.

to regulation, Congress in 1990 established a specific list of 189 hazardous air pollutants in the CAA itself and ordered the EPA to issue lists of categories and subcategories of "major sources" emitting any of the listed toxic pollutants.[5] For each category listed, the EPA is to formulate appropriate emissions standards.[6]

Another significant change enacted by Congress in 1990 is the creation of Title V of the CAA, which establishes a detailed permitting program that is reminiscent of the permitting program found in the Federal Clean Water Act.[7] These provisions require states to enact an the EPA-approved state permit program for all stationary sources—including existing sources—no later than November 15, 1994. New York's permitting scheme, described in detail in the following section, had already required existing sources to obtain permits. Nevertheless, New York's permitting scheme was amended in 1993 to ensure conformity with the 1990 Amendments.

Library References:

West's Key No. Digests, Health and Environment ⚖=25.6(3.1).

§ 15.21 Air Pollution Control—New York State Requirements

As contemplated under the Federal CAA, New York State is responsible for devising, implementing and enforcing air pollution requirements to achieve NAAQS. However, New York State, in some ways, regulates matters that go beyond what is required by the CAA. For example, Article 19 of the Environmental Conservation Law, which regulates air pollution, defines "air contaminant" more broadly than the CAA to include noise.[1] In addition, New York required permits for existing stationary sources before such permits were mandated by the CAA Amendments of 1990.

The New York State Department of Environmental Conservation has been delegated authority by the EPA to issue permits to construct

---

5. 42 U.S.C.A. §§ 7412(b), (c). EPA may promulgate rules adding toxics to this list and any person may petition EPA to modify the statutory list, including deleting a substance from the list, if the petitioner can present adequate data to support a showing that "emissions, ambient concentrations, bioaccumulation, or deposition of the substance may not reasonably be anticipated to cause any adverse effects to the [sic] human health or adverse environmental effects." 42 U.S.C.A. § 7412(b)(3).

6. 42 U.S.C.A. § 7412(c)(2). Maximum achievable control technology ("MACT") is required for new and existing sources. However, the MACT standard may differ for new and existing sources. For new sources, MACT will be the most stringent limitation achieved by any single source in that category, while for existing sources the standard must not be less stringent than either the average emission limitation achieved by the best performing twelve percent of the existing sources, or the average emission limitation achieved by the best performing five sources. 42 U.S.C.A. §§ 7412(d)(3)(A), (B).

7. See supra, § 15.9.

§ 15.21

1. ECL § 19–0107(2).

new or modified stationary sources subject to the NSPS,[2] or in accordance with the EPA's National Emissions Standards for Hazardous Air Pollutants ("NESHAPS").[3] The DEC has also been delegated permitting authority for construction of new or modified stationary sources in accordance with Federal Prevention of Significant Deterioration ("PSD") requirements.[4]

The 1990 CAA Amendments require states to permit both existing and new or modified stationary sources as air pollution.[5] Although New York already required existing sources to obtain permits, the New York Legislature enacted extensive amendments to Environmental Conservation Law Article 19 in 1993, instructing the DEC to establish an operating permit program for all sources subject to Title V of the CAA.[6] These amendments direct the DEC to:

> review and revise, as necessary, to be consistent with the [CAA] and other applicable federal and state laws, existing regulations to provide for adequate streamlined and reasonable procedures for processing permit applications ...[7]

The DEC may not promulgate a regulation that contains a requirement that is stricter than what is required by the CAA unless the DEC issues a statement explaining the reason for exceeding the federal standard and analyzing the cost-effectiveness of the rule; however, a valid reason for enacting a more stringent regulation includes "protecting public health and the environment."[8] Other amendments to bring the state into conformity with the dictates of the 1990 CAA Amendments were also enacted by the New York State Legislature in 1993.[9]

The CAA Amendments of 1990 allow states to adopt California's stricter motor vehicle emissions standards and the DEC has promulgated regulations requiring that motor vehicles sold in New York meet these stricter standards.[10] After clearing numerous judicial challenges these regulations took effect beginning with the 1996 model year vehicles.[11]

2. See supra, § 15.19.

3. 6 NYCRR § 200.10. The federal NSPS are set forth at 40 C.F.R. Pt. 60 and the NESHAPS are set forth at 40 C.F.R. Pt. 61.

4. 6 NYCRR § 200.10(d). The federal PSD requirements can be found at 40 C.F.R. § 52.21.

5. 42 U.S.C.A. § 7661; see supra, § 15.20.

6. ECL § 19–0311. Permit issuance, modification and renewal are governed by Title 5 of Article 19 and DEC's uniform hearing rules at 6 NYCRR Part 621.

7. ECL § 19–0311(2)(a).

8. ECL § 19–0303(4).

9. E.g., ECL §§ 19–0315 (creation of small business stationary source compliance panel), 19–0317 (creation of biennial assessment of State programs proposed or adopted to implement the CAA), 19–0319 (creation of clean-fuel program for fleet vehicles).

10. 6 NYCRR Pt. 218.

11. Motor Vehicle Mftrs. Assn. of U.S. v. New York State Dep't of Environmental Conservation, 17 F.3d 521 (2d Cir.1994), on remand 869 F.Supp. 1012 (N.D.N.Y.1994), affirmed 79 F.3d 1298 (2d Cir.1996) (court holds that New York scheme is not prohibited by CAA, but cannot take effect until 1996 model year).

Library References:

West's Key No. Digests, Health and Environment ⟹25.6(2).

§ 15.22 Air Pollution Control—Enforcement

Article 71 of the ECL provides that the DEC may bring administrative enforcement actions for any violation of ECL Article 19, rule, regulation or DEC order to enjoin the violation and/or assess civil penalties.[1] Penalties can be as high as $10,000 per day for a first violation and up to $15,000 per day for a second violation.[2] In what will probably be the wave of the future for the DEC civil penalty assessments, a 1993 amendment to Article 71 outlines factors that the DEC or a court should consider when imposing a civil penalty, including "the economic impact of a penalty on a business, the compliance history of a violator, good faith efforts of a violator to comply, any economic benefit obtained from noncompliance, the amount of risk or damage to public health or the environment" and other factors "as justice may require."[3]

In addition, Article 71 also provides for criminal sanctions for willful violations of Article 19.[4] The Attorney General has the duty, at the request of the DEC, to bring an action for injunctive relief for any violations of Article 19.[5] These enforcement powers are in addition to the power of the Attorney General, political subdivisions of the state or individuals to bring public nuisance actions to abate air pollution.[6]

The CAA, like the other major federal environmental statutes, allows for citizen enforcement of the Act. Section 304 of the CAA allows any person to commence a civil action against any person "who is alleged to have violated," or "to be in violation" of an "emission standard or limitation" under the Act or an order issued by the EPA or a state "with respect to such a standard or limitation."[7] Citizen suits may also be brought against the EPA for an alleged failure to perform any nondiscretionary act or duty under the Act, or against any person who proposes to construct or constructs "any new or modified major emitting facility without a permit" or is alleged to have violated or be in violation of any permit condition.[8] The CAA's citizen suit provision, amended by Congress in 1990, explicitly provides that citizens may bring action against any person who is "alleged to have violated" the Act. This alters—for CAA citizen suits—the rule, enunciated by the United States Supreme Court in *Gwaltney of Smithfield Ltd.v. Chesapeake Bay Foun-*

---

§ 15.22

1. ECL § 71–2103.
2. *Id.* A person who violates regulations, permits or orders issued pursuant to ECL § 19–0304, regulating the burning of hazardous wastes, may be liable for civil penalties of up to $25,000 per day for a first violation and up to $50,000 per day for a second violation. ECL § 71–2113.
3. ECL § 71–2115.
4. ECL §§ 71–2105, 71–2113(2).
5. ECL § 71–2107.
6. ECL § 19–0703; *see infra*, § 15.32.
7. 42 U.S.C.A. § 7604(a)(1).
8. 42 U.S.C.A. § 7604(a)(2), (3).

dation,[9] prohibiting citizen suits based upon past violations that are not ongoing at the time the citizen suit is commenced.

To maintain a citizen suit for violation of an emission standard or limitation, a plaintiff must allege a violation of "a specific strategy or commitment" in a SIP promulgated under the Act and "describe, with some particularity, the respects in which compliance with the provision is deficient."[10] However, the failure to obtain NAAQS is not a violation of an emission standard or limitation and thus not a proper basis of a citizen suit.[11] NAAQS are not considered specific SIP strategies, but rather are the goals to be achieved through implementation of strategies in a SIP.[12] The Title V permit program, added by the CAA Amendments of 1990, requiring permits for emissions from all major stationary sources is likely to lead to greater enforcement under the CAA. This is because a permit issued pursuant to Title V's requirements—even if issued by a state pursuant to its enforcement program—may be enforced by the EPA and citizens, as well as states, under the CAA.

As with the citizen suit provisions contained in other federal environmental statutes, no CAA citizen suit may be commenced before providing prior notice to government agencies and the alleged violator, and no action may be brought if the EPA or a state "has commenced or is diligently prosecuting a civil action in a court of the United States or a State to require compliance with the standard, limitation, or order."[13]

Library References:

West's Key No. Digests, Health and Environment ⚖25.6(9).

§ 15.23 Regulation of Solid and Hazardous Waste

The generation, handling, transport and disposal of solid and hazardous wastes are subject to concurrent federal and state regulation. In addition, neither federal nor state law preempts additional local regulation in this area.[1] The Federal Resource Conservation and Recovery Act ("RCRA") was enacted by Congress in 1976 and was substantially amended by the Hazardous and Solid Waste Amendments of 1984.[2]

---

9. 484 U.S. 49, 108 S.Ct. 376, 98 L.Ed.2d 306 (1987).

10. Council of Commuter Organizations v. Metropolitan Transportation Authority, 683 F.2d 663, 670 (2d Cir.1982).

11. Wilder v. Thomas, 854 F.2d 605, 613–14 (2d Cir.1988), cert. denied 489 U.S. 1053, 109 S.Ct. 1314, 103 L.Ed.2d 583 (1989).

12. 854 F.2d at 613–15.

13. 42 U.S.C.A. § 7604(b)(1)(A), (B). EPA regulations governing prior notice for CAA citizen suits are set forth at 40 C.F.R. Pt. 54. For a further discussion of the notice requirement and diligent prosecution defense in federal citizen suits, see supra, § 15.11, notes 12–18.

§ 15.23

1. 42 U.S.C.A. § 6904 (1995); ECL § 27–0711.

2. Pub. L. 89–272, October 20, 1965, 79 Stat. 992 and Pub. L. 98–616, November 8, 1984, 98 Stat. 3268. RCRA was added to the Solid Waste Disposal Act ("SWDA") at 42 U.S.C.A. §§ 6901 et seq., though the entire act is more commonly referred to as RCRA and will be done so here.

RCRA defines "solid waste" broadly to include any solid, semi-solid, liquid or gaseous material that is "discarded."[3] Solid and dissolved materials in domestic sewage and irrigation return flows are exempted under this definition. The definition of "waste" under New York State law mirrors the federal statutory definition of solid waste.[4]

Hazardous waste, as defined in RCRA and the New York State Environmental Conservation Law, is a subset of solid waste. Specifically, hazardous waste is defined as a solid waste or combination thereof that cause or significantly contribute to an increase in mortality or serious illness or pose a substantial present or potential hazard to human health or the environment when improperly treated, stored, transported or disposed of.[5] The EPA has promulgated a list of substances that are deemed hazardous, as well as criteria to determine whether other, unlisted substances are considered hazardous waste under RCRA.[6]

Solid waste treatment and disposal facilities, such as landfills, incinerators, transfer stations and materials recycling facilities ("MRFs"), are concurrently regulated under RCRA and Article 27 of the ECL. RCRA requires that states create solid waste management plans, and prohibits the open dumping of solid and hazardous wastes.[7]

In New York, the State Department of Environmental Conservation ("DEC") has broad authority to regulate the transport, handling and disposal of solid waste.[8] The ECL requires that all transporters have a DEC-issued permit. In addition, the DEC has promulgated extensive regulations, set forth at 6 NYCRR Part 360, governing the operation of solid waste management facilities.[9] These regulations require an operator to apply for or obtain a DEC-issued permit for any new or existing solid waste facility. These regulations also set forth the procedure and requirements to obtain a Part 360 operating permit.[10] The Part 360 regulations include subparts that contain specific dictates applicable to every type of solid waste management facility.[11] RCRA and the regulations promulgated thereto also require that any person owning or operating an existing facility, or planning to construct a new facility, for

---

3. 42 U.S.C.A. § 6903(27); 40 C.F.R. § 261.2.

4. ECL § 27–0303(7).

5. 42 U.S.C.A. § 6903(5).

6. 40 C.F.R. § 261.30. In addition, the criteria for determining whether a waste is considered hazardous is whether it exhibits any of the characteristics identified in 40 C.F.R. §§ 261.20–261.24: ignitability, corrosivity, reactivity or toxicity. *See* Connecticut Coastal Fishermen's Assoc. v. Remington Arms Co., Inc., 989 F.2d 1305, 1316 (2d Cir.1993).

7. 42 U.S.C.A. §§ 6946, 6945. The EPA has promulgated regulations relating to state Solid Waste Management plans and the open dumping prohibition at 40 C.F.R. §§ 256 and 241, respectively.

8. ECL §§ 27–0305, 27–0707.

9. Solid waste management facilities are defined at ECL § 27–0701(2).

10. 6 NYCRR § 360.2.

11. 6 NYCRR §§ 360.2 (landfills), 360.3 (incinerators), 360.4 (land application facilities), 360.5 (composting facilities), 360.6 (liquid storage), 360.11 (transfer stations). Other specific provisions apply to construction and demolition landfills, landfills located on Long Island, medical waste facilities, recyclables handling and recovery facilities and waste tire storage facilities.

§ 15.23 ENVIRONMENTAL LAW Ch. 15

the treatment, storage or disposal of hazardous waste must obtain an EPA permit.[12]

Library References:

West's Key No. Digests, Health and Environment ⇔25.5(5, 5.5).

§ 15.24 Regulation of Solid and Hazardous Waste— New York Hazardous Waste Regulation

RCRA[1] empowers the EPA to authorize states to implement their own hazardous waste program for facilities located within their borders and conduct taking place therein. New York has applied for and received the EPA approval to administer its own program that is consonant with RCRA's dictates.[2] Thus, the DEC is charged with implementing RCRA's "cradle to grave" regulation of hazardous waste.[3] The preamble to Title 9 of the ECL states that "it is the purpose of this title to regulate the management of hazardous waste (from its generation, storage, transportation, treatment and disposal) ... in a manner that is consistent" with RCRA and that in no way is the DEC authorized to adopt or amend any rule or regulation "in a manner less stringent than provided in RCRA."[4]

One of the essential elements of the federal-state regulatory scheme is the hazardous waste manifest system that identifies and tracks the transport of hazardous wastes from the generator through to the ultimate disposal of the waste.[5] Under the EPA and the DEC regulations, a generator of solid waste is responsible for determining whether that waste is a hazardous waste.[6] If a waste is deemed hazardous under the regulations, the generator must obtain an EPA identification number before treating, storing (for greater than ninety days), disposing or transporting such hazardous waste.[7] Before transporting the waste, the generator is responsible for properly labelling such waste with the generator's name and the EPA number and to prepare a hazardous waste manifest in accordance with state regulations.[8] Manifests must be

---

12. RCRA § 3005; 42 U.S.C.A. § 6925.

§ 15.24

1. *See supra*, § 15.23.

2. RCRA § 3006(b); 42 U.S.C.A. § 6926(b).

3. *See* B.F. Goodrich v. Murtha, 958 F.2d 1192, 1201 (2d Cir.1992).

4. ECL § 27–0900.

5. ECL § 27–0905. The DEC's regulations are contained at 6 NYCRR Pt. 372. EPA's regulations are contained at 40 C.F.R. § 262.20.

6. 6 NYCRR § 372.2(a)(2); 40 C.F.R. § 262.11.

PRACTICE POINTER: Extensive RCRA counseling can rarely be done effectively without the help of an experienced environmental consultant who is familiar with the accepted methods for determining whether waste streams are deemed hazardous under the applicable regulations. However, the counseling attorney should be extremely familiar with the regulations and dictates concerning such waste streams and not rely upon even a knowledgeable consultant in determining what actions are required to comply with the federal-state regulatory scheme.

7. 6 NYCRR § 372.2(a)(3).

8. CAVEAT: The DEC has issued a Uniform Hazardous Waste manifest. However, if the hazardous waste is to be shipped out of state and that state provides a manifest, the generator is to use that manifest. 6 NYCRR § 372.2(b). Most generators rely

retained by the generator for at least three years after the waste is released and the generator must also file annual reports with the DEC.[9] The generator is also prohibited from offering hazardous waste to transporters or treatment, storage and disposal facilities ("TSDFs"), unless such facilities have the EPA identification numbers and have obtained permits.[10]

A small quantity generator is defined in the federal and state regulations as a generator of less than 1,000 kilograms of non-acute hazardous waste in a calendar month.[11] The federal-state regulatory scheme exempts these "small quantity generators" from some (though not all) of the regulations relating to hazardous wastes.

There are two classifications of small quantity generators. The EPA and the DEC regulations provide that a generator who generates less than a total of 100 kilograms of hazardous waste per month, or less than one kilogram of an acute hazardous waste per month, is a "conditionally exempt" small quantity generator.[12] A conditionally exempt small quantity generator is not subject to the hazardous waste regulations that apply to other generators, except that such generators must ensure that their waste is sent to a facility permitted or otherwise authorized by the regulations to receive such wastes.[13]

A small quantity generator who generates greater than 100 kilograms but less than 1,000 kilograms of non-acute hazardous waste per month, is subject to less stringent restrictions than what is required for larger generators, but more stringent restrictions than what is required for "conditionally exempt" small quantity generators. For example, these generators may accumulate non-acute hazardous waste on-site for up to 180 days, rather than the 90 days applicable to regular generators.[14] However, small quantity generators must ensure that the quantity of waste accumulated on-site never exceeds 6,000 kilograms of non-acute hazardous waste.[15] If waste does exceed this amount, the generator is

upon environmental compliance firms and transporters to complete manifests and other activities in connection with hazardous waste transport and there are many firms that specialize in this area. However, this obligation independently rests upon the generator, who relies upon transporters or consultants at his or her peril. At a minimum, the generator should regularly audit its hazardous waste transport and manifesting procedures to ensure compliance.

9. 6 NYCRR § 372.2(c).

10. 6 NYCRR § 372.2(b); 40 C.F.R. § 262.12(c).

11. 6 NYCRR § 370.2(164); 49 C.F.R. § 260.10.

12. 40 C.F.R. § 261.5.

13. 6 NYCRR § 371.1(f)(7); 40 C.F.R. § 261.5(g)(3).

CAVEAT: The conditionally exempt generator must still undertake an analysis of its waste streams to determine which are hazardous and take steps to avoid storing over 1,000 kilograms of hazardous waste on-site. If the generator does store over 1,000 kilograms any one month, the generator will be subject to the special regulations applicable to generators of between 100 and 1,000 kilograms of hazardous waste per month. 40 C.F.R. § 262.11; 6 NYCRR § 371.1(f)(7)(ii).

14. 40 C.F.R. § 262.34(d); 6 NYCRR §§ 370.2(164), 372.2(a)(8)(iii).

15. 40 C.F.R. § 262.34(d); 6 NYCRR § 372.2(a)(8)(iii)(a). Small quantity generators must also comply with, among other

considered an operator of a TSDF and is subject to the requirements of Part 373 of the DEC's TSDF regulations.[16]

Transporters of hazardous waste must (1) obtain a permit pursuant to 6 NYCRR Part 364 to transport hazardous waste; (2) obtain an EPA identification number; and (3) maintain the requisite number of copies of the hazardous waste manifest in the transportation vehicle when the waste is in transit.[17]

TSDFs are regulated pursuant to the very detailed requirements relating to such facilities set forth at 6 NYCRR Part 373. A TSDF is any facility that treats, stores or disposes of hazardous waste on site.[18] Owners or operators who store (in containers or tanks) hazardous waste that was generated on-site are exempt from regulation as a TSDF as long as such waste is stored for a period not exceeding 90 days (or 180 days for small quantity generators).[19] Conditionally exempt small quantity generators are exempt from the TSDF regulations.[20]

Library References:
West's Key No. Digests, Health and Environment ⚖25.5(5.5).

§ 15.25 Regulation of Solid and Hazardous Waste—Enforcement

RCRA[1] provides the EPA with the usual panoply of enforcement options. The EPA is empowered to issue administrative compliance orders, revoke permits and impose civil penalties that can be as high as $25,000 per day of noncompliance for each violations of the Act.[2] RCRA authorizes criminal penalties for "knowing" violations of RCRA's hazardous waste rules, including knowingly transporting or causing to be transported hazardous waste to an unpermitted facility, knowingly treating, storing, or disposing of hazardous waste without a permit or in

---

things, DEC regulations relating to the storage of these wastes and emergency response. See 6 NYCRR § 372.2(a)(8)(iii).

16. 6 NYCRR § 372.2(a)(8)(v).
17. 6 NYCRR § 372.3.
18. 6 NYCRR § 373-1.1(b).
19. 6 NYCRR § 373-1.1(d)(1)(ii). A small quantity generator is allowed to accumulate non-acute hazardous waste on-site for up to 270 days if the generator must transport, or offer the waste for transport, over a distance of 200 miles or more for off-site treatment, storage or disposal. 6 NYCRR § 372.2(a)(8)(iv).

CAVEAT: Generators are highly susceptible to unwittingly transforming their manufacturing facilities into TSDFs by running afoul of the time limitation for storing hazardous wastes. These generators should be counseled to continually monitor the storage of hazardous wastes at their facility to ensure that the maximum storage time is not exceeded. Extensions of up to thirty additional days from the DEC are available if the wastes must remain on site due to "unforeseen, temporary and uncontrollable circumstances." 6 NYCRR § 373-1.1(e). A major facility should consider conducting an environmental audit, either in-house or with environmental consultants, to ensure that hazardous wastes are not stored for greater than the applicable period and to assess the facility's compliance with the myriad regulations governing the storage, generation and disposal of hazardous wastes.

20. 6 NYCRR § 373-1.1(d)(1)(i).

§ 15.25

1. See supra, § 15.23.
2. 42 U.S.C.A. § 6928(a).

knowing violation of such permit or interim status regulation, or knowingly omitting information or making a false statement on a hazardous waste manifest.[3]

In addition, pursuant to Section 7003 of RCRA, the EPA may commence an action in federal district court upon evidence that the past or present handling, storage, treatment, transportation or disposal of any solid waste or hazardous waste may present an imminent and substantial endangerment to health or the environment.[4] Such actions may be brought against *any* person, including past or present generators, past or present transporters, or past or present owners or operators of a TSDF,[5] who have "contributed or who is contributing to such handling, storage, treatment or disposal."[6] The use of the word "may," as a preface to this standard of liability, has been seized on by courts as proof of Congressional intent "to confer upon the Courts the authority to grant affirmative, equitable relief to the extent necessary to eliminate *any* risk posed by toxic wastes."[7] In order to establish imminent harm, a plaintiff need not establish that actual harm will occur immediately.[8] Instead, imminence has been interpreted to mean the "nature of the threat rather than identification of the time when the endangerment initially arose."[9] Establishing liability only requires a finding of imminent and substantial endangerment and does not require proof of actual harm.[10] Unlike most of RCRA, Section 7003 goes beyond RCRA's primary focus on regulating activities relating to the handling, transport storage and disposal of solid waste prospectively, and is often employed by the EPA, in conjunction with the Comprehensive Environmental Response, Compensation and Liability Act ("CERCLA"), to compel the remediation of sites by parties whose past conduct has contributed to present hazardous conditions.[11]

Section 7002(a)(1)(A) of RCRA also allows citizen suits against "any person alleged to be in violation of any permit, standard, regulation,

---

3. 42 U.S.C.A. § 6928(d)(1)-(7). United States v. Laughlin, 10 F.3d 961 (2d Cir. 1993), cert. denied 511 U.S. 1071, 114 S.Ct. 1649, 128 L.Ed.2d 368 (1994) (government need not prove that the defendant was aware of the applicable regulations, or that no permit was issued, in order to establish RCRA and CERCLA violations for knowing disposal of hazardous waste).

4. 42 U.S.C.A. § 6973(a).

5. *See supra*, § 15.24.

6. *Id. See* United States v. Aceto Agricultural Chemicals Corp., 872 F.2d 1373, 1384 (8th Cir.1989) (plain meaning of "contributing to is to have a share in any act or effect").

7. Dague v. City of Burlington, 935 F.2d 1343, 1355 (2d Cir.1991), rev'd in part on other grounds 505 U.S. 557, 112 S.Ct. 2638, 120 L.Ed.2d 449 (1992) (emphasis in original) (quoting United States v. Price, 688 F.2d 204, 213–14 (3d Cir.1982)).

8. 935 F.2d at 1356.

9. *Id.*

10. *Id. See also*, United States v. Waste Industries, Inc., 734 F.2d 159 (4th Cir. 1984), on remand 16 ELR 20501 (E.D.N.C. 1985).

11. United States v. Waste Industries, 734 F.2d at 164–65; United States v. Northeastern Pharmaceutical & Chemical Co., Inc., 810 F.2d 726, 737 (8th Cir.1986), cert. denied 484 U.S. 848, 108 S.Ct. 146, 98 L.Ed.2d 102 (1987).

condition, requirement, prohibition or order" under the Act.[12] The 1984 Amendments to RCRA added Section 7002(a)(1)(B), which gave citizens the additional right to commence citizen suits for conditions that "may present an imminent and substantial endangerment to health or the environment."[13] The United States Supreme Court has held, however, that, unlike CERCLA, RCRA Section 7002(a)(1)(B) does not provide an owner of contaminated property a remedy to recover past costs incurred to clean up the property.[14] Reversing a decision by the Ninth Circuit Court of Appeals, the Supreme Court found that RCRA Section 7002(a)(1)(B) pertains to endangerments that threaten to occur immediately, not to the prior clean up of wastes that no longer pose an imminent and substantial danger.[15] No action may be commenced under either subsection until after the plaintiff has given the requisite notice (sixty days for actions under Section 7002(a)(1)(A) and ninety days for actions under Section 7002(a)(1)(B)) of the alleged violation to the EPA, to the state in which the violation occurred and to the alleged violator.[16] Failure to provide such notice will result in the dismissal of the citizen suit.[17] A citizen action cannot be maintained when the EPA or a state has commenced and is diligently prosecuting a civil or criminal action in a court of the United States or a state for the same violation alleged in the citizen suit.[18]

New York State law provides for monetary penalties for violation of State laws relating to solid hazardous wastes. For violations of laws and regulations relating to solid waste, the DEC is empowered to impose civil and administrative penalties of up to $2,500 for each violation and up to $1,000 for each day such violation continues.[19] The ECL also provides for criminal sanctions for violations committed with the requisite criminal intent and for additional sanctions of up to $5,000 for violations relating to construction and demolition facilities.[20]

Violations of the laws and regulations relating to hazardous waste are punishable by extremely high civil and administrative sanctions—as much as $25,000 per day for each violation.[21] Criminal violations of the

12. 42 U.S.C.A. § 6972(a)(1)(A).

13. 42 U.S.C.A. § 6972(a)(1)(B).

14. Meghrig v. KFC Western, Inc., ___ U.S. ___, 116 S.Ct. 1251, 134 L.Ed.2d 121 (1996), on remand 83 F.3d 1174 (9th Cir. 1996).

15. Id.

16. 42 U.S.C.A. § 6972(b)(1)(A). EPA regulations governing the contents and service of prior notice are set forth at 40 C.F.R. Pt. 254.

17. Hallstrom v. Tillamook County, 493 U.S. 20, 31, 110 S.Ct. 304, 311, 107 L.Ed.2d 237 (1989), rehearing denied 493 U.S. 1037, 110 S.Ct. 761, 107 L.Ed.2d 777 (1990) (holding RCRA's notice and delay requirements are "mandatory conditions precedent to commencing a citizen suit").

18. 42 U.S.C.A. § 6972(b)(1)(B).

19. ECL § 71–2703(1).

20. ECL § 71–2703(2), (3). See also, Ginsberg, Weinberg, et al., Environmental Law and Regulation in New York (West 1996) Ch. 18 "Criminal Enforcement of Environmental Law."

21. ECL § 71–2705.

State's hazardous waste laws are similarly punishable by penalties of up to $25,000 per day and/or by imprisonment of not more than one year.[22]

The ECL also establishes crimes for the unlawful possession of hazardous wastes in the first and second degree.[23] The DEC is also authorized to issue, without a prior hearing, summary abatement orders whenever the Commissioner finds that any person is causing, engaging in or maintaining a condition or activity that "presents an imminent danger to the health or welfare of the people of the state or results in or is likely to result in irreversible or irreparable damage to natural resources."[24]

Library References:

West's Key No. Digests, Health and Environment ⚖️25.5(10).

§ 15.26 Regulation of Underground Storage Tanks and Petroleum Storage Tanks—Federal Law

Like other areas subject to environmental regulations, the storage of petroleum products and other substances in underground storage tanks ("USTs") is subject to local overlapping federal and state regulations. These federal and state regulations differ in the scope of coverage and type of requirements imposed on USTs and, in some instances, above-ground storage tanks ("ASTs"). Thus, a practitioner must be aware of both federal and state law requirements when navigating through the maze of requirements that may be applicable to tanks storing petroleum and other hazardous substances.

The use of USTs for storage of petroleum and other hazardous substances is regulated by the federal government pursuant to Subchapter IX of the Resource Conservation and Recovery Act, or RCRA.[1] The detailed federal regulations apply to any USTs with a capacity of at least 110 gallons used to store a substance defined as hazardous under CERCLA,[2] as well as petroleum.[3] Unlike the state regulations governing petroleum storage, tanks used for storing oil used for space heating are

---

22. Id.

23. ECL §§ 71–2707, 71–2709.

24. ECL § 71–0301. See e.g., State of New York v. Brookhaven Aggregates, Ltd., 121 A.D.2d 440, 503 N.Y.S.2d 413 (2d Dep't 1986) (dumping of solid waste at landfill subsequent to the DEC's issuance of summary abatement order entitles state to preliminary injunction without showing that irreparable injury will result in absence of such injunction).

§ 15.26

1. 42 U.S.C.A. §§ 6991–6991i. See also, supra, § 15.23.

2. See 40 C.F.R. Pt. 302. See also, supra, § 15.25.

3. Congress gave EPA the authority to regulate USTs, including requirements for registration of USTs and establishing technical performance standards, when it passed the Hazardous and Solid Waste Amendments of 1984. Pub. L. 89–272, Title II, § 9001, as added, Pub. L. 98–616, Title VI, § 601(a), November 8, 1984, 98 Stat. 3277. 42 U.S.C.A. §§ 6991a, 6991b.

exempt from regulation.[4] RCRA also requires that owners of existing USTs subject to regulation notify the appropriate state or local agency—designated by each state pursuant to RCRA—of each UST's size, type, location and purpose no later than May 1986.[5] USTs installed after May 1986 must be registered no later than 30 days from the time of installation and the seller of a UST must apprise the buyer of these notification requirements.[6]

The EPA has issued technical performance criteria for USTs pursuant to RCRA, that became effective as of December 22, 1988.[7] USTs installed after that date must meet detailed the EPA requirements for design, construction and installation. These rules include requirements that tanks include spill and overfill prevention equipment, be equipped with leak or release detection monitors, and be made of materials that are compatible with the substance to be stored within the tank. USTs installed prior to December 22, 1988 must meet other, less stringent, regulations that provide for overfill prevention and tank tightness testing to ensure leak detection.[8] However, by no later than December 22, 1998, preexisting USTs must comply with the EPA's new performance requirements, or be upgraded to meet the EPA standards for corrosion protection and spill/overfill prevention.[9] Thus, existing tanks must be either closed, upgraded or replaced by that time. The EPA's UST regulations also set forth the proper procedures for the temporary and permanent closure of USTs.[10]

Library References:

West's Key No. Digests, Health and Environment ☞25.5(5.5).

§ 15.27 Regulation of Underground Storage Tanks and Petroleum Storage Tanks—New York Law

The storage of petroleum—in USTs and ASTs[1]—is also regulated pursuant to New York State law.[2] The New York State Department of Environmental Conservation (DEC) has promulgated detailed regulations governing the use of USTs for storing petroleum products within the state. Petroleum is defined very broadly and, unlike the federal

---

4. 40 C.F.R. § 280.12. This Section and Section 280.10 contain numerous other exemptions, including exemptions for emergency spill protection tanks, farm and residential tanks with a volume of not more that 1,100 gallons used for storing fuel for private use, septic tanks.

5. RCRA § 6991a(a)(1); 40 C.F.R. § 280.22.

6. 42 U.S.C.A. § 6991a(a)(3).

7. 42 U.S.C.A. § 6991b(e); 40 C.F.R. §§ 280.20, 280.42.

8. 42 U.S.C.A. § 6991b(c); 40 C.F.R. §§ 280.40, 280.41.

9. 40 C.F.R. § 280.21.

10. 40 C.F.R. Pt. 280.

§ 15.27

1. See supra, § 15.26.

2. ECL § 17–1001. New York also regulates USTs/ASTs used for storing hazardous substances pursuant to the Hazardous Substances Bulk Storage Act. ECL § 40–0111; 6 NYCRR Pt. 597.

requirements, includes heating oil.[3] The DEC regulations cover a "petroleum storage facility," which includes ASTs, USTs, or a combination of both, with a storage capacity of over 1,100 gallons of petroleum. Such facilities must be registered with the DEC by the owner of the facility.[4] This registration requirement includes "out-of-service" facilities that have not been properly closed pursuant to state regulations.[5] The tank registrations must be renewed every five years from the time of the last valid registration.[6] New facilities must be registered before being put in service.[7] The owner of the facility must include, along with the application for registration or renewal, a five-year fee for each facility. This fee differs depending on the size of the UST facility being registered.[8]

The DEC regulations also mandate performance standards for both existing AST and UST petroleum storage facilities (facilities that were constructed and capable of being operated as of January 26, 1985)[9] and for any new or "substantially modified" facility, which includes all facilities that are not considered existing facilities.[10]

The DEC regulations for existing facilities place certain requirements on the owner of the UST/AST facility exclusively, while other requirements apply to either the owner *or* operator of the facility. Strictly operational requirements apply to either the owner/operator, while requirements for installation of additional equipment fall upon the owner. For example, the regulations require that the owner *or* operator permanently mark all fill ports to identify the product inside the tank, but that the owner is responsible to install shut-off valves for motor fuel dispensing units, as well as provide gauges and secondary containment for ASTs.[11] The owner and operator are both required to maintain all gauges, valves and other spill prevention equipment in good working order.[12]

The DEC regulations require that operators conduct inventory monitoring and owners conduct periodic tightness testing for USTs (but not

3. Navigation Law § 172(15); 6 NYCRR § 612.1(b)(21).

4. 6 NYCRR § 612.2(a)(1).

5. *Id*. This provision is very important, and has tripped up many site owners who have abandoned USTs located on their property that have not been removed or properly closed pursuant to the DEC's regulations (filled with an inert material such as concrete or sand). The DEC maintains that the failure to register such tanks, even though they may not have been used for years, is a violation of its regulations and may give rise to penalties under the ECL. Thus, it is important for any owner or potential purchaser of industrial property to survey the site for the existence of improperly closed or abandoned USTs that may be located at the site.

6. 6 NYCRR at § 612.2(a)(2).

7. 6 NYCRR at § 612.2(b).

8. 6 NYCRR § 612.3(a). The fee is $50 per facility for UST systems with less than 2,000 gallons of storage capacity, $150 per facility for facilities with greater than 2,000 gallons and less than 5,000 gallons of storage capacity, and $250 per facility for facilities with storage capacity greater than 5,000 gallons.

9. 6 NYCRR §§ 612.1(c)(9), 612.4.

10. 6 NYCRR § 612.1(c)(13).

11. 6 NYCRR § 613.3(c).

12. 6 NYCRR § 613.3(d).

ASTs) to ensure that the tank systems are not leaking.[13] The age when a tank first must be tested depends upon whether the tank has corrosion protection and the degree of that protection. Once tank testing is required, the tank must be retested every five years.[14] These UST testing requirements do not apply to USTs with capacity of less than 1,100 gallons, USTs that are used to store No. 5 or No. 6 heating oil, USTs that are corrosion resistant and have a leak monitoring system, or USTs that comply with the new performance standards contained in Part 614 of the DEC regulations.[15]

The DEC regulations also require monthly and ten year inspections of ASTs and the maintenance of inspection reports.[16] The regulations also set out the accepted procedures for the temporary and permanent closure of ASTs and USTs.[17] Permanent closures must be reported to the DEC thirty days prior to such closure.[18]

The New York State standards for all new or substantially modified USTs and ASTs that store petroleum are set forth in Part 614 of the DEC regulations. These provisions were promulgated by the DEC on November 27, 1985 and became effective one year later. Similar to the federal regulations, these provisions set forth the composition of new USTs, how they shall be installed and the minimum level of secondary containment and leak monitoring that must be included.[19] Minimum standards for reconditioning USTs are also set forth.[20] Minimum performance standards for ASTs relating to the composition of these tanks and how they are to be installed are also included.[21]

Pursuant to the State Navigation Law, the DEC also regulates major onshore facilities ("MOSFs"), which include any petroleum storage facility with a total combined storage capacity of 400,000 gallons or more.[22] This law requires that MOSFs register with the DEC, pay a fee per barrel of petroleum at such facility, and submit a cleanup and removal plan showing that the MOSF has the capability—either in house or through a service contract—to address a petroleum discharge from such facility.[23] MOSFs must also have a spill prevention and control plan in place, which shall meet all requirements of a Spill Prevention Control and Countermeasure plan ("SPCC plan") required by the United States Coast Guard under federal regulations.[24]

13. 6 NYCRR §§ 613.4, 613.5.
14. 6 NYCRR § 613.5(a)(1)(v).
15. 6 NYCRR § 613.5(a)(2). The DEC also does not require a tightness test where the tank exceeds 50,000 gallons, or where it is impossible to perform such a test. In such instances, the DEC requires that an alternative test or inspection that it deems acceptable be performed.
16. 6 NYCRR § 613.6.
17. 6 NYCRR § 613.9.
18. 6 NYCRR § 613.9(c).
19. 6 NYCRR § 614.2.
20. 6 NYCRR § 614.6.
21. 6 NYCRR § 614.8.
22. Navigation Law § 174; 6 NYCRR Pt. 610.
23. Navigation Law § 174(4); 6 NYCRR §§ 610.2(j), 610.4(a).
24. 6 NYCRR § 610.4(a)(4).

The DEC regulations also require that any person with knowledge of a spill, leak or discharge of petroleum report such incident to the DEC spill hotline within two hours of discovery of the incident.[25] This includes leaks detected through inventory monitoring and tank tightness testing. The cleanup of a petroleum spill is governed by the Navigation Law, which empowers the DEC to take action to remediate the spill and holds any person responsible for the discharge strictly liable, without regard to fault, for all cleanup and removal costs and all direct and indirect damages incurred as a result of the discharge.[26] The Navigation Law also creates private right of action that holds a discharger strictly liable for "any claim by any injured person for the costs of cleanup and removal and direct and indirect damages."[27]

§ 15.28 Regulation of Inactive Hazardous Waste Sites—CERCLA[1]

The reckless dumping of toxic chemicals—sometimes years or even decades earlier—often can pose a significant and continuing threat to human health when such chemicals subsequently leach and pollute ground and surface water. Concern about this threat crystallized in the late 1970s with public outcry and media attention over the contamination at Love Canal, located in upstate New York. This controversy, and others like it, fueled efforts by Congress and the New York State Legislature to address the threats created by decades of uncontrolled disposal of hazardous substances. These efforts resulted in the enactment of regulatory schemes designed to investigate and clean up these sites, as well as to impose liability on persons responsible for these conditions.

Congress enacted CERCLA, sometimes known as Superfund, in 1980 to provide a comprehensive response to the release of hazardous substances into the environment.[2] One federal court in New York has stated CERCLA's overall purpose as ensuring "that those responsible for problems caused by the disposal of chemical poisons bear the costs and responsibility for remedying the harmful conditions they created."[3]

---

25. Navigation Law § 175; 6 NYCRR § 613.8.

26. Navigation Law §§ 176, 181(1).

27. Navigation Law § 181(5). See White v. Long, 85 N.Y.2d 564, 626 N.Y.S.2d 989, 650 N.E.2d 836 (1995), appeal after remand 229 A.D.2d 178, 655 N.Y.S.2d 176 (1997).

§ 15.28

1. See supra, § 15.25.

2. 42 U.S.C.A. §§ 9601 et seq.; City of New York v. Chemical Waste Disposal Corp., 836 F.Supp. 968, 971 (E.D.N.Y.1993). CERCLA was significantly amended in 1986 by the Superfund Amendments and Reauthorization Act, commonly known as the SARA amendments. Pub. L. 99-499 (Oct. 17, 1986). CERCLA is a very complicated, poorly drafted statute that has engendered a tremendous amount of litigation between the government and private parties and between private parties to apportion liability under the Act. A detailed discussion of the myriad issues under CERCLA is well beyond the scope of this discussion. For a more detailed discussion of issues under CERCLA, see A. Topol & R. Snow, *Superfund Law & Procedure* (West 1992).

3. City of New York v. Exxon Corp., 744 F.Supp. 474, 485 (S.D.N.Y.1990).

The term Superfund derives from the Hazardous Substance Trust Fund, or Superfund, created by CERCLA for the clean up of toxic dump sites where few or no financially solvent liable parties exist. This fund was created and financed through a tax imposed on petroleum products, certain inorganic chemicals and from general appropriations.[4] However, the federal government funds cleanups from the Superfund only when it is unable to find any solvent party deemed liable under CERCLA to fund or undertake the clean up of the site.

CERCLA provides for two different types of actions to address toxic contamination: short term "removal" actions to abate an immediate threat to human health or the environment and long term "remedial" actions to design and implement a permanent remedy to address the contamination at the site.[5] CERCLA also requires the EPA to establish a priority among the nation's inactive hazardous waste sites based on their potential threat to human health and the environment and to place the priority sites on a National Priorities List ("NPL").[6] To qualify for a "remedial action," a site must be on the NPL.[7]

In any removal or remedial action under CERCLA, the EPA has the discretion to either (1) undertake the clean up itself with monies from the Superfund and pursue responsible parties for reimbursement later; or (2) to compel the responsible parties to undertake the clean up itself.[8] When conditions at the site are not in need of immediate attention, and financially viable persons or entities exist who are liable under the Act, the EPA will seek to compel the clean up by those persons or entities.

Library References:

West's Key No. Digests, Health and Environment ⚖25.5(5.5).

§ 15.29 Regulation of Inactive Hazardous Waste Sites—CERCLA Section 107(a)

CERCLA[1] casts a notoriously wide liability net. Section 107(a) of the Act establishes four classes of responsible parties liable for the costs of

---

4. In addition to its original commitment of $11.6 billion, Congress allocated no more than $8.5 billion for the five-year period beginning October 17, 1986, and an additional $5.1 billion for a three-year period commencing October 1, 1991. *See* 42 U.S.C.A. § 9611.

5. 42 U.S.C.A. §§ 9601(23) (defining removal action), 9601(24) (defining remedial action); *see* City of New York v. Exxon Corp., 633 F.Supp. 609, 614 (S.D.N.Y.1986) (Weinfeld, J.) (CERCLA " 'removal' actions are primarily those intended for the short term abatement of toxic waste hazards while remedial actions are typically those intended to restore long-term environmental quality.").

6. 42 U.S.C.A. § 9605(a). The NPL, which EPA must update annually, is set forth at 40 C.F.R. Pt. 300, App. B.

7. 42 U.S.C.A. § 9611.

8. 42 U.S.C.A. § 9606(a).

§ 15.29

1. *See supra*, § 15.25.

responding to releases or threatened releases of hazardous substances.[2] These parties include past and present owners or operators of facilities, transporters of hazardous substances to such facilities, and those who generate or arrange for the treatment or disposal of hazardous substances.[3]

CERCLA provides two mechanisms, one public and one private, that work together to provide for cleanup, compensation and liability for sites where there is a threat posed by the disposal of hazardous substances.[4] Section 106 of CERCLA empowers the EPA to issue administrative orders necessary to protect public health and welfare and the environment because there may be an imminent and substantial endangerment caused by an actual or threatened release of hazardous substances.[5] The EPA may bring a Section 106 enforcement action against any party liable pursuant to Section 107(a) of CERCLA. In addition, CERCLA does not provide for pre-enforcement judicial review of the EPA's Section 106 orders.[6]

Section 107(a) provides that the federal, state and local government, or private party, may sue for the recovery of the costs of response to conditions caused by the release or threatened release of hazardous substances.[7] In order to establish a *prima facie* cause of action for liability under CERCLA for response costs incurred, the federal government or a state must establish that: (1) the site is a "facility" as defined by CERCLA; (2) there is a "release" or "threatened release" of hazardous substances at the facility; (3) the defendant fits into at least one of the four classes of responsible parties set forth in Section 107(a); and (4) the party has incurred costs responding to the release or threatened

---

2. 42 U.S.C.A. § 9607. The EPA refers to parties that fall within one of the classes of parties liable under Section 107(a) as potentially responsible parties, or PRPs. Thus, in the CERCLA lexicon, the term PRP is used to refer to parties found liable under Section 107(a).

3. *Id*; B.F. Goodrich v. Murtha, 958 F.2d 1192, 1198 (2d Cir.1992).

4. City of New York v. Chemical Waste Disposal Corp., 836 F.Supp. 968, 971 (E.D.N.Y.1993).

5. 42 U.S.C.A. § 9606.

PRACTICE POINTER: Section 106 is, without doubt, the most potent weapon in the government's CERCLA enforcement arsenal. When EPA commences a Section 106 enforcement action, it will seek solvent PRPs to compel to undertake the cleanup pursuant to an order on consent. If a PRP refuses to undertake the cleanup, EPA can undertake the cleanup itself (which will invariably cost more than if the cleanup was undertaken by the private party directly); moreover, the noncomplying PRP is subject to severe penalties for failure to comply with a Section 106 order. A non-complying party may be subject to fines of up to $25,000 for each day of noncompliance (42 U.S.C.A. § 9606(b)(1)), as well as punitive treble damages on the amount of costs incurred by the Superfund as a result of such non-compliance (42 U.S.C.A. § 9607(c)(3)). Thus, it is ill-advised, to say the least, for a PRP to refuse to cooperate with an EPA Section 106 enforcement order. If a PRP believes EPA has overreached, the PRP should contest liability only after financing all or part of the cleanup. Nevertheless, even if a party is caught in CERCLA's liability net, there may be other solvent PRPs that EPA has not pursued who can be brought in by the PRP through a private cost recovery action or action for contribution.

6. *See* Wagner Seed Co. v. Daggett, 800 F.2d 310 (2d Cir.1986).

7. *See e.g.*, Chemical Waste, 836 F.Supp. at 972.

release that are not inconsistent with the National Contingency Plan ("NCP").[8] The elements are the same for a private party or local government action, except that a private party must establish that the response costs incurred were consistent with the NCP, rather than merely "not inconsistent" with the NCP.[9]

The term "facility" is broadly defined to mean any structure or place where a "hazardous substance" has been placed.[10] "Hazardous substance" is also broadly defined.[11] Moreover courts have held that liability is based on the presence *in any form* of listed hazardous substances. Thus, when a mixture or waste stream contains hazardous substances, that mixture is itself hazardous under CERCLA and there is no *de minimis* exception under the Act.[12] "Release" is similarly broadly defined to mean "any spilling, leaking, pumping, pouring, emitting, emptying, discharging, injecting, escaping, leaching, dumping or disposing into the environment" of a hazardous substance.[13] As stated previously, merely the "threat" of a release is sufficient to establish this element under Section 107(a) of CERCLA.

Section 107(a) of CERCLA provides for strict liability.[14] Moreover, strict liability for clean up costs is applied to multiple defendants jointly and severally, unless a defendant can demonstrate that the harm it caused is divisible from the harm caused by others.[15] To make matters

8. 42 U.S.C.A. § 9607(a). State of New York v. Shore Realty, 759 F.2d at 1043. The NCP consists of detailed regulations outlining the proper procedures to be followed for a removal or remedial action under CERCLA. *See* 40 C.F.R. Pts. 300 *et seq.*

9. One court in New York has held that a local government, when functioning in the role of the federal or state government, is also entitled to the benefit of only having to prove that its actions are "not inconsistent" with the NCP. City of New York v. Exxon Corp., 697 F.Supp. 677, 686 (S.D.N.Y.1988). *But see* City of New York v. Chemical Waste Disposal Corp., 836 F.Supp. at 977–78.

10. 42 U.S.C.A. § 9601(9).

11. CERCLA's definition of hazardous substance includes, among other things, substances identified by EPA pursuant to Section 102 of the Act, as well as any substance designated as hazardous under the Federal Clean Water Act ("CWA") (*see supra*, § 15.8) (33 U.S.C.A. § 1321(b)(2)(A)) or any hazardous waste listed pursuant to the Section 3001 of the Resource Conservation and Recovery Act (RCRA) (*see supra*, § 15.23) (42 U.S.C.A. § 6921). Many CERCLA hazardous substances are listed in regulations promulgated by EPA under CERCLA, RCRA and the CWA. *See* 40 C.F.R. Part 261 and 40 C.F.R. Pt. 116. Congress has, however, explicitly excluded petroleum from CERCLA's definition of hazardous substance. 42 U.S.C.A. § 9601(14).

12. B.F. Goodrich v. Murtha, 958 F.2d at 1201; City of New York v. Exxon Corp., 744 F.Supp. at 483–484. The Murtha court went on to note that whether such substance is a consumer product, a manufacturing byproduct, or an element of a waste stream is irrelevant for the purposes of determining whether that substance is a CERCLA hazardous substance.

13. 42 U.S.C.A. § 9601(22). "The continuing leaching and seepage from ... earlier spills and leaking drums all constitute 'releases.'" State of New York v. Shore Realty, 759 F.2d at 1045.

14. B.F. Goodrich v. Murtha, 958 F.2d at 1198.

15. *Id.* United States v. Alcan Aluminum Corp. ("Alcan II"), 990 F.2d 711, 722 (2d Cir.1993), on remand 1996 WL 637559 (N.D.N.Y.1996) (court found that defendant was entitled to the opportunity to establish that government's response costs were capable of some reasonable apportionment). *See also*, United States v. Alcan Aluminum Corp. ("Alcan I"), 964 F.2d 252 (3d Cir. 1992).

worse for PRPs, CERCLA provides only three very limited statutory defenses to liability under Section 107(a)—when the release or threat of release has been caused solely by an act of God, an act of war, or the act or omission of a third party other than one with whom the defendant has a contractual relationship.[16]

In order to establish CERCLA's "third party" defense, the party asserting the defense must also establish that he or she exercised due care with respect to the hazardous substance concerned and took precautions against any foreseeable acts or omissions by any third parties and the consequences that could foreseeably result from such acts or omissions.[17] The scope of the "third party" defense, however, is limited because it does not apply when the "act or omission occurs in connection with a contractual relationship, existing directly or indirectly with the defendant."[18] Thus, the defense is unavailable if the third party is the employee or agent of the defendant. Moreover, CERCLA Section 101(35)[19] defines "contractual relationship" to include "land contracts, deeds or other instruments transferring title," thereby making the defense unavailable if the third party responsible for the release or threatened release is a lessee, or the seller of the contaminated property.[20]

An exception to this rule is if the buyer can establish that it was an "innocent landowner," an extension of the third-party defense added by Congress in the 1986 SARA amendments. This amendment amended the definition of "contractual relationship" to expressly exclude a landowner who can demonstrate that at the time the landowner acquired the property, he or she had no knowledge or *reason to know* of the disposal of hazardous substances at the facility.[21] However, the burden is on the landowner to establish this defense, including that he or she made "all

PRACTICE POINTER: Perhaps even more significantly, the Second Circuit in Alcan II went beyond the issue of joint and several liability to hold that Alcan could escape all liability for response costs under CERCLA if it can prove that its waste, "when mixed with other wastes, did not contribute to the release and the response costs that followed . . ." 990 F.2d at 722.

16. 42 U.S.C.A. § 9607(b).

17. New York v. Lashins Arcade Co., 91 F.3d 353 (2d Cir.1996) (present owner of shopping center is entitled to third-party defense because the shopping center was contaminated 15 years prior to the current owner's purchase of the property, the sales contract was with the prior owners and was not tied to the handling of hazardous substances, and the defendant had demonstrated that it had exercised "due care" at the site).

18. 42 U.S.C.A. § 9607(b)(3).

19. 42 U.S.C.A. § 9601(35).

20. In Westwood Pharmaceuticals v. National Fuel Gas Distribution Corp., 964 F.2d 85, 89–91 (2d Cir.1992), the Second Circuit held that a prior owner of a contaminated property is precluded from using CERCLA's third-party defense "only if the contract between the landowner and the third-party is somehow connected with the handling of hazardous substances" or "if the contract allows the landowner to exert some control over the third-party's actions so that the landowner fairly can be held liable for the release or threatened release of hazardous substances." *See also,* New York v. Lashins Arcade Co., 91 F.3d at 360.

21. 42 U.S.C.A. § 9601(35)(A) (emphasis added).

appropriate inquiry into the previous ownership and uses of the property consistent with good commercial or customary practice in an effort to minimize liability."[22] Although defendants have tried, most courts have found CERCLA to mean what it says and have held that no other defenses besides the three enumerated in the statute are relevant to whether a party is liable under Section 107(a).[23]

§ 15.30 Regulation of Inactive Hazardous Waste Sites—Lender Liability, Contribution and Indemnification Under CERCLA[1]

Because current and former owners of land where there is a release or threatened release of hazardous substances are liable, regardless of fault, CERCLA is of significant concern to banks and other real estate lenders who hold security interests in real property. CERCLA purports to exempt such parties from owner liability under the Act by excluding from its definition of owner any "person, who, without participating in the management of a vessel or facility, holds indicia of ownership primarily to protect his security interest ..."[2] However, this provision is not as air tight as it first may appear because some courts have found lenders liable as current owners responsible for clean up costs when, in order to protect its security interest, the lender gets actively involved in the borrower's operations. One case, *United States v. Fleet Factors Corp.*, stunned the real estate lending community by holding that a lender could be found to have participated in management, thereby forfeiting its exemption from liability as a current owner, "if its involvement with the management of the facility is sufficiently broad to support the inference that it *could* affect hazardous waste decisions if it so chose."[3] The EPA attempted to resolve the controversy over the *Fleet* decision when it promulgated a rule that specifically delineated what actions a lender may take without losing the secured creditor exemption under CERCLA. This rule, however, was struck down by the District of Columbia Court of Appeals because the EPA lacked the statutory author-

22. *Id*; Westwood Pharmaceuticals v. National Fuel Gas Distribution Corp., 964 F.2d at 90.

PRACTICE POINTER: The parameters of CERCLA's "innocent landowner" defense are still being defined by the courts. The best approach for purchasers of sites that may contain hazardous substances remains undertaking the type of "environmental due diligence" that has become a standard for real estate transactions involving commercial properties. A record of this due diligence must be maintained to show that the purchaser made reasonable inquiries into the environmental conditions of the property *before* it acquired it. *Id*.

23. United States v. Alcan, 990 F.2d at 721; City of New York v. Chemical Waste Disposal Corp., 836 F.Supp. at 972.

PRACTICE POINTER: Although other equitable defenses are not relevant to whether a party is a CERCLA PRP, these defenses—such as whether and to what degree the party was actually responsible for causing or exacerbating the hazardous condition—are relevant at the equitable apportionment stage of a litigation involving multiple PRPs. *See infra*, § 15.30 notes 6 and 7.

§ 15.30

1. *See supra*, § 15.25.

2. 42 U.S.C.A. § 9601(20)(A).

3. 901 F.2d 1550, 1558 (11th Cir.1990), cert. denied 498 U.S. 1046, 111 S.Ct. 752, 112 L.Ed.2d 772 (1991) (emphasis added).

ity to restrict by regulation the private right of action arising under CERCLA.[4]

Congress stepped into the vacuum in 1996 and amended CERCLA's definition of "owner or operator" to exclude from liability a lender who, prior to foreclosure, "did not participate in management of a ... facility" and who, after foreclosure, attempted to sell or release the property "at the earliest practicable, commercially reasonable terms."[5] The amendments also redefines the term "participates in management" and lists nine activities that do not constitute "participation in management" sufficient to trigger CERCLA liability as an owner/operator.

When facing liability for a clean up, a PRP should immediately search for all other responsible parties who may have funds to commit to the response action. When Congress amended CERCLA in 1986, it specifically provided a statutory cause of action for contribution, pursuant to CERCLA Section 113(f)(1), from any other person who is liable under Section 107(a).[6] A PRP may commence a contribution action during or following any civil action under Section 106 or 107 of the Act.[7] CERCLA does not, however, provide much guidance to courts on how to allocate response costs allocated among liable parties, except to provide that the court may consider "such equitable factors as the court deems appropriate."[8] Moreover, in order to promote settlement of government

---

4. Kelley v. E.P.A., 15 F.3d 1100 (D.C.Cir.1994), cert. denied 513 U.S. 1110, 115 S.Ct. 900, 130 L.Ed.2d 784 (1995). The Circuit Court also found that the EPA's lender liability rule was not an interpretative rule entitled to deference by courts. 15 F.3d at 1108.

5. Pub. L. No. 104–208, §§ 2501–2505 (codified at 42 U.S.C.A. §§ 9601(2)(E)-(G), 9007(n), 6991(h)).

6. 42 U.S.C.A. § 9613(f)(1). Before 1986, most courts had found an implied right to contribution under Section 107(a).

7. *Id*. **CAVEAT:** Ordinarily, a contribution action is combined with a private cost recovery action under Section 107(a) against all other PRPs. However, some courts have held that a PRP may not commence a 107(a) action against other PRPs, but only an action for contribution. United States v. Colorado & Eastern Railroad Co., 50 F.3d 1530, 1536 (10th Cir.1995); Akzo Coatings, Inc. v. Aigner Corp., 30 F.3d 761, 765 (7th Cir.1994), on remand 881 F.Supp. 1202 (D.Ind.1994); Redwing Carriers, Inc. v. Saraland Apartments, 94 F.3d 1489 (11th Cir.1996); Town of New Windsor v. Tesa Tuck, Inc., 919 F.Supp. 662 (S.D.N.Y.1996). *But see* Velsicol Chemical Corp. v. Enenco, Inc., 9 F.3d 524, 528–30 (6th Cir.1993); Idylwoods Assocs. v. Mader Capital, Inc., 915 F.Supp. 1290 (W.D.N.Y.1996). This is not merely a distinction without a difference, because in a contribution action a party is only liable for its equitable share of the damages, while liability under Section 107(a) is joint and several. *Restatement (Second) Torts*, § 886A(2) (1979). Thus, whether a PRP may maintain a private cost recovery action under Section 107(a) will determine who will be responsible for any orphan share of liability. In addition, the statute of limitations applicable to the action will also be affected. United Technologies Corp. v. Browning-Ferris Industries, 33 F.3d 96 (1st Cir.1994), cert. denied 513 U.S. 1183, 115 S.Ct. 1176, 130 L.Ed.2d 1128 (1995).

8. 42 U.S.C.A. § 9613(f)(1). In apportioning liability, courts generally follow the comparative fault approach outlined in the *Restatement of Torts*, § 886A, and apportion liability based on factors such as relative fault, volume of waste deposited and relative toxicity of waste. *See* United States v. Conservation Chemical, 628 F.Supp. 391, 401 (W.D.Mo.1985). Some courts also examine factors outlined in the Gore Amendment, which was passed by the House of Representatives on September 23, 1980, but dropped in the final compromise bill adopted by Congress in December 1980. 126

§ 15.30   ENVIRONMENTAL LAW   Ch. 15

enforcement actions, Section 113(f)(2) of CERCLA provides a party who has resolved its liability in an administrative or judicially-approved settlement protection from subsequent contribution actions.[9]

Private parties may allocate CERCLA responsibility through private contractual indemnification agreements; but such agreements cannot alter a party's liability pursuant to Section 107 of CERCLA.[10] Courts have found that an indemnification agreement entered before CERCLA was enacted will not bar CERCLA claims unless the terms of such agreement "unequivocally show that the parties intended to resolve all their disputes regarding any type of claim."[11] Courts have also found that if the indemnity agreement contains express provisions, then its terms must "unequivocally establish the clear transfer or release of future 'CERCLA-like' liabilities."[12]

§ 15.31   Regulation of Inactive Hazardous Waste Sites— New York Law

Title 13 of Article 27 of the New York Environmental Conservation Law (ECL) also provides for a regulatory program, somewhat modeled on CERCLA,[1] that requires the DEC to maintain a registry of inactive hazardous waste disposal sites and oversee and enforce the clean up of sites on the Registry that pose "a significant threat to the environment."[2] However, there are certain significant distinctions between New York law and CERCLA. First, there is no private right of action to recover response costs under Article 27; thus, only the state can seek the clean up of sites on the State Registry and seek reimbursement for clean up costs incurred. Moreover, the state definition of "hazardous waste," is not coextensive with CERCLA's definition of "hazardous substances."[3]

The DEC's procedures for listing and classifying sites, selecting clean up remedies, and de-listing or reclassifying a site are set in 6 NYCRR Part 375. The DEC's Registry should include all inactive hazardous waste sites within the state "at which a consequential amount of hazardous waste has been disposed."[4] The mere presence of hazardous

Cong. Rec. H9461, 26, 781 (September 23, 1990). *See generally*, Russo, "Contribution Under CERCLA: Judicial Treatment After SARA," 14 Colum. J. Envtl. L. 267 (1989).

9. 42 U.S.C.A. § 9613(f)(2).

10. 42 U.S.C.A. § 9607(e)(1). Commander Oil Corp. v. Advance Food Service Equipment, 991 F.2d 49 (2d Cir.1993).

11. 55 Motor Avenue Co v. Liberty Industrial Finishing Corp., 1994 WL 241104 at *3 (E.D.N.Y. 1994); Purolator Products Corp. v. Allied-Signal, Inc., 772 F.Supp. 124, 131 (W.D.N.Y.1991).

12. 55 Motor Avenue, *supra* note 11; *see also*, Mobay Corp. v. Allied-Signal,, Inc., 761 F.Supp. 345, 357–58 (D.N.J.1991).

§ 15.31

1. *See supra*, § 15.25.

2. ECL § 27–1313(3)(a).

3. ECL § 27–1301(1).

4. 6 NYCRR § 375–1.8(a)(1). The DEC defines an inconsequential amount of hazardous waste as an amount "which does not presently constitute a significant threat to the environment ... and is not reasonably foreseeable to ever constitute a significant threat to the environment." *Id*.

268

waste is not sufficient, standing alone, to determine that the site constitutes a significant threat to the environment.[5]

Once the DEC determines to list a site, that site must be classified pursuant to the severity of risk to health or the environment posed by the site.[6] A Class 1 site is a site that constitutes a significant threat to the environment and is causing or is in imminent danger of causing irreparable damage to the environment. Class 2 sites—the vast majority of site listed in New York—are sites where hazardous waste poses a significant threat to public health or the environment.[7] The DEC also classifies sites as Class 2A, a designation that is not contained in the Part 375 regulations, but is used for sites where there is not enough information to determine whether the hazardous wastes present on those sites pose a significant threat.[8]

If a site has been designated as a Class 2A site, DEC will further investigate the site, or have the owner fund an investigation.[9] The DEC regulations also provide that the current or former owner or operator of a site may petition the DEC to delete a site from the Registry, reclassify the site, or modify information on the site that is listed on the Registry.[10]

If a property is found to pose a significant threat to public health or the environment, the DEC will commence what is usually a long and costly Remedial Investigation and Feasibility Study ("RI/FS").[11] The goal of the remedial program is to "restore the site to pre-disposal conditions, to the extent feasible."[12] The DEC's regulations also allow interim remedial measures ("IRMs") to be implemented. IRMs are designed to be short-term actions that should be taken to prevent, mitigate, or

5. 6 NYCRR § 375–1.4(c).

6. 6 NYCRR § 375–1.8.

7. Class 3 sites are sites that contain hazardous wastes but which have been found not to pose a significant threat to public health or the environment and Classes 4 and 5 are sites that have been remediated or closed.

8. **PRACTICE POINTER:** DEC also uses an internal "P" designation for unlisted sites where the presence of hazardous waste is suspected.

9. As a practical matter, the same procedure generally applies for sites internally designated as "P" sites by DEC.

PRACTICE POINTER: The general procedure employed by the state for these site assessments is to first conduct a preliminary site assessment that consists of a historical review of uses at the site, visual inspection of the site, and usually soil and water sampling in order to further delineate potential areas and types of contamination present. At the conclusion of this assessment, a 2A site will either be reclassified as a Class 2 site or delisted. A "P" site will either be listed or not investigated further.

10. 6 NYCRR § 375–1.9. The DEC sends a computer printout containing the site classification and information on the site to the listed owner of the site. If a current or former owner or operator files a petition, DEC must respond to the petition within 45 days with a decision on the petition, or convene an adjudicatory hearing to commence not more than 90 days after receipt of the petition. *Id.*

11. The RI/FS is a comprehensive environmental study that often takes several years to complete. It is designed to further investigate the contamination—the remedial investigation—and then propose a remedy to address the toxic contamination—the feasibility study. The RI/FS process comes from the NCP promulgated by EPA for cleanups pursuant to CERCLA.

12. 6 NYCRR § 375–1.10(b).

remedy imminent environmental damage.[13] The final remediation must not be inconsistent with the NCP and the remedy chosen is subject to a thirty-day public comment period and a public hearing.[14] The final remedy selected for a site is set forth in a Record of Decision ("ROD") issued by the DEC Commissioner.[15]

§ 15.32 Relevant Common Law Doctrines—Nuisance

Before there were any federal or state statutes or regulations governing a person's use (and abuse) of the environment, there was the law of nuisance. The common law torts of public and private nuisance, as well as trespass, are additional non-statutory devices still used by the government—as well as private parties—to obtain injunctive relief and damages for alleged environmental wrongs.[1] These common law causes of action are often used to supplement the myriad statutory enforcement mechanisms available to government and private parties. These doctrines have been invoked—with varying degrees of success—to curb or cure many types of different environmental concerns, including air pollution, noise, oil spills, and even siting of controversial public facilities like homeless shelters. These doctrines continue to be widely used and remain a potent weapon in the arsenal of the government, as well as the private plaintiff. The legal concept of nuisance—referred to as an "impenetrable jungle" by the New York Court of Appeals—is indeed a complicated and often misunderstood area of the law.[2] One reason is that the term "nuisance" encompasses two distinct causes of action—public and private nuisance. A private nuisance "threatens one person or a relatively few," with "an essential feature being an interference with the use or enjoyment of land."[3] It is actionable by the person or persons whose rights have disturbed.[4] A public nuisance, on the other hand, "is an offense against the State and is subject to abatement or prosecution

---

13. 6 NYCRR at § 375–1.3(n).

PRACTICE POINTER: IRMs are exempt from comprehensive public participation requirements and can be undertaken without extensive investigation and evaluation activities, and sometimes without obtaining the required DEC permits. Thus, sometimes a site owner can utilize IRMs to effectuate a quick, DEC-approved cleanup of contamination at a site in lieu of a full blown RI/FS. If possible, this option should be explored with the DEC when negotiating a remedy.

14. 6 NYCRR at § 375–1.5(c)(2). The regulations provide that a citizen participation program be developed before the RI/FS that will provide affected and interested citizens with information and documents relating to the RI/FS. *Id.*

15. 6 NYCRR at § 375–1.10(d). The ROD is borrowed from the EPA procedures relating to CERCLA cleanups. 40 C.F.R. § 300.430.

§ 15.32

1. In some instances, public nuisance concepts have been codified in state regulations and local laws. *See e.g.*, N.Y.C.Admin. Code, §§ 7–701 *et seq.* (1995); 6 NYCRR § 211.2 (DEC regulations prohibiting air emissions that "unreasonably interfere with the comfortable enjoyment of life or property").

2. Copart Industries, Inc. v. Consolidated Edison Co. of New York, Inc., 41 N.Y.2d 564, 565, 394 N.Y.S.2d 169, 170, 362 N.E.2d 968, 969 (1977).

3. *Id.* (citations omitted).

4. *Id.* (citations omitted).

on application of the proper government agency."[5] Public nuisances are conduct or omissions that

> offend, interfere with or cause damage to the public in the exercise of rights common to all in a manner such as to offend public morals, interfere with use by the public of a public place or endanger or injure the property, health, safety or comfort of a considerable number of persons."[6]

Although the term public nuisance "is incapable of any exact of comprehensive definition,"[7] its essence is the interference of public right or privilege common to every person, or where an aggregation of private injuries becomes so great and extensive as to constitute a wrong against the community.[8]

The state has standing to bring public nuisance actions in its role as guardian of the environment and such actions brought by the State Attorney General. Moreover, the Attorney General's authority to seek injunctive relief under Article 71 of the Environmental Conservation Law does not preclude an action to enjoin a public nuisance.[9] Public nuisance actions may not be maintained by a private individual, unless the individual can establish that he or she suffered "special damage" from a public nuisance.[10] A person is liable for maintenance of a public nuisance regardless of negligence or fault.[11] All that needs to be established is that the defendant's conduct is unreasonable and materially interferes with the general well-being health or property rights of neighbors or people generally.[12]

The harm or threat of harm to the public and the environment caused by the disposal of hazardous wastes is often the subject of public (as well as private) nuisance actions.[13] One court has found that a chemical manufacturer who contracted for the disposal of various chemical wastes at a site, where such wastes later were found to be seeping into a public water supply, can be found to have caused a public nuisance.[14] A landowner maybe found liable for a public nuisance or

5. Id. (citations omitted).

6. Id. (citations omitted).

7. State v. Waterloo Stock Car Raceway, 96 Misc.2d 350, 355, 409 N.Y.S.2d 40, 43 (Sup.Ct., Seneca County, 1978).

8. Id. (quoting Judge Cardozo in People v. Rubenfeld, 254 N.Y. 245, 247, 172 N.E. 485, 486 (1930)).

9. State of New York v. Monarch Chemicals, Inc., 90 A.D.2d 907, 456 N.Y.S.2d 867 (3d Dep't 1982).

10. Copart at 565, 394 N.Y.S.2d at 170, 362 N.E.2d at 969.

11. McFarlane v. City of Niagara Falls, 247 N.Y. 340, 343, 160 N.E. 391, 391 (1928); State of New York v. Shore Realty, 759 F.2d 1032, 1051 (2d Cir.1985).

12. See Copart at 568, 394 N.Y.S.2d at 172, 362 N.E.2d at 971.

13. PRACTICE POINTER: A public (and, if appropriate, private) nuisance claim is invariably included in any action brought by the state or a private party pursuant to the Federal Superfund Law, 42 U.S.C.A. §§ 9606, 9607(a). See e.g., State of New York v. Shore Realty, 759 F.2d 1032 (2d Cir.1985).

14. State v. Schenectady Chemicals, Inc., 103 A.D.2d 33, 36, 479 N.Y.S.2d 1010, 1013 (3d Dep't 1984).

§ 15.32   ENVIRONMENTAL LAW   Ch. 15

private nuisance on its property—regardless of whether it created the harmful condition—once that person learns or should have learned of the conditions causing the nuisance and has had a reasonable opportunity to abate it.[15]

A person is liable for a private nuisance when such person's conduct "is a legal cause of the invasion of the interest in the private use and enjoyment of land and such invasion is (1) intentional and unreasonable, (2) negligent or reckless, or (3) actionable under the rules governing liability for abnormally dangerous activities."[16] A great deal of confusion has been caused over the relationship between negligence and nuisance. Although negligence is not always an essential element to establish nuisance, " 'whenever a nuisance has its origin in negligence', negligence must be proven and a plaintiff 'may not avert the consequences of his [or her] own contributory negligence by affixing to the negligence of the wrongdoer the label of nuisance.' "[17]

Although a nuisance is a continuing tort that accrues each day of the wrong, an action seeking monetary damages based on a continuing nuisance that causes the exposure of property to hazardous wastes must be brought within three years of the time the exposure is first discovered or should be discovered under New York's "discovery rule." This rule provides that the Statute of Limitations for actions for personal injury or injury to property caused by the latent effects of exposure to any substance will be calculated from the date of discovery of the injury by the plaintiff, or the date when it should have reasonably been discovered by the plaintiff.[18] Therefore, any action for monetary damages caused by such nuisance must be brought within three years of the time the property owner learned of the contamination.[19] The discovery rule, however, does not apply to actions for injunctive relief.[20]

An injunction for a private nuisance will not be granted when a defendant can establish that the plaintiff can be adequately compensated

15. State of New York v. Shore Realty Corp., 759 F.2d at 1050–51, citing *Restatement (Second) of Torts* § 839 comment d (1979) ("Shore is liable for maintenance of a *public* nuisance irrespective of negligence or fault").

16. Copart, 41 N.Y.2d at 569, 394 N.Y.S.2d at 172, 362 N.E.2d at 991 (citations omitted).

17. 41 N.Y.2d at 569, 394 N.Y.S.2d at 173, 362 N.E.2d at 972 (quoting McFarlane v. City of Niagara Falls, 247 N.Y. at 344–45).

18. CPLR 214–c.

19. Jensen v. General Electric Co., 82 N.Y.2d 77, 83, 603 N.Y.S.2d 420, 422, 623 N.E.2d 547, 549 (1993).

CAVEAT: CPLR 214–c effectively extends the Statute of Limitations for non-continuing torts that cause latent health effects because it begins to run from date of a plaintiff's reasonable discovery of the harm, rather than the date when the wrong occurred. However, the Court of Appeals' decision in Jensen effectively shortens the Statute of Limitations for continuing torts like nuisance and trespass because, prior to this decision, courts had found that the Statute of Limitations for nuisance and trespass actions continued to accrue each day of the wrong. *See* Schnectady Chemicals, 103 A.D.2d at 37–38, 479 N.Y.S.2d at 1014.

20. Jensen, 82 N.Y.2d at 90, 603 N.Y.S.2d at 426, 623 N.E. 2d at 553.

in damages and restraint could result in great public inconvenience.[21] Thus, even when a private nuisance is established, an injunction enjoining the activity causing the nuisance will not automatically be granted. Instead, courts will apply a risk/utility balancing test that examines the harm to the plaintiff by the activity causing the nuisance against the social usefulness of the defendant's activity.[22] The risk/utility test was explained in detail by the Court of Appeals in the seminal case *Boomer v. Atlantic Cement Co.*[23] In that case, the court found that, although the plaintiff had established that the defendant's operation of its cement plant created a private nuisance, no order enjoining operation of the plant would issue because of the large disparity in economic consequences between the damage caused by its nuisance and the cost of granting the injunction.[24] Instead, the court directed the defendant to pay monetary damages to compensate the plaintiff's injury.[25]

Library References:

West's Key No. Digests, Health and Environment ⚖=26–29.

§ 15.33 Common Law Doctrines—Trespass

A trespass, often described as an intentional invasion of a person's interest in land,[1] is invoked, with mixed results, in actions seeking damages and injunctive relief for contamination of property.[2] It often goes hand in hand with actions alleging public and private nuisance. In order to establish the requisite intent to establish trespass, a plaintiff need not demonstrate that the trespasser intended or expected the damaging consequences of the intrusion. All that must be shown is that the defendant intended the act which amounts to or produces the unlawful invasion, notwithstanding that the act was done by mistake,

---

21. See Schwarzenbach v. Oneonta Light & Power Co., 144 A.D. 884, 129 N.Y.S. 384, modified on other grounds 207 N.Y. 671, 100 N.E. 1134 (1911).

22. Little Joseph Realty, Inc. v. Town of Babylon, 41 N.Y.2d 738, 745, 395 N.Y.S.2d 428, 433, 363 N.E.2d 1163, 1168 (1977).

23. 26 N.Y.2d 219, 309 N.Y.S.2d 312, 257 N.E.2d 870 (1970).

24. 26 N.Y.2d at 223, 309 N.Y.S.2d at 315, 257 N.E.2d at 872.

25. *Id.* A key consideration in the Boomer case was the court's finding that there was no reasonable technical improvement that the defendant could implement to abate the nuisance: "techniques to eliminate dust and other annoying by-products of cement making are unlikely to be developed by any research the defendant can undertake within any short period, but will depend on the total resources of the cement industry nationwide and throughout the world." 26 N.Y.2d at 225–26, 309 N.Y.S.2d at 317, 257 N.E.2d at 873.

§ 15.33

1. Copart Industries v. Consolidated Edison Co. Inc., 41 N.Y.2d 564, 570, 394 N.Y.S.2d 169, 173 362 N.E.2d 968, 972 (1977).

2. *See* State of New York v. Fermenta ASC Corp., 166 Misc.2d 524, 630 N.Y.S.2d 884 (Sup.Ct., Suffolk County, 1995), affirmed 656 N.Y.S.2d 342 (1997) ("[t]he term trespass in its broadest sense has been held to mean any misfeasance, transgression or offense which damages another's person, health, reputation or property (*see* Serota v. M & M Utilities Inc., 55 Misc.2d 286, 285 N.Y.S.2d 121 (1967)").

inadvertence, or that the resulting damage is neither intended nor expected.[3] Thus, a manufacturer of an herbicide that was lawfully applied to soils may be liable for trespass for the invasion of contaminants from such herbicide into groundwater because the manufacturer intended and advised consumers to apply the herbicide to soil. However, courts have repeatedly found that the underground travel of petroleum products from a defendant's land that contaminates wells off-site does not constitute a trespass because the plaintiff could not establish that the defendant intended for the petroleum product to travel onto plaintiff's property.[4]

Library References:

West's Key No. Digests, Trespass ⚖1–15.

§ 15.34 Regulatory Takings

The increase in the number and scope of environmental regulations affecting the use of private property has given rise to numerous claims that such regulations run afoul of the Fifth Amendment of the United States Constitution, which prohibits the taking of private property without just compensation.[1] Since Justice Holmes' decision in *Pennsylvania Coal Co. v. Mahon*[2] in 1922, the United States Supreme Court has held that the Fifth Amendments "Takings Clause" reach beyond a direct appropriation of private property by the government. However it is only relatively recently that the Court has attempted to provide further guidance in this amorphous area of constitutional law about when a regulation will "go too far" to constitute a taking requiring just compensation.

3. Ivancic v. Olmstead, 66 N.Y.2d 349, 352, 497 N.Y.S.2d 326, 328, 488 N.E.2d 72, 74 (1985); Phillips v. Sun Oil Co., 307 N.Y. 328, 121 N.E.2d 249 (1954); State of New York v. Fermenta ASC Corp., 162 Misc.2d 288, 293, 616 N.Y.S.2d 702, 705 (Sup.Ct., Suffolk County, 1994), appeal dismissed 656 N.Y.S.2d 342 (1997).

4. Phillips v. Sun Oil Co, 307 N.Y. at 329, 121 N.E.2d at 250. *See also*, Drouin v. Ridge Lumber, Inc., 209 A.D.2d 957, 958, 619 N.Y.S.2d 433, 435 (4th Dep't 1994); Leone v. Leewood Service Station, Inc., 212 A.D.2d 669, 624 N.Y.S.2d 610, 612 (2d Dep't 1995).

PRACTICE POINTER: Although off-site contamination caused by petroleum spills may not constitute trespass, a plaintiff will have a cause of action pursuant to Section 181 of the New York Navigation Law. *See infra*, § 15.25. Moreover, in any type of off-site contamination case, a plaintiff may still be able to recover damages pursuant to a nuisance theory or negligence if the plaintiff can establish that the defendant failed to exercise due care and that such conduct proximately caused the off-site contamination. *E.g.*, Meehan v. State of New York, 95 Misc.2d 678, 408 N.Y.S.2d 652 (Ct.Cl.1978), aff'd sub nom. Kiley v. State of New York, 74 A.D.2d 917, 426 N.Y.S.2d 78 (2d Dep't 1980) (state liable for injuries caused because of salt-contaminated well water because contamination was caused by the state's negligent storage of large piles of rock salt).

§ 15.34

1. The Fifth Amendment applies to the states through the Fourteenth Amendment. Lucas v. South Carolina Coastal Council, 505 U.S. 1003, 112 S.Ct. 2886, 2887, 120 L.Ed.2d 798 (1992).

2. 260 U.S. 393, 43 S.Ct. 158, 67 L.Ed. 322 (1922).

In *Lucas v. South Carolina Coastal Council*,[3] the owner of beachfront property had purchased two residential lots on a barrier beach upon which he wished to build single family homes. Two years after he purchased the property, South Carolina enacted the Beachfront Management Act, which barred Lucas from building on his property. Lucas brought an action contending that, even though the regulation may have been a lawful exercise of the state's police power, the ban on construction deprived him of all economically viable use of his property and therefore constituted a regulatory taking under the Fifth and Fourteenth Amendments of the Constitution.[4]

The trial court agreed with Lucas, finding that the new law rendered his parcel valueless. However, the State Supreme Court, citing old Supreme Court precedent, reversed, holding that when a regulation is designed to prevent serious public harm or "noxious use," no compensation under the Takings Clause is required regardless of the effect of the new regulation on the property's value.[5] The United States Supreme Court reversed the State Supreme Court, finding that the new law violated the Takings Clause because it deprived the owner of all economically beneficial use of his property.[6] The Court also rejected the State Supreme Court's reliance on the objective of the regulation as a rationale for not providing compensation, finding that the " 'noxious use' logic cannot serve as a touchstone to distinguish regulatory 'takings'—which require compensation—from regulatory deprivations that do not require compensation."[7] Instead, the Court enunciated a new formulation of the test to determine whether a regulation that deprives land of all economically beneficial use can resist compensation under the Takings Clause. That test provides that, unless the new regulation imposes a limitation "that background principles of the State's law of property and nuisance already place upon land ownership," such regulation will have to provide just compensation under the Takings Clause.[8] In other words, the new law or regulation must "do no more than duplicate the result that could have been achieved in the courts—by adjacent landowners (or other uniquely affected persons) under the state's law or private nuisance, or by the state under its complementary power to abate nuisances that affect the public generally, or otherwise."[9] Under this test, the court found that, because common-law principles would not have prevented the building of homes on Lucas' property, the new regulation effected a taking without just compensation.

In a pre-*Lucas* case, *Seawall Associates v. City of New York*, the New York Court of Appeals found that a City ordinance that required private owners to rent their rooms or be subject to severe penalties would

---

3. 505 U.S. 1003, 112 S.Ct. 2886, 120 L.Ed.2d 798.
4. 112 S.Ct. at 2887.
5. 112 S.Ct. at 2890.
6. 112 S.Ct. at 2895.
7. 112 S.Ct. at 2899.
8. 112 S.Ct. at 2900.
9. *Id.*

§ 15.34 ENVIRONMENTAL LAW Ch. 15

constitute a *per se* physical taking of private property, as well as a regulatory taking, that would not be allowed without just compensation.[10] In interpreting the Taking Clause of the United States Constitution, the Court of Appeals reasoned that a "burden shifting regulation of the use of private property" will constitute a taking when it "denies an owner economically viable use of his property *or* ... if it does not substantially advance legitimate State interests."[11] In a post-*Lucas* case, the Court of Appeals has reaffirmed that "failure to measure up to either criterion can invalidate a governmental incursion or encumbrance on private property rights."[12]

However, a landowner who claims that land regulation has effected a taking "bears the heavy burden of overcoming the presumption of constitutionality that attaches to the regulation and of proving every element of his claim beyond a reasonable doubt."[13] To establish that a regulation has denied a landowner "economically viable use of his property, New York courts require that the owner show by "dollars and cents" evidence that under no use permitted by the regulation under attack will the properties be capable of producing a reasonable return; the economic value, or all but a bare residue of the economic value, of the parcels must have been destroyed by the regulations at issue."[14]

The New York Court of Appeals has interpreted *Lucas* as setting forth a *per se* regulatory taking "only in the relatively rare situation where 'the owner of the real property has been called upon to sacrifice *all* economically beneficial uses in the name of the common good ...' "[15] Thus, new rent regulations enlarging the class of family members entitled to succeed to a rent regulated apartment was held to not constitute a regulatory taking because the new rules did not affect an owner's right to receive a reasonable return from their property.[16] Moreover, in order to constitute a *per se* regulatory taking based on total loss of economic value, the plaintiff must sustain the "heavy burden of

---

10. 74 N.Y.2d 92, 107, 544 N.Y.S.2d 542, 549, 542 N.E.2d 1059, 1066, cert. denied 493 U.S. 976, 110 S.Ct. 500, 107 L.Ed.2d 503 (1989).

11. *Id.*

12. Manocherian v. Lenox Hill Hospital, 84 N.Y.2d 385, 392, 618 N.Y.S.2d 857, 860, 643 N.E.2d 479, 482 (1994), cert. denied 514 U.S. 1109, 115 S.Ct. 1961, 131 L.Ed.2d 853 (1995) (courts holds that state law requiring owner of rent-stabilized apartments to offer renewal leases to hospital for apartments occupied by some of the hospital's employees did not advance any legitimate state interest warranting the "indeterminate and unjustifiable burden draped disproportionately" on owners). 84 N.Y.2d at 394, 618 N.Y.S.2d at 861, 643 N.E.2d at 479.

13. de St. Aubin v. Flacke, 68 N.Y.2d 66, 76, 505 N.Y.S.2d 859, 865, 496 N.E.2d 879, 885 (1986) (citing Northern Westchester Professional Park Assoc. v. Town of Bedford, 60 N.Y.2d 492, 500, 470 N.Y.S.2d 350, 354, 458 N.E.2d 809, 813 (1983)).

14. Flacke, 68 N.Y.2d at 77, 505 N.Y.S.2d at 865, 496 N.E.2d at 885 (citations omitted).

15. Rent Stabilization Association of New York City,. Inc. v. Higgins, 83 N.Y.2d 156, 173, 608 N.Y.S.2d 930, 937, 630 N.E.2d 626 (1993), cert. denied 512 U.S. 1213, 114 S.Ct. 2693, 129 L.Ed.2d 823 (1994), quoting Lucas, 505 U.S. at 1015, 112 S.Ct. at 2893.

16. *Id.*

showing that the property, as restricted, has lost its economic value, or all but a bare residue of it."[17] Thus, a party who was denied a wetlands permit to construct a single family home under the state wetlands law is not entitled to compensation where a court found the parcel had not lost all value and was acquired after he had been put on notice of the limits imposed by the wetlands regulations at issue.[18] Another court has found that a town resolution designating a solid waste disposal complex as the sole facility for delivery of all solid waste generated within the town did not constitute a taking because the plaintiffs did not have "property right, vested or otherwise," in the continuation of its solid waste collecting activities.[19]

The *Lucas* decision is likely to spawn a multitude of challenges to any new environmental laws or regulations that affect private property rights in the state; however, it is doubtful that *Lucas* will enhance a private property owner's ability to limit new governmental regulation of their property (or obtain compensation for such regulation) in cases other than where they can establish a total loss in economic value.

Library References:

West's Key No. Digests, Eminent Domain ⚞2(5).

§ 15.35 Drafting Checklist—Clean Water Act Citizen Suit Notice Letter

1. Contents of Notice. Notice of alleged continuing violation of an effluent standard or limitation or order under the CWA.[1] (*See* § 15.8)

2. Reference to information sufficient to permit recipient to identify specific standard, limitation or order alleged to have been violated, the activity alleged to constitute such violation, the person(s) responsible for the alleged violation, location of alleged violation, the date(s) of violation and identification of person giving notice.[2]

3. Service of notice by certified mail upon alleged violator, with copy to EPA, EPA region where alleged violation occurred, and chief administrative officer of water pollution control agency in state where alleged violation occurred.[3]

---

17. Gazza v. New York State Department of Environmental Conservation, 159 Misc.2d 591, 605 N.Y.S.2d 642, 644 (Sup. Ct., Suffolk County, 1993), aff'd 217 A.D.2d 202, 634 N.Y.S.2d 740 (2d Dep't 1995).

18. *Id. See also,* Save the Pine Bush v. Common Council of the City of Albany, 188 A.D.2d 969, 591 N.Y.S.2d 897 (3d Dep't 1992) (SEQRA requirement that developer take hard look at configuration of development necessary to ensure survival of Pine Bush ecology is not a regulatory taking because SEQRA requirement advances a significant State interest).

19. Vinnie Montes Waste System, Inc. v. Town of Oyster Bay, 150 Misc.2d 109, 113, 567 N.Y.S.2d 335, 338 (Sup.Ct., Nassau County, 1991), aff'd on other grounds 199 A.D.2d 493, 606 N.Y.S.2d 41 (2d Dep't 1993).

§ 15.35

1. *See* 40 C.F.R. § 135.3.

2. *See id.*

3. *See* 40 C.F.R. § 135.2.

§ 15.35   ENVIRONMENTAL LAW   Ch. 15

Library References:

West's Key No. Digests, Health and Environment ⟲25.15(3.1).

§ 15.36 Drafting Checklist—Clean Water Act and Resource Conservation and Recovery Act Citizen Suit Notice Letter

1. Requirements for CWA notice letter. (See §§ 15.8, 15.35)

2. Contents of RCRA Violation. Notice regarding alleged violation of a permit, standard, regulation, condition, requirement, or order under RCRA.[1] (See § 15.23)

3. Reference to sufficient information to permit recipient to identify specific permit, standard etc. which has allegedly been violated, the activity alleged to constitute the violation, the person(s) responsible for alleged violation, date(s) of alleged violation and identification of person giving such notice.[2]

4. Notice of failure to perform a non-discretionary act or duty by EPA shall identify provision of statute requiring such non-discretionary act or duty and action taken or not taken by EPA that constitutes the failure to perform the act or duty.[3]

5. Service of notice by registered mail upon alleged violator, with copy to EPA, EPA region where alleged violation occurred, and chief administrative officer of solid waste management agency in state where alleged violation occurred.[4]

Library References:

West's Key No. Digests, Health and Environment ⟲25.15(3.1).

§ 15.37 Drafting Checklist—Clean Water Act Complaint

1. Notice of violations sent to governmental regulators and defendant. (See § 15.11)

2. Sixty days have elapsed since notice sent. (See § 15.11)

3. No diligent prosecution by governmental regulators of the violations that are the subject of the complaint. (See § 15.11)

4. Action not barred by any prior administrative penalty action brought pursuant to 33 U.S.C.A. § 1319(g). (See § 15.11)

5. Plaintiffs' use and interest in cleanliness of affected waterways.

§ 15.36
1. 40 C.F.R. § 254.3.
2. Id.
3. 40 C.F.R. § 254.3(b).
4. See 40 C.F.R. § 254.2.

6. Defendant *currently* in violation of effluent standard, limitation or order issued pursuant to CWA.[1] (*See* §§ 15.8, 15.11)

Library References:

West's Key No. Digests, Health and Environment ⚖25.15(3.3).

§ 15.38 Drafting Checklist—Nuisance and Trespass Complaint

1. Defendant's use of its property has contaminated air/water located on plaintiff's property. (*See* § 15.32–15.33)

2. Defendant's use of its property unreasonably interferes with plaintiff's use of its property. (*See* § 15.32)

3. Defendant's use of its property has proximately caused damage to plaintiff's property. (*See* § 15.32)

4. Defendant's use of its property poses a continuing threat to public health and enjoyment and have proximately caused damage to the public in the exercise of rights common to all (public nuisance only). (*See* § 15.32)

5. Plaintiff has suffered special damages (public nuisance only). (*See* § 15.32)

6. Defendant's knowing and intentional conduct proximately caused an invasion of, and interference with, plaintiff's exclusive possessory interest in its property (trespass). (*See* § 15.33)

7. The invasion and interference of property proximately caused damages (trespass). (*See* § 15.33)

8. Continuing violation causing irreparable harm (for injunction).

Library References:

West's Key No. Digests, Nuisance ⚖84; Trespass ⚖40.

§ 15.39 Drafting Checklist—Oil Spill Complaint

1. Defendant's conduct has resulted in the release of a petroleum product into the environment. (*See* §§ 15.10, 15.27)

2. The release has proximately caused contamination that has caused plaintiff to incur direct and indirect damages. (*See* § 15.27 notes 24–25)

3. Defendant's conduct is ultrahazardous activity that proximately caused contamination that has caused plaintiff to sustain damages.

4. Defendant's conduct causing spill has proximately caused an invasion and interference with plaintiff's use of property constituting a trespass. (*See* § 15.33)

§ 15.37
1. 33 U.S.C.A. § 1311.

§ 15.39   ENVIRONMENTAL LAW   Ch. 15

5. Defendant's actions and non-actions have proximately and unreasonably interfered with plaintiff's use of property. (*See* § 15.32)

6. Defendant's had duty to exercise reasonable care in handling and storage of petroleum and breached this duty by negligently allowing the release of petroleum products that proximately caused plaintiff to sustain damages.

Library References:

West's Key No. Digests, Health and Environment ⊕25.15(3.3).

§ 15.40   Forms—Clean Water Act Citizen Suit Notice Letter

BY CERTIFIED MAIL

President
ABC Condominium Company
c/o XYZ Management, Inc.
301 Main Street
Scenic Junction, New York

    Re: 60 Day Notice Pursuant to Clean Water Act: ABC Condominiums

Dear Sir or Madam:

Citizens For Cleaner Condos ("CFCC") believes that the ABC Condominium Wastewater Treatment Facility (the "ABC Plant" located at 301 Main Street, Scenic Junction, New York), has been violating and continues to violate its State Pollutant Discharge Elimination System ("SPDES") permit, No. NY–01000000. The ABC Plant discharges into an unnamed tributary of the Pristine Stream, which in turn flows into the Picturesque River. CFCC is concerned about these violations because the ABC Plant is located near the residences and businesses of its members, who use both the Pristine Stream and the Picturesque River for recreational purposes.

CFCC believes that the ABC Plant is violating its SPDES permit in two ways. First, the ABC Plant is not meeting the effluent limits set forth in its SPDES permit. The discharge monitoring reports ("DMRs") for the ABC Plant, filed with the Scenic County Health Department from January through December 19—demonstrate that the ABC Plant has violated its permit limits for ammonia, BOD, suspended solids and fecal coliform. The attached schedule I lists the violations reported in the ABC Plant's DMRs. On the basis of the DMRs, CFCC believes that the ABC Plant has violated its SPDES permit and will continue to do so unless corrective actions are taken.

Second, CFCC believes that the ABC Plant is not being properly maintained and operated, in violation of the General Conditions of its SPDES permit. This permit requires that ABC "properly operate and maintain all facilities and systems of treatment and control." SPDES Permit, General Condition 9.1(b). The permit further provides that "proper operation and maintenance ... includes a preventative/corrective program and a specific operation and maintenance manual for routine use and training of new operators."

On _____, 19__, an inspector for the Department of Environmental Conservation ("DEC") notified ABC of several serious maintenance and operation conditions at the ABC Plant. Specifically, the DEC inspectors stated that "several unauthorized bypasses" of the ABC Plant's sand filters were observed and that there was evidence that such bypasses were routinely occurring. DEC inspectors also observed ... [list additional specific problems relating to plant operation].

CFCC believes that these operation and maintenance problems have not been corrected and are contributing to the ABC Plant's inability to meet the limits required by the plant's SPDES permit. If left unabated, these problems will lead to future violations. CFCC believes that these problems will continue unless ABC takes corrective action.

The ABC Plant's failure to comply with its SPDES permit, as outlined above, violates the Federal Water Pollution Control Act (the "Clean Water Act" or "CWA") 33 U.S.C.A. §§ 1251 *et seq.* CFCC is a "person" authorized under the CWA to bring suit in federal court to enforce the Act's requirements against alleged violators. 33 U.S.C.A. § 1365(a). The CWA requires that notice be provided to you, the alleged violator, as well as the Federal Environmental Protection Agency and the State in which the violation is alleged to be occurring 60 days before filing a citizen suit pursuant to Section 1365(a). 33 U.S.C.A. § 1365(b). This letter constitutes such notice. We reserve our rights to include other violations in the complaint.

If you would like to discuss these violations further, I can be reached at the above number.

Sincerely,

cc: Administrator[1]
United States Environmental
Protection Agency
401 Main Street, A–100
Washington, D.C. 20460

U.S.E.P.A. Regional
Administrator
Region II
290 Broadway
New York, New York 10007

---

§ 15.40

1. *See* 40 C.F.R. § 135.2 for regulations concerning service of notices of intent to sue. *See also*, 40 C.F.R. Pt. 254 (notice for RCRA citizen suits) (*see supra*, § 15.25).

Commissioner
New York State Department
of Environmental Conservation
50 Wolf Road
Albany, New York 12233

New York State Department
of Environmental Conservation
Region—
_____, New York

Library References:
West's Key No. Digests, Health and Environment ⟳25.15(3.1).

§ 15.41 Forms—Clean Water Act and Resource Conservation and Recovery Act Citizen Suit Notice Letter

Re: Notice of Intent to Sue for Violations of the Resource Conservation and Recovery Act (RCRA) and the Clean Water Act at property located at Scenic Junction, New York

Dear Sir or Madam:

This letter is a notice filed on behalf of the [*Village of Scenic Junction*] (the "Village") of its intent to commence a citizen suit pursuant to the Resource Conservation and Recovery Act ("RCRA"), 42 U.S.C.A. § 6901 *et seq.* and the Clean Water Act, 33 U.S.C.A. § 1251 against [*Fred & Barney Transfer Station*]. This citizen suit is based upon conditions presently existing at the site formerly operated by the [*Heavy Metal Industrial Company*] at [*1 Wetland Road, Village of Scenic Junction*], New York (the "Heavy Metal site"), presently owned and operated by [*Fred & Barney, Inc.*]

The [*Village*] will maintain its citizen suit pursuant to Section 7002(a)(1)(A) and Section 7002(a)(1)(B) of RCRA, 42 U.S.C.A. §§ 6972(a)(1)(A), 6972(a)(1)(B). Section 7002(a)(1)(A) authorizes citizen suits against any person "who is alleged to be in violation of any permit, standard, regulation, condition requirement, prohibition or order" under RCRA. Section 7002(a)(1)(B) authorizes a citizen suit against any person "who has contributed or who is contributing to the past or present handling, storage, treatment, transportation, or disposal of any solid or hazardous waste which may present an imminent and substantial endangerment to health or the environment."

Specifically, the [*Village*] will allege that conditions in and around the [*Heavy Metal*] site, where approximately [*700 drums of solid and liquid wastes, as well as 10,000 cubic yards of solid waste and other debris*] have been abandoned, violates Section 4005 of RCRA, 42 U.S.C.A.

§ 6945, which prohibits any solid waste management practice or disposal that constitutes the open dumping of solid waste.

In addition, the [Heavy Metal] site also may present an imminent and substantial endangerment to health and the environment in violation of RCRA. In an environmental assessment conducted by the Department of Health, soil contaminated with [list contaminants] was discovered at the [Heavy Metal] Site.

The [Village] will claim that [Fred & Barney], as the current owner and operator of the [Heavy Metal] site, is liable for the aforementioned violations of RCRA that have occurred or are occurring on the [Heavy Metal] Site. Moreover, the [Village] maintains that [Fred & Barney], as the current owner and operator of the site, has contributed and continues to contribute to the handling, storage or disposal of solid and/or hazardous wastes that may present an imminent and substantial endangerment to human health and the environment.

The [Village] will also allege violations of Section 505 of the CWA, 33 U.S.C.A. § 1365, which authorizes a person to bring a suit against any person who is "alleged to be in violation of an effluent standard or limitation" under the CWA. The [Village] contends that [Fred & Barney] have violated and continue to violate the CWA by discharging pollutants from point sources located on the [Heavy Metal] site into the [Picturesque River] without a CWA permit.

Specifically, the [Village] contends that the current owner and operator of the [Heavy Metal] site are allowing leachate from the piles of debris and toxic material located at the site to discharge into the [Picturesque River]. These discharges occur from culverts and ditches located at the site that discharge into the [Picturesque River].

The leachate discharged from the [Heavy Metal] site contains, among other things [list contaminants] and other "pollutants" within the meaning of Section 502(6) of the CWA, 33 U.S.C.A. § 1362(6). Moreover, the ditches, culverts and other discrete conveyances that convey the leachate from the [Heavy Metal] site into the [Picturesque River] are "point sources" within the meaning of Section 502(14) of the CWA, 33 U.S.C.A. § 1362(14) and the [Picturesque River] constitutes "navigable waters" as that term is defined in Section 502(7) of the CWA, 33 U.S.C.A. § 1362(7). These discharges violate Section 301 of the CWA, 33 U.S.C.A. § 1311, because no permit has been issued pursuant to Section 402(a) of the CWA, 33 U.S.C.A. § 1342(a), authorizing the past or continuing discharges at the [Heavy Metal] site.

Unless you take immediate action to remedy these ongoing violations, the [Village] will commence a lawsuit against you pursuant to CWA Section 505 RCRA Sections 7002(a)(1)(A) and 7002(a)(1)(B). If you would like to discuss this matter, please contact me at the above number.

Sincerely,

cc: Administrator[1]
United States Environmental
Protection Agency
401 Main Street, A–100
Washington, D.C. 20460

U.S.E.P.A. Regional
Administrator
Region II
290 Broadway
New York, New York 10007

Commissioner
New York State Department
of Environmental Conservation
50 Wolf Road
Albany, New York 12233

New York State Department
of Environmental Conservation
Region—
_____, New York

Library References:

West's Key No. Digests, Health and Environment ⛤25.15(3.1).

§ 15.42 Forms—Clean Water Act Complaint

UNITED STATES DISTRICT COURT
_____ DISTRICT OF NEW YORK

_____, Plaintiff, -against- _____, Defendant.	Civil Action No. (xxx) COMPLAINT

Plaintiff, by its attorneys, alleges as follows:

---

§ 15.41

1. See 40 C.F.R. § 135.2 for regulations concerning service of notices of intent to sue. See also, 40 C.F.R. Pt. 254 (notice for RCRA citizen suits) (see supra, § 15.25).

1. Plaintiff brings this citizen enforcement action against the above-named defendant to abate violations of the Clean Water Act, ("CWA") 33 U.S.C.A. § 1251 *et seq.* at a facility located at _____, New York (the "Facility"). Specifically, since _____, defendant has permitted the continuing illegal discharge of pollutants from its facility in to the _____ River, in excess of its State Pollutant Discharge Elimination System ("SPDES") permit at the Facility. Defendant also has violated the CWA by allowing the discharge of pollutants from point sources located on its property without first obtaining a SPDES permit as required under the CWA.

JURISDICTION

2. This Court has jurisdiction over this action pursuant to the Clean Water Act, 33 U.S.C.A. § 1365(a) and 28 U.S.C.A. § 1331 (federal question jurisdiction).

3. On _____, plaintiff sent a notice of intent to commence an action based upon the CWA violations alleged in this complaint to the Administrator of the Environmental Protection Agency ("EPA"), the New York State Department of Environmental Conservation ("DEC") and to the defendant, in accordance with the requirements of the CWA, 33 U.S.C.A. § 1365(b) and 40 C.F.R. Part 135.

4. More than sixty days have passed since the plaintiff delivered its notice and the violations outlined therein have not ceased.

5. Neither the United States nor the State of New York has commenced and is diligently prosecuting a civil or criminal court action in a Court of the United States, or of New York State for, the violations that are alleged in this complaint and thus, this action is not barred pursuant to 33 U.S.C.A. § 1365(b).

6. This action is not barred by any prior administrative penalty proceeding brought by EPA or DEC pursuant to 33 U.S.C.A. § 1319(g) or a comparable State Law.

7. As of the date that this complaint was filed the violations alleged herein are ongoing, continuous and have not ceased.

VENUE

8. Venue is proper in the _____ District of New York because the violations alleged occurred and continue to occur within this judicial district.

PARTIES

9. Plaintiff is an organization organized to protect the land and waters of the State of New York and to work to ensure that the environmental resources of the State are preserved and improved. Many of plaintiff's members use the waters of this State, including the _____

River, for recreational purposes such as fishing, swimming and canoeing. Other members of the organization also engage in commercial fishing in New York State and will be adversely impacted if defendant's pollution is allowed to continue.

10. Defendant is a corporation organized pursuant to the laws of the State of _____, with its principal place of business in _____, New York. Defendant is engaged in, among other things, the manufacturing of _____ at the facility.

FACTS OF THE CASE

11. As part of its manufacturing process at the facility, defendant discharges approximately __ gallons per day of effluent from its facility through four outfalls that flow directly into the _____ River.

12. The effluent discharged by defendant from these outfalls contains numerous pollutants, including but not limited to [*list pollutants*].

13. On _____, the DEC issued to defendant a SPDES permit to discharge certain levels of the above-referenced pollutants into the _____ River. Specifically, defendant's SPDES permit provided, in relevant part, that [*list relevant requirements of permit*].

14. Defendant's SPDES permit required it to test its effluent at regular intervals to ensure that the limits of its permit were not exceeded and to submit the results of these tests on Discharge Monitoring Reports ("DMRs") filed with the DEC.

15. The DMRs filed with the DEC report the following violations of the limits set forth in defendant's SPDES permit:

[*outline all reported violations in complaint or on an attached and incorporated schedule*].

16. Discharges from defendant's facility continue to exceed the SPDES permit limits for _____.

17. Defendant also discharges pollutants through a series of ditches, culverts and other discrete conveyances located near defendant's facility.

18. These conveyances discharge pollutants from defendant's property into the _____ River, including [*list pollutants*].

19. On _____, the effluent discharged from defendant's drainage system was collected, tested and found to contain, among other things, the following: [*list pollutants detected*].

20. At no time has Defendant applied for or received a SPDES permit for the discharge of pollutants from those ditches, culverts and/or other discrete conveyances into the _____ River.

FIRST CLAIM FOR RELIEF

21. Defendants are "persons" pursuant to 33 U.S.C.A. § 1362(5).

Ch. 15   **CLEAN WATER ACT COMPLAINT**   **§ 15.42**

22. [*identify contents of effluent*] are "pollutants" pursuant to 33 U.S.C.A. § 1362(6).

23. The outfalls that discharge into the _____ River are "point sources" pursuant to 33 U.S.C.A. § 1362(14).

24. The _____ River is a "navigable water" pursuant to 33 U.S.C.A. § 1362(7).

25. The discharges outlined above are in excess of the limits set forth in defendant's SPDES permit.

26. Defendant owns and operates a facility that has discharged and continues to discharge pollutants from a point source into navigable waters in excess of the limits of the SPDES permit issued to it. Defendant, therefore, is violating the CWA, 33 U.S.C.A. § 1311(a).

SECOND CLAIM FOR RELIEF

27. Plaintiff repeats and reincorporates the allegations set forth in paragraphs 1 through 22 of the complaint.

28. Defendant discharges _____ through ditches, culverts and other discrete conveyances into the _____ River.

29. These ditches, culverts and other discrete conveyances located on defendant's property are "point sources" pursuant to 33 U.S.C.A. § 1362(14).

30. [*identify contents of effluent*] are "pollutants" pursuant to 33 U.S.C.A. § 1362(6).

31. Defendant does not have a SPDES permit for the discharges of these pollutants from the ditches, culverts and other discrete conveyances located on its property.

32. Defendant owns and operates a facility that has discharged and continues to discharge pollutants from a point source into navigable waters without a SPDES permit issued pursuant to CWA, 33 U.S.C.A. § 1342. Defendant, therefore, is violating the CWA, 33 U.S.C.A. § 1311(a).

PRAYER FOR RELIEF

WHEREFORE, plaintiff respectfully requests that this Court enter an Order and Mandatory Injunction:

A. Declaring that Defendant is violating the CWA by discharging pollutants from a point source into the _____ River in excess of its SPDES permit;

B. Declaring that Defendant is violating the CWA by discharging pollutants from point sources into the _____ River without a permit in violation of the CWA, 33 U.S.C.A. § 1311(a);

§ 15.42　ENVIRONMENTAL LAW　Ch. 15

C. Ordering Defendant to cease discharging pollutants into the _____ River in violation of the CWA.

D. Ordering Defendant to pay civil penalties of $25,000 per day for each violation of the CWA pursuant to 33 U.S.C.A. § 1365(d).

E. Awarding Plaintiff its costs of litigation, including but not limited to reasonable attorney and expert witness fees, as authorized by 42 U.S.C.A. § 1365(d).

F. Awarding such other and further relief that this Court deems just and proper.

Dated: New York, New York
　　　[date]

　　　　　　　　　　　　　　　　[FIRM NAME]

　　　　　　　　　　　　　　　　By: _____
　　　　　　　　　　　　　　　　_____, Esq.

　　　　　　　　　　　　　　　　[Attorney's initials and last four digits of attorney's social security number]
　　　　　　　　　　　　　　　　[address and phone]

To: [Name and address of opposing counsel]

Library References:

West's Key No. Digests, Health and Environment ⚖25.15(3.3).

§ 15.43　Forms—Nuisance and Trespass—Complaint

SUPREME COURT OF THE STATE OF NEW YORK
COUNTY OF _____

_____,	)
Plaintiff,	)
	) [Pleading]
-against-	)
	) Index No. _____
_____,	)
Defendant.	)

_____, by its attorneys, alleges as follows:

1. [ABC Corporation ("ABC Corp.")], is a corporation organized and existing under the laws of the State of New York with its principal

place of business at _____. [ABC Corp.] owns certain property located at _____.

2. On information and belief, defendant [XYZ Corporation ("XYZ Corp.")] is a corporation organized and existing under the laws of the State of New York with its principal place of business at _____. On information and belief, [XYZ Corp.] is presently engaged in the business of [describe general business operations].

3. [XYZ Corp.] operates a manufacturing facility in _____, New York, adjacent to headquarters of [ABC Corp.] Located within this manufacturing facility are _____ buildings and associated structures on approximately [40] acres of land. Also located at the site are _____ above ground and underground storage tanks used for storing wastes containing hazardous chemicals, as well as heating and fuel oil.

4. _____, staff members of the New York State Department of Environmental Conservation ("DEC"), reported to plaintiff that groundwater in the general area of its property had been contaminated with [list contaminants]. Subsequent testing conducted by plaintiff and the _____ County Department of Health confirm the presence of [list contaminants] within the drinking water wells located on plaintiff's property.

5. Subsequent studies conducted by DEC have confirmed that discharges from the underground storage tanks located on defendant's property and discharges associated with defendant's manufacturing processes are the source of this area-wide groundwater contamination.

6. The contaminants detected within the groundwater beneath plaintiff's property and in plaintiff's wells include chemicals used in defendant's manufacturing operations.

AS AND FOR A FIRST CAUSE OF ACTION
(Private Nuisance)

7. Plaintiff repeats and realleges the allegations set forth in paragraphs [1] through [6] of the Complaint.

8. The defendant has willfully, wantonly, intentionally, and negligently created and permitted to continue conditions at the Site that present a threat to human health and the environment.

9. The defendant's actions and non-actions unreasonably interfere with plaintiff's use of it property have proximately caused, among other things, the contamination of groundwater and soils beneath the plaintiff's property.

10. The contamination proximately caused by defendant's conduct has also diminished the value of plaintiff's property.

AS AND FOR A SECOND CAUSE OF ACTION
(Public Nuisance)

11. Plaintiff repeats and realleges the allegations set forth in paragraphs [1] through [10] of the Complaint.

12. The present conditions at defendant's facility pose a continuing threat to human health and enjoyment, as well as the environment, and have proximately caused damage to the public in the exercise of rights common to all. Therefore, defendant is operating its facility as public nuisance.

13. Defendant's actions and non-actions have proximately caused contamination of drinking water in the area surrounding defendant's property, thereby causing a threat to public health.

14. Plaintiff has suffered special damages because the conditions at defendant's facility directly interfere with plaintiff's use and enjoyment of its property, including, but not limited to use of groundwater as a potable water supply, and by diminishing the value of plaintiff's property due to this contamination.

AS AND FOR A THIRD CAUSE OF ACTION
(Trespass)

15. Plaintiff repeats and realleges the allegations set forth in paragraphs [1] through [14] of the Complaint.

16. Defendant willfully, wantonly, knowingly, intentionally, and negligently failed to use proper care in handling, storing and disposing of hazardous chemicals at its facility. Defendant's handling, storage and disposal of hazardous chemicals at its facility have proximately caused the contamination and continued contamination at the Site, thus causing a continued invasion of and interference with plaintiff's exclusive possessory interest in its property.

17. This invasion and interference constitutes a trespass, that has proximately caused, and/or will proximately cause plaintiff to suffer irreparable harm and damages and to incur expenditures arising from its cleanup of the Site in excess of $_____.

WHEREFORE, plaintiff respectfully requests that a judgment be made and entered:

A. Declaring defendant's facility a private nuisance and ordering defendant to remediate its Site and all areas that are contributing to the ongoing contamination of plaintiff's property;

B. Declaring defendant's facility a public nuisance and ordering defendant to take all action necessary to prevent further contamination of groundwater and soils, as well as all actions necessary to clean up existing contamination caused by the release of hazardous substances;

C. Awarding plaintiff damages in an amount to be determined at trial for all costs incurred by plaintiff due to the contamination of its property;

D. Awarding plaintiff damages for the diminution in value of its property due to the contamination proximately caused by defendant; and

E. Such other and further relief as the Court may deem proper, just, together with cost and disbursements of this action.

Dated: New York, New York
_____, 19__

[*Indorsement/Signature Block*]

Library References:

West's Key No. Digests, Nuisance ⌾84; Trespass ⌾40.

§ 15.44 Forms—Oil Spill: Complaint

SUPREME COURT OF THE STATE OF NEW YORK
COUNTY OF _____

_____,	)
Plaintiff,	)
	) [Pleading]
-against-	)
	) Index No. _____
_____,	)
Defendant.	)

_____, by its attorneys, alleges as follows:

1. [*ABC Associates, L.P. ("ABC Associates")*] is a New York limited partnership. [*ABC Associates*] owns a shopping center located at _____, New York (the "Shopping Center").

2. Defendant [*XYZ Corporation ("XYZ Corp.")*] is a corporation organized and existing under the laws of the State of New York with its principal place of business at _____. [*XYZ*] operates an automotive service station and fuel dispensing business at _____, which is located on a portion of the shopping center owned by [*ABC Associates*] (the "Site").

3. On _____, 19__, [*ABC Associates*] and [*XYZ Corp.*] entered into a five-year lease for the Site commencing on _____. This lease was renewed on _____.

4. As part of its operations at the Site, [*XYZ Corp.*] operates and maintains four _____ gallon underground storage tanks ("USTs") that it installed for the purpose of storing gasoline that it sells at the Site.

5. On or about _____, 19__, [*XYZ Corp.*] tested the USTs located at the Site. The test disclosed that two of the USTs were severely corroded and were leaking petroleum product from the tanks into the environment.

6. Subsequent investigations have disclosed that the discharges of petroleum from these tanks has caused significant contamination of soils and groundwater on the Site and adjoining areas within the Shopping Center.

AS AND FOR A FIRST CAUSE OF ACTION
(Navigation Law)

7. Defendant's acts and omissions relating to the Site have resulted in the release of oil by Defendant from an underground storage tank located at the Site owned and operated by it through the time of release.

8. This release has proximately caused the contamination of groundwater and surface water waters at the Site and in areas adjoining the Site.

9. Section 181(1) of the New York State Navigation Law provides that "[a]ny person who has discharged petroleum shall be strictly liable, without regard to fault, for all cleanup and removal costs and all direct and indirect damages, no matter by whom sustained, as defined in this section."

10. Section 181(5) of the New York State Navigation law provides that "any injured person" may bring a claim for the costs of cleanup and removal and direct and indirect damages based on the strict liability imposed by Section 181 "directly against the person who has discharged the petroleum."

11. Defendant is strictly liable to plaintiff, without regard to fault, for all damages incurred or that will be incurred by plaintiff for the containment, cleanup and remediation of the contamination caused by the discharge if petroleum from defendant's underground storage tank.

AS AND FOR A SECOND CAUSE OF ACTION
(Strict Liability in Conducting an Ultrahazardous and/or Abnormally Dangerous Activity)

12. Plaintiff repeats the allegations of paragraphs [1] through [11] and incorporates them here.

13. In the course of its operations at the Site, Defendant brought to the premises, generated, created, stored, maintained, collected, used,

spilled, discharged and disposed of petroleum products dangerous to human health and environment.

14. Defendant's acts and failures to act at the Site thereby constituted ultrahazardous and/or abnormally dangerous activities.

15. As a result of Defendant's abnormally dangerous activities, the Site and the adjoining [*Shopping Center*] has become and continues to be contaminated by petroleum and its by-products.

16. As a result of the continuing contamination of the premises, plaintiff has suffered and will continue to incur damages.

17. Defendant is strictly liable for the past and future damages suffered by plaintiff.

AS AND FOR A THIRD CAUSE OF ACTION
(Willful and Wanton Misconduct)

18. Plaintiff repeats the allegations of paragraphs [1] through [17] and incorporates them here.

19. Defendant was engaged in handling, storage, and disposal of petroleum and knew that such activity would, in all certainty, result in damage to persons and property if permitted to escape.

20. Defendant failed to use proper care in handling, storing and disposing of petroleum at the Site, thus causing spills, discharges, and disposal of petroleum at the Site and other portions of the [*Shopping Center*].

21. Defendant, by and through its agents, servants and employees, knew, or in the exercise of ordinary and reasonable care should have known, that its acts and failures to act in the handling, storage and disposal of petroleum presented a grave risk of harm to Plaintiff, the general public, and the environment and that the acts and failures to act by Defendant represented a willful, wanton, knowing, intentional, and reckless disregard for, and indifference to, the health, well-being and general rights and safety of Plaintiff and the general public.

22. As a result of Defendant's willful and wanton misconduct, Plaintiff has suffered and will continue to suffer irreparable and continuing harm and incur damages.

AS AND FOR A FOURTH CAUSE OF ACTION
(Trespass)

23. Plaintiff repeats the allegations of paragraphs [1] through [22] and incorporates them here.

24. Defendant willfully, wantonly, knowingly, intentionally, and negligently failed to use proper care in handling, storing and disposing of petroleum at the Site.

25. Defendant's handling, storage, and disposal of petroleum at the Site contaminated and continues to contaminate the Site, thus causing a continued invasion of and interference with Plaintiff's exclusive possessory interests in the Site and the other portions of the [Shopping Center].

26. This invasion and interference constitutes trespass, has proximately caused, and/or will proximately cause Plaintiff to suffer irreparable harm and damages and to incur expenditures arising from remediation of the Site and adjoining portions of the [Shopping Center].

AS AND FOR A FIFTH CAUSE OF ACTION
(Private Nuisance)

27. Plaintiff repeats the allegations of paragraphs [1] through [26] and incorporates them here.

28. Defendant willfully, wantonly, intentionally and negligently created and permitted to remain at the Site petroleum which has been and continues to be highly dangerous to human health and the environment.

29. Defendant's actions and non-actions have proximately and unreasonably interfered with Plaintiff's use of the [Shopping Center].

30. Defendant knew, or in the exercise of ordinary and reasonable care should have known, that its discharge and spillage of petroleum at the Site would cause a continuing private nuisance, yet Defendant has failed to abate the private nuisance or cause it to be abated.

31. The presence of petroleum disposed of and spilled by Defendant at the Site caused and causes irreparable harm and damages to Plaintiff in the exercise of its rights, and substantially injures and interferes with Plaintiff's interest, enjoyment, and utilization of the [Shopping Center].

32. Defendant is strictly liable for abatement of the private nuisance and the damages, including lost profits resulting therefrom, incurred by Plaintiff.

AS AND FOR A SIXTH CAUSE OF ACTION
(Negligence)

33. Plaintiff repeats the allegations of paragraphs [1] through [32] and incorporates them here.

34. Defendant had a duty to exercise reasonable care in order to prevent risks to human health and the environment caused by its use, spills, discharges, and the disposal of petroleum at the Site.

35. Defendant breached its duty by releasing and/or permitting the release of petroleum, and this breach of duty has proximately caused, and/or will proximately cause, Plaintiff to incur expenditures arising from cleanup and related activities.

36. As a result of Defendant's negligence, Plaintiff has been and continues suffer damages.

WHEREFORE, Plaintiff [ABC Associates] demands the following judgment:

1. Declaring that [XYZ Corp.] is liable pursuant to sections 181(1) and 181(5) of the New York State Navigation Law for the costs and damages incurred or that will be incurred by [ABC Associates] due to the contamination caused by [XYZ Corp.'s] discharge of petroleum at the Site.

2. Declaring that [XYZ Corp.] is liable to [ABC Associates] of all costs and damages that have been incurred or that will be incurred by it due to the contamination of the Site and adjoining areas caused by Defendant's discharge of petroleum at the Site.

3. For such other and further relief as this Court may deem just and proper, together with the costs and disbursements of this action.

Dated: New York, New York
_____, 19__

[Indorsement/Signature Block]

Library References:

West's Key No. Digests, Health and Environment ⚖25.15(3.3).

Chapter 16

LAND USE LAW

by
John R. Nolon
and
Jayne E. Daly*

Table of Sections

16.1	Scope Note.
16.2	Strategy.
16.3	Local Land Use Law.
16.4	___ Delegated Authority.
16.5	___ Enabling Acts.
16.6	___ ___ New York City.
16.7	___ Home Rule Authority.
16.8	___ ___ Flexibility.
16.9	___ ___ Floating Zone.
16.10	___ Summary.
16.11	Comprehensive Plan.
16.12	___ Judicial Definition.
16.13	___ Statutory Definition.
16.14	___ Preparation and Adoption.
16.15	___ Protects Zoning Against Challenge.
16.16	___ Summary.
16.17	Substantive Limits—Illustrative Case.
16.18	___ Substantive Due Process.
16.19	___ Procedural Due Process.
16.20	___ Equal Protection.
16.21	___ *Ultra Vires*.
16.22	___ Regulatory Takings.
16.23	___ Vested Rights.
16.24	___ Preemption.
16.25	___ First Amendment.
16.26	___ Summary.
16.27	Local Process.
16.28	___ Structure of Local Regulations.
16.29	___ Adoption.
16.30	___ Amendment.
16.31	___ Other Regulations/Official Map.

* The authors would like to thank John B. Kirkpatrick of Kirkpatrick & Silverberg and Linda B. Whitehead of MuCullough, Goldberger & Staudt for their helpful suggestions for making this chapter useful to the busy land use practitioner.

16.32	___ Building Regulations and Permits.
16.33	___ Summary.
16.34	Local Boards and Practices.
16.35	___ Local Legislature.
16.36	___ Planning Board.
16.37	___ Zoning Board of Appeals.
16.38	___ Freedom of Information.
16.39	___ Open Meetings.
16.40	___ Conflict of Interests.
16.41	___ Summary.
16.42	Judicial Review.
16.43	___ Procedures.
16.44	___ Standards.
16.45	___ ___ Local Legislature.
16.46	___ ___ Zoning Board of Appeals.
16.47	___ ___ Planning Board.
16.48	___ Standing.
16.49	___ Exhaustion.
16.50	___ Remedies.
16.51	___ Summary.
16.52	Local Environmental Review.
16.53	___ Actions Subject to SEQRA.
16.54	___ ___ Building Permits.
16.55	___ ___ Variances.
16.56	___ ___ Subdivisions.
16.57	___ ___ Site Plans.
16.58	___ ___ Rezoning.
16.59	___ Summary.
16.60	Zoning Law—In General.
16.61	As of Right Use.
16.62	Nonconforming Use—Definition and Application.
16.63	___ Changes.
16.64	___ Reconstruction and Restoration.
16.65	___ Enlargement, Alteration or Extension.
16.66	___ Changes to Another Nonconforming Use.
16.67	___ Termination.
16.68	___ Abandonment.
16.69	___ Amortization.
16.70	___ Transfer of Ownership.
16.71	___ Procedures.
16.72	___ Summary.
16.73	Use Variance.
16.74	___ Statutory Standard.
16.75	___ ___ Reasonable Return.
16.76	___ ___ Unique Hardship.
16.77	___ ___ Protect Essential Neighborhood Character.
16.78	___ ___ Self–Created Hardship.
16.79	___ Minimum Variance Needed.
16.80	___ Procedure.
16.81	___ Summary.
16.82	Area Variance.

Sec.	
16.83	___ Statutory Balancing Test.
16.84	___ ___ Guiding Principles from Case Law.
16.85	___ ___ Balancing Factors.
16.86	___ Minimum Variance Needed.
16.87	___ Procedure.
16.88	___ Summary.
16.89	Conditions Imposed on Use and Area Variances.
16.90	Special Use Permits.
16.91	___ Imposition and Use of Standards.
16.92	___ Findings and Determination of Board.
16.93	___ Limitation on Imposition of Conditions.
16.94	___ Procedure.
16.95	___ Summary.
16.96	Subdivision Approval.
16.97	___ Procedure.
16.98	___ ___ How Affected By SEQRA.
16.99	___ Provision of Essential Services.
16.100	___ Parkland.
16.101	___ Decisions and Conditions.
16.102	___ Summary.
16.103	Site Plans.
16.104	___ Responsible Agency.
16.105	___ ___ Procedure.
16.106	___ ___ Standards for Review.
16.107	___ ___ Conditions Imposed.
16.108	___ Summary.
16.109	Particularized Actions.
16.110	___ Spot Zoning.
16.111	___ ___ Challenge Dismissed.
16.112	___ ___ Challenge Successful.
16.113	___ Rezoning.
16.114	___ ___ Conditions.
16.115	___ ___ Contract Zoning.
16.116	___ ___ Development Agreements.
16.117	___ Summary.
16.118	Special Regulations.
16.119	___ Accessory Uses.
16.120	___ Accessory Apartments.
16.121	___ Home Offices.
16.122	___ Definition of Family.
16.123	___ Affordable Housing.
16.124	___ Mobile Homes.
16.125	___ Aesthetics.
16.126	___ ___ Architectural Review.
16.127	___ ___ Historic Preservation.
16.128	___ Public Uses.
16.129	___ ___ Public Utilities.
16.130	___ ___ Cellular Transmission Facilities.
16.131	___ ___ Religious Uses.
16.132	___ Summary.
16.133	Forms—Environmental Assessment—Short Form.

16.134 ____ Environmental Assessment—Long Form.

WESTLAW Electronic Research

See WESTLAW Electronic Research Guide preceding the Summary of Contents.

§ 16.1 Scope Note

This chapter covers the local regulation of private land use in New York State. Land use law, broadly defined, encompasses the full range of laws and regulations that influence or affect the development and conservation of land. This law is intensely intergovernmental and interdisciplinary. In land use law there are countless intersections among federal, state, regional and local statutes and regulations; it is significantly influenced by other legal regimes such as environmental,[1] administrative[2] and municipal law,[3] to name a few.

Chapter 16 discusses the aspects of this larger land use control system that have been delegated to cities, towns and villages by the State Legislature. These state enabling acts are covered in Sections 16.3 through 16.10; they include a discussion of the separate authority delegated to these municipalities under the Municipal Home Rule Law.

New York law establishes that the predicate of local land use regulation is comprehensive planning. This requirement, since it is so fundamental, reappears throughout the chapter in addition to the basic description of it found in Sections 16.11 through 16.16. The failure of zoning to conform to comprehensive planning will result in its invalidation. This amounts to a substantive limitation on the authority of local governments to regulate land use. Other substantive limitations, including due process, equal protection, regulatory takings, fundamental freedoms and vested rights, are covered in Sections 16.17 through 16.26.

The local legislature in a city, town or village is responsible for deciding whether and how extensively to regulate land use. It adopts the comprehensive plan and zoning ordinance, for example, and creates the administrative bodies that enforce their provisions. The local process of adopting local land use controls is discussed in Sections 16.27 through 16.33. The principal local land use agencies and the requirements under which they operate are set forth in Sections 16.34 through 16.41.

The procedures that aggrieved parties must follow to appeal the decisions of local land use actions to the courts are discussed in Sections 16.42 through 16.51. These Sections cover the standards used by the courts in reviewing local determinations, who has standing to sue,

---

§ 16.1

1. *See* Chapter 15 "Environmental Law," *supra*.
2. *See* Chapter 4 "Administrative Law," *supra*.
3. *See* Chapter 3 "Municipal Law," *supra*.

§ 16.1   LAND USE LAW   Ch. 16

requirements for the exhaustion of local administrative remedies, the remedies that courts afford and when they are available.

Although Chapter 15 contains a full treatment of Environmental Law, Sections 16.52 through 16.59 of this chapter discuss in some detail the applicability of state statutes requiring a review of the impact on the environment of local land use actions. This treatment is included here because of the fundamental way in which these environmental review requirements alter the time periods and standards otherwise applicable to local land use review and approval processes.

Several basic aspects of local zoning are covered beginning with Section 16.60. These include a brief discussion of as-of-right zoning uses, and in Section 16.61 an extensive treatment of nonconforming uses, their continuance, limitations and termination in Sections 16.62 through 16.72. Sections 16.73 through 16.81 discuss use variances; 16.82 through 16.88, area variances; and Section 16.89, the imposition of conditions on variances granted by a local zoning board of appeals. Special use permits are required for certain uses that are declared by the local legislature to be compatible with permitted as-of-right uses, but which are sufficiently different to merit individual project review. The standards and processes typically applicable to the permitting of special uses are covered in Sections 16.90 through 16.95.

The subdivision of large land parcels and the development of individual plots of land may be regulated by local governments. Cities, towns and villages have been delegated the authority to review and approve land subdivision if, and to the extent, they decide to do so. Subdivision review and approval matters are covered in Sections 16.96 through 16.102. The development of individual sites may also be subject to further regulation at the local level in the discretion of the local legislature. The procedures and standards applicable to local site plan review authority are discussed in Sections 16.103 through 16.108.

Local land use laws typically single out and regulate specifically a variety of uses and subjects including accessory uses, accessory apartments, home offices, nontraditional families, mobile homes and aesthetic aspects of building and development. The special rules and procedures that attend these more specific local land use regulations are discussed in Sections 16.118 through 16.127.

Local zoning provisions often regulate certain uses that are considered to be in the public interest; normally, this requires that zoning impose fewer restrictions on such uses than on wholly private uses. Constitutionally, and under the delegated police power, zoning must either accommodate, or be careful not to exclude, governmental, hospital, airport, utility, religious, educational and charitable uses. The chapter concludes in Sections 16.128–16.132 with a discussion of the standards and limitations applicable to local regulations of these public uses.

§ 16.2 Strategy

The material in this chapter reveals that many local land use decisions are highly discretionary. Most are clothed with a presumption of validity; courts typically defer to the judgment of local legislatures and administrative bodies regarding local land use matters. Although the statutes frequently require decisions to be made within certain periods, these deadlines may often be extended by mutual consent, or to allow additional material to be submitted or facts to be gathered. In this environment, the practitioner must be highly sensitive to the particular practices and predilections of individual administrative and legislative agencies.

Offsetting this local discretion and administrative flexibility are requirements that local decisions be based on facts found on the record of the proceedings and that they not be arbitrary or capricious. This suggests that the gathering and presentation of solid factual information supporting a client's position is essential.

As important is sensitivity to the real and justifiable concerns of adjacent and neighboring property owners. With most land use decisions, one of the cognizable concerns is the effect of the project on nearby properties, the neighborhood and the community. It is not sufficient for decisions to be based on the perceptions and fears of neighbors and citizens, but facts showing negative impacts on them and their properties are highly relevant to local decisions and whether they will be sustained if challenged.

Local land use agencies are not subject to the requirements of the State Administrative Procedures Act. Rather, they are governed by particular requirements regarding notice, hearing and procedure contained in the various enabling acts that authorize them to act with respect to particular land use matters. Often, these statutes contain substantive provisions as well. As a consequence, the practitioner must know how to find and interpret the particular authorizing statute under which a local land use action is to be taken.

One critical step in representing clients before local land use decisionmaking bodies is to gather and understand all the facts. This includes the critical information regarding the impacts of the proposed project on surrounding properties and neighborhoods. These impacts include economic, visual, health and environmental matters. Quite often, the client cannot provide all the relevant facts. Accordingly, the practitioner is required to develop strategies for accessing and evaluating these impacts in a quick and efficient fashion.

Another step is to identify and understand the statutory and case law standards that must be met by the particular local decisionmaking body. For example, if a client must obtain a variance from the application of a zoning ordinance's provisions, the practitioner must know that New York statutes require that function to be delegated to the local zoning board of appeals and that those statutes contain both the standards that the board must apply and the burden of proof that is placed on the applicant. If the client needs a variance from the use provisions of the zoning ordinance, that client must prove four specific matters to the board of appeals. If, on the other hand, the variance needed is an area variance, the board itself must balance a number of factors in arriving at its decision. In this latter case, the practitioner's job is to be certain that the appropriate facts are before the board when it conducts the statutorily required balancing.

Clients must understand the sensitivity of local boards to offsite impacts of land use decisions and be counseled to investigate all possible means of mitigating those impacts. Quite often, a favorable decision will depend on the ability of the client to mitigate the demonstrable impacts of a project or proposal. Routinely, mitigation conditions are imposed as a condition of granting a variance, rezoning a property, or approving an application for a special permit, subdivision or site plan. Effective legal counselling on this subject may mean the difference between success and failure for a client seeking local approval to improve real property.

Attorneys representing the opponents of development projects should counsel their clients that local boards must respect the property rights of their applicants and as a result, the board will need much more than the well orchestrated opposition of the project's neighbors to disapprove of, or substantially limit, a development proposal. The protection provided property owners by the New York and U.S. Constitutions require that local boards proceed in a careful and objective fashion and understand that their ability to deny or limit development proposal is constrained by the substantive limitations on their authority discussed in this chapter.

Increasingly, the critical skill needed by the attorney representing the private owner, opposing neighbor or the municipal agency, is the ability to find and negotiate an acceptable solution to development matters that is sensitive to the demonstrable needs and rights of the parties and within the authority of the municipal board involved. Taking this broader view of each local land use matter at the onset of representing a client will greatly aid the attorney in effecting suitable solutions to what are often very difficult and time consuming efforts to win, or block, a local approval.

§ 16.3 Local Land Use Law

Land use law, broadly defined, encompasses the full range of laws and regulations that influence or affect the development and conservation of the land. This law is intensely intergovernmental and interdisciplinary. In land use law there are countless intersections among federal, state, regional and local statutes; it is significantly influenced by other legal regimes such as environmental,[1] administrative[2] and municipal law,[3] to name a few.

While noting these influences, it is appropriate for a chapter such as this to focus entirely on local land use regulation. At the base of the pyramid of land use law is the delegated authority of local governments. Its exercise, over time, dictates the broad patterns of land development and conservation.

By dividing their jurisdictions into zoning districts and providing for the uses allowed in, and the development specifications pertaining to, each district, local governments create a blueprint for the future development of each community. The aggregate effect of these blueprints, when aligned on an inter-municipal basis, is the plan for the future development of the region. These patterns evolve as local boards and agencies review, approve and condition applications for site plans,[4] subdivisions,[5] and special permits;[6] they change as the local legislature rezones discrete areas[7] and as property owners are awarded variances[8] from the strict application of the zoning ordinance.

Many of the intersecting laws and regulations of higher levels of government are adopted, in the first instance, either to influence or remedy the consequences of local land use planning and regulation. This is true particularly in the area of environmental law where state and federal agencies shape and sometimes preempt local decision-making in the interest of protecting shared natural resources such as rivers and aquifers. Nonetheless, it is the decisions made by boards and agencies at the village, town and city level that constitute the primary regulatory influence on the land.

Library References:

West's Key No. Digests, Zoning and Planning ⚖1–14.

§ 16.4 Local Land Use Law—Delegated Authority

Pursuant to the New York Constitution, the State Legislature is given the authority to pass laws to protect the public health, safety, morals and general welfare of the people.[1] In the wisdom of the Legislature, significant authority to regulate land use in the public interest has been delegated to the local level: the over 1,600 villages, towns and cities in the state.[2] The state has retained authority to regulate certain aspects

§ 16.3

1. *See* Chapter 15 "Environmental Law," *supra*.
2. *See* Chapter 4 "Administrative Law," *supra*.
3. *See* Chapter 3 "Municipal Law," *supra*.
4. *See infra*, § 16.103.
5. *See infra*, § 16.96.
6. *See infra*, § 16.96.
7. *See infra*, § 16.113.
8. *See infra*, §§ 16.73, 16.82.

§ 16.4

1. N.Y. State Constitution Art. III, § 1.
2. *See infra*, §§ 16.27, 16.34.

of land use,[3] delegated some authority to county or regional agencies,[4] and in certain instances has shared land use authority with local governments.[5] Occasionally, the Legislature withdraws this delegated authority by enacting legislation that preempts the local role.[6]

Villages, towns and cities therefore have no inherent authority to control land use, but are limited by the authority specifically delegated to them.[7] A provision enacted by a local legislature "for which legislative delegation of power cannot be found is *ultra vires* and void."[8] The authority to enact zoning regulations is derived from and limited by the enabling acts.[9] This delegated authority is broadly interpreted by the courts, however, when reasonably exercised at the local level.[10]

Library References:

West's Key No. Digests, Zoning and Planning ⚖=5.1.

§ 16.5 Local Land Use Law—Enabling Acts

The structure of the enabling acts that delegate land use authority is similar for all three types of local governments in New York: villages, towns and cities.

First, local governments are authorized to regulate the development of the land:

> For the purpose of promoting the health, safety, morals or the general welfare of the community, the town board is hereby empowered by ordinance to regulate and restrict the height, number of stories and size of buildings and other structures, the percentage of lot that may be occupied, the size of yards, courts, and other open spaces, the density of population, and the location and use of

---

3. N.Y. State Uniform Fire Prevention and Building Code Act, Executive Law § 377, provides that its extensive provisions shall regulate the construction of buildings throughout the state.

4. *See* General Municipal Law § 239–m providing for county and regional agency review of local land use decisions and Executive Law §§ 800–820 creating the Adirondack Park Agency.

5. *See* ECL § 24–1509. Local governments are free to regulate freshwater wetlands so long as such regulations are "at least as protective of freshwater wetlands as the regulations in effect pursuant to the provisions of" the State Freshwater Wetlands Act. *Id.*

6. *See infra*, § 16.24.

7. Kamhi v. Planning Bd. of Yorktown, 59 N.Y.2d 385, 465 N.Y.S.2d 865, 452 N.E.2d 1193 (1983).

8. FGL & L Property Corp. v. City of Rye, 66 N.Y.2d 111, 115, 495 N.Y.S.2d 321, 324, 485 N.E.2d 986, 989 (1985).

9. Barron v. Getnick, 107 A.D.2d 1017, 486 N.Y.S.2d 528 (4th Dep't 1985).

10. Rodgers v. Village of Tarrytown, 302 N.Y. 115, 96 N.E.2d 731 (1951): "[a] decision as to how a community shall be zoned or rezoned, as to how various properties shall be classified or reclassified, rests with the local legislative body; its judgment and determination will be conclusive, beyond interference from the courts, unless shown to be arbitrary." 302 N.Y. at 121, 96 N.E.2d at 733.

buildings, structures and land for trade, industry, residence or other purposes.[1]

The language of the statutes delegating this authority to cities is different but of similar effect.[2] Villages are similarly empowered, but may act only by local law, not by ordinance.[3]

Second, the enabling acts authorize local governments to regulate land use by dividing the municipality into districts, within which uniform zoning regulations apply:

> [T]he board of trustees may divide the village into districts of such number, shape and area as may be deemed best suited to carry out the purposes of this article; and within such districts it may regulate and restrict the erection, construction, reconstruction, alteration, repair or use of buildings, structures or land. All such regulations shall be uniform for each class or kind of buildings throughout each district but the regulations in one district may differ from those in another.[4]

Nearly identical language is used to empower towns to create and regulate zoning districts.[5] The statute delegating this authority to cities uses different language but with similar effect.[6]

Third, the statutes use nearly identical language to authorize villages, towns and cities to adopt comprehensive plans.[7] Further, they require zoning regulations to be in accordance with those plans.[8]

Library References:

West's Key No. Digests, Zoning and Planning ⚖5.1.

§ 16.6 Local Land Use Law—Enabling Acts—New York City

When the authority of cities to enact and enforce land use regulations is discussed in this chapter, citations are to the General Cities Law, frequently to Article 5–A. That article, and other provisions of this law, specify that they do not apply to cities having a population in excess of

§ 16.5

1. Town Law § 261.
2. General City Law § 20(24).

PRACTICE POINTER: City charters may contain specific provisions dealing with zoning authority. The original city charter, approved by the New York State Legislature, may add to the city's authority under the enabling act; local amendments to the charter may alter, but not add to, the zoning authority of the city.

3. Village Law § 7–700. When this chapter refers to a zoning "ordinance" of a village it uses that term in its non-technical sense. Villages may adopt zoning provisions only by local law.

4. Village Law § 7–702.
5. Town Law § 262.
6. General City Law §§ 20(24), (25).
7. Village Law § 7–722, Town Law § 272–a, General City Law § 28–a. See infra, § 16.11.
8. Village Law § 7–704, Town Law § 261, General City Law § 20(25). See infra, § 16.13.

§ 16.6 LAND USE LAW

one million.[1] New York City is the only city in this state exceeding that threshold and many of the matters discussed in this chapter are governed by provisions of its city charter and adopted regulations.

The adoption and amendment of New York City zoning provisions, for example, are regulated under the charter.[2] Many of the procedures relating to the implementation of zoning regulations are contained in the Uniform Land Use Review Procedure, also found in the charter.[3] Applications for variances and special permits in New York City are made to the Board of Standards and Appeals,[4] created by the charter.[5]

Responsibility for planning for the orderly growth and development of the city is delegated to the City Planning Commission.[6] This responsibility is shared with community and borough boards that may be involved in initiating plans and must be involved in reviewing them.[7] New York City has promulgated its own regulations governing the environmental review of the actions of its agencies.[8] The alteration or demolition of historic properties is regulated under the city's administrative code.[9] Its Landmarks Preservation Commission was created under the charter.[10]

§ 16.7 Local Land Use Law—Home Rule Authority

In addition to state delegated authority, Article IX of the New York Constitution specifically grants various "home rule" powers to local governments.[1] It specifies, for example, that "every local government shall have power to adopt and amend local laws not inconsistent with the provisions of this constitution or any general law relating to its property, affairs or government."[2] Since this article was adopted in 1964, the

§ 16.6

1. General City Law § 81–e.
2. *See* New York City Charter § 200.
3. New York City Charter § 197–c.
4. *See* New York City Charter § 668.
5. New York City Charter § 659.
6. New York City Charter § 192.
7. *Id.*
8. Executive Order No. 91, August 24, 1977.
9. N.Y.C. Admin. Code §§ 25–301 *et seq.*
10. New York City Charter § 3020.

§ 16.7

1. N.Y. State Constitution Art. IX.
2. N.Y. State Constitution Art. IX. at § 2(c)(1). **CAVEAT:** Section 10 of the Municipal Home Rule law states that "[e]very local government shall also have the power to adopt and amend local laws where and to the extent that its legislative body has power to act by ordinance, resolution, rule or regulation." Municipal Home Rule Law § 10(2). Since towns and cities may adopt zoning provisions by ordinance and villages by local law, all three may adopt such provisions by local law. This statute further prescribes the procedures by which local laws must be adopted with its own provisions for notice and hearing. *Id.* § 20. Still further, the statute authorizes towns and villages to supersede the town and village law as it applies to them. *Id.* § 10(1)(ii)(d), (e). Where a village, town or city adopts or amends a zoning provision in a manner that does not conform to the provisions prescribed in the enabling sections of the village, town or city law, it is necessary to determine whether it followed the provisions of Section 20 of the Municipal Home Rule law or, in the case of a village or town, whether it followed the procedures prescribed by a local law that specifically su-

courts have narrowly construed the authority granted to local governments by limiting the scope of the term "property, affairs or government." Conversely, the courts have increased the scope of issues that are deemed of "statewide concern" where the State Legislature has evidenced a clear authority to act and have held that the State Legislature has preempted local authority.[3]

Article IX also requires the State Legislature to enact a statute of local governments granting powers to local governments.[4] Under the statute of local governments, villages, towns and cities are given the "power to adopt, amend and repeal zoning regulations"[5] and to "perform comprehensive or other planning work relating to [their] jurisdiction."[6] This statute stipulates that these powers are subject to "such purposes, standards and procedures as the legislature may have heretofore prescribed or may hereafter prescribe."[7] Since the zoning and planning acts do precisely that, it is doubtful that these provisions add greatly to the authority of local governments to regulate land use.

Library References:

West's Key No. Digests, Zoning and Planning ⇒4.

§ 16.8 Local Land Use Law—Home Rule Authority—Flexibility

What constitutes a valid zoning regulation has been the subject of much debate. The restrictive view holds that zoning is a rigid, district bound technique and that a locality is constrained by a literal reading of the enabling statutes.[1] This view asserts, additionally, that zoning can regulate only the "use," not the "user" of property.[2]

The breadth of the statutes delegating zoning authority to local governments and the presumption of validity accorded zoning regulations by the courts[3] have made it possible, however, for localities to create a variety of zoning mechanisms not referred to in the statutes. Until the early 1990s, the statutes did not mention or specifically delegate authority to grant variances, special permits, site plan approv-

---

persedes the provisions of the enabling statutes.

3. J. Nolon, *The Erosion of Home Rule Through the Emergence of State-Interests in Land Use Control*, Pace Env. Law Review, Vol. 10, No. 2, Spring, 1993 at 512–530.

4. N.Y. State Constitution Art. IX, § 2(b)(1).

5. Statute of Local Governments § 10(6).

6. *Id.* at § 10(7).

7. *Id.* at § 10.

§ 16.8

1. *See infra,* § 16.9 discussing the vigorous dissent in Rodgers v. Village of Tarrytown where the Court of Appeals upheld the use of a "floating zone."

2. *See* Dexter v. Town Bd. of Town of Gates, 36 N.Y.2d 102, 365 N.Y.S.2d 506, 324 N.E.2d 870 (1975). "The fundamental rule [is] that zoning deals basically with land use and not with the person who owns or occupies it." *Id.* at 105, 365 N.Y.S.2d at 508, 324 N.E.2d at 871.

3. *See infra,* § 16.18, note 3.

§ 16.8   LAND USE LAW

als, density bonuses, or transferable development rights, all techniques long employed by local governments.[4]

Despite the lack of specifics in the delegating statutes, the courts have upheld an impressive variety of techniques used by local governments that allow them to provide for the orderly development of their communities. The case law has established, for example, that:

1. zoning districts can be created and "float" subject to a request by a qualifying landowner for their application to his property;[5]

2. in proper cases, zoning can specify the attributes of people who can build, own, and live in certain types of developments;[6]

3. rezoning can be conditioned on the proposed development meeting requirements demonstrably within the public interest, but not contained in the ordinance itself;[7]

4. uses can be allowed by special permit, also subject to such conditions;[8]

5. waivers of requirements can be given in the interest of achieving a planned unit development that integrates diverse land uses in an otherwise single-use district;[9] and

6. variances from zoning requirements may be granted if the "spirit" of the law is achieved by them.[10]

These devices have been sustained by the courts particularly when they meet the illusive requirement of being "in accordance with the comprehensive plan."[11]

§ 16.9   Local Land Use Law—Home Rule Authority—Floating Zone

The extent of the implied authority enjoyed by localities to achieve the objective of a balanced and orderly community through zoning became apparent in 1951 when the Court of Appeals decided *Rodgers v.*

---

4. Village Law § 7–712(1), Town Law § 267(1), General City Law § 81–b (defining "variances"); Village Law § 7–725–a(1), Town Law § 274–a(1), General City Law § 27–a (defining "site plan"); Village Law § 7–725–b(1), Town Law § 274–b(1), General City Law § 27–b (defining "special use permit"); Village Law § 7–701(1)(d), Town Law § 261–a(1)(d), General City Law § 20–f (defining "transfer of development rights"); Village Law § 7–703(1)(c), Town Law § 261–b(1)(e), General City Law § 81–d (defining "incentive zoning").

5. *See* Rodgers v. Village of Tarrytown, 302 N.Y. 115, 96 N.E.2d 731 (1951). *See infra*, § 16.9.

6. *See* Maldini v. Ambro, 36 N.Y.2d 481, 369 N.Y.S.2d 385, 330 N.E.2d 403 (1975).

7. *See* Church v. Town of Islip, 8 N.Y.2d 254, 203 N.Y.S.2d 866, 168 N.E.2d 680 (1960).

8. *See* Penny Arcade, Inc. v. Town Bd. of Town of Oyster Bay, 75 A.D.2d 620, 427 N.Y.S.2d 52 (2d Dep't 1980).

9. *See* Ahearn v. Zoning Bd. of App. of Town of Shawangunk, 158 A.D.2d 801, 551 N.Y.S.2d 392 (3d Dep't 1990).

10. *See* Aucello v. Moylan, 60 Misc.2d 1094, 304 N.Y.S.2d 765 (Sup.Ct., Westchester County, 1969).

11. *See infra*, § 16.15.

Village of Tarrytown,[1] which approved a "floating zone" created by the village. In that case, a neighboring owner questioned the validity of amendments to the village zoning ordinance that created a new district permitting multiple-family dwellings in single-family districts.[2]

Tarrytown's floating zone mechanism involved three separate steps to be followed prior to rezoning a parcel of land from single-family to multi-family. First, the village board created a new zoning district. Instead of amending the zoning map to designate these districts, however, the district's boundaries were "to be fixed by amendment of the official building zone map" when future applications for this district were reviewed and approved.[3] Standards specifying the size and physical layout of developments under this zoning were prescribed.[4] Second, the planning board was authorized to review applications from owners of parcels of at least ten acres for the inclusion of their land in the floating multi-family district. Third, upon recommendation of the planning board, the village board would amend the zoning map to include the parcel officially in the district.

At the time, this mechanism was untested and the village board's authority to adopt it was questionable. Nonetheless, it survived a host of challenges. The dissent, for example, argued several points. First, it posited that the "plain language" of the Village Law made it essential that "physical boundaries" be established for the district, that the reference to "districts" or "zones" in the ordinance was meaningless without the creation of specified boundaries.[5] Second, the dissent stressed that the action of the board could not be considered as "in accordance with a comprehensive plan."[6] The floating zone was illegal, in the dissent's view, either as spot-zoning[7] that benefited only private owners, the inappropriate creation of a non-conforming use in an established zone,[8] or a variance[9] awarded improperly by the board of trustees instead of the zoning board of appeals.[10]

The majority disagreed and upheld the floating zone. It stated that "[w]hile stability and regularity are undoubtedly essential to the operation of zoning plans, zoning is by no means static" when "[c]hanged or changing conditions call for changed plans."[11] The court stressed: "[a]

§ 16.9

1. 302 N.Y. 115, 96 N.E.2d 731 (1951).

2. *Id. See infra*, § 16.32 and Village Law § 7–700 requiring regulations to be uniform for each class of buildings throughout each district.

3. 300 N.Y. at 120, 96 N.E.2d at 732.

4. *Id.*, 96 N.E.2d at 732–33. For example, this amended ordinance designated maximum building height, setback requirements and ground area of the plots to be occupied by the buildings. *Id.*

5. *Id.* at 127, 96 N.E.2d at 737.

6. *Id.* at 128, 96 N.E.2d at 737 (quoting Village Law § 7–704).

7. *See infra*, § 16.110.

8. *See infra*, § 16.62.

9. *See infra*, §§ 16.73, 16.82.

10. 300 N.Y. at 128, 96 N.E.2d at 737.

11. *Id.* at 121, 96 N.E.2d at 733. Private interests must bow to public concerns if contrary to such classification since "the power of a village to amend its basic zoning

decision as to how a community shall be zoned or rezoned, as to how various properties shall be classified or reclassified, rests with the local legislative body; its judgment and determination will be conclusive, beyond interference from the courts, unless shown to be arbitrary."[12] Therefore, "[i]f the validity of the legislative classification ... be fairly debatable, the legislative judgment must be allowed to control."[13]

§ 16.10 Local Land Use Law—Summary

Land use law, broadly defined, encompasses the full range of laws and regulations that influence or affect the development and conservation of the land. This law is intensely intergovernmental and interdisciplinary. In land use law there are countless intersections among federal, state, regional and local statutes; it is significantly influenced by other legal regimes such as environmental,[1] administrative[2] and municipal law,[3] to name a few.

Pursuant to the New York Constitution, the State Legislature is given the authority to pass laws to protect the public health, safety, morals and general welfare of the people.[4] In the wisdom of the legislature, significant authority to regulate land use in the public interest, has been delegated to the local level: the over 1,600 villages, towns and cities in the state.[5] The state has retained authority to regulate certain aspects of land use, delegated some authority to county or regional agencies, and in certain instances has shared land use authority with local governments. Occasionally, the legislature withdraws this delegated authority by enacting legislation that preempts the local role.

Through the adoption of zoning ordinances, local governments divide their jurisdictions into districts and provide for the uses allowed in, and the development specifications pertaining to, each district, thereby creating a blueprint for the future development of each community. The aggregate effect of these blueprints, when aligned on an inter-municipal basis, is the plan for the future development of the region. These patterns evolve as local boards and agencies review, approve and condition applications for site plans,[6] subdivisions,[7] and special permits;[8] they change as the local legislature rezones discrete areas[9] and as property owners are awarded variances[10] from the strict application of the zoning ordinance.

ordinance ... to promote the general welfare cannot be questioned." Id.

12. Id.
13. Id.

§ 16.10

1. See Chapter 15 "Environmental Law," supra.
2. See Chapter 4 "Administrative Law," supra.
3. See Chapter 3 "Municipal Law," supra.
4. N.Y. State Constitution Art. III, § 1.
5. See supra, § 16.4 and infra § 16.27.
6. See infra, § 16.103.
7. See infra, § 16.96.
8. See infra, § 16.90.
9. See infra, § 16.113.
10. See infra, §§ 16.73, 16.82.

§ 16.11 Comprehensive Plan

The enabling statutes require that the provisions of zoning ordinances must be "in accordance with a comprehensive plan"[1] or "in accord[ance] with a well considered plan."[2] The Court of Appeals has stated that planning "is the essence of zoning."[3] Comprehensive planning is society's insurance that the public welfare is served by land use regulation.[4]

In 1922, the U.S. Department of Commerce published a model statute, the Standard State Zoning Enabling Act, to promote zoning.[5] The model act, with certain variations, was adopted by most states as a method of encouraging and guiding their municipalities in adopting zoning ordinances.[6] Zoning, according to one view, was intended to be an end in itself.[7] However, the drafters of the zoning enabling act suggested that more was needed.[8]

A second model act, the Standard City Planning Enabling Act,[9] promulgated in 1928, promoted the adoption of a local comprehensive land use plan as a document separate and distinct from a zoning ordinance.[10] This act, and its adoption by the states, gave rise in some

---

§ 16.11

1. Village Law § 7–704, Town Law § 263.

2. General City Law § 20(25).

3. Udell v. Haas, 21 N.Y.2d 463, 469, 288 N.Y.S.2d 888, 893, 235 N.E.2d 897, 900–01 (1968). The court also references "[t]he almost universal statutory requirement that zoning conform to a 'well considered plan.'" *Id.*

4. *Id.*, 288 N.Y.S.2d at 893–94, 235 N.E.2d at 900–01.

5. The 1926 version of the Standard State Zoning Enabling Act (U.S. Dep't of Commerce) is reprinted in E. Ziegler, Jr., 5 *Rathkopf's The Law of Zoning and Planning*, app. A. (1988). R. Fishman ed., *Housing for All Under Law* 328 (1978).

6. *Housing for All Under Law* at 331. The Standard City Planning Enabling Act ("SPEA") defined the purpose of the master plan as:

> Guiding and accomplishing a coordinated, adjusted, and harmonious development of the municipality and its environs which will, in accordance with present and future needs, best promote health, safety, order, morals, convenience, prosperity, and general welfare as well as efficiency and economy in the process of development, including, among other things, adequate provision for traffic, the provision of safety from fire and other dangers, adequate provisions for light and air, the promotion of good civic design, wise and efficient expenditure of public funds, and the adequate provision of public utilities and other public requirements.

Id. at 329 (quoting SPEA § 7).

7. The "unitary" view of zoning holds that the zoning ordinance itself contains comprehensive planning principles and can exist independently from a comprehensive plan without violating the legal requirement that zoning be "in accordance with" a comprehensive plan. *Housing for All Under Law* at 332.

8. Alfred Bettman, *The Present State of Court Decisions on Zoning*, 2 City Plan. 24, 26–27 (1926):

> By zoning is meant the comprehensive zone plan based on a comprehensive survey; and if the zone plan be part of a more comprehensive city plan, it derives from that fact an additional element of reasonableness and therefore has additional constitutional support.

Id. at 34.

9. Standard City Planning Enabling Act (U.S. Dep't of Commerce 1928).

10. D. Arnold *et al.* eds., *The Practice of Local Government Planning* 40 (1979).

quarters to the notion that comprehensive land use planning should precede the zoning ordinance and serve as its predicate.[11]

In the promulgation of the model acts and the progress of local land use regulation, however, zoning came first. Many states adopted the Standard City Planning Enabling Act, but after they had created the legal framework for zoning.[12] Most failed in any meaningful way to prescribe how zoning and planning were to be integrated. In New York, for example, state statutes require that zoning regulations conform to a comprehensive plan;[13] however, they do not require localities to adopt comprehensive plans.[14] Where local governments have not adopted comprehensive plans, or have failed to keep them current, an enigmatic situation is created which has required the courts to be creative in discovering and interpreting the "required," but often missing, incomplete or out-of-date, comprehensive plan.

Library References:

West's Key No. Digests, Zoning and Planning ⊂⇒30.

§ 16.12 Comprehensive Plan—Judicial Definition

Where local governments have not adopted a comprehensive plan, or have not kept it current, the judiciary has been called upon to confront the enigma of statutes which require zoning regulations to conform to the comprehensive plan but do not require localities to adopt such a plan. Judicial decisions have provided the following guidelines:

1. zoning can be legal even in the absence of a written plan;[1]

2. the statutes are satisfied if, implicit in the zoning ordinance itself, there is evidence of rational planning;[2]

---

11. The danger is that [zoning] may be considered a substitute for city planning and that, a zoning plan having been adopted, enthusiasm and interest may die out. Zoning is not a substitute for a city plan; it is an essential part of a comprehensive plan.
H. Lewis, 1 *Planning the Modern City*, 261–62 (1949).

12. *Housing for All Under Law* at 49.

13. Village Law § 7–704, Town Law § 263, General City Law § 20(25). These provide that zoning "regulations shall be made in accordance with a comprehensive plan." The provisions in the General City Law require that the regulations shall be "in accord with a well considered plan." General City Law § 20(25).

14. Village Law § 7–722(7), Town Law § 272–a(7), General City Law § 28–a(7), (local legislative body "may" adopt a comprehensive plan).

§ 16.12

1. *See* Daum v. Meade, 65 Misc.2d 572, 318 N.Y.S.2d 199 (Sup.Ct., Nassau County, 1971), aff'd 37 A.D.2d 691, 323 N.Y.S.2d 670 (2d Dep't 1971). The plaintiff challenged an action as "not made in accord with a 'comprehensive plan' and argued that the term 'comprehensive plan' as stated in Section 263 of the Town Law meant the 'master plan' that was commissioned by the Town Board." The court disagreed, stating that the plan can "be garnered from any available source." 65 Misc.2d at 576, 318 N.Y.S.2d at 204.

2. *See* Randolph v. Town of Brookhaven, 37 N.Y.2d 544, 375 N.Y.S.2d 315, 337 N.E.2d 763 (1975).

3. once a plan is adopted, it does not have to be kept current; in such cases, courts will not require "slavish servitude to any particular comprehensive plan," but look rather for "comprehensiveness of planning;"[3] and

4. in the absence of any plan or the presence of an out-dated one, courts will "examin[e] all relevant evidence" of comprehensive planning found in previous land use decisions of the locality, including the zoning ordinance itself.[4]

In *Udell v. Haas*,[5] a property owner contested the reclassification of his property from a business to a residential use by the village. The court began its analysis by looking for the village's comprehensive plan. It understood that "the comprehensive plan is the essence of zoning."[6]

The court noted two defects in land use regulation that occur when comprehensive planning is missing. The first is that "[w]ithout [a plan], there can be no rational allocation of land use. It is the insurance that the public welfare is being served and that zoning does not become nothing more than just a Gallup poll."[7] The second is that "the 'comprehensive plan' protects the landowner from arbitrary restrictions on the use of his property which can result from the pressures which outraged voters can bring to bear on public officials."[8]

The village had not adopted a "comprehensive master plan;" therefore, there was no single document that could constitute a "comprehensive plan."[9] As a result, the court was forced to deal with the enigmatic nature of the New York State land use system. Since planning is not required, and what constitutes a plan was not specified by law, the court had to define a judicial strategy for determining whether this rezoning conformed, as required, to a comprehensive plan.[10]

This was the moment in the historical development of New York's planning law for the highest court to determine how to interpret the "in accordance with" requirement. Did the zoning ordinance itself constitute the plan?[11] Did zoning have to conform to a separate, independent,

---

3. *See* Town of Bedford v. Village of Mount Kisco, 33 N.Y.2d 178, 188, 351 N.Y.S.2d 129, 136, 306 N.E.2d 155, 159 (1973).

4. Udell v. Haas, 21 N.Y.2d 463, 471–72, 288 N.Y.S.2d 888, 895–96, 235 N.E.2d 897, 902 (1968).

5. 21 N.Y.2d 463, 288 N.Y.S.2d 888, 235 N.E.2d 897 (1968).

6. *Id.* at 469, 288 N.Y.S.2d at 893, 235 N.E.2d at 900–01. The court also references "[t]he almost universal statutory requirement that zoning conform to a 'well considered plan.'" *Id.*, 288 N.Y.S.2d at 893, 235 N.E.2d at 900.

7. *Id.*, 288 N.Y.S.2d at 893–94, 235 N.E.2d at 901.

8. *Id.*, 288 N.Y.S.2d at 894, 235 N.E.2d at 901. "[T]here is a danger that zoning, considered as a self-contained activity rather than as a means to a broader end, may tyrannize individual property owners." *Id.*

9. 21 N.Y.2d at 472, 288 N.Y.S.2d at 896, 235 N.E.2d at 902.

10. *Id.* at 472–76, 288 N.Y.S.2d at 896–99, 235 N.E.2d at 902–05.

11. For an early New York case taking this view, *see* Harris v. Village of Dobbs Ferry, 208 App.Div. 853, 204 N.Y.S. 325 (2d Dep't 1924).

§ 16.12 LAND USE LAW Ch. 16

comprehensive planning document?[12] Was evidence of comprehensive planning in the adoption of zoning enough to satisfy the requirement?

The Court of Appeals began its analysis by "examining all relevant evidence."[13] In the absence of an adopted plan, it looked at the zoning ordinance and zoning map for evidence of comprehensive planning. It also reviewed a 1958 zoning amendment that was entitled a "Development Policy" for the village. This policy articulated a vision of the village as a low-density, single-family community with commercial development only in peripheral areas. The plaintiff's land was in such an area and had been classified by the zoning ordinance, prior to the contested rezoning, as business property.[14]

Having discovered the plan for the community in this piecemeal fashion, adopting in the process the "evidence of comprehensive planning" standard for interpreting the "in accordance with" requirement,[15] it was not hard for the court to determine that the rezoning, which diminished plaintiff's property value by sixty percent, was not in conformance with the comprehensive plan.[16] In constitutional terms, the land use action of the village violated substantive due process;[17] it was not designed to accomplish a valid public objective.[18] In statutory terms, the action was beyond the powers of the village since it did not conform to the plan.[19] "Hence [the] ordinance ... must be held to be *ultra vires*[20] as not meeting the requirements of ... the Village Law that zoning be 'in conformance with a comprehensive plan.'"[21]

In *Town of Bedford v. Village of Mount Kisco*,[22] Bedford challenged Mount Kisco's adoption of a resolution rezoning a parcel from one-family residential housing to six-story residential housing.[23] The parcel in

---

12. *See* Fasano v. Board of County Comm'rs of Washington County, 264 Or. 574, 507 P.2d 23 (Or.1973) superseded by statute as stated in Menges v. Board of County Commissioners, 44 Or.App. 603, 606 P.2d 681 (1980).

13. 21 N.Y.2d at 471, 288 N.Y.S.2d at 895, 235 N.E.2d at 902. Development policies "may be garnered from any available source, most especially the master plan of the community, if any has been adopted, the zoning law itself and the zoning map." *Id.* at 472, 288 N.Y.S.2d at 896, 235 N.E.2d at 902.

14. *Id.* at 466–67, 288 N.Y.S.2d at 891–92, 235 N.E.2d at 899.

15. *Id.* at 472, 288 N.Y.S.2d at 896, 235 N.E.2d at 902. This interpretation of the "in accordance with" requirement is that there must exist evidence of comprehensive planning in the adoption of zoning, which would satisfy the requirement.

16. 21 N.Y.2d at 476, 288 N.Y.S.2d at 899, 235 N.E.2d at 904–05.

17. *See infra,* § 16.18.

18. 21 N.Y.2d at 475–76, 288 N.Y.S.2d at 898–99, 235 N.E.2d at 904–05.

19. *Id.* at 476, 288 N.Y.S.2d at 899, 235 N.E.2d at 905.

20. The Latin phrase *"ultra vires"* (beyond the power) is frequently used by the courts to characterize a local land use regulation taken outside of the local government's authority. *See* Moriarty v. Planning Board, 119 A.D.2d 188, 506 N.Y.S.2d 184 (2d Dep't 1986).

21. 21 N.Y.2d at 476, 288 N.Y.S.2d at 899, 235 N.E.2d at 905.

22. 33 N.Y.2d 178, 351 N.Y.S.2d 129, 306 N.E.2d 155 (1973).

23. *Id.* at 182, 351 N.Y.S.2d at 130–31, 306 N.E.2d at 156.

question was in an isolated northern section of Mount Kisco, bounded on three sides by Bedford.[24]

The town challenged this zoning change as "arbitrary and capricious," pointing out that it was inconsistent with a comprehensive plan adopted by Mount Kisco in 1958.[25] The matter had been disapproved by Mount Kisco's own planning board and had been objected to by the county planning department, as well as by neighboring landowners.[26] The issue before the Court of Appeals was whether, as a matter of law, the decision of the village board was "arbitrary and capricious."[27] It found that although there had been no formal amendment to the comprehensive plan since 1958, there were a number of factors that justified the zoning amendment.[28] The zoning resolution itself included a finding that changes in the area since 1958 rendered the newly adopted use in conformity with that plan.[29]

The court stated that "zoning changes must indeed be consonant with [the] total planning strategy, reflecting consideration of the needs of the community."[30] Thus, "[w]hat is mandated is that there be [current] comprehensiveness of planning, rather than special interest, irrational ad hocery."[31] Most importantly, the court stressed that "[t]he obligation is support of comprehensive planning, not slavish servitude to any particular comprehensive plan."[32] Therefore, the proper standard is "current comprehensiveness of planning."[33] Given this standard, it was not an arbitrary determination by the village board of trustees to consider the welfare and economic stability of Mount Kisco as its first concern.[34]

§ 16.13 Comprehensive Plan—Statutory Definition

The judicial definitions of the community's "comprehensive plan" were all framed before the enabling acts were amended to add a

---

24. *Id.* at 183, 351 N.Y.S.2d at 132, 306 N.E.2d at 157.

CAVEAT: The village's rezoning exemplifies the external impacts that one municipality's land use actions can have on another. This decision also illustrates how frustrating it is for impacted communities, like Bedford in this instance, as they struggle to exercise any influence over their neighbors' decisions.

25. *Id.* at 182–83, 186, 351 N.Y.S.2d at 131, 135, 306 N.E.2d at 156, 159.

26. *Id.* at 186, 351 N.Y.S.2d at 134, 306 N.E.2d at 158.

27. *Id.*

28. *Id.* at 189, 351 N.Y.S.2d at 136, 306 N.E.2d at 160. The village board had clearly stated its findings in an adopted, formal resolution. These findings contained the public interest justifications for its action. They included the need for revitalization of the affected area, the increased growth and population in the community, the need for housing to serve increased jobs in the area, and the lack of adverse effects upon the neighborhood. *Id.* at 187, 351 N.Y.S.2d at 135, 306 N.E.2d at 159.

29. *Id.*

30. *Id.* at 188, 351 N.Y.S.2d at 136, 306 N.E.2d at 159.

31. *Id.*

32. *Id.*

33. *Id.* at 188, 351 N.Y.S.2d at 136, 306 N.E.2d at 160.

34. *Id.* at 189, 351 N.Y.S.2d at 136–37, 306 N.E.2d at 160. Moreover, "there was nothing in the record [to] suggest ... the action taken resulted from favoritism for the owners or any other extraneous influence." *Id.* at 189, 351 N.Y.S.2d at 137, 306 N.E.2d at 160.

statutory definition.[1] The statutory definitions were designed to encourage villages, towns and cities to adopt comprehensive plans. They did so with the following language:

> Among the most important powers and duties granted by the legislature to a [local] government is the authority and responsibility to undertake [local] comprehensive planning and to regulate land use for the purpose of protecting the public health, safety and general welfare of its citizens. The development and enactment by the [local] government of a [local] comprehensive plan which can be readily identified, and is available for use by the public, is in the best interest of the people of each [locality]. It is the intent of the legislature to encourage, but not to require, the preparation and adoption of a comprehensive plan.[2]

These amendments effect several important changes in the statutes. In addition to defining the comprehensive plan, they provide guidance to localities in the preparation of their plans by listing 15 topics that may be included in the plan. Among these topics are a consideration of regional needs and affordable housing, often noted as critical defects in local planning and zoning.[3] The amendments state that, in addition to zoning provisions, all "land use regulations must be in accordance with a comprehensive plan."[4] Land use regulations are defined to include "zoning, subdivision, special use permit or site plan regulation or any other regulation which prescribes the appropriate use of property or the scale, location, and intensity of development."[5] Localities are instructed to provide, "as a component of such proposed comprehensive plan, the

---

§ 16.13

1. Village Law § 7–722(2)(a), Town Law § 272–a(2)(a), General City Law § 28–a(3)(a).

2. Village Law § 7–722(1)(b), (c), (h), Town Law § 272–a(1)(b), (c), (h), General City Law § 28–a(2)(b), (c), (h).

3. *See infra*, § 16.123. Localities are encouraged, as well, to consider the official plans of other government units and agencies within the region. Village Law § 7–722(3)(b), (h), Town Law § 272–a(3)(b), (h), General City Law § 28–a(4)(b),(h).

PRACTICE POINTER: The amendments note that one effect of the adoption of a comprehensive plan is that "[a]ll plans for capital projects of another governmental agency on land included in the [local] comprehensive plan adopted pursuant to this section shall take such plan into consideration." This language appears to give local comprehensive plans some extraterritorial effect, for example, on the capital planning activities of state departments and agencies.

4. Village Law § 7–722(11), Town Law § 272–a(11), General City Law § 28–a(12). The specific language of this subsection is: "Effect of adoption of the [local] comprehensive plan. All [local] land use regulations must be in accordance with a comprehensive plan adopted pursuant to this section." *Id.*%

CAVEAT: The apparent effect of this language is to require all subsequent local land use regulations, as defined, to conform to any comprehensive plan adopted after the effective date of the subsection, July 1, 1995. A separate subsection of these amendments provides that they shall not "be deemed to affect the status or validity of existing master plans, comprehensive plans, or land use plans." Village Law § 7–722(1)(h), Town Law § 272–a(1)(h), General City Law § 28–a(2)(h).

5. Village Law § 7–722(2)(b), Town Law § 272–a(2)(b), General City Law § 28–a(3)(b).

maximum intervals at which the adopted plan shall be reviewed."[6]

§ 16.14 Comprehensive Plan—Preparation and Adoption

The local legislature may prepare a proposed comprehensive plan.[1] Alternatively, if authorized by resolution of the legislature, the planning board, or a special board consisting of one or more members of the planning board and other members appointed by the legislature, may prepare a proposed comprehensive plan.[2]

During the preparation phase, whether conducted by the legislature, the planning board or a special board, one or more public hearings must be held along with other meetings necessary to assure full opportunity for citizen participation.[3] When the plan is proposed by the planning board or a special board, that body must adopt a resolution containing its recommendations to the legislature regarding the plan.[4]

If the plan is prepared by the planning board or a special board, then the legislature must hold a public hearing within 90 days of receiving the board's recommendations on the proposed plan.[5] When the plan is prepared by the legislature or a special board, it must be submitted to the planning board for review and recommendation before action on the plan is taken by the legislature.[6] Before adoption, a proposed plan must be referred to the county, metropolitan or regional planning agency for review and recommendation.[7] The plan may be adopted by the local legislature by resolution.[8] These procedures apply equally to the preparation and adoption of amendments to a comprehensive plan.

§ 16.15 Comprehensive Plan—Protects Zoning Against Challenge

Dur-Bar Realty Co. v. City of Utica[1] illustrates how compliance with a comprehensive plan will protect burdensome land regulations from

6. Village Law § 7-722(10), Town Law § 272-a(10), General City Law § 28-a(11).

§ 16.14

1. Village Law § 7-722(4), Town Law § 272-a(4), General City Law § 28-a(5).

2. *Id. See* Village Law § 7-722(2)(c), Town Law § 272-a(2)(c), General City Law § 28-a(3)(c) defining "special board."

3. Village Law § 7-722(6), Town Law § 272-a(6), General City Law § 28-a(7).

4. Village Law § 7-722(4)(b), Town Law § 272-a(4), General City Law § 28-a(5).

5. Village Law § 7-722(6)(b), Town Law § 272-a(6)(b), General City Law § 28-a(7)(b).

6. Village Law § 7-722(5)(b), Town Law § 272-a(5)(b), General City Law § 28-a(6)(b).

7. *Id. See also,* General Municipal Law § 239-m.

8. Village Law § 7-722(7), Town Law § 272-a(7), General City Law § 28-a(8).

§ 16.15

1. 57 A.D.2d 51, 394 N.Y.S.2d 913 (4th Dep't 1977).

§ 16.15   LAND USE LAW   Ch. 16

challenge. In *Dur-Bar*, the plaintiff sought to invalidate portions of the city zoning ordinance that created a "Land Conservation District."[2] The subject parcel was located completely within the flood plain of a river classified as a "Land Conservation District" by the city zoning ordinance.[3] The plaintiff made two applications for special permits, but both were denied because the location within the flood plain required large amounts of landfill.[4] Subsequently, the plaintiff brought suit, claiming that the ordinance was not "in accord with a well considered plan."[5]

The pivotal issue for the appellate division was whether the denial of the special permit furthered the "well considered plan." The court found the city ordinance to be "comprehensive ... containing detailed use provisions and a carefully drawn map" that demonstrated "orderly and painstaking forethought."[6] The ordinance also contained evidence that it was "based on the Master Plan for the City of Utica."[7] The "Land Conservation District" was created after carefully assessing the character of the land in light of protecting the public from hazards that would result from "intensive development" of the area.[8] The district presented a number of problems, such as drainage and topography, that could have jeopardized the health and safety of the community. In addition, adequate standards existed to guide the Board in issuing special permits.[9] The court held that where adequate standards exist in issuing special permits for specific areas to further the comprehensive planning strategy of the community, the zoning ordinance will not be invalidated for

2. *Id.* at 52, 394 N.Y.S.2d at 915.

3. *Id.* Utica's ordinance created fourteen zoning districts. The "Land Conservation District" permitted only limited special uses: (1) farm and other agricultural operations; (2) parks, golf courses, athletic facilities; (3) essential services; (4) disposal facilities and landfill operations; and (5) marinas. *Id.* at 52–53, 394 N.Y.S.2d at 915.

4. *Id.* at 53, 394 N.Y.S.2d at 915. This required a permit from the New York Department of Environmental Conservation, but this agency advised the planning board that the permit would never be issued due to the location of the parcels within the flood plain. *Id. See also,* Chapter 15 "Environmental Law," *supra*.

5. *Id.* at 53, 394 N.Y.S.2d at 915–16 (quoting General City Law § 20(25)).

6. *Id.* at 54–55, 394 N.Y.S.2d at 916.

7. *Id.*

8. *Id.* at 54–55, 394 N.Y.S.2d at 916.

CAVEAT: The principle established in Dur–Bar may not extend too far beyond the facts of the case. *See* Marshall v. Village of Wappingers Falls, 28 A.D.2d 542, 542, 279 N.Y.S.2d 654, 655–56 (2d Dep't 1967) (holding that regulating development by special permit in a Planned Residential District is not comprehensive planning, but simply a procedure providing for decisions on a lot-by-lot basis). The Dur–Bar court distinguished this case because the character of the district in Wappingers Falls was not so unusual in topography or location as to justify special use permits. The Wappingers Falls procedure was a substitute for "comprehensive planning," while the procedure used in Utica "was chosen in furtherance of comprehensive planning." 57 A.D.2d at 55, 394 N.Y.S.2d at 916–17.

9. 57 A.D.2d at 55–56, 394 N.Y.S.2d at 917. The proposed use was required to be

'designed, located, and ... be operated [so] that the public health, safety, welfare, and convenience will be protected'; that the use not substantially injure the value of the neighboring property; that it be compatible with adjoining development and the proposed character of the district; and that it conform to 'all applicable regulations governing the district where located.'

Id. at 56, 394 N.Y.S.2d at 917.

failure to conform to a well considered plan.[10]

Other cases illustrate the point that conformance with a comprehensive plan or evidence of comprehensive planning attending the adoption of restrictive zoning provisions help to insulate them from attack. This was apparent in a case challenging a town's adoption of an ordinance requiring mobile home lots to be at least one-acre in size.[11] The court stated that "the requirements of the enabling statute are met if implicit in the ordinance there is the element of planning which is both rational and consistent with the basic land use policies of the community."[12] In another case, the court upheld a village's creation of a unique multi-family zone against a charge that it constituted illegal spot-zoning, finding that it conformed to the comprehensive plan.[13] The relevant inquiry was not "whether the particular zoning under attack consist[ed] of areas fixed within larger areas of different use, but whether it was accomplished for the benefit of individual owners rather than pursuant to a comprehensive plan for the general welfare of the community."[14]

In two other cases, the reasonableness of a controversial mixed-use zoning ordinance was upheld because there was evidence of forethought in planning,[15] and a major rezoning withstood the attack of the neighbors because there was evidence that there was a comprehensive planning rationale for the approval.[16] In a final illustrative case,[17] the continued residential zoning of plaintiff's land in an area bounded on two sides by commercial and industrial zoning was upheld because the plaintiff did "not demonstrate that the Town ha[d] so deviated from its original plan that a comprehensive plan [was] no longer in existence."[18]

§ 16.16 Comprehensive Plan—Summary

The enabling statutes require that the provisions of zoning ordinances must be "in accordance with a comprehensive plan" or "in accordance with a well considered plan."[1] Where localities have not adopted a comprehensive plan, or not kept it current, the courts will examine all of the land use policies and actions of the municipality, including the zoning ordinance itself, for evidence of the comprehensive plan to which zoning actions must conform.

---

10. Id. at 54–55, 394 N.Y.S.2d at 916–17.

11. McBride v. Town of Forestburgh, 54 A.D.2d 396, 388 N.Y.S.2d 940 (3d Dep't 1976).

12. Id.

13. Rodgers v. Tarrytown, 302 N.Y. 115, 96 N.E.2d 731 (1951). See supra, § 16.9.

14. Id. at 124, 96 N.E.2d at 735.

15. Randolph v. Town of Brookhaven, 37 N.Y.2d 544, 375 N.Y.S.2d 315, 337 N.E.2d 763 (1975).

16. Place v. Hack, 34 Misc.2d 777, 230 N.Y.S.2d 583 (Sup.Ct., Wayne County, 1962).

17. Tilles Investment Co. v. Town of Huntington, 74 N.Y.2d 885, 547 N.Y.S.2d 835, 547 N.E.2d 90 (1989).

18. Id. See J. Nolon, *Comprehensive Land Use Planning: Learning How and Where to Grow*, Pace Law Review, Vol. 13, No. 2, Fall 1993 at 351.

§ 16.16

1. See supra, § 16.13.

The statutes now encourage villages, towns and cities to adopt comprehensive plans. While adoption of a plan is not mandatory, the amendments provide guidance to localities in the preparation of plans by listing fifteen topics that may be included.[2]

§ 16.17 Substantive Limits—Illustrative Case

There are several legal doctrines that limit the authority of local governments to enact and enforce land use regulations. The first of these is substantive due process which requires that such regulations serve a legitimate public purpose.[1] Secondly, the administrative process by which regulations are adopted and enforced must meet the requirements of procedural due process.[2] Third, by classifying land uses, dividing land into districts and regulating it accordingly, local land use regulations may raise equal protection problems.[3] Fourth, since local governments in New York may exercise only those powers delegated to them by the State Legislature, land use regulations may be attacked as *ultra vires* if the action of the municipality is not undertaken pursuant to specific legislative authority.[4] Fifth, local land use regulations must not effect a taking of private property without just compensation in violation of the "takings" provisions of the state and federal constitutions.[5] Sixth, the doctrine of vested rights limits the authority of municipalities in certain cases to impose regulations on existing investments in land development.[6] Seventh, local land use regulations are not permitted to control matters whose regulation has been preempted by the State Legislature.[7] Finally, local regulations must not abridge First Amendment freedoms of expression and the exercise of religion.[8]

In *Udell v. Haas*,[9] the seminal case in New York that defined the comprehensive plan and its importance to the validation of zoning actions, the Court of Appeals explored four substantive limits on the exercise of local zoning authority. The plaintiff complained that the rezoning of his property was *ultra vires* and violated his right to equal protection of the law and procedural and substantive due process.

In statutory terms, the court held that the rezoning of the plaintiff's property was beyond the powers of the village since it did not conform to the local comprehensive plan.[10] "Hence [the] ordinance ... must be held

---

2. See supra, § 16.13.

§ 16.17

1. See infra, § 16.18.
2. See infra, § 16.19.
3. See infra, § 16.20.
4. See infra, §§ 16.21, 16.4.
5. See infra, § 16.22.
6. See infra, § 16.23.
7. See infra, § 16.24.
8. See infra, § 16.25.

9. 21 N.Y.2d 463, 288 N.Y.S.2d 888, 235 N.E.2d 897 (1968). See supra, § 16.11.

10. Id. at 476, 288 N.Y.S.2d at 899, 235 N.E.2d at 905. "Such [zoning] regulations shall be made in accordance with a comprehensive plan.... " Village Law § 7–704, Town Law § 263, General City Law § 20(25). The language in this latter section is similar, but not identical. See supra, § 16.11.

to be *ultra vires*[11] as not meeting the requirements of ... the Village Law that zoning be 'in conformance with a comprehensive plan.' "[12] In constitutional terms, the land use action of the village violated substantive due process; it was not designed to accomplish a valid public objective.[13]

The plaintiff also complained that the reclassification of his land violated his right to equal protection of the law.[14] The court used a narrow inquiry to review this allegation. "The issue is the propriety of the treatment of the subject parcel as compared to neighboring properties."[15] The evidence provided by the plaintiff established that other similarly situated properties were allowed to be used for business uses, leading the court to agree that the rezoning was discriminatory.[16] "Discrimination," said the Court, "is a wrong done to the community's land use control scheme."[17]

The Court also found fault with the process by which the rezoning was accomplished. It wrote, "the process by which a zoning revision is carried out is important in determining ... [its] validity...."[18] The facts showed that the development policies of the community were clear when, on the morning of June 21, 1960, the plaintiff's representative appeared at the village offices with a plan for the business development of the property.[19] That evening, the village planning board recommended a change in zoning from business to residential use.[20] Within a month, the rezoning was accomplished.[21]

The Court characterized this process as a "rush to the statute books,"[22] and found that the rezoning was not "accomplished in a proper, careful and reasonable manner."[23] "The amendment was not the result of a deliberate change in community policy and was enacted without sufficient forethought or planning."[24] This amounted to a violation of procedural guarantees.[25] Planning is more than the substantive result. It is also a process, aptly described by the court as "careful,

---

11. The Latin phrase *"ultra vires"* (beyond the power) is frequently used by the courts to characterize a local land use regulation taken outside of the local government's authority. *See* Moriarty v. Planning Board, 119 A.D.2d 188, 196, 506 N.Y.S.2d 184, 189 (2d Dep't 1986), *infra* § 16.21.

12. 21 N.Y.2d at 476, 288 N.Y.S.2d at 899, 235 N.E.2d at 905. *See supra*, § 16.13.

13. 21 N.Y.2d at 475–76, 288 N.Y.S.2d at 898–99, 235 N.E.2d at 904–05. *See infra*, § 16.18.

14. *Id. See infra*, § 16.20.

15. *Id.*

16. *Id.* at 476–77, 288 N.Y.S.2d at 899–900, 235 N.E.2d at 905.

17. *Id.* at 476, 288 N.Y.S.2d at 899, 235 N.E.2d at 905.

18. *Id.* at 474, 288 N.Y.S.2d at 897, 235 N.E.2d at 903.

19. *Id.* at 473, 288 N.Y.S.2d at 896–97, 235 N.E.2d at 903.

20. *Id.*, 288 N.Y.S.2d at 897, 235 N.E.2d at 903.

21. *Id.*

22. *Id.* at 474, 288 N.Y.S.2d at 897, 235 N.E.2d at 903.

23. *Id.* at 475, 288 N.Y.S.2d at 899, 235 N.E.2d at 904.

24. *Id.*

25. *See infra*, § 16.19.

reasonable and deliberate."[26] The failure to plan properly by the village led to a finding that the rezoning violated procedural due process guarantees.[27]

The village's failure to conform its regulation of the plaintiff's land to its comprehensive plan led to the invalidation of the contested action on four separate grounds. It did not meet either substantive[28] or procedural due process tests,[29] it was beyond the village's legal authority,[30] and it was discriminatory, in violation of the plaintiff's equal protection rights.[31]

The message is clear. Over thirty years ago, the courts gave landowners a checklist to use in analyzing whether land use actions are proper. All of them emanate from the comprehensive plan. If a plan is developed in an orderly way, if it is reasonable, and if it can be shown that the regulation achieves one of its objectives, it is more likely that a contested regulation will withstand attack on all four of these grounds. A showing that a regulation conforms to the comprehensive plan will help insulate it as well from regulatory takings challenges. These points are further illustrated in the next five sections of this chapter.

§ 16.18 Substantive Limits—Substantive Due Process

The *Udell* case demonstrates that a land use regulation must not be arbitrary or capricious; it must be reasonably related to the achievement of a valid public purpose to comply with substantive due process guarantees of the Fifth Amendment of the Federal Constitution.[1] In the seminal zoning case, *Village of Euclid v. Ambler Realty Co.*,[2] the U.S. Supreme Court established the standard of review to be used by the courts when

---

26. 21 N.Y.2d at 469–70, 288 N.Y.S.2d at 894, 235 N.E.2d at 901.

27. *Id.* at 474, 288 N.Y.S.2d at 903, 235 N.E.2d at 897.

28. *Id.* at 476, 288 N.Y.S.2d at 899, 235 N.E.2d at 905. *See infra,* § 16.18.

29. *Id.* at 473–74, 288 N.Y.S.2d at 896–97, 235 N.E.2d at 903. *See infra,* § 16.19.

30. *Id.* at 476, 288 N.Y.S.2d at 899, 235 N.E.2d at 905. *See infra,* § 16.21.

31. *Id.* at 477, 288 N.Y.S.2d at 900, 235 N.E.2d at 906. *See infra,* § 16.20.

§ 16.18

1. The Fifth Amendment states that "no person shall ... be deprived of life, liberty, or property without due process of law." U.S. Const. amend. V. A similar limitation on government action is applied to the states through the Fourteenth Amendment. U.S. Const. amend. XIV. In New York, this "due process" requirement is contained in the New York Constitution, using language virtually identical to that of the U.S. Constitution. N.Y. Constitution art. I, § 6. Due process has been characterized as both substantive and procedural. Substantive due process is concerned with the essential fairness of the action of government. *Black's Law Dictionary* 1429 (6th ed. 1990). In the property regulation field, the issues are whether the regulation is designed to accomplish a valid public purpose and is reasonable and fair. Procedural due process concerns the "process" that is followed in the adoption of regulations that affect property rights. Apart from the substantive content of the regulation, it must be adopted and administered in a way that treats affected interests fairly, giving them notice and a reasonable chance to be heard before an accessible and impartial tribunal. D. Mandelker, *Land Use Law* 58–60 (2d ed. 1988).

2. 272 U.S. 365, 47 S.Ct. 114, 71 L.Ed. 303 (1926).

the wisdom of a regulatory scheme is challenged on due process grounds. "[T]he reasons [must be] sufficiently cogent to preclude us from saying, as it must be said before the ordinance can be declared unconstitutional, that such provisions are clearly arbitrary and unreasonable, having no substantial relation to the public health, safety, morals, or general welfare."[3] Failure to conform with a comprehensive plan risks violating this standard of review.

In *McMinn v. Town of Oyster Bay*,[4] the substantive due process tests of a land use regulation were reviewed. The case is a reminder that a land use regulation must meet a two part test to satisfy substantive due process. First, the zoning ordinance "must have been enacted in furtherance of a legitimate governmental purpose."[5] Second, "there must be a reasonable relation between the end sought to be achieved by the regulation and the means used to achieve that end."[6]

The Oyster Bay zoning ordinance restricted the occupancy of single-family housing to any number of persons related by blood, marriage or adoption, or to two persons not so related but who are sixty-two years of age or older.[7] The plaintiffs had rented their four-bedroom home to four unrelated young men. The dispositive issue was whether the zoning ordinance could restrict the use of single-family homes in this fashion.[8] The Court of Appeals found that there was a "legitimate governmental purpose" in preserving the "character of traditional single-family neighborhoods, reduction of parking and traffic problems, control of population density and prevention of noise and disturbance."[9] However, the Court found that the means of achieving this purpose were not reasonably related to that end. The provision was characterized as a violation of the plaintiff's due process rights; restrictions based on the size of the household were reasonably related to the achievement of the town's

---

3. *Id.* at 395, 47 S.Ct. at 121. *See* Goldblatt v. Town of Hempstead, 369 U.S. 590, 594–95, 82 S.Ct. 987, 990, 8 L.Ed.2d 130 (1962).

> Indulging in the usual presumption of constitutionality, ... we find no indication that the ... Ordinance ... is unconstitutional.... [T]his court has often said that 'debatable questions as to reasonableness are not for the courts but for the legislature.'

This United States Supreme Court standard of review has been adopted in New York for zoning cases challenged on due process grounds:

> [D]ecision as to how a community shall be zoned or rezoned, as to how various properties shall be classified or reclassified, rests with the local legislative body; its judgment and determination will be conclusive, beyond interference from the courts, unless shown to be arbitrary, and the burden of establishing such arbitrariness is imposed upon him who asserts it.

Rodgers v. Village of Tarrytown, 302 N.Y. 115, 121, 96 N.E.2d 731, 733 (1951).

4. 66 N.Y.2d 544, 498 N.Y.S.2d 128, 488 N.E.2d 1240 (1985).

5. *Id.* at 549, 498 N.Y.S.2d at 130, 488 N.E.2d at 1242.

6. *Id.*, 498 N.Y.S.2d at 130–31, 488 N.E.2d at 1242.

7. *Id.* at 547–48, 498 N.Y.S.2d at 130, 488 N.E.2d at 1241–42.

8. *Id.* at 547, 498 N.Y.S.2d at 129, 488 N.E.2d at 1241.

9. *Id.* at 549, 498 N.Y.S.2d at 131, 488 N.E.2d at 1243.

legitimate purpose, but those based on the type of relations among the occupants of a house were not.[10]

In *Kraizberg v. Shankey*,[11] the plaintiffs sought an extension of the existing town sewer district to serve their property, but were denied based upon an alleged lack of capacity at the town's central sewage plant and attendant infiltration and inflow problems. The supreme court annulled the town board's denial because the findings were not supported by the evidence.[12] The appellate division affirmed this holding. In addition, the appellate division found that even though the town board had the power to create sewer improvement districts,[13] its decision was not based upon "a determination of the public interest but upon the desire of town residents and the Board to minimize development."[14] The Board's determination was thus "arbitrary and capricious," lacking support by substantial evidence.[15]

In *Walus v. Millington*,[16] the failure to show reasons for deviating from the plan constituted spot zoning and was fatal to the rezoning of an individual parcel.[17] The plaintiffs challenged the validity of a zoning ordinance reclassifying the defendant's parcel from single-family residential to general business.[18] Other than a few nonconforming uses within the general vicinity, the area was primarily developed as a single-family residential neighborhood. The application for reclassification was to allow the construction of a restaurant and eventually a motel.[19]

The appellate division invalidated the rezoning because it was not in accordance with the "comprehensive plan" of the community. The court stated that "an underlying purpose [of comprehensive planning is] to control land uses for the benefit of the whole community based upon consideration of the community's problems and ... a general policy to obtain a uniform result."[20] In addition, "it requires a consideration of the individual parcel's relationship to the community as a whole."[21] "[T]he requirement is that a plan be implicit in the zoning regulation as a whole and that the amendments be consistent with such [a] plan and

---

10. Id.

11. 167 A.D.2d 370, 561 N.Y.S.2d 600 (2d Dep't 1990).

12. Id. at 371, 561 N.Y.S.2d at 601.

13. Id. (noting Town Law § 190).

14. Id. See also, Town of Orangetown v. Magee, 156 Misc.2d 881, 594 N.Y.S.2d 951 (Sup.Ct., Rockland County, 1992), opinion amended on reargument 218 A.D.2d 733, 631 N.Y.S.2d 166 (2d Dep't 1995), affirmed in part, reversed in part on other grounds, 626 N.Y.S.2d 511 (reversing denial of a building permit because of clear evidence that the denial was based on the local officials' desire to placate constituents rather than to further legitimate public purposes).

15. 167 A.D.2d at 371, 561 N.Y.S.2d at 601.

16. 49 Misc.2d 104, 266 N.Y.S.2d 833 (Sup.Ct., Oneida County, 1966).

17. Id. at 108, 266 N.Y.S.2d at 389. See Rodgers v. Village of Tarrytown, 302 N.Y. 115, 96 N.E.2d 731 (1951) (single parcel rezoning is not illegal spot zoning if it is in accord with sound planning principles).

18. 49 Misc.2d at 105, 266 N.Y.S.2d at 836.

19. Id.

20. Id. at 108, 266 N.Y.S.2d at 839; see also, Cannon v. Murphy, 196 A.D.2d 498, 600 N.Y.S.2d 965 (2d Dep't 1993).

21. Id. at 109, 266 N.Y.S.2d at 839.

not be enacted on a piecemeal or haphazard basis."[22] Therefore, if the amendment benefits the community as a whole, any incidental benefit or detriment to the owners or neighboring property does not invalidate the legislation.

These three cases, *McMinn*,[23] *Kraizberg*,[24] and *Walus*,[25] illustrate the vulnerability of regulations that are not clearly connected to the advancement of an objective of a comprehensive plan.[26] In *McMinn*, there was no evidence that the regulatory means chosen by the town advanced a valid planning objective. In *Kraizberg*, the dangers of not integrating local plans, such as the capital infrastructure budget, the official map and the comprehensive plan were demonstrated. In *Walus*, it was fatal to a regulation that it was not part of the planning whole but was instead enacted on a piecemeal or haphazard basis. In each of these cases, there was no evidence that the regulations were enacted to further a specific public planning objective. The courts in these cases advised municipalities to regulate with clear public objectives in mind, being certain that the regulatory means chosen advanced those objectives.

Library References:

West's Key No. Digests, Constitutional Law ⚖︎278.2(1).

§ 16.19 Substantive Limits—Procedural Due Process

Land use regulations must adhere to procedural guarantees secured by the Due Process Clause of the Fifth Amendment of the U.S. Constitution.[1] Procedural due process concerns the "process" that is followed in the adoption of regulations that affect property rights. Apart from the substantive content of a regulation, it must be adopted and administered in a way that treats affected interests fairly, giving them notice and a reasonable chance to be heard before a tribunal that is accessible and impartial.

The failure of an agency to follow an orderly and logical process in enacting a land use regulation can be fatal to a regulation's validity. Recall that in *Udell v. Haas*, the rezoning was not "accomplished in a proper, careful and reasonable manner."[2]

---

22. *Id.*

23. McMinn v. Town of Oyster Bay, 66 N.Y.2d 544, 498 N.Y.S.2d 128, 488 N.E.2d 1240 (1985).

24. Kraizberg v. Shankey, 167 A.D.2d 370, 561 N.Y.S.2d 600 (2d Dep't 1990).

25. Walus v. Millington, 49 Misc.2d 104, 266 N.Y.S.2d 833 (Sup.Ct., Oneida County, 1966).

26. *See also*, South Gwinnett Venture v. Pruitt, 491 F.2d 5 (5th Cir.), cert. denied 419 U.S. 837, 95 S.Ct. 66, 42 L.Ed.2d 64 (1974). "It necessarily follows that upon a factual showing of arbitrariness there must be some basis in fact and law to justify the zoning action as consistent with reasonableness." 491 F.2d at 7.

§ 16.19

1. *See supra*, § 16.18, note 1.
2. *See supra*, § 16.17.

Similarly, in *Pokoik v. Silsdorf*,[3] the town's dilatory tactics resulted in the invalidation of the rezoning of plaintiff's property. The plaintiff sought to annul the decision of the building inspector and town zoning board of appeals that denied a building permit.[4] The plaintiff's application for a building permit to construct two additional bedrooms was originally rejected because of previous zoning violations.[5] The plaintiff revised the building plans, but the building inspector did not act upon them. A court order compelling the building inspector's action on the application was granted nine months later, but the application was denied three months after issuance of the order.[6] The plaintiff appealed to the zoning board of appeals, but was forced to reschedule the hearing because no one appeared on behalf of the town. Meanwhile, the town board of trustees amended the zoning ordinance, limiting one-family residences to four bedrooms. This was a new requirement that would be violated by the plaintiff's revised plans.[7] The ordinance became effective prior to the plaintiff's hearing, resulting in the denial of the building permit. The special term annulled this decision, but the appellate division reversed, finding the amended ordinance controlling because it was effective at the time of the hearing.[8]

The Court of Appeals held that the amended ordinance could not apply and that the dilatory tactics of the town board and building inspector were a "special facts exception" to the rule that zoning amendments may be made at anytime in the public interest.[9] The plaintiff's full compliance with the zoning requirements at the time of the revised application created a right to the permit. The plaintiff was denied his right to begin construction before the effective date of the amendment because of the "abuse of administrative procedure" by the village officials.[10] The Court held that where a town board has abused administrative procedures in amending its zoning ordinance, that amendment may not be used to invalidate an application for a permit.[11]

---

3. 40 N.Y.2d 769, 390 N.Y.S.2d 49, 358 N.E.2d 874 (1976).

4. *Id.* at 770, 390 N.Y.S.2d at 50, 358 N.E.2d at 875.

5. *Id.* Plaintiff violated the zoning restrictions by renting rooms in a residential district without a license. Moreover, the application for a building permit did not explain why plaintiff needed the additional room. Thus, the application was rejected. *Id.*

6. *Id.*

7. *Id.* at 771, 390 N.Y.S.2d at 50, 358 N.E.2d at 875.

8. *Id.* at 772, 390 N.Y.S.2d at 51, 358 N.E.2d at 876.

9. *Id.* at 772-73, 390 N.Y.S.2d at 51, 358 N.E.2d at 876.

CAVEAT: The faulty proceedings in the Pokoik case are symptomatic of what happens when land use is regulated in the absence of systematic planning, clear objectives and a determined and demonstrable strategy to achieve them. Operating in a planning void heightens the risk of having a court characterize the operating method as dilatory and abusive, a violation of the guarantee of procedural due process. This reinforces the historical reliance on planning before regulation and proceeding according to that plan.

10. *Id.* at 773, 390 N.Y.S.2d at 51, 358 N.E.2d at 876.

11. *Id.*, 390 N.Y.S.2d at 51-52, 358 N.E.2d at 876-77. *See also,* Golisano v. Town Bd. of Town of Macedon, 31 A.D.2d 85, 296 N.Y.S.2d 623 (4th Dep't 1968). The absence of comprehensive planning principles to justify a rezoning was transparent in the court's analysis of the denial of the

§ 16.20 Substantive Limits—Equal Protection

Udell v. Haas further established that a land use regulation may not discriminate unfairly against a particular owner or class of owners in violation of the Equal Protection Clause of the Fourteenth Amendment of the Federal Constitution.[1] This guarantee provides a landowner with the ability to attack the validity of a land use regulation in two ways, either by attacking the regulation on its face or by attacking the regulation as applied to a plaintiff's land.[2]

In *Osiecki v. Town of Huntington*,[3] a regulation that departed from the comprehensive plan was invalidated for failure to articulate sufficient reasons for the deviation. In this 1991 case, the plaintiffs challenged the low-density residential classification of their five and one-half acre parcel. The plaintiffs claimed a violation of their equal protection rights, pointing to nearby properties that were zoned and developed commercially in conformance with a master plan adopted in 1965.[4] The plan designated the entire block, including the subject property, for commercial development.[5]

Using the vocabulary of other comprehensive plan cases, the town argued that it was not obligated to "slavish servitude to the master plan" and that it could change the use of the plaintiffs' property.[6] A search of the record showed no reason articulated by the town justifying a departure from the adopted plan. As a result, the zoning of plaintiffs'

---

plaintiff's application for a building permit. The court noted that the town board had cited fifteen reasons for denial of the permit, but these were "groping" and without merit because no rationale for rezoning to increase the size of a building lot was given. The town board "abused administrative procedure" by trying to conceal its desire to delay the application with insufficient reasons for denial. Due to this abuse, the court invoked the "special facts exception." It held that where a town board has abused administrative procedures in the exercise of its zoning powers, this "special facts exception" will prevent a subsequent zoning amendment from justifying a denial of the plaintiff's application for a permit. Thus, the amended ordinance did not apply and the arbitrary decision of the board was annulled. *Id.* at 88, 296 N.Y.S.2d at 627.

§ 16.20

1. 21 N.Y.2d 463, 477–78, 288 N.Y.S.2d 888, 900–01, 235 N.E.2d 897, 906. The Fourteenth Amendment states that "[n]o state shall make or enforce any law ... nor deny to any person within its jurisdiction the equal protection of the laws." U.S. Const. Amend. XIV; *see also* N.Y. State Constitution Art. I, § 11. Owners may contest the regulation of their property if they have evidence that similarly situated properties are not so affected. Equal protection attacks may also be brought on other grounds, such as race, poverty or age. Equal protection attacks on land use regulation are often intertwined with charges that such regulations violate the plaintiff's constitutional due process rights.

2. If there is no logical difference between plaintiff's property and an adjacent property which was classified more favorably, then the regulation is attacked as applied to plaintiff's land.

3. 170 A.D.2d 490, 565 N.Y.S.2d 564 (2d Dep't 1991).

4. *Id.* at 490, 565 N.Y.S.2d at 565.

5. *Id.* at 491, 565 N.Y.S.2d at 565.

6. *Id.*

property was voided since it was not in compliance with comprehensive planning. Otherwise, "[t]o accept the Town's contention that it is free to determine that the master plan should no longer be followed, without articulating a reason for that determination, would invite the kind of ad hoc and arbitrary application of zoning power that the comprehensive planning requirement was designed to avoid."[7]

Library References:

West's Key No. Digests, Constitutional Law ⚖228.2.

§ 16.21 Substantive Limits—*Ultra Vires*

Finally, the illustrative case of *Udell v. Haas* demonstrated that the enactment of a land use regulation must be within the powers that have been delegated to the regulator through an enabling statute.[1] Similarly, in *Moriarty v. Planning Board of the Village of Sloatsburg*,[2] the power of a planning board to review a site plan was strictly construed, so as to deny the board powers that were expressly granted to the building inspector.

In *Moriarty*, the plaintiff proposed to build a metal fabricating plant on a vacant parcel of industrially-zoned property.[3] The existing zoning ordinance required site plan approval by the village planning board before any building permit could be issued. After submitting an application, the site plan was denied because of inadequate fire protection mechanisms. The question on appeal was not the "reasonableness" of the planning board's actions, but whether the planning board was empowered to deny site plan approval because of fire protection concerns.[4]

The court, strictly interpreting the scope of delegated powers,[5] found that the planning board was not empowered to deny the building permit because fire code requirements were not met. The court stated that "[z]oning laws are ... in derogation of common-law property rights and thus are subject to the long-standing rule requiring their strict construction."[6] Because the State Legislature did not empower the board to assume the powers of local fire inspectors in denying building permits

7. *Id.*

§ 16.21

1. 21 N.Y.2d at 469, 288 N.Y.S.2d at 893–94, 235 N.E.2d at 900–01. See supra, § 16.17.

2. 119 A.D.2d 188, 506 N.Y.S.2d 184 (2d Dep't 1986).

3. *Id.* at 189, 506 N.Y.S.2d at 185.

4. *Id.* at 189–90, 506 N.Y.S.2d at 185.

5. The court held that:

[A] planning board may not vary zoning regulations at all without explicitly being delegated such power, nor may it deny site plan approval on the ground that the proposed use is not permitted under the zoning ordinance because the power to interpret the zoning ordinance is vested in the building inspector and the Zoning Board of Appeals.

Id. at 196–97, 506 N.Y.S.2d at 190.

6. *Id.* at 195, 506 N.Y.S.2d at 188–89.

due to inadequate fire protection, the court annulled the board's denial of the application.[7]

Library References:
West's Key No. Digests, Zoning and Planning ⇌4.

§ 16.22 Substantive Limits—Regulatory Takings

One important claim not advanced by the plaintiff in *Udell* was that the rezoning of his property constituted a regulatory taking in violation of provisions of the U.S. and New York Constitutions.[1] Seeds of confusion in distinguishing a regulation from a taking of property under the Fifth Amendment were first sown in 1922, when Justice Holmes stated "while property may be regulated to a certain extent, if regulation goes too far it will be recognized as a taking."[2] For a half century thereafter, the Court entertained no occasion to explain how to determine when a regulation could become a taking by going too far. Beginning in 1978[3] and continuing through 1987 in a trilogy of cases,[4] the Court struggled with this issue, piercing little of its enigmatic nature.[5]

Since the U.S. Supreme Court decided *Euclid v. Ambler* in 1926, it has reviewed challenges to regulations that arbitrate burdens and benefits among property owners giving great deference to the regulator, striking down regulations rarely and only when the challenger can prove conclusively that the regulation in question has "no substantial relation to the public health, safety, morals, or general welfare"[6] or that the

---

7. Id. at 199, 506 N.Y.S.2d at 191.

§ 16.22

1. U.S. Const. amend. V; U.S. Const. amend. XIV; *see* Chicago, Burlington & Quincy R.R. v. City of Chicago, 166 U.S. 226, 241, 17 S.Ct. 581, 41 L.Ed. 979 (1897) (applying the Just Compensation Clause of the Fifth Amendment through the Fourteenth Amendment to the states and their instrumentalities); N.Y. State Constitution Art. I, § 7.

2. Pennsylvania Coal Co. v. Mahon, 260 U.S. 393, 415, 43 S.Ct. 158, 160, 67 L.Ed. 322 (1922).

3. Penn Central Transp. Co. v. City of New York, 438 U.S. 104, 98 S.Ct. 2646, 57 L.Ed.2d 631 (1978).

4. Nollan v. California Coastal Comm'n, 483 U.S. 825, 107 S.Ct. 3141, 97 L.Ed.2d 677 (1987); First English Evangelical Lutheran Church v. County of Los Angeles, 482 U.S. 304, 107 S.Ct. 2378, 96 L.Ed.2d 250 (1987); and Keystone Bituminous Coal Ass'n v. DeBenedictis, 480 U.S. 470, 107 S.Ct. 1232, 94 L.Ed.2d 472 (1987).

5. "Even the wisest lawyers would have to acknowledge great uncertainty about the scope of [the] Court's takings jurisprudence." Nollan, 483 U.S. at 866, 107 S.Ct. at 3163 (Stevens, J., dissenting).

6. Village of Euclid v. Ambler Realty Co., 272 U.S. 365, 388, 47 S.Ct. 114, 118, 71 L.Ed. 303 (1926) ("If the validity of the legislative classification for zoning purposes be fairly debatable, the legislative judgment must be allowed to control."). *Compare* Gorieb v. Fox, 274 U.S. 603, 608, 47 S.Ct. 675, 677, 71 L.Ed. 1228 (1927) ("[C]ity councils ... are better qualified than the courts [to make these determinations].") *and* Zahn v. Board of Public Works, 274 U.S. 325, 328, 47 S.Ct. 594, 595, 71 L.Ed. 1074 (1927) ("[I]t is impossible for us to say that [this zoning decision] was clearly arbitrary and unreasonable."), where regulations were upheld using this approach, *with* Nectow v. City of Cambridge, 277 U.S. 183, 188, 48 S.Ct. 447, 448, 72 L.Ed. 842 (1928), where a challenger overcame this presumption of validity by proving affirmatively that the regulation bore no relation to advancing a public interest.

§ 16.22 LAND USE LAW Ch. 16

regulation results in a denial of "all economically beneficial or productive use of the land."[7]

It was in the context of a case challenging a rezoning of the plaintiff's property that the Supreme Court articulated the test by which regulations are judged to determine whether they are takings. In *Agins v. City of Tiburon*,[8] which involved a landowner's challenge to the city's zoning ordinance, the Court framed a two-pronged test, drawing from two of its earlier cases. Zoning "effects a taking if the ordinance (1) 'does not substantially advance a legitimate state interest' or (2) if it 'denies an owner economically viable use of his land.' "[9]

Applying the test articulated in *Agins*, other federal and state court opinions provide a set of considerations to be utilized when determining whether a regulation constitutes an unconstitutional taking.

1. On its face, is the " 'justice and fairness' guaranteed by the Fifth and Fourteenth amendments" respected by the regulation?[10]

2. The principal indicator of fairness is "in essence, a determination that the public at large, rather than a single owner, must bear the burden."[11]

3. An additional indicator that fairness is effected is that the regulation involves reciprocal benefits to the landowner and the public.[12]

4. Since "no precise rule determines when property has been taken, the question necessarily requires a weighing of private and public interests,"[13] particularly in close cases.

5. The public "benefits must be considered along with any diminution in market value" of the affected property.[14]

6. Determinations of the legislature regarding the legitimacy of the public interest pursued by a regulation will be "clothed with a

---

7. Lucas v. South Carolina Coastal Council, 505 U.S. 1003, 1015, 112 S.Ct. 2886, 2893, 120 L.Ed.2d 798 (1992).

8. 447 U.S. 255, 100 S.Ct. 2138, 65 L.Ed.2d 106 (1980).

9. Id. at 260, 100 S.Ct. at 2141.

10. Id. at 263, 100 S.Ct. at 2143.

The question here, as in any case where government action is challenged as violative of the right to just compensation, is whether the uncompensated obligations and restrictions imposed by the governmental action force individual property owners to bear more than a just share of obligations which are rightfully those of society at large.

Seawall Associates v. City of New York, 74 N.Y.2d 92, 101, 544 N.Y.S.2d 542, 545, 542 N.E.2d 1059, 1062 (1989), appeal after remand 223 A.D.2d 416, 636 N.Y.S.2d 767 (1996).

11. Id. at 260, 100 S.Ct. at 2141; Lucas v. South Carolina Coastal, 505 U.S. 1003, 1071, 112 S.Ct. 2886, 2923, 120 L.Ed.2d 798 (1992) (Stevens, J., dissenting). Justice Stevens characterized this notion as follows: "Perhaps the most familiar application of this principle of generality arises in zoning cases. A diminution of value caused by a zoning regulation is far less likely to constitute a taking if it is part of a general and comprehensive land use plan." 505 U.S. at 1071, 112 S.Ct. at 2923.

12. 447 U.S. at 262, 100 S.Ct. at 2142.

13. Id.

14. Id.

strong presumption of constitutionality."[15]

7. Implicit in the presumption of validity is that the challenger of the regulation must bear the burden of proving its invalidity.[16] This is particularly difficult, with respect to the first prong of *Agins*, due to the presumption.

These rules, derived from seminal cases, demonstrate the operating method adopted by a court that perceives itself to be working within the "stable core" of regulatory takings law.[17] That operating method is deferential to a legislature that is pursuing a comprehensive plan for the municipality, meting out burdens on landowners generally for the overall benefit of the community. The court's sense of justice is not offended by a severe and demonstrated diminution in value, or by the methods used or objectives pursued by the regulators.

To the extent that the legislative body has tied a regulation to a clearly stated plan, one that spells out the public interest pursued, the regulation will have a better chance of surviving whatever level of scrutiny a court decides to apply. In fact, it can be argued that a court is likely to select the standard of review it will apply, depending on its sense of the seriousness of the public purpose advanced by the regulation. The plan, if drafted with integrity and properly advanced by the regulation, can greatly influence such matters.

Library References:

West's Key No. Digests, Eminent Domain ⊱2(1.2).

15. *See* Curtiss–Wright Corp. v. Town of East Hampton, 82 A.D.2d 551, 553, 442 N.Y.S.2d 125, 127 (2d Dep't 1981). In Village of Euclid v. Ambler Realty Co., 272 U.S. 365, 395, 47 S.Ct. 114, 121, 71 L.Ed. 303 (1926), the Court wrote:

If these reasons ... do not demonstrate the wisdom ... of those restrictions ..., at least the reasons are sufficiently cogent to preclude us from saying, as it must be said before the ordinance can be declared unconstitutional, that such provisions are clearly arbitrary and unreasonable, having no substantial relation to the public health, safety, morals or general welfare.

Id.

16. A landowner who claims that land regulation has effected a taking of his property bears the heavy burden of overcoming the presumption of constitutionality that attaches to the regulation and of proving every element of his claim beyond a reasonable doubt.... That burden remains upon him throughout the case and never shifts to the State.

de St. Aubin v. Flacke, 68 N.Y.2d 66, 76, 505 N.Y.S.2d 859, 865, 496 N.E.2d 879, 885 (1986).

17. For a more detailed discussion of regulatory takings law, *see* J. Nolon, *Footprints in the Shifting Sands of the Isle of Palms: A Practical Analysis of Regulatory Takings Cases*, 8 J. Land Use & Envtl. L. 1 (1992).

PRACTICE POINTER: Outside this stable core of cases, the courts' operating method changes, particularly when the regulation requires, for example, the conveyance of an interest in the regulated property. Such was the case in Nollan v. California Coastal Commission, 483 U.S. 825, 107 S.Ct. 3141, 97 L.Ed.2d 677 (1987), where the U.S. Supreme Court first articulated the "essential nexus" requirement, and in Dolan v. City of Tigard, 512 U.S. 374, 114 S.Ct. 2309, 129 L.Ed.2d 304 (1994), on remand 319 Or. 567, 877 P.2d 1201 (1994), where it formulated and applied the "rough proportionality" test for the first time.

§ 16.23 Substantive Limits—Vested Rights

Doctrines that protect property owners from the impacts of new regulations that are so onerous as to constitute regulatory takings are similar to those that protect investments in land development from changes in applicable regulations. The law protecting existing developments, or nonconforming uses, from changes in zoning provisions, for example, is based on the legal notion that property owners have a vested right in those uses, subject to certain limitations.[1]

Questions arise when landowners secure permits from local authorities to build upon their land, undertake construction and then are subjected to a change in applicable regulations. Is their right to a development in progress vested as it would be if completed? When the landowner has received a local subdivision approval he is protected, to a degree, by statutory vesting. The legislature has provided that certain approved residential subdivisions, filed in the county land records office, are exempt for a period from zoning changes that impose different dimensional requirements, such as lot line set back or lot area provisions.[2] The exemption period ranges from one to three years depending on whether the municipality had a zoning ordinance and a planning board at the time the subdivision was filed.[3]

These statutory provisions add to the common law of vested rights that existed in New York prior to their adoption. That law stated that:

> [W]here a more restrictive zoning ordinance is enacted, an owner will be permitted to complete a structure or development which an amendment has rendered nonconforming only where the owner has undertaken substantial construction and made substantial expenditures prior to the effective date of the amendment.[4]

As with nonconforming uses, these vested rights can be lost by abandonment or where there is an overriding benefit to the public to be derived from the enforcement of an amendment to the zoning ordinance.[5]

Library References:

West's Key No. Digests, Constitutional Law ⇌92; Zoning and Planning ⇌465.

§ 16.23

1. *See infra,* § 16.62.
2. Village Law § 7–708(2), Town Law § 265–a, General City Law § 83–a.
3. Village Law § 7–708(2)(b), Town Law § 265–a(2), General City Law § 83–a(2).
4. Schoonmaker Homes v. Village of Maybrook, 178 A.D.2d 722, 725, 576 N.Y.S.2d 954, 956 (3d Dep't 1991).

PRACTICE POINTER: Schoonmaker involved a phased development project which had been partially developed. The later phases were said to be vested under what the court characterized as the "single integrated project theory." That theory vests an owner's right to develop an undeveloped phase of a multi-phased project where substantial expenditures on parcels involved in earlier phases benefit or have some connection with the undeveloped parcel. *Id.* at 724, 576 N.Y.S.2d at 956.

5. Putnam Armonk v. Town of Southeast, 52 A.D.2d 10, 382 N.Y.S.2d 538 (2d Dep't 1976). *See infra,* §§ 16.67–16.68.

§ 16.24 Substantive Limits—Preemption

Even where the State Legislature has granted authority to act to local governments, that power is not absolute. For example, the state has reserved to itself the power to enact laws relating to matters of state concern[1] and matters other than the property, affairs or government of a municipality.[2] An illustration of the preemptive power of the state is the Adirondack Park Agency Act, which created a state agency and delegated to it many of the functions associated with local land use regulation.[3] In sustaining this Act, the Court of Appeals stated:

> Of course, the Agency Act prevents localities within the Adirondack Park from freely exercising their zoning and planning powers. That indeed is its purpose and effect, not because the motive is to impair home rule but because the motive is to serve a supervening state concern transcending local interests.[4]

Courts have found local zoning preempted where they have found an intention on the part of the State Legislature to occupy a particular field. For example, the Court found that the State Legislature had intended to occupy and control the field of providing drug abuse facilities as a matter of state policy.[5] In another, a city's zoning was held to violate the State Mental Hygiene Law[6] because it was inconsistent with a state legislative scheme for providing housing for the mentally ill.[7] In another case, a statutory provision that all duly licensed "community residential facilities" shall constitute family units overrode conflicting local zoning regulations.[8]

In *Albany Area Builders v. Town of Guilderland*,[9] the Court of Appeals explored the limiting effect of preemptive state laws on local authority to exercise powers otherwise granted to them under the Municipal Home Rule Law and other enabling statutes.[10] The Court

---

§ 16.24

1. N.Y. State Constitution Art. IX, § 3(a)(3); Statute of Local Governments Law §§ 2—11.

2. N.Y. State Constitution Art. IX, § 2(b)(2). The state here further retains power to act with respect to matters of local property, affairs or government by general law, or by special law where both local and state interests are involved.

3. Executive Law §§ 800–820.

4. Wambat Realty Corp. v. New York, 41 N.Y.2d 490, 494–95, 393 N.Y.S.2d 949, 952, 362 N.E.2d 581, 584 (1977).

5. People v. St. Agatha Home, 47 N.Y.2d 46, 416 N.Y.S.2d 577, 389 N.E.2d 1098 (1979); Unitarian Universalist Church of Central Nassau v. Shorten, 63 Misc.2d 978, 314 N.Y.S.2d 66 (Sup.Ct., Nassau County, 1970).

6. Mental Hygiene Law § 141.34.

7. Community Resource Center for the Developmentally Disabled, Inc. v. City of Yonkers, 140 Misc.2d 1018, 532 N.Y.S.2d 332 (Sup.Ct., Westchester County, 1988).

8. Zubli v. Community Mainstreaming Assocs., 102 Misc.2d 320, 423 N.Y.S.2d 982 (Sup.Ct., Nassau County, 1979), aff'd 50 N.Y.2d 1024, 431 N.Y.S.2d 813, 410 N.E.2d 746 (1980). See also, Incorporated Village of Old Field v. Introne, 104 Misc.2d 122, 430 N.Y.S.2d 192 (Sup.Ct., Suffolk County, 1980).

9. 74 N.Y.2d 372, 547 N.Y.S.2d 627, 546 N.E.2d 920 (1989).

10. In 1976 the State Legislature amended the Municipal Home Rule Law, Section 10, to provide towns with a limited exception to the general rule that local laws

reviewed the legality of a locally enacted Transportation Impact Fee Law ("TIFL") adopted by the Town of Guilderland. The TIFL required that developers of certain types of projects pay a transportation impact fee as a condition for the town's permission to build. The funds collected were to be spent on capital improvement and expansion of the roads and transportation facilities within the town necessitated by the additional traffic projected to be generated by the new developments.[11]

In defending its transportation initiative, the town cited the grant of home rule powers in the Constitution and various sections of the Municipal Home Rule Law as authority. The Court stated, however, that there was no need to consider whether TIFL fell within the delegated powers because the general area had been preempted by state law. The power to adopt local laws is limited by the preemption doctrine, which the court in *Albany Area Builders* described as "a fundamental limitation on home rule powers."[12] It applies when a local law is in conflict with a state law and when the legislature "has evidenced its intent to occupy ... the field."[13]

may not be inconsistent with a general law. Municipal Home Rule Law § 10(1)(ii)(d)(3). The amendment allows towns to amend or supersede:

any provisions of the Town Law relating to its property, affairs or government or to other matters in relation to which and to the extent to which it is authorized to adopt local laws by this section, notwithstanding that such provision is a general law, unless the legislature expressly shall have prohibited the adoption of such a local law.

The supersession authority allows a town to use its delegated powers "in a narrow, well-demarcated area of purely local concern", to meet those needs. Kamhi v. Town of Yorktown, 74 N.Y.2d 423, 430, 548 N.Y.S.2d 144, 150, 547 N.E.2d 346, 349 (1989). Section 10(1)(ii)(e)(3) of Municipal Home Rule Law confers similar supersession powers on villages.

The Court in *Kamhi* recognized the Legislature's grant of supersession authority to towns and villages, while at the same time noting the limitations of the supersession authority and its application to matters of a purely local nature.

We conclude that the Town had the power to adopt a local law requiring parkland-or-money exactions in connection with site plan approval for R-3 developments. This is hardly License for an 'arrogation of undelegated power' or a 'profound change ... giving municipalities virtually unconstrained authority to act'.... Rather, our conclusion represents a faithful application of the dictates of the Municipal Home Rule Law, which—within narrow confines—permits the Town of Yorktown to adjust a provision of the Town Law so that in its local application it will have exactly the effect intended by the Legislature.

74 N.Y.2d at 434, 548 N.Y.S.2d at 150, 547 N.E.2d at 352.

The Court ultimately held that because the Town had failed to comply with the formal requirements of the Municipal Home Rule Law with respect to exercising its supersession authority, Local Law No. 6 was invalid. The Town had failed to declare with "definiteness and explicitness" its intention to supersede the Town Law, as required by Section 22 of the Municipal Home Rule Law. 74 N.Y.2d at 434, 548 N.Y.S.2d at 150, 547 N.E.2d at 352.

11. Albany Area Builders Ass'n v. Town of Guilderland, 74 N.Y.2d 372, 547 N.Y.S.2d 627, 546 N.E.2d 920 (1989).

12. 74 N.Y.2d at 377, 547 N.Y.S.2d at 629, 546 N.E.2d at 922. "Where the State has preempted the field, a local law regulating the same subject matter is deemed inconsistent with the State's transcendent interest, whether or not the terms of the local law actually conflict with a State-wide statute." *Id.*

13. *Id.* The Court noted that the Town Law § 107(3) and Highway Law § 271 provided comprehensive and detailed regula-

If an intent to occupy the field can be ascertained from the nature of the subject matter regulated, the purpose and scope of the state legislative scheme and the need for statewide uniformity in a given area, then local laws in the subject area are preempted,[14] whether or not the legislature has expressly restricted the local government from legislating regarding the subject.[15]

Library References:
West's Key No. Digests, Zoning and Planning ⚖14.

§ 16.25 Substantive Limits—First Amendment

In both the U.S. and New York constitutions, freedom of religion is guaranteed.[1] Consequently, courts have declared that the construction of churches, synagogues and other religious structures are beneficial to the public interest and somewhat protected from zoning and other land use restrictions.[2] Since land use regulations are justified by their pursuit of the public interest, where their effect is to impede the practice of religion, guaranteed by the constitution, they are of dubious constitutionality.[3] This notion has been characterized as a rebuttable presumption that religious uses will have a beneficial effect on an area, including residential neighborhoods.[4]

Zoning ordinances that totally exclude religious institutions from a residential district are invalid since they serve no purpose related to the public health, welfare, safety or morals.[5] The protection of religious institutions extends to their treatment by planning boards and zoning boards of appeal. With respect to applications before these bodies, "every

---

tions on the budgeting and financing of roadway improvements, and on the manner in which the moneys were to be expended for those improvements. The Court stated that the "purpose, number and specificity of these statutes make clear that the State perceived no real distinction between the particular needs of any one locality and other parts of the State with respect to the funding of roadway improvements, and thus created a uniform scheme to regulate this subject matter." Id. at 378–379, 547 N.Y.S.2d at 630, 546 N.E.2d at 923. The Court concluded that this uniform and comprehensive scheme evidenced the legislature's intent to occupy the field; therefore, the TIFL was preempted.

14. See Town of Islip v. Cuomo, 147 A.D.2d 56, 541 N.Y.S.2d 829 (2d Dep't 1989), for an example of a special law of the state affecting local property, affairs and government that was upheld because it related to a matter of state concern: the siting of solid waste facilities.

15. It has been noted that the Court severely limited the scope of home rule authority by holding that the legislature's intent to preempt a field can be ascertained through judicial construction rather than by requiring the legislature to expressly restrict the field.

§ 16.25

1. U.S. Constitution, amend. I, N.Y. State Constitution, Art. I, § 3.

2. Holy Spirit Ass'n for Unification of World Christianity v. Rosenfeld, 91 A.D.2d 190, 458 N.Y.S.2d 920 (2d Dep't 1983).

3. American Friends of Society of St. Pius v. Schwab, 69 A.D.2d 646, 417 N.Y.S.2d 991 (2d Dep't 1979).

4. Neddermeyer v. Town of Ontario Planning Bd., 155 A.D.2d 908, 548 N.Y.S.2d 951 (4th Dep't 1989).

5. Cornell University v. Bagnardi, 68 N.Y.2d 583, 510 N.Y.S.2d 861, 503 N.E.2d 509 (1986).

effort to accommodate the religious use must be made."[6] The failure to grant a variance from dimensional requirements of the zoning ordinance or the denial of a special permit regarding the construction of religious structures routinely are overturned in the absence of clear evidence that the proposed use will be detrimental to the area.[7] This evidentiary requirement is a substantial one; localities, for example, may not deny variances for religious uses on the basis of factors which would justify the exclusion or restriction of commercial uses.[8]

Similar doctrines protect the posting of signs from burdensome land use regulation. The regulation of noncommercial and commercial content of signs posted on private property is subject to restriction because of the free speech clause of the constitution. In the mid-1970's, the U.S. Supreme Court extended the historical protection of noncommercial speech to commercial expression.[9]

Most free speech cases, in the land use context, relate to the regulation of commercial signs. As to these, the U.S. Supreme Court reviews their constitutionality using a four-part test adopted in 1980:

> At the outset, we must determine whether the expression is protected by the First Amendment. For commercial speech to come within that provision, it at least must concern lawful activity and not be misleading. Next, we ask whether the asserted governmental interest is substantial. If both inquiries yield positive answers, we must determine whether the regulation directly advances the governmental interest asserted, and whether it is not more extensive than is necessary to serve that interest.[10]

New York cases exhibit rulings consistent with this approach. Prohibiting noncommercial signs but permitting commercial ones, for example, is invalid.[11] Permitting some noncommercial messages, but allowing others, is unconstitutional.[12] An ordinance that excludes billboards except those advertising goods made on the premises is also invalid.[13] These regulations are not neutral as to the content of the message that

---

6. Genesis Assembly of God v. Davies, 208 A.D.2d 627, 628, 617 N.Y.S.2d 202, 203 (2d Dep't 1994).

7. Islamic Society of Westchester & Rockland, Inc. v. Foley, 96 A.D.2d 536, 464 N.Y.S.2d 844 (2d Dep't 1983), overturning the denial of an area variance; North Syracuse First Baptist Church v. Village of North Syracuse, 136 A.D.2d 942, 524 N.Y.S.2d 894 (4th Dep't 1988), reversing the denial of a special permit.

8. Islamic Society of Westchester & Rockland, Inc. v. Foley, 96 A.D.2d 536, 464 N.Y.S.2d 844 (2d Dep't 1983).

9. Bigelow v. Virginia, 421 U.S. 809, 95 S.Ct. 2222, 44 L.Ed.2d 600 (1975); Virginia State Bd. of Pharmacy v. Virginia Citizens Consumer Council, 425 U.S. 748, 96 S.Ct. 1817, 48 L.Ed.2d 346 (1976).

10. Central Hudson Gas & Electric Corp. v. Public Service Commission, 447 U.S. 557, 566, 100 S.Ct. 2343, 2351, 65 L.Ed.2d 341 (1980).

11. Incorporated Village of Hempstead v. Carlson, 129 Misc.2d 537, 493 N.Y.S.2d 280 (Sup.Ct., Nassau County, 1985).

12. Carmel v. Suburban Outdoor Advertising Co., 127 A.D.2d 204, 514 N.Y.S.2d 387 (2d Dep't 1987).

13. Id.

is regulated and, therefore, more highly suspect as violations of free speech.

Municipalities have attempted to regulate adult theaters and businesses through regulations which do not prohibit them, or regulate the content of expression on the premises, but restrict the time, place or manner of such enterprises. In *Islip v. Caviglia*,[14] the Court of Appeals reviewed a town ordinance enacted to address the proliferation of adult businesses in the downtown area. It applied a test set out by the U.S. Supreme Court to determine if the ordinance impinged upon the freedom of speech guaranteed by the First Amendment.

> Municipalities [may] regulate [adult uses] through the zoning power if they can establish that (1) the predominant purpose of the ordinance is not to control the content of the material purveyed but to control the secondary effects of such uses on the surrounding community, (2) the ordinance is designed to serve a substantial governmental interest, (3) it is narrowly tailored to affect only a category of uses that produce the unwanted effects and (4) it allows for reasonable alternative avenues of expression.[15]

The petitioner in *Caviglia* also argued that his right to free speech guaranteed under the New York Constitution, which provides greater protection than the Federal Constitution, was violated.[16] The Court of Appeals agreed that, "New York has a long history and tradition of fostering freedom of expression, often tolerating and supporting works which in other states would be found offensive to the community."[17] However, it disagreed that the ordinance was inconsistent with that history, stating that "a municipality may, under the circumstances presented, restrict adult business uses to certain areas of the community without violating the State Constitution."[18]

The Court of Appeals found that the town ordinance was content neutral because it did not mention the nature of the material purveyed, since the challenged ordinance defined the uses regulated only to include those which exclude minors by reasons of age. It further found that the ordinance, which restricted the location of adult entertainment businesses to certain districts, was no broader than necessary to achieve its purpose of eradicating the effects of urban blight and enhancing the quality of life of the town's residents. The court mentioned with favor that the ordinance provided ample alternative locations for the regulated enterprises.

---

14. 73 N.Y.2d 544, 542 N.Y.S.2d 139, 540 N.E.2d 215 (1989).

15. Renton v. Playtime Theatres, 475 U.S. 41, 106 S.Ct. 925, 89 L.Ed.2d 29 (1986).

16. N.Y. State Constitution, Art. I, § 8 provides: "Every citizen may freely speak, write and publish his sentiments on all subjects, being responsible for the abuse of that right; and no law shall be passed to restrain or abridge the liberty of speech or of the press."

17. 73 N.Y.2d at 556, 542 N.Y.S.2d at 145, 540 N.E.2d at 221.

18. *Id.*

This case demonstrates the critical importance of tying regulations to a comprehensive plan,[19] which, in this case was preceded by an extensive study conducted by the town. The court turned to the study and found evidence that the adult uses had a negative effect on the downtown area and that the trend toward increased criminal activity and deterioration of property values would continue. The comprehensive plan was crafted based upon the study's findings and the ordinance enacted to accomplish the goals of the plan. The court held that "[the town] was not required to wait before acting until its business areas became wastelands."[20]

Library References:

West's Key No. Digests, Constitutional Law ⚖90.1(1).

§ 16.26 Substantive Limits—Summary

There are several legal doctrines that limit the authority of local governments to enact and enforce land use regulations.

- First, substantive due process requires that such regulations serve a legitimate public purpose.[1]

- Second, the administrative process by which regulations are adopted and enforced must meet the requirements of procedural due process.[2]

- Third, by classifying land uses, dividing land into districts and regulating it accordingly, local land use regulations may improperly discriminate among similar parcels or against types of land users and violate equal protection guarantees of the state or federal constitution.[3]

- Fourth, since local governments in New York may exercise only those powers delegated to them by the State Legislature, land use regulations may be attacked as *ultra vires* if the municipal action is not undertaken pursuant to specific legislative authority.[4]

- Fifth, local land use regulations must not effect a taking of private property without just compensation in violation of the "takings" provisions of the state and federal constitutions.[5]

- Sixth, the doctrine of vested rights limits the authority of municipalities in certain cases to impose overly burdensome regulations

---

19. See supra, § 16.11.
20. Town of Islip v. Caviglia, 73 N.Y.2d at 553–554, 542 N.Y.S.2d at 143, 540 N.E.2d at 219.

§ 16.26
1. See supra, § 16.18.

2. See supra, § 16.19.
3. See supra, § 16.20.
4. See supra, § 16.21.
5. See supra, § 16.22.

on existing investments in land, such as completed structures or projects under construction.[6]

- Seventh, local land use regulations are not permitted to control matters whose regulation has been preempted by the State Legislature.[7]

- Eighth, local regulations must not abridge First Amendment freedoms of expression and the exercise of religion.[8]

§ 16.27 Local Process

The local process of land use regulation begins with the delegation of authority in particular areas such as zoning, subdivision control and site plan review. Regulations in each of these areas may be adopted by the local legislative body. In each case, the local legislature specifies the local administrative body responsible for implementation and enforcement of the provisions of the regulations.

In most municipalities, the principal bodies employed to carry out these zoning and related regulations are the planning board, the zoning board and the building inspector. The procedures to be followed by these administrative agencies are found in the specific enabling statutes discussed in this chapter; local administrative bodies are not subject to the provisions of the State Administrative Procedures Act.[1]

§ 16.28 Local Process—Structure of Local Regulations

In general, provisions of New York statutory law delegating land use authority to local governments are permissive rather than mandatory. They provide villages, towns and cities the authority to adopt a wide variety of regulations in their discretion. Whether a municipality is to adopt a zoning ordinance, comprehensive plan, or regulations regarding subdivisions, site plans, special permits and related matters is a matter of local discretion. This statutory scheme is explained elsewhere in this chapter.[1]

Local land use regulations may be structured in a wide variety of ways. Zoning ordinances, depending on local needs, may contain relatively few provisions or be extensive in their coverage. They may contain the municipality's provisions for subdivision control, site plan review and the

---

6. *See supra*, § 16.23 and *infra*, §§ 16.62–16.72.
7. *See supra*, § 16.24.
8. *See supra*, § 16.25.

§ 16.27
1. 1777 Penfield Road Corp. v. Morrison-Vega, 116 A.D.2d 1035, 498 N.Y.S.2d 653 (4th Dep't 1986). *See* Chapter 4 "Administrative Law," *supra*.

§ 16.28
1. The authority of local governments in the land use area and the flexibility of the state legislative scheme are discussed at §§ 16.3–16.9 *supra*; the comprehensive plan at §§ 16.11–16.15 *supra*; subdivision authority at §§ 16.96–16.102 *infra*; site plan control at §§ 16.103–16.108 *infra* and special permits at §§ 16.90–16.95 *infra*.

§ 16.28 LAND USE LAW Ch. 16

issuance of special permits. Alternatively, subdivision, site plan and special permit regulations may be contained in separate laws or ordinances adopted by the local legislature as discrete documents.

The local zoning ordinance divides the municipality into districts that are reflected in a zoning map which is also adopted by the local legislature. Within each district, certain land uses such as single-family housing or neighborhood commercial buildings are permitted as a matter of right.[2] Uses that are accessory to the as-of-right uses,[3] such as garages or storage buildings, are permitted in each district as well. Other uses may be allowed by special permit which are awarded only after application and review by a local administrative body.[4] If uses in existence at the time of the adoption or amendment of the zoning ordinance are not in conformance with its provisions, they may be continued in most cases subject to various controls contained in the ordinance.[5]

Most zoning ordinances contain a table of bulk and dimensional requirements. This table is normally divided by zoning district and type of permitted use. It contains various mandatory dimensional requirements applicable in each district and to each use. These include, for example, the permitted height of structures, the percent of the building lot upon which structures may be constructed, provisions requiring structures to be set back from front, side and rear lot lines by a specified number of feet and the number of parking spaces required for commercial or industrial buildings.

Subdivision regulations govern the division of larger parcels of land into approved lots for building purposes.[6] They go beyond the use and dimensional requirements of zoning and regulate the location of ingress and egress, roads and the placement of water, sewer and electrical service within the subdivision. When a municipality has adopted subdivision controls, property owners may not record the sale of a subdivided lot unless the subdivision was duly approved pursuant to the provisions of the local subdivision regulations.[7]

Site plan regulations govern the development of individual sites and require local board approval of the placement, and other specifications, of buildings, roads and infrastructure on the parcel, ingress and egress, landscaping, drainage and architecture, among other site features.[8] If a parcel has been recently subdivided, its development normally will have been approved under the local subdivision regulations and be exempt from further review. Site plan control provides additional authority for

---

2. *See infra,* § 16.61.

3. Accessory uses are discussed at § 16.119, *infra.*

4. The issuance of special permits is treated at *infra* §§ 16.90–16.95.

5. The treatment of prior nonconforming uses is discussed at §§ 16.62–16.72, *infra.*

6. Subdivision control is discussed at §§ 16.96–16.102, *infra.*

7. RPL § 333(1–e)(ii)(8)(b).

8. Site plan regulations are discussed at §§ 16.103–16.108, *infra.*

§ 16.29 Local Process—Adoption

The original adoption of zoning ordinances is provided for by state statute.[1] To exercise the zoning authority conferred upon a town or village, the legislative body must appoint a zoning commission to recommend the boundaries of zoning districts and the use and dimensional regulations applicable within each district.[2] Where a planning board has already been established, it may serve as the zoning commission.[3] The commission must prepare a preliminary report, hold one or more public hearings on the report and submit a final report to the local legislative body.[4] Cities are not required to appoint, and receive the report of, a zoning commission prior to adopting an initial zoning ordinance.

The local legislature in a town or village, after receipt of the commission's report, "shall provide for the manner in which [zoning] regulations, restrictions and boundaries of such districts including any amendments thereto shall be determined, established and enforced."[5] No zoning regulation may be adopted until after a public hearing, held upon at least 10 days notice.[6] Failure to conduct the required hearing, after notice, renders the zoning ordinance invalid.[7] The provisions of the State Environmental Quality Review Act are applicable to the initial adoption of a zoning ordinance.[8] This requirement applies equally to towns, villages and cities.

Where zoning ordinances are adopted by local law, a majority of the whole membership of the legislative body is required.[9] Where referral to a county or regional planning board is required, its disapproval of the ordinance can be reversed only by a vote of a majority plus one member of the local legislative body.[10]

§ 16.29

1. Village Law § 7–710, Town Law § 266.

2. Id.

3. Village Law § 7–710(2), Town Law § 266(2).

4. Id.

5. Village Law § 7–706, Town Law § 264.

6. Id. Towns and villages may elect to adopt zoning ordinances under the provisions of these specific enabling acts and, if they do, they must follow the notice and hearing requirements that the enabling statutes contain. They may, alternatively, adopt or amend zoning ordinances by local law under the provisions of Section 20 of the Municipal Home Rule Law, in which case the more specific provisions of that law regarding voting, notice and hearing apply. General Municipal Law § 20(5). See supra, § 16.4, notes 2–4.

7. Estabrook v. Chamberlain, 240 App. Div. 899, 267 N.Y.S. 425 (2d Dep't 1933), affirmed 240 A.D. 1006, 268 N.Y.S. 1015 (1933).

8. ECL §§ 8.0101–8.0117. The adoption of a zoning ordinance is declared to be a Type I action under SEQRA which normally mandates the preparation, review and adoption of a full Environmental Impact Statement. See infra, §§ 16.52–16.59 and Chapter 15 "Environmental Law," supra.

9. Municipal Home Rule Law § 20(5).

10. General Municipal Law § 239–m.

§ 16.30 Local Process—Amendment

In towns, villages and cities, zoning ordinances may be amended by the vote of a simple majority of the local legislative body.[1] A three-fourths majority is required, however, if the legislative body receives a written protest signed by the owners of 20% or more of the land area affected by such change, or of the land immediately adjacent to the affected area, or of the land directly opposite the affected area.[2] Where the amendment is subject to referral to a county or regional planning board, disapproval of the amendment can be reversed only by a vote of a majority plus one member of the local legislative body.[3] The provisions of zoning ordinances may be amended or repealed only after notice and public hearing.[4]

Library References:

West's Key No. Digests, Zoning and Planning ⟸191–199.

§ 16.31 Local Process—Other Regulations/Official Map

A number of other local regulations may be adopted to complement zoning, subdivision, site plan and special permit regulations. These include historic preservation district regulations,[1] landmark regulations,[2] wetlands regulations,[3] other environmental constraints ordinances and the protection of open spaces,[4] among others. The adoption and enforcement of these regulations involves a mix of delegated and implied authority which has been clarified and interpreted by case law.[5]

If there is a blueprint that physically organizes these diverse local land use regulations, it is the official map of the locality. Such a map may be adopted by the local legislative body in a village, town or city and show the physical layout of public infrastructure, including roads,

§ 16.30

1. Village Law § 7–708, Town Law § 265, General City Law § 83.

2. Village Law § 7–708(1), Town Law § 265(1), General City Law § 83(2).

3. General Municipal Law § 239–m.

4. Village Law § 7–708, Town Law § 265, General City Law § 83.

§ 16.31

1. The designation of historic preservation districts, the protection of landmarks and the creation of historic district boards or commissions is discussed at § 16.127, *infra*.

2. *Id.*

3. ECL § 24–1509. Local governments are free to regulate freshwater wetlands so long as such regulations are "at least as protective of freshwater wetlands as the regulations in effect pursuant to the provisions of" the State Freshwater Wetlands Act. *Id*. See Chapter 15 "Environmental Law," § 15.15, *supra*.

4. General Municipal Law, Art. 12–F. This article authorizes local governments to create Conservation Advisory Councils which may be used to review the impact of zoning, subdivision, site plan and other actions on the community's open space and natural resources.

5. Beyond the sections cited, a complete discussion of these types of regulations is beyond the scope of this chapter.

streets, highways, drainage systems, parks and public buildings, both current and projected.[6] The clerk of every municipality that adopts an official map must file a certificate of the adoption with the county clerk.[7]

The official map provides a partial framework which assists local boards and agencies in reviewing individual subdivision and construction proposals to determine whether they comport with the efficient and orderly growth and development of the community.

§ 16.32 Local Process—Building Regulations and Permits

The enforcement of the zoning ordinance may be delegated to the a zoning administrator or the local building inspector.[1] In addition, building permits, certifying that proposed construction is in compliance with the Fire Prevention and Building Code, are to be issued by the building inspector.[2] These are related but separate functions.

Local practice with respect to zoning and building matters may vary considerably. The separate functions of reviewing and approving building permit applications for conformance with the fire and building code and of reviewing and certifying the proposed development's compliance with the complex provisions of zoning, subdivision, site plan and special permit regulations are often separated administratively in larger or more experienced communities. In such localities, there may be a building department, on one hand, and a separate zoning administrator, office or department, on the other. In these situations, the building department or office refuses to issue building permits until the approval of the zoning administrator, office or department, is secured.

Library References:
West's Key No. Digests, Zoning and Planning ⚖=431–446.

§ 16.33 Local Process—Summary

The local process of land use regulation begins with the delegation of authority in particular subject matter areas such as zoning, subdivision control and site plan review. Regulations in these areas may be adopted by the local legislative body. In each case, the local legislature specifies the local administrative body responsible for implementation and enforcement of the provisions of the regulations.

---

6. Village Law § 7–724, Town Law § 270, General City Law § 26.

CAVEAT: Do not confuse the Official Map, although it is sometimes called the "official plan," with the comprehensive plan provided for in separate sections of the enabling statutes: Village Law § 7–722, Town Law § 272–a, General City Law § 28–a. *See supra*, § 16.11.

7. Village Law § 7–724, Town Law § 270, General City Law § 26.

§ 16.32

1. Town Law § 138.

2. *Id. See* N.Y. State Uniform Fire Prevention and Building Code Act, Executive Law § 377 which regulates the construction of buildings throughout the state.

§ 16.33   LAND USE LAW   Ch. 16

In most municipalities, the principal bodies employed to carry out these zoning and related regulations are the planning board, the zoning board and the building department or inspector. The procedures to be followed by these administrative agencies are found in the specific enabling statutes discussed in this chapter; local administrative bodies are not subject to the provisions of the State Administrative Procedures Act.[1]

§ 16.34   Local Boards and Practices

When an application for a building permit is submitted to the local building inspector or department, the inspector must ascertain before issuing the permit that the proposed construction is in compliance with the zoning ordinance. This determination of compliance with zoning may be delegated to the building inspector or department, or to a separate zoning administrator or department of local government.

If the proposed development is not in compliance with the use and dimensional requirements, then the permit must be denied. This denial may be appealed to the Zoning Board of Appeals[1] which may issue a use or area variance in conformance with the standards of state law.[2] If, on the other hand, the proposed development requires subdivision, site plan, special permit or other approval, the applicant will be referred to the appropriate administrative agency for its review and determination.

Library References:

West's Key No. Digests, Zoning and Planning ⟜351.

§ 16.35   Local Boards and Practices—Local Legislature

The role of the local legislative body is the pivotal one in the field of local land use control. It is within the authority of the local legislature to adopt and amend the zoning ordinance[1], subdivision regulations,[2] site plan controls[3] and special permit provisions,[4] in addition to other regulatory regimes such as wetlands ordinances,[5] historic district protections[6] and open space plans.

It is within the authority of the legislative body to create other local boards and agencies such as the planning board[7] and zoning board of

§ 16.33
1. *See* Chapter 4 "Administrative Law," *supra*.

§ 16.34
1. *See infra*, § 16.37.
2. These standards are discussed at §§ 16.73–16.88, *infra*.

§ 16.35
1. *See supra*, §§ 16.28–16.29.

2. *See infra*, §§ 16.96–16.102.
3. *See infra*, §§ 16.103–16.108.
4. *See infra*, §§ 16.90–16.95.
5. *See* Chapter 15 "Environmental Law," §§ 15.12–15.17, *supra*.
6. *See infra*, § 16.127.
7. *See infra*, § 16.36.

344

appeals,[8] among others, and to determine what authority to delegate to them. Further, the legislature is responsible for adopting and amending the official map[9] and the comprehensive plan of the community.[10] In other words, the local legislature is responsible for the substantive provisions that effect land use controls and creates the procedures and agencies that implement and enforce those controls.

Library References:

West's Key No. Digests, Zoning and Planning ⚖︎355.

§ 16.36 Local Boards and Practices—Planning Board

Planning boards are created by act of the legislative body and may have from five to seven members.[1] This authority to create planning boards is permissive, not mandatory. Members of the legislative body may not be appointed as members of the planning board.[2] Appointments to the planning board are made by the legislative body in the case of towns, by the mayor in the case of villages and, in the case of cities, by the mayor or "other duly authorized appointing authority."[3]

Typically, the local legislature delegates to the planning board the authority to review and dispose of applications for land subdivision[4] and site plan approval.[5] Frequently, the planning board is delegated the responsibility for awarding special permits.[6]

The advisory functions of the planning board include making recommendations to the local legislature regarding the adoption of regulations concerning matters within the jurisdiction of the planning board,[7] the adoption and amendment of the comprehensive plan[8] and other matters that are referred to it by direction of the legislative body.[9]

Library References:

West's Key No. Digests, Zoning and Planning ⚖︎351.

8. See infra, § 16.37.
9. See supra, § 16.31.
10. See supra, § 16.11.

§ 16.36

1. Village Law § 7–718(1), Town Law § 271(1), General City Law § 27(1).
2. Village Law § 7–718(3), Town Law § 271(3), General City Law § 27(3).
3. Village Law § 7–718(1), Town Law § 271(1), General City Law § 27(1).
4. See infra, §§ 16.96–16.102.
5. See infra, §§ 16.103–16.108. The legislative body may delegate subdivision and site plan approval authority to the planning board or other administrative body. Village Law § 7–725–a(2), b(2), Town Law § 274– a(2), b(2), General City Law § 27–a(2), b(2). Special permit issuance authority may be delegated to another "responsible agency." Village Law § 7–725–a, Town Law § 274–a, General City Law § 27–a.

6. See infra, §§ 16.96–16.102. The legislative body may delegate special permit issuance authority to another "responsible agency," Village Law § 7–725–a, Town Law § 274–a, General City Law § 27–a.

7. Village Law § 7–718(13), Town Law § 271(13), General City Law § 27(13).

8. See supra, § 16.14.

9. Village Law § 7–718(14), Town Law § 271(14), General City Law § 27(14).

§ 16.37 Local Boards and Practices—Zoning Board of Appeals

When the local legislature adopts a zoning ordinance, it is required to establish a zoning board of appeals consisting of three or five members.[1] Appointments to the board of appeals are made by the legislative body, in the case of a village or town, and by the mayor or other duly authorized appointing authority, in the case of a city.[2] Members of the legislative body may not be appointed to the zoning board of appeals.[3]

The principal function of the zoning board of appeals is to grant variances from the strict application of the ordinance's provisions.[4] It may also reverse or affirm decisions, orders and determinations made by the administrative official charged with the enforcement of the zoning ordinance.[5] Separate authority may be conferred on the zoning board of appeals to hear and determine applications for subdivision and site plan approval and to issue special permits.

The jurisdiction of the board to interpret the zoning ordinance and grant variances is appellate only; it is limited to hearing and deciding appeals from, and reviewing the decisions, orders and determinations of, the administrative official charged with the enforcement of the zoning ordinance.[6] A majority of the members of the board must concur to reverse any such decision, order or determination.[7]

The jurisdiction of the board of appeals regarding the decisions, orders and determinations of the administrative official may be invoked by any person aggrieved or by an officer, department, board or bureau of the municipality.[8] Appeals must be filed by such persons within 60 days of the filing of the disputed decision, order or determination.[9] This is accomplished by filing with the administrative official and the board of appeals a notice of appeal, specifying its grounds and relief sought.[10] The board of appeals must hold a hearing on the appeal and give at least five days public notice of the hearing.[11]

Decisions of these appeals to the board must be rendered within 62 days of the hearing, unless extended by mutual consent of the appellant and the board.[12] Decisions of the zoning board of appeals may be subject

---

§ 16.37

1. Village Law § 7–712(2), Town Law § 267(2), General City Law § 81(1).
2. Id.
3. Village Law § 7–712(3), Town Law § 267(3), General City Law § 81(2).
4. Village Law § 7–712–b, Town Law § 267–b, General City Law § 81–b. See infra, §§ 16.73–16.88.
5. Id.
6. Village Law § 7–712–a(4), Town Law § 267–a(4), General City Law § 81–a(4).
7. Id.
8. Id.
9. Village Law § 7–712–a(5), Town Law § 267–a(5), General City Law § 81–a(5).
10. Id.
11. Village Law § 7–712–a(7), Town Law § 267–a(7), General City Law § 81–a(7).
12. Village Law § 7–712–a(8), Town Law § 267–a(8), General City Law § 81–a(8).

to environmental review under the State Environmental Quality Review Act.[13]

Library References:

West's Key No. Digests, Zoning and Planning ⚖354.

§ 16.38 Local Boards and Practices—Freedom of Information

Although local land use agencies are not subject to the State Administrative Procedures Law,[1] they are governed by the State Freedom of Information Law (FOIL)[2] which provides public access to governmental records. Agencies subject to its provisions are defined to include municipalities of the State of New York.[3]

The records that are subject to public access are defined broadly. Of great relevance to local land use matters, they include photos, maps, designs, drawings, rules, regulations, codes, manuals as well as reports, files and opinions.[4] The provisions of FOIL that establish methods of access, periods of time for compliance and provisions for payment for records reproduction are beyond the scope of this chapter.[5]

Library References:

West's Key No. Digests, Records ⚖30–35.

§ 16.39 Local Boards and Practices—Open Meetings

Local public bodies are also governed by the provisions of the Open Meetings Law[1] if the local body requires a quorum to do business and consists of two or more members.[2] The meetings of the local legislature and planning board, therefore, are subject to the provisions of this state law. Although the Open Meetings Law does not apply to "quasi-judicial proceedings,"[3] all meetings of the zoning board of appeals are subject to its provisions.[4]

The purpose of the Open Meetings Law is to insure "the performance of public business in an open and public manner, with the public able to attend and listen to the deliberations and decisions that go into the making of public policy."[5] All gatherings of these local land use

---

13. Village Law § 7–712–a(11), Town Law § 267–a(11), General City Law § 81–a(11). See infra, §§ 16.52–16.59.

§ 16.38

1. Public Officers Law §§ 95—106.
2. Public Officers Law, Art. 6.
3. Public Officers Law § 86(3).
4. Public Officers Law § 86(4).
5. See Chapter 3, "Municipal Law," supra.

§ 16.39

1. Public Officers Law, Art. 7.
2. Public Officers Law § 102(2).
3. Public Officers Law § 108(1).
4. Village Law § 7–712–a(1), Town Law § 267–a(1), General City Law § 81–a(1).
5. Matter of Sciolino v. Ryan, 81 A.D.2d 475, 477, 440 N.Y.S.2d 795, 797 (4th Dep't 1981).

§ 16.39　　　　　　　LAND USE LAW　　　　　　　Ch. 16

bodies are covered, therefore, including site visits conducted by the local legislature, planning boards and zoning boards of appeals and special meetings with applicants or opponents attended by members of the board.

When a town board adopted amendments to the zoning ordinance after a closed session in which the public was not involved, its action was nullified by the court for failure to conform to the open meetings provisions.[6] Courts have the discretion to declare void any action taken in violation of these provisions, "upon good cause shown."[7] Where the deliberations are held in private and the public permitted to know only the result of the deliberations, both the letter and spirit of the Open Meetings Law is violated.[8]

The Open Meetings Law contains extensive provisions governing notice of meetings to the public and media, barrier free access and the conduct of executive sessions[9] that are exempt from its provisions. These matters are beyond the scope of this chapter.[10]

Library References:
West's Key No. Digests, Zoning and Planning ⊜359.

§ 16.40　Local Boards and Practices—Conflict of Interests

State law prohibits municipal officers from participating in public matters in which they have a private conflict of interest.[1] Municipal officers governed by these provisions include members of "any administrative board, commission or other agency" of the municipality.[2] These conflict of interest provisions prohibit a municipal officer from having an interest in any "contract" with the municipality when the officer has the power to approve the "contract."[3]

This statute has been interpreted to prohibit planning and zoning board members from deliberating and voting on matters in which they have a private interest. For example, where a member of a local planning board has a 25% interest in the land subject to a subdivision application,

---

6. Gernatt Asphalt Products v. Town of Sardinia, 208 A.D.2d 139, 622 N.Y.S.2d 395 (4th Dep't 1995).

7. Matter of New York Univ. v. Whalen, 46 N.Y.2d 734, 735, 413 N.Y.S.2d 637, 638, 386 N.E.2d 245, 246 (1978).

8. Gernatt Asphalt Products v. Town of Sardinia, 208 A.D.2d 139, 622 N.Y.S.2d 395 (4th Dep't 1995).

9. Courts will scrutinize the propriety of executive sessions "lest the ... mandate be thwarted by thinly veiled references to the areas delineated thereunder." Daily Gazette Co. v. Town of Cobleskill, 111 Misc.2d 303, 303, 444 N.Y.S.2d 44, 45 (Sup.Ct., Schoharie County, 1981).

10. See Chapter 3 "Municipal Law," supra.

§ 16.40

1. See generally, General Municipal Law, Art. 18, Conflicts of Interests of Municipal Officers and Employees and Chapter 3 "Municipal Law," §§ 3.22–3.23, supra.

2. General Municipal Law § 800(5).

3. General Municipal Law § 801.

that member has a conflict of interest.[4] On the other hand, there is no conflict of interest when a planning board member is the president of a supply company that does a few hundred dollars of business with the applicant for subdivision approval.[5]

State law provides that every application for "a variance, amendment, change of zoning, approval of a plat, ... or permit, pursuant to the provisions of any ordinance, local law, rule or regulation constituting the zoning and planning regulations of a municipality" must provide full information regarding "the nature and extent of the interest" of any municipal officer in the matter presented.[6]

Library References:

West's Key No. Digests, Zoning and Planning ⚖︎360, 436.1, 543.

§ 16.41 Local Boards and Practices—Summary

When an application for a building permit is submitted to the local building inspector or department, the administrator must ascertain before issuing the permit that the proposed construction is in compliance with the zoning ordinance. This determination of compliance with zoning may be delegated to the building inspector or to a separate zoning administrator or department of local government.

If the proposed development is not in compliance with the ordinance's use and dimensional requirements, the permit must be denied. This denial may be appealed to the Zoning Board of Appeals which may issue a use or area variance in conformance with the standards of state law.[1] If, on the other hand, the proposed development requires subdivision, site plan, special permit or other approval, the applicant must be referred to the appropriate administrative agency for its review and determination. Once compliance with all local regulations is assured, a building permit may be issued, but only if the construction plans conform to the requirements of the fire protection and building code.

§ 16.42 Judicial Review

The judicial review of local land use decisions involves the doctrine of separation of powers between the judicial and legislative branches of government. It is governed by special statutory provisions that limit both actions against governmental bodies, in general, and against local land use decisions, in particular. The rules of judicial review may change depending on the type of local body involved and the action challenged.

4. Keller v. Morgan, 149 A.D.2d 801, 539 N.Y.S.2d 589 (3d Dep't 1989).

5. Parker v. Town of Gardiner Planning Bd., 184 A.D.2d 937, 585 N.Y.S.2d 571 (3d Dep't 1992).

6. General Municipal Law § 809.

§ 16.41

1. These standards are discussed at §§ 16.73–16.88, *infra*.

Judicial review of local land use decisions involves several key issues: What are the procedures that must be used to invoke the jurisdiction of the courts?[1] What standards does the judiciary use to review the decisions of local legislatures, zoning boards of appeals and planning boards?[2] Who has standing to challenge these decisions?[3] What prerequisites must be met before the challenge is ripe for judicial review?[4] Finally, what remedies are the courts willing to use when local actions are found to be invalid?[5]

Library References:

West's Key No. Digests, Zoning and Planning ⚖561–593.

§ 16.43 Judicial Review—Procedures

The actions of public bodies are reviewable principally under Article 78 of the Civil Practice Law and Rules.[1] These provisions allow aggrieved parties to obtain writs of certiorari and mandamus against the final determinations of public officers and bodies.[2] Such actions must be brought in the supreme court of the appropriate county.[3]

In general, the Statute of Limitations for the filing of a proceeding under Article 78 is four months after the decision to be reviewed becomes final and binding on the petitioner.[4] With respect to many local land use decisions, this Statute of Limitations has been shortened to thirty days. This applies in villages, towns and cities when the determination challenged is a use or area variance[5] or a decision regarding an application for a site plan,[6] subdivision[7] or special permit approval.[8] Decisions of local boards of appeals are subject to this shortened 30 day Statute of Limitations.[9]

These shorter Statute of Limitation periods begin to run, generally, from the date the decision is filed in the office of the municipal clerk. The statutes require that these decisions be filed promptly, usually within five business days.[10] It has been determined that the filing with

§ 16.42

1. See infra, § 16.43.
2. See infra, §§ 16.44–16.47.
3. See infra, § 16.48.
4. See infra, § 16.49.
5. See infra, § 16.50.

§ 16.43

1. CPLR 7801 et seq.
2. CPLR 7801.
3. CPLR 7804.
4. CPLR 217.
5. Village Law § 7-712-c, Town Law § 267-c, General City Law § 81-c. The latter of these three provisions applies to decisions regarding use and area variances, specifically; the former apply to decisions of a village or town board of appeals, in general.

6. Village Law § 7-725-a, Town Law § 274-a, General City Law § 27-a.

7. Village Law § 7-740, Town Law § 282, General City Law § 38.

8. Village Law § 7-725-b, Town Law § 274-b, General City Law § 27-b.

9. Village Law § 7-712-c, Town Law § 267-c, General City Law § 81-c.

10. "Decisions of the board of appeals on appeals shall be filed within five business days after the day such decision is rendered." Village Law § 7-712-a(9), Town

§ 16.44 Judicial Review—Standards

Courts exercise considerable restraint in reviewing the decisions of local land use bodies, including the local legislature, zoning board of appeals and the planning board. In general, they presume that such local decisions are valid, impose a heavy burden of proof on those who challenge them, and sustain them if there is a rational basis for the decision which is supported by substantial evidence.[1]

This judicial deference is extended to the decisions of zoning and planning boards:

> The crux of the matter is that the responsibility for making zoning decisions has been committed primarily to quasi-legislative, quasi-

---

the village clerk of the minutes of a board of appeals meeting was sufficient to start the running of the Statute of Limitations.[11] The minutes would not suffice, however, if they did not contain the final decision of the board.[12]

Library References:

West's Key No. Digests, Zoning and Planning ⌾581–593.

Law § 267–a(9), General City Law § 81–a(9). This latter section permits the decision to be filed, alternatively, in the zoning office of a city, if one has been established. Decisions of the authorized board regarding special use permits shall be filed within five business days after such decision is rendered. Village Law § 7–725(b)(6), Town Law § 274–b(6), General City Law § 27–b(6). Resolutions approving both preliminary subdivision plats (Village Law § 7–728(5)(g), Town Law § 276(5)(g), General City Law § 32(5)(g)) and final subdivision plats (Village Law § 7–728(9), Town Law § 276(9), General City Law § 32(9)) must be filed within five business days of their adoption. The decision of the authorized board shall be filed within five business days of a site plan decision. Village Law § 7–725–a(7), Town Law § 274–a(7), General City Law § 27–a(7).

11. DeBellis v. Luney, 128 A.D.2d 778, 513 N.Y.S.2d 478 (2d Dep't 1987).

12. Town of Clinton v. Dumais, 69 A.D.2d 836, 415 N.Y.S.2d 81 (2d Dep't 1979).

PRACTICE POINTER: The decisions of local boards may be reversed if they are not supported by substantial evidence on the record of their proceedings. These provisions requiring the filing of decisions within five business days put pressure on local boards to file a record of their decision promptly and this starts the running of the statute. If the full basis for the decision is missing from the filing, will it be available to an aggrieved party if the record of the proceeding is not yet available for inspection? If not, how will aggrieved parties determine whether to bring an Article 78 proceeding and what the grounds for that action are? Whether a memorandum of decision, board resolution or the minutes of the meeting are filed, they should contain the board's findings and the evidence on which those findings are based, or else be otherwise available to the public in some fashion. This is the intent, if not the letter of these filing requirements.

§ 16.44

1. Esselte Pendaflex Corp. v. Incorporated Village of Garden City, 216 A.D.2d 519, 629 N.Y.S.2d 59 (2d Dep't 1995).

[I]t is well settled that zoning ordinances ... enjoy a strong presumption of constitutionality and if there is a reasonable relationship between the end sought to be achieved and the means adopted to achieve it, the regulation will be upheld. The party challenging a zoning ordinance must establish its unconstitutionality beyond a reasonable doubt. Moreover, the role of the courts is limited to determining whether the ordinance bears at least a minimal relationship to a legitimate, governmental objective.

§ 16.44 LAND USE LAW Ch. 16

administrative boards composed of representatives from the local community. Local officials, generally, possess the familiarity with local conditions necessary to make the often sensitive planning decisions which affect the development of their community. Absent arbitrariness, it is for locally selected and locally responsible officials to determine where the public interest in zoning lies.[2]

This deference expresses itself as a limitation on the power of judicial review in these matters:

Judicial review of local zoning decisions is limited; not only in our court but in all courts. Where there is a rational basis for the local decision, that decision should be sustained. It matters not whether, in close cases, a court would have, or should have, decided the matter differently. The judicial responsibility is to review zoning decisions but not, absent proof of arbitrary and unreasonable action, to make them.[3]

When reviewing a challenge to a local land use decision, the courts, in general,

must apply a local government's zoning ordinance as it exists at the time of judicial review, unless there is proof of 'special facts' which indicate that the local government acted in bad faith in delaying the landowner's application for a building permit while the zoning law was changed.[4]

Where the issuance of a building permit was delayed and, during such delay, the zoning law was amended to apply greater restrictions to petitioner's property, the new restrictions were held to apply in the absence of any special facts showing "malice, oppression, manipulation or corruption."[5] Where, however, the planning board improperly delayed the application and presented unsatisfactory reasons for the delay, the board was held to be precluded from relying on newly added, more restrictive provisions under the "special facts" exception to the rule.[6]

Library References:

West's Key No. Digests, Zoning and Planning ⚖︎601–626.

§ 16.45 Judicial Review—Standards—Local Legislature

An Article 78 proceeding is not the appropriate vehicle to challenge

216 A.D.2d at 519, 629 N.Y.S.2d at 60.

2. Matter of Cowan v. Kern, 41 N.Y.2d 591, 599, 394 N.Y.S.2d 579, 584, 363 N.E.2d 305, 310 (1977).

3. Id.

4. Wiehe v. Town of Babylon, 169 A.D.2d 728, 728–729, 564 N.Y.S.2d 193, 194 (2d Dep't 1991).

5. Id. at 729, 564 N.Y.S.2d at 194.

6. Miller v. Southold Town, 190 A.D.2d 672, 593 N.Y.S.2d 74 (2d Dep't 1993).

the constitutionality of a local legislature's zoning decision.[1] The denial of a request for a change in zoning, for example, may be reviewed in a declaratory judgment action, not in an Article 78 proceeding.[2] The court is not required to do so, especially when "the allegations in the petition [are] insufficient to make out a valid cause of action."[3] If a declaratory judgment action could have been "resolved through a form of action or proceeding for which a specific limitation period is statutorily provided, that limitation period governs the declaratory judgment action."[4] However, where the challenge to the local legislature's action is to the procedure followed, not the constitutional validity of the enactment, an Article 78 proceeding is the appropriate vehicle.[5]

§ 16.46 Judicial Review—Standards—Zoning Board of Appeals

In reviewing a decision of the zoning board of appeals, a court may reverse or affirm, wholly or partly, or may modify the decision brought up for review.

> Concededly, the court's review power is limited. A board determination may not be set aside in the absence of illegality, arbitrariness or abuse of discretion. Moreover, the reviewing court may not conduct a trial de novo on an issue already decided by the zoning board on the basis of substantial evidence. Within those limitations, however, the court may appropriately modify the decision brought up for review if the zoning board's determination was illegal, arbitrary or an abuse of its discretion.[1]

The court, in these cases, is concerned primarily with whether there is substantial evidence on the record in support of the board's decision.[2] "The local zoning board has discretion in considering applications for variances and its determination will be sustained if it has a rational basis and is supported by substantial evidence in the record."[3]

§ 16.45

1. Save the Pine Bush, Inc. v. City of Albany, 70 N.Y.2d 193, 518 N.Y.S.2d 943, 512 N.E.2d 526 (1987).

2. CPLR 103(c); *see also*, Vezza v. Bauman, 192 A.D.2d 712, 597 N.Y.S.2d 418 (2d Dep't 1993).

3. Rodriques v. McCluskey, 156 A.D.2d 369, 548 N.Y.S.2d 323 (2d Dep't 1989).

4. Save the Pine Bush, Inc. v. City of Albany, 70 N.Y.2d 193, 518 N.Y.S.2d 943, 512 N.E.2d 526 (1987).

5. *Id.*

§ 16.46

1. St. Onge v. Donovan, 71 N.Y.2d 507, 519, 527 N.Y.S.2d 721, 727, 522 N.E.2d 1019, 1025 (1988). In Cohen v. Hahn, 155 A.D.2d 969, 547 N.Y.S.2d 780 (4th Dep't 1989) "[i]t was error for the court to order a hearing de novo in Supreme Court on petitioner's application for a use variance. The determination whether to grant a variance lies within the discretion of the zoning authorities and a reviewing court may not conduct a trial de novo." *Id.* at 970, 547 N.Y.S.2d at 781.

2. Friendly Ice Cream Corp. v. Barrett, 106 A.D.2d 748, 483 N.Y.S.2d 782 (3d Dep't 1984).

3. Segal v. Zoning Board of Appeals of Town of Bethel, 191 A.D.2d 873, 873, 594 N.Y.S.2d 459, 460 (3d Dep't 1993).

§ 16.47 Judicial Review—Standards—Planning Board

In reviewing subdivision applications, it is within the discretion of the planning board to determine whether to approve or disapprove.[1] The role of the courts is limited to deciding whether the planning board's decision is illegal or arbitrary and capricious.[2]

> The reviewing court should not disturb the [p]lanning [b]oard's determination absent illegality, irrationality, or an abuse of discretion, nor should the court substitute its judgment for that of the Board. Moreover, where conflicting inferences may be drawn from the record before the [b]oard, it is the function of the [b]oard, not the court, to weigh and reconcile that conflicting evidence.[3]

In reviewing the record of a planning board's proceedings, evidence supporting the findings of the board is very significant. Without such evidence, the findings can be seen as lacking factual support and hence an arbitrary and capricious exercise of the board's authority.[4] The findings are sufficient when they show grounds for a decision and provide the basis for judicial review.[5] Where the only "findings" on the record are conclusory statements of the planning board, such statements fail to provide the evidentiary basis needed to support the board's decision.[6] When the board fails to make sufficient findings, the proper disposition by the court is remand.[7]

§ 16.48 Judicial Review—Standing

When the standing of a party to challenge a local land use decision is raised, the basic inquiry is whether that party can demonstrate an adverse effect different from that of the public at large and that the interest asserted is within the zone of interest to be protected by the statute under which the decision was made. The court's require a "threshold showing" that a person has sustained "special damage, different in kind and degree from the community generally."[1] Although courts sometimes say that this special damage must be pleaded and proved, this is softened by the judicial policy that, in land use litigation, it is desirable that "disputes be resolved on their own merits rather than

---

§ 16.47

1. Thomas v. Brookins, 175 A.D.2d 619, 572 N.Y.S.2d 557 (4th Dep't 1991).

2. Id.

3. Id. at 619, 572 N.Y.S.2d at 558.

4. McDonald's Corporation v. Rose, 111 A.D.2d 850, 490 N.Y.S.2d 588 (2d Dep't 1985).

5. Masten v. Baldauf, 147 A.D.2d 566, 537 N.Y.S.2d 860 (2d Dep't 1989).

6. Leibring v. Planning Board of Town of Newfane, 144 A.D.2d 903, 534 N.Y.S.2d 236 (4th Dep't 1988).

7. Greene v. Johnson, 121 A.D.2d 632, 503 N.Y.S.2d 656 (2d Dep't 1986).

§ 16.48

1. Sun–Brite Car Wash, Inc. v. Board of Zoning and Appeals of Town of North Hempstead, 69 N.Y.2d 406, 413, 515 N.Y.S.2d 418, 421, 508 N.E.2d 130, 133 (1987).

by preclusive, restrictive standing rules."[2]

That the "special damage" test of standing has meaning is demonstrated in a case where the petitioners challenged the issuance of a construction permit to a discount store based on the failure of the local permitting agency to comply with the environmental review requirements of state law.[3] The court held that the ownership of property one half mile from the store was not enough, in itself, to confer standing. Petitioner's status was protected, however, by his showing that changes in the hydrogeologic formations and patterns of stormwater drainage beneath the site would adversely affect his private drinking water well. "A direct impact on one's drinking water supply is a concern that is plainly within the zone of interest that [the environmental review statute] was designed to protect."[4]

The ownership of adjacent property is often sufficient to show the required special injury, but not always.[5] Where the plaintiffs contested the issuance of a temporary certificate of occupancy to an adult entertainment establishment, the proximity of their properties to the contested business was sufficient to confer standing on them.[6] Since the objective of the operative statute was to protect surrounding properties from adverse effects, their properties were within the zone of interest to be protected, as well. Where a nearby property owner challenged a

---

2. Id. at 413, 515 N.Y.S.2d at 421, 508 N.E.2d at 133. The court further held that "proof of special damage or in-fact injury is not required in every instance to establish that the value or enjoyment of one's property is adversely affected." Id.

3. Many v. Village of Sharon Springs Board of Trustees, 218 A.D.2d 845, 629 N.Y.S.2d 868 (3d Dep't 1995).

4. 218 A.D.2d at 845, 629 N.Y.S.2d at 870. In another case where petitioner challenged the agency's failure to comply with state environmental review requirements, standing was denied. Society of the Plastics Industry, Inc., v. County of Suffolk, 77 N.Y.2d 761, 570 N.Y.S.2d 778, 573 N.E.2d 1034 (1991).

In land use matters especially, we have long imposed the limitation that the plaintiff, for standing purposes, must show that it would suffer direct harm, injury that is in some way different from that of the public at large. The doctrine grew out of a recognition that, while directly impacting particular sites, governmental action affecting land use in another sense may aggrieve a much broader community. The location of a gas station may, for example, directly affect its immediate neighbors but indirectly affect traffic patterns, noise levels, air quality and aesthetics throughout a wide area. The concept of a plaintiff's aggrievement, generally necessary to secure judicial review, was therefore refined and restricted by the courts in such matters to require that plaintiffs have a direct interest in the administrative action being challenged, different in kind or degree from that of the public at large.

Id. at 774–775, 570 N.Y.S.2d at 786, 573 N.E.2d at 1042.

5. "The status of neighbor does not, however, automatically provide the entitlement or admission ticket to judicial review in every instance. Petitioner, for example, may be so far from the subject property that the effect of the proposed change is no different from that suffered by the public generally." Sun–Brite Car Wash, 69 N.Y.2d at 414, 570 N.Y.S.2d at 422, 573 N.E.2d at 134.

6. Golden v. Steam Heat, Inc., 216 A.D.2d 440, 628 N.Y.S.2d 375 (2d Dep't 1995). In this case, the borough president was denied standing as a plaintiff because he was acting on behalf of the borough's residents whose interests in the matter are not different in kind or degree from those of the public at large.

§ 16.48 LAND USE LAW Ch. 16

variance to allow a small building addition, however, adjacency was not sufficient to confer standing in the absence of some allegation that the proposed addition would cause some injury in fact.[7]

Standing is not conferred to property owners whose only injury is increased business competition. Even where the plaintiff's property is adjacent to the business benefited by a favorable land use decision, he may lack standing where his injury is solely economic.[8] This interest is not within the zone of interest protected by the operative land use statute.

Numerous standing issues are raised when an association challenges a local land use decision. Would the members of the association have standing, some special injury within the statute's zone of interest, if they brought the action individually?[9] Is the association fairly representative of the aggrieved community?[10] Does the association have the legal capacity and authority to bring the suit?[11] Are the interests the association asserts in the litigation germane to its purposes?[12]

Library References:

West's Key No. Digests, Zoning and Planning ⚖571.

§ 16.49 Judicial Review—Exhaustion

Inherent in a petitioner's Article 78 challenge is that the local land use decision is "final."[1] If a land use decision is not ripe, that is, if its effect on the petitioner is not direct and immediate, it lacks this requisite finality. Similarly, if an aggrieved party has not exhausted the administrative remedies available to him, a court will not entertain his Article 78 petition.

Plaintiffs who have subdivision applications pending before a local planning board, for example, may not challenge a recreation fee imposed by the locality on each approved subdivision lot because the effect of the

---

7. Hoxsie v. Zoning Board of Appeals of City of Saratoga Springs, 129 Misc.2d 493, 493 N.Y.S.2d 535 (Sup.Ct., Saratoga County, 1985).

8. Kemp v. Zoning Bd. of Appeals of Village of Wappingers Falls, 216 A.D.2d 466, 628 N.Y.S.2d 187 (2d Dep't 1995).

9. Otsego 2000 v. Planning Bd. of Town of Otsego, 171 A.D.2d 258, 575 N.Y.S.2d 584 (3d Dep't 1991).

10. Friends of Woodstock, Inc. v. Woodstock Planning Board, 152 A.D.2d 876, 543 N.Y.S.2d 1007 (3d Dep't 1989).

11. Darlington v. City of Ithaca Bd. of Zoning Appeals, 202 A.D.2d 831, 609 N.Y.S.2d 378 (3d Dep't 1994). The local Conservation Advisory Council did not have the capacity to sue under the local law creating it.

12. Society of the Plastics Industry, Inc. v. County of Suffolk, 77 N.Y.2d 761, 570 N.Y.S.2d 778, 573 N.E.2d 1034 (1991). A national trade association was held not to have, as one of its purposes, the objective of protecting individual members from local conditions such as air quality and traffic congestion.

§ 16.49

1. Article 78 of the Civil Practice Law and Rules allows aggrieved parties to obtain writs of certiorari and mandamus against the "final" determinations of public officers and bodies. CPLR 7801.

disputed fee schedule on the plaintiffs is not immediate.[2] They must wait until the fee is imposed on their approved subdivision to challenge its validity. Similarly, plaintiffs "do not show that the [b]oard's action has a 'direct and immediate' impact upon them or that the harm they perceive to have suffered at the hands of the [b]oard will not subsequently be prevented or cured" until they have exhausted their administrative remedies by applying for a variance.[3]

The failure to exhaust administrative remedies is not a bar to judicial relief where the administrative body could not provide adequate relief to the plaintiffs.[4] Where the plaintiffs suffer special injury from ongoing construction and seek an injunction alleging the violation of the local zoning ordinance, an appeal directly to the court is permissible since the administrative agency may not issue "adequate and complete relief" in the form of an injunction.[5] Similarly, where the only question at issue is one of law, the plaintiff need not exhaust his administrative remedies.[6]

Library References:

West's Key No. Digests, Zoning and Planning ☞562.

§ 16.50 Judicial Review—Remedies

A writ of certiorari under Article 78 of the CPLR is the appropriate vehicle to secure judicial review of a local board or agency decision. Parties aggrieved, for example, by a local board determination regarding a variance,[1] special permit,[2] site plan[3] or subdivision application,[4] engage the jurisdiction of the court by bringing an Article 78 proceeding in the nature of a writ of certiorari.

When the plaintiff seeks to compel an administrative agency or officer to perform an official duty, the appropriate vehicle is an Article 78 proceeding in the nature of a writ of mandamus. A zoning board of

2. Weingarten v. Town of Lewisboro, 77 N.Y.2d 926, 569 N.Y.S.2d 599, 572 N.E.2d 40 (1991).

3. Stone v. McGowan, 157 A.D.2d 882, 550 N.Y.S.2d 153, (3d Dep't 1990). "At this juncture there is no identifiable harm to them for there has been no actual interference. ... If petitioners apply for a variance and that application is denied, the effect of the Board's interpretation that the variance is required can then be reviewed." Id. at 883, 550 N.Y.S.2d at 154.

4. Haddad v. Salzman, 188 A.D.2d 515, 591 N.Y.S.2d 193 (2d Dep't 1992).

5. Id. at 516, 591 N.Y.S.2d at 194.

6. Sievers v. City of New York, Dep't of Buildings, 146 A.D.2d 473, 536 N.Y.S.2d 441 (1st Dep't 1989), appeal after remand 182 A.D.2d 580, 582 N.Y.S.2d 722 (1992).

§ 16.50

1. Black v. Board of Appeals of Incorp. Village of Westbury, 33 A.D.2d 916, 308 N.Y.S.2d 302 (2d Dep't 1969).

2. Cunningham v. Planning Bd. and Bd. of Appeals of Town of Brighton, 157 N.Y.S.2d 698 (1956), rev'd and vacated in part on other grounds 4 A.D.2d 313, 164 N.Y.S.2d 601 (4th Dep't 1957).

3. Elle v. Neennan, 68 Misc.2d 725, 327 N.Y.S.2d 706 (Sup.Ct., Ontario County, 1972).

4. Walton v. Town of Brookhaven, 41 Misc.2d 798, 246 N.Y.S.2d 985 (Sup.Ct., Suffolk County, 1964).

appeals, for example, can be directed to issue a determination that the use of the petitioner's property is a permitted use.[5] Similarly, the building inspector can be compelled to issue a building permit where a variance has been granted and the inspector has no discretion to deny the requested permit.[6] Courts very rarely employ mandamus relief that effects a legislative result, such as the rezoning of a plaintiff's property. In the case of discriminatory treatment of like parcels, and in the case of exclusionary zoning, however, exceptions to this general rule have been created.[7]

An Article 78 proceeding is not an appropriate vehicle for challenging the legislative actions of a village board of trustees, a city council or the town board, such as the validity of the zoning ordinance.[8] An action for a declaratory judgment is more commonly brought to challenge the validity of legislative actions such as the adoption or amendment of the zoning ordinance[9] or subdivision regulations.[10] Such an action is brought under separate provisions of the Civil Practice Law and Rules.[11]

Injunctions are appropriately sought, in conjunction with actions for declaratory judgments, to enjoin the enforcement or application of an ordinance declared to be invalid.[12] Injunctions are also used routinely to remove structures that are found to be in violation of local requirements or to otherwise require property owners to comply with land use regulations.[13]

5. Levada v. Board of Zoning Appeals of Incorporated Village of Freeport, 199 A.D.2d 504, 605 N.Y.S.2d 397 (2d Dep't 1993).

6. Charter Land Development v. Hartmann, 170 A.D.2d 600, 566 N.Y.S.2d 375 (2d Dep't 1991).

7. See Berenson v. Town of New Castle, 67 A.D.2d 506, 415 N.Y.S.2d 669 (2d Dep't 1979) where the court directed the town to rezone plaintiff's property for multi-family use. The court noted:

[z]oning and land use regulations were deemed to be legislative functions, to be exercised by and within the particular expertise of the local legislative body. Thus, with the single exception of discriminatory zoning of similarly situated parcels, in which case the obvious remedy was to treat like parcels alike, a judicial declaration that a zoning ordinance was invalid was never accompanied by a declaration which actually rezoned that property or placed it within a particular use classification.

Id. at 515, 415 N.Y.S.2d at 674.

8. Janiak v. Town of Greenville, 203 A.D.2d 329, 610 N.Y.S.2d 286 (2d Dep't 1994); Putcha v. Beattie, 129 A.D.2d 918, 514 N.Y.S.2d 559 (3d Dep't 1987).

9. Abbott House v. Tarrytown, 34 A.D.2d 821, 312 N.Y.S.2d 841 (2d Dep't 1970).

10. Levine v. Town Bd. of Carmel, 34 A.D.2d 796, 311 N.Y.S.2d 691 (2d Dep't 1970)

11. CPLR 3001, 3017(b).

12. North Shore Beach Property Owners Ass'n v. Brookhaven, 115 N.Y.S.2d 670 (1952).

13. Incorporated Village of Williston Park v. Argano, 197 A.D.2d 670, 602 N.Y.S.2d 878 (2d Dep't 1993). The defendants were compelled to remove an extension to their home found to be in violation of the zoning ordinance. See also, Village Law § 7–714:

In case any building or structure is erected, constructed, reconstructed, altered, repaired, converted, or maintained; or any building, structure or land is used, or any land is divided into lots, blocks or sites in violation of this act, or of any local law or other regulation made under authority conferred thereby, the proper local authorities of the village, in addition

Library References:
West's Key No. Digests, Zoning and Planning ⚖ 721–729.

§ 16.51 Judicial Review—Summary

Judicial review of local land use decisions involves the doctrine of separation of powers between the judicial and legislative branches of government. It is governed by special statutory provisions that limit both actions against governmental bodies, in general, and against local land use decisions, in particular. The applicable rules of judicial review depend on the type of local body that is involved and the type of action that is challenged.

Several key issues are implicated when a local land use decision is reviewed by a court of law:

- What are the procedures that must be used to invoke the jurisdiction of the courts?
- What standards does the judiciary use to review the decisions of local legislatures, zoning boards of appeals and planning boards?
- Who has standing to challenge these decisions?
- What prerequisites must be met before a challenge is ripe for judicial review?
- What remedies are the courts willing to grant when local actions are found to be invalid?

§ 16.52 Local Environmental Review

The State Legislature has declared that all state, county and local agencies "are stewards of the air, water, land and living resources" and "have an obligation to protect the environment for the use and enjoyment of this and all future generations."[1] Therefore, most actions of local governmental agencies that affect the use of the land may not be taken officially until those agencies have conducted a thorough review of their potential environmental impact.

The extensive provisions setting forth the procedures and requirements for the environmental review of local land use actions are found in the Environmental Conservation Law, Article 8, commonly referred to as the State Environmental Quality Review Act, or SEQRA. Further details

---

to other remedies, may institute any appropriate action or proceedings to prevent such unlawful erection ... to restrain, correct or abate such violation, to prevent the occupancy of said building, structure or land or to prevent any illegal act, conduct, business or use in or about such premises.

Similar wording is found in Town Law § 268.

§ 16.52

1. ECL § 8–0103(8). See also, 6 NYCRR § 617.1(b). "Agencies" whose actions are regulated by Article 8 of the ECL and required by it to perform environmental impact assessments of those actions are defined to include "local" agencies. See ECL § 8–0105(3).

regarding these requirements are set forth in the regulations of the Commissioner of the State Department of Environmental Conservation.[2]

Under SEQRA, a local agency must determine whether an action it is considering may have a significant adverse environmental impact.[3] If an action has such potential, the agency must first prepare an Environmental Impact Statement (EIS).[4] Failure to follow the procedures required by SEQRA will render the action invalid.[5] The procedural steps required by SEQRA, and the time periods within which they must be taken, have been determined to take precedence over other statutory provisions regulating the land use actions of local governments.[6]

SEQRA requires local agencies to "use all practicable means to realize the policies" of this legislation and to choose alternative actions, where practicable to "minimize or avoid adverse environmental effects, including effects revealed in the environmental impact statement."[7] The Court of Appeals has held that this language imposes substantive, in addition to procedural, obligations on local decisionmakers that force them to take effective action to protect the environment.[8]

Library References:

West's Key No. Digests, Health and Environment ⚖25.10(1)–25.10(8).

§ 16.53 Local Environmental Review—Actions Subject to SEQRA

SEQRA applies to a wide variety of local agency actions that affect the environment. These include projects or physical activities that are

---

2. The regulations of the Commissioner are found in 6 NYCRR Part 617. A more thorough review of SEQRA's requirements is set forth in Chapter 15 "New York Environmental Law," §§ 15.2–15.6, *supra*.

3. 6 NYCRR § 617.7(a).

4. *Id.*

5. Chinese Staff and Workers Association v. City of New York, 68 N.Y.2d 359, 509 N.Y.S.2d 499, 502 N.E.2d 176 (1986).

The appropriate remedy for violations of the statutory mandate imposed by SEQRA ... is to ... declare the special permit null and void. The suggestion in the dissenting opinion that the omission here can be cured by an amended negative declaration ... would effectively allow the municipality to comply with SEQRA only as an afterthought following a successful challenge to [a] prior action. Indeed it would allow a project to be initially approved without the benefit of a valid environmental review.

Id. at 369, 509 N.Y.S.2d at 505, 502 N.E.2d at 182.

6. Sun Beach Real Estate Development Corp. v. Anderson, 62 N.Y.2d 965, 479 N.Y.S.2d 341, 468 N.E.2d 296 (1984). The court held that an application for preliminary approval of a subdivision plat was not complete until the procedural steps required under SEQRA have been taken.

PRACTICE POINTER: This case involved a clash between the time periods governing the review by a local planning board of a subdivision application contained in Section 276 of the Town Law and those set forth in SEQRA, which can take considerably more time to complete. The court held that the legislature intended the more onerous requirements of SEQRA to govern the planning board's review of subdivision applications. By implication, this holding applies to the resolution of clashes between the time periods prescribed for other local land use actions and those required by SEQRA.

7. ECL § 8–0109(1).

8. Matter of Jackson v. New York State Urban Dev. Corp., 67 N.Y.2d 400, 503 N.Y.S.2d 298, 494 N.E.2d 429 (1986).

directly undertaken by the agency or require agency approval, planning and policy making activities of agencies and the adoption of rules, regulations and resolutions.[1]

The regulations issued under SEQRA assist local agencies in classifying their actions to determine whether they must first conduct environmental reviews. For land use purposes, there are three relevant classes of actions: Type I, Type II and Unlisted Actions. Unlisted Actions are those not included on the Type I and Type II lists contained in the regulations.[2] Type II actions are not subject to the review requirements of SEQRA. Type I actions are more likely than Unlisted Actions to require a full review of the potential environmental impact of the project or policy under consideration.

The regulations state that Type II actions do not have a significant environmental impact or are otherwise precluded from environmental review.[3] The Type II list includes:

    1. the replacement, rehabilitation or reconstruction of existing structures or facilities;

    2. the construction of non-commercial structures involving less than 4,000 square feet of gross floor area and not involving a change in zoning or a use variance;

    3. the construction or expansion of a single-family, two-family or three-family residence on an improved lot or a structure accessory to a residential use;

    4. the granting of an area variance for single-family, two-family or three-family residences;

    5. the issuance of building permits and historic preservation permits predicated solely upon the applicant's compliance with local building or preservation codes;

    6. the adoption of a moratorium on land development or construction; or

    7. a local legislative decision to not entertain a request to rezone property.[4]

Type I actions "are more likely to require the preparation of an Environmental Impact Statement" than Unlisted Actions.[5] If an action is directly undertaken, funded or approved by a local agency it is classified as a Type I action if it involves:

    1. the adoption of a municipality's land use plan and the initial adoption of comprehensive zoning regulations;

§ 16.53
1. 6 NYCRR § 617.2(b).
2. 6 NYCRR § 617.2(ak).
3. 6 NYCRR § 617.5.
4. Id.
5. 6 NYCRR § 617.4.

§ 16.53 LAND USE LAW Ch. 16

2. changes in zoning regulations that affect 25 acres or more or that exceed thresholds contained elsewhere in the listing of Type I actions;

3. the construction of residential structures exceeding stipulated thresholds;[6] or

4. the construction of non-residential facilities that exceed stipulated thresholds.[7]

The inclusion of an action on this Type I list "carries with it the presumption that it is likely to have a significant adverse impact on the environment and may require an [Environmental Impact Statement]."[8] This presumption increases the burden on a local agency when it determines whether the action may have a significant adverse environmental impact as required by SEQRA.[9]

Library References:
West's Key No. Digests, Health and Environment ⊱25.10(2.1).

§ 16.54 Local Environmental Review—Actions Subject to SEQRA—Building Permits

The general notion that the issuance of a building permit is a ministerial act, exempt from SEQRA's requirements, was challenged in *Pius v. Bletsch*.[1] In this case, the Director of Engineering of the Town of Huntington had been delegated site plan approval powers coupled with the authority to make certain case-by-case judgments on site plan design and construction materials issues. Due to these discretionary powers, the Director was entitled to require that an Environmental Impact Statement ("EIS") be submitted as a precondition to the issuance of a permit.[2]

A subsequent case stated that the "pivotal inquiry" is whether the information contained in the environmental impact statement may form the basis for a decision whether to approve the building permit.[3] The court held that

> In determining whether an agency decision falls within SEQRA's purview ... the courts cannot rely on a mechanical distinction between ministerial and discretionary acts alone. When an agency has some discretion, but that discretion is circumscribed by a

---

6. *Id.* at § 617.4(b)(5).
7. *Id.* at § 617.4(b)(6).
8. *Id.* at § 617.4(a)(1).
9. 6 NYCRR § 617.7.

§ 16.54
1. 70 N.Y.2d 920, 524 N.Y.S.2d 395, 519 N.E.2d 306 (1987).
2. The applicant in Pius relied on Filmways Communications v. Douglas, 106 A.D.2d 185, 484 N.Y.S.2d 738 (4th Dep't 1985), where it was held that the building inspector's function was ministerial and excluded from SEQRA review because there was no provision in the building code that gives the building inspector a latitude of choice.

3. Incorporated Village of Atlantic Beach v. Gavalas, 81 N.Y.2d 322, 599 N.Y.S.2d 218, 615 N.E.2d 608 (1993).

narrow set of criteria which do not bear any relationship to the environmental concerns that may be raised in an [Environmental Impact Statement], its decisions will not be considered actions for purposes of SEQRA's EIS requirements.[4]

In this case, the building inspector was authorized to require and review architectural and engineering reports and was vested with some discretion to deny or approve the building permit based on those reports. The reports, however, were required solely to determine whether the proposed construction met building code requirements and did not pertain to SEQRA's broader environmental concerns. In this context, the court held that the preparation of an environmental impact statement would be a meaningless act. The information contained in the environmental impact statement would not be relevant to the building inspector's discretionary inquiry.[5]

§ 16.55 Local Environmental Review—Actions Subject to SEQRA—Variances

SEQRA regulations stipulate that area variances for single-family, two-family and three-family residences and the granting of individual setback and lot line variances are Type II actions, not subject to environmental review.[1] Use variances and area variances not included in the Type II list must be classified either as Type I actions, if the applicable thresholds are exceeded, or as Unlisted Actions. When applications for these types of variances are made, the zoning board of appeals will classify the action under the SEQRA regulations and make its determination of significance accordingly.

In *Concerned Citizens of Westbury v. Board of Appeals of Incorporated Village of Westbury*,[2] an application was made for an area variance to allow an existing restaurant to double in size. Under SEQRA regulations this would not be a Type II action, and a determination of significance would have to be made by the zoning board of appeals. A local citizens group challenged the zoning board's action for failure to comply with SEQRA's requirements. However, since the matter was not raised during the administrative review process, the court refused to entertain the SEQRA challenge.

The issuance of a use variance was challenged for failure to comply with SEQRA in *Crepeau v. Zoning Board of Appeals of Village of Cambridge*.[3] The variance allowed the property to be used for parking

---

4. Id. at 326, 599 N.Y.S.2d at 219–20, 615 N.E.2d at 609–10.

5. Id. at 328, 599 N.Y.S.2d at 221, 615 N.E.2d at 611.

§ 16.55
1. 6 NYCRR § 617.5(12), (13).

2. 173 A.D.2d 615, 570 N.Y.S.2d 314 (2d Dep't 1991).

3. 195 A.D.2d 919, 600 N.Y.S.2d 821 (3d Dep't 1993).

§ 16.56 Local Environmental Review—Actions Subject to SEQRA—Subdivisions

In *Save the Pine Bush, Inc. v. Planning Board of Town of Guilderland*,[1] the applicant sought approval to subdivide a parcel of land into 65 lots. The planning board did not require the applicant to submit a full Environmental Impact Statement ("EIS") even though the action was listed as a Type I action. A citizens group challenged that decision arguing that SEQRA had been violated because no EIS was required. The court held "an EIS is not a per se requirement of all Type I actions"[2] and that the planning board's review of the reports regarding the potential impacts was sufficient for it to issue a declaration that no adverse environmental impacts were raised by the subdivision application.[3]

SEQRA may not be used to alter the jurisdiction of public agencies.[4] In a challenge to the approval of a subdivision application, the petitioner claimed that the local planning board erred in applying SEQRA by not requiring the applicant to meet state agency sewer placement regulations.[5] The court held that it is the State's Department of Health, not the town planning board, that is statutorily directed to supervise and regulate the sanitary aspects of sewage disposal. It noted that

> SEQRA does not alter the jurisdiction between or among State agencies. So long as the lead agency identifies the relevant areas of environmental concern, takes a "hard look" at them to determine whether there may be a significant effect on the environment and sets forth in writing the basis for its determination of significance, it has met its SEQRA obligation. That the proposed action does not comport with Department of Health regulations does not, in and of itself, mandate SEQRA denial.[6]

In this case, however, the planning board action was invalidated, because it had issued a preliminary subdivision approval before determining that the action would have no significant negative impact on the environment.[7]

§ 16.56

1. 217 A.D.2d 767, 629 N.Y.S.2d 124 (3d Dep't 1995).
2. 217 A.D.2d at 768, 629 N.Y.S.2d at 125.
3. 217 A.D.2d at 770, 629 N.Y.S.2d at 126.
4. ECL § 8-0103(6).
5. Ames v. Johnston, 169 A.D.2d 84, 571 N.Y.S.2d 831 (3d Dep't 1991).
6. *Id.* at 86, 571 N.Y.S.2d at 833.
7. *Id.* at 86–7, 571 N.Y.S.2d at 833–4.

§ 16.57 Local Environmental Review—Actions Subject to SEQRA—Site Plans

In *WEOK Broadcasting Corp. v. Planning Board of Town of Lloyd*,[1] the petitioner's application for site plan approval for a radio transmission tower was denied based on aesthetic factors. The planning board determined, after SEQRA review, that the petitioner had "failed to adequately minimize or avoid adverse environmental effects to the maximum extent practicable."[2] The Court of Appeals held that "aesthetic considerations are a proper area of concern in [SEQRA] balancing analysis inasmuch as the Legislature has declared that the "maintenance of a quality environment ... that at all times is healthful and pleasing to the senses" is a matter of State-wide concern."[3]

However, the Court dismissed the board's allegation that its determination was based upon an alleged failure of the site plan to conform to zoning regulation and held that SEQRA review may not serve as a vehicle for adjudicating "legal issues concerning compliance with local government zoning."[4] The Court found that the evidence submitted in the Environmental Impact Statement by the petitioner was unrefuted by substantial evidence on the record. It held that "negative aesthetic impact considerations, alone, however, unsupported by substantial evidence, may not serve as a basis for denying approval of a proposed action pursuant to SEQRA review."[5]

§ 16.58 Local Environmental Review—Actions Subject to SEQRA—Rezoning

When the local legislature amends the zoning ordinance to provide for land uses that will be subject to separate approvals and SEQRA review at a later time, it must, nonetheless, conduct an environmental review of the zoning amendments themselves. In *Eggert v. Town Board of Town of Westfield*,[1] the town board classified a zoning amendment as a Type I action but found that the amendment itself would not have a significant impact on the environment as the rezoning required property owners to apply for special permits before developing under the amendments.

The town board in *Eggert* acknowledged that there would be adverse environmental impacts to be considered at that time, but reasoned that such impacts could be adequately addressed when applications for special

---

§ 16.57

1. 79 N.Y.2d 373, 583 N.Y.S.2d 170, 592 N.E.2d 778 (1992).

2. *Id.* at 377, 583 N.Y.S.2d at 171, 592 N.E.2d at 779.

3. *Id.* at 381, 583 N.Y.S.2d at 173, 592 N.E.2d at 781.

4. *Id.* at 382, 583 N.Y.S.2d at 174, 592 N.E.2d at 782.

5. *Id.* at 385, 583 N.Y.S.2d at 176, 592 N.E.2d at 784.

§ 16.58

1. 217 A.D.2d 975, 630 N.Y.S.2d 179 (4th Dep't 1995).

§ 16.58   LAND USE LAW   Ch. 16

permits were submitted. The court rejected this argument stating, "[t]o comply with SEQRA, the [t]own [b]oard must consider the environmental concerns that are reasonably likely to result from, or are dependent on, the amendments ... at least on a conceptual basis."[2]

In *Cannon v. Murphy*,[3] the town board rezoned the applicant's property, allowing him to build 108 houses, a 100 percent increase in density. The board did not require an Environmental Impact Statement to be submitted and found that the development would not have a negative impact on the environment. The court invalidated the rezoning because there was information on the record that the action might have potential large impacts on water, threatened or endangered species, aesthetic resources and transportation. The declaration by the board that there would be no significant environmental impact was not supported by sufficiently detailed information.[4]

The degree of detail required in a SEQRA review depends on the circumstances involved. In *Valley Realty Development Co, Inc. v. Town of Tully*,[5] a rezoning of land in a mining district to residential use was upheld as in compliance with SEQRA. The court stated that:

> In reviewing an agency's issuance of a negative declaration, a court's inquiry is limited to whether the relevant areas of concern were identified, whether a hard look was given to those areas and whether a reasoned elaboration was given for the negative declaration. In making such review, the agency's obligations under SEQRA must be viewed in light of a rule of reason. The degree of detail required will vary with the circumstances and the nature of the zoning proposal.[6]

Here, there was no evidence that the elimination of mining would harm, rather than benefit the environment. "In the totality of the circumstances, we conclude that respondents gave the necessary hard look at the effects of the zoning change and otherwise complied with SEQRA."[7]

§ 16.59 Local Environmental Review—Summary

Most actions of local governmental agencies that affect the use of the land may not be taken officially until those agencies have conducted a thorough review of their potential environmental impact. The State Legislature has declared that all state, county and local agencies are stewards of the air, water, land and living resources and have an obligation to protect the environment for the use and enjoyment of this and all future generations.

2. 217 A.D.2d at 976, 630 N.Y.S.2d at 181.

3. 196 A.D.2d 498, 600 N.Y.S.2d 965 (2d Dep't 1993).

4. *Id.* at 501, 600 N.Y.S.2d at 968.

5. 187 A.D.2d 963, 590 N.Y.S.2d 375 (4th Dep't 1992).

6. *Id.* at 963–64, 600 N.Y.S.2d at 376.

7. *Id.* at 964, 600 N.Y.S.2d at 376–77.

The extensive provisions that set forth the procedures and requirements for the environmental review of local land use actions are found in the Environmental Conservation Law, Article 8, commonly referred to as the State Environmental Quality Review Act, or SEQRA. Under SEQRA, a local agency must first determine whether an action it is considering may have a significant adverse environmental impact. If an action has such potential, the agency must prepare an Environmental Impact Statement (EIS) prior to making a determination on the land use action.

The failure to follow the procedures required by SEQRA will render the action invalid. The procedural steps required by SEQRA and the time periods within which they must be taken have been determined to take precedence over other statutory provisions regulating the land use actions of local governments.

SEQRA requires local agencies to use all practicable means to realize the policies of this legislation and to choose alternative actions, where practicable, to minimize or avoid adverse environmental effects, including effects revealed in the environmental impact statement. The Court of Appeals has held that this language imposes substantive, in addition to procedural, obligations on local decision makers that force them to take effective action to protect the environment.

§ 16.60 Zoning Law—In General

In general, the improvement and development of real property is categorized by New York State law into five types of land uses. Each triggers a different procedure under local law and is governed by different substantive standards. These five categories are as follows:

1. As-of-Right Uses: Where the zoning ordinance specifically permits a proposed use of land without the imposition of special conditions, the proposed activity is denominated an "as of right use."[1]

2. Non–Conforming Use: Where the actual use of the property predates the imposition of zoning restrictions and those restrictions do not permit that use, it is called a "non-conforming use."[2]

3. Variance: If a proposed use of property does not conform to applicable zoning restrictions it may be authorized by a "use or area variance" under certain circumstances.[3]

4. Special Permit: Other proposed uses are authorized by the zoning ordinance, but are subject to the imposition of special conditions that protect the public interest; these uses are approved by a "special permit."[4]

§ 16.60
1. See infra, § 16.61.
2. See infra, §§ 16.62–16.72.
3. See infra, §§ 16.73–16.88.
4. See infra, §§ 16.90–16.95.

5. Rezoning: Finally, where a proposed use is not otherwise permitted under local law, the property owner may request that the local government rezone the property, making the proposed activity an "as of right" use under that rezoning.[5]

Once the proposed use of land is authorized under one of the foregoing techniques, it may still be subject to further review and approval under "subdivision regulations"[6] which govern the subdivision of land parcels or "site plan regulations"[7] which apply to the actual development of individual land parcels.

State law governing these land uses, and the local procedures that apply to them, are a blend of case and statutory law. In recent years, the statutory law has been amplified significantly; many needed definitions have been added, much of the prior case law has been codified, and many of the statutory gaps have been filled.

§ 16.61 As of Right Use

Municipal zoning ordinances separate the land within the community's jurisdiction into districts within which stipulated uses are permitted as of right. For example, the zoning ordinance may say that, in all residentially zoned districts in the municipality, a detached one-family dwelling shall be permitted as a matter of right.[1] When a use is permitted in this way, an administrative agency generally does not have the authority to deny an applicant the right to use its property for such uses, based on its determination that the use will have a negative impact on the neighborhood. This determination has been made by the local legislative body and it is beyond the authority of a subordinate administrative agency to deny a landowner that use.

A zoning district that does not permit some viable economic uses on an as of right basis is suspect. Where a zone was created within which development was permitted exclusively by special permit, where all uses were subject to discretionary review and approval of an administrative agency, the court found the provisions violative of the requirement that zoning conform to comprehensive planning.[2] The court held that this procedure, of allowing for a discretionary review on a lot-by-lot basis within the district, was an invalid substitute for the requirement that zoning be in furtherance of comprehensive planning.

---

5. See infra, §§ 16.113–16.116.
6. See infra, §§ 16.96–16.102.
7. See infra, §§ 16.103–16.108.

§ 16.61

1. See § 154–20, Code of the Town of Patterson.
2. Marshall v. Village of Wappingers Falls, 28 A.D.2d 542, 279 N.Y.S.2d 654 (2d Dep't 1967). In a subsequent case, such a procedure was sustained where the subject parcel was located entirely in a flood plain; in that circumstance, a discretionary review of each application for approval and the absence of an "as of right use" were deemed to be in conformance with the comprehensive planning requirement. Dur-Bar Realty Co. v. City of Utica, 57 A.D.2d 51, 394 N.Y.S.2d 913 (4th Dep't 1977). See supra, §§ 16.11–16.16.

§ 16.62 Nonconforming Use—Definition and Application

A nonconforming use is created when a zoning ordinance is adopted or amended to prohibit a particular use that lawfully existed prior to the enactment or amendment. Nonconforming land uses are not defined by New York State statutes but may be defined in the local ordinance. A typical local ordinance may provide as follows: a nonconforming use is any use, whether of a building or tract of land or both, existing on the effective date of this chapter, which does not conform to the use regulations of the district in which it is located.[1]

Typically, nonconforming use issues are created upon the initial adoption of the zoning ordinance which, for example, restricts land use in a given district to residential development, thereby rendering all existing nonresidential uses nonconforming. Subsequent amendments to the zoning ordinance, however, may have the same effect. When property owners propose the improvement, expansion, rebuilding or other change in their nonconforming property use, they must be certain to comply with local regulations governing those uses. Normally, these regulations are found in a discrete article of the local zoning ordinance.

Provisions that protect existing uses in which property owners have a significant investment or business interest save zoning ordinances from violating constitutionally protected property rights. Provisions that constrain changes in nonconforming uses, or that require such uses to be terminated over time, balance the municipality's interest in eliminating nonconforming uses with constitutionally protected property rights.

Library References:

West's Key No. Digests, Zoning and Planning ⌦321–338.

§ 16.63 Nonconforming Use—Changes

The expansion, enlargement, extension, alteration, reconstruction, restoration, increase in use or a change in the type or location of a nonconforming use typically is restricted by the local zoning ordinance. The case law clarifies that these provisions encourage the disappearance of nonconforming uses in zoning districts.[1]

Normally, such prohibitions do not extend to structural maintenance and repair, or internal alterations, that do not increase the degree of, or create any new, noncompliance with the locality's zoning regulations. In some cases, they do not extend to improvements needed to

§ 16.62

1. Code of Town of Ossining, Chapter 200, § 36(a) (1985).

§ 16.63

1. Cave v. Zoning Bd. of Appeals of Village of Fredonia, 49 A.D.2d 228, 373 N.Y.S.2d 932 (4th Dep't 1975).

modernize a nonconforming business, even when the number of customers served will be increased.[2]

These provisions may vary considerably from one locality to another. A municipality, particularly intent on eliminating nonconforming uses may prohibit any physical expansion of a building; another may favor property use by allowing, for example, the construction of an additional story because it does not increase the footprint, or lot coverage, of the structure.

Library References:

West's Key No. Digests, Zoning and Planning ⚖327, 328.

§ 16.64 Nonconforming Use—Reconstruction and Restoration

The local zoning ordinance may provide that a nonconforming structure that suffers physical damage shall not be restored, other than for a use which conforms to the zoning ordinance, if that damage exceeds a certain percentage of the structure's value. Typical standards range from 25% to 50%. These provisions are premised on the theory that owners do not have a vested right to reconstruct a nonconforming building after damage by fire, weather, natural disaster or otherwise.[1] In such a case, their property rights are destroyed by the disaster, rather than by the ordinance.

Restrictions on reconstruction can raise interesting issues of interpretation. For example, if two separate apartment buildings that are operated as a single enterprise are damaged by fire, how would a local ordinance be applied that prohibits reconstruction if the nonconforming use is damaged by 50% or more? If the damage to one of the buildings exceeded the 50% standard, but the damage to the enterprise did not, could the locality prohibit the reconstruction of the heavily damaged building? New York courts tend to look at the economic and functional interdependence of the properties in such a case and have held that the locality must permit reconstruction.[2]

Library References:

West's Key No. Digests, Zoning and Planning ⚖335.

2. Tartan Oil v. Board of Zoning Appeals of the Town of Brookhaven, 213 A.D.2d 486, 623 N.Y.S.2d 902 (2d Dep't 1995); Ruhm v. C.P. Craska, Inc., 59 A.D.2d 1016, 399 N.Y.S.2d 749 (4th Dep't 1977); Gilmore v. Beyer, 46 A.D.2d 208, 361 N.Y.S.2d 739 (3d Dep't 1974).

§ 16.64

1. Bobandal Realties, Inc. v. Worthington, 21 A.D.2d 784, 250 N.Y.S.2d 575 (2d Dep't 1964).

2. *Id. See* Pelham Esplanade, Inc. v. Board of Trustees of the Village of Pelham Manor, 77 N.Y.2d 66, 563 N.Y.S.2d 759, 565 N.E.2d 508 (1990).

§ 16.65 Nonconforming Use—Enlargement, Alteration or Extension

Similarly, local ordinances often prohibit the enlargement, alteration or extension of a nonconforming use. To allow such activity would defeat the underlying policy of the nonconforming use provision, which is to eliminate them. Courts have upheld prohibitions on the construction of an awning over a courtyard outside a restaurant on the theory that it would create additional space for patrons to congregate and, in this sense, increase the degree of the nonconforming use.[1] Similarly, the prohibition imposed upon the conversion of seasonal bungalows to year-round residences has been upheld as an acceptable method of preventing the enlargement of a nonconforming use.[2]

Where nonconforming business operations are proposed to be extended, the case law is somewhat less clear. Where roads and structures built on a parcel used as a gravel mining operation exhibited the owner's intention to use the entire parcel, the Court held that expanding the mining operation to another location on the property was permitted.[3] The addition of a body-toning operation to the premises containing a nonconforming beauty parlor, however, was considered a prohibited extension of the prior nonconforming use.[4] The court's interest in protecting the owner's demonstrated investment in the gravel mining operation could explain the difference between these cases.

Library References:
West's Key No. Digests, Zoning and Planning ⚖329–331.

§ 16.66 Nonconforming Use—Changes to Another Nonconforming Use

The property owner's vested right to continue a nonconforming use does not extend to a materially different use.[1] The pivotal inquiry is what constitutes a material change in use such as to render the prior non-conforming use terminated or abandoned. One could argue, on behalf of a property owner, that the change of a nonconforming use from one commercial use to another, for example, should not be prohibited by the zoning ordinance: to change a building's occupancy from a dairy plant to a business that rents machinery simply shifts the type of nonconformance from one commercial category to another. It has been

---

§ 16.65

1. Country Sam Inc. v. Bennett, 192 A.D.2d 448, 597 N.Y.S.2d 13 (1st Dep't 1993).

2. Castore v. Breite, 167 A.D.2d 799, 563 N.Y.S.2d 361 (3d Dep't 1990).

3. Syracuse Aggregate Corp. v. Weise, 51 N.Y.2d 278, 434 N.Y.S.2d 150, 414 N.E.2d 651 (1980).

4. Traveler Real Estate, Inc. v. Cain, 160 A.D.2d 1214, 555 N.Y.S.2d 217 (3d Dep't 1990).

§ 16.66

1. Town of Carmel v. Meadowbrook National Bank of Nassau County, 15 Misc.2d 789, 182 N.Y.S.2d 465 (Sup.Ct., Putnam County, 1959).

held, however, that it is not only a change in the volume of business conducted but in the character of that business that determines whether one business use is a continuation of another.[2] This is true despite the generic similarity between the old and new proposed use.[3]

Occasionally, courts hold that changes from one use to another within the same category of use are permitted. In one case, for example, the owner was allowed to establish a storage business in a building that had been occupied as a nursery and florist enterprise.[4] Determinations in these cases turn on the particular facts involved, the court's interpretation of how material the change will be, and the specific language of the local ordinance which regulates changes in nonconforming uses.

Library References:

West's Key No. Digests, Zoning and Planning ⚖327.

§ 16.67 Nonconforming Use—Termination

Local ordinances provide for the termination of nonconforming uses in a variety of ways. Provisions that prohibit the reconstruction of destroyed nonconforming structures is one such method. In addition, zoning ordinances may provide that nonconforming uses shall not be reestablished if discontinued for a specified period of time, ranging from a few months to a year or more. Further, nonconforming uses that are particularly offensive to other uses in the zoning district may be required to be amortized, or discontinued, within a specific time period, depending on how offensive they are considered to be. Under certain circumstances, a local ordinance may terminate a nonconforming use upon the transfer of the property from one owner to another.

Library References:

West's Key No. Digests, Zoning and Planning ⚖321.

§ 16.68 Nonconforming Use—Abandonment

A property owner's right to continue a nonconforming use may be lost by abandonment. Originally, this required a voluntary, completed act of abandonment by the owner.[1] It was said that there must be the concurrence of an intention to abandon and some act, or failure to act, which implies a lack of interest on the part of the owner to retain the use. Time was considered relevant to the issue of abandonment, but not

---

2. Hustis v. City of White Plains, 201 N.Y.S.2d 909 (1960).

3. Oreiro v. Board of Appeals of the City of White Plains, 204 A.D.2d 964, 612 N.Y.S.2d 509 (3d Dep't 1994); Calcagni Constr. Co. v. Zoning Bd. of Appeals, Town & Vil. of Harrison, 56 A.D.2d 845, 392 N.Y.S.2d 86 (2d Dep't 1977).

4. Prudence v. Town of Ithaca Zoning Board of Appeals, 195 A.D.2d 662, 599 N.Y.S.2d 749 (3d Dep't 1993).

§ 16.68

1. City of Binghamton v. Gartell, 275 App.Div. 457, 90 N.Y.S.2d 556 (3d Dep't 1949).

enough, alone, to establish it; further, the mere failure to continue the nonconforming use was not sufficient to establish abandonment.[2]

Today, local zoning ordinances frequently stipulate that any discontinuance of the nonconforming use for a specified period constitutes abandonment. Courts hold that such provisions are sufficient to establish the owner's intent to abandon the nonconforming use as a matter of law. Where the established period is reasonable, discontinuance of the use for that time amounts to an abandonment of the use.[3] In *Darcy v. Zoning Board of Appeals of the City of Rochester*, the court upheld a local determination that a nonconforming use was abandoned when evidence showed discontinuance for at least 20 months, well beyond the six month period specified in the ordinance.[4] It has also been held that local discontinuance periods apply even when the owner can prove that it did not actually intend to abandon the nonconforming use.[5]

Library References:
West's Key No. Digests, Zoning and Planning ⇐336–338.

§ 16.69 Nonconforming Use—Amortization

Some local ordinances require certain nonconforming uses to be amortized, that is terminated, after a specified period. The Court of Appeals has upheld such provisions "where the benefit to the public has been deemed of greater moment than the detriment to the property owner."[1] In *Modjeska Sign Studies, Inc. v. Berle*, the Court of Appeals noted that the test for when an amortization period is reasonable is

> a question that must be answered in the light of the facts of each particular case. Certainly, a critical factor is the length of the amortization period in relation to the investment.... The critical question, however, ... is whether the public gain achieved by the exercise of the police power outweighs the private loss suffered by the owners of the nonconforming uses.[2]

Contexts in which amortization provisions are likely to be upheld are:

1. When the common law of nuisance would allow neighboring property owners to enjoin the continuation of a nonconforming use. For example, a gravel pit, auto wrecking operation, or junkyard, harmful to children in a developing residential area, might be enjoined under a

---

2. Id.

3. Town of Islip v. P.B.S. Marina, Inc., 133 A.D.2d 81, 518 N.Y.S.2d 427 (2d Dep't 1987).

4. Darcy v. Zoning Board of Appeals of the City of Rochester, 185 A.D.2d 624, 586 N.Y.S.2d 44 (4th Dep't 1992).

5. Spicer v. Holihan, 158 A.D.2d 459, 550 N.Y.S.2d 943 (2d Dep't 1990).

§ 16.69

1. Harbison v. City of Buffalo, 4 N.Y.2d 553, 559, 176 N.Y.S.2d 598, 600, 152 N.E.2d 42, 44 (1958).

2. Modjeska Sign Studios, Inc. v. Berle, 43 N.Y.2d 468, 479, 402 N.Y.S.2d 359, 367, 373 N.E.2d 255, 262 (1977).

private nuisance action.[3] Likewise, a zoning ordinance can legally require such a nonconforming use to be terminated in an appropriate case. If an amortization provision is challenged, the municipality can show that the owner's property interest is slight because of its vulnerability to a nuisance action. In this context, however, the label "amortization" is inapt. The grace period, if any, allowed by the local statute is gratuitous if, in fact, the owner's use may be enjoined as a nuisance.

2. When the nonconforming use is somewhat noxious and the owner has little investment in it.[4] For example, a provision requiring the owner to cease raising pigeons on the roof or to remove an old outdoor sign might withstand challenge because of the minimal nature of the owner's investment and the significant harm done to the zoning scheme if the owner's activity is allowed to continue. Harder cases are presented when the owner has a significant investment in the use and the public interest in removing it is clear but where the threat to public health and safety is not imminent.

§ 16.70 Nonconforming Use—Transfer of Ownership

Local ordinances may provide that a nonconforming use must terminate upon the transfer of ownership of property. In *Village of Valatie v. Smith*, such a local provision was challenged.[1] The zoning ordinance required the termination of a nonconforming use upon the transfer of title to a mobile home or to the land on which it is situated. The Court of Appeals upheld the provision finding that it was appropriate for the village to use a nonfinancial interest of the owner, such as not being displaced involuntarily, as the standard for measuring when a nonconforming use must be terminated.[2]

Library References:

West's Key No. Digests, Zoning and Planning ⟐321.

§ 16.71 Nonconforming Use—Procedures

Nonconforming use issues arise most frequently when a property owner seeks a building permit which is denied by the building inspector because the improvements proposed are not permitted under local zoning provisions governing nonconforming uses. Counsel for the owner must investigate the applicable zoning ordinance and determine the property's history to judge whether the building inspector has ruled

---

3. It has long been a maxim of property law that owners may not use their own property to injure that of another. *Sic utere tuo ut alienum non laedas*. Private nuisance claims are tort actions brought by private parties where a neighboring landowner seeks to have the court enjoin the noxious use of property by claiming that the defendant's use is such that it prevents the plaintiff from the quiet enjoyment of his property.

4. *Id.*

§ 16.70

1. 83 N.Y.2d 396, 610 N.Y.S.2d 941, 632 N.E.2d 1264 (1994).

2. *Id.*

appropriately.[1] If the inspector has erred in determining that the property fails to conform to the zoning ordinance, or that the improvements are prohibited by the ordinance, an appeal to the zoning board of appeals may be taken, challenging the inspector's ruling.[2]

If the inspector's determinations are correct, the owner can apply for a variance from the application of the ordinance to the property which will free it from the constraints of the nonconforming use provisions of the ordinance. For such an application to be successful, all the requirements for obtaining a variance under state and local law must be met.[3]

§ 16.72 Nonconforming Use—Summary

Trigger:

1. Property owner seeks to use or continue to use property which use is prohibited under the zoning ordinance; or

2. Property owner is denied building permit because proposed modification to nonconforming use is not permitted under the zoning ordinance.[1]

Considerations:

1. Nonconforming uses are given constitutional protection if the use was substantial, existing and lawful at the time the zoning ordinance was adopted or amended;[2]

2. Restrictions on expansion, enlargement, alteration, reconstruction, increase in use or change in type or location of nonconforming use can vary significantly from municipality to municipality;[3]

3. Termination of nonconforming use can occur through:

   • prohibition on reconstruction of destroyed structures;[4]

   • property owner's abandonment or discontinuance of nonconforming use for a specified period of time;

   • requirement that nonconforming use be required to be amortized over a specific period of time;[5] or

§ 16.71
1. See supra, § 16.32.
2. See supra, § 16.37.
3. See infra, §§ 16.73–16.88.

§ 16.72
1. See supra, § 16.62.

2. See supra, § 16.62.
3. See supra, §§ 16.63–16.65.
4. See supra, § 16.64.
5. See supra, § 16.68.

- enactment of ordinance extinguishing right to nonconforming use on transfer of ownership of the property.[6]

Options:

1. Property owner can challenge the rejection of a building permit by appealing directly to the zoning board of appeals within 60 days of rejection;[7] or
2. Property owner may apply to the zoning board of appeals for a variance from application of the zoning ordinance.[8]

§ 16.73 Use Variance

Use variances are defined and the standards for their issuance are stipulated by uniform New York State statutes applicable to villages, towns and cities.[1] The local zoning board of appeals may grant a use variance which "shall mean the authorization by the zoning board of appeals for the use of land in a manner or for a purpose which is otherwise not authorized or is prohibited by the applicable zoning regulations."[2] This authority is specifically provided to the board of appeals by statute.[3]

In establishing standards that boards of appeals must follow in issuing use variances, the statutes codify previous case law requirements which developed in the absence of specific statutory authority.[4] Since the terms used in the statutes are similar to those used in previous seminal cases, the interpretation of the rules guiding boards of appeals requires a knowledge of both case and statutory law.[5]

Typically, issues involving use variances arise when a property owner is denied a building permit by the building inspector because the proposed use of the property is not permitted, or is prohibited, by zoning provisions applicable to the property. The statutes provide that "[t]he board of appeals, on appeal from the decision or determination of the administrative official charged with the enforcement of such ordinance or local law, shall have the power to grant use variances, as defined herein."[6]

---

6. See supra, § 16.70.
7. See supra, § 16.71.
8. See infra, §§ 16.73–16.81.

§ 16.73

1. Village Law § 7–712, Town Law § 267, General City Law § 81–b.

2. Village Law § 7–712(1)(a), Town Law § 267(1)(a), General City Law § 81–b(1)(a).

3. Village Law § 7–712–b(2)(a), Town Law § 267–b(2)(a), General City Law § 81–b(3)(a). See supra, § 16.37.

4. See People ex rel. Fordham Manor Reformed Church v. Walsh, 244 N.Y. 280, 155 N.E. 575 (1927); Otto v. Steinhilber, 282 N.Y. 71, 24 N.E.2d 851 (1939).

5. See infra, §§ 16.75–16.78.

6. Village Law § 7–712–b(2)(a), Town Law § 267–b(2)(a), General City Law § 81–b(3)(a).

Under the statutes, the board of appeals may grant a use variance only when the property owner can show that applicable zoning regulations have caused an unnecessary hardship.[7] The burden of proving this hardship is placed on the applicant. To meet that burden, the owner must demonstrate to the board that all four of the following statutory conditions are met:[8]

1. The owner cannot realize a reasonable return;[9]

2. The hardship is unique to the owner's property and not applicable to a substantial portion of the zoning district;[10]

3. Granting the variance will not alter the essential character of the neighborhood;[11] and

4. The hardship is not self-created.[12]

The statute instructs the board to grant the minimum variance necessary to address the hardship to the owner while protecting the character of the neighborhood and the community.[13]

Library References:

West's Key No. Digests, Zoning and Planning ⟜481–518.

§ 16.74 Use Variance—Statutory Standard

In New York, a zoning board of appeals can grant a use variance only upon a showing by the property owner that the application of the zoning regulation causes an unnecessary hardship.[1] This requirement imposes a heavy burden of proof upon the applicant for a use variance, since that applicant is asking the board to alter the determination of the local legislature as to the uses that are appropriate in a particular zoning district.

Since uniformity and predictability of the uses of property within districts was essential to the early constitutional underpinnings of zoning, variances from those provisions were not to be given lightly. In 1939, the Court of Appeals set out three of the criteria now found in the statutes[2] that must be demonstrated by the applicant to establish unnecessary hardship: no reasonable return, unique hardship and protection of the essential character of the neighborhood.[3]

---

7. Village Law § 7–712–b(2)(b), Town Law § 267–b(2)(b), General City Law § 81–b(3)(b).
8. *Id.*
9. *See infra,* § 16.75.
10. *See infra,* § 16.76.
11. *See infra,* § 16.77.
12. *See infra,* § 16.78.
13. Village Law § 7–712–b(2)(c), Town Law § 267–b(2)(c), General City Law § 81–b(3)(c).

§ 16.74

1. People ex rel. Fordham Manor Reformed Church v. Walsh, 244 N.Y. 280, 155 N.E. 575 (1927).

2. Village Law § 7–712–b, Town Law § 267–b, General City Law § 81–b.

3. Otto v. Steinhilber, 282 N.Y. 71, 24 N.E.2d 851 (1939).

§ 16.75 Use Variance—Statutory Standard—Reasonable Return

New York statutes require an applicant for a use variance to demonstrate that it cannot realize a reasonable return on its property under the provisions of the ordinance and that this lack of return is substantial as demonstrated by competent financial evidence.[1]

Owners are often inclined to prove that the zoning ordinance prevents them from using their property in a particular or desired way and that the returns allowed under the ordinance are substantially less than the returns they would realize if allowed to use their property in this particular way. Such proof fails to address the required burden of proof. "A zoning ordinance is confiscatory and unreasonable only if it prevents a plaintiff from using his property for any purpose for which it is reasonably adapted."[2]

This standard presents an obstacle to an owner who seeks a variance because he cannot expand a nonconforming use.[3] For example, in a case where the owner of a gasoline station needed to modernize and expand his operations to compete with nearby stations, proof of that particular hardship, based on the difficulty of competing with nearby modernized stations, was inadequate. The court held that the appropriate inquiry was whether the owner could realize a reasonable return on the property as developed or on any permitted use of the property.[4]

The statutes codify the case law with respect to the type of proof required of an applicant.[5] That the applicant cannot realize a reasonable return, and that the lack of return is substantial, must be demonstrated by competent financial evidence.[6] This requires the applicant to disclose relevant aspects of the property's finances and may include investments, mortgages and incumbrances, taxes and charges, expenses and income and appraisals.[7] Statements indicating that developers or purchasers for

---

§ 16.75

1. Village Law § 7–712–b(2)(b)(1), Town Law § 267–b(2)(b)(1), General City Law § 81–b(3)(b)(i).

2. Williams v. Town of Oyster Bay, 32 N.Y.2d 78, 81, 343 N.Y.S.2d 118, 121, 295 N.E.2d 788, 790 (1973). Everhart v. Johnston, 30 A.D.2d 608, 290 N.Y.S.2d 348 (3d Dep't 1968). "The applicant must demonstrate that the return from the property would not be reasonable for each and every permitted use under the ordinance." 30 A.D.2d at 609, 290 N.Y.S.2d at 350. Bath Beach Health Spa of Park Slope, Inc. v. Bennett, 176 A.D.2d 874, 575 N.Y.S.2d 344 (2d Dep't 1991). "The applicable standard is not whether a higher rate of return is possible with the grant of the use variance, but whether a reasonable return can be realized without the variance." 176 A.D.2d at 878, 575 N.Y.S.2d at 345.

3. *See supra,* § 16.65.

4. Crossroads Recreation v. Broz, 4 N.Y.2d 39, 172 N.Y.S.2d 129, 149 N.E.2d 65 (1958).

5. Village Law § 7–712(2)(b), Town Law § 267–b(2)(b), General City Law § 81–b(3)(b).

6. Village Law § 7–712(2)(b)(1), Town Law § 267–b(2)(b)(1), General City Law § 81–b(3)(b)(i).

7. Crossroads Recreation v. Broz, 4 N.Y.2d 39, 172 N.Y.S.2d 129, 149 N.E.2d 65 (1958).

the property cannot be found are insufficient unless they indicate a good faith effort to sell and are supported by competent evidence.[8]

Library References:

West's Key No. Digests, Zoning and Planning ⚖498.

§ 16.76 Use Variance—Statutory Standard—Unique Hardship

In addition to establishing that the applicant cannot realize a reasonable return under the ordinance, the statutes require that he must establish that "the hardship is unique and does not apply to a substantial portion of the district or neighborhood."[1] The Court of Appeals has held that the applicant must prove that his "particular property suffers a singular disadvantage through the operation of the zoning ordinance."[2] However, "uniqueness does not require that only the parcel of land in question and none other be affected by the condition which creates the hardship."[3]

If the hardship suffered by the applicant is not unique in the zoning district, it calls into question the legitimacy of the role of the board of appeals with respect to such conditions. Generally prevailing conditions were taken into account when the local legislature created the zoning ordinance, and the generally applicable zoning provisions represent the judgment of that legislative body regarding the exercise of its police power. If commonly occurring conditions have arisen since the ordinance was adopted, they justify a legislative amendment to the ordinance, not a host of use variances granted by the board as an administrative body.[4]

Library References:

West's Key No. Digests, Zoning and Planning ⚖496.

§ 16.77 Use Variance—Statutory Standard—Protect Essential Neighborhood Character

In addition to proving no reasonable return and unique hardship,[1] an applicant for a use variance must also establish that the requested

8. Shiner v. Board of Estimate of the City of New York, 95 A.D.2d 831, 463 N.Y.S.2d 872 (2d Dep't 1983).

§ 16.76

1. Village Law § 7–712(2)(b)(2), Town Law § 267–b(2)(b)(2), General City Law § 81–b(3)(b)(ii).

2. Hickox v. Griffin, 298 N.Y. 365, 370 83 N.E.2d 836, 838 (1949).

3. Douglaston Civic Association v. Klein, 51 N.Y.2d 963, 965, 435 N.Y.S.2d 705, 706, 416 N.E.2d 1040, 1041 (1980); Jayne Estates v. Raynor, 22 N.Y.2d 417, 293 N.Y.S.2d 75, 239 N.E.2d 713 (1968).

4. Clark v. Board of Zoning Appeals of Town of Hempstead, 301 N.Y. 86, 92 N.E.2d 903 (1950).

§ 16.77

1. *See supra*, §§ 16.75–16.76.

use variance will not alter the essential character of the neighborhood.[2] This requirement also focuses on the legitimate administrative role of the board of appeals.[3] If the use variance will alter the essential character of the neighborhood, it may be at odds with the legislatively adopted zoning ordinance itself. For example, where a neighborhood is undeveloped, but zoned residential, the granting of a use variance for a cemetery would alter the zoned, if not the actual, character of the district and the variance should be properly denied.[4]

In determining whether the essential character of the neighborhood will be changed, one reliable indicator is the intensity of use of the proposed development as compared to the intensity of present and permitted uses in the neighborhood.[5] Where the proposed use would create a "commercial atmosphere" in a residential neighborhood, the district's character would be altered.[6] In contrast, a use variance to permit construction of an apartment building in a single-family neighborhood where several such buildings already exist may not be denied on the ground that it would alter the area's character.[7]

Library References:

West's Key No. Digests, Zoning and Planning ⚖489.

§ 16.78 Use Variance—Statutory Standard—Self–Created Hardship

The fourth required element of proof for a use variance is that "the hardship has not been self-created."[1] This element was first discussed in *Clark v. Board of Zoning Appeals of Town of Hempstead*, where the Court of Appeals held that "one who thus knowingly acquires land for a prohibited use, cannot thereafter have a variance on the ground of 'special hardship.'"[2] This concept is now codified in the statutes.[3]

It is possible for the property owner to commit acts that cause the hardship, as when the owner creates an unapproved subdivision, leaving

---

2. Village Law § 7–712(2)(b)(3), Town Law § 267–b(2)(b)(3), General City Law § 81–b(3)(b)(iii).

3. When the variance violates the general purpose of the ordinance, the board of appeals invades the province of the legislative body, and the grant is invalid for want of authority. Reed v. Board of Standards and Appeals of City of N.Y., 255 N.Y. 126, 174 N.E. 301 (1931).

4. Holy Sepulchre Cemetery v. Board of Appeals of Town of Greece, 271 App.Div. 33, 60 N.Y.S.2d 750 (4th Dep't 1946).

5. Rostlee Associates, Ltd. v. Amelkin, 121 A.D.2d 725, 503 N.Y.S.2d 902 (2d Dep't 1986).

6. Fiore v. Zoning Bd. of Appeals of Town of Southeast, 21 N.Y.2d 393, 288 N.Y.S.2d 62, 235 N.E.2d 121 (1968).

7. Guadagnolo v. Mamaroneck Bd. of Appeals, 52 A.D.2d 902, 383 N.Y.S.2d 377 (2d Dep't 1976).

§ 16.78

1. Village Law § 7–712(2)(b)(4), Town Law § 267–b(2)(b)(4), General City Law § 81–b(3)(b)(iv). *See supra*, §§ 16.75–16.76.

2. Clark v. Board of Zoning Appeals of Town of Hempstead, 301 N.Y. 86, 89, 92 N.E.2d 903 (1950).

3. Village Law § 7–712–b(2)(b)(4), Town Law § 267–b(2), (4), General City Law § 81–b(3)(b)(iv).

one parcel undevelopable because of significant wetlands.[4] But where an owner undertakes improvements under an approved site plan, which improvements are later determined to not conform to the zoning regulations, the hardship will not be construed to have been self created, but rather created in good faith reliance on the assurance of town officials.[5]

Library References:

West's Key No. Digests, Zoning and Planning ⚖497.

§ 16.79 Use Variance—Minimum Variance Needed

The board of appeals, in granting a use variance, "shall grant the minimum variance that it shall deem necessary and adequate to address the unnecessary hardship proven by the applicant, and at the same time preserve and protect the character of the neighborhood and the health, safety and welfare of the community."[1] As distinguished from the previous four statutory criteria,[2] this requirement imposes a responsibility on the board rather than a burden of proof on the applicant.

The board may tailor use variances to meet this statutory requirement. "It is settled that a zoning board may impose conditions in conjunction with granting a variance, as long as the conditions are reasonable."[3] The statutory language clarifies the purposes for which conditions may be imposed and aids in determining whether they are reasonable in nature.[4]

Library References:

West's Key No. Digests, Zoning and Planning ⚖486.

§ 16.80 Use Variance—Procedure

A use variance issue arises when a property owner wishes to undertake a land use that is not permitted or is prohibited by the local zoning ordinance. Upon the filing of a building permit, the local building administrator will reject the permit and inform the applicant that the use of the property for which the permit is sought is not in accordance with the uses permitted by the parcel's zoning classification.[1] If the

---

4. Amco Development, Inc. v. Zoning Board of Appeals of the Town of Perinton, 185 A.D.2d 637, 586 N.Y.S.2d 50 (4th Dep't 1992).

5. La Dirot Associates v. Smith, 169 A.D.2d 896, 564 N.Y.S.2d 620 (3d Dep't 1991).

§ 16.79

1. Village Law § 7–712–b(2)(c), Town Law § 267–b(2)(c), General City Law § 81–b(3)(c).

2. See supra, §§ 16.75–16.78.

3. Finger v. Levenson, 163 A.D.2d 477, 558 N.Y.S.2d 163, 164 (2d Dep't 1990).

4. The power to impose conditions affirmed in the case law has been set forth explicitly in the statutes. Village Law § 7–712–b(4), Town Law § 267–b(4), General City Law § 81–b(5). See infra, § 16.89.

§ 16.80

1. See supra, § 16.37.

applicant disagrees with the administrator's interpretation of the ordinance, the administrator's ruling can be appealed to the local zoning board of appeals. Such an appeal must be taken within 60 days. Alternatively, the applicant can apply directly to the board of appeals for a use variance.[2]

Along with the required use variance application form, the applicant, in most localities, will be required to submit an environmental review form so that the board of appeals can determine whether the variance, if granted, might have a negative impact on the environment.[3] New York State regulations define an approval of a project that may affect the environment by changing the use of any natural resource or structure as an "action" subject to environmental review.[4] If the board's determination on this subject is that the action may have a negative impact on the environment, then all of the procedural steps and substantive requirements of the State Environmental Quality Review Act and regulations adopted pursuant to it must be followed.[5]

The board must hold a hearing, after public notice, on the application and environmental impact statement, if required, and make a final determination on the application within 62 days of the hearing. The board's determination on the matter must be filed with the municipal clerk within five days.[6]

Library References:

West's Key No. Digests, Zoning and Planning ⚖=531–549.

§ 16.81 Use Variance—Summary

Trigger: Property owner is denied building permit because proposed use is not permitted by zoning ordinance.

Standard: Applicant must prove regulation causes unnecessary hardship.[1]

Factors: To demonstrate unnecessary hardship, applicant must demonstrate all four factors:

1. Owner cannot realize a reasonable return on property as zoned;[2]
2. The hardship is unique to the property;[3]
3. The variance will not alter the essential character of the neighborhood;[4] and

---

2. Id.
3. See supra, §§ 16.52–16.59 and Chapter 15 "Environmental Law."
4. 6 NYCRR § 617.2.
5. ECL, Art 8, Title 6, Part 617.
6. Village Law § 7–712–a, Town Law § 267–a, General City Law § 81–a. See supra, § 16.37.

§ 16.81
1. See supra, § 16.74.
2. See supra, § 16.75.
3. See supra, § 16.76.
4. See supra, § 16.77.

4. The hardship is not self-created.[5]

Options:

1. Property owner can appeal the building inspector's determination to zoning board of appeals within 60 days of rejection;[6] or

2. Property owner can apply for a use variance.[7]

Procedure for Use Variance:

1. Submit application for variance to zoning board of appeals;[8]

2. Submit environmental review form, if required;[9]

3. Zoning board of appeals must hold public hearing on application for variance;[10]

4. Zoning board must make determination on application within 62 days of hearing (time may be extended if full SEQRA review is required);[11]

5. Zoning board's determination must be filed within 5 days after decision is rendered.[12]

§ 16.82 Area Variance

An area variance is defined by New York State statutes as "the authorization by the zoning board of appeals for the use of land in a manner which is not allowed by the dimensional or physical requirements of the applicable zoning regulations."[1] The distinction between an area and use variance is fundamental.

An area variance exempts the parcel's owner from one or more of the ordinance's requirements regarding, for example, the height or set back of a building or its placement on the site; a use variance allows the parcel to be used in a manner different than surrounding parcels, such as allowing a light industrial use in a neighborhood retail district.

In general, the award of an area variance is less detrimental to the surrounding area than a use variance. "When the variance is one of area only, there is no change in the character of the zoned district and the

---

5. See supra, § 16.78.
6. See supra, § 16.37.
7. See supra, §§ 16.73–16.79.
8. See supra, § 16.37.
9. See supra, §§ 16.52–16.59 and Chapter 15 "Environmental Law."

10. See supra, §§ 16.37, 16.80.
11. Id.
12. Id.

§ 16.82

1. Village Law § 7–712(1)(b), Town Law § 267(1)(b), General City Law § 81–b(1)(b).

neighborhood considerations are not as strong as in a use variance."[2] As a consequence, the case and statutory law requirements governing the award of an area variance are less stringent.[3] Instead of demonstrating an unnecessary hardship, which is the standard for a use variance,[4] applicants for area variances must only convince the board of appeals that the benefits of the requested variance, in balance, outweigh the detriment it will cause to the health, safety and welfare of the neighborhood.

Library References:

West's Key No. Digests, Zoning and Planning ⚖=503.

§ 16.83   Area Variance—Statutory Balancing Test

When presented with an application for an area variance, the statutes require the zoning board of appeals to weigh the benefit to the applicant against the detriment to the neighborhood: a balancing test.[1] The statutes contain five factors that must be considered by the board of appeals in making its determination in each case:

    1. Whether an undesirable change will be produced in the character of the neighborhood or a detriment to nearby properties will be created by the granting of the area variance;

    2. Whether the benefit sought by the applicant can be achieved by some method, feasible for the applicant to pursue, other than an area variance;

    3. Whether the requested area variance is substantial;

    4. Whether the proposed variance will have an adverse effect or impact on the physical or environmental conditions in the neighborhood or district; and

    5. Whether the alleged difficulty was self-created, which consideration shall be relevant to the decision of the board of appeals, but shall not necessarily preclude the granting of the area variance.[2]

Library References:

West's Key No. Digests, Zoning and Planning ⚖=503.

§ 16.84   Area Variance—Statutory Balancing Test— Guiding Principles from Case Law

The courts established a balancing test, and directed boards of appeals to consider several factors in making their determinations, well

---

2. Hoffman v. Harris, 17 N.Y.2d 138, 144, 269 N.Y.S.2d 119, 123, 216 N.E.2d 326, 330 (1966).

3. Id.

4. See supra, §§ 16.73–16.81.

§ 16.83

1. Village Law § 7–712(1)(b), Town Law § 267(1)(b), General City Law § 81–b(1)(b).

2. Village Law § 7–712–b(3)(b), Town Law § 267–b(3)(b), General City Law § 81–b(4)(b).

before this approach was codified.[1] Other cases created difficult, particular requirements for boards to apply, including whether the ordinance caused the owner "practical difficulties,"[2] whether the owner suffered "significant economic injury"[3] and whether the owner's difficulties or injury were "self-created."[4]

How binding and determinative these particular tests were in each case was difficult to know. Two instances in which owners applied for variances from building set back requirements in a residential zone illustrate the point. In one case, a variance to build a front-entrance enclosure to prevent respiratory ailments suffered by the applicant's children was rejected as having no nexus to the property and because it was a personal convenience not amounting to a practical difficulty.[5] In another, a variance to allow a cat-walk to be built to accommodate a disabled resident was allowed by balancing the personal needs of the applicant against the detriment to the community.[6]

The statutes do not incorporate the practical difficulty and economic injury requirements of the case law.[7] Rather, by stating that self-created difficulties need not preclude the granting of an area variance and by listing five factors that must be considered in balancing applicant benefit against public detriment, the statutes clarify the standard to be followed.[8]

§ 16.85 Area Variance—Statutory Balancing Test—Balancing Factors

One method of understanding the statutory balancing test is to view the evidence presented to the board of appeals regarding an area variance as arranged in two columns. In one column are those factors that demonstrate the benefits to the applicant of the variance. In the other are factors that demonstrate the public purposes for denying the application. Although the statutes require a balancing test and specify

§ 16.84

1. Wachsberger v. Michalis, 19 Misc.2d 909, 191 N.Y.S.2d 621 (Sup.Ct., Nassau County, 1959), aff'd 18 A.D.2d 921, 238 N.Y.S.2d 309 (1963).

2. Village of Bronxville v. Francis, 1 A.D.2d 236, 150 N.Y.S.2d 906 (2d Dep't 1956), aff'd 1 N.Y.2d 839, 153 N.Y.S.2d 220, 135 N.E.2d 724 (1956).

3. Fulling v. Palumbo, 21 N.Y.2d 30, 286 N.Y.S.2d 249, 233 N.E.2d 272 (1967), rev'd in part Doyle v. Amster, 79 N.Y.2d 592, 584 N.Y.S.2d 417, 594 N.E.2d 911 (1992).

4. Conley v. Town of Brookhaven Zoning Board of Appeals, 40 N.Y.2d 309, 386 N.Y.S.2d 681, 353 N.E.2d 594 (1976).

5. Fuhst v. Foley, 45 N.Y.2d 441, 410 N.Y.S.2d 56, 382 N.E.2d 756 (1978).

6. Welch v. Law, 121 A.D.2d 808, 504 N.Y.S.2d 790 (3d Dep't 1986).

7. Village Law § 7–712–b(3)(b), Town Law § 267–b(3)(b), General City Law § 81–b(4)(b).

8. Vilardi v. Roth, 192 A.D.2d 662, 597 N.Y.S.2d 86 (2d Dep't 1993).

§ 16.85 LAND USE LAW Ch. 16

the factors to be balanced, they do not guide the board of appeals in weighing individual factors or in making its ultimate determination.[1]

Historically, courts have not overturned the decisions of boards of appeals if they are rational and supported by substantial evidence in the record.[2] The emphasis in litigation under the balancing test, then, will be on whether the board based its determination on substantial evidence found in the record of the proceeding and whether that determination is rational rather than arbitrary.[3]

In *Sasso v. Osgood*, the Court of Appeals addressed the issue of whether "by failing to include the phrase 'practical difficulties' in the new statute, the Legislature ... eliminated the requirement that the applicant for an area variance make that showing."[4] By referring to the bill jacket for the law, the Court found that it was the intent of the legislature to "clarify and establish, in statute, the powers of the [z]oning [b]oard as already defined by jurisprudence."[5] Accordingly, it held that the statute requires a balancing test of the factors it contains and that "an applicant need not show 'practical difficulties.'"[6] However, although the practical difficulties and economic injury tests of previous case law were omitted from the statutes, evidence of them can be considered in determining the benefits to the applicant of the variance.

To the extent that the applicant does show that dimensional requirements cause serious economic injury, the board of appeals must consider the general rules courts use to review whether land use regulations effect a taking of property without just compensation.[7] In that area of law, when an owner shows significant economic hardship bordering on deprivation of economic use of the property, courts tend to look harder at the public purpose to be served by the regulation and defer less to the board's determination to deny the variance.

Since dimensional and physical regulations tend to be less relevant to preserving public health, safety and welfare than use regulations, boards should examine the evidence before them carefully to determine whether there is sufficient evidence of detriment to the community in granting the variance and whether, in balance, this outweighs the

§ 16.85

1. Several of the cases applying the balancing test codified by the statute called upon the board of appeals to determine "whether strict application of the ordinance will serve a valid public purpose which outweighs the injury to the property owned." Friendly Ice Cream Corporation v. Barrett, 106 A.D.2d 748, 749, 483 N.Y.S.2d 782, 783 (3d Dep't 1984). See Iannone v. Zoning Board of Appeals of the Village of Wappingers Falls, 161 A.D.2d 1101, 557 N.Y.S.2d 659 (3d Dep't 1990); Lund v. Town Board of Town of Philipstown, 162 A.D.2d 798, 557 N.Y.S.2d 712 (3d Dep't 1990).

2. See supra, § 16.46.

3. Fulling v. Palumbo, 21 N.Y.2d 30, 286 N.Y.S.2d 249, 233 N.E.2d 272 (1967) rev'd in part Doyle v. Amster, 79 N.Y.2d 592, 584 N.Y.S.2d 417, 594 N.E.2d 911 (1992).

PRACTICE POINTER: Since the statutes direct the board to base its decision on all five of the factors it lists, the record should reveal that all five factors were considered and contain the findings of the board with respect to each.

4. 86 N.Y.2d 374, 633 N.Y.S.2d 259, 657 N.E.2d 254 (1995).

5. *Id.* at 4.

6. *Id.* at 5.

7. See supra, § 16.22.

significant economic harm to the applicant. This interpretation is consistent with the historical purpose of variances and nonconforming use provisions: to protect zoning from vulnerability to property owner charges that the ordinance arbitrarily violates their constitutional right to the reasonable use of their property.[8]

It may be equally true that, where an owner argues for an area variance because of serious economic injury, the board may regard self-created hardship as a more significant factor in its balancing exercise. If it can be shown that the owner is responsible for the demonstrated economic injury, it is less likely that his property rights have been offended by the local regulation itself.

The importance of this type of contextual application of the balancing factors suggests that boards of appeals cannot avoid altogether the complexities of the former case law that arose when the practical difficulties and economic injury requirements were developed and applied. In some contexts, cases decided before codification of the balancing test involved complicated rules shifting the burden of proof from the applicant to the board and back.[9] Although the statute does not codify this process, it is imperative, for example, that the board have on the record credible evidence of the public detriment, once the applicant competently demonstrates the benefit of the variance to the property.[10]

§ 16.86 Area Variance—Minimum Variance Needed

Finally, the statutes provide that the board of appeals, "in the granting of area variances, shall grant the minimum variance that it shall deem necessary and adequate and at the same time preserve and protect the character of the neighborhood and the health, safety and welfare of the community."[1] That the board may tailor area variances to meet this statutory requirement is clear. "It is well settled that a zoning board may impose conditions in conjunction with granting a variance, as long as the conditions are reasonable."[2] The statutory language clarifies the purposes for which conditions may be imposed and aids in determining whether they are reasonable in nature.

---

8. *See supra,* §§ 16.62, 16.75, 16.82.

9. Fulling v. Palumbo, 21 N.Y.2d 30, 286 N.Y.S.2d 249, 233 N.E.2d 272 (1967), rev'd in part Doyle v. Amster, 79 N.Y.2d 592, 584 N.Y.S.2d 417, 594 N.E.2d 911 (1992); Stevens v. Town of Huntington, 20 N.Y.2d 352, 283 N.Y.S.2d 16, 229 N.E.2d 591 (1967).

10. In Gillings v. Fernan, 204 A.D.2d 450, 612 N.Y.S.2d 49 (2d Dep't 1994) and Brous v. Planning Bd. of Village of Southampton, 191 A.D.2d 553, 594 N.Y.S.2d 816 (2d Dep't 1993) the courts reverted to the pre-statutory practice of expressing the exercise as one involving a shifting of the balance of proof from the applicant to the board.

§ 16.86

1. Village Law § 7–712–b(3)(c), Town Law § 267–b(3)(c), General City Law § 81–b(4)(c).

2. Finger v. Levenson, 163 A.D.2d 477, 558 N.Y.S.2d 163, 164 (2d Dep't 1990). The power to impose conditions affirmed in the case law has been set forth explicitly in the statutes. Village Law § 7–712–b(4), Town Law § 267–b(4), General City Law § 81–b(5).

§ 16.87 Area Variance—Procedure

Normally, an area variance issue arises when a property owner wishes to improve a parcel but finds that the improvements violate certain dimensional requirements of the local zoning ordinance. Upon the filing of a building permit, the local building administrator will reject the permit and inform the applicant that the improvements are not allowed under applicable zoning requirements.[1] If the applicant disagrees with the administrator's interpretation of the ordinance, the administrator's ruling can be appealed to the local zoning board of appeals. Such an appeal must be taken within 60 days of the administrator's ruling. Alternatively, the applicant can apply directly to the board of appeals for an area variance.[2]

If a property owner cannot receive a special permit,[3] or subdivision[4] or site plan[5] approval because of noncompliance with a dimensional or physical requirement, the statutes provide that the owner may proceed directly to the board of appeals for an area variance without making application to the building administrator.[6]

Along with the required application form, the applicant, in most localities will be required to submit an environmental review form so that the board of appeals can determine whether the variance, if granted, might have a negative impact on the environment.[7] State regulations define an approval of a project that may affect the environment by changing the use of any natural resource or structure as an "action" subject to environmental review.[8] If the board's determination on this subject is that the action may have a negative impact on the environment, then all of the procedural steps and substantive requirements of the State Environmental Quality Review Act,[9] and regulations adopted pursuant to it must be followed.

The board must hold a public hearing, after notice, on the application and environmental impact statement, if required, and make a final determination on the area variance application within 62 days of the

§ 16.87
1. *See supra,* § 16.32.
2. *See supra,* § 16.37.
3. *See infra,* §§ 16.90–16.95.
4. *See infra,* §§ 16.96–16.102.
5. *See infra,* §§ 16.103–16.108.
6. For special permits *see* Village Law § 7–725–b(3), Town Law § 274–b(3), General City Law § 81–b(3). For subdivisions *see* Village Law § 7–730(6), Town Law § 277(6), General City Law § 33(6). For site plans *see* Village Law § 7–725–a(3), Town Law § 274–a(3), General City Law § 27–a(3).

7. *See supra,* §§ 16.52–16.59 and Chapter 15 "Environmental Law."
8. 6 NYCRR § 617.2
9. ECL, Art. 8, Title 6, Part 617.

hearing. The board's determination on the matter must be filed with the municipal clerk within five days.[10]

Library References:

West's Key No. Digests, Zoning and Planning ⚖️531–549.

§ 16.88 Area Variance—Summary

Trigger: Property owner is denied building permit because the request violates dimensional requirements of the zoning ordinance.[1]

Standard: Balancing test—zoning board of appeals must determine that the benefit of the variance to the property outweighs the detriment it will cause to the health, safety and welfare of the neighborhood.[2]

Factors: Five factors must be considered by zoning board in making its determination on the variance application:

1. Will the variance cause an undesirable change in the neighborhood's character or a detriment to nearby properties;
2. Can the benefit of the variance be achieved by another feasible method;
3. Is the variance substantial;
4. Will the variance have an adverse physical or environmental effect on the neighborhood; and
5. Is the difficulty self-created.[3]

Options:

1. Property owner can challenge the rejection of the building permit by appealing directly to the zoning board of appeals within 60 days of rejection;[4] or
2. Property owner can apply for an area variance.[5]

Procedure for Area Variance:

1. Submit application for variance to zoning board of appeals;[6]
2. Submit environmental review form, if required;[7]

---

10. *See* Village Law § 7–712–a, Town Law § 267–a, General City Law § 81–a.

§ 16.88
1. *See supra,* § 16.82.
2. *See supra,* § 16.83.
3. *See supra,* § 16.85.

4. *See supra,* § 16.37.
5. *See supra,* §§ 16.82–16.87.
6. *See supra,* § 16.87.
7. *See supra,* §§ 16.52–16.59 and Chapter 15 "Environmental Law."

3. Zoning board of appeals must hold public hearing on application for variance;[8]

4. Zoning board must make determination on application within 62 days of hearing (time may be extended if full SEQRA review is required);

5. Zoning board's determination must be filed within 5 days after decision is rendered.[9]

§ 16.89 Conditions Imposed on Use and Area Variances

New York State statutes require a zoning board of appeals to "grant the minimum variance that it shall deem necessary."[1] Since the applicant for a variance petitions the board of appeals to exempt his property from one or more specific provisions of the zoning ordinance, boards utilize various techniques to minimize the impact of a wholesale exemption. Frequently, they employ conditions for this purpose. The courts have held that the imposition of conditions on variances is proper because they are "corrective measures designed to protect neighboring properties against the possible adverse effects" of the use of the property favored by the variance.[2]

The statutes grant boards of appeals this power to condition variances explicitly.

> The board of appeals shall, in the granting of both use variances and area variances, have the authority to impose such reasonable conditions and restrictions as are directly related to and incidental to the proposed use of the property. Such conditions shall be consistent with the spirit and intent of the zoning ordinance or local law, and shall be imposed for the purpose of minimizing any adverse impact such variance may have on the neighborhood or community.[3]

The types of conditions that withstand challenge are those that relate directly to the parcel exempted from the ordinance's requirements and bear a clear relationship to lessening the impact of that exemption on surrounding properties. Such conditions include various property improvement requirements such as:

> fences, safety devices, landscaping, screening, and access roads relating to period of use, screening, outdoor lighting and noises, and enclosure of buildings and relating to emissions of odors, dust,

---

8. See supra, §§ 16.37, 16.80.
9. Id.

§ 16.89
1. Regarding use variances, see Village Law § 7-712-b(2)(c), Town Law § 267-b(2)(c), General City Law § 81-b(3)(c); regarding area variances, see Village Law § 7-712-b(3)(c), Town Law § 267-b(3)(c), General City Law § 81-b(4)(c).

2. St. Onge v. Donovan, 71 N.Y.2d 507, 527 N.Y.S.2d 721, 522 N.E.2d 1019 (1988).

3. Village Law § 7-712-b(4), Town Law § 267-b(4), General City Law § 81-b(5).

smoke, refuse matter, vibration noise and other factors incidental to comfort, peace, enjoyment, health or safety of the surrounding area.[4]

The types of conditions that may be imposed by a board of appeals has been limited by case law. For example, courts have held that conditions must not be vague and ambiguous,[5] will not be inferred, and should be stated clearly.[6] Further, the zoning board may not condition a variance upon a property owner's agreement to dedicate land that is not the subject of the variance application.[7] Similarly, it is not proper to require a parcel's owner to provide off-street parking.[8] Conditions imposed must relate to the use of the property approved by the variance.

Perhaps the most significant limitation imposed by New York courts is that the condition must be "directly related to and incidental to the proposed use of the property."[9] This calls into question conditions that relate to the owner, personally,[10] or that attempt to regulate the details of the operations conducted on the land.[11] These holdings are based on the "fundamental rule that zoning deals basically with land use and not with the person who owns or occupies it."[12] Variances, and the conditions imposed on them, are not personal matters but run with the title to the land from one owner to the next and allow owners to use the property as authorized by zoning, but not in violation of any conditions imposed.[13]

4. St. Onge v. Donovan, 71 N.Y.2d 507, 516, 527 N.Y.S.2d 721, 725, 522 N.E.2d 1019, 1023 (1988).

5. Pearson v. Shoemaker, 25 Misc.2d 591, 202 N.Y.S.2d 779 (Sup.Ct., Rockland County, 1960) (conditions which are ambiguous and vague are of no value for the protection of the comfort, health and welfare of the community and the rights of nearby residents).

6. Sabatino v. Denison, 203 A.D.2d 781, 610 N.Y.S.2d 383 (3d Dep't 1994). "[I]t was the Zoning Board's obligation to clearly state the conditions it required petitioners to adhere to in connection with the approval." 203 A.D.2d at 783, 610 N.Y.S.2d at 383.

7. Gordon v. Zoning Bd. of Appeals of Town of Clarkstown, 126 Misc.2d 75, 481 N.Y.S.2d 275 (Sup.Ct., Rockland County, 1984) (condition requiring dedication of portion of front yard was held invalid where variance sought related to side yard requirements); Allen v. Hattrick, 87 A.D.2d 575, 447 N.Y.S.2d 741 (2d Dep't 1982)(conditions unrelated to relief requested in variance was held invalid).

8. Titus St. Paul Property Owners Ass'n v. Board of Zoning Appeals of Town of Irondequoit, 205 Misc. 1083, 132 N.Y.S.2d 148 (Sup.Ct., Monroe County, 1954).

9. Pearson v. Shoemaker, 25 Misc.2d 591, 202 N.Y.S.2d 779 (Sup.Ct., Rockland County, 1960); St. Onge v. Donovan, 71 N.Y.2d 507, 527 N.Y.S.2d 721, 522 N.E.2d 1019 (1988).

10. Dexter v. Town Board of the Town of Gates, 36 N.Y.2d 102, 365 N.Y.S.2d 506, 324 N.E.2d 870 (1975). "[S]uch conditions and safeguards must be reasonable and relate only to the real estate involved without regard to the person who owns or occupies it." 36 N.Y.2d at 105, 365 N.Y.S.2d at 508, 324 N.E.2d at 871.

11. Summit School v. Neugent, 82 A.D.2d 463, 442 N.Y.S.2d 73 (2d Dep't 1981)(conditions regulating details of the operation of a private school invalid); Schlosser v. Michaelis, 18 A.D.2d 940, 238 N.Y.S.2d 433 (2d Dep't 1963)(conditions regulating details of a wholesale florist business invalid).

12. Dexter v. Town Board of the Town of Gates, 36 N.Y.2d 102, 105, 365 N.Y.S.2d 506, 508, 324 N.E.2d 870, 871 (1975).

13. Balodis v. Fallwood Park Homes, Inc., 54 Misc.2d 936, 283 N.Y.S.2d 497 (Sup.Ct., Nassau County, 1967).

§ 16.89 LAND USE LAW

Whether a board of appeals may impose a durational requirement on a variance has been dealt with both in the courts and statutorily. The New York statute originally giving boards their authority to impose conditions authorized them to impose conditions related to the "duration" of the variance. This explicit wording was removed from the statute by the legislature implying that a durational limitation, by itself, may be improper.[14] However, there is authority indicating that a board may provide for a variance to lapse upon the occurrence of an event that relates to the property itself.[15]

Library References:

West's Key No. Digests, Zoning and Planning ⚖=501.

§ 16.90 Special Use Permits

Local zoning ordinances contain provisions for certain land uses to be approved by special use permit. These uses are allowed in specific districts by the local legislature. They are declared compatible uses in the district, subject to conditions that may be imposed to mitigate any negative impact on surrounding properties. Examples of land uses that are subject to special permit approval are adult homes, day care centers, drive in services, nursing homes, video arcades, gas stations, shopping centers, convenience stores, professional offices and churches.

In contrast to as-of-right uses of land, special uses breathe flexibility into the ordinance and afford a degree of discretion in reviewing, imposing conditions on and approving land uses. If an as-of-right use meets the specific requirements of the zoning regulations, it must be permitted.[1] The legislature may designate certain standards and conditions that special uses must meet to insure that they are in harmony with the neighborhood. Unless the applicant for a special use permit demonstrates that the proposed use adequately meets the standards and conditions in the law, the permit need not be approved.

A special use permit is defined by New York statutes as

> an authorization of a particular land use which is permitted in a zoning ordinance or local law, subject to requirements imposed by

---

14. Subd. 4. L.1993, c. 208, s 14, eff. July 6, 1993, deleted authority to impose conditions and restrictions concerning duration of variance.

15. Holthaus v. Zoning Board of Appeals of Town of Kent, 209 A.D.2d 698, 619 N.Y.S.2d 160 (2d Dep't 1994). "A zoning board may grant a limited variance which will lapse if not acted upon within a specified time." 209 A.D.2d at 699, 619 N.Y.S.2d at 161. Douglaston Civic Assn., Inc. v. Board of Standards & Appeals of City of N.Y., 278 A.D. 659, 102 N.Y.S.2d 582 (2d Dep't 1951) (conditions upon which a variance may lapse must be related to the property itself and may not be conditioned upon continued ownership by the grantee).

§ 16.90

1. See supra, § 16.61.

such zoning ordinance or local law to assure that the proposed use is in harmony with such zoning ordinance or local law and will not adversely affect the neighborhood if such requirements are met.[2]

The statutes provide that the local legislature may authorize the planning board or other administrative body, such as the zoning board of appeals, to approve applications for special use permits.[3] The legislature has the inherent power to retain special use approval power itself.[4]

The significant characteristic of a special use permit, as opposed to a variance, is that it is expressly permitted by the ordinance.[5] If a planning board finds that an application complies with all the standards and conditions contained in the zoning ordinance regarding the special use, then the permit must be granted.[6] As with variances, the approval agency may impose "reasonable conditions and restrictions as are directly related to and incidental to the proposed special use permit."[7] Once awarded, special use permits run with title to the land and are not personal to the owner.[8] The statutes specify the procedures reviewing bodies must follow and require public notice and hearing.[9]

Library References:

West's Key No. Digests, Zoning and Planning ⟐371–394.

2. Village Law § 7–725–b(1), Town Law § 274–b(1), General City Law § 27–b(1). General City Law § 27–b(12) stipulates that the provisions of Section 27–b regarding approval of special use permits do not apply to any city having a population of more than one million.

3. Village Law § 7–725–b(2), Town Law § 274–b(2), General City Law § 27–b(2).

4. Zeifman v. Board of Trustees of the Village of Great Neck, 40 Misc.2d 130, 242 N.Y.S.2d 738 (Sup.Ct., Nassau County, 1963).

5. Matter of North Shore Steak House v. Board of Appeals of Inc. Vil. of Thomaston, 30 N.Y.2d 238, 331 N.Y.S.2d 645, 282 N.E.2d 606 (1972).

A variance is an authority to a property owner to use property in a manner forbidden by the ordinance while a special exception allows the property owner to put his property to a use expressly permitted by the ordinance. The inclusion of the permitted use in the ordinance is tantamount to a legislative finding that the permitted use is in harmony with the general zoning plan and will not adversely affect the neighborhood.

30 N.Y.2d at 244, 331 N.Y.S.2d at 649, 282 N.E.2d at 609.

6. North Shore Equities, Inc. v. Fritts, 81 A.D.2d 985, 440 N.Y.S.2d 84 (3d Dep't 1981).

From our examination of the record, we are of the view that petitioner complied with the standards outlined in the ordinance. Furthermore, there was no proof offered to contravene that of petitioner's three experts. Consequently, there is not substantial evidence to support respondent's findings [concluding that the application should be denied].

81 A.D.2d at 986, 440 N.Y.S.2d at 85.

7. Village Law § 7–725–b(4), Town Law § 274–b(4), General City Law § 27–b(4).

8. Dexter v. Town Board of Town of Gates, 36 N.Y.2d 102, 365 N.Y.S.2d 506, 324 N.E.2d 870 (1975); St. Onge v. Donovan, 71 N.Y.2d 507, 527 N.Y.S.2d 721, 522 N.E.2d 1019 (1988).

9. Village Law § 7–725–b(6), (7), Town Law § 274–b(6), (7), General City Law § 27–b(6), (7).

§ 16.91 Special Use Permits—Imposition and Use of Standards

Unless the legislative body is to retain special use permit authority, the zoning ordinance must contain reasonably clear standards to guide the planning board or other administrative body in determining whether to grant a special permit. Where, for example, a board was given the authority to issue permits for uses serving "educational, religious or eleemosynary purposes," but was guided by no standards to make its decisions, the Court determined that the standards were too vague, giving the board unfettered and unrestricted discretion to approve or reject proposed educational uses.[1] Numerous cases have invalidated special permit provisions because of this deficiency.[2] On the other hand, an ordinance is not invalid where the standards guiding the permitting body are stated in general terms.[3]

Where the legislative body retains special permit issuance authority, however, there need not be formulated standards to guide and limit its discretion.[4] In such a case, judicial standards that limit the discretion of administrative bodies do not apply. Local legislatures enjoy "untrammeled discretion" to deny special use permits where they have not precluded themselves from doing so in the zoning ordinance and where this discretion is not exercised capriciously.[5] However, where the legislative body heard no expert testimony or scientific evidence, its denial of a permit was reversed where it was shown that the subject property would produce no greater noise, traffic and fumes than neighboring uses.[6]

Where the legislative body has established standards by which applications for special use permits are to be reviewed, the administrative body may not deny the permit because of considerations that are not

§ 16.91

1. Concordia Collegiate Institute v. Miller, 301 N.Y. 189, 93 N.E.2d 632 (1950).

2. Little v. Young, 299 N.Y. 699, 87 N.E.2d 74 (1949)(failure of Town to prescribe standards for zoning board of appeals to follow in granting special permits invalidates board's power to review.); Small v. Moss, 279 N.Y. 288, 18 N.E.2d 281 (1938)(commissioner of licenses had no power to deny license to a theater on grounds that traffic and parking problems would be created since no such policy or standard was declared in the statute).

3. Aloe v. Dassler, 278 App.Div. 975, 106 N.Y.S.2d 24 (2d Dep't 1951). The provisions were upheld because they

confer no power on the Board of Appeals which may not be lawfully delegated to an administrative body. Standards are provided which, though stated in general terms are capable of a reasonable application and are sufficient to limit and define the Board's discretionary powers.

278 App.Div. at 975, 106 N.Y.S.2d at 25.

4. Green Point Savings Bank v. Board of Zoning Appeals of Town of Hempstead, 281 N.Y. 534, 24 N.E.2d 319 (1939); Larkin Co. v. Schwab, 242 N.Y. 330, 151 N.E. 637 (1926).

5. 4M Club, Inc. v. Andrews, 11 A.D.2d 720, 204 N.Y.S.2d 610 (2d Dep't 1960)(zoning authority did not act capriciously in denying permit for water pool by considering other factors not specifically set forth in the ordinance). Larkin Co. v. Schwab, 242 N.Y. 330, 151 N.E. 637 (1926)(council acted within its discretion in denying license for gasoline storage tanks even though similar owners had been granted licenses).

6. J.P.M. Properties, Inc. v. Town of Oyster Bay, 204 A.D.2d 722, 612 N.Y.S.2d 634 (2d Dep't 1994).

included in the established standards. For example, where a theater was denied a special permit based on traffic dangers, the denial was reversed because the legislature did not designate traffic as a standard applicable to the special use.[7]

Another basis for reversing the denial of a special use permit is that the impact or intensity of use of the subject property is no greater than that of uses that are unconditionally permitted in the zoning district.[8] "[T]he denial of a special use permit on the basis of traffic congestion may be arbitrary and capricious unless the evidence establishes that the proposed use would have a greater impact on traffic than would other unconditionally permitted uses."[9]

§ 16.92 Special Use Permits—Findings and Determination of Board

The denial of a special use permit by an administrative body must be rational and based on substantial evidence in the record.[1] If the decision is made by the legislative body, however, formal findings are not necessary and must be disclosed only if challenged in court.[2]

Where the administrative body determined that a dining facility was incompatible with surrounding commercial uses and denied the requested permit, the court reversed, noting that the decision lacked a rational basis, was not supported by substantial evidence and was conclusory in nature.[3] Similarly, testimony of community residents regarding their

---

7. Small v. Moss, 279 N.Y. 288, 18 N.E.2d 281 (1938). See Holmes & Murphy, Inc. v. Bush, 6 A.D.2d 200, 176 N.Y.S.2d 183 (4th Dep't 1958)(concluding it was improper for village to deny permit on grounds that excessively heavy trucks would be used on site because no such consideration was contained in the ordinance). Diocese of Rochester v. Planning Board of Town of Brighton, 1 N.Y.2d 508, 154 N.Y.S.2d 849, 136 N.E.2d 827 (1956)(several jurisdictions have held it is arbitrary and unreasonable to deny a permit to a church because of possible traffic hazards).

8. Robert Lee Realty Co. v. Village of Spring Valley, 61 N.Y.2d 892, 474 N.Y.S.2d 475, 462 N.E.2d 1193 (1984); Markowitz v. Town Board of Town of Oyster Bay, 200 A.D.2d 673, 606 N.Y.S.2d 705 (2d Dep't 1994).

9. Serota v. Town Board of Town of Oyster Bay, 191 A.D.2d 700, 701, 595 N.Y.S.2d 525, 526 (2d Dep't 1993), opinion after remand 198 A.D.2d 507, 605 N.Y.S.2d 930 (1993).

§ 16.92

1. Pluto's Retreat, Inc. v. Granito, 80 A.D.2d 899, 437 N.Y.S.2d 112 (2d Dep't 1981) "An examination of the record, however, fails to reveal any support for the findings of the Board of Appeals." 80 App. Div. at 900, 437 N.Y.S.2d at 114. See Ferman v. Board of Appeals, Inc. Vil. of Sea Cliff, 69 A.D.2d 882, 415 N.Y.S.2d 469 (2d Dep't 1979).

2. Zeifman v. Board of Trustees of the Village of Great Neck, 40 Misc.2d 130, 242 N.Y.S.2d 738 (Sup.Ct., Nassau County, 1963). "[I]t is settled law that where the Board 'empowered to grant consent is the same body which enacted the ordinance,' no findings need be made in support of the determination." 40 Misc.2d at 132, 242 N.Y.S.2d at 740. Lemir Realty Corp. v. Larkin, 8 A.D.2d 970, 190 N.Y.S.2d 952 (2d Dep't 1959)(there is no requirement that findings be made on the record, it is sufficient if the reasons are forthcoming in the answer).

3. Burke v. Denison, 203 A.D.2d 642, 609 N.Y.S.2d 959 (3d Dep't 1994).

fears about the use of property does not constitute substantial evidence supporting a denial.[4]

Library References:

West's Key No. Digests, Zoning and Planning ⚖︎439.

§ 16.93 Special Use Permits—Limitations on Imposition of Conditions

Under the statutes, the approval agency may impose such "reasonable conditions and restrictions as are directly related to and incidental to the proposed special use permit."[1] Conditions imposed, however, "cannot go beyond the ordinance, which is the source of the [b]oard's power."[2] The administrative body cannot impose conditions relating to the occupants of the property and the hours of operation because they are unrelated to the zoning use and apply to the details of operation of the business.[3]

Conditions must be directly related and incidental to the proposed use of the property,[4] and the conditions stated must be sufficiently clear and definite that the permittee and his neighbors are not left in doubt concerning the extent of the use permitted.[5] Moreover, the factual basis for the Board's determination to impose a condition must be stated, so that the court will have an intelligent basis for review.[6]

Library References:

West's Key No. Digests, Zoning and Planning ⚖︎382–382.6.

---

4. C.B.H. Properties, Inc. v. Rose, 205 A.D.2d 686, 613 N.Y.S.2d 913 (2d Dep't 1994)(residents testimony and evidence of effect cabaret had on neighborhood was insufficient itself to determine that cabaret was the sole source of the neighborhood disturbances); Master Billiard Co., Inc. v. Rose, 194 A.D.2d 607, 599 N.Y.S.2d 68 (2d Dep't 1993)(testimony by residents that billiard parlor would constitute a hang-out for kids did not establish that the use would have a greater impact on neighborhood than other unconditionally permitted uses).

§ 16.93

1. Village Law § 7–725–b(4), Town Law § 274–b(4), General City Law § 27–b(4).

2. Bernstein v. Board of Appeals, Village of Matinecock, 60 Misc.2d 470, 473, 302 N.Y.S.2d 141, 146 (Sup.Ct., Nassau County, 1969).

3. Id. See also, Old Country Burgers v. Town of Oyster Bay, 160 A.D.2d 805, 553 N.Y.S.2d 843 (2d Dep't 1990) (court reversed conditions that required the use of a drive-through window during breakfast, lunch and dinner hours to mitigate traffic pressures because such a condition relates to the details of the particular business and not the use of the land).

4. Conmar Bldrs. v. Board of Appeals, 43 Misc.2d 577, 251 N.Y.S.2d 521 (Sup.Ct., Nassau County, 1964); Oakwood Is. Yacht Club v. Board of Appeals of the City of New Rochelle, 32 Misc.2d 677, 223 N.Y.S.2d 907 (Sup.Ct., Westchester County, 1961); Pearson v. Shoemaker, 25 Misc.2d 591, 202 N.Y.S.2d 779 (Sup.Ct., Rockland County, 1960).

5. Conmar Bldrs. v. Board of Appeals, 43 Misc.2d 577, 251 N.Y.S.2d 521 (Sup.Ct., Nassau County, 1964); Pearson v. Shoemaker, 25 Misc.2d 591, 202 N.Y.S.2d 779 (Sup.Ct., Rockland County, 1960).

6. Pearson v. Shoemaker, 25 Misc.2d 591, 202 N.Y.S.2d 779 (Sup.Ct., Rockland County, 1960).

§ 16.94 Special Use Permits—Procedure

Under New York statutes, the reviewing agency must conduct a public hearing within sixty-two days from the day the special use permit application is received.[1] Public notice must be printed in a newspaper of general circulation at least five days prior to the hearing. The agency must decide upon the application within sixty-two days of the hearing. The time within which the decision must be rendered may be extended by mutual consent of the applicant and the agency. The decision must be filed within five business days after it is rendered and a copy must be mailed to the applicant.

The statutes cross reference other requirements which, if not met, can create jurisdictional defects resulting in the reversal of action on a permit application. Notice to a county, metropolitan or regional planning agency, as required under Section 239–m of the General Municipal Law, is required to be sent at least ten days before the public hearing. Compliance with the State Environmental Quality Review Act is also required.[2]

§ 16.95 Special Use Permits—Summary

Trigger: Property owner is denied building permit because proposed use is listed as requiring a special permit under the ordinance.[1]

Standard: Applicant must establish that proposed use complies with all standards and conditions contained in the ordinance regarding the special use.[2]

Grounds for Challenging a Denial of Special Use Permit:

1. Ordinance contains no standards for administrative body to follow;[3]
2. Administrative body considered factors not specified in the ordinance;[4]
3. Impact of special permitted use is no greater than other unconditionally permitted uses;[5]
4. Decision of administrative body is irrational and not based on substantial evidence on the record;[6]
5. Conditions imposed do not relate to the proposed use of

---

§ 16.94
1. Village Law § 7–725–b(6), Town Law § 274–b(6), General City Law § 27–b(6).
2. Village Law § 7–725–b(8), Town Law § 274–b(8), General City Law § 27–b(8).

§ 16.95
1. See supra, § 16.90.

2. Id.
3. See supra, § 16.91.
4. Id.
5. Id.
6. See supra, § 16.92.

the property.[7]

Procedure for Special Use Permit:

1. Submit application for special use permit to zoning board of appeals;[8]
2. Submit environmental review form, if required;[9]
3. Zoning board of appeals must hold public hearing on application for special use permit;[10]
4. Zoning board must make determination on application within 62 days of hearing (time may be extended if full SEQRA review is required);[11]
5. Zoning board's determination must be filed within 5 days after decision is rendered;[12]
6. Notice must be given to county, metropolitan or regional planning agency, if required.[13]

§ 16.96 Subdivision Approval

The authority of local governments to regulate and approve the subdivision of land is a central community planning function. Either by itself, or in conjunction with the adoption of a comprehensive plan, zoning ordinance and official map, this authority is to be used "[f]or the purpose of providing for the future growth and development of the [municipality] and affording adequate facilities for the housing, transportation, distribution, comfort, convenience, safety, health and welfare of the population."[1]

Subdivision authority is such a central function that it was used by the Court of Appeals to uphold the adoption of local growth control ordinances.[2] The Court stated that subdivision control "reflects, in essence, a legislative judgment that the development of unimproved areas be accompanied by provision of essential facilities."[3] State law, consequently, delegates subdivision approval authority to local governments to assure that land proposed for development "can be used safely for building purposes without danger to health or peril from fire, flood,

---

7. *See supra,* § 16.93.
8. *See supra,* §§ 16.37, 16.94.
9. *See supra,* §§ 16.52–16.59, Chapter 15 "Environmental Law."
10. *See supra,* §§ 16.37, 16.94.
11. *See supra,* §§ 16.52–16.59, 16.94, Chapter 15 "Environmental Law."
12. *See supra,* §§ 16.37, 16.94.
13. *See supra,* § 16.94.

§ 16.96

1. Village Law § 7-728(1), Town Law § 276(1), General City Law § 32(1).

2. Golden v. Planning Bd. of Town of Ramapo, 30 N.Y.2d 359, 334 N.Y.S.2d 138, 285 N.E.2d 291 (1972).

3. 30 N.Y.2d at 147, 334 N.Y.S.2d at 298, 285 N.E.2d at 372.

drainage or other menace to neighboring properties or the public health, safety or welfare."[4]

Under local subdivision regulations, subdividers may be required to show the location of water, sewer, electrical, drainage, transportation, landscaping and other site features on a plat, or map, of the subdivided parcel that they then submit for review.[5] By carefully reviewing, modifying and conditioning the features of a subdivision plat, the locality seeks to insure that new development is cost effective, properly designed and has a favorable, rather than negative, impact on the neighborhood.

The local legislature may decide to exercise this authority or allow market forces to dictate raw land development. When it chooses to regulate subdivisions, the local legislature may retain that authority or delegate it to the local planning board.[6] Once the planning board is delegated this authority it may, after a public hearing on the matter, adopt regulations specifying how its jurisdiction is to be exercised.[7] These subdivision regulations are subject to the approval of the local legislature.[8]

The local subdivision regulations may exempt a subdivision that creates just a few lots from the approval process, and may specify whether minor and major subdivisions, as defined locally, are to be treated differently, whether lot line alterations are controlled by the subdivision regulations, and whether subdivision applicants must go through a preliminary and final approval process or be subjected only to final approval. Further, each locality, in adopting subdivision regulations to guide the local review process, can specify how detailed subdivision applications must be and how many factors the submitted subdivision plat must contain. How the local planning board determines these matters dictates how complicated and lengthy the subdivision process will be for applicants in each community.

Once subdivision approval procedures have been established by a municipality, the sale of a parcel of land may not be recorded in the county land records office unless the subdivision of the land has been approved by the locality.[9] The ability of land owners to sell and record the transfer of land titles is implicated by the subdivision process in this way.

§ 16.97 Subdivision Approval—Procedure

One typical procedure adopted locally is to require a subdivider of land to submit both a preliminary plat or map of the proposed subdivi-

---

4. Village Law § 7-730(1), Town Law § 277(1), General City Law § 33(1).

5. *See generally*, Village Law § 7-730, Town Law § 277, General City Law § 33.

6. Village Law § 7-728(1), Town Law § 276(1), General City Law § 32(1).

7. Village Law § 7-718(13), Town Law § 271(13), General City Law § 17(13).

8. *Id.*

9. RPL § 333(1-e)(ii)(8)(b).

sion and then a final plat. When this procedure is adopted by the local regulations, the planning board shall hold a hearing within 62 days of the submission of the preliminary plat, subject to public notice being published at least five days prior to the hearing.[1] The planning board's decision must be made within 62 days after the close of the public hearing. The statutes require that public hearings be closed within 120 days of the date they are opened.[2]

Where the decision is to approve the plat, that decision must be filed with the planning board and municipal clerk within five days of the decision.[3] Where the decision is to approve but modify the preliminary plat, the grounds for modification must be stated upon the record of the board and the board must state in writing any modifications it deems necessary for submission of the plat in its final form.[4]

Within six months after an approval, the applicant must submit his final plat for review.[5] If he fails to do so, the preliminary approval may be revoked.[6] Where the final plat is in substantial agreement with the approved preliminary plat, the planning board must approve or disapprove the final plat within 62 days of its submission to the clerk of the planning board.[7] Within five business days of the adoption of the resolution granting approval of the final plat, the plat must be certified by the clerk of the planning board, filed in that clerk's office as well as in the office of the municipal clerk.[8] The approval of the planning board shall expire within 62 days from the date of approval, or the date certified, if not filed by the property owner in the office of the county clerk or register.[9] The failure of the planning board to take action within the established periods is declared an approval by default.[10]

This brief description of the subdivision approval process is deceptive. It is necessary to read the statutes and local regulations very carefully to understand the many variations in this procedure that may be applicable in a given circumstance. For example, local regulations may not provide for preliminary plat submission and approval. In such a case, a public hearing, subject to notice, must be held regarding the submis-

§ 16.97

1. Village Law § 7–728(5)(d)(i), (e)(i), Town Law § 276(5)(d)(i), (e)(i), General City Law § 32(5)(d)(i), (e)(i).

2. Village Law § 7–728(5)(d)(ii), (e)(ii), Town Law § 276(5)(d)(ii), (e)(ii), General City Law § 32(5)(d)(ii), (e)(ii).

3. Village Law § 7–728(5)(g), Town Law § 276(5)(g), General City Law § 32(5)(g).

4. Village Law § 7–728(5)(d)(iv), (e)(iv), Town Law § 276(5)(d)(iv), (e)(iv), General City Law § 32(5)(d)(iv), (e)(iv). Similarly, if the preliminary plat is disapproved the grounds must be stated on the record.

5. Village Law § 7–728(5)(h), Town Law § 276(5)(h), General City Law § 32(5)(h).

6. Id.

7. Village Law § 7–728(6)(b), Town Law § 276(6)(b), General City Law § 32(6)(b).

8. Village Law § 7–728(9), Town Law § 276(9), General City Law § 32(9).

9. Village Law § 7–728(11), Town Law § 276(11), General City Law § 32(11).

10. Village Law § 7–728(8), Town Law § 276(8), General City Law § 32(8).

sion of the final plat.[11] A public hearing, on notice, is also required when the submitted final plat is not in substantial agreement with the approved preliminary plat.[12] Further, the application may be subject to review by the county planning agency under Section 239–m of the General Municipal Law; failure to submit the application to the county in the required circumstance creates a jurisdictional defect in the subsequent local action on the application.[13]

Library References:

West's Key No. Digests, Zoning and Planning ⟽431–446.

§ 16.98 Subdivision Approval—Procedure—How Affected by SEQRA

Further complications arise when the planning board or other lead agency determines that the subdivision application is subject to review under the State Environmental Quality Review Act ("SEQRA").[1] Regulations adopted under SEQRA make it clear that a subdivision approval is a discretionary action affecting the environment that is subject to environmental review.[2] The statutes governing subdivision approval attempt to coordinate the procedures required for the review of the subdivision with those required by SEQRA.[3]

One method used by the statutes to coordinate these procedures is to stipulate that a subdivision plat submission is not deemed complete until the reviewing agency has determined that the subdivision will not have a negative impact on the environment or until it has completed an environmental impact statement.[4] The time periods contained in the subdivision statutes do not begin to run until one of these two events has occurred.[5]

Another method by which the two processes are coordinated by the subdivision statutes is to require that a planning board which is a lead

---

11. Village Law § 7–728(6), Town Law § 276(6), General City Law § 32(6).

12. Village Law § 7–728(6)(d), Town Law § 276(6)(d), General City Law § 32(6)(d). *See* Hickey v. Planning Board of the Town of Kent, 173 A.D.2d 1086, 571 N.Y.S.2d 105 (3d Dep't 1991) (no additional public hearing was necessary when the developer modified its plat to reduce the subdivision from six to five lots when it was done based on planning board suggestions from the first hearing).

13. Village Law § 7–728(10), Town Law § 276(10), General City Law § 32(10) require the planning board clerk to submit all applicable plats to the county, if the county has authority to review.

§ 16.98

1. Village Law § 7–728(5)(b), Town Law § 276(5)(b), General City Law § 32(5)(b). *See* Twin Lakes Farms Associates v. Town of Bedford, 215 A.D.2d 667, 628 N.Y.S.2d 310 (2d Dep't 1995)(complete compliance with State Environmental Quality Review Act (SEQRA) was required before final plat approval). *See supra*, §§ 16.52–16.59 and Chapter 15 "Environmental Law."

2. *See* ECL § 8–0109, 6 NYCRR Pt. 617.

3. These procedures are set forth at length in 6 NYCRR Pt. 617.

4. Village Law § 7–728(5)(c), Town Law § 276(5)(c), General City Law § 32(5)(c).

5. *Id.*

agency for SEQRA purposes hold a single public hearing on the subdivision application in compliance with the hearing requirements under both the SEQRA and subdivision regulations.[6] Where an agency other than the planning board is the lead agency on the subdivision application, the statutes provide for the planning board and the lead agency to hold their public hearings jointly.[7] Where the public hearing is held to comply with SEQRA's requirements, 14 days advance notice of the public hearing is required.[8]

§ 16.99 Subdivision Approval—Provision of Essential Services

The Court of Appeals has stated that the local adoption of subdivision control "reflects, in essence, a legislative judgment that the development of unimproved areas be accompanied by provision of essential facilities."[1] Statutorily, the planning board "shall require" that the land shown on an applicant's plat can be used "without danger to health or peril" or "other menace to neighboring properties or the public health, safety and welfare." The statutes further require that the planning board insure that the streets and highways on plats be of "sufficient width and suitable grade" and "suitably located."[2]

State law requires local subdivision control to insure that a variety of essential site services are installed in accordance with standards acceptable to municipal departments, or that a performance bond be furnished, until such installation occurs.[3] Specifically mentioned in the statute are such site improvements as street signs, sidewalks, street lighting standards, curbs, gutters, street trees, water mains, fire alarm signal devices, sanitary sewers and storm drains.[4] Further, the statutes authorize the planning board to require the applicant to reserve land for park, playground or other recreational purposes on the plat or to require the payment of a sum of money in lieu of such a reservation.[5]

Where a planning board has been authorized to review and approve subdivisions but has not adopted subdivision regulations, it may use the specific language of the state statutes regarding essential services as the basis for its subdivision review. In this relatively rare event, the plan-

---

6. See Village Law § 7-728(5)(d), Town Law § 276(5)(d), General City Law § 32(5)(d). Public hearings are allowed, but not required, under SEQRA regulations.

7. Village Law § 7-728(5)(e), Town Law § 276(5)(e), General City Law § 32(5)(e).

8. Village Law § 7-728(5)(d)(ii), Town Law § 276(5)(d)(ii), General City Law § 32(5)(d)(ii).

§ 16.99
1. Golden v. Planning Bd. of Town of Ramapo, 30 N.Y.2d 359, 334 N.Y.S.2d 138, 285 N.E.2d 291(1972).

2. Village Law § 7-730(1), Town Law § 277(1), General City Law § 33(1).

3. Village Law § 7-730(2), Town Law § 277(2), General City Law § 33(2).

4. Id.

5. Village Law § 7-730(4), Town Law § 277(4), General City Law § 33(4).

ning board must clearly base its findings, modifications and decisions on a carefully constructed record justifying its actions. Where planning boards do adopt regulations, they may go beyond the specifics of the state statutes and clearly state the services that must be provided and the standards that must be met by subdividers to insure that the public health, safety and welfare is served.[6]

Site improvements required on approved plats are to be provided directly by the subdivider. Alternatively, their installation can be secured by a performance bond posted by the subdivider.[7] The municipality may elect to provide one or more platted improvements directly or through the creation of an improvement district.[8]

§ 16.100 Subdivision Approval—Parkland

One of the few statutory provisions that specifically allows a municipality to require the set aside of private land for a specific purpose or to exact money in lieu thereof is in the law governing subdivisions.[1] The State Legislature has authorized planning boards to insure that the recreational needs of the occupants of residential subdivisions be met by requiring land to be set aside where a municipal study shows that there is now or will be an unmet need for recreational facilities in the municipality. The planning board may only require a financial contribution in lieu of a land reservation where it specifically determines that, in a particular case, the subdivision is not of a sufficient size or adequate character to create a suitable recreational area for the subdivision's occupants.[2]

This statutory provision is carefully designed to meet the need for recreational facilities of the residents of the subdivision and their guests, not to provide recreational facilities for the public at large. This was clarified by the Court of Appeals in setting aside a local requirement that the reserved recreational area be dedicated to the town for park purposes.[3]

The courts and legislature have made it clear that this authority to require land reservation for recreation, or the payment of money in lieu thereof, must be exercised on a case-by-case basis and may not be

---

6. Koncelik v. Planning Bd. of Town of East Hampton, 188 A.D.2d 469, 590 N.Y.S.2d 900 (2d Dep't 1992)(planning board had authority to require adequate means of access for emergency vehicles and to impose conditions in order to protect extensive area of undisturbed forest and numerous important plant species).

7. Village Law § 7–730(9), Town Law § 277(9), General City Law § 33(8).

8. Village Law § 7–730(10), Town Law § 277(10). There is no analogous provision in the General City Law.

§ 16.100

1. Village Law § 7–730(4), Town Law § 277(4), General City Law § 33(4).

2. Id.

3. Kamhi v. Planning Bd. of Town of Yorktown, 59 N.Y.2d 385, 465 N.Y.S.2d 865, 452 N.E.2d 1193 (1983).

administered under fixed formulas applicable to all development.[4] In each case, a two step process must be followed. First, the planning board must determine that the subdivision under review will add to the present or future unmet recreational needs of the municipality.[5] If it will not, an appropriate case for land reservation cannot be made. Second, based on a review of the particular plat before it, the planning board must determine whether it contains adequate and suitable space for recreational facilities. Only if it finds that such space does not exist may the planning board require the subdivider to make a cash contribution. All such contributions must be deposited into a trust fund to be used by the municipality exclusively for recreational purposes.[6]

§ 16.101 Subdivision Approval—Decisions and Conditions

As with most local land use decisions, courts will not overturn planning board determinations regarding subdivision applications when that determination has a rational basis supported by substantial evidence.[1] Determinations should be supported by impartial evidence present on the record of the planning board's proceedings.[2]

Where a subdivision application was denied because of its negative impact on the historical integrity of the neighborhood, the board's determination was reversed where the only relevant evidence on the record was an archeological survey that concluded that the development would not have any impact on the cultural resources in the area.[3]

Conditions imposed on subdivision approvals must bear a reasonable relationship with the impact on the community of the subdivision itself. Where prohibition of the development of a second story on a residential development had no measurable impact on the area, this condition was annulled.[4] Similarly, conditioning a subdivision approval of a particular site on the prohibition of development of other property owned by the

---

4. Village Law § 7–730(4), Town Law § 277(4), General City Law § 33(4). Bayswater Realty v. Planning Bd. of Town of Lewisboro, 76 N.Y.2d 460, 560 N.Y.S.2d 623, 560 N.E.2d 1300 (1990).

5. Bayswater Realty v. Planning Bd., 76 N.Y.2d 460, 560 N.Y.S.2d 623, 560 N.E.2d 1300 (1990). In determining whether a subdivider must reserve land or pay money, the Court of Appeals noted that the planning board must consider "whether there is a need for additional facilities in the immediate neighborhood," implying that even though there may be a community-wide need, this particular subdivision may not contribute to it. 76 N.Y.2d at 471, 560 N.Y.S.2d at 629, 560 N.E.2d at 1306.

6. Village Law § 7–730(4), Town Law § 277(4), General City Law § 33(4).

§ 16.101

1. M & M Partnership v. Sweenor, 210 A.D.2d 575, 619 N.Y.S.2d 802 (3d Dep't 1994). See supra, § 16.47.

2. See Village Law § 7–728(5)(d)(iv), Town Law § 276(5)(d)(iv), General City Law § 32(5)(d)(iv).

3. Fitzner v. Beach, 174 A.D.2d 798, 571 N.Y.S.2d 119 (3d Dep't 1991).

4. Brous v. Planning Bd. of Village of Southampton, 191 A.D.2d 553, 594 N.Y.S.2d 816 (2d Dep't 1993).

applicant was set aside since it did not mitigate demonstrable defects in the subdivision under review.[5]

Generalized complaints by local residents are insufficient to justify the denial of a preliminary plat application.[6] Subdivision approval cannot be withheld based solely on conclusory allegations that the subdivision is not in keeping with the character of the neighborhood, where the plat meets all the applicable requirements of local law.[7]

A planning board may properly waive the application of certain stated subdivision requirements where they are deemed to be unnecessary as applied to the application under review. The statutes provide for waivers of requirements, if reasonably granted, when the planning board finds that the requirements are not "requisite in the interest of the public health, safety, and general welfare or inappropriate because of inadequacy or lack of connecting facilities adjacent to or in proximity to the subdivision."[8]

Library References:

West's Key No. Digests, Zoning and Planning ⚖382.1–382.6.

§ 16.102 Subdivision Approval—Summary

Trigger: Property owner wishes to divide a single piece of property into multiple parcels.[1]

Standard: Planning board must find that the land as shown on the subdivision plat can be used without danger to the health, safety and welfare of neighboring properties.[2]

Factors: for review of subdivision plat:

1. Essential services must be provided;[3]
2. Planning board can require that parkland be reserved or the payment of money in lieu of reservation.[4]

Sample Procedure for Subdivision Approval[5]

Ordinance Requires Submission of Preliminary Plat:

1. Preliminary plat review:
   - Preliminary plat is submitted for review to planning board;

---

5. Black v. Summers, 151 A.D.2d 863, 542 N.Y.S.2d 837 (3d Dep't 1989).
6. Fitzner v. Beach, 174 A.D.2d 798, 571 N.Y.S.2d 119 (3d Dep't 1991).
7. Brucia v. Planning Bd. of Town of Huntington, 157 A.D.2d 657, 549 N.Y.S.2d 757 (2d Dep't 1990).
8. Village Law § 7-730(7), Town Law § 277(7), General City Law § 33(7).

§ 16.102
1. *See supra,* § 16.96.
2. *Id.*
3. *See supra,* § 16.99.
4. *See supra,* § 16.100.
5. *See supra,* § 16.97.

§ 16.102   LAND USE LAW   Ch. 16

- Planning board must hold a public hearing (on 5 days notice) within 62 days of the submission of the preliminary plat;
- Hearing cannot exceed 120 days;
- Planning board decision must be rendered within 62 days after hearing closes;
- Decision of planning board must be filed within 5 days of determination;
- If decision is to require modifications to plat or to reject preliminary plat, grounds must be stated on the record, with written notice of any required modifications given to the applicant.

2. Final plat review:
   - Final plat must be submitted for review within 6 months after preliminary plat determination;
   - If final plat is in substantial agreement with preliminary plat, planning board determination on application must be made within 62 days;
   - Certification and filing by planning board of decision must be made within 5 days of determination;
   - Approval expires within 62 days after determination if plat not filed with the county by property owner.

Possible Variations:

1. Ordinance does not require preliminary plat approval—public hearing is required prior to final plat approval;
2. Final plat is not in substantial agreement with preliminary plat—public hearing is required on final plat;
3. County planning agency may have authority to review plat;
4. Local subdivision regulations contain further or different requirements.

State Environmental Quality Review Act (SEQRA) Compliance:[6]

1. Submission of subdivision plat for review is not complete until reviewing agency determines that the application will not have a negative environmental impact or

---

6. *See supra,* §§ 16.52–16.59, 16.96 and Chapter 15 "Environmental Law."

the applicant has submitted an environmental impact statement.

2. If planning board is lead agency for SEQRA review, it may hold a single public hearing for plat approval and SEQRA review.

3. If planning board is not the lead agency for SEQRA review, the lead agency and planning board can agree to hold a joint public hearing to coordinate SEQRA and subdivision review.

§ 16.103 Site Plans

State statutes delegate authority to villages, towns and cities to review and approve site plans, also called site development plans.[1] This authority supplements municipal authority to adopt comprehensive plans,[2] zoning ordinances[3] and land subdivision regulations.[4] Site plan review and approval authority is used to regulate the development or redevelopment of individual parcels of land. It is often used in conjunction with adopted zoning ordinances; however, municipalities that have not adopted zoning ordinances may adopt site plan regulations to govern the improvement of individual sites.

The general purposes of adopting standards and procedures for site plan review and approval are to assure that the development of individual sites does not affect surrounding properties negatively and that the community develops in an orderly and cost-effective fashion. State law does not require localities to adopt site plan regulations, but rather allows them to do so, subject to compliance with the provisions of the state statutes.

A "site plan" is defined as a drawing, prepared in accordance with local specifications, that shows the "arrangement, layout and design of the proposed use of a single parcel of land."[5] Narrative elements can be added to this graphic presentation to explain how the development plan complies with the requirements of local law and the general purposes of site plan regulations. Often, the local specifications are found in the municipality's zoning ordinance. Alternatively, they may be adopted separately by the local legislature as a local law.[6]

State law requires that local site plan provisions "specify the land uses that require site plan approval and the elements to be included on

§ 16.103

1. Village Law § 7-725-a, Town Law § 274-a, General City Law § 27-a. The provisions of the General City Law regarding site plan review and approval are not applicable to any city having a population of more than one million. General City Law § 27-a(13).

2. See supra, §§ 16.11-16.16.

3. See supra, §§ 16.60-16.95.

4. See supra, §§ 16.96-16.102.

5. Village Law § 7-725-a(1), Town Law § 274-a(1), General City Law § 27-a(1).

6. Id.

plans."[7] For example, local legislatures may choose to require site plan approval only in flood hazard areas, historic districts, coastal zones or other natural resource areas. Alternatively, they may provide for such review only in certain zoning districts where individual parcel development may raise particular problems. A third approach is to require all new land use activities on individual parcels to receive site plan approval except for certain types of development such as one and two family dwellings, accessory structures, and specified low impact uses.

Elements that may be required to be shown on the site plan include, "where appropriate, those related to parking, means of access, screening, signs, landscaping, architectural features, location and dimensions of building, adjacent land uses and physical features meant to protect adjacent land uses."[8] The local zoning ordinance or local law may include additional elements in the local legislature's discretion.[9]

The scale of the proposed site development may dictate the scope of the site plan submission and the intensity of the review process. Small projects typically raise immediate on-site issues and involve limited off-site impacts, primarily on adjacent properties, roads and facilities. Larger projects often raise issues about their impact on more remote environmental features, neighborhoods, transportation facilities and other municipal services.

Library References:

West's Key No. Digests, Zoning and Planning ⇔372.1–372.6, 381.5, 382–382.6.

§ 16.104 Site Plans—Responsible Agency

The statutes provide that site plan review and approval authority may be delegated by the local legislature to the local planning board or other administrative body, such as the zoning board of appeals.[1] Alternatively, the legislature may retain that authority. In most municipalities, the planning board is vested with site plan authority.[2]

Where the planning board, zoning board of appeals, or other administrative body is delegated site plan authority, the legislature must be careful to articulate standards to guide the decision making process, so that it is not wholly discretionary.[3] Where the legislature retains site

---

7. Village Law § 7–725–a(2)(a), Town Law § 274–a(2)(a), General City Law § 27–a(2)(a).

8. Id.

9. Id.

§ 16.104

1. Village Law § 7–725–a(2), Town Law § 274–a(2), General City Law § 27–a(2).

2. Site Development Plan Review, Procedures and Guidelines, James A. Coon Local Government Technical Series, N.Y Department of State, at 3.

3. Under the general rules of administrative law, delegation of authority by a legislative body to an administrative body must be accompanied by sufficient standards to guide the administrative body's decisions. Holy Sepulchre v. Town of Greece, 191 Misc. 241, 79 N.Y.S.2d 683 (Sup.Ct., Monroe County, 1947), aff'd 273 App.Div. 942, 79 N.Y.S.2d 863 (4th Dep't

plan authority, there is no delegation of legislative authority, hence such standards are not required to be included in the local site plan law.[4]

In all cases, the local site plan law must specify the elements that are to be included in site plan applications submitted for approval.[5] The local legislature may empower the responsible agency to waive any requirements for approval where it finds that such requirements are inappropriate to a particular site plan or not required to protect the public interest.[6]

§ 16.105 Site Plans—Responsible Agency—Procedure

A proposed land use that requires site plan approval must be described in a site plan that meets state and local requirements and be submitted to the responsible agency.[1] The statutes provide that the local legislature, in adopting site plan procedures, may require the responsible agency to hold a public hearing on the site plan submission prior to acting on it.[2] If a public hearing is not required, the responsible agency can, in its discretion, decide to conduct a public hearing in a particular case.[3]

If a public hearing is required, it must be held within sixty-two days from the date the application is received.[4] Mail notice of the hearing must be sent to the applicant at least ten days before the hearing and public notice must be given in a local newspaper of general circulation at least five days prior to the date of the public hearing.[5] The responsible agency has sixty-two days from the date of the hearing to make its decision on the application, although this time may be extended by mutual consent of the agency and the applicant.[6] If the agency fails to

---

1948). See supra, Chapter 4 "New York Administrative Law," § 4.68.

4. Larkin Co. v. Schwab, 242 N.Y. 330, 151 N.E. 637 (1926).

5. Village Law § 7–725–a(2)(a), Town Law § 274–a(2)(a), General City Law § 27–a(2)(a).

PRACTICE POINTER: Many responsible agencies develop and provide a checklist of the components of an application that meets local and state site plan submission standards.

6. Village Law § 7–725–a(5), Town Law § 274–a(5), General City Law § 27–a(5).

§ 16.105

1. **PRACTICE POINTER:** Local practice varies significantly with respect to filing, reviewing and deciding upon a site plan submission. In some instances, localities may create a multi-phase application process including as many as three separate phases: presubmission review, preliminary submission and final submission. In others, a single phase may be provided and involve the submission and review of a site plan containing the required elements. Within the same municipality, smaller-scale site plans may be subjected to simpler procedures and larger-scale projects required to follow more complex procedures. Responsible agencies may proceed with various degrees of formality from one locality to another. Check carefully the local site plan regulations to determine what procedures apply to a particular project.

2. Village Law § 7–725–a(7), Town Law § 274–a(8), General City Law § 27–a(8).

3. Id.

4. Id.

5. Id.

6. Id.

act within the allotted time frame, the site plan is deemed approved.[7]

Responsible agency determinations regarding site plan applications are "actions" under the State Environmental Quality Review Act (SEQRA).[8] Because SEQRA contains its own time periods for environmental review of public agency actions, it may require the responsible agency to extend the time periods found in state statutes applicable to site plan review and approval.[9]

State statutes require that certain actions, including site plan approvals, may not be taken by local agencies unless they are first referred to a metropolitan, regional or county planning board, and that board has 30 days to review the matter.[10] Notice, including a full statement of the site plan application being considered, must be sent to the county planning board if the land subject to the approval is within 500 feet of a municipal boundary, an existing or proposed county or state highway or park, or of an existing or proposed stream channel owned by the county, or of existing or proposed county or state owned land on which a public building is situated.[11] Where such referral is required, it must be submitted ten days prior to a public hearing held on the matter; if no public hearing is held, the referral must be made before final action is taken by the responsible agency.[12] The time period for local review and decision does not begin to run until the county planning board has been heard from, or thirty days have passed from the date of referral.[13]

The decision of the responsible agency may be to approve the submitted site plan, approve it with modifications, or disapprove the submission.[14] Disapproval requires the resubmision of a new application if the applicant is interested in having the responsible agency consider

---

7. Figgie Intern., Inc. v. Town of Huntington, 203 A.D.2d 416, 610 N.Y.S.2d 563 (2d Dep't 1994). In Figgie, the planning board's failure to act within the 45 days required by the local ordinance resulted in an automatic approval of petitioner's site plan. *Id.*

8. WEOK Broadcasting Corporation v. Planning Bd. of Town of Lloyd, 79 N.Y.2d 373, 583 N.Y.S.2d 170, 592 N.E.2d 778 (1992). *See supra,* §§ 16.52–16.59 and Chapter 15 "Environmental Law."

9. Sun Beach Real Estate Development Corp. v. Anderson, 98 A.D.2d 367, 469 N.Y.S.2d 964 (2d Dep't 1983), aff'd 62 N.Y.2d 965, 479 N.Y.S.2d 341, 468 N.E.2d 296 (1984).

10. Village Law § 7–725–a(8), Town Law § 274–a(8), General City Law § 27–a(8).

11. General Municipal Law § 239–m.

CAVEAT: The failure to provide notice and the required submission under this section amounts to a jurisdictional defect in the responsible agency's ultimate action on the site plan submission. Old Dock Associates v. Sullivan, 150 A.D.2d 695, 541 N.Y.S.2d 569 (2d Dep't 1989).

PRACTICE POINTER: The full statement required to be sent with notice under this section encompasses the completed site plan application including any environmental impact forms and information. *See* Ferrari v. Town of Penfield Planning Board, 181 A.D.2d 149, 585 N.Y.S.2d 925 (4th Dep't 1992).

12. Village Law § 7–725–a(8), Town Law § 274–a(8), General City Law § 27–a(8).

13. *Id. See* King v. Chmielewski, 76 N.Y.2d 182, 556 N.Y.S.2d 996, 556 N.E.2d 435 (1990) where analogous provisions contained in General Municipal Law § 239–n were involved.

14. Village Law § 7–725–a(2)(a), Town Law § 274–a(2)(a), General City Law § 27–a(2)(a).

the plan further. The statutes provide that the decision of the responsible agency must be filed in the office of the municipal clerk within five business days after its decision is rendered, and a copy mailed to the applicant.[15]

Library References:
West's Key No. Digests, Zoning and Planning ⚖︎431–446.

§ 16.106 Site Plans—Responsible Agency—Standards for Review

In adopting site plan regulations and delegating authority to a responsible agency, the municipal legislature should provide standards to guide the agency's review of a site plan application.[1] The applicant must carry the burden of showing that he meets the applicable standards. When that burden is met, the site plan application must be approved.[2] If that burden is not met, the application must be denied.[3]

Site plan review standards generally contain both qualitative and quantitative measures. For example, they may authorize the responsible agency to review the adequacy of the arrangement of trees, shrubs and other landscaping—a qualitative standard. They may require that no septic tank be located within 50 feet of any shoreline—a quantitative standard that supplements the requirements of the zoning ordinance. Both types of standards are permissible and are sufficient to guide the responsible agency in coming to a decision on the application.

The types of standards for review that may be included in site plan regulations are extensive. They include a long list of specific elements contained in the state statute and "any additional elements specified" by the local legislature.[4] Decisions of the responsible agency must be based on the specific elements enumerated in the state statute and the local legislature.

In evaluating the responsible agency's decision on a site plan application, the courts will look for and require a rational basis for that decision.[5] If the denial is not supported by objective or expert evidence but only, for example, by generalized fears and conclusions, it will not be sustained.[6] Reference by the responsible agency on the record to specific design and layout features of the site plan that offend the public health,

15. Village Law § 7–725–a(7), Town Law § 274–a(7), General City Law § 27–a(7).

§ 16.106

1. *See supra,* § 16.104, note 3.

2. North Shore Equities, Inc. v. Fritts, 81 A.D.2d 985, 440 N.Y.S.2d 84 (3d Dep't 1981).

3. Fornaby v. Feriola, 18 A.D.2d 215, 239 N.Y.S.2d 185 (2d Dep't 1963).

4. Village Law § 7–725–a(2)(a), Town Law § 274–a(2)(a), General City Law § 27–a(2)(a).

5. Janiak v. Planning Bd. of Town of Greenville, 159 A.D.2d 574, 552 N.Y.S.2d 436 (2d Dep't 1990). *See supra,* §§ 16.44–16.47.

6. Dodson v. Planning Bd. of Town of Highlands, 163 A.D.2d 804, 558 N.Y.S.2d 1012 (3d Dep't 1990).

§ 16.106 LAND USE LAW Ch. 16

safety or welfare or fail to meet specific standards in the local regulations is helpful to judicial ratification of agency action.[7] Aesthetic grounds for denial or modification may be used, but they, too, must be based on substantial evidence and not on general concerns or values.[8]

In some instances, local legislatures add language to the effect that the responsible agency may consider "such other elements as may be reasonably related to the health, safety and general welfare of the community." The denial or required modification of an application based on this general language can be upheld where it is not arbitrary or capricious. Where the record shows that the denial or modification is related to protecting public safety, for example, the agency's determination will be upheld.[9]

Occasionally, responsible agencies base a denial or modification on this general police power language and are reversed because they are acting beyond their authority. If, for example, a denial is based on the inadequacy of the water supply for fire protection purposes, it may be reversed because fire protection is expressly regulated under the fire and building code under the authority of the local fire and building inspector.[10] Similarly, a denial based on the failure of the proposed land use to comply with the zoning ordinance is *ultra vires*;[11] that determination must be made by the local building inspector and the zoning board of appeals.[12]

Library References:

West's Key No. Digests, Zoning and Planning ⚖606.

§ 16.107 Site Plans—Responsible Agency—Conditions Imposed

State statutes authorize the responsible agency to impose reasonable conditions and restrictions on its approval of a site plan application when they are directly related and incidental to the proposed plan.[1] A responsible agency, however, is without authority to impose conditions that are unrelated to the legitimate purposes of the laws governing site plan

---

7. J & R Esposito Builders, Inc. v. Coffman, 183 A.D.2d 828, 584 N.Y.S.2d 73 (2d Dep't 1992). *See* Rex Realty of Conn., Inc. v. Broderick, 215 A.D.2d 664, 628 N.Y.S.2d 500 (2d Dep't 1995) where court struck down Village of Harrison Planning Board determination to deny site plan approval finding that the Board's contention that its determination was based on public health, safety and general welfare was unsupported by the record.

8. Exxon Corp. v. Gallelli, 192 A.D.2d 706, 597 N.Y.S.2d 139 (2d Dep't 1993).

9. Grossman v. Planning Bd. of Town of Colonie, 126 A.D.2d 887, 510 N.Y.S.2d 929 (3d Dep't 1987).

10. Moriarty v. Planning Bd. of Village of Sloatsburg, 119 A.D.2d 188, 506 N.Y.S.2d 184 (2d Dep't 1986).

11. *See supra,* § 16.21.

12. Figgie Intern., Inc. v. Town of Huntington, 203 A.D.2d 416, 610 N.Y.S.2d 563 (2d Dep't 1994).

§ 16.107

1. Village Law § 7–725–a(4), Town Law § 274–a(4), General City Law § 27–a(4).

review and approval.[2] Once such conditions are imposed on an approved site plan, they must be met in conjunction with the issuance of a building permit by the municipal building inspector.

Conditions imposed on site plan approvals will not be sustained if they are not supported by empirical evidence contained in the record of the proceeding regarding the proposed site development.[3] For example, limiting the recreational users of a proposed hunting preserve to the use of shotguns was sustained because the planning board properly considered the impact of the proposed use on adjacent properties.[4] On the other hand, the imposition of a requirement that a proposed commercial project include the construction of permanent fountains with drainage retention basins was overturned because the record did not show how fountains would make the development aesthetically pleasing in the proposed location.[5]

If the site plan proposes the construction of residential units, the responsible agency can require it to show a park or parks suitably located for playground or other recreational purposes.[6] Such a requirement may not be imposed unless the responsible agency has found that there is a need for such recreational facilities in the municipality.[7] Additionally, where the agency finds that the proposed site is not suitable for the location of needed recreational facilities, it may require a sum of money in an amount established by the local legislature.[8] All such funds must be held in a trust fund for recreational purposes.[9]

§ 16.108 Site Plans—Summary

Trigger: Property owner proposes land use of an individual site that is subject to site plan approval under local law.

Standard: Applicant must show that his site plan application meets the requirements of the local site plan regulations and applicable state law.

Procedure:

1. Local legislature adopts site plan regulations.[1]
2. Local legislature retains review and approval authority

---

2. Clinton v. Summers, 144 A.D.2d 145, 534 N.Y.S.2d 473 (3d Dep't 1988).

3. Castle Properties Company v. Ackerson, 163 A.D.2d 785, 558 N.Y.S.2d 334 (3d Dep't 1990).

4. Janiak v. Planning Board of the Town of Greenville, 159 A.D.2d 574, 552 N.Y.S.2d 436 (2d Dep't 1990).

5. Castle Properties Company v. Ackerson, 163 A.D.2d 785, 558 N.Y.S.2d 334 (3d Dep't 1990).

6. Village Law § 7–725–a(6)(a), Town Law § 274–a(6)(a), General City Law § 27–a(6)(a)

7. Village Law § 7–725–a(6)(b), Town Law § 274–a(6)(b), General City Law § 27–a(6)(b)

8. Village Law § 7–725–a(6)(c), Town Law § 274–a(6)(c), General City Law § 27–a(6)(c)

9. Id.

§ 16.108

1. See supra, § 16.103.

or delegates it to any local body.[2]

3. Local legislature may authorize responsible body to waive requirements when they are inappropriate.[3]

4. Local legislature or responsible agency may require a public hearing on application.[4]

5. Hearing must be held within 62 days of receipt of application; 10 day prior mail notice to applicant; five day public notice.[5]

6. Responsible agency must comply with SEQRA and referral requirements to metropolitan, regional or county planning board.[6]

7. Referral to metropolitan, regional or county planning board must be 10 days before public hearing, or the time period for local review and approval does not start to run until 30 days after referral. These requirements may extend the time period for agency review and determination.[7]

8. Responsible agency may approve, approve with modifications or disapprove application.[8]

9. Agency decision must be filed with municipal clerk within 5 days after it is rendered.[9]

Standards:

1. Agency decision must be based on specific elements required in a site plan submission.[10]

2. Decision must meet rational basis test and be based on evidence on the record.[11]

3. Basis for decision must be within authority of the responsible agency, not another local body.[12]

4. Reasonable conditions may be imposed on approvals.[13]

5. Conditions must be related to and incidental to the proposed land use and supported by evidence on the record.[14]

---

2. *See supra,* § 16.104.
3. *Id.*
4. *See supra,* § 16.105.
5. *Id.*
6. *Id.*
7. *Id.*
8. *Id.*
9. *Id.*
10. *See supra,* § 16.106.
11. *Id.*
12. *Id.*
13. *See supra,* § 16.107.
14. *Id.*

6. Agency may require residential site plan developer to provide recreation facilities or sum of money as established by the local legislature.[15]

§ 16.109 Particularized Actions

The "essence of zoning," according to the Court of Appeals, is comprehensive planning.[1] When zoning actions are based on a comprehensive plan for the community, they confer reciprocal benefits and burdens on all property owners. It is that reciprocity of advantage that often gives zoning its fundamental fairness and insulates it from attack. The statutes, however, give the village, town and city legislatures discretion to rezone property, which rezoning may be broad based or focus on a particular parcel.[2]

A common, but unexamined, assumption about zoning is that actions that treat particular parcels differently from others in a zoning district undermine the "foundation on which comprehensive zoning depends by destroying uniformity within use districts."[3] When zoning decisions affect one or a few parcels, the query is whether they, and their owners, are unduly burdened or benefitted.

Complaints about particularized actions have two different applications. The first is that an owner who is "unduly burdened" by a land use regulation may request judicial relief from its application.[4] The second is that where one or a few owners are particularly benefitted by a land use action, the owners of surrounding properties may challenge the decision. Stating that the purpose of zoning is to achieve public benefits, these neighboring owners allege that particularized actions which benefit individual owners confer private benefits, instead.

§ 16.110 Particularized Actions—Spot Zoning

Generally, plaintiffs in spot zoning cases claim that a land use action which benefits one or a few property owners lacks the essential character of a proper police power action: protecting the public interest.[1] The

---

15. *Id.*

§ 16.109

1. Udell v. Haas, 21 N.Y.2d 463, 469, 288 N.Y.S.2d 888, 893, 235 N.E.2d 897, 902 (1968). *See supra,* §§ 16.11–16.16.

2. Village Law § 7-708, Town Law § 265, General City Law § 83. An amendment to the zoning ordinance may be accomplished through rezoning (*see infra,* § 16.113), conditional rezoning (*see infra,* § 16.114) or development agreements (*see infra,* § 16.116). Local legislatures may not, however, engage in contract zoning (*see infra,* § 16.115).

3. Collard v. Incorporated Village of Flower Hill, 52 N.Y.2d 594, 439 N.Y.S.2d 326, 421 N.E.2d 818 (1981).

4. Armstrong v. United States, 364 U.S. 40, 80 S.Ct. 1563, 4 L.Ed.2d 1554 (1960), on remand 287 F.2d 577 (Ct.Cl. 1961). *See supra,* §§ 16.42–16.51.

§ 16.110

1. Although it is usually the neighbors of parcels benefited by particularized zoning actions who bring spot zoning actions, there have been cases brought by landowners who allege that unfavorable treatment of their own properties is spot zoning. These are seldom successful since spot zon-

§ 16.110 LAND USE LAW Ch. 16

challengers typically seek a judgment declaring that the zoning action is illegal spot zoning and enjoining its implementation.

In *Rodgers v. Tarrytown*, the seminal case on the subject, spot zoning is defined as

> the process of singling out a small parcel of land for a use classification totally different from that of the surrounding area, for the benefit of the owner of such property.... The relevant inquiry is not whether the particular zoning under attack consists of areas fixed within larger areas of different use, but whether it was accomplished for the benefit of individual owners rather than pursuant to a comprehensive plan for the general welfare of the community.[2]

In the *Rodgers* case, the context of the dispute was the adoption of a "floating zone."[3] The village board created a garden apartment zone and, instead of amending the zoning map to indicate where the use applied, gave the planning board the discretion to approve sites meeting stated conditions for garden apartment use. After planning board approval, the village board amended the zoning map accordingly, one parcel at a time, hence the allegation of spot zoning. Other contexts in which spot zoning challenges arise include the granting of special permits[4] and individual parcel rezoning.[5]

Plaintiffs who bring spot zoning challenges bear a heavy burden of proof as zoning actions are presumed to be constitutional.[6] Further, New York law holds that zoning is not invalid *per se* merely because only a single parcel is benefited[7] and that persons who own property in a particular use district "enjoy no eternally vested right to that classification if the public interest demands otherwise."[8]

---

ing is the illegal singling out of parcels "for the benefit of the owner of such property." *See* Solow v. City of New York, 49 A.D.2d 414, 375 N.Y.S.2d 356 (1st Dep't 1975), aff'd 43 N.Y.2d 700, 401 N.Y.S.2d 207, 372 N.E.2d 41 (1977); Taylor v. Incorporated Village of Head of the Harbor, 104 A.D.2d 642, 480 N.Y.S.2d 21 (2d Dep't 1984).

2. Rodgers v. Village of Tarrytown, 302 N.Y. 115, 123–124, 96 N.E.2d 731, 734–735 (1951). *See supra*, § 16.9.

3. *See* Beyer v. Burns, 150 Misc.2d 10, 567 N.Y.S.2d 599 (Sup.Ct., Albany County, 1991). In Carnat Realty v. Town of Islip, 34 A.D.2d 780, 311 N.Y.S.2d 239 (2d Dep't 1970), the court on a motion for summary judgment reviewed a zoning ordinance that contained descriptions of two business districts; however, those districts were not specifically located on the zoning map and would only be located upon application by an individual property owner. The court held that "these are not 'floating zones' where new or specialized uses are contemplated but had not been considered at the time the districts were originally drawn." 34 A.D.2d at 781, 311 N.Y.S.2d at 241.

4. Kravetz v. Plenge, 84 A.D.2d 422, 446 N.Y.S.2d 807 (4th Dep't 1982). *See supra*, §§ 16.90–16.95.

5. Mahoney v. O'Shea Funeral Homes, Inc., 45 N.Y.2d 719, 408 N.Y.S.2d 470, 380 N.E.2d 297 (1978). *See infra*, § 16.113.

6. Kravetz v. Plenge, 84 A.D.2d 422, 446 N.Y.S.2d 807 (4th Dep't 1982).

7. Mahoney v. O'Shea Funeral Homes, 45 N.Y.2d 719, 408 N.Y.S.2d 470, 380 N.E.2d 297 (1978).

8. Rodgers v. Village of Tarrytown, 302 N.Y. 115, 121, 96 N.E.2d 731, 733 (1951).

§ 16.111 Particularized Actions—Spot Zoning—Challenge Dismissed

Several factors have been cited by courts in dismissing spot zoning challenges:

1. The zoning action was adopted after careful study and consultation with experts and extensive hearings;[1]

2. The challenged zoning was accomplished in a proper, careful and reasonable manner;[2]

3. Although an action deviated from an adopted comprehensive plan, a study was done before the action was taken and the evidence showed that numerous other properties were treated similarly;[3]

4. Although an action deviated from an adopted comprehensive plan, there was evidence that there were intervening changes in property use since the plan's adoption that made the alleged spot zoning reasonable;[4]

5. The alleged spot zoning was not arbitrary in view of evidence that there were, in the area, other uses similar to the one approved by the challenged action;[5] and

6. Other properties in the area benefit from the zoning amendment that is being challenged.[6]

In *Rodgers v. Tarrytown*, the plaintiff complained that the village board had arbitrarily changed the zoning of an adjacent parcel from single-family to multi-family zoning. The Court of Appeals responded by stating:

> [t]he Tarrytown board of trustees was entitled to find that there was a real need for additional housing facilities; that the creation of Residence B–B districts for garden apartment developments would prevent young families, unable to find accommodations in the village, from moving elsewhere; would attract business to the community; would lighten the tax load of the small home owner, ... and

---

§ 16.111

1. Thomas v. Town of Bedford, 11 N.Y.2d 428, 230 N.Y.S.2d 684, 184 N.E.2d 285 (1962).

2. Rodgers v. Village of Tarrytown, 302 N.Y. 115, 96 N.E.2d 731 (1951).

3. Century Circuit, Inc. v. Ott, 65 Misc.2d 250, 317 N.Y.S.2d 468, (Sup.Ct., Nassau County, 1970), aff'd 37 A.D.2d 1044, 327 N.Y.S.2d 829 (2d Dep't 1971).

4. Town of Bedford v. Village of Mount Kisco, 33 N.Y.2d 178, 351 N.Y.S.2d 129, 306 N.E.2d 155 (1973).

5. Mahoney v. O'Shea Funeral Homes, Inc., 45 N.Y.2d 719, 408 N.Y.S.2d 470, 380 N.E.2d 297 (1978).

6. Kravetz v. Plenge, 84 A.D.2d 422, 446 N.Y.S.2d 807 (4th Dep't 1982). *See* Century Circuit v. Ott, 65 Misc.2d 250, 317 N.Y.S.2d 468 (Sup.Ct., Nassau County, 1970), aff'd 37 A.D.2d 1044, 327 N.Y.S.2d 829 (2d Dep't 1971).

would develop otherwise unmarketable and decaying property. The village's zoning aim being clear, the choice of methods to accomplish it lay with the board.[7]

§ 16.112 Particularized Actions—Spot Zoning—Challenge Successful

In *Cannon v. Murphy*,[1] the town board doubled the density on a large parcel at the request of the property owner and accepted the owner's offer to limit density on a remote parcel in exchange. Surrounding property owners challenged the individual parcel's rezoning as illegal spot zoning. The court considered several factors important in invalidating the town's action:

1. It was not part of a well-considered and comprehensive plan calculated to serve the general welfare of the community;

2. There was no evidence that the board had carefully studied, prepared and considered the comprehensive plan in granting the amendment;

3. The planning departments involved had found that the amendment was inconsistent with the town's comprehensive plan;

4. The rezoning would have negative effects on the neighboring properties; and

5. These negative effects were not taken into account by the board.

Where the only benefit discernable in a rezoning accrues to the property owner, illegal spot zoning will be found.[2] Where the evidence shows that there is significant incompatibility between surrounding uses and the use approved on a single parcel, that incompatibility is further evidence that the benefit of a rezoning accrues to the property owner and not the public.[3]

§ 16.113 Particularized Actions—Rezoning

The statutes give village, town and city legislatures the authority, in

---

7. Rodgers v. Village of Tarrytown, 302 N.Y. 115, 122, 96 N.E.2d 731, 733–34 (1951).

§ 16.112
1. 196 A.D.2d 498, 600 N.Y.S.2d 965 (2d Dep't 1993).
2. Dexter v. Town Bd. of Town of Gates, 36 N.Y.2d 102, 365 N.Y.S.2d 506, 324 N.E.2d 870 (1975); Mazzara v. Town of Pittsford, 34 A.D.2d 90, 310 N.Y.S.2d 865 (4th Dep't 1970).
3. Levine v. Town of Oyster Bay, 26 A.D.2d 583, 272 N.Y.S.2d 171 (2d Dep't 1966).

PRACTICE POINTER: In Rogers v. Tarrytown, 302 N.Y. 115, 96 N.E.2d 731 (1951), the challenged action approved a multi-family use in a single-family district, arguably incompatible with one another. The village board, however, imposed certain restrictions on the multi-family project to render it compatible with the surrounding uses, including landscaping, lot line set backs and a minimum parcel size. Counsel should be attentive to this more subtle aspect of incompatibility.

their discretion, to amend zoning ordinances.[1] In most situations, local legislatures are not required to entertain rezoning applications.[2] In cities, however, the legislature must consider and vote on a zoning change where it is requested by a petition signed and acknowledged by the owners of at least fifty percent of the frontage in any district.[3]

If the local legislature considers an application for rezoning and summarily denies the applicant's request, the property owner may challenge such refusal as arbitrary. However, it is well established that, in rezoning, the legislature is acting in its legislative capacity and there is no requirement that the legislature set out its reasons for denying the application.[4] An applicant may also challenge a legislature's refusal to rezone on the grounds that is constitutes exclusionary zoning,[5] is discriminatory or is confiscatory.[6]

When a local legislature chooses to grant a rezoning application, challengers bear the burden of proving the invalidity of the action which is presumed to be constitutional and valid.[7] Local rezoning approval, however, is subject to attack on various grounds, some procedural, others substantive.

Procedural grounds for challenging rezoning actions include inadequate public notice,[8] failure to notify the county planning board as required by statute,[9] failure to comply with environmental review requirements,[10] and failure to enact the rezoning ordinance by a super-

§ 16.113

1. Village Law § 7-708, Town Law § 265, General City Law § 83.

2. Village Law § 7-708, Town Law § 265. See Rodriques v. McCluskey, 156 A.D.2d 369, 548 N.Y.S.2d 323 wherein the court held that there is no duty on the town to act on each and every application for zoning change. This applies as well to cities where the petition to rezone lacks the required signatures. General City Law § 83.

3. General City Law § 83(1). See Society of New York Hospital v. Del Vecchio, 70 N.Y.2d 634, 518 N.Y.S.2d 781, 512 N.E.2d 302 (1987), where the court held that ownership of 100% of the parcel for which the rezoning is sought is insufficient. "The proper interpretation of [§ 83] is that the common council must consider and vote on a petition by owners of 50% of the frontage of the entire district or of the portion of the district in which the property is located." 70 N.Y.2d at 636, 518 N.Y.S.2d at 783, 512 N.E.2d at 304. Note: The General City Law does not apply to cities with populations of over one million.

4. Litz v. Town Bd. of Guilderland, 197 A.D.2d 825, 602 N.Y.S.2d 966 (3d Dep't 1993). See Municipal Home Rule Law § 20.

5. Berenson v. Town of New Castle, 38 N.Y.2d 102, 378 N.Y.S.2d 672, 341 N.E.2d 236 (1975).

6. These last two infirmities were raised without success to challenge the denial of an application to rezone a parcel of the applicant's land in Seggio v. Town of West Seneca, 145 A.D.2d 956, 536 N.Y.S.2d 328 (4th Dep't 1988).

7. Coutant v. Town of Poughkeepsie, 69 A.D.2d 506, 419 N.Y.S.2d 148 (2d Dep't 1979); Town of Bedford v. Village of Mount Kisco, 33 N.Y.2d 178, 351 N.Y.S.2d 129, 306 N.E.2d 155 (1973).

8. Coutant v. Town of Poughkeepsie, 69 A.D.2d 506, 419 N.Y.S.2d 148 (2d Dep't 1979).

9. General Municipal Law § 239-m.

10. Valley Realty Development Co., Inc. v. Town of Tully, 187 A.D.2d 963, 590 N.Y.S.2d 375 (4th Dep't 1992). See supra, §§ 16.52–16.59 and Chapter 15 "Environmental Law."

§ 16.113   LAND USE LAW   Ch. 16

majority vote where required by statute.[11] Substantive grounds include charges that the action is illegal spot zoning,[12] inconsistent with the comprehensive plan,[13] or unlawful contract zoning.[14]

Library References:

West's Key No. Digests, Zoning and Planning ⟐151–172.

§ 16.114 Particularized Actions—Rezoning—Conditions

Conditional rezoning occurs when the local legislature imposes conditions on its grant of an application for rezoning. Conditional rezoning has been defined as

> a means of achieving some degree of flexibility in land-use control by minimizing the potentially deleterious effect of a zoning change on neighboring properties; reasonably conceived conditions harmonize the landowner's need for rezoning with the public interest and certainly fall within the spirit of the enabling legislation.[1]

The logic behind conditional rezoning is that if it is initially proper to rezone the property without the imposition of restrictive conditions, it is equally proper to grant the rezoning subject to conditions that mitigate its impact on the surrounding area.[2] Like zoning itself, conditional zoning may be amended in the future; the legislature is free to modify or abandon the terms of conditional rezoning when changed circumstances dictate that the restrictions are no longer in the public interest.[3]

Under certain circumstances, conditions imposed on rezoning actions are invalidated. Where, for example, the condition limits the benefit of the rezoning solely to the applicant, it is invalid.[4] Conditions imposed on rezoning actions should be reasonable, related and incidental to the use of the property and not personal to its user.[5] A condition that operated *in futuro*, which was proposed by the applicants and adopted *in*

---

11. Baader v. Town Board of the Town of Aurelius, 171 A.D.2d 1046, 568 N.Y.S.2d 991 (4th Dep't 1991). See Village Law § 7–708(1)-(3), Town Law § 265(1)(a)-(c), General City Law § 83(2)(a)-(c).

12. See *supra*, §§ 16.110–16.112.

13. Los–Green, Inc. v. Weber, 156 A.D.2d 994, 548 N.Y.S.2d 832 (4th Dep't 1989). See *supra*, §§ 16.11–16.16.

14. Cram v. Geneva, 190 A.D.2d 1028, 593 N.Y.S.2d 651 (4th Dep't 1993). See *infra*, § 16.115.

§ 16.114

1. Church v. Town of Islip, 8 N.Y.2d 254, 203 N.Y.S.2d 866, 168 N.E.2d 680 (1960).

2. Collard v. Village of Flower Hill, 52 N.Y.2d 594, 439 N.Y.S.2d 326, 421 N.E.2d 818 (1981).

3. Thomas v. June, 194 A.D.2d 842, 598 N.Y.S.2d 615 (3d Dep't 1993).

4. Dexter v. Town of Gates, 36 N.Y.2d 102, 365 N.Y.S.2d 506, 324 N.E.2d 870 (1975).

5. Cram v. Town of Geneva, 190 A.D.2d 1028, 593 N.Y.S.2d 651 (4th Dep't 1993)

toto by the town board, was reason, by itself, for the court to strike the zoning amendment.[6]

Library References:
West's Key No. Digests, Zoning and Planning ⌐160.

§ 16.115 Particularized Actions—Rezoning—Contract Zoning

The term "contract zoning" is sometimes used to describe a situation where a property owner agrees to record a document restricting the property's use or provide other "consideration" in exchange for the municipality's agreement to rezone the property. These bilateral agreements can be distinguished from conditional rezoning, where the legislature unilaterally imposes a zoning condition.[1] In certain instances, bilateral agreements may be attacked as an illegal bargaining away of the municipality's zoning power.

There are no cases in New York where the courts have invalidated bilateral arrangements with property owners because they constitute an illegal selling, or bargaining away, of zoning authority.[2] In *Church v. Town of Islip*,[3] the Court of Appeals entertained a challenge that a zoning change constituted contract zoning. In this case, as with most such local arrangements, the condition on the property owner was imposed as part of the municipality's rezoning action: simultaneous occurrences.

Where the conditions, as in *Islip*, are found to be imposed for the benefit of surrounding property owners and the public, they are upheld. The Court noted that there is nothing unconstitutional about the imposition of conditions in this context to achieve the public good. It further stated that "incidentally, the record does not show any agreement in the sense that the owners made an offer accepted by the board."[4]

Library References:
West's Key No. Digests, Zoning and Planning ⌐160.

§ 16.116 Particularized Actions—Rezoning—Development Agreements

Municipalities may enter into contracts with developers to which both parties are bound. In general, municipalities are free to contract as

---

6. Levine v. Town of Oyster Bay, 26 A.D.2d 583, 272 N.Y.S.2d 171 (2d Dep't 1966).

§ 16.115

1. *See supra,* § 16.114.

2. *But see* City of New York v. 17 Vista Associates 84 N.Y.2d 299, 618 N.Y.S.2d 249, 642 N.E.2d 606 (1994) where an exchange of money from the developer for a promise to expedite the local review and approval process was struck as violative of public policy.

3. 8 N.Y.2d 254, 203 N.Y.S.2d 866, 168 N.E.2d 680 (1960).

4. 8 N.Y.2d at 259, 203 N.Y.S.2d at 869, 168 N.E.2d at 683.

private parties and are bound by the terms of their contracts.[1] Where, however, an agreement binds the legislature to act in a certain way in the future or bargains away zoning authority, unique legal questions are raised.

Development agreements are bilateral agreements between a developer and a municipality that obligate the developer to comply with a variety of conditions. Some agreements attempt to safeguard the developer from changes in applicable zoning and permitting standards. To the extent that required zoning changes and permits are awarded simultaneously with the developer's agreement to abide by conditions imposed, they do not run afoul of the prohibition of bargaining away the municipality's zoning power. In this instance, there is no evidence of a bargain being struck today to benefit the developer by zoning adjustments to be made in the future.

Development agreements that obligate the legislature to refrain from changing zoning and permit arrangements for a fixed period or that compromise its regulatory standards or procedure, however, raise serious questions about whether they constitute illegal bargaining away of future municipal prerogatives. An agreement by a municipality to refrain from altering its approvals or permits may induce a developer, in certain cases, to invest the considerable sums necessary to bring a project to the point of construction. Case law does not protect such investments from changes in applicable zoning laws until construction has begun and a substantial investment has been made.[2]

An agreement entered into between a municipality and a developer to expedite requisite permits was struck by the Court of Appeals as violative of public policy. In *City of New York v. 17 Vista Associates*,[3] a developer paid a predetermined sum of money to the City in exchange for an expedited and favorable determination regarding the status of a building which was the subject of a real estate contract. In striking the agreement as violative of public policy, the Court held, "The City is restricted from bargaining and agreeing to schemes or arrangements beyond public policy and procedures prescribed by the law, under the guise of 'public good.'"[4]

Development agreements that do not implicate the future legislative and regulatory prerogatives of the municipality have been upheld and enforced. In *Sun Company v. City of Syracuse Industrial Development Agency* ("SIDA"), the appellate division upheld an agreement between SIDA, a municipal public benefit corporation, and a developer, Pyramid, whereby SIDA exercised its power of eminent domain and condemned

§ 16.116

1. Halleran v. City of New York, 132 Misc. 73, 228 N.Y.S. 116 (Sup.Ct., N.Y. County, 1928).

2. *See supra*, § 16.23.

3. 84 N.Y.2d 299, 618 N.Y.S.2d 249, 642 N.E.2d 606 (1994).

4. 84 N.Y.2d at 306, 618 N.Y.S.2d at 252, 642 N.E.2d at 609.

property on which a retail mall was to be constructed. The developer agreed to pay the total costs incurred in acquisition of the property and all environmental review expenses in exchange for the right to develop the retail property. In this context, the court held that SIDA did not "contract away its power of eminent domain for value given by Pyramid. [Rather] SIDA intended to condemn the property and entered into an agreement ... to ensure that the property would be developed in the anticipated beneficial manner."[5] Additionally, certain development agreements have been held to be enforceable by third party beneficiaries of the arrangement.[6]

§ 16.117 Particularized Actions—Summary

Trigger: Amendment of the zoning map whereby land use designation of one or a few parcels within a single use district are changed.

Procedure:

1. Rezoning: application is made by property owner to the local legislature requesting a change in use designation for a particular parcel of property. (*See* § 16.128)

2. Conditional Rezoning: application is made by property owner to the local legislature. The rezoning is granted subject to the unilateral imposition of conditions that mitigate its impact on the surrounding area. (*See* § 16.129)

3. Development Agreement: bilateral agreement made between a developer and a municipality that obligates the developer to comply with agreed upon conditions. (*See* § 16.131)

Challenges:

1. Spot Zoning: allegation that the change in zoning is solely for the benefit of the property owner.[1]

Challengers may be successful if the rezoning:[2]

- is not part of a comprehensive plan for the community;
- is inconsistent with the comprehensive plan;
- would negatively effect neighboring properties; and
- results in negative effects on adjacent parcels and such effects were not adequately considered prior to rezoning.

---

5. 209 A.D.2d 34, 46, 625 N.Y.S.2d 371, 379, appeal dismissed 86 N.Y.2d 776, 631 N.Y.S.2d 603, 655 N.E.2d 700 (1995).

6. 6–8 Pelham Parkway Corp. v. Rusciano & Son Corp., 170 A.D.2d 497, 565 N.Y.S.2d 843 (2d Dep't 1991).

§ 16.117

1. *See supra,* § 16.113.
2. *See supra,* § 16.112.

Challengers are less likely to succeed when the rezoning:[3]

- is adopted after careful study and consultation with experts;
- is preceded by a study that demonstrated the rezoning was in conformity with the development of the area;
- is in conformity with other uses in the area; and
- will result in a benefit to other neighboring properties.

2. Contract Zoning: challenge to conditional rezoning or development agreement where the property owner agrees to record a document restricting the use of the property or provides other consideration to a municipality in exchange for a change in zoning designation.[4]

Challengers may be successful if the agreement:

- violates public policy; and
- bargains away the municipality's future prerogative regarding land use decisions.[5]

Challengers are less likely to succeed if the rezoning can be shown to be a valid conditional rezoning or development agreement.[6]

§ 16.118 Special Regulations

Local zoning regulations often contain provisions that allow special land uses but impose limits on them. Construction of sheds, garages and boat houses, for example, may be permitted as uses accessory to the principal permitted use. Within a dwelling, an accessory apartment or home office may be allowed, but carefully regulated. Municipalities are constrained by law not to exclude nontraditional families, affordable housing and mobile homes. Regulations may be adopted to protect the aesthetic quality of a district or promote architectural or historic integrity.

Zoning regulates uses that are considered to be in the public interest in a less restrictive fashion than it does wholly private uses. Constitutionally, and under the delegated police power, zoning must either accommodate, or be careful not to exclude, governmental uses, hospitals, airports, utilities, and religious, educational and charitable uses. Local governments encounter stricter standards when they attempt to regulate these publicly beneficial uses.

3. *See supra*, § 16.111.
4. *See supra*, § 16.115.
5. *See supra*, § 16.115.
6. *See supra*, §§ 16.114–16.115.

§ 16.119 Special Regulations—Accessory Uses

An accessory use is incidental to the main use of the property that is subject to zoning restrictions. Typically, an accessory use is defined as one that is incidental or subordinate to, and customary in connection with, the principal building or use on the same lot.[1]

The basis for permitting accessory uses in local zoning ordinances is that:

> during the formative period of comprehensive zoning it became evident that districts could not be confined to principal uses only. It had always been customary for occupants of homes to carry on gainful employment as something accessory and incidental to residential use ... The earliest zoning ordinances took communities as they existed and did not try to prevent customary practices that met with no objection from the community.[2]

If the zoning ordinance codifies permissible accessory uses, however, property owners may be limited to those accessory uses enumerated in the ordinance.[3] Where, for example, the zoning ordinance enumerates permitted accessory uses to a hotel and the list does not include a car rental business, such a business may not be conducted as accessory to the principal use.[4] Similarly, where an owner's land is already developed for its permitted use, an application to add an accessory use that is allowed in the district only by a special permit may be denied.[5]

If the ordinance does not codify specific accessory uses and simply permits uses "incidental and customarily found" in connection with the principal use, it must be determined whether the use has, in fact, "commonly, habitually and by long practice been established as reasonably associated with the primary use."[6] Where, for example, the zoning board denied a gasoline station owner a permit to operate a convenience store as an accessory use, the court reversed. It found that the type of store proposed by the owner is commonly and customarily found in

---

§ 16.119

1. For a different definition, one particularly applicable to commercial zoning districts, see Del Vecchio v. Lalla, 136 A.D.2d 820, 523 N.Y.S.2d 654 (3d Dep't 1988), where the City of Cortland defined accessory uses as "those uses customarily incidental to the principal uses and including customary services within the building, provided that such services are for patrons of the principal use of the building and there is no external evidence of such services or signs advertising the same." 136 A.D.2d at 821, 523 N.Y.S.2d at 655.

2. Gray v. Ward, 74 Misc.2d 50, 56, 343 N.Y.S.2d 749, 755 (Sup.Ct., Nassau County, 1973), aff'd 44 A.D.2d 597, 354 N.Y.S.2d 591 (2d Dep't 1974).

3. **PRACTICE POINTER:** The typical local zoning ordinance will contain a provision stating, for example, that "all uses not expressly enumerated are deemed prohibited." See, e.g., Aim Rent A Car, Inc. v. Zoning Bd. of Appeals of Village of Montebello, 156 A.D.2d 323, 548 N.Y.S.2d 275 (2d Dep't 1989).

4. Id.

5. Del Vecchio v. Lalla, 136 A.D.2d 820, 523 N.Y.S.2d 654 (3d Dep't 1988).

6. Gray v. Ward, 74 Misc.2d 50, 52, 343 N.Y.S.2d 749, 751 (Sup.Ct., Nassau County, 1973), aff'd 44 A.D.2d 597, 354 N.Y.S.2d 591 (2d Dep't 1974).

connection with and incidental to the principal use of an automotive service station.[7] Other accessory uses that have been found to be customarily incidental to their principal uses include a skateboard ramp in a residential neighborhood,[8] a homeless shelter in a church,[9] and a swimming pool near a school.[10]

Owners have been denied accessory uses where they have failed to prove that they put the property to the principal use permitted under the ordinance,[11] where the proposed accessory use is incompatible with surrounding uses[12] and where there is no evidence that the use is customary in the neighborhood.[13]

Library References:

West's Key No. Digests, Zoning and Planning ⇔301.

§ 16.120   Special Regulations—Accessory Apartments

An accessory apartment has been defined as:

> a second housekeeping unit located within a structure designed originally as a single-family house. The accessory unit is subordinate to the primary unit in terms of size, location, and appearance. The main structure is usually divided so that the subordinate unit can function independently of the main living unit in terms of access, kitchen, bedroom and bathroom facilities.... It should also be noted that some municipalities permit accessory apartments in a structure that is physically separate from the main house on a lot. Examples include garages, former carriage houses, or former servant's quarters.[1]

There are a variety of reasons that prompt municipalities to permit accessory apartments in single-family use districts. These include giving older homeowners extra income so that they can continue to live in their family homes, encouraging younger homeowners to live in the community by allowing them extra rental income to pay for their home mortgages

---

7. Exxon Corp. v. Board of Standards and Appeals of City of New York, 151 A.D.2d 438, 542 N.Y.S.2d 639 (1st Dep't 1989).

8. Collins v. Lonergan, 198 A.D.2d 349, 603 N.Y.S.2d 330 (2d Dep't 1993).

9. Greentree at Murray Hill Condominium v. Good Sheperd Episcopal Church, 146 Misc.2d 500, 550 N.Y.S.2d 981 (Sup.Ct. N.Y. County, 1989).

10. Lawrence School Corp. v. Lewis, 174 A.D.2d 42, 578 N.Y.S.2d 627 (2d Dep't 1992).

11. Moody Hill Farms, Inc. v. Zoning Bd. of Appeals of Town of North East, 199 A.D.2d 954, 605 N.Y.S.2d 560 (3d Dep't 1993); Sinon v. Zoning Bd. of Appeals of Town of Shelter Island, 117 A.D.2d 606, 497 N.Y.S.2d 952 (2d Dep't 1986).

12. Town of Brookhaven v. Spadaro, 204 A.D.2d 533, 612 N.Y.S.2d 175 (2d Dep't 1994).

13. Porianda v. Amelkin, 115 A.D.2d 650, 496 N.Y.S.2d 487 (2d Dep't 1985).

§ 16.120

1. A Guide to Accessory Apartment Regulations, The Westchester Experience, Westchester County Planning Board, March, 1989, p. 2.

and providing a source of affordable housing to the accessory apartment residents.[2]

There are two possible characterizations of an accessory unit in a single-family zone. The first is that it is an accessory unit that meets all the standards applicable to, and should be permitted as, an accessory use.[3] These standards hold that the accessory use must be "incidental," "subordinate," "minor," "attendant," "concomitant" and "customarily found in connection with" the principal use: single-family housing.[4] The second is that this independent living unit renders the primary use impermissible two-family housing, particularly where it is used for auxiliary income. As such, to be permitted, the municipality must adopt a zoning provision allowing accessory apartments by, for example, special permit.[5]

Where accessory apartments are allowed by special permit, a variety of conditions may be imposed. These include, for example, limitations on the permit's duration, requirements that the owner of the property occupy either the main or accessory unit or be a resident of the community, maximum size limitations, design requirements, parking restrictions and safety standards. The court upheld the denial of a special permit for an accessory apartment where the grounds included the inadequacy of buffering and setbacks, traffic circulation, road access and incompatibility with surrounding uses.[6]

Where accessory apartment laws impose residency or owner-occupancy requirements, they are often countered with the oft-quoted generalization that zoning must regulate the use of the property, not its user. Although this generalization is often apt, it has been held inapplicable to accessory apartment regulations. In one case, the court held that the

---

2. Kasper v. Town of Brookhaven, 142 A.D.2d 213, 535 N.Y.S.2d 621 (2d Dep't 1988).

3. *See* Stafford v. Village of Sands Point, 200 Misc. 57, 102 N.Y.S.2d 910 (Sup.Ct., Nassau County, 1951). The court held permissible in a single-family district the occupancy of a large house containing two kitchens by a son, his family, his mother and sister.

4. Gray v. Ward, 74 Misc.2d 50, 343 N.Y.S.2d 749 (Sup.Ct., Nassau County, 1973), aff'd 44 A.D.2d 597, 354 N.Y.S.2d 591 (2d Dep't 1974). *See* Glick v. Summer, 213 A.D.2d 403, 623 N.Y.S.2d 323 (2d Dep't 1995), where the court upheld the zoning board's failure to renew a temporary permit for a small guest house used for visiting relatives as an accessory use.

PRACTICE POINTER: Most zoning ordinances enumerate permissible accessory uses in single-family zones. The omission of an accessory apartment from that list makes it difficult to argue that such a unit should be permitted as a customary accessory use. *See supra,* §§ 16.90–16.95.

5. PRACTICE POINTER: There are other ways to provide for accessory apartments in a local zoning ordinance. They may be included on the enumerated list of permitted accessory uses, but only in certain residential districts. Applications to permit accessory apartments could be submitted to the zoning board of appeals which could approve a use variance. (*But, see supra,* §§ 16.74–16.78 for statutory requirements applicable to use variances.) In some communities, special licensing provisions have been adopted. A Guide to Accessory Apartment Regulations, The Westchester Experience, Westchester County Planning Board, March 1989, p. 22.

6. L & M Realty v. Village of Millbrook Planning Board, 207 A.D.2d 346, 615 N.Y.S.2d 434 (2d Dep't 1994).

public purpose of an accessory apartment law was to "aid occupying homeowners in retaining and maintaining their properties" and therefore the owner occupancy requirement "is an integral component of the town's legislative strategy."[7] In another, the court upheld a three year residency requirement for an owner to qualify for a special permit for an accessory apartment.[8] In a third case, the court upheld a series of conditions on the award of a special permit for an accessory apartment, including termination upon the death of the owner or the transfer of the property, as well as an owner occupancy requirement.[9]

Library References:

West's Key No. Digests, Zoning and Planning ⚖=302.

§ 16.121 Special Regulations—Home Offices

Home offices may be permitted as accessory uses in residentially zoned districts. As with accessory apartments,

> [i]t had always been customary for occupants of homes to carry on gainful employment as something accessory and incidental to residential use * * * The earliest zoning ordinances took communities as they existed and did not try to prevent customary practices that met with no objection from the community.[1]

Most zoning ordinances codify this custom and enumerate the types of home occupations that are allowed as accessory uses in a residential zone, often restricting them to single-family districts.

Litigation often focuses on the limitations on permissible home occupations contained in the zoning ordinance. For example, a lawyer challenged a zoning board's interpretation that he could not practice in a single family zoned building because he did not live on the premises. The zoning ordinance defined a home occupation as "any use customarily conducted entirely within a dwelling and carried on by the inhabitants

---

7. Kasper v. Town of Brookhaven, 142 A.D.2d 213, 535 N.Y.S.2d 621 (2d Dep't 1988). *See also,* Maldini v. Ambro, 36 N.Y.2d 481, 369 N.Y.S.2d 385, 330 N.E.2d 403 (1975) where the Court of Appeals upheld an ordinance that regulated users stating: "[t]hat the 'users' of the retirement community district have been considered in creating the zoning classification does not necessarily render the amendment suspect, nor does it clash with traditional 'use' concepts of zoning. Including the needs of potential users cannot be disassociated from sensible community planning." 36 N.Y.2d at 487, 369 N.Y.S.2d at 391, 330 N.E.2d at 407.

8. Hazzard v. Moraitis, 172 A.D.2d 753, 569 N.Y.S.2d 140 (2d Dep't 1991).

CAVEAT: No reason was offered by the court to explain how this condition accomplished a legitimate public interest. For a contrary view in a different context, *see* Allen v. Town of N. Hempstead, 103 A.D.2d 144, 478 N.Y.S.2d 919 (2d Dep't 1984) classifying a local residency requirement for senior citizen housing as unconstitutionally exclusionary, and finding no compelling local government interest in restricting occupancy to local residents.

9. Sherman v. Frazier, 84 A.D.2d 401, 446 N.Y.S.2d 372 (2d Dep't 1982).

§ 16.121

1. Gray v. Ward, 74 Misc.2d 50, 56, 343 N.Y.S.2d 749, 755 (Sup.Ct., Nassau County, 1973), aff'd 44 A.D.2d 597, 354 N.Y.S.2d 591 (2d Dep't 1974).

thereof, which use is clearly incidental and secondary to the use of the dwelling for dwelling purposes." The court upheld the board's interpretation because the home occupation use was not incidental to the lawyer's use of the property for residential purposes.[2]

Where the ordinance provides that a home occupation must be "customarily carried on in a dwelling unit," the intensity of the occupation becomes relevant to a determination of whether it is "customary" and, therefore, permissible. A zoning board was sustained in its determination that a dance studio, where 160 students were trained each week and classes were held five days per week was not customary in the district.[3]

Some local definitions of "home occupation" are very broad, including, for example, "an occupation or profession which is customarily carried on in a dwelling unit, or in an attached building, provided no commodity is sold upon the premises."[4] An attempt to preclude a dentist from installing equipment to see a few patients each week failed where the definition of home occupation was a broad one.[5] A family therapist was also allowed to conduct her business from home where the home occupation definition allowed "any profession or customary home occupation."[6]

Other ordinances employ narrow definitions, limiting home occupations to, for example, "a physician, lawyer, architect, teacher or similar professional person residing on the premises."[7] Where a management consultant did not present evidence demonstrating that he was a "professional person" such as those listed in the ordinance, the court upheld a denial of permission to conduct that business in a room in the owner's dwelling.[8]

Library References:

West's Key No. Digests, Zoning and Planning ⚖302.

2. Criscione v. City of Albany Bd. of Zoning Appeals, 185 A.D.2d 420, 585 N.Y.S.2d 821 (3d Dep't 1992). *See also*, Elichar Realty Corp. v. Eastchester, 150 A.D.2d 444, 541 N.Y.S.2d 53 (2d Dep't 1989) a basement office in an apartment building was not permitted to be rented to a person who was not a resident of the apartment building.

3. Baker v. Polsinelli, 177 A.D.2d 844, 576 N.Y.S.2d 460 (3d Dep't 1991).

PRACTICE POINTER: In this case, the court held that the board's determination that the home occupation was not "incidental" to the primary use as a dwelling was not supported by factual evidence on the record of the board's proceedings. This illustrates the importance of tying board determinations to factual evidence on the record, a fairly frequent failure noted in the cases.

4. *See* Klingaman v. Miller, 168 A.D.2d 856, 564 N.Y.S.2d 526 (3d Dep't 1990).

5. Winnie v. O'Brien, 171 A.D.2d 997, 567 N.Y.S.2d 943 (3d Dep't 1991).

6. Osborn v. Planning Bd. of Town of Colonie, 146 A.D.2d 838, 536 N.Y.S.2d 244 (3d Dep't 1989).

7. People v. Cully Realty, Inc., 109 Misc.2d 169, 442 N.Y.S.2d 847 (9th and 10th Judicial Districts, 1981). This narrow definition was held to be constitutional.

8. Simon v. Board of Appeals on Zoning of City of New Rochelle, 208 A.D.2d 931, 618 N.Y.S.2d 729 (2d Dep't 1994).

§ 16.122 Special Regulations—Definition of Family

In addition to restricting land uses in residential districts to dwellings and permitted accessory uses, zoning ordinances typically define the type of family that may occupy a dwelling. In doing so, municipalities often distinguish between two types of families, the "traditional" family, related by blood, marriage or adoption, and the "non-traditional" family, whose members are not related in these ways. In a non-traditional family, the bonds may be friendship, profession, age, disability or other attractions. These bonds may create a single housekeeping unit that seeks to secure housing in the community.

In 1975, the United States Supreme Court sanctioned the differential treatment by zoning ordinances of these two types of households. In *Village of Belle Terre v. Boraas*, the village's definition of family was attacked as violative of the equal protection clause of the Fourteenth Amendment.[1] The local provision limited the occupancy of single-family dwellings to any number of persons related by blood, marriage or adoption but not more than two unrelated persons, living as a single housekeeping unit.[2]

The plaintiffs in *Belle Terre* were property owners who had rented their single family home in the village to six unrelated college students. In rejecting their arguments, the Court upheld the provision as a valid exercise of the police power noting:

> A quiet place where yards are wide, people few, and motor vehicles restricted are legitimate guidelines in a land-use project addressed to family needs. The police power is not confined to the elimination of filth, stench, and unhealthy places. It is ample to lay out zones where family values, youth values, and the blessings of quiet seclusion and clean air make a sanctuary for people.[3]

In interpreting the due process clause of the New York Constitution,[4] the Court of Appeals has taken a different view of these provisions.

---

§ 16.122

1. 416 U.S. 1, 94 S.Ct. 1536, 39 L.Ed.2d 797 (1974).

2. The Village of Belle Terre's zoning ordinance defined family as:

One or more persons related by blood, adoption, or marriage, living and cooking together as a single housekeeping unit, exclusive of housekeeping servants. A number of persons, but not exceeding two (2), living and cooking together as a single housekeeping unit though not related by blood, adoption or marriage shall be deemed to constitute a family.

416 U.S. at 2, 94 S.Ct. at 1537.

3. 416 U.S. at 3, 94 S.Ct. at 1541. See Moore v. City of East Cleveland, 431 U.S. 494, 97 S.Ct. 1932, 52 L.Ed.2d 531 (1977) where the U.S. Supreme Court found to be unconstitutional a local definition of family as a nuclear family consisting primarily of a parent and their children. "When the government intrudes on choices concerning family living arrangements, this Court must examine carefully the importance of the governmental interests advanced and the extent to which they are served by the challenged regulation." Id. at 499, 97 S.Ct. at 1936.

4. N.Y. Constitution, Due Process Clause.

In *McMinn v. Town of Oyster Bay*,[5] the Court invalidated a town ordinance that allowed any number of related persons to constitute a family, but limited the definition of family to "two persons not related by blood, marriage or legal adoption, living and cooking on the premises together as a single, non-profit housekeeping unit, both of whom are 62 years of age or over."[6] In *Baer v. Town of Brookhaven*,[7] the Court of Appeals invalidated a town provision that limited single family home occupancy to four or fewer individuals "living and cooking together as a single housekeeping unit."[8]

In *McMinn*, the court recognized the legitimacy of the objective sought to be achieved by the ordinance which included the "preservation of the character of traditional single-family neighborhoods, reduction of parking and traffic problems, control of population density and prevention of noise and disturbance."[9] It focused, instead, on the validity of the means chosen, the contested definition of family, as a reasonable method of achieving that objective. In invalidating the definition the court held:

> [m]anifestly, restricting occupancy of single-family housing based generally on the biological or legal relationships between its inhabitants bears no reasonable relationship to the goals of reducing parking and traffic problems, controlling population density and preventing noise and disturbance.[10]

McMinn and *Baer* were based on previous case law that invalidated similar restrictions on the occupancy of single-family housing by various groups of occupants. In *City of White Plains v. Ferraioli*,[11] the Court of Appeals held that a married couple, their two children and ten foster children, constituted a single housekeeping unit and fitted the local definition of family. In subsequent cases, the courts have held that group homes for mentally retarded children[12] and mentally retarded young women[13] were permissible in single-family districts. The Court of Appeals has held that a group home for the foster care of disturbed children by two permanent surrogate parents was "the functional and factual equiv-

---

5. 66 N.Y.2d 544, 498 N.Y.S.2d 128, 488 N.E.2d 1240 (1985). The McMinns had rented their single family home to four unrelated young men who were friends, co-workers and had grown up in the community and could not afford rental units available in the community.

6. 66 N.Y.2d at 547, 498 N.Y.S.2d at 129, 488 N.E.2d at 1243.

7. 73 N.Y.2d 942, 540 N.Y.S.2d 234, 537 N.E.2d 619 (1989). The plaintiffs were five elderly women living together in a single-family home.

8. 73 N.Y.2d at 943, 540 N.Y.S.2d at 234, 537 N.E.2d at 619.

9. 66 N.Y.2d at 549, 498 N.Y.S.2d at 131, 488 N.E.2d at 1243.

10. *Id.*, 498 N.Y.S.2d at 131, 488 N.E.2d at 1243.

11. 34 N.Y.2d 300, 357 N.Y.S.2d 449, 313 N.E.2d 756 (1974).

12. Little Neck Community Association v. Working Organization for Retarded Children, 52 A.D.2d 90, 383 N.Y.S.2d 364 (2d Dep't 1976).

13. Incorporated Village of Freeport v. Association for the Help of Retarded Children, 94 Misc.2d 1048, 406 N.Y.S.2d 221 (Sup.Ct., Nassau County, 1977), aff'd 60 A.D.2d 644, 400 N.Y.S.2d 724 (2d Dep't 1977).

alent of a natural family" and its exclusion from a residential area served no valid public purpose.[14]

§ 16.123 Special Regulations—Affordable Housing

New York law imposes some requirements on localities with respect to meeting the need for affordable housing in their regions. The Court of Appeals held in *Berenson v. Town of New Castle*[1] that "in determining the validity of an ordinance excluding multi-family housing as a permitted use, we must consider the general purposes which the concept of zoning seeks to serve."[2]

The Court of Appeals established a two-pronged test to be applied to local ordinances when they are attacked as unconstitutionally exclusionary. First, whether the municipality has provided a properly balanced and well ordered plan for the community—that is, are the present and future housing needs of the community's residents met;[3] and second, whether regional needs were considered.[4]

The Court of Appeals has defined exclusionary zone as "a form of racial or socioeconomic discrimination which we have repeatedly condemned."[5] In a subsequent case, a court noted that the municipality's "contention" that Berenson and its progeny eschew any requirement of affordability is simply wrong.[6]

In other cases, the state courts have invalidated as unconstitutionally exclusionary a local residency requirement for senior citizen housing,[7]

---

14. Group House of Port Washington v. Town of North Hempstead, 45 N.Y.2d 266, 272, 408 N.Y.S.2d 377, 379–80, 380 N.E.2d 207, 209 (1978).

PRACTICE POINTER: The cases cited in this section limit, but do not prevent, localities from imposing requirements on the occupancy of single-family dwellings. Drafting and enforcement problems abound, but the decisions do not prohibit regulations that are clearly directed at achieving stability and at limiting all families from unduly congesting a single family neighborhood. In its Group House decision, for example, the court made it clear that its holding was limited to households "which serve as the functional equivalent of a family." 45 N.Y.2d at 274, 408 N.Y.S.2d at 381, 380 N.E.2d at 211.

§ 16.123

1. 38 N.Y.2d 102, 378 N.Y.S.2d 672, 341 N.E.2d 236 (1975).

2. 38 N.Y.2d at 109, 378 N.Y.S.2d at 680, 341 N.E.2d at 241.

3. 38 N.Y.2d at 110, 378 N.Y.S.2d at 680–81, 341 N.E.2d at 242.

4. 38 N.Y.2d at 110, 378 N.Y.S.2d at 681, 341 N.E.2d at 242.

5. Asian Ams. for Equality v. Koch, 72 N.Y.2d 121, 133, 531 N.Y.S.2d 782, 788, 527 N.E.2d 265, 271 (1988). *See also*, Suffolk Hous. Servs. v. Town of Brookhaven, 70 N.Y.2d 122, 517 N.Y.S.2d 924, 511 N.E.2d 67, (1987):

[W]e note that today's decision (should not) be read as revealing hostility to breaking down even unconstitutional zoning barriers that frustrate the deep human yearning of low-income and minority groups for decent housing they can afford in decent surroundings.

70 N.Y.2d at 131, 517 N.Y.S.2d at 927, 511 N.E.2d at 71.

6. Continental Building v. Town of North Salem, 211 A.D.2d 88, 94, 625 N.Y.S.2d 700, 704 (3d Dep't 1995), appeal dismissed 86 N.Y.2d 818, 634 N.Y.S.2d 432, 658 N.E.2d 209 (1995).

7. Allen v. Town of N. Hempstead, 103 A.D.2d 144, 478 N.Y.S.2d 919 (2d Dep't 1984). The court found no compelling local government interest in restricting occupancy to local residents while ignoring regional needs that were not met.

established that it would be unconstitutional to adopt a zoning provision that has an "exclusionary purpose,"[8] and invalidated zoning where it was shown that only upper income families could be expected to afford housing under the municipality's zoning.[9]

Courts have rejected exclusionary zoning challenges where the plaintiff cannot show that the municipality failed to consider regional needs, and that such needs are unsatisfied,[10] where the plaintiff "failed to demonstrate that the efforts of [the municipality] caused the claimed shortage of shelter,"[11] where the attack was against one zone that was allegedly exclusionary within the larger community[12] and where the municipality is not a "developing municipality."[13]

§ 16.124 Special Regulations—Mobile Homes

Mobile homes are often subject to special governmental regulation because of the judicially recognized difference between them and other forms of housing.[1] Whereas, the construction of single-family homes, permitted in single family districts, is regulated by the local and the state building code,[2] mobile home manufacture is regulated under federal law.[3] State and local regulation of the manufacture of mobile homes is preempted by these federal provisions.[4]

A use variance granted to a landowner to place a mobile home on his land outside a designated mobile home park was annulled by the court reasoning that:

> although a mobile home is certainly capable of use as a dwelling, it is not a single-family dwelling as that term is used in the Village Code and is not a permitted use in a residential district. The ordinance specifically excludes a mobile home from the definition of

---

8. Kurzius v. Village of Upper Brookville, 51 N.Y.2d 338, 346, 434 N.Y.S.2d 180, 184, 414 N.E.2d 680, 684 (1980).

9. Continental Building v. Town of North Salem, 211 A.D.2d 88, 94, 625 N.Y.S.2d 700, 704 (3d Dep't 1995), appeal dismissed 86 N.Y.2d 818, 634 N.Y.S.2d 432, 658 N.E.2d 209 (1995).

10. Kurzius v. Village of Upper Brookville, 51 N.Y.2d 338, 434 N.Y.S.2d 180, 414 N.E.2d 680 (1980). In this context, the court upheld the villages five acre minimum lot size provision.

11. Suffolk Hous. Servs. v. Town of Brookhaven, 70 N.Y.2d 122, 130, 517 N.Y.S.2d 924, 926, 511 N.E.2d 67, 70 (1987).

12. Asian Ams. for Equality v. Koch, 72 N.Y.2d 121, 133, 531 N.Y.S.2d 782, 788, 527 N.E.2d 265, 271 (1988).

13. "In view of the fact that the Town of Pompey, unlike New Castle, is concededly not a developing community . . . we agree that the Berenson test need not be applied in the instant case." Town of Pompey v. Parker, 53 A.D.2d 125, 127, 385 N.Y.S.2d 959, 962, (1976), aff'd 44 N.Y.2d 805, 406 N.Y.S.2d 287, 377 N.E.2d 741(1978).

§ 16.124

1. Kyritsis v. Fenny, 66 Misc.2d 329, 330, 320 N.Y.S.2d 702, 704 (Sup.Ct., Dutchess County, 1971).

2. Executive Law Article 19–AA.

3. Housing and Community Development Act of 1974, Title IV. Under this statute, known as the National Mobile Home Construction and Safety Standards Act of 1974, mobile home construction standards were promulgated in June, 1976.

4. 42 U.S.C.A. § 5403(d). See Rivers v. Corron, 160 Misc.2d 968, 608 N.Y.S.2d 977 (Sup.Ct., Clinton County, 1993).

a single family dwelling and it cannot be thwarted by removing the vehicle's mobile apparatus and affixing it to the land.[5]

Additionally, mobile homes are distinct from modular homes.

A mobile home is a single entity, which when placed on a building site, is completed and needs no further installation of a heating system or materials. A modular home is transported to the construction site in several pieces. Moreover, a modular home is indistinguishable in appearance from conventionally built homes while a mobile home cannot be easily mistaken from a conventional dwelling. It appears that the average cost of a modular home is at least twice that of a mobile home.[6]

The operation of mobile home parks is regulated under a state law entitled the Mobile Home Owners Bill of Rights.[7] The rationale provided by the Court of Appeals further reflects on the special nature of mobile homes that are located in discrete parks owned and operated by entrepreneurs who make mobile homes or lots for siting such homes available to their owners or occupants.

Mobile home owners are not apartment or condominium dwellers; nor are they campers. They have different needs and distinct concerns. Whatever the economic and qualitative benefits of year-round mobile home living, the fact remains that, nomenclature notwithstanding, the homes themselves are relatively immobile. Once 'planted' and 'plugged in' they are not easily relocated. Yet they lack the protective enclosure of apartment buildings. As a result, owners and operators of mobile home parks are in a unique position to take advantage of a more or less captive audience.[8]

Because of the comprehensive nature and detailed regulatory scheme of this statute, it has been held to preempt further regulation of mobile home park operations at the municipal level.[9]

Municipal governments in New York have the authority under their delegated zoning powers to regulate, but not to exclude, mobile homes.[10]

---

5. Village Bd. of Trustees of Village of Malone v. Zoning Bd. of Appeals of Village of Malone, 164 A.D.2d 24, 562 N.Y.S.2d 973 (3d Dep't 1990).

6. Kyritsis v. Fenny, 66 Misc.2d 329, 330 320 N.Y.S.2d 702, 704 (Sup.Ct., Dutchess County, 1971).

7. RPL § 233.

8. Miller v. Valley Forge Village, 43 N.Y.2d 626, 628–629, 403 N.Y.S.2d 207, 208–209, 374 N.E.2d 118, 120 (1978).

9. Ba Mar v. County of Rockland, 164 A.D.2d 605, 566 N.Y.S.2d 298 (2d Dep't 1991), appeal dismissed 78 N.Y.2d 877, 573 N.Y.S.2d 67, 577 N.E.2d 58 (1991). "[T]he statute regulates many, if not all, of the rights, duties, obligations and responsibilities of mobile home park owners/operators and those who reside in mobile home parks." 164 A.D.2d at 609–610, 566 N.Y.S.2d at 301. While it appears that municipalities cannot regulate affairs within mobile home parks, mobile park owners can. See Miller v. Valley Forge Village, 43 N.Y.2d 626, 403 N.Y.S.2d 207, 374 N.E.2d 118 (1978) where the Court of Appeals upheld mobile park regulations prohibiting "For Sale" signs and air conditioners.

10. Koston v. Town of Newburgh, 45 Misc.2d 382, 256 N.Y.S.2d 837 (Sup.Ct., Orange County, 1965), 10 Opinion State

Mobile homes may be subjected to different and stricter regulation than conventional dwellings where the regulation is reasonably related to the health, safety and welfare of the community.[11] Further, mobile homes can be excluded from certain residential districts[12] and they may be confined to parks, or courts.[13]

Library References:

West's Key No. Digests, Zoning and Planning ⚭83, 281, 391, 512.

§ 16.125 Special Regulations—Aesthetics

It is constitutionally permissible for local governments to adopt zoning ordinances to achieve aesthetic objectives.

The concept of the public welfare is broad and inclusive. The values it represents are spiritual as well as physical, aesthetic as well as monetary. It is within the power of the legislature to determine that the community should be beautiful as well as healthy.[1]

In *People v. Stover*,[2] the Court of Appeals sustained, solely on aesthetic grounds, an ordinance that prohibited the erection of clotheslines in a front or side yard abutting a street. This case removed some of

Comptroller 254, 11 Op.St. Compt. 619, 20 Op.St. Compt. 527, 19 Op.St. Compt. 337.

11. Servatius v. Town of Verona, 112 A.D.2d 706, 491 N.Y.S.2d 879 (4th Dep't 1985).

CAVEAT: Where there is no local zoning ordinance dealing specifically with mobile homes, the Court of Appeals has held that mobile homes may become realty and be included within the definition of buildings for zoning purposes. Willets v. Schnell, 16 N.Y.2d 686, 261 N.Y.S.2d 888, 209 N.E.2d 547 (1965). In Servatius, however, where there was a zoning ordinance that specifically defined and restricted the use of a mobile home, to successfully attack it, a petitioner had to establish that the ordinance had no reasonable basis. *See supra*, Chapter 3 "Municipal Law."

12. Casella v. Stumpf, 29 Misc.2d 460, 217 N.Y.S.2d 709 (Sup.Ct., Chautauqua County, 1961); Stevens v. Smolka, 11 A.D.2d 896, 202 N.Y.S.2d 783 (4th Dep't 1960).

13. Mobile Home Owners Protective Assn. v. Chatham, 33 A.D.2d 78, 305 N.Y.S.2d 334 (3d Dep't 1969); People v. Clute, 47 Misc.2d 1005, 263 N.Y.S.2d 826 (Washington County Ct., 1965), aff'd 18 N.Y.2d 999, 278 N.Y.S.2d 231, 224 N.E.2d 734 (1966).

CAVEAT: While authorization to develop or expand a mobile home site may be reasonably regulated and withheld, the municipality must be careful to not base its decision on community pressure. Sullivan v. Town Bd. of Town of Riverhead, 102 A.D.2d 113, 476 N.Y.S.2d 578 (2d Dep't 1984); Pleasant Valley Home Construction v. Van Wagner, 41 N.Y.2d 1028, 395 N.Y.S.2d 631, 363 N.E.2d 1376 (1977). Localities are further cautioned when requiring mobile home developers to obtain the consent of their neighbors, to check the case law, which tends to limit the use of consent provisions to land use activities that have nuisance-like effects. "[T]he proposed use of property as a mobile home park or for placement of a mobile home does not qualify as an offensive use because it has been said that the use is residential in nature and not potentially dangerous to other residential uses." Town of Gardiner v. Stanley Orchards, Inc., 105 Misc.2d 460, 467, 432 N.Y.S.2d 335, 340 (Sup.Ct., Ulster County, 1980).

§ 16.125

1. Berman v. Parker, 348 U.S. 26, 33, 75 S.Ct. 98, 102, 99 L.Ed. 27 (1954).

2. 12 N.Y.2d 462, 240 N.Y.S.2d 734, 191 N.E.2d 272 (1963). The court held that "the ordinance ... though based on what may be termed aesthetic considerations, proscribes conduct which offends sensibilities and tends to debase the community and reduce real estate values." 12 N.Y.2d at 466, 240 N.Y.S.2d at 737, 191 N.E.2d at 274.

the previous ambiguity that existed in the area of aesthetic regulation. Prior to *Stover*, for example, local regulation of signs had never been sustained solely on the basis of aesthetic control, requiring instead some basis in public health, safety or welfare. After *Stover*, the Court of Appeals determined that sign regulation "for aesthetic purposes alone, constitutes a valid exercise of the police power."[3]

The public interest in aesthetic regulations "is not necessarily as strong as in those cases involving threats to the public safety."[4] For example, the denial of an area variance was overturned because of a lack of evidence that the zoning board had the authority to reject variances on aesthetic grounds.[5]

Other cases illustrate the limitations municipalities encounter when they restrict private property use based on aesthetic considerations. An ordinance prohibiting a certain type of gate in the community, an aesthetic regulation, was held unconstitutional when it was applied retroactively.[6] In another case, the city's attempt to deny a parking variance on aesthetic grounds was thwarted where the petitioner had otherwise proved he was eligible for the variance.[7] The denial of site plan approval under the municipality's environmental review authority was overturned where it was based solely on negative aesthetic impact considerations.[8] A village was ordered to pay the costs associated with the placement of a utility's transmission facility under the street where the only basis for the requirement was beautification of the neighborhood.[9]

Municipalities fare somewhat better when they impose conditions on land use approvals to achieve aesthetic purposes. A condition on the

---

3. Suffolk Outdoor Advertising Co. v. Hulse, 43 N.Y.2d 483, 402 N.Y.S.2d 368, 373 N.E.2d 263 (1977).

PRACTICE POINTER: Local sign regulations can be part of the zoning ordinance of the community or they can be enacted by discrete ordinance under Village Law § 4-412, Town Law § 130, General City Law § 20, Second Class Cities Law § 30 and Municipal Home Rule Law § 10. Local ordinances that regulate signs may still encounter resistance on First Amendment, freedom of expression, grounds; however, they are more likely to be sustained when they are enacted under delegated zoning authority. *See e.g.*, Gibbons v. O'Reilly, 44 Misc.2d 353, 253 N.Y.S.2d 731 (Sup.Ct., Westchester County, 1964); Huntington v. Estate of Schwartz, 63 Misc.2d 836, 313 N.Y.S.2d 918 (Dist.Ct., Suffolk County, 1970).

4. De Sena v. Board of Zoning Appeals of Incorp. Village of Hempstead, 45 N.Y.2d 105, 408 N.Y.S.2d 14, 379 N.E.2d 1144 (1978).

5. Id.

6. Village of Hempstead v. SRA Realty Corp., 160 Misc.2d 819, 611 N.Y.S.2d 441 (Sup.Ct., Nassau County, 1994), aff'd 208 A.D.2d 713, 617 N.Y.S.2d 794 (2d Dep't 1994). The benefits gained by aesthetic improvement were held not to outweigh the damage or loss suffered by those property owners adversely effected.

7. Sanzone v. City of Rome, 170 A.D.2d 977, 565 N.Y.S.2d 666 (4th Dep't 1991), appeal dismissed 77 N.Y.2d 988, 571 N.Y.S.2d 911, 575 N.E.2d 397 (1991).

8. WEOK Broadcasting Corp. v. Planning Bd. Town of Lloyd, 79 N.Y.2d 373, 583 N.Y.S.2d 170, 592 N.E.2d 778 (1992).

9. Rochester Telephone Corp. v. Village of Fairport, 84 A.D.2d 455, 446 N.Y.S.2d 823 (4th Dep't 1982). Here, the village was operating in its enterprise capacity of reconstructing the streets.

award of a variance requiring that the exterior design and appearance of a building not be altered was upheld.[10] Requiring the mitigation of negative visual impacts through the use of muted exterior colors has been upheld as a valid condition under the locality's environmental review authority.[11]

Property owners also have a difficult time obtaining variances for aesthetic purposes. Where the applicant demonstrated no practical difficulty beyond his inability to accommodate a chosen aesthetic design, an area variance may not be awarded.[12] In a similar case, the court held that aesthetic difficulties of this type are self created.[13] Where area variances were sought on the basis of aesthetic considerations, the court found that the zoning ordinance provides no authority to the zoning board to apply aesthetics as a standard in considering applications for area variances.[14] Where variances are awarded on purely aesthetic grounds, the neighbors can have them set aside.[15]

With respect to the regulation of satellite television antennas, localities have been preempted by federal law, unless they comply with federal prescriptions. Federal Communication Commission regulations require that:

> state and local zoning or other regulations that differentiate between satellite receive only antennas and other types of antenna facilities are preempted unless such regulations: (a) have a reasonable and clearly defined health, safety or aesthetic objective; and (b) do not operate to impose unreasonable limitations on, or to prevent, reception of satellite delivered signals ... or to impose costs on the users ... that are excessive.[16]

Where a municipality had defined satellite dishes as an accessory use and limited their height to 15 feet, one court held that the locality had failed to articulate a clear and permissible reason for distinguishing between satellite dishes and other types of antenna as required by the preemptive federal regulations.[17] In a similar case the court held that:

> [t]he planting of screening foliage would make the plaintiff's reception of all satellite signals virtually impossible. An ordinance may

---

10. Proskin v. Donovan, 150 A.D.2d 937, 541 N.Y.S.2d 628 (3d Dep't 1989).

11. Macchio v. Planning Bd. Town of East Hampton, 152 Misc.2d 622, 578 N.Y.S.2d 355 (Sup.Ct., Suffolk County, 1991). See supra, §§ 16.52–16.59 and Chapter 15 "Environmental Law."

12. Levine v. Korman, 185 A.D.2d 323, 586 N.Y.S.2d 620 (2d Dept 1992).

13. Grando v. Town of Islip, 172 A.D.2d 663, 568 N.Y.S.2d 635 (2d Dep't 1991).

14. Zwitzer v. Zoning Bd. of Appeals of Town of Canandaigua, 144 A.D.2d 1023, 534 N.Y.S.2d 298 (4th Dep't 1988), aff'd 74 N.Y.2d 756, 545 N.Y.S.2d 81, 543 N.E.2d 724 (1989). See supra, §§ 16.82–16.88.

15. Miller v. Messina, 150 A.D.2d 535, 541 N.Y.S.2d 121 (2d Dep't 1989); Gottlieb v. Board of Appeals of City of Rye, 139 A.D.2d 617, 527 N.Y.S.2d 258 (2d Dep't 1988).

16. 47 C.F.R. § 25.104 (1990) known as "Preemption of Local Zoning of Earth Stations."

17. Kessler v. Town of Niskayuna, 774 F.Supp. 711 (N.D.N.Y.1991).

§ 16.125 LAND USE LAW Ch. 16

not limit reception by requiring an antenna to be screened so that the line of sight is obscured.[18]

Library References:
West's Key No. Digests, Zoning and Planning ⟲36.

§ 16.126 Special Regulations—Aesthetics—Architectural Review

Local architectural control ordinances may be adopted to maintain the visual and architectural integrity of the community. They are a specific form of regulation to achieve aesthetic objectives and are sustained in much the same way as other aesthetic regulations.[1] The U. S. Supreme Court, in *Saveland Park Holding Corp. v. Wieland*, upheld a local ordinance that prohibited the issuance of a building permit if the building was so at variance with existing structures in the neighborhood as to cause a substantial depreciation in property values.[2]

To control architectural quality, municipalities typically adopt a design review ordinance under which a design review board or architectural review board is created. The ordinance can specify the zoning districts or types of construction that are to be regulated and can require board approval of the design of new construction and building improvement projects before the building inspector is authorized to issue a building permit.[3]

There is no specific enabling legislation to guide villages, towns and cities in adopting and enforcing design review ordinances. Their authority is based on a passage in the General Municipal Law which permits the local legislative body to regulate districts, sites and buildings having "aesthetic interest or value."[4] Such regulations "may include appropriate and reasonable control of the use or appearance of neighboring private property within public view, or both."[5]

---

18. Cawley v. City of Port Jervis, 753 F.Supp. 128 (S.D.N.Y.1990).

PRACTICE POINTER: The degree to which FCC regulations preempt local control of these matters varies with the apparatus and communications subject matter involved. For example, in People v. Krimko, 145 Misc.2d 822, 548 N.Y.S.2d 615 (Sup.Ct., Nassau County, 1989), the court held that the local height restrictions were reasonable, and not preempted, where they applied to plaintiff's amateur radio communication tower.

§ 16.126

1. See supra, § 16.125.

2. 350 U.S. 841, 76 S.Ct. 81, 100 L.Ed. 750 (1955).

3. The New Castle ordinance challenged in Old Farm Road, Inc. v. Town of New Castle, 26 N.Y.2d 462, 311 N.Y.S.2d 500, 259 N.E.2d 920 (1970) conferred authority upon the Board of Architectural Review to disapprove of a building permit application if it found that the structure "would, if erected or altered, be so detrimental to the desirability, property values or development of the surrounding areas as to provide one or more harmful effects ... by reason of ... excessive similarity ... excessive dissimilarity ... or ... inappropriateness in relation to the established character of other structures in the immediate area or neighboring areas." 26 N.Y.2d at 463, 311 N.Y.S.2d at 501, 259 N.E.2d at 920–921.

4. General Municipal Law § 96–a.

5. *Id.*

In *Old Farm Road v. New Castle*,[6] the Court of Appeals entertained a frontal assault on the town's design review law. The plaintiff claimed that the ordinance provided no standards to guide the architectural board's determination, exceeded the bounds of the police power, was unconstitutionally vague and ambiguous and that it was confiscatory. The Court affirmed the lower court's determination that the action was premature and confined the plaintiff to its administrative remedy, noting that a decision rendered prior to the denial of a building permit would be reached in a vacuum.

§ 16.127 Special Regulations—Aesthetics—Historic Preservation

Under the General Municipal Law, villages, towns, and cities are authorized to enact regulations to protect, enhance and perpetuate districts, sites and buildings of special historical interest or value.[1] The law provides a framework for municipalities to manage their historic and cultural properties for future generations and to conduct their activities, plans and programs in a manner that is consistent with the preservation and enhancement of historic and cultural properties.[2]

These enabling laws make it clear that the authority to protect the municipality's historical legacy is in addition to its power to regulate by planning or zoning laws.[3] For these purposes, local governments may establish a landmark or historic preservation board or commission with powers "to carry out all or any of the authority possessed by the municipality for a historic preservation program."[4]

The Court of Appeals agrees that there is a significant difference between how municipal zoning and historic district regulation maintain the character of an area. In *Penn Central v. New York*, the Court noted that:

> the difference generally is that zoning does this largely by regulating construction of new buildings, while historic district regulation concentrates instead on preventing alteration or demolition of existing structures. In each case, owners although burdened by the restrictions also benefit, to some extent, from the furtherance of a general community plan.[5]

This tendency of historic district regulation to reciprocally benefit and burden the owners of affected properties within the historic district

---

6. 26 N.Y.2d 462, 311 N.Y.S.2d 500, 259 N.E.2d 920 (1970).

§ 16.127
1. General Municipal Law § 96–a.
2. General Municipal Law § 119aa, bb, cc, dd.
3. General Municipal Law § 96–a.
4. General Municipal Law § 119dd(2).
5. Penn Central Transportation Co. v. City of New York, 42 N.Y.2d 324, 397 N.Y.S.2d 914, 366 N.E.2d 1271 (1977).

was central to the U.S. Supreme Court's determination to sustain New York City's historic district regulations.

> Unless we are to reject the judgment of the New York City Council that the preservation of landmarks benefits all New York citizens and all structures, both economically and by improving the quality of life in the city as a whole—which we are unwilling to do—we cannot conclude that the owners of the [affected property] have in no sense been benefited by the Landmarks Law.[6]

The fact that the local law applied to a vast number of structures in the city convinced the court to reject the plaintiff's argument that it was solely burdened and unbenefited by the regulations.[7]

Under state law, municipalities have two methods for protecting historic properties. They are authorized to adopt historic district ordinances to maintain the historic character of the entire district. This was the route chosen by New York City that was challenged in *Penn Central*. Such ordinances designate the district or districts to be regulated and establish an historic district board or commission to review all proposals to alter or demolish existing buildings or to construct new buildings within the district. The approval of the commission is a prerequisite to the issuance of a building permit by the local building inspector.

Another form of regulation to maintain the historic integrity of a community involves the creation of a landmarks commission whose duties include the designation of specific buildings of historic value throughout the entire community. Typically, landmarks commissions conduct surveys of buildings of historic significance, recommend designations of some of these buildings to the local legislature and then review proposals to alter or demolish the legislatively designated buildings.

Both types of historic property regulation have been challenged as discriminatory and confiscatory. The Court of Appeals has sustained such regulations against claims that they are discriminatory:

> Landmark restrictions are designed to prevent alteration or demolition of a single piece of property. To this extent, such restrictions resemble 'discriminatory' zoning restrictions, properly condemned, affecting properties singled out in a zoning district for more restrictive or more liberal zoning limitations. There is, however, a significant difference. Discriminatory zoning is condemned because there is no acceptable reason for singling out one particular parcel for different and less favorable treatment. When landmark regulation is involved, there is such a reason: the cultural, architectural, historical or social significance attached to the affected parcel.[8]

---

6. Penn Central Transportation Co. v. City of New York, 438 U.S. 104, 98 S.Ct. 2646, 57 L.Ed.2d 631 (1978).

7. Id.

8. Penn Central Transportation Co. v. City of New York, 42 N.Y.2d 324, 397 N.Y.S.2d 914, 366 N.E.2d 1271 (1977).

"Even when regulation is designed to achieve such an acceptable purpose, however, the landowner must be allowed a reasonable return or equivalent private use of his property."[9] Where the affected property is used for a charitable purpose, however, the standard is different. The court invalidates the regulation only if "it does not physically or financially prevent or seriously interfere with the carrying out of the charitable purpose."[10]

There are limits imposed on the structure of local historic character ordinances. They may not, for example, impose requirements regarding the form of ownership of regulated properties.[11] They may not impose costly rehabilitation requirements.[12] A requirement that the Historical Area Board grant variances from the zoning ordinance regarding properties in the historic district was set aside as a violation of Section 267(5) of the Town Law which gives that authority to the zoning board of appeals.[13] The appeal of a denial of a building permit based on a determination of a landmarks preservation commission, however, is directly to the courts, not to the zoning board of appeals.[14]

Library References:

West's Key No. Digests, Health and Environment ⚖=25.5(8).

§ 16.128 Special Regulations—Public Uses

Federal, state and local activities may be exempt from the application of local zoning regulations, in the strict sense. When a local government is developing a municipal building,[1] a court, a highway garage, traffic sign, lights on a baseball field,[2] school,[3] fire department or police building, it may locate the project where the public interest

---

9. Id.

10. Society for Ethical Culture v. Spatt, 51 N.Y.2d 449, 434 N.Y.S.2d 932, 415 N.E.2d 922 (1980); Lutheran Church in America v. City of New York, 35 N.Y.2d 121, 359 N.Y.S.2d 7, 316 N.E.2d 305 (1974).

11. FGL & L Property Corp. v. City of Rye, 66 N.Y.2d 111, 495 N.Y.S.2d 321, 485 N.E.2d 986 (1985).

12. Id.

13. Burdick v. Bryant, 111 Misc.2d 756, 444 N.Y.S.2d 997 (Sup.Ct., Rockland County, 1981).

14. Academy Mews, Inc. v. Kane, 143 A.D.2d 960, 533 N.Y.S.2d 620 (2d Dep't 1988), appeal dismissed 73 N.Y.2d 906, 539 N.Y.S.2d 292, 536 N.E.2d 621 (1989).

§ 16.128

1. Dunn v. Town of Warwick, 146 A.D.2d 601, 537 N.Y.S.2d 174 (2d Dep't 1989).

2. Armenia v. Luther, 152 A.D.2d 928, 543 N.Y.S.2d 832 (4th Dep't 1989).

3. Lawrence School Corp. v. Lewis, 174 A.D.2d 42, 578 N.Y.S.2d 627 (2d Dep't 1992). The local zoning board denied school's application to construct two swimming pools. The court noted:

> [T]his appeal provides the opportunity to remind municipalities that because educational institutions presumptively serve a beneficial public purpose, local governments may not unreasonably prohibit accessory uses of school premises.... Educational and religious institutions are generally entitled to locate on their property facilities for such social, recreational, athletic and other accessory uses as are reasonably associated with their educational or religious purposes.

174 A.D.2d at 43, 578 N.Y.S.2d at 628.

demands, whether or not it complies with the provisions of the locality's zoning ordinance.[4]

When the state desires to locate facilities for governmental functions in a community, it has relative freedom from local zoning in locating structures serving those functions. The familiar applications of this power are the construction of state facilities such as educational institutions,[5] utilities,[6] prisons, state office buildings, roads,[7] bridges, sewers, and similar projects.

With regard to these state actions, the courts generally apply a "superior sovereign" test, the result of which is to immunize state activities from the restrictions of local zoning. This doctrine applies where the legislature's intention to preempt local zoning is direct and where the action is one taken directly by a state agency.[8]

In a variety of contexts, the courts in New York have found an implied intention to preempt local zoning. When the declaration of intent to preempt is indirect, the court proceeds with a bit more caution. Instead of deferring to the state, as it does in applying the superior sovereign test, it balances the interests of the state with those of the affected locality. This test was applied in *Matter of City of Rochester*[9] which exempted a county airport expansion project from local land use jurisdiction.[10]

After reviewing a variety of factors, the Court in *Monroe* exempted the county's project from local land use oversight. Among the factors considered by the Court were the county's own procedures providing for public notice and hearing, the importance of the project to the locality and the state, the lack of other appropriate locations, lack of evidence of

---

4. *See supra*, § 16.124 for an example of federal preemption of local land use authority regarding the siting of satellite dishes on individual parcels of land.

5. Education Law §§ 401, 407, 408; 8 NYCRR §§ 14, 155; *see* Board of Education of City of Buffalo v. City of Buffalo, 32 A.D.2d 98, 302 N.Y.S.2d 71 (4th Dep't 1969) where a city ordinance that restricted construction of schools was preempted by state law. *See also*, Wiltwyck School for Boys, Inc. v. Hill, 11 N.Y.2d 182, 227 N.Y.S.2d 655, 182 N.E.2d 268 (1962) and Summit School v. Neugent, 82 A.D.2d 463, 442 N.Y.S.2d 73 (2d Dep't 1981).

6. *See e.g.*, New York State Elec. & Gas Corp. v. McCabe, 32 Misc.2d 898, 224 N.Y.S.2d 527 (Sup.Ct., Westchester County, 1961) and Consolidated Edison Co. v. Village of Briarcliff Manor, 208 Misc. 295, 144 N.Y.S.2d 379 (Sup.Ct., Westchester County, 1955).

7. Mair Realty Corp. v. Siegel, 34 A.D.2d 735, 310 N.Y.S.2d 680 (2d Dep't 1970).

8. *See* Washington County Cease, Inc. v. Persico, 120 Misc.2d 207, 465 N.Y.S.2d 965 (Sup.Ct., Washington County, 1983), aff'd 99 A.D.2d 321, 473 N.Y.S.2d 610 (1984).

9. 72 N.Y.2d 338, 533 N.Y.S.2d 702, 530 N.E.2d 202 (1988). In this case the Court of Appeals discarded the long-used distinction between the governmental activities of the superior sovereign, which were found to preempt local zoning, and its proprietary activities, which subjected them to local review. The usefulness of this distinction was called "outlived." 72 N.Y.2d at 341, 533 N.Y.S.2d at 703, 530 N.E.2d at 203.

10. This balancing approach subjects the encroaching governmental unit in the first instance, in the absence of an expression of contrary legislative intent, to the zoning requirements of the host governmental unit where the extraterritorial land use would be employed.

72 N.Y.2d at 343, 533 N.Y.S.2d at 704, 530 N.E.2d at 204.

negative impact on adjacent owners, and the fact that the project involved the expansion of an existing county use.

Monroe involved a two tier analysis of the preemption issue. The first inquiry is whether the activity is expressly immune from local control. Where it is not, the project is subjected to local land use scrutiny with the court using the balancing of interest test to determine the reasonableness of the local determination with respect to the project.

Implied preemption of local zoning has been found even regarding the projects of agencies that are not creatures of state government, but whose activities are simply aided by the state. In one case, the court found that the State Legislature had intended to occupy and control the field of providing drug abuse facilities as a matter of state policy.[11] In another, a city's zoning was held to violate the Mental Hygiene Law[12] because it was inconsistent with a state legislative scheme for providing housing for the mentally ill.[13] In another case, a statutory provision that all duly licensed "community residential facilities" shall constitute family units overrode conflicting local zoning regulations.[14]

§ 16.129 Special Regulations—Public Uses—Public Utilities

Public utility facilities may be permitted as-of-right,[1] considered accessory uses[2] or allowed by special permit,[3] subject to reasonable conditions. The services provided by public utilities, which include electricity, gas and telephone are deemed to be in the public interest. The providers of these services are publicly regulated. Often their licenses, issued by federal or state agencies, require them to provide adequate service to the public.

The extent to which localities may regulate public utilities through zoning is limited in comparison with wholly private commercial uses. Facilities needed for the safe and adequate provision of these public services cannot be excluded from communities. Discrete regulation of them is permitted,[4] but it must be tempered by the public necessity

---

11. People v. St. Agatha Home, 47 N.Y.2d 46, 416 N.Y.S.2d 577, 389 N.E.2d 1098 (1979); Unitarian Universalist Church of Central Nassau v. Shorten, 63 Misc.2d 978, 314 N.Y.S.2d 66 (Sup.Ct., Nassau County, 1970).

12. Mental Hygiene Law § 141.34.

13. Community Resource Center for the Developmentally Disabled, Inc. v. City of Yonkers, 140 Misc.2d 1018, 532 N.Y.S.2d 332 (Sup.Ct., Westchester County, 1988).

14. Zubli v. Community Mainstreaming Assocs., 102 Misc.2d 320, 423 N.Y.S.2d 982 (Sup.Ct., Nassau County, 1979), aff'd 50 N.Y.2d 1024, 431 N.Y.S.2d 813, 410 N.E.2d 746 (1980). See also, Incorporated Village of Old Field v. Introne, 104 Misc.2d 122, 430 N.Y.S.2d 192 (Sup.Ct., Suffolk County, 1980).

§ 16.129

1. See supra, § 16.61.
2. See supra, § 16.119.
3. See supra, §§ 16.90–16.95.
4. Long Island Lighting Co. v. Griffin, 272 App.Div. 551, 74 N.Y.S.2d 348 (2d Dep't 1947), aff'd 297 N.Y. 897, 79 N.E.2d 738 (1948).

§ 16.129   LAND USE LAW   Ch. 16

incident to the provision and expansion of the utility's service to meet the demand of the public.

In *Consolidated Edison Company of New York, Inc. v. Hoffman*,[5] the Court of Appeals reviewed a denial by a village zoning board of a request for a variance by Consolidated Edison to modify its nuclear generating plant by adding a wet cooling tower. The Court noted:

> It has long been held that a zoning board may not exclude a utility from a community where the utility has shown a need for its facilities. However, this has never meant that a utility may place a facility wherever it chooses within the community. To be granted a use variance, the utility should be required to show that denial of the variance would cause unnecessary hardship, but not in the sense required of other applicants. Instead, the utility must show that modification (of the plant) is a public necessity in that it is required to render safe and adequate service, and that there are compelling reasons, economic or otherwise, which make it more feasible to modify the plant than to use alternative sources of power such as may be provided by other facilities.[6]

In a subsequent case,[7] a court defined the burden of proof that a utility company must meet in applying the Court of Appeals' test to qualify for a variance. First, the utility must show that construction is necessary to provide safe and adequate service. Second, it must show that the proposed activities, for which the variance is requested, are necessary to that needed construction. Finally, there must be a showing that the service could not be rendered safe and adequate by some other means. The court held that there was no express or implied preemption of local zoning and, therefore, the utility was required to prove the unnecessary hardship.

Library References:

West's Key No. Digests, Zoning and Planning ⚖=238.

§ 16.130 Special Regulations—Public Uses—Cellular Transmission Facilities

In New York, providers of cellular telephone service are regulated as public utilities and defined as such for zoning purposes. The Court of Appeals, in *Cellular Telephone Company v. Rosenberg*, ruled specifically that a cellular telephone company is a public utility and that the construction of an antenna tower for power transmission is a public

---

5. 43 N.Y.2d 598, 403 N.Y.S.2d 193, 374 N.E.2d 105 (1978).

6. 43 N.Y.2d at 610, 403 N.Y.S.2d at 199, 374 N.E.2d at 111.

7. Zagoreos v. Conklin, 109 A.D.2d 281,

utility building.[1] In reversing the zoning board's denial of an application for a variance, the Court held that the utility had made the requisite showing that the installation would have a negligible impact on the surrounding neighborhood, that the cell site would not affect humans, animals or other organisms and that the petitioner had proven the site was a requisite public necessity by showing that the erection of the cell would enable it to remedy gaps in existing service. Therefore, the court found there existed no rational basis for the Board's determination denying the use variance.[2]

In *Consolidated Edison Company of New York, Inc. v. Hoffman*,[3] the Court of Appeals held that the factors normally applicable to the review of a requested variance are not appropriate when the entity requesting the variance is a public utility.

> Instead, the utility must show that modification is a public necessity in that it is required to render safe and adequate service, and that there are compelling reasons, economic or otherwise.... Where the intrusion or burden on the community is minimal, the showing required by the utility should be correspondingly reduced.[4]

When a city planning board denied a petitioner's application for site plan approval to install a cellular transmission facility, the court held that the proposed cell site presented a minimal intrusion into the community.[5] It noted that the cellular company is mandated to provide its service and the facility was necessary to fill gaps in the grid, so that service could be adequately provided. Given the minimal intrusion into the community, the cellular company's showing was sufficient to warrant granting of its application. The planning board's denial was held to be arbitrary and capricious.

A local moratorium, prohibiting the use of property for the erection of cellular transmission antennas due to the potential health effects of radio frequency transmission, was held invalid since:

> there is not a scintilla of evidence in the record indicating that the installation of cellular antennas in accordance with the plaintiff's

---

491 N.Y.S.2d 358 (2d Dep't 1985).

§ 16.130

1. 82 N.Y.2d 364, 604 N.Y.S.2d 895, 624 N.E.2d 990 (1993). "A public utility has been defined to mean a private business, often a monopoly, which provides services so essential to the public interest as to enjoy certain privileges such as eminent domain and be subject to such governmental regulation as fixing of rates and standards of services." 82 N.Y.2d at 371, 604 N.Y.S.2d at 898, 624 N.E.2d at 993. The Court also noted that nothing in the amendment to Village Law § 7-712-b(2), regarding the standards governing the award of variances, (see supra, §§ 16.73–16.88) supports the conclusion that the legislature intended to overrule Matter of Consolidated Edison, 82 N.Y.2d at 372, 604 N.Y.S.2d at 899, 624 N.E.2d at 994.

2. 82 N.Y.2d at 373, 604 N.Y.S.2d at 900, 624 N.E.2d at 995.

3. 43 N.Y.2d 598, 403 N.Y.S.2d 193, 374 N.E.2d 105 (1978).

4. 43 N.Y.2d at 610, 403 N.Y.S.2d at 199, 374 N.E.2d at 111.

5. Cellular Telephone Company v. Meyer, 200 A.D.2d 743, 607 N.Y.S.2d 81 (2d Dep't 1994).

§ 16.130   LAND USE LAW   Ch. 16

proposed plan will be inimical to the well-being of the Village citizenry. Rather, the overwhelming and unrefuted medical and scientific evidence is to the contrary.[6]

In the absence of any supporting proof, a legislative body can not rely on the speculative and unfounded perception of health risks as a basis to declare a moratorium. However, a 90 day municipal moratorium on the review or approval of cellular telephone antenna facilities was upheld where the stated purpose was "to regulate cellular telephone facilities within the Town and provide the Town with adequate criteria by which it can be reviewed."[7] The court held:

> [L]ocal land use officials are charged with imposing reasonable zoning regulations that do not conflict with the law, but further land appropriate for their community. An imposition of a moratorium of brief duration and for the rational purpose of instituting comprehensive zoning regulations which reasonably regulate an ever present technology which could significantly impact the Town such as cellular telephone antenna facilities, is a logical response to a municipality's duty in this area.[8]

Library References:
West's Key No. Digests, Zoning and Planning ⚍238.

§ 16.131 Special Regulations—Public Uses—Religious Uses

Municipal determinations regarding the use of land by religious organizations arises in a variety of contexts from local rulings on applications for subdivisions,[1] variances,[2] and special permits,[3] to whether the proposed religious activity constitutes an accessory use.[4] Objections to religious land uses most often arise in residential districts when local boards are urged to exclude or carefully control them by their neighbors.

It is old law in New York that it is not:

---

6. Cellular Telephone Company v. Village of Tarrytown, 209 A.D.2d 57, 67, 624 N.Y.S.2d 170, 176 (2d Dep't 1995).

7. Cellular Telephone Company v. Town-Village of Harrison, (Sup.Ct., Westchester County, Justice Cowhey) N.Y.L.J., 11/30/95, p.35, col.3.

8. Id.

§ 16.131

1. Diocese of Rochester v. Planning Bd. of Town of Brighton, 1 N.Y.2d 508, 154 N.Y.S.2d 849, 136 N.E.2d 827, (1956). See supra, §§ 16.96–16.102.

2. Islamic Society Of Westchester and Rockland, Inc. v. Foley, 96 A.D.2d 536, 464 N.Y.S.2d 844 (2d Dep't 1983). See supra, §§ 16.73–16.88.

3. Neddermeyer v. Town of Ontario Planning Board, 155 A.D.2d 908, 548 N.Y.S.2d 951 (4th Dep't 1989); Harrison Orthodox Minyan, Inc. v. Town Board of Harrison, 159 A.D.2d 572, 552 N.Y.S.2d 434 (2d Dep't 1990); Province of Meribah Soc. of Mary, Inc. v. Village of Muttontown, 148 A.D.2d 512, 538 N.Y.S.2d 850 (2d Dep't 1989). See supra, §§ 16.90–16.95.

4. Greentree at Murray Hill Condominium v. Good Sheperd Episcopal Church, 146 Misc.2d 500, 550 N.Y.S.2d 981 (Sup.Ct., N.Y. County, 1989). See supra, § 16.119.

a proper function of government to interfere in the name of the public to exclude churches from residential districts for the purpose of securing to adjacent landowners the benefits of exclusive residential restrictions.[5]

In one case, the denial of a permit for the erection of a church on the ground that it would negatively affect property values and tax revenues was invalidated.[6] The Court of Appeals stated flatly that neither ground was an appropriate reason for denying the subdivision application, noting further that:

> the paramount authority of this State had declared a policy that churches and schools are more important than local taxes, and that it is in furtherance of the general welfare to exclude such institutions from taxation. This being the case, it cannot be seriously argued that the decision of respondents denying this permit because of a loss of tax revenue is in furtherance of the general welfare.[7]

Subsequent cases have held that religious structures enjoy a constitutionally protected status. Considerations of the surrounding area "are outweighed by the constitutional prohibition against the abridgement of the free exercise of religion."[8] The power to regulate them has not been eliminated, but considerations appropriate to the denial of development permits for commercial activities in residential districts cannot be used to exclude religious uses. Where the impacts of such uses on surrounding properties are at issue, they may be used to condition or minimize the religious use, but not when such conditions irreconcilably conflict with the proposed use by the religious organization.[9]

Religious uses are not confined to areas dedicated to worship. They include a homeless shelter,[10] day care center[11] and church-related nonprofit organization.[12] However, "affiliation with or supervision by religious organizations does not, per se, transform institutions into religious ones."[13]

Library References:

West's Key No. Digests, Zoning and Planning ⌐76, 288, 388, 508.

5. Diocese of Rochester v. Planning Board of Town of Brighton, 1 N.Y.2d 508, 524, 154 N.Y.S.2d 849, 860, 136 N.E.2d 827, 835 (1956).

6. Id.

7. 1 N.Y.2d at 525, 154 N.Y.S.2d at 861, 136 N.E.2d at 836.

8. Westchester Reform Temple v. Brown, 22 N.Y.2d 488, 496–497, 293 N.Y.S.2d 297, 303–304, 239 N.E.2d 891, 896 (1968).

9. Id.

10. Greentree at Murray Hill Condominium v. Good Sheperd Episcopal Church, 146 Misc.2d 500, 550 N.Y.S.2d 981 (Sup.Ct., N.Y. County, 1989).

11. Siegert v. Luney, 111 A.D.2d 854, 491 N.Y.S.2d 15 (2d Dep't 1985).

12. Catholic Charities of Roman Catholic Diocese of Syracuse v. Zoning Bd. of Appeals of City of Norwich, 187 A.D.2d 903, 590 N.Y.S.2d 918 (3d Dep't 1992).

13. Yeshiva & Mesivta Toras Chaim v. Rose, 136 A.D.2d 710, 523 N.Y.S.2d 907 (2d Dep't 1988).

§ 16.132 Special Regulations—Summary

Local zoning regulations often contain provisions that allow special land uses but impose limits on them. Construction of sheds, garages and boat houses, for example, may be permitted as uses accessory to the principal permitted use.[1] Within a dwelling, an accessory apartment or home office may be allowed, but carefully regulated.[2] Municipalities are constrained by law not to exclude nontraditional families, affordable housing and mobile homes.[3] Regulations may be adopted to protect the aesthetic quality of a district or promote architectural or historic integrity.[4]

Zoning regulates uses that are considered to be in the public interest in a less restrictive fashion than it does wholly private uses. Constitutionally, and under the delegated police power, zoning must either accommodate, or be careful not to exclude, governmental uses, hospitals, airports, utilities, and religious, educational and charitable uses.[5] Local governments encounter stricter standards when they attempt to regulate these publicly beneficial uses.

§ 16.133 Forms—Environmental Assessment—Short Form

617.20
State Environmental Quality Review
For UNLISTED ACTIONS Only

PART I–PROJECT INFORMATION (To be completed by Applicant or Project sponsor)

1. APPLICANT/SPONSOR   2. PROJECT NAME
   _____   _____

3. PROJECT LOCATION:
   Municipality _____ County _____

4. PRECISE LOCATION (Street address and road intersection, prominent landmarks, etc., or provided map)
   _____

5. IS PROPOSED ACTION:
   ___ New ___ Expansion ___ Modifications/alterations

6. DESCRIBE PROJECT BRIEFLY:

7. AMOUNT OF LAND AFFECTED:
   Initially _____ acres Ultimately _____ acres

---

§ 16.132
1. See supra, § 16.119.
2. See supra, §§ 16.120–16.121.
3. See supra, §§ 16.122–16.24.
4. See supra, §§ 16.125–16.127.
5. See supra, §§ 16.128–16.131.

8. WILL PROPOSED ACTION COMPLY WITH EXISTING ZONING OR OTHER EXISTING LAND USE RESTRICTIONS:
___ Yes ___ No   If No, describe briefly.

9. WHAT IS PRESENT LAND USE IN VICINITY OF PROJECT?
___ Residential ___ Industrial ___ Commercial ___ Agriculture
___ Park/Forest/Open space ___ Other
Describe:

10. DOES ACTION INVOLVE A PERMIT APPROVAL, OR FUNDING, NOW OR ULTIMATELY FROM ANY OTHER GOVERNMENTAL AGENCY (FEDERAL, STATE OR LOCAL)?
___ Yes ___ No   If yes, list agency(s) and permit/approvals

11. DOES ANY ASPECT OF THE ACTION HAVE A CURRENTLY VALID PERMIT OR APPROVAL?
___ Yes ___ No   If yes, list agency name and permit/approval

12. AS A RESULT OF PROPOSED ACTION WILL EXISTING PERMIT/APPROVAL REQUIRE MODIFICATION?
___ Yes ___ No
I CERTIFY THAT THE INFORMATION PROVIDED ABOVE IS TRUE TO THE BEST OF MY KNOWLEDGE

Applicant/sponsor name: _____   Date: _____

Signature: _____

If the action is in the Coastal Area, and you are a state agency, complete the Coastal Assessment Form before proceeding with this assessment

PART II–ENVIRONMENTAL ASSESSMENT (To be completed by Agency)

A. DOES ACTION EXCEED ANY TYPE I THRESHOLD IN 6 NYCRR, PART 617.12? If yes, coordinate the review process and use the FULL EAF.
___ Yes ___ No

B. WILL ACTION RECEIVE COORDINATED REVIEW AS PROVIDED FOR UNLISTED ACTIONS IN 6 NYCRR, PART 617.6? If No, a negative declaration may be superseded by another involved agency.
___ Yes ___ No

C. COULD ACTION RESULT IN ANY ADVERSE EFFECTS ASSOCIATED WITH THE FOLLOWING (Answers may be handwritten, if legible)

C1. Existing air quality, surface or groundwater quality or quantity, noise levels, existing traffic patterns, solid waste production or disposal, potential for erosion, drainage or flooding problems? Explain briefly:

C2. Aesthetic, agricultural, archaeological, historic, or other natural or cultural resources, or community or neighborhood character? Explain briefly.

C3. Vegetation or fauna, fish, shellfish or wildlife species, significant habitats, or threatened or endangered species? Explain briefly.

C4. A community's existing plans or goals as officially adopted, or a change in use or intensity of use of land or other natural resources? Explain briefly.

C5. Growth, subsequent development, or related activities likely to be induced by the proposed action? Explain briefly.

C6. Long term, short term, cumulative, or other effects not identified in C1–C5? Explain briefly.

C7. Other impacts (including changes in use of either quantity or type of energy)? Explain briefly.

D. WILL THE PROJECT HAVE AN IMPACT ON THE ENVIRONMENTAL CHARACTERISTICS THAT CAUSED THE ESTABLISHMENT OF A CEA?

___ Yes ___ No

E. IS THERE, OR IS THERE LIKELY TO BE, CONTROVERSY RELATED TO POTENTIAL ADVERSE ENVIRONMENTAL IMPACTS?

___ Yes ___ No   If Yes, explain briefly

PART III–DETERMINATION OF SIGNIFICANCE (To be completed by Agency)

INSTRUCTIONS: For each adverse effect identified above, determine whether it is substantial, large, important or otherwise significant. Each effect should be assessed in connection with its (a) setting (i.e., urban or rural); (b) probability of occurring; (c) duration; (d) irreversibility; (e) geographic scope; and (f) magnitude. If necessary, add attachments or reference supporting materials. Ensure that explanations contain sufficient detail to show that all relevant adverse impacts have been identified and adequately addressed. If question D of Part II was checked yes, the determination and significance must evaluate the potential impact of the proposed action on the environmental characteristics of the CEA.

___ Check this box if you have identified one or more potentially large or significant adverse impacts which **MAY** occur. Then proceed directly to the FULL EAF and/or prepare a positive declaration.

___ Check this box if you have determined, based on the information and analysis above and any supporting documentation, that the proposed action **WILL NOT** result in any significant ad-

Ch. 16   ENVIRONMENTAL ASSESSMENT—LONG FORM §16.134

verse environmental impacts **AND** provide on attachments as necessary, the reasons supporting this determination:

Name of Lead Agency

Print or Type Name of Responsible Officer in Lead Agency

Title of Responsible Officer

Signature of Responsible Officer in Lead Agency

Signature of Preparer (if different from responsible officer)

Date

§ 16.134   Forms—Environmental Assessment—Long Form

617.20 SEQR

Appendix A

State Environmental Quality Review

Purpose: The full EAF is designed to help applicants and agencies determine, in an orderly manner, whether a project or action may be significant. The question of whether an action may be significant is not always easy to answer. Frequently, there are aspects of a project that are subjective or unmeasurable. It is also understood that those who determine significance may have little or no formal knowledge of the environment or may be technically expert in environmental analysis. In addition, many who have knowledge in one particular area may not be aware of the broader concerns affecting the question of significance.

The full EAF is intended to provide a method whereby applicants and agencies can be assured that the determination process has been orderly, comprehensive in nature, yet flexible to allow introduction of information to fit a project or action.

Full EAF Components: The full EAF is comprised of three parts:

Part 1: Provides objective data and information about a given project and its site. By identifying basic project data, it assists a reviewer in the analysis that takes place in Parts 2 and 3.

Part 2: Focuses on identifying the range of possible impacts that may occur from a project or action. It provides guidance as to whether an impact is likely to be considered small to moderate or whether it is a potentially large impact. The form also identifies whether an impact can be mitigated or reduced.

Part 3: If any impact in Part 2 is identified as potentially large, then Part 3 is used to evaluate whether or not the impact is actually important.

DETERMINATION OF SIGNIFICANCE—
Type 1 and Unlisted Actions

Identify the Portions of EAF completed for this project:

___ Part 1 ___ Part 2 ___ Part 3

Upon review of the information recorded on this EAF (Parts 1 and 2 and 3, if appropriate), and any other supporting information, and considering both the magnitude and importance of each impact, it is reasonably determined by the lead agency that:

___ A. The project will not result in any large and important impact(s) and, therefore, is one which **will not** have a significant impact on the environment, therefore **a negative declaration will be prepared.**

___ B. Although the project could have a significant effect on the environment, there will not be a significant effect for this Unlisted Action because the mitigation measures described in PART 3 have been required, therefore **a CONDITIONED negative declaration will be prepared.***

___ C. The project may result in one or more large and important impacts that may have a significant impact on the environment, therefore **a positive declaration will be prepared.**

Name of Action

Name of Lead Agency

Print or Type Name of Responsible Officer in Lead Agency

Title of Responsible Officer

Signature of Responsible Officer in Lead Agency

Signature of Preparer (if different from responsible officer)

Date

* A Conditioned Negative Declaration is only valid for Unlisted Actions

Ch. 16   ENVIRONMENTAL ASSESSMENT—LONG FORM § 16.134

PART 1—PROJECT INFORMATION
Prepared by Project Sponsor

NOTICE: This document is designed to assist in determining whether the action proposed may have a significant effect on the environment. Please complete the entire form, Parts A through E. Answers to these questions will be considered as part of the application for approval and may be subject to further verification and public review. Provide any additional information you believe will be needed to complete Parts 2 and 3.

It is expected that completion of the full EAF will be dependent on information currently available and will not involve new studies, research or investigation. If information requiring such additional work is unavailable, so indicate and specify each instance.

NAME OF ACTION
_____

LOCATION OF ACTION (include Street Address, Municipality and County)
_____

NAME OF APPLICANT/SPONSOR   BUSINESS TELEPHONE
                                                    (   )
_____

ADDRESS
_____

CITY/PO   STATE   ZIP CODE
_____

NAME OF OWNER (if different)   BUSINESS TELEPHONE
                                                    (   )
_____

ADDRESS
_____

CITY/PO   STATE   ZIP CODE
_____

DESCRIPTION OF ACTION
_____

Please Complete Each Question—Indicate N.A. if not applicable

A. Site Description

Physical setting of overall project, both developed and undeveloped areas.

1. Present land use: ___Urban ___Industrial ___Commercial ___Residential (suburban) ___Rural (non-farm) ___Forest ___Agriculture ___Other _____

2. Total acreage of project area _____ acres.

APPROXIMATE ACREAGE	PRESENTLY	AFTER COMPLETION
Meadow or Brushland (Non-agricultural)	_____ acres	_____ acres
Forested	_____ acres	_____ acres
Agricultural (includes orchards, cropland, pasture, etc.)	_____ acres	_____ acres
Wetland (Freshwater or tidal as per Articles 24, 25 of ECL)	_____ acres	_____ acres
Water Surface Area	_____ acres	_____ acres
Unvegetated (Rock, earth or fill)	_____ acres	_____ acres

§ 16.134   LAND USE LAW   Ch. 16

      Roads, buildings and other paved surfaces _____ acres _____ acres
      Other (indicate type) _____ _____ acres _____ acres

3. What is predominant soil type(s) on project site? _____
   a. Soil drainage. __Well drained _____ % of site
   __Moderately well drained _____ % of site
   __Poorly drained _____ % of site
   b. If any agricultural land is involved, how many acres of soil are classified within soil group 1 through 4 of the NYS Land Classification System? _____ acres. (See 1 NYCRR 370)

4. Are there bedrock outcroppings on project site? __Yes __No
   a. What is depth to bedrock? _____
   (in feet)

5. Approximate percentage of proposed project site with slopes:
   __0–10%_____% __10–15%_____% __15% or greater _____%

6. Is project substantially contiguous to, or contain a building, site, or district, listed on the State or the National Registers of Historic Places? __Yes __No.

7. Is project substantially contiguous to a site listed on the Register of National Natural Landmarks? __Yes __No

8. What is the depth of the water table? _____ (in feet)

9. Is site located over a primary, principal, or sole source aquifer? __Yes __No

10. Do hunting, fishing or shell fishing opportunities presently exist in the project area? __Yes __No

11. Does project site contain any species of plant or animal life that is identified as threatened or endangered?
    __Yes __No According to _____
    Identify each species _____

12. Are there any unique or unusual land forms on the project site? (i.e., cliffs, dunes, other geological formations)
    __Yes __No Describe _____

13. Is the project site presently used by the community or neighborhood as an open space or recreation area?
    __Yes __No If yes, explain _____

14. Does the present site include scenic views known to be important to the community?
    __Yes __No

15. Streams within or contiguous to project area: _____
    a. Name of Stream and name of River to which it is tributary _____

16. Lakes, ponds, wetland areas within or contiguous to project area:
    a. Name _____ b. Size (In acres) _____

17. Is the site served by existing public utilities? __Yes __No
    a) If Yes, does sufficient capacity exist to allow connection? __Yes __No
    b) If Yes, will improvements be necessary to allow connection? __Yes __No

18. Is the site located in an agricultural district certified pursuant to Agriculture and Markets Law, Article 25–AA, Section 303 and 304? __Yes __No

19. Is the site located in or substantially contiguous to a Critical Environmental Area designated pursuant to Article 8 of the ECL, and 6 NYCRR 617? __Yes __No

20. Has the site ever been used for the disposal of solid or hazardous wastes? __Yes __No

B. Project Description
1. Physical dimensions and scale of project (fill in dimensions as appropriate)
   a. Total contiguous acreage owned or controlled by project sponsor _____ acres.

Ch. 16   ENVIRONMENTAL ASSESSMENT—LONG FORM §16.134

    b. Project acreage to be developed: _____ acres initially; _____ acres ultimately.
    c. Project acreage to remain undeveloped _____ acres.
    d. Length of project, in miles: _____ (If appropriate)
    e. If the project is an expansion, indicate percentage of expansion proposed _____%;
    f. Number of off-street parking spaces existing _____; proposed _____.
    g. Maximum vehicular trips generated per hour _____ (upon completion of project)?
    h. If residential: Number and type of housing units:

	One Family	Two Family	Multiple Family	Condominium
Initially				
Ultimately				

    i. Dimensions (in feet) of largest proposed structure _____ height; _____ width; _____ length.
    j. Linear feet of frontage along a public thoroughfare project will occupy is? ___ ft.

2. How much natural material (i.e., rock, earth, etc.) will be removed from the site? _____ tons/cubic yards
3. Will disturbed areas be reclaimed? ___Yes ___No ___N/A
    a. If yes, for what intended purpose is the site being reclaimed? _____
    b. Will topsoil be stockpiled for reclamation?   ___Yes ___No
    c. Will upper subsoil be stockpiled for reclamation? ___Yes ___No
4. How many acres of vegetation (trees, shrubs, ground covers) will be removed from site?
    _____ acres
5. Will any mature forest (over 100 years old) or other focally-important vegetation be removed by this project? ___Yes ___No
6. If single phase project: Anticipated period of construction _____ months, (including demolition).
7. If multi-phased:
    a. Total number of phases anticipated _____ (number).
    b. Anticipated date of commencement phase 1 _____ month _____ year. (including demolition)
    c. Approximate completion date of final phase _____ month _____ year.
    d. Is phase 1 functionally dependent on subsequent phases? ___Yes ___No
8. Will blasting occur during construction? ___Yes ___No
9. Number of jobs generated: during construction _____; after project is complete _____
10. Number of jobs eliminated by this project _____
11. Will project require relocation of any projects of facilities? ___Yes ___No
    If yes, explain _____
12. Is surface liquid waste disposal involved? ___Yes ___No
    a. If yes, indicate type of waste (sewage, industrial, etc.) and amount _____
    b. Name of water body into which effluent will be discharged_____
13. Is subsurface liquid waste disposal involved? ___Yes ___No Type _____
14. Will surface area of an existing water body increase or decrease by proposal? ___Yes ___No
    Explain _____
15. Is project or any portion of project located in a 100 year flood plain? ___Yes ___No
16. Will the project generate solid waste? ___Yes ___No
    a. If yes, what is the amount per month _____ tons
    b. If yes, will an existing solid waste facility be used? ___Yes ___No

§ 16.134   LAND USE LAW   Ch. 16

    c. If yes, give name _____; location _____
    d. Will any water **not** go into a sewage disposal system or into a sanitary landfill?
       ___Yes ___No
    e. If yes, explain _____
17. Will the project involve the disposal of solid waste? ___Yes ___No
    a. If yes, what is the anticipated rate of disposal? _____ tons/month.
    b. If yes, what is the anticipated site life? _____ years.
18. Will project use herbicides or pesticides? ___Yes ___No
19. Will project routinely produce odors (more than one hour per day)? ___Yes ___No
20. Will project produce operating noise exceeding the local ambient noise levels? ___Yes ___No
21. Will project result in an increase in energy use? ___Yes ___No
    If yes, indicate type(s) _____
22. If water supply is from wells, indicate pumping capacity _____ gallons/minute.
23. Total anticipated water usage per day _____ gallons/day.
24. Does project involve Local, State or Federal funding? ___Yes ___No
    If yes, explain _____
25. **Approvals Required:**

		Type	Submittal Date
City, Town, Village Board	___Yes ___No		
City, Town, Village Planning Board	___Yes ___No		
City, Town Zoning Board	___Yes ___No		
City, County Health Department	___Yes ___No		
Other Local Agencies	___Yes ___No		
Other Regional Agencies	___Yes ___No		
State Agencies	___Yes ___No		
Federal Agencies	___Yes ___No		

C. **Zoning and Planning Information**
1. Does proposed action involve a planning or zoning decision? ___Yes ___No
    If Yes, indicate decision required:
    ___ zoning amendment ___ zoning variance ___ special use permit ___ subdivision ___ site plan ___ new/revision of master plan ___ resource management plan ___ other _____
2. What is the zoning classification(s) of the site?
   _____

3. What is the maximum potential development of the site if developed as permitted by the present zoning?
   _____

4. What is the proposed zoning of the site? _____

5. What is the maximum potential development of the site if developed as permitted by the proposed zoning?
   _____

6. Is the proposed action consistent with the recommended uses in adopted local land use plans? ___Yes ___No

7. What are the predominant land use(s) and zoning classifications within a ¼ mile radius of proposed action? _____

8. Is the proposed action compatible with adjoining/surrounding land uses within a ¼ mile?
    ___Yes ___No

Ch. 16   ENVIRONMENTAL ASSESSMENT—LONG FORM § 16.134

9. If the proposed action is the subdivision of land, how many lots are proposed? _____
   a. What is the minimum lot size proposed? _____
10. Will proposed action require any authorization(s) for the formation of sewer or water districts?
    ___Yes ___No
11. Will the proposed action create a demand for any community provided services (recreation, education, police, fire protection)? ___Yes ___No
    a. If yes, is existing capacity sufficient to handle projected demand? ___Yes ___No
12. Will the proposed action result in the generation of traffic significantly above present levels?
    ___Yes ___No
    a. If yes, is the existing road network adequate to handle the additional traffic? ___Yes ___No

D. Informational Details

Attach any additional information as may be needed to clarify your project. If there are or may be any adverse impacts associated with your proposal, please discuss such impacts and the measures which you propose to mitigate or avoid them.

E. Verification

I certify that the information provided above is true to the best of my knowledge.

Applicant/Sponsor Name _____   Date _____

Signature _____
Title _____

If the action is in the Coastal Area, and you are a state agency, complete the Coastal Assessment Form before proceeding with this assessment.

Part 2—PROJECT IMPACTS AND THEIR MAGNITUDE

Responsibility of Lead Agency

General Information (Read Carefully)

- In completing the form the reviewer should be guided by the question: Have my responses and determinations been **reasonable**? The reviewer is not expected to be an expert environmental analyst.

- Identifying that an impact will be potentially large (column 2) does not mean that it is also necessarily **significant**. Any large impact must be evaluated in PART 3 to determine significance. Identifying an impact in column 2 simply asks that it be looked at further.

- The **Examples** provided are to assist the reviewer by showing types of impacts and wherever possible the threshold of magnitude that would trigger a response in column 2. The examples are generally applicable throughout the State and for most situations. But, for any specific project or site other examples and/or lower thresholds may be appropriate for a Potential Large Impact response, thus requiring evaluation in Part 3.

§ 16.134   LAND USE LAW   Ch. 16

- The impacts of each project, on each site, in each locality, will vary. Therefore, the examples are illustrative and have been offered as guidance. They do not constitute an exhaustive list of impacts and thresholds to answer each question.
- The number of examples per question does not indicate the importance of each question.
- In identifying impacts, consider long term, short term and cumulative effects.

Instructions (Read Carefully)

a. Answer each of the 19 questions in PART 2. Answer **Yes** if there will be **any** impact.

b. **Maybe** answers should be considered as **Yes** answers.

c. If answering **Yes** to a question then check the appropriate box (column 1 or 2) to indicate the potential size of the impact. If impact threshold equals or exceeds any example provided, check column 2. If impact will occur but threshold is lower than example, check column 1.

d. If reviewer has doubt about size of the impact then consider the impact as potentially large and proceed to PART 3.

e. If a potentially large impact checked in column 2 can be mitigated by change(s) in the project to a small to moderate impact, also check the **Yes** box in column 3. A **No** response indicates that such a reduction is not possible. This must be explained in Part 3.

	1 Small to Moderate Impact	2 Potential Large Impact	3 Can Impact Be Mitigated By Project Change
IMPACT ON LAND 1. Will the proposed action result in a physical change to the project site? ___ NO ___ YES **Examples** that would apply to column 2 • Any construction on slopes of 15% or greater, (15 foot rise per 100 foot of length), or where the general slopes in the project area exceed 10%. • Construction on land where the depth to the water table is less than 3 feet. • Construction of paved parking area for 1,000 or more vehicles. • Construction onland where bedrock is exposed or generally within 3 feet of existing ground surface. • Construction that will continue for more than 1 year or involve more than one phase or stage. • Excavation for mining purposes that would remove more than 1,000 tons of natural material (i.e., rock or soil) per year. • Construction or expansion of a sanitary landfill. • Construction in a designated floodway. • Other impacts: _____			

Ch. 16 ENVIRONMENTAL ASSESSMENT—LONG FORM § 16.134

	1 Small to Moderate Impact	2 Potential Large Impact	3 Can Impact Be Mitigated By Project Change

2. Will there be an effect to any unique or unusual land forms found on the site? (i.e., cliffs, dunes, geological formations, etc.) ___ NO ___ YES
   - Specific land forms: _____

IMPACT ON WATER

3. Will proposed action affect any water body designated as protected? (Under Articles 15, 24, 25 of Environmental Conservation Law, ECL) ___ NO ___ YES
   Examples that would apply to column 2
   - Developable area of site contains a protected water body.
   - Dredging more than 100 cubic yards of material from channel of a protected stream.
   - Extension of utility distribution facilities through a protected water body.
   - Construction in a designated freshwater or tidal wetland.
   - Other impacts: _____

4. Will proposed action affect any non-protected existing or new body of water? ___ NO ___ YES
   Examples that would apply to column 2
   - A 10% increase or decrease in the surface area of any body of water or more than a 10 acre increase or decrease.
   - Construction of a body of water that exceeds 10 acres of surface area.
   - Other impacts: _____

5. Will Proposed Action affect surface or groundwater quality or quantity? ___ NO ___ YES
   Examples that would apply to column 2
   - Proposed Action will require a discharge permit.
   - Proposed Action requires use of a source of water that does not have approval to serve proposed (project) action.
   - Proposed Action requires water supply from wells with greater than 45 gallons per minute pumping capacity.
   - Construction or operation causing any contamination of a water supply system.
   - Proposed Action will adversely affect groundwater.
   - Liquid effluent will be conveyed off the site to facilities which presently do not exist or have inadequate capacity.
   - Proposed Action would use water in excess of 20,000 gallons per day.
   - Proposed Action will likely cause siltation or other discharge into an existing body of water to the extent that there will be an obvious visual contrast to natural conditions.
   - Proposed Action will require the storage of petroleum or chemical products greater than 1,100 gallons.
   - Proposed Action will allow residential uses in areas without water and/or sewer services.
   - Proposed Action locates commercial and/or industrial uses which may require new or expansion of existing waste treatment and/or storage facilities.
   - Other impacts: _____

6. Will proposed action alter drainage flow or patterns, or surface water runoff? ___ NO ___ YES
   Examples that would apply to column 2
   - Proposed Action would change flood water flows.
   - Proposed Action may cause substantial erosion.

§ 16.134 　　　　LAND USE LAW　　　　Ch. 16

	1 Small to Moderate Impact	2 Potential Large Impact	3 Can Impact Be Mitigated By Project Change

- Proposed Action will allow development in a designated floodway.
- Other impacts: _____

IMPACT ON AIR

7. Will proposed action affect air quality? ___ NO ___ YES

    Examples that would apply to column 2
    - Proposed Action will induce 1,000 or more vehicle trips in any given hour.
    - Proposed Action will result in the incineration of more than 1 ton of refuse per hour.
    - Emission rate of total contaminants will exceed 5lbs per hour or a heat source producing more than 10 million BTU's per hour.
    - Proposed Action will allow an increase in the amount of land committed to industrial use.
    - Proposed Action will allow an increase in the density of industrial development within existing industrial areas.
    - Other impacts: _____

IMPACTS ON PLANTS AND ANIMALS

8. Will Proposed Action affect any threatened or endangered species? ___ NO ___ YES

    Examples that would apply to column 2
    - Reduction of one or more species listed on the New York or Federal list, using the site, over or near site or found on site.
    - Removal of any portion of a critical or significant wildlife habitat.
    - Application of pesticide or herbicide more than twice a year, other than for agricultural purposes.
    - Other impacts: _____

9. Will Proposed Action substantially affect non-threatened or non-endangered species? ___ NO ___ YES

    Examples that would apply to column 2
    - Proposed Action would substantially interfere with any resident or migratory fish, shellfish, or wildlife species.
    - Proposed Action requires the removal of more than 10 acres of mature forest (over 100 years of age) or other locally important vegetation.

IMPACT ON AGRICULTURAL LAND RESOURCES

10. Will Proposed Action affect agricultural land resources? ___ NO ___ YES

    Examples that would apply to column 2
    - The proposed action would sever, cross or limit access to agricultural land (includes cropland, hayfields, pasture, vineyard, orchard, etc.)
    - Constructional activity would excavate or compact the soil profile of agricultural land.
    - The proposed action would irreversibly convert more than 10 acres of agricultural land or, if located in an Agricultural District, more than 2.5 acres of agricultural land.
    - The proposed action would disrupt or prevent installation of agricultural land management systems (e.g., subsurface drain lines, outlet ditches, strip cropping); or create a need for such measures (e.g. cause a farm field to drain poorly due to increased runoff).

Ch. 16 ENVIRONMENTAL ASSESSMENT—LONG FORM §16.134

	1 Small to Moderate Impact	2 Potential Large Impact	3 Can Impact Be Mitigated By Project Change

- Other impacts: _____

IMPACT ON AESTHETIC RESOURCES

11. Will proposed action affect aesthetic resources? ___ NO ___ YES
    (If necessary, use the Visual EAF Addendum in Section 617.21, Appendix B.)
    Examples that would apply to column 2
    - Proposed land uses, or project components obviously different from or in sharp contrast to current surrounding land use patterns, whether man-made or natural.
    - Proposed land uses, or project components visible to users of aesthetic resources which will eliminate or significantly reduce their enjoyment of the aesthetic qualities of that resource.
    - Project components that will result in the elimination or significant screening of scenic view known to be important to the area.
    - Other impacts: _____

IMPACT ON HISTORIC AND ARCHAEOLOGICAL RESOURCES

12. Will Proposed Action impact any site or structure of historic, prehistoric or paleontological importance? ___ NO ___ YES
    Examples that would apply to column 2
    - Proposed Action occurring wholly or partially within or substantially contiguous to any facility or site listed on the State or National Register of historic places.
    - Any impact to an archaeological site or fossil bed located within the project site.
    - Proposed Action will occur in an area designated as sensitive for archaeological sites on the NYS Site Inventory.
    - Other impacts: _____

IMPACT ON OPEN SPACE AND RECREATION

13. Will Proposed Action affect the quantity or quality of existing or future open spaces or recreational opportunities? ___ NO ___ YES
    Examples that would apply to column 2
    - The permanent foreclosure of a future recreational opportunity.
    - A major reduction of an open space important to the community.
    - Other impacts: _____

IMPACT ON CRITICAL ENVIRONMENTAL AREAS

14. Will Proposed Action impact the exceptional or unique characteristics of a critical environmental area (CEA) established pursuant to subdivision 6 NYCRR 617.14(g)? ___ NO ___ YES
    List the environmental characteristics that caused the designation of the CEA.
    _____
    _____
    _____

    Examples that would apply to column 2

§ 16.134   LAND USE LAW   Ch. 16

	1 Small to Moderate Impact	2 Potential Large Impact	3 Can Impact Be Mitigated By Project Change

- Proposed Action to locate within the CEA?
- Proposed Action will result in a reduction in the quantity of the resource?
- Proposed Action will result in a reduction in the quality of the resource?
- Proposed Action will impact the use, function or enjoyment of the resource?
- Other impacts: _____

IMPACT ON TRANSPORTATION

15. Will there be an effect to existing transportation systems? __ NO __ YES
    Examples that would apply to column 2
    - Alteration of present patterns of movement of people and/or goods.
    - Proposed Action will result in major traffic problems.
    - Other impacts: _____

IMPACT ON ENERGY

16. Will proposed action affect the community's sources of fuel or energy supply? __ NO __ YES
    Examples that would apply to column 2
    - Proposed Action will cause a greater than 5% increase in the use of any form of energy in the municipality.
    - Proposed Action will require the creation or extension of an energy transmission or supply system to serve more than 50 single or two family residences or to serve a major commercial or industrial use.
    - Other impacts: _____

NOISE AND ODOR IMPACT

17. Will there be objectionable odors, noise, or vibration as a result of the Proposed Action? __ NO __ YES
    Examples that would apply to column 2
    - Blasting within 1,500 feet of a hospital, school or other sensitive facility.
    - Odors will occur routinely (more than one hour per day).
    - Proposed Action will produce operating noise exceeding the local ambient noise levels for noise outside of structures.
    - Proposed Action will remove natural barriers that would act as a noise screen.
    - Other impacts: _____

IMPACT ON PUBLIC HEALTH

18. Will Proposed Action affect public health and safety? __ NO __ YES
    Examples that would apply to column 2
    - Proposed Action may cause a risk of explosion or release of hazardous substances (i.e. oil, pesticides, chemicals, radiation, etc.) in the event of accident or upset conditions, or there may be a chronic low level discharge or emission.
    - Proposed Action may result in the burial of "hazardous wastes" in any form (i.e. toxic, poisonous, highly reactive, radioactive, irritating, infectious, etc.)
    - Storage facilities for one million or more gallons of liquified natural gas or other flammable liquids.

Ch. 16   ENVIRONMENTAL ASSESSMENT—LONG FORM §16.134

	1 Small to Moderate Impact	2 Potential Large Impact	3 Can Impact Be Mitigated By Project Change

- Proposed Action may result in the excavation or other disturbance within 2,000 feet of a site used for the disposal of solid or hazardous waste.
- Other impacts: _____

IMPACT ON GROWTH AND CHARACTER OF COMMUNITY OR NEIGHBORHOOD

19. Will Proposed Action affect the character of existing community? ___ NO ___ YES
    Examples that would apply to column 2
    - The permanent population of the city, town or village in which the project is located is likely to grow by more than 5%.
    - The municipal budget for capital expenditures or operating services will increase by more than 5% per year as a result of this project.
    - Proposed Action will conflict with officially adopted plans or goals.
    - Proposed Action will cause a change in the density of land use.
    - Proposed Action will replace or eliminate existing facilities, structures or areas of historic importance to the community.
    - Development will create a demand for additional community services (e.g. schools, police and fire, etc.)
    - Proposed Action will set an important precedent for future projects.
    - Proposed Action will create or eliminate employment.
    - Other impacts: _____

20. Is there likely to be, public controversy related to potential adverse environmental impacts? ___ NO ___ YES

If Any Action in Part 2 Is Identified as a Potential Large Impact or If You Cannot Determine the Magnitude of Impact, Proceed to Part 3

Part 3—EVALUATION OF THE IMPORTANCE OF IMPACTS
Responsibility of Lead Agency

Part 3 must be prepared if one or more impact(s) is considered to be potentially large, even if the impact(s) may be mitigated.

Instructions

Discuss the following for each impact identified in Column 2 of Part 2:

1. Briefly describe the impact.

2. Describe (if applicable) how the impact could be mitigated or reduced to a small to moderate impact by project change(s).

3. Based on the information available, decide if it is reasonable to conclude that this impact is **important**.

   To answer the question of importance, consider:
   - The probability of the impact occurring

- The duration of the impact
- Its irreversibility, including permanently lost resources of value
- Whether the impact can or will be controlled
- The regional consequences of the impact
- Its potential divergence from local needs and goals
- Whether known objections to the project relate to this impact

(Continue on attachments)

Ch. 16 ENVIRONMENTAL ASSESSMENT—LONG FORM § 16.134

617.20

Appendix B

State Environmental Quality Review

Visual EAF Addendum

This form may be used to provide additional information relating to Question 11 of Part 2 of the Full EAF.

(To be completed by Lead Agency)

Visibility

Distance Between Project and Resource (in Miles)

	0–¼	¼–½	½–3	3–5	5+
1. Would the project be visible from:					
• A parcel of land which is dedicated to be available to the public for the use, enjoyment and appreciation of natural or man-made scenic qualities?	—	—	—	—	—
• An overlook or parcel of land dedicated to public observation, enjoyment and appreciation of natural or man-made scenic qualities?	—	—	—	—	—
• A site or structure listed on the National or State Registers of Historic Places?	—	—	—	—	—
• State Parks?	—	—	—	—	—
• The State Forest Preserve?	—	—	—	—	—
• National Wildlife Refuges and state game refuges?	—	—	—	—	—
• National Natural Landmarks and other outstanding natural features?	—	—	—	—	—
• National Park Service lands?	—	—	—	—	—
• Rivers designated as National or State Wild Scenic or Recreational?	—	—	—	—	—
• Any transportation corridor of high exposure, such as part of the Interstate System, or Amtrak?	—	—	—	—	—
• A governmentally established or designated interstate or inter-county foot trail, or one formally proposed for establishment or designation?	—	—	—	—	—
• A site, area, lake, reservoir or highway designated as scenic?	—	—	—	—	—
• Municipal park, or designated open space?	—	—	—	—	—
• County road?	—	—	—	—	—
• State?	—	—	—	—	—
• Local road?	—	—	—	—	—

2. Is the visibility of the project seasonal? (i.e., screened by summer foliage, but visible during other seasons?) __ Yes __ No

3. Are any of the resources checked in question 1 used by the public during the time of year during which the project will be visible? __ Yes __ No

DESCRIPTION OF EXISTING VISUAL ENVIRONMENT

4. From each item checked in question 1, check those which generally describe the surrounding environment.

	Within * ¼ mile	* 1 mile
Essentially undeveloped	—	—
Forested	—	—

§ 16.134 LAND USE LAW Ch. 16

Agricultural	——	——
Suburban residential	——	——
Industrial	——	——
Commercial	——	——
Urban	——	——
River, Lake, Pond	——	——
Cliffs, Overlooks	——	——
Designated Open Space	——	——
Flat	——	——
Hilly	——	——
Mountainous	——	——
Other	——	——

NOTE: add attachments as needed

5. Are there visually similar projects within:
   * ½ mile ___ Yes ___ No
   * 1 mile ___ Yes ___ No
   * 2 miles ___ Yes ___ No
   * 3 miles ___ Yes ___ No
   * Distances from project site are provided for assistance. Substitute other distances as appropriate.

EXPOSURE

6. The annual number of viewers likely to observe the proposed project is _____.
   NOTE: When user data is unavailable or unknown, use best estimate.

CONTEXT

7. The situation or activity in which the viewers are engaged while viewing the proposed action is

FREQUENCY

Activity	Daily	Weekly	Holidays/Weekends	Seasonally
Travel to and from work	——	——	——	——
Involved in recreational activities	——	——	——	——
Routine travel by residents	——	——	——	——
At a residence	——	——	——	——
At worksite	——	——	——	——
Other _____	——	——	——	——

Chapter 17

EMPLOYMENT LAW

by
Wayne N. Outten
and
Jack A. Raisner

Table of Sections

17.1	Scope Note.
17.2	Strategy.
17.3	___ Plaintiff's Counsel's Investigation.
17.4	___ Defendant's Counsel's Investigation.
17.5	___ Pre-litigation Settlement Process.
17.6	___ Negotiating With Opposing Counsel.
17.7	___ Alternative Dispute Resolution ("ADR").
17.8	___ ___ Mediation.
17.9	___ ___ Arbitration.
17.10	___ Settlement and Severance Agreements.
17.11	___ ___ Older Workers Benefit Protection Act ("OWBPA").
17.12	___ ___ COBRA.
17.13	___ ___ Pay.
17.14	___ ___ Income Taxes.
17.15	___ ___ Benefits.
17.16	___ Other Severance Issues.
17.17	___ Independent Contractor vs. Employee.
17.18	___ Checklist: Initial Considerations for Plaintiff.
17.19	___ Checklist: Terminating an Employee.
17.20	Causes of Action.
17.21	___ Tort–Assault.
17.22	___ ___ Battery.
17.23	___ ___ Conspiracy.
17.24	___ ___ Conversion.
17.25	___ ___ Defamation.
17.26	___ ___ False Imprisonment; Malicious Prosecution.
17.27	___ ___ Fraud, Negligent Misrepresentation and Fraudulent Inducement.
17.28	___ ___ Intentional Infliction of Emotional Distress.
17.29	___ ___ Interference with Business Relations.
17.30	___ ___ Negligence.
17.31	___ ___ *Prima Facie* Tort.
17.32	___ ___ Wrongful Discharge.
17.33	___ Contract.

17.34	____ ____ Express Promises.
17.35	____ ____ Implied Promises.
17.36	____ ____ Estoppel.
17.37	Statutory Causes of Action—Age Discrimination.
17.38	____ Anti-reprisal Provisions of Various Statutes.
17.39	____ Arrest Records.
17.40	____ Bankruptcy.
17.41	____ Convictions.
17.42	____ Credit Information.
17.43	____ Disability.
17.44	____ Equal Pay.
17.45	____ Family and Medical Leave Act (FMLA).
17.46	____ Health Plan Coverage (COBRA).
17.47	____ Legal Off Duty Activities.
17.48	____ Marital Status Discrimination.
17.49	____ Discrimination on the Basis of Race, Color or National Origin.
17.50	____ Pension Plans.
17.51	____ Plant Closing, Mass Layoffs.
17.52	____ Polygraphs.
17.53	____ Public Employees.
17.54	____ Pregnancy.
17.55	____ Privacy.
17.56	____ Religious Discrimination.
17.57	____ Sex Discrimination, Harassment.
17.58	____ Sexual Orientation Discrimination.
17.59	____ Title VII, Burdens of Proof.
17.60	____ Unemployment Insurance.
17.61	____ Unionization, Rights Within Unions.
17.62	____ Unsafe Workplace.
17.63	____ Wages; Unpaid Compensation; Overtime.
17.64	____ Whistleblowing/*Qui Tam*.
17.65	____ Workers' Compensation.
17.66	Procedure—Anti-discrimination Agency Practice.
17.67	____ Filing and Responding to Administrative Charges.
17.68	____ Election of Remedies.
17.69	____ Statutes of Limitations and Prerequisites to Private Lawsuits.
17.70	Private Lawsuits.
17.71	____ Discovery—General Considerations.
17.72	____ ____ Plaintiff's Strategy.
17.73	____ Summary Judgment.
17.74	____ Trial.
17.75	____ Fee Application.
17.76	____ Post–Trial Motions and Appeal.
17.77	____ Checklist: Statutes of Limitations.
17.78	____ Checklist: Commencement of New York State Actions.
17.79	____ Checklist: Commencement of Federal Court Actions.
17.80	Miscellaneous Practice Issues—OFCCP/Glass Ceiling Audits.
17.81	____ Employment Policies and Handbooks.
17.82	Drafting the Complaint.
17.83	Drafting Checklist—Complaint.
17.84	Drafting the Answer.

17.85 Drafting Checklist—Answer
17.86 Forms—Client (Plaintiff) Intake Questionnaire.
17.87 ___ Severance/Release Agreement.
17.88 ___ Letter to EEOC Requesting "Mohasco" Waiver of State Processing.
17.89 ___ Charge of Discrimination—New York State Division of Human Rights (Official Form).
17.90 ___ Information Sheet—New York State Division of Human Rights (Official Form).
17.91 ___ SDHR Information Sheet.
17.92 ___ Charge of Discrimination—Equal Employment Opportunity Commission (Official Form).
17.93 ___ Affidavit for a Charge of Discrimination—Equal Employment Opportunity Commission (Official Form).
17.94 ___ EEOC Filing Cover Letter Requesting EEOC Processing of Dual-filed Charge.
17.95 ___ Letter Requesting Administrative Convenience Dismissal from State or City Administrative Agency.
17.96 ___ Pleadings—New York State Complaint.
17.97 ___ ___ New York State Answer.
17.98 ___ ___ Federal Complaint.
17.99 ___ ___ Federal Answer.

WESTLAW Electronic Research

See WESTLAW Electronic Research Guide preceding the Summary of Contents.

§ 17.1 Scope Note

This chapter is designed to help the practitioner face the bewildering array of causes of action and procedural hurdles that tend to leap out from behind employment law questions. Even seemingly simple workplace problems can become a convergence point for causes of action sounding in tort, contract, violation of numerous statutes, and, at times, the Constitution. The emphasis of the chapter is on rights and responsibilities of employers and employees in the private, non-union sector. Counsel to employers or employees in the governmental or union setting may find some of the material on statutory rights presented here useful, but unique substantive and procedural rules apply in government and unionized workplaces and are only alluded to here.

Section 17.2 begins with a discussion of the steps counsel should take upon first learning of a possible employment dispute, as well as what to consider in the subsequent investigation. The chapter discusses counsel's strategies when initially evaluating the strengths and weaknesses of cases and the best routes toward their resolution.

Today, a large part of employment law practice involves working towards negotiated resolutions, using alternative dispute resolution

§ 17.1 EMPLOYMENT LAW Ch. 17

("ADR") devices such as mediation and conferences between counsel; Section 17.6 reviews commonly used methods of avoiding litigation.

To successfully represent either employers or employees in negotiating a settlement agreement, counsel must be aware of the "tools of the trade", *i.e.*, the component parts of settlement agreements. These are discussed beginning in Section 17.10 of this chapter. The initial strategy portion of this chapter ends in Section 17.17 with a discussion of the important difference between employees and non-employees (*e.g.*, independent contractors) that must be considered before determining whether various causes of action apply.

A discussion of the causes of action available to employees in New York begins in Section 17.20 and extends through Section 17.65. This portion of the chapter looks first at tort claims, then contract-based claims, and finally, statutory causes of action. The list of statutory claims are alphabetical. In each cause of action, the elements of the claim, and of common defenses, are enumerated and discussed.

The chapter continues at Section 17.66 with a guide through the preliminary exhaustion requirements of the anti-discrimination laws, federal, state and local (New York City), that often bedevil the expert and novice alike. The chapter continues at Section 17.70 with a discussion of the important strategic and procedural steps that should be considered when taking an employment case through litigation and trial.[1]

The chapter notes the basic steps of filing and serving pleadings[2] and walks the practitioner through the drafting of a complaint and answer.[3] It also addresses glass ceiling reviews[4] and ends with a series of essential forms that will help the practitioner shepherd a case through the administrative agency "thickets" and into court, when necessary.

Employment disputes become legal problems when the expectations of an employee or applicant are not met and the employer's "business-as-usual" responses do not make the dispute go away. At that point, both employers and employees increasingly seek legal counsel.

Often, an employee's decision to seek counsel is prompted by a perception of having been treated unfairly. This perception may be based not only on the fact of an adverse action, such as termination, but also on the manner of termination, such as a sudden pronouncement, a demeaning encounter, or defamatory remarks. By the same token, the employer may feel that the employee's claims and the law itself create an unfair intrusion into its discretion. The employer may perceive the employee as disloyal and motivated by greed.

§ 17.1
1. *See infra*, §§ 17.70—17.79.
2. *See infra*, §§ 17.79.
3. *See infra*, §§ 17.82–17.85.
4. *See infra*, § 17.80, employee handbook, *see infra* § 17.81.

§ 17.2 Strategy

The initial task of employee's and employer's counsel is to evaluate the case. This can happen even before an adverse job action occurs, such as when the employer senses that the employee will not be happy with an upcoming announcement, or when the employee sees "the writing on the wall." The client often will make the initial legal contact at the point when an important managerial decision is to be made. In the case of the employer, it may be a crucial decision for the organization. In the case of an employee, it may be the most important decision of his or her career. Counsel's task is not to make the decision, but to explain to the client how the law views the circumstances in question and to explain the probable legal consequences so a well thought out conclusion may be reached.

In short, this means that counsel should be prepared for the curtain to rise on a drama of conflicting stories, profound interests, and high emotions when sitting down with a client for the first time. Counsel may often be called on at this point to lend business and even psychological advice, but the prime task, of course, is to clarify the legal issues at hand and to point out their strengths and weaknesses.

Usually, the initial consultation involves several in-depth interviews with the client, both to gather the facts and to see whether the client's expectations and objectives may reasonably be met. Plaintiff's counsel must get a sense of the client's relevant personal strengths and weaknesses. Defendant's counsel must gauge the employee-relations atmosphere of the organization. Next, each attorney must carefully evaluate all potential causes of action and their possible outcome (*e.g.*, damages). This process is especially important in New York State because employees have so few common law remedies available to them; as a consequence, plaintiff's counsel must analyze the facts carefully and creatively.

Both sides should attempt to resolve the dispute before initiating litigation. Sometimes, the employer is unaware of the employee's feelings or the extent of the wrong suffered by the employee. On the other hand, the employee may be oblivious to his or her own shortcomings or to the difficulties the employer may be experiencing. Occasionally, making each party aware of the other's point of view can enable them to reach a settlement instead of proceeding to litigation. At this juncture, the parties should seriously consider alternative dispute resolution ("ADR") procedures, such as mediation and arbitration.

If these strategies fail and the decision to litigate is made, certain strategic considerations, such as choice of forum, must be resolved immediately. Thereafter, the principal objectives of the employee's counsel in litigation, generally, are to assert as many meritorious causes of action as possible, to get through discovery as expeditiously as possible, and, whenever possible, to try the case before a jury.

§ 17.2 EMPLOYMENT LAW Ch. 17

Defendant's counsel may recognize the value of reaching an early disposition, whether or not the merits favor its position. Where possible, defeating the plaintiff's claim through a motion to dismiss or a motion for summary judgment would avoid the need for a trial. Alternatively, the employer's strategy may be to employ its greater resources to fight, and ultimately survive, a war of attrition.

§ 17.3 Strategy—Plaintiff's Counsel's Investigation

Plaintiff's counsel must make a thorough investigation before commencing a lawsuit based on employment matters. Indeed, a thorough investigation is necessary before representing a potential plaintiff or before advising a client about the merits of a potential claim. Similarly, defendant's counsel must take these steps when considering any counterclaims against the employee.[1]

Initial Interview. The first and most important step in the investigation is the initial interview with the employee. Plaintiff's counsel should ask the client to bring to this interview all potentially useful documents, including copies of correspondence and memoranda, job evaluations, personnel manuals, summary plan descriptions, diary notes and, where possible, personnel records. Additionally, it is often helpful for the client to prepare and bring to the initial interview: (1) a chart describing key players and their relationships to each other and the employee; and (2) a concise statement of the sequence of events. The client should provide the names of individuals as well as documents that may be used to corroborate information. If time allows, counsel may wish to contact these individuals to determine whether supporting affidavits or other evidence can be obtained and used.

At the initial interview, plaintiff's counsel must ascertain the relevant facts, analyze them critically and objectively, and determine whether they support a claim or negotiation strategy. Moreover, counsel must examine the interviewee critically and objectively in order to evaluate him or her as a prospective client, litigant, and witness.

While the interview questions and techniques are too numerous and variable to enumerate here, questions and subjects useful in evaluating the facts and the client include the following, some of which are contained in the sample intake questionnaire (*See* Forms § 17.86):

§ 17.3

1. PRACTICE POINTER: A good faith, in-depth inquiry is required by the Federal Rules of Civil Procedure. Under Rule 11, plaintiff's counsel must sign the complaint and defendant's counsel must sign the answer, thereby certifying that to the best of the person's knowledge, information, and belief, formed after an inquiry reasonable under the circumstances,—

(1) it is not being presented for any improper purpose, such as to harass or to cause unnecessary delay or needless increase in the cost of litigation;

(2) the claims, defenses, and other legal contentions therein are warranted by existing law or by a nonfrivolous argument for the extension, modification, or reversal of existing law or the establishment of new law;

(3) the allegations and other factual contentions have evidentiary support or, if specifically so identified, are likely to have evidentiary support after a reasonable opportunity for further investigation or discovery; and

(4) the denials of factual contentions are warranted on the evidence or, if specifically so identified, are reasonably based on a lack of information or belief.

- Is the person a private sector employee, unionized employee, government/civil servant employee, or independent contractor? *(See infra,* § 17.17)
- How many employees does the employer have?
- What adverse personnel action has been taken?
- When (earliest notice)?
- What reason(s), if any, did the employer give for taking the adverse personnel action? What does the employee believe are the *real* reasons? If asked by a neutral third-party, what reasons would the employer probably give?
- Does the client *believe* he or she was discriminated against for illegal reasons, *i.e.*, on the basis of sex, race, religion, national origin, age? Why?
- What are the worst things the employer may say about the employee or his/her work?
- What is the employee's work record with the employer? (All past positions, promotions, evaluations, problems, etc.) Were there performance appraisals; and, if so, what did they say?
- Who are the key managers/decision-makers involved in the adverse personnel action?
- What are the relevant personality, political, and power factors affecting the situation?
- Who are potential witnesses? Former employees? Others? Are they "friendly"? Can they be contacted?
- What records does the employer have? Where? Who controls them? Are they likely to help or hurt the claim?
- Were there any warnings regarding the relevant adverse personnel action? Any witnesses?
- Who is left on the job? What happened to the client's work? Were younger employees kept or hired?
- What damages does the employee believe he or she has sustained? (Back pay, benefits, pension, front pay, emotional distress, etc.) Has the employee mitigated damages (*e.g.*, sought re-employment). Kept records of efforts?
- What steps, if any, has the employee already taken to seek redress? Discussions with line managers or personnel managers? Administrative filings? Unemployment insurance sought? What happened?
- What does the employee want? Are the objectives reasonable? Realistic? (If not, the potential exists for serious attorney-client problems.)

- If the employee has not been terminated, can he or she keep the job? How important is the job? Is it better to resign or be fired (unemployment compensation will be affected)? Should the employee purchase mortgage insurance (premiums are typically 2.5% to 4% of monthly mortgage payments, there is a waiting period, and some job classifications may be excluded)?

- What steps might be taken, short of litigation, to try to obtain the objectives?

- What kind of retainer arrangements are appropriate and workable?

Review Claims and Strategy Options. After making these types of inquiries, plaintiff's counsel should then discuss with the potential client the strengths and weaknesses of the claims. (Many of the most common claims are described at §§ 17.20 *et seq.*) This discussion often leads to a mutual recognition that some or all claims lack sufficient actual or potential merit to warrant their assertion. Sometimes, the decision may be to investigate further, which may entail gathering further documentation, interviewing potential witnesses, having additional interviews with the client, and researching legal issues.[2]

In any event, plaintiff's counsel and the client should explore non-litigation avenues for the client to achieve his or her objectives.[3] Finally, assuming that such measures do not result in a satisfactory result and that the investigation supports the viability of a claim, plaintiff's counsel and the client must determine the litigation strategy most suitable to the situation. A good plaintiff's attorney will press the client to articulate his or her ultimate goals and interests. Doing so helps the client separate anger-driven, self-destructive motivations from constructive, realistic goals. These refined goals should be the criteria against which the available strategies are evaluated.

Gathering Information. An employee may be able to collect evidence that will be helpful to a case. In an initial conference, the employee may ask for advice with respect to procuring copies of documents or making secret tape recordings in an attempt to collect admissions or contradictory statements. In general, this evidence will be admissible; but, the employee takes the risk of being caught and then disciplined or discharged. Although it is legal in New York to tape record secretly a conversation in which one is a participant, the attorney who advocates or assists the employee may be acting unethically, depending upon the circumstances.[4]

---

2. PRACTICE POINTER: If emotional distress is an issue, and the client is not receiving counseling, it may be appropriate to suggest such counseling or even refer the client to a psychologist or psychiatrist.

3. This process is described in greater detail in § 17.6, *infra.*

4. *See* Heller v. Champion Int'l Corp., 891 F.2d 432 (2d Cir.1989) (employee has right to surreptitiously tape an in-person conversation with employer); Miano v. AC

§ 17.4 Strategy—Defendant's Counsel's Investigation

When a dispute arises, defense counsel's factual checklist must include many of the same "5-W" (who, what, when, where, and why) questions as found in plaintiff's counsel's checklist. One important difference, however, is that defense counsel must address the sometimes difficult issue of, who is the client? Although the Second Circuit has held that managers and supervisors cannot be held individually liable under Title VII,[1] they may be named as defendants in tort and other statutory claims. Undertaking multiple representation can lead to conflicts of interest throughout the representation. At the outset, it should be clearly stated that defense counsel will be conducting its investigation on behalf of the employer, not as counsel for individual managers. Generally, when the preliminary investigation reveals a meritless claim, the employer will want to defend any named individuals.[2] If it reveals intentional unlawful conduct by individual managers, however, the employer often will choose to distance itself and recommend separate representation. A checklist of considerations involved in a termination is set forth below at Section 17.19.

§ 17.5 Strategy—Pre-litigation Settlement Process

There are good reasons, whether from the outset or at some subsequent time, why each side in employment disputes should seriously consider settlement. Employment disputes are usually highly emotional affairs that tend to become extremely costly in terms of time, money, and stress when they go to litigation. The factual and legal issues are often complex, thus requiring significant expenditures for lawyers on both sides. The recovery, or lack thereof, is often unpredictable. The impact of litigation on the life of the plaintiff and the employer is likely to be very disruptive and burdensome.

Although proposing settlement may be a "sign of weakness" in other areas of litigation, most employment advocates now agree that the potential to achieve an outcome that will better serve clients, at substantial cost savings, legitimizes the proposal to settle no matter how weak or strong the respective legal positions may be. Many times, a settlement can be reached before the legal fees, and bitter feelings, begin to escalate. Given these advantages, it has become increasingly common practice for counsel to discuss the possibility of a settlement in employment disputes

& R Advertising, 148 F.R.D. 68, adopted and approved 834 F.Supp. 632 (S.D.N.Y. 1993) (counsel has an ethical duty not to participate in tape recording, but can advise client of the legal right to tape).

§ 17.4

1. Tomka v. The Seiler Corp., 66 F.3d 1295 (2d Cir.1995).

2. **PRACTICE POINTER:** If joint representation is chosen, counsel should issue a waiver letter confirming the arrangement to the individual defendants. The letter should disclose the conflict of interest risks, advise them of the possibility of withdrawal of counsel in the event of a conflict, and seek a limited waiver of any attorney-client privileges and other rights associated with exclusive representation, as may be needed.

from the outset. Counsel for each side should prepare for this process by having frank discussions with the client that explain the value of a settlement and that clarify the client's essential interests. Counsel should review the pros and cons of the case and disabuse the client of unrealistic expectations. Plaintiff's counsel should calculate the past and future damages suffered, the damages likely to be awarded, and the cost of litigation to reach that point. Once the client has been given a rough road map of the costs, risks, and possible rewards of litigation and has given the attorney some direction, counsel should attempt to negotiate.

§ 17.6 Strategy—Negotiating With Opposing Counsel

As a matter of strategy, it sometimes makes sense for the client personally to undertake initial settlement discussions. The presence of counsel in early discussions may create unhelpful wariness or hostility. In such circumstances, plaintiff's counsel should simply guide the client in developing and implementing a settlement strategy. At other times, it may be best for plaintiff's counsel to commence negotiations.

Perhaps the most common means by which plaintiff's counsel initiate discussions is through a demand letter. An effective demand letter will spell out the essential elements of the plaintiff's claim, the strength of the evidence, the extent of the damages, and the likelihood of recovery. Generally, it will end with an invitation to discuss settlement before the plaintiff takes the next step in pursuing the claim. Where the plaintiff has set forth realistic claims, and the employer is a reputable organization represented by experienced counsel, it is likely that the demand letter will generate a comprehensive response. If the defense's approach is to ignore or brush off the initial demand letter, plaintiff's counsel may decide to emphasize the seriousness of the plaintiff's intention to litigate by sending a follow-up letter with a draft complaint attached. This "shot across the bow" should not be undertaken casually, for the plaintiff's attorney places his or her credibility on the line when threatening litigation. Nevertheless, sending a draft complaint often aids in the process of settlement. Issues are framed and the possibility of litigation, with the attendant expenses in both time and money, becomes more of a reality. At this stage, before positions become hardened, a settlement may be possible.

Usually, defense counsel's written response to the demand letter will outline the employer's position by taking issue with the allegations or theories advanced by the plaintiff. Additionally, it may communicate facts that the plaintiff may not have known or shared with counsel. At this point, the parties may even exchange key documents or affidavits that constitute material evidence.

In furtherance of the settlement discussions, plaintiff's counsel should be ready to detail the client's actual damages, including lost compensation (*e.g.*, salary, wages, bonuses, severance, and the value of other benefits). Counsel should also be able to support any claim for emotional distress or punitive damages by referring to out-of-pocket expenses and to awards in similar cases.

For negotiation to be successful at the outset, or at any time during the litigation, counsel on both sides should maintain a credible, professional demeanor. This will facilitate discussions that are meaningful between the attorneys and perhaps even the parties. If the personality or styles of the parties or their counsel are not conducive to direct settlement negotiations, they should seriously consider employing some form of alternative dispute resolution ("ADR").

§ 17.7 Strategy—Alternative Dispute Resolution ("ADR")

Employment law practitioners who represent employees or employers recognize the value of ADR in helping their clients avoid the protracted and bitterly fought litigation associated with employment disputes. Broadly speaking, ADR encompasses a wide spectrum of opportunities to resolve disputes in a manner other than through judicial proceedings. ADR might be more accurately described as the *"primary"* means of problem solving or dispute resolution. It should be considered in place of, and not merely as an alternative to, litigation.

Employment-related disputes do not always require or warrant litigation, which is simply too expensive, slow, inefficient, and inflexible for many such disputes. Nonetheless, litigation is a necessary alternative (perhaps the "last resort") when other mechanisms fail to avoid or resolve the dispute. The availability of litigation is, of course, sometimes essential to spur parties to engage seriously in ADR procedures.

The most informal approach to ADR is the direct negotiation route described in Section 17.6, *supra*. If this does not work, the plaintiff should consider escalating the confrontation in the least adversarial manner possible until progress can be achieved. The benefits of this approach are that disputes often can be resolved faster, better, with less aggravation for all concerned, than may occur when parties rush into more adversarial forums.

Internal grievance or review mechanisms in the organization may provide a suitable forum in which the parties, at the very least, learn about the strengths and weaknesses of each other's positions. If the company is serious about such programs and takes care to design and run them in a way that assures fair procedures, plaintiff's counsel may be willing to recommend that the client use them. Of course, if the employer uses such programs merely as litigation avoidance schemes, and employees perceive them as unfair, prejudicial, or futile, the process will probably go unused.

Once an employee decides to take the dispute "outside" the company, various alternatives are available. In employment discrimination cases, of course, the employee may go to the EEOC, or to a state or local human rights agency. Such agencies are beginning to turn in earnest to ADR techniques, particularly mediation, to reduce their backlog of cases.

§ 17.8 Strategy—Alternative Dispute Resolution—Mediation

Mediation is an increasingly popular ADR procedure for employment disputes. The key benefit of mediation is its voluntariness and non-binding result. The parties can design the process to suit the dispute, choose the mediator, and retain control over whether and how to settle. Mediation, done correctly, can resolve disputes not settled through direct negotiations, relatively quickly and amicably. Virtually any employment dispute is a good candidate for mediation. Prime candidates are cases involving on-going relationships (*e.g.*, an employee still working for the company), emotional or sensitive issues (*e.g.*, with a potential for bad publicity), and problems with non-financial aspects that may lend themselves to creative problem-solving. Examples include sexual harassment and reasonable accommodation for a disability.

Perhaps the most important role for counsel in mediation is to select an effective mediator. A good mediator is essential; however, not everyone can be effective in this role. Although retired judges may meet the standard, they do not *necessarily* make effective mediators. The important characteristics for a mediator are good interpersonal and listening skills, creative problem-solving skills, and credibility with the parties. Substantive knowledge of the law is helpful, but is not usually essential. Rather than merely taking the parties' opening settlement figures and pushing toward a compromise, the mediator should be able to use his or her knowledge of litigation risks and outcomes in order to focus attention on the weaknesses of each party's case, the burdens of litigation, and the risks of failure in court. Sensitive counsel and good mediators, who are aware that emotional scars often becloud the clients' vision, can use the mediation forum to ease them through the psychological barriers that sometimes, more than the issue of dollars, impede a beneficial settlement.

In preparing for the mediation, it is important that each party have present a decision-maker with full authority to settle the matter. The mediation agreement, which generally includes a confidentiality stipulation, is usually supplied by the mediator. It should be reviewed and explained to the client. Mediators differ with respect to requiring preliminary briefs or documentation. Whether or not a brief has been drafted, the lawyer, prior to mediation, should organize the facts and legal arguments and be prepared to make a persuasive presentation. The objective in mediation is not to convince or persuade the mediator as one would a judge or arbitrator. Its purpose is to convince the other side, through the mediator, of the risks of going forward. To maximize the chances of reaching a favorable settlement in mediation, counsel should not pull punches. The most effective arguments and evidence should be presented to the mediator. There may be occasions when it is tactically premature to disclose one's whole case to the other side. Nevertheless, counsel should come to the mediation prepared to tell the mediator the full story and to present important exhibits. These can be shared with the mediator on a non-disclosure basis for the purpose of communicating through the mediator, however obliquely, the true potential of the case.

Pre-mediation preparation should include a careful explanation of the process to the client. In particular, the client may be unaware that the mediator is not a decision-maker, but merely a negotiation facilitator who offers suggestions and who conveys facts, arguments, and ideas between the parties. The client should be told that the process may entail hearing allegations that are upsetting and that the pitch may become so intense as to be emotionally distressing. Nonetheless, considering the risks of going to trial, and the costs associated with litigating through judgment and possibly appeal, the client will often conclude that the relatively little time spent in mediation (in comparison to a trial) is well worth the effort. Roughly 85% percent of mediations lead to a settlement, often within one day.

The mediator usually begins by laying down certain ground rules to both parties. Often, with the opposing side still present, counsel for each side will make an opening statement that outlines the case and sells it, not to the mediator necessarily, but to the individuals on the other side, who may have never before heard the unfiltered story of their adversary. Generally, the mediator then excuses one party from the room and "caucuses" with the remaining party to discuss the merits of the case and the parties' interests and positions. The mediator then will "shuttle" back and forth, caucusing with each party, until a mutually acceptable resolution is worked out or an impasse is reached. The settlement agreement should be comprehensive and be in writing—and initialled by the parties—before the mediation is completed, even if it cannot be put in final form and signed. It will usually include a release and follow along the lines of the severance agreement terms discussed in § 17.10, *infra* (Strategy—Settlement and Severance Agreements).

§ 17.9 Strategy—Alternative Dispute Resolution—Arbitration

Binding arbitration raises a set of considerations that are different from those associated with mediation. Of course a dispute may be submitted to non-binding arbitration, which could be considered a hybrid of mediation and arbitration—the object being to facilitate a consensual agreement on settlement terms. Binding arbitration, however, entails

§ 17.9

surrendering to a neutral third-party the authority to resolve the dispute. The case, essentially, is tried as in court, and the arbitrator, similar to a judge, imposes a resolution in the form of a decision. The decision may, or may not, be explained, and it is not appealable.

Although the courts have approved so-called "pre-dispute" mandatory arbitration agreements in certain areas of employment, principally in the securities industry, it has triggered vociferous criticism.[1] Arbitration may be suitable for employment claims if, and only if, the parties enter into the agreement to arbitrate knowingly and voluntarily. Thus, an employee, with aid of counsel, could agree with the employer to submit such a dispute to arbitration if the employee decides that the procedures are fair.

Plaintiffs' attorneys assert that so-called "pre-dispute" mandatory arbitration programs—those imposed by the employer on employees as a condition of employment before a dispute has arisen—are not the product of a knowing and voluntary choice by an employee with a comparable bargaining position (except perhaps in the case of senior executives, professionals, etc.). Moreover, such programs sometimes do not provide full and fair procedures (*e.g.*, discovery) and remedies required of discrimination cases.

By the same token, counsel for the employer may want to consider carefully whether avoiding a possible "runaway" jury justifies an attempt to impose mandatory arbitration of all claims.[2] Providing ready access to arbitration may entail an increase in overall employee-related claims, thereby increasing the amount of employee litigation. Moreover, arbitrators purportedly sometimes "split the baby," which could favor an employee with a weak case. In cases where employees have meritorious

---

§ 17.9

1. Since the U.S. Supreme Court construed the Federal Arbitration Act to hold that discrimination claims are arbitrable under standard securities arbitration agreements, a plethora of decisions have applied these agreements to employment disputes. Gilmer v. Interstate/Johnson Lane Corp., 500 U.S. 20, 111 S.Ct. 1647, 114 L.Ed.2d 26 (1991). New York courts have upheld these mandatory agreements against challenge. See Fletcher v. Kidder, Peabody & Co., 184 A.D.2d 359, 584 N.Y.S.2d 838 (1st Dep't 1992), aff'd 81 N.Y.2d 623, 601 N.Y.S.2d 686, 619 N.E.2d 998 (1993), cert. denied 510 U.S. 993, 114 S.Ct. 554, 126 L.Ed.2d 455 (1993) (N.Y.State Human Rights Law); Bird v. Shearson Lehman/American Express, 926 F.2d 116 (2d Cir.1991), cert. denied 501 U.S. 1251, 111 S.Ct. 2891, 115 L.Ed.2d 1056 (1991) (ERISA). Nevertheless, a backlash against the use of these agreements especially for claims under the Civil Rights Act of 1991, has been growing. In February 1996, for example, one of the nation's largest providers of arbitration and mediation services, JAMS/Endispute, followed the urging of the EEOC and employee groups in refusing to arbitrate employment claims under mandatory arbitration programs. (See JAMS/Endispute, *Six Principles of Neutrality and Fairness for Employment Dispute Resolution Practice* (1996)).

2. **PRACTICE POINTER:** In drafting their mandatory arbitration agreements, many employers in the securities industry have specified that the law of the State of New York would govern, under which punitive damages are generally proscribed in arbitration. The U.S. Supreme Court defeated this strategy by holding that, under federal common law, punitive damages will be available even under New York law. Mastrobuono v. Shearson Lehman Hutton, 514 U.S. 52, 115 S.Ct. 1212, 131 L.Ed.2d 76 (1995).

claims that might otherwise have been resolved judicially, full-blown arbitration can be nearly indistinguishable from litigation. To the extent that the employer seeks to "streamline" arbitrations by limiting discovery and eliminating other due process safeguards, the employer may find that the process is unenforceable, to say nothing of the employee relations problems that may arise.

§ 17.10 Strategy—Settlement and Severance Agreements

Severance negotiations are akin to those surrounding the settlement of a dispute. The most common scenario is that the employee is fired and is given the employer's severance letter or agreement. Sometimes, the fired employee is not given a severance package and decides to negotiate for one. Occasionally, the departure is subject to negotiation from the start. In any event, the process of negotiating will bear a resemblance to the dispute settlement process discussed in Section 17.6 above. The final agreement, assuming one can be reached, will usually be comprehensive, involve a release, and entail certain formal requirements under federal law, as detailed below.

From the employee's standpoint, one question frequently faced is whether to attempt to negotiate for a severance package or for an enhancement. Generally, the answer is "yes." It doesn't hurt to ask. Employers may have the right to rescind or withdraw the package if the employee asks for more, but this virtually never happens.[1]

Counsel for the employee must consider who should do the negotiating, the client or counsel, and with whom to negotiate. Ideally, someone can be identified in the company who has the authority, the willingness to negotiate, and an inclination to help the employee. Counsel must also consider the employee's negotiating leverage. Does the employee have a legal claim that is strong? "Viable?" "Colorable?" Even absent such a legal claim—or before asserting one—the employee can try to "push the buttons" of the employer. The "buttons" include fairness, guilt (which can be a great motivator), fear (*e.g.*, bad publicity, government intrusion, higher management scrutiny), friendship, and so on. In some companies, it works. This is especially true where proposed changes in benefits will cost the employer little or no money while helping the employee.

Typically, it is harder to negotiate potential changes in the context of a "reduction in force" ("RIF") or large-company standard severance policy. The employer will argue that it cannot, or will not, make changes that could undermine the standard or create a bad precedent. Even in the face of such a mindset, changes can be obtained—even substantial ones—through creative approaches (discussed below).

§ 17.10

1. **PRACTICE POINTER:** Under the Older Workers Benefit Protection Act, 29 U.S.C.A. § 626(f) (*see* below), the employer probably cannot withdraw the proposed agreement during the 21/45 days consideration period.

§ 17.11 Strategy—Settlement and Severance Agreements—Older Workers Benefit Protection Act ("OWBPA")

OWBPA amends the Age Discrimination Employment Act ("ADEA") by creating strict requirements for waiver of ADEA rights or claims. Under OWBPA, an individual *may* not waive any ADEA right or claim "unless the waiver is knowing and voluntary";[1] and "a waiver *may* not be considered knowing and voluntary unless" it meets certain minimum requirements. In other words, any purported waiver of ADEA rights or claims will be totally ineffective unless it meets the minimum requirements.[2] The minimum requirements for a valid release under the OWBPA are:[3]

(1) the agreement must be written "in a manner calculated to be understood by such individual or by the average individual eligible to participate";

(2) the agreement must specifically refer to "rights or claims arising under" ADEA;

(3) there must be no waiver of rights or claims "that may arise after the date the waiver is executed";

(4) the waiver must be made "only in exchange for consideration *in addition to* anything of value to which the individual already is entitled"[4];

(5) the employee must be advised *in writing* to consult with an attorney prior to executing the agreement;

(6) the employee must be given *at least* 21 days within which to consider the agreement; and

(7) the employee must be given at least 7 days to revoke the agreement after signing.

Where the waiver is requested "in connection with an exit incentive or other employment termination program offered to a group or class of employees":

§ 17.11

1. This codifies the well-established principle that waiver of any statutory rights must be knowing and voluntary to be effective.

2. Emphasis supplied.

PRACTICE POINTER: A waiver that fails to comply with OWBPA can still waive non-ADEA rights and claims.

3. PRACTICE POINTER: Under a literal interpretation of the language of OWBPA, a waiver that fails to meet even one of these requirements is ineffective. Thus, an employee could take the benefits and still assert ADEA rights. In that event, it is uncertain whether the employer can require the employee to restore the consideration. The employer may wish, therefore, to include explicit language that states that the consideration has to be returned in the event the employee does so.

4. Emphasis supplied.

PRACTICE POINTER: An ADEA waiver would be ineffective if signed to get a standard severance package. But if there is enhanced severance for a release, the consideration requirement is met. Many companies now have a standard package available without a release, plus an enhanced package with a release. Some companies have stated that they provide no severance pay ... but will give severance in exchange for a release.

(1) the consideration period is 45 days, not 21;[5] and

(2) the employer must inform the individual *in writing* as to

    (a) any class, unit, or group of individuals covered by such program, any eligibility factors for such program, and any time limits applicable to such program; and

    (b) the job titles and ages of all individuals eligible or selected for the program, and the ages of all individuals in the same job classification or organization unit who are not eligible or selected for the program.[6]

§ 17.12 Strategy—Settlement and Severance Agreements—COBRA

A discharged employee has the right under COBRA[1] to continue group health/medical insurance coverage, with the existing coverage and rates, for up to 18 months after the off-payroll date (up to 29 months if the employee is disabled under Social Security standards).[2] The employer may require the employee to pay up to 102% of the applicable premium.[3]

Library References:

West's Key No. Digests, Pensions ⟐121.

§ 17.13 Strategy—Settlement and Severance Agreements—Pay

The basic choices for severance pay are lump sum and salary continuation. Typically, benefits end when a lump sum is paid and some

---

5. PRACTICE POINTER: Presumably, the employer cannot withdraw the proposed agreement during the 21/45 day consideration period.

6. PRACTICE POINTER: It is unclear whether this information requirement is triggered when 2 or 3 persons are fired at the same time and are provided a standard employment package, and whether the failure to comply invalidates the waiver.

§ 17.12

1. 29 U.S.C.A. §§ 1161–1168. While many COBRA rules are incorporated in ERISA, other COBRA provisions are found in the Internal Revenue Code (26 U.S.C.A. § 4980B) and the Public Health Service Act (42 U.S.C.A. § 300bb–1).

2. PRACTICE POINTER: Employees fired for "gross misconduct" do not qualify for COBRA continuation. Under New York State Insurance Law, however, employers are required to offer COBRA-like continuation coverage for six months and there is no "misconduct" exemption. Insurance Law § 3221(m). Employers, who are often the plan administrators, violate New York law if they withhold all notification on misconduct grounds.

3. PRACTICE POINTER: Plaintiff's counsel should routinely inquire whether the terminated employee has received notice of COBRA continuation coverage. The employer must give notice to the plan administrator of coverage termination within 60 after the "qualifying event" (*e.g.*, discharge). Within 14 days of receiving such notice, the plan administrator must provide notice of the right to elect COBRA continuation coverage for each person who might otherwise lose coverage. From the date that coverage would otherwise end (or if later, from the date of receiving notice from the plan administrator that coverage will soon end), the employee has at least 60 days to elect COBRA coverage. 29 U.S.C.A. §§ 1165, 1166.

483

benefits continue during a continuation period, though exceptions occur both ways. Employers will sometimes negotiate a switch from one to the other at the employee's request. The choices may further affect benefits as follows. During a severance continuation period, employers often will continue to pay for health/medical benefits on the same terms as during active employment, though the employer may require the employee to pay up to 102% of the cost. Employers sometimes will continue other benefits, such as life insurance coverage, pension/401(k) contributions and accruals, and accruals under stock plans. Employers generally do not continue disability benefits or vacation/sick day accruals during a salary continuation period, though sometimes the latter can be negotiated.

Termination of Severance Pay. An important negotiating point is whether salary continuation will end when the employee gets a new job. Some severance arrangements so provide, with a forfeiture of pay and benefits thereafter; such a provision may, or may not, impose a duty to mitigate on the employee. Other arrangements provide that the employee may choose to cease severance pay, obtain a lump sum payment for the balance upon starting a new job or merely upon request.[1]

An employee who is concerned about the prospect of running out of severance pay before finding a new job may try to negotiate a trade-off; trading a fixed amount or duration of severance pay for a potentially larger variable amount or duration, depending on when the employee gets a job. In such a situation, the employer will usually insist on an outside deadline or ceiling and a duty to mitigate.[2]

Base Pay. Severance pay is typically based on base salary and does not include such remuneration as bonuses, incentive pay, or commissions. Nonetheless, employees should be alert to opportunities to lay claim to such compensation. Such claims have special merit toward the end of the business year when the compensation would normally accrue or be paid, especially if the employee has met most or all of the standards for the extra compensation.[3]

§ 17.13

1. **PRACTICE POINTER:** Of course, if the proposed agreement contains a defeasance or mitigation provision or lacks an option to choose a lump sum payment, the plaintiff's lawyer may try to negotiate for a change.

2. **PRACTICE POINTER:** For example, in lieu of fixed severance pay of 26 weeks, an employee may prefer to receive severance until (and only until) reemployment, which could happen after only 10 weeks or after 40 weeks. Sometimes a combination of fixed and variable pay is negotiated, providing a floor and a ceiling.

PRACTICE POINTER: A modified arrangement sometimes is negotiated to meet the employee's security objectives (*i.e.*, limiting the risk of missing paydays), while meeting the employer's concern that the employee won't try hard enough to find a job. Thus, for example, under a variable payment arrangement with an outside date, the employee may receive pay until reemployment and then split (50/50%) with the employer the amount of severance covered by the remainder of the severance period. This shares risks and benefits.

3. **PRACTICE POINTER:** When an employer refuses to alter a standard severance pay amount or period, the plaintiff's lawyer should look for creative ways to improve the package "around the edges" while leaving the core intact.

Leave Pay. Plaintiff's counsel should ascertain the employee's entitlement or potential claim to accrued but unused vacation or other leave pay.[4] Sometimes, the employee can get the whole year's allotment; other times, all he or she can get is the pro rata portion. Counsel should check the employer's manuals and policies and ascertain what other employees have gotten. Increasing the amount of vacation pay is a way to enhance the package without "breaking the mold" of the standard package.

Offsets. Employers are not allowed to offset unilaterally against "wages" any amount that the employer contends the employee owes the employer (*e.g.*, cash advances, loans, alleged thefts).[5]

Library References:

West's Key No. Digests, Master and Servant ⊛68–82.

§ 17.14 Strategy—Settlement and Severance Agreements—Income Taxes

Severance pay is subject to income taxes, as is accrued vacation or other leave pay. Moreover, such pay is subject to payroll taxes (*e.g.*, FICA/Medicare) and deductions (*e.g.*, withholding of income taxes).

Under certain circumstances, amounts received for settlement of claims can be free of income taxes and wage taxes and deductions, but those circumstances are now quite limited in the employment context. Before August 20, 1996, settlements of tort-type claims for personal injuries (*e.g.*, emotional distress damages under Title VII) could be tax-free under Internal Revenue Code Section 104(a)(2). The Small Business Job Protection Act amended that statute as of August 20, 1996 to limit such tax-free treatment to instances in which the plaintiff has suffered personal *physical* injury or disease. As a practical matter, that will occur in very few employment cases (*e.g.*, assault and battery).

Examples:

(1) Defer the effective date of the termination. This could be in the form of a "notice period" or simply continued employment. If the off-payroll date is postponed, the employee gets paid longer before getting the standard package. It may be understood (or better, stated) that the employee will not be expected to perform any or much service during all or part of the extended period, presumably while looking for a new job.

(2) Add a consulting agreement (discussed later).

(3) Convert some unimportant benefit to cash. For example, if the employee does not need proffered outplacement services, occasionally an employer will allow the cost of that service to be "traded in" for severance pay; this can be as much a 15% of the employee's salary. Similarly, if the employee does not need medical coverage (*e.g.*, when covered under a spouse's plan), the cost of such coverage might be traded in.

(4) Get increased vacation or sick leave pay.

4. PRACTICE POINTER: The employer's failure to pay vacation and other accrued benefits may violate New York Labor Law § 198(1–a), and give rise to a cause of action that includes liquidated damages and attorneys' fees.

5. Labor Law § 193.

§ 17.14 EMPLOYMENT LAW Ch. 17

Nonetheless, where a tort-type claim has been asserted, amounts paid as damages for the costs of medical care can be received tax-free.[1] Thus, for example, a sexual harassment victim's expenditures for medical or psychiatric treatment could be reimbursed tax-free as part of a settlement or award. As to such amounts, no Form W-2 or Form 1099 tax report would be issued.

Other ways of structuring and allocating settlements of employment cases to achieve tax benefits include the following: (a) the employer's purchase of an annuity for the benefit of the (former) employee; (b) maximizing payments, accruals and vesting in pension and 401(k) accounts; (c) the employer's payment of attorneys' fees (and issuance of a Form 1099) directly to the employee's attorney;[2] (d) the employer's payment of consideration as a fee to cancel an employment agreement for fixed term;[3] and (e) the payment of emotional distress damages or punitive damages.[4]

Library References:

West's Key No. Digests, Taxation ⊕1096.

§ 17.15 Strategy—Settlement and Severance Agreements—Benefits

As discussed in § 17.12, *supra,* COBRA provides rights regarding medical coverage, and some benefits are commonly extended during a salary continuation period. In any event, as to all benefits, the employee should gather all pertinent information as soon as possible, including benefit and account statements, plan documents, summary plan descriptions, etc. This is especially applicable to any severance plan documents. With these documents, the employee and counsel can assess the effects of the severance on those benefits—what is being preserved and what may be lost (*e.g.*, due to inadequate accrual or vesting). This process can lead to identification of problems, clarification of ambiguities, and improvements that can benefit the employee, often without substantial cost to the employer.[1]

§ 17.14

1. I.R.C. § 104(a)(2).

2. This approach can be employed *only* when the employee has asserted and is settling a claim under a fee-shifting statute (*e.g.*, Title VII). Even then, this approach has not been the subject of any regulations or cases, so its viability is untested.

3. Although such a payment is subject to income taxes, it is not subject to wage taxes or withholdings. *See* Rev. Ruling 58–301; *cf.* Rev. Rulings 74–252 and 75–44.

4. Although such a payment is subject to income taxes, it is not subject to wage taxes or withholdings.

§ 17.15

1. **PRACTICE POINTER**: Employee's counsel should be alert to the remote possibility that the employer might be terminating the employee for the purpose of preventing the employee from obtaining a benefit (*e.g.*, vesting in a pension). While obviously hard to prove, such a purpose would violate ERISA § 510.

Where the employee is close to a date for vesting or accruing some benefit, counsel should try to negotiate a way to bridge to that date. This is especially applicable to pensions, 401(k)s, and stock plans. Ways to do that include: getting a longer severance period; spreading the same severance pay over a longer period; getting an authorized leave of absence (*i.e.*, continuing employment status without pay); or getting credit for some prior service. Sometimes an employer can be persuaded to provide some cash in lieu of the forfeited benefit. Under non-qualified plans, the employer can even accelerate or waive vesting and accrual requirements.

§ 17.16 Strategy—Other Severance Issues

Consulting. Sometimes, it is advantageous for both the employer and employee to enter into a consulting agreement after the end of employment. The employer may have use for the employee's expertise and contacts, and the employee can obtain additional income that may not interfere with other employment. Sometimes, a consulting agreement is a way for the employer to assure the employee's good will/non-disparagement in the trade. Thus, a consulting agreement is a way for the employee to obtain additional money in exchange for something of real value to the employer.[1]

Consulting agreements are especially useful when the employer does not want to alter a standard package but is otherwise willing to improve the deal.

Outplacement Services. Some employers offer professional outplacement services. If this option is not offered and the employee could benefit from it, the employee's lawyer should ask for it. If the employee doesn't need or want such professional help, the employer may be willing to trade in the cost for cash. Some employers refuse to do so, however, taking the position that outplacement service is offered to help the employee find a new job/career and the employee can take it or leave it.

In the absence of professional outplacement, the employee may ask for assistance from the employer in looking for a job. The employer may provide the use of a company office, secretarial and reception services, a telephone and photocopying privileges. This type of help can be a substantial benefit, especially when it helps preserve the appearance that the employee is "looking for a job from a job."

Personal Property and Perquisites. The employee's counsel should be alert to issues over personal property, such as the employee's

---

§ 17.16

1. **PRACTICE POINTER:** Sometimes, a "no-show" consultancy can be arranged. For example, the employee may be paid to "be available" or to be "on call."

CAVEAT: The employee should be careful to assure that the consultancy agreement is not drafted in a way that imposes real, significant obligations as a condition for payment, if that is not the intent; otherwise, the employer could stop payments for alleged non-performance.

§ 17.16   EMPLOYMENT LAW   Ch. 17

rolodex, personal papers and files, copies of some "business" documents, or office furnishings. As to documents, ascertain whether a confidentiality agreement is already in place. Employers sometimes allow employees to keep (or purchase at a reduced price) such company property as the employee's personal office computer, home fax machine, cellular telephone, or even a company car.

The employee should try to obtain all personal belongings and material that could not be removed before the separation, including books, awards, pictures, and any personal documents that may be on the computer system. If there is concern over any negative information that may be in the employee's personnel file, counsel may try to review it and then have it destroyed, sealed, or removed. Employers generally seek a provision requiring the employee to return all property belonging to the employer. Counsel will have to consider to whom the property belongs, such as employee manuals or other documents that set forth employee policies.

Confidentiality. Whenever an employee obtains a non-standard severance package, the employer almost always wants its terms to be kept confidential. Generally, as long as the financial terms are acceptable, an employee should have no problem with such a request. Confidentiality provisions obviously make it more difficult for other employees (and their attorneys) to learn about enhanced severance terms; that is the goal from the employer's perspective.

The typical clause may contain some exceptions to confidentiality, but they usually are incomplete. The employee should seek the following exceptions to the confidentiality clause: (a) the employee's professional advisors (attorney, accountant, financial planner, etc.); (b) the employee's immediate family (and perhaps other specified family, friends, etc.); (c) use in any proceeding arising under or pertaining to the severance agreement; (d) disclosure in response to any subpoena or other compulsory legal process (though employers sometimes ask/insist that the employee give notice of any such process received, so the employer can move to quash).[2]

Releases/Waivers. When an employer provides an enhanced severance package, it invariably insists on a release of any and all claims and rights by the employee against the employer (and its agents, representatives, successors, assigns, etc.). For adequate consideration, that is fair and appropriate.[3]

---

2. PRACTICE POINTER: The employee should be careful to not agree to a confidentiality clause that forbids discussion with prospective employers of all aspects of the employee's tenure, inasmuch as communicating accomplishments and other "marketing" information may be essential to obtaining a new job.

PRACTICE POINTER: A review of case law reveals that confidentiality clauses are very, very seldom the subject of litigation.

3. CAVEAT: A waiver that does not conform to the requirements of the OWBPA is ineffective as to ADEA rights. (*See supra*, § 17.11 OWBPA). It would still be effective as to all other rights and claims, assuming

Releases in typical severance agreements are often unduly broad, probably unknowingly. For example, read literally, such releases often would encompass an employee's rights under benefit plans, vested or otherwise. Such a release would undoubtedly be unenforceable as to vested rights, but the release language should be clarified anyway. In any event, it should specifically exclude from the scope of the release all excludable benefits.

From the employee's standpoint, a release by the employer of any rights and claims against the employee may be desirable or even essential. Employers generally resist such releases, especially in a typical severance situation. When they are agreed to, employers sometimes want an exception for after-discovered claims, such as any claim for defalcation or theft against the employee. To protect the employee, such exceptions should be narrowly tailored. Moreover, the employee's counsel should obtain a representation that the employer is unaware of any such claims.

In the release, the employee's counsel should be careful not to forfeit reimbursement for business expenses. The employee should submit the expenses and get reimbursed before signing the agreement, or at least reserve the ability to submit the expenses for reimbursement.

Reasons for Termination/References/Non–Disparagement. The terminology used to describe a separation can have an impact on the employee's ability to get a new job. Obviously, the employee will want the least pejorative-sounding reasons. For the employer, there may be no downside in accommodating the employee, since any concern that the employee will somehow use the more favorable reason against the employer probably has been precluded by the release made part of the separation agreement.[4]

A good job reference can be very valuable to an employee. Forestalling a bad job reference can be even more valuable. An agreed upon form of reference letter is a good idea. Often, the employee can draft a reasonable proposed letter that the employer should accept, and then negotiate from that draft. Many employees prefer to have the agreed upon letter annexed to the severance agreement. The letter can be used in two forms: as a "To Whom It May Concern" letter that the employee can use any time, and as the standard letter to be sent out by the employer in response to any requests. The content of the letter can also be the script for any oral references given.[5]

---

it is otherwise knowing and voluntary and does not violate some other statutory limitation (such as the one in the Fair Labor Standards Act as to minimum wage and overtime pay claims).

4. PRACTICE POINTER: Among the commonly used terms are: resignation, employee wishes to "pursue other opportunities," reductions in force, reorganization, restructuring, retrenchment, personal reasons, disagreement over philosophy, practices, etc., and strictly confidential.

5. PRACTICE POINTER: It is advisable to name specific individuals who are deemed acceptable/trustworthy to respond to any call for a reference; obtain assur-

In the absence of the foregoing, the employee should try to obtain agreement that, in response to any reference request, the employer will state that, pursuant to standard company policy, it can only confirm limited employment information (such as last position held and dates of employment).

Prohibition on Re–Applying for Employment. Employers often demand a provision that the employee never apply for employment with the company. In the case of a large, diversified company, the employee's counsel should be careful that the provision not be drawn too broadly to include all successors or affiliates, as this might unwittingly foreclose numerous employment opportunities, especially if acquisitions or mergers follow.

Restrictive Covenants. In some contexts, employers try to include in severance agreements restrictive covenants, such as a covenant not to solicit employees or customers ("non-solicitation"), a covenant not to compete for a period of time within certain geographic and/or business parameters ("non-competition"), or a covenant not to disclose confidential or proprietary information ("non-disclosure"). Sometimes, an employee may already be subject to such restrictions, in which event the employer may ask to confirm their continued validity or to extend their scope, or the employee may seek to narrow or eliminate them.

Non-competition covenants present obvious limitations on an employee's ability to earn a living after leaving the employer. A logical argument can be made that such restrictions should not extend beyond the end of the severance pay period; or put another way, that severance pay should be paid for the entire duration of any such restrictions.

Generally, non-competition and non-solicitation covenants are enforceable in New York to the extent that they are reasonable in time, place, and scope. In New York, unreasonable provisions can be "blue-pencilled" to make them reasonable. Such covenants are treated differently in other states. Some places (*e.g.*, Florida) consider such covenants as promoting public policy and encourage them by statute or common law; others, like California, consider such covenants to be against public policy and therefore, for the most part, unenforceable; some states declare any unreasonable provision to be unenforceable, without "blue-pencilling" to preserve reasonable aspects.

One way of handling an employer's legitimate non-competition or non-solicitation concern is to be very specific about what is prohibited. For example, the employee may covenant not to solicit *named* employees or customers for a period of time or not to compete as to *named* clients; a list can be attached as an exhibit to the agreement.[6]

---

ances that no one else will handle such a call.

6. CAVEAT: It is important to keep in mind the difference between non-solicitation and non-hire or non-competition. A

Cooperation. Employers sometimes want to assure that former employees will cooperate in the future if necessary for a lawsuit or claim as to which the employee has knowledge. For example, the employer's counsel may want to interview the employee or to have the employee available for an affidavit, deposition, or as a witness at a trial. While the employee is receiving severance benefits, the employer may have some self-help remedies. Otherwise, the employer may wish to obtain a written assurance of cooperation.

If the employee is willing to assure future cooperation, some ground rules are appropriate. For example, it may be agreed that the employee will be available only outside business hours (so as not to interfere with a subsequent job), or only up to a certain amount of time. Moreover, it is often advisable to negotiate a *per diem* or per hour compensation arrangement for such services, sometimes with a small amount of time (say, one day) provided free, plus assurance of reimbursement for all expenses.

Attorneys' Fees/Liquidated Damages. The employee may attempt to convince the employer to pay attorneys fees. Some employers view counsel's participation as a moderating influence, and view the fees as a vendor payment. Sometimes, the employee's attorneys' fees may be traded off against other amounts that would be subject to income taxes and/or FICA, thereby saving some taxes for both parties.

Many agreements contain a clause stating that, in the event of a breach, attorneys' fees will be or may be paid to the prevailing party. Employees are usually strongly opposed to any provision imposing liquidated damages in the event of a breach, except perhaps, if it is mutual.

Unemployment Insurance ("UI"). The employee's counsel should always remind the terminated employee of the right to collect UI benefits. Those benefits are not payable until the employee applies. UI benefits are not payable to employees who quit without sufficient reason or are fired for misconduct. If there is a doubt about what the employer will tell the UI office about the termination, the employee should try to get that straightened out beforehand and acknowledged in the agreement.

Strictly speaking, UI benefits generally are not payable while an employee remains on the payroll receiving variable severance pay, but are payable despite a lump sum severance payment or while receiving a fixed amount of severance pay. It appears that these rules are not uniformly applied. If an employee is denied UI benefits improperly, an appeal should be filed; initial determinations are routinely reversed on

clause that prohibits an employee from soliciting co-workers to leave the employer would not prohibit the employee from actually hiring a co-worker who approaches the employee. The same thing applies to customers and clients.

appeal in New York.[7]

§ 17.17 Strategy—Independent Contractor vs. Employee

Before determining whether the rights of a worker have been violated, the question of whether the worker is an employee, independent contractor, government employee, and/or labor union member must be answered. Many of the rights that apply to members of one group may not apply to others. The distinction between an employee or independent contractor is crucial because most statutory protections that apply to employees (*e.g.*, civil rights law, FLSA, FMLA) do not apply to independent contractors. If the statute does not set forth specific criteria, the courts generally use a 20–factor test in which the extent of the employer's right to control the means and manner in which the employee performs the work is the most decisive indicator of status.[1] The rights that pertain to government or civil service employees (as defined by the relevant statutes) and labor union members are beyond the scope of this chapter.

Library References:

West's Key No. Digests, Master and Servant ⚖1.

§ 17.18 Strategy—Checklist: Initial Considerations for Plaintiff

1. What are the applicable causes of action?

2. What type of action is appropriate (*e.g.*, lawsuit or special proceeding)?

3. If bringing a tort claim against a municipality, public agency, authority or corporation, does a notice of claim need to be filed within 90 days of the claim arising? In which court will jurisdiction and venue be proper (*i.e.*, based on the dollar amount of the damages claim, location of parties, etc.)?

---

7. PRACTICE POINTER: New York unemployment insurance law prohibits an attorney from charging a fee for handling an UI proceeding, except as ordered by the ALJ. Presumably, however, an attorney who is helping an employee preserve and enforce rights under discrimination laws or under the common law (*e.g.*, contract claims) can help the employee with the UI proceeding in aid of the other claims.

PRACTICE POINTER: For help in New York, an employee can be referred to the Unemployment Action Center, (212) 533-7744.

§ 17.17

1. PRACTICE POINTER: The only antidiscrimination law that applies to certain independent contractors is the New York City Human Rights Law. N.Y.C.Admin. Code § 8–102(5).

See Nationwide Mutual Ins. Co. v. Darden, 503 U.S. 318, 112 S.Ct. 1344, 117 L.Ed.2d 581 (1992)(common law agency test).

4. What methods of personal service are available to acquire jurisdiction over the defendant?
5. What time limitations are applicable?
6. What administrative processing is required before commencing the action? (*See* § 17.67)
7. What other exhaustion requirements must be satisfied? (*See* § 17.69)

§ 17.19 Strategy—Checklist: Terminating an Employee

1. Review all relevant documents including personnel files, handbooks, policies and procedures. (*See* § 17.3)
2. Conduct thorough investigation of the facts relating to the dismissal. (*See id.*)
3. Did the employee raise any statutory complaint for which the termination may be perceived as retaliatory? (*See* §§ 17.32–17.38)
4. Does the documentation support the termination, *i.e.*, a legitimate and non-discriminatory reason? (*See* § 17.4)
5. Are any statutory or common law causes of action implicated by the termination? (*See* §§ 17.20–17.65)
6. Is the termination consistent with company policies and customs?
7. Did the employee have notice of the consequences of his/her actions leading to termination? Does the employee understand the reasons for the termination?
8. Has a COBRA letter been prepared? Has the employee been notified of any appeal or grievance procedures or outplacement opportunities that are available? (*See* § 17.12)
9. Has property been returned?
10. Are there alternatives to termination?
11. Given all the circumstances, would the termination appear "fair" to an impartial observer?

§ 17.20 Causes of Action

If the dispute is not resolved through settlement, then the employee's counsel will plan a litigation strategy. This section describes the major common law and statutory causes of action that may be available.

In litigation, the principal objectives of employee's counsel generally are to sustain as many meritorious causes of action as possible, to get through discovery as expeditiously as possible, and to get to a jury whenever possible. Defendant's counsel may seek to derail the case on procedural grounds, if possible, or with substantive defenses—such as that the plaintiff cannot prove the necessary elements of the cause of action, or that an affirmative defense negates liability. The following overview highlights the salient elements and defenses, but of course, counsel should consult the cases cited and statutory authority before asserting these claims and defenses in litigation.

This overview focuses mainly on the possible claims arising out of the non-union *private* workplace. Although brief mention is made, the topics of labor law and public employment are outside the scope of this discussion. Generally speaking, the New York courts construe the common law rights of individual private employees very narrowly, and the State Legislature has been unwilling to expand these rights significantly.

§ 17.21 Causes of Action—Tort—Assault

A cause of action for assault might arise in connection with sexual harassment, an internal investigation, a confrontation between the employee and a supervisor, or an ejection of a terminated employee from the premises. In order for an assault to occur, the plaintiff must be placed in imminent apprehension of harmful or offensive contact.

Civil assault is defined generally as an intentional attempt or threat to do injury or commit a battery.[1] Not all courts require that an assault be based on fear of physical harm. "An action for an assault need not involve physical injury, but only a grievous affront or threat to the person of the plaintiff."[2] In *Leahy v. Federal Express Corp.*,[3] an employee alleged he was placed in apprehension of immediate harm when an investigator revealed a firearm. While the court found that he had made out a *prima facie* case, the jury denied recovery at the trial.

Library References:

West's Key No. Digests, Assault and Battery ⚖1–18.

§ 17.22 Causes of Action—Tort—Battery

A battery is an intentional, wrongful and unprivileged physical contact with another person, without consent. In order to recover damages for battery, the plaintiff must establish that there was bodily contact, that the contact was offensive, and that the defendant intended to make contact.[1] An example of a privileged battery is a lawful involuntary commitment to a mental institution.[2]

Library References:

West's Key No. Digests, Assault and Battery ⚖1–18.

§ 17.21

1. Rubenstein v. Benedictine Hospital, 790 F.Supp. 396, 412 (N.D.N.Y.1992).

2. DiGilio v. William J. Burns International Detective Agency, Inc., 46 A.D.2d 650, 359 N.Y.S.2d 688, 689 (2d Dep't 1974).

3. 609 F.Supp. 668, 673 (E.D.N.Y.1985).

§ 17.22

1. *See* Laurie Marie M. v. Jeffrey T.M., 159 A.D.2d 52, 559 N.Y.S.2d 336, (2d Dep't 1990), appeal denied 77 N.Y.2d 803, 568 N.Y.S.2d 15, 569 N.E.2d 874 (1991).

2. Rubenstein v. Benedictine Hospital, 790 F.Supp. 396, 411 (N.D.N.Y.1992).

Ch. 17   CAUSES OF ACTION—TORT—DEFAMATION   § 17.25

§ 17.23 Causes of Action—Tort—Conspiracy

Under New York law, conspiracy in itself does not constitute a tort.[1] The plaintiff must plead specific wrongful acts that might constitute an independent tort.[2]

An allegation of conspiracy can, however, connect nonactors, who otherwise might escape liability, with acts of their co-conspirators.[3] A claim of conspiracy may arise if the defendants are alleged to have conspired to violate another's right to "equal protection of the laws."[4]

Library References:
West's Key No. Digests, Conspiracy ⇔1–14.

§ 17.24 Causes of Action—Tort—Conversion

Employers who are sued by discharged employees sometimes assert counterclaims that sound in conversion, based on the employee's alleged theft or overuse of fringe benefits, such as expense accounts or vacation days. Conversion may be defined as an employee's assumption and exercise of the right of ownership, without authorization, over property belonging to the employer.

Library References:
West's Key No. Digests, Trover and Conversion ⇔1–12.

§ 17.25 Causes of Action—Tort—Defamation

Defamation is defined as the publication of false and derogatory statements about an individual which injures that person's reputation. Derogatory statements often occur in the employment context when an employer tells co-workers or outsiders why an employee was terminated or disciplined or when an employer gives employment references to outsiders (prospective employers or credit or employment agencies).[1]

§ 17.23

1. Noble v. Creative Technical Services, Inc., 126 A.D.2d 611, 511 N.Y.S.2d 51 (2d Dep't 1987)(dismissing claim that defendants conspired to fabricate a reason to terminate plaintiff as legally insufficient); Gould v. Community Health Plan of Suffolk, Inc., 99 A.D.2d 479, 470 N.Y.S.2d 415 (2d Dep't 1984); 117 East 24th Street Associates v. Karr, 95 A.D.2d 735, 464 N.Y.S.2d 473 (1st Dep't 1983); but see Arlinghaus v. Ritenour, 622 F.2d 629 (2d Cir.1980), cert. denied 449 U.S. 1013, 101 S.Ct. 570, 66 L.Ed.2d 471.

2. Raymond Corp. v. Coopers & Lybrand, 105 A.D.2d 926, 482 N.Y.S.2d 377 (3d Dep't 1984).

3. Burns Jackson Miller Summit & Spitzer v. Lindner, 88 A.D.2d 50, 452 N.Y.S.2d 80 (2d Dep't 1982), aff'd 59 N.Y.2d 314, 464 N.Y.S.2d 712, 451 N.E.2d 459 (1983); Danahy v. Meese, 84 A.D.2d 670, 446 N.Y.S.2d 611 (4th Dep't 1981).

4. 42 U.S.C.A. § 1985(3). See Calder v. Planned Community Living, Inc., 1995 WL 456400, 68 Fair Empl.Prac.Cas. (BNA) 1012 (S.D.N.Y.1995).

§ 17.25

1. See Rohnke v. National Broadcasting Co., Inc., 186 A.D.2d 436, 588 N.Y.S.2d 564 (1st Dep't 1992), leave to appeal denied, 81 N.Y.2d 702, 610 N.E.2d 389, 594 N.Y.S.2d 716 (1993); Buffolino v. Long Island Savings Bank, 126 A.D.2d 508, 510 N.Y.S.2d

The elements of defamation are:

(a) a false statement of fact;

(b) reduction of the plaintiff in the estimation of others;

(c) publication; and

(d) special (economic) damages.

Fact vs. Opinion. While pure opinions are protected from defamation claims, one who states the reasons for an employee's termination in the form of an opinion may still face an action if the language used implies facts about the employee's performance.[2] In *Kraus v. Brandstetter*,[3] the court held that a hospital newsletter stating that the medical staff board was unanimous in a vote of no confidence with regard to a nursing services officer was actionable in libel. The board created the impression that the conclusion was based upon facts that justified its opinion. These facts were not known to those reading the article, however, creating a "mixed opinion," thereby damaging the plaintiff's professional reputation.[4]

Defamation Per Se. At common law, derogatory statements in the context of one's profession, trade or business are considered libel *per se*.[5] Therefore, employees are often relieved of having to prove the fourth element of the prima facie case, special damages, because their defamation claims tend to involve disparaging statements about their profession, trade or business. The mere expression of dissatisfaction with an employee's performance will not be considered libelous *per se*.[6]

Publication. Any communication to a third party of the derogatory statement may constitute publication.[7] Some communications, however, are privileged.

---

628 (2d Dep't 1987)(reference letter that merely set forth dates of former employment, along with a statement that it was the policy of the company not to provide further information, was not defamatory; it specifically provided that the failure to comment on character was no reflection on the former employee); Kraus v. Brandstetter, 167 A.D.2d 445, 562 N.Y.S.2d 127 (2d Dep't 1990).

2. Afftrex, Ltd. v. General Electric Company, 161 A.D.2d 855, 555 N.Y.S.2d 903, 904–05 (3d Dep't 1990)(statement that the plaintiff was fired for being "an evil man" is actionable because it "implies a justifiable basis in facts unknown to the listener ... which may support [the] opinion and are detrimental.").

3. 167 A.D.2d 445, 562 N.Y.S.2d 127 (2d Dep't 1990).

4. *See also,* Kovacs v. Briarcliffe School, Inc., 208 A.D.2d 686, 617 N.Y.S.2d 804 (2d Dep't 1994)(memorandum distributed informing faculty of hiring of new department chairman and assuring improved quality of department was sufficient to defame terminated chairman, even though he was not mentioned).

5. *Restatement (Second) of Torts,* §§ 573 *et seq.*

6. *See* McDowell v. Dart, 201 A.D.2d 895, 607 N.Y.S.2d 755 (4th Dep't 1994); Noble v. Creative Technical Services, Inc., 126 A.D.2d 611, 511 N.Y.S.2d 51 (2d Dep't 1987).

7. Carney v. Memorial Hospital & Nursing Home, 64 N.Y.2d 770, 485 N.Y.S.2d 984, 475 N.E.2d 451 (1985); *see also* Pirre v. Printing Developments, Inc., 468 F.Supp. 1028 (S.D.N.Y.), aff'd 614 F.2d 1290 (2d Cir.1979).

Qualified Privilege. Employers have a qualified privilege, however, to disseminate derogatory information (*e.g.*, information concerning theft of company property) about employees to interested persons, which means persons who have a legitimate need to know the information.[8] In New York, the privilege is lost if the defendant acted with malice or recklessness, or exceeded the scope of the privilege (*e.g.*, overbroad dissemination).[9]

Punitive Damages. In New York State, defamation claims, where provable, may provide one of the most complete forms of relief, especially where plaintiff can be awarded punitive damages. Punitive damages are recoverable, however, only if the employer authorizes, participates in, consents to, or ratifies the conduct giving rise to the liability.[10]

Self-publication. Employees may be able to recover under the doctrine of self-publication. That doctrine is an exception to the rule that the originator of a defamatory statement is not liable for the defamed person's voluntary disclosure of that statement to a third party. The doctrine holds that the originator may be liable for the defamed person's own republication of the defamatory matter "if the defamed person's transmission of the communication to the third person was made ... without an awareness of the defamatory nature of the matter and if the circumstances indicated that the communication to a third party would be likely."[11]

Several federal courts in New York have adopted the doctrine of self publication, although New York's State courts have generally rejected it.[12] One district court in the Second Circuit has stressed that, under the

---

8. Turner v. Halliburton Co., 240 Kan. 1, 722 P.2d 1106 (Kan.1986) (qualified privilege concerning theft of company property for communications among managerial employees and for communications between past and prospective employers). *See* McDowell, *supra*; Pappas v. Air France, 652 F.Supp. 198 (E.D.N.Y.1986); *but see* Carter v. Willert Home Products Inc., 714 S.W.2d 506 (Mo.1986) (whether employee acted beyond scope of employment duties in stating allegedly defamatory material about co-employee to credit company presents question of fact for jury).

9. *See* Liberman v. Gelstein, 80 N.Y.2d 429, 590 N.Y.S.2d 857, 605 N.E.2d 344 (1992)(the qualified privilege is defeated if the plaintiff demonstrates that the defendant acted with constitutional or common law malice); Harris v. Hirsh, 161 A.D.2d 452, 555 N.Y.S.2d 735 (1st Dep't 1990), appeal after remand 196 A.D.2d 425, 601 N.Y.S.2d 275 (1993)(employer's knowing false accusation that employee used drugs provided evidence of malice to destroy the qualified privilege); Brown v. Albany Citizens Council on Alcoholism Inc. et al., 199 A.D.2d 904, 605 N.Y.S.2d 577 (3d Dep't 1993); Mock v. LaGuardia Hospital–Hip Hospital, Inc., 117 A.D.2d 721, 498 N.Y.S.2d 446 (2d Dep't 1986).

10. *See* Loughry v. Lincoln First Bank, 67 N.Y.2d 369, 494 N.E.2d 70, 502 N.Y.S.2d 965 (1986). In addition, statements made in the course of a judicial or quasi-judicial proceeding are privileged. *See* Pappas v. Air France, 652 F.Supp. 198 (E.D.N.Y.1986).

11. Restatement (Second) of Torts, § 577, comment m.; *see* Lewis v. Equitable Assurance Society, 389 N.W.2d 876, 886 (Minn.1986).

12. *E.g.,* Elmore v. Shell Oil Co., 733 F.Supp 544 (S.D.N.Y.1988); *contra,* Wieder v. Chemical Bank, 202 A.D.2d 168, 608 N.Y.S.2d 195 (1st Dep't 1994). *But see* Wright v. Guarinello, 165 Misc.2d 720, 635 N.Y.S.2d 995 (Sup.Ct., Kings County, 1995).

doctrine, plaintiffs must show a foreseeable compulsion to disclose.[13]

Some New York federal courts have refused to rule on or to accept the doctrine absent recognition of it by New York State's courts.[14]

Pleading with Particularity. The particularity requirement set forth in CPLR 3016(a) mandates that, when pleading a defamation cause of action, the allegedly defamatory words must be quoted verbatim.

Library References:

West's Key No. Digests, Libel and Slander ⚖=1–33.

§ 17.26 Causes of Action—Tort—False Imprisonment; Malicious Prosecution

False Imprisonment. Unreasonable detention might arise in connection with sexual harassment, an internal investigation, or a confrontational termination. To establish a false imprisonment claim, plaintiff must show that:

(a) defendant intended to confine plaintiff;

(b) plaintiff was conscious of the confinement;

(c) plaintiff did not consent to the confinement; and

(d) the confinement was not otherwise privileged.[1]

Imprisonment, unconsented to, may nevertheless be lawful if it is privileged, such as involuntary commitment to a mental institution under Article 9 of the Mental Hygiene Law.[2]

Defenses to false imprisonment may include a legal justification, such as reasonable suspicion that the employee is involved in a loss under investigation. If the detention was caused by an agent or employee

---

13. *See* J. Crew Group, Inc. v. Griffin, 1990 WL 193918 (S.D.N.Y.1990).

14. *E.g.*, Mendoza v. SSC & B Lintas, 799 F.Supp. 1502 (S.D.N.Y.1992) (the court discussed the doctrine but did not rule on it because the tort is not recognized in New York); Metchick v. Bidermann Industries Corp., 1993 WL 106139, 8 IER 1204 (S.D.N.Y.1993) (the court concluded that the doctrine would be rejected in New York); McNabb v. MacAndrews & Forbes, 1991 WL 284104 (S.D.N.Y.1991), aff'd without opinion 972 F.2d 1328 (2d Cir.1992) (declined to predict that the New York Court of Appeals will recognize the doctrine of self-publication).

§ 17.26

1. *See* Broughton v. State, 37 N.Y.2d 451, 456, 373 N.Y.S.2d 87, 93, 335 N.E.2d 310, 314, cert. denied 423 U.S. 929, 96 S.Ct. 277, 46 L.Ed.2d 257 (1975); Parvi v. Kingston, 41 N.Y.2d 553, 555, 394 N.Y.S.2d 161, 163, 362 N.E.2d 960 (1977); Leahy v. Federal Express Corp., 609 F.Supp. 668, 672 (E.D.N.Y.1985) (employee, who alleged he was prevented from leaving the room during a security investigation made out *prima facie* case). *See also,* Kaminski v. United Parcel Service, 120 A.D.2d 409, 501 N.Y.S.2d 871 (1st Dep't 1986)(*see* Intentional Infliction of Emotional Distress, *infra* at § 17.28).

2. Rubenstein v. Benedictine Hospital, 790 F.Supp. 396, 409 (N.D.N.Y.1992).

acting outside the scope of employment, the employer may defend itself by claiming it is not vicariously liable.

False Arrest and Malicious Prosecution. Employers occasionally attempt to buttress their grounds for discharging employees based on alleged criminal conduct by pressing charges or having the employee arrested. The employee may make a false arrest claim if the employer knowingly, or with malicious intent, makes charges without legal justification that result in an arrest, followed by the dismissal of the charges.

The elements of malicious prosecution are:

(a) commencement or continuation of a criminal proceeding by defendant;

(b) termination of proceeding in favor of plaintiff;

(c) absence of probable cause for the criminal proceeding; and

(d) actual malice.[3]

Library References:

West's Key No. Digests, False Imprisonment ⇐1–15(3); Malicious Prosecution ⇐1–14.

§ 17.27 Causes of Action—Tort—Fraud, Negligent Misrepresentation and Fraudulent Inducement

The elements of proof necessary to prove fraud are:

(a) material misrepresentation of an existing fact;

(b) falsity;

(c) scienter;

(d) deception; and

(e) injury.[1]

When pleading fraud and misrepresentation, the particularity requirement set forth in CPLR 3016(b) means that the circumstances must be stated in detail. At trial, the plaintiff has the burden of proving fraud by clear and convincing evidence, not mere preponderance of the evidence.[2]

Fraud and Contract Claims. An action for fraudulent misrepresentation, independently pleaded, can constitute a cause of action that

---

3. *See* Witcher v. Children's Television Workshop, 187 A.D.2d 292, 589 N.Y.S.2d 454 (1st Dep't 1992).

§ 17.27

1. *See* Channel Master Corp. v. Aluminium Limited Sales, Inc., 4 N.Y.2d 403, 406–07, 176 N.Y.S.2d 259, 262, 151 N.E.2d 833, 835 (1958); Alanthus Corporation v. Travelers Insurance Company, 92 A.D.2d 830, 460 N.Y.S.2d 549 (1st Dep't 1983). *See* Stewart v. Jackson Nash, 976 F.2d 86 (2d Cir.1992).

2. Abrahami v. Lee, 224 A.D.2d 231, 638 N.Y.S.2d 11 (1st Dep't 1996).

may be pleaded in addition, or as an alternative, to an action for breach of contract.[3]

"Absent a present intent to deceive, a statement of future intentions, promises or expectations is not actionable on the grounds of fraud."[4]

Scienter. Scienter includes not only knowing misrepresentations, but also "reckless indifference to error, a pretense of knowledge, and the misrepresentation of a material fact susceptible of accurate knowledge, but stated as true on personal knowledge of the representer."[5]

Negligent Misrepresentation. A cause of action for *negligent* misrepresentation may lie, "[w]hen the parties' relationship suggests a closer degree of trust and reliance than that of ordinary buyer and seller."[6]

Fraudulent Inducement. The Third and Fourth Departments have sustained claims of fraudulent inducement to contract in the employment context. In *Navaretta v. Group Health, Inc.*,[7] the plaintiff was induced to accept a position after being assured that she would not have to pass post-training exams. Although she resigned, the court held that she stated a claim of fraudulent misrepresentation, since the employer did not deny that she would have been fired.[8] Applying New York law in a diversity case, the Second Circuit upheld a fraud claim in *Stewart v. Jackson & Nash*,[9] where an associate left a law firm to join the defendant firm in reliance on allegedly false representations about

---

3. *See* North Shore Bottling Co., Inc. v. Schmidt & Sons, Inc., 22 N.Y.2d 171, 179, 292 N.Y.S.2d 86, 92, 239 N.E.2d 189, 193 (1968); Shaitelman v. Phoenix Mutual Life Ins., Co., 517 F.Supp. 21,22 (S.D.N.Y.1980); DuSesoi v. United Refining Co., 540 F.Supp. 1260 (W.D.Pa.1982); Brudnicki v. General Electric Co., 535 F.Supp. 84 (N.D.Ill.1982). *But see* Grant v. DCA Food Industries, Inc., 124 A.D.2d 909, 508 N.Y.S.2d 327 (3d Dep't 1986) (plaintiff employee's fraud claim dismissed because a cause of action for fraud does not arise when "the only fraud charged relates to a breach of contract"); Dalton v. Union Bank of Switzerland, 134 A.D.2d 174, 520 N.Y.S.2d 764, 767 (1st Dep't 1987) (same).

4. Adams v. Clark, 239 N.Y. 403, 146 N.E. 642 (1925); Brown v. Lockwood, 76 A.D.2d 721, 731–732, 432 N.Y.S.2d 186, 194 (2d Dep't 1980).

5. Morse v. Swank, Inc., 459 F.Supp. 660, 667 (S.D.N.Y.1978); PVM Oil Futures, Inc. v. Banque Paribas, 161 A.D.2d 220, 554 N.Y.S.2d 606 (1st Dep't 1990); Coolite Corp. v. American Cyanamid Co., 52 A.D.2d 486, 384 N.Y.S.2d 808, 811 (1st Dep't 1976).

6. Coolite Corp., *supra*, 52 A.D.2d at 488, 384 N.Y.S.2d at 811; Morse, *supra*, 459 F.Supp. at 667 "... [G]enerally, a negligent statement may be the basis for recovery of damages, where there is carelessness in imparting words upon which others were expected to rely and upon which they did act or failed to act to their damage ..., but such information is not actionable unless expressed directly, with knowledge or notice that it will be acted upon, to one to whom the author is bound by some relation of duty, arising out of contract or otherwise, to act with care if he acts at all"; White v. Guarente, 43 N.Y.2d 356, 362–363, 401 N.Y.S.2d 474, 478, 372 N.E.2d 315, 319 (1977) (accountant for limited partnership held liable to limited partners for negligent performance of auditing and tax return services).

7. 191 A.D.2d 953, 595 N.Y.S.2d 839 (3d Dep't 1993).

8. *See* Steigerwald v. Dean Witter Reynolds, Inc., 107 A.D.2d 1026, 486 N.Y.S.2d 516 (4th Dep't 1985).

9. 976 F.2d 86 (2d Cir.1992).

the firm's clients and practice. The First Department has not yet recognized this cause of action in an employment context.[10]

The essential elements of a cause of action for fraudulent inducement or misrepresentation in the making of a contract are:

(a) false representation of a material fact;

(b) reliance on that fact by the plaintiff to the detriment of the plaintiff.[11]

There has been a split of authority on whether a claim for fraud relating to a contract may be interposed in a complaint together with a claim for breach of contract—specifically whether the addition of an allegation that the defendant never intended to perform the promises made in the contract would sustain a fraud claim. The Court of Appeals has held, however, that a "false statement of intention is sufficient to support an action for fraud, even where that statement relates to an agreement between the parties."[12]

Any fact likely to influence the decision-making process is material.[13] Actual detrimental reliance on the part of the plaintiff must be shown, *i.e.*, the misrepresentation must be the inducement for the injured party to have entered into the agreement.[14]

Punitive damages are available only if the plaintiff can demonstrate egregious tortious conduct, *and* a pattern of similar conduct directed at the public generally.[15] This standard may be met also where a "very high threshold of moral culpability is satisfied."[16]

Library References:

West's Key No. Digests, Fraud ⟺1–30.

§ 17.28 Causes of Action—Tort—Intentional Infliction of Emotional Distress

"One who by extreme and outrageous conduct intentionally or recklessly causes severe emotional distress to another is subject to liability for such emotional distress.... Liability has been found only

---

10. *See* Dalton v. Union Bank of Switzerland, 134 A.D.2d 174, 520 N.Y.S.2d 764 (1st Dep't 1987); *see also* Silver v. Mohasco Corp., 94 A.D.2d 820, 462 N.Y.S.2d 917 (3d Dep't 1983), affirmed 62 N.Y.2d 741, 476 N.Y.S.2d 822, 465 N.E.2d 361 (1984); Sivel v. Readers Digest, Inc., 677 F.Supp. 183 (S.D.N.Y.1988).

11. Goodridge v. Harvey Group, Inc., 778 F.Supp. 115 (S.D.N.Y.1991); *See generally* Sabo v. Delman, 3 N.Y.2d 155, 143 N.E.2d 906, 164 N.Y.S.2d 714 (1957).

12. Graubard Mollen Dannett & Horowitz v. Moskovitz, 86 N.Y.2d 112, 629 N.Y.S.2d 1009, 653 N.E.2d 1179 (1995).

13. *See* Ettman v. Equitable Life Assurance Society, 6 A.D.2d 697, 174 N.Y.S.2d 553 (2d Dep't 1958), aff'd 5 N.Y.2d 1005, 158 N.E.2d 124, 185 N.Y.S.2d 262 (1959); Seyfried v. Greenspan, 92 A.D.2d 563, 459 N.Y.S.2d 316 (2d Dep't 1983).

14. Leasco Corp. v. Taussig, 473 F.2d 777 (2d Cir.1972).

15. Rocanova v. Equitable Life Assurance Soc. of U.S., 83 N.Y.2d 603, 612 N.Y.S.2d 339, 634 N.E.2d 940 (1994).

16. Giblin v. Murphy, 73 N.Y.2d 769, 536 N.Y.S.2d 54, 532 N.E.2d 1282 (1988).

where the conduct has been so outrageous in character, and so extreme in degree, as to go beyond all possible bounds of decency, and to be regarded as atrocious, and utterly intolerable in a civilized community."[1]

In New York, discharged employees who claim intentional infliction of emotional distress have been hampered by the fear that such claims will be substituted for wrongful discharge actions. For example, in *Murphy v. American Home Products Corp.*,[2] the Court of Appeals stated that a plaintiff should not be allowed to "subvert the traditional at-will contract rule by casting his cause of action in terms of a tort of intentional infliction of emotional distress." Nevertheless, the lower courts have sustained such causes of action in the termination of at-will employees. In *Kaminski v. United Parcel Service*,[3] the First Department held that the plaintiff stated a claim for intentional infliction of emotional distress based on defendant's coercion in obtaining plaintiff's resignation, his relinquishment of pension, health, and hospital benefits, and his statements admitting that he stole from the company. The defendant's agents held plaintiff in a room for three hours, threatening him with criminal prosecution and a prison term, accompanied by loud, aggressive, profane and obscene language and gestures.[4]

Sexual Harassment Claims. In both *Collins v. Willcox, Inc.*,[5] and *O'Reilly v. Executone of Albany, Inc.*,[6] the courts sustained claims for intentional infliction of emotional distress from sexual harassment that forced the plaintiffs to resign.

By contrast, other courts have declined to allow such claims, even when faced with allegations of egregious conduct.

§ 17.28

1. *Restatement (Second) of Torts*, § 46(1) and Comment d; Fischer v. Maloney, 43 N.Y.2d 553, 557, 402 N.Y.S.2d 991, 992, 373 N.E.2d 1215, 1217 (1978); Collins v. Willcox Inc., 158 Misc.2d 54, 600 N.Y.S.2d 884 (1992).

2. 58 N.Y.2d 293, 303, 461 N.Y.S.2d 232, 236, 448 N.E.2d 86 (1983).

3. 120 A.D.2d 409, 501 N.Y.S.2d 871 (1st Dep't 1986).

4. *E.g.*, Huzar v. The State of New York, the State of New York Department of Corrections and the Great Meadow Correctional Facility, 156 Misc.2d 370, 590 N.Y.S.2d 1000 (1992) (threatening correction officer and his family that officer would be dismissed unless stress related disability claim was dropped was not actionable); Navarro v. Federal Paper Board Company Inc., 185 A.D.2d 590, 586 N.Y.S.2d 381 (3d Dep't 1992) (union official being arrested in front of fellow workers not actionable); Buffolino v. Long Island Savings Bank, 126 A.D.2d 508, 510 N.Y.S.2d 628 (2d Dep't 1987) (requiring employee to submit to polygraph tests, following bank's discovery of sizable cash shortage at branch in which plaintiff worked, held not outrageous); Lapidus v. New York City Chapter of the New York State Association for Retarded Children, Inc., 118 A.D.2d 122, 504 N.Y.S.2d at 629 (1st Dep't 1986) (humiliation of being "thrown out in the middle of a working day and told not to go back to [his] office" not actionable); Seneca Knitting Mills Corp. v. Wilkes, 120 A.D.2d 955, 502 N.Y.S.2d 844 (4th Dep't 1986) (employee's allegation that he was escorted out of company does not rise to necessary level of outrageous conduct); Bradley v. Consolidated Edison of New York, Inc., 657 F.Supp. 197 (S.D.N.Y. 1987) (negative evaluations, harassment, job assignments and disparaging statements insufficient to sustain claim for intentional infliction of emotional distress).

5. 158 Misc.2d 54, 600 N.Y.S.2d 884 (Sup.Ct., N.Y. County, 1992).

6. 121 A.D.2d 772, 503 N.Y.S.2d 185 (3d Dep't 1986).

Ch. 17 INTERFERENCE WITH BUSINESS RELATIONS § 17.29

Library References:

West's Key No. Digests, Damages ⚖48–56.20.

§ 17.29 Causes of Action—Tort—Interference With Business Relations

Disparagement or Injurious Falsehood. This tort arises from interference with an advantageous business relation by means of publishing a matter derogatory to plaintiff's title to his property, the quality of the property, or plaintiff's business in general. It is similar to defamation, but defamation reflects upon the plaintiff's personal conduct or character, whereas disparagement reflects upon the quality or nature of plaintiff's business. The plaintiff must prove that the published statement was false and that special damages were sustained resulting from the loss of a present or prospective advantage.[1]

Intentional Interference with Contractual Relations. The elements are:

(a) the existence of a valid contract;

(b) defendant's knowledge of that contract;

(c) defendant's intentional and improper procuring of the breach of that contract; and

(d) damages.[2]

Factors to be considered in determining whether the interference was "improper" include: the nature of the conduct of the interferer, the interests of the party interfered with, the relationship between the parties, the motive and interests sought to be advanced by the one who interferes, the social interests in protecting the freedom of action of that person as well as the contractual interests of the party interfered with, and the proximity or remoteness to the interference of the alleged wrongful conduct.[3]

Usually, an employer's breach of his contract with an employee is not a basis for this tort.[4] Nonetheless, a parent company or individual

---

§ 17.29

1. L.W.C. Agency, Inc. v. St. Paul Fire and Marine, 125 A.D.2d 371, 509 N.Y.S.2d 97 (2d Dep't 1986); SRW Associates v. Bellport Beach Property Owners, 129 A.D.2d 328, 517 N.Y.S.2d 741 (2d Dep't 1987).

2. *See Restatement (Second) Torts*, § 766; Guard–Life Corp. v. S. Parker Hardware Mfg. Corp., 50 N.Y.2d 183, 428 N.Y.S.2d 628, 406 N.E.2d 445 (1980); Wegman, *supra*, 50 A.D.2d at 114, 376 N.Y.S.2d at 736; Reale v. IBM, 34 A.D.2d 936, 311 N.Y.S.2d 767 (1st Dep't 1970), aff'd 28 N.Y.2d 912, 322 N.Y.S.2d 735, 271 N.E.2d 565 (1971); *Prosser on Torts*, 4th Edition, § 129; Savage v. Pacific Gas and Electric Company, 21 Cal.App.4th 434, 26 Cal. Rptr.2d 305 (1993); Manor Investment Co., Inc. v. F.W. Woolworth, Inc., 159 Cal. App.3d 586, 206 Cal.Rptr. 37 (1984).

3. Guard-Life Corp., *supra*, 50 N.Y.2d at 189–90, 428 N.Y.S.2d at 631–32; Rossi v. Kelly, 96 A.D.2d 451, 465 N.Y.S.2d 1, 4–5 (1st Dep't 1983); *see also* Cappiello v. Ragen Precision Industries Inc., 192 N.J.Super. 523, 471 A.2d 432 (1984).

4. WFB Telecommunications, Inc. v. NYNEX Corporation, 188 A.D.2d 257, 590 N.Y.S.2d 460 (1st Dep't 1992); Bradford v. Weber, 138 A.D.2d 860, 525 N.Y.S.2d 968

defendants may be liable for interference.[5]

The New York Court of Appeals has indicated that employees-at-will cannot obtain relief under the intentional interference with contractual relations theory. In *Ingle v. Glamore Motor Sales, Inc.*,[6] the court dismissed an action brought by an employee who was terminated by the close corporation in which he was a minority shareholder. The court held that he could not "evade the employment-at-will rule" by claiming tortious interference with his employment. Similarly, in *Kaminski v. United Parcel Service*,[7] the First Department held that an employee-at-will could not maintain an action for tortious interference with contract against the individual defendants, because the termination of the plaintiff's employment did not constitute a breach.[8] Prior to *Ingle*,[9] however, one appellate court in New York held that improper interference with an employment contract terminable at will may be actionable.[10] At least two federal courts have held that employment-at-will is not a bar to a tortious interference claim.[11]

Intentional Interference with Prospective Advantage. This is similar to intentional interference with contractual obligations, except that the contract need not have been entered into yet. Although the nature of the interference is different from intentional interference with contractual relations, it picks up where that tort leaves off. The plaintiff must show that the defendant intended to interfere with his business, that the action was unjustifiable and the interference had the intended result.[12]

Courts have held that "[t]he essence of this tort is interference by a third party which is fraudulent, deceitful or illegal ... [and] the unlawful means which the party has employed must be alleged."[13] Failure to plead special damages will not defeat this cause of action; "interests of justice" have been the basis for granting leave to amend pleadings.[14]

(3d Dep't 1988); Manley v. Pandick Press, Inc., 72 A.D.2d 452, 424 N.Y.S.2d 902 (1st Dep't 1980); Greyhound Corp. v. Commercial Casualty Insurance Co., 259 App.Div. 317, 19 N.Y.S.2d 239 (1st Dep't 1940); Kay v. Sussel, 22 Misc.2d 627, 199 N.Y.S.2d 180, 181 (Sup.Ct., N.Y. County, 1960).

5. Agugliaro v. Brooks Brothers, Inc., 802 F.Supp. 956 (S.D.N.Y.1992).

6. 73 N.Y.2d 183, 538 N.Y.S.2d 771, 535 N.E.2d 1311 (1989).

7. 120 A.D.2d 409, 501 N.Y.S.2d 871 (1st Dep't 1986).

8. *See also,* Graham v. Dim–Rosy U.S.A. Corp., 128 A.D.2d 417, 512 N.Y.S.2d 700 (1st Dep't 1987).

9. Ingle, *supra* note 6.

10. Mansour v. Abrams, 120 A.D.2d 933, 502 N.Y.S.2d 877 (4th Dep't 1986).

11. Agugliaro v. Brooks Brothers, Inc., 802 F.Supp. 956, 963 (S.D.N.Y.1992); Calder v. Planned Community Living, Inc., 1995 WL 456400, 68 FEP Cas. (BNA) 1012, 1019 (S.D.N.Y.1995).

12. *See* Buckaloo v. Johnson, 14 Cal.3d 815, 122 Cal.Rptr. 745, 537 P.2d 865 (1975) (distinguishing intentional interference with contractual relations from intentional interference with prospective advantage).

13. Marino Ind. Corp. v. Kahn Lumber, 70 A.D.2d 629, 416 N.Y.S.2d 642 (2d Dep't 1979) (mem.); *see* Prosser on Torts, Fourth Edition, p. 954.

14. *See, e.g.,* Sommer v. Kaufman, 59 A.D.2d 843, 399 N.Y.S.2d 7 (1st Dep't 1977).

This tort has been applied to an at-will employment relationship[15] despite the fact that the Court of Appeals has indicated that employees-at-will cannot obtain relief under the intentional interference with contractual relations theory.[16]

Interference with a Prospective Business Relationship. This cause of action arises when a contract would have been entered into had it not been for the malicious conduct of a third person.[17]

Employer's Action Against Employee. Although an employee may compete with a former employer, an employee may be subject to claims of interfering with the employer's business relationships as a result of competing with the employer (1) while the employee is still employed, or (2) using secret information, or (3) in violation of a covenant not to compete.[18]

Library References:
West's Key No. Digests, Torts ⇐10(1)–10(5).

§ 17.30 Causes of Action—Tort—Negligence

Negligent Performance Appraisal; Maintenance of Records. Negligence entails a legal duty to act reasonably. Outside of New York State, courts have imposed such a duty on employers with respect to performance appraisals.[1] These duties of care have not been recognized in New York.

Negligent Retention of Unfit Supervisor. This arises where an employee injures a co-worker or third party and the employer is not automatically, or vicariously, liable because the employee's tort, typically a violent one, occurred outside the scope of employment. The employer may nevertheless be held liable for failing to take reasonable care in hiring or retaining the employee if a background check would have revealed a propensity for violence or other misconduct. In *Loughry v. Lincoln First Bank, N.A.*,[2] the Court of Appeals stated that punitive damages were available against a corporation for the intentional wrongdoing of its employees where "management has authorized, participated

---

15. Herlihy v. Metropolitan Museum of Art, 214 A.D.2d 250, 633 N.Y.S.2d 106 (1st Dep't 1995)(at-will museum officer stated a claim against subordinates who allegedly defamed her, causing her loss of employment).

16. Ingle v. Glamore Motor Sales, Inc.,73 N.Y.2d 183, 538 N.Y.S.2d 771, 535 N.E.2d 1311 (1989).

17. *See* A.S. Rampell, Inc. v. Hyster Co., 3 N.Y.2d 369, 165 N.Y.S.2d 475, 144 N.E.2d 371 (1957).

18. *See generally*, N.Y.Jur., Employment Relations § 214.

§ 17.30

1. *See* Chamberlain v. Bissell, Inc., 547 F.Supp. 1067 (W.D.Mich.1982) (employer negligent in failing to give long-term employee honest appraisals and warning of possible termination based on poor performance); regarding the maintenance of records, *see* Bulkin v. Western Kraft East, Inc., 422 F.Supp. 437 (E.D.Pa.1976) (private employer provided inaccurate employment reference to outsider due to negligent maintenance of records).

2. 67 N.Y.2d 369, 502 N.Y.S.2d 965, 494 N.E.2d 70 (1986).

in, consented to or ratified the conduct giving rise to such damages, or deliberately retained the unfit servant."[3] In a case involving an allegation that a hospital improperly supervised an alcoholic surgeon, the court stated: "A question of fact exists as to whether a breach of its duty to supervise, if there was such a breach, was the proximate cause of Plaintiff's injury."[4] Under this theory, employees harmed by their unfit supervisors may have an actionable claim.[5]

Library References:

West's Key No. Digests, Negligence ⚖1-15.

§ 17.31 Causes of Action—Tort—*Prima Facie* Tort

This tort arises when there is an infliction of intentional harm resulting in damages, without excuse or justification, by an act or series of acts that would otherwise be lawful. The elements that the plaintiff must prove are:

(a) intentional infliction of harm;

(b) causing special damages;

(c) without excuse or justification;

(d) by an act or series of acts that would otherwise be lawful.[1]

The plaintiff must allege and prove malice and special damages.[2] Liability depends on the causing of actual damages, which may not be presumed from the intention or act of the tortfeasor.[3]

In *Murphy v. American Home Products Corp.*,[4] the Court of Appeals stated that "this cause of action cannot be allowed in circumvention of the unavailability of a tort claim for wrongful discharge or the contract rule against liability for discharge of an at-will employee." Nevertheless,

---

3. 67 N.Y.2d at 378, 502 N.Y.S.2d at 969.

4. Bush v. St. Clare's Hospital, 82 N.Y.2d 738, 602 N.Y.S.2d 324, 621 N.E.2d 691 (1993), rev'g 192 A.D.2d 772, 596 N.Y.S.2d 203 (3d Dep't 1993).

5. *See* Calder v. Planned Community Living, Inc., 68 FEP Cs. (BNA) 1012, 1019, 1995 WL 456400 (S.D.N.Y.1995)(motion to dismiss denied where plaintiff alleged that employer knew or should have known that the supervisor was permitting illegal conduct and was grossly negligent in failing to adequately supervise).

§ 17.31

1. *See* Curiano v. Suozzi, 63 N.Y.2d 113, 117, 480 N.Y.S.2d 466, 469, 469 N.E.2d 1324, 1326 (1984); Riddell Sports, Inc. v. Brooks, 872 F.Supp. 73 (S.D.N.Y.1995).

2. Dalton v. Union Bank of Switzerland, 134 A.D.2d 174, 520 N.Y.S.2d 764 (1st Dep't 1987).

3. ATI, Inc. v. Ruder & Finn, 42 N.Y.2d 454, 398 N.Y.S.2d 864, 368 N.E.2d 1230 (1977); Mahoney v. Temporary Commission of Investigation of the State of New York, 165 A.D.2d 233, 565 N.Y.S.2d 870 (3d Dep't 1991); McCullough v. Certain Teed Prod. Corp., 70 A.D.2d 771, 417 N.Y.S.2d 353 (4th Dep't 1979); Wegman v. Dairylea Co-op., Inc., 50 A.D.2d 108, 376 N.Y.S.2d 728 (4th Dep't 1975), app. dism'd 38 N.Y.2d 918, 382 N.Y.S.2d 979, 346 N.E.2d 817 (1976); O'Keefe v. Niagara Mohawk Power Corp., 714 F.Supp. 622 (N.D.N.Y.1989); Shaitelman v. Phoenix Mutual Life Ins. Co., 517 F.Supp. 21 (S.D.N.Y.1980).

4. 58 N.Y.2d 293, 304, 461 N.Y.S.2d 232, 237, 448 N.E.2d 86, 91 (1983).

a cause of action for *prima facie* tort may still be viable in New York if the employer's conduct goes far beyond that which often accompanies a discharge (*e.g.*, a pattern of intentional harassment or an outrageously humiliating manner of discharge). In *Kostaras v. United Airlines Inc.*,[5] the court sustained such a claim but without setting forth legal rational.

Library References:

West's Key No. Digests, Torts ⚖1, 10(1)–10(5).

§ 17.32 Causes of Action—Tort—Wrongful Discharge

The New York State Courts have flatly rejected the tort of wrongful or abusive discharge.[1] It has been held that "[a]n individual employed without express contractual guarantees of job security may be discharged for no reason or for any reason not specifically proscribed by constitutional or statutory law."[2] The Court of Appeals has been quick to state that any changes in this area are to be made by the Legislature.[3]

The statutory exceptions that have been created, including the so-called Whistleblower Protection Statute (section 740 of the Labor Law), have seldom been used to enforce the rights of employees. Of the more than twenty four cases raising the issue of "whistleblower protection" under Section 740 that have been brought since its passage in 1984, only a few have been sustained by the courts.[4]

Public Policy. At least one federal court in New York has recognized a public policy exception where the employee was fired for investigating and reporting wrongful or unlawful acts, which investigation

---

5. 650 F.Supp. 576 (S.D.N.Y.1986).

§ 17.32

1. *See* Wieder v. Skala, 80 N.Y.2d 628, 609 N.E.2d 105, 593 N.Y.S.2d 752 (1992); Sabetay v. Sterling Drug, Inc., 69 N.Y.2d 329, 514 N.Y.S.2d 209, 506 N.E.2d 919 (1987); Murphy v. American Home Products Corp., 58 N.Y.2d 293, 295, 461 N.Y.S.2d 232, 233, 448 N.E.2d 86, 87 (1983) ("This Court has not and does not now recognize a cause of action in tort for abusive or wrongful discharge of an employee; such recognition must await action of the Legislature").

2. O'Donnell v. NPS Corp., 133 A.D.2d 73, 518 N.Y.S.2d 418 (2d Dep't 1987). *See also,* O'Reilly v. Citibank, 198 A.D.2d 270, 603 N.Y.S.2d 572 (2d Dep't 1993).

3. Wieder, *supra* note 1, 80 N.Y.2d at 633, 593 N.Y.S.2d at 757; Sabetay, 69 N.Y.2d at 336, 514 N.Y.S.2d at 213; Murphy, *supra* note 1, 58 N.Y.2d at 295, 461 N.Y.S.2d at 235.

4. *See* Kraus v. New Rochelle Hospital Medical Center, 216 A.D.2d 360, 628 N.Y.S.2d 360, leave to app. denied, 86 N.Y.2d 885, 635 N.Y.S.2d 950, 659 N.E.2d 773 (1995)(retaliatory dismissal of nurse who complained of unsafe and illegal practices); Scaduto v. Restaurant Associates Industries, Inc., 180 A.D.2d 458, 579 N.Y.S.2d 381 (1st Dep't 1992) (chef threatened to disclose alleged health violations at Mamma Leone's); Majer v. MTA, 1990 WL 212928, 6 IER Cases (BNA) 78 (S.D.N.Y.1990) (employee who complained of kickbacks and purchases of unsafe railroad equipment). *See also,* Keleher v. American Airlines, Inc., 132 A.D.2d 949, 518 N.Y.S.2d 276 (4th Dep't 1987), leave to app. denied, 70 N.Y.2d 614, 519 N.E.2d 622, 524 N.Y.S.2d 676 (1988) (no cause of action for wrongful discharge will lie for at-will employee who failed to exhaust the employer's grievance procedure).

impliedly was part of the employee's contract.[5] New York State courts have refused to recognize a public policy exception to employment-at-will, even when the employee was fired for refusing to commit a wrongful or unlawful act.[6]

Library References:

West's Key No. Digests, Master and Servant ⚖=34–46.

§ 17.33 Causes of Action—Contract

General Principles. Contractual promises may be express, implied-in-fact, or implied-in-law. In an express promise, the terms are stated by the parties; in an implied promise, the terms are not stated. The term "implied" has been used to refer to two types of promises: implied-in-fact and implied-in-law. The New York Court of Appeals recognized this distinction in *Miller v. Schloss*.[1]

In the employment context, the New York State courts have applied these traditional principles narrowly, especially in connection with the employment-at-will doctrine. The courts recognize that an express promise may limit the presumption of employment-at-will in certain circumstances. With the exception of *Wieder v. Skala*,[2] however, the courts have not recognized an implied-in-fact promise, or an implied-in-law covenant of good faith and fair dealing, as limiting the presumption of employment-at-will. In *Wieder*, the plaintiff brought an action against his employer/law firm for breach of contract and abusive discharge. The court held that, because of the plaintiff's status as an attorney, there was an implied covenant of good faith that he would not be fired for acting in a manner consistent with the precepts of the Code of Professional Responsibility. In rejecting the claim of abusive discharge, the court may have limited its holding to associates in law firms only: "It is in this distinctive relationship between a law firm and a lawyer hired as an associate that plaintiff finds the implied-in-law obligation on which he founds his claims."[3] Federal courts have been more liberal in their

---

5. *See* Calder v. Planned Community Living, Inc., 1995 WL 456400, 68 FEP Cas. (BNA) 1012 (S.D.N.Y.1995) (Schwartz,J.)(court denied motion to dismiss plaintiff's breach of contract claim, holding that public policy prohibits retaliatory discharge of whistleblower who had an affirmative duty to report abuse of mental patients); *see* Contract Causes of Action, §§ 17.33, *supra, et seq.*

6. *See* Murphy v. American Home Products, 58 N.Y.2d 293, 461 N.Y.S.2d 232, 448 N.E.2d 86 (1983); *see* Sabetay v. Sterling Drug, Inc., 69 N.Y.2d 329, 514 N.Y.S.2d 209, 506 N.E.2d 919 (1987).

§ 17.33

1. 218 N.Y. 400, 113 N.E. 337 (1916).

2. 80 N.Y.2d 628, 593 N.Y.S.2d 752, 609 N.E.2d 105 (1992).

3. 80 N.Y.2d at 635, 593 N.Y.S.2d at 755, 609 N.E.2d at 108. *See, e.g.*, Mulder v. Donaldson, Lufkin & Jenrette, 208 A.D.2d 301, 623 N.Y.S.2d 560 (1st Dep't 1995)(Wieder doctrine does not extend to non-attorney who reported a money-laundering scheme to his superior). *Compare* Weiner v. McGraw-Hill, 57 N.Y.2d 458, 443 N.E.2d 441, 457 N.Y.S.2d 193 (1982), with Sabetay v. Sterling Drug, Inc., 69 N.Y.2d 329, 506 N.E.2d 919, 514 N.Y.S.2d 209

interpretation of state contract law.[4]

It is important that the employee's attorney look for a contractual basis for job security (*i.e.*, to overcome the employment-at-will doctrine), and for any contractual entitlements that may be available upon termination. Considering that New York courts are reluctant to find meaningful contractual limits on employment-at-will, the most that employees can often seek is a good package on the way out the door; this includes severance pay, medical benefits (*e.g.*, COBRA), pension benefits, and other fringes, plus outplacement services. A contractual claim to severance pay may arise not only under a formal written policy, but also under an informal but consistent policy or practice, on which the employee relied (though the contractual claim might be preempted by ERISA if more than a lump sum payment is involved).[5]

Library References:

West's Key No. Digests, Master and Servant ⇒34–46.

§ 17.34 Causes of Action—Contract—Express Promises

Written Contracts. In *Weiner v. McGraw-Hill, Inc.*,[1] the Court of Appeals held that an employer's express promise not to terminate employment can be enforceable under certain circumstances and can limit the presumption of employment-at-will. The court found four factors that, taken together, constituted sufficient evidence of a contract and a breach:

(a) the defendant induced the plaintiff to leave his prior employment with the assurance that he would not be discharged without cause;

(b) the defendant's assurance appeared in the employment application;

(c) the plaintiff rejected other employment offers in reliance on the defendant's assurance; and

(d) the defendant instructed supervisors to comply strictly with the corporate manual in recommending dismissal of subordinates because employees could be discharged only for cause.

Subsequently, the courts had to determine whether the *Weiner* holding required an employee to present all four factors delineated there,

---

(1987), and Murphy v. American Home Products Corp., 58 N.Y.2d 293, 461 N.Y.S.2d 232, 448 N.E.2d 86 (1983).

4. *See, e.g.*, the Wakefield v. Northern Telecom cases at 769 F.2d 109 (2d Cir.1985) and 813 F.2d 535 (2d Cir.1987), discussed in § 17.35, *infra*.

5. Morschauser v. American News Company, 6 A.D.2d 1028, 178 N.Y.S.2d 279 (1st Dep't 1958)(cause of action arises if employer engaged in a practice of making severance payments and employees relied on this practice in accepting or continuing their employment). *See also*, Smith v. New York State Electric and Gas Corp., 155 A.D.2d 850, 548 N.Y.S.2d 117 (3d Dep't 1989).

§ 17.34

1. 57 N.Y.2d 458, 457 N.Y.S.2d 193, 443 N.E.2d 441 (1982).

§ 17.34 EMPLOYMENT LAW Ch. 17

or whether an employee could succeed in limiting the presumption of employment-at-will based upon a general "totality of the circumstances" standard.

The federal courts have been generally more liberal than the state courts. A unanimous Court of Appeals for the Second Circuit stated: "*Weiner* . . . stands for the proposition that the merits of a claim alleging breach of an employment contract are not to be determined by application of a formula or checklist; instead, the totality of the facts giving rise to the claim must be considered."[2] In the Second Circuit, the courts have continued to follow the "totality of the circumstances" approach.[3]

After the Court of Appeals slammed the door shut on most implied contract exceptions to at-will employment in *Sabetay v. Sterling Drug, Inc.*,[4] state courts have generally applied *Weiner* narrowly by emphasizing the facts in *Weiner* and demanding that plaintiffs show an express agreement to limit employment-at-will;[5] several decisions have sustained *Weiner*-type claims.[6]

2. Gorrill v. Icelandair/Flugleidir, 761 F.2d 847, 853 (2d Cir.1985).

3. *See* Knudsen v. Quebecor Printing (U.S.A.), Inc., 792 F.Supp. 234 (S.D.N.Y. 1992); Melnyk v. Adria Laboratories, 799 F.Supp. 301 (W.D.N.Y.1992). *See also*, Poklitar v. CBS, Inc., 652 F.Supp. 1023 (S.D.N.Y.1987). *But see* Leathem v. Research Foundation of the City University of New York, 658 F.Supp. 651 (S.D.N.Y.1987); Blair v. CBS, Inc., 662 F.Supp. 947 (S.D.N.Y.1987).

4. 69 N.Y.2d 329, 514 N.Y.S.2d 209, 506 N.E.2d 919 (1987).

5. *See, e.g.*, O'Reilly v. Citibank, N.A., 198 A.D.2d 270, 603 N.Y.S.2d 572 (2d Dep't 1993); Hager v. Union Carbide Corp., 106 A.D.2d 348, 483 N.Y.S.2d 261 (1st Dep't 1984).

6. *See* Skelly v. Visiting Nurse Association of the Capital Region, Inc., 210 A.D.2d 683, 619 N.Y.S.2d 879 (3d Dep't 1994)(breach of just-cause contract based on oral assurances as to post-probation status and manual's outline of progressive discipline, but failure to reserve employer's employment-at-will rights); Evans v. Ithaca Urban Renewal Agency, 205 A.D.2d 844, 613 N.Y.S.2d 446 (3d Dep't 1994) (termination of plaintiff after she took a one-year leave violated promise of reappointment found in company's employment manual); Nice v. Combustion Engineering, Inc., 193 A.D.2d 1088, 599 N.Y.S.2d 205 (4th Dep't 1993) (court denied employer summary judgment since an express limitation of employment-at-will might be imported from handbook provisions regarding pretermination warnings and written performance reviews); Gibouleau v. Society of Women Engineers, 127 A.D.2d 740, 511 N.Y.S.2d 932 (2d Dep't 1987) (denying employer's motion for summary judgment where plaintiff alleged existence of employment handbook containing provision prohibiting termination without just cause and due warning, that she was informed of the provision, and that she relied upon it in accepting employment and in not pursuing other employment); Battaglia v. Sisters of Charity Hospital, 124 A.D.2d 987, 508 N.Y.S.2d 802 (4th Dep't 1986); Wernham v. Moore, 121 A.D.2d 297, 504 N.Y.S.2d 3 (1st Dep't 1986)(denying summary judgment where handbook provided for just cause dismissal); *see also*, Aharanwa v. Trustees of Columbia University, 163 A.D.2d 8, 557 N.Y.S.2d 76 (1st Dep't 1990) (trial required to determine whether disclaimer supersedes handbook's just cause provision). Both the First and Third Departments have used the totality of the circumstances test. *See* Lapidus v. New York City Chapter of the New York State Association for Retarded Children, Inc., 118 A.D.2d 122, 504 N.Y.S.2d 629 (1st Dep't 1986); Dicocco v. Capital Area Community Health Plan, Inc., 135 A.D.2d 308, 525 N.Y.S.2d 417 (3d Dep't 1988); *but see* DiCocco v. Capital Area Community Health Plan, Inc., 159 A.D.2d 119, 559 N.Y.S.2d 395 (3d Dep't 1990), appeal denied 77 N.Y.2d 802, 566 N.Y.S.2d 587, 567 N.E.2d 981 (1991) (reversing lower court verdict for plaintiff due

Handbooks. The presence of express conditions set forth in an employer's handbook may limit employment-at-will. The Second Circuit found a handbook's job security provisions sufficient to form a contract, even though the employee signed an agreement at the time of hire providing that employment was terminable at-will. The court found that the handbook provisions concerning work force reduction were stated in mandatory and unqualified terms, but nevertheless dismissed the complaint, concluding that they had not been breached.[7] In *Criado v. ITT Corp.*,[8] the court upheld a jury award of $250,000 to an employee based on his claim that a code of conduct (together with an accompanying letter and oral assurances) limited the employment-at-will doctrine. If the employee neither knew about nor relied upon the handbook terms in accepting an offer of employment, no contract will be formed.[9]

Contract. When an employee has a written contract for a term of years, the employment generally is not terminable at-will, and the focus is on the contractual provisions governing when the employee can be terminated. If the contract provides that the employee must perform "satisfactorily," the employer can successfully defend a wrongful discharge action by producing evidence showing a good faith basis for dissatisfaction with the employee's work. The employee has the burden of proving that the dissatisfaction was not genuine.[10]

Oral Promises. The possibility of *oral* contract claims should not be overlooked. Both the state and federal courts have held oral promises of employment enforceable notwithstanding the Statute of Frauds.[11] In *Ohanian v. Avis Rent A Car*,[12] the court held that an employer's promise to dismiss an employee only for cause ("his future was secure in the company, unless ... he screwed up badly") did not violate the Statute of Frauds. The court reasoned that a contract that may rightfully be terminated by either party within a year, without there having been a breach of that contract by the other party, is outside of the Statute of

to lack of sufficient evidence of detrimental reliance).

7. Mycak v. Honeywell, 953 F.2d 798 (2d Cir.1992).

8. 1993 WL 322837, 8 IER Cases (BNA) 1267 (S.D.N.Y.1993).

9. *See* Blair v. CBS, Inc., 662 F.Supp. 947 (S.D.N.Y.1987) (suggesting that, to survive a summary judgment motion, plaintiff must, at a minimum, allege reliance on the handbook); *see also* DiCocco v. Capital Area Community Health Plan, Inc., 159 A.D.2d 119, 559 N.Y.S.2d 395 (3d Dep't 1990), appeal denied 77 N.Y.2d 802, 566 N.Y.S.2d 587, 567 N.E.2d 981 (1991)(detrimental reliance by forsaking other employment must be demonstrated).

10. *See* Golden v. Worldvision Enterprises, Inc., 133 A.D.2d 50, 519 N.Y.S.2d 1 (1st Dep't 1987).

11. *E.g.*, Cooper v. Manufacturers Hanover Trust Co., 185 A.D.2d 150, 586 N.Y.S.2d 6 (1st Dep't 1992) (bank's oral promise of lifetime work could suffice as an express agreement); Skelly v. Visiting Nurse Association of the Capital Region, Inc., 210 A.D.2d 683, 619 N.Y.S.2d 879 (3d Dep't 1994)(oral assurances made by executive director, combined with written personnel and procedures manuals providing for grounds for dismissal, raised a question of fact as to whether employer limited its authority to terminate at-will).

12. 779 F.2d 101 (2d Cir.1985).

Frauds. For example, under *Ohanian*, adverse business conditions could warrant dismissal within a year, without a breach of the contract by the employee.[13]

To overcome the Statute of Frauds defense, it may be possible to construct a sufficient "writing" from an assortment of documents.[14] In *Crabtree v. Elizabeth Arden*,[15] the court held that the signed notation on the employer's memorandum that the employee had "2 years to make good" on the expense account could be read in conjunction with the employer's payroll cards (stating "per contractual arrangement with Miss Arden"), and that the two documents, read together, were sufficient to allow the court to conclude that the plaintiff had a two-year contract. To satisfy the Statute of Frauds, the writings, when taken together, should contain one document signed by the party to be charged that either incorporates or refers to another document that contains the essential terms of the contract.[16]

The evidence used to prove the oral promise need not, as in *Ohanian*, consist of trial testimony. In *Sivel v. Readers Digest*,[17] the employee alleged he had accepted the job on assurances from company officials that he could be terminated only for a serious mistake, and that the performance evaluation described in the handbook would be used to determine the existence of just cause. The court denied the defendant's motion for summary judgment even though the only evidence of the oral promise was the plaintiff's own affidavit as to the assurances made by the employer. The defendant did not submit affidavits confirming or denying plaintiff's version of the facts. The court held that "plaintiff's own testimony, if believed, may furnish evidence of the express limitation required to rebut the at-will presumption."[18]

---

13. *See* Weiner v. McGraw Hill, 57 N.E.2d at 463, 457 N.Y.S.2d at 196 (the Statute of Frauds does not bar an oral contract for "as long as you do a good job," or "for as long as you live," or for some other indefinite period, because those terms are capable of being performed within one year); Lucy-Turner v. Builders Bonds Limited, 160 A.D.2d 484, 554 N.Y.S.2d 148 (1st Dep't 1990); Jones v. Dunkirk Radiator Corp., 21 F.3d 18, 9 IER Cas. (BNA) 610 (2d Cir.1994), *but see* Guterman v. RGA Accessories, 196 A.D.2d 785, 602 N.Y.S.2d 116 (1st Dep't 1993)(oral agreement not capable of performance within a year is therefore unenforceable under Statute of Frauds).

14. General Obligations Law § 5–701; Crabtree v. Elizabeth Arden, 305 N.Y. 48, 110 N.E.2d 551 (1953).

15. 305 N.Y. 48, 110 N.E.2d 551 (1953).

16. *See also,* Dickerson v. Robert Kaplan and RK Associates, 763 F.Supp. 694, aff'd 963 F.2d 1522 (2d Cir.1992) (letter which did not provide starting date or duration of employment was deemed sufficient to constitute a writing to satisfy the Statute of Frauds); Kalfin v. United States Olympic Committee, 209 A.D.2d 279, 618 N.Y.S.2d 724 (1st Dep't 1994)(although memorandum was insufficient to satisfy Statute of Frauds insofar as the agreement could not be performed within one year, it did support claims for unjust enrichment and *quantum meruit* because it evidenced the fact of plaintiff's employment by defendant); Mirchel v. RMJ Securities Corp., 205 A.D.2d 388, 613 N.Y.S.2d 876 (1st Dep't 1994)(letter confirming amount of earned bonus satisfied the writing requirement under the Statute of Frauds).

17. 677 F.Supp. 183 (S.D.N.Y.1988).

18. *Id.* at 187.

In *Mirchel v. RMJ Securities Corp.*,[19] the First Department held that the Statute of Frauds did not bar a claim for an unpaid bonus. In *Mirchel*, the plaintiff resigned before the end of the year; the bonus, however, was anticipated on the basis of a course of dealings between the parties. As a consequence, an implied promise to pay the bonus was created. Note, if the benefits or compensation sought have been earned, the plaintiff may demand additional relief pursuant to Labor Law § 198(1–a) for attorneys' fees and, where non-payment is willful, for liquidated damages.

§ 17.35 Causes of Action—Contract—Implied Promises

Implied Contracts/Covenants. New York courts have declined to distinguish between implied-in-fact and implied-in-law contracts in the employment-at-will area, although they do recognize the distinction in other areas.[1] Therefore, while an implied-in-fact contract may be actionable based on handbooks or other assurances with respect to certain job entitlements, such as severance benefits, it will not be upheld with respect to continued employment.[2]

An implied-in-law covenant, also called a quasi contract, is not a contract at all. Rather, it is an obligation "imposed by the law for the purpose of bringing about justice without reference to the intention of the parties." The only limit on quasi contracts is that the "obligation in question more closely resembles those created by contract than those created by tort."[3]

Although the law implies in every contract a covenant of good faith and fair dealing,[4] the New York Court of Appeals has rejected the idea that this covenant can limit the employment-at-will doctrine.[5]

---

19. 205 A.D.2d 388, 613 N.Y.S.2d 876 (1st Dep't 1994).

§ 17.35

1. *Compare* Sabetay v. Sterling Drug, Inc., 69 N.Y.2d 329, 514 N.Y.S.2d 209, 506 N.E.2d 919 (1987) (in an employment case, court declined to recognize any implied contractual limit on employment at will), with Brown Brothers Electric Contractors v. Beam Construction Corp., 41 N.Y.2d 397, 393 N.Y.S.2d 350, 361 N.E.2d 999 (1977)(contractor case recognizing an implied-in-fact promise).

2. *See* Saunders v. Big Brothers, Inc., 115 Misc.2d 845, 454 N.Y.S.2d 787, 789 (Civ.Ct., N.Y. County, 1982) (Booth Glen, J.)(personnel manual's promise of severance pay held an implied part of employment contract and binding; Methe v. General Electric Co., 169 A.D.2d 864, 564 N.Y.S.2d 593 (3d Dep't 1991)(plaintiff was induced to continue her employment by promises of certain post-termination benefits). Defenses to claims for implied-in-fact benefits include lack of reliance by the plaintiff. Gallagher v. Ashland Oil, Inc. 183 A.D.2d 1033, 583 N.Y.S.2d 624 (3d Dep't), appeal denied 80 N.Y.2d 758, 589 N.Y.S.2d 309, 602 N.E.2d 1125 (1992)(that employee continued employment after severance pay policy was instituted was insufficient to establish reliance).

3. S. Williston, *A Treatise on the Law of Contracts*, § 1:6 (4th ed. 1990).

4. *See Restatement (Second) of Contracts* § 205.

5. *See* Sabetay v. Sterling Drug, Inc., 69 N.Y.2d 329, 514 N.Y.S.2d 209, 506 N.E.2d 919 (1987); Murphy v. American Home Products Corp., 58 N.Y.2d 293, 461 N.Y.S.2d 232, 448 N.E.2d 86 (1983).

Federal courts have been more willing to imply covenants of good faith and fair dealing. In *Wakefield I*,[6] the Second Circuit held that an agreement to pay the employee commissions contained an implied covenant of good faith and fair dealing not to terminate the employee to avoid paying the commissions otherwise owed. The court reasoned that "an unfettered right to avoid payment of commissions in the principal or employer creates incentives counterproductive to the purpose of this contract itself in that the better the performance by the employee, the greater the temptation to terminate."[7] Even though the New York Court of Appeals has virtually closed the door on implied contracts modifying employment-at-will,[8] courts within the Second Circuit continue to recognize that terminations in avoidance of paying commissions may violate the implied covenant of good faith and fair dealing.[9]

Obligations based on professional ethical standards create implied understandings that implicate the covenant of good faith and fair dealing. In *Wieder v. Skala*,[10] the court allowed a claim that the implied covenant of good faith was violated when a lawyer was dismissed for insisting that his firm comply with the Code of Professional Responsibility. This doctrine may not apply, however, to other professions.[11]

Punitive damages. Generally, when contracts are breached in bad faith, plaintiffs may, in an extreme case, seek punitive damages.[12] In a notable decision, the First Department held that punitive damages can be obtained in a breach of contract case where there is evidence of bad faith or a dishonest failure to carry out a contract.[13]

Library References:

West's Key No. Digests, Implied and Constructive Contracts ⊙1–4.

§ 17.36 Causes of Action—Contract—Estoppel

"An estoppel" rests upon the word or deed of one party upon which another rightfully relies and, so relying, changes his position to his injury. "It is imposed by law in the interest of fairness to prevent the

---

6. Wakefield v. Northern Telecom, Inc., 769 F.2d 109, 112–113 (2d Cir.1985).

7. *See also,* Wakefield II, Wakefield v. Northern Telcom, Inc., 813 F.2d 535 (2d Cir.1987).

8. *See* Gallagher v. Lambert, 74 N.Y.2d 562, 549 N.Y.S.2d 945, 549 N.E.2d 136 (1989).

9. Knudsen v. Quebecor Printing (U.S.A.) Inc., 792 F.Supp. 234 (S.D.N.Y. 1992).

10. 80 N.Y.2d 628, 593 N.Y.S.2d 752, 609 N.E.2d 105 (1992); *see also* Calder v. Planned Community Living, Inc., 1995 WL 456400, 68 FEP Cas. (BNA) 1012 (S.D.N.Y. 1995) (Schwartz,J.)(court denied motion to dismiss plaintiff's breach of contract claim, holding that public policy prohibits retaliatory discharge of whistleblower who had an affirmative duty to report abuse of mental patients).

11. *See* Mulder v. Donaldson Lufkin & Jenrette, 208 A.D.2d 301, 623 N.Y.S.2d 560 (1st Dep't 1995) (Wieder doctrine does not extend to non-attorney employee).

12. *See* Hudson Motor Partnership v. Crest Leasing Enterprises Inc. and Metro Auto Leasing Inc., 93–CV–5642 (E.D.N.Y. 1994), cited in N.Y.L.J., 3/3/94, p.1 col.3.

13. Mulder v. Donaldson, Lufkin & Jenrette, 208 A.D.2d 301, 623 N.Y.S.2d 560 (1st Dep't 1995).

enforcement of rights which would work fraud or injustice upon the person against whom enforcement is sought and who, in justifiable reliance upon the opposing party's words or conduct, has been misled into acting upon the belief that such enforcement would not be sought."[1]

Promissory estoppel can be used as a substitute for consideration,[2] or to bar assertion of the Statute of Frauds.[3] New York courts have applied the doctrine very narrowly as a substitute for consideration.[4] Under New York law, promissory estoppel claims require a clear and unambiguous promise, reasonable and foreseeable reliance by the party to whom the promise is made, and injuries sustained by reason of the reliance.[5]

Generally, a change of job or residence, by itself, is insufficient to invoke the promissory estoppel doctrine.[6] In *Cunnison*,[7] an employee alleged that she had an oral five year contract of employment; the claim was dismissed under the Statute of Frauds. The court held that the promissory estoppel doctrine did not defeat the Statute of Frauds defense, though the plaintiff alleged that she had moved from Toronto to New York and had rejected other job offers based on the defendant's promises. The court concluded that, on the facts presented, the plaintiff did not suffer any cognizable harm.[8]

Library References:

West's Key No. Digests, Estoppel ⚖52–62.8.

§ 17.37 Statutory Causes of Action—Age Discrimination

In New York, an employee may be protected by as many as three different statutes. They differ somewhat with respect to coverage, remedies, and procedural requirements; otherwise, the substance of the statutory protections are almost identical.

Age Discrimination in Employment Act of 1967 ("ADEA") 29 U.S.C.A. §§ 621 et seq. ADEA prohibits discrimination on the basis of age in all aspects of employment. ADEA applies to employers with 20 or more employees, and protects all applicants or employees who are at

§ 17.36

1. Nassau Trust Co. v. Montrose Concrete Prod., 56 N.Y.2d 175, 184, 451 N.Y.S.2d 663, 667, 436 N.E.2d 1265 (1982).

2. *Restatement (Second) Contracts*, § 90.

3. *Restatement (Second) Contracts*, § 217(a). Swerdloff v. Mobil Oil Corp., 74 A.D.2d 258, 427 N.Y.S.2d 266, 268 (2d Dep't 1980).

4. *Id.*

5. R.G. Group, Inc. v. Horn & Hardart Co., 751 F.2d 69 (2d Cir.1984).

6. Cunnison v. Richardson Greenshields Securities, Inc., 107 A.D.2d 50, 485 N.Y.S.2d 272 (1st Dep't 1985).

7. *Id.*

8. *See also*, Dalton v. Union Bank of Switzerland, 134 A.D.2d 174, 520 N.Y.S.2d 764, 767 (1st Dep't 1987); Ginsberg v. Fairfield-Noble Corp., 81 A.D.2d 318, 321, 440 N.Y.S.2d 222, 225 (1st Dep't 1981); *but see* Hager v. Union Carbide Corp., 106 A.D.2d 348, 483 N.Y.S.2d 261, 264 (1st Dep't 1984) (dissenting opinion). *See also, supra* § 17.27.

least 40 years old. A plaintiff may bring a case of disparate treatment based on direct or circumstantial evidence. The following must be alleged in order to make out a *prima facie* case:

(a) that the plaintiff was 40 years of age or older;

(b) that the plaintiff was qualified for the job;

(c) that the plaintiff was rejected, terminated or denied entitlement;

(d) that the position remained open or was filled by a younger person (or in a reduction in force [RIF], and the plaintiff was not offered other openings).[1]

Claims also may be brought under the theory of disparate impact, based on statistical evidence.[2] ADEA contains several statutory defenses such as that the employment decision was based on "reasonable factors other than age," on a "bona fide employee benefit plan," or a "bona fide seniority system."[3] To bring an action, the plaintiff must first file a charge with the EEOC or the state or city agency alleging age discrimination, and must follow the procedures required for Title VII actions (*see infra*, Sections 17.66, *et seq.*). A jury trial is available. Damages under ADEA are different than under Title VII. The prevailing ADEA claimant may be entitled to backpay, frontpay, reinstatement, liquidated damages of double the backpay for "willful violations,"[4] fringe benefits, and injunctive relief. Damages for pain and suffering or emotional distress are not provided by ADEA.

New York State Human Rights Law ("NYSHRL").[5] Section 296.3–a(a) of the Executive Law covers employees 18 years of age and older working in organizations with four or more employees (Executive Law § 292(5)). The elements of the plaintiff's cause of action are the same as those under ADEA.[6] The employer's defenses are also similar.[7] Under NYSHRL, the plaintiff may file a charge with the New York State Division of Human Rights ("SDHR") to commence an investigation. If the SDHR finds probable cause of discrimination, it will move the case toward a hearing before an administrative law judge. That process currently takes at least 4–6 years to complete. The plaintiff, instead, may avoid administrative processing and commence a lawsuit in state court (or in federal court if there is pendant jurisdiction) within three years of the discriminatory conduct. A jury trial is available as to legal claims

§ 17.37

1. *See* Cronin v. Aetna Life Ins. Co., 46 F.3d 196, 203 (2d Cir.1995) (summarizing law regarding elements of ADEA case); EEOC v. Doremus, 921 F.Supp. 1048, 69 FEP Cas. (BNA) 449 (S.D.N.Y.1995)(elements of prima facie case in RIF-transfer).

2. *See* Geller v. Markham, 635 F.2d 1027, 1032 (2d Cir.1980).

3. 29 U.S.C.A. § 623(f).

4. Hazen Paper Co. v. Biggins, 507 U.S. 604, 113 S.Ct. 1701, 123 L.Ed.2d 338 (1993).

5. For a more comprehensive discussion of this statute, *see supra*, Chapter 18 "Civil Rights Law."

6. *See* Vaughn v. Mobil Oil Corp., 708 F.Supp. 595 (S.D.N.Y.1989).

7. Executive Law §§ 296(3–a)(d) *et seq.*

only.[8] The remedies under NYSHRL include: hiring/reinstatement, backpay, frontpay, and compensatory damages. Punitive damages and attorneys' fees are not available. If a plaintiff has filed with the SDHR and wishes to bring a private lawsuit, the election of forum provision of the NYSHRL may be a barrier,[9] though an "administrative convenience dismissal" from the agency can revive the right to sue in court.

New York City Human Rights Law ("NYCHRL").[10] The NYCHRL covers employees of any age. Substantively and procedurally, the age discrimination provisions under the New York City law are similar to those under NYSHRL, except that, to initiate agency proceedings, filing is with the New York City Commission on Human Rights. Under the New York City law, however, both attorneys' fees and punitive damages are available, unlike under the state law.[11]

Library References:
West's Key No. Digests, Civil Rights ⚖168–172.

§ 17.38 Statutory Causes of Action—Anti-reprisal Provisions of Various Statutes

The following statutes contain provisions prohibiting reprisals against employees reporting violations of, or asserting rights under, those statutes:

- Age Discrimination in Employment Act of 1967, 29 U.S.C.A. § 623;
- Americans with Disabilities Act, 42 U.S.C.A. § 12203(a);
- Asbestos School Hazard Detection & Control Act, 20 U.S.C.A. § 3608;
- Civil Rights Act of 1964, Title VII, 42 U.S.C.A. § 2000e–3;
- Civil Rights of Institutionalized Persons Act, 42 U.S.C.A. § 1997(d);
- Civil Service Reform Act of 1978, 5 U.S.C.A. §§ 2301, 2302, 7102, 7116;
- Clean Air Act Amendments of 1977, 42 U.S.C.A. §§ 7401, 7622;
- Comprehensive Environmental Response, Comp. & Liability Act of 1980, 42 U.S.C.A. § 9610;
- Conspiracy to Obstruct Justice Act, 15 U.S.C.A. § 1985(2);
- Consumer Credit Protection Act of 1968, 15 U.S.C.A. § 1674;
- Employee Polygraph Protection Act, 29 U.S.C.A. §§ 2001, *et seq.*;

8. Murphy v. American Home Products Corp., 136 A.D.2d 229, 527 N.Y.S.2d 1 (1st Dep't 1988).

9. *See infra,* § 17.68.

10. N.Y.C.Admin. Code § 8–107(1). For a more comprehensive discussion of this statute *see infra,* Chapter 18 "Civil Rights Law."

11. For a discussion of agency charges or litigation, generally, *see infra,* §§ 17.66–69, and for a discussion of burdens of proof, *see infra,* § 17.59.

§ 17.38   EMPLOYMENT LAW   Ch. 17

- Employee Retirement Income Security Act of 1974, 29 U.S.C.A. §§ 1140, 1141;
- Energy Reorganization Act Amendment of 1978, 42 U.S.C.A. § 5851;
- Equal Pay Act, 29 U.S.C.A. § 215(a)(3);
- Fair Labor Standards Act, 29 U.S.C.A. § 215;
- False Claims Act, 31 U.S.C.A. § 3730;
- Federal Mine Safety and Health Act Amendment of 1977, 30 U.S.C.A. §§ 815, 820(b);
- Family and Medical Leave Act, 29 U.S.C.A. § 2615;
- Federal Railroad Safety Act Amendment, 45 U.S.C.A. § 441;
- Federal Water Pollution Control Act of 1972, 33 U.S.C.A. § 1367;
- International Safe Container Act of 1977, 46 U.S.C.A. § 1506;
- Jury Duty Act, 28 U.S.C.A. § 1875;
- Longshoremen's and Harbor Workers' Compensation Act of 1972, 33 U.S.C.A. § 948(a);
- Migrant and Seasonal Agricultural Worker Protection Act of 1983, 29 U.S.C.A. § 1855;
- National Labor Relations Act, 29 U.S.C.A. § 158;
- New York City Human Rights Law, N.Y.C. Administrative Code § 8–107(19);
- New York State Human Rights Law, Executive Law § 296;
- New York State Labor Law (unsafe workplace), Labor Law § 215;
- Occupational Safety and Health Act of 1970, 29 U.S.C.A. § 660;
- Railroad Employers Act of 1908, 45 U.S.C.A. § 60;
- Safe Drinking Water Act of 1974, 42 U.S.C.A. § 300j–9;
- Solid Waste Disposal Act of 1976, 42 U.S.C.A. § 6972;
- Surface Mining Control & Reclamation Act of 1977, 30 U.S.C.A. §§ 1201, 1293; and
- Toxic Substances Control Act of 1976, 15 U.S.C.A. § 2622.

Library References:

West's Key No. Digests, Master and Servant ⇐30(6.5)–30(6.35).

§ 17.39   Statutory Causes of Action—Arrest Records

Arrests cannot be used as a basis for denial of a job or other employment entitlements.[1] To establish a claim without direct evidence,

§ 17.39   1. Executive Law § 296(16).

the employee should set forth the following elements in the *prima facie* case:

(a) plaintiff's application for employment;

(b) arrest or criminal accusation;

(c) defendant's inquiry and knowledge that plaintiff had been arrested and cleared; and

(d) defendant's refusal to hire, or other adverse treatment.

The plaintiff may initiate a proceeding or lawsuit according to the provisions of the NYSHRL and be entitled to the remedies generally available to prevailing discrimination plaintiffs under that law.[2] For a discussion of agency charges or litigation, generally, *see infra,* Sections 17.66–69; for a discussion of burdens of proof, *see infra,* Section 17.59.

§ 17.40 Statutory Causes of Action—Bankruptcy

The Federal Bankruptcy Act[1] prohibits the denial of employment on the basis of the applicant's bankruptcy or indebtedness. A plaintiff who has been denied employment based solely on his declaration of bankruptcy, or nonpayment of debts dischargeable in bankruptcy would be entitled to actual damages, including back pay, fringe benefits, as well as hiring and/or reinstatement.[2]

§ 17.41 Statutory Causes of Action—Convictions

The New York State Human Rights Law makes it unlawful to discriminate against an individual based on a prior criminal conviction.[1] Article 23–A of the Correction Law prohibits the denial of employment based on a criminal conviction unless there is a "direct relationship" between the employment sought and the specific offense, or the granting of employment would create "an unreasonable risk to property" or "human safety."[2] According to the Fourth Department, Executive Law § 296(15) apparently protects employees from discrimination after they have been hired.[3]

---

2. Executive Law §§ 297 (4)(c) *et seq; see* Sheriff's Department v. State Div. of Human Rights, 129 A.D.2d 789, 514 N.Y.S.2d 779 (2d Dep't 1987).

§ 17.40

1. 11 U.S.C.A. § 525.

2. *See* In re Sweeney, 113 B.R. 359 (Bankr.N.D.Ohio 1990) (though couched in terms of concern for financial imprudence, employer's discharge of employee solely because of his insolvency, bankruptcy filing, and discharge of debt was discriminatory.); In re Vaughter, 109 B.R. 229 (Bankr.W.Tex. 1989) (employer's failure to offer participation of debtor in commission program after debtor had filed for bankruptcy violated anti-discrimination provision of Bankruptcy Code).

§ 17.41

1. Executive Law § 296(15).

2. Correction Law § 752(2).

3. In State Div. of Human Rights on Complaint of Maymi v. Sorrento Cheese Co., 115 A.D.2d 323, 495 N.Y.S.2d 865 (4th Dep't 1985), the First Department indicated that these provisions may apply to only the denial of a job at the application stage.

See also, Green v. Wells Fargo Alarm Service, 192 A.D.2d 463, 596 N.Y.S.2d 412

§ 17.42 Statutory Causes of Action—Credit Information

New York State and federal law protect job applicants' and employees' rights with respect to employers' use of credit reports.[1]

The Federal Fair Credit Reporting Act, as amended by the Consumer Credit Reporting Reform Act of 1996 ("FCRA"),[2] imposes strict conditions on the use of credit reports by employers. Before obtaining a standard credit report on a current or prospective employee, an employer must provide a written disclosure statement to the person and must secure the person's written authorization for the report. Moreover, before obtaining an *investigative* report (*i.e.*, one based on interviews with neighbors, friends, etc.), the employer must provide a more comprehensive disclosure, including a summary of rights under the FCRA and notice of the right to obtain, upon request, a "complete and accurate" written disclosure of the nature and scope of the investigation.

An employer cannot take any "adverse action" (*i.e.*, "denial of employment or any other decision for employment purposes that adversely affects any current or prospective employee") based, in whole or in part, on a credit report, unless the employer first provides the employee/applicant with a copy of the report and a written summary of rights. Moreover, the affected person has the right, upon request within 60 days of the adverse action, to dispute the accuracy or completeness of the information in the report by calling or writing the credit reporting agency.

The New York State General Business Law[3] also regulates consumer credit reports, though less stringently than the FCRA, as amended. Under the General Business law or the FCRA, the plaintiff may recover actual damages sustained as a result of defendant's failure to comply with the law, including loss of wages, benefits, and promotional opportunities, and possibly punitive damages for defendant's willful and knowing failure to comply.[4] Costs of the action, together with reasonable attorneys' fees, are also available.

(1st Dep't 1993)(Section 296 applies only to persons applying for employment previously convicted of a criminal offense); Bonacorsa v. Van Lindt, 71 N.Y.2d 605, 528 N.Y.S.2d 519, 523 N.E.2d 806 (1988) (presumption of rehabilitation created by certificate of good conduct applies even when applicant's prior conviction directly relates to license or employment sought).

§ 17.42

1. For further discussion of consumer credit, *see* Chapter 7 "Consumer Law," *supra*.

2. 15 U.S.C.A. §§ 1681a, *et seq.*

3. General Business Law § 380–b(b).

4. *See* Comeaux v. Brown & Williamson Tobacco Co., 915 F.2d 1264 (9th Cir.1990) (knowingly and willfully obtaining information from consumer reporting agency under false pretenses gives rise to civil liability).

§ 17.43 Statutory Causes of Action—Disability

A plaintiff may be covered by several separate disability discrimination statutes in New York.

Americans with Disabilities Act ("ADA").[1] The ADA prohibits discrimination in all aspects of employment in workplaces with 15 or more employees. The ADA protects from discrimination persons with disabilities who are able to perform the essential functions of a job, with or without a reasonable accommodation, without undue hardship and without imposing a direct threat to health and safety. A disability is defined as an "impairment, physical or mental, that substantially limits a major life activity." An individual who has a disability, has a record of disability, or is perceived to have a disability, is covered. The key ADA burden placed on employers is the duty to provide a reasonable accommodation.[2] The ADA is limited in that it does not apply to federal government employees and damages are capped under the Civil Rights Act of 1991. Procedurally, the plaintiff must comply with the filing requirements of Title VII.

Rehabilitation Act. Section 504 of the Rehabilitation Act prohibits discrimination against otherwise qualified handicapped individuals "solely because of their handicap" in "any program or activity receiving federal financial assistance or under any program or activity conducted by any Executive agency or by the United States Postal Service."[3] The Rehabilitation Act, similar to the ADA, requires employers to make reasonable accommodations. While § 504 confers a direct private right of action, a plaintiff should determine whether there are any agency administrative channels that can or must be exhausted before commencing a lawsuit.[4]

New York State Human Rights Law ("NYSHRL"). Unlike the ADA or the NYCHRL,[5] the NYSHRL does not impose an affirmative duty on employers to reasonably accommodate persons with disabilities. However, the NYSHRL prohibits an employer from discriminating if the employee can perform the duties of the job "in a reasonable manner."[6] Because the New York State Human Rights Law does not impose a duty on the employer to make a reasonable accommodation to known disabilities of an otherwise qualified individual,[7] plaintiffs must be careful to assert claims under the Americans with Disabilities Act or the New York

---

§ 17.43

1. 42 U.S.C.A. §§ 12101–17 *et seq.*

2. *See* 42 U.S.C.A. §§ 12112(b)(5)(A), (B); Lyons v. Legal Aid Society, 68 F.3d 1512 (2d Cir.1995).

3. 29 U.S.C.A. § 794.

4. *See* Borkowski v. Valley Central School District, 63 F.3d 131 (2d Cir.1995).

5. Executive Law § 296.1(a).

6. McEniry v. Landi, 84 N.Y.2d 554, 620 N.Y.S.2d 328, 644 N.E.2d 1019 (1994) (evidence showed that plaintiff's termination was unlawful where it was causally related to alcoholism and plaintiff had completed a rehabilitation program and was performing his job satisfactorily).

7. *See* City of New York v. Cole, 48 N.Y.2d 707, 708, 422 N.Y.S.2d 367, 397 N.E.2d 1171 (1979).

City Human Rights Law, if applicable, if they seek a reasonable accommodation or can perform the essential functions of their job only with a reasonable accommodation.

New York City Human Rights Law ("NYCHRL"). The NYCHRL provides more expansive protection than either the ADA or the NYSHRL in that it protects from discrimination anyone with a "physical, medical, mental or psychological impairment," even if that impairment does not "substantially limit a major life activity."[8] Moreover, like the ADA, but unlike the NYSHRL, the New York City law imposes a duty upon employers to reasonably accommodate disabilities. The NYCHRL, unlike the ADA, imposes that duty not only when the disability is known,[9] but also when the employer *should have* known about it.[10]

Library References:

West's Key No. Digests, Civil Rights ⊜173–175.

§ 17.44 Statutory Causes of Action—Equal Pay

Federal Equal Pay Act ("EPA").[1] The EPA prohibits pay discrimination "between employees on the basis of sex" when they perform "equal work," that is, jobs requiring "equal skill, effort, and responsibility, and which are performed under similar working conditions." Liability will not be found if the jobs are not equal, or if any wage differential is the result of a seniority system, merit system, quantity or quality measurement system, or based on any factor other than sex.[2]

New York State Equal Pay Violation Act.[3] New York State's Equal Pay law is found in the Labor Law. As under federal law, the key issue is whether the jobs in question are, indeed, equal or "substantially equivalent."[4]

New York City Human Rights Law. Unlike the Equal Pay Act or the New York State Labor Law, the New York City Human Rights Law may be interpreted as broadening the equal pay right from equal work to

8. N.Y.C.Admin. Code § 8–102(16)(a).

9. *See* 42 U.S.C.A. § 12112(b)(5)(A).

10. N.Y.C.Admin. Code § 8–107(15)(a). For a discussion of agency charges or litigation, generally, *see infra,* §§ 17.66–69; for a discussion of burdens of proof, *see infra,* § 17.59.

§ 17.44

1. 29 U.S.C.A. § 206(d).
2. *Id.* at § 206(d)(1).
3. Labor Law § 194.

4. *See* Mize v. State Div. of Human Rights, 38 A.D.2d 278, 328 N.Y.S.2d 983, aff'd 31 N.Y.2d 1032, 342 N.Y.S.2d 65, 294 N.E.2d 851 (1973) (plaintiffs were entitled to equal pay because the evidence showed that the "job" was the guarding of prisoners in the cell block at police headquarters, not the job of policemen, and the plaintiffs performed substantially the same duties as the male guards. Back pay was not awarded because the difference in pay was not due to underpayment of matrons, but the assignment of overqualified personnel to the position of turnkey.).

Ch. 17   HEALTH PLAN COVERAGE ("COBRA")   § 17.46

"comparable work."[5] In *Pagan*,[6] the NYCCHR indicated that claims can be made for unequal pay for *comparable*, as opposed to merely equal, work; the Equal Pay Act and the NYSHRL have been interpreted to cover claims for equal work only.[7]

Library References:

West's Key No. Digests, Labor Relations ⚖1333.

§ 17.45 Statutory Causes of Action—Family and Medical Leave Act ("FMLA")

The Family and Medical Leave Act ("FMLA")[1] requires employers who employ 50 or more employees to grant up to 12 weeks of leave during any 12-month period to any eligible employee under the following circumstances: (1) following the birth or adoption of a child; (2) to care for a seriously sick spouse, child, or parent; or (3) due to the employee's own serious health condition (illness, injury, or impairment, or a physical or mental condition involving either inpatient care or continuing treatment by a healthcare provider). There has been considerable discussion in the federal rules over the definition of a "serious medical condition."[2] Leave for birth or placement of a child for adoption or foster care may be taken intermittently or on a reduced leave schedule, while leave to care for seriously ill family members or one's own health condition is permitted whenever it is "medically necessary."[3] Except for certain "key" employees who take FMLA leave, upon return from FMLA leave, the employer must restore the employee to his or her original job or its equivalent without loss of pay or benefits. Employees whose FMLA rights have been violated have the choice of filing a civil lawsuit or a complaint with the Secretary of Labor. Remedies include equitable relief such as reinstatement, compensatory damage, liquidated damages (equal to the sum of actual damages), and reasonable attorneys' and expert witness fees.

Library References:

West's Key No. Digests, Civil Rights ⚖173.1.

§ 17.46 Statutory Causes of Action—Health Plan Coverage ("COBRA")

COBRA. The Consolidated Omnibus Budget Reconciliation Act of 1985, or COBRA, applies to employers—both private and public—with

---

5. *See* Pagan v. Technical Career Institutes, Inc., Decision and Order NYCCHR Compl. No. 7771–EP (Aug. 29, 1980).

6. *Id.*

7. *E.g.,* Mize v. State Div. of Human Rights, 38 A.D.2d 278, 328 N.Y.S.2d 983, aff'd 31 N.Y.2d 1032, 342 N.Y.S.2d 65, 294 N.E.2d 851 (1973).

§ 17.45

1. 29 U.S.C.A. §§ 2601 *et seq.*

2. *See* 29 U.S.C.A. § 2612(a)(1)(D); 29 CFR § 825.114(a).

3. 29 U.S.C.A. § 2612(b).

20 or more employees.[1] COBRA provides that employees and their families who would otherwise lose health insurance coverage under an employer's group health plan have the right, under certain circumstances, to elect to continue that coverage for at least 18 months and possibly up to 36 months, at the employee's own cost. The right to COBRA continuation is triggered by loss of coverage due to (1) death of the covered employee; (2) termination of employment (except for gross misconduct); (3) reduction of hours; (4) divorce or legal separation; (5) eligibility for Medicare benefits; or (6) dependent children ceasing to meet the plan's definition of dependent.[2] When a triggering or qualifying event occurs that causes the employee to lose coverage, the plan administrator must be notified. Within 14 days of receiving such notice, the plan administrator must provide notice of the right to elect COBRA continuation coverage. From the date that coverage would otherwise end (or if later, from the date of receiving notice from the plan administrator that coverage will soon end), the employee or family members have at least 60 days to elect COBRA coverage. Payment of the first premium must be made within 45 days after COBRA coverage is elected. If the employer fails to notify the employee or family member of the right of COBRA election, or wrongfully fails to continue COBRA benefits, the employee has a right to sue.

New York Insurance Law.[3] The Insurance Law of New York provides health plan coverage continuation rights that are similar to COBRA with two major distinctions: under Insurance Law § 3221(m), employers with less than 20 employees are covered as are employees who are discharged for "gross misconduct."

Library References:

West's Key No. Digests, Pensions ⚖121.

§ 17.47 Statutory Causes of Action—Legal Off Duty Activities

New York Labor Law § 205–d prohibits discrimination against employees for off duty conduct of the following types: (i) legal use of consumable substances (*e.g.*, smoking); (ii) engaging in legal "recreational activities;" (iii) engaging in such political activities as fundraising and running for office; and (iv) engaging in union activities.[1] The statute

---

§ 17.46
1. 29 U.S.C.A. § 1161(b).
2. 29 U.S.C.A. § 1163.
3. Insurance Law § 3221(m).

§ 17.47
1. *See, e.g.*, State of New York v. Wal–Mart Stores, Inc., 207 A.D.2d 150, 621 N.Y.S.2d 158 (3d Dep't 1995) ("dating" is not "recreational activity" under Section 201–d, so termination of two employees for violating employer's anti-fraternization policy was lawful); *but see* Pasch v. Katz Media Corp., 1995 WL 469710, 10 IER Cas. (BNA) 1574 (S.D.N.Y.1995) (rejecting the Wal–Mart analysis, "cohabitation" is protected "recreational activity").

provides for equitable remedies and compensatory damages, but not attorneys' fees.

§ 17.48 Statutory Causes of Action—Marital Status Discrimination

New York State Human Rights Law.[1] Unlike Title VII, New York State protects marital status from being used as a basis for employment decisions unless it can be shown to be a *bona fide* occupational qualification at the point of hiring.[2] While the fact of one's marital status cannot be considered by employers, anti-nepotism rules that forbid married employees from working together are nevertheless enforceable because the focus is not on the marital status, but the individual relationship.[3]

New York City Human Rights Law.[4] The New York City Human Rights Law prohibits discrimination based on actual or perceived marital status. For a discussion of agency charges or litigation, generally, *see infra,* Sections 17.66–17.69; for a discussion of burdens of proof, *see infra,* Section 17.59.

Library References:

West's Key No. Digests, Civil Rights ⚷141.

§ 17.49 Statutory Causes of Action—Discrimination on the Basis of Race, Color or National Origin

Title VII. Employers with fifteen or more employees may not discriminate on the basis of a person's race, color or national origin.[1] For the purposes of Title VII, national origin means both the country in which a person was born or from which his or her ancestors came, as well as the physical, cultural or linguistic characteristics of a national origin group.[2] For a discussion of bringing agency charges or litigation, generally, *see infra,* Sections 17.66–69; for a discussion of burdens of proof, *see infra,* Section 17.59.

§ 17.48

1. Executive Law § 296.1(a); Pasch v. Katz Media Corp., 1995 WL 469710 (1995).

2. Executive Law § 296(1)(d). *See generally* Belanoff v. Grayson, 98 A.D.2d 353, 356, 471 N.Y.S.2d 91, 93 (1st Dep't 1984) (evidence that employer changed his attitude toward plaintiff after she announced her engagement to be married created an issue of fact supporting a claim of marital status discrimination).

3. In Manhattan Pizza Hut, Inc. v. New York State Human Rights Appeal Bd., 51 N.Y.2d 506, 434 N.Y.S.2d 961, 415 N.E.2d 950 (1980), the Court of Appeals held that employer's anti-nepotism rule and application did not constitute discrimination attributable to an individual's "marital status." Employee was not dismissed for being married; the record showed that had employee been married to another person other than a supervisor employed in the same establishment she would not have been discharged.

4. N.Y.C.Admin. Code § 8–107(1)(a).

§ 17.49

1. 42 U.S.C.A. § 2000e–2.

2. *See* 29 C.F.R. §§ 1606.1 *et seq.* for regulatory guidelines.

Section 1981. The Civil Rights Act of 1866 ("Section 1981"),[3] which prohibits discrimination on the basis of race, may apply where "national origin" is synonymous with "race." "Race," which has been held to include Arabs, Jews, and possibly Germans and English, is defined for Section 1981 purposes as an "identifiable class of persons who are subjected to intentional discrimination solely because of their ancestry or ethnic characteristics."[4] The advantages of litigating under Section 1981 are the three-year Statute of Limitations, lack of EEOC filing requirements, and uncapped damages. For a discussion of burdens of proof, *see infra*, Section § 17.59.

***Immigration Reform Control Act ("IRCA")*.**[5] IRCA makes it unlawful for an employer to hire individuals who are not legally authorized to work in the United States. It also contains a provision that forbids discrimination based on national origin (that is not otherwise covered by Title VII) and citizenship.[6] IRCA applies to all employers with four or more employees. Complaints are filed with the Department of Justice and must be pursued through administrative channels; there is no direct private right of action.

New York State Human Rights Law ("NYSHRL").[7] Race and national origin discrimination litigation under state law tracks Title VII, although under the NYSHRL, employers can use the *bona fide* occupational qualification ("BFOQ") defense against only applicants in the hiring context.[8] Once the employee is hired, however, employers may not claim that being of a certain national origin is a business necessity, even under the NYSHRL. For a discussion of agency charges or litigation, generally, *see infra*, Sections 17.66–69; for a discussion of burdens of proof, *see infra*, Section 17.59.

New York City Human Rights Law ("NYCHRL"). In addition to prohibiting discrimination on the basis of race, color,[9] and national origin,[10] the NYCHRL forbids discrimination based on actual or perceived "alienage or citizenship status."[11] "Alienage or citizenship status" is defined as "(a) the citizenship of any person, or (b) the immigration status of any person who is not a citizen or national of the United States." This prohibition would apply to "citizen only" or "green card

---

3. 42 U.S.C.A. § 1981.

4. Saint Francis College v. Al–Khazraji, 481 U.S. 604, 107 S.Ct. 2022, 95 L.Ed.2d 582 (1987); Shaare Tefila Congregation v. Cobb, 481 U.S. 615, 107 S.Ct. 2019, 95 L.Ed.2d 594 (1987).

5. 8 U.S.C.A. § 1324 a, b.

6. 8 U.S.C.A. § 1324b(a)(1).

7. Executive Law § 296(1)(a).

8. Executive Law § 296(1)(d). *See* Holland v. Edwards, 282 App.Div. 353, 122 N.Y.S.2d 721, aff'd 307 N.Y. 38, 119 N.E.2d 581 (1954) (the court held that inquiries about nationality and religion of applicants by an employment agency constituted an unlawful employment practice).

9. Discrimination on the basis of race or color is prohibited in accordance with the framework outlined § 17.59, *infra*.

10. N.Y.C.Admin. Code § 8–107(1)(a).

11. N.Y.C.Admin. Code § 8–107(14), (21).

only" employment rules.[12] For a discussion of agency charges or litigation, generally, *see infra,* Sections 17.66–69; for a discussion of burdens of proof, *see infra,* Section 17.59.

Library References:
West's Key No. Digests, Civil Rights ⚖142.

§ 17.50 Statutory Causes of Action—Pension Plans

***ERISA.*[1]** The Employee Retirement Income Security Act ("ERISA") protects the interests of workers who participate in pension plans, and their beneficiaries. While the provisions of ERISA are complex and beyond the scope of this chapter, the essence of ERISA is that it confers a legal right to obtain "vested" benefits, and makes it illegal for employers to interfere with the attainment of any right under a benefit or pension plan or statute.[2] A plan participant may also bring an action (called a "Section 504" claim) against plan administrators or trustees under the theory of breach of fiduciary duty.[3] Depending on the nature of the action, legal or equitable remedies will be available. A jury trial is generally not available.

Section 510 claims do not depend on an interpretation of the benefit plan; rather they commonly arise when an employer discharges an employee prior to the vesting of plan benefits or when a self-insured employer learns that the plaintiff is about to incur substantial medical costs. Generally, the relief sought is "make-whole"; the awarding of attorneys' fees is discretionary based on the merits. A jury trial may be available because the claim is legal in terms of the statutory rights and claims for damages. Claims must be brought in federal district court.

ERISA may apply to welfare benefits, including severance benefits (other than lump sum payment benefits),[4] disability insurance, life insurance, and other benefits.[5]

When filing a Section 501(a)(1)(B) ERISA complaint that seeks to enforce the terms of a plan, copies of the complaint must be served by

12. *See generally* Kramer v. World Zionist Organization-American Section, Decision and Order NYCCHR Compl. No. 11061–GP (Apr. 30, 1986).

§ 17.50

1. 29 U.S.C.A. §§ 1001 *et seq.*

2. 29 U.S.C.A. § 1140 (also known as "Section 510").

3. 29 U.S.C.A. §§ 1104(a)(1); *See* Mullins v. Pfizer, Corp., 23 F.3d 663 (2d Cir. 1994), on remand 899 F.Supp. 69 (D.C.Conn.1995) (plaintiff entitled to jury trial based on employer's affirmative misrepresentations and failure to disclose early retirement plan under consideration); Katsaros v. Cody, 568 F.Supp. 360 (E.D.N.Y. 1983), aff'd remanded, 744 F.2d 270 (2d Cir.1984)(failure of plan trustees to investigate $2 million loan breached the prudent person standard). The provisions governing the bringing of an ERISA action are set forth under Section 502, 29 U.S.C.A. § 1132(a)(1).

4. *See, e.g.,* Reichelt v. Emhart Corp., 921 F.2d 425 (2d Cir.1990), cert. den. 501 U.S. 1231, 111 S.Ct. 2854, 115 L.Ed.2d 1022 (1991).

5. *See* ERISA § 3(1), 29 C.F.R. § 2510.3–2(b).

§ 17.50 EMPLOYMENT LAW Ch. 17

certified mail on both the Secretary of Labor and the Secretary of the Treasury, who may then intervene.[6]

Library References:

West's Key No. Digests, Pensions ⚍21–32.

§ 17.51 Statutory Causes of Action—Plant Closing, Mass Layoffs

The Worker Adjustment and Retraining Notification Act ("WARN")[1] requires the employer to notify affected employees or their union 60 days before an anticipated plant closing or a termination of a substantial number of jobs in the workplace. If the employer fails to give this notice, it is obligated to give the affected employees backpay for the period they would have been employed during the 60–day notification period had the employer not shut down.[2] WARN applies only to businesses with 100 or more employees. There is no government agency overseeing the enforcement of WARN. Employees who believe their rights have been violated may bring a lawsuit in federal court on behalf of themselves and others similarly affected, and may recover their backpay, benefits, and attorneys' fees.[3] The statute and its interpretive guidance should be consulted for further WARN definitions, exemptions, and duties.[4]

§ 17.52 Statutory Causes of Action—Polygraphs

The Employee Polygraph Protection Act[1] generally prohibits the use of polygraphs in employment, and sets forth a limited exemption for ongoing investigations, and establishes procedures for the protection of employees in the use of polygraphs.

An employer may use a polygraph if there is an ongoing investigation involving economic loss or injury to the employer's business, such as theft, embezzlement, misappropriation, industrial espionage or sabotage. In addition to carrying out such an investigation, the employer must have a reasonable suspicion that the employee was involved in the

---

6. 29 U.S.C.A. § 502(h). The Secretary of Labor may be served by sending the complaint to: Secretary of Labor, Attention: Associate Solicitor, Plan Benefits Security Division, U.S. Department of Labor, 200 Constitution Ave. N.W., Washington, D.C. 20210.

The Secretary of Treasury may be served by sending the complaint to: Secretary of Treasury, Internal Revenue Service, Attention: Employee Plans Division, 1111 Constitution Ave., N.W., Washington, D.C. 20224.

§ 17.51

1. 29 U.S.C.A. §§ 2102 *et seq.*

2. *See* Gonzalez v. AMR Services Corp., 68 F.3d 1529 (2d Cir.1995) (transfer of employees to new division did not constitute employment loss triggering WARN notification duties).

3. Finnan v. L.F. Rothschild & Co., 726 F.Supp. 460 (S.D.N.Y.1989) (backpay and benefits are exclusive remedies).

4. *See* 29 C.F.R. § 639.3.

§ 17.52

1. 29 U.S.C.A. § 2006(d)(1).

incident and must present "additional supporting evidence," other than the polygraph test analysis or the refusal to take the test, in order to discriminate against the employee. Otherwise, the employee may not be denied employment or adversely treated based on his/her refusal to submit to a polygraph or based on the results of a polygraph.

The complaint should set forth:

(a) employer's demand that plaintiff take a polygraph test;

(b) employer's lack of reasonable suspicion that plaintiff was engaged in causing an economic loss or injury to its business;

(c) plaintiff's refusal to submit to the polygraph examination; and

(d) defendant's discharge, discipline or other discrimination against plaintiff because plaintiff refused to submit to the polygraph test or complained, testified or participated in a proceeding under the statute.

§ 17.53 Statutory Causes of Action—Public Employee

Civil Service Law of New York. Although many causes of action outlined here are available to public sector employees, such as the antidiscrimination laws,[1] counsel must look to the Civil Service Law to determine how such claims are processed. In addition, depending on the status of the employee, the Civil Service Law is likely to provide other substantive and procedural due process rights to the state or local employee who has been adversely treated on the job.

The Civil Service Law categorizes employees as "unclassified" or "classified." Unclassified positions, listed in section 35 of the Civil Service Law, include certain legislative officers, department chiefs, and various educational positions. These positions are generally filled by appointment. The "classified service" encompasses the balance of positions. Four categories exist in the classified service:

(a) exempt class—examination or other qualification requirements are not "practicable" for these positions, which are listed in rules of the State Department of Civil Service and in local agency rules;[2]

(b) noncompetitive class—noncompetitive examination, followed by appointment;[3]

(c) labor class—unskilled laborers whose positions are filled by appointment (no examinations) as long as minimum requirements are met;[4]

---

§ 17.53
1. Federal workers are covered by the Rehabilitation Act, not the Americans with Disabilities Act. *See supra,* § 17.43.

2. Civil Service Law § 41(2).
3. Civil Service Law § 42.
4. *Id.*

(d) competitive class—competitive examinations determine merit and fitness of applicants.[5]

In seeking a position within these classifications, the applicant will find various mechanisms for challenging determinations, such as to fitness.[6] Employees who wish to challenge discipline or discharge may look to Civil Service Law § 75, which sets forth due process requirements for many classes of employees. Teachers, on the other hand, will find similar provisions in the Education Law.[7] Note: Section 75–b of Civil Service Law provides whistleblower protection that permits employees to commence a private lawsuit to challenge retaliatory discharges.[8]

CPLR Article 78. Employees who exhaust their remedies under Section 75 ultimately may seek to challenge a final determination of the Civil Service Commission by instituting a judicial review proceeding under CPLR Article 78. Article 78 generally allows a court to review whether an agency determination was arbitrary and capricious, was made in bad faith, or was otherwise illegal.[9] Dismissal or discipline that is so disproportionate to the offense that it "shocks" one's sense of fairness may also be challenged.[10] Article 78 may provide an avenue of recourse for public sector employees not covered by the due process requirements of Section 75, such as those in probationary or confidential, noncompetitive positions.[11] The Statute of Limitations for commencing an Article 78 proceeding is four months after the final agency determination.[12]

Collective Bargaining Law. The Public Employees Fair Employment Act ("the Taylor Law")[13] regulates the collective bargaining process between state and municipal employers and employee organizations. The Taylor Law also created the Public Employment Relations Board ("PERB"), which oversees the administration and effectuates the goals of the Taylor Law.

Library References:

West's Key No. Digests, Officers and Public Employees ⚖60–71.5.

§ 17.54 Statutory Causes of Action—Pregnancy

Title VII. Title VII was amended by the Pregnancy Discrimination

---

5. Civil Service Law § 44.

6. *E.g.,* Civil Service Law § 50(4) provides an opportunity to submit facts prior to disqualification in the competitive class.

7. Education Law § 3020–a.

8. Civil Service Law § 75–b.

9. York v. McGuire, 63 N.Y.2d 760, 480 N.Y.S.2d 320, 469 N.E.2d 838 (1984).

10. Pell v. Board of Education, 34 N.Y.2d 222, 356 N.Y.S.2d 833, 313 N.E.2d 321 (1974).

11. *See* Scherbyn v. Wayne–Finger Lakes Bd. of Cooperative Education Services, 77 N.Y.2d 753, 570 N.Y.S.2d 474, 573 N.E.2d 562 (1991).

12. CPLR 217.

13. Civil Service Law §§ 200 *et seq.*

Ch. 17 STATUTORY CAUSES OF ACTION—PRIVACY § 17.55

Act of 1978[1] to explicitly prohibit discrimination on the basis of pregnancy. Employers may not make adverse decisions simply because a woman is pregnant, or is likely to become pregnant. Nor may employers differentiate between pregnancy-related disabilities and other disabilities or treat leave for pregnancy differently from leave for other disabilities.[2] Pregnancy-related benefits offered to female employees must also be offered to the pregnant spouses of covered male employees.[3] Fetal protection policies may discriminate against women on the basis of pregnancy and must meet the requirements of a BFOQ (*bona fide* occupational qualification) to be valid.[4] Basic Title VII litigation practice, procedures and remedies apply to pregnancy discrimination.[5]

New York State Human Rights Law. Denial of sick leave benefits for pregnancy-related disabilities, when they are provided for other forms of disability, also constitutes impermissible discrimination under the Human Rights Law.[6] The rights generally comport with those under Title VII, though the remedies are narrower.

New York City Human Rights Law ("NYCHRL"). For a discussion of agency charges or litigation under the NYCHRL and generally, see *supra*, Sections 17.66–69; for a discussion of burdens of proof, see *supra*, Section 17.59.[7]

Library References:
West's Key No. Digests, Civil Rights ⚖=162.

§ 17.55 Statutory Causes of Action—Privacy

In New York, there is no state common law or statute protecting the right to be free from intrusions into one's seclusion (the right to be "left alone"). Instead, there are various provisions of the Constitution and various statutes that provide a thin patchwork of protection from certain types of intrusive conduct by employers. New York State does recognize

§ 17.54

1. 42 U.S.C.A. § 2000e(k).

2. *See* Quaratino v. Tiffany & Co., 71 F.3d 58 (2d Cir.1995); *see also*, Family and Medical Leave Act of 1993 (discussed *supra*, § 17.45)

3. Newport News Shipbuilding & Dry Dock v. EEOC, 462 U.S. 669, 103 S.Ct. 2622, 77 L.Ed.2d 89 (1983).

4. United Auto. Workers v. Johnson Controls, Inc., 499 U.S. 187, 111 S.Ct. 1196, 113 L.Ed.2d 158 (1991).

5. *See* § 17.59 (burden-shifting); §§ 17.66 *et seq.* (procedures and remedies).

6. Binghamton GHS Employees Federal Credit Union v. State Division of Human Rights, 77 N.Y.2d 12, 563 N.Y.S.2d 385, 564 N.E.2d 1051 (1990)(pregnancy may not be treated differently than other disabilities); Brooklyn Union Gas Co. v. New York State Human Rights Appeal Bd., 41 N.Y.2d 84, 390 N.Y.S.2d 884, 359 N.E.2d 393 (1976) (holding that compliance with provisions of Disability Benefits Law, which exempts disabilities caused by or arising in connection with pregnancy from minimum benefits mandated by law does not relieve private employers with more than three (3) employees from compliance with provisions of the Human Rights Law prohibiting discrimination based on sex in employment cases).

7. Elaine W. v. Joint Diseases Gen. Hospital, 81 N.Y.2d 211, 597, N.Y.S.2d 617, 613 N.E.2d 523 (1993) (policy denying drug treatment to pregnant women based solely on pregnancy violates NYCHRL).

the right to control the use of one's name and likeness,[1] but claims under these provisions rarely arise in the workplace.

Public Sector: Searches, Testing. Government employees in New York are protected by the Fourth Amendment of the United States Constitution, and Article 1, Section 12 of the New York State Constitution, from unreasonable searches and seizures. These may include desk/file searches,[2] and, to a limited degree, drug testing.[3] Federal constitutional-based claims may be brought in federal court under 42 U.S.C.A. § 1983. The Federal and State Constitutions may also protect a "zone of privacy" with respect to invasive questioning by employers.[4] New York State employees may be constrained to bring an Article 78 (CPLR) petition and should be aware of the four month Statute of Limitations under that provision. *See supra,* Section 17.53.

The First Amendment provides free speech and other protections to public sector employees.[5]

Electronic Eavesdropping. The Electronic Communications Privacy Act prohibits anyone's surreptitious monitoring of electronically transmitted conversations, including telephone conversations.[6] Section 2520 limits damages to $100 per day for each day of violation, or $10,000, whichever is greater, although punitive damages are available and are uncapped. The plaintiff should attempt to allege separate violations for each affected person and for acts of interception as separate from dissemination. New York's General Business Law prohibits the use of viewing devices in restrooms.[7] The Penal Law prohibits various types of electronic interceptions with private communications.[8] Generally, the

§ 17.55

1. Civil Rights Law §§ 50, 51. *See also,* Chapter 18 "Civil Rights Law," *infra.*

2. *See* O'Connor v. Ortega, 480 U.S. 709, 107 S.Ct. 1492, 94 L.Ed.2d 714 (1987)(psychiatrist's right of privacy as to belongings in office).

3. Seelig v. Koehler, 76 N.Y.2d 87, 556 N.Y.S.2d 832, 556 N.E.2d 125, cert. denied 498 U.S. 847, 111 S.Ct. 134, 112 L.Ed.2d 102 (1990)(upholding random drug testing of uniformed correction officers).

4. *See* Thorne v. City of El Segundo, 726 F.2d 459(9th Cir.1983), cert. denied 469 U.S. 979, 105 S.Ct. 380, 83 L.Ed.2d 315 (1984)(questioning police applicant about her sexual activities violated constitutional rights).

5. *See* Waters v. Churchill, 511 U.S. 661, 114 S.Ct. 1878, 128 L.Ed.2d 686 (1994); Jeffries v. Harleston, 52 F.3d 9 (2d Cir.1995)(university department chairman's First Amendment rights were not violated when college officials limited his appointment term after he made a controversial speech at off-campus event, when officials reasonably believed his speech was disruptive) (speech); Roberts v. United States Jaycees, 468 U.S. 609, 104 S.Ct. 3244, 82 L.Ed.2d 462 (1984) (association); Rutan v. Republican Party of Illinois, 497 U.S. 62, 110 S.Ct. 2729, 111 L.Ed.2d 52 (1990)(political activities).

6. 18 U.S.C.A. §§ 2510–20. *See* Deal v. Spears, 980 F.2d 1153 (8th Cir.1992)(court held that business use of telephone extension exemption did not apply to employer's eavesdropping and recording of employee's private telephone conversations, because recorder was not provided by telephone company or connected to phone line and the interception was beyond ordinary course of business.) *See also,* Abel v. Bonfanti, 625 F.Supp. 263, 269–71 (S.D.N.Y.1985)(interception of employee's phone calls without consent using tape recorder stated claim).

7. General Business Law § 395–b.

8. Penal Law §§ 250.05, 250.25.

tape recording of conversations by one party, without the consent of the other, is permitted whether over telephone or in person[9]

Personal Records. Mirroring federal law, New York State has two statutes which allow persons to obtain records or other types of information from the government. Like the federal Freedom of Information Act ("FOIA"),[10] New York's Freedom of Information Law ("FOIL"),[11] allows persons to request various kinds of information from government files, subject to a list of exemptions to disclosure.[12]

The Personal Privacy Protection Law ("PPPL")[13] is analogous to the Federal Privacy Act.[14] Subject to certain exemptions, the statute allows individuals to obtain and correct government records about themselves.[15]

AIDS. In New York State, the disclosure of the results of HIV tests to anyone except health care personnel and certain other persons is prohibited without the consent of the tested person.[16] Disclosure by a government entity of AIDS-related information may give rise to a constitutional claim.[17]

For further privacy-related claims, see Polygraphs (*supra,* Section 17.52), Credit Information (*supra,* Section 17.42), and Legal Off Duty Activities (*supra,* Section 17.47).

§ 17.56 Statutory Causes of Action—Religious Discrimination

Title VII. Discrimination because of religion or creed is prohibited under 42 U.S.C.A. § 2000e–2. The standard disparate treatment analysis under Title VII, which prohibits discrimination because of one's religion focuses on adverse decisions and harassment.[1] In addition, employers have an affirmative duty to reasonably accommodate employees whose sincerely-held religious beliefs and practices conflict with workplace policies and rules.[2] While the duty is minimal under Title VII, it may be weightier under NYSHRL and NYCHRL.[3]

---

9. Heller v. Champion Int'l Corp., 891 F.2d 432 (2d Cir.1989).

10. 5 U.S.C.A. § 552.

11. Public Officers Law §§ 84 *et seq.*

12. Public Officers Law § 89.

13. Public Officers Law §§ 91 *et seq.*

14. 5 U.S.C.A. § 552a.

15. *See* Lochner v. Surles, 149 Misc.2d 243, 564 N.Y.S.2d 673 (Sup.Ct., Albany County, 1990).

16. Public Health Law § 2782.

17. *See* Doe v. City of New York, 15 F.3d 264, 9 IER Cas. (BNA) 360 (2d Cir. 1994) (HIV-infected city human rights commission complainant has right to privacy which was violated when the conciliation agreement he entered into was publicized by agency).

§ 17.56

1. Philbrook v. Ansonia Board of Education, 925 F.2d 47 (2d Cir.), cert. denied 501 U.S. 1218, 111 S.Ct. 2828, 115 L.Ed.2d 998 (1991); Peck v. Sony Music Corp., 1995 WL 505653, 68 FEP Cas. (BNA) 1025 (S.D.N.Y.1995)(hostile environment created when plaintiff was repeatedly called "a sinner" who had to "repent").

2. 42 U.S.C.A. § 2000e-j.

3. Trans World Airlines v. Hardison, 432 U.S. 63, 84, 97 S.Ct. 2264, 2277, 53 L.Ed.2d 113 (1977)(to establish an undue hardship, the employer is required only to

New York State Human Rights Law. Under the Executive Law,[4] employers bear a heavier duty to accommodate employees' religious practices than under Title VII. "Undue economic hardship," according to the Court of Appeals, is a "significant" or "palpable increase in costs," as opposed to the "more than de minimis" federal standard.[5] For a discussion of agency charges or litigation, generally, *see infra,* Sections 17.66–69; for a discussion of burdens of proof, *see infra,* Section 17.59.

New York City Human Rights Law ("NYCHRL"). Discrimination based on one's actual or perceived creed or religion is unlawful.[6] Moreover, NYCHRL makes it unlawful for an employer to interfere with one's sabbath or "any other religious custom or usage," or "to impose upon a person as a condition of obtaining or retaining employment any terms or conditions, compliance with which would require such person to violate, or forego a practice of, his or her creed or religion ..."[7]

The "reasonable accommodation" duty includes an "undue hardship" standard that placed a burden of proof on the employer to show a hardship, but the scope of that duty is unclear due to the lack of published decisions on this point.

Religious Entity exclusion. Title VII, NYSHRL, and NYCHRL all contain similar provisions partially exempting religious organizations from the religious discrimination laws.[8]

Library References:

West's Key No. Digests, Civil Rights ⚖151.

§ 17.57 Statutory Causes of Action—Sex Discrimination, Harassment

Sex Discrimination Generally. Sex discrimination litigation has given rise to several variations on the standard theories of disparate treatment discrimination. These are outlined below. Otherwise, the litigation framework for sex discrimination, whether under Title VII, NYSHRL, or NYCHRL, conforms with the general Title VII rules explained *infra,* at § 17.59.

Sexual Harassment. Two types of sexual harassment have been

show that the accommodation would cause it to incur more than a *de minimis* cost).

4. Executive Law § 296(10)(c).

5. *See* Genesee Hospital v. State Division of Human Rights, 50 N.Y.2d 917, 431 N.Y.S.2d 523, 409 N.E.2d 995 (1980)(employer failed to attempt to accommodate the known religious beliefs of its employees or to prove that such efforts would be futile); State Div. of Human Rights v. Carnation Co., 42 N.Y.2d 873, 397 N.Y.S.2d 781, 366 N.E.2d 869 (1977)(employer required to reasonably accommodate a religious day as long as it does not incur a palpable increase in costs).

6. N.Y.C.Admin. Code § 8–107(1),(2).

7. NYCHRL § 8–107(3)(a), (b).

8. *See* 42 U.S.C.A. § 2000e–1; Executive Law § 296(11), and N.Y.C.Admin. Code § 8–107(9), (12).

identified: *quid pro quo*, and hostile work environment[1] Hostile work environment harassment is applicable to race, religion, and other forms of discrimination.

The elements of a claim for *quid pro quo* sexual harassment are:

(a) the employee is a member of a protected group;

(b) the employee was subject to unwelcome sexual harassment;

(c) the harassment complained of was based upon sex;

(d) the harassment affected tangible aspects of the employee's compensation, terms, conditions, or privileges of employment; and

(e) *respondeat superior*.[2]

While *quid pro quo* harassment often involves allegations of requests by supervisors for sexual favors, the court in *Bridges v. Eastman Kodak Co.* pointed out that "other verbal or physical conduct of a sexual nature is actionable under the *quid pro quo* theory such as where a supervisor hold[s] out the employer's benefits as an inducement to the employee to submit to the sexually harassing conduct."[3] If employees are compelled to withstand sexual advances, requests for sexual favors, or any verbal or physical conduct of a sexual nature by an employer or supervisor, and if the purpose or effect of this behavior is to unreasonably hinder an individual's work performance or create an intimidating working environment, it constitutes actionable sexual harassment.[4]

Unlike a claim of *quid pro quo* harassment, the elements of a hostile work environment claim need not include an allegation of *respondeat superior* as long as the employer is alleged to have known of the sexual harassment, or should have known of it. The elements, therefore, are that:

(a) the harassment was severe or pervasive;

(b) it altered the conditions of employment;

(c) it created an intimidating, hostile or offensive working environment;

(d) it was unwelcome;

(e) the employer was aware (or should have been aware) of the harassment, or a supervisor was aided by his or her apparent

---

§ 17.57

1. *See generally* Meritor Savings Bank v. Vinson, 477 U.S. 57, 106 S.Ct. 2399, 91 L.Ed.2d 49 (1986).

2. Bridges v. Eastman Kodak Co., 822 F.Supp. 1020 (S.D.N.Y.1993).

3. *Id.* at 1026, 1028; *see* Harris v. Forklift Systems, Inc., 510 U.S. 17, 114 S.Ct. 367, 126 L.Ed.2d 295 (1993); Karibian v. Columbia University, 14 F.3d 773 (2d Cir. 1994).

4. *See* Rudow v. New York City Commission on Human Rights, 123 Misc.2d 709, 474 N.Y.S.2d 1005 (Sup.Ct., N.Y. County, 1984), aff'd 109 A.D.2d 1111, 487 N.Y.S.2d 453 (1st Dep't 1985).

authority in carrying out the harassment.[5]

Where the nature of the harassment is egregious and not known to the employer, or especially egregious (e.g., rape by co-workers), the assertion may be made that the act is beyond the scope of the employment of the offending employees and, as a consequence, the employer is not liable. Co-workers, it should be noted, may not be held personally liable as "employers" under Title VII.

Where the employer did not and could not know of the hostile work environment, a key defense to negate liability is that the employer took "prompt remedial action" upon learning of the harassment.

New York State Human Rights Law. The NYSHRL (N.Y. Executive Law § 296(1)(a)) generally follows the guidelines for sexual harassment litigation formulated under Title VII.[6]

New York City Human Rights Law. N.Y.C. Administrative Code § 8–602 appears to follow the Title VII guidelines concerning sexual harassment.[7]

Library References:

West's Key No. Digests, Civil Rights ⚖158–167.

§ 17.58 Statutory Causes of Action—Sexual Orientation Discrimination

Federal Law. Sexual orientation is not protected under Title VII. Federal employees may be protected, however, under the Fifth and Fourteenth Amendments.[1]

New York State Human Rights Law. NYSHRL does not specifically protect sexual orientation. Employees seeking benefits for same-sex spouses have proceeded under NYSHRL's marital status discrimination provision.

New York City Human Rights Law. Section 8–107(2) of the N.Y.C. Administrative Code prohibits discrimination relating to actual or

---

5. *See* Karibian v. Columbia University, 14 F.3d 773 (2d Cir.1994).

6. *See* Rudow v. New York City Commission on Human Rights, 123 Misc.2d 709, 474 N.Y.S.2d 1005, aff'd 109 A.D.2d 1111, 487 N.Y.S.2d 453 (1st Dep't 1985).

7. *See, e.g.,* Ruiz v. Arcade Cleaning Corp., Rec. Dec. and Order NYCCHR Compl. No. EM 00465–08/29/88 (and related cases)(Dec. 5, 1994)($300,000 compensation for mental anguish awarded to plaintiffs for various acts of sexual harassment, including attempted rape); Lebron v. Caterair International, Rec. Dec. and Order NYCCHR Compl. No. E90–02061 (Jan. 28, 1994), Dec. and Order (Mar. 16, 1994)($75,000 in mental anguish compensation awarded against company based on co-worker hostile work environment sexual harassment); Polster v. American Society for the Prevention of Cruelty to Animals, Rec. Dec. and Ord. NYCCHR Compl. No. EM02423–02/16/90–DE (Feb. 15, 1995)(female humane officer unlawfully harassed and terminated because she was female and a lesbian).

§ 17.58

1. *See* Pruitt v. Cheney, 963 F.2d 1160 (9th Cir.1991) (discharged lesbian Army reservist could make equal protection claim); *but see* Shahar v. Bowers, 114 F.3d 1097 (11th Cir.1997).

perceived sexual orientation, which is defined as heterosexuality, homosexuality, or bisexuality.[2]

Transsexualism. Employees undergoing sex changes may be protected, not as a matter of sexual orientation, but rather on the basis of gender.[3]

Library References:

West's Key No. Digests, Civil Rights ⚖164.

§ 17.59 Statutory Causes of Action—Title VII, Burdens of Proof

Various theories protect discrimination claimants under Title VII and the New York State and New York City Human Rights Laws. Substantively, discrimination litigation under the New York State and New York City Human Rights laws generally follows the same shifting-burden frameworks and guidelines followed under federal law.[1]

Disparate Treatment. The employee must show that he or she was discriminated against intentionally because of his or her protected characteristic (*e.g.*, race). The employee bears this burden of proof, although the burden of production shifts to the employer if the employee has satisfied the pleading requirements of the *prima facie* case.

The employer need not have based the decision solely on the protected characteristic in order to be held liable. If there is direct evidence of discriminatory intent, the employee will not only satisfy the initial burden but also will shift an affirmative burden onto the employer to show that it would have made the same decision even in the absence of the discriminatory intent revealed by the direct evidence. This is a "mixed-motives" analysis. If the employer can prove that, even absent the discriminatory motive, it would have taken the same action, the employee will not achieve reinstatement or win any damages, but will be entitled to attorneys' fees, declaratory relief, and certain injunctive relief.[2]

---

2. *See generally*, Polster v. American Society for the Prevention of Cruelty to Animals, Rec. Dec. and Order. NYCCHR Compl. No. EM 02423 02/16/90-DE (Feb. 15, 1995)(humane officer unlawfully harassed and terminated because she was a female and a lesbian).

3. Maffei v. Kolaeton Industry, Inc., 164 Misc.2d 547, 626 N.Y.S.2d 391 (Sup.Ct., N.Y. County, 1995).

§ 17.59

1. *See* Miller Brewing Co. v. State Division of Human Rights, 66 N.Y.2d 937, 489 N.E.2d 745, 498 N.Y.S.2d 776 (1985)(applying Title VII's shifting burden or proof framework to the NYSHRL); Pace College v. City Commission on Human Rights, 38 N.Y.2d 28, 377 N.Y.S.2d 471, 339 N.E.2d 880 (1975) (applying Title VII's shifting burden or proof framework to the NYCHRL).

2. Civil Rights Act of 1991 §§ 107(b)(3)(B)(i), (ii).

If the employee does not have direct evidence, as most do not, the employee is able to establish a *prima facie* case with circumstantial evidence. In most cases, the pleading requirements follow those set forth in *McDonnell Douglas v. Green*.[3] The plaintiff's *prima facie* case would require the following allegations:

(a) plaintiff's membership in a protected group (*e.g.* race);

(b) plaintiff was qualified for the position;

(c) adverse treatment of plaintiff (*e.g.*, rejection, termination); and

(d) employer kept the position open or replaced plaintiff with non-member of a protected group.

Once the *prima facie* case has been established, the employer has the burden to rebut it by offering a legitimate and nondiscriminatory reason for the adverse employment decision. The employer need not prove the legitimate, nondiscriminatory reason; he need only articulate it. The employer would be well advised, however, to have some substantiation so as to guard against the argument that the response was fabricated in order to rebut the plaintiff's allegation.

The third stage of analysis requires the employee to prove that the employer's stated reason for the action is merely pretextual and conceals the real discriminatory reason. The plaintiff must, in other words, prove that the employer's "proffered explanation is unworthy of credence."[4] This three-stage pleading framework often comes to a head at the summary judgment stage, at which time the court weighs whether the plaintiff has gathered sufficient evidence to satisfy its burden to persuade a jury that the employer's assertions of legitimate and nondiscriminatory behavior are unworthy of credence.[5]

Additional defenses against claims of disparate treatment available under Title VII include the "BFOQ" or *bona fide* occupational qualification defense to overtly discriminatory practices upon which a business depends.[6]

Pattern and Practice. When discrimination can be proved to have occured systematically to a large group, the plaintiffs may bring a class action in which liability can be established for the group and individualized proof will be forestalled until the damages stage. Usually these cases are built on statistics.[7]

---

3. 411 U.S. 792, 93 S.Ct. 1817, 36 L.Ed.2d 668 (1973).

4. St. Mary's Honor Ctr. v. Hicks, 509 U.S. 502, 113 S.Ct. 2742, 125 L.Ed.2d 407 (1993).

5. *See* Quaratino v. Tiffany & Co., 71 F.3d 58, 68 FEP Cas. (BNA) 507 (2d Cir. 1995), citing Gallo v. Prudential Residential Services, Ltd., Partnership, 22 F.3d 1219 (2d Cir.1994)(setting forth the Title VII pleading thresholds in the Second Circuit). *See also* Fisher v. Vassar College, 114 F.3d 1332 (2d Cir.1997)(en banc).

6. 42 U.S.C.A. § 2000e–2(e)(1).

7. *See, e.g.*, Ottaviani v. State University of New York at New Paltz, 679 F.Supp. 288, 297 (S.D.N.Y.), aff'd 875 F.2d 365 (2d Cir.1989) cert. den. 493 U.S. 1021, 110 S.Ct. 721, 107 L.Ed.2d 740 (1990)(finding of classwide discrimination based on statistics

Harassment. *See* discussion of Sex Discrimination and Harassment at Section 17.57.

Retaliation. Under Title VII (42 U.S.C.A. § 2000e–3(a)), it is unlawful to discriminate against an employee or applicant because that person has either:

(a) opposed any employment practice made unlawful by Title VII, or

(b) filed a charge under Title VII, or

(c) participated (*e.g.*, by testifying, assisting, etc.) in any manner in an investigation, proceeding, or hearing under Title VII.

The NYSHRL and NYCHRL contain similar provisions. Filing a state or city law complaint of discrimination will serve as a predicate for Title VII's anti-retaliation protection.[8]

Disparate Impact. These claims proceed on the theory that neutral employment rules or policies that adversely affect certain protected groups violate Title VII or state and local anti-discrimination laws.[9] The employer may defend against a *prima facie* showing of disparate impact by proving that the employment policy causing the significant statistical disparity is consistent with business necessity.[10]

Unlike Title VII, the plaintiff pleading a disparate impact cause of action under the New York City Human Rights Law does not have to identify the particular practice that created the statistical disparity.[11]

Library References:

West's Key No. Digests, Civil Rights ⟲377.1–380.

§ 17.60 Statutory Causes of Action—Unemployment Insurance

Unemployment insurance provides salary replacement benefits to those who have become unemployed through no fault of their own. To be eligible, the claimant must have worked as an employee, not as an

creates rebuttable presumption of discriminatory treatment under practice and pattern aspects of Title VII).

8. *See* Mays v. New York City Police Dept., 701 F.Supp. 80 (S.D.N.Y.1988). *See* list of anti-reprisal provisions *supra* at § 17.38.

9. Griggs v. Duke Power Co., 401 U.S. 424, 91 S.Ct. 849, 28 L.Ed.2d 158 (1971); State Div. of Human Rights v. Kilian Mfg. Corp., 35 N.Y.2d 201, 360 N.Y.S.2d 603, 318 N.E.2d 770 (1974) (statistical evidence as to the members of minority groups resident in the area, which was the largest source of employer's employees, and as to the percentage of minority workers employed by the employer, as well as its recruitment practices, shows that the Human Rights Division had sufficient reason to conclude that there was constructive discrimination in employer's hiring practices despite the absence of proof of subjective motive on the part of the employer to produce such results).

10. *See* 42 U.S.C.A. § 2000e–2(k), as amended by the Civil Rights Act of 1991; N.Y.C.Admin. Code § 8–107(17)(a) ("significant business objective").

11. N.Y.C.Admin. Code § 8–107(17)(a)(2).

§ 17.60   EMPLOYMENT LAW   Ch. 17

independent contractor or self-employed person.[1] The issue of employee status turns on the degrees of control over the performance of the work and related factors.[2] The claimant must be able to, and available for, work and have had at least 20 weeks of employment in the twelve months preceding the filing of the claim.[3] Generally, benefits are paid up to a maximum benefit of $300 per week, for up to 26 weeks in a given benefit year.[4] Additional benefits of up to 13 weeks may also be available.[5]

To receive benefits, the claimant may file an application at the state employment office serving the area in which he or she worked or resides.[6] The Commissioner of Labor then requests information from the former employer in order to determine the claimant's entitlement to benefits.[7] An initial determination is made, which can then be contested by the employer or the claimant at a hearing before an administrative law judge.[8] An appeal from the hearing officer's findings can be made by either party to the Unemployment Insurance Appeal Board, followed by an appeal directly to the Appellate Division, Third Department, in Albany. See Chapter 37 "Civil Appellate Practice Before the Appellate Division and Other Intermediate Appellate Courts," *infra*.

The most common grounds for the denial of benefits are that the employee voluntarily left employment without good cause[9] or was terminated for misconduct.[10] Misconduct generally entails gross negligence or an intentional disregard for the employer's business, particularly after warnings are given. Mere inefficiency or the commission of an error of judgment are usually not enough to render the claimant ineligible. In other words, the issue is whether the employee would have reasonably known that the conduct would lead to discharge.[11]

Library References:

West's Key No. Digests, Social Security and Public Welfare ⚖︎251–281.

§ 17.61   Statutory Causes of Action—Unionization, Rights Within Unions

The National Labor Relations Act of 1935 (the "NLRA" or "Wagner Act"), which was amended by the Labor Management Relations Act of

§ 17.60

1. Labor Law § 511.
2. *See, e.g*, Matter of Interglobal Travel Service, Inc., 156 A.D.2d 849, 549 N.Y.S.2d 849 (3d Dep't 1989).
3. Labor Law § 527(1).
4. Labor Law § 590(4), (5).
5. Labor Law § 601(3).
6. Labor Law § 596(1).
7. Labor Law § 597(1).
8. Labor Law § 620(1).
9. Labor Law § 593(1); *see, e.g.*, In re Nelson, 173 A.D.2d 995, 569 N.Y.S.2d 513 (3d Dep't 1991).
10. Labor Law § 593(3).
11. *See, e.g.*, In re Benitez, 165 A.D.2d 924, 560 N.Y.S.2d 366 (3d Dep't 1990)(denial of benefits for misconduct based on termination for absenteeism and tardiness after warnings).

Ch. 17   UNIONIZATION, RIGHTS WITHIN UNIONS   § 17.61

1947 ("LMRA" or "Taft–Hartley Act"), and the Labor Management Reporting and Disclosure Act of 1959 ("LMRDA" or "Landrum–Griffin Act"), constitutes the basis of federal labor law. The basic purposes of the three laws and some of the major provisions affecting employees are discussed briefly here. A more substantive review is beyond the scope of this chapter; labor law authority should be consulted.

National Labor Relations Act.[1] The NLRA sets out basic procedures for establishing a collective bargaining relationship. It gives workers protection against discrimination for engaging in concerted[2] activity, and it established the National Labor Relations Board, which is the agency administering the NLRA. The NLRA applies only to private employers. Public employees are covered under the Federal Labor Management and Employee Relations Law[3] or the New York Public Employees' Fair Employment Act ("Taylor Law") (*see* this section, below).

Section 7 of the NLRA protects nonsupervisors who engage in, or who do not wish to engage in, concerted activities.[4] For union members, such activities are those taken for the "mutual aid or protection" of workers.[5] In the nonunion context, the terms refer to employee activities engaged in with or on the authority of other employees, and not solely on behalf of the employee himself.[6]

Section 8 of the NLRA, as amended by the LMRA, sets forth actions that will be considered "unfair labor practices" when engaged in by the employer[7] or by the union.[8]

An employee whose Section 7 rights have been violated by an employer may file an unfair labor practice ("ULP" charge), pursuant to Section 8(a) of the NLRA, with the regional National Labor Relations Board ("NLRB").[9] The NLRB is empowered to prevent any person from engaging in unfair labor practices (listed in Section 158 of Title 29) affecting commerce.[10] The charge must be filed within six months of the incident on which the charge is based. Any person aggrieved by a final order of the Board may appeal to the United States Court of Appeals "wherein the [ULP] in question was alleged to have been engaged in or wherein such person resides or transacts business, . . . by filing a written

§ 17.61

1. 29 U.S.C.A. §§ 151 *et seq.*

2. Meyers Industries, Inc., 1984 WL 35992, 268 N.L.R.B. 493, 497 (1984) ("Meyers I"); Meyers Industries, Inc., 1986 WL 54414, 281 N.L.R.B. 882 (1986) ("Meyers II"), enf'd sub nom Prill v. N.L.R.B., 835 F.2d 1481 (D.C.Cir.1987); Ewing v. N.L.R.B., 861 F.2d 353, 361 n. 4 (2d Cir.1988)("Individual action will be considered 'concerted' because sufficient nexus exists between the act in question and the collective action. For example, a lone act is concerted if it stems from prior 'concerted activity' or if an individual acts, formally or informally, on behalf of a group.").

3. 5 U.S.C.A. §§ 7101 *et seq.*

4. 29 U.S.C.A. § 157.

5. N.L.R.B. v. City Disposal Systems, Inc., 465 U.S. 822, 104 S.Ct. 1505, 79 L.Ed.2d 839 (1984).

6. *Id.*

7. 29 U.S.C.A. § 158(a).

8. 29 U.S.C.A. § 158(b).

9. 29 U.S.C.A. § 158.

10. 29 U.S.C.A. § 160.

§ 17.61 EMPLOYMENT LAW Ch. 17

petition praying that the order of the Board be modified or set aside."[11] There is no private right of action under the NLRA.

Labor Management Relations Act. The LMRA imposes limitations on the power of unions to pressure employers and employees in various circumstances. One notable feature is that it grants jurisdiction to federal courts to enforce collective bargaining agreements on behalf of employers, unions, or individual union members.[12] This right to sue on the basis of contract has given rise to "hybrid" actions in which aggrieved union members sue both their employer and their union (under the "duty of fair representation") for failing to comply with the collective bargaining agreement.[13]

Labor Management Reporting and Disclosure Act. The LMRDA concerns the internal governance of unions. In addition to regulating union elections in detail, it protects democracy within unions by affording members equal votes in elections[14] and free speech protections when criticizing union officials,[15] and by imposing duties of trust on union officials who spend union funds.[16]

New York State Public Employment and Labor Law. The New York State Employment Relations Act[17] ("NYSERA") is similar in scope to the National Labor Relations Act. The Act is administered by the State Employment Relations Board and addresses issues not covered by federal law. Discussion of the NYSERA is outside the scope of this chapter.

Public employment in New York State is covered by the provisions of the Civil Service Law, principally, the Public Employees' Fair Employment Act ("Taylor Law").[18] New York City has its own collective bargaining law.[19] The rules and regulations governing public employment are complex and extensive. Guidance for questions relating to these labor laws should be sought from the appropriate authorities.

Library References:

West's Key No. Digests, Labor Relations ⚖=81–151.

11. 29 U.S.C.A. § 160(f).
12. 29 U.S.C.A. § 185; see Vaca v. Sipes, 386 U.S. 171, 87 S.Ct. 903, 17 L.Ed.2d 842 (1967).
13. Clayton v. Automobile Workers, 451 U.S. 679, 101 S.Ct. 2088, 68 L.Ed.2d 538 (1981); DelCostello v. Teamsters, 462 U.S. 151, 103 S.Ct. 2281, 76 L.Ed.2d 476 (1983). Members may also sue their unions or union officials for breach of their union's constitution. Shea v. McCarthy, 953 F.2d 29 (2d Cir.1992).
14. 29 U.S.C.A. § 411(a)(1).
15. 29 U.S.C.A. § 411(a)(2). See Salzhandler v. Caputo, 316 F.2d 445 (2d Cir. 1963), cert. denied 375 U.S. 946, 84 S.Ct. 344, 11 L.Ed.2d 275 (1963); Petramale v. Laborers Union, 736 F.2d 13 (2d Cir.1984), cert. denied 469 U.S. 1087, 105 S.Ct. 593, 83 L.Ed.2d 702 (1984).
16. 29 U.S.C.A. § 501(a).
17. Labor Law §§ 700 et seq.
18. Civil Service Law §§ 200 et seq.
19. See N.Y.C.Admin. Code, ch. 3.

§ 17.62 Statutory Causes of Action—Unsafe Workplace

Federal Occupational Safety and Health Act.[1] This law does not create a private right of action for employees. Rather, it established an administrative mechanism by which employees may complain about, and sometimes refuse to work in, unsafe workplaces. The Occupational Safety and Health Administration ("OSHA"), a division of the U.S. Department of Labor, sets safety standards, inspects workplaces and enforces the law, often on behalf of employees affected by unsafe conditions. Section 11(c) of the Act provides anti-retaliation protection for any person discriminated against because he has instituted a proceeding, testified, or exercised any right afforded by the Act. The employee must file a complaint with the regional OHSA office within 30 days of the violation. If an investigation reveals a violation, an action will be brought on the employee's behalf in federal court. Relief may include backpay and reinstatement.[2] The employer compliance provisions are beyond the scope of this chapter.

Retaliation against employees who complain about unsafe workplaces that violate New York State Labor Law is prohibited.[3] Unlike the federal law, it does provide a private right of action to employees who make complaints or institute proceedings stemming from unsafe work conditions.[4]

Library References:
West's Key No. Digests, Labor Relations ⚖9.5–9.8.

§ 17.63 Statutory Causes of Action—Wages; Unpaid Compensation; Overtime

Unpaid Compensation. The Labor Law of New York protects an employee's right to be paid and to receive all forms of earned compensation, including vacation benefits.[1] It applies to both wage earning and salaried employees. An employee who prevails in a "wage claim" under the Labor Law can recover attorneys' fees and, if the failure to pay was willful, can recover liquidated damages of 25%. An employer cannot withhold earned compensation as a self-help remedy when the employee breaches a duty owed to the employer.[2]

Overtime. Under the Fair Labor Standards Act ("FLSA"),[3] employees are entitled to overtime pay after 40 hours of work in the workweek.

§ 17.62

1. 29 U.S.C.A. §§ 651 *et seq.*
2. 29 U.S.C.A. § 11(3).
3. Labor Law § 215; generally, see Labor Law §§ 200 *et seq.*
4. *See* R.A. Givens, *Practice Commentaries*, Labor Law § 740, p. 545 (main volume); p. 117 (1996 Supp.) (general whistleblower protection).

§ 17.63

1. Labor Law §§ 198(1–a), 198–c.
2. *See* P & L Group, Inc. v. Garfinkel, 150 A.D.2d 663, 541 N.Y.S.2d 535 (2d Dep't 1989); *cf.* Bon Temps Agency, Ltd. v. Greenfield, 184 A.D.2d 280, 584 N.Y.S.2d 824 (1st Dep't), appeal dismissed 81 N.Y.2d 759, 594 N.Y.S.2d 718, 610 N.E.2d 391 (1992).
3. 29 U.S.C.A. § 207(a)(1).

The overtime pay rate must be at least one-and-a-half times the regular rate. Exempt employees include a litany of job titles specified in the FLSA, as well as salaried executives, administrators, professionals, or outside salespersons.[4] To be "salaried" for the purposes of these exemptions, the employee must receive full weekly pay without regard to the number of days or hours worked. The four categories are further defined as follows:

(a) Executive—whose primary (at least 50% of time) duty is management; customarily directs the work of two or more employees, and has responsibility for hiring, firing, and evaluating employees.[5]

(b) Administrator—whose primary duty requires exercise of discretionary and independent judgment; performance of office work directly relates to management policies or business operations (routine clerical work, such as bookkeeping, is not administrative).[6]

(c) Professional—whose primary duty is performance of learned, artistic or educational activities (e.g., medicine, law, theater, teaching.) In addition, the professional must exercise discretion and judgment in the performance of his or her work.[7]

(d) Outside salesperson—(1) who regularly works away from the employer's premises while making sales; and (2) spends no more than 20% of the work week engaged in other activities.[8]

Minimum Wage. The Federal Fair Labor Standards Act mandates that employees be paid a minimum rate of compensation for "hours worked."[9] Hours worked generally includes time spent on job-related activities. Generally, excluded are commuting, washing and changing, doing voluntary work, or on-call time when the employee must be available, but is not restricted in his or activities.

Child Labor. The Federal Fair Labor Standards Act[10] and New York law regulate the employment of "minors" under the age of 18 years. While federal law may add enforcement power and penalties, the standards governing the eligibility of minors to work in New York is found in New York Labor Law §§ 130–144. In general, all working minors must have a work permit or employment certificate. The availability of a permit may depend upon the age of the minor, the nature of the work, whether school is in session, whether the student is in good academic standing, and the need for parental consent. Restrictions are also placed on the number of hours minors can work. Violations of New

---

4. 29 U.S.C.A. § 213(1); 29 C.F.R. § 541.1–3.
5. 29 C.F.R. § 541.103.
6. 29 C.F.R. § 541.2(e)(2).
7. 29 C.F.R. § 541.3(a)-(c).
8. 29 C.F.R. § 541.5(a).
9. 29 U.S.C.A. § 206.
10. 29 U.S.C.A. § 212.

York's child labor law may result in severe penalties, as well as federal liability.

Claims under Fair Labor Standards Act. Claims and questions may be taken to the local wage and hour office of the Department of Labor. An FLSA compliance officer may investigate the complaint to determine if the employer's practices comply with the FLSA. If an FLSA official finds a violation, the Department may attempt to bring the employer into compliance, including the payment of backpay. If the employer refuses to comply, the Secretary of Labor may sue for backpay and liquidated damages in an amount equal to the backpay. The employee may file a private lawsuit for backpay and an equal amount of liquidated damages for "willful" violations, plus attorneys' fees and costs. The suit must be commenced within two years of a nonwillful violation or within three years of a willful violation.[11] "Willfulness" is shown by the employer's knowing or reckless disregard for the matter of whether its conduct was prohibited by the Act.[12] The FLSA contains an anti-retaliation provision.[13]

New York State Wage and Hour Laws. New York State Labor Law provides overtime, minimum wage, and other regulations that are mostly concurrent with the FLSA.[14] Most of the New York law overlaps the federal law; however, differences exist which may provide employees with additional rights and coverage. Employers and employees with wage claims should therefore consult both federal and state law. A full review of the New York State law is beyond the scope of this chapter.

Library References:

West's Key No. Digests, Labor Relations ⌾1081–1107.

§ 17.64 Statutory Causes of Action—Whistleblowing/*QUI TAM*

State Law: Private Sector "Whistleblower Protection" Law. The so-called Whistleblower Protection Statute[1] provides protection for employees who "blow the whistle" on employer conduct that both (i) violates a law, rule, or regulation and (ii) creates and presents a substantial and specific danger to public health or safety.[2] This narrow statute has provided very limited protection for New York employees; of the dozens of cases raising the issue of "whistleblower protection" under Section 740 that have been brought since its passage in 1984, only a few have been sustained by the courts.[3]

11. 29 U.S.C.A. § 216.
12. 29 U.S.C.A. § 255(a).
13. 29 U.S.C.A. § 215(a)(3).
14. Labor Law §§ 652, 657.

§ 17.64

1. Labor Law § 740.

2. *Id.*

3. *See, e.g.,* Rogers v. Lenox Hill Hospital, 211 A.D.2d 248, 626 N.Y.S.2d 137 (1st Dep't 1995) (Section 740 does not require the plaintiff to have personal knowledge of the violation of law or that there be more than a single incident); Granser v. Box Tree

One of the most important considerations for the plaintiff to bear in mind in determining whether to bring a Section 740 claim is the exclusive remedy provision of Section 740(7). Under this provision, the plaintiff may not assert any other claims arising out of the events on which the Section 740 claim is based. This harsh, compulsory waiver operates whether relief is sought in state or federal court.[4] The only type of claim that can survive despite this waiver provision is a constitutional claim.[5]

State Law: Public Employees. A public employee who is fired for disclosing a violation of law, rule or regulation may have a cause of action under New York Civil Service Law § 75–b. Public employees may also bring First Amendment claims when they are discharged in retaliation for complaining about potential corrupt practices.[6]

Federal False Claims Act ("FFCA").[7] The Federal False Claims Act provides whistleblower protection and relief to employees who report to the federal government an employer (or its agents) who "knowingly presents, or causes to be presented, to an officer or employee of the United States Government or a member of the Armed Forces of the United States, a false or fraudulent claim for payment or approval."[8] The terms "knowing" or "knowingly" mean that the person who presents the claim did so with actual knowledge of the falsity of the information,[9] acted in deliberate ignorance of the truth or falsity of the information, or acted in reckless disregard of the truth or falsity of the information.[10] No proof of specific intent is required.[11]

The *"qui tam"* provisions of the FFCA have prompted a considerable amount of litigation in recent years. Under the False Claims Act, individuals are authorized to bring a civil action for a violation of Section 3729 for the person and for the United States Government.[12] The action is brought in the name of the government; the government may either intervene and prosecute the action or allow the original plaintiff—the

---

South Ltd., 164 Misc.2d 191, 623 N.Y.S.2d 977 (Sup.Ct., N.Y. County, 1994) (violations creating hazardous fire conditions sufficiently threatened public health and safety to support a Section 740 cause of action); *Cf.* Bordell v. General Electric, 208 A.D.2d 219, 622 N.Y.S.2d 1001 (3d Dep't 1995), aff'd 88 N.Y.2d 869, 644 N.Y.S.2d 912, 667 N.E.2d 922 (1996) (nuclear reactor employee's reasonable belief there was a radiation leak held insufficient to trigger protection inasmuch as Section 740 requires an actual violation of law, rule or regulation, not supposition that one as occurred).

4. *See* U.S. *ex rel.* Mikes v. Straus, 846 F.Supp. 21 (S.D.N.Y.1994); U.S. *ex rel.* Mikes v. Straus, 853 F.Supp. 115 (S.D.N.Y. 1994).

5. Fischer v. Homes for the Homeless, Inc., 1994 WL 319166 (S.D.N.Y.1994) (Section 1983 cause of action was not waived by assertion of whistleblower claim).

6. *See, e.g.,* Lundgren v. Curiale, 836 F.Supp. 165 (S.D.N.Y. 1993) (employee's suit alleging that he was fired for complaining about practices in ex-Governor Cuomo's office survived the defendant's summary judgment motion).

7. 31 U.S.C.A. § 3729(a)(1).

8. United States v. O'Connell, 890 F.2d 563, 569 (1st Cir.1989).

9. 31 U.S.C.A. § 3729(b)(1).

10. *See* 31 U.S.C.A. § 3729(b)(2).

11. 31 U.S.C.A. § 3729(b)(3).

12. 31 U.S.C.A. § 3730(b)(1).

qui tam relator—to proceed with the suit under Section 3730(b)(4)(B).[13] The action may be dismissed only if the court and the Attorney General give written consent to the dismissal and their reasons for consenting.[14]

If the Government decides to proceed with the action, "it shall have the primary responsibility for prosecuting the action, and shall not be bound by an act of the person bringing the action. Such person shall have the right to continue as a party to the action, subject to the limitations set forth in paragraph (2)."[15]

If the Government pursues the action with the *qui tam* plaintiff, the plaintiff shall receive "at least 15 percent but not more than 25 percent of the proceeds of the action or settlement of the claim, depending upon the extent to which the person substantially contributed to the prosecution of the action."[16] If the Government does not proceed with the action, however, "the person bringing the action or settling the claim shall receive an amount the court decides is reasonable for collecting the civil penalty and damages. The amount shall not be less than 25 percent and not more than 30 percent . . . ."[17]

Library References:

West's Key No. Digests, Master and Servant ⟐30(6.35).

§ 17.65 Statutory Causes of Action—Workers' Compensation

As in most states, employees in New York are automatically covered by workers' compensation and can receive compensation for injuries "arising out of and in the course" of employment.[1] Negligence and fault are irrelevant; however, in return for guaranteed compensation, the employee relinquishes any common law right to sue for negligence. Although workers' compensation is an exclusive remedy, employees still retain the right to sue negligent third parties, such as manufacturers,[2] or even the employer if he or she causes intentional or reckless harm.[3]

Whether the claimant is an employee or an independent contractor is a determination made by the Workers' Compensation Board based on

---

13. U.S. *ex rel.* Kreindler & Kreindler v. United Technologies Corp., 985 F.2d 1148, 1153 (2d Cir.1993), cert. denied 508 U.S. 973, 113 S.Ct. 2962, 125 L.Ed.2d 663 (1993).

14. 31 U.S.C.A. § 3730(b)(1).

15. 31 U.S.C.A. § 3730(c)(1).

16. *Id.* § 3730(d)(1).

17. *Id.* § 3730(d)(2).

§ 17.65

1. Workers' Compensation Law §§ 2(7), 10(1). *See generally* Chapter 32 "Workers' Compensation," *infra.*

2. *Id.* § 29(1).

3. *See* Morris v. United Parcel Service, 134 A.D.2d 840, 521 N.Y.S.2d 591 (4th Dep't 1987)(injuries from false imprisonment). For a fuller discussion of Workers' Compensation, *see* Chapter 32 "Workers' Compensation," *infra.*

numerous factors including, for example, the extent of control over the performance of the work, the method of payment, and the furnishing of tools.[4] Once it is determined that the claimant is an employee, a causal connection must be shown between the injury and the job which, in turn, gives rise to the presumption that the injury is compensable.[5] The employer may rebut this presumption by presenting substantial evidence that, for example, the injury was the result of (1) personal pursuits, (2) intent to injure oneself or another, (3) intoxication, or (4) activity unrelated to work.[6] Occupational diseases[7] and psychological injuries are compensable, even if there is no physical component.[8]

An employee must report his or her injury to the employer within 30 days of the accident. Failure to do so will cause a forfeiture of the claim.[9] A claim for workers' compensation must be filed with the Workers' Compensation Board within two years after the date of the accident.[10] An employer may not discriminate against an employee because he or she has filed a claim or has participated in a proceeding.[11] The schedule of payments and other procedures are beyond the scope of this chapter.

Library References:

West's Key No. Digests, Workers' Compensation ⟬1–73.

§ 17.66 Procedure—Anti-discrimination Agency Practice

One of the most important decisions employees have to make when challenging discrimination is whether to file agency charges, and if so, with which body. Up to three agencies may receive the initial charge: the Equal Employment Opportunity Commission ("EEOC"), the New York State Division of Human Rights ("NYSDHR"), or a local commission, such as the New York City Commission on Human Rights ("NYCCHR").[1] The main advantages of filing agency charges are: (1) the low entry barrier (an employee can initiate proceedings without counsel or financial expenditure); (2) the possibility that the agency will investigate the matter, find "probable cause" of discrimination, and either pressure the employer to settle the matter or undertake further proceed-

---

4. See, e.g., Hopkins v. Players' Three, Inc., 99 A.D.2d 912, 472 N.Y.S.2d 519 (3d Dep't 1984).

5. Workers' Compensation Law § 21(1).

6. See, e.g., Richardson v. Fiedler Roofing, Inc., 67 N.Y.2d 246, 502 N.Y.S.2d 125, 493 N.E.2d 228 (1986).

7. Workers' Compensation Law §§ 3(2), 37–49.

8. La Mendola v. Butler, 179 A.D.2d 862, 578 N.Y.S.2d 280 (3d Dep't 1992)(personality disorder caused by excessive work stress).

9. Workers' Compensation Law § 18.

10. Id. § 28.

11. Id. § 120.

§ 17.66

1. PRACTICE POINTER: The public-sector employee may be governed by an additional or alternative regulatory complaint system. The discussion in this section is applicable to private-sector employees; counsel for a public sector employee must consider whether other filing and exhaustion requirements exist.

ings on behalf of the complainant; and (3) to preserve the right to sue under Title VII (by filing an EEOC charge). The main disadvantage of filing charges is the possibility that the agency may issue a no probable cause determination and dismiss the proceeding. When the EEOC does so, the employee must initiate a federal lawsuit under Title VII within 90 days or be foreclosed from any remedy; when the NYSDHR or the NYCCHR does so, the complainant has no further remedy under state or city law (unless he or she obtained an "administrative convenience" dismissal).

The main advantage of *not* filing agency charges, from the employee's standpoint, is that he or she will not be barred from going to court pursuant to the "election of remedies" provisions of state and local law. The employee will enjoy a three year Statute of Limitations period within which to file a lawsuit under state or local law. The disadvantage, however, is that, by failing to file a charge with the EEOC, the employee will forego relief under the federal statutes, which require EEOC filing (*i.e.*, Title VII, ADEA, and ADA). The failure to file limits the employee to litigation under state and local laws. Given these choices, an employee's counsel must carefully compare the statutes and decide which law affords the greatest advantage to the client.

The best time for the employee and counsel to sort through the strategy options is when the claim arises. The reality, however, is that many employees first seek legal counsel only after they have started down one path or another. Some employees file agency charges or even lawsuits *pro se* before they realize the need for legal assistance. Others allow the Statutes of Limitations or filing deadlines to run before seeking help. The task for counsel, therefore, often entails not only selecting the best route for the plaintiff, but also getting the client on the right track by undoing what may have already been done. Unfortunately, even more than 30 years after the passage of Title VII, the rules governing the interaction between anti-discrimination laws, and particularly the work-share arrangements between the agencies, are still somewhat unclear and subject to change. Even seasoned employment lawyers often find themselves befuddled by byzantine complexities in agency policies and practices. It is beyond the scope of this chapter to anticipate every circumstance that might arise. Instead, the basic filing procedures and problems commonly faced when shifting from agency to court will be outlined and explored.

§ 17.67 Procedure—Filing and Responding to Administrative Charges

EEOC. Before a plaintiff can file a lawsuit under Title VII or ADA, he or she must (1) file a charge of discrimination with the EEOC, (2) allow 180 days for processing,[1] and (3) receive a "right to sue" letter from the EEOC. After receipt of the right to sue letter, the complainant has ninety days to file the lawsuit.

In New York, the charge should be filed within 240 days from the date the employee learns of the discriminatory act. An outside limit of 300 days is available, however, if the complainant who files after 240 days receives a waiver of processing from the New York State Division of Human Rights ("SDHR"). This waiver is necessary because the New York State Division of Human Rights has exclusive jurisdiction over Title VII charges for at least 60 days; during those 60 days, the charge will not be considered active in the EEOC for the purpose of tolling the 300 day filing deadline. If the EEOC receives the charge within 240 days, it will defer it to the SDHR and receive it back within the 300 days. If the EEOC receives the charge after 240 days, it will not be able to activate processing before 300 days have elapsed unless the SDHR waives its processing which, in turn, activates EEOC processing.[2]

The filing of an ADEA charge differs in that, while filing with the EEOC (or SDHR) is necessary, a right to sue letter is not required. The complainant may commence an ADEA lawsuit 60 days after filing the EEOC charge, but the ADEA lawsuit may not be filed if any processing in the SDHR has not been completed. Since SDHR processing is an obstacle to filing the lawsuit, it behooves the complainant to file the ADEA charge with the EEOC, not the SDHR, and to request that the EEOC activate and investigate it and seek a waiver of SDHR processing, so that no SDHR proceedings are commenced.[3] As with a Title VII or

§ 17.67
1. **CAVEAT**: A complainant may request the EEOC to issue a right to sue letter less than 180 days after the filing of the charge. If the EEOC determines that it will not be able to process the complaint within 180 days (which it does routinely), it may issue the right to sue notice before the 180 days have elapsed. The complainant who files a lawsuit based on such an "early" right to sue letter risks possible dismissal by the court based on the defense that the suit is premature until the 180 days have elapsed. *See* Henschke v. New York Hospital–Cornell Medical Center, 821 F.Supp. 166 (S.D.N.Y.1993) (180 days must expire before court has jurisdiction to hear a claim based on a right-to-sue letter).

2. **PRACTICE POINTER**: It is extremely important that plaintiff's counsel specifically request the EEOC to obtain a SDHR waiver of processing for any charge filed after 240 days of the discriminatory act. The EEOC can do this orally in a telephone call to the SDHR, so that, with diligent follow-up, a charge filed with the EEOC at the last minute can be made timely.

PRACTICE POINTER: If the complainant has filed a Title VII, ADA, or ADEA charge *with the SDHR* after 240 days from the date of the discriminatory act, the SDHR should defer it to the EEOC immediately with a transmittal notice waiving SDHR processing so that it leaves the exclusive jurisdiction of the SDHR and arrives at the EEOC within the 300 day limit.

3. **PRACTICE POINTER**: If the complainant includes an age discrimination complainant under the NYSHRL that he or she wishes to bring in federal court, it is imperative that the EEOC be instructed to seek an SDHR waiver. If the EEOC defers the charge to the SDHR for processing, it may be considered an "election" of an administrative remedy that will preclude the bringing of the state law claim in court, unless the complainant can have the SDHR proceeding dismissed on the grounds of administrative convenience. (*See* § 17.68 Election of Remedies) Despite New York State's

ADA claim, the ADEA lawsuit must be commenced within 90 days after the date of receipt of notice that the EEOC has terminated its processing.

The EEOC charge consists of an intake form and an affidavit. The complainant checks off the type of discrimination claimed and, in a sworn (not required for an ADEA claim) statement, sets forth a "clear and concise statement of the facts" constituting the unlawful conduct. The EEOC will notify the employer of the charge within ten days and then investigate it.

The employer generally responds to the EEOC charge by submitting a "position statement" that outlines the facts from the employer's perspective and identifies probative witnesses. The EEOC investigator may conduct on on-site investigation or subpoena documents or witnesses in order to determine whether there is "reasonable cause" to believe that the charge of discrimination is true. If EEOC determines that reasonable cause exists, it will attempt to conciliate the charge through informal discussions or conferences. If conciliation fails, the EEOC may sue on behalf of the complainant. If it does not find reasonable cause, or reach a conciliation, or commence litigation itself, the EEOC will issue a right to sue letter to the complainant. After receipt, the complainant has fourteen days within which to request a review by the EEOC's Washington, D.C., office.

SDHR. The filing of charges under the NYSHRL with the SDHR is not a prerequisite for commencing a NYSHRL lawsuit in either state or federal court. While filing such charges is inevitable when they are ancillary to EEOC charges, the only purpose of filing these charges is to commence administrative proceedings, which should be avoided if litigation may be sought. If litigation is not an option, however, SDHR offers a viable forum, especially in cases where no federal protection is available.[4]

The complainant may file the NYSHRL charge either at the SDHR or EEOC. The prior commencement of an NYSHRL action in court will preclude a SDHR filing. The complaint must describe the alleged unlawful discriminatory conduct and must be notarized. Complaints must be filed with the SDHR within one year of the discriminatory act or practice.

Once an SDHR complaint is filed, the employer is notified and usually submits a position statement. The SDHR investigation, like that of the EEOC, may include fact-finding conferences, and some discovery for the purpose of determining whether there is probable cause to believe

---

election of remedies rule, the complainant's filing of a Title VII charge with the EEOC does not constitute an "election" of a state administrative remedy when the EEOC defers the complaint to the SDHR. Executive Law § 297(9).

4. PRACTICE POINTER: The scope of the NYSHRL is in some respects broader than Title VII. NYSHRL covers employers with four or more employees, not fifteen. It also proscribes discrimination based on marital status and against persons under 40 years of age (but over eighteen).

that the employer has engaged in an unlawful discriminatory practice. If no probable cause is found, the SDHR will dismiss the complaint; this will preclude any further action on the NYSHRL claims other than an appeal of the dismissal. If the SDHR finds probable cause, the parties may mutually elect to go to arbitration or wait for the case to reach a hearing before an administrative law judge wherein the SDHR will represent the complainant. Currently, this administrative process may take over five years.

Instead of filing an SDHR charge, the complainant may elect to sue in court. The period of limitations is three years from the discriminatory act. The election to go to court cannot be made, however, if the SDHR has dismissed an administrative complaint. If the SDHR is processing a charge based on the same incident, the complainant must have the SDHR grant an administrative convenience dismissal, or else be subject to the election-of-remedies defense, which will block the court action.[5]

NYCCHR. Employees and certain independent contractors within New York City may file charges of discrimination with the New York City Commission on Human Rights. Employers with four or more employees are covered. The scope of the NYCHRL exceeds both Title VII and the NYSHRL in its protection of sexual orientation, citizenship and alienage, and certain aspects of disability discrimination. When filing charges with the NYCCHR, the complainant can request dual filing with the EEOC. Once NYCHRL processing begins, however, its jurisdiction will be considered exclusive. If the complainant wishes to bring a court action, an administrative convenience dismissal from the NYCCHR will be required.

A complaint with the NYCCHR must be filed within one year of the discriminatory act. The NYCCHR will serve it on the respondent, who must file an answer within 30 days after receipt. As in the SDHR, a complaint in the NYCCHR will be investigated. On-site visits and fact-finding conferences may be conducted. Attempts at mediation or conciliation may be made. Following the investigation, the NYCCHR will determine whether probable cause exists to believe that the covered entity has engaged in unlawful discrimination. If no probable cause is found, the NYCCHR will dismiss the complaint. The dismissed complainant may request that the chairperson of the Commission review the determination. If probable cause is found, the NYCCHR will take the complaint to a hearing before an administrative law judge.

Library References:
West's Key No. Digests, Civil Rights ⚖︎442–446.

§ 17.68 Procedure—Election of Remedies

The complainant who has filed a charge under the NYSHRL or the NYCHRL with the SDHR or NYCCHR, relinquishes the right to bring a

---
[5.] *See infra,* Election of Remedies, § 17.68.

Ch. 17   PROCEDURE—ELECTION OF REMEDIES   **§ 17.68**

private action in court regarding the same alleged unlawful conduct.[1] In order to avoid this election of remedies, the prospective litigant must obtain an administrative convenience dismissal ("ACD") of the charges being processed by the SDHR or NYCCHR. The grant of an ACD is discretionary.[2]

If the administrative complaint was originally filed with the EEOC and then deferred to SDHR, it need not be dismissed before bringing a federal court action. Executive Law § 297(9) provides: "A complaint filed by the equal employment opportunity commission ... shall not constitute the filing of a complaint within the meaning of this subdivision." Nevertheless, as a precaution, a plaintiff who intends to commence a legal action should seek to have a pending complaint with the SDHR dismissed for administrative convenience if New York State Human Rights Law claims were asserted along with the federal claims in the EEOC filing.

The grounds upon which the SDHR will dismiss a complaint for administrative convenience are a matter of controversy. The SDHR's regulations state that the Division has discretion, not subject to review, to dismiss the complaint on the grounds of administrative convenience if, among other reasons, the "complainant has initiated or wants to initiate an administrative agency proceeding or court action based on the same grievance."[3] It would appear from this regulation that a plaintiff who seeks to assert a NYSHRL claim, in either federal or state court, would ordinarily be entitled to have the SDHR dismiss the complaint for administrative convenience. Nevertheless, the courts have held, particularly in cases where the Division has already extensively investigated a charge of discrimination, that an administrative convenience dismissal may be denied.[4] Thus, a plaintiff who seeks a dismissal for administrative convenience for the purpose of commencing a bare NYSHRL claim,

---

§ 17.68

1. This obstacle to filing claims under the New York State Human Rights Law exists due to New York's exclusive remedy provision which requires that, when a private action is commenced, no complaint of discrimination can be pending with, or have been dismissed on the merits (*i.e.*, finding of no probable cause) by the SDHR. Executive Law § 297(9). The NYCCHR contains a similar provision. N.Y.C.Admin. Code § 8–502(a).

2. *See* 9 NYCRR § 465.5(d)(1); N.Y.C.Admin. Code § 8–113(a).

PRACTICE POINTER: Contrary to the SDHR's rules which provide that the ACD grant is unreviewable, it may be reviewed if it is purely arbitrary or contrary to agency rules. Pan American Airways, Inc. v. New York State Human Rights Appeal Bd., 61 N.Y.2d 542, 475 N.Y.S.2d 256, 463 N.E.2d 597 (1984). Moreover, an appeal from a SDHR administrative convenience dismissal, if any, may also have to be completed before the claim is considered fully out of the administrative system and ripe for private action. High v. AMR Services Corp., 1995 WL 362419 (E.D.N.Y.1995).

3. 9 NYCRR § 465.5(d)(2)(vi).

4. CAVEAT: If the employer fails to challenge the Division's grant of an administrative convenience dismissal, it will likely be precluded from raising an election of remedies contention in a subsequent lawsuit even if the dismissal was arguably defective. *See* Ryan v. New York State Thruway Authority, 889 F.Supp. 70 (N.D.N.Y. 1995).

in state or federal court, could have the ACD denied by the agency or challenged and nullified in court.[5]

A complaint may be dismissed for administrative convenience in the NYCCHR if the request is made either before the answer is received or before the complaint has been actively investigated if the respondent will not be "unduly prejudiced," or where the public interest will not be served by prosecution of the complaint.[6] These rules make legal action difficult for the complainant who has filed charges with these non-federal agencies. Plaintiffs, therefore, would be well-advised to avoid filing complaints with the SDHR or the NYCCHR if they wish to go to court.

The NYCHRL offers several features that may be attractive to plaintiffs. First, like the NYSHRL, it allows for a generous three year period in which to commence a private right of action and does not require an administrative filing as a prerequisite to suit. It therefore provides a safety net to those who fail to make timely EEOC (300 days), NYSDHR (one year), or NYCCHR (one year) administrative filings. Second, the NYCHRL also provides for uncapped damages, including punitive damages, which makes it superior to the Civil Rights Act of 1991.[7] Moreover, the NYCHRL protects the widest spectrum of employees, including coverage for sexual orientation, and contains a broadened definition of "disability." In addition, individual employees can be held liable for employment discrimination under the NYCHRL.[8]

Library References:

West's Key No. Digests, Election of Remedies ⚖︎1–16.

5. *See* Marine Midland Bank, N.A. v. New York State Division of Human Rights, 75 N.Y.2d 240, 246, 552 N.Y.S.2d 65, 67, 551 N.E.2d 558, 560 (1989) (pre-regulation case annulling SDHR order granting complainant's request for an administrative convenience dismissal); Matter of AMR Services Corp. v. New York State Division of Human Rights, 214 A.D.2d 665, 625 N.Y.S.2d 583 (2d Dep't 1995) (SDHR "policy" of issuing ACD's only when a complainant has federal claims in addition to state claims and when appeals from Division dismissals have been completed); Chachra v. Katharine Gibbs School, Inc., 828 F.Supp. 176 (E.D.N.Y.1993) (legal action barred where ACD is sought to change litigation strategy, rather than truly for administrative convenience); *see also* Ryan v. New York Thruway Authority, 889 F.Supp. 70 (S.D.N.Y.1995).

6. N.Y.C.Admin. Code § 8–113(c).

CAVEAT: It is noteworthy, however, that the grounds listed under N.Y.C.Admin. Code § 8–113(c), while non-exclusive, do not include the initiation of legal action by the complainant.

Given the uncertainty of gaining an ACD in order to permit a NYCHRL cause of action to be brought in state or federal court, a plaintiff who wishes to keep alive the right to file a court action under the NYCHRL is probably best advised to avoid filing administrative charges with the NYCCHR or to seek an ACD before the NYCCHR investigation has progressed too far.

7. Bracker v. Cohen, 204 A.D.2d 115, 612 N.Y.S.2d 113 (1st Dep't 1994). Punitive damages may be unavailable under the NYCHRL in federal court, however, where an age discrimination claim is pendent to an ADEA claim. Chambers v. Capital Cities/ABC, 851 F.Supp. 543 (S.D.N.Y.1994).

8. Falbaum v. Pomerantz, 891 F.Supp. 986 (S.D.N.Y.1995).

§ 17.69 Procedure—Statutes of Limitations and Prerequisites to Private Lawsuits

Complainants have up to three years from the discriminatory act to bring a private lawsuit under the NYSHRL and the NYCHRL.[1] Before commencing a private cause of action under the NYCHRL, the plaintiff must serve copies of the complaint on the New York City Commission on Human Rights and the City's Corporation Counsel.[2] Failure to do so may result in the claims being dismissed, even if commenced in federal court as pendent to federal discrimination claims.[3]

Library References:

West's Key No. Digests, Civil Rights ⌭448.1.

§ 17.70 Private Lawsuits

If the plaintiff has satisfied any internal or administrative exhaustion prerequisites, and if any settlement discussions have failed the plaintiff's next step is to file a complaint. Although this steeply escalates the confrontation, the commencement of litigation may induce new settlement discussions. If it does not, the plaintiff should be prepared to undertake the detailed, and often complex, pre-trial preparation necessary to win an employment case. The defendant's main goal, in the early

---

§ 17.69

1. Murphy v. American Home Products Corp., 58 N.Y.2d 293, 461 N.Y.S.2d 232, 448 N.E.2d 86 (1983); N.Y.C.Admin. Code § 8–502(d).

CAVEAT: While that period will be tolled during agency processing, it will not be tolled where the administrative charge is dismissed for administrative convenience due to the complainant's "malfeasance, misfeasance or recalcitrance." N.Y.C.Admin. Code § 8–502(e).

2. N.Y.C.Admin. Code § 8–502(c).

3. There is conflicting authority as to whether the service of the complaint on the NYCCHR and Corporation Counsel is a prerequisite to bringing a lawsuit. The view that it was a prerequisite was shared by the federal courts. Robins v. Max Mara, U.S.A., Inc., 923 F.Supp. 460 (S.D.N.Y.1996); Walsh v. Lincoln Savings Bank, 1995 WL 66639 (S.D.N.Y.1995); Monaco v. Lincoln Savings Bank, 1995 WL 66643 (S.D.N.Y.1995); Lightfoot v. Union Carbide Corp., 1994 WL 184670 (S.D.N.Y.1994).

However, after the First Department held to the contrary, federal district courts took the position that such service need not be a predicate. See Robins v. Max Mara, U.S.A., Inc., 923 F.Supp. 460 (S.D.N.Y.1996); Bernstein v. 1995 Associates, 217 A.D.2d 512, 630 N.Y.S.2d 68, 72 (1st Dep't 1995) (the language of § 8–502(c) was designed not to create a condition precedent, but to serve as a device by which the [City Commission] and the [Corporation Counsel] would be apprised of any actions commenced under Title 8); McIlwain v. Korbean Int'l Investment Corp., 896 F.Supp. 1373, 1384 (S.D.N.Y.1995). In McIlwain, the defendants moved to dismiss the plaintiff's NYCHRL claim on the ground that she had not served the Corporation Counsel and City Commission on Human Rights with her complaint. Upon plaintiff's submission of an affidavit stating that she had since served the agencies with the complaint, the court found that § 8–502(c) was satisfied—that is, the agencies had received sufficient notice—even though service of the complaint was made after plaintiff commenced her lawsuit. Id. at 1384. See also, Dirschel v. Speck, 1994 WL 330262 (S.D.N.Y.1994) (plaintiff's failure to allege that she had served her amended complaint on the specified agencies did not require dismissal of an NYCHRL claim where the plaintiff's counsel certified in a letter to the court that the service had been made).

§ 17.70 EMPLOYMENT LAW Ch. 17

stages, will often be to position the case for dismissal on a motion for summary judgment.

Most, though not all, employment discrimination cases in New York are brought under federal law in federal court, sometimes with pendent state claims. Other kinds of employment cases are typically brought in state court, unless diversity of citizenship exists.

§ 17.71 Private Lawsuits—Discovery—General Considerations

General Considerations. The plaintiff relies on discovery more than the defendant in employment litigation. The plaintiff's initial focus is on the defendant's document production. Employers are often careful not to express anything that suggests unlawful conduct, especially in depositions. Nevertheless, a paper trail may have been left that supports inferences of discrimination, implied contractual promises, or assertions of unlawful pay practices. Employers generally maintain and control all of the relevant paperwork. The strength of the plaintiff's case can depend upon obtaining those documents in discovery.

Employers rarely can expect to obtain helpful evidence from the plaintiff by way of document production. The best discovery device for the employer is the deposition of the plaintiff. The examination will be critical to limiting the plaintiff and foreclosing claims and theories.[1]

Library References:

West's Key No. Digests, Pretrial Procedure ⚖11–46.

§ 17.72 Private Lawsuits—Discovery—Plaintiff's Strategy

Document production. The plaintiff should serve a document request (to the extent documents are not fully produced under the mandatory production rules in FRCP 26(a)) and review the documents before proceeding to depositions. In addition to requesting hard copies of documents, computer files (especially e-mail) may provide useful information. Additionally, discovery requests that seek "erased" computer files are becoming common and should be considered. Optimally, the plaintiff will seek documents that contain admissions. In discrimination cases, the plaintiff will have to find evidence that bolsters the *prima facie* case and shows that the defendant's articulated legitimate and nondiscriminatory reasons for the adverse action are pretextual. Inconsistencies, such as positive statements about the plaintiff's qualifications

---

§ 17.71

1. **PRACTICE POINTER:** When applicable, both parties should seek access to the investigatory files of the EEOC, SDHR, or NYCCHR. This is done by a request under the Freedom of Information Act (EEOC) or Freedom of Information Law (SDHR or NYCCHR).

or performance[1] that contrast with the reasons for the adverse action, can help to establish the pretextual nature of the defendant's assertions.

Comparisons between the plaintiff and similarly situated "comparators" may also provide the support required for a claim of discrimination based on indirect proof. In such cases, or in cases dealing with a practice or pattern of intentional or disparate impact (unintentional) discrimination, the plaintiff may seek to compel company-wide disclosure, usually over the defendant's objection.[2]

Items to be considered in drafting the plaintiff's document request include written employment policies, handbooks and manuals, evaluations, communications regarding the plaintiff's termination, and the personnel files of the plaintiff and any similarly situated employees. For the employer's request, documents commonly demanded include notes and diaries, documents taken by the plaintiff from the company, documents relating to efforts to locate new employment, and medical documentation relating to emotional distress.

Interviewing Witnesses. A case based upon an employer's statements revealing an unlawful animus toward the plaintiff may hinge on whether other employees who may have heard the remarks will testify in the litigation. Although plaintiff's counsel should diligently explore this evidence, it should be carried out with the understanding that the rules of professional conduct preclude contact with opposing parties known to have counsel, without the prior consent of the opposing attorney.[3] A key question will be whether the employee to be interviewed is an "alter ego" of the corporation.[4]

Defendant's Deposition. The main function of the deposition of the defendant is to gain a thorough understanding of the employer's practices and procedures, and how they were applied in the instant case. To do this, plaintiff's counsel will have to first gather all of the relevant documentation that can be obtained, and then ask the defendant to explain the meaning, purpose, and surrounding circumstances of each document so that a complete picture is formed. Unless direct, inculpatory evidence surfaces, which is rare, plaintiff's counsel must focus on inconsistencies, gaps, and other unexplained actions that evince unfair treatment or a pretextual cover-up.

§ 17.72

1. Performance reviews may be a source of such information.
2. Among the factors that may be used to determine the breadth of discovery is whether the extent of the alleged decision maker's influence and authority was department-wide or company-wide.
3. DR § 7–104(a)(1).
4. The court's inquiry will be guided by the balancing test set forth in Niesig v. Team I, 76 N.Y.2d 363, 559 N.Y.S.2d 493, 558 N.E.2d 1030 (1990). The actions or omissions under scrutiny must be of a corporate employee whose statements would be binding on the corporation, would be imputed to the corporation for liability purposes, or would reflect the advice of corporate counsel. Former employees of the corporation are fair game for plaintiff's counsel.

§ 17.72 EMPLOYMENT LAW Ch. 17

Ex Parte Contacts. The employer should be on guard with respect to communications between the plaintiff and prospective witnesses in the company. The rules concerning contact with the defendant's employees prohibit the plaintiff's lawyer from communicating, without prior consent from the opposing attorney, with a "person" (including a corporation) known to have counsel.[5]

Document Production. Contrary to common belief, plaintiffs often have documents relevant to the case. Before deposing the plaintiff, the employer might request any relevant documents that the plaintiff created or retains, including notes, diaries, pay stubs, expense vouchers, and tape recordings. In some cases, however, the defendant will forego document production and interrogatories, preferring to take plaintiff's deposition as quickly as possible in order to ascertain the theory of the action before the plaintiff is "educated" by the defendant's answer and discovery requests.

Plaintiff's Deposition. This is the most crucial discovery tool at the employer's disposal. Its main purpose is to foreclose the plaintiff's claims that have no basis and to prevent the possibility that plaintiff's story will change. Questions should be geared to gain admissions that negate elements of the plaintiff's *prima facie* case; show the employer was fair; pinpoint witnesses who heard discriminatory remarks; show an absence of evidence that the employer's reasons for adverse action were pretextual; establish that plaintiff understood the company rules; and show consistent treatment by the employer. Defense counsel may also inquire into the plaintiff's past bad acts, terminations, other lawsuits filed or workplace complaints reported, and medical/psychological history before and after the events in question.

Medical/Psychological Examination of the Plaintiff. CPLR 3121 and FRCP 35(a) set forth the circumstances under which a court may allow an examination of a party when a physical or mental condition is in issue. If the plaintiff merely seeks compensatory damages for discriminatory treatment that includes mental distress, a court is likely to find that mental condition has not been put in controversy, and that Rule 35 discovery may be unavailable. If the plaintiff brings a tort claim, such as intentional infliction of emotional distress, or if the plaintiff claims severe mental injury, a court is more likely to allow the defendant to conduct a mental evaluation.[6] Requests for medical records may be

---

5. PRACTICE POINTER: Potential witnesses within the company may be requested to keep defense counsel advised of any requests by opposing counsel to discuss the matter; additionally, they may be asked not to communicate directly with opposing counsel without a company representative present.

6. Most courts take a restrictive approach to Rule 35 examinations. See Bridges v. Eastman Kodak Co., 850 F.Supp. 216 (S.D.N.Y.1994) (limiting inquiry to effect of harassment); O'Quinn v. New York University Medical Center, 163 F.R.D. 226, 68 FEP Cas. (BNA) 1798 (S.D.N.Y.1995)("boilerplate" mental anguish assertion in complaint did not put mental condition in controversy to warrant an examination); Burger v. Litton Industries, Inc., 1995 WL 363741, 68 FEP Cas.

subject to similar restrictions.[7]

Interrogatories. Plaintiff may use interrogatories to complete the picture of the employer's personnel practices, employee demographics, and decision-makers. The employer can use them to gain definitive information about the plaintiff's background and claims. Local rules should be consulted, such as the Southern District of New York's Local Rule 64, which confines the scope of interrogatories to identification of relevant witnesses, documents, and damages-related information.

§ 17.73 Private Lawsuits—Summary Judgment

Plaintiffs move for summary judgment far less frequently than defendants. If the defendant makes the motion, the plaintiff may wish to cross-move to seek dismissal of any frivolous counterclaims. In cases that involve contracts, or statutory interpretation, the plaintiff may want to initiate the summary judgment if the court's interpretation of pertinent language will resolve the issue in question.

Defendants rely on summary judgment to stop the litigation before it reaches trial, especially where a jury will be able to award substantial damages.[1] In the typical intentional discrimination case, the plaintiff must show both that the employer's stated reason for the adverse action was false and that discrimination was the real reason.[2] The burden is on the plaintiff to come forward with admissible evidence on both of these issues to create a question of material fact as to the employer's intent. The Second Circuit has recognized that the intent to discriminate usually entails a question of fact that precludes summary judgment, as long as evidence from which a jury could find intent has been submitted.[3] The defendant will argue that plaintiff's demonstration of proof of intent, including any failure to negate the defendant's stated reasons with evidence of pretext, compels dismissal.[4]

(BNA) 737 (S.D.N.Y.1995)(limiting length of psychological exam in age and sex claim).

PRACTICE POINTER: The plaintiff should inform defense counsel that plaintiff's counsel or a stenographer will attend the deposition, or that it will be video-or audio-taped. Although the examiner may have a legitimate right to conduct the examination without interference, and plaintiff's counsel does not have the right to be present, defendant will have difficulty arguing that a tape recorder will be disruptive. Recording and preserving the examination will curb any potential abuses and be useful when deposing or cross-examining the doctor.

7. *See* Alden v. Time Warner, Inc., 1995 WL 679238 (S.D.N.Y.1995)(barring request for medical records from personal physician based on supposition that records would reveal other sources of mental distress).

§ 17.73

1. *See generally*, Meloff v. New York Life Ins. Co., 51 F.3d 372 (2d Cir.1995).

2. St. Mary's Honor Center v. Hicks, 509 U.S. 502, 113 S.Ct. 2742, 125 L.Ed.2d 407 (1993).

3. Gallo v. Prudential Residential Services, 22 F.3d 1219 (2d Cir.1994) (ADEA); Quaratino v. Tiffany, 71 F.3d 58 (2d Cir.1995)(Title VII pregnancy discrimination).

4. Woroski v. Nashua Corp. 31 F.3d 105 (2d Cir.1994).

Although it is difficult to show that no material question of fact exists in discrimination cases, defendants may have other reasons to move for summary judgment. The cost of the motion itself may have strategic importance in stimulating settlement discussions. Nevertheless, courts will not be receptive to motions that are ill-founded and intended to harass. The court may be receptive, however, to a motion for partial summary judgment attempting to streamline the case for trial. The defendant also will find it advantageous to move if the determination of a legal issue can resolve or narrow the case, such as personal liability for employees' acts or an affirmative defense such as a qualified privilege in a claim of defamation. Counsel should consult the local rules of the federal district court where the action is to be tried to determine whether, and when, a Rule 56 motion (summary judgment) may be made.[5]

Library References:
West's Key No. Digests, Judgment ⚖178–190.

§ 17.74 Private Lawsuits—Trial

Generally. The plaintiff's purpose at trial is to convince the fact-finder that the employer has violated the law. This is accomplished by highlighting the evidence that the employer acted in an unfair or inexplicable manner. In jury trials, plaintiff's counsel must choose a simple and persuasive theme, knowing that juries decide cases with their heads and their hearts. Defendants, on the other hand, must persuade the fact-finder to rely on hard evidence and will try to personalize the corporate employer and show the reasonableness of its actions. While a defense strategy of characterizing the plaintiff as greedy and non-credible may prove useful, defendant's counsel will have to proceed cautiously if the plaintiff's case would engender sympathy.

Pre-Trial Order. In federal court, the local district court rules of practice, in conjunction with FRCP 16, will set forth the requirements for the joint pre-trial order. The process is designed to narrow the factual disputes, disclose the witnesses and exhibits, and identify the legal issues. Each party drafts a version and discusses the contents with the other side and, sometimes, with the court. The final pre-trial order is agreed to by both sides. Failure to raise an issue in the final pre-trial order will normally preclude bringing the issue to the jury.

Motions in Limine. Advance rulings on the admissibility of evidence can be obtained by a motion *in limine*. If the case hinges on key evidence, such as an overheard remark of the supervisor, the trial can turn on this motion. The motion can be made to either admit or exclude

---

5. PRACTICE POINTER: Although seeking leave to bring the motion is not required under the Federal Rules of Civil Procedure, some judges require that a conference or written submission precede the serving of the motion in order to reduce unwarranted motion practice.

the particular evidence or witness. The subject of such motions in employment litigation can include actions taken against other employees that may be unrelated, hearsay, lay opinions, stray remarks by decisionmakers, statistics as to comparators or patterns of discrimination, events outside the Statute of Limitations, expert testimony, agency determinations, medical/psychiatric or other expert testimony, as well as general questions of probative/prejudicial value under Rule 403 of the Federal Rules of Evidence.

Jury Selection. The prime objective of jury selection is to pick favorably-disposed jurors and eliminate undesirables. The secondary objective is to begin to convince the jury of the merits of one's case. In federal court, the judge usually conducts the *voir dire* or closely oversees the process. In state court practice, the attorneys have more of an opportunity to talk to the jury, usually in the absence of the court.

In preparing for *voir dire*, whether conducted by the court or counsel, the attorneys in an employment case should probe each potential juror's experience in, and attitudes toward, the workplace. In discrimination cases, it is essential that the parties explore and try to reveal hidden biases.[1]

Typical *voir dire* questions include whether the juror has: (a) had personal experience in a similar case or incident; (b) friends or relatives who were involved in a similar case; (c) ever been terminated, filed charges or had a dispute with an employer; (d) a friend or relative who is disabled; (e) been a supervisor; (f) difficulty applying the employment-at-will rule; or (g) difficulty deciding in favor of a large damage award.

Opening Statements. The plaintiff should establish the theme of the case with a strong opening statement that attracts the attention and moves the emotions of the jury. Counsel should be careful not to overstate the case because unproven claims will be used against the plaintiff in the defendant's closing argument. Most lawyers use the opening statement to tell the plaintiff's story in terms so compelling that a lasting impression is created that can be reinforced throughout the remainder of the trial. Themes that can resonate through the jury deliberations include the sense of helplessness associated with being a victim of discrimination; the fact that everyone ages or might become disabled; the heartlessness of impersonal corporations; and the perception of worthlessness inherent in discriminatory decisions. A powerful metaphor may effectively evoke these themes, such as Willy Loman's comparison between an employee with many years at a firm and a fruit, where the employer eats the meat and discards the skin.

---

§ 17.74

1. **PRACTICE POINTER**: In jury selection, each side is allowed three peremptory challenges. 28 U.S.C.A. § 1870, CPLR 4109. Jurors may not be stricken on the basis of race or gender. Batson v. Kentucky, 476 U.S. 79, 106 S.Ct. 1712, 90 L.Ed.2d 69 (1986). To avoid running afoul of Batson, counsel must be able to articulate a neutral, non-discriminatory explanation for striking the juror in question.

Defendants will use opening argument to personalize themselves and to present counter-themes that will be reinforced by the evidence showing a decision-making process that was fair, caring, and reasonable. Simple assertions that "we did not discriminate" will be insufficient. Counsel for plaintiff and defendant must be wary of making "promises" as to evidentiary presentations that will not be kept.

Presentation of Evidence. Trial lawyers often debate the best order of the witnesses. The conventional wisdom is that the plaintiff should be the first witness, so the jury can hear the story and make up their minds whether they believe him or her. As the chief fact witness, only the plaintiff can paint the whole picture so that the jury understands the entire case. The plaintiff generally puts on supporting fact witnesses in the chronological order of the "story" being told. The plaintiff's chances of winning are diminished if the jury is confused. Of course, good reasons may exist for having the plaintiff testify later in the case. If the plaintiff can put on a corroborating witness who can tell the story, counsel may wish to save the plaintiff for the end of the case-in-chief, and may even want to call the defendant's key witnesses first, so the plaintiff can finish strongly. When in doubt, counsel on either side should choose the safest route, which is to present witnesses so that the jurors' interest will remain high and they will be able to assimilate the testimony and integrate it into the big picture or theme being created by the attorney.

Demonstrative Exhibits. Lawyers who represent employees generally agree that charts and other graphic presentations of the evidence are essential. Employment cases often involve complex organizational "trees," or comparisons between different employees or groups with respect to various aspects of the job. The way to persuade jurors of these often subtle distinctions is through visual images, which can become embedded in the jurors' minds to a far greater degree than fleeting oral testimony. Charts that show lost earnings or other damages-related information are also essential. Plaintiffs who win the graphics "contest" against defendants have an edge in the jury deliberation room. Judges hearing a bench trial can also benefit from good visual presentations of the evidence.[2]

Expert Witnesses. In addition to fact witnesses, the plaintiff and defendant may call expert witnesses to offer relevant opinions. The use of experts is governed in federal court by Rule 702 of the Federal Rules of Evidence, and by common law rules in the state courts where the state has not adopted a code of evidence. New York has not adopted a code of evidence. Under the federal rule, the opinion of an expert will be admissible if it is relevant and would assist or be helpful to the jury to

---

2. *See* the excellent treatment of this subject in Haig, *et al., Commercial Litigation in New York State Courts* (West 1995), Ch. 35 "Graphics and Other Demonstrative Evidence."

"understand the evidence or to determine a fact in issue."[3] The competence of the expert's testimony will be governed according to the leading case, *Daubert v. Merrell Dow Pharmaceuticals*,[4] which diminishes the offeror's need to show that the expert's opinion would be accepted by the scientific community, but allows a court to restrict the expert's testimony on relevance grounds.[5] For example, an unconventional social scientist might be found competent to testify as to stereotypical thinking, but may nevertheless be barred from testifying if the judge finds his testimony will not help the jury decide an issue of fact in the case.

Plaintiffs have used experts in cases of hostile work environment and sexual harassment in order to define the impact of offensive conduct on the working conditions, and on the opportunities for women in general, since this may not be evident to the jurors through the plaintiff's own experiences.[6] In disability discrimination, both parties commonly use expert medical and vocational witnesses to explain the nature of the plaintiff's disability in relation to the job functions at issue. Experts are essential disparate treatment cases where a pattern and practice of discrimination is based on statistics.

Finally, the plaintiff often uses an expert to establish damages. Typically, an economist or financial expert will calculate the plaintiff's lost earnings, past and future, perhaps based on the expert testimony of a job counselor who will assess the marketability of the plaintiff's skills. A medical or psychological witness may testify as to any injuries that are part of the damages demand.[7]

Jury Charges. In federal court, each party will submit jury instruction requests to the court in the pre-trial order. The court will generally use these submissions as the basis for the final instructions. The court may give the parties the opportunity to brief the issues of law raised by the competing instructions. While each side competes for the most favorable instructions, care must be taken not to overreach. In jury trials where the plaintiff's case is likely to be compelling, plaintiff's counsel

---

3. CAVEAT: Courts have held that doubts about helpfulness of expert testimony are to be resolved in favor of admissibility. In re Agent Orange Product Liability Litigation, 611 F.Supp. 1223, affirmed, 818 F.2d 187 (2d Cir.1987), cert. denied Lombardi v. Dow Chemical Co., 487 U.S. 1234, 108 S.Ct. 2898, 101 L.Ed.2d 932 (1988).

4. 509 U.S. 579, 113 S.Ct. 2786, 125 L.Ed.2d 469 (1993).

5. In state court, the expert testimony must similarly assist the jurors, but the guidelines are less clear. People v. Mooney, 76 N.Y.2d 827, 560 N.Y.S.2d 115, 559 N.E.2d 1274 (1990). *See* Barker and Alexander, *Evidence in New York State and Federal Courts* (West 1995) § 702.1.

6. *See* Robinson v. Jacksonville Shipyards, Inc., 760 F.Supp. 1486 (M.D.Fla. 1991).

7. PRACTICE POINTER: Counsel considering the use of experts should be wary of a battle-of-the-experts that results in confusing and, perhaps even worse, boring the jury. Counsel should also avoid using any expert who is patronizing. Jurors cannot help but dislike any party that puts on an arrogant expert, especially after they hear testimony revealing the expert's hourly fees, which should always be elicited on cross examination to diminish credibility. The ideal expert testimony is forceful, clear, and brief.

§ 17.74 EMPLOYMENT LAW Ch. 17

may find that giving in to the defendant's instruction requests may be wise. Experience shows that jurors are less sensitive to the legal nuances that are the grist for appellate review. Accepting the defendant's instuctions may reduce the risk that the defendant will appeal the successful jury verdict on the basis of defective instructions.

If objections to the adversary's proposed instructions are not made at the pre-trial order stage, objections may be stated on the record at the charge conference or immediately after the judge has given the charge to the jury. Failure to object to the charge will generally be considered a waiver of the objection.

Summation. Both parties must make the best use of the closing argument to persuade the fact-finder. The appeal will be more emotional in a jury trial than a bench trial. The attorneys should take advantage of the freer rein given in closing to make arguments that track the evidence. Counsel should talk in "pictures." Logic should be used to put disparate pieces of evidence together into a convincing and emphatic statement of what happened and why. Themes, such as human dignity or fairness, that were set forth in the opening should be reinvoked. Many "closers" adhere to the short and sweet approach, avoiding numbing recapitulations of the evidence. The attorneys should attempt to frame the issues favorably. For example, the plaintiff's attorney should anticipate resistance to high damages; the jurors should be asked to think of damages in terms of what is fair, considering the amount of suffering sustained by the plaintiff. Plaintiffs sometimes propose damages figures to the jurors, although this approach is not risk-free.

§ 17.75 Private Lawsuits—Fee Application

Several statutes allow the prevailing plaintiff to collect attorneys' fees from the defendant. Victories under statutes without fee-shifting provisions may also provide a basis for fee shifting if the plaintiff has secured a common benefit for a class or group.[1] The amount of the attorneys' fees request will usually be based on the "lodestar" figure constituting the number of hours spent multiplied by the attorneys' hourly rates, plus costs and expenses. Multipliers of the lodestar are now rare. The application generally takes the form of a post-trial motion for attorneys' fees. The plaintiff's attorney's affidavit should include a summary of the case, a description of the type and quality of services, the difficulty of the case, the extent of success, the attorneys' backgrounds and qualifications, the hourly rates, a summary of the hours

§ 17.75
1. Hall v. Cole, 412 U.S. 1, 93 S.Ct. 1943, 36 L.Ed.2d 702 (1973)(*see e.g.,* 29 U.S.C.A. § 411(a)(2)).

spent (itemizing the time billed based on contemporaneously-kept time records), and an itemization of the costs and expenses.[2]

The application should include a memorandum of law that sets forth the standards for award setting in civil rights cases. The leading cases focus on whether the plaintiff was the prevailing party on "any significant issue," whether there were "excellent results," and whether the fee request is reasonable.[3]

Defendants typically challenge the request on several grounds, including lack of contemporaneous time records, the records' lack of clarity, lack of success on certain aspects of the case, and unreasonably high rates or amounts of time spent on the case.

Library References:
West's Key No. Digests, Costs ⚖=198.

§ 17.76 Private Lawsuits—Post–Trial Motions and Appeal

The rules regarding post-trial motions to challenge the verdict or bench decision in employment cases are no different than those in civil litigation generally.[1]

§ 17.77 Private Lawsuits—Checklist: Statutes of Limitations

Four Months: Article 78 proceedings.

Six Months: NLRB, Duty of fair representation. (29 U.S.C.A. § 301(a))

240–300 Days: EEOC/ADA Charge (Lawsuit: 90 days after Right to Sue Letter to bring action).

300 Days: ADEA (Lawsuit: 60 days from filing until 90 days after final notice of review by agency).

One Year:

    (a) Filing complaint with NYSDHR. (*See* § 17.67)

    (b) Filing complaint with NYCCHR. (*See* § 17.67)

    (c) Tort claims, defamation, IIED, malicious prosecution, false imprisonment (personal injury). (*See* §§ 17.20 *et seq.*)

---

2. *See, e.g.*, New York Ass'n for Retarded Children, Inc. v. Carey, 711 F.2d 1136 (2d Cir.1983).

3. *See* City of Riverside v. Rivera, 477 U.S. 561, 106 S.Ct. 2686, 91 L.Ed.2d 466 (1986); Hensley v. Eckerhart, 461 U.S. 424, 103 S.Ct. 1933, 76 L.Ed.2d 40 (1983); Grant v. Martinez, 973 F.2d 96 (2d Cir.1992).

PRACTICE POINTER: Fees do not need to be proportional to the amount of recovery to be reasonable. Riverside v. Rivera, 477 U.S. 561, 106 S.Ct. 2686, 91 L.Ed.2d 466 (1986)(award of $250,000 even though plaintiff recovered only $34,000).

§ 17.76

1. *See* FRCP 50, 59; CPLR 4404.

§ 17.77　　　　　　EMPLOYMENT LAW　　　　　　Ch. 17

 (d) Whistleblower claims under New York Labor Law. (*See* § 17.64; and Civil Service Law, *see* § 17.53)

***Two Years*:**

 (a) FLSA, EPA, FMLA proceedings (non-willful violations). (*See* §§ 17.44, 17.45, 17.63)

 (b) Workers' Compensation claims. (*See* § 17.65)

***Three Years*:**

 (a) FLSA, EPA, FMLA proceedings (willful violations). (*See* §§ 17.44, 17.45, 17.63)

 (b) Filing of suit under NYSHRL or NYCHRL. (*See* § 17.67)

 (c) ERISA fiduciary claims. (*See* § 17.50)

 (d) 42 U.S.C.A. §§ 1981, 1983, 1985. (*See* § 17.51)

 (e) Rehabilitation Act claims. (*See* § 17.43)

***Four Years*:**

 (a) Sales claims under UCC, *e.g.*, employer's failure to pay for computer program or other goods sold to employer as part employment.

***Six Years*:**

 (a) Breach of contract actions. (*See* § 17.33)

 (b) Tortious interference with contractual relations. (*See* § 17.29)

 (c) Wage claims under New York Labor Law. (*See* § 17.66)

§ 17.78　Private Lawsuits—Checklist: Commencement of New York State Actions

1. Initial considerations:

- Consider the facts, as revealed by a thorough inquiry, and the availability of admissible evidence.
- Determine the nature of the employment relationship: private or public-sector? Unionized? Is the client a member of a protected class?
- Analyze the applicable laws that govern the type of conduct and harm in question.
- Determine which causes of action can be supported by the facts and under which statutes the client may claim relief.
- Check Statute of Limitations for each prospective cause of action.
- Determine whether any administrative steps or the internal exhaustion of remedies are prerequisites to suit.

Ch. 17   CHECKLIST: FEDERAL COURT ACTIONS   § 17.79

- Forum selection, administrative agencies vs. court, and, if in court, state vs. federal court.
- Choose the venue for the suit.
- Identify the proper parties, considering liability, authority, political and settlement factors, and judgment enforceability.

2. Preparation of the complaint.
   - Does it require verification by the plaintiff? (*e.g.*, CPLR Art. 78 petition or where a non-profit organization is a defendant).[1]

3. Administrative convenience dismissal.
   - Determine whether it is necessary to secure an administrative convenience dismissal from the NYSHRD or NYCCHR..

4. Filing Requirements.
   - File the summons and complaint with the clerk of the court in which the action is brought, and pay the filing fee for the purchase of an index number. In the case of an Article 78 proceeding, file the petition, notice of petition, and a Request for Judicial Intervention ("RJI"), along with payment for filing fees.

5. Service of process.
   - Serve the summons and complaint, or summons with notice, within 120 days of purchasing the index number, unless the applicable Statute of Limitations for the cause of action is four months or less (*e.g.*, CPLR Article 78) in which case service must be made not later than 15 days after the Statute of Limitations expires. (If the plaintiff has not served the summons and complaint a second 120-day period, during which the Statute of Limitations continues to be tolled, is available with the purchase of a second index number.).[2]

6. Service of complaint on New York City Agency.
   - If the action includes a NYCHRL-based claim, serve the complaint on the NYCCHR and the New York City Corporation Counsel.[3] (*See* § 17.69)

§ 17.79   Private Lawsuits—Checklist: Commencement of Federal Court Actions

1. Initial considerations:
   - What are the applicable causes of action?

§ 17.78
1. CPLR 3016(h).

2. CPLR 306–b(b)
3. *See* N.Y.C.Admin. Code § 8–502(c).

§ 17.79 EMPLOYMENT LAW Ch. 17

- In which court (state or federal) will jurisdiction and venue be proper?
- What method of personal service to acquire jurisdiction over the defendant is available?
- What time limitations are applicable?
- What administrative processing is required in order to commence the action?
- What other exhaustion of remedies requirements must be satisfied?

2. Federal requirements.
   - Does federal law require leave to bring the complaint?[1]

3. Complaint.
   - Preparation of the complaint, signed by a member of the bar of the district in which the action is to be filed.

4. Filing requirements.
   - Filing of the summons and complaint with the clerk of the district court along with filing fee for the purchase of an index number The current filing fee to institute any civil action is $120.[2] A summons form can be obtained from the court, along with any cover sheets the district may require to be completed.

5. 120 days to complete service.
   - Completion of service of the summons and complaint within 120 days after filing of the complaint and before the expiration of the applicable statute of limitations. The plaintiff may request waiver of service of the defendant in order to save process-serving costs pursuant to FRCP 4(d).[3]

6. Agency filing requirements.
   - Filing complaint or sending copies to authorities as stipulated by various statutes, *e.g.*, ERISA.[4] (*See* §§ 17.50, 17.69)

7. Filing proof of service.
   - Filing of proof of service within the defendant's answering time. Filing of papers, thereafter, before or reasonably after their service.

8. Responsive pleadings.

§ 17.79

1. *See, e.g.*, 29 U.S.C.A. § 501(b).
2. 28 U.S.C.A. § 1914.
3. *See* Official Forms 1A and 1B, in the Appendix of Forms to the Federal Rules of Civil Procedure.
4. 29 U.S.C.A. § 502(h); N.Y.C.Admin. Code § 8–502(c).

Ch. 17   EMPLOYMENT POLICIES AND HANDBOOKS   § 17.81

- Service of answer or other responsive pleadings, 20 days after service of the complaint.

§ 17.80 Miscellaneous Practice Issues—OFCCP/Glass Ceiling Audits

The U.S. Department of Labor's Office of Federal Contract Compliance Programs ("OFCCP") reviews the affirmative action efforts of federal contractors on an ongoing basis.[1] Of the estimated 200,000 federal contractors under its purview, the OFCCP reviews only about 2% annually. Two of the most significant strategies the OFCCP has pursued recently are "glass ceiling" reviews and mega-construction project reviews. The glass ceiling reviews target obstacles impeding women and minorities from advancing to executive level positions. Mega-construction project reviews focus on efforts by general contractors on major federally funded construction projects to recruit and train women and minorities for skilled jobs.

In a glass ceiling review, as in all compliance reviews, the OFCCP generally starts with a desk audit. The OFCCP will request and review data to determine the management level at which the presence of women and minorities declines. The OFCCP will attempt to ascertain the type of positions that remain unfilled by women or minorities at that level, the proportion of women or minorities in "feeder" positions to those management jobs, and the selection and developmental strategies of the company that allow or prevent the movement of women or minorities in the feeder pool positions to the top level jobs.

If the OFCCP's desk audit has identified a "marked decline" in presence of women/minorities in management, it will conduct an on-site review. This will entail a more thorough analysis of the racial and gender make up of those above and below the "glass ceiling." The OFCCP will determine whether the employer has made a good faith effort to identify and eliminate barriers to women/minority opportunities and whether there has been unlawful discrimination. Under the OFCCP's remedial powers, the Department of Labor can seek term debarment, undertake conciliation for back pay awards, or commence a discrimination action in federal court.

§ 17.81 Miscellaneous Practice Issues—Employment Policies and Handbooks

Policies. An employer should have policies and procedures in place to manage the key personnel decisions that can give rise to legal actions.

---

§ 17.80

1. PRACTICE POINTER: The authority for carrying out affirmative action compliance reviews is set forth in Section 202(1) of Executive Order 11246. Failure to comply with this Executive Order may lead to debarment or other penalties. Debarment is an action undertaken to exclude a contractor from government contracting for a reasonable, specified period of time. *See e.g.*, 48 C.F.R. § 9.403(b). A discussion of the affirmative action requirements for federal contractors in these guidelines is beyond the scope of this chapter.

§ 17.81

The purpose of these policies is to guide managers; therefore, they are distributed among managers only and are not given to other employees. Nevertheless, the employer must create these policies with disclosure in mind, since they will be subject to discovery requests if they are in writing, or may be testified to in depositions. While many personnel actions and functions must be carefully managed, the ones that give rise to the most disputes involve:

(a) hiring/screening/interviewing;

(b) performance evaluation of employees;

(c) compensation/benefits allocation;

(d) promotion decisions;

(e) discipline for misconduct;

(f) handling of medical records;

(g) sexual harassment and investigations;

(h) termination.

Broadly speaking, good procedures for handling these aspects of employment will entail one or more levels of oversight to prevent actions that are arbitrary or unnecessarily unfair or that violate contractual, tort, or statutory rights. The procedure will also require that sufficient documentation be on file to support the decision whenever possible.

Handbooks. The purpose of distributing personnel manuals or handbooks to employees is to provide ready answers to common questions and to inform employees of their benefits and workplace rules. One of the risks, however, is that the employer will inadvertently create enforceable rights in a handbook. Care must therefore be taken in drafting the handbook.[1]

The common elements of a handbook include:

(a) introduction to the company;

(b) EEO statement and at-will disclaimer (if appropriate);

(c) classification of employment (*e.g.*, full/part-time);

(d) work hours;

(e) pay procedures;

(f) overtime pay policy;

---

§ 17.81

1. PRACTICE POINTER. Some employers ask that employees sign a statement that they have received the handbook or manual and have read it. This may provide the employer with support for a claim against the employee who, for example, breaches the confidentiality policy that prohibits non-disclosure of proprietary information. On the other hand, the employer should be wary that doing so may turn the handbook, as a whole, into a contractual agreement, which employers generally want to avoid. The better practice may be to design a separate confidentiality agreement, if the nature of the job is that sensitive, while maintaining the non-contractual character of the handbook.

Ch. 17 DRAFTING THE COMPLAINT § 17.82

(g) performance evaluations;

(h) vacation policy;

(i) holidays; sick days; personal days;

(j) family and medical leave;

(k) leaves of absence: medical/personal/military;

(*l*) bereavement;

(m) jury duty;

(n) health insurance: hospitalization/major medical/dental;

(o) life insurance;

(p) disability leaves;

(q) COBRA;

(r) Workers' Compensation;

(s) pension/401(k) plans;

(t) educational assistance;

(u) appropriate conduct/misconduct/discipline procedures;

(v) absenteeism/tardiness;

(w) complaint procedures;

(x) smoking policy;

(y) drug free workplace;

(z) confidentiality of information;

(aa) conflict of interests;

(ab) health and safety;

(ac) termination of employment; and

(ad) policy on sexual (and other) harassment and complaint procedures.

§ 17.82 Drafting the Complaint

State Court Complaints, Generally. Pursuant to CPLR 3013, New York State Court complaints and answers must (1) give the court and parties notice of the transactions and occurrences intended to be proved and the material elements of each cause of action or defense. They must do so in plain and concise statements. While the CPLR does not specify a precise format for the pleadings, the structure provided by the CPLR Appendix of Official Forms is commonly followed, as it is here.[1]

---

§ 17.82

1. PRACTICE POINTER: In New York State Court, the pleadings are to be printed on letter size paper. CPLR 2101(a). The paper must be white, but need not have colored lines down the margins. They

§ 17.82　　　　EMPLOYMENT LAW　　　　Ch. 17

Federal Court Complaints, Generally. The components of a pleading in federal court are set forth in the Federal Rules of Civil Procedure (*See* Rule 8(a) and in the appendix of forms to the rules). As with the CPLR, however, there is no precise structure that the pleadings must follow. Individual district courts and circuits promulgate local civil rules, which, of course, must be consulted.

Caption—New York State Complaints and Answers. The following information must appear in the captions of complaints and answers filed in New York State Courts:

(a) Name of the court. The front page of the pleading must contain a caption at the top. The uppermost lines state the name and county (venue) of the court in capital letters.

(b) Names of the parties. The names of all the parties, and, if applicable, their capacities, must appear in a boxed area at the left side of the front page.

(c) Index number and title. To the right is the index number and, if a judge has been assigned, the name of the judge.[2] Below, is the title of the pleading, which is usually underlined.

Caption—The Federal Complaints and Answers. The caption should include the name of the court, the parties, their capacities, the docket number, and the title of the papers. Once the complaint is filed and a docket number and judge are assigned, the number and initials of the judge must appear to the right of the caption.

Introductory Statement. In New York State and federal courts, an introductory statement is not required but helps orient the reader before the elements of the cause(s) of action(s) are alleged. The first part introduces the party whose pleading it is, and the second part is a brief preliminary statement:

(a) Name of party. *E.g.*, "[NAME OF PLAINTIFF] (in capital letters), by [his/her] attorneys [name of firm], as and for [his/her] complaint, alleges as follows:"

(b) Preliminary Statement. Create a heading by centering and underlining (or otherwise emboldening) the words "PRELIMINARY STATEMENT." Such headings are optional and are employed to guide the reader through the pleading. Beneath this heading, the first numbered paragraph summarizes the action. (*E.g.*, "This is an action for breach of contract and violation of New York State Labor

---

must be printed in black and written in English (foreign language attachments are to be translated). CPLR 2101(b). The body of the pleading is to be set forth in consecutively numbered paragraphs. CPLR 3014. All signatures are to be followed by the printed name of the signatory. CPLR 2101(a). Any attachments to a pleading are considered incorporated into the pleading (*e.g.*, a contract). Pleadings are usually prepared with backs that contain the caption and the name and address of the attorney who prepared and served the pleading.

2.　22 NYCRR § 202.5.

Law arising from the termination of plaintiff, [name of plaintiff]'s employment as [title] of [defendant's name] on [date]). After introducing the names of the parties and other frequently used names or objects, practitioners must state in parentheses any shorthand substituted name that will be used, *e.g.*, '[surname],' or ['the Contract']. The introductory statement can also include one or more separate paragraphs setting forth a summary of the types of relief sought."

The Parties: New York State and Federal Complaints. The practitioner must identify the parties and characterize their capacities and corporate status, if necessary.[3] Commonly, one paragraph is used to describe the plaintiff, another, the defendant, and so on. The plaintiff's place of residence should be stated, particularly when needed to support jurisdiction or venue.[4] In the case of multiple parties, create subsections to describe each of the parties within the paragraph. If standing to sue under a statute requires that certain criteria be met, *e.g.*, "employer" or "employee," state that the parties meet the requirement. State any factual allegations needed to support the status, *e.g.*, "as [plaintiff]'s supervisor, [individual defendant] has the power to make personnel decisions regarding [plaintiff]'s employment."[5]

Jurisdictional Allegations. Although this is not always required under the CPLR in New York State complaints, the basis for jurisdiction should be pleaded, especially when it rests on special circumstances.[6] In New York, the state courts have jurisdictional limits. Here, state that the amount of damages claimed is within the limits of the court, where a higher court might otherwise have jurisdiction; or, when bringing a tort claim against a government entity, state that a timely notice of claim has been filed. Any filing prerequisites can alternatively be stated at the end of the recitation of the facts or, preferably, just prior to the Demand for Relief, see "Procedural Requirements," discussed below in this section.

---

3. CPLR 3015.

4. **PRACTICE POINTER**. Significantly, the NYCHRL has been held applicable to claims arising from conduct that does not necessarily occur in New York City, as long as the defendant maintains offices in New York City. The plaintiff must also be a resident of New York City.

5. **PRACTICE POINTER**. In naming parties, the plaintiff must choose whether to name individual managers or supervisors in their official or individual capacities. In discrimination cases, this decision turns in part on whether the manager may be held individually liable under the particular law. The Second Circuit has held that supervisors are not subject to personal liability for discrimination under Title VII because Title VII covers only employers of fifteen or more individuals, while agents, in their individual capacities, do not do so. Tomka v. Seiler Corp., 66 F.3d 1295 (2d Cir.1995). This rationale would presumably preclude personal liability for managers under the Americans with Disabilities Act as well. Employees who seek to sue their supervisors individually may proceed under the New York State Human Rights Law, Executive Law § 296(6), which makes it "unlawful for any person to aid, abet, incite, compel or coerce the doing of any of the acts forbidden under this article." Such a claim could be raised in conjunction with a Title VII cause of action in either federal or state court as long as the jurisdictional requirement as between the individual defendant and the plaintiff are otherwise met. Managers can also be held individually liable under the New York City Human Rights Law and under 42 U.S.C.A. § 1981.

6. *See generally*, CPLR 301.

Federal complaints, unlike most New York State complaints, require a detailed jurisdictional statement.

Class Action Allegations. New York State discrimination claims are rarely brought as class actions. Class action claims of discrimination under the NYSHRL can nevertheless be brought using the procedural mechanism for establishing a class action set forth in CPLR Article 9.[7] This vehicle is somewhat unpredictable in that the determination of class action status rests in the discretion, *i.e.*, the "attitude" of the trial judge.[8]

Federal procedural law is more hospitable to class action claims.[9] The allegations for certification of a class include: the scope of the class, the number in the class, the claims that are typical of the class, that there are questions of law common to the members of the class, and that the class representatives are able to fairly and adequately represent the class interests.[10]

Factual Allegations. This is the first time to tell the plaintiff's story. If there is only one cause of action, set forth, sequentially, the material facts that constitute the cause of action. In New York (and federal) complaints, every material element of the cause of action should be set forth in a separate paragraph.[11] Each paragraph should contain, if practicable, a single allegation.[12]

Although the CPLR generally favors "liberality in pleading," matter that is prejudicial and unnecessary may be stricken from a pleading.[13] Irrelevant, scandalous, and otherwise immaterial assertions in the pleadings may lead to a motion to strike, such as allegations of settlement discussions which are inadmissible as evidence of liability.[14]

In New York, several causes of action relevant to employment law require pleading with "particularity."[15] The particularity requirement in defamation cases, for example, mandates that the allegedly defamatory words be quoted verbatim. In fraud, misrepresentation, breach of trust, and undue influences cases, the particularity requirement simply means

---

7. *See also,* 9 NYCRR § 465.3(a)(4)(permitting class actions); *but see* Consolidated Edison Co. v. State Human Rights Appeal Bd., 65 A.D.2d 546, 409 N.Y.S.2d 141 (2d Dep't 1978), aff'd 49 N.Y.2d 944, 428 N.Y.S.2d 945, 406 N.E.2d 800 (1980)(precluding class-wide relief to individuals not party to the proceedings).

8. *See* D. Siegel, *New York Practice* § 142 (2d ed.1991).

9. *See* FRCP 23(a), (b)(2).

10. Under the ADEA (29 U.S.C.A. § 216(b)), a "similarly situated" criteria replaces the certification requirement in FRCP 23, and there are special rules for "opting-in" in class action age discrimination cases that should be consulted. *See* Heagney v. European American Bank, 122 F.R.D. 125 (E.D.N.Y.1988).

11. CPLR 3013.

12. CPLR 3014.

13. CPLR 3024(b). *See* D. Siegel, *Practice Commentaries*, C3024:4.

14. *See* Sabin–Goldberg v. Horn, 179 A.D.2d 462, 578 N.Y.S.2d 187 (1st Dep't 1992).

15. CPLR 3016.

that the circumstances must be stated in detail.[16]

In federal complaints, each cause of action should be pleaded as a separate count. Within each count, recite the pertinent facts that support that cause of action.[17] Placing a prayer for damages within each cause of action is a matter of style; these requests may be saved for the prayer for relief.

Procedural Requirements. If administrative processing, filing of a notice of claim, or mandatory service of the complaint on administrative entities are necessary predicates to commencing the action, the facts that constitute satisfaction of the requirement must be alleged. This paragraph can follow the Jurisdictional Statement, described above in this Section.

Cause of Action Denomination. The heart of the complaint is the pleading of the cause(s) of action. The essential component of the cause of action is the recitation of the factual allegations that, taken together, satisfy the elements of the cause of action.[18] As long as the requisite factual elements have been alleged, the cause of action has been pleaded, even if the name of the cause of action has never been mentioned, or the wrong name of the cause of action has been set forth. Nevertheless, for the sake of clarity, it is better practice to state the name given to the particular cause of action. The first time this can be done is in the introductory statement. The next opportunity may be a heading over the factual allegations relating to the particular cause of action.

The third time to mention the cause of action may be in a concluding allegation in which the plaintiff alleges that the defendant is liable under the alleged cause of action.

For many causes of action (*e.g.*, fraud), one of the substantive elements of the claim will be that the plaintiff has suffered an injury compensable by an award of damages. To satisfy this element, the final sentence of the cause of action usually alleges that the violation of law caused the plaintiff to suffer damages in excess of a specified amount. If such an allegation is omitted in the cause of action section, it should be stated in the "wherefore" or "*ad damnum*" clause at the end of the complaint, discussed immediately below in "Demand for Relief."

Pleading alternative, inconsistent, or hypothetical causes of action is expressly permitted in New York.[19] This means that the plaintiff may

---

16. PRACTICE POINTER: A further "particularity" requirement relates to claims against non-profit organizations. CPLR 3106(f). Besides verifying the complaint, it provides that the plaintiff in such cases must aver whether or not gross negligence or intentionally harmful conduct is being alleged.

17. *See generally*, FRCP 8.

18. *See* CPLR 3013 ("Statements in a pleading shall be sufficiently particular to give the court and parties notice of the transactions, occurrences, or series of transactions or occurrences, intended to be proved and *the material elements of each cause of action or defense.*" [emphasis added]).

19. CPLR 3014.

§ 17.82   EMPLOYMENT LAW   Ch. 17

assert multiple causes of action based upon the same set of facts. Moreover, the fact that these causes of action may be inconsistent does not render the complaint defective. These rules are generally applicable to federal complaints.

Demand for Relief. In an unnumbered paragraph at the end of the complaint, beginning with the capitalized word "WHEREFORE," set forth a monetary or other demand or prayer for relief. In New York, a monetary or other demand for relief is required in every complaint, except in medical and dental malpractice actions and actions against municipalities.[20] The dollar amount of the demand limits the judgment only if exceeding the limit will cause prejudice to the defendant, and any limitation can be avoided by stating the demand in the form " ... damages not less than $_____."[21] If the demand includes various forms of relief, set them forth in numbered subsections of the *ad damnum* clause for purposes of clarity. Include a demand for interest, costs, disbursements and attorneys' fees where applicable. If a jury trial is sought, that request may be made in this section and should also be made in the Note of Issue in actions pending in supreme and county courts.[22] The right to a jury trial will be waived, however, if equitable relief, as opposed to strictly legal relief, is sought anywhere in the complaint.

The demand for relief should be subdivided according to type, *i.e.*, legal or equitable, with each claim preceded by a small letter for numbering purposes (*e.g.*, a., b., etc.). They should loosely track the causes of action. If only certain damages are sought against certain defendants, that should also be stated.

A basic checklist of some, but not all, possible claims for relief would include:

1. Legal relief

    • Actual damages for loss of wages, benefits, and promotional opportunities and bonuses, including an award of front pay for loss of future compensation;

---

20. CPLR 3017.

21. Loomis v. Civetta Corinno Construction Corp., 54 N.Y.2d 18, 444 N.Y.S.2d 571, 429 N.E.2d 90 (1981)(plaintiff permitted to retain verdict in excess of demand in complaint where defendant was not prejudiced; but when a defendant relies on a low demand in litigating, prejudice might occur).

22. CPLR 4102(a); Uniform Rule 202.21.

CAVEAT: Claims for equitable relief may result in a forfeiture of the right to a jury trial for New York law claims. In New York State courts, jury trials are available where the plaintiff seeks only legal relief (*i.e.*, monetary damages). CPLR 4102. Any claim for equitable relief, such as reinstatement or an injunction against future discrimination, may be considered a waiver of the right to jury trial in a discrimination proceeding. *See* Kaplan v. Long Island University, 116 A.D.2d 508, 509, 497 N.Y.S.2d 378, 378 (1st Dep't 1986); *but see*, Davila v. New York Hospital, 1995 WL 115598, 67 FEP Cas. (BNA) 861, (S.D.N.Y. 1995)(inclusion of equitable relief claim in action for damages under Executive Law § 296 did not constitute a jury trial waiver in federal court).

Ch. 17   DRAFTING THE COMPLAINT   § 17.82

- Compensatory damages for mental anguish, humiliation, emotional distress, loss of enjoyment of life;[23]
- Punitive damages to the fullest extent permitted by law.[24]

2. Equitable relief.
   - An order prohibiting defendant from continuing or maintaining the policy or practice of [state practice, *e.g.*, denying opportunities to minorities];
   - An order enjoining defendants from all [state nature of conduct, *e.g.*, discriminatory, harassing] conduct;
   - Reinstatement [or promotion] of [plaintiff] to [position].

3. Costs.
   - Costs of this action, together with plaintiff's reasonable attorneys' fees.
   - Such other and further relief as this court deems necessary and just.

Jury Demand. FRCP 38(b) provides that a jury demand (which must be made if a jury trial is sought) can be indorsed in the pleadings. In general, jury trials are available in all discrimination causes of action in federal or state court, except where no intentional discrimination is alleged (*i.e.*, disparate impact).[25] With regard to ERISA claims, allegations of an equitable nature, such as denial of benefits[26] or fiduciary breach, are tried exclusively by the court; while those arising under ERISA's interference section[27] have been deemed legal remedies and may be tried by a jury.

Signature Block/Verification: New York Complaints. CPLR 2101(d) provides: "Each paper served or filed shall be indorsed with the name, address and telephone number of the attorney for the party serving or filing the paper, or if the party does not appear by attorney, with the name, address and telephone number of the party." Accordingly, the signature of the plaintiff or the attorney is not required, unless

---

23. Under Title VII, as amended by the CRA 1991 (42 U.S.C.A. § 1981a(b)(3)), compensatory and punitive damages are capped. These caps also apply to actions under the Americans With Disabilities Act. Each plaintiff under these statutes is limited to an amount of total of compensatory (*e.g.*, pain, suffering, emotional anguish) and punitive damages depending on the number of employees working for the defendant (economic damages, *e.g.*, back and front pay are not subject to these caps), as follows:

Employees	Damages may not exceed
15–100	$ 50,000
101–200	$100,000
201–500	$200,000
501+	$300,000

24. Punitive damages under Title VII as amended by the CRA 1991 are unavailable against public sector employers, but may be available against individuals acting in their official capacity. 42 U.S.C.A. §§ 1981a(b)(1), 1983, 1985.

25. CAVEAT: Plaintiffs in New York State Courts must be wary not to demand equitable relief if they wish to preserve their right to a jury trial.

26. 29 U.S.C.A. § 502.

27. 29 U.S.C.A. § 510.

the complaint is to be verified, and then only on the affidavit of verification.[28]

Verification of the complaint is usually optional. In certain employment law actions, however, it is required, such as complaints involving the performing of labor,[29] or gross negligence or intentional infliction of harm by certain directors, officers or trustees of certain corporations, associations, organizations or trusts, such as non-profit corporations.[30] Once a pleading is verified, each subsequent pleading must be verified.[31] In certain instances, an answer must be verified.[32]

Federal Complaint Signature Block. FRCP 11 provides that the pleadings must be signed by the attorney of record (or by the *pro se* party). In addition, in the Southern and Eastern Districts of New York, the attorney's name, together with his/her initials (without middle initial) and the final four digits of his/her Social Security number, are required for identification purposes.[33] The Western and the Northern Districts do not have this requirement.

Certain statutory causes of action specify that the complaint or other papers must be verified.[34]

§ 17.83 Drafting Checklist—Complaint

These basic components of an employment law complaint are discussed at § 17.82, *supra* and elsewhere in this chapter, as noted below.

1. Caption.

    - Index number, judge's name (N.Y.) or initials (federal).

2. Preliminary statement (optional but recommended).

3. Jurisdiction.

    - Mandatory in federal court, optional in New York;[1]
    - Statutes may confer jurisdiction on certain courts.

4. Venue.

    - Venue is generally where employee worked.

5. Parties.

    - Defendants named in their official or individual capacities (or both);

---

28. CPLR 3021.
29. CPLR 3016(f).
30. CPLR 3016(h).
31. CPLR 3020(a).
32. CPLR 3020(b).

33. Local Rule 1(b) of the United States District Courts for the Southern and Eastern Districts.
34. *See, e.g.*, 29 U.S.C.A. § 501(b).

§ 17.83
1. CPLR 301.

Ch. 17 **DRAFTING THE ANSWER** **§ 17.84**

- Class action allegations. (*See* § 17.82)

6. Factual statement.
   - State facts common to all causes of action;
   - Five "W's," *prima facie* elements;
   - Procedural prerequisites such as exhaustion of internal or administrative remedies (*See* §§ 17.67, 17.69).

7. Causes of action: (track *prima facie* elements) (*See* §§ 17.20–17.65):
   - Plead certain causes of action (*e.g.*, fraud) with "particularity" (*see supra*, §§ 17.26, 17.28);
   - State that defendants' actions were the cause of damages so that each cause of action contains a prayer for relief, and specifies whether damage is continuing (or not).

8. Demand for relief.
   - Legal damages (*e.g.*, actual damages for loss of wages, benefits, and promotional opportunities and bonuses, including an award of front pay for loss of future compensation);
   - Compensatory damages for mental anguish, humiliation, emotional distress, loss of enjoyment of life;
   - Punitive damages;
   - Liquidated damages;
   - Equitable relief (*e.g.*, order prohibiting defendant from continuing or maintaining the policy or practice, promotion, order enjoining defendants, declaratory relief, reinstatement, restraining future violations)[2]
   - Attorneys' Fees;
   - Costs;
   - Such other and further relief as court deems necessary and just;
   - Jury demand;
   - Signature block (federal complaints must be signed, New York State complaints need not be signed unless verified);
   - Verification (if applicable).

§ 17.84 Drafting the Answer

Before answering, the defendant must contemplate whether to move

---

2. CAVEAT: In New York State actions, asserting these claims will prevent a jury trial, *see supra*, § 17.82 (Demand for relief).

§ 17.84   EMPLOYMENT LAW   Ch. 17

to dismiss the complaint,[1] move to strike,[2] move to remove the action to federal or state court, or to answer.

New York State and Federal Captions. The caption of the answer generally follows that of the complaint. (*See* above.)

Denial of Allegations. The manner in which answers are made is set forth at CPLR 3018(a). "A party shall deny those statements known or believed by him to be untrue. He shall specify those statements as to the truth of which he lacks knowledge or information sufficient to form a belief and this shall have the effect of a denial. All other statements of a pleading are deemed admitted, except that where no responsive pleading is permitted they are deemed denied or avoided."[3]

Rule 8 of the Federal Rules of Civil Procedure sets forth the general rules of pleading with respect to, among other things, defenses and forms of denials. As in the case of all pleadings, subsection (e)(1) of Rule 8 states that each averment be "simple, concise, and direct" and that "[n]o technical forms of pleading or motion are required."

Affirmative Defenses. In New York State, as in federal civil practice, affirmative defenses must be included in a responsive pleading.[4] FRCP 8(c) specifies certain affirmative defenses that should be pleaded as well as "any other matter constituting an avoidance or affirmative defense," just as CPLR 3018(b) gives several examples of affirmative defenses. For example, the employer met with a claim for unpaid wages would have to plead the affirmative defense of payment in order to preserve the defense. Many of the typical affirmative defenses pleaded in New York employment litigation can apply to both New York and federal pleadings. Other affirmative defenses relate to specific causes of action that arise from certain New York or federal statutes. Typical affirmative defenses are failure to exhaust remedies (internal or administrative), Statute of Limitations, written at-will provisions, Statute of Frauds, defamation privileges, mandatory arbitration, individuals as improper defendants, preemption, and failure to mitigate damages.[5]

---

§ 17.84

1. FRCP 12(b)(6) (federal); CPLR 3211 (New York).

2. **PRACTICE POINTER**: Although the CPLR generally favors "liberality in pleading," matter that is prejudicial and unnecessary may be stricken from a pleading. CPLR 3024(b).

See D. Siegel, *Practice Commentaries*, C3024:4, p. 322. Irrelevant, scandalous, and otherwise immaterial assertions in the pleadings may lead to a motion to strike. Allegations regarding settlement discussions which are inadmissible as evidence of liability, would likewise be subject to motions to strike. *See* Sabin–Goldberg v. Horn, 179 A.D.2d 462, 578 N.Y.S.2d 187 (1st Dep't 1992).

3. CPLR 3018(a).

4. *See* CPLR 3018(b).

5. **PRACTICE POINTER**: After a finding of unlawful discharge, the burden of showing that the employee failed to mitigate damages is on the defendant. The defendant must demonstrate that the discharged employee did not use due diligence and that the efforts to find comparable employment were insufficient.

The burden is also on the employer to prove any set-offs to back pay damages. For example, unemployment benefits may offset back pay. *See* EEOC v. Enterprise Asso-

Counterclaims. Employers are asserting counterclaims with increasing frequency. Some typical grounds for counterclaims include breach of duty of loyalty, disclosure of confidential or proprietary information to competitors, speaking derogatorily of employer, failure to return documents or property, abuse of expense account, conversion, interference with business relations, and other forms of self-dealing. FRCP 13 sets forth both mandatory and permissive counterclaims.[6] In federal court, if the court's jurisdiction rests on the grounds pleaded in the complaint, no statement of jurisdiction need accompany the counterclaims. Allege the facts in a counterclaim in the same manner as setting forth the allegations in a complaint.[7]

Reply to Counterclaims. Plaintiff is required to "serve a reply to a counterclaim in the answer within 20 days after service of the answer."[8] Plaintiff's counsel should treat the counterclaims as a separate and distinct lawsuit against the plaintiff.

Answer Demand for Relief. Although the answer is not an affirmative request for relief, defendants commonly demand judgment dismissing the complaint. Such a demand is probably unnecessary (*see* Official Form 20, promulgated by the Advisory Committee on Civil Rules of the Judicial Conference of the United States accompanying the Federal Rules of Civil Procedure.) If counterclaims are asserted, a demand for damages and other relief must be set forth.

Verification. If the complaint is verified, the answer must be verified. Under certain circumstances, the answer must be verified independent of the complaint.[9]

§ 17.85 Drafting Checklist—Answer

These basic components of an answer to an employment law claim are discussed at Section 17.82 and elsewhere in this chapter, as noted below.

1. Response to each allegation: admit; deny; or, if a party is without knowledge or information sufficient to form a belief as to the truth of an averment, the party shall so state; such a statement is equivalent to a denial.

2. Defenses and affirmative defenses (those with asterisks are generally considered affirmative defenses which must be pleaded in order not to be waived):

---

ciation Steamfitters, 542 F.2d 579 (2d Cir. 1976), cert. denied 430 U.S. 911, 97 S.Ct. 1186, 51 L.Ed.2d 588 (1977); *but see* Maturo v. National Graphics, Inc., 722 F.Supp. 916 (D.Conn.1989).

6. *See also* CPLR § 3019.
7. *See* FRCP 12(b).
8. FRCP 12(a).

PRACTICE POINTER: Every defense to a counterclaim must be asserted in the reply except for those which can be raised by motion, such as lack of subject matter jurisdiction. FRCP 12(a).

9. *See* CPLR 3020.

§ 17.85 EMPLOYMENT LAW Ch. 17

- Failure to state a cause of action.
- Subject matter jurisdiction.
- Improper forum.
- Lack of personal jurisdiction.*
- Expiration of Statute of Limitations. (*See* § 17.77)*
- Discharge in bankruptcy.*
- Exclusivity of remedies (*e.g.,* Workers' Compensation Law). (*See* § 17.65)*
- Election of remedies. (*See* § 17.68)*
- Preemption. (*See* § 17.50)*
- Failure to exhaust internal or administrative remedies. (*See* §§ 17.67–17.69)*
- *Res judicata* or collateral estoppel.*
- *Bona fide* seniority system or occupational qualification. (*See* § 17.59)*
- Reasonable factors other than age, sex, religion, etc. (*See* § 17.37)
- Claims barred by release, waiver, estoppel. (*See* §§ 17.10–17.11)*
- Unclean hands.*
- Reasons for discharge not pretextual. (*See* § 17.59)
- Failure to establish qualifications for job. (*See* § 17.59)*
- Failure to state claim of retaliation. (*See* §§ 17.38, 17.59)
- Failure to mitigate damages.*
- Qualified privilege. (*See* § 17.25)
- Lack of knowledge of disability or other protected class membership. (*See* § 17.43)*
- No entitlement to punitive damages/injunctive relief. (*See* § 17.82)
- Consistent with business necessity. (*See* § 17.59)*
- Claims subject to arbitration. (*See* § 17.9)*
- Inability to reasonably perform duties (NYSHRL-disability discrimination defense). (*See* § 17.43)*
- Exempt employee. (*See* § 17.63)*
- Statute of Frauds. (*See* §§ 17.33 *et seq.*)*

3. Counterclaims.
4. Demand for relief.

5. Signature block/verification (if applicable).

§ 17.86 Forms—Client (Plaintiff) Intake Questionnaire

CONSULTATION INFORMATION SHEET

Date _____

Name (please print) _____

Address _____

_____

Home phone ( ) _____ Work phone ( ) _____

Social Security number _____ Date of birth _____

Referred to this office by _____

Employer (or former employer) _____

(Former) Employer's address _____

_____

How many employees does it have? _____

Job title _____ Supervisor _____

How long with employer? _____

Labor union _____

    Address _____

_____ Phone _____

Salary: _____ Other benefits:

    Medical _____ Pension _____ Other _____

Nature of Dispute (why are your seeking legal advice) _____

_____

_____

If terminated from employment:

    Date notified of termination _____

    Date actually terminated _____

    Severance received _____

    Does/did your employer evaluate you? ___ What evaluations were you given _____

    Were you ever given a raise, promotion, bonus, demotion? If so, describe. _____

    Were you ever disciplined? If so, for what? _____

Have you filed any grievances, complaints, proceedings or actions?

_____

Are there witnesses to the incidents relating to the job action taken against you? If so, describe. _____

_____

If you were terminated, have you sought reemployment? _____

_____

Itemize the salary and benefits that you have lost due to the job action. _____

_____

Have you sought medical or psychological treatment/care as a result of the job action? If yes, describe the nature of the ailment and treatment. _____

_____

§ 17.87 Forms—Severance/Release Agreement

SEVERANCE AGREEMENT AND RELEASE

This Severance Agreement and Release (the "Agreement") is made and entered into this [*date*] by and between [*Employee*], [*address*], and [*Name of Company*] and all its officers, directors, owners and employees ("*Short name of company*"), [*address*].

WHEREAS [*Employee*] has served as the [*position*] of [*Company*] since [*year*]; and

WHEREAS [*Company*] and [*Employee*] mutually agree that [*Employee*]'s relationship with [*Company*] shall terminate effective the close of business on [*date*];

NOW THEREFORE, in consideration of the promises and covenants hereinafter set forth, [*Employee*] and [*Company*] agree as follows:

I. In consideration of [*Employee*]'s consent to the release set forth in Paragraph II, below, and the representations and agreements set forth in this Agreement, [*Company*] agrees to pay [*Employee*] on [*date*] the severance compensation of [$_____], less all applicable federal, state and local withholding taxes (the "severance payment"). [*Company*] further agrees that on [*date*], or the seventh day following [*Employee's*] execution and delivery of this Agreement, such severance payment will be hand delivered to [*Employee or attorney*].

II. In consideration of the compensation described in Paragraph I, above, [*Employee*] voluntarily, knowingly and willingly releases and forever discharges [*Company*], its parents, subsidiaries and affiliates, together with its and their respective officers, directors, owners, partners, shareholders, employees, agents, successors and assigns (collectively the "Related Persons"), from any and all charges, complaints, claims, promises, agreements, controversies, causes of action and demands of any nature whatsoever which against any of them [*Employee*], [*his/her*] heirs, executors, administrators, successors or assigns ever had, now have or hereafter can, shall or may have by reason of any matter, cause or thing whatsoever arising out of or pertaining to Employee's employment up to the time he/she signs this agreement. This release includes, but is not limited to, any rights or claims relating in any way to [*Employee*]'s employment relationship with [*Company*], or the termination thereof, or under any statute, including the federal Age Discrimination in Employment Act, Title VII of the Civil Rights Act, the Americans With Disabilities Act, the New York Human Rights Law, and any other federal, state or local law.

III. [*Employee*] represents that he/she has not filed against [*Company*] or its parents, subsidiaries, affiliates or any Related Persons, any complaints, charges or law suits arising out of his/her employment by [*Company*], or any other matter arising on or prior to the date hereof. [*Employee*] covenants and agrees that he/she will not seek recovery against [*Company*] or any of its parents, subsidiaries, affiliates or any Related Person arising out of any of the matters set forth in this paragraph or in paragraph II.

IV. In consideration of the release contained in paragraph II, [*Company*] voluntarily, knowingly and willingly releases and forever discharges [*Employee*], together with his/her agents, successors, heirs and assigns, from any and all charges, complaints, claims, controversies and causes of action arising out of or pertaining to Employee's employment, including any comments or remarks, whether written or oral, made by [*Employee*] regarding the [*Company*] or any related persons, or this Agreement, up to the date of this Agreement.

V. Nothing set forth in this Agreement shall prevent [*Employee*] or [*Company*] from enforcing the terms of this Agreement.

VI. The parties shall keep the terms of this Agreement confidential (except for Exhibits A and B) and shall not disclose the terms to anyone other than their professional advisers, or, for [*Employee*], his/her immediate family, or as they may be compelled by law or legal process, or in connection with an action to enforce this Agreement. The parties agree that if either receives any inquiry in connection with [*Employee*]'s departure, whether written or oral, they will respond in a manner consistent with Exhibit "B" hereto.[1]

VII. Simultaneously with the execution of this Agreement, [*Employee*] shall receive from [*Company*] a letter of reference in the form

§ 17.87

1. The purpose of this language is to avoid mention of the dispute or settlement terms arising from the termination. Example: "The employment was terminated on mutually agreeable terms, 'or' The job was eliminated as part of a [downsizing, outsourcing, etc.], 'or' The proceeding was discontinued by agreement of all parties."

§ 17.87   EMPLOYMENT LAW   Ch. 17

annexed hereto as Exhibit "A".[2] All inquiries regarding [Employee]'s employment with [Company], whether written or oral, will be directed to [Name of Executive]. [Executive] will respond to such inquiries by providing only the information set forth in Exhibit "A".

VIII. Simultaneously with the execution of this Agreement, [Employee] shall receive from [Company] a departure letter in the form annexed hereto as Exhibit "B". [Company] agrees that on or before [date], it will send a copy of the departure letter to those parties indicated on Exhibit B.

IX. [Employee] agrees that from the date of this Agreement up to and including [date], he/she shall perform his/her duties as set forth in Exhibit "C" annexed hereto.

X. [Employee] and [Company] acknowledge that this Agreement is voluntarily entered into and each party has had an opportunity to consult with an attorney or other advisor (at that party's cost) and has done so.

XI. This Agreement embodies the entire agreement of [Employee] and [Company] and supersedes all prior negotiations, understandings, and agreements concerning the subject matter of this Agreement. This Agreement may not be modified, terminated or discharged, nor may any of its provisions be waived, except by an express written agreement between these parties.

XII. The parties agree that whatever rights to which [Employee] is entitled under COBRA and any applicable state insurance continuation laws shall continue under, and be binding upon, [Company] and any successor to [Company] to the extent provided by law. Nothing in this Agreement shall be construed to provide [Employee] with any additional rights other than those provided him/her under COBRA and any applicable state insurance continuation laws.

XIII. This Agreement shall be governed by and construed in accordance with the internal laws of the State of New York (without giving effect to conflict of law rules).

XIV. This Agreement shall inure to the benefit of and be binding upon each of the parties and their respective assigns, successors, heirs and representatives.

---

2. Typically, employers provide neutral references that are limited to the employee's dates of employment and positions held. This practice has become so uniform that a glowing reference letter may be a tip-off that the employment ended in a dispute which was settled. The typical language of a neutral letter is as follows: TO WHOM IT MAY CONCERN: Pursuant to the policy of [employer], we write to confirm that [employee] was an employee of [employer] from [date] to [date]. His/her last title was [title] and his/her last salary was [amount]. [Optional: cause of separation, e.g. He/She submitted a letter of resignation, or His/Her job was eliminated as part of a downsizing]

Sincerely, [officer of employer].

Ch. 17 **LETTER REQUESTING "MOHASCO"** **§ 17.88**

XV. If any provision or part of a provision of this Agreement is found to be in violation of law or otherwise unenforceable in any respect, the parties agree that the remaining provisions or part of a provision shall remain unaffected and the Agreement shall be reformed and construed to the maximum extent possible as if such provision or part of a provision had never been contained herein, giving maximum possible effect to the release of claims set forth herein.

XVI. By executing this Agreement, [*Employee*] acknowledges that he/she has been advised, and is hereby so advised, that he/she has a period of 21 days from the date of delivery of a copy of this Agreement within which to consider this Agreement. Therefore, [*Employee*] shall have until the ___ day of _____, 19__ to consider this Agreement and to deliver to [*Company*] an executed copy. In addition, [*Employee*] shall have seven days following his/her execution and delivery to [*Company*] of a copy of this Agreement to revoke this Agreement (the "Revocation Period"). Such a revocation must be in writing and delivered to [*Company*] by hand. This Agreement will not be effective or enforceable until the Revocation Period has expired.

[*Print name of employee under signature*]

[*Insert date of employee's signature*]

[*Print name and title of person signing for the employer*]

[*Insert date signed by employer's representative*]

§ 17.88 Forms—Letter to EEOC Requesting "Mohasco" Waiver of State Processing[1]

BY HAND

[*Name of EEOC Manager of Deferrals*]
U.S. Equal Employment
Opportunity Commission
[*Address*]

Re: [*Charging Party / Defendant*]

---

§ 17.88

1. *See supra,* § 17.67.

Dear [*Name of officer*]:

Enclosed for filing and processing is a Charge of Discrimination in the above-captioned case, alleging a violation of Title VII [*and/or the Americans with Disabilities Act*].

Since the date of the most recent discriminatory act was _____, 19__, the 300–day limitations period will expire on Friday, _____, 19__. Accordingly, we urgently request that the Commission ask the New York State Division of Human Rights for a waiver of the Division's 60–day period for processing, pursuant to *Mohasco Corp. v. Silver*, 447 U.S. 807, 100 S.Ct. 2486, 65 L.Ed.2d 532 (1980). We specifically ask that this request be made by fax, due to the unreliability of the mails, and we ask to be copied on the request.

If you have any questions, please telephone me immediately.

Sincerely yours,

[*Charging Party's Attorney*]

§ 17.89 Forms—Charge of Discrimination—New York State Division of Human Rights (Official Form)

STATE OF NEW YORK: EXECUTIVE DEPARTMENT
STATE DIVISION OF HUMAN RIGHTS

State Division of Human Rights
on the Complaint of

        Complainant) EXEC. LAW ART. 15
) SDHR COMPLAINT
   -against-

        Respondents.

TITLE VII EEOC CHARGE NO: ____

I, _____
Residing at _____
Tel No. _____, charge the above named respondent(s) whose address(es) (is/are), _____ with an unlawful discriminatory practice relating to _____ in violation of Article 15 of the Executive Law of the State of New York (Human Rights Law) because of Race/Color ( ) National Origin ( ) Creed ( ) Age ( ) Sex ( ) Disability ( ) Marital Status ( ) Arrest Record(s) ( ) Criminal Conviction(s) ( ) Retaliation ( ).

Ch. 17 DISCRIMINATION (OFFICIAL FORM) § 17.89

Date most recent or continuing discrimination took place was _____. (month, date, year)

The particulars are:

[set forth particulars]

AFFIDAVIT

SDHR COMPLAINT NO: _____
EEOC CHARGE NO: _____

[TITLE VII and/or ADEA]

COMPLAINANT: _____
RESPONDENT(S): _____

"I have not commenced any other civil or criminal action, nor do I have an action pending before any administrative agency under any other law of this state based upon this same unlawful discriminatory practice."

[ ] I also charge the above-named respondent(s) with violating Title VII of the Civil Rights Act of 1964, as amended (covers race, color, creed, national origin, sex relating to employment), and I hereby authorize SDHR to accept this verified complaint on behalf of EEOC subject to the statutory limitations contained in Title VII.

STATE OF NEW YORK)
) ss:
COUNTY OF _____   )

_____
(Signature of Complainant)

_____, being duly sworn, deposes and says: that he/she is the complainant herein; that he/she has read (or had read to him/her) the foregoing complaint and knows the contents thereof; that the same is true to his/her own knowledge except as to the matters therein stated on information and belief; and that as to those matters, he/she believes the same to be true.

_____
(Signature of Complainant)

Subscribed and sworn to before me this ___ day of _____, 19__

_____
(Signature of Notary Public)

§ 17.90 Forms—Information Sheet—New York State Division of Human Rights (Official Form)

NYS EXECUTIVE DEPARTMENT DIVISION OF HUMAN RIGHTS

CONFIDENTIAL

PERSONAL INFORMATION SHEET

Please fill in the information requested and return this sheet to our office.

Social Security No:

Name:

Address:

Home Phone Number:

Date of Birth:

Marital Status:

Race:

Place of Birth:

Education—Highest year completed:

Present Employer–

   Name:

   Address:

   Telephone Number:

   No. of years employed:

   Salary/wages:

   Occupation:

Contact Person—(Someone who will always know how to contact you)

   Name:

   Address:

   Telephone Number(s):

If you are not presently employed, are you receiving unemployment insurance benefits and how much?

§ 17.91 Forms—SDHR Information Sheet

STATE OF NEW YORK—DIVISION OF HUMAN RIGHTS

COMPLAINANT'S INFORMATION SHEET

REGIONAL OFFICE

COMPLAINANT(S): _____

Ch. 17   FORMS—SDHR INFORMATION SHEET   § 17.91

RESPONDENT(S): _____

I, _____, the complainant in the above matter, acknowledge the following:

____ 1. I have been advised that, according to the Division's Rules of Practice;

(a) The Division or I shall be able to reasonably amend my complaint.

(b) This complaint may voluntarily be withdrawn in writing by me at any time before the service of a Notice of Public Hearing. The original must be signed by me and be verified before a Notary Public or other person duly authorized by Law to make acknowledgments.

(c) If this matter is conciliated, I will be given fifteen days in which to agree to or object to the terms of conciliation.

(d) At a public hearing I may be present and be allowed to present testimony in person or by counsel and cross-examine witnesses in this matter.

____ 2. I have been informed that a copy of my complaint and/or the determination in this matter will be sent to _____. (The local Human Rights commission, or referral agency of my choice.)

____ 3. I have been informed of my right to retain private counsel.

____ 4. (a) I understand that I, or my attorney, may review the Division's file in this matter.

(b) I also understand that I, or my attorney, may copy by hand any material in the file, or obtain photocopies at a nominal charge.

____ 5. I have been informed that in cases where it appears that the Regional Office may dismiss my complaint, I must have an opportunity to review and rebut the investigative material.

____ 6. I am to notify the Division of Human Rights of any change in my address, telephone number, or place of employment which may occur during the course of the Division's proceedings. I understand that failure to do so may jeopardize my rights.

____ 7. Except for emergency situations, I shall give the Division's Regional Office four days' notice in the event that I cannot attend any scheduled conference at which my presence has been requested.

____ 8. I acknowledge receipt of a copy of the complaint and a copy of the Complainant's Information Sheet in the above-entitled matter.

____ 9. I have been informed as follows:

"The Division has entered into contracts to protect your federal rights with the following agencies: U.S. Department of Housing & Urban Development (HUD) covering

Title VIII, the federal fair housing law; U.S. Equal Employment Opportunity Commission (EEOC) covering title VII and the Age Discrimination in Employment Act (ADEA). Where your complaint with the Division shows a violation of federal law, the contracts permit the Division with your written authorization, to send this complaint to HUD or EEOC as appropriate for filing with the appropriate agency to invoke your federal rights. We call this dual-filing. In order to avoid duplication of work and expenses, the SDHR will actively investigate your complaint and the federal agency will suspend its investigation to await the results of the SDHR investigation. The federal agency, however, may activate its own investigation if it determines that SDHR is unable to process the complaint. In such a case the federal agency will notify you of such action, but SDHR will not be divested of jurisdiction."

_____ 10. I understand that if my complaint alleges discrimination based on race, creed, color, national origin or sex, and I have filed a similar complaint with the EEOC under Title VII, then it may be possible for an attorney engaged to represent me in proceedings before the Division on this complaint, where the complaint is subsequently sustained, to sue the respondent in Federal Court to collect the fee for such representation from the respondent. *See* U.S. Supreme Court decision in *New York Gaslight Club, Inc. v. Carey*, 447 U.S. 54, 100 S.Ct. 2024, 64 L.Ed.2d 723 (1980).

_____ 11. I understand that if my complaint alleges discrimination based on age and I have filed a similar complaint with the EEOC under the Age Discrimination in Employment Act (ADEA), then I may sue for recovery of back pay, an equal amount as liquidated damages, appropriate make-whole relief, attorney's fees and court cost of injunctive relief so long as a charge is filed with EEOC within 300 days of the alleged discrimination and so long as the lawsuit is filed within two years of the alleged discrimination (this statute of limitations is extended to three years if the violation is proven to be willful). I also understand that in order to protect my right to pursue a lawsuit, I must file a complaint in Federal Court before the two year statute of limitation has run.

_____   _____
        (Date)   *(Complainant's Signature)*

(Complainant is asked to initial each numbered space where indicated).

Ch. 17 DISCRIMINATION CHARGE (OFFICIAL FORM) § 17.92

§ 17.92 Forms—Charge of Discrimination—Equal Employment Opportunity Commission (Official Form)

CHARGE OF DISCRIMINATION

This form is affected by the Privacy Act of 1974; see Privacy Act Statement on reverse before completing this form.

ENTER CHARGE NUMBER
[ ] FEPA
[ ] EEOC

_____ and EEOC
(State or local Agency, if any)

_____
NAME (Indicate Mr., Ms., or Mrs.)   Telephone No. (include area code)

| STREET ADDRESS | CITY | STATE | ZIP |

NAMED IS THE EMPLOYER, LABOR ORGANIZATION, EMPLOYMENT AGENCY, APPRENTICESHIP COMMITTEE, STATE OR LOCAL GOVERNMENT AGENCY WHO DISCRIMINATED AGAINST ME (If more than one list below)

| NAME | NO. OF EMPLOYEES/MEMBERS | TELEPHONE NO. (including area code) |

| STREET ADDRESS | CITY | STATE | ZIP |

CAUSE OF DISCRIMINATION BASED ON (Check appropriate box(es))
[ ] RACE   [ ] COLOR   [ ] SEX   [ ] RELIGION   [ ] NATIONAL ORIGIN
[ ] AGE   [ ] RETALIATION   [ ] OTHER (Specify)

DATE MOST RECENT OR CONTINUING DISCRIMINATION TOOK PLACE

_____ _____ _____
Month   Day   Year

THE PARTICULARS ARE (If additional space is needed, attached extra sheet(s)):

[ ] I also want this charge filed with the EEOC. I will advise the agencies if I change my address or telephone number and I will cooperate fully with them in the processing of my charge in accordance with their procedures.

I declare under penalty of perjury that the foregoing is true and correct.

_____   _____
Date   Charging Party (Signature)

NOTARY—(When necessary to meet State and Local Requirements)

I swear or affirm that I have read the above charge and that it is true to the best of my knowledge, information and belief.

SIGNATURE OF COMPLAINANT

SUBSCRIBED AND SWORN TO BEFORE ME THIS DATE

_____ (Day, month, and year)

§ 17.93 Forms—Affidavit for a Charge of Discrimination—Equal Employment Opportunity Commission (Official Form)

Instruction for Taking Affidavits and Revised Format

The Charging Party's affidavit is the one document that must be relied upon to provide the investigator with a clear description of the harm complained about and the pertinent facts surrounding the alleged harm that will form the basis for conducting a proper investigation. It is therefore essential that affidavits are prepared accurately with full disclosure by the Charging Party of the pertinent facts. It is incumbent upon the investigator to be in charge of the interview and to ask the relevant questions to ensure a high quality affidavit. We cannot rely on the Charging Party alone to provide the information that is necessary. The following guidance and format will help investigators in framing questions to obtain all of the relevant information from Charging Parties during the interview and reducing those responses into an affidavit that organizes the information in an appropriate sequential order.

If the Charging Party does not have information concerning any of the items, include a statement to that effect. Not applicable (N/A) is not normally to be used under any of the 10 subject areas. If there is nothing of relevance to include, then record the Charging Party's answer in response to the inquiry, *e.g.*, "I cannot identify any witness who saw what occurred," or "I have no other relevant information to offer."

EEOC Affidavit

1. Respondent's business.

    The nature and size of the Respondent's business activity, including description of the Charging Party's department, its function, and the unit supervisor and decision maker who caused the alleged harm to the Charging Party. If the Respondent is not an employer, *e.g.*, union or employment agency, indicate the Charging Party's relationship and involvement with the Respondent.

Ch. 17　　EEOC AFFIDAVIT (OFFICIAL FORM)　　§ 17.93

2. Charging Party's relevant work history.

   A description of the Charging Party's education, training, work experience, job duties and responsibilities that relate to the allegation of harm.

3. Personal harm.

   A description of the personal harm, *i.e.*, what happened; when did it happen; who did it; how did it happen; where did it happen? Also include the sequence of events leading to the personal harm.

4. Respondent's explanations for the alleged harm and its policies and practices.

   The Respondent's explanations to the Charging Party for the harm, and a description of Respondent's policies or practices that relate to the allegations of harm.

5. Charging Party's rational basis for believing there was discrimination.

   A detailed explanation as to why the Charging Party believes that she/he was a victim of discrimination. Since discrimination means a difference in treatment, elicit from the Charging Party how she/he was treated differently or less favorably than others who were similarly situated, or how the alleged discriminator had some animosity toward the class represented by the Charging Party, or other reasons for believing there was discrimination.

Note: The information to be obtained about the Charging Party's reasons for believing discrimination occurred is the most important part of the affidavit as it plays a key role in guiding the investigation.

6. Comparators names, titles, and how similarly situated.

   A listing of all persons (include job titles) who are similarly situated to the Charging Party, *e.g.*, in a similar position under the same levels of supervision and/or subject to the same policies and practices of the Respondent, and how they were treated under similar circumstances as those complained of by the Charging Party. The Charging Party should be asked why she/he believes that named or identified individuals are the ones to be properly compared with him/her.

   Also obtain information as to how the Charging Party knows about the comparators.

7. Witness identification.

Have the Charging Party identify by name and position those people who have direct knowledge or information that is relevant to the charge. Also indicate how or why the identified witnesses have pertinent information, and specifically, what the information is to which they will attest.

8. Remedy.

A description of the remedy or terms of settlement that the Charging Party is seeking in filing the charge, and the Charging Party's calculation or rational basis supporting the resolution that he/she desires.

9. Class harm. (Optional: Use only when applicable to the allegation raised in the charge)

Identification of others who were allegedly harmed by the same Respondent's policies, practices, or procedures as the Charging Party or other class aspects of employment with an explanation for the Charging Party's belief that there was discrimination and other pertinent information described in other items of this format that pertain to the class charge.

10. Other relevant information.

Any other relevant information that pertains to the individual or class harm that was not captured in any item above.

STATE OF _____   CASE NAME VS _____
CITY/COUNTY OF _____   CASE NUMBER _____

AFFIDAVIT

I, _____, (Name) being first duly sworn upon my oath affirm and hereby say:

I have been given assurances by an Agent of the U.S. Equal Employment Opportunity Commission that this Affidavit will be considered confidential by the United States Government and will not be disclosed as long as the case remains open unless it becomes necessary for the Government to produce the affidavit in a formal proceeding. Upon the closing of this case, the Affidavit may be subject to disclosure in accordance with Agency policy.

I am _____ years of age, my gender is _____ (sex) and my racial identity is _____ (race).

I reside at _____, (Number/Street) _____.

Subscribed and sworn to before me this _____ day of _____.

§ 17.94 Forms—EEOC Filing Cover Letter Requesting EEOC Processing of Dual-filed Charge

[DATE]

Equal Employment Opportunity Commission

[ADDRESS]

re: [Name of complainant] v. [Name of respondent]

Dear Sir or Madam:

This firm represents the above-named charging party on whose behalf we enclose an executed Charge of Discrimination. Also enclosed is his/her affidavit in support of his/her charge.

We understand that pursuant to EEOC regulations and the worksharing agreement between EEOC and the New York State Division of Human Rights (the "Division"), your office will automatically file this EEOC charge with the Division. Please advise us within 30 days if that filing is not made with the Division.

Although we understand that the EEOC will file the charge with the Division, the charging party does not thereby elect an administrative remedy under Section 297(9) of the New York Executive Law; indeed, the charging party hereby elects to reserve the right to bring a judicial action under said Section 297(9). In addition, it is the charging party's preference that any investigation of this matter be handled by the EEOC, and not deferred to the Division.

Please assure that this office receives a copy of all future correspondence in this matter. If you have any questions regarding the enclosed or this letter, please feel free to call or write to me. Thank you for your cooperation.

Sincerely,

[Name of complainant's attorney]

§ 17.95 Forms—Letter Requesting Administrative Convenience Dismissal From State or City Administrative Agency

[Name of Manager]

New York State Division of Human Rights
[or *New York City Commission on Human Rights*
40 Rector Street New York, NY 10006]
55 West 125th Street, 12th Floor
New York New York 10027

Dear _____,

Please be advised that this firm has been retained by the persons listed below to file Age Discrimination in Employment Act [or *Title VII or ADA*] actions in federal court against defendant [*name*], with pendent state claims against these defendants brought under Sections 296 and 297(9) of the Executive Law.

Our clients have not filed complaints with the New York State Division of Human Rights ("the Division"), but their EEOC charges were deferred to the Division by EEOC. Our clients have elected their court remedies under New York law, and request dismissal of the charges deferred to the Division by EEOC on the grounds of administrative convenience.

The persons we represent, for whom we make this request, filed the EEOC charges listed below next to their names:

[*Name of charging party—EEOC charge number*]

We are grateful for your assistance in this matter.

Sincerely yours,

[*Attorney of charging party*]

§ 17.96   Forms—Pleadings—New York State Complaint

SUPREME COURT OF THE STATE OF NEW YORK
COUNTY OF NEW YORK

[*Name(s) of Plaintiff(s)*],	)
Plaintiff,	) Index No.
-against-	) Judge [*Name of judge*]
[*Name(s) of Defendant(s)*],	) COMPLAINT
Defendant.	)

[*Name of plaintiff*]("Plaintiff" or "[*surname*]"), by [*his/her*] attorneys, [*name of law firm*], as and for [*his/her*] complaint, alleges as follows:

PRELIMINARY STATEMENT

—. This is an action for [*state cause(s) of action, e.g., breach of contract, fraudulent misrepresentation, and violation of New York State*

Ch. 17 PLEADINGS—NEW YORK STATE COMPLAINT § 17.96

Labor Law] arising from [*state adverse job action, e.g., the termination*] of [*plaintiff*]'s employment as [*job title*] of [*defendant*]("defendant" or "[corporate name]"), on [*date*]. [*Insert a one or two sentence factual description of the case reflecting the key themes to be pursued.*]

THE PARTIES

—. [*Plaintiff*] served as the [*job title*] of [*defendant*] from [*dates*], when he/she was removed from his/her employment duties by [*defendant*]. [*Plaintiff*] resides at [*address*].

—. [*If plaintiff is suing under a statute, then allege appropriate status, e.g., at all relevant times herein, [plaintiff] was an "employee" of [defendant] within the meaning of the New York State Human Rights Law.*]

—. [*Defendant*] is a [*state of incorporation, type of corporation, e.g., New York non-profit*] corporation engaged in [*describe defendant's business*]. [*Defendant*] has, and at all relevant times had, its principal place of business at [*address*].

—. [*If plaintiff is suing under a statute, then allege appropriate status under it, e.g., At all relevant times herein, [defendant] was an "employer" within the meaning of the New York State Human Rights Law.*].

[*If business owners or supervisors are being sued in their individual capacities, allege as follows:*]

—. Defendant [*supervisor 1*] is, upon information and belief a fe/male citizen of the State of New York residing in [*county*]. At all times relevant herein, [*supervisor 1*] has been employed by [*defendant*], most recently as its [*position*].

—. As [*plaintiff*]'s supervisor during his/her employment at [*defendant*], [*supervisor 1*] had the power to make personnel decisions regarding [*plaintiff*]'s employment.*

—. Defendant [*supervisor 2 . . . etc.*]

JURISDICTION AND VENUE (optional)

[*State grounds for personal jurisdiction over each defendant and if, applicable, subject matter jurisdiction, e.g.:*]

—. This Court has personal jurisdiction over [*defendant*] because its principal place of business is in New York and it is doing business in this jurisdiction.

—. This Court has personal jurisdiction over defendants [*supervisor 1*] and [*supervisor 2*] because, upon information and belief, they are New York residents.

—. This Court has subject matter jurisdiction over this action by virtue of the New York Human Rights Law, N. Y. Executive Law §§ 290 *et seq.*

[*State grounds for venue, e.g.:*]

—. Venue is proper before this Court because [*defendant*]'s principal place of business, and the office at which [*plaintiff*] worked, is located in [*county*] and, upon information and belief, defendants [*supervisor 1*] and [*supervisor 2*] reside in [*county*.]

THE FACTS

—. [*If there are two or more causes of action, here state the facts that are common to them. A chronological recitation of those facts will usually work best. If there is only one cause of action, begin the allegation of facts with or without the heading immediately below.*]

[PROCEDURAL REQUIREMENTS]

[*At the end of the recitation of facts, state facts showing the satisfaction of procedural requirements. For example, if the state Human Rights Law claim is being brought in federal court, state that*]:

—. A charge of discrimination was filed on plaintiff's behalf with the New York State Division of Human Rights (the "SDHR"). Plaintiff's complaint of discrimination to the SDHR was ordered dismissed by the SDHR on the grounds of administrative convenience on [*date*], stating:

> Processing the complaint will not advance the State's Human Rights goals inasmuch as the matter is presently being litigated in federal court in which forum all the issues concerning the question of race discrimination can be resolved.

FIRST CAUSE OF ACTION

[*Here, state Name of Cause of Action, e.g., Breach of Contract*]

—. [*Plaintiff*] repeats and realleges each and every allegation contained in paragraphs 1 through—as if set forth herein.

—. [*Here allege any additional facts constituting the basis of the first cause of action, including the resulting injury.*]

SECOND CAUSE OF ACTION

[*Here, state Name of Cause of Action*]

—. [*Plaintiff*] repeats and realleges each and every allegation contained in paragraphs 1 through—as if fully set forth herein.

—. [*Here allege any additional facts constituting the basis of the second cause of action, including the resulting injury.*]

WHEREFORE, [*plaintiff*] demands judgment against [*defendant*], [*supervisor 1*], and [*supervisor 2*], as follows:

Ch. 17   PLEADINGS—NEW YORK STATE COMPLAINT § 17.96

1. Under the [*First, Second, etc.*] Cause(s) of Action, damages [*itemize compensatory damages components*] in an aggregate amount of not less than [*amount or to be determined at trial*].

2. Under the [*First, Second, etc.*] Cause(s) of Action, punitive damages to the full extent permitted by law, and in an amount [*not less than $_____ to be determined at trial*];

3. Under the [*First, Second, etc.*] Cause(s) of Action, [*describe any injunctive relief sought*] [1];

4. Interest on all the amounts due;

5. [*Plaintiff*]'s costs of this action, together with his/her reasonable attorneys' fees to the full extent permitted by law; and

6. Punitive damages to the full extent permitted by law, and in an amount [*not less than $(amount) to be determined at trial*]; and

7. Such other and further relief as this Court may deem just and proper.

Dated: [*County of plaintiff*], New York
    [*Date*]

> [*NAME OF PLAINTIFF'S ATTORNEY(S) LAW FIRM*]
> Attorneys for plaintiff
> [*Address*]
> [*Telephone number*]

[Optional]

OF COUNSEL:
[*Name of individual attorney(s) of the firm, if different than named above*]

[If the complaint is to be verified by the party:]

STATE OF NEW YORK)
) ss:
COUNTY OF _____   )

I, [*plaintiff*], being duly sworn, state:

I am the plaintiff in this action. The foregoing complaint is true to my own knowledge, except as to matters therein stated to be alleged upon

---

§ 17.96

1. **CAVEAT**: Under CPLR 4101, the inclusion of claims for equitable relief constitutes a waiver of the right to a jury trial. (*See supra*, § 17.82 "Demand for Relief.")

information and belief and, as to those matters, I believe them to be true.

(*Signature of plaintiff*)

Printed name of plaintiff

Sworn to before me
this day of [*month*] 19___

Notary Public

§ 17.97 Forms—Pleadings—New York State Court Answer

SUPREME COURT OF THE STATE OF NEW YORK
COUNTY OF NEW YORK

[*Name of Plaintiff*],

        Plaintiff,

    -against-

[*Name of Defendant*]

        Defendant.

Index No.

Judge [*Name of judge*]

ANSWER AND COUNTERCLAIMS

[*Name of defendant*] ("Defendant" or "[*corporate name*]"), by its attorneys, [*name of law firm*], for its answer to [*plaintiff*]'s ("plaintiff" or "[*name*]") complaint:

1. [*Admit the allegations, deny the allegations, or deny knowledge or information sufficient to form a belief as to the truth of the allegations of any preliminary statements or factual allegations common to multiple causes of action in the complaint.*]

ANSWERING FIRST CAUSE OF ACTION

—. [*For clarity's sake, answer the allegations of each cause of action under a separate heading.*]

FIRST AFFIRMATIVE DEFENSE

—. [*State each affirmative defense.*]

FIRST COUNTERCLAIM

—. [*Here allege facts constituting a cause of action in the manner of a complaint.*]

SECOND COUNTERCLAIM

—. [*Defendant*] repeats and realleges the allegations of paragraphs 1 through—.

—. [*Here allege facts constituting a cause of action in the manner of a complaint.*]

WHEREFORE, [*defendant*] demands judgment dismissing the complaint with prejudice, together with the costs and disbursements of this action, and granting judgment on the counterclaims as follows:

A. On the first counterclaim, [*state damages amount*];

B. On the second cause of action, [*state damages amount*];

C. [*Defendant*]'s attorneys' fees, costs and disbursements incurred in this action; and

D. Such other and further relief as is just and proper.

Dated: [*Name of city*], New York
[*Date*]

                        [*Attorney or law firm*]
                        [*Address*]
                        Attn.:[*Attorney's name*]
                        [*Telephone number*]

OF COUNSEL

[*Name of individual attorney[s] is different than firm named above.*]

§ 17.98 Forms—Pleadings—Federal Complaint

UNITED STATES DISTRICT COURT
_____ DISTRICT OF NEW YORK [1]

[*NAME OF PLAINTIFF*],

                    Plaintiff,

                    Civ. ____ (XXX)

            -against-

                    COMPLAINT AND JURY

[*NAME OF DEFENDANT*], individually   TRIAL DEMAND
and as [*Title of Position*], and [*Name of Defendant Organization*]

                  Defendants.

---

§ 17.98

1. Set forth either SOUTHERN, EASTERN, NORTHERN OR WESTERN DISTRICT.

§ 17.98 EMPLOYMENT LAW Ch. 17

Plaintiff [*NAME OF PLAINTIFF*]["Plaintiff" or "Short name"], as and for his/her complaint, by his/her undersigned counsel, alleges as follows:

INTRODUCTION

1. This is an action to remedy violations of the rights of [*plaintiff*] under [*state name(s) of statutes that are the basis of the claims, if applicable*]. [*Summarize the cause of action in one sentence*].

JURISDICTION and VENUE

—. The jurisdiction of the Court is invoked pursuant to [*cite the statutory provisions which give the court jurisdiction for each statute*]. [*If federal jurisdiction is also based on diversity or citizenship, state the diverse citizenship and that the damages, exclusive of interest and costs, are in excess of fifty thousand dollars.*] [*If state claims are included, state that "This Court's pendent jurisdiction is also invoked pursuant to (statutory reference)."*]

—. The unlawful employment practices alleged herein were committed in whole or in part in the _____ District of New York.

CLASS ACTION ALLEGATIONS (if any)

—. [*Here allege the scope of the class, their number, the claims that are typical of the class, that there are questions of law common to the members of the class, the failure of defendant to make appropriate relief with respect to the class.*]

PARTIES

—. Since [*date*], [*plaintiff*] has been employed by [*defendant*].

—. Plaintiff served as the [*job title*] of [*defendant*] from [*dates*], when he/she was removed from his/her employment duties by [*defendant*]. Plaintiff resides at [*address*].

—. [*If plaintiff is suing under a statute, then allege appropriate status, e.g., At all relevant times herein, [plaintiff] was an "employee" of [defendant] within the meaning of 42 U.S.C.A. §§ 2000e et seq.*]

—. [*Defendant*] is a [*state of incorporation, type of corporation, e.g., New York non-profit*] corporation. [*Here, describe defendant's business*]. [*Defendant*] has, and at all relevant times had, its principal place of business at [*address*].

[*If business owners or supervisors are being sued in their individual capacities, allege as follows:*[2]]

—. Defendant [*supervisor 1*], upon information and belief, resides at [address]. At all times relevant herein, [*supervisor 1*] has been employed by [*defendant*], most recently as its [*position*].

—. As [*plaintiff*]'s supervisor during most of his/her employment at [*defendant*], [*supervisor 1*] had the power to make personnel decisions regarding [*plaintiff*]'s employment.

—. Defendant [*supervisor 2*] . . . etc.

(*If there are any unnamed defendants, e.g., "John/Jane Doe," describe who or what they are to the extent possible*).

—. [*If plaintiff is suing under a statute, then allege appropriate status for defendant*], e.g., At all relevant times herein, [*defendant was an "employer" of* [plaintiff] *within the meaning of 42 U.S.C.A. §§ 2000e et seq.*]

FACTS

—. [*Here state the facts that form the basis of one or more cause(s) of action.*]

PROCEDURAL REQUIREMENTS

—. [*Plaintiff*] has satisfied all procedural requirements prior to commencing this action. (*Where there are required administrative proceedings [i.e, the issuance of an EEOC right to sue letter] or other administrative exhaustion required before commencing suit, state that they have been satisfied.*)

2. The Second Circuit has held that supervisors are not subject to personal liability for discrimination under Title VII because Title VII covers only employers of fifteen or more individuals while agents, in their individual capacities, do not do so. Tomka v. Seiler Corp., 66 F.3d 1295 (2d Cir.1995). This rationale would presumably preclude personal liability for managers under the Americans with Disabilities Act as well. Employees who seek to sue their supervisors individually may proceed under the New York State Human Rights Law, Executive Law § 296, which makes it "unlawful for any person to aid, abet, incite, compel or coerce the doing of any of the acts forbidden under this article." Such a claim could be raised in conjunction with a Title VII cause of action in either federal or state court, as long a the jurisdictional requirement as between the individual defendant and the plaintiff are otherwise met.

AS AND FOR A FIRST CAUSE OF ACTION

(Name of statute under which claim arises, [e.g., "Title VII § 704(a)]")

—. [Here reallege any previous factual allegations, by their paragraph.]

—. [Here allege the factual allegations that constitute the particular cause of action, or any additional facts not previously alleged that are particular to this cause of action.]

—. By engaging in the foregoing conduct, [*defendant*] has violated [*plaintiff*]'s rights under [*state relevant statutory provision*].

—. By acting as described, [*defendant*] acted with malice or with reckless disregard for [*plaintiff*]'s rights, causing [*plaintiff*] [*state injuries*] and entitling [*plaintiff*] to [*state remedies sought, e.g., damages in the amount of (amount)*].

[*Repeat in this manner, as necessary, for each additional cause of action*]

PRAYER FOR RELIEF

WHEREFORE, [*plaintiff*] prays that this Court enter judgment against the [*defendant*] as follows:

(a) under the First Cause of Action, ordering the individual defendants to [*state demand for monetary relief*];

(b) under each Cause of Action, granting any injunctive relief as may be appropriate;

(c) (if applicable) under the each Cause of Action, awarding plaintiff costs and, under the First Cause of Action, reasonable attorneys' fees; and

(d) directing such other and further relief as the Court may deem proper.

JURY DEMAND

Plaintiff demands a jury of six persons on all claims stated herein.

Dated: [*City and State*
       Month, day, year]

[*NAME OF LAW FIRM*]
Attorneys for Plaintiff

Ch. 17   FEDERAL ANSWER   § 17.99

By: _____
[Name of Attorney][ID #]
A Member of the Firm
[address]
[telephone]

Verification (if needed)

STATE OF NEW YORK   )
) ss:
COUNTY OF _____   )

[NAME OF PLAINTIFF], being duly sworn, deposes and says:

I am the plaintiff in this action. I have read the foregoing complaint and know the content thereof; the same is true to my knowledge, except as to matters therein stated to be alleged upon information and belief, and as to those matters I believe them to be true.

_____
[Name of Plaintiff]

[Jurat, if verified]
Sworn to before me this
day of _____, 199__.

_____
Notary Public

§ 17.99 Forms—Pleadings—Federal Answer

UNITED STATES DISTRICT COURT
_____ DISTRICT OF NEW YORK [1]

[NAME OF PLAINTIFF],)	
)	
Plaintiff,)	
)	
-against-)	Civ. ____ (XXX)
)	
[NAME OF DEFENDANT], individually)	ANSWER
and as [Title of Position], and [Name of)	
Defendant Organization])	
)	
Defendants.)	

§ 17.99
1. Set forth either SOUTHERN, EASTERN, NORTHERN or WESTERN DISTRICT.

[NAME OF CORPORATE DEFENDANT]("[Short name]"), and [NAME OF INDIVIDUAL DEFENDANT] ["Short name"], by their attorneys, [law firm name] as and for their Answer to Complaint allege as follows:

1. [Admit, deny, deny knowledge and information sufficient to form a belief as to the truth or falsity, or respectfully refer all questions of law to the Court, the allegations of each paragraph 1.]

FIRST AFFIRMATIVE DEFENSE

—. [Here state any affirmative defense, e.g., "The complaint fails to state a claim against defendant upon which relief can be granted."].

FIRST COUNTERCLAIM

[Here state any claim as if pleading a cause of action in a complaint.]

WHEREFORE, [Defendants] demand judgment dismissing the Complaint together with their costs and disbursements and such other relief as may be just.

Dated: [City and State
      Month, day, year]

                              NAME OF LAW FIRM
                              Attorneys for Defendants

                              By: _____
                                     [Name of Attorney][ID #]
                                     A Member of the Firm
                                     [address]
                                     [telephone]

Chapter 18

CIVIL RIGHTS LAW

by
Marilyn Trautfield Sugarman

Table of Sections

18.1 Scope Note.
18.2 Strategy.
18.3 ___ Checklist.
18.4 Overview of New York and Federal Civil Rights Provisions.
18.5 Jurisdiction over Civil Rights Actions.
18.6 New York Bill of Rights.
18.7 ___ Overview.
18.8 ___ Comparison With Federal Bill of Rights.
18.9 ___ Search and Seizure.
18.10 ___ ___ Civil Liability.
18.11 ___ ___ Return of Seized Property.
18.12 ___ Rights of Persons Accused of Crimes.
18.13 ___ ___ Public Trial/Closure of Courtroom.
18.14 ___ ___ Exclusion of Public or Press.
18.15 ___ Rights of Jurors.
18.16 General Federal Civil Rights Provisions.
18.17 ___ 42 U.S.C.A. § 1981.
18.18 ___ 42 U.S.C.A. § 1983.
18.19 ___ Other Federal Civil Rights Provisions.
18.20 Police and Prosecutorial Misconduct.
18.21 ___ Excessive Force.
18.22 ___ False Arrest.
18.23 ___ False Imprisonment.
18.24 ___ Search and Seizure.
18.25 ___ Malicious Prosecution.
18.26 First Amendment.
18.27 ___ Freedom of Speech.
18.28 ___ Freedom of Religion.
18.29 Rights of Prisoners.
18.30 Defenses to Federal Actions.
18.31 ___ Absolute Immunity.
18.32 ___ Qualified Immunity.
18.33 ___ Eleventh Amendment.
18.34 ___ *Monell* and Its Progeny.
18.35 ___ *Respondeat Superior*.
18.36 ___ Abstention.

18.37	___ *Res Judicata* and Collateral Estoppel.
18.38	___ Statute of Limitations.
18.39	Housing.
18.40	___ Prohibition Against Discrimination in Publicly Assisted Housing.
18.41	___ ___ Owners and Lessors.
18.42	___ ___ Real Estate Agents and Brokers.
18.43	___ ___ Remedies for Discrimination.
18.44	___ Prohibition Against Discrimination in Private Housing.
18.45	___ ___ Owners and Lessors.
18.46	___ ___ Real Estate Agents and Brokers.
18.47	___ ___ Cooperatives.
18.48	___ ___ Remedies for Discrimination.
18.49	___ ___ ___ Administrative Proceedings.
18.50	___ ___ ___ Actions in State and Federal Court.
18.51	___ *Prima Facie* Case and Burden of Proof.
18.52	___ Summary of Procedure for Filing an Administrative Claim and Challenging an SDHR Order.
18.53	Education.
18.54	Equal Rights in Places of Public Accommodation and Amusement.
18.55	___ General Provisions.
18.56	___ Private Clubs.
18.57	___ Persons With Disabilities Accompanied by a Guide Dog, Hearing Dog or Service Dog.
18.58	___ Remedies for Discrimination.
18.59	Employment Discrimination Provisions Exclusive to the New York Civil Rights Law.
18.60	___ In General.
18.61	___ Persons With Disabilities.
18.62	___ Persons With Genetic Disorders.
18.63	Right of Privacy.
18.64	___ Generally.
18.65	___ Police Officers, Corrections Officers and Firefighters.
18.66	___ Victims of Sex Offenses.
18.67	Changing One's Name.
18.68	___ Procedure for Petition to Change Name.
18.69	___ ___ Contents of Petition.
18.70	___ ___ Special Procedures for Infants.
18.71	___ Factors to Be Considered by the Court.
18.72	___ Publication Requirement.
18.73	___ Checklist.
18.74	Heart Balm Statute.
18.75	___ Penalty for Bringing Action.
18.76	___ Action for Return of Gifts Made in Contemplation of Marriage.
18.77	___ ___ Procedure.
18.78	Miscellaneous Rights and Immunities.
18.79	___ Frivolous Litigation.
18.80	___ ___ Protection from SLAPP Suits.
18.81	___ Libel and Slander.
18.82	___ ___ Defenses.
18.83	___ Breast Feeding.
18.84	___ Suspension of Rights Due to Imprisonment.

Ch. 18 **SCOPE NOTE** **§ 18.1**

18.85 ____ Shield Law.
18.86 ____ Performing Abortion.
18.87 ____ "Good Samaritan" Law Provisions.
18.88 Drafting Checklists.
18.89 ____ Framing the Federal Court § 1983 Complaint.
18.90 ____ Petition to Change One's Name.
18.91 Forms.
18.92 ____ Complaint for False Arrest, False Imprisonment and Malicious Prosecution.
18.93 ____ Complaint for Excessive Force.
18.94 ____ Complaint for Return of Seized Property.
18.95 ____ Complaint Against Landlord for Housing Discrimination.
18.96 ____ Complaint Against Cooperative for Discrimination.
18.97 ____ Notice of Commencement of Action for Discrimination.
18.98 ____ Complaint for Discrimination in Place of Public Accommodation.
18.99 ____ Petition to Change Name.

WESTLAW Electronic Research

See WESTLAW Electronic Research Guide preceding the Summary of Contents.

§ 18.1 Scope Note

This chapter deals primarily with civil rights practice in New York State courts. While New York State has a statute designated as the Civil Rights Law,[1] laws with respect to civil rights are also found in Article 15 of the Executive Law, which is referred to as the Human Rights Law, and in the New York State Constitution and Bill of Rights.

Section 11 of Article I of the New York State Constitution provides that "[n]o person shall be denied the equal protection of the laws of this state or any subdivision thereof. No person shall, because of race, color, creed or religion, be subjected to any discrimination in his civil rights by any other person or by any firm, corporation or institution, or by the state or any agency or subdivision of the state."[2] This clause, however, is not self executing, and prohibits discrimination only with respect to civil rights which are "elsewhere declared" by Constitution, statute or common law.[3]

While the great majority of civil rights cases are brought in the federal courts pursuant to various amendments to the United States Constitution and the reconstruction era civil rights statutes,[4] as this chapter demonstrates, causes of action should also be asserted under the

§ 18.1
1. Civil Rights Law.
2. N.Y. State Constitution, Art. I, § 11.
3. Dorsey v. Stuyvesant Town Corp., 299 N.Y. 512, 531, 87 N.E.2d 541, 548 (1949), cert. denied 339 U.S. 981, 70 S.Ct. 1019, 94 L.Ed. 1385 (1950).
4. 42 U.S.C.A. §§ 1981, *et seq.*

§ 18.1 CIVIL RIGHTS LAW Ch. 18

New York State Constitution and laws since there are occasions where the state may provide greater protections for its citizens than are provided in the Federal Constitution.

Throughout the chapter, references are made to analogous federal statutes and constitutional provisions and, where appropriate, federal provisions are discussed in greater detail. Local agencies, such as the New York City Commission on Human Rights, which also deal with civil rights issues, are also discussed.

The chapter begins with an overview of New York and federal civil rights provisions and a comparison of the New York Bill of Rights with the Federal Bill of Rights. *See* Sections 18.4 through 18.8. A few of the more important rights, such as the freedom from unreasonable searches and seizures and rights of persons accused of crimes, are discussed in more detail in sections 18.9 through 18.14. The rights of jurors are discussed in Section 18.15, particularly as their rights impact on attorneys during jury selection.

Federal civil rights provisions are discussed in general in Sections 18.16 through 18.19. Some of the common civil rights claims, such as claims of excessive force, false arrest, false imprisonment, search and seizure and malicious prosecution are discussed in greater detail in Sections 18.20 through 18.25.

This chapter does not purport to provide a comprehensive treatment of civil rights subjects which are almost exclusively within the domain of federal litigation, such as First Amendment issues of freedom of speech and religion. These subjects are discussed briefly in Sections 18.26 through 18.28, primarily in the context of state court litigation. Federal prisoner rights litigation is discussed in general in the sections dealing with the federal civil rights statutes (*see infra*, Sections 18.16—18.18) and also in Section 18.29, which discusses state court prisoner litigation. Defenses to Section 1983 claims and other federal causes of action are discussed in Sections 18.30 through 18.38.

The chapter then proceeds to discuss the subject matters encompassed in the Civil Rights Law and other state and federal statutes. Housing discrimination is discussed in Sections 18.39 through 18.52. Claims involving education, including both discrimination claims and challenges to school disciplinary proceedings, are examined in Section 18.53. The protection of civil rights in places of public accommodation and amusement, which is contained in both the Civil Rights Law and Human Rights Law, is discussed in Sections 18.54 through 18.58.

This chapter will not deal with employment discrimination, which is discussed in the chapter entitled "Employment Law,"[5] except to discuss

---

5. *See* Chapter 17, "Employment Law," *supra*.

those areas that are unique to the New York Civil Rights Law with respect to employment discrimination.[6]

The chapter concludes with subjects that are unique to the Civil Rights Law. The right of privacy, which is contained in Article 5 of the Civil Rights Law, is covered in Sections 18.63 through 18.66. The statutory procedure for changing one's name is detailed in Sections 18.67 through 18.73. Article 8 of the Civil Rights Law, referred to as the heart balm statute, which eliminated the causes of action for alienation of affection and breach of contract to marry, is discussed in Sections 18.74 through 18.77. The text of the chapter concludes with a review of Article 7 of the Civil Rights Law, which is entitled "Miscellaneous Rights and Immunities," and includes, *inter alia*, the prohibition against frivolous litigation, the Shield Law, protection from libel and slander actions, and protection for good samaritans.[7]

At the end of the chapter are form complaints for some of the more common civil rights actions, such as claims of police misconduct arising out of false arrest, false imprisonment and excessive force. Also included are two form complaints which set forth common causes of action for housing discrimination claims—a complaint appropriate for discrimination in rental property is set forth in Section 18.95 while a complaint against a cooperative is set forth in Section 18.96. A form complaint for discrimination in a place of public accommodation is set forth in Section 18.98. The forms conclude with a form that is unique to the Civil Rights Law, that of the form for a petition to change one's name, which is set forth in Section 18.99. A drafting checklist for the name-changing petition is set forth in Section 18.90 and a drafting checklist for a Section 1983 complaint is set forth in Section 18.89.

§ 18.2 Strategy

The most important initial strategical considerations are where to file a civil rights claim. First, counsel must decide whether to file an administrative claim or proceed directly to court. If the decision is to bypass the administrative remedies, the next decision is whether the claim should be filed in state or federal court.

Regardless of whether a civil rights action is filed in state or federal court, causes of action should be asserted under the New York State Constitution,[1] Civil Rights Law[2] and Human Rights Law,[3] if appropriate,

---

6. *See infra*, §§ 18.59–18.62.
7. *See* §§ 18.78—18.87.

§ 18.2
1. *See, e.g.*, §§ 18.9, 18.12, 18.26—18.28. *See also*, form complaints set forth *infra* §§ 18.92, 18.94.
2. *See, e.g., infra*, §§ 18.9, 18.12, 18.40—18.43, 18.47, 18.50, 18.54, 18.55, 18.57—18.66. *See also*, form complaints set forth *infra* §§ 18.92, 18.94, 18.96, 18.98.
3. *See, e.g., infra*, §§ 18.40, 18.41, 18.45—18.47, 18.49, 18.50, 18.52—18.54, 18.57, 18.58, 18.62. *See also* form complaints set forth *infra* §§ 18.95, 18.96, 18.98.

§ 18.2

since there are occasions where the state may provide greater protections for its citizens than are provided in the Federal Constitution.

In choosing between state and federal court, the following factors, *inter alia*, should be considered: the composition of the court and the likelihood of being assigned a judge sympathetic toward your client's claim; the differences between the Civil Practice Law and Rules and the Federal Rules of Civil Procedure and local rules of the district court with respect to motion practice and discovery; and the composition of the jury pool.[4]

It is also important to determine whether there are any differences in the development of the law in the subject matter being litigated. While New York's federal district courts must follow the precedents handed down by the United States Court of Appeals for the Second Circuit, state courts in New York are not required to follow decisions of the Second Circuit nor accord these decisions any deference.[5] Accordingly, an unfavorable decision of the Second Circuit could be avoided by commencing the action in state court.

Another important strategical consideration in deciding which claims to raise is the availability of attorney's fees. A party who prevails in an action asserting claims under the federal civil rights statutes[6] is entitled to an award of attorney's fees pursuant to 42 U.S.C.A. § 1988. There are also other federal statutes which specifically provide for prevailing party fees.[7]

The Statute of Limitations is another factor to be considered in determining which claims to include in the complaint. The limitations period for civil rights claims generally ranges from one to three years, depending upon the nature of the claim. These differences may be significant, particularly in, for example, a housing discrimination claim, where the Statute of Limitations under the Human Rights Law is one year; the Statute of Limitations under the Federal Fair Housing Act, 42 U.S.C.A. § 3613(a)(1)(A), is two years; and the Statute of Limitations under 42 U.S.C.A. § 1981 is three years.

The defendant may be precluded from asserting a particular defense depending upon the forum selected. For example, the Eleventh Amend-

---

4. As Justice Brennan stated in Felder v. Casey, 487 U.S. 131, 150, 108 S.Ct. 2302, 2313, 101 L.Ed.2d 123 (1988), "[l]itigants who choose to bring their civil rights action in state courts presumably do so in order to obtain the benefit of certain procedural advantages in those courts, or to draw their juries from urban populations. Having availed themselves of these benefits, civil rights litigants must comply as well with those state rules they find less to their liking."

Cf., Svaigsen v. City of New York, 203 A.D.2d 32, 609 N.Y.S.2d 894 (1st Dep't 1994), the court held that a state court should follow the federal law with respect to discovery in Section 1983 claims.

5. S. Steinglass, *Section 1983 Litigation in State Courts*, § 5.4 (1989).

6. 42 U.S.C.A. §§ 1981, *et seq.*

7. *See infra*, §§ 18.19, 18.43, 18.48. For example, the Federal Fair Housing Act specifically provides for attorney's fees to the prevailing party. *See* 42 U.S.C.A. § 3613(c)(2).

ment only applies to actions brought in federal court. Similarly, since questions of privilege in a federal court action are governed by federal law, the protections of Civil Rights Law § 50-a are inapplicable to discovery in a federal civil rights action alleging police misconduct.[8]

It is probably preferable to bring claims of employment discrimination in federal court, particularly since the federal courts are more familiar with some of the newer statutes, such as the Americans With Disabilities Act of 1990, 42 U.S.C.A. §§ 12101 *et seq.* Moreover, some of the provisions concerning employment discrimination that are contained in the Civil Rights Law, such as the prohibition of discrimination against individuals with genetic disorders, do not provide for a private right of action for the recovery of damages.

§ 18.3 Strategy—Checklist

Set forth below are some of the factors that should be considered by counsel in deciding where to file a civil rights claim.

1. Should an administrative claim be filed, or should plaintiff proceed directly to court? (*See* §§ 18.48, 18.49.) Has the time period within which to file an administrative claim lapsed? (*See, e.g.*, § 18.49.) Are fees an issue?

2. If the decision is to bypass the administrative forum, should the action be filed in state or federal court? What are the respective compositions of the trial courts? What is the likelihood of being assigned a judge sympathetic toward your client's claim? What is the composition of the appellate court?

3. Are the procedures set forth in the Civil Practice Law and Rules or the Federal Rules of Civil Procedure with respect to motion practice and discovery more favorable to the action? (*See* §§ 18.55, 18.85.)

4. Would the jury pool in the state or federal court tend to be more sympathetic to plaintiff's claim?

5. Are there any state or federal court precedents that are more favorable toward plaintiff's claim? (*See, e.g.*, §§ 18.8, 18.9.) Are there any precedents plaintiff would seek to avoid? Which court would be more familiar with the type of claim being asserted?

6. Are there any other advantages plaintiff would have over the defendant if the action were commenced in a particular court? Are any defenses unavailable in a particular forum?

7. Is there a cause of action under the New York State Constitution? (*See, e.g.*, §§ 18.9, 18.12, 18.26—18.28. *See also*, form complaints set forth in §§ 18.92, 18.94.) Is there a cause of action under the Civil Rights Law? (*See, e.g.*, §§ 18.9, 18.12, 18.40—18.43, 18.47, 18.50, 18.54, 18.55, 18.57—18.66. *See also*, form complaints set forth in

---

8. King v. Conde, 121 F.R.D. 180 (E.D.N.Y.1988).

§§ 18.92, 18.94, 18.96, 18.98.) Is there a cause of action under the Human Rights Law? (*See, e.g.,* §§ 18.40, 18.41, 18.45—18.47, 18.49, 18.50, 18.52—18.54, 18.57, 18.58, 18.62. *See also,* form complaints set forth in §§ 18.95, 18.96, 18.98.) Is there a cause of action under the Federal Constitution or the federal civil rights statutes? (*See* §§ 18.10, 18.17—18.19.) Are there any other specific state or federal statutes that are applicable to the type of claim being asserted? (*See* §§ 18.40—18.48, 18.53, 18.58.)

8. What are the Statutes of Limitations for each of the possible causes of action? (*See, e.g.,* §§ 18.38, 18.50.) Are there any statutory prerequisites to bringing a particular action, such as a Notice of Claim or Notice of Commencement of Action? (*See* §§ 18.43, 18.55, 18.58, 18.60.)

9. Are any special damages available? (*See, e.g.,* §§ 18.49, 18.79.) Are attorneys' fees available? (*See, e.g.,* §§ 18.25, 18.66, 18.80.)

§ 18.4 Overview of New York and Federal Civil Rights Provisions

New York civil rights provisions are set forth in the New York Constitution's Bill of Rights and primarily in the Civil Rights Law and the Human Rights Law.[1] Federal civil rights provisions are primarily found in Title 42 of the United States Code.[2] Other federal statutes are discussed in Section 18.19, *infra.*

Library References:
West's Key No. Digests, Civil Rights ⚖101–135.

§ 18.5 Jurisdiction over Civil Rights Actions

Both the New York State courts and the federal courts have concurrent jurisdiction over civil rights actions.[1] Actions under Section 1983 may be brought in either state or federal court. Most statutory causes of action may be brought in either state or federal court; any exceptions are set forth in the text of the statute.[2] In *Brown v. State of New York*,[3] the Court of Appeals held for the first time that the state may be sued for monetary damages for violations of certain state constitutional rights in the Court of Claims. While no state statute authorizes a civil remedy for

---

§ 18.4

1. *See* Article 15 of the Executive Law.
2. *See* 42 U.S.C.A. §§ 1981, et seq., 42 U.S.C.A. §§ 2000, et seq.

§ 18.5

1. Felder v. Casey, 487 U.S. 131, 108 S.Ct. 2302, 101 L.Ed.2d 123 (1988); Svaigsen v. City of New York, 203 A.D.2d 32, 609 N.Y.S.2d 894 (1st Dep't 1994).

2. For example, Title VII of the Civil Rights Act, as amended, § 2000e–5(f), provides that an action for employment discrimination brought pursuant to the statute may only be commenced in the appropriate federal district court, and cannot be brought in state court.

3. 89 N.Y.2d 172, 652 N.Y.S.2d 223, 674 N.E.2d 1129 (1996).

so-called "constitutional torts," the court found that the statutory jurisdiction of the Court of Claims is broad enough to include an implied right of recovery to hear "damage claims against the state based on violations of the State Constitution," regardless of whether they are linked to a common law tort.[4] The court in *Brown* held that a direct action for violations of the New York State Constitution's Bill of Rights may now be brought in the Court of Claims so long as the provisions are self-executing. Specifically, a cause of action may now be brought against the state in the Court of Claims under Article I, Section 11 of the New York State Constitution relating to equal protection, and Article I, section 12 which prohibits unreasonable searches and seizures.

§ 18.6 New York Bill of Rights

Article I of the New York Constitution is entitled the "Bill of Rights." Similarly, Civil Rights Law §§ 2–15, are also referred to as the Bill of Rights. In some areas, the Bill of Rights provides even greater protection in areas that were not contemplated by the framers of the Federal Constitution. For example, in *O'Neill v. Oakgrove Constr., Inc.*,[1] the Court of Appeals noted that "[t]he protection afforded by the guarantees of free press and speech in the New York Constitution is often broader than the minimum required by the First Amendment."

The provisions of the New York Bill of Rights are discussed in the next section. Immediately following Section 18.7 is a comparison of the New York Bill of Rights with the Federal Bill of Rights.

§ 18.7 New York Bill of Rights—Overview

Article I, Section 1 of the New York Constitution provides in part that "[n]o member of this state shall be disenfranchised, or deprived of any of the rights or privileges secured to any citizen thereof, unless by the law of the land, or the judgment of his peers, ..." Section 2 reaffirms the right to a jury trial, but provides that a jury trial may be waived by the parties in all civil cases in the manner to be prescribed by law, and may be waived by a defendant in a criminal case, except a case in which the crime charged may be punishable by death. Section 3 sets forth the right of freedom of religion. *See infra*, Section 18.28.

Sections 4 through 6 concern criminal defendants. Section 4 provides that the privilege of a writ of *habeas corpus* shall not be suspended unless the public safety requires it in case of rebellion or invasion. Excessive bail is prohibited in Article I, § 5, which further provides that cruel and unusual punishments shall not be inflicted, nor shall witnesses be unreasonably detained. Section 6 concerns grand jury indictments. The section continues by providing that the party accused shall be

---

4. Brown v. State, 89 N.Y.2d 172, 183, 652 N.Y.S.2d 223, 230, 674 N.E.2d 1129 (1996).

§ 18.6
1. 71 N.Y.2d 521, 528 note 3, 528 N.Y.S.2d 1, 4 note 3, 523 N.E.2d 277 (1988).

§ 18.7   CIVIL RIGHTS LAW   Ch. 18

allowed to appear and defend in person and with counsel as in civil actions and shall be informed of the nature and cause of the accusation and be confronted with the witnesses against him. Section 6 also protects against double jeopardy and self-incrimination.[1] The section concludes with the language "[n]o person shall be deprived of life, liberty or property without due process of law."

Article I, § 7 provides that private property shall not be taken for public use without just compensation. Section 8 contains the protections of freedom of speech and of the press. The section provides that "[e]very citizen may freely speak, write and publish his sentiments on all subjects, ... and no law shall be passed to restrain or abridge the liberty of speech or of the press." Section 9 provides for the right peaceably to assemble and to petition the government.

Section 11 protects against discrimination, by providing that "[n]o person shall be denied the equal protection of the laws of this state or any subdivision thereof." This section further states that "[n]o person shall, because of race, color, creed or religion, be subjected to any discrimination in his civil rights by any other person or by any firm, corporation, or institution, or by the state or any agency or subdivision of the state." Section 12 protects against unreasonable searches and seizures. *See infra*, Section 18.9.

Section 16 provides that "the right of action now existing to recover damages for injuries resulting in death, shall never be abrogated; and the amount recoverable shall not be subject to any statutory limitation."

Sections 17 and 18 concern labor. Section 17 affirms that labor "is not a commodity nor an article of commerce and shall never be so considered or construed." The section then continues by providing rules for limiting the hours of a laborer employed in the performance of any public work, and the wages the worker may be paid. The section concludes by reaffirming that employees have the right to organize and to bargain collectively. Finally, Article I, § 18 refers to workers' compensation.

§ 18.8   New York Bill of Rights—Comparison With Federal Bill of Rights

To a large extent, the provisions contained in the New York Bill of Rights provide the same guaranties as do the provisions in the Federal Constitution or Federal Bill of Rights. Both the State and Federal Bill of Rights provide that no one shall be disenfranchised, or deprived of any of the rights or privileges secured to any citizen, unless by the law of the

---

§ 18.7

1. There is an exception for public officials.

land, or the judgment of his peers.[1] Both provide for trial by jury.[2] Both provide protection for the free exercise and enjoyment of religious profession and worship.[3] The prohibition against suspending the privilege of a writ of *habeas corpus* is set forth in Article I, § 4 of the New York Constitution and the second clause of Article I, § 9 of the Federal Constitution. Prohibitions against excessive bail and fines and the ban on cruel and unusual punishments are set forth in Article I, § 5.[4]

Section 6 of Article I of the New York Constitution concerns grand jury indictment prior to a criminal prosecution and further provides that the defendant shall be informed of the nature and cause of the accusation and be confronted with the witnesses against him. The same section contains the prohibition against double jeopardy and self-incrimination.[5] Section 6 concludes with the language that "[n]o person shall be deprived of life, liberty or property without due process of law." These protections are nearly identical to those contained in the Fifth Amendment and Sixth Amendment.[6] The protection against taking private property for public use without just compensation is set forth in Article I, § 6, and is similar to the United States Constitution's Fifth Amendment.

One area in which the New York State provides greater protections than the Federal Constitution is with respect to freedom of speech and of the press. Article I, § 8 provides that "[e]very citizen may freely speak,

§ 18.8

1. Compare N.Y. State Constitution, Art. I, § 1 with U.S. Constitution, amend. V and XIV and U.S. Constitution, Art. 4, § 2 cl. 1.

2. Compare N.Y. State Constitution, Art. I, § 2 with U.S. Constitution Art. 3, § 2, cl. 3 and U.S. Constitution, amend. VI and VII. The New York Constitution further sets forth that "the legislature may provide, however, by law, that a verdict may be rendered by not less than five-sixths of the jury in any civil case. A jury trial may be waived by the defendant in all criminal cases, except those in which the crime charged may be punishable by death, by a written instrument signed by the defendant in person in open court before and with the approval of a judge or justice of a court having jurisdiction to try the offense. The legislature may enact laws, not inconsistent herewith, governing the form, content, manner and time of presentation of the instrument effectuating such waiver."

3. Compare N.Y. State Constitution, Art. I, § 3 with U.S. Constitution, amend. I. The First Amendment provides that "Congress shall make no law respecting an establishment of religion, or prohibiting the free exercise thereof." The New York constitutional provision is more explicit: "The free exercise and enjoyment of religious profession and worship, without discrimination or preference, shall forever be allowed in this state to all mankind; and no person shall be rendered incompetent to be a witness on account of his opinions on matters of religious belief; but the liberty of conscience hereby secured shall not be so construed as to excuse acts of licentiousness, or justify practices inconsistent with the peace or safety of this state."

4. This provision is repeated in Civil Rights Law § 11, and both are similar to the provision contained in the Eighth Amendment to the United States Constitution.

5. There is an exception to the self-incrimination provision with respect to defendants who are public officials.

6. *See* U.S. Constitution, amend. V (double jeopardy; self-incrimination; grand jury indictment; due process); U.S. Constitution, amend. VI (confrontation clause; nature and cause of accusation); U.S. Constitution, amend. XIV (due process). Similarly, Civil Rights Law § 12 contains provisions with respect to confrontation of witnesses and the nature of the accusation.

write and publish his sentiments on all subjects, being responsible for the abuse of that right; and no law shall be passed to restrain or abridge the liberty of speech or of the press." This provision provides greater protections than the First Amendment.[7] Article I, § 9 provides that "[n]o law shall be passed abridging the rights of the people peaceably to assemble and to petition the government, or any department thereof... ," which is similar to the protections in the First Amendment.

The New York Constitution's equivalent to the Federal Equal Protection Clause of the Fourteenth Amendment specifically sets forth that "[n]o person shall, because of race, color, creed or religion, be subjected to any discrimination in his civil rights by any other person or by any firm, corporation, or institution, or by the state or any agency or subdivision of the state."[8]

"The right of the people to be secure in their persons, houses, papers and effects, against unreasonable searches and seizures" is protected in Article I, § 12. The first paragraph of Section 12 is identical to the Fourth Amendment to the United States Constitution. *See infra*, Section 18.9. The second paragraph of Section 12 provides an additional protection against unreasonable interception of telephone and telegraph communications.

Other sections of the New York Constitution have no federal constitutional counterpart, and provide protections which were not protected under federal law until they were enacted as statutes much later. For example, Article I, § 17 provides protection to laborers and provides for the right to organize and to bargain collectively[9] and Article I, § 18 refers to workers' compensation. Additionally, Article I, § 16 provides that "the right of action now existing to recover damages for injuries resulting in death, shall never be abrogated; and the amount recoverable shall not be subject to any statutory limitation."

---

7. *See* Goetz v. Kunstler, 164 Misc.2d 557, 625 N.Y.S.2d 447, 451 (Sup.Ct., N.Y. County, 1995) (recognizing that the framers of the New York State Constitution made a "deliberate choice" not to follow the language of the First Amendment, but instead, elected "to set forth our basic democratic ideal of liberty of the press in strong affirmative terms.")(citation omitted); *see also*, O'Neill v. Oakgrove Constr., Inc., 71 N.Y.2d 521, 528 note 3, 528 N.Y.S.2d 1, 4 note 3, 523 N.E.2d 277 (1988), in which the Court of Appeals noted that "[t]he protection afforded by the guarantees of free press and speech in the New York Constitution is often broader than the minimum required by the First Amendment."

8. Compare N.Y. State Constitution, Art. I, § 11 with U.S. Constitution, amend. XIV.

9. The text of the section provides in part that

[l]abor of human beings is not a commodity nor an article of commerce and shall never be so considered or construed.

No laborer, workman or mechanic, in the employ of a contractor or subcontractor engaged in the performance of any public work, shall be permitted to work more than eight hours in any day or more than five days in any week, except in cases of extraordinary emergency; nor shall he be paid less than the rate of wages prevailing ...

Employees shall have the right to organize and to bargain collectively through representatives of their own choosing.

§ 18.9 New York Bill of Rights—Search and Seizure

Section 8 of the New York Civil Rights Law provides that "[t]he right of the people to be secure in their persons, houses, papers and effects, against unreasonable searches and seizures, shall not be violated; and no warrants can issue but upon probable cause supported by oath or affirmation, and particularly describing the place to be searched, and the persons or things to be seized." This provision was enacted in 1909, prior to the enactment of an essentially identical provision as part of the New York Bill of Rights in 1938.[1]

A claim for monetary damages for an unlawful search and seizure may be brought against the appropriate officials in either state or federal court, pursuant to the Civil Rights Law § 8 and Art. I, § 12 of the New York Constitution and 42 U.S.C.A. § 1983 and the Fourth and Fourteenth Amendments to the United States Constitution.[2] Both the state and federal causes of action should be pleaded since, as the United States Supreme Court has noted, it is possible that state constitutional provisions may afford more protections against searches and seizures than the does the Federal Constitution.[3] An action solely to recover property

---

§ 18.9

1. In fact, aside from differences in punctuation, Civil Rights Law § 8 is essentially identical to both the first paragraph of N.Y. State Constitution Art. I, § 12 and the Fourth Amendment to the United States Constitution. The only difference in language is that Section 8 states that "no warrants *can* issue" while the other provisions state that "no warrants *shall* issue."

The second paragraph of Art. I, § 12 of the New York Constitution provides an additional protection against unreasonable interception of telephone and telegraph communications.

2. **PRACTICE POINTER**: With respect to the federal causes of action, care must be given to plead more than mere negligence to allege a viable claim under Section 1983. *See infra*, § 18.18. Additionally, the defense of qualified immunity may be available to the defendants with respect to the federal claims, whereas such a defense is unavailable as to the state claims. *See infra*, § 18.32. A factual inquiry may be necessary to determine whether the qualified immunity defense is available, which may involve additional discovery or even a trial. Stipo v. Town of North Castle, 205 A.D.2d 608, 613 N.Y.S.2d 407 (2d Dep't 1994).

In addition to alleging a claim of unlawful search and seizure, consideration should be given to alleging causes of action for false arrest and false imprisonment as part of the same incident, if appropriate under the circumstances. *See infra*, §§ 18.22, 18.23.

CAVEAT: If municipal defendants are named in the action, it may be necessary to serve a Notice of Claim against the city. *See* General Municipal Law § 50–e(1)(a). The Notice of Claim requirement does not apply, however, to a claim under Section 1983. Felder v. Casey, 487 U.S. 131, 108 S.Ct. 2302, 101 L.Ed.2d 123 (1988); Zurat v. Town of Stockport, 142 A.D.2d 1, 534 N.Y.S.2d 777 (3d Dep't 1988). Moreover, since the statute of limitation set forth in General Municipal Law § 50–i(1)(c) is one year and ninety days and the Statute of Limitation set forth in CPLR 215 is one year, an action alleging a state law claim should be commenced within one year of the act alleged.

If the claim is against the state police, the action should be brought against the State of New York in the Court of Claims.

3. *See* California v. Greenwood, 486 U.S. 35, 43, 108 S.Ct. 1625, 1630, 100 L.Ed.2d 30 (1988) (holding that the Fourth Amendment does not prohibit the warrantless search of garbage left for collection by the curb, but leaving open the possibility that individual states, through their own constitutions, "might impose more stringent constraints on police conduct than does the Federal Constitution."); New Jersey v. T.L.O., 469 U.S. 325, 343 note 10, 105 S.Ct. 733, 744 note 10, 83 L.Ed.2d 720 (1985).

§ 18.9   CIVIL RIGHTS LAW

seized by the police should be brought in state court. *See infra*, Section 18.11.

Library References:

West's Key No. Digests, Searches and Seizures ⚖︎11–129.

§ 18.10   New York Bill of Rights—Search and Seizure—Civil Liability

The Fourth Amendment standard governs civil actions challenging illegal searches and seizures.[1] Although the conduct of private individuals is not subject to Fourth Amendment scrutiny,[2] in addition to law enforcement officials, the Fourth Amendment has been applied to school officials[3] and public employers.[4]

The threshold question in a search and seizure case is whether the plaintiff has an expectation of privacy in the area and items to be searched. "An expectation of privacy does not give rise to Fourth Amendment protection, however, unless society is prepared to accept that expectation as objectively reasonable."[5] Thus, for example, courts have allowed warrantless searches of public employees' work spaces and belongings by their employers on the grounds that public employees have a more diminished expectation of privacy due to the special needs of public employment.[6]

The second inquiry is the appropriate standard of reasonableness applicable to the search. This entails " 'balancing the nature and quality of the intrusion on the individual's Fourth Amendment interests against the importance of the governmental interests alleged to justify the intrusion.' "[7] Put another way, the determination of the reasonableness of a search involves (1) whether the search was justified at its inception and (2) whether the search as conducted "was reasonably related in scope to the circumstances which justified the interference in the first place."[8] For example, in *New Jersey v. T.L.O.*,[9] which involved the warrantless search by a school principal of a female student's pocketbook, the court said the search would be "justified at its inception" if there were "reasonable grounds for suspecting that the search will turn up evidence that the student has violated or is violating either the law or

---

§ 18.10

1. O'Connor v. Ortega, 480 U.S. 709, 714, 107 S.Ct. 1492, 1496, 94 L.Ed.2d 714 (1987).

2. People v. Mendoza, 211 A.D.2d 493, 621 N.Y.S.2d 553 (1st Dep't 1995).

3. New Jersey, § 18.9, *supra* note 3.

4. O'Connor, *supra* note 1.

5. California, § 18.9, *supra* note 3, 486 U.S. at 39–40, 108 S.Ct. at 1628.

6. O'Connor, *supra* note 1; Moore v. Constantine, 191 A.D.2d 769, 594 N.Y.S.2d 395 (3d Dep't 1993).

7. O'Connor, *supra*, note 1, 480 U.S. at 719, 107 S.Ct. at 1498 (citations omitted).

8. New Jersey, *supra*, § 18.9, note 3, 469 U.S. at 341, 105 S.Ct. at 742 (quoting Terry v. Ohio, 392 U.S. 1, 20, 88 S.Ct. 1868, 1879, 20 L.Ed.2d 889 (1968)).

9. 469 U.S. 325, 105 S.Ct. 733, 83 L.Ed.2d 720 (1985).

the rules of the school."[10] The scope of such a search is permissible if the extent of the search is reasonably related to its objectives and the search is not excessively intrusive in view of the age and sex of the student and the nature of the infraction.[11]

An additional inquiry is whether the individual has consented to the search. Implied or expressed consent to a search may vitiate an otherwise valid claim for unlawful search and seizure. Validity of consent depends on a totality of the circumstances.[12]

Searches where there is no individualized suspicion have also been allowed under certain circumstances. For example, claims brought by attorneys and other visitors challenging electronic searches of all persons entering courthouses have been denied on the grounds that such searches are reasonable under the Fourth Amendment and Article I, § 12 of the New York Constitution.[13]

Library References:

West's Key No. Digests, Searches and Seizures ⚖85.

§ 18.11 New York Bill of Rights—Search and Seizure—Return of Seized Property

If a client has had property seized by the New York City Police during a search or at the time of an arrest, there is a special procedure to be followed to seek the return of the property. Pursuant to the terms of a federal civil rights class action,[1] the City must provide written notice of the demand procedure to those from whom property is seized. If the property was seized in connection with criminal charges, and the criminal charges are ultimately dismissed, a demand for return of the seized property should be made to the police property clerk within ninety days of the dismissal of the charges.[2] The City must return the property if a

---

10. New Jersey, *supra*, § 18.9, note 3, 469 U.S. at 342, 105 S.Ct. at 743 (footnote omitted).

11. *Id.* (footnote omitted).

12. Ruggiero v. Krzeminski, 928 F.2d 558 (2d Cir.1991).

13. Bozer v. Higgins, 204 A.D.2d 979, 613 N.Y.S.2d 312 (4th Dep't 1994); Legal Aid Society of Orange Co. v. Crosson, 784 F.Supp. 1127 (S.D.N.Y.1992).

§ 18.11

1. *See* McClendon v. Rosetti, 369 F.Supp. 1391 (S.D.N.Y.1974), discussed in Moreno v. City of New York, 69 N.Y.2d 432, 515 N.Y.S.2d 733, 508 N.E.2d 645 (1987) and Butler v. Castro, 896 F.2d 698, 701–02 note 1 (2d Cir.1990).

CAVEAT: As the Second Circuit noted in Butler, *supra*, the actual procedures followed by the City of New York are not set forth in the Administrative Code. Indeed, to this day, the Administrative Code has not been amended to reflect the procedures in effect.

2. *See supra*, McClendon, note 1; *see also*, Administrative Code of the City of New York § 14–140.

Section 14–140(e) of the Administrative Code provides that money seized by the police that remains in the custody of the property clerk for more than ninety days without a lawful claim being made shall be paid into the Police Pension fund. Property other than abandoned vehicles is sold at public auction and the proceeds are paid into the same fund. Alternatively, property may be used or converted to use for any governmental agency or for charitable purpose. Accordingly, every effort should be

§ 18.11 CIVIL RIGHTS LAW Ch. 18

demand is made within ninety days of the disposition of criminal charges, or a release is issued by the District Attorney, whichever is sooner. If the City does not believe the claimant is a "lawful claimant," the City must commence an action to retain the property within ten days of the demand.[3] If the claimant makes a proper demand, the property should be returned immediately without resorting to litigation.

If the property clerk nevertheless refuses to honor the demand, or an untimely demand is made, an Article 78 proceeding may be commenced to challenge the decision to refuse the demand.[4] Alternatively, a common law action for replevin may be commenced for the return of seized property.[5] According to the Administrative Code, in an action or proceeding against the property clerk, a claimant must establish that he or she has a lawful title or property right in the money or property, lawfully obtained possession of the money or property, and held and used the property in a lawful manner.[6]

Library References:

West's Key No. Digests, Searches and Seizures ⚖84.

§ 18.12 New York Bill of Rights—Rights of Persons Accused of Crimes

Both the Federal and State Constitutions provide protections for persons accused of crimes. Section 12 of the Civil Rights Law parallels the Sixth Amendment to the United States Constitution and Art. I, § 6 of the New York State Constitution by providing that a criminal defendant has a right to a speedy and public trial, an impartial jury, to be informed of the nature and cause of the accusation, to be confronted with the witnesses against him, and to subpoena witnesses in his favor.

---

made to make the demand within ninety days, since after ninety days, the property may no longer be recoverable.

3. See supra, McClendon, note 1; see also, Administrative Code of the City of New York § 14–140.

4. DeBellis v. New York City Prop. Clerk, 79 N.Y.2d 49, 580 N.Y.S.2d 157, 588 N.E.2d 55 (1992); Boyle v. Kelley, 42 N.Y.2d 88, 91, 396 N.Y.S.2d 834, 836, 365 N.E.2d 866 (1977).

5. Moreno v. City of New York, 69 N.Y.2d 432, 515 N.Y.S.2d 733, 508 N.E.2d 645 (1987).

CAVEAT: General Municipal Law § 50–e(1)(a) requires that in any action founded upon a tort against a municipal corporation, a Notice of Claim must be filed within ninety days after the claim arises. Some courts have held that notice must be given before bringing an action for the return of property. Beck v. City of New York, 133 Misc.2d 265, 507 N.Y.S.2d 129 (Sup.Ct., Richmond County, 1986). Although leave to file a late Notice of Claim may be granted by the court (see General Municipal Law § 50–e(5)), it is a better practice to timely serve the Notice of Claim. Additionally, General Municipal Law § 50–i(1)(c) provides that any action against a city, county, town, village, fire district or school district must be commenced "within one year and ninety days after the happening of the event upon which the claim is based." See also, CPLR 215(1) (action against a sheriff must be commenced within one year). The Notice of Claims provisions of the General Municipal Law are discussed in "Municipal Law," Chapter 3, supra.

6. Administrative Code of the City of New York § 14–140(f); but see supra, Butler, note 1.

Criminal defendants have the right to be present at all phases of their trial, including pre-trial hearings[1] and *voir dire*.[2] A defendant's rights are not denied, however, if the defendant is not present during the conference in which challenges are exercised.[3]

§ 18.13 New York Bill of Rights—Rights of Persons Accused of Crimes—Public Trial/Closure of Courtroom

Criminal trials are presumptively open to the public and the press. Temporary closure of the courtroom does not necessarily violate a defendant's rights. A courtroom may be ordered closed to allow an undercover police officer to testify, particularly where the undercover officer is testifying with respect to threats to the officer's safety and the danger if the officer's identity were to be revealed.[1] Prior to closing the courtroom, the judge must make a sufficient inquiry to determine whether such closure is warranted. The Court of Appeals has cautioned that the court's discretion in closing the courtroom should be used sparingly and "only when unusual circumstances necessitate it."[2] Any closure over the objection of the accused must meet the following test:

§ 18.12

1. People v. Monclavo, 87 N.Y.2d 1029, 643 N.Y.S.2d 470, 666 N.E.2d 175 (1996) (defendant has right to be present at preliminary Sandoval hearing).

2. People v. Antommarchi, 80 N.Y.2d 247, 590 N.Y.S.2d 33, 604 N.E.2d 95, rearg. denied 81 N.Y.2d 759, 594 N.Y.S.2d 720, 610 N.E.2d 393 (1992) (right to attend sidebars and conferences). The Court of Appeals curbed the right to attend jury selection sidebars in a single decision involving four separate criminal appeals, People v. Vargas; People v. Pondexter; People v. Hutton; People v. Wilson, 88 N.Y.2d 363, 645 N.Y.S.2d 759, 668 N.E.2d 879 (1996). In Pondexter, the defendant elected not to attend sidebars during voir dire because the trial judge had directed that if defendant wanted to attend sidebars, he would be surrounded with court officers, and the defendant feared this would make him appear guilty. The Court of Appeals rejected defendant's claim of coercion, but cautioned that "trial courts should be vigilant not to overbear with activity that might constitute legally coercive or offensive rulings."

3. People v. Todd, 209 A.D.2d 652, 619 N.Y.S.2d 121 (2d Dep't 1994). This right was violated when a defendant and his counsel were not present in the courtroom when the judge responded to a note from the jury. People v. Bici, 211 A.D.2d 804, 621 N.Y.S.2d 666 (2d Dep't 1995).

§ 18.13

1. People v. Reece, 204 A.D.2d 495, 612 N.Y.S.2d 61 (2d Dep't 1994). The Second Circuit has held that an undercover officer is not automatically entitled to have a courtroom closed when testifying. Ayala v. Speckard, 89 F.3d 91, 96 (2d Cir.1996) ("Judges must consider courtroom closure on a case-by-case basis, allowing the public to be excluded only if the moving party establishes a 'substantial probability' of prejudice.").

PRACTICE POINTER: The court in Ayala noted that judges must consider other less drastic alternatives, such as having the witness testify behind a screen, before closing the courtroom. Counsel should be prepared to propose these and other alternatives if the defendant does not want the courtroom closed.

2. People v. Hinton, 31 N.Y.2d 71, 334 N.Y.S.2d 885, 286 N.E.2d 265 (1972), cert. denied 410 U.S. 911, 93 S.Ct. 970, 35 L.Ed.2d 273 (1973). In People v. Jones, 47 N.Y.2d 409, 418 N.Y.S.2d 359, 391 N.E.2d 1335 (1979), the Court of Appeals stopped short of requiring a court to hold an evidentiary hearing, but made it clear that a careful inquiry must be made before ordering a courtroom closed. Failure to make such an inquiry is grounds for reversal. People v. Rivera, 195 A.D.2d 389, 600 N.Y.S.2d 248 (1st Dep't 1993).

(1) the party seeking to close the hearing must set forth an overriding interest that is likely to be prejudiced; (2) the closure must be no broader than necessary to protect that interest; (3) the court must consider reasonable alternatives to closure; and (4) the court must make findings to support the decision to close the courtroom.[3]

In a factually unique case, the Second Circuit held that the brief inadvertent closure of the courtroom does not violate a defendant's Sixth Amendment rights.[4]

Library References:

West's Key No. Digests, Criminal Law ⚖635.

§ 18.14 New York Bill of Rights—Rights of Persons Accused of Crimes—Exclusion of Public or Press

A court may also impose a "gag" order on the participants in a criminal trial to insure that pretrial publicity does not prejudice the defendant. Before doing so, the court should allow members of the news media an opportunity to be heard and must make factual findings which demonstrate that the gag order is necessary to protect the defendant, or it may be struck down as an invalid prior restraint of speech.[1] The defendant has the burden of demonstrating that his right to a fair trial will be compromised if the courtroom is not closed to the press and the public.[2]

Library References:

West's Key No. Digests, Criminal Law ⚖635.

---

3. Waller v. Georgia, 467 U.S. 39, 48, 104 S.Ct. 2210, 2216, 81 L.Ed.2d 31 (1984). For example, in Cosentino v. Kelly, 926 F.Supp. 391 (S.D.N.Y.), aff'd, 102 F.3d 71 (2d Cir.1996), cert. denied __ U.S. __, 117 S.Ct. 1821, 137 L.Ed.2d 1029 (1997), the court denied a writ of *habeas corpus* and upheld the partial closure of a courtroom during a retrial of a defendant because of legitimate concerns about disorder in the courtroom that could cause a second mistrial. The decision to close the courtroom was not based on speculation but on the actual events of the first trial. Conversely, in Guzman v. Scully, 80 F.3d 772 (2d Cir.1996), the court granted a writ of *habeas corpus* and ordered a retrial because the trial judge had excluded friends and relatives of a defendant based solely on a prosecutor's unsubstantiated contention that spectators would intimidate a prosecution witness. The trial judge failed to satisfy the Waller requirements since he never inquired of the witness whether he would be intimidated.

4. Peterson v. Williams, 85 F.3d 39 (2d Cir.), cert. denied __ U.S. __, 117 S.Ct. 202, 136 L.Ed.2d 138 (1996). In Peterson, the courtroom inadvertently remained closed for 20 minutes during defendant's testimony following the lawful closure for the testimony of an undercover officer.

§ 18.14

1. Matter of Gannett Co., Inc. v. DePasquale, 43 N.Y.2d 370, 401 N.Y.S.2d 756, 372 N.E.2d 544 (1977); New York Times Co., Inc. v. Rothwax, 143 A.D.2d 592, 533 N.Y.S.2d 73 (1st Dep't 1988).

2. Matter of Associated Press v. Bell, 70 N.Y.2d 32, 517 N.Y.S.2d 444, 510 N.E.2d 313 (1987).

§ 18.15 New York Bill of Rights—Rights of Jurors

Jury service is a civil right accorded all New York State citizens.[1] Section 13 of the Civil Rights Law provides that "[n]o citizen ..., shall be disqualified to serve as a grand or petit juror in any court of this state on account of race, creed, color, national origin or sex,...." This section further provides that any person who excludes or fails to summon any citizen for jury duty based on race, creed, color, national origin or sex may be charged with a misdemeanor and may be subject to a fine of not less than $100 nor more than $500 or imprisoned for not less than 30 days nor more than 90 days or both.

The New York Court of Appeals has held that Section 13 applies not only to the jury commission, but also prohibits purposeful racial discrimination in the exercise of peremptory challenges by criminal defense attorneys.[2] In subsequent criminal cases, courts have also prohibited the exercise of peremptory challenges based on gender[3] and disability[4] as violative of the New York Constitution and civil rights laws.

In 1991, the Supreme Court extended the prohibition to civil cases as well, holding that state action doctrine applied to prohibit private civil litigants from using peremptory challenges to exclude jurors based on race.[5] Three years later, the court further extended the rule to prohibit gender-based discrimination, holding that the use of peremptory challenges to exclude men from a jury violates the Equal Protection Clause.[6] One New York court has ruled that the use of peremptory challenges based on religion is barred by the New York Constitution.[7] Another court has barred the discriminatory use of peremptory challenges against Italian–Americans.[8]

Accordingly, attorneys must exercise caution in using peremptory challenges and should be prepared to articulate a neutral and nondiscriminatory reason for the exercise of the challenge.[9] As a penalty for

---

§ 18.15

1. N.Y. State Constitution Art. I, §§ 1, 11.

2. People v. Kern, 75 N.Y.2d 638, 555 N.Y.S.2d 647, 554 N.E.2d 1235, cert. denied 498 U.S. 824, 111 S.Ct. 77, 112 L.Ed.2d 50 (1990); see also, Georgia v. McCollum, 505 U.S. 42, 112 S.Ct. 2348, 120 L.Ed.2d 33 (1992) (prohibition applies to defendants as well as prosecutors).

3. See, e.g., People v. Blunt, 162 A.D.2d 86, 561 N.Y.S.2d 90 (2d Dep't 1990) (prosecutor prohibited from using peremptory challenges to exclude women).

4. People v. Green, 148 Misc.2d 666, 561 N.Y.S.2d 130 (Sup.Ct., Westchester County, 1990).

5. Edmonson v. Leesville, Concrete Co., Inc., 500 U.S. 614, 111 S.Ct. 2077, 114 L.Ed.2d 660 (1991).

6. J.E.B. v. Alabama ex rel. T.B., 511 U.S. 127, 114 S.Ct. 1419, 128 L.Ed.2d 89 (1994).

7. People v. Langston, 167 Misc.2d 400, 641 N.Y.S.2d 513 (Sup.Ct., Queens County, 1996).

8. People v. Rambersed, 170 Misc.2d 923, 649 N.Y.S.2d 640 (Sup.Ct., Bronx County, 1996).

9. See People v. Payne; People v. Jones; People v. Lowery, 88 N.Y.2d 172, 643 N.Y.S.2d 949, 666 N.E.2d 542 (1996). In People v. Payne, the court upheld the trial court's disallowance of two peremptory challenges by defense counsel, finding that proffered explanation was pretextual.

the improper use of peremptory challenges, a court could order that the panel be disbanded and a new jury be selected;[10] it is also conceivable that attorneys could be subject to disciplinary action or fined for engaging in purposeful discrimination.[11] Additionally, attorneys should ensure that they do not ask discriminatory questions on *voir dire* and do not single out certain members of the jury panel in asking particular questions.

§ 18.16 General Federal Civil Rights Provisions

The most common civil rights claim asserted in federal court is a claim under 42 U.S.C.A. § 1983.[1] Section 1983 provides that

> [e]very person who, under color of any statute, ordinance, regulation, custom, or usage, ... , subjects, or causes to be subjected, any citizen of the United States or other person within the jurisdiction thereof to the deprivation of any rights, privileges, or immunities secured by the Constitution and laws, shall be liable to the party injured in at action an law, suit in equity, or other proper proceeding for redress.

Section 1983 is referred to as a remedial statute, the prime focus of which is to insure "a right of action to enforce the protection of the Fourteenth Amendment and the federal laws enacted pursuant thereto."[2]

Section 1981 is more limited in scope in that it applies to discrimination based on race and applies only to contractual relations. Section 1981 provides, in relevant part, that:

> All persons within the jurisdiction of the United States shall have the same right ... to make and enforce contracts, to sue, be parties, give evidence, and to the full and equal benefit of all laws and proceedings for the security of persons and property as is enjoyed by white citizens, and shall be subject to like punishment, pains,

The New York Court of Appeals has made clear that there is no particular procedure for the conduct of the inquiry, referred to as a Batson hearing, after the Supreme Court decision in Batson v. Kentucky, 476 U.S. 79, 106 S.Ct. 1712, 90 L.Ed.2d 69 (1986). *See* People v. Hameed, 88 N.Y.2d 232, 644 N.Y.S.2d 466, 666 N.E.2d 1339 (1996) (defendants not entitled to cross-examine prosecutors in Batson hearing).

10. O'Neill v. City of New York, 160 Misc.2d 1086, 612 N.Y.S.2d 303 (Civ.Ct., N.Y. County, 1994).

CAVEAT: Objections to the use of peremptory challenges are waived unless they are made before the end of jury selection.

McCrory v. Henderson, 82 F.3d 1243 (2d Cir.1996).

11. *See* Siriano v. Beth Israel Hosp. Center, 161 Misc.2d 512, 614 N.Y.S.2d 700 (Sup.Ct., N.Y. County, 1994).

§ 18.16

1. It is beyond the scope of this chapter to provide a comprehensive treatment of § 1983. For a more exhaustive treatment of Section 1983, *see* Schwartz & Kirklin, *Section 1983 Litigation: Claims, Defenses and Fees* (2d ed. 1991 and 1995).

2. Chapman v. Houston Welfare Rights Organization, 441 U.S. 600, 611, 99 S.Ct. 1905, 1913, 60 L.Ed.2d 508 (1979).

penalties, taxes, licenses, and exactions of every kind, and to no other. . . .

For the purposes of this section, the term 'make and enforce contracts' includes the making, performance, modification, and termination of contracts, and the enjoyment of all benefits, privileges, terms, and conditions of the contractual relationship. . . .

The rights protected by this section are protected against impairment by nongovernmental discrimination and impairment under color of State law.

Both of these statutes provide important safeguards for civil rights claims.

§ 18.17 General Federal Civil Rights Provisions—42 U.S.C.A. § 1981

Section 1981 prohibits intentional racial discrimination in the making and enforcing of contracts. Unlike a claim under Section 1983, state action is not required to assert a claim under Section 1981. *See* Section 18.18. Since Section 1981 involves an allegation of intentional discrimination, a plaintiff must be able to show that defendant's conduct was racially motivated and was purposely discriminatory.[1]

A plaintiff's burden of proof for a Section 1981 claim is essentially the same as that which was articulated by the Supreme Court for employment discrimination cases under Title VII actions. *See* "Employment Law" § 17.59. Plaintiff has the burden of proving by a preponderance of the evidence a *prima facie* case of discrimination. Once this burden is satisfied, the burden shifts to defendant to articulate a legitimate, non-discriminatory reason for its determination. If this burden is met, plaintiff must show by a preponderance of the evidence that the reason was not a true reason but was merely a pretext for discrimination.[2]

The law is unclear as to whether a Section 1981 claim may be asserted against a municipality for actions of its employees. In *Jett v. Dallas Indep. Sch. Dist.*,[3] the United States Supreme Court held that Section 1983 provides the exclusive federal remedy when a claim is presented against a state actor. Part of *Jett's* holding was overruled by the Civil Rights Act of 1991, which specifically provides that a Section 1981 claim may be brought for violations "under color of state law."[4]

---

§ 18.17

1. Section 1981 also prohibits discrimination against caucasians (McDonald v. Santa Fe Trail Transp. Co., 427 U.S. 273, 96 S.Ct. 2574, 49 L.Ed.2d 493 (1976)) and covers claims based on ethnicity as well. Saint Francis College v. Al-Khazraji, 481 U.S. 604, 609–12, 107 S.Ct. 2022, 2026–28, 95 L.Ed.2d 582 (1987).

2. *See* Harvey v. NYRAC, Inc., 813 F.Supp. 206 (E.D.N.Y.1993) (citations omitted).

3. 491 U.S. 701, 109 S.Ct. 2702, 105 L.Ed.2d 598 (1989).

4. 42 U.S.C.A. § 1981(c).

§ 18.17 CIVIL RIGHTS LAW Ch. 18

Recent cases have questioned, however, whether the 1991 amendment to Section 1981 should also allow causes of action under Section 1981 against state municipalities.[5]

Library References:

West's Key No. Digests, Civil Rights ⚖118.

§ 18.18 General Federal Civil Rights Provisions—42 U.S.C.A. § 1983

To state a claim under Section 1983, a plaintiff must allege (1) that he or she was deprived of a right, privilege or immunity secured by the Constitution or laws of the United States and (2) that the conduct was attributable at least in part by someone acting under color of state law.[1] Plaintiff bears the burden of proof of both of these elements.[2]

Section 1983 itself creates no substantive rights. Accordingly, a Section 1983 complaint must allege a violation of the Federal Constitution or laws. "Violations of state procedural rules ..., do not of their own accord deprive an individual of a federally protected liberty interest, and therefore do not give rise to an actionable claim under 42 U.S.C.A. § 1983."[3] For example, a claim of violation of due process rights would be asserted under the Fourteenth Amendment and Section 1983, not merely under Section 1983 standing alone.

The second element of a Section 1983 claim is the requirement of "state action." Generally, the defendants must be state or municipal government officials or employees.[4] In order to maintain a Section 1983 action against a private party, the conduct must be "fairly attributable to the State."[5]

---

5. See, e.g., Philippeaux v. North Central Bronx Hosp., 871 F.Supp. 640, 654 (S.D.N.Y.1994) (holding that Jett still applies to bar vicarious liability with respect to municipalities and that in order to state a Section 1981 claim against a municipality, plaintiff must also allege a violation of Section 1983 and must meet the requirements of Monell); see also, infra, § 18.34.

§ 18.18

1. See Dahlberg v. Becker, 748 F.2d 85, 89, (2d Cir.1984), cert. denied 470 U.S. 1084, 105 S.Ct. 1845, 85 L.Ed.2d 144 (1985); see also, Dwares v. City of New York, 985 F.2d 94 (2d Cir.1993).

2. Baker v. McCollan, 443 U.S. 137, 144 note 3, 99 S.Ct. 2689, 2694 note 3, 61 L.Ed.2d 433 (1979).

3. Smallwood–El v. Coughlin, 589 F.Supp. 692, 699 (S.D.N.Y.1984). Violations of procedural rules "place no substantive limitations on official discretion and thus create no liberty interest entitled to protection under the Due Process Clause." Olim v. Wakinekona, 461 U.S. 238, 249, 103 S.Ct. 1741, 1747, 75 L.Ed.2d 813 (1983).

4. A claim against federal officials is not brought under Section 1983. Rather, such a claim is brought under Bivens v. Six Unknown Named Agents of Federal Bureau of Narcotics, 403 U.S. 388, 91 S.Ct. 1999, 29 L.Ed.2d 619 (1971), which provides for the commencement of an action against defendants who act under color of federal law. Claims brought under Bivens are analyzed in the same manner as claims brought under Section 1983 and courts generally apply the holdings in Section 1983 actions to Bivens actions. Chin v. Bowen, 833 F.2d 21, 23 (2d Cir.1987).

5. Lugar v. Edmondson Oil Co., 457 U.S. 922, 937, 102 S.Ct. 2744, 2753–54, 73 L.Ed.2d 482 (1982). In Lugar, the court stated the test is that the deprivation must

There are certain pleading requirements unique to a Section 1983 claim. To state a claim under Section 1983, the complaint must allege more than mere conclusory allegations. Rather, the complaint must set forth "specific instances of misconduct" in order to survive a motion to dismiss.[6] Section 1983 requires more than mere negligence; negligence alone does not rise to level of a Section 1983 violation.[7]

A Section 1983 complaint must name a "person" as a defendant.[8] It is generally insufficient to merely name a government agency or department. *See infra*, Section 18.34.

Additionally, a claim may only be asserted against a defendant who was "personally involved" in the acts alleged.[9] The doctrine of *respondeat superior* does not apply to Section 1983 actions. See *infra*, Section 18.35.

To obtain an award of compensatory damages under Section 1983, a plaintiff must prove that his or her injuries were proximately caused by the constitutional violation alleged. Compensatory damages may be awarded only up to the amount plaintiff can prove.[10] "[T]he abstract

be caused by the exercise of a right or privilege created by the state or by a rule of conduct imposed by the state or by a person for whom the state is responsible **and** the person must have either acted together with a state actor, obtained significant aid from a state official or have engaged in conduct that is otherwise chargeable to the state. *See also,* Singer v. Fulton County Sheriff, 63 F.3d 110, 119 (2d Cir.1995); Chan v. City of New York, 1 F.3d 96, 106 (2d Cir.1993) ("Actions by a private party are deemed state action if 'there is a sufficiently close nexus between that State and the challenged action' that the actions by the private parties 'may be fairly treated as that of the State itself.'" (citations omitted)).

6. Martin v. New York State Dept. of Mental Hygiene, 588 F.2d 371, 372 (2d Cir. 1978)("It is well settled in this Circuit that a complaint consisting of nothing more than naked assertions, and setting forth no facts upon which a court could find a violation of the Civil Rights Act, fails to state a claim under rule 12(b)(6)."); San Filippo v. U.S. Trust Co., 737 F.2d 246, 256 (2d Cir. 1984), cert. denied 470 U.S. 1035, 105 S.Ct. 1408, 84 L.Ed.2d 797 (1985); Contemporary Mission, Inc. v. U.S. Postal Service, 648 F.2d 97 (2d Cir. 1981).

7. Daniels v. Williams, 474 U.S. 327, 106 S.Ct. 662, 88 L.Ed.2d 662 (1986); Davidson v. Cannon, 474 U.S. 344, 106 S.Ct. 668, 88 L.Ed.2d 677 (1986).

8. A state, a state agency or a state official sued in his or her official capacity is not considered a "person" under Section 1983. Will v. Michigan Dept. of State Police, 491 U.S. 58, 109 S.Ct. 2304, 105 L.Ed.2d 45 (1989). When a state official is named in his official capacity in a claim for injunctive relief, the official is considered a "person," but is not considered a "person" with respect to claims for retroactive relief. In Hafer v. Melo, 502 U.S. 21, 25, 112 S.Ct. 358, 362, 116 L.Ed.2d 301 (1991), the Supreme Court held that state officials may be personally liable for damages under Section 1983 for actions taken in their official capacities provided they are named as defendants in their individual capacities.

PRACTICE POINTER: The effect of these pleading requirements is that it is generally insufficient to solely name the governmental agency or department in a § 1983 action. Rather, the complaint must name one or more officials of the agency, and must seek more than retroactive relief. If monetary damages are sought, the official should also be named in his or her individual capacity.

9. Wright v. Smith, 21 F.3d 496 (2d Cir.1994).

10. Gibeau v. Nellis, 18 F.3d 107 (2d Cir.1994); Miner v. City of Glens Falls, 999 F.2d 655, 660 (2d Cir.1993). For example, the Supreme Court has held that to recover damages for an unreasonable search under Section 1983, a plaintiff must prove the

§ 18.18   CIVIL RIGHTS LAW   Ch. 18

value of a constitutional right may not form the basis for § 1983 damages."[11] Only nominal damages of $1.00 may be awarded based upon the abstract value or importance of the constitutional rights involved.[12]

Library References:

West's Key No. Digests, Civil Rights ⚖ 108–135.

§ 18.19   General Federal Civil Rights Provisions—Other Federal Civil Rights Provisions

For a claim under Section 1985(3), plaintiffs must allege that (1) they are members of a protected class; (2) the defendants conspired to deprived them of their constitutional rights; (3) defendants acted with a racial or otherwise "class-based invidious discriminatory animus" toward them;[1] and (4) that they suffered injury as a result of defendants' actions. Plaintiff must also allege that defendants engaged in an act in furtherance of the conspiracy.[2] In addition, the defendants may not work for the same entity and the actions in furtherance of the conspiracy must be outside the scope of their employment.[3]

Section 1986 provides a cause of action against a person who had the power to prevent or aid in preventing a wrong mentioned in Section 1985 but knowingly refused to do so. A claim under this section presupposes a valid claim under Section 1985.[4]

Section 504 of the Rehabilitation Act, 29 U.S.C.A. § 794 provides that "[n]o otherwise qualified individual with handicaps ... shall, solely

---

search was unlawful and caused an actual, compensable injury. Heck v. Humphrey, 512 U.S. 477, 114 S.Ct. 2364, 129 L.Ed.2d 383 (1994).

11. Memphis Community Sch. Dist. v. Stachura, 477 U.S. 299, 308, 106 S.Ct. 2537, 2543, 91 L.Ed.2d 249 (1986).

12. Carey v. Piphus, 435 U.S. 247, 98 S.Ct. 1042, 55 L.Ed.2d 252 (1978); Smith v. Coughlin, 748 F.2d 783, 789 (2d Cir.1984).

§ 18.19

1. Griffin v. Breckenridge, 403 U.S. 88, 102, 91 S.Ct. 1790, 1798, 29 L.Ed.2d 338 (1971). It is well established that blacks are members of a protected class under the statute. In Bray v. Alexandria Women's Health Clinic, 506 U.S. 263, 113 S.Ct. 753, 122 L.Ed.2d 34 (1993), the Supreme Court had the occasion to consider the definition of "other class-based discriminatory animus" and concluded that women seeking abortions did not constitute such a class. The court left for another day to determine whether women constituted a class. At least one district court in New York has subsequently held that persons with disabilities may be considered a class protected under Section 1985(3). Trautz v. Weisman, 819 F.Supp. 282 (S.D.N.Y.1993).

2. A conspiracy may also be pleaded under Section 1983. See Dwares, § 18.18, supra note 1; Ostrer v. Aronwald, 567 F.2d 551, 553 (2d Cir.1977) (where allegations of conspiracy in civil rights complaints are not supported by factual detail in the form of specific instances of alleged wrongdoing, dismissal is required).

PRACTICE POINTER: In deciding whether to allege a conspiracy claim under Section 1983 or Section 1985(3), counsel should bear in mind that a conspiracy under Section 1983 need not allege any class-based animus.

3. See Herrmann v. Moore, 576 F.2d 453, 459 (2d Cir.1978), cert. denied 439 U.S. 1003, 99 S.Ct. 613, 58 L.Ed.2d 679 (1978).

4. Dwares, § 18.18, supra note 1.

CAVEAT: The Statute of Limitations for a claim under Section 1986 is only one year

by reason of her or his handicap, be excluded from the participation in, be denied the benefits of, or be subjected to discrimination under any program or activity receiving Federal financial assistance ..."[5] To establish a claim under the Rehabilitation Act, a plaintiff must show that he or she (1) meets the definition of a "handicapped person" under the Act; (2) is "otherwise qualified" to participate in the program or activity or to enjoy the services offered; (3) is being excluded solely by reason of the handicap; and (4) the entity denying participation receives federal financial assistance.[6]

Similarly, the Americans With Disabilities Act of 1990, 42 U.S.C.A. §§ 12131 et seq., which took effect in 1992, prohibits discrimination based on disabilities. The requirements for establishing a claim under the ADA are essentially the same as those under the Rehabilitation Act, namely a plaintiff must show that he or she (1) is a "qualified individual with a disability;" (2) is being discriminated against by being excluded from participation in or being denied the benefits of a service program or activity by reason of a disability; and (3) is being denied this service program or activity by a place of public accommodation.[7]

These causes of action should be pleaded in state or federal court complaints where appropriate.[8]

§ 18.20 Police and Prosecutorial Misconduct

In filing a case alleging false arrest, false imprisonment, malicious prosecution or the use of force, the most important decision may be

after the cause of action has accrued. 42 U.S.C.A. § 1986.

5. 29 U.S.C.A. § 794; see Alexander v. Choate, 469 U.S. 287, 105 S.Ct. 712, 83 L.Ed.2d 661 (1985).

6. Rothschild v. Grottenthaler, 907 F.2d 286, 289–90 (2d Cir.1990).

CAVEAT: Since there is no Statute of Limitations period set forth for a claim under the Act, a court is required to apply the most analogous state Statute of Limitations. In Morse v. University of Vermont, 973 F.2d 122 (2d Cir.1992), the Second Circuit held for the first time that the state Statute of Limitations applicable to personal injury actions should control (i.e., in New York, three years).

7. See Clarkson v. Coughlin, 898 F.Supp. 1019 (S.D.N.Y.1995).

8. CAVEAT: The practice of asking a federal court to entertain state law claims, which was formerly referred to as the exercise of "pendent jurisdiction," is now referred to as "supplemental jurisdiction." 28 U.S.C.A. § 1367(a). This section provides that if the state law claim raises a novel or complex issue of state law, the federal court may decline to exercise supplemental jurisdiction. 28 U.S.C.A. § 1367(c)(1). Even though the federal and state claims may arise from the same set of operative facts, a federal court may refuse to consider state court claims, particularly if there are unresolved questions of state law. See Support Ministries for Persons With AIDS, Inc. v. Village of Waterford, N.Y., 799 F.Supp. 272 (N.D.N.Y.1992). Therefore, counsel should weigh carefully the strength of the federal versus the state causes of action in determining first, whether to bring the action in state or federal court and second, if the action is brought in federal court, whether the state causes of action satisfy the test for the exercise of supplemental jurisdiction.

PRACTICE POINTER: Prior to commencing an action, a practitioner may consider notifying the state attorney general, who has the power to bring an action to enforce provisions of the federal as well as state statutes prohibiting discrimination. People by Vacco v. Mid Hudson Medical

where to file the case and whether to proceed under the state causes of action, under Section 1983, or both. The differences between the state law and federal law causes of action include the Statute of Limitations,[1] the elements of each cause of action, Notice of Claim requirements[2] and the defenses available. For example, the doctrines of absolute immunity (*see* infra, Section 18.31) or qualified immunity (see *infra*, Section 18.32) may bar an otherwise valid federal claim.[3]

Library References:

West's Key No. Digests, Civil Rights ⚖132–135.

§ 18.21 Police and Prosecutorial Misconduct—Excessive Force

Claims of excessive force by police officers may be brought under Section 1983 and the Fourth Amendment. The United States Supreme Court held in *Graham v. Connor*,[1] that claims of excessive force should be analyzed under the Fourth Amendment's reasonableness standard. A determination of the reasonableness of the use of force during an arrest requires balancing the "nature and quality of the intrusion on the individual's Fourth Amendment interests against the countervailing governmental interests at stake."[2] This necessarily involves a case-by-case analysis as to whether under the particular facts, the amount of force used was excessive and unreasonable.

Group, P.C., 877 F.Supp. 143 (S.D.N.Y. 1995).

§ 18.20

1. The Statute of Limitation for a Section 1983 claim for all of these actions is three years while the Statute of Limitations for the state law actions is only one year. *See* CPLR 215.

2. CAVEAT: If the claim is going to be brought in state court against the City of New York, a notice of claim must be filed within ninety days of the date of the arrest. *See* General Municipal Law § 50–e(1)(a). *See generally*, Chapter 3 "Municipal Law," *supra*. Similarly, if the claim is against the State of New York, a Notice of Claim must be filed with the state, and the action would then be commenced in the Court of Claims. DeBonis v. State of New York, 37 A.D.2d 878, 325 N.Y.S.2d 215 (3d Dep't 1971). While leave to file a late Notice of Claim may be granted by the supreme court (with respect to a claim against the City) or by the Court of Claims (with respect to a claim against the state), the decision to grant or deny leave depends on the factual circumstances of each case. *See* Grullon v. City of New York, 222 A.D.2d 257, 635 N.Y.S.2d 24 (1st Dep't 1995); Court of Claims Act §§ 8, 9.

PRACTICE POINTER: If a client does not seek advice of counsel within the ninety day period, and the allegations meet the standard for a Section 1983 claim, the best course of action would be to commence the action against the state or municipal actors in federal court to avoid the problem of a late Notice of Claim. The Notice of Claim requirement does not apply to claims asserted under Section 1983, whether filed in state or federal court. Felder v. Casey, 487 U.S. 131, 108 S.Ct. 2302, 101 L.Ed.2d 123 (1988); *see supra*, § 18.9 note 2.

3. *See* discussion in Pinaud v. County of Suffolk, 52 F.3d 1139, 1146 (2d Cir.1995) concerning the fact that some of plaintiff's state law claims were valid while the federal claims were barred by the doctrine of absolute immunity.

§ 18.21

1. 490 U.S. 386, 109 S.Ct. 1865, 104 L.Ed.2d 443 (1989).

2. Lennon v. Miller, 66 F.3d, 416, 425 (2d Cir.1995) (quoting Graham, 490 U.S. at 396, 109 S.Ct. at 1872).

The defense of qualified immunity (*see infra*, Section 18.32) is available to claims of excessive force.[3] The Statute of Limitations for a claim of excessive force begins to run on the date of plaintiff's confrontation with the police officers.

Library References:

West's Key No. Digests, Civil Rights ⊙132.1, 133.

§ 18.22 Police and Prosecutorial Misconduct—False Arrest

A false arrest claim will lie under Section 1983 if it also encompasses a violation of federal statutory or constitutional rights.[1] The elements of a false arrest claim under Section 1983 are substantially identical to the state law tort of false arrest in that plaintiff must show that there was a lack of probable cause for the arrest.[2]

Based on a recent Supreme Court decision, a claim of false arrest should be pleaded under the Fourth Amendment and Section 1983,

---

3. *Id.* at 425 citing Finnegan v. Fountain, 915 F.2d 817, 822–23 (2d Cir.1990). The proper inquiry is whether a reasonable officer could have believed that the use of force was objectively reasonable under the factual circumstances. *Id.* (citations omitted). In Lennon, the Second Circuit found that the defense of qualified immunity was available since the officers' action of forcibly removing plaintiff from her car to effect her arrest constituted a limited intrusion on plaintiff's Fourth Amendment rights.

PRACTICE POINTER: The plaintiff in Lennon also alleged supplemental state law claims of assault, unlawful imprisonment and malicious prosecution, which were also dismissed. The case demonstrates that where the amount of force used is not "shocking" and where plaintiff's injuries are minimal (here, treatment for a wrist injury and no other physical injury), commencing an action in state court is a more prudent choice. Where, however, a plaintiff has been beaten, recovery is available for intentional infliction of emotional distress. *See* O'Neill v. Krzeminski, 839 F.2d 9, 13 (2d Cir.1988).

§ 18.22

1. Lennon v. Miller, 66 F.3d 416, 423 (2d Cir.1995) (citations omitted).

2. Raysor v. Port Authority of New York and New Jersey, 768 F.2d 34, 39 (2d Cir.1985)(stating that a tort action for false arrest is "substantially the same" as a Section 1983 claim), cert. denied 475 U.S. 1027, 106 S.Ct. 1227, 89 L.Ed.2d 337 (1986). In Raysor, the court stated that plaintiff need not prove malice or lack of probable cause; rather, defendant has the burden of proving that there was probable cause for the arrest.

In a later case, the Second Circuit stated that the tort of false arrest is synonymous with the tort of false imprisonment, and cited with approval the decision of the New York Court of Appeals in Broughton v. State, 37 N.Y.2d 451, 373 N.Y.S.2d 87, 335 N.E.2d 310, cert. denied sub nom. 423 U.S. 929, 96 S.Ct. 277, 46 L.Ed.2d 257 (1975) for the definition of the state law tort of false arrest or imprisonment:

> The action for false imprisonment is derived from the ancient common-law action of trespass and protects the personal interest of freedom from restraint of movement. Whenever a person unlawfully obstructs or deprives another of his freedom to choose his own location, that person will be liable for that interference (Restatement, 2d, Torts, § 35, comment H). To establish this cause of action the plaintiff must show that: (1) the defendant intended to confine him, (2) the plaintiff was conscious of the confinement, (3) the plaintiff did not consent to the confinement and (4) the confinement was not otherwise privileged....

Posr v. Doherty, 944 F.2d 91, 96–97 (2d Cir.1991) (quoting Broughton, *supra*, 37 N.Y.2d at 456, 457, 373 N.Y.S.2d at 93).

§ 18.22

rather than under the Fourteenth Amendment.[3]

The defense of qualified immunity (*see infra*, Section 18.32) is available to defendants in a false arrest action if it was objectively reasonable for them to believe they had probable cause to arrest the plaintiff or if officers of reasonable competence could differ as to whether there was probable cause for the arrest.[4] This determination entails reviewing the elements of the particular offense for which plaintiff was arrested.

Library References:

West's Key No. Digests, Civil Rights ⚖133.

§ 18.23 Police and Prosecutorial Misconduct—False Imprisonment

The cause of action for false imprisonment, which is derived from the ancient common law action of trespass, protects the plaintiff from freedom of restraint of movement.[1] To state a cause of action for false imprisonment in New York, plaintiff must demonstrate that "(1) the defendant intended to confine him, (2) the plaintiff was conscious of the confinement, (3) the plaintiff did not consent to the confinement and (4) the confinement was not otherwise privileged."[2]

False imprisonment is distinguished from malicious prosecution (*see infra*, Section 18.25) by the absence of a warrant. If an arrest is made pursuant to a warrant, the appropriate cause of action is malicious prosecution, not false imprisonment.[3] The defendant has the burden to prove legal justification by showing that there was probable cause for the arrest and confinement.

3. Albright v. Oliver, 510 U.S. 266, 114 S.Ct. 807, 127 L.Ed.2d 114, reh. denied 510 U.S. 1215, 114 S.Ct. 1340, 127 L.Ed.2d 688 (1994); Lennon, *supra* note 1, 66 F.3d at 423 note 2.

4. Lennon, *supra* note 1 (citing Wachtler v. County of Herkimer, 35 F.3d 77, 80 (2d Cir.1994)). "'Probable cause to arrest exists when the authorities have knowledge or reasonably trustworthy information sufficient to warrant a person of reasonable caution in the belief that an offense has been committed by the person to be arrested.'" Lennon, 66 F.3d at 424 (quoting Golino v. City of New Haven, 950 F.2d 864, 870 (2d Cir.1991), cert. denied 505 U.S. 1221, 112 S.Ct. 3032, 120 L.Ed.2d 902 (1992)); Eagleston v. Guido, 41 F.3d 865, 872 (2d Cir.1994).

§ 18.23

1. Broughton v. State, 37 N.Y.2d 451, 373 N.Y.S.2d 87, 335 N.E.2d 310, cert. denied 423 U.S. 929, 96 S.Ct. 277, 46 L.Ed.2d 257 (1975).

2. *Id.* at 456, 373 N.Y.S.2d at 93, 335 N.E.2d at 314 (citing *Restatement 2d Torts*, § 35).

In at least one case, the Second Circuit has seemingly blurred any distinction between the torts of false arrest and false imprisonment. See *supra*, Posr, § 18.22, note 2.

3. Colon, *supra* note 1; Broughton, § 18.22, *supra* note 2, 37 N.Y.2d at 457, 373 N.Y.S.2d at 94, 335 N.E.2d at 314–15 ("When an unlawful arrest has been effected by a warrant an appropriate form of action is malicious prosecution.").

Ch. 18 MALICIOUS PROSECUTION § 18.25

The Supreme Court recently held in *Heck v. Humphrey*,[4] that a claim of unlawful imprisonment under Section 1983 does not lie until the plaintiff's conviction or sentence has been "officially" voided.[5] Accordingly, the Statute of Limitations begins to run on that date.[6] Damages for false imprisonment are designed to compensate plaintiff for his or her freedom from restraint of movement, and are measured only up to the time of plaintiff's arraignment or indictment, whichever is earlier.[7]

Library References:

West's Key No. Digests, Civil Rights ⚖114.

§ 18.24 Police and Prosecutorial Misconduct—Search and Seizure

A discussion of search and seizure under the New York Bill of Rights is set forth at Sections 18.9 through 18.11, *supra*.

Library References:

West's Key No. Digests, Civil Rights ⚖132.1.

§ 18.25 Police and Prosecutorial Misconduct—Malicious Prosecution

To establish a state law claim of malicious prosecution, a plaintiff must demonstrate that "(1) the defendant either commenced or continued a criminal proceeding against him; (2) that the proceeding terminated in his favor; (3) that there was no probable cause for the criminal proceeding; and (4) that the criminal proceeding was instituted with actual malice."[1] Favorable termination of a prosecution is a prerequisite

---

4. 512 U.S. 477, 114 S.Ct. 2364, 129 L.Ed.2d 383 (1994).

5. 512 U.S. at 477, 114 S.Ct. at 2374. Under Heck, the Statute of Limitations for a Section 1983 claim for false imprisonment would not begin to run until the conviction or sentence has been invalidated. Thus, if a state prisoner's conviction is reversed by an appellate court, the Statute of Limitations would begin to run on the date of the reversal. Woods v. Candela, 47 F.3d 545, 546 (2d Cir.1995).

6. **CAVEAT:** If asserting a state law claim against the City of New York or the State of New York in state court, *see supra*, § 18.20, note 2.

7. Colon, *supra* note 1. These damages would include compensation for humiliation, mental anguish and lost earnings. While the court in Colon stated that a recovery for attorney's fees would be available, the amount of fees is limited to the time up to the arraignment or indictment.

PRACTICE POINTER: In addition to bringing an action for false arrest and imprisonment, Court of Claims Act § 8–b provides "innocent persons who have been wrongly convicted of crimes ... an available avenue of redress over and above the existing tort remedies to seek compensation for damages." The statute provides that plaintiff must demonstrate his or her innocence "by clear and convincing evidence." The statute sets forth in detail the requirements of the claim and if the court finds that claimant is entitled to a judgment, "it shall award damages in such sum of money as the court determines will fairly and reasonably compensate [claimant]."

§ 18.25

1. Russo v. New York, 672 F.2d 1014 (2d Cir.1982), modified on other grounds, 721 F.2d 410 (2d Cir.1983) (per curiam) (quoting Martin v. City of Albany, 42 N.Y.2d 13, 16, 396 N.Y.S.2d 612, 614, 364

§ 18.25　　　　　　CIVIL RIGHTS LAW　　　　　　Ch. 18

to the action for malicious prosecution.[2]

The Second Circuit has traditionally applied the state law standard to a Section 1983 claim for malicious prosecution, with the added requirement that a cause of action for malicious prosecution will lie under Section 1983 only if plaintiff's federal constitutional or statutory rights are implicated.[3]

The limitations period for a Section 1983 claim based on malicious prosecution begins to run when the underlying criminal action is conclusively terminated, rather than at time of arrest.[4]

Compensatory damages for a malicious prosecution claim include any damages that are "the direct, natural and proximate results of the criminal prosecution, and may include damages for suffering the indigni-

---

N.E.2d 1304 (1977)); *see also*, Bernard v. United States, 25 F.3d 98, 104 (2d Cir. 1994); Broughton, § 18.22 *supra* note 2, 37 N.Y.2d at 457, 373 N.Y.S.2d at 93, 335 N.E.2d at 314; Loeb v. Teitelbaum, 77 A.D.2d 92, 432 N.Y.S.2d 487 (2d Dep't 1980).

2. Janetka v. Dabe, 892 F.2d 187, 189 (2d Cir.1989)(citing Munoz v. City of New York, 18 N.Y.2d 6, 10, 271 N.Y.S.2d 645, 649, 218 N.E.2d 527, 529 (1966)) ("It is kind of a pre-condition to the later action, the *sine qua non* ...") Dismissal of the indictment with leave to replead does not constitute a termination of the proceeding in plaintiff's favor. Russell v. Smith, 68 F.3d 33, 36 (2d Cir.1995).

Similarly, if a prosecution is never commenced, a claim will not lie. A claim of malicious prosecution only arises after an arraignment or indictment. Stile v. City of New York, 172 A.D.2d 743, 569 N.Y.S.2d 129 (2d Dep't 1991).

CAVEAT: If alleging a state law malicious prosecution claim against the City of New York, State of New York or another municipality, a Notice of Claim must be filed within ninety days of the date that the charges against plaintiff are dismissed. *See supra*, § 18.20, note 2.

3. Lennon, § 18.22 *supra* note 1, 66 F.3d at 425; *see also*, *supra*, Heck, § 18.23, note 4, 114 S.Ct. at 2372.

CAVEAT: The recent Supreme Court decision in Albright v. Oliver, § 18.22 *supra* note 3, forecloses the assertion of malicious prosecution claims as a substantive due process claim under Section 1983. In Singer v. Fulton County Sheriff, 63 F.3d 110 (2d Cir. 1995), the Second Circuit recognized that Albright left available the remedy of asserting a federal claim for malicious prosecution under the Fourth Amendment but stated that "the extent of those rights ... remains to be defined by the Court." 63 F.3d at 115. The court recognized that to state a claim under Section 1983 and the Fourth Amendment, plaintiff must show a "deprivation of liberty consistent with the concept of a 'seizure.'" 63 F.3d at 116. Since, however, the lower courts have not yet grappled with Albright, the Second Circuit has cautioned that the effect of Albright on malicious prosecution claims is unclear. *See supra*, Pinaud, § 18.20, note 3.

4. Murphy v. Lynn, 53 F.3d 547, 548 (2d Cir.1995). This comports with the nature of a malicious prosecution claim, which is a challenge to the post-arraignment deprivation of liberty, as opposed to a false arrest claim, which concerns the arrest and imprisonment before a judicial proceeding has been commenced. *See* discussion in Singer v. Fulton County Sheriff, 63 F.3d 110, 117 (2d Cir.1995) and Broughton, § 18.22 *supra* note 2, 37 N.Y.2d at 456–57, 373 N.Y.S.2d at 93, 335 N.E.2d at 314.

PRACTICE POINTER: Although the claim of malicious prosecution under Section 1983 is governed by state law (Russell v. Smith, 68 F.3d 33 (2d Cir.1995)) there is one important difference, which may be the deciding factor in determining whether to bring a malicious prosecution claim under Section 1983 or whether to bring a common law claim. While the Statute of Limitations for a malicious prosecution claim under Section 1983 is three years (*see supra*, Murphy), the Statute of Limitations under CPLR 215 is only one year.

ties of arrest and imprisonment, injury to reputation and compensation for attorney's fees expended in the defense of the criminal prosecution."[5]

The defense of absolute immunity is available to prosecutors in a malicious prosecution claim.[6] *See infra*, Section 18.31. Qualified immunity is also available as a defense to a malicious prosecution claim, under the same standard as a false arrest claim. *See infra*, Section 18.32

Library References:

West's Key No. Digests, Civil Rights ⬯114, 134.

§ 18.26 First Amendment

The First Amendment to the United States Constitution provides in pertinent part that "Congress shall make no law respecting an establishment of religion, or prohibiting the free exercise thereof; or abridging the freedom of speech, or of the press...."[1] Similar protection of freedom of speech, freedom of the press and freedom of religion are contained in the New York Constitution. Article I, section 8 of the New York Constitution provides that:

> Every citizen may freely speak, write and publish his sentiments on all subjects, being responsible for the abuse of that right; and no law shall be passed to restrain or abridge the liberty of speech or of the press. In all criminal prosecutions or indictments for libels, the truth may be given in evidence to the jury; and if it shall appear to the jury that the matter charged as libelous is true, and was published with good motives and for justifiable ends, the party shall be acquitted; and the jury shall have the right to determine the law and the fact.

The guarantee of freedom of religion is set forth in Article I, Section 3 of the New York Constitution, which states:

> The free exercise and enjoyment of religious profession and worship, without discrimination or preference, shall forever be allowed in this

---

5. Colon, § 18.23 *supra* note 1, 37 N.Y.2d at 459, 373 N.Y.S.2d at 96, 335 N.E.2d at 315; Loeb v. Teitelbaum, 77 A.D.2d 92, 432 N.Y.S.2d 487, 496 (2d Dep't 1980). Punitive damages are also available in an action for malicious prosecution if defendant was motivated by actual malice or in reckless disregard for plaintiff's rights. *Id.*

6. The defense is available, depending upon the nature of the function the prosecutors performed (*see infra*, § 18.31), even where prosecutors act in a "disgraceful" manner. Pinaud, § 18.20 *supra* note 3, 52 F.3d at 1147.

PRACTICE POINTER: It may be possible to avoid the absolute immunity defense by naming the county as a defendant. To do so, the complaint must allege deficiencies in the management of the district attorney's office (Walker v. City of New York, 974 F.2d 293, 301 (2d Cir.1992), cert. denied 507 U.S. 961, 113 S.Ct. 1387, 122 L.Ed.2d 762 (1993)) or that the district attorney's office had a "long history of negligent disciplinary practices regarding law enforcement personnel, which gave rise to the individual defendant's conduct in promoting the malicious prosecution" in the case. Gentile v. County of Suffolk, 926 F.2d 142 (2d Cir. 1991). Essentially, the complaint must allege that the way in which the prosecutor's office is administered somehow led to the malicious prosecution.

§ 18.26

1. U.S. Constitution, amend. I.

§ 18.26　　　　　CIVIL RIGHTS LAW　　　　　Ch. 18

state to all mankind; and no person shall be rendered incompetent to be a witness on account of his opinions on matters of religious belief; but the liberty of conscience hereby secured shall not be so construed as to excuse acts of licentiousness, or justify practices inconsistent with the peace or safety of this state.

These provisions are discussed in the next two sections, which concern "First Amendment"–type actions in state court.

§ 18.27　First Amendment—Freedom of Speech

In *O'Neill v. Oakgrove Constr., Inc.*,[1] the Court of Appeals noted that "[t]he protection afforded by the guarantees of free press and speech in the New York Constitution is often broader than the minimum required by the First Amendment" and further noted that the expansive language in the New York State Constitution was adopted prior to the application of the First Amendment to the states.[2] New York has a history of affording protection to the press, as noted in decisions of the Court of Appeals[3] and by the adoption of statutes which provide specific guarantees.[4]

In New York, the guarantee of freedom of speech seemingly collides with the common law action for libel and slander. *See also,* discussion of libel and slander, Sections 18.81 and 18.82 *infra*. Expressions of "pure opinion" are accorded greater protection under New York law than under federal law.[5]

Freedom of speech issues also arise in challenges to certain criminal statutes. Challenges to New York Penal Law § 240.30(2), the crime of aggravated harassment, on the basis that the statute violates both the New York and United States Constitutions because it prohibits constitutionally protected speech, have failed in the Court of Appeals.[6] Similarly,

---

§ 18.27

1. 71 N.Y.2d 521, 528 note 3, 528 N.Y.S.2d 1, 4 note 3, 523 N.E.2d 277 (1988).

2. *See also,* Immuno AG. v. Moor-Jankowski, 77 N.Y.2d 235, 248–49, 566 N.Y.S.2d 906, 913, 567 N.E.2d 1270 (recognizing that as the "cultural center for the Nation," New York has a rich tradition in freedom of speech and of the press), cert. denied 500 U.S. 954, 111 S.Ct. 2261, 114 L.Ed.2d 713 (1991); Goetz v. Kunstler, 164 Misc.2d 557, 625 N.Y.S.2d 447, 451 (Sup. Ct., N.Y. County, 1995) (recognizing that the framers of the New York State Constitution made a "deliberate choice" not to follow the language of the First Amendment, but instead, elected "to set forth our basic democratic ideal of liberty of the press in strong affirmative terms.")(citation omitted).

3. *See supra,* Immuno AG., note 2.

4. *See, e.g.,* the Shield Law, which is set forth in § 79–h of the Civil Rights Law. *See infra,* § 18.85.

5. Guarneri v. Korea News, Inc., 214 A.D.2d 649, 625 N.Y.S.2d 291 (2d Dep't), leave to appeal denied 86 N.Y.2d 706, 632 N.Y.S.2d 500, 656 N.E.2d 599 (1995) (citing Steinhilber v. Alphonse, 68 N.Y.2d 283, 289–90, 508 N.Y.S.2d 901, 903–04, 501 N.E.2d 550 (1986)).

6. People v. Shack, 86 N.Y.2d 529, 634 N.Y.S.2d 660, 658 N.E.2d 706 (1995)(rejecting facial and "as applied" challenge to statute under First and Fourteenth Amendments to Federal Constitution and Article I, § 8 of New York Constitution).

local laws prohibiting soliciting or begging in the subway have been upheld under both the United States and New York Constitutions.[7]

Generally, courts will not enjoin speech, since prior restraints on speech are prohibited under both the First Amendment and the New York Constitution. Special provisions apply, however, with respect to children, such as in divorce cases, in which courts may restrict parents' speech if it is in the best interest of the child.[8]

Library References:

West's Key No. Digests, Constitutional Law ⟜90–90.4(6).

§ 18.28 First Amendment—Freedom of Religion

As set forth above (see supra, § 18.26) the free exercise clause is contained in Article I, Section 3 of the New York Constitution. While it seemingly provides even greater protection than the First Amendment of the United States Constitution,[1] there are a dearth of freedom of religion cases brought in the New York state courts; overwhelmingly, cases dealing with the free exercise of religion are in the federal courts.[2]

Nevertheless, there are some discrete areas within the subject of religious freedom which are more commonly brought in the state courts.[3] The most frequently litigated of these issues concerns the refusal to undergo medical treatment due to religious belief. So long as a plaintiff has sincerely-held religious beliefs, a competent adult cannot be forced to undergo medical treatment which would violate his or her religious

---

7. Young v. New York City Transit Authority, 903 F.2d 146 (2d Cir.), cert. denied 498 U.S. 984, 111 S.Ct. 516, 112 L.Ed.2d 528 (1990); People v. Schrader, 162 Misc.2d 789, 617 N.Y.S.2d 429 (Crim.Ct., N.Y. City, 1994); but see Loper v. New York City Police Dept., 999 F.2d 699 (2d Cir.1993)(finding that begging is protected speech and declaring that Penal Law § 240.35(1) violates the Federal Constitution).

8. See discussion in Stephanie L. v. Benjamin L., 158 Misc.2d 665, 602 N.Y.S.2d 80 (Sup.Ct., N.Y. County, 1993).

§ 18.28

1. See Williams v. Bright, 167 Misc.2d 312, 632 N.Y.S.2d 760, 761 (Sup.Ct., N.Y. County, 1995), which notes that while the First Amendment prohibits the federal government and the states from any official action which would either restrict the free exercise of religion or do anything to establish or promote it, the New York Constitution proclaims that the free exercise and enjoyment of religion shall forever be allowed in the state to all persons "without discrimination or preference."

2. A recently enacted federal statute also provides protection for the exercise of one's religious beliefs. The Freedom of Religion Restoration Act of 1993, 42 U.S.C.A. §§ 2000bb, et seq. ("RFRA") restores the "compelling state interest test" to cases involving the free exercise of religion. RFRA provides that the government may substantially burden one's exercise of religion only upon a demonstration that the burden furthers a compelling governmental interest and is the least restrictive means of furthering that interest. 42 U.S.C.A. § 2000bb–2.

3. Religious freedom issues may arise in the context of an Article 78 proceeding. In Matter of Griffin v. Coughlin, 88 N.Y.2d 674, 649 N.Y.S.2d 903, 673 N.E.2d 98 (1996), discussed in § 18.29, infra, an inmate successfully challenged a prison determination under the Establishment Clause of the First Amendment to the United States Constitution.

precepts except in the face of overriding compelling state interests.[4]

The cases tend to reach a different result, however, where children are involved. Where a parent refuses to provide medical treatment for children based on the parent's religious beliefs, courts have exercised the inherent power of the state to insure the health and welfare of children and have ordered treatment where necessary[5] and have made findings of neglect for failure to provide medical treatment.[6]

The other cases which arise involve issues under state law. For example, in *Williams v. Bright*,[7] the court grappled with an issue of apparent first impression in New York: whether in assessing damages in a personal injury case, the jury could consider the fact that plaintiff's religious beliefs prohibited her from undergoing blood transfusions, and that had she agreed to the transfusions, her recovery would have been lessened and her prognosis for recovery would have been better. After reviewing the law on religion and mitigation of damages in other jurisdictions, and considering the principle that defendants must take their victims as they find them, the court held that plaintiff was not required to mitigate damages by undergoing a transfusion which would have violated her religious beliefs.

In *LaRocca v. Lane*,[8] the Court of Appeals held that a court was within its power to order a defense attorney, who was also a Roman Catholic priest, to change his clerical garb prior to the commencement of a criminal jury trial.

---

4. *See generally*, Rivers v. Katz, 67 N.Y.2d 485, 504 N.Y.S.2d 74, 495 N.E.2d 337 (1986) (establishing procedure for determining consent for an involuntarily committed mental patient for use of antipsychotic drugs); *see* Rockland Psychiatric Ctr. v. Virginia G., 166 Misc.2d 659, 634 N.Y.S.2d 648 (Sup.Ct., Rockland County, 1995) (authorizing use of psychotropic drugs where patient offered no evidence that she had been a practicing Christian Scientist, patient lacked the capacity to make a reasoned decision regarding the proposed treatment, and the proposed treatment is narrowly tailored to serve the patient's interests).

5. Matter of Sampson, 65 Misc.2d 658, 317 N.Y.S.2d 641 (Fam.Ct., Ulster County, 1970) (ordering child's surgical procedure to go forward and authorizing blood transfusions over the mother's religious objections), aff'd 37 A.D.2d 668, 323 N.Y.S.2d 253, (3d Dep't), appeal denied 29 N.Y.2d 486, 325 N.Y.S.2d 1026, 275 N.E.2d 339 (1971).

But see Public Health Law § 2164, which requires children to receive certain immunizations before they may be admitted to attend school. Section 2164(9) provides an exception for children "whose parent, parents, or guardian hold genuine and sincere religious beliefs which are contrary to the practices herein required, and no certificate shall be required as a prerequisite to such children being admitted or received into school or attending school." If a parent's objections to vaccinations are not predicated on sincerely held religious beliefs, the exemption will not apply. Matter of Christine M., 157 Misc.2d 4, 595 N.Y.S.2d 606 (Fam.Ct., Kings County, 1992) (finding that parent's objection to vaccination was not based on religious convictions).

6. *See* Family Court Act § 1012(f) for the definition of a neglected child; *see also*, Matter of Christine M., 157 Misc.2d 4, 595 N.Y.S.2d 606 (Fam.Ct., Kings County, 1992)(finding of neglect for refusing to provide immunizations); Matter of Gregory S., 85 Misc.2d 846, 380 N.Y.S.2d 620 (Fam.Ct., Kings County, 1976)(same).

7. Williams, *supra* note 1.

8. 37 N.Y.2d 575, 376 N.Y.S.2d 93, 338 N.E.2d 606 (1975), cert. denied 424 U.S. 968, 96 S.Ct. 1464, 47 L.Ed.2d 734 (1976).

In *Trietley v. Board of Ed. of City of Buffalo*,[9] the court found that the Board of Education had no authority to permit a proposed bible club to meet in a public school, but that even if there were such authority, allowing such a club to meet would violate the First Amendment. The United States Supreme Court, however, held in *Lamb's Chapel v. Center Moriches Union Free School District*,[10] that the school district does have the authority to allow a church's request to use school facilities to show religious oriented films on family values and child rearing. The court held that it was not an establishment of religion to allow the films to be shown, but reaffirmed support for *Trietley*.

Library References:

West's Key No. Digests, Constitutional Law ⚖84–84.5(19).

§ 18.29 Rights of Prisoners

While no discussion of civil rights would be complete without mentioning the rights of prisoners, a thorough discussion of rights of pretrial detainees and convicted inmates is beyond the scope of the confines of this chapter. A few cautionary points, however, are set forth in this section in the event the reader is wholly unfamiliar with prisoner rights litigation in New York State.

If counsel is representing a convicted inmate in the state correctional system who plans to bring an action against officers or employees of the Department of Correctional Services in their personal capacities, the action may only be commenced in the appropriate federal district court or in the Court of Claims. Correction Law § 24 prohibits a civil action from being brought against officers or employees of the Department in any court of the state, except that an action for damages may be brought against the State of New York in the Court of Claims. The only actions or proceedings that are appropriately commenced in the New York State supreme court are cases brought under Article 78 of the CPLR and actions solely seeking declaratory and injunctive relief.[1]

Accordingly, a claim for monetary damages for a state inmate should be brought either in federal district court under Section 1983 and the appropriate constitutional amendments[2] or should be filed in the Court of Claims against the State of New York.

---

9. 65 A.D.2d 1, 409 N.Y.S.2d 912 (4th Dep't 1978).

10. 508 U.S. 384, 113 S.Ct. 2141, 124 L.Ed.2d 352 (1993).

§ 18.29

1. *See, e.g.*, Matter of Griffin v. Coughlin, 88 N.Y.2d 674, 649 N.Y.S.2d 903, 673 N.E.2d 98 (1996). In Griffin, the court held that the Establishment Clause of the United States Constitution prohibited the Department of Correctional Services from denying an atheist or agnostic inmate the opportunity to participate in family visitation privileges based on the inmate's refusal to participate in an alcohol and drug addiction program that adopts the religious-oriented practices of Alcoholics Anonymous.

2. Claims for a convicted inmate may be brought either under the Eighth or Fourteenth Amendments. A claim on behalf of a pre-trial detainee, however, cannot be

§ 18.30 Defenses to Federal Actions

While there are some defenses that are common to claims asserted under both federal and state law, some defenses are only appropriately asserted in response to a federal court action or may only be asserted as a defense to a federal cause of action in either state or federal court. For example, the Eleventh Amendment defense (*see infra*, Section 18.33) only applies to an action pending in federal court. While qualified immunity may be pleaded as a defense to an action in either state or federal court, qualified immunity only applies if a defendant violates a federal statutory or constitutional right; it does not apply to a violation of state law. *See infra*, Section 18.32. These and other common defenses to federal claims are set forth in Sections 18.31 through 18.39.

§ 18.31 Defenses to Federal Actions—Absolute Immunity

"Absolute immunity from liability has been accorded to a few types of government officials whose duties are deemed as a matter of public policy to require such protection to enable them to function independently and effectively, without fear or harassment."[1] Among those entitled to assert the defense of absolute immunity are judges,[2]

brought under the Eighth Amendment, and is only appropriately brought under the Fourteenth Amendment.

§ 18.31

1. Barrett v. United States, 798 F.2d 565, 571 (2d Cir.1986).

2. Under federal law, judges are entitled to absolute immunity for acts performed in the exercise of their judicial function, Pierson v. Ray, 386 U.S. 547, 87 S.Ct. 1213, 18 L.Ed.2d 288 (1967), but not for administrative decisions, Forrester v. White, 484 U.S. 219, 108 S.Ct. 538, 98 L.Ed.2d 555 (1988), or for acts undertaken in the absence of any jurisdiction. In Mireles v. Waco, 502 U.S. 9, 112 S.Ct. 286, 116 L.Ed.2d 9 (1991) the Supreme Court granted a judge absolute immunity for allegedly ordering police officers to bring an attorney before him, even though the judge ordered the officers to use excessive force to seize the attorney and bring him to the courtroom.

The New York courts similarly afford judges absolute immunity, except for those acts performed in the absence of their jurisdiction. Lombardoni v. Boccaccio, 121 A.D.2d 828, 504 N.Y.S.2d 260 (3d Dep't 1986) (even though judge may have exceeded his jurisdiction by authorizing plaintiff's arrest, judge is still entitled to absolute immunity since his actions were not in complete absence of jurisdiction).

In addition to judges, other court personnel have been granted absolute immunity for their roles in assisting the judiciary by performing quasi-judicial functions. Oliva v. Heller, 839 F.2d 37 (2d Cir.1988) (extending the absolute immunity granted to judges to law clerks assisting judges in the performance of their duties); Scott v. Dixon, 720 F.2d 1542, 1546 (11th Cir.1983), cert. denied 469 U.S. 832, 105 S.Ct. 122, 83 L.Ed.2d 64 (1984) (according absolute immunity to court clerks who perform discretionary acts of a judicial nature); Bettencourt v. Board of Registration in Medicine, 904 F.2d 772, 784–85 (1st Cir.1990) (extending absolute immunity to staff members of a state disciplinary board).

Witnesses in a judicial proceeding are also accorded absolute immunity. Briscoe v. LaHue, 460 U.S. 325, 330–334, 103 S.Ct. 1108, 1112–13, 75 L.Ed.2d 96 (1983). In Antoine v. Byers & Anderson, Inc., 508 U.S. 429,

Ch. 18 ABSOLUTE IMMUNITY § 18.31

prosecutors,[3] legislators[4] and certain high executive officers engaged in prosecutorial-like or quasi-judicial functions.[5] Like qualified immunity, (*see infra*, Section 18.32), absolute immunity only protects a defendant from an award of damages; the defendant is not immune from an award of injunctive relief. Since absolute immunity is an affirmative defense, it can be waived if not pleaded in an answer or motion.[6] If a district court denies the defense, the denial is immediately appealable to the Second Circuit

113 S.Ct. 2167, 124 L.Ed.2d 391 (1993), the Supreme Court held court reporters are not entitled to absolute immunity for failure to produce the transcript from a federal criminal trial.

3. There continues to be extensive litigation with respect to the circumstances under which a prosecutor may be entitled to the absolute immunity defense. Essentially, the defense only applies when performing prosecutorial functions. Imbler v. Pachtman, 424 U.S. 409, 96 S.Ct. 984, 47 L.Ed.2d 128 (1976); Pinaud, § 18.20 *supra* note 3, 52 F.3d 1139 (absolute immunity extends to bail applications and a decision to arrange for prisoner's transfer from federal to state custody to facilitate state prosecution but does not extend to decision to keep plaintiff in custody for three weeks after dismissal of charges against him). When a prosecutor's role is more akin to that of an investigator or police officer, courts decline to shield their conduct in the cloak of absolute immunity. *See* Buckley v. Fitzsimmons, 509 U.S. 259, 113 S.Ct. 2606, 125 L.Ed.2d 209 (1993)(prosecutor not entitled to absolute immunity when conducting investigative work and for allegedly making false statements when announcing an indictment); Burns v. Reed, 500 U.S. 478, 111 S.Ct. 1934, 114 L.Ed.2d 547 (1991) (no absolute immunity to prosecutor when giving legal advice to police concerning investigative technique); Hill v. City of New York, 45 F.3d 653 (2d Cir.1995) (no absolute immunity for acts of investigation or administration); Dory v. Ryan, 25 F.3d 81, 83 (2d Cir.1994) (role of district attorney insofar as he performed as an investigator is not entitled to absolute immunity); Day v. Morgenthau, 909 F.2d 75, 77 (2d Cir.1990) (no immunity for assisting in search and seizure or arrest). Similarly, when a prosecutor acts manifestly beyond the jurisdiction of a prosecutor, there is no immunity. Doe v. Phillips, 81 F.3d 1204 (2d Cir.1996) (no immunity for prosecutor who threatened continued prosecution of a criminal case unless a woman swore her innocence on a bible in church).

The New York courts also afford prosecutors absolute immunity. Arteaga v. State of New York, 72 N.Y.2d 212, 217 note 1, 532 N.Y.S.2d 57, 60 note 1, 527 N.E.2d 1194 (1988); Rosen & Bardunias v. County of Westchester, 158 A.D.2d 679, 552 N.Y.S.2d 134 (2d Dep't 1990) (prosecutor absolutely immune notwithstanding allegations that he acted with malice). Where, however, a prosecutor acts outside of his or her authority, New York courts also refuse to accord absolute immunity. Della Pietra v. State, 71 N.Y.2d 792, 796, 530 N.Y.S.2d 510, 512, 526 N.E.2d 1 (1988); Claude H. v. County of Oneida, 214 A.D.2d 964, 626 N.Y.S.2d 933 (4th Dep't 1995) (no absolute immunity for directing police to make arrest).

4. Eastland v. United States Servicemen's Fund, 421 U.S. 491, 95 S.Ct. 1813, 44 L.Ed.2d 324 (1975).

5. Butz v. Economou, 438 U.S. 478, 515–17, 98 S.Ct. 2894, 2915–16, 57 L.Ed.2d 895 (1978); Rudow v. City of New York, 822 F.2d 324, 327–28 (2d Cir.1987); Matter of Kaczmarek v. Conroy, 218 A.D.2d 97, 635 N.Y.S.2d 310 (3d Dep't 1995) (local legislators have absolute immunity for legislative acts done in their official capacities and unsubstantiated allegations of improper motivation are insufficient to defeat immunity).

The Second Circuit recently resolved a conflict among the district courts by holding that the official who reviews administrative appeals from prison disciplinary hearings is not entitled to absolute immunity. Young v. Selsky, 41 F.3d 47 (2d Cir. 1994), cert. denied sub nom. Selsky v. Young, 514 U.S. 1102, 115 S.Ct. 1837, 131 L.Ed.2d 756 (1995). Similarly, there is no absolute immunity for prison disciplinary hearing officers. Tulloch v. Coughlin, 50 F.3d 114 (2d Cir.1995). There is absolute immunity, however, for parole commissioners. *See, e.g.*, Quartararo v. Catterson, 917 F.Supp. 919 (E.D.N.Y.1996).

6. Satchell v. Dilworth, 745 F.2d 781, 784 (2d Cir.1984).

§ 18.32 Defenses to Federal Actions—Qualified Immunity

Public officials are entitled to immunity from lawsuits for monetary damages arising out of the performance of their discretionary official acts "insofar as their conduct does not violate clearly established statutory or constitutional rights of which a reasonable person would have known."[1] For a legal right to be "clearly established" at the time that the plaintiff's right is allegedly violated, "[t]he contours of the right must be sufficiently clear that a reasonable official would understand that what he is doing violates that right."[2]

The Second Circuit has cautioned that "[w]hen addressing a claim of qualified immunity, a court must take care not to pose the issue in terms

---

7. 28 U.S.C.A. § 1291; Cohen v. Beneficial Indus. Loan Corp., 337 U.S. 541, 69 S.Ct. 1221, 93 L.Ed. 1528 (1949); see also, Mitchell v. Forsyth, 472 U.S. 511, 105 S.Ct. 2806, 86 L.Ed.2d 411 (1985). Similarly, in a state court action, the denial of an absolute immunity defense is also immediately appealable. CPLR 5701(a); see also, Rodrigues v. City of New York, 193 A.D.2d 79, 602 N.Y.S.2d 337 (1st Dep't 1993).

§ 18.32

1. Harlow v. Fitzgerald, 457 U.S. 800, 818 102 S.Ct. 2727, 2738, 73 L.Ed.2d 396 (1982); Richardson v. Selsky, 5 F.3d 616, 621 (2d Cir.1993) (qualified immunity protects public officials if it was "objectively reasonable for them to believe that their acts did not violate clearly established rights") (citing Anderson v. Creighton, 483 U.S. 635, 638–40, 107 S.Ct. 3034, 3038–39, 97 L.Ed.2d 523 (1987)).

A threshold inquiry is whether plaintiff has alleged a constitutional violation at all. Siegert v. Gilley, 500 U.S. 226, 111 S.Ct. 1789, 114 L.Ed.2d 277 (1991). Qualified immunity does not apply to violations of state law or regulations. Davis v. Scherer, 468 U.S. 183, 104 S.Ct. 3012, 82 L.Ed.2d 139, reh. denied 468 U.S. 1226, 105 S.Ct. 26, 82 L.Ed.2d 919 (1984). "An official who violates state regulations may be held liable in damages under 42 U.S.C. § 1983 only if he also violates federal constitutional or statutory rights clearly established at the time of his actions." Deane v. Dunbar, 777 F.2d 871, 876 (2d Cir.1985) (citing Davis, 468 U.S. at 197, 104 S.Ct. at 3020).

CAVEAT: As set forth in the text, qualified immunity only applies to claims for monetary damages; it does not apply to claims for injunctive relief. Additionally, the defense only applies to claims against defendants named in their individual capacities; it does not apply when defendants are named in their official capacities. See Rodriguez v. City of New York, 72 F.3d 1051 (2d Cir.1995).

Qualified immunity is an affirmative defense that must be pleaded. Failure to assert the defense up to and including trial may constitute a waiver of the defense. Blissett v. Coughlin, 66 F.3d 531 (2d Cir. 1995). If qualified immunity is denied, an immediate interlocutory appeal cannot be taken if the denial is based on a determination that there are genuine issues of material fact. Johnson v. Jones, 515 U.S. 304, 115 S.Ct. 2151, 132 L.Ed.2d 238 (1995).

2. Anderson, supra, note 1, 483 U.S. at 640, 107 S.Ct. at 3039. As the Second Circuit has noted, when considering the defense of qualified immunity,"the inquiry is not whether plaintiff has alleged a violation of an abstract legal standard, but whether under the particular circumstances alleged, defendants could have reasonably believed that they did not violate plaintiff's constitutional rights." Gittens v. LeFevre, 891 F.2d 38, 42 (2d Cir.1989); see also, Fox v. Coughlin, 893 F.2d 475, 477 (2d Cir.1990).

that are too general or abstract."[3] In order to defeat a defendant's claim of qualified immunity, a plaintiff must demonstrate that "in the light of pre-existing law the unlawfulness [of defendants' acts] must be apparent."[4] Further, the determination of whether a right was clearly established when the defendants' acts occurred is based on the decisional law of the Supreme Court and the Second Circuit; decisions of other circuits do not clearly establish the law.[5]

Qualified immunity should be decided "at the earliest possible stage in litigation."[6] Sometimes qualified immunity may be decided on a motion to dismiss, if the issue of immunity is purely a question of law.[7] If factual issues need to be resolved, the issue may be decided on summary judgment, after discovery.[8] Additionally, the United States Supreme Court has warned against "routinely plac[ing] the question of immunity in the hands of the jury. Immunity ordinarily should be decided by the court long before trial.... [In addition], the court should ask whether

---

3. Mozzochi v. Borden, 959 F.2d 1174, 1177 (2d Cir.1992). "[T]he boundaries of the supposed 'right' must be sufficiently definite so that the official understood that his actions violated it or ... the unlawfulness of his actions was evident." Fox, 893 F.2d at 477 (quoting Eng v. Coughlin, 858 F.2d 889, 895 (2d Cir.1988)). The defense is not overcome "when those federal rights exist only generally in the air, so to speak." Eng v. Coughlin, 858 F.2d at 895.

4. Anderson, *supra* note 1, 483 U.S. at 640, 107 S.Ct. at 3039. "An officers' actions are objectively unreasonable when no officer of reasonable competence could have made the same choice in similar circumstances." Lennon v. Miller, 66 F.3d 416, 420–21 (citing Malley v. Briggs, 475 U.S. 335, 341, 106 S.Ct. 1092, 1096, 89 L.Ed.2d 271 (1986)).

5. Francis v. Coughlin, 891 F.2d at 46 (citing Anderson); *see also,* Soares v. State of Connecticut, 8 F.3d 917, 922 (2d Cir. 1993).

In Weber v. Dell, 804 F.2d 796, 803 (2d Cir.1986), cert. denied sub nom. 483 U.S. 1020, 107 S.Ct. 3263, 97 L.Ed.2d 762 (1987), the Second Circuit held that a right will be clearly established even if there is no Second Circuit or Supreme Court decision establishing a right if other circuits have decided the issue and there is "supportive language" in any Second Circuit decisions concerning the issue. Qualified immunity was rejected in Weber since there had been seven decisions in other circuits holding the very conduct at issue unconstitutional and several Second Circuit decisions had condemned the practice at issue. Conversely, in Shabazz v. Coughlin, 852 F.2d 697 (2d Cir. 1988), which concerned an inmate's claim that he was unconstitutionally disciplined for leading group prayer in the prison yard, qualified immunity did lie because there was a "legitimate question" as to whether a prisoner had a right to engage in prayer in the prison yard. Although a prisoner's right to engage in religious practices was generally accepted, the Second Circuit had not then nor since directly addressed the constitutionality of restrictions on group prayer and prayer in prison yards. Since there were no decisions in the circuit clearly foreshadowing a ruling on the constitutionality of the restrictions at issue, nor were there cases in other circuits condemning or condoning such practices, qualified immunity was available to defendants. 852 F.2d at 700–01.

6. Hunter v. Bryant, 502 U.S. 224, 227, 112 S.Ct. 534, 536, 116 L.Ed.2d 589 (1991). In Mitchell v. Forsyth, 472 U.S. 511, 525–26, 105 S.Ct. 2806, 2814–15, 86 L.Ed.2d 411 (1985), the court observed that "[u]nless the plaintiff's allegations state a claim of violation of clearly established law, a defendant pleading qualified immunity is entitled to dismissal before the commencement of discovery."

7. Molinelli v. Tucker, 901 F.2d 13 (2d Cir.1990).

8. Warren v. Dwyer, 906 F.2d 70, 76 (2d Cir.), cert. denied 498 U.S. 967, 111 S.Ct. 431, 112 L.Ed.2d 414 (1990)(court should decide qualified immunity on motion for summary judgment or on motion for a directed verdict).

the [officials] acted reasonably under settled law in the circumstances, not whether another reasonable, or more reasonable, interpretation of the events can be constructed . . . after the fact."[9]

In *Robison v. Via*,[10] the Second Circuit enumerated three methods whereby the defense of qualified immunity may be established. The first basis for establishing qualified immunity is if, at the time the defendant officials acted, "it was unclear whether plaintiff's asserted interests were protected by federal law."[11] Second, qualified immunity would also be available if defendants show that "even if the interest asserted by the plaintiff was clearly of a type generally protected by federal law . . . it was not clear at the time of the acts at issue that an exception did not permit those acts."[12] A third basis upon which a defense of qualified immunity could lie is that "even if the contours of the plaintiff's federal rights and the official's permissible actions were clearly delineated at the time of the acts complained of, . . . it was objectively reasonable for [defendants] to believe that [their] acts did not violate those rights."[13]

If the defendant's conduct is objectively reasonable but an unconstitutional subjective intent is alleged, plaintiff must come forward with particularized evidence of direct or circumstantial facts supporting the claim of improper motive in order to defeat summary judgment. This "particularized evidence" may include expressions by public officials regarding their state of mind, circumstances suggesting that plaintiff was singled out, or the unusual nature of actions taken.[14]

Library References:

West's Key No. Digests, Civil Rights ⚖=214(1)–214(9).

§ 18.33 Defenses to Federal Actions—Eleventh Amendment

Under the Eleventh Amendment to the United States Constitution, an unconsenting state is immune from suit in federal court.[1] Even

---

9. Hunter v. Bryant, 502 U.S. 224, 228, 112 S.Ct. 534, 537, 116 L.Ed.2d 589 (1991) (citations omitted).

10. 821 F.2d 913 (2d Cir.1987).

11. *Id.* at 920.

12. *Id.* at 921.

13. *Id.* The Second Circuit has emphasized that summary judgment is available, even under this third alternative, if the defendant can elicit such facts so that " 'no reasonable jury, looking at the evidence in the light most favorable to, and drawing all inferences most favorable to, the plaintiff[], could conclude that it was objectively unreasonable for the defendant[]' to believe that he was acting in a fashion that did not clearly violate an established federally protected right." *Id.* (quoting Halperin v. Kissinger, 807 F.2d 180, 189 (D.C.Cir.1986)).

14. Blue v. Koren, 72 F.3d 1075 (2d Cir.1995).

§ 18.33

1. Seminole Tribe of Florida v. Florida, 517 U.S. 44, ___, 116 S.Ct. 1114, 1122, 134 L.Ed.2d 252 (1996); United States v. Lopez, 514 U.S. 549, 115 S.Ct. 1624, 131 L.Ed.2d 626 (1995); Edelman v. Jordan, 415 U.S. 651, 663–64, 94 S.Ct. 1347, 1355–56, 39 L.Ed.2d 662 (1974); Trotman v. Palisades Interstate Park Comm'n, 557 F.2d 35, 40 (2d Cir.1977) (New York is an unconsenting state).

though a state is not named as a party, a suit will nonetheless be barred where the defendant is an agency of the state[2] or the defendant is a state official sued in his official capacity for damages,[3] since such actions are deemed to be against the state.

The Eleventh Amendment also bars recovery of an award of retroactive monetary relief against the state or an agency of the state,[4] but does not preclude an award of prospective injunctive relief.[5]

Library References:

West's Key No. Digests, Federal Courts ⌕265.

§ 18.34 Defenses to Federal Actions—*Monell* and Its Progeny

In *Monell v. New York City Dep't of Soc. Servs.*,[1] the Supreme Court held that municipalities and other local governments cannot be held liable under Section 1983 "unless action pursuant to official municipal policy of some nature caused a constitutional tort."[2]

To hold a municipality liable for the conduct of employees below the level of policy makers (*e.g.*, police officers), plaintiff must demonstrate that "the violation of his constitutional rights resulted from a municipal

The Eleventh Amendment does not apply in the state courts. Nevada v. Hall, 440 U.S. 410, 99 S.Ct. 1182, 59 L.Ed.2d 416 (1979).

2. Pennhurst State School & Hospital v. Halderman, 465 U.S. 89, 100, 104 S.Ct. 900, 907, 79 L.Ed.2d 67 (1984); Quern v. Jordan, 440 U.S. 332, 99 S.Ct. 1139, 59 L.Ed.2d 358 (1979); Alabama v. Pugh, 438 U.S. 781, 98 S.Ct. 3057, 57 L.Ed.2d 1114 (1978); Santiago v. New York State Dep't of Correctional Servs., 945 F.2d 25, 28 note 1 (2d Cir.1991), cert. denied 502 U.S. 1094, 112 S.Ct. 1168, 117 L.Ed.2d 414 (1992).

3. Ying Jing Gan v. City of New York, 996 F.2d 522 (2d Cir.1993).

CAVEAT: In Ying Jing Gan, the Second Circuit noted that " '[i]n many cases,' a complaint against public officials 'will not clearly specify whether officials are sued personally, in their official capacity or both,' " Ying Jing Gan, *supra*, 996 F.2d at 530 (citations omitted). To avoid confusion and possible dismissal of claims, counsel should indicate that defendants are being sued in either their individual or official capacities or both in the caption of the complaint and/or in the body of the complaint in which the parties are described.

4. Pennhurst, *supra* note 2, 465 U.S. at 103, 104 S.Ct. at 909; Edelman, 415 U.S. at 663–64, 94 S.Ct. at 1356; *see also*, McClary v. O'Hare, 786 F.2d 83, 89–90 (2d Cir.1986); Eshun v. New York State Dep't of Social Services, 652 F.Supp. 455, 459 (S.D.N.Y. 1987). Under a similar theory, the Supreme Court has held that a Section 1983 claim against a state agency must fail since an agency is not a "person" within the meaning of Section 1983. Will v. Michigan Department of State Police, 491 U.S. 58, 109 S.Ct. 2304, 105 L.Ed.2d 45 (1989).

5. Ex parte Young, 209 U.S. 123, 156, 28 S.Ct. 441, 452, 52 L.Ed. 714 (1908); Minotti v. Lensink, 798 F.2d 607, 609 (2d Cir.1986), cert. denied 482 U.S. 906, 107 S.Ct. 2484, 96 L.Ed.2d 376 (1987).

§ 18.34

1. 436 U.S. 658, 98 S.Ct. 2018, 56 L.Ed.2d 611 (1978).

2. Monell, *supra* note 1, 436 U.S. at 691, 98 S.Ct. at 2036. The court concluded that "a local government may not be sued under Section 1983 for an injury inflicted solely by its employees or agents. Instead, it is when execution of a government's policy or custom, whether made by its lawmakers or by those whose edicts or acts may fairly be said to represent official policy, inflicts the injury that the government as an entity is responsible under § 1983." *Id.* at 694, 98 S.Ct. at 2037–38.

custom or policy."[3] A municipality's failure to adequately train its police officers can provide a basis for liability for injuries if plaintiff can show that the inadequate training constitutes "deliberate indifference" to the rights of the public.[4] The focus on such a case must be on the adequacy of the training program and there must be a close relationship between the flaw in the training program and the resulting injury to plaintiff.

An outgrowth of *Monell* is the decision in *DeShaney v. Winnebago County Dep't of Social Servs.*,[5] in which the Supreme Court held that the county had no duty to protect a child against beatings by his father, notwithstanding the fact that the government had received reports of such abuse. *DeShaney* stands for the proposition that generally, a cause of action will not lie based on an allegation that defendants simply failed to act to protect the plaintiff. If, however, plaintiff can allege that defendants acted in a way to increase the danger to the plaintiff, such as, for example, assisting in creating the danger to plaintiff, this could be sufficient to hold defendants liable.[6]

Library References:

West's Key No. Digests, Civil Rights ⚖206(3).

3. Ricciuti v. New York City Transit Auth., 941 F.2d 119, 122 (2d Cir.1991). In Ricciuti, the court went on to state that a single incident alleged in a complaint is insufficient to show a municipal policy and to hold the municipality liable. What is necessary is an allegation that the municipality "so failed to train its employees as to display a deliberate indifference to the constitutional rights of those within its jurisdiction" or "evidence that the municipality had notice of but repeatedly failed to make any meaningful investigation into charges that police officers had used excessive force in violation of the complainants' civil rights." Ricciuti, 941 F.2d at 123 (citations omitted); *see also*, Town of Orangetown v. Magee, 88 N.Y.2d 41, 48–49, 643 N.Y.S.2d 21, 25, 665 N.E.2d 1061, 1065 (1996).

CAVEAT: In Dwares v. City of New York, 985 F.2d 94 (2d Cir.1993), the court found insufficient an allegation that the city "knowingly, recklessly, negligently failed to, and was deliberately indifferent to the need to provide adequate training, monitoring and supervision of the defendant police officers with respect to their obligation to protect citizens engaged in protected First Amendment activity from unlawful and unjustified intrusions on the exercise of those rights." *Id.* at 100. In Leatherman v. Tarrant County Narcotics Intelligence & Coordination Unit, 507 U.S. 163, 113 S.Ct. 1160, 122 L.Ed.2d 517 (1993), however, the Supreme Court, rejected a "heightened pleading standard" for municipal liability claims under Section 1983. The court stated that there is no requirement that a plaintiff must do more than plead a single instance of misconduct to establish municipal liability. 507 U.S. at 167, 113 S.Ct. at 1162. Although at least two district courts have recognized that Leatherman apparently changes the law in the Second Circuit, the Second Circuit has not had an opportunity to address the effect of Leatherman on Monell-type claims. *See* Javid v. Scott, 913 F.Supp. 223 (S.D.N.Y.1996); Simpkins v. Bellevue Hosp., 832 F.Supp. 69, 74 note 3 (S.D.N.Y.1993).

PRACTICE POINTER: Punitive damages are not available against a municipality in a Section 1983 action. City of Newport v. Fact Concerts, 453 U.S. 247, 271, 101 S.Ct. 2748, 2762, 69 L.Ed.2d 616 (1981).

4. City of Canton v. Harris, 489 U.S. 378, 109 S.Ct. 1197, 103 L.Ed.2d 412 (1989).

5. 489 U.S. 189, 109 S.Ct. 998, 103 L.Ed.2d 249 (1989).

6. *See supra*, Dwares, § 18.18, *supra*, note 1, in which the defendant police officers were alleged to have actually played a part in assisting or increasing the danger to

§ 18.35 Defenses to Federal Actions—*Respondeat Superior*

A defendant's personal involvement in an alleged deprivation is a prerequisite to an award of damages under Section 1983.[1] A defendant cannot be held liable under a theory of *respondeat superior* since the doctrine of *respondeat superior* does not apply to civil rights actions.[2] A supervisory official may be personally involved in a constitutional deprivation within the meaning of Section 1983 in four ways: (1) the official may have directly participated in the violation; (2) the official, after learning of the violation through a report or appeal, may have failed to remedy the wrong; (3) the official may be liable because he or she created a policy or custom under which unconstitutional practices occurred, or allowed such a policy or custom to continue; or (4) the official may be personally liable if he or she was grossly negligent in managing subordinates who caused the unlawful condition or event.[3]

Library References:

West's Key No. Digests, Civil Rights ⊘=205(1, 2), 206(2.1).

§ 18.36 Defenses to Federal Actions—Abstention

The doctrine of abstention, which is derived from fundamental principles of federalism and comity, counsels against the federal court's involvement in areas that are committed to the jurisdiction of state bodies.[1] In *Younger v. Harris*,[2] the Supreme Court recognized that "courts of equity should not act to restrain a criminal prosecution, when the moving party has an adequate remedy at law."[3]

plaintiff by aiding and abetting in the assault against him.

§ 18.35

1. Moffitt v. Town of Brookfield, 950 F.2d 880, 886 (2d Cir.1991); Barbera v. Smith, 836 F.2d 96, 99 (2d Cir.1987), cert. denied 489 U.S. 1065, 109 S.Ct. 1338, 103 L.Ed.2d 808 (1989); Gill v. Mooney, 824 F.2d 192, 196 (2d Cir.1987); Williams v. Smith, 781 F.2d 319, 323 (2d Cir.1986), cert. denied sub nom. Patterson v. McKinnon, 434 U.S. 1087, 98 S.Ct. 1282, 55 L.Ed.2d 792 (1978).

2. Al–Jundi v. Estate of Rockefeller, 885 F.2d 1060, 1065 (2d Cir.1989); Ayers v. Coughlin, 780 F.2d 205, 210 (2d Cir.1985) (mere "linkage in the prison chain of command" insufficient).

CAVEAT: A complaint should set forth specific instances or concrete examples of the alleged wrongdoing on the part of defendants. The Second Circuit has cautioned that "a complaint consisting of nothing more than naked assertions, and setting forth no facts upon which a court could find a violation of the Civil Rights Act, fails to state a claim under rule 12(b)(6)." Martin v. New York State Dept. of Mental Hygiene, 588 F.2d 371, 372 (2d Cir.1978); *see also*, San Filippo v. U.S. Trust Co., 737 F.2d 246, 256 (2d Cir.1984), cert. denied 470 U.S. 1035, 105 S.Ct. 1408, 84 L.Ed.2d 797 (1985); Contemporary Mission, Inc. v. U.S. Postal Service, 648 F.2d 97 (2d Cir.1981); Louis v. Ward, 444 F.Supp. 1107, 1109 (S.D.N.Y.1978)(without concrete instances or examples of the challenged practices, complaint is insufficient and must be dismissed).

3. *See supra*, Williams, note 1, 781 F.2d at 323–24.

§ 18.36

1. *See* Railroad Commission of Texas v. Pullman Co., 312 U.S. 496, 498, 61 S.Ct. 643, 644, 85 L.Ed. 971 (1941).

2. 401 U.S. 37, 91 S.Ct. 746, 27 L.Ed.2d 669 (1971).

3. Id., 401 U.S. at 43, 91 S.Ct. at 750.

In *Younger*, the Supreme Court held that a federal district court could not enjoin an ongoing state criminal proceeding in order to entertain constitutional challenges to the criminal statute under which the defendant was being prosecuted when such arguments could be heard and decided in the state proceeding. The *Younger* abstention doctrine has been extended to include civil proceedings and state administrative proceedings provided "the State's interests in the proceeding are so important that exercise of the federal judicial power would disregard the comity between the states and the national government."[4]

The Second Circuit has articulated three questions which must be answered affirmatively in order for a court to abstain under *Younger*: "(1) is there an ongoing state proceeding; (2) is an important state interest implicated; and (3) does the plaintiff have an avenue open for review of constitutional claims in the state court?"[5]

Abstention is also appropriate if the case involves complex state law questions bearing on substantial policy issues. This is referred to as "Burford abstention," after the Supreme Court decision in *Burford v. Sun Oil Co.*[6] A third category of abstention, "Pullman abstention," after the Supreme Court decision in *Railroad Comm'n of Texas v. Pullman Co.*,[7] provides that abstention is appropriate when the case involves an interpretation of state law. Pullman abstention is warranted when (1) there is an unclear state statute or uncertain state law issue; (2) the determination of the federal issue depends on the resolution of that provision of state law; and (3) the state law provision is susceptible to an interpretation that would avoid or modify the federal constitutional question at issue.[8]

---

4. Pennzoil Co. v. Texaco, Inc., 481 U.S. 1, 11, 107 S.Ct. 1519, 1526, 95 L.Ed.2d 1 (1987); CECOS International, Inc. v. Jorling, 895 F.2d 66, 70 (2d Cir.1990); *see also*, Ohio Civil Rights Comm'n v. Dayton Christian Schools, Inc., 477 U.S. 619, 627–29, 106 S.Ct. 2718, 2722–23, 91 L.Ed.2d 512 (1986) (state administrative civil rights proceedings); Middlesex County Ethics Comm. v. Garden State Bar Ass'n, 457 U.S. 423, 432–34, 102 S.Ct. 2515, 2521–22, 73 L.Ed.2d 116 (1982)(state attorney disciplinary proceedings); Moore v. Sims, 442 U.S. 415, 99 S.Ct. 2371, 60 L.Ed.2d 994 (1979) (state proceedings related to child abuse); Trainor v. Hernandez, 431 U.S. 434, 97 S.Ct. 1911, 52 L.Ed.2d 486 (1977) (state civil action seeking a return of welfare payments alleged to have been wrongfully received).

5. CECOS International Inc., *supra* note 4, 895 F.2d at 70. There are three exceptions to the Younger doctrine which will prohibit its application—a bad faith prosecution, patently unconstitutional state laws or the absence of an adequate state forum in which to raise the constitutional issues. Carr v. Axelrod, 798 F.Supp. 168, 175 (S.D.N.Y.1992). The Supreme Court has stated that there may be circumstances in which state court procedures "were so deficient that the Younger abstention is inappropriate." Pennzoil Co., *supra* note 4, 481 U.S. at 17, 107 S.Ct. at 1529.

6. 319 U.S. 315, 63 S.Ct. 1098, 87 L.Ed. 1424 (1943); *see* Tribune Company v. Abiola, 66 F.3d 12 (2d Cir.1995)(affirming denial of Burford abstention).

7. 312 U.S. 496, 61 S.Ct. 643, 85 L.Ed. 971 (1941).

8. Ohio Bureau of Employment Servs. v. Hodory, 431 U.S. 471, 477, 97 S.Ct. 1898, 1902, 52 L.Ed.2d 513 (1977) (Pullman abstention "involves an inquiry focused on the possibility that the state courts may interpret a challenged state statute so as to eliminate, or at least to alter materially, the constitutional question presented."); Planned Parenthood of Dutchess–Ulster,

Ch. 18 RES JUDICATA & COLLATERAL ESTOPPEL § 18.37

Library References:

West's Key No. Digests, Federal Courts ⚖=41–65.

§ 18.37 Defenses to Federal Actions—*Res Judicata* and Collateral Estoppel

"Collateral estoppel, or 'issue preclusion,' prevents a party from relitigating only those 'issues *actually adjudicated*, and essential to the judgment in a prior litigation ...'"[1] *Res judicata*, or claim preclusion, provides that "a final judgment on the merits of an action precludes the parties or their privies from relitigating issues that were or could have been raised in that action."[2] Although the distinction between them is often blurred, different rules apply to the two doctrines.[3]

Among the factors to be considered in determining whether the parties had a full and fair opportunity to litigate and whether collateral estoppel applies are: "the nature of the forum and the importance of the claim in the prior litigation, the incentive and initiative to litigate and the actual extent of litigation, the competence and expertise of counsel, the availability of new evidence, the differences in the applicable law and the foreseeability of future litigation."[4] Plaintiff bears the burden of establishing that he or she did not have a full and fair opportunity to litigate in the prior forum.[5]

Under some circumstances, decisions of administrative agencies are also given preclusive effect.[6] Generally, administrative decisions will be given preclusive effect if the administrative adjudication was rendered by the agency "employing procedures substantially similar to those used in a court of law."[7]

A section 1983 action will not be precluded because plaintiff has brought an Article 78 proceeding, since an Article 78 proceeding does not

Inc. v. Steinhaus, 60 F.3d 122 (2d Cir.1995) (reversing district court and refusing to apply both Pullman and Burford abstention doctrines).

§ 18.37

1. Clarke v. Frank, 960 F.2d 1146, 1150 (2d Cir.1992)(citation omitted).

2. Allen v. McCurry, 449 U.S. 90, 94, 101 S.Ct. 411, 414, 66 L.Ed.2d 308 (1980).

3. For a discussion of the difference between the two doctrines, *see* Burgos v. Hopkins, 14 F.3d 787 (2d Cir.1994).

4. Ryan v. New York Telephone Co., 62 N.Y.2d 494, 501, 478 N.Y.S.2d 823, 826, 467 N.E.2d 487 (1984) (citations omitted).

5. Schwartz v. Public Administrator of County of Bronx, 24 N.Y.2d 65, 71, 298 N.Y.S.2d 955, 960, 246 N.E.2d 725 (1969); *see also*, Allen, *supra*, note 2, 449 U.S. at 94, 101 S.Ct. at 414–15.

6. University of Tennessee v. Elliott, 478 U.S. 788, 106 S.Ct. 3220, 92 L.Ed.2d 635 (1986). *See* Chapter 4, "Administrative Law," *supra*, at § 4.25.

7. Ryan v. New York Telephone Co., 62 N.Y.2d 494, 499, 478 N.Y.S.2d 823, 826, 467 N.E.2d 487, 490 (1984).

In Colon v. Coughlin, 58 F.3d 865 (2d Cir.1995), the Second Circuit recently opined that "there is a substantial question as to whether, under New York law, collateral estoppel should ever apply to fact issues determined in a prison disciplinary hearing and reviewed for substantial evidence in an Article 78 proceeding, given the 'procedural laxity' of such prison hearings ... and the limited nature of substantial evidence review." 58 F.3d at 869 (citations omitted).

provide the same incentive to litigate and since monetary damages are not generally awarded in an Article 78 proceeding.[8]

Under *res judicata*, a federal court must accord state court judgments the same preclusive effect as would a New York State court.[9] New York has adopted a transactional approach to *res judicata*, which bars a later claim arising out of the same factual grouping as an earlier litigated claim, even if the second claim is based on different legal theories or seeks different relief.[10]

Library References:

West's Key No. Digests, Judgment ⟐540–581.

§ 18.38 Defenses to Federal Actions—Statute of Limitations

The Statute of Limitations for cases brought pursuant to 42 U.S.C.A. § 1983 is three years.[1] Thus, for a federal court Section 1983 complaint to be timely, it must be filed with the district court[2] no more than three years from the date the cause of action accrued.[3] Federal law

---

8. Colon v. Coughlin, 58 F.3d 865 (2d Cir.1995); Davidson v. Capuano, 792 F.2d 275 (2d Cir.1986); Nelson v. Coughlin, 115 A.D.2d 131, 495 N.Y.S.2d 528 (3d Dep't 1985).

9. Migra v. Warren City School District, 465 U.S. 75, 81, 104 S.Ct. 892, 896, 79 L.Ed.2d 56 (1984); Kremer v. Chemical Constr. Corp., 456 U.S. 461, 102 S.Ct. 1883, 72 L.Ed.2d 262 (1982).; U.S. Constitution Art. IV, § 1; 28 U.S.C.A. § 1738.

10. Smith v. Russell Sage College, 54 N.Y.2d 185, 445 N.Y.S.2d 68, 429 N.E.2d 746 (1981).

§ 18.38

1. Owens v. Okure, 488 U.S. 235, 251, 109 S.Ct. 573, 582, 102 L.Ed.2d 594 (1989); Day v. Morgenthau, 909 F.2d 75, 79 (2d Cir.1990) (on rehearing).

2. In the Second Circuit, a *pro se* Section 1983 complaint is deemed timely if it is received by the *Pro Se* office of the district court within three years of the date of accrual. Toliver v. County of Sullivan, 841 F.2d 41, 42 (2d Cir.1988).

Upon the enactment of the 1992 amendments to the CPLR, New York adopted the same rule as the federal courts for determining the timeliness of an action. New York changed the event that marked the commencement of an action from service of the summons and the complaint to the filing of the summons and complaint. CPLR 203(c), 304.

3. PRACTICE POINTER: When the complaint is filed, every effort should be made to insure that all defendants are named or that a "John Doe" defendant is named if the identity of a defendant is unknown at the time of filing, particularly if the Statute of Limitations is due to expire. If after discovery, the identity of new possible defendants arises, and the Statute of Limitations has run, a federal district court will only allow an amended pleading which adds a new defendant if (1) the claim asserted arose out of the conduct, transaction or occurrence in the original pleading and (2) the new defendant "knew or should have known that, but for a mistake concerning the identity of the proper party, the action would have been brought against the party." Fed. R. Civ. P. 15(c)(3)(B), referred to as the "relation back doctrine"; *see also*, Schiavone v. Fortune, 477 U.S. 21, 29, 106 S.Ct. 2379, 2384, 91 L.Ed.2d 18 (1986); Barrow v. Wethersfield Police Dept., 66 F.3d 466 (2d Cir.1995)(amendment substituting individual named police officers for "John Doe" defendants did not relate back to original complaint); *but see* Soto v. Brooklyn Correctional Facility, 80 F.3d 34 (2d Cir.1996) (remanding to district court to determine whether individual officers would be prejudiced by amendment naming them as defendants when complaint mistakenly only named municipal entity without any allegation of improper policy or practice).

determines when a federal claim accrues. A Section 1983 claim accrues when a plaintiff "knows or has reason to know" of the harm he or she has suffered.[4] The accrual date depends on the nature of the claim.[5]

The Statute of Limitations for a Section 1983 claim may also be subject to equitable tolling if the defendant fraudulently concealed his or her wrongful conduct. Under such circumstances, plaintiff must proffer "non-conclusory evidence of a conspiracy or other fraudulent wrong *which precluded his possible discovery of the harms that he suffered.*"[6] Under circumscribed conditions, this period may be longer, such as where there is a continuous course of treatment[7] or a "continuing violation."[8]

The state court relation back doctrine, codified at CPLR 203(f), provides that "[a] claim asserted in an amended pleading is deemed to have been interposed at the time the claims in the original pleading were interposed, unless the original pleading does not give notice of the transactions, occurrences, or series of transactions or occurrences, to be proved pursuant to the amended pleading."

4. Cullen v. Margiotta, 811 F.2d 698, 725 (2d Cir.), cert. denied 483 U.S. 1021, 107 S.Ct. 3266, 97 L.Ed.2d 764 (1987).

5. For example, a claim based on malicious prosecution begins to run when the underlying criminal action is conclusively terminated, rather than at time of arrest. Murphy v. Lynn, 53 F.3d 547 (2d Cir.1995). A claim of false arrest, however, accrues at the time of the arrest, not when the arrest is later proved "false." Singleton v. City of New York, 632 F.2d 185, 191–93 (2d Cir. 1980), cert. denied 450 U.S. 920, 101 S.Ct. 1368, 67 L.Ed.2d 347 (1981).

6. Pinaud v. County of Suffolk, 52 F.3d 1139, 1157 (2d Cir.1995) (citation omitted, emphasis in original). Merely alleging a conspiracy claim will not forestall the commencement of the Statute of Limitations period. Singleton v. City of New York, 632 F.2d 185 (2d Cir.1980), cert. denied 450 U.S. 920, 101 S.Ct. 1368, 67 L.Ed.2d 347 (1981). However, there may be a delay in the accrual of a cause of action if a Monell claim is alleged. See supra, § 18.34. A cause of action against a municipality accrues "when it is clear, or should be clear, that the harmful act is the consequence of a county 'policy or custom.'" Pinaud, supra, 52 F.3d at 1157 (quoting Monell, 436 U.S. at 694, 98 S.Ct. at 2037).

7. The continuous course of treatment doctrine provides that the time to commence an action is stayed "when the course of treatment which includes the wrongful acts or omissions has run continuously and is related to the same original condition or complaint." McDermott v. Torre, 56 N.Y.2d 399, 405, 452 N.Y.S.2d 351, 353, 437 N.E.2d 1108 (1982) (quoting Borgia v. City of New York, 12 N.Y.2d 151, 155, 237 N.Y.S.2d 319, 320, 187 N.E.2d 777 (1962)); see also, Ulrich v. Veterans Administration Hospital, 853 F.2d 1078, 1080–81 (2d Cir.1988). This doctrine could apply, for example, to an inmate's Section 1983 claim alleging deliberate indifference to serious medical needs.

8. The continuing violation doctrine provides that if a complaint is filed "that is timely as to any incident of discrimination in furtherance of an ongoing policy of discrimination, all claims of acts of discrimination under that policy will be timely even if they would be untimely standing alone." Lambert v. Genesee Hosp., 10 F.3d 46, 53 (2d Cir.1993) (citations omitted), cert. denied 511 U.S. 1052, 114 S.Ct. 1612, 128 L.Ed.2d 339 (1994); cf. Gleason v. McBride, 715 F.Supp. 59, 63 (S.D.N.Y.1988) ("In a section 1983 action involving separate wrongful acts, each claim must be analyzed separately to determine when it occurred and when the limitations period ran."), modified on other grounds, 869 F.2d 688 (2d Cir.1989). Courts in the Second Circuit "consistently have looked unfavorably on continuing violation arguments" and only "compelling circumstances will warrant application of the exception to the Statute of Limitations." Blesedell v. Mobil Oil Co., 708 F.Supp. 1408, 1415 (S.D.N.Y.1989).

§ 18.39 Housing[1]

Various federal and state statutes prohibit discrimination in either public or private housing accommodations based on race, color, sex, religion, national origin, ancestry, familial status and disability. Since some statutes are broader than others in prohibiting certain types of discrimination, both the federal and state statutes should be analyzed to determine whether the type of discrimination at issue is covered under one or both statutory schemes.

Library References:

West's Key No. Digests, Civil Rights ⚖131.

§ 18.40 Housing—Prohibition Against Discrimination in Publicly Assisted Housing

Both the New York Civil Rights Law and the Human Rights Law contain separate provisions with respect to discrimination in publicly-assisted housing accommodations. Indeed, the Civil Rights Law contains a section which specifically states that the provision concerning publicly-assisted housing accommodations "shall not apply to privately owned housing accommodations."[1] The federal fair housing statutes, however, do not differentiate between private and public housing.[2]

§ 18.41 Housing—Prohibition Against Discrimination in Publicly Assisted Housing—Owners and Lessors

New York Civil Rights Law § 18–a provides that it is unlawful to discriminate "because of race, color, religion, national origin or ancestry in any publicly assisted housing accommodations." It is unlawful for an owner of a publicly assisted housing accommodation to refuse to rent or lease or otherwise deny a housing accommodation based on these factors or to discriminate in the terms, conditions or privileges of any publicly assisted housing accommodation or in the furnishing of facilities or services provided.[1] Finally, it is unlawful for any person to make an oral or written inquiry with respect to race, color, religion, national origin or

---

§ 18.39

1. *See generally*, Finkelstein and Ferrara, *Landlord and Tenant Practice in New York* (West 1997).

§ 18.40

1. Civil Rights Law § 18–e.

2. The federal fair housing statutes are set forth at 42 U.S.C.A. §§ 3601, *et seq. See also*, 42 U.S.C.A. §§ 2000d, *et seq.*, which prohibits discrimination based on race, color or national origin in federally-assisted programs. Sections 2000d, *et seq.* should be pleaded in conjunction with Section 3601, if appropriate.

§ 18.41

1. Civil Rights Law §§ 18–c(1), (2). Note that discrimination based on sex, disability and familial status are not prohibited under this provision.

ancestry of a person seeking to rent or lease any publicly assisted housing accommodation.[2]

New York's Human Rights Law further provides that it is unlawful for the owner, lessee, sub-lessee, assignee, or managing agent of publicly assisted housing accommodations: (a) to refuse to rent or lease or otherwise deny anyone such accommodation based on race, creed, color, disability, national origin, age, sex or marital status; (b) to discriminate against any person in the terms, conditions or privileges of any publicly-assisted housing accommodation or in the furnishing of facilities based on race, creed, color, disability, national origin, age, sex or marital status; or (c) to make a written or oral inquiry or record concerning the race, creed, color, disability, national origin, age, sex or marital status of a person seeking to rent or lease any publicly assisted housing accommodation.[3] It is also unlawful to refuse to make a reasonable modification to the existing premises, at the expense of the person with a disability, if the modification may be necessary to afford the person full enjoyment of the premises.[4]

The New York City Administrative Code also specifically prohibits discrimination in publicly assisted housing.[5]

Federal housing statutes do not distinguish between public and privately owned housing. Title 42 U.S.C.A. § 3604(a) makes it unlawful "[t]o refuse to sell or rent after the making of a *bona fide* offer, or to refuse to negotiate for the sale or rental of, or otherwise make unavailable or deny, a dwelling to any person because of race, color, religion, sex, familial status, or national origin." A separate section provides that it is unlawful "[t]o discriminate against any person in the terms, conditions, or privileges of sale or rental of a dwelling, or in the provision of services or facilities in connection with such dwelling, because of a handicap of that person."[6] This includes refusing to make a "reasonable accommodation" if necessary to afford the individual an equal opportunity to use and enjoy a dwelling.[7] The federal statutes are also discussed in Sections 18.43 and 18.50, *infra*.

§ 18.42 Housing—Prohibition Against Discrimination in Publicly Assisted Housing—Real Estate Agents and Brokers

New York Civil Rights Law § 18–c, as well as 42 U.S.C.A. § 3604, also prohibits real estate agents and brokers from engaging in discrimination.

2. Civil Rights Law § 18–c(3).
3. Executive Law § 296(2–a)(a)-(c).
4. Executive Law § 296(2–a)(d).
5. N.Y.C. Adm. Code § 8–107(3).
6. 42 U.S.C.A. § 3604(f)(2)(A).
7. 42 U.S.C.A. § 3604(f)(3)(B).

§ 18.43 Housing—Prohibition Against Discrimination in Publicly Assisted Housing—Remedies for Discrimination

The specific remedy under the New York Civil Rights Law for discrimination in publicly assisted housing is found in Section 18–d, which provides for money damages or equitable remedies "including such affirmative relief as may be necessary to undo the effects of such violation."[1] A claim may also be brought in either state or federal court under 42 U.S.C.A. § 1983, since public housing necessarily constitutes state action.[2] *See*, Section 18.18, *supra*.

Additionally, claims may be asserted in state or federal court under Title VIII of the Civil Rights Act of 1968, 42 U.S.C.A. §§ 3601, *et seq.*, which is referred to as the Fair Housing Act;[3] if the discrimination is based on race, causes of action may also be brought under 42 U.S.C.A. § 1981, which prohibits racial discrimination in the making of contracts, and 42 U.S.C.A. § 1982, which prohibits racial discrimination in the sale or rental of property. These remedies, which are also applicable to private housing, and the administrative remedies that are also available, are discussed in greater detail in Sections 18.49 and 18.50, *infra*.

§ 18.44 Housing—Prohibition Against Discrimination in Private Housing

As stated above, the New York Civil Rights Law only prohibits discrimination in the rental or leasing of publicly assisted housing; it does not contain any provisions concerning the rental or leasing of privately owned housing.[1] The New York Human Rights Law, however, fills this void, in that it contains prohibitions for discrimination in the rental and sale of property and co-operative apartments. While the Civil Rights Law does not contain any provisions with respect to discrimination in the sale of individual homes, it does address discrimination in the sale of co-operative apartments.

§ 18.43

1. **CAVEAT:** Section 18–d(3) mandates that "[a]t or before the commencement of any action," notice of the action must be served on the Attorney General. A sample form for the notice is set forth in § 18.97, *infra*.
2. Colon v. Tompkins Square Neighbors, Inc., 289 F.Supp. 104 (S.D.N.Y.1968).
3. Federal criminal penalties for interference or intimidation in connection with the sale or rental of a dwelling are set forth in 42 U.S.C.A. § 3631. This section provides for the imposition of fines or imprisonment for not more than one year, or both. If bodily injury results from the acts committed or if dangerous weapons, explosives or fire are used or threatened, the term of imprisonment may be up to ten years. An indeterminate term of imprisonment up to and including life shall be imposed if the unlawful discriminatory conduct results in death, or if the conduct includes kidnapping, aggravated sexual abuse or any attempt to commit these offenses.

§ 18.44

1. *See supra*, § 18.41.

§ 18.45 Housing—Prohibition Against Discrimination in Private Housing—Owners and Lessors

The Human Rights Law provides that it is unlawful for the owner, lessee, sub-lessee, assignee, managing agent, or any person having the right to sell, rent or lease a housing accommodation (1) to refuse to sell, rent, lease or deny in any way a housing accommodation based on race, creed, color, national origin, sex, age, disability, marital status, or familial status (2) to discriminate in the terms, conditions or privileges of the sale, rental, lease or furnishing of the housing accommodation based on race, creed, color, national origin, sex, age, disability, marital status or familial status; or (3) to either directly or indirectly express any limitation, specification or discrimination in an advertisement or publication or make any record or inquiry with respect to race, creed, color, national origin, sex, age, disability, marital status, or familial status.[1] These provisions do not apply under certain limited circumstances set forth in the statute.[2] Discrimination in the sale, rental or lease of commercial space is prohibited as well.[3]

It is unlawful for a landlord to refuse to rent a dwelling, or, once rented, seek to evict a couple who are unmarried.[4]

It is also unlawful for a landlord to terminate a lease for a violation of a "no pet" clause when a tenant needs a dog due to a disability.[5]

In addition to being held liable directly, landlords may be held vicariously liable for discrimination by real estate brokers or agents they employ, even if the landlord specifically instructs the broker not to

---

§ 18.45

1. Executive Law § 296(5)(a); *see, e.g.*, Dunn v. Fishbein, 123 A.D.2d 659, 507 N.Y.S.2d 29 (2d Dep't 1986) (action against building superintendent for race discrimination); *see also*, 42 U.S.C.A. § 3604(a). As set forth in §§ 18.40, 18.41, *supra*, the federal statutes apply to public and private housing accommodations.

2. The prohibited activity set forth in Section 296(5)(a) does not apply to (1) a two-family house if the owner of the property resides in one of the housing accommodations; (2) a single-sex rental accommodation; (3) the rental of a room or rooms in a housing accommodation, if the rental is by the occupant of the housing accommodation or by the owner and the owner or members of the owner's family live in the housing accommodation; or (4) rental or lease of housing accommodations designed exclusively to persons fifty-five year of age or older, and the person's spouse.

3. *See* Executive Law § 296(5)(b).

4. Munroe v. 344 East 76th Realty Corp., 113 Misc.2d 155, 448 N.Y.S.2d 388 (Sup.Ct., N.Y. County, 1982). In Hudson View Props. v. Weiss, 59 N.Y.2d 733, 463 N.Y.S.2d 428, 450 N.E.2d 234 (1983), the New York Court of Appeals held that a lease restriction against occupancy by persons who have no familial relationship does not constitute discrimination based on "marital status," since the applicability of the lease provision did not actually depend on marital status. In response to this holding, the Legislature enacted Real Property Law § 235–f, referred to as the "roommate law," which was designed to extend the protection of the Human Rights Law to unrelated persons sharing a dwelling. See 425 Realty Co. v. Herrera, 146 Misc.2d 790, 559 N.Y.S.2d 442 (App. Term., 1st Dep't 1990). *See also*, Finkelstein and Ferrara, *New York Landlord and Tenant Practice* (West 1997).

5. Ocean Gate Assocs. Starrett Systems, Inc. v. Dopico, 109 Misc.2d 774, 441 N.Y.S.2d 34 (Sup.Ct., Kings County, 1981).

discriminate, under the theory that a principal is liable for the wrongful acts of its agent.[6]

§ 18.46 Housing—Prohibition Against Discrimination in Private Housing—Real Estate Agents and Brokers

It is unlawful for a real estate broker, real estate salesperson or employee or agent to refuse to sell, rent or lease or negotiate for the sale, rental or lease of any housing accommodation, or misrepresent that any housing accommodation is no longer available when it is or otherwise deny or withhold any housing accommodation because of race, creed, color, national origin, sex, age, disability, marital status or familial status of any person or group of persons.[1] Directing members of certain groups to buildings and neighborhoods occupied by members of their same racial or ethnic group and away from those buildings and neighborhoods occupied by individuals of different racial and ethnic groups, which perpetuates patterns of racial segregation, is referred to as "racial steering."[2]

It is also unlawful to print or circulate an advertisement or publication or use an application in connection with the prospective purchase, rental or lease of any housing accommodation which expresses, directly or indirectly, any limitation, specification, or discrimination as to race, creed, color, national origin, sex, age, disability, marital status or family status.[3]

It is also unlawful for a real estate broker or salesperson to represent that a change has occurred or will or may occur in the composition of the owners or occupants of a neighborhood or block with respect to race, creed, color, national origin or marital status and to represent that this change will or may result in undesirable consequences, including but not limited to a decrease in property values, increase in criminal or antisocial behavior, or a decline in the quality of schools or other facilities.[4] This unlawful practice, referred to as "blockbusting," is enforced by the Secretary of State, who can prohibit real estate brokers from soliciting in certain neighborhoods as a remedy for blockbusting and may, if appro-

6. Cabrera v. Jakabovitz, 24 F.3d 372, 385–89 (2d Cir.1994).

§ 18.46

1. Executive Law § 296(5)(c)(1); see, e.g., Van Cleef Realty, Inc. v. New York State Div. of Human Rights, 216 A.D.2d 306, 627 N.Y.S.2d 744 (2d Dep't 1995); Alverson v. State Div. of Human Rights, 181 A.D.2d 1019, 581 N.Y.S.2d 953 (4th Dep't 1992) (upholding SDHR determination and award of $7,500 to each plaintiff after finding that real estate broker discriminated based on race and color by refusing to show a house that had been listed for rent). See also, 42 U.S.C.A. § 3604(a), (d).

The provisions with respect to age do not apply to a housing accommodation for individuals fifty-five and over and their spouses.

2. Cabrera v. Jakabovitz, 24 F.3d 372, 378 note 2 (2d Cir.1994) (citation omitted).

3. Executive Law § 296(5)(c)(2); see also, 42 U.S.C.A. § 3604(c).

4. Executive Law § 296(3-b); see also, 42 U.S.C.A. § 3604(e), which prohibits discrimination based on sex, handicap and familial status as well.

§ 18.47 Housing—Prohibition Against Discrimination in Private Housing—Cooperatives

Cooperative corporations are similarly precluded from discrimination. Section 19–a of the Civil Rights Law provides that the tenants, shareholders and management of a housing cooperative are prohibited from withholding consent to the sale or proposed sale of certificates of stock or other evidence of ownership of an interest in the cooperative corporation because of the race, creed, national origin, or sex of the purchaser.[1] Section 19–b provides that not only the prospective purchaser, but "[a]ny person" aggrieved by the withholding of consent, including but not limited to a bank or other lending institution, may commence an action for damages and equitable relief. Thus, the seller of the cooperative apartment should also have a remedy under the Civil Rights Law for the cooperative's failure to approve the proposed purchaser.[2]

---

5. Real Property Law § 441–c, 441–h; see also, discussion in New York State Ass'n of Realtors, Inc. v. Shaffer, 27 F.3d 834 (2d Cir.1994).

§ 18.47

1. Civil Rights Law § 19–a. Although Section 19–a is contained in Article 2–A, entitled "Equal Rights to Publicly–Aided Housing," this provision applies to private cooperatives. The sections concerning cooperatives were enacted in 1971. Note that in contrast to Section 18–c, which was enacted in 1950, Section 19–a prohibits discrimination based on sex.

While there is no separate provision concerning discrimination in the sale of condominiums, boards of directors of condominiums generally do not have the authority to withhold consent to the sale of an individual unit. If the owner of a condominium unit discriminates in the sale of the unit, the prohibitions with respect to owners of private homes would apply.

2. Cf. Faiola v. Jac Towers Apartments, Inc., 147 Misc.2d 630, 558 N.Y.S.2d 478 (Sup.Ct., Queens County, 1990)(although cooperative owner has a claim under Civil Rights Law § 19–a, owner is not a person aggrieved under Executive Law § 296(2–a)).

CAVEAT: A claim of discrimination or bad faith is an exception to the general rule enunciated by the Court of Appeals in Levandusky v. One Fifth Avenue Apartment Corp., 75 N.Y.2d 530, 554 N.Y.S.2d 807, 553 N.E.2d 1317 (1990). In Levandusky, the court held that so long as the board of directors of a cooperative acts for the purposes of the cooperative, within the scope of its authority and in good faith, no court should substitute its judgment for that of the board. When asserting a claim against a cooperative for refusing to approve a prospective purchaser, the complaint must allege more than mere conclusory allegations to withstand the business judgment rule. For example, rather than merely alleging that "plaintiff was denied approval to purchase shares based on her race," the complaint must set forth specific facts in support of the claim, such as examples of discriminatory questions during the interview. Otherwise, plaintiff's allegations will not raise a triable issue of fact. See Hunter v. Board of Directors of Grymes Hill Owners Corp., 204 A.D.2d 395, 614 N.Y.S.2d 182 (2d Dep't 1994)(memorandum). See also, infra, § 18.96.

PRACTICE POINTER: In addition to naming the cooperative corporation as a defendant, the managing agent, individual members of the board of directors, and any other individuals or entities involved should be named as defendants. See Sanders v. Winship, 57 N.Y.2d 391, 456 N.Y.S.2d 720, 442 N.E.2d 1231 (1982) (liberally construing Civil Rights Law § 19–a to allow a cause of action to proceed against the wife of a shareholder who allegedly engaged in discrimination against prospective shareholders).

If your practice involves representing cooperatives, you should advise the co-op that

§ 18.47 CIVIL RIGHTS LAW Ch. 18

Under city, state and federal law, cooperatives are also required to make reasonable accommodations for disabled or handicapped individuals.[3]

§ 18.48 Housing—Prohibition Against Discrimination in Private Housing—Remedies for Discrimination

An individual who believes he or she has a claim under any of the aforementioned statutes has a choice, which is referred to as an "election of remedies." A charge may be filed with any of the administrative agencies that have jurisdiction over the particular type of housing discrimination. As set forth below, various agencies are empowered to investigate the charge and award damages and other relief, if appropriate. Alternatively, an individual may bypass the administrative proceeding and commence an action in either state or federal court. Once an administrative proceeding is commenced, however, an individual forfeits his or her right to commence an action directly in court.[1]

§ 18.49 Housing—Prohibition Against Discrimination in Private Housing—Remedies for Discrimination—Administrative Proceedings

The federal, state and local statutes that prohibit discrimination all provide that certain federal, state and local agencies are empowered to review and determine administrative complaints of discrimination in housing. Each respective governmental agency has its own procedures and regulations, which are discussed below.

New York State Division of Human Rights. A prospective tenant or purchaser who believes he or she is the victim of discrimination may file a charge of discrimination with the New York State Division of Human Rights ("SDHR" or "the Division"), within one year after the alleged unlawful discriminatory practice.[1] The verified complaint is re-

the best defense to a discrimination claim is to establish standard criteria that are applied to all applicants regarding their financial suitability and be able to document this practice. See R. Siegler, *Cooperatives and Condominiums*, N.Y.L.J., 1/8/96, p.3, col.1.

3. 42 U.S.C.A. § 3604(f)(3)(B); Executive Law § 296(18); N.Y.C. Admin. Code §§ 8–102(18), 8–107(5), 8–107(15); see Shapiro v. Cadman Towers, Inc., 51 F.3d 328 (2d Cir.1995)(duty of reasonable accommodation requires cooperative to provide a parking space to handicapped apartment owner near her apartment); United Veterans Mutual Housing No. 2 Corp. v. New York City Comm'n on Human Rights, 207 A.D.2d 551, 616 N.Y.S.2d 84 (2d Dep't 1994).

§ 18.48

1. Executive Law § 297(9). The only exception is if the Division dismisses the complaint on the grounds of "administrative convenience," all rights are still retained as if no administrative complaint had been filed.

§ 18.49

1. Executive Law § 297(5).

quired to state the name and address of the person alleged to have committed the unlawful discriminatory practice (referred to as the respondent) and provide details of the acts alleged. With respect to housing discrimination claims, the Division is required to serve a copy of the complaint on the respondent and any other persons it deems to be necessary parties within thirty (30) days of filing. Within one hundred (100) days after a housing discrimination complaint is filed, the Division is required to determine whether it has jurisdiction and, if so, whether there is probable cause to believe that the respondent has engaged in an unlawful discriminatory practice.[2]

At any time during the proceedings before the Division, the Commissioner of the Division may apply to the supreme court for an order requiring respondent to show cause why it should not be enjoined from engaging in any conduct which would tend to render ineffectual any order the Division may eventually enter.[3]

The Division may attempt to eliminate the discriminatory practice through "conference, conciliation and persuasion."[4] If the conciliation process fails, the SDHR will direct the respondent to answer the charges and will schedule a public hearing on the complaint.[5] The Division has broad powers, including the power to subpoena witnesses to compel their attendance and may require the production of records for examination.[6]

The complainant's case may be presented by an attorney or agent for the Division and/or by the complainant's attorney.[7] The statute provides that "[t]he hearing examiner shall not be bound by the strict rules of evidence prevailing in courts of law or equity."[8]

Within one hundred eighty (180) days after the commencement of the hearing, the Division is required to make a determination which sets forth findings of fact and issue an order based on these findings.[9] If upon all the evidence the Commissioner finds respondent has not engaged in

2. Executive Law § 298(2)(b). For all other types of discrimination claims, the Division has one hundred eighty (180) days to investigate. *See* Executive Law § 298(2)(a).

If the Division finds that it lacks jurisdiction or that no probable cause exists with respect to part or all of the complaint, it issues an order dismissing the complaint or dismissing the claims against a particular respondent.

3. Executive Law § 297(6). For example, if the complainant is the proposed purchaser of a cooperative apartment, the Division may seek to preserve the status quo by seeking an order prohibiting the board of directors from authorizing a sale to another individual.

4. Executive Law § 298(3)(a).

5. Executive Law § 297(4)(a)(i). The Division is required to serve the notice and copy of the complaint on the respondent within two hundred seventy days after the complaint is filed. The respondent must file its answer at least two business days prior to the scheduled hearing. A voluntary arbitration procedure has also been established. *See* Executive Law § 297(4)(a)(ii). Both subsections (a)(i) and (a)(ii) expire June 30, 1997.

6. Executive Law § 295(7).

7. Executive Law § 297(4)(a).

8. *Id. See* Chapter 4, "Administrative Law" § 4.15, *supra*.

9. Executive Law § 297(4)(c).

§ 18.49 CIVIL RIGHTS LAW Ch. 18

an unlawful discriminatory act, the Commissioner will issue an order dismissing the complaint. If, however, the Commissioner finds that respondent has engaged in any discriminatory housing practices, the Commissioner has broad remedial powers and may award any of the following forms of relief: a cease and desist order; an order requiring respondent to extend full, equal and unsegregated accommodations, advantages, facilities and privileges; compensatory damages for economic losses, mental and emotional distress and any physical illness[10] and punitive damages, not to exceed $10,000.[11]

Any person aggrieved by an order of the Division may bring a proceeding to review a determination of the SDHR in the county in which the unlawful discriminatory practice occurred or where the respondent transacts business within sixty (60) days after service of the order.[12] The Division is required to file a written transcript of the record of the prior proceedings. Absent extraordinary circumstances, the court will not consider any objections that were not first raised before the Division. The decision will be upheld if the SDHR's determination is "conclusive if supported by sufficient evidence on the record considered as a whole."[13] The court may enter an order enforcing, modifying, enforcing as modified, or setting aside in whole or in part the Division's order. If the determination is not found to be supported by sufficient evidence and the determination is set aside, the matter will be remanded to the SDHR for a new determination.[14] An appeal from the judgment of the court is required to be reviewed as expeditiously as possible and receives precedence over other matters.

10. PRACTICE POINTER: The complainant should be prepared with some proof of damages, including medical treatment, if any, and ability to substantiate mental or emotional damages by showing, *inter alia*, loss of sleep, that interpersonal relationships or employment were adversely affected, etc. Economic losses would include, *inter alia*, broker fees, mortgage fees, difference between rent and utility bills at new location, etc.

See Portee v. Hastava, 853 F.Supp. 597 (E.D.N.Y.1994); Van Cleef Realty, Inc. v. New York State Div. of Human Rights, 216 A.D.2d 306, 627 N.Y.S.2d 744 (2d Dep't 1995) (reducing SDHR's award against realtors for racial steering from $30,000 to $5,000 since there was no evidence of prolonged mental anguish); State Div. of Human Rights v. Muia, 176 A.D.2d 1142, 575 N.Y.S.2d 957 (3d Dep't 1991); Moore v. SDHR, 154 A.D.2d 823, 546 N.Y.S.2d 487 (3d Dep't 1989)(reducing SDHR award of $25,000 to $2,500 for lack of proof of damages).

11. Punitive damages are available only in housing discrimination cases. Executive Law § 297(4)(c). *See*, Van Cleef Realty Inc., *supra*, note 10, (refusing to disturb punitive damage award of $10,000 in light of SDHR's broad remedial powers).

12. The proceeding may be transferred to the Appellate Division, pursuant to Executive Law § 298, if the order sought to be reviewed was made as a result of a public hearing. *See, e.g.*, Alverson v. State Div. of Human Rights, 181 A.D.2d 1019, 581 N.Y.S.2d 953 (4th Dep't 1992).

13. Executive Law § 298.

14. Bachman v. SDHR, 104 A.D.2d 111, 481 N.Y.S.2d 858 (1st Dep't 1984) (granting petition to annul SDHR determination of no probable cause to believe that cooperative discriminated where investigation was inadequate and remanding to SDHR for a full and thorough investigation).

Ch. 18 ACTIONS IN STATE & FEDERAL COURT **§ 18.50**

New York City Commission on Human Rights. If the alleged discrimination concerns housing within New York City, a charge of discrimination may be filed with the New York City Commission on Human Rights, which has essentially the same powers as the SDHR.[15] A decision of the Commission may be reviewed in supreme court.[16]

Secretary of Housing and Urban Development. Similarly, 42 U.S.C.A. § 3610 provides that within one year after an alleged discriminatory housing practice has occurred or terminated, a complaint may be filed with the Secretary of Housing and Urban Development, who may either investigate the charge, file a complaint on his or her own initiative, or authorize the Attorney General to commence an action.[17] If the Secretary retains jurisdiction, the procedure is similar to the procedure followed by the SDHR. If the aggrieved individual is not satisfied with the Secretary's decision, a petition for review may be filed in the circuit where the alleged discrimination occurred.[18]

§ 18.50 Housing—Prohibition Against Discrimination in Private Housing—Remedies for Discrimination—Actions in State and Federal Court

In lieu of filing an administrative claim, an action may be commenced in state supreme court or in federal district court in the first instance, alleging violations of the appropriate provisions of the Civil Rights Act and/or Executive Law.[1] Additionally, 42 U.S.C.A. § 3613(a) provides that an action may be commenced in state or federal court under within two years of the occurrence or termination of any alleged discriminatory housing practice. If the discrimination is based on race, causes of action may also be brought under the general federal civil

---

15. *See* N.Y.C. Admin. Code §§ 8–101 *et seq.*

16. N.Y.C. Admin. Code § 8–123; *see, e.g.,* Application of 119–121 East 97th Street Corp. v. New York City Comm'n on Human Rights, 220 A.D.2d 79, 642 N.Y.S.2d 638 (1st Dep't 1996) (upholding $100,000 award by City Commission to tenant whose landlord tried to oust him because he is HIV positive); Fugardi v. Angus, 216 A.D.2d 85, 628 N.Y.S.2d 77 (1st Dep't 1995)(modifying Commission's award of compensatory damages against homeowner for discrimination in refusing to show to plaintiff, a West Indian black).

17. *See* 42 U.S.C.A. § 3610(e). If, however, the matter is within the jurisdiction of a state or local agency, the complaint will be referred to it without any action. 42 U.S.C.A. § 3610(f).

For example, in Shapiro, § 18.47 *supra* note 3, plaintiff filed a complaint with HUD. After an investigation, HUD issued a charge of discrimination. Plaintiff elected to have her claims addressed in federal court. The United States then filed a separate case under 42 U.S.C.A. § 3612(*o*) and the cases were consolidated.

18. 42 U.S.C.A. § 3612(i). *See, e.g.,* Soules v. U.S. Dep't of Hous. & Urban Devel., 967 F.2d 817 (2d Cir.1992). The standard of review is substantial evidence.

§ 18.50

1. CAVEAT: As set forth above, the decision to file an administrative charge rather than proceed directly to court is referred to as an election of remedies. Once a decision is made to file an administrative claim, the aggrieved party cannot commence an action in court alleging the same claim, except to seek review of the administrative determination. Jiminez v. Southridge Cooperative, Section I, Inc., 626 F.Supp. 732 (E.D.N.Y.1985).

rights provisions, 42 U.S.C.A. § 1981, which prohibits racial discrimination in the right to contract, and 42 U.S.C.A. § 1982, which prohibits racial discrimination in the sale or rental of property.[2]

If the plaintiff is already residing as a tenant in a dwelling and the landlord seeks to evict the tenant for a discriminatory reason, the tenant can wait until the landlord brings a holdover proceeding in housing court and can then affirmatively allege the discrimination as a defense.[3] It would be appropriate in such a case to move for a temporary restraining order and preliminary injunction to block the attempted eviction. Alternatively, the tenant could initiate a proceeding in supreme court in the first instance alleging discrimination under Executive Law § 297(9) and seek monetary damages as well as injunctive relief.

Rather than commencing an action directly against a real estate broker or salesperson, claims of discrimination by real estate brokers and salespersons may be brought to the attention of the Attorney General, who has the authority to commence an action,[4] or to the Secretary of State, who is responsible for licensing brokers and salespersons and may revoke or suspend a license or impose a fine.[5]

---

2. *See* Robinson v. 12 Lofts Realty, 610 F.2d 1032 (2d Cir.1979), in which a black plaintiff brought an action pursuant to 42 U.S.C.A. §§ 3601–31 and 42 U.S.C.A. §§ 1981 and 1982 seeking damages and a preliminary injunction directing a housing cooperative to permit him to consummate the sale and restraining the cooperative from taking any action to interfere with his purchase. The district court found that plaintiff had proven a prima facie case of discrimination but that defendants met their burden of showing substantial justification for their decision denying the transfer of shares. The Second Circuit, however, stated that once a *prima facie* case is established, the claim cannot be defeated by defendants' reliance on mere hypothetical reasons for a prospective purchaser's rejection, and that for the cooperative corporation to prevail, the district court must find that racial motivation did not play any role in the decision. 610 F.2d at 1043.

See also, Murphy v. 253 Garth Tenants Corp., 579 F.Supp. 1150 (S.D.N.Y.1983), brought under 42 U.S.C.A. §§ 3601–31 and Executive Law § 296(5)(a), in which a woman claimed a cooperative and its president discriminated against her based on sex and national origin. Although the court found that improper motive did not play a role in the denial of the application, it nevertheless determined that consent was unreasonably withheld and ordered the transfer of shares.

CAVEAT: The Statute of Limitations for commencing a civil action under the Federal Fair Housing Act is two years (42 U.S.C.A. § 3613(a)(1)(A)) while the Statute of Limitations for a claim under the general civil rights statutes (42 U.S.C.A. §§ 1981 and 1982) is three years. The advantage of asserting a federal claim is that the prevailing party may be awarded attorneys' fees and costs. *See* Sections 3613(c)(2), 1988.

3. Leonedas Realty Corp. v. Brodowsky, 115 Misc.2d 88, 454 N.Y.S.2d 183 (Civ.Ct., Queens County, 1982).

4. *See, e.g.,* People of State of New York by Abrams v. Merlino, 694 F.Supp. 1101 (S.D.N.Y.1988), in which the New York State Attorney General brought an action in federal court under 42 U.S.C.A. §§ 1981, 1982, 3604(a)—(d), 3617; Executive Law § 296(5)(a) and Civil Rights Law § 40–c based on race and sex discrimination against real estate brokers and salespersons.

Local governments may also have standing to commence an action against realtors under the federal or state statutes if they can demonstrate an injury as a result of discrimination. City of N.Y. v. Fillmore Real Estate, Ltd., 665 F.Supp. 178 (E.D.N.Y. 1987).

5. *See* Real Prop. Law § 441–c.

§ 18.51 Housing—*Prima Facie* Case and Burden of Proof

The burden of proof in a housing discrimination case is essentially the same as the "shifting burden" articulated by the United States Supreme Court in an employment discrimination case, *Texas Dep't of Community Affairs v. Burdine*.[1] The plaintiff has the burden of establishing a *prima facie* case of discrimination. A plaintiff alleging housing discrimination establishes a *prima facie* case by showing that: (1) plaintiff is a member of the class protected by the statute; (2) plaintiff sought and was qualified for the property sought to be owned or rented; (3) plaintiff was denied the opportunity to rent or own the dwelling or property; and (4) the property remained available thereafter.[2] Once the *prima facie* case is established, the burden shifts to defendants to articulate a legitimate, non-discriminatory reason for their determination. If defendants meet this burden, plaintiff must then show that the reasons offered by defendants were not their true reasons but were a pretext for discrimination.[3]

§ 18.52 Housing—Summary of Procedure for Filing an Administrative Claim and Challenging an SDHR Order

When filing an administrative claim with the Division, the following procedures should be followed:

1. File a claim of discrimination within one year of the alleged unlawful discriminatory practice.[1]

   The verified complaint must state

   (a) the name and address of the person alleged to have committed the unlawful discriminatory practice (referred to as the respondent) and

   (b) details of the acts alleged.[2]

2. The Division serves a copy of the complaint on the respondent and any other persons it deems to be necessary parties within thirty days of filing.

---

§ 18.51

1. 450 U.S. 248, 253, 101 S.Ct. 1089, 1093, 67 L.Ed.2d 207 (1981). *See also*, Chapter 17, "Employment Law" at § 17.59.

2. *See* Cabrera v. Jakabovitz, 24 F.3d 372, 381 (2d Cir.1994).

3. *See* Hitter v. Rubin, 208 A.D.2d 480, 617 N.Y.S.2d 730 (1st Dep't 1994), in which plaintiff failed to meet her burden to show that the co-op's articulated reason that it rejected her prospective purchase because of her exaggerated financial statement and dishonesty in altering documents was a pretext for age discrimination.

PRACTICE POINTER: For an excellent discussion on burdens of proof and how to frame the jury charge in a housing discrimination case, *see*, Cabrera, *supra*, note 2.

§ 18.52

1. Executive Law § 297(5).

2. Executive Law § 297(1).

(a) If the Division determines it has jurisdiction, it then determines whether there is probable cause to believe that the respondent has engaged in an unlawful discriminatory practice.[3]

(b) If the Division finds that it lacks jurisdiction or that no probable cause exists with respect to part or all of the complaint, an order will be issued dismissing the complaint or dismissing the claims against a particular respondent.[4]

3. If the Division elects to proceed with "conference, conciliation and persuasion,"[5] the parties will meet with a representative from the Division in an attempt to resolve the dispute without further proceedings. If the conciliation process fails, the Division will direct the respondent to answer the charges and will schedule a public hearing on the complaint.[6] The respondent must file its answer at least two business days prior to the scheduled hearing.

4. The Division may subpoena witnesses and require the production of records for examination.[7] The complainant's case may be presented by an attorney or agent for the Division and/or by the complainant's attorney.[8]

5. The complainant should be prepared to come forward with proof of damages, including medical expenses, evidence to show mental or emotional damages and other economic losses. Also be prepared with evidence as to why punitive damages should be awarded.[9]

6. Within one hundred eighty (180) days after the commencement of the hearing, the Division will make a determination setting forth findings of fact and issue an order based on these findings.[10]

7. If the Commissioner finds respondent has not engaged in an unlawful discriminatory act, the order will dismiss the complaint. If, however, the Commissioner finds that respondent has engaged in any discriminatory housing practices, the Commissioner may award any of the following forms of relief: a cease and desist order; an order requiring respondent to extend full, equal and unsegregated accommodations, advantages, facilities and privileges; compensatory damages for economic losses, mental and emotional distress and any physical illness.

---

3. Executive Law § 297(2)(b).
4. Executive Law § 297(2)(b).
5. Executive Law § 298(3)(a).
6. Executive Law § 297(4)(a)(i).
7. Executive Law § 295(7).
8. Executive Law § 297(4)(a).
9. Executive Law § 297(4)(c).
10. Executive Law § 297(4)(c).

8. To challenge an order of the Division, bring a proceeding in supreme court in the county in which the unlawful discriminatory practice occurred or where the respondent transacts business within sixty (60) days after service of the order.[11]

9. The proceeding may be transferred to the appellate division if the order sought to be reviewed was made as a result of a public hearing.[12]

10. The Division is required to file a written transcript of the record of the prior proceedings.

11. The court may enter an order enforcing, modifying, enforcing as modified, or setting aside in whole or in part the Division's order. If the determination is not found to be supported by sufficient evidence and the determination is set aside, the matter will be remanded to the SDHR for a new determination. An appeal from the judgment of the court is required to be reviewed as expeditiously as possible and receives precedence over other matters.

§ 18.53 Education

Claims of civil rights violations in education may be brought under any of the applicable state or federal statutes. For example, a claim of discrimination against a student by a public school or state or municipal college may be brought under 42 U.S.C.A. § 1983, since the element of state action is present.[1] *See*, Section 18.18, *supra*. A claim for discrimination based on race may also be brought under 42 U.S.C.A. § 1981.[2] *See*, Section 18.17, *supra*. A claim of discrimination based on race, color, religion, disability, national origin, age or marital status against a public, non-sectarian educational institution may also be brought under the New York Human Rights Law.[3] Claims of discrimination based on a

---

11. Executive Law § 298.

12. *Id.*

§ 18.53

1. Gant v. Wallingford Bd. of Educ., 69 F.3d 669 (2d Cir.1995)(challenge to demotion of child from first grade to kindergarten based on his race); Clements v. County of Nassau, 835 F.2d 1000 (2d Cir.1987) (unsuccessful claim of discrimination against county college under Section 1983 alleging bad faith in grading and evaluating student which led to her failure to graduate).

Under some circumstances, it is possible that a cause of action may lie under Section 1983 even with respect to private educational institutions. *See, e.g.,* Coleman v. Wagner College, 429 F.2d 1120 (2d Cir. 1970); *but see* Albert v. Carovano, 851 F.2d 561 (2d Cir.1988) (en banc) (a private college's decision to discipline students does not constitute state action merely because a state statute requires private colleges to adopt disciplinary procedures and file them with the state). *See also, supra,* § 18.18.

2. As set forth in § 18.17, *supra*, a complaint must set forth more than mere conclusory allegations and must allege that the institution's conduct was the result of purposeful race-based discrimination, or the claim will fail. *See* Odom v. Columbia Univ., 906 F.Supp. 188 (S.D.N.Y.1995).

3. Executive Law § 296(4) provides that "[i]t shall be an unlawful discriminatory practice for an education corporation or association which holds itself out to the public to be non-sectarian and exempt from taxation pursuant to the provisions of article

§ 18.53 CIVIL RIGHTS LAW Ch. 18

disability may also be brought against either public or private institutions under the Rehabilitation Act or the ADA.[4] *See*, Section 18.19, *supra*.

A claim may also lie under the Individuals With Disabilities Education Act ("IDEA"), formerly referred to as the Education of the Handicapped Act, a federal statute which guarantees children with disabilities a free and appropriate public education.[5] A claim under the IDEA may be brought in either state or federal court, once all administrative remedies are exhausted.[6]

Claims of sex discrimination may be brought under Title IX of the Education Amendments of 1972, 20 U.S.C.A. §§ 1681–88 (1988). Title IX provides that no person shall be excluded from participation in, denied benefits of, or be subjected to discrimination under any education program or activity receiving federal funding. A successful Title IX claim

---

four of the real property tax law to deny the use of its facilities to any person otherwise qualified, by reason of his race, color, religion, disability, national origin, age or marital status."

PRACTICE POINTER: Proof that a plaintiff is "otherwise qualified" is a required element to a successful cause of action. *See* Brown v. Albert Einstein Coll. of Medicine of Yeshiva Univ., 172 A.D.2d 197, 568 N.Y.S.2d 61 (1st Dep't 1991)(affirming dismissal of age discrimination claim in denial of admission to medical school because plaintiff was not "otherwise qualified" for admission in that his grades and test scores were significantly lower than those of students who were accepted for admission). The court further noted in Brown that in matters of academic judgment, a court's review is limited "to the issue of whether the institution has acted in good faith or irrationally or arbitrarily." *Id.*, 172 A.D.2d at 198, 568 N.Y.S.2d at 62 (citations omitted).

4. Morse v. Univ. of Vermont, 973 F.2d 122 (2d Cir.1992)(unsuccessful claim of failure to accommodate student's handicap of hypothyroidism under the Rehabilitation Act); Rothschild v. Grottenthaler, 907 F.2d 286 (2d Cir.1990) (successful challenge under Rehabilitation Act to require school district to provide and pay for sign language interpreter to deaf parents of non-hearing impaired students at certain school activities).

5. 20 U.S.C.A. §§ 1400, *et seq. See also*, Mrs. C. v. Wheaton, 916 F.2d 69 (2d Cir. 1990); Mrs. W. v. Tirozzi, 832 F.2d 748 (2d Cir.1987).

CAVEAT: The IDEA is a comprehensive statutory scheme. Prior to bringing a claim under the IDEA, the plaintiff must exhaust his or her state administrative remedies, or the claim will be dismissed for lack of subject matter jurisdiction. 20 U.S.C.A. § 1415; Education Law § 4404; *see also*, Schlude v. Northeast Cent. School Dist., 892 F.Supp. 560 (S.D.N.Y.1995); Hope v. Cortines, 872 F.Supp. 14 (E.D.N.Y.1995). Although there is an exception where exhaustion would be futile, the practitioner should not rely upon the futility exception. *Id.*; *cf.* Mason v. Schenectady City School Dist., 879 F.Supp. 215 (N.D.N.Y.1993) (not requiring plaintiffs to exhaust because defendants persistently failed to inform plaintiff of the safeguards available to her).

Moreover, Section 1415(f) of the IDEA provides that before an action is filed under the Constitution, the Rehabilitation Act or other federal statutes seeking relief that is also available under the IDEA, plaintiff must exhaust his or her remedies to the same extent as would be required under the IDEA. Based on this provision, the court in Hope, *supra* concluded that the ADA, § 1983 and Title VI claims could not stand and dismissed the entire complaint.

6. 20 U.S.C.A. § 1415(e)(2).

CAVEAT: The IDEA contains no Statute of Limitations. Depending upon the nature of the claim, some courts have held that the four month limitations period applicable to an Article 78 proceeding should apply, *see* Heldman v. Sobol, 962 F.2d 148, 158 note 10 (2d Cir.1992), while other courts have held that the three year limitations period applicable to personal injury actions should apply. *See, e.g.*, Mason v. Schenectady

requires a showing of intentional discrimination. So, for example, to satisfy the elements of a Title IX claim of discrimination in disciplinary actions, plaintiff must allege "a particularized allegation relating to a causal connection between the flawed outcome and gender bias" and must point to "particularized circumstances" which support an inference of gender bias, such as statements by members of the disciplinary panel or school officials or patterns of decisions demonstrating the influence of gender.[7] Without allegations of selective enforcement in academic standards or that the decision was inconsistent with those standards, the complaint will be deficient.

A new federal statute, Section 40302 of the 1994 Violence Against Women Act, 42 U.S.C.A. § 13981, provides that an action may be commenced in federal or state court by a victim of a crime of violence motivated by gender. The statute provides that the plaintiff may recover compensatory and punitive damages together with injunctive and declaratory relief against any person, including a person who acts under color of state law. The law was declared unconstitutional in July 1996, in connection with the first civil action brought under the statute.[8]

It is well established that the right to public education may not be taken away without appropriate due process, which includes notice and an opportunity to be heard.[9] If a student is disciplined without adequate due process safeguards, he or she may have a civil rights claim under Section 1983.[10] Alternatively, a state court challenge may also be brought under Article 78 of the CPLR.[11] The Court of Appeals has cautioned,

---

School Dist., 879 F.Supp. 215 (N.D.N.Y. 1993).

7. Murray v. New York Univ. College of Dentistry, 57 F.3d 243, 251 (2d Cir.1995) (quoting Yusuf v. Vassar College, 35 F.3d 709, 715 (2d Cir.1994)).

8. Brzonkala v. Virginia Polytechnic and State Univ., 935 F.Supp. 779 (W.D.Va. 1996). The action was brought by a female student at Virginia Polytechnic & State University sought damages after she was allegedly raped by two students. The lawsuit also challenged the disciplinary system used by the school to deal with student offenses. The statute was upheld in Doe v. Doe, 929 F.Supp. 608 (D.Conn.1996).

9. Goss v. Lopez, 419 U.S. 565, 95 S.Ct. 729, 42 L.Ed.2d 725 (1975).

The right to public education only includes education through the twelfth grade. There is no statutory or constitutional right to a state financed higher education. Weinbaum v. Cuomo, 219 A.D.2d 554, 631 N.Y.S.2d 825 (1st Dep't 1995) (holding that Sections 6201 and 6221 of the Education Law, which concern the financing of the city university system, do not create private rights of action).

10. *See* Ross v. Disare, 500 F.Supp. 928 (S.D.N.Y.1977)(granting temporary restraining order for deficient hearing).

11. PRACTICE POINTER: Since under Section 1983 there is no requirement to exhaust administrative remedies, there is a longer Statute of Limitations and the possibility of an award of attorneys' fees, it is probably preferable to bring the claim under Section 1983.

CAVEAT: In at least one case, however, a court dismissed a cause of action for intentional infliction of emotional distress and breach of contract brought by a student against a law school and in so doing, observed that plaintiff's claim would be redressable only in an Article 78 proceeding, but refused to convert the action to an Article 78 proceeding since plaintiff had failed to exhaust his administrative remedies and was now barred from doing so. Silverman v. New York Univ. School of Law, 193 A.D.2d 411, 597 N.Y.S.2d 314 (1st Dep't 1993).

§ 18.53 CIVIL RIGHTS LAW Ch. 18

however, that a claim which merely alleges that a student was dismissed from school because of purely deficient academic performance is not actionable since "[s]trong policy considerations militate against the intervention of courts in controversies relating to an educational institution's judgment of a student's academic performance."[12]

Library References:
West's Key No. Digests, Civil Rights ⚖127.1, 128.

§ 18.54 Equal Rights in Places of Public Accommodation and Amusement

Section 40 of the Civil Rights Law prohibits discrimination in places of public accommodation, resort or amusement to any persons based on race, creed, color or national origin.[1] The phrase "places of public accommodation, resort or amusement" includes, *inter alia*, inns, taverns, road houses, hotels, restaurants or any place where food is sold for consumption on the premises, any store or park where spirituous or malt liquors are sold, any store where ice cream, fruit preparations or beverages are sold for consumption on their premises, retail stores, barber shops, theatres, schools and public libraries supported in whole or in part by public funds or by contributions from the general public; garages, public conveyances, public halls or elevators in buildings occupied by two or more tenants.[2]

The Human Rights Law also prohibits discrimination based in public accommodations.[3] The Human Rights Law definition of public accommodation differs from the definition in the Civil Rights Law.[4]

---

12. Matter of Susan M. v. New York Law School, 76 N.Y.2d 241, 245, 557 N.Y.S.2d 297, 299, 556 N.E.2d 1104, 1106 (1990) (dismissing Article 78 petition seeking reinstatement to law school brought by petitioner who complained of "irrational testing and grading procedures" and that she had been retaliated against for complaining about professors). The Court of Appeals further explained that its review of cases concerning grading disputes is strictly limited to the question of whether the challenged determination was arbitrary and capricious, irrational, made in bad faith, or contrary to law, and that this standard has rarely been satisfied.

§ 18.54

1. The statute does not apply to corporations. Jews for Jesus, Inc. v. Jewish Community Relations Council of New York, Inc., 968 F.2d 286 (2d Cir.1992).

2. *See* Civil Rights Law § 40 for a complete list of the places included.

3. Executive Law § 296(2)(a). Unlike the Civil Rights Law provision, which only prohibits discrimination based on race, creed, color or national origin, the Human Rights Law also prohibits discrimination in public accommodations based on sex, disability and marital status. *See also,* Title II of the Civil Rights Act of 1964, 42 U.S.C.A. §§ 2000a, *et seq*. Section 2000a(a) prohibits discrimination in places of public accommodation based on race, color, religion or national origin.

A public or private accommodation may, however, bar a person based on sex if the SDHR grants an exemption based on bona fide considerations of public policy. Executive Law § 296(2)(b).

4. *Compare* Executive Law § 292(9) *with* Civil Rights Law § 40. The Court of Appeals has noted that the definition of public accommodation under the Executive Law should be interpreted broadly. United States Power Squadrons v. State Human Rights App. Bd., 59 N.Y.2d 401, 409, 465 N.Y.S.2d 871, 875, 452 N.E.2d 1199, rearg. dismissed 60 N.Y.2d 702, 468 N.Y.S.2d 1027, 455 N.E.2d 1267 (1983).

Library References:

West's Key No. Digests, Civil Rights ⚖119–124.

§ 18.55 Equal Rights in Places of Public Accommodation and Amusement—General Provisions

A "legitimate theater," burlesque theater, music hall, opera house, concert hall or circus may refuse to admit a person or may exclude a person "whose conduct or speech ... is abusive or offensive" or who is "engaged in any activity which may tend to be a breach of the peace."[1] This provision only applies to the enumerated places, and does not apply to movie theatres or other places of public entertainment or amusement that are not enumerated in the statute.[2]

Section 40–c provides that all persons are entitled to equal protection of the laws of the state and any subdivision and further prohibits discrimination or harassment[3] by any person, firm, corporation, institution, the state or any political subdivision based on race, creed, color, national origin, sex, marital status or disability.[4] Any person who violates Section 40–c, Penal Law § 240.30(3)[5] or § 240.31[6] or who aids or incites in the violation of these statutes is subject to a penalty of not less than one hundred dollars nor more than five hundred dollars for each viola-

In Cahill v. Rosa, 89 N.Y.2d 14, 651 N.Y.S.2d 344, 674 N.E.2d 274 (1996), the Court of Appeals held that a private dental office is a place of public accommodation under the Human Rights Law, even though a dental office is not listed as a place of public accommodation in the statutory definition. While the dental offices were in privately-owned premises, and the dentists operated on an "appointment-only" basis, the court determined that dental offices fell within the definition of "establishments dealing with goods or services of any kind."

§ 18.55

1. Civil Rights Law § 40–b.

2. Impastato v. Hellman Enterprises, Inc. 147 A.D.2d 788, 537 N.Y.S.2d 659 (3d Dep't 1989)(movie theater); Mandel v. Brooklyn Nat. League Baseball Club, 179 Misc. 27, 37 N.Y.S.2d 152 (Sup.Ct., Bronx County, 1942) (baseball stadium). In Impastato, plaintiffs also alleged a cause of action for intentional and negligent infliction of emotional distress, which failed as well.

3. "Harassment" as defined by Penal Law § 240.26, provides:

A person is guilty of harassment in the second degree when, with intent to harass, annoy or alarm another person: (1) He or she strikes, shoves, kicks or otherwise subjects such other person to physical contact, or attempts or threatens to do the same; or (2) He or she follows a person in or about a public place or places; or (3) He or she engages in a course of conduct or repeatedly commits acts which alarm or seriously annoy such other person and which serve no legitimate purpose.

4. Section 40–c has been upheld against First Amendment challenges. See, e.g., People v. Miccio, 155 Misc.2d 697, 589 N.Y.S.2d 762 (Crim.Ct., Kings County, 1992).

5. Section 240.30(3) provides that a person is guilty of aggravated harassment in the second degree when, with intent to harass, annoy, threaten or alarm another person, a person "strikes, shoves, kicks, or otherwise subjects another person to physical contact, or attempts or threatens to do the same because of the race, color, religion or national origin of such person." Aggravated harassment in the second degree is a class A misdemeanor.

6. Penal Law § 240.31, aggravated harassment in the first degree, is a class E felony. Section 240.31 covers the destruction of religious property and also individuals who have previously been convicted of aggravated harassment in the second degree.

tion, to be recovered by the person aggrieved.[7] A violation of Section 40–c is also a class A misdemeanor.

A plaintiff alleging discrimination in a place of public accommodation must establish a *prima facie* case of discrimination. The burden then shifts to the defendant to rebut the presumption of discrimination by putting forth legitimate, nondiscriminatory reasons for the difference in treatment. Once the presumption of discrimination is rebutted, the plaintiff must show that the proffered reasons were not true but were merely a pretext for discrimination.[8]

§ 18.56 Equal Rights in Places of Public Accommodation and Amusement—Private Clubs

An institution, club or place of accommodation which is in its nature "distinctively private" is exempt. In any action against a club, the club has the burden of proof to show that it is private. In determining whether a club is private, the following factors should be considered: (1) whether there is an established screening procedure for prospective members, (2) whether the use of facilities and services of the organization are limited to members and their guests, (3) whether the members control the club, (4) whether it is nonprofit and operated solely for the benefit of its members, and (5) whether it directs its publicity exclusively and only to members.[1]

---

7. See Civil Rights Law § 40–d. See also, People v. Dieppa, 158 Misc.2d 584, 601 N.Y.S.2d 786 (Sup.Ct., Kings County, 1993).

CAVEAT: Section 40–d requires that "[a]t or before the commencement of any action under this section, notice thereof shall be served upon the attorney general." While the notice requirement is not a condition precedent to the District Attorney's commencement of a criminal prosecution under the Penal Law (People v. Fuller, 155 Misc.2d 812, 590 N.Y.S.2d 159 (Crim.Ct., Kings County, 1992)), it is a condition precedent where both federal and state causes of action are asserted, regardless of whether the action is brought in state or federal court. Harvey v. NYRAC, Inc., 813 F.Supp. 206 (E.D.N.Y.1993); Silver v. Equitable Life Assur. Soc., 168 A.D.2d 367, 563 N.Y.S.2d 78 (1st Dep't 1990). See infra, § 18.97 for the form of the notice.

8. Matter of North Shore Univ. Hosp. v. Rosa, 86 N.Y.2d 413, 633 N.Y.S.2d 462, 657 N.E.2d 483 (1995); Elaine W. v. Joint Diseases North General Hospital, Inc., 81 N.Y.2d 211, 597 N.Y.S.2d 617, 613 N.E.2d 523 (1993) (holding that unless hospital can demonstrate it is medically unsafe to treat all pregnant women at its inpatient drug treatment program, its blanket exclusion of pregnant women would constitute discrimination based on sex); Brown v. Daytop Village, Inc., 161 Misc.2d 248, 613 N.Y.S.2d 1021 (Sup.Ct., Bronx County, 1994) (residential drug treatment facility met burden of showing that its regulation requiring residents to cut their hair was based on legitimate medical reasons and did not discriminate based on religious belief).

§ 18.56

1. United States Power Squadrons v. State Human Rights Appeal Bd., 59 N.Y.2d 401, 465 N.Y.S.2d 871, 452 N.E.2d 1199, rearg. dismissed 60 N.Y.2d 702, 468 N.Y.S.2d 1027, 455 N.E.2d 1267 (1983).

In 1984, the City of New York adopted an amendment to its Human Rights Law which provides that any institution, club or place of accommodation, other than a religious corporation or benevolent order, is not considered private if it has more than 400 members, provides regular meals and receives regular payment directly or directly from or on behalf of non-members. The law was upheld under the First and Fourteenth Amendments in New York State Club Ass'n v. City of New York, 487 U.S. 1, 108 S.Ct. 2225, 101 L.Ed.2d 1 (1988).

§ 18.57 Equal Rights in Places of Public Accommodation and Amusement—Persons With Disabilities Accompanied by a Guide Dog, Hearing Dog or Service Dog

Pursuant to Civil Rights Law § 47(1), no person may be denied admission to or equal use and enjoyment of any public facility solely because that person is accompanied by a guide dog, hearing dog or service dog. "Public facility" includes places in which the general public is normally invited, for example, all forms of transportation, housing accommodations, educational facilities, restaurants, theatres and entertainment facilities. Although part of a building may be considered "public," other areas may not be for the purposes of this statute.[1]

A provision of the Human Rights Law also prohibits discrimination against a blind or hearing impaired person or person with a disability based on the use of a guide dog, hearing dog or service dog.[2]

Library References:
West's Key No. Digests, Civil Rights ⚖107(2).

§ 18.58 Equal Rights in Places of Public Accommodation and Amusement—Remedies for Discrimination

In addition to the remedies set forth in the Civil Rights Law (*see*, Sections 18.54, 18.55, *supra*), an action for discrimination in places of public accommodation may be brought under the Human Rights Law,[1] either by filing an action directly in court or by filing an administrative claim. An action may also be commenced under Title II of the Civil Rights Act of 1964.[2]

§ 18.57

1. *See, e.g.*, Perino v. St. Vincent's Medical Center of Staten Island, 132 Misc.2d 20, 502 N.Y.S.2d 921 (Sup.Ct., Richmond County, 1986). In Perino, the court noted that although some areas of a hospital would be considered a "public facility," the labor and delivery room were not, since the general public was not normally invited there. Accordingly, the court held that the hospital did not discriminate against a blind expectant father by prohibiting him from bringing his seeing eye dog into the delivery room.

2. Executive Law § 296(14). This provision is more comprehensive than Civil Rights Law § 47, since it applies to "any person engaged in any activity covered by [§ 296]," not only public accommodations.

§ 18.58

1. Executive Law § 296(2)(a).

2. 42 U.S.C.A. §§ 2000a, *et seq.*

PRACTICE POINTER: The only remedy available under the federal statute is injunctive relief. O'Connor v. 11 West 30th Street Rest. Corp., 1995 WL 354904 (S.D.N.Y.1995). Therefore, the state law causes of action should be asserted as well.

CAVEAT: Since New York has a state statute prohibiting discrimination in public accommodations, Section 2000a–3(c) requires a plaintiff to give written notice to

Section 47–c of the New York Civil Rights Law provides that any person or legal entity violating the provisions contained in Sections 47, 47–a or 47–b shall be guilty of a violation, which is punishable under the Penal Law. There is no provision in the Civil Rights Law which provides a private right of action for damages for individuals with disabilities who are denied admission to a public facility because the individual is accompanied by a guide dog. A private right of action does lie, however, under Executive Law § 296(14). The aggrieved individual may file a complaint with the State Division of Human Rights (*see*, Section § 18.49, *supra*) or may file an action in state or federal court. A claim may also lie under the Americans With Disabilities Act of 1990.[3]

§ 18.59 Employment Discrimination Provisions Exclusive to the New York Civil Rights Law

There are numerous state and federal statutes prohibiting discrimination in employment, including Title VII of the Civil Rights Act of 1964,[1] the Equal Pay Act,[2] and the Age Discrimination in Employment Act[3] which are discussed in Chapter 17, "Employment Law." These provisions are generally known to practitioners and actions under these sections are common. There are also very specific statutes unique to the New York Civil Rights Law, that are not as well known and are not commonly pleaded. These statutes are discussed in the two sections, below.

Library References:

West's Key No. Digests, Civil Rights ⇐141.

§ 18.60 Employment Discrimination Provisions Exclusive to the New York Civil Rights Law—In General

Section 40–a of the Civil Rights Law prohibits schools, Boards of Education, or any other official responsible for hiring persons seeking employment or an official position in the public schools of the State of New York from either directly or indirectly asking, indicating or transmitting orally or in writing the religion or religious affiliation of any person seeking employment in the public schools.[1]

Section 42 of the Civil Rights Law prohibits a public utility company from refusing to employ any person in the operation or maintenance of a

---

the State of New York or its designated agency prior to commencing an action in federal court.

3. 42 U.S.C.A. §§ 12131, *et seq.*

§ 18.59

1. 42 U.S.C.A. §§ 2000e, *et seq.*

2. 29 U.S.C.A. §§ 206, *et seq.*

3. 29 U.S.C.A. §§ 621, *et seq.*

§ 18.60

1. Civil Rights Law § 40–a.

public service based on race, creed, color or national origin.[2] Section 43 prohibits labor organizations from denying membership to or treating any person differently based on race, creed, color or national origin.[3] Section 44 provides that it is unlawful for any person, firm or corporation engaged in the production, manufacture or distribution of military or naval material, equipment or supplies for the state or federal government to refuse to employ any person based on race, color, creed or national origin.[4] The provisions of Sections 42, 43 and 44 may be enforced by the Commissioner of the Department of Labor.

Additionally, Section 41 provides for civil and criminal penalties for a violation of Section 40–a, Section 40–b, Section 42 and Section 43.[5] For each violation, the penalty is not less than one hundred dollars nor more than five hundred dollars. The action may be commenced in any court of competent jurisdiction in the county in which the plaintiff or the defendant resides. In addition to the civil penalty, the employer, manager, owner or officer of the defendant company, agency, bureau, association or corporation shall be deemed guilty of a misdemeanor for each offense and upon conviction, shall be fined between $100 and $500, or shall be imprisoned for not less than thirty days nor more than ninety days, or be subject to both fine and imprisonment.[6]

Library References:

West's Key No. Digests, Civil Rights ⚷141.

§ 18.61 Employment Discrimination Provisions Exclusive to the New York Civil Rights Law—Persons With Disabilities

It is unlawful to discriminate by refusing to employ a person with a disability who is accompanied by a guide dog, hearing dog or service dog,

2. Civil Rights Law § 42.

3. Civil Rights Law § 43.

4. Civil Rights Law § 44. Given the specific nature of the conduct prohibited in this section, it is not surprising that there is only one reported decision discussing discrimination under this section. See Matter of Board of Higher Education of the City of New York v. Carter, 14 N.Y.2d 138, 250 N.Y.S.2d 33, 199 N.E.2d 141 (1964).

5. Section 41 does not provide a civil penalty for a violation of Section 44, the prohibition of discrimination in employment by those engaged in the manufacture of military or naval equipment or supplies. Section 44–a, however, provides a criminal penalty for a person who excludes an individual from employment in any capacity in an industry engaged in defense contracts based on race, color, creed or national origin. A person violating Section 44–a is guilty of a misdemeanor, and is subject to a fine of not less than $50 nor more than $500.

6. **CAVEAT:** At or before the commencement of an action under Civil Rights Law § 41, notice of commencement of the action shall be served on the Attorney General. See infra, § 18.97 for the form for the notice.

PRACTICE POINTER: There are a dearth of reported decisions concerning these provisions. In the event the practitioner finds that one of these provisions applies to a prospective plaintiff, the statutory cause of action should be pleaded in conjunction with those causes of action which provide more complete relief.

§ 18.61 CIVIL RIGHTS LAW Ch. 18

unless it can be clearly shown that the disability would prevent that individual from performing the particular job. Any person who violates this provision is guilty of a violation.[1]

Library References:

West's Key No. Digests, Civil Rights ⚖=173–175.

§ 18.62 Employment Discrimination Provisions Exclusive to the New York Civil Rights Law—Persons With Genetic Disorders

New York also has a separate statute providing that it is unlawful to discriminate in employment because a person has the sickle cell trait or is a carrier of Tay-Sachs disease or Cooley's anemia, unless it can be clearly shown that the person would be prevented from performing the particular job based on the genetic disorder.[1] Any person or entity violating this provision is guilty of a violation.[2]

Since the Civil Rights Law does not provide for a private right of action for the recovery of damages under this section, a claim for relief on behalf of an individual with a genetic disorder should be brought in state or federal court under the Human Rights Law or the Americans With Disabilities Act of 1990.[3]

Library References:

West's Key No. Digests, Civil Rights ⚖=173–175.

§ 18.63 Right of Privacy

New York does not recognize a common law tort of invasion of privacy.[1] While some other jurisdictions have expanded the law with respect to privacy rights,[2] the New York Legislature has consistently rejected proposed bills to expand the law to cover new areas.[3] New York's

---

§ 18.61

1. Civil Rights Law § 47–c.

§ 18.62

1. Civil Rights Law §§ 48, 48–a.

2. Civil Rights Law § 48–b.

3. 42 U.S.C.A. §§ 12101, et seq. See Jones v. Inter–County Imaging Centers, 889 F.Supp. 741 (S.D.N.Y.1995).

§ 18.63

1. Howell v. New York Post Co., 81 N.Y.2d 115, 123, 596 N.Y.S.2d 350, 354, 612 N.E.2d 699 (1993). See generally, Haig, et al., Commercial Litigation in New York State Courts (West 1995) Ch. 64 "Right of Publicity Claims."

2. See supra, Howell, 81 N.Y.2d at 123, 596 N.Y.S.2d at 354, discussing three other "privacy torts" recognized by a number of other states: (1) unreasonable publicity given to another's private life; (2) unreasonable intrusion upon seclusion; and (3) publicity that unreasonably places another in a false light. See also, Waldron v. Ball Corp., 210 A.D.2d 611, 619 N.Y.S.2d 841 (3d Dep't 1994); Groden v. Random House, Inc., 61 F.3d 1045 (2d Cir.1995), which both note that New York does not recognize a cause of action for reporting inaccurate but not defamatory information.

3. Howell, supra note 1.

privacy protection for individuals[4] is found solely in Civil Rights Law §§ 50 and 51.

Section 50 provides that

> [a] person, firm or corporation that uses for advertising purposes, or for the purposes of trade, the name, portrait or picture of any living person without having first obtained the written consent of such person, or if a minor of his or her parent or guardian, is guilty of a misdemeanor.

The civil remedy is found in Section 51, which provides in pertinent part that

> [a]ny person whose name, portrait or picture is used within the state for advertising purposes or for the purposes of trade without the written consent first obtained as [provided in § 50] may maintain an equitable action in the supreme court of this state against the person, firm or corporation so using his name, portrait or picture, to prevent and restrain the use thereof; and may also sue and recover damages for any injuries sustained by reason of such use and if the defendant shall have knowingly used such person's name, portrait or picture in such manner as is forbidden or declared to be unlawful by section fifty of this article, the jury, in its discretion, may award exemplary damages. . . .

These sections were enacted in 1909 as a legislative response to a Court of Appeals decision which denied a cause of action to a minor whose picture was used without her consent for advertising purposes[5] and have consistently been strictly construed since the statutes are "in derogation of the common law."[6] While the statutes sometimes seemingly conflict with the First Amendment (*see*, Section 18.64, *infra*), the rights protected are separate and apart from federal copyright protection and are not

---

4. The statutes only provide protection for "persons." Protection for non-profit organizations is found in General Business Law § 397.

5. Roberson v. Rochester Folding Box Co., 171 N.Y. 538, 64 N.E. 442 (1902). For a history of the statutes, *see* Shields v. Gross, 58 N.Y.2d 338, 344, 461 N.Y.S.2d 254, 257, 448 N.E.2d 108 (1983); *see also, supra,* Howell, note 1, 81 N.Y.2d at 122–23, 596 N.Y.S.2d at 354.

6. Shields, *supra*, note 5, 58 N.Y.2d at 345, 461 N.Y.S.2d at 257; *see also*, Arrington v. New York Times Co., 55 N.Y.2d 433, 449 N.Y.S.2d 941, 434 N.E.2d 1319 (1982) (stating that §§ 50 and 51 "were drafted narrowly to encompass only the commercial use of an individual's name or likeness and no more").

Claims for any other type of "invasion of privacy" are routinely dismissed. *See, e.g.*, Hurwitz v. United States, 884 F.2d 684 (2d Cir.1989) (Unauthorized opening and copying of another's mail does not give rise to a cause of action for invasion of privacy).

PRACTICE POINTER: If the use of plaintiff's name or photograph does not fall within the statutory cause of action, plaintiff could still possibly state a cause of action for intentional infliction of emotional distress. While the Second Circuit has recognized a limited constitutional right of privacy, Doe v. City of New York, 15 F.3d 264 (2d Cir.1994), such a claim is unavailable unless there is state action. Arrington, *supra*, 55 N.Y.2d at 443, 449 N.Y.S.2d at 946; *see supra*, § 18.18.

Alternatively, counsel should consider bringing the action in a jurisdiction which recognizes a more general tort of invasion of privacy.

§ 18.63 CIVIL RIGHTS LAW Ch. 18

preempted by federal law, since the right of privacy is qualitatively different from a copyright infringement claim.[7]

Library References:

West's Key No. Digests, Constitutional Law ⚷82(7).

§ 18.64 Right of Privacy—Generally

In order to state a cause of action under Section 51, plaintiff must allege and prove (1) use of plaintiff's name, portrait or picture, (2) for the purpose of advertisement or trade, (3) without plaintiff's consent.[1] The statute further provides that the usage must have occurred within the State of New York.[2] All of these allegations should be pled in the complaint.[3]

Although the statutes prohibit the use of a "name, portrait or picture," other representations are also prohibited, provided that plaintiff is recognizable. Use of a person's voice without consent, however, is not protected.[4]

While the statutes state that the use must be for "advertising purposes or for the purposes of trade," these terms are not defined. The cases are clear that "a picture illustrating an article on a matter of public interest is not considered used for the purpose of trade or advertising ... unless it has no real relationship to the article ... or unless the article is an advertisement in disguise."[5] Similarly, a news article, even if false, will not be the basis for a viable claim under the

---

7. *See* Shamsky v. Garan, Inc., 167 Misc.2d 149, 632 N.Y.S.2d 930, 935 (Sup. Ct., N.Y. County, 1995) (citing 17 U.S.C.A. § 301(b)(3), which provides that states may regulate activities that are not "equivalent" to rights within the general scope of copyright).

§ 18.64

1. Civil Rights Law § 51; *see also*, Cohen v. Herbal Concepts, 63 N.Y.2d 379, 384, 482 N.Y.S.2d 457, 459, 472 N.E.2d 307 (1984).

2. CAVEAT: The complaint should contain an allegation that the use of plaintiff's name, portrait or picture was used "within the State of New York."

3. PRACTICE POINTER: If one of these elements is not satisfied, defendant should move to dismiss or should move for summary judgment. Only if a material issue of fact is found will summary judgment be precluded. Titan Sports, Inc. v. Comics World Corp., 870 F.2d 85 (2d Cir.1989)(question of fact as to whether the photographs are for use of trade); Da Silva v. Time Incorporated, 908 F.Supp. 184 (S.D.N.Y.1995) (genuine issue of material fact as to whether plaintiff's new reputation could have been tainted as a result of published photograph and caption).

4. Maxwell v. N.W. Ayer, Inc. 159 Misc.2d 454, 605 N.Y.S.2d 174 (Sup.Ct., N.Y. County, 1993).

5. Finger v. Omni Publications, 77 N.Y.2d 138, 142, 564 N.Y.S.2d 1014, 1016, 566 N.E.2d 141 (1990) (citation omitted) (affirming dismissal of claim by parents on their own behalf and on behalf of their six children for the use of a family photograph accompanying an article on research related to fertility, since it was not a commercial publication); *see also*, Howell, *supra*, § 18.63, note 1 (affirming dismissal of claim by mental patient for use of a photograph of plaintiff with another patient to accompanying a news article about the other patient); Arrington, *supra*, § 18.63, note 6, 449 N.Y.S.2d 941.

Civil Rights Law.[6]

The statutes are "designed to protect a person's identity, not merely a property interest in his or her 'name,' 'portrait' or 'picture'...."[7] To prevail, plaintiff must be recognizable and identifiable.[8] Since the cause of action protects the individual, it is limited to any living person and ceases upon the person's death.[9]

It is also essential to prove that the use was without plaintiff's consent. If plaintiff has given prior consent but that consent has expired, a cause of action will lie.[10]

The action must be commenced within one year of the date of the first publication.[11] Plaintiff can seek compensatory and punitive damages, and an injunction to discontinue the prohibited use.[12] If products were sold, plaintiff should request an accounting.[13] Section 51 is in a sense a "strict liability" statute, at least insofar as recovery for compensatory damages and equitable relief. Section 51 provides that knowing use is only required for an award of exemplary (punitive) damages.[14]

Nevertheless, there are defenses available. Set forth in the text of Section 51 are four statutory exceptions. The first provides that a person, firm or corporation is not prohibited from "selling or otherwise transferring any material containing such name, portrait or picture in whatever medium to any user of such name, portrait or picture, or to any third party for sale or transfer directly or indirectly to such a user, for use in a manner lawful under this article." A second exception allows professional photographers to exhibit samples of their work unless the person being portrayed has given written notice objecting to such use of photographs. The third exception allows for the use of the name, picture

---

6. Cruz v. Latin News Impacto Newspaper, 216 A.D.2d 50, 627 N.Y.S.2d 388 (1st Dep't 1995)(no tort for inaccurate but not defamatory information).

7. Cohen v. Herbal Concepts, 63 N.Y.2d 379, 384, 482 N.Y.S.2d 457, 459, 472 N.E.2d 307 (1984).

8. *Id.*, noting however that there is no requirement that a photograph must show plaintiff's face in order for plaintiff to prevail.

9. Smith v. Long Island Jewish–Hillside Medical Center, 118 A.D.2d 553, 499 N.Y.S.2d 167 (2d Dep't 1986)(a cause of action for use of an infant's picture without parental permission abates upon the infants's death).

10. Welch v. Mr. Christmas Inc., 57 N.Y.2d 143, 148, 454 N.Y.S.2d 971, 974, 440 N.E.2d 1317 (1982)("use after expiration of the effective period of consent is no less an invasion of privacy than is use without consent").

11. CPLR 215(3). *Cf.* Russo v. Huntington Town House, Inc., 184 A.D.2d 627, 584 N.Y.S.2d 883 (2d Dep't 1992) (allowing action to proceed since it was brought within one year of continuing use of photograph, but limiting damages to those sustained within the previous year).

CAVEAT: Since the Statute of Limitations is an affirmative defense, it must be pleaded by defendant in the answer or in a motion to dismiss.

12. *See* Cohen *supra*, note 7, 63 N.Y.2d at 383, 482 N.Y.S.2d at 459. For a form complaint for unlawful use of a photograph, *see* Haig, *et al.*, *Commercial Litigation in New York State Courts*, (West 1995) § 64.9, pp. 719–21.

13. *See* Shamsky v. Garan, Inc., 167 Misc.2d 149, 632 N.Y.S.2d 930 (Sup.Ct., New York County, 1995).

14. Welch v. Mr. Christmas Inc., 57 N.Y.2d 143, 150, 454 N.Y.S.2d 971, 975, 440 N.E.2d 1317 (1982).

§ 18.64   CIVIL RIGHTS LAW   Ch. 18

or portrait of a manufacturer or dealer in connection with goods and merchandise being sold. Fourth, the statute permits the use of the name, portrait or picture of an author, composer or artist in connection with his or her work.

Other defenses have developed under the case law. One such defense is the "newsworthy" exception, which applies to news stories and matters of public interest, including social trends and fashion. The Court of Appeals has held that the defense should be "liberally construed."[15]

Another defense is the "incidental use" exception. This exception provides that a news disseminator is entitled to use a person's name or likeness in distribution or advertising.[16] This defense is available (1) when the reproduced item is newsworthy and (2) the advertised material is related to the product and to the use for which the reproduced material first appeared.[17] This defense flows from the First Amendment protection given to news disseminators and is construed broadly.[18] The defense is not lost if the plaintiff did not give permission for the original use of his or her likeness.[19]

Additional issues arise if plaintiff is bringing an action with respect to fictionalized or factually-based works. A cause of action will not lie for a fictionalized account of a true story if plaintiff's name or photograph is not used.[20] In *Time, Inc. v. Hill*,[21] the Supreme Court held that the Federal Constitutional guarantees of freedom of the press and freedom of speech "preclude the application of the New York statute to redress false reports of matters of public interest in the absence of proof that the

15. Arrington, *supra*, § 18.63, note 6; see also, Howell, *supra*, § 18.63, note 1; Finger v. Omni, *supra*, note 5;. The defense is premised on the media's First Amendment protection.

16. See Stern v. Delphi Internet Servs. Corp., 165 Misc.2d 21, 626 N.Y.S.2d 694 (Sup.Ct., N.Y. County, 1995)(use of Howard Stern's name and photograph from a previously published advertisement by a computer network's bulletin board constitutes "incidental use"); Groden v. Random House, Inc., 61 F.3d 1045 (2d Cir.1995)(use of plaintiff's name and photograph in publisher's advertisement for another author's book on the same topic was "incidental use" and did not violate Sections 50 and 51).

17. Stern, *supra*, note 16, 165 Misc.2d at 30, 626 N.Y.S.2d at 700 (citation omitted).

18. Stern, *supra*, note 16, 626 N.Y.S.2d at 697–98. See also, Rand v. Hearst Corp., 31 A.D.2d 406, 408–09, 298 N.Y.S.2d 405, 409–10 (1st Dep't 1969), aff'd 26 N.Y.2d 806, 309 N.Y.S.2d 348, 257 N.E.2d 895 (1970). In Rand, the Appellate Division noted that the words "advertising purposes" and for the "purposes of trade" must be "construed narrowly and not used to curtail the right of free speech, or free press, or to shut off the publication of matters newsworthy or of public interest, or to prevent comment on matters in which the public has an interest or the right to be informed." The court went on to state that "no cause of action will lie when the name or photograph of a public figure is used unless the publication is knowingly false or may be considered a blatant selfish, commercial exploitation of plaintiff's personality." *Id.*, 31 A.D.2d at 409, 298 N.Y.S.2d at 410.

19. Stern, *supra*, note 16,165 Misc.2d at 27, 626 N.Y.S.2d at 698.

20. Hampton v. Guare, 195 A.D.2d 366, 600 N.Y.S.2d 57 (1st Dep't), leave to appeal denied 82 N.Y.2d 659, 605 N.Y.S.2d 5, 625 N.E.2d 590 (1993).

21. 385 U.S. 374, 87 S.Ct. 534, 17 L.Ed.2d 456 (1967).

defendant published the report with knowledge of its falsity or in reckless disregard of the truth."[22] Before recovery will lie for a claim by a public figure for an unauthorized presentation of his life, plaintiff must show that the portrayal is "infected with material and substantial falsification and that the work was published with knowledge of such falsification or with a reckless disregard for the truth."[23]

§ 18.65 Right of Privacy—Police Officers, Corrections Officers and Firefighters

Defendants in criminal cases generally subpoena personnel records of the arresting officers. Similarly, a plaintiff in a civil rights action claiming police misconduct or an inmate alleging excessive force by corrections officers may seek discovery of defendants' personnel files. Section 50–a(1) of the Civil Rights Law provides in relevant part that "[a]ll personnel records, used to evaluate performance toward continued employment or promotion" of police officers, firefighters, paramedics and corrections officers "shall be considered confidential and not subject to inspection or review without the express written consent of such [individual] except as may be mandated by lawful court order."

The individual seeking the records must present a "clear showing of facts sufficient to warrant the judge to request records for review."[1] If the judge concludes there is a sufficient basis, the statute provides that the judge shall sign an order requiring that the records be sealed and sent directly to the judge, who will review them and determine whether the documents are "relevant and material" to the pending action.[2]

The documents requested must be "relevant to the merits of the case and not sought to conduct 'a fishing expedition to gain information to impeach a witness's general credibility.'"[3] Conclusory allegations of negligent training and supervision are insufficient.[4]

Whether a document qualifies as a personnel record depends upon its nature and its use in evaluating an officer's performance, not its physical location or the custodian of the records.[5]

---

22. 385 U.S. at 387–88, 87 S.Ct. at 542.

23. Spahn v. Julian Messner, Inc., 21 N.Y.2d 124, 127, 286 N.Y.S.2d 832, 834, 233 N.E.2d 840, 842 (1967).

§ 18.65

1. Civil Rights Law § 50–a(2).

2. Civil Rights Law § 50–a(3).

3. Flores v. City of New York, 207 A.D.2d 302, 303, 615 N.Y.S.2d 400, 402 (1st Dep't 1994) (citation omitted); People v. Scott, 212 A.D.2d 477, 623 N.Y.S.2d 212 (1st Dep't 1995). Where, however, the outcome of the case may depend on the credibility of the officers, courts may require the records be produced.

4. *See supra*, Flores.

5. Matter of Prisoners' Legal Servs. of N.Y. v. New York State Dept. of Corr. Servs., 73 N.Y.2d 26, 31, 538 N.Y.S.2d 190, 192, 535 N.E.2d 243 (1988); Matter of Capital Newspapers Div. of the Hearst Corp. v. Burns, 109 A.D.2d 92, 95, 490 N.Y.S.2d 651, 653 (1985), aff'd 67 N.Y.2d 562, 505 N.Y.S.2d 576, 496 N.E.2d 665 (1986)(record of sick days and absences not protected).

§ 18.65 CIVIL RIGHTS LAW Ch. 18

With respect to cases brought in federal court, since questions of privilege are governed by federal law, Section 50–a is inapplicable in federal civil rights actions.[6] Therefore, there is no requirement that the court conduct an *in camera* review.[7] However, "the purposes of the state privilege law should be respected in the direct discovery of police personnel records in federal civil rights cases."[8]

Section 50–a has been strictly construed and held not to apply to any officials other than those enumerated in the statute.[9] In 1992, the Legislature enacted Civil Rights Law § 50–d, which provides similar protections to court officers and in 1993, the Legislature enacted Section 50–e, which provides similar protections to bridge and tunnel officers, sergeants and lieutenants.

The provisions of Sections 50–a, 50–d and 50–e do not apply to any grand jury or any government agency which requires the records in the furtherance of their official duties.[10]

§ 18.66 Right of Privacy—Victims of Sex Offenses

Sections 50–b and 50–c of the Civil Rights Law provide special protection to victims of sex offenses. Section 50–b provides that any documents that would tend to reveal the identity of the victim are not to be made available for public inspection.[1] The statute only protects the personal right of a sex offense victim to confidentiality of his or her identity. It does not protect against the release of medical reports or statements.[2] The rights of the accused are protected insofar as the statute specifically provides that it should not be construed so as to

---

6. King v. Conde, 121 F.R.D. 180 (E.D.N.Y.1988).
7. Askew v. Rigler, 130 F.R.D. 26 (S.D.N.Y.1990).
8. King, *supra*, note 6, 121 F.R.D. 180.

PRACTICE POINTER: In deciding whether to commence an action in state or federal court, plaintiff's counsel should consider whether it is preferable to proceed in a forum which mandates *in camera* review of such documents or whether it is preferable to proceed under the Federal Rules of Civil Procedure and local court rules concerning discovery.

If the action is in federal court, the attorney representing the officers should prepare a stipulation of confidentiality with respect to the documents that are ordered to be produced, as the court ordered to be done in Askew, have the plaintiff's attorney sign it and have the court "so order" the stipulation. The stipulation should provide that the documents are not to be disclosed to anyone; that no copies are to be made; and that the set of copies supplied be returned to counsel upon the conclusion of the litigation. *See, e.g.*, Askew v. Rigler, 130 F.R.D. 26, 27 (S.D.N.Y.1990).

9. McKinney v. State, 111 Misc.2d 382, 444 N.Y.S.2d 386 (Ct.Cl.1981) (holding that Section 50–a does not apply to court officers).

10. Civil Rights Law §§ 50–a(4), 50–d(3), 50–e(4).

§ 18.66

1. Civil Rights Law § 50–b(1). The statute provides exceptions for the person charged with the sex offense; counsel or guardian of that person; any government employee charged with investigating, prosecuting or record keeping; a necessary witness; any person who is legally responsible for the care of the victim, provided the victim consents in writing; and any other person who makes an application to the court for disclosure, if good cause is shown.

2. People v. Burton, 189 A.D.2d 532, 597 N.Y.S.2d 488 (3d Dep't 1993).

require the court to exclude the public from any stage of the criminal proceeding.[3]

Section 50–c creates a private right of action for the victim of a sex offense whose identity is disclosed and any other person injured by the disclosure. The statute further provides that the court may award attorneys' fees to a prevailing plaintiff.

§ 18.67 Changing One's Name

There is no requirement that a legal proceeding be commenced in order for an individual to change his or her name. Under common law, a person may change his or her name, without obtaining a court order, merely by assuming and using a new name, provided that "the new name is used consistently and without intent to defraud."[1] Upon marriage, either the man or the woman may elect to assume a new name; upon divorce, either the man or woman may resume a former name.[2]

Nevertheless, for the client who wishes a court-ordered name change, Article 6 of the Civil Rights Law sets forth the statutory procedure for an individual to change his or her name.[3] A party need not be a citizen to change one's name.[4] Applications brought by current or former prison inmates, however, have been subject to greater scrutiny and in some cases, have been denied.[5]

Library References:

West's Key No. Digests, Names ⚖20.

3. Civil Rights Law § 50–b(4).

§ 18.67

1. Civil Rights Law § 65(4). Indeed, even children of sufficient age and intelligence may change their names without judicial proceedings. Application of Shipley, 26 Misc.2d 204, 205 N.Y.S.2d 581 (Sup.Ct., Nassau County, 1960).

2. Civil Rights Law § 65(1), DRL § 15 (marriage); Civil Rights Law § 65(2), DRL § 240–a (divorce).

PRACTICE POINTER: In the case of a divorce, it would be prudent to ensure that the separation agreement set forth both a provision for the names of the children and a provision prohibiting one parent from unilaterally changing the names of the children without the other parent's consent. This way, unless consent is given, neither parent may unilaterally change a child's name without court permission. See, e.g., Gershowitz v. Gershowitz, 112 A.D.2d 67, 491 N.Y.S.2d 356 (1st Dep't 1985). See generally infra, Chapter 21, "Domestic Relations."

3. Civil Rights Law §§ 60–65. For changing a corporate name, see Business Corporation Law § 801 and see generally, supra, Chapter 1, "Business Organizations: Corporations"; for change of name in adoption, see DRL § 114 and Matter of Adoption of J.O.T., 120 Misc.2d 817, 466 N.Y.S.2d 636 (Fam.Ct., Kings County, 1983) and see generally, infra, Chapter 20, "Adoptions"; for changing one's name in a naturalization proceeding, see 8 U.S.C.A. §§ 1447, 1454.

4. Matter of Novogorodskaya, 104 Misc.2d 1006, 429 N.Y.S.2d 387 (Civ.Ct., Kings County, 1980).

5. Matter of Washington, 216 A.D.2d 781, 628 N.Y.S.2d 837 (3d Dep't 1995) (remitting for hearing on notice of Department of Correctional Services and Division of Criminal Justice Services); Matter of Mendelson, 151 Misc.2d 367, 572 N.Y.S.2d 1014 (Civ.Ct., Kings County, 1991); Application of Rouson, 119 Misc.2d 1069, 465 N.Y.S.2d 155 (Sup.Ct., Schoharie County, 1983).

§ 18.68 Changing One's Name—Procedure for Petition to Change Name

A petition to change one's name should be brought in the supreme court of the county in which the individual resides. If the petitioner resides in New York City, the proceeding may alternatively be brought in civil court.[1] The family court has no statutory jurisdiction over the proceeding to change one's name.[2]

The petition to change the name of an infant may be brought by the infant "through his next friend, or by either of his parents, or by his general guardian, or by the guardian of his person."[3] *See*, Section 18.70, *infra*.

§ 18.69 Changing One's Name—Procedure for Petition to Change Name—Contents of Petition

The petition should be prepared by setting forth the specific grounds of the application.[1] The petition must include petitioner's current name; date and place of birth; age and residence; petitioner's proposed new name; whether or not petitioner has been convicted of a crime or been adjudicated a bankrupt; whether there are any judgments or liens of record against petitioner and the details of any such judgments or liens; and whether there are any actions or proceedings pending in which petitioner is a party and the details of any such actions or proceedings.[2]

If petitioner is an infant, include additional allegations setting forth how the change would be beneficial to the child. (*See*, Section 18.70, *infra*) If petitioner was born in New York State, attach to the petition a copy of petitioner's birth certificate or certified transcript or certificate of the commissioner or local board of health that none is available.[3]

The petition must be signed and verified.[4]

§ 18.68

1. Civil Rights Law § 60.

2. In the Matter of Maria E. v. Anthony E., 125 Misc.2d 933, 481 N.Y.S.2d 227 (Fam.Ct., Bronx County, 1984); Matter of Adoption of J.O.T., § 18.67, *supra* note 3.

3. Civil Rights Law § 60.

§ 18.69

1. **PRACTICE POINTER:** If a petitioner desires to change a name from one that is obviously male to female or female to male, the petition should contain sufficient facts and appropriate supportive evidence to substantiate that the individual has in fact undergone a sex change operation, or the court is likely to deny the petition. Matter of Application of Anonymous, 155 Misc.2d 241, 587 N.Y.S.2d 548 (Civ.Ct., Queens County, 1992); Matter of Anonymous, 153 Misc.2d 893, 582 N.Y.S.2d 941 (Civ.Ct., Queens County, 1992).

2. Civil Rights Law § 61.

3. Civil Rights Law § 61.

4. Civil Rights Law § 61.

PRACTICE POINTER: If a petitioner desires to change a name from one that is obviously male to female or female to male, the petition should contain sufficient facts and appropriate supportive evidence to substantiate that the individual has in fact undergone a sex change operation, or the court is likely to deny the petition. Matter of Application of Anonymous, 155 Misc.2d 241, 587 N.Y.S.2d 548 (Civ.Ct., Queens County, 1992); Matter of Anonymous, 153 Misc.2d 893, 582 N.Y.S.2d 941 (Civ.Ct., Queens County, 1992).

§ 18.70 Changing One's Name—Procedure for Petition to Change Name—Special Procedures for Infants

Either parent may petition to change the name of an infant. If the petition is brought by one parent, notice of the time and place when and where the petition will be presented must be served, in the same manner as a Notice of Motion, upon the other parent. If the application is made by someone other than the parents, notice must be served on both parents. Notice must also be served on a guardian, if there is one.[1] If the parent(s) or guardian reside outside New York State, the notice must be sent by registered mail to the last known address. If the parent(s) or guardian cannot be located with due diligence, the court may dispense with the notice provision or may require notice to be given in another manner, such as by publication.[2]

Petitions on behalf of infants are afforded greater judicial scrutiny than those of adults.[3] The primary factor in determining whether to change a child's surname is whether the proposed change is in the best interests of the child.[4] Accordingly, the application should state that the child will suffer harassment, embarrassment, alienation or confusion if the change is not granted and also set forth how the change would be beneficial to the child.

Interestingly, and in an apparent conflict with the special statutory protections set forth for name changes of infants, Civil Rights Law § 64 provides that if the surname of a parent is legally changed pursuant to the Civil Rights Law, "any minor child of such parent at the time of such change may thereafter assume such changed surname."[5]

§ 18.71 Changing One's Name—Factors to Be Considered by the Court

The power of the court to review the petition is limited. The statute provides that the court "shall authorize the petitioner to assume the name proposed" if it is satisfied that the petition is true and there is no reasonable objection to the proposed name change.[1] The court is charged with " 'examining whether the name sought to be assumed will be a source of or instrumentality for fraud, evasion or interference with the

---

§ 18.70

1. Civil Rights Law § 62.
2. *Id.*; Application of DeJesus, 44 Misc.2d 833, 254 N.Y.S.2d 23 (Civ.Ct., N.Y. County, 1964).
3. Application of Sakaris by Sakaris, 160 Misc.2d 657, 610 N.Y.S.2d 1007 (Civ.Ct., Richmond County, 1993).
4. Bell v. Bell, 116 A.D.2d 97, 500 N.Y.S.2d 387 (3d Dep't 1986); Application of Robinson, 74 Misc.2d 63, 344 N.Y.S.2d 147 (Civ.Ct., N.Y. County, 1972).
5. Civil Rights Law § 64.

§ 18.71

1. Civil Rights Law § 63.

§ 18.71   CIVIL RIGHTS LAW   Ch. 18

rights of others.' "[2]

Confusion alone is an insufficient ground upon which to deny the application.[3] However, courts will not grant a change of name which would amount to a judicial endorsement to an illegality or fraud, since to do so would violate public policy considerations.[4] Similarly, courts will not sanction a change of name for other improper or frivolous reasons.[5]

§ 18.72   Changing One's Name—Publication Requirement

The order shall contain a provision directing that it be published at least once, within twenty (20) days, in a designated newspaper within the county.[1] If, however, the court finds that petitioner's safety would be jeopardized by the publication of the changed name, the publication requirements shall be waived and the court shall order the records of the proceeding to be sealed.[2]

Within forty (40) days after the making of the order, an affidavit of the publication of the order must be filed in the clerk's office in the county in which the order is entered.[3] Once this is done, the petitioner shall be known by the name which the court has authorized petitioner to assume.[4] The clerk of court is required to certify that the order has been complied with and to enter the order in the clerk's minutes of the proceeding.

§ 18.73   Changing One's Name—Checklist

1. Where to file the proceeding? The proceeding may be filed in supreme court or, if client resides in New York City, in Civil Court. (*See* § 18.68)

2. Matter of Application of Stempler, 110 Misc.2d 174, 441 N.Y.S.2d 800, 801 (Sup.Ct., Nassau County, 1981) (citations omitted).

3. Matter of Alvarado, 166 A.D.2d 932, 560 N.Y.S.2d 586 (4th Dep't 1990); *cf.* Matter of Miller, 162 Misc.2d 527, 617 N.Y.S.2d 1024 (Civ.Ct., N.Y. County, 1994) (denying application to change first and last name to a new one-word name).

4. Application of B., 81 Misc.2d 284, 366 N.Y.S.2d 98 (Sup.Ct., Wayne County, 1975)(dismissing a woman's petition to change her surname to that of a married man with whom she was living since to allow the name change would foster misrepresentation and condone adultery, which is a misdemeanor); Matter of A., 126 Misc.2d 43, 480 N.Y.S.2d 996 (Sup.Ct., Queens County, 1984) (denying a woman's petition to change her surname to that of her lover who is married to another woman).

5. Applications of Greenfield, 66 Misc.2d 733, 322 N.Y.S.2d 276 (Civ.Ct., N.Y. County, 1970) (denying application of husband and wife who wanted to change their "Jewish-sounding" name in order to vacation in the Middle East).

§ 18.72

1. Civil Rights Law § 63. The form for the notice is contained in the text of Section 63.

2. Civil Rights Law § 64-a.

3. Civil Rights Law § 64.

4. **CAVEAT**: A client should be cautioned before a legal proceeding is commenced that, pursuant to Civil Rights Law § 64, once a name change is judicially ordered, it cannot be changed again except by a like decree.

PRACTICE POINTER: Advise client to notify the Social Security Administration, Board of Elections and other government agencies of the name change.

2. Was petitioner born in New York State? If so, obtain a copy of petitioner's birth certificate or certified transcript or certificate of the commissioner or local board of health that none is available.[1] (See § 18.69)

3. Is the petitioner an infant? If so, serve notice of the time and place when and where the petition will be presented. The notice must be served in the same manner as a notice of motion.[2] (See § 18.70)

4. If the petition is granted, publish notice of the order within twenty (20) days of the date of the order.[3] (See § 18.72)

5. File Affidavit of Publication, certifying that the publication requirement has been complied with, in the clerk's office within forty (40) days of the date of the order.[4]

6. Obtain certified copies of the entered order for client and files.

§ 18.74 Heart Balm Statute

Section 80–a of the New York Civil Rights Law, sometimes referred to as the "heart balm" statute, abolished all causes of action for alienation of affections, criminal conversation, seduction or breach of contract to marry. The statute plainly provides that "[n]o contract to marry made or entered into in this state shall operate to give rise, ... to any cause or right of action for its breach." Although these torts were originally abolished in 1935 under Sections 61–b and 61–d of the former Civil Practice Act, questions still arise today as to whether these causes of action or similar causes of action are valid.[1]

Library References:
West's Key No. Digests, Husband and Wife ⚛323.1, 341.

§ 18.75 Heart Balm Statute—Penalty for Bringing Action

Sections 81 and 83 provide the mechanisms for enforcing a violation of Section 80–a. Section 81 states that it is unlawful for an attorney or

---

§ 18.73
1. Civil Rights Law § 61.
2. Civil Rights Law § 62.
3. Civil Rights Law § 63.
4. Civil Rights Law § 64.

§ 18.74
1. **CAVEAT:** While it might seem appropriate to bring a cause of action for intentional infliction of emotional distress in lieu of the abolished causes of action, the practitioner should exercise caution. Such alternative theories have been rejected as well on public policy grounds, since to allow such a cause of action would circumvent the statute's abolition of these type of cases.

Sanders v. Rosen, 159 Misc.2d 563, 605 N.Y.S.2d 805, 811 (Sup.Ct., N.Y. County, 1993); Weicker v. Weicker, 22 N.Y.2d 8, 290 N.Y.S.2d 732, 237 N.E.2d 876 (1968), rearg. denied 22 N.Y.2d 827, 292 N.Y.S.2d 1031, 239 N.E.2d 659; *but cf.*, Murphy v. Murphy, 109 A.D.2d 965, 486 N.Y.S.2d 457 (3d Dep't 1985) (allowing, over two dissents, a cause of action by a common law wife for intentional infliction of severe emotional distress). A cause of action may also lie for fraud or deceit against someone who knowingly fraudulently deceives someone into marriage. Tuck v. Tuck, 14 N.Y.2d 341, 251 N.Y.S.2d 653, 200 N.E.2d 554 (1964).

party "to file, serve or cause to be filed or served, or threaten to file, serve or cause to be filed or served, any process or pleading, ... , setting forth or seeking to recover a sum of money upon any cause of action abolished by this article ..." Section 83 provides that "[a]ny person who violates any of the provisions of this article shall be guilty of a felony which shall be punishable by a fine of not less than one thousand dollars nor more than five thousand dollars, or by imprisonment for a term of not less than one year nor more than five years, or by both such fine and imprisonment, in the discretion of the court." An attorney may also be subject to sanctions pursuant to Judiciary Law § 476 and §§ 130–1.1 *et seq.* of Title 22 of the New York Code of Rules and Regulations.[1]

§ 18.76 Heart Balm Statute—Action for Return of Gifts Made in Contemplation of Marriage

Keeping in mind the prohibition against bringing certain actions, if a man gives his fiancée an engagement ring, and the engagement is broken off, may the fiancée keep the ring? Although the cause of action for breach of promise to marry has been abolished, either party to the broken engagement may nevertheless recover real or personal property, money or securities "when the sole consideration for the transfer of the chattel, money or securities or real property was a contemplated marriage which has not occurred."[1]

Thus, the answer to the above question is "no," regardless of who was at fault for the breakup. While some older cases held that a woman could keep her engagement ring if the man who gave her the ring broke the engagement,[2] under more recent cases the "fault" determination seems to have been abolished.[3] The only issue should be whether the ring was given in contemplation of marriage; if it was, the ring may be recovered.[4] If the ring is not recoverable, the value of the ring may be recovered.[5]

§ 18.75
1. 22 NYCRR §§ 130–1.1, *et seq.*

§ 18.76
1. Civil Rights Law § 80–b. For a brief legislative history of this provision, *see* Gaden v. Gaden, 29 N.Y.2d 80, 323 N.Y.S.2d 955, 272 N.E.2d 471 (1971). *See also* Scheinkman, *et al., New York Law of Domestic Relations* (West 1996) Ch. 4 "Courtship."

2. Cohen v. Bayside Federal Savings and Loan Ass'n, 62 Misc.2d 738, 309 N.Y.S.2d 980, 982 (Sup.Ct., Queens County, 1970) (allowing fiancée to keep engagement ring after fiancée was killed in automobile accident); Lowe v. Quinn, 27 N.Y.2d 397, 318 N.Y.S.2d 467, 267 N.E.2d 251 (1971) (barring action by man who was already married from recovering engagement ring even though woman changed her mind one month after receiving the ring, presumably on public policy grounds, since he was unable to marry).

3. In recent cases where one party is already married, courts have continued to adhere to the "fault" determination, presumably on public policy grounds. Leemon v. Wicke, 216 A.D.2d 272, 627 N.Y.S.2d 761 (2d Dep't 1995); Witkowski v. Blaskiewicz, 162 Misc.2d 66, 615 N.Y.S.2d 640 (Civ.Ct., Queens County, 1994).

4. Gagliardo v. Clemente, 180 A.D.2d 551, 580 N.Y.S.2d 278, 279 (1st Dep't 1992).

5. Goldstein v. Rosenthal, 56 Misc.2d 311, 288 N.Y.S.2d 503 (Civ.Ct., Bronx County, 1968).

Similarly, other gifts exchanged between an engaged couple during the engagement period may be recoverable if they were expressly given in contemplation of the upcoming marriage.[6] If a man and woman contemplating marriage buy property together, or if one transfers property to the other but the marriage never takes place, the purchase or transfer may be rescinded, providing it is clear the purchase or transfer was conditioned upon the contemplated marriage.[7] If there is a mortgage involved, the rescission could be conditioned upon the discharge and release from liability on the mortgage.

Gifts given by others in contemplation of marriage may be recovered, but money given for wedding expenses may not.[8]

§ 18.77 Heart Balm Statute—Action for Return of Gifts Made in Contemplation of Marriage—Procedure

The proper procedure for the return of gifts made in contemplation of marriage is to bring an action for replevin[1] seeking return of the ring or other property. Alternatively, the complaint should seek compensation for the value of the property.[2]

§ 18.78 Miscellaneous Rights and Immunities

Article 7 of the Civil Rights Law, entitled "Miscellaneous Rights and Immunities," contains an amalgam of privileges and rights ranging from protection against vexatious lawsuits, and protection against libel to "good samaritan" statutes and the consequences of imprisonment.

§ 18.79 Miscellaneous Rights and Immunities—Frivolous Litigation

Section 70 of the Civil Rights Law provides a cause of action to recover damages against any person who vexatiously or maliciously commences an action or proceeding in the name of another but without that person's consent. Both the person whose name was used without his or her consent and the defendant in the lawsuit which was improperly brought may bring suit under this provision. In order to prevail, the adverse party or person whose name was used improperly must have

---

6. Passeri v. Katzenstein, 183 A.D.2d 817, 586 N.Y.S.2d 523 (2d Dep't 1992)(memorandum) (return of money toward purchase of automobile); Lewis v. Permut, 66 Misc.2d 127, 320 N.Y.S.2d 408 (Civ. Ct., Queens County, 1971).

7. Mancuso v. Russo, 132 A.D.2d 533, 517 N.Y.S.2d 539, 540 (2d Dep't 1987).

8. Bruno v. Guerra, 146 Misc.2d 206, 549 N.Y.S.2d 925, 926 (Sup.Ct., N.Y. County, 1990).

§ 18.77

1. *See generally* CPLR Art. 71.

2. PRACTICE POINTER: Since fault has been abolished, a motion for summary judgment demanding return of the ring or other property should lie. If return of the property is impossible or the fiancée refuses to return it, a trial may be necessary only for the determination of damages, unless there is agreement as to the property's value.

§ 18.79

evidence that the defendant (the plaintiff in the vexatious action) commenced or continued a proceeding without another's consent.[1]

If the action is brought by the adverse party, and that person prevails, he or she is entitled to recover treble damages; if the action is brought by the person whose name was improperly used, that person may recover his or her actual damages plus $250.[2] The person who brings the vexatious or malicious lawsuit may also be found guilty of a misdemeanor and be sentenced to a term of imprisonment for up to six months.[3]

There are other federal and state statutes and rules which provide remedies against parties and attorneys for frivolous litigation.[4]

§ 18.80 Miscellaneous Rights and Immunities—Frivolous Litigation—Protection From SLAPP Suits

Section 70–a of the Civil Rights law provides protection for defendants named in actions involving public petition and participation. An "action involving public petition and participation" is defined as an "action, claim, cross–claim or counterclaim for damages that is brought by a public applicant or permittee, and is materially related to any efforts of the defendant to report on, comment on, rule on, challenge or oppose such application or permission."[1] A defendant may bring an action, claim, cross-claim or counterclaim to recover damages from any person who commences such an action, which is referred to as a SLAPP suit. "SLAPP" stands for Strategic Lawsuit Against Public Participation. SLAPP suits are essentially actions without substantial merit that are designed to "stop citizens from exercising their political rights

---

§ 18.79

1. Oceanside Enterprises, Inc. v. Capobianco, 146 A.D.2d 685, 537 N.Y.S.2d 190 (2d Dep't 1989). The meager number of reported cases in this area focus on actions brought on behalf of corporations. Since a president or director of a corporation is entitled to bring suit on behalf of the corporation, no cause of action will lie under Section 70 for bringing an action in the name of the corporation. Fischer v. Maloney, 43 N.Y.2d 553, 402 N.Y.S.2d 991, 373 N.E.2d 1215 (1978); DiDominici v. Parmet, 118 A.D.2d 618, 499 N.Y.S.2d 768 (2d Dep't 1986).

2. Civil Rights Law § 71.

3. Civil Rights Law § 70.

4. See, e.g., CPLR 8303–a, which provides for costs and fees of up to $10,000 against the party or the party's attorney or both, who commence or continue frivolous claims or counterclaims in actions to recover damages for personal injury, injury to property and wrongful death; Judiciary Law § 476, which provides that an attorney who knowingly lends his or her name to an action and the person who uses the attorney's name are both required to pay $50 to the party against whom the action was brought; 22 NYCRR §§ 130–1.1 et seq., which provides for the imposition of costs and sanctions for frivolous litigation; 28 U.S.C.A. § 1927, which provides that an attorney may be required to satisfy personally the excess costs, expenses and attorneys' fees incurred because of his or her unreasonable and vexatious conduct; and Fed.R.Civ.P. 11, which provides that sanctions may be awarded against an attorney or unrepresented party who signs a pleading or files papers in contravention of the rule.

§ 18.80

1. Civil Rights Law § 76–a(1)(a).

or to punish them for having done so."[2] The purpose of a SLAPP suit is to retaliate against persons who take part in governmental decision-making on issues of public interest. The SLAPP suit forces a defendant to expend time and money defending the action in an effort to punish the defendant for past conduct or to deter the defendant from a future course of conduct.

In an effort to curb the abusive nature of SLAPP suits, damages and attorney's fees are available.[3] Compensatory damages are only available upon a showing that the action was "commenced or continued for the purpose of harassing, intimidating, punishing or otherwise maliciously inhibiting the free exercise of speech, petition or association rights."[4] If harassment, intimidation or punishment was the sole purpose for commencement of the action, punitive damages are also recoverable.[5] Costs and attorney's fees may be recovered upon demonstrating only that the action was commenced or continued without a substantial basis in fact and law and could not be supported by a substantial argument for the extension, modification or reversal of existing law.

Library References:
West's Key No. Digests, Torts ⟜14.

§ 18.81 Miscellaneous Rights and Immunities—Libel and Slander

While libel and slander are common law actions, these torts are addressed under "Miscellaneous Rights and Immunities." The Civil

---

2. Gordon v. Marrone, 155 Misc.2d 726, 590 N.Y.S.2d 649, 656 (Sup.Ct., Westchester County, 1992) (citations omitted).

3. In addition to obtaining damages under the Civil Rights Law, sanctions and attorneys' fees may also be available under CPLR 8303–a and 22 NYCRR Part 130.

CAVEAT: One court has cautioned that a plaintiff's attorney in a SLAPP suit needs to consider the ethical issues involved. Representing plaintiffs in a SLAPP suit could subject counsel to charges of violating DR 7–102, which prohibits lawyers from taking action merely to harass or maliciously injure and DR 2–109(A)(1) requires an attorney to decline such an offer of employment. See Entertainment Partners Group v. Davis, 155 Misc.2d 894, 590 N.Y.S.2d 979 (Sup.Ct., N.Y. County, 1992). The attorney defending the SLAPP suit may wish to consider bringing the Davis decision to the attention of plaintiff's counsel.

4. Civil Rights Law § 70–a(1)(b). Section 76–a(2) provides that damages may only be recovered if the plaintiff establishes by clear and convincing evidence that any communication which gives rise to the action was made with knowledge of its falsity or with reckless disregard of whether it was false, where the truth or falsity of such communication is material to the cause of action at issue.

5. In Greenwich Citizens Committee Inc. v. Counties of Warren and Washington Industrial Development Agency, 77 F.3d 26 (2d Cir.1996), the Second Circuit held for the first time that where a government entity is charged with trying to chill the First Amendment rights of citizens, plaintiffs must establish retaliatory intent in order to prevail. Plaintiffs in Greenwich Citizens alleged that the counties' counterclaims constituted unlawful SLAPP litigation. The court announced a new state-of-mind requirement, holding that plaintiffs must demonstrate that the counterclaims were filed "not as a legitimate response to litigation, but as a form of retaliation, with the purpose of deterring the exercise of First Amendment freedoms."

Rights Law enumerates certain statutory causes of action and procedures with respect to libel and slander actions.

Section 77 provides that "[i]n an action of slander of a woman imputing unchastity to her, it is not necessary to allege or prove special damages."[1] For other types of actions not covered by the statute or considered defamatory *per se* by common law,[2] plaintiff must allege and prove special damages.[3] Damages are available not only for injury to plaintiff's reputation, but also for humiliation, mental anguish and any other financial losses directly attributable to the defamation. Punitive damages are also available.[4]

Plaintiff has the burden of proving the falsity of the statement.[5] A cause of action for slander or libel must be commenced within one year.[6]

Any criticism of public figures or public officials is governed by the "actual malice" standard enunciated by the Supreme Court in *New York Times Co. v. Sullivan.*[7]

Library References:

West's Key No. Digests, Libel and Slander ⚖1–33.

§ 18.81

1. Civil Rights Law § 77. This section is strictly construed in that the words must actually convey unchaste behavior. James v. Gannett Co., Inc., 40 N.Y.2d 415, 386 N.Y.S.2d 871, 353 N.E.2d 834 (1976). Note that the statute only mentions "slander" and does not include "libel." Rejent v. Liberation Publications, Inc., 197 A.D.2d 240, 611 N.Y.S.2d 866, 868 (1st Dep't 1994). In Rejent, the Appellate Division commented that "the notion that while the imputation of sexual immorality to a woman is defamatory per se, but is not so with respect to a man, has no place in modern jurisprudence. Such a distinction, having its basis in a gender-based classification, would violate constitutional precepts." *Id.*, 611 N.Y.S.2d at 868–69.

2. Other types of slander or libel are considered defamatory *per se*, but are not set forth in the statute. For example, statements that impute the commission of a crime, statements that injure or adversely affect plaintiff in his or her occupation or profession, and statements that plaintiff has contracted a loathsome disease are considered defamatory *per se*. Liberman v. Gelstein, 80 N.Y.2d 429, 590 N.Y.S.2d 857, 605 N.E.2d 344 (1992); Matherson v. Marchello, 100 A.D.2d 233, 473 N.Y.S.2d 998, 1001 (2d Dep't 1984).

3. Liberman, *supra*, note 2.

4. The Court of Appeals has cautioned that the standard for punitive damages for a defamation action requires more than a finding of "actual malice," as that term is defined in the landmark defamation case New York Times Co. v. Sullivan, 376 U.S. 254, 84 S.Ct. 710, 11 L.Ed.2d 686 (1964). Rather, in Prozeralik v. Capital Cities Communications, Inc., 82 N.Y.2d 466, 479–80, 605 N.Y.S.2d 218, 226, 626 N.E.2d 34 (1993), the Court of Appeals reaffirmed that an award of punitive damages requires a higher level of outrage.

5. Immuno AG. v. Moor–Jankowski, 77 N.Y.2d 235, 245, 566 N.Y.S.2d 906, 911, 567 N.E.2d 1270, cert. denied 500 U.S. 954, 111 S.Ct. 2261, 114 L.Ed.2d 713 (1991).

6. CPLR 215(3).

7. 376 U.S. 254, 84 S.Ct. 710, 11 L.Ed.2d 686 (1964)(holding that a public figure may only recover damages if he or she can show both that the defamatory statement was false and that it was uttered with "'actual malice'—that is, with knowledge that it was false or with reckless disregard of whether it was false or not") *Id.* at 279, 84 S.Ct. at 725.

§ 18.82 Miscellaneous Rights and Immunities—Libel and Slander—Defenses

The Civil Rights Law also enumerates statutory defenses to an action for libel or slander. Section 74 provides that a civil action cannot be maintained "for the publication of a fair and true report of any judicial proceeding, legislative proceeding or other official proceeding, or for any heading of the report which is a fair and true headnote of the statement published." Under Section 74, a statement is absolutely privileged if it is a "substantially accurate" reporting of an official proceeding.[1] The phrase "substantially accurate" is liberally interpreted, and the test is whether "the published account of the proceeding would have a different effect on the reader's mind than the actual truth, if published."[2] The absolute privilege is extended only to a speaker who is officially participating in the proceeding and discharging a public function.[3]

Section 75 provides that a television or radio station is not liable for damages for a defamatory statement published or uttered by any "legally qualified candidate for public office." To qualify for this absolute privilege, the radio or television station must announce at the beginning and end of each broadcast of more than five minutes duration that the remarks "are not to be construed as reflecting the opinions or beliefs of the station, its ownership or management."[4]

Section 78 codifies the general common law rule that a defendant may prove "mitigating circumstances." These include "the sources of [defendant's] information and the grounds for [defendant's] belief," whether or not defendant pleads a defense. Section 76 permits a defendant to demonstrate that plaintiff has already recovered damages or has or will receive damages with respect to a libel of a similar nature.

Other defenses derive from common law and are not set forth in the statute. For example, New York recognizes the public interest and common interest privileges.[5] Additionally, under New York law, a libel

---

§ 18.82

1. See Daniel Goldreyer, Ltd. v. Van De Wetering, 217 A.D.2d 434, 630 N.Y.S.2d 18, 22 (1st Dep't 1995) and cases cited therein; see also, Glendora v. Gannett Suburban Newspapers, 201 A.D.2d 620, 608 N.Y.S.2d 239 (2d Dep't 1994).

2. Daniel Goldreyer, Ltd., supra 630 N.Y.S.2d at 22 (citation omitted).

3. 600 West 115th St. Corp. v. Von Gutfeld, 80 N.Y.2d 130, 135, 589 N.Y.S.2d 825, 827, 603 N.E.2d 930, rearg. denied 81 N.Y.2d 759, 594 N.Y.S.2d 720, 610 N.E.2d 393 (1992), cert. denied 508 U.S. 910, 113 S.Ct. 2341, 124 L.Ed.2d 252 (1993). Only a qualified privilege attaches to remarks made by a speaker who does not hold an official position, e.g., a member of the public who speaks at a public hearing.

In Caplan v. Winslett, 218 A.D.2d 148, 637 N.Y.S.2d 967 (1st Dep't 1996), the First Department held that the privilege extends to remarks made by counsel to opposing counsel upon leaving the courthouse following a conference.

4. Civil Rights Law § 75.

5. Brady v. Ottaway Newspapers, Inc., 63 N.Y.2d 1031, 484 N.Y.S.2d 798, 473 N.E.2d 1172 (1984) (public interest privilege); Garson v. Hendlin, 141 A.D.2d 55, 60, 532 N.Y.S.2d 776, 779 (2d Dep't 1988), app. denied 74 N.Y.2d 603, 543 N.Y.S.2d 396,

§ 18.82   CIVIL RIGHTS LAW   Ch. 18

action will not lie for publication of a statement of opinion. Whether a statement is considered fact or opinion is an issue of law to be determined by the court. The test is whether a reasonable reader could conclude that the statement was conveying facts about the plaintiff. Among the factors a court will consider in making this determination are "(1) whether the specific language in issue has a precise meaning which is readily understood; (2) whether the statements are capable of being proven true or false; and (3) whether either the full context of the communication in which the statement appears or the broader social context and surrounding circumstances are such as to 'signal * * * readers or listeners that what is being read or heard is likely to be opinion, not fact.' "[6]

Finally, truth is an absolute bar to a libel or slander action. If a challenged statement is true or substantially true, a motion to dismiss or a summary judgment motion should lie.[7]

Library References:

West's Key No. Digests, Libel and Slander ⚖=34–51(5).

541 N.E.2d 425 (1989) (common interest privilege). The common interest privilege arises when "a person makes a bona fide communication upon a subject in which he or she has an interest, or a legal, moral, or social duty to speak, and the communication is made to a person having a corresponding interest or duty." Garson, 141 A.D.2d at 60, 532 N.Y.S.2d at 779.

6. Gross v. New York Times Co., 82 N.Y.2d 146, 153, 603 N.Y.S.2d 813, 817, 623 N.E.2d 1163 (1993)(citations omitted, ellipsis in original). There is a further distinction between a statement of opinion that implies a basis in facts which are not disclosed to the reader or listener (which is actionable) and a statement of opinion that is accompanied by a recitation of the facts on which it is based or one that does not imply the existence of undisclosed underlying facts (which is not actionable). Id., 82 N.Y.2d at 153–54, 603 N.Y.S.2d at 818. In Immuno AG. v. Moor–Jankowski, 77 N.Y.2d 235, 254, 566 N.Y.S.2d 906, 917, 567 N.E.2d 1270 (1991), the Court of Appeals endorsed an analysis beginning by looking at the content of the entire communication, including its tone and apparent purpose. Gross and Immuno AG were endorsed by the First Department in Caplan, supra note 3, as the test for what constitutes opinion under New York law.

CAVEAT: In Milkovich v. Lorain Journal Co., 497 U.S. 1, 110 S.Ct. 2695, 111 L.Ed.2d 1 (1990), the Supreme Court rejected the "wholesale defamation exemption" accorded to statements of opinion but reaffirmed that immunity lies for "statements of opinion relating to matters of public concern that do not contain a provably false factual connotation." Immuno AG. v. Moor–Jankowski, 77 N.Y.2d at 242, 566 N.Y.S.2d at 909 (quoting Milkovich, supra, 497 U.S. at 20, 110 S.Ct. at 2705–06). Following the decision in Milkovich, other courts have articulated the "opinion" test under the First Amendment as whether the statement (1) addresses matters of public concern; (2) is expressed in a manner that is provably true or false; and (3) can be reasonably interpreted as intended to convey actual facts about a person. Coliniatis v. Dimas, 848 F.Supp. 462, 467 (S.D.N.Y.1994) and cases cited therein.

7. See Rinaldi v. Holt, Rinehart & Winston, 42 N.Y.2d 369, 384, 397 N.Y.S.2d 943, 952, 366 N.E.2d 1299 (1977), cert. denied 434 U.S. 969, 98 S.Ct. 514, 54 L.Ed.2d 456 (1977); Goetz v. Kunstler, 164 Misc.2d 557, 625 N.Y.S.2d 447 (Sup.Ct., N.Y. County 1995); King v. Tanner, 142 Misc.2d 1004, 539 N.Y.S.2d 617, rearg. denied 144 Misc.2d 1073, 545 N.Y.S.2d 649 (Sup.Ct., Westchester County, 1989) (DNA test proving that plaintiff was actually the father of defendant's child established truth as an absolute defense to the slander claim).

§ 18.83 Miscellaneous Rights and Immunities—Breast Feeding

A 1994 amendment to the Civil Rights Law provides that "a mother may breast feed her baby in any location, public or private, where the mother is otherwise authorized to be, irrespective of whether or not the nipple of the mother's breast is covered during or incidental to the breast feeding."[1] The statute does not set forth any penalties for its violation, nor does it expressly provide for a private right of action.

§ 18.84 Miscellaneous Rights and Immunities—Suspension of Rights Due to Imprisonment

A series of statutes in the Civil Rights Law concerns the rights inmates retain and the forfeiture of certain other rights. A person sentenced to a term of imprisonment forfeits any public office and during the term of imprisonment, all civil rights, private trusts, authority or powers are suspended.[1] Section 79(2) provides that an inmate may commence an action or proceeding in any court or before any administrative agency, but may not appear in an action or proceeding outside the correctional facility unless a subpoena is issued on two days' notice to the correctional facility.[2] The statute sets forth the provisions for transporting and lodging inmates, and contains a proviso that if an inmate recovers a judgment or settlement in his or her favor, the court may direct the inmate to pay out of the recovery all or part of any sum expended by the state.[3]

Section 79–a(1) provides that a person sentenced to a term of life imprisonment is deemed "civilly dead," and forfeits the right to marry. A marriage entered into by an inmate serving a life sentence is void from its inception.[4] Section 79–a(2) removed the disqualification of persons serving life terms from bringing an action in court.

A convicted inmate is specifically protected under Section 79–c, which states that a convicted inmate is "under the protection of the law, and any injury to his person, not authorized by law, is punishable in the same manner as if he were not sentenced or convicted." Conversely, a person injured during the commission of a felony for which the perpetrator is later convicted and sentenced, is deemed a creditor of the inmate

---

§ 18.83

1. Civil Rights Law § 79–e. Public exposure of a female's breast for the purpose of breast feeding infants is expressly excluded from the definition of the offense of "exposure" set forth in Penal Law § 245.01.

§ 18.84

1. Civil Rights Law § 79(1).

2. Civil Rights Law § 79(2).

3. Civil Rights Law § 79(3)(b).

4. Ferrin v. Department of Corr. Servs., 71 N.Y.2d 42, 523 N.Y.S.2d 485, 517 N.E.2d 1370 (1987).

§ 18.84 CIVIL RIGHTS LAW Ch. 18

and may bring an action for damages against the inmate or the inmate's estate after his death.[5]

Library References:

West's Key No. Digests, Convicts ⊙1.

§ 18.85 Miscellaneous Rights and Immunities—Shield Law

The Shield Law, Civil Rights Law § 79–h, protects journalists and newscasters from the compulsory disclosure of their sources and from being found in contempt. In practice, the Shield Law frequently arises in the context of a criminal proceeding in which the defendant seeks to compel production of information obtained by the media. The Court of Appeals held in *Matter of Beach v. Shanley*,[1] that the protection against disclosure is not affected by the fact that "the information concerns criminal activity and, indeed, even when revealing the information to the reporter might itself be a criminal act."

The privilege may be either qualified or unqualified. An unqualified or absolute privilege exists if there was an understanding or expectation of confidentiality.[2] The burden of proving confidentiality is on the journalist seeking protection.[3]

If the product sought to be protected is from a nonconfidential source, or has not been broadcast or published, the protection afforded is only "qualified."[4] The person seeking to overcome the qualified privilege to compel the disclosure of any non-broadcast news or notes must satisfy the test set forth in the statute, which requires that "the party seeking such news ... ma[k]e a clear and specific showing that the news: (i) is highly material and relevant; (ii) is critical or necessary to the maintenance of the party's cost, defense or proof of an issue material thereto; and (iii) is not obtainable from any alternative source."[5] If alternative

---

5. Civil Rights Law § 79–d.

§ 18.85

1. 62 N.Y.2d 241, 245, 476 N.Y.S.2d 765, 766, 465 N.E.2d 304 (1984).

2. Civil Rights Law § 79–h(b); People v. Korkala, 99 A.D.2d 161, 472 N.Y.S.2d 310 (1st Dep't 1984).

3. Lipinski v. Skinner, 781 F.Supp. 131, 136 (N.D.N.Y.1991).

4. O'Neill v. Oakgrove Const., 71 N.Y.2d 521, 527–29, 528 N.Y.S.2d 1, 3–4, 523 N.E.2d 277 (1988).

5. Civil Rights Law § 79–h(c). This tripartite test, which was added to the statute in a 1990 amendment, is a codification of the Court of Appeals decision in O'Neill v. Oakgrove Constr., Inc., 71 N.Y.2d 521, 528 N.Y.S.2d 1, 523 N.E.2d 277 (1988). In O'Neill, the court held both the First Amendment to the Federal Constitution and Art. I, § 8 of the New York Constitution provide a qualified privilege that extends to nonconfidential materials obtained by journalists during the course of newsgathering activities, and refused to compel disclosure of photographs which were kept as resource materials and never published.

For cases applying the statutory three-part test, *see* Matter of Sullivan, 167 Misc.2d 534, 635 N.Y.S.2d 437 (Sup.Ct., Queens County, 1995) (denying motion to quash subpoena and finding that criminal defendant satisfied all three prongs of the test); In re Grand Jury Subpoenas to Maguire, 161 Misc.2d 960, 615 N.Y.S.2d 848 (Sup.Ct., Westchester County, 1994) (grant-

sources may be available from outside the media, such as depositions of other witnesses, these avenues must be pursued.[6]

There is no federal law analogous to the Shield Law. When material is sought in a federal court action alleging violations of federal law, the privilege had been analyzed under federal common law and not under the Shield Law.[7] More recently, the Second Circuit, in a diversity case, refused to order production of outtakes of a television interview and specifically noted that it was applying a standard "identical to that embodied in the New York Shield Law."[8]

The privilege is rarely overcome and in at least one case, certain material was redacted before a subpoenaed videotape was turned over.[9] One significant difference is that the Shield Law applies only to professional journalists, while under federal common law, the privilege has been extended to student journalists.[10]

---

ing motion to quash grand jury subpoenas duces tecum on the ground that prosecutor failed to satisfy the second prong of the test); People v. Cheche, 151 Misc.2d 15, 571 N.Y.S.2d 992 (Sup.Ct., Cayuga County, 1991) (denying motion to quash subpoenas ad Testificandum and requiring reporters to testify).

6. Blum v. Schlegel, 150 F.R.D. 42, 45–46 (W.D.N.Y.1993) (federal common law privilege against disclosure of journalist's sources not overcome when plaintiff could take deposition of interview subject); Application of Behar, 779 F.Supp. 273 (S.D.N.Y. 1991).

7. Blum v. Schlegel, supra, 150 F.R.D. at 44 (citing von Bulow by Auersperg v. von Bulow, 811 F.2d 136, 141 (2d. Cir.1987)), cert. denied 481 U.S. 1015, 107 S.Ct. 1891, 95 L.Ed.2d 498 (1987). Although Fed. R.Evid. 501 provides that "with respect to an element of a claim or defense as to which State law supplies the rule of decision, the privilege of a witness ... shall be determined in accordance with State law," the Shield Law does not create a state privilege. See PPM America, Inc. v. Marriott Corp., 152 F.R.D. 32, 34 (S.D.N.Y.1993). The court in Blum noted though that the underlying principles of the Shield Law "are congruent with the federal courts' recognition of a journalist's privilege." Id. (citing von Bulow, 811 F.2d at 144). The test is essentially identical. In the Second Circuit, " 'disclosure may be ordered only upon a clear and specific showing that the information is: highly material and relevant, necessary or critical to the maintenance of the claim, and not obtainable from other sources.' " Blum, 150 F.R.D. at 44 (quoting In re Petroleum Products Antitrust Litigation, 680 F.2d 5, 7 (2d Cir.), cert. denied 459 U.S. 909, 103 S.Ct. 215, 74 L.Ed.2d 171 (1982)); see also, PPM America, Inc., supra.

8. In re Application to Quash Subpoena to National Broadcasting Co., Inc. v. Graco Children Products Inc., 79 F.3d 346 (2d Cir.1996). The court refused to order production of outtakes, finding they were neither necessary nor critical, particularly since Graco had not sought other sources for the unbroadcast information and there was no basis for concluding that the outtakes would establish any inconsistencies.

9. United States v. Sanusi, 813 F.Supp. 149 (E.D.N.Y.1992).

PRACTICE POINTER: The Sanusi case demonstrates that the party seeking the material should ask the court to review the material in camera. After reviewing the videotape sought in Sanusi, the court recognized that it contained potentially exculpatory evidence. The court ordered the tape to be produced, but permitted the television station to obscure the identity of a confidential source on the tape.

10. Blum, supra note 6, 150 F.R.D. at 44–45.

§ 18.86 Miscellaneous Rights and Immunities—Performing Abortion

Section 79–i of the Civil Rights Law, entitled "Discrimination against person who refuses to perform certain act prohibited," provides that someone who refuses to perform or assist in an abortion because it is contrary to the person's conscience or religious beliefs may not be discriminated against for the refusal. Any person or entity violating this provision is guilty of a misdemeanor. The statute further provides that an action for negligence or malpractice cannot be brought against a person who refuses to perform an abortion based on the refusal.

Library References:

West's Key No. Digests, Abortion and Birth Control ⇐1–16.

§ 18.87 Miscellaneous Rights and Immunities—"Good Samaritan" Law Provisions

The Civil Rights Law contains two separate provisions which limit the liability of persons who render assistance to others. Section 79–f provides that the state, a state agency or a political subdivision of the state will hold harmless an individual who renders assistance to a police officer upon being lawfully commanded to do so, provided the individual does not act in a manner that is grossly negligent or that results in bodily injury or property damage. The protection afforded by this section is not triggered unless the person who renders the assistance delivers a copy of the summons, complaint or pleading to the chief legal officer of the state, state agency or political subdivision within ten (10) days of the time he is served with a complaint as a defendant.[1]

This statute does not provide a basis for a "good samaritan" who is injured to sue the government directly.[2] A provision of the General Municipal Law, however, permits a cause of action directly against the municipal corporation employing a police officer in the event a person who is commanded to aid a police or peace officer in effectuating or securing an arrest or in the prevention of the commission of an offense is killed or injured or suffers property damage.[3]

A second provision of the Civil Rights Law grants immunity from liability for damages to any person who voluntarily assists in the event of

§ 18.87

1. **CAVEAT:** Failure to adhere to the ten day notice provision constitutes a waiver. Corbett v. Sherwood, 84 A.D.2d 571, 443 N.Y.S.2d 443 (2d Dep't 1981).

2. Prior Aviation Serv., Inc. v. State of New York, 100 Misc.2d 237, 418 N.Y.S.2d 872 (Ct.Cl.1979).

3. General Municipal Law § 71–a. See Schiaroli v. Ellenville, 111 A.D.2d 947, 490 N.Y.S.2d 43 (3d Dep't 1985). This provision does not apply to the state, however, since the term "municipal corporation" includes only a county, town, city or village. General Municipal Law § 2; Ast v. State of New York, 123 Misc.2d 200, 474 N.Y.S.2d 174 (Ct.Cl.1984).

an accident or emergency situation involving the use of compressed gases or liquified petroleum gases, provided the individual was not grossly negligent.[4]

Library References:

West's Key No. Digests, Negligence ⚖8.

§ 18.88 Drafting Checklists

Before filing a Section 1983 complaint or a petition to change a client's name, review the following checklists. Samples of form complaints for civil rights actions and a sample petition for a court-ordered name change pursuant to Article 6 of the Civil Rights Law follow in Sections 18.92—18.99. The forms should be adapted to the specific facts of plaintiff's case, and only those claims that are legally cognizable should be asserted.

§ 18.89 Drafting Checklists—Framing the Federal Court § 1983 Complaint

In preparing a federal civil rights complaint alleging a claim under 42 U.S.C.A. § 1983, and any other applicable federal or state statutes, the following items should be included in the allegations:

1. An introductory paragraph setting forth a short statement of the claim.

2. A statement of jurisdiction, which sets forth the statute(s) under which the case is being brought (*E.g.*, Section 1983 and any other applicable federal and/or state statutes.) Since Section 1983 itself does not create any substantive rights, the paragraph should allege a violation of the Federal Constitution or laws of the United States. This paragraph should also include a reference to 28 U.S.C.A. § 1331, which provides the basis for subject matter jurisdiction.

3. A statement demonstrating that venue is proper in the district court in which the case is filed.[1]

4. A description of the parties. The description of the plaintiff should include residence and, if necessary to other statutes asserted, citizenship as well. The description of the defendant(s) should include a reference to

---

4. Civil Rights Law § 79-k.

§ 18.89

1. The venue provision for an action brought pursuant to Section 1983 is found in 28 U.S.C.A. § 1391(b) which provides that "a federal action not founded solely on diversity of citizenship may be brought only in (1) a district where any defendant resides if they all reside in the same state; (2) a district where a substantial part of the events giving rise to the claim occurred; or (3) a district where any defendant may be found, if there is no other district where the case may be brought." 28 U.S.C.A. § 1391(b).

where defendant(s) reside(s), particularly if this is the basis for establishing venue. The description of any governmental defendants should state that they were acting under color of state law and should state whether the defendant(s) is being sued individually and/or in their official capacities.[2] (*See* § 18.18)

5. A statement that any jurisdictional prerequisites have been satisfied. For example, although Section 1983 does not require exhaustion of remedies or the filing of a notice before commencement of the action, if another statute plaintiff is proceeding under requires service of a Notice of Claim or Notice of Commencement of the Action (*see* §§ 18.43, 18.55, 18.58, 18.60), a statement that the requirement has been satisfied should be set forth in the section describing the parties or in the statement of jurisdiction.

6. Factual allegations setting forth in a clear manner exactly what happened to the plaintiff and how each defendant was involved. Care should be taken to name each defendant individually, and not to merely state that "defendants struck plaintiff." The factual allegations must demonstrate that plaintiff suffered injuries as a result of each defendant's conduct.

7. Separate causes of action setting forth how each defendant violated a particular statutory or common law cause of action.

8. A prayer for relief setting forth the damages plaintiff seeks, including compensatory damages, punitive damages, attorney's fees, and any other relief as may be appropriate, including declaratory and injunctive relief.

9. The federal court complaint must be signed.[3]

Library References:

West's Key No. Digests, Civil Rights ⟐234–238.

§ 18.90 Drafting Checklists—Petition to Change One's Name

1. The petition must set forth:

   • The specific grounds of the application

   • Current name, date and place of birth, age and residence of petitioner

2. Alternatively, the caption of the complaint may include the phrase "named in their individual and official capacities" immediately before the word "Defendants."

3. The signature of an attorney signifies that he or she has read the complaint, that the allegations are true to the best of his or her knowledge, the claims are not being interposed in bad faith and are in accordance with the existing law or are seeking a reasonable extension of existing law. Fed. R.Civ.P. 11.

- Petitioner's proposed new name
- Whether or not petitioner has been convicted of a crime or been adjudicated a bankrupt
- Whether or not there are any judgments or liens of record against petitioner; if there are, the petition must set forth descriptive details sufficient to readily identify the matter
- Whether or not there are any actions or proceedings pending in which petitioner is a party; if there are, the petition must set forth descriptive details sufficient to readily identify the actions or proceedings;
- (If petitioner was born in New York State) a copy of petitioner's birth certificate or certified transcript or certificate of the commissioner or local board of health that none is available (*See* § 18.69); and
- If petitioner is an infant, include additional allegations setting forth how the change would be beneficial to the child. (*See* § 18.70)

2. The petition must be signed by the petitioner and verified.[1]

Library References:

West's Key No. Digests, Names ⇐20.

§ 18.91 Forms

Set forth in the following sections are form complaints for some of the civil rights actions and proceedings discussed in the chapter, including actions for police and prosecutorial misconduct (*see* Sections 18.92—18.94), housing discrimination (*see* Sections 18.95 and 18.96), discrimination in a place of public accommodation (*see* Section 18.98), the notice of commencement of certain actions under the Civil Rights Law (*see* Section 18.97) and a petition to change one's name (*see* Section 18.99). The practitioner should carefully adapt the form pleading in accordance with the particular facts of the client's case and should only allege legally cognizable statutory and constitutional causes of action.

§ 18.90

1. Civil Rights Law § 61. **PRACTICE POINTER:** If a petitioner desires to change a name from one that is obviously male to female or female to male, the petition should contain sufficient facts and appropriate supportive evidence to substantiate that the individual has in fact undergone a sex change operation, or the court is likely to deny the petition. Matter of Application of Anonymous, 155 Misc.2d 241, 587 N.Y.S.2d 548 (Civ.Ct., Queens County, 1992); Matter of Anonymous, 153

§ 18.92   CIVIL RIGHTS LAW   Ch. 18

§ 18.92 Forms—Complaint for False Arrest, False Imprisonment and Malicious Prosecution[1]

UNITED STATES DISTRICT COURT
SOUTHERN DISTRICT OF NEW YORK

JANE SMITH,	)
Plaintiff,	) Dkt. No. _____
-against-	) **COMPLAINT**
THOMAS TROOPER; JOHN MANAGER; SAM SECURITY; and FIRST CITY BANK,	) JURY TRIAL) DEMANDED
Defendants.	)

INTRODUCTORY STATEMENT

1. This is a civil action seeking to redress violations of plaintiff's rights under the Constitution and laws of the United States and the State of New York for defendants' conduct in falsely arresting and imprisoning plaintiff, coercing plaintiff to confess to a crime she did not commit, and subjecting her to malicious prosecution.

JURISDICTION

2. This action is brought pursuant to 42 U.S.C.A. §§ 1983 and 1988 and the Fourth, Fifth and Fourteenth Amendments to the United States Constitution. Plaintiff also invokes this Court's supplemental jurisdiction to assert claims under Article I, § 12 of the New York State Constitution, § 8 of the New York Civil Rights Law and the State law claims of false arrest, false imprisonment and malicious prosecution.

3. This Court has jurisdiction pursuant to 28 U.S.C.A. §§ 1331 and 1343, since this claim arises under the Constitution and laws of the United States and since defendants acted under color of state law.[2]

VENUE

4. Venue lies in this District pursuant to 28 U.S.C.A. § 1391(b)(2) since the events giving rise to the claim occurred in the Southern District.

---

§ 18.92

1. This form complaint is adapted from the complaint in Niemann v. Whalen, 93 Civ. 7576 (WCC), which was filed in the United States District Court for the Southern District of New York. See Niemann v. Whalen, 911 F.Supp. 656 (S.D.N.Y.1996). Misc.2d 893, 582 N.Y.S.2d 941 (Civ.Ct., Queens County, 1992).

2. This complaint contains allegations charging private parties with violations of 42 U.S.C.A. § 1983. See supra, § 18.18, for the requirements for maintaining a Section 1983 action against private persons.

PARTIES

5. Plaintiff Jane Smith is a resident of Rye, New York. At the time of the events alleged, she resided in the city of Beacon in Dutchess County in the State of New York.

6. Defendant Thomas Trooper is a resident of Putnam County in the State of New York. At the time of the events alleged in this complaint, defendant Trooper was employed as a Trooper by the New York State Police and was acting under color of state law. Trooper is named in his individual capacity.[3]

7. Defendant John Manager is the Regional Manager of the First City Bank in the office in Fishkill, New York and is an agent of First City Bank.

8. Defendant Sam Security is employed as the Assistant Security Officer of the First City Bank.

9. Defendant First City Bank (the "Bank") is a banking corporation duly organized under the State of New York, with a branch office in Fishkill, New York and conducts business within the Southern District of New York.

FACTUAL ALLEGATIONS

10. Plaintiff began working at the Bank in January 1985. In September 1992, at the time of the events alleged, plaintiff was employed as the head teller of the Bank's branch in Fishkill, New York.

11. Plaintiff was an exemplary employee and had always received excellent performance evaluations. Plaintiff had never been disciplined and had no prior record of embezzling or stealing money from the Bank.

12. On September 2, 1992, plaintiff telephoned the branch to advise her supervisor that she would not be coming in that day because her son was sick.

13. On September 3, 1992, defendant Manager telephoned plaintiff and asked her to come to his office in Fishkill the next morning to read some memoranda concerning plaintiff's upcoming transfer to another Bank branch.

14. Plaintiff arrived at the Fishkill office at 9:30 a.m. on September 4, 1992 with her son. When plaintiff arrived, Manager told her he was not ready for her and directed her to take her son to a sitter and then go home and wait for his call.

---

3. As set forth in § 18.18, *supra*, claims for money damages cannot be brought against state officials sued in their official capacities. Rather, the defendants must be named in their individual capacities. Only in complaints in which declaratory or injunctive relief is sought is it appropriate to name the officials in their official capacities.

15. At approximately 11:30 a.m., defendant Manager telephoned plaintiff and directed her to return to his office.

16. When plaintiff entered Manager's office, defendants Trooper and Security were already seated. Defendant Manager introduced defendants Trooper and Security as friends of his. Defendant Trooper did not identify himself as a police officer.

17. Defendant Manager asked plaintiff to wait outside until they were ready for her. Approximately twenty minutes later, plaintiff was called into the office.

18. Defendants Manager, Trooper and Security kept plaintiff in Manager's office and interrogated plaintiff concerning an alleged theft of money from the vault in the Fishkill branch of the Bank.

19. Throughout the questioning, defendants conferred with each other and frequently passed each other notes while plaintiff was talking.

20. Defendant Security threatened plaintiff that if she did not confess to the theft, he would tell her husband's employer that her husband helped her steal the money; would have her house searched; have her taken away in handcuffs in front of her child; and have her child taken away from her.

21. Defendants Manager, Trooper and Security refused to let plaintiff use the telephone to call her husband or her lawyer and refused to let her leave the room. Plaintiff's request to use the bathroom was denied.

22. Plaintiff was never advised of her Miranda rights.

23. Defendants Manager and Trooper told plaintiff she could not leave the room until she signed a confession admitting that she had taken the money from the vault.

24. Defendant Trooper stated that if she signed a confession, plaintiff would not be arrested.

25. Defendant Trooper prepared a one page document which he told plaintiff was a confession to the alleged theft.

26. After four hours of defendants' threats, intimidations and questioning, plaintiff signed the one page document without reading it.

27. Plaintiff signed the document under duress, and was coerced into signing it by defendants Manager, Trooper and Security.

28. Defendants Manager, Trooper and Security failed to conduct an appropriate investigation into the alleged theft and did not have probable cause to arrest plaintiff for the alleged theft. Defendants did not have any reasonable or trustworthy information to believe that plaintiff had been involved in the alleged theft.

29. The confession plaintiff signed was false.

30. Immediately after plaintiff signed the false confession, she was advised by defendant Manager that she was fired, and was then permitted to leave.

31. On September 9, 1992, plaintiff was arrested by defendant Trooper at her home for the crime of grand larceny in the third degree.

32. Plaintiff was taken to the State Trooper Barracks and was fingerprinted and photographed.

33. Plaintiff was brought to the town courthouse, where she was arraigned before the Honorable Judy Justice and was released on $1,000 bail. During the pendency of the proceeding, plaintiff was prohibited from leaving the State as a condition of her bail.[4]

34. The District Attorney never presented the case to the grand jury. On or about October 1, 1993, Judge Justice dismissed the charge of grand larceny in the third degree upon the Government's failure to prosecute.

35. Plaintiff expended approximately $15,000 in legal fees to defend the baseless charges levied against her.

36. As a proximate result of defendants' conduct, plaintiff suffered humiliation, embarrassment, pain and suffering, mental anguish, restrictions on her freedom to travel and loss of consortium.

37. As a proximate result of defendants' conduct, plaintiff was fired and lost wages and other benefits from September 4, 1992 through present.

AS AND FOR A FIRST CAUSE OF ACTION

38. Plaintiff repeats and realleges the allegations contained in paragraphs "1" through "37" as if more fully set forth herein.

39. Defendants Manager, Security, Trooper and First City Bank, through its agents violated plaintiff's rights under the Fourth Amendment and 42 U.S.C.A. § 1983 by falsely imprisoning her.

AS AND FOR A SECOND CAUSE OF ACTION

40. Plaintiff repeats and realleges the allegations contained in paragraphs "1" through "37" as if more fully set forth herein.

---

4. In the Niemann case, plaintiff had actually been released on her own recognizance. The district court dismissed the malicious prosecution claim, stating that "[w]ithout any indication that plaintiff was subject to restrictions on her liberty—such as travel restrictions or posting bail—in violation of her Fourth Amendment right to be free from unreasonable seizure of her person, she may not maintain a § 1983 claim for malicious prosecution" and granted defendants' motion to dismiss this claim. Niemann, *supra* note 1, 911 F.Supp. at 671.

41. Defendants Manager, Security, Trooper and First City Bank, through its agents violated plaintiff's rights under the Fourth Amendment and 42 U.S.C.A. § 1983 by falsely arresting her.

AS AND FOR A THIRD CAUSE OF ACTION

42. Plaintiff repeats and realleges the allegations contained in paragraphs "1" through "37" as if more fully set forth herein.

43. Defendants Manager, Security, Trooper and First City Bank, through its agents violated plaintiff's rights under the Fifth and Fourteenth Amendments and 42 U.S.C.A. § 1983 by coercing plaintiff's confession.

AS AND FOR A FOURTH CAUSE OF ACTION

44. Plaintiff repeats and realleges the allegations contained in paragraphs "1" through "37" as if more fully set forth herein.

45. Defendants Manager, Security, Trooper and First City Bank, through its agents violated plaintiff's rights under the Fourth Amendment and 42 U.S.C.A. § 1983 by maliciously prosecuting her.

AS AND FOR A FIFTH CAUSE OF ACTION

46. Plaintiff repeats and realleges the allegations contained in paragraphs "1" through "37" as if more fully set forth herein.

47. Defendants Manager, Security, Trooper and First City Bank, through its agents violated plaintiff's rights under the Fourth Amendment and 42 U.S.C.A. § 1983 by conspiring to falsely imprison her.

AS AND FOR A SIXTH CAUSE OF ACTION

48. Plaintiff repeats and realleges the allegations contained in paragraphs "1" through "37" as if more fully set forth herein.

49. Defendants Manager, Security, Trooper and First City Bank, through its agents violated plaintiff's rights under the Fourth Amendment and 42 U.S.C.A. § 1983 by conspiring to falsely arrest her.

AS AND FOR A SEVENTH CAUSE OF ACTION

50. Plaintiff repeats and realleges the allegations contained in paragraphs "1" through "37" as if more fully set forth herein.

51. Defendants Manager, Security, Trooper and First City Bank, through its agents violated plaintiff's rights under the Fifth and Fourteenth Amendments and 42 U.S.C.A. § 1983 by conspiring to coerce plaintiff's confession.

AS AND FOR AN EIGHTH CAUSE OF ACTION

52. Plaintiff repeats and realleges the allegations contained in paragraphs "1" through "37" as if more fully set forth herein.

53. Defendants Manager, Security, Trooper and First City Bank, through its agents violated plaintiff's rights under the Fourth Amendment and 42 U.S.C.A. § 1983 by conspiring to maliciously prosecute her.

AS AND FOR A NINTH CAUSE OF ACTION

54. Plaintiff repeats and realleges the allegations contained in paragraphs "1" through "37" as if more fully set forth herein.

55. Defendants Manager, Security, Trooper and First City Bank, through its agents violated plaintiff's rights under the Constitution and laws of the State of New York by falsely imprisoning her.

AS AND FOR A TENTH CAUSE OF ACTION

56. Plaintiff repeats and realleges the allegations contained in paragraphs "1" through "37" as if more fully set forth herein.

57. Defendants Manager, Security, Trooper and First City Bank, through its agents violated plaintiff's rights under the Constitution and laws of the State of New York by falsely arresting her.

AS AND FOR AN ELEVENTH CAUSE OF ACTION

58. Plaintiff repeats and realleges the allegations contained in paragraphs "1" through "37" as if more fully set forth herein.

59. Defendants Manager, Security, Trooper and First City Bank, through its agents violated plaintiff's rights under the Constitution and laws of the State of New York by coercing plaintiff's confession.

AS AND FOR A TWELFTH CAUSE OF ACTION

60. Plaintiff repeats and realleges the allegations contained in paragraphs "1" through "37" as if more fully set forth herein.

61. Defendants Manager, Security, Trooper and First City Bank, through its agents violated plaintiff's rights under the Constitution and laws of the State of New York by maliciously prosecuting her.

WHEREFORE, plaintiff demands judgment against defendants, jointly and severally:

(a) Awarding plaintiff compensatory damages in an amount to be determined by the jury;

(b) Awarding plaintiff punitive damages in an amount to be determined by the jury;

(c) Awarding plaintiff reasonable attorneys' fees, costs and disbursements pursuant to 42 U.S.C.A. § 1988; and

(d) such other and further relief as may be just and proper.

§ 18.93 Forms—Complaint for Excessive Force[1]

UNITED STATES DISTRICT COURT
SOUTHERN DISTRICT OF NEW YORK

ROGER ROE,

        Plaintiff,

-against-

OTTO OFFICER; and VILLAGE OF PIERREPONT,

        Defendants.

Dkt. No. _____

COMPLAINT

JURY TRIAL DEMANDED

INTRODUCTORY STATEMENT

1. This is a civil action seeking to redress violations of plaintiff's rights under the Constitution and laws of the United States and the State of New York for defendants' conduct under color of state law in which excessive force was used, causing substantial and permanent injuries to the plaintiff Roger Roe.

JURISDICTION

2. This action is brought pursuant to 42 U.S.C.A. §§ 1983 and 1988 and the Fourth and Fourteenth Amendments to the United States Constitution. Plaintiff also invokes this Court's supplemental jurisdiction to assert the State law claims of assault and battery.

3. This Court has jurisdiction pursuant to 28 U.S.C.A. §§ 1331 and 1343, since this claim arises under the Constitution and laws of the United States and since defendants acted under color of state law.

VENUE

4. Venue lies in this District pursuant to 28 U.S.C.A. § 1391(b)(2) since the events giving rise to the claim occurred in the Southern District.

PARTIES

5. Plaintiff Roger Roe is a resident of New York City, in the State of New York and resided there at the time of the events alleged.

---

§ 18.93
[1]. This form complaint is adapted from the amended complaint in Javid v. Scott, 92 Civ. 4476 (WCC), which is pending in the United States District Court for the Southern District of New York. *See*, Javid v. Scott, 913 F.Supp. 223 (S.D.N.Y.1996).

6. Defendant Otto Officer is employed as a Police Officer by the Village of Pierrepont, in the State of New York and was acting under color of state law. Officer is named in his individual and official capacities.[2]

7. Defendant Village of Pierrepont is a municipality duly organized and existing under the laws of the State of New York. The Village of Pierrepont maintains a police department, which employs defendant Officer.

8. On or about March 1, 1995, a Notice of Claim was served on the Village of Pierrepont by delivering a copy of the Notice of Claim to the Village Clerk and Village Attorney, pursuant to the requirements of the General Municipal Law.[3]

FACTUAL ALLEGATIONS

9. On or about January 1, 1995 at approximately 2:30 a.m., plaintiff was driving a motor vehicle which was duly registered to plaintiff in the area of Route 22 and Route 43 when defendant Officer was driving a police vehicle in pursuit of plaintiff.

10. Officer fired his police firearm several times from his vehicle, which resulted in a puncture to the left rear tire of plaintiff's vehicle and injuries to plaintiff.

11. After plaintiff pulled the car over, Officer approached the vehicle and fired two more shots through the window. At the time of the shooting, plaintiff was not armed and defendant Officer had no reason to believe that the use of such force was either necessary or required.

12. Plaintiff's shooting by defendant Officer was in violation of standard police policies and practices in general and specifically, in violation of the regulation of the Village of Pierrepont Police Department which provides that a police officer shall not discharge a firearm at or from a moving vehicle except as the ultimate measure of self-defense when a suspect is using deadly physical force by means other than the vehicle.

13. Defendant Officer's conduct was performed knowingly and intentionally and with callous disregard for plaintiff's rights.

14. Plaintiff Roe suffered injuries to his head, arms and neck; endured three operations; was hospitalized for over eight months; does not have the use of his arms and legs and is confined to a wheelchair.

AS AND FOR A FIRST CAUSE OF ACTION

15. Plaintiff repeats and realleges the allegations contained in paragraphs "1" through "14" as if more fully set forth herein.

---

2. Since declaratory and injunctive relief is sought, Officer is named in both his individual and official capacities.

3. *See supra,* § 18.9, note 2.

16. Defendant Officer violated plaintiff's rights under 42 U.S.C.A. § 1983 and the Fourth Amendment to the United States Constitution by subjecting plaintiff to excessive force.

AS AND FOR A SECOND CAUSE OF ACTION

17. Plaintiff repeats and realleges the allegations contained in paragraphs "1" through "14" as if more fully set forth herein.

18. Defendant Officer violated plaintiff's rights under State law by assaulting him.

AS AND FOR A THIRD CAUSE OF ACTION

19. Plaintiff repeats and realleges the allegations contained in paragraphs "1" through "14" as if more fully set forth herein.

20. Defendant Officer violated plaintiff's rights under State law by inflicting a battery upon him.

AS AND FOR A FOURTH CAUSE OF ACTION

21. Plaintiff repeats and realleges the allegations contained in paragraphs "1" through "14," "16," "18" and "20" as if more fully set forth herein.

22. At all times relevant to this action, it was a policy of defendant Village of Pierrepont to either fail to ascertain or to inadequately take into account the temperament and character of its police officers, prior to, at, and subsequent to the time when it employed them, and, as a consequence of this policy, defendant Village of Pierrepont failed to take reasonable and necessary measures to prevent officers with unfit temperament or character from serving on its Police Department.

23. Defendant Village of Pierrepont was grossly negligent in failing to make appropriate inquiries with respect to the temperament and character of defendant Officer prior to, at, or subsequent to the time it employed him as a police officer.

24. If defendant Village of Pierrepont had properly inquired into the character of defendant Officer, the Village of Pierrepont would have learned that defendant Officer had a mean, violent and unstable temperament and was unsuitable to the position of police officer.

25. It was also a policy of the Village of Pierrepont to improperly and inadequately train and instruct the police officers employed by the Village of Pierrepont Police Department, including defendant Officer, in the appropriate manner of apprehending a suspect and effectuating an arrest.

26. Defendant Village of Pierrepont was aware of the deficiencies in its policy prior to the acts alleged in this complaint, since on August 1,

1991, another police officer, Officer Kopp, was found liable in the matter *Jones v. Kopp* for causing the death of plaintiff Jones during the course of a high speed chase.

27. Despite the knowledge of the deficiencies in its policies, the Village of Pierrepont has failed to take corrective measures to train its police officers in the manner of pursuing a suspect, effectuating an arrest and in the proper exercise of apprehending a suspect.

28. The policies of the Village of Pierrepont were a proximate cause of the injuries to plaintiff in that but for the defendant Village of Pierrepont's policies, the acts alleged would not have occurred.

29. Defendant Village of Pierrepont violated plaintiff's rights under the Fourth Amendment to the United States Constitution and 42 U.S.C.A. § 1983 by subjecting plaintiff to excessive force.[4]

WHEREFORE, plaintiff demands judgment against defendants, jointly and severally:

(a) Awarding plaintiff compensatory damages against defendants Officer and Village of Pierrepont, jointly and severally, in an amount to be determined by the jury;

(b) Awarding plaintiff punitive damages against defendant Officer[5] in an amount to be determined by the jury;

(c) Awarding plaintiff reasonable attorneys' fees, costs and disbursements pursuant to 42 U.S.C.A. § 1988;

(d) Declaring that the conduct of defendants Officer and Village of Pierrepont violated plaintiff's rights under the Fourth Amendment to the United States Constitution;

(e) Granting such other and further relief as may be just and proper.

---

[4]. *See* discussion in § 18.34, *supra*, with respect to the impact of the Supreme Court's decision in Leatherman v. Tarrant County Narcotics Intelligence & Coordination Unit, § 18.34 *supra* with respect to the standard for pleading municipal liability claims under Section 1983. In Javid, the district court permitted the claim to proceed against the municipality to allow plaintiff to develop the claim after further discovery. Javid v. Scott, 913 F.Supp. 223 (S.D.N.Y.1996).

[5]. Punitive damages are not available against a municipality. *See supra*, § 18.34.

§ 18.94   CIVIL RIGHTS LAW   Ch. 18

§ 18.94   Forms—Complaint for Return of Seized Property[1]

SUPREME COURT OF THE STATE OF NEW YORK
NEW YORK COUNTY

CHARLES CARR,

                     Plaintiff,   Index No. _____

       -against-   **COMPLAINT**

THE CITY OF NEW YORK; NEW YORK   JURY TRIAL
CITY POLICE PROPERTY CLERK; and   DEMANDED
PATRICK POLICEMAN,

                   Defendants.

INTRODUCTORY STATEMENT

1. This is a civil action seeking to redress violations of plaintiff's rights under the Fourteenth Amendment to the United States Constitution; 42 U.S.C.A. §§ 1983 and 1988; Article 1, § 6 and Article 1, § 12 of the New York Constitution; § 8 of the Civil Rights Law and the common law of the State of New York for defendants' conduct in depriving plaintiff of his property without due process of law.

PARTIES

2. Plaintiff Charles Carr is a resident of New York City, in the State of New York and resided there at the time of the events alleged.

3. Defendant City of New York is a municipal corporation organized under the laws of the State of New York and at all relevant times alleged herein maintains a police department, which employs defendants Police Property Clerk and Policeman.

4. Defendant Patrick Policeman is a Police Officer employed by the Police Department of the City of New York.

5. Defendant Property Clerk is employed by the Police Department of the City of New York and is responsible for performing the duties set forth in § 14–140 of the Administrative Code of the City of New York. At all times the Property Clerk served as an agent and employee of the City of New York Police Department.

---

§ 18.94

[1] This form complaint is adapted from the complaint in Tartaglione v. City of New York, 96 Civ. 1681 (LLS), which is pending in the United States District Court for the Southern District of New York.

6. On or about October 30, 1995, a Notice of Claim was served on the City of New York in the manner specified by the General Municipal Law.[2] Additionally, that same date, plaintiff, through his counsel, made a formal demand for the return of his property, or the fair market value of the property, to the Property Clerk. The Property Clerk rejected the demand.

FACTUAL ALLEGATIONS

7. On July 1, 1995, defendant Policeman arrested plaintiff Carr on Canal Street in Manhattan, outside the Holland Tunnel, on a charge of possession and sale of fireworks. At the time of the arrest, Carr was in his automobile, a 1994 Lexus, Vehicle Identification Number 1A2B3C4D5E.

8. Policeman transported plaintiff to the 1st Precinct where he was issued a desk appearance ticket.

9. Policeman seized the automobile as incidental to the arrest. At the time of the arrest, the automobile was valued at approximately $50,000.

10. Policeman also seized certain personal property belonging to plaintiff which was contained in the automobile, specifically a cellular telephone and camera equipment valued at $5,000.

11. Policeman did not give plaintiff a voucher for the automobile and property.

12. Plaintiff returned the next day to obtain a voucher for the automobile and his property. He was given a voucher which indicated that the automobile had been categorized as "arrest evidence."

13. Plaintiff inquired as to how he could reclaim his automobile and property; he was advised by an officer at the desk that the automobile and property might be needed as evidence and that he would need a District Attorney's release.

14. Plaintiff then proceeded to the Office of the District Attorney for New York County. Upon showing the voucher to an employee at the main desk, he was advised he could not get his automobile and property until his criminal case was concluded.

15. Plaintiff received a certified letter, dated July 7, 1995, from the New York City Police Department Auto Pound advising him that his car had been impounded and that he needed a District Attorney's release to reclaim the automobile and property.

16. Plaintiff again attempted to obtain the required release and was again told that he could not obtain a property release until his criminal case was concluded.

2. See supra, § 18.9.

17. On August 1, 1995, plaintiff's counsel telephoned the Auto Pound and was advised that the automobile would not be released without a release from the District Attorney.

18. On September 20, 1995, plaintiff appeared in Criminal Court before the Honorable L. Judge. Plaintiff was sentenced to one day of community service and received a conditional discharge. Judge advised plaintiff that upon completion of the community service, he could reclaim his automobile.

19. The next day, September 21, 1995, plaintiff obtained a District Attorney's release for the automobile, voucher #A1234-95.

20. Plaintiff went to the Auto Pound later that day to retrieve his automobile. The police officer in charge informed plaintiff that the automobile had been sold at auction two weeks before.

21. Plaintiff was told he would receive a letter advising him how he could obtain the proceeds from the sale.

22. On October 6, 1995, plaintiff received a letter from the Property Clerk Division, Auction Proceeds Claims, advising him that the automobile had been sold at auction on September 6, 1995 and that he would be entitled to the proceeds from the sale, $9,000, after executing a release.

23. As a result of defendants' conduct, plaintiff has suffered the loss of his property, mental distress and anguish.

AS AND FOR A FIRST CAUSE OF ACTION

24. Plaintiff repeats and realleges the allegations contained in paragraphs "1" through "23" as if more fully set forth herein.

25. The conduct of defendants City of New York, Property Clerk and Policeman deprived plaintiff of property without due process of law, in violation of Article 1, § 6 and Article 1, § 12 of the New York Constitution and § 8 of the Civil Rights Law.

AS AND FOR A SECOND CAUSE OF ACTION

26. Plaintiff repeats and realleges the allegations contained in paragraphs "1" through "23" as if more fully set forth herein.

27. The conduct of defendants Policeman and Property Clerk deprived plaintiff of property without due process of law, in violation of the Fourteenth Amendment to the United States Constitution and 42 U.S.C.A. § 1983.

AS AND FOR A THIRD CAUSE OF ACTION

28. Plaintiff repeats and realleges the allegations contained in paragraphs "1" through "23," "25" and "27" as if more fully set forth herein.

29. At all times relevant to this action, defendant City of New York had actual knowledge of the fact that the procedures and practices of the New York City Police Property Clerk result in unlawful and unconstitutional deprivations of property.

30. Specifically, defendant City of New York has had actual knowledge since the decision in McClendon v. Rosetti, 460 F.2d 111 (2d Cir.1972) and more recently, since the decision in Butler v. Castro, 896 F.2d 698 (2d Cir.1990) that the Property Clerk's failure to notify persons before their property is sold at auction is a violation of their due process rights under the United States Constitution.

31. Defendant City of New York was grossly negligent in failing to take corrective measures in view of court-ordered findings of unconstitutional procedures.

32. Despite the knowledge of the deficiencies in its policies, defendant City of New York has taken no affirmative steps to ensure that the unlawful and unconstitutional practices cease. Instead, defendant City of New York has ratified its institutionalized practices by (a) failing to create a system whereby plaintiff would have received notice prior to the sale of his automobile at auction and (b) failing to ensure that plaintiff had been given correct information in order to retrieve his property.

33. If defendant City of New York had established procedures and practices with respect to notifying persons of the proper method for retrieving their property and had established procedures and practices to notify persons prior to the sale of property at auction, plaintiff would not have been deprived of property without due process of law.

34. Defendant City of New York's failure to establish procedures and practices was a proximate cause of the injuries to plaintiff in that but for the defendant City of New York's conduct, the acts alleged would not have occurred.

35. Defendant City of New York violated plaintiff's rights under the Fourteenth Amendment to the United States Constitution and 42 U.S.C.A. § 1983 by depriving him of property without due process of law.[3]

WHEREFORE, plaintiff demands judgment against defendants, jointly and severally:

(a) Awarding plaintiff compensatory damages against defendants City of New York, Policeman and Property Clerk, jointly and severally, in an amount to be determined by the jury;

---

[3]. *See* discussion in § 18.34 with respect to the impact of the Supreme Court's decision in Leatherman v. Tarrant County Narcotics Intelligence & Coordination Unit, *supra* with respect to the standard for pleading municipal liability claims under Section 1983.

(b) Awarding plaintiff punitive damages against defendants Policeman and Property Clerk, jointly and severally, in an amount to be determined by the jury;[4]

(c) Awarding plaintiff reasonable attorneys' fees, costs and disbursements pursuant to 42 U.S.C.A. § 1988;

(d) Declaring that the conduct of defendants City of New York, Policeman and Property Clerk violated plaintiff's rights under the Fourteenth Amendment to the United States Constitution; Article 1, § 6 and Article 1, § 12 of the New York Constitution and § 8 of the Civil Rights Law; and

(e) Granting such other and further relief as may be just and proper.

§ 18.95 Forms—Complaint Against Landlord for Housing Discrimination[1]

SUPREME COURT OF THE STATE OF NEW YORK
NEW YORK COUNTY

THOMAS TENANT,

    Plaintiff,

    -against-

LARRY LANDLORD,

    Defendant.

Index No. _____

COMPLAINT

INTRODUCTORY STATEMENT

1. This is a civil action seeking to redress violations of plaintiff Thomas Tenant's rights under Executive Law § 296(5)(a) (the Human Rights Law) and 42 U.S.C.A. §§ 3604(a) and 3604(b) (the Fair Housing Act) against his landlord, Larry Landlord, for discrimination against him because he has a child. Jurisdiction lies for the claims asserted under the Fair Housing Act pursuant to 42 U.S.C.A. § 3613(a). Plaintiff seeks a preliminary and permanent injunction to enjoin defendant from evicting him from the apartment, damages and attorneys' fees.

---

4. Punitive damages are not available against a municipality. *See supra*, § 18.34.

§ 18.95

1. This form complaint is adapted from the complaint in Filicori v. Jossel, Sup.Ct., New York County.

PARTIES

2. Plaintiff Thomas Tenant is a resident of New York City, in the State of New York. Plaintiff is a residential tenant at 123 Caraway Street, Apartment A (the "Apartment"), New York, New York.

3. Defendant Larry Landlord is a resident of the State of New York and is the owner of the six unit apartment building at 123 Caraway Street, New York, New York (the "Building").

FACTUAL ALLEGATIONS

4. On or about September 1, 1985, defendant Larry Landlord executed a lease for the Apartment to plaintiff. Plaintiff moved in on September 5, 1985. At that time, he was single and had no children.

5. On December 18, 1993, plaintiff's girlfriend, the former Tina Occupant, gave birth to their daughter Tanya Tenant. On February 14, 1994, plaintiff married his girlfriend, who is now referred to as Tina Tenant.

6. Prior to plaintiff's marriage, he informed defendant Landlord that he was getting married and that his wife and daughter would be moving into the Apartment. Defendant Landlord objected to plaintiff's plans and told plaintiff he would not be able to continue to live in the Apartment.

7. On February 28, 1994, plaintiff's wife, Tina Tenant, and his daughter, Tanya Tenant, moved into the Apartment.

8. From on or about February 28, 1994 through the present, defendant Landlord has engaged in acts of harassment and discrimination toward plaintiff.

9. On numerous occasions, including but not limited to March 17, 1994, June 16, 1994 and August 27, 1994, defendant and his agents and employees have requested access to the Apartment unnecessarily.

10. Defendant has refused to perform certain requested repairs to plaintiff's apartment including but not limited to painting and repairs to the garbage disposal.

11. Defendant has harassed, threatened and intimidated plaintiff, his family and their guests.

12. Defendant has gained access to the Apartment and have rifled through the possessions of plaintiff and his family.

13. Defendant has refused to provide certain essential services to the Apartment, including heat and hot water.

14. Defendant has refused to install window guards in the Apartment, as plaintiff requested, for the safety of his daughter.

15. Defendant instituted baseless legal proceedings against plaintiff in order to evict him from the Apartment.

16. On or about November 15, 1994, defendant caused to be served on plaintiff a Notice of Petition and Petition commencing a holdover proceeding.

17. The holdover proceeding was decided in plaintiff's favor by decision entered on December 20, 1995.

18. Upon information and belief, defendant commenced the holdover proceeding against plaintiff solely because he did not wish to have a child living in the Building.

19. All of the above-mentioned conduct occurred after plaintiff's wife and child moved into the Apartment and continues to the present.

20. In the years prior to plaintiff's marriage and prior to the birth of his child, plaintiff had no difficulties with defendant Landlord.

21. There are no other children living in the building.

22. Upon information and belief, defendant has never rented an apartment in the Building to a tenant or tenants with a child or children.

23. Upon information and belief, defendant has only rented the other apartments in the Building to single men or women, in an effort to avoid having children in the Building.

24. Defendant does not behave toward the other tenants in the building who do not have children as he has behaved toward plaintiff.

AS AND FOR A FIRST CAUSE OF ACTION

23. Plaintiff repeats and realleges the allegations contained in paragraphs "1" through "24" as if more fully set forth herein.

24. Defendant Larry Landlord violated plaintiff's rights under Executive Law § 296(5)(a), the Human Rights Law, by discriminating against plaintiff in the terms, conditions or privileges of the rental of a housing accommodation based on familial status.

AS AND FOR A SECOND CAUSE OF ACTION

25. Plaintiff repeats and realleges the allegations contained in paragraphs "1" through "24" as if more fully set forth herein.

26. Defendant Larry Landlord violated plaintiff's rights under 42 U.S.C.A. § 3604(a), the Federal Fair Housing Act, by discriminating against plaintiff in that defendant expressed his intention to refuse to continue to rent the Apartment to plaintiff and has otherwise made unavailable or denied the Apartment to plaintiff based on familial status.

AS AND FOR A THIRD CAUSE OF ACTION

27. Plaintiff repeats and realleges the allegations contained in paragraphs "1" through "24" as if more fully set forth herein.

28. Defendant Larry Landlord violated plaintiff's rights under 42 U.S.C.A. § 3604(b), the Federal Fair Housing Act, by discriminating against plaintiff in the terms, conditions or privileges of the rental of the Apartment, and in the provision of services or facilities in connection with the Apartment based on familial status.

WHEREFORE, plaintiff demands judgment against defendant in his favor:

(a) Declaring that the conduct of defendant in discriminating against plaintiff violated his rights under Executive Law § 296(5), 42 U.S.C.A. § 3604(a) and § 3604(b);

(b) Granting a preliminary and permanent injunction barring defendant from seeking a judgment of possession in Landlord v. Tenant, New York Civil Court L & T Index No. 12345/94, or from taking any further steps to evict him from the Apartment;

(c) Granting a preliminary and permanent injunction barring defendant from discriminating against plaintiff in the terms and conditions of the rental of his apartment based on familial status;

(d) Awarding plaintiff compensatory damages against defendant Landlord in the amount of $1,000,000;

(e) Awarding plaintiff punitive damages against defendant Landlord in the amount of $1,000,000;

(f) Awarding plaintiff reasonable attorneys' fees and costs pursuant to 42 U.S.C.A. § 3613(c)(2); and

(g) Granting such other and further relief as may be just and proper.

§ 18.96 Forms—Complaint Against Cooperative for Discrimination

SUPREME COURT OF THE STATE OF NEW YORK
COUNTY OF _____

SONIA SINGLE,

          Plaintiff,

  -against-   Index No. _____

COUPLES CORPORATION; PETER PRESIDENT; SAM SECRETARY; and THOMAS TREASURER,

          Defendants.

COMPLAINT

§ 18.96

INTRODUCTORY STATEMENT

1. This is an action brought pursuant to Civil Rights Law §§ 19–a and 19–b; Executive Law § 296(5)(a); 42 U.S.C.A. §§ 1981, 1982 and 1988; and 42 U.S.C.A. §§ 3604(a), 3604(b) and 3613(c)(2) to redress violations of plaintiff's rights for defendants' conduct in unlawfully discriminating against her in the proposed sale of a cooperative apartment.

PARTIES

2. Plaintiff Sonia Single is an unmarried black female. She is a citizen of the United States and resides in New York, New York.

3. Defendant Couples Corporation (the "Corporation") is a corporation organized and existing under the laws of the State of New York for the purpose of cooperative ownership of real estate within the State of New York. The Corporation is the owner of the building located at 123 Noah's Ark Way, New York, New York, which is a cooperative apartment building (the "Building").

4. Defendant Peter President is the President of the Board of Directors of the Corporation. Upon information and belief, defendant President is caucasian and married. Defendant President voted to reject plaintiff's proposed purchase of the shares to the Apartment.

5. Defendant Sam Secretary is the Secretary of the Board of Directors of the Corporation. Upon information and belief, defendant Secretary is caucasian and unmarried. Defendant Secretary voted to reject plaintiff's proposed purchase of the shares to the Apartment. 6. Defendant Thomas Treasurer is the Treasurer of the Board of Directors of the Corporation. Upon information and belief, defendant Treasurer is caucasian and unmarried. Defendant Secretary voted to reject plaintiff's proposed purchase of the shares to the Apartment.

FACTUAL ALLEGATIONS

7. On or about April 20, 1995, plaintiff entered into a contract of sale with Sidney and Sally Sellers, the owners of the shares of the Corporation that corresponded to Apartment 3–G of the Building. The contract was contingent upon plaintiffs obtaining financing and consent of a majority of the Board of Directors for the transfer of shares. Upon execution of the contract, plaintiff tendered $25,000, ten percent of the purchase price, as a down payment.

8. Plaintiff immediately set about to obtain financing. Plaintiff submitted an application to First City Bank, together with the loan processing fees of $500.00.

9. Once plaintiff obtained a loan commitment, she completed the required application, given to her by the Corporation's managing agent,

to seek Board approval. The completed application was submitted on June 10, 1995.

10. An interview was scheduled with a subcommittee of the Board of Directors on June 30, 1995. The Board members present, defendants President, Secretary and Treasurer, were all white males and, upon information and belief, all were married.

11. At the interview, plaintiff was questioned regarding her annual income and her savings. President requested for the first time that plaintiff submit copies of her income tax returns for the previous three years. Plaintiff was also requested to submit two references from prior neighbors. None of this information was requested on the printed application form.

12. During the interview, defendant Secretary inquired as to how plaintiff would feel being the only minority owner in the building. Defendant Treasurer inquired as to whether plaintiff attended church. Defendant Treasurer also asked plaintiff about her social life and specifically inquired as to whether she had any boyfriends and whether they would be staying overnight. Defendant President then asked where plaintiff's relatives resided, and whether plaintiff anticipated receiving many guests.

13. Plaintiff felt awkward and uncomfortable responding to these questions, but did her best to reply to the apparent concerns raised by the Board members.

14. On or about July 6, 1995, plaintiff submitted the additional information requested during the interview. Plaintiff also inquired of the Managing Agent for the Building whether any other prospective purchasers had been asked to submit copies of tax returns and references, but plaintiff received no response to this question.

15. On or about July 12, 1995, plaintiff was requested, through the Corporation's managing agent, to obtain a guaranty from her parents which would provide that they would pay the maintenance for the Apartment in the event plaintiff were unable to pay it.

16. Plaintiff inquired through the Managing Agent as to whether any prospective male purchasers or caucasian purchasers had ever been requested to submit the same type of guaranty. Plaintiff never received a response to her question.

17. On or about July 17, 1995, before plaintiff had the opportunity to submit the requested guaranty, plaintiff was advised, through the Corporation's managing agent, that the Board of Directors had refused to give its consent to plaintiff's proposed purchase of the cooperative Apartment.

18. Although plaintiff requested a reason for her disapproval, no reason was given.

19. Upon information and belief, defendant Corporation and the members of the Board of Directors have never requested caucasian, male or married purchasers to submit copies of their tax returns, references from prior neighbors, or a guaranty for the maintenance. Upon further information and belief, prospective caucasian, male or married purchasers have not been asked about their social life and whether they would be receiving guests.

20. Upon information and belief, defendant Corporation and the members of the Board of Directors treated plaintiff differently in the terms and conditions of the proposed sale of shares in the defendant Corporation and ultimately withheld their consent of plaintiff's proposed purchase because plaintiff is an unmarried black female.

21. Upon information and belief, the cooperative apartment is still vacant.

AS AND FOR A FIRST CAUSE OF ACTION

22. Plaintiff repeats and realleges each and every allegation set forth in paragraphs "1" through "21" as if more fully set forth herein.

23. By withholding consent for the transfer of shares for the proposed purchase of the Apartment to plaintiff, the defendant Corporation and defendants President, Secretary and Treasurer, violated Civil Rights Law § 19–a, which prohibits discrimination in the sale of an interest in the cooperative corporation based on sex.

AS AND FOR A SECOND CAUSE OF ACTION

24. Plaintiff repeats and realleges each and every allegation set forth in paragraphs "1" through "21" as if more fully set forth herein.

25. By withholding consent for the transfer of shares for the proposed purchase of the Apartment to plaintiff, the defendant Corporation and defendants President, Secretary and Treasurer, violated Civil Rights Law § 19–a, which prohibits discrimination in the sale of an interest in the cooperative corporation based on race.

AS AND FOR A THIRD CAUSE OF ACTION

26. Plaintiff repeats and realleges each and every allegation set forth in paragraphs "1" through "21" as if more fully set forth herein.

27. By discriminating against plaintiff in the terms and conditions of the proposed transfer of shares for the purchase of the Apartment, the defendant Corporation and defendants President, Secretary and Treasurer, violated Executive Law § 296(5)(a)(2), which prohibits discrimination against any person because of sex in the terms or conditions of a housing accommodation.

AS AND FOR A FOURTH CAUSE OF ACTION

28. Plaintiff repeats and realleges each and every allegation set forth in paragraphs "1" through "21" as if more fully set forth herein.

29. By discriminating against plaintiff in the terms and conditions of the proposed transfer of shares for the purchase of the Apartment, the defendant Corporation and defendants President, Secretary and Treasurer, violated Executive Law § 296(5)(a)(2), which prohibits discrimination against any person because of race in the terms or conditions of a housing accommodation

AS AND FOR A FIFTH CAUSE OF ACTION

30. Plaintiff repeats and realleges each and every allegation set forth in paragraphs "1" through "21" as if more fully set forth herein.

31. By discriminating against plaintiff in the terms and conditions of the proposed transfer of shares for the purchase of the Apartment, the defendant Corporation and defendants President, Secretary and Treasurer, violated Executive Law § 296(5)(a)(2), which prohibits discrimination against any person because of marital status in the terms or conditions of a housing accommodation

AS AND FOR A SIXTH CAUSE OF ACTION

32. Plaintiff repeats and realleges each and every allegation set forth in paragraphs "1" through "21" as if more fully set forth herein.

33. By discriminating against plaintiff in the terms and conditions of the proposed transfer of shares for the purchase of the Apartment, and by prohibiting plaintiff from fulfilling the terms of the contract entered into on April 20, 1995 between plaintiff and Sidney and Sally Sellers, the defendant Corporation and defendants President, Secretary and Treasurer, violated 42 U.S.C.A. § 1981, which prohibits racial discrimination in the right to contract.

AS AND FOR A SEVENTH CAUSE OF ACTION

34. Plaintiff repeats and realleges each and every allegation set forth in paragraphs "1" through "21" as if more fully set forth herein.

35. By discriminating against plaintiff in the terms and conditions of the proposed transfer of shares for the purchase of the Apartment, and by prohibiting plaintiff from fulfilling the terms of the contract entered into on April 20, 1995 between plaintiff and Sidney and Sally Sellers, the defendant Corporation and defendants President, Secretary and Treasurer, violated 42 U.S.C.A. § 1982, which prohibits racial discrimination in the sale of property.

AS AND FOR A SEVENTH CAUSE OF ACTION

36. Plaintiff repeats and realleges each and every allegation set forth in paragraphs "1" through "21" as if more fully set forth herein.

37. By withholding consent for the transfer of shares for the proposed purchase of the Apartment to plaintiff, the defendant Corporation and defendants President, Secretary and Treasurer violated 42 U.S.C.A. § 3604(a) which provides that it is unlawful to make unavailable or otherwise deny a dwelling to any person because of race.

AS AND FOR AN EIGHTH CAUSE OF ACTION

38. Plaintiff repeats and realleges each and every allegation set forth in paragraphs "1" through "21" as if more fully set forth herein.

39. By withholding consent for the transfer of shares for the proposed purchase of the Apartment to plaintiff, the defendant Corporation and defendants President, Secretary and Treasurer violated 42 U.S.C.A. § 3604(a) which provides that it is unlawful to make unavailable or otherwise deny a dwelling to any person because of sex.

AS AND FOR A NINTH CAUSE OF ACTION

40. Plaintiff repeats and realleges each and every allegation set forth in paragraphs "1" through "21" as if more fully set forth herein.

41. By withholding consent for the transfer of shares for the proposed purchase of the Apartment to plaintiff, the defendant Corporation and defendants President, Secretary and Treasurer violated 42 U.S.C.A. § 3604(b) which provides that it is unlawful to discriminate against any person in the terms, conditions, or privileges of the sale of a dwelling to any person because of race.

AS AND FOR A TENTH CAUSE OF ACTION

42. Plaintiff repeats and realleges each and every allegation set forth in paragraphs "1" through "21" as if more fully set forth herein.

43. By withholding consent for the transfer of shares for the proposed purchase of the Apartment to plaintiff, the defendant Corporation and defendants President, Secretary and Treasurer violated 42 U.S.C.A. § 3604(b) which provides that it is unlawful to discriminate against any person in the terms, conditions, or privileges of the sale of a dwelling to any person because of sex.

AS AND FOR AN ELEVENTH CAUSE OF ACTION

44. Plaintiff repeats and realleges each and every allegation set forth in paragraphs "1" through "21" as if more fully set forth herein.

45. By withholding consent for the transfer of shares for the proposed purchase of the Apartment to plaintiff, the defendant Corporation and defendants President, Secretary and Treasurer caused plaintiff severe emotional distress, which manifest itself by loss of appetite, loss of sleep and poor performance at work.

46. Plaintiff also expended legal fees of $4,000 in connection with the proposed purchase of the shares and fees of $1,000 in connection with the loan and application process.

WHEREFORE, plaintiff demands judgment against defendants as follows:

(a) Compensatory damages in the amount of $1,000,000;

(b) Punitive damages in the amount of $1,000,000;

(c) A preliminary injunction ordering defendants to refrain from giving consent to the transfer of shares to another prospective purchaser during the pendency of this action.

(d) An order requiring defendants to order the transfer of shares to plaintiff

(e) An award of attorney's fees pursuant to 42 U.S.C.A. §§ 1988 and 3613(c)(2)

(f) Such other and further relief as this court may deem just and proper.

§ 18.97 Forms—Notice of Commencement of Action for Discrimination[1]

SUPREME COURT OF THE STATE OF NEW YORK
COUNTY OF _____

HARRY HUNGRY and STEVEN STARVING,

        Plaintiffs,

    -against-

THE DISCRIMINATING PALATE and MICHAEL MAITRE'D,

        Defendants.

Index No. _____

NOTICE OF COMMENCEMENT OF ACTION

PLEASE TAKE NOTICE that pursuant to Civil Rights Law §§ 40–d and 41, plaintiffs are serving notice on the Attorney General of the State

---

§ 18.97

1. This form is for an action alleging discrimination under Civil Rights Law § 40–d, alleging discrimination in a public accommodation. Since Section 18–d and Section 41 (for an action under Sections 40, 40–a, 40–b, 42 and 43) also require this notice to be served, the same notice may be served, substituting Section 18–c for Section 40–c and Section 18–d for Section 40–d or the appropriate statute (Section 40, Section 40–a, Section 40–b, Section 42 and Section 43) for Section 40–c and Section 41 for Section 40–d. Additionally, since this notice must also be served if action is commenced in federal court, the same form may be used by changing the caption.

§ 18.97

of New York that plaintiffs will be commencing an action pursuant to Civil Rights Law § 40–c.

[Alternatively, if the complaint is being filed simultaneously, you may annex a copy of the complaint to the notice, and change the language of the notice to:]

PLEASE TAKE NOTICE that pursuant to Civil Rights Law § 40–d, plaintiff is serving notice on the Attorney General of the State of New York that plaintiff is commencing an action pursuant to Civil Rights Law § 40–c. A copy of the complaint is annexed hereto as Exhibit 1.

§ 18.98 Forms—Complaint for Discrimination in Place of Public Accommodation

SUPREME COURT OF THE STATE OF NEW YORK
COUNTY OF _____

HARRY HUNGRY and STEVEN STARVING,

Plaintiffs,

-against-

THE DISCRIMINATING PALATE and
MICHAEL MAITRE'D,

Defendants.

Index No. _____

COMPLAINT

INTRODUCTORY STATEMENT

1. This is an action brought pursuant to Civil Rights Law §§ 40, 40–c, 40–d, 41; Executive Law § 296(2)(a); 42 U.S.C.A. §§ 1981, 1988 and 2000a, *et seq.* to redress violations of plaintiff's rights for defendants' conduct in unlawfully discriminating against him by refusing to serve him in defendant's restaurant.

2. In accordance with the provisions of Civil Rights Law § 40–d and 41 and in accordance with the provisions of 42 U.S.C.A. § 2000a–3(c), written notice of commencement of this action has been served on the Attorney General and on the State of New York Division of Human Rights.

PARTIES

3. Plaintiff Harry Hungry is a black male citizen of the United States and resides in New York, New York.

4. Plaintiff Steven Starving is a black male citizen of the United States and resides in New York, New York.

5. Defendant The Discriminating Palate is a restaurant located in New York, New York. At all times relevant to this action, The Discriminating Palate was a place of public accommodation as that term is defined in Civil Rights Law § 40; Human Rights Law § 292(9) and 42 U.S.C.A. § 2000a.

6. Defendant Michael Maitre'd was at all times the Maitre'd at the Discriminating Palate.

FACTUAL ALLEGATIONS

7. On or about April 20, 1995, plaintiffs entered The Discriminating Palate. Plaintiffs had an 8:00 p.m. dinner reservation, which plaintiff Hungry confirmed that morning.

8. Despite the fact that plaintiffs had a confirmed reservation, plaintiffs were forced to wait at the bar for over twenty minutes. While plaintiffs waited, they observed a number of other patrons being seated.

9. At approximately 8:25 p.m., plaintiffs were led to a table adjacent to the kitchen and station for busing tables.

10. After plaintiffs saw the table, they asked the maitre'd if they could have another table. The Maitre'd replied that this was the only table available and that it would be over thirty minutes before another table would become available. Based on this comment, plaintiffs took the table.

11. It was not until ten minutes after plaintiffs were seated that a waiter took their order. Plaintiffs observed other patrons being seated and ordering more quickly.

12. While plaintiffs waited for their food, they observed at least four tables in more desirable locations become available.

13. Plaintiff Starving attempted to summon the maitre'd to advise him that they wished to change tables. After five minutes, the Maitre'd appeared.

14. When plaintiff asked about changing tables, their request was denied.

15. Plaintiffs' food did not arrive until more than thirty minutes after they ordered. Plaintiffs observed many other patrons, all of whom were caucasian, order and receive their food before plaintiffs received their food.

16. Plaintiffs asked to see the Maitre'd and complained about the service. When the Maitre'd arrived at the table, he told plaintiffs that if they were not happy with the service, they could leave.

17. Upon information and belief, plaintiffs were the only black patrons in the restaurant.

18. Later that night, plaintiff Hungry related his experience to two of his black friends. Both of these friends indicated that they had experienced similar behavior at The Discriminating Palate in the past.

19. As a result of defendants' conduct, plaintiffs suffered humiliation and severe emotional distress.

20. Upon information and belief, defendant restaurant treated plaintiffs differently than caucasian customers in that plaintiffs were not afforded equal treatment in a place of public accommodation.

21. Defendants' conduct was willful and intentional in that they knowingly refused to treat plaintiffs in the same manner as their caucasian customers.

AS AND FOR A FIRST CAUSE OF ACTION

22. Plaintiffs repeat and reallege each and every allegation set forth in paragraphs "1" through "21" as if more fully set forth herein.

23. The conduct of defendants violated §§ 40 and 40–c of the Civil Rights Law, which prohibits racial discrimination in a place of public accommodation, based on race.

AS AND FOR A SECOND CAUSE OF ACTION

24. Plaintiffs repeat and reallege each and every allegation set forth in paragraphs "1" through "21" as if more fully set forth herein.

25. The conduct of defendants violated Executive Law § 296(2)(a), which prohibits racial discrimination in a place of public accommodation.

AS AND FOR A THIRD CAUSE OF ACTION

26. Plaintiffs repeat and reallege each and every allegation set forth in paragraphs "1" through "21" as if more fully set forth herein.

27. The conduct of defendants violated 42 U.S.C.A. § 1981, which prohibits racial discrimination in the making and enforcement of contracts.

AS AND FOR A FOURTH CAUSE OF ACTION

28. Plaintiffs repeat and reallege each and every allegation set forth in paragraphs "1" through "21" as if more fully set forth herein.

29. The conduct of defendants violated 42 U.S.C.A. § 2000a, which prohibits racial discrimination in a place of public accommodation.

AS AND FOR A FIFTH CAUSE OF ACTION

30. Plaintiffs repeat and reallege each and every allegation set forth in paragraphs "1" through "21" as if more fully set forth herein.

Ch. 18 PETITION TO CHANGE NAME § 18.99

31. Defendants have engaged in a pattern and practice of discriminatory conduct by their conduct which is designed to discourage blacks from patronizing The Discriminating Palate.

WHEREFORE, plaintiffs demand judgment against defendants as follows:

(a) The maximum statutory penalty under Civil Rights Law §§ 40 and 41

(b) Compensatory damages in the amount of $1,000,000;

(c) Punitive damages in the amount of $1,000,000;

(d) A preliminary and permanent injunction ordering defendants to refrain from engaging in conduct that discriminates against plaintiffs and other black patrons of the defendant restaurant;

(e) An award of attorneys' fees; and

(f) Such other and further relief as this court may deem just and proper.

§ 18.99 Forms—Petition to Change Name

SUPREME COURT OF THE STATE OF NEW YORK
COUNTY OF _____[1]

IN THE MATTER OF THE APPLICATION)
OF ZELDA ZYZENLUBERSTEIN)
)
Petitioner,) Index No. _____
)
For an Order, pursuant to Article 6 of) **PETITION TO**
the Civil Rights Law,) **CHANGE NAME**
)
To Change Her Name to)
ZELDA STEIN.)

1. Petitioner is a citizen of the State of New York, County of New York and resides at 884 East 86th Street, New York, New York.

2. Petitioner was born on January 8, 1975 and is currently 21 years of age.[2]

3. Petitioner was born in New York City, New York. Annexed

---

§ 18.99

1. If petitioner resides in New York City, the petition may be brought in Civil Court. See Civil Rights Law § 60.

2. If petitioner is an infant, the petition should state that it is brought by a parent on the infant's behalf and should allege that notice has been made pursuant to Civil Rights Law § 62. The Petition should also allege facts with respect to the infant's parents and specific reasons why the change would be in the best interests of the child.

hereto as Exhibit A is a copy of petitioner's birth certificate.[3]

4. Petitioner wishes to change her name to Zelda Stein.

5. The grounds for this petition are as follows:

For years, plaintiff has suffered ridicule as a result of her name. Plaintiff is studying acting and intends to pursue a modeling and acting career. Plaintiff wishes to legally change her name to the name she plans to use professionally, to avoid confusion.

6. Petitioner has never been convicted of a crime.[4]

7. Petitioner has never been adjudicated a bankrupt.[5]

8. There are no judgments or liens of record against petitioner.[6]

9. There are no actions or proceedings pending to which petitioner is a party.[7]

10. No prior application for this or other similar relief has been made.

WHEREFORE, your petitioner seeks an order granting the within petition changing petitioner's name from Zelda Zyzenluberstein to Zelda Stein and such other and further relief as this court may deem just and proper.

VERIFICATION

STATE OF NEW YORK   )
) ss.:
COUNTY OF _____   )

ZELDA ZYZENLUBERSTEIN, being duly sworn, deposes and says:

I am the petitioner in the within proceeding. I have read the foregoing Petition and know the contents thereof. The statements contained therein are true to my own knowledge.

ZELDA ZYZENLUBERSTEIN

---

3. A copy of the birth certificate is required to be annexed to the Petition if petitioner was born in New York State. Alternatively, counsel may attach a certified transcript or certificate of the commissioner or local board of health that the birth certificate is unavailable.

4. If petitioner has been convicted of a crime or adjudicated a bankrupt, or there are judgments or liens of record or actions or proceedings pending to which petitioner is a party, the petition should set forth "descriptive details in connection therewith sufficient to readily identify the matter referred to." Civil Rights Law § 61. For example, the petition might state that "petitioner was named as a defendant in an action entitled _____ v. _____, Index No. _____/___, which is pending in the Supreme Court, _____ County." Counsel should also consider including a paragraph in the Petition offering to give notice of the change of name to the parties to any such actions or proceedings.

5. Id.

6. Id.

7. Id.

Chapter 19

IMMIGRATION AND NATIONALITY LAW—PERMANENT RESIDENCE APPLICATIONS

by
David Grunblatt
and
Roxanne Levine

Table of Sections

19.1	Scope Note.
19.2	Strategy.
19.3	____ Flowchart.
19.4	Overview of the U.S. Immigration System.
19.5	____ Numerical Limitations on Immigrant Selection.
19.6	____ Implementation: Foreign State Chargeability and Quota Allocation.
19.7	Family–Based Immigration.
19.8	____ Immediate Relative Categories.
19.9	____ Family Preference Categories.
19.10	____ Qualifying as a Relation.
19.11	____ ____ "Child" and "Parent" Issues.
19.12	____ ____ "Marriage" Issues.
19.13	____ Petitioning Procedures and Documentation.
19.14	____ ____ I–130 Petition.
19.15	____ Orphans and Amerasians.
19.16	____ Abused Spouse and Children.
19.17	Employment–Based Immigration.
19.18	____ First Employment Preference Applicants (Priority Workers).
19.19	____ ____ Extraordinary Ability Aliens.
19.20	____ ____ Outstanding Professors and Researchers.
19.21	____ ____ Managerial or Executive Intracompany Transferees.
19.22	____ Second Employment Preference Applicants.
19.23	____ ____ Exceptional Ability Aliens.
19.24	____ ____ Advanced Degree Professionals.
19.25	____ ____ The Role of "National Interest."
19.26	____ Third Employment Preference Applicants.
19.27	____ ____ Professional and Skilled Workers.
19.28	____ ____ Unskilled Workers.
19.29	____ I–140 Petition, Procedures and Documentation.
19.30	____ ____ Checklist.
19.31	____ Labor Certification.

IMMIGRATION AND NATIONALITY LAW — Ch. 19

19.32	___ ___	Procedures.
19.33	___ ___	Legal Issues.
19.34	___ ___	Job Description.
19.35	___ ___	Business Necessity.
19.36	___ ___	Recruitment.
19.37	___ ___	Approvals.
19.38	___ ___	Notices of Findings.
19.39	___ ___	Denials and Administrative Appeal.
19.40	___	Fourth Employment Preference Applicants.
19.41	___ ___	Religious Workers and Ministers.
19.42	___	Fifth Employment Preference Applicants (Immigrant Investors).
19.43	___ ___	Petition Procedures and Requirements.
19.44	___ ___	Special Immigrant Investor Programs.
19.45		Special Categories.
19.46	___	The Diversity (Lottery) Program.
19.47	___	Registry.
19.48	___	Cancellation of Removal.
19.49	___	Legislatively Created Programs.
19.50	___	Asylum and Refugee Status.
19.51		Applying for Permanent Residence.
19.52	___	Exclusionary Grounds.
19.53	___	Immigrant Visa Processing.
19.54	___ ___	Framework of the Immigrant Visa Processing System.
19.55	___ ___	Special Requirements, Public Law No. 103–317.
19.56	___ ___	Checklist of Required Documents.
19.57	___	Adjustment of Status.
19.58	___ ___	General Requirements.
19.59	___ ___	Special Provisions of Section 245(i).
19.60	___ ___	Discretionary Factors.
19.61	___ ___	Application Process.
19.62	___ ___	Concurrent Filing of Petition and Adjustment of Status.
19.63	___ ___	Completion of the Process.
19.64	___ ___	Administrative and Judicial Review.
19.65	___ ___	Checklist.
19.66	___	Tactical Considerations.
19.67	___ ___	Nonimmigrant Status as a Factor.
19.68	___ ___	Immigrant Visa Processing Versus Adjustment of Status.
19.69	___ ___	Flowchart.
19.70		The Green Card and its Limitations.
19.71	___	Conditional Residence.
19.72	___ ___	Marriage Cases, Removal of Condition.
19.73	___ ___	Immigrant Investors, Removal of Condition.
19.74	___	Unconditional Permanent Residence.
19.75		Forms.
19.76	___	Form I–130.
19.77	___	Form I–140.
19.78	___	Form I–485.
19.79	___	Form OF–230.

§ 19.1 Scope Note

WESTLAW Electronic Research

See WESTLAW Electronic Research Guide preceding the Summary of Contents.

§ 19.1 Scope Note

This chapter covers that body of federal law, both substantive and procedural, relating to the process of qualifying for and obtaining permanent residence in the United States for non-U.S. citizens. Numerical limitations on immigration, including worldwide and national quota limitations, are discussed in Sections 19.5 and 19.6.

Two major substantive grounds for eligibility for permanent residence are family reunification and eligibility relating to employment. The specific substantive categories for qualifying for permanent residence based upon family reunification, and the procedures and forms required to file an initial petition to establish such qualification, are discussed in Sections 19.7 through 19.16.

Sections 19.17 through 19.39 cover employment-based immigration categories and their related petitions.

Sections 19.40 through 19.50 cover a variety of alternative means for qualifying for permanent residence in the U.S., including qualifying as a religious worker or minister, as an investor, through the Diversity (lottery) program, through Registry and Cancellation of Removal for individuals who have been in the U.S. for an extended period of time, through asylum and refugee status, and other specially created legislative programs.

The actual process of applying for a green card, either through immigrant visa processing at U.S. Embassies overseas or through adjustment of status at a local office of the Immigration and Naturalization Service ("INS") are covered in Sections 19.51 through 19.65. Tactical considerations in choosing the appropriate method of applying are discussed in Sections 19.66 through 19.69.

The significance of having a green card, and its limitations, are covered in Sections 19.70 through 19.74.

This chapter will not address in detail the many areas of practice which do not relate directly to applying for permanent residence in the U.S., such as those provisions relating to non-immigrant visas;[1] grounds for inadmissability and removal;[2] employer sanctions;[3] citizenship and

---

§ 19.1

1. Immigration and Nationality Act § 101(a)(15) (8 U.S.C.A. § 1101(a)(15)) (1952, as amended) (hereinafter "INA" or "the Act").

2. INA §§ 212(a), 240, 240A; 8 U.S.C.A. §§ 1182(a), 1251.

3. INA § 274A; 8 U.S.C.A. § 1324(a).

§ 19.1   IMMIGRATION AND NATIONALITY LAW   Ch. 19

naturalization, and related issues.[4]

Although issues of U.S. Constitutional law on the rare occasion will arise in the context of immigration practice,[5] the plenary power of a nation to control its borders has served as the basis for the statutory scheme that has evolved, mitigated by principles developed over time with reference to equal protection and due process.[6]

The principal statute governing immigration practice is the Immigration and Nationality Act of 1952, as amended and codified in Title 8 of the U.S. Code.[7]

Principal enforcement and adjudicative responsibility is assigned to the Attorney General,[8] whose responsibility is generally delegated to the Immigration and Naturalization Service ("INS"), a division of the Department of Justice.[9] The INS is responsible both for enforcement and adjudications.[10]

The Department of State, through its Embassies and Consulates has responsibility for visa issuance, visa processing and other aspects of immigration law.[11] The U.S. Information Agency has responsibility for exchange visitor programs to the U.S.[12]

The U.S. Department of Labor is responsible for preliminary adjudications relating to temporary employment of aliens in the U.S.[13] In addition, the Department implements the "labor certification" program to qualify certain employees for permanent residence in the U.S.[14]

Some responsibilities related to the labor certification process are delegated to the State Employment Service agencies.[15]

As noted, the practitioner is expected to deal with a number of federal and state agencies while practicing immigration and nationality law; he or she must be sensitive as well to the fact that other areas of substantive law impact directly on immigration law practice and vice

---

4. INA §§ 301–357; 8 U.S.C.A. §§ 1401–1489.

5. *See* Chinese Exclusion Case, Chae Chan Ping v. United States, 130 U.S. 581, 9 S.Ct. 623, 32 L.Ed. 1068 (1889).

6. For a thorough discussion of these issues *see* Aleinikoff, *Immigration: Process and Policy*,(Martin and Motomura, 3d ed. 1995) pp. 1–40.

7. *See* 8 U.S.C.A. §§ 1101, et seq.

8. INA § 103; 8 U.S.C.A. § 1103.

9. 8 C.F.R. § 2.1. Regulations relating to practice before the Immigration and Naturalization Service can be found at Title 8 of the Code of Federal Regulations.

10. Administrative proceedings relating to enforcement generally come under the authority of another agency with the Department of Justice, the Executive Office for Immigration Review. 8 C.F.R. §§ 3.1–3.41.

11. 22 C.F.R. Pts. 40, 41, 42.

12. 22 C.F.R. Pt. 514.

13. 20 C.F.R. Pt. 655.

14. 20 C.F.R. Pt. 656. A more detailed discussion of the labor certification program and its role in the process of applying for permanent residence is found in this chapter at §§ 19.31—19.39.

15. 20 C.F.R. 656.21(a)-(h). State employment service offices are delegated responsibility with regard to recruitment of U.S. workers as mandated in the "labor certification" process. *See infra,* §§ 19.31 and 19.32 for a detailed description of this program.

versa. Criminal convictions can affect an alien's admissibility and eligibility for permanent residence.[16] Permanent residence status directly relates to the ability of an employer to hire, and can impact on discrimination claims.[17] Eligibility for certain government benefits is related to permanent residence status,[18] and domestic relations proceedings relating to adoption, divorce, and annulment may directly impact certain relatives' eligibility for permanent residence status.[19]

There are a number of primary sources cited in this chapter that are unique to the practice of immigration law and with which the practitioner should become familiar.

The Board of Immigration Appeals ("BIA"),[20] and the Administrative Appeals Unit ("AAU")[21] are administrative bodies which hear appeals on various immigration matters, and a number of their decisions are designated as precedents. These decisions are known as Interim Decisions.[22]

The Board of Alien Labor Certification Appeals ("BALCA") publishes decisions relating to applications for labor certification,[23] and on occasion informal opinions are issued by INS Washington headquarters or the State Department's Visa Office.[24]

---

16. INA §§ 212(a)(2), 237(a)(2); 8 U.S.C.A. §§ 1182(a)(2), 1251 (a)(2). *See generally* Chapter 33 "Local Criminal Court Practice," *infra*.

17. INA §§ 274A, B; 8 U.S.C.A. §§ 1324a, 1324b. *See* Chapter 17 "Employment Law," *supra*.

18. *See* Chapter 23 "Elder Law," *infra*.

19. *See infra*, §§ 19.10—19.16. *See also*, Chapters 20 "Adoptions," and 21 "Domestic Relations," *infra*.

20. *See infra*, § 19.12, note 23, for a description of the Board of Immigration Appeals and its jurisdiction.

21. Rules relating to the function of the Administrative Appeals Unit are found at 8 C.F.R. § 103.3. The scope of its appellate authority is outlined at 8 C.F.R. § 103.1(f)(3)(E)(iii).

22. Bound volumes of precedent decisions, "Administrative Decisions under Immigration and Nationality Laws of the United States," are available for purchase from the Superintendent of Documents, U.S. Government Printing Office, Washington, D.C. 20402. Interim Decisions are available prior to being bound in volumes from the Superintendent of Documents on a yearly subscription basis. Citations to the bound volumes follow the format of Matter of John Smith, 10 I & N Dec. 551 (AAU, 1964). Unpublished or unbound decisions will be cited by case number, name, and/or date, depending upon the information available. These are reported to other publications by private attorneys personally familiar with the cases involved.

23. *See infra*, § 19.36, note 1, for a description of BALCA. BALCA decisions are reported by year and number in the format: Matter of ___, 89–INA–173 (BALCA, Jan. 9, 1991). A number of publications report BALCA decisions, such as Matthew Bender's Immigration Reporter, but there is no central, complete source for BALCA decisions at the present time. Services and computer programs that have BALCA decisions available are cited or advertised in the two major periodicals that report on immigration law. These two publications are: the Monthly Mailing of the American Immigration Lawyers Association, which can be contacted at its headquarters at: AILA, 1400 Eye Street, N.W., Suite 1200, Washington, D.C. 20005 (1–202–371–9377); and the principal newsletter in the field, Interpreter Releases, published by Federal Publications, which can be contacted at: Federal Publications Inc., 1120 20th Street, N.W., Suite 500 South, Washington, D.C. 20036 (1–619–377–3532).

24. *See* AILA Monthly Mailing or Interpreter Releases.

Of great value in understanding the policies and procedures of INS and the U.S. Embassies and Consulates are the internal instructions of these agencies relating to immigration law. The INS publishes Operations Instructions,[25] and the State Department publishes the Foreign Affairs Manual.[26]

§ 19.2 Strategy

The practitioner may encounter the non-resident alien in almost any legal context, and it would not be unusual for that individual to broach the subject of permanent residence in the U.S. to the general practitioner, perhaps the first legal expert he or she has confronted in the U.S. A full review of the individual's personal and family background is an essential prerequisite to a determination as to whether immigration benefits are available.

The first order of business is to identify whether the applicant is, in fact, a non-resident alien. The possibility that the applicant, unknowingly, is in fact a U.S. citizen must first be eliminated.[1]

Next, it must be determined whether the individual really requires permanent residence in the U.S. or perhaps can fulfill his objective by remaining or entering the U.S. within one of the non-immigrant categories.[2] The individual must be made aware of the income and estate tax implications of becoming a permanent resident of the U.S.[3]

If, after this initial review, the practitioner concludes that the individual is in fact not a U.S. citizen and does require the benefit of permanent residence, the practitioner must review the individual's background to assure that he or she is not inadmissable or subject to removal from the U.S. pursuant to one of the categories enumerated by statute, *e.g.*, past criminal convictions, immigration fraud, etc.[4] If the client is

---

25. The Operations Instructions are cited to the particular federal regulation to which they relate. Accordingly, an Operations Instruction related to adjustment of status, which is found in 8 C.F.R. Pt. 245, would be found at O.I. 245. The Operations Instructions are available at the reading room of the INS and are reproduced in a number of treatises and computer programs.

26. Volume 9 of the Foreign Affairs Manual covers visa processing and its sections parallel State Department regulations found at Title 22 of the Code of Federal Regulations. The Foreign Affairs Manual is available from the Government Printing Office and is reproduced in a number of treatises and computer programs.

§ 19.2

1. PRACTICE POINTER: Particularly useful are charts published by the INS listing how historically children may have derivatively acquired U.S. citizenship, often unbeknownst to them. *See Basic Guide to Naturalization and Citizenship* (Publication M230) 89–93. This publication may be acquired from the Federal Government Printing Office.

2. INA § 101(a)(15); 8 U.S.C.A. § 1101(a)(15).

3. *See* I.R.C., 26 U.S.C.A. §§ 7701, 871(a), (b), 897, 2501(a).

4. If such a disability exists, is there potential for a waiver of the ground of excludability based upon equitable considerations? *See* INA §§ 212, 240A, 244; 8 U.S.C.A. §§ 1182, 1251, 1254.

inadmissable or subject to removal, it may not be possible to apply for permanent residence at all.

If the client is not inadmissable or subject to removal, the practitioner can proceed to explore whether a substantive ground of eligibility for permanent residence is available. One must identify the status of each first level relative, parent, spouse, sibling and offspring to determine whether they fit within one of the categories enumerated in Sections 19.8 and 19.9, *infra,* and whether the requisite legal relationship can be documented pursuant to the rules discussed in Sections 19.8 and 19.9, *infra*.[5] If one or more of the qualifying relationships does exist, what is the visa availability and quota backlog in that particular category?[6]

The practitioner then must identify the educational and employment background of the applicant to determine whether there is potential to qualify under the employment-based provisions enumerated in Sections 19.17 through 19.44, *infra.*

Once all the sources of potential eligibility for residence in these categories have been identified, the relative merits of applying must be determined through reference to current quota allocation backlogs, as published by the Department of State[7] and by identifying processing backlogs by contacting the local offices of the relevant federal and state government agencies.[8]

The picture of eligibility is still not complete. Counsel must consider whether there are any extraordinary relief provisions or special categories which might be applicable.[9] Home country conditions and the circumstances of the individual in that home country may qualify an applicant for asylum or refugee status.[10]

---

5. CAVEAT: It is not sufficient to be able to identify the nature of the relation. One also must be able to document it. Be alert to the fact that obtaining documentation from certain countries can be extremely difficult. Volume 9 of the Foreign Affairs Manual of the Department of State, which can be obtained from the Department, provides, at Appendix C, a detailed listing as to the availability of documents and services worldwide, by country.

6. *See infra,* § 19.6 which details the quota allocation system and those categories which are quota exempt.

PRACTICE POINTER: It is also important to identify potential changes in status that would be helpful, *e.g.,* a spouse who is a permanent resident of the U.S. who is eligible to apply for U.S. citizenship, or a U.S. citizen child who will become 21 years of age in the near future. *See infra,* § 19.11.

7. *See infra,* § 19.6. **PRACTICE POINTER:** The Department of State publishes on a monthly basis a Visa Bulletin which individuals may obtain or subscribe to. The Department of State's Bureau of Consular Affairs "Visa Bulletin" is on the Internet. The Internet address to access the Bulletin is DOSFAN.LIB.UIC.EDU. It may also be obtained by fax, by dialing 1–202–647–3000 and following the prompts. Alternatively, one may be placed on the Department of State's Visa Bulletin mailing list by writing to: Visa Bulletin, Visa Office, Department of State, Washington, DC 20522–0113.

8. CAVEAT: Processing time at various government agency offices can be quite substantial and are subject to fluctuation and change. Specialty bar associations, such as the American Immigration Lawyers' Association, may be able to provide data and publications as to these varying backlogs.

9. *See infra,* §§ 19.45—19.49.

10. *See infra,* § 19.50.

§ 19.2   IMMIGRATION AND NATIONALITY LAW   Ch. 19

It is important to note that the various categories are not necessarily mutually exclusive, and an individual might qualify under more than one category. Therefore, it might be advisable, tactically, to file petitions in more than one category, so that more options for completing the process remain available.[11]

Once eligibility is assessed, a strategy for completing the process must be identified. Given the relevant quota, the bureaucratic backlog, and the personal circumstances of the individual and family members, counsel must determine whether the application process should be completed at a local office of the INS within the U.S.,[12] or at a U.S. Embassy or Consulate overseas.[13]

Having gathered the information, ascertained eligibility, and determined a strategy, the practitioner must continue to monitor the strategy and revisit it, since one or more of the significant variables may change. Quota or bureaucratic backlogs may increase or decrease, personal or employment circumstances may change, and of course, the statutory authority and implementing regulations may be modified in the interim.

§ 19.3   Strategy—Flowchart

The flowchart that follows illustrates the analysis of a permanent residence application.

DETERMINING THE CLASSIFICATION
OF INTENDING IMMIGRANTS

---

[11]. **PRACTICE POINTER:** The most obvious and even simplest petition procedure is not always the best, *e.g.*, an individual recently married to a U.S. citizen may qualify directly for permanent residence through the petition of his or her U.S. citizen spouse, but would obtain permanent residence status, which is subject to a condition subsequent, requiring the filing of an additional petition two years later. *See infra*, § 19.72. However, the same individual, as a priority worker might be required to present considerably more documentation at the onset, but if the petition is approved and the application for residence granted, would not be subject to any conditions subsequent. *See infra*, § 19.18.

[12]. *See infra*, §§ 19.57—19.65.

[13]. *See infra*, §§ 19.53—19.56.

Ch. 19 OVERVIEW OF U.S. IMMIGRATION SYSTEM § 19.4

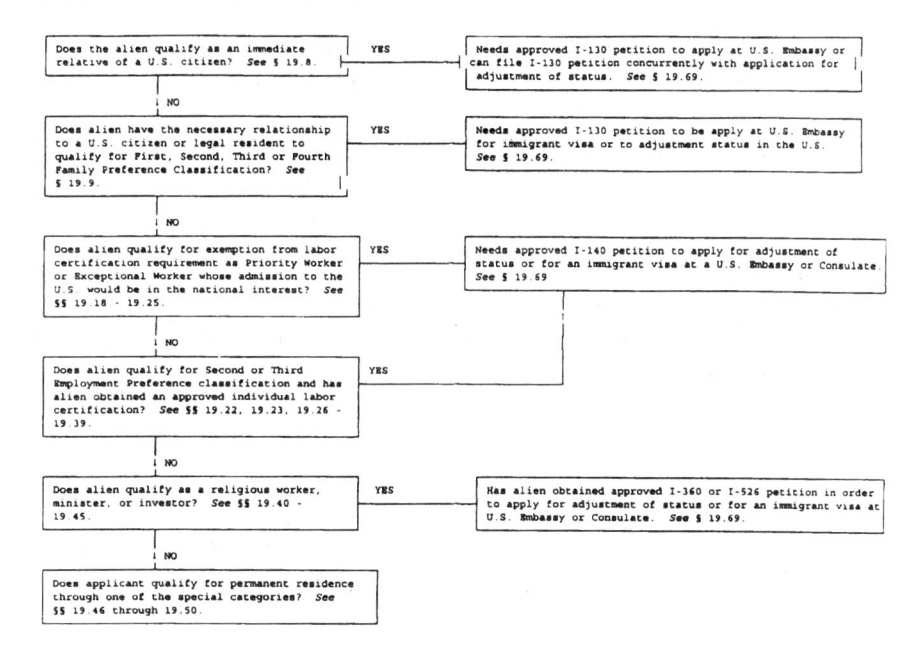

```
┌─────────────────────────────────┐ YES  ┌─────────────────────────────────┐
│ Does the alien qualify as an    │─────▶│ Needs approved I-130 petition   │
│ immediate relative of a U.S.    │      │ to apply at U.S. Embassy or     │
│ citizen? See § 19.8.            │      │ can file I-130 petition         │
└─────────────────────────────────┘      │ concurrently with application   │
              │ NO                       │ for adjustment of status.       │
              ▼                          │ See § 19.69.                    │
                                         └─────────────────────────────────┘
┌─────────────────────────────────┐ YES  ┌─────────────────────────────────┐
│ Does alien have the necessary   │─────▶│ Needs approved I-130 petition   │
│ relationship to a U.S. citizen  │      │ to be apply at U.S. Embassy     │
│ or legal resident to qualify    │      │ for immigrant visa or to        │
│ for First, Second, Third or     │      │ adjustment status in the U.S.   │
│ Fourth Family Preference        │      │ See § 19.69.                    │
│ Classification? See § 19.9.     │      └─────────────────────────────────┘
└─────────────────────────────────┘
              │ NO
              ▼
┌─────────────────────────────────┐ YES  ┌─────────────────────────────────┐
│ Does alien qualify for exemption│─────▶│ Needs approved I-140 petition   │
│ from labor certification        │      │ to apply for adjustment of      │
│ requirement as Priority Worker  │      │ status or for an immigrant visa │
│ or Exceptional Worker whose     │      │ at a U.S. Embassy or Consulate. │
│ admission to the U.S. would be  │      │ See § 19.69.                    │
│ in the national interest? See   │      └─────────────────────────────────┘
│ §§ 19.18 - 19.25.               │
└─────────────────────────────────┘
              │ NO
              ▼
┌─────────────────────────────────┐ YES
│ Does alien qualify for Second   │─────┐
│ or Third Employment Preference  │     │
│ classification and has alien    │     │
│ obtained an approved individual │     │
│ labor certification? See §§     │     │
│ 19.22, 19.23, 19.26 - 19.39.    │     │
└─────────────────────────────────┘     │
              │ NO                      │
              ▼                         ▼
┌─────────────────────────────────┐ YES  ┌─────────────────────────────────┐
│ Does alien qualify as a         │─────▶│ Has alien obtained approved     │
│ religious worker, minister, or  │      │ I-360 or I-526 petition in      │
│ investor? See §§ 19.40 - 19.45. │      │ order to apply for adjustment   │
└─────────────────────────────────┘      │ of status or for an immigrant   │
              │ NO                       │ visa at U.S. Embassy or         │
              ▼                          │ Consulate. See § 19.69.         │
                                         └─────────────────────────────────┘
┌─────────────────────────────────┐
│ Does applicant qualify for      │
│ permanent residence through one │
│ of the special categories? See  │
│ §§ 19.46 through 19.50.         │
└─────────────────────────────────┘
```

§ 19.4 Overview of the U.S. Immigration System

Lawful permanent residence is "the status of having been lawfully accorded the privilege of residing permanently in the U.S. as an immigrant in accordance with the immigration laws, such status not having changed."[1] Permanent residents of the U.S. are issued the so-called "green card," properly known as the Alien Registration Receipt Card, Form I-551. The card itself is principally an identification document.[2] However, without it, even a *bona fide* permanent resident of the U.S. may be unable to prove his or her status or obtain employment because of Employer Sanctions restrictions.[3]

Although all non-U.S. citizens seeking entry to the U.S. are presumed to be intending immigrants unless they prove to the contrary,[4] no individual will qualify for immigrant or permanent resident status[5] unless he or she qualifies under a specific provision of the Immigration and Nationality Act and complies with all necessary procedures to obtain that status.

§ 19.4

1. INA § 101(a)(20); 8 U.S.C.A. § 1101(a)(20).

2. United States v. Campos–Serrano, 404 U.S. 293, 92 S.Ct. 471, 30 L.Ed.2d 457 (1971).

3. 8 C.F.R. § 274a.2(b)(1)(v)(A)(5).

4. INA § 291; 8 U.S.C.A. § 1361.

5. The terms "immigrant" and "permanent resident" are often used interchangeably, in that an intending immigrant is one seeking entry into the U.S. to reside permanently.

741

§ 19.4   IMMIGRATION AND NATIONALITY LAW   Ch. 19

The provisions of the immigration selection system are set forth in Sections 201–206 of the Act (8 U.S.C.A. §§ 1151—1156), which consists of the following components:

- permanent residence through family member petitions, including immediate family members of U.S. citizens exempt from numerical limitation[6] and other family members subject to annual numerical limitations imposed both by family member category and country of origin;[7]
- employment-based immigration, including a hierarchy of categories of workers with employment offers in the U.S., investors, all subject to numerical limitations based upon category and country of origin;[8]
- diversity immigrants, consisting of a group of applicants identified by a random selection procedure from "low-admission countries" to increase the diversity of the U.S. immigration pool.[9]

Although these provisions are intended to constitute the complete structure of the system for applying for permanent residence, there are a number of alternative routes leading to permanent resident status provided in the statute to accommodate special circumstances. Aliens who qualify as refugees or asylees pursuant to Sections 207 and 208 of the Act (8 U.S.C.A. §§ 1157 and 1158) may apply for and be granted permanent residence after a statutory waiting period.[10]

One can qualify for cancellation of removal under Section 240A of the Act by establishing the requisite physical presence in the U.S. and the appropriate humanitarian considerations before an immigration judge during the cancellation of removal proceedings.[11] Or, one can qualify for "registry," pursuant to Section 249 of the Act,[12] by establishing entry into the U.S. prior to January 1, 1972, and continuous residency in the U.S. thereafter.[13]

However, the heart and soul of the system remains the immigrant selection system enumerated in Sections 201–206 of the Act.[14]

§ 19.5   Overview of the U.S. Immigration System—Numerical Limitations on Immigrant Selection

The immigrant selection system is essentially a "quota allocation" system which imposes a "cap" or limitation on the various visa catego-

6. INA § 201(b)(2)(A)(i); 8 U.S.C.A. § 1151(b)(2)(A)(i).

7. INA §§ 201(a)(1), 203(a); 8 U.S.C.A. §§ 1151(a)(1), 1153(a).

8. INA §§ 201(a)(2), 203(b); 8 U.S.C.A. §§ 1151(a)(2), 1153(b).

9. INA §§ 201(a)(3), 203(c); 8 U.S.C.A. §§ 1151(a)(3), 1153(c).

10. See § 209 of the Immigration and Nationality Act (8 U.S.C.A. § 1159), which provides for an adjustment of status procedure quite similar to the one for normal immigrants enumerated in Section 245 of the Act (8 U.S.C.A. § 1255). See infra, § 19.57.

11. See infra, § 19.48.

12. 8 U.S.C.A. § 1259.

13. See infra, § 19.47.

14. 8 U.S.C.A. §§ 1151—1156.

Ch. 19 NUMERICAL LIMITATIONS ON SELECTION § 19.5

ries and, in addition, a per-country limit for preference immigrants. The cap for family-sponsored immigrants is 480,000 per annum, plus an additional visa allocation using those numbers not allocated in the prior fiscal year to the employment-based preferences.[1]

Immediate relatives of U.S. citizens[2] are not subject to a numerical limitation. They are included, however, in the overall cap and reduce availability in the other family-sponsored immigrant categories. The statute provides, however, that the total number of visas available to the other family-sponsored categories cannot be reduced below 226,000 per annum.[3] The family-sponsored preference categories are allocated as follows:[4]

First: Unmarried Sons and Daughters of Citizens: 23,400, plus any numbers not required for fourth preference.

Second: Spouses and Children, and Unmarried Sons and Daughters of Permanent Residents: 114,200, plus the number (if any) by which the worldwide family preference level exceeds 226,000, and any unused first preference numbers:

   A. Spouses and Children: 77% of the overall second preference limitation, of which 75% are exempt from the per-country limit;

   B. Unmarried Sons and Daughters (21 years of age or older): 23% of the overall second preference limitation.

Third: Married Sons and Daughters of Citizens: 23,400, plus any numbers not required by first and second preferences.

Fourth: Brothers and Sisters of Adult Citizens: 65,000, plus any numbers not required by first three preferences.

The limit for employment-based immigration is established at 140,000 per annum,[5] allocated per category as follows:[6]

First: Priority Workers: 28.6% of the worldwide employment-based preference level, plus any numbers not required for fourth and fifth preferences.

Second: Members of the Professions Holding Advanced Degrees or Persons of Exceptional Ability: 28.6% of the worldwide employment-based preference level, plus any numbers not required by first preference.

---

§ 19.5

1. INA § 201(c); 8 U.S.C.A. § 1151(c).

2. For a description of this category, *see infra*, § 19.8.

3. INA § 201(c)(1)(B)(ii); 8 U.S.C.A. § 1151(c)(1)(B)(ii).

4. As published in the U.S. Department of State, Bureau of Consular Affairs Visa Bulletin.

5. INA § 201(d); 8 U.S.C.A. § 1151(d).

6. As published in the U.S. Department of State, Bureau of Consular Affairs Visa Bulletin.

Third: Skilled Workers, Professionals, and Other Workers: 28.6% of the worldwide level, plus any numbers not required by first and second preferences, not more than 10,000 of which to "Other Workers."

Fourth: Certain Special Immigrants: 7.1% of the worldwide level.

Fifth: Employment Creation: 7.1% of the worldwide level, not less than 3,000 of which reserved for investors in a targeted rural or high-unemployment area, and 300 set aside for investors in regional centers by Sec. 610 of P.L. 102–395.

The annual cap for "diversity" immigrant visas is 55,000 per annum.[7]

Library References:

West's Key No. Digests, Aliens ⊛51.5.

§ 19.6 Overview of the U.S. Immigration System—Implementation: Foreign State Chargeability and Quota Allocation

The statutory caps mandated for the various preference categories, taken together with the statutory limitations on visa allocation per country, produce an inevitable result—quota backlogs. The Visa Bulletin[1] published monthly by the Department of State lists those preference categories which are current, unavailable, or oversubscribed, as illustrated by the two schedules reproduced below, published for the month of December 1995.

SCHEDULE ONE: FAMILY PREFERENCE

Family	All Chargeability Areas Except Those Listed	CHINA-Mainland born	INDIA	MEXICO	PHILIPPINES
1st	C	C	C	01Apr95	24Jan86
2A*	01Aug92	01Aug92	01Aug92	22Feb92	01Aug92
2B	15Jul90	15Jul90	15Jul90	15Jul90	15Jul90
3rd	15Apr93	15Apr93	15Apr93	15Jul87	01May94
4th	15Sep95	15Sep85	01May84	01Dec84	15Sep77

* NOTE: For DECEMBER, 2A numbers *EXEMPT from per-country limit* are available to applicants from all countries with priority dates *earlier* than 22FEB92. 2A numbers *SUBJECT to per-country limit* are available to applicants chargeable to all countries EXCEPT MEXICO with priority dates beginning 22FEB92 and earlier than 01AUG92. (2A numbers subject to per-country limit are "unavailable" for applicants chargeable to MEXICO.) (The three-year transition program which had provided additional visas for spouses/children of legalization beneficiaries has ended; petitions approved on behalf of such spouses/children continue to accord them status in the Family 2A preference, however.)

7. INA § 201(e); 8 U.S.C.A. § 1151(e).

§ 19.6

1. U.S. Department of State, Bureau of Consular Affairs.

SCHEDULE TWO: EMPLOYMENT PREFERENCES

	All Chargeability Areas Except Those Listed	CHINA-Mainland born	INDIA	MEXICO	PHILIPPINES
Employment-Based					
1st	C	C	C	C	C
2nd	C	C	C	C	C
3rd	C	C	C	C	01May94
Other Workers	01Mar91	01Mar91	01Mar91	01Mar91	01Mar91
4th	C	C	C	C	16Dec93
Certain Religious Workers	C	C	C	C	16Dec93
5th	C	C	C	C	C
Targeted Employment Areas/ Regional Centers	C	C	C	C	C

Foreign state chargeability and the cutoff date for oversubscribed categories are determined by the Visa Office of the State Department, generally based upon the country of birth of the applicant, not the country of citizenship.[2]

There are three exceptions to the rule that chargeability is attributable to the place of birth: (1) a spouse or child may be charged to the foreign state of the principal applicant that the spouse or child is accompanying or following to join in the U.S.;[3] (2) an alien born in the U.S. who loses his U.S. citizenship or was never accorded U.S. citizenship may be allocable to the country where he or she is currently a citizen or subject;[4] and (3) an alien born in a foreign state where neither of his parents is a resident, if the parents were temporarily visiting that place or were stationed there temporarily by a country or foreign employer, may be charged to his or her country of nationality.[5]

In the great majority of cases, foreign state chargeability will be determined according to the place of birth of the applicant.[6]

---

2. INA § 202(b); 8 U.S.C.A. § 1152(b). See also 22 C.F.R. § 42.12(a).

3. INA § 202(b)(2),(1); 8 U.S.C.A. § 1152(b)(2), (1). See also 22 C.F.R. §§ 42.12(c), (b).

4. INA § 202(b)(3); 8 U.S.C.A. § 1152(b)(3). See also 22 C.F.R. § 42.12(d).

5. 22 C.F.R. § 42.12(e).

6. PRACTICE POINTER: These rules which allow an individual to allocate out from his or her place of birth (called in the practice "cross-chargeability") are an extremely important tool. Any time an applicant is from one of the few countries whose quota allocation is worse than the rest of the world, (*e.g.*, in the December 1995 chart, natives of China (mainland born), India, Mexico, or the Philippines) the applicant may be able to obtain a more preferable quota allocation if his or her spouse is from another country. The State Department and the INS have accepted the princi-

§ 19.6   IMMIGRATION AND NATIONALITY LAW   Ch. 19

Applications for immigrant visas and permanent residence are considered chronologically, and accordingly when a quota category is oversubscribed, a cutoff date is established and only those applicants with a "priority date" prior to the cutoff date would be eligible to complete the process of applying for permanent residence during that month. The "priority date," the applicant's place on line, so to speak, is generally established when the appropriate visa petition is filed with the INS.[7] For employment-based petitions, it will generally be the date the petition is filed, unless a labor certification is required, in which case the date of the filing of the application for labor certification will become the "priority date."[8] The labor certification process is discussed, *infra*, at Section 19.31.

The spouse and children of an applicant who are eligible for derivative status (who are accompanying or following to join the principal applicant)[9] may use the original priority date of the principal beneficiary.[10]

The following example, using the December, 1995, Visa Bulletin, illustrates how the quota system and nationality allocation system are implemented:

John Doe, born in Mexico, is married to Jane Doe and is the adult child of a U.S. citizen father. In December 1995 he asks his attorney to determine if he is eligible to complete the process of applying for permanent residence. According to the December 1995 Visa Bulletin, only petitions filed prior to July 15, 1987 would be available for the month of December. If John Doe's wife were a citizen of the United Kingdom, pursuant to the principles of cross-chargeability,[11] a petition filed prior to April 15, 1993 would authorize visa issuance or the grant of permanent residence during the month of December 1995. Were the petition to have been filed later than that date, the applicant would have to wait month to month until the Visa Office reported that the quota was current for Mexico or that John Doe's priority date was earlier than the published cutoff date.

Accordingly, the processing time of an application for permanent residence in the U.S. is dependant upon a number of variables, including: (1) bureaucratic backlogs in processing the petitions and applications; (2) the particular preference category under which the applicant is

---

ple that in the case of spouses, either spouse can cross-charge. In other words, the couple may apply under the quota of the individual that has the better allocation. *See* 22 C.F.R. § 40.1(a); 9 F.A.M. 40.1, note 6.

7. With reference to family relationship petitions, *see* 22 C.F.R. § 42.53(a) and 8 C.F.R. § 204.1(c), (d), (e).

8. 8 C.F.R. § 204.5(d).
9. INA § 203(d); 8 U.S.C.A. § 1153(d).
10. 22 C.F.R. § 42.53(d).
11. *See supra*, note 6.

eligible for permanent residence in the U.S.; and (3) the foreign state chargeability of the applicant and relevant family members.

Library References:

West's Key No. Digests, Aliens ⊗51.5.

§ 19.7 Family–Based Immigration

The family reunification categories constitute some of the most frequently utilized provisions of U.S. immigration law. The filing of a visa petition by a U.S. citizen or permanent resident "petitioner" is the prerequisite step to an alien "beneficiary" making application for permanent resident status.

The following family-based categories are eligible for permanent residence:

- immediate relatives of U.S. citizens—these include spouses, minor children and parents of U.S. citizens;
- unmarried adult sons and daughters of U.S. citizens;
- married sons and daughters of U.S. citizens;
- spouses and unmarried sons and daughters of U.S. permanent resident aliens;
- brothers and sisters of U.S. citizens.

Library References:

West's Key No. Digests, Aliens ⊗51.5.

§ 19.8 Family–Based Immigration—Immediate Relative Categories

Immediate relatives of U.S. citizens enjoy the privilege of qualifying for permanent residence without numerical restrictions. "Immediate relative" is defined to include the spouse and unmarried children under the age of 21 of U.S. citizens, and the parents of adult U.S. citizens.[1]

The spouse of a deceased U.S. citizen who was married to the citizen for at least two years at the time of the citizen spouse's death, qualifies as an immediate relative, provided the couple were not legally separated at the time of death and the alien spouse files an immediate relative petition within two years of the death and while still unmarried.[2]

Aliens born to permanent resident parents during a "temporary visit" of the parents abroad, and aliens born to an alien issued an immediate relative visa after the issuance of the visa, but before the visa

---

§ 19.8

1. INA § 201(b)(2)(A)(i); 8 U.S.C.A. § 1151(b)(2)(A)(i).

2. Id.

is used to apply for admission to the U.S., also qualify for permanent residence without quota restriction.[3]

The exemption from numerical restrictions extends only to the immediate relative beneficiary himself, and does not confer derivative immediate relative status on the family members of the immediate relative beneficiary.[4] However, some family members of an immediate relative beneficiary may themselves be entitled to immediate relative status by virtue of their direct relationship to the petitioner (*e.g.*, stepchildren). In such a case, a separate visa petition must be filed for each immediate relative.[5]

Immediate relative status is granted to alien spouses of U.S. citizens. To qualify as a spouse, it must be established that a marriage is legally valid at its inception and that it has not been entered into for the purpose of evading immigration laws, *i.e.*, as a fraudulent or sham marriage.[6] Fraudulent or sham marriages are impermissible as bases for conferring an immigration benefit and can lead to the deportation of the alien or even imposition of criminal penalties against the alien entering into such a marriage. Special provisions to protect against the conferral of immigration benefits in the case of sham marriages were enacted as part of the Immigration Marriage Fraud Amendments of 1986 ("Marriage Fraud Act").[7] The requirements to establish a viable marriage and of the Marriage Fraud Act generally are discussed, *infra*, at Sections 19.12 and 19.72.

Children of U.S. citizens are also eligible to immigrate under the immediate relative provisions. The child must be unmarried and under the age of 21 years at the time the benefit will be conferred. Legitimate children will automatically qualify for immediate relative treatment. "Legitimacy" is determined by the law in the country of the applicant's birth at the time of birth.[8] Natural-born children of U.S. citizen mothers also qualify, even if illegitimate.[9] Natural-born children of U.S. citizen fathers will qualify for immediate relative treatment if paternity is established by clear evidence and a legitimate parent-child relationship exists as evidenced by factors including the provision of documentation establishing financial support of the child or continued residence of the child with the parent.[10] Adopted children may also qualify, but only if the

---

3. INA §§ 201(b)(2)(A)(ii), (b)(2)(B); 8 U.S.C.A. § 1151(b)(2)(A)(ii), (b)(2)(B).

4. INA § 201(b); 8 U.S.C.A. § 1151(b).

5. PRACTICE POINTER: Where a remarriage of an alien to a U.S. citizen occurs and there are children from the first marriage of the alien under the age of 18 at the time of the remarriage, separate I-130 petitions should be filed by the U.S. citizen spouse on behalf of each child, thus qualifying each child as an immediate relative of the stepparent.

6. Matter of Kitsalis, 11 I & N Dec. 613 (BIA 1966).

7. INA § 216(b); 8 U.S.C.A. § 1186a(b).

8. Matter of Rivers, 17 I & N Dec. 419 (I.D. 2802, BIA 1980).

9. Matter of B.S., 6 I & N Dec. 305 (A.G. 1955).

10. Matter of Chambers, 17 I & N Dec. 117 (I.D. 2730, BIA 1979).

adoption was finalized prior to the child's 16th birthday and procedural requirements regarding the adoption have been satisfied.[11] Step-children may qualify for immediate relative treatment where the step-relationship was established prior to the child's 18th birthday.

Special provisions are applicable to children of alien widows or widowers and battered children of U.S. citizens.[12] These are discussed, *infra*, at Sections 19.11 and 19.16.

§ 19.9 Family–Based Immigration—Family Preference Categories

The preference category applicants are subject to numerical limitations. The spouse and children of a principal alien qualifying for "preference qualification" are entitled to immigrate with him or her, and are charged against the visa allotment in the same preference as the principal alien.[1]

The first family-sponsored preference includes unmarried adult sons and daughters of U.S. citizens.[2] This preference is allotted 23,400 annual visas, plus any visas not used by the fourth family-sponsored preference (for brothers and sisters of U.S. citizens).[3]

The second family-sponsored preference is set aside for two groups: 2A, spouses and children of permanent residents; and 2B, unmarried adult sons and daughters of residents.[4]

The third family-sponsored preference is set aside for married sons and daughters of U.S. citizens.[5]

The fourth family-sponsored preference is comprised of brothers and sisters of U.S. citizens, provided the U.S. citizen is at least 21 years old.[6]

Validity of a visa petition based on these preference categories depends upon the establishment of the requisite relationship, and a visa petition cannot be approved if such relationship is terminated, even if the termination occurred after the visa petition was filed.[7] Where a petitioner withdraws a visa petition on behalf of a spouse, son or daughter, there is no bar to the submission of a second petition on behalf of the same beneficiary.[8]

---

11. Matter of Bautista, 17 I & N Dec. 122 (I.D. 2731, BIA 1979).

12. Violent Crime Control and Law Enforcement Act of 1994 (Pub.L.No. 103–322), § 40701.

§ 19.9

1. INA § 203(a); 8 U.S.C.A. § 1153(a).

2. INA § 203(a)(1); 8 U.S.C.A. § 1153(a)(1).

3. INA § 203(a)(4); 8 U.S.C.A. § 1153(a)(4).

4. INA § 203(a)(2)(A); 8 U.S.C.A. § 1153(a)(3); INA § 203(a)(2)(B); 8 U.S.C.A. § 1153(a)(3)(B).

5. INA § 203(a)(3); 8 U.S.C.A. § 1153(a)(3).

6. INA § 203(a)(4); 8 U.S.C.A. § 1153(a)(4).

7. INA § 205; 8 U.S.C.A. § 1155.

8. Matter of Isber, 20 I & N Dec. (I.D. 3203, BIA 1993).

§ 19.9   IMMIGRATION AND NATIONALITY LAW   Ch. 19

In general, where status is sought on the basis of either the petitioner's U.S. citizenship or lawful permanent resident status, an unexpired U.S. passport, birth certificate establishing that the petitioner was born in the U.S., certificate of citizenship or certificate of naturalization, alien registration receipt ("green card") forms I–151 or I–551, or other proof given by the INS that evidences the petitioner's lawful status is generally accepted to establish eligibility of a petitioner to qualify the beneficiary for immigration benefits.

§ 19.10   Family–Based Immigration—Qualifying as a Relation

Most petitions for family-based immigration are filed on Form I–130. Petitions for orphans are filed on Form I–600, and petitions to qualify as an immediate relative by widow or widowers of U.S. citizens are filed on Form I–360. Visa petition regulations provide that copies of documents may be submitted without submitting the originals, and copies need not be certified.[1]

It is well-established that the petitioner bears the burden of proving[2] that the claimed familial relationship actually exists. The evidence required to prove immigration or nationality status of the petitioner is described at 8 C.F.R. § 204.1(g). The evidence required to prove the different family relationships is described in subsections of 8 C.F.R. § 204.2[3] and is discussed at Section 19.14 *infra*.

The authoritative source of availability of foreign documents is the U.S. Department of State *Foreign Affairs Manual*, Appendix B/C/A/ to Volume 9 ("FAM"). The FAM notes on each country indicate whether a particular document required is available, whether civil or religious documents will be acceptable, how to request documents from appropriate agencies, and what fees, if any, are to be charged. The INS will generally not accept a substitute in lieu of the officially available document as indicated by the FAM. Where a petition is not submitted without primary evidence to establish the claimed relationship, the petitioner will be required to explain why it was not obtained and why secondary evidence was submitted. Foreign language documents must be submitted with an English translation, certified by a competent translator.[4]

§ 19.10

1. 8 C.F.R. § 103.2(b)(4); 8 C.F.R. § 204.1(f)(2).

2. Matter of MA, Int.Dec. 3160 (BIA 1991). The standard required to meet the burden of proof in familial relationships is "clear and convincing" evidence. INA § 291; 8 U.S.C.A. § 1361.

3. Where primary documentation, such as a birth certificate, marriage certificate or passport are unavailable, secondary evidence in the form of affidavits of family members, school records, tax records or other indicia of the claimed status depending on the relationship that must be proved will be accepted by the INS. *See* 8 C.F.R. § 204.1(g)(2).

4. 8 C.F.R. § 204.1(f)(3).

§ 19.10 QUALIFYING AS A RELATION

U.S. citizenship may be established as follows:

- a birth certificate from one of the 50 states, Guam or Puerto Rico;
- a naturalization or citizenship certificate;
- a valid U.S. passport bearing petitioner's photograph.[5]

Where primary evidence is unavailable, secondary evidence may be submitted in the form of a baptismal certificate with the seal of the church, showing the date and place of birth in the U.S. and date of baptism, affidavits sworn to by persons living at the time and having personal knowledge of the events to which they attest, early school records evidencing the child's admission to the school, date and place of birth, and name(s) and place(s) of birth of the parent(s), census records evidencing name, date and place of birth or age of petitioners; or where it is determined that it would cause unusual delay or hardship to obtain documentary proof of birth in the U.S., a U.S. citizen petitioner who is a member of the Armed Forces and who is serving outside the U.S. may submit a statement from the appropriate authority of the Armed Forces. The statement should attest to the fact that personnel records of the Armed Forces evidence that petitioner was born in the U.S. on a certain date.[6]

Petitioners may establish lawful permanent residence status with: (1) Alien Registration Card, Form I–551 or Form I–151[7] (an earlier form of Form I–551), or (2) other proof provided by INS of evidence of lawful permanent residence status.[8]

8 C.F.R. § 204.2(a)(2) provides that in all spousal cases, the following documents must be submitted to prove the relationship:

- a marriage certificate issued by a civil governmental authority (not one issued by a religious entity);
- proof of termination of any and all prior marriages of petitioner and/or beneficiary;
- the petitioner may, in some circumstances, be requested to prove not only the existence of the marriage, but also that the marriage was legal at the place of inception, or that it is a *bona fide* marriage.[9]

Marriages present particular problems of proof. There may be a need to prove termination of prior marriages, including proving the law of the jurisdiction and establishment of customary divorces. A common request by the INS is for proof that the marriage was *bona fide* at its inception. Documentation such as birth certificates for children born to the petitioner and beneficiary, wedding pictures, joint bank accounts,

---

5. 8 C.F.R. § 204.1(g)(1)(ii).
6. 8 C.F.R. § 204.1(g)(2).
7. These are different versions of the so-called "green card."
8. 8 C.F.R. § 204.1(g)(1)(vii).
9. 8 C.F.R. § 204.2(a)(1)(i), (ii).

joint leases or evidence of the purchase of real estate, income tax returns evidencing joint filings and acknowledgment from an employer to indicate that an alien spouse has been included as a beneficiary in the employee's insurance coverage would generally evidence the *bona fides* of the marriage at its inception.

Documentation in support of an I–130 petition by a U.S. citizen mother on behalf of her child would include the child's birth certificate evidencing the mother's name. If the mother's name on the certificate is different from her name on the petition, proof of name change, in the form of marriage certificate and change of name decree must be submitted. In this petition process the child need not show legitimacy.[10]

Where a father petitions for a child born in wedlock, the following documents should be submitted:

- the child's birth certificate containing at least the maiden name of mother, and preferably, names of both parents;
- the parents' marriage certificate, if any;
- proof of termination of any and all previous marriages of both mother and father, if parents are married to each other;
- proof of any change or variation in either petition or beneficiary's surname.[11]

Petitions involving children legitimated through the marriage of their parents must include proof that the marriage took place before the child turned 18. If legitimation was based on changes in the law, the change must have taken place before the child turned 21. If based upon the law in the father's place of residence, the INS position is that the father must have moved to that jurisdiction before the child turned 18.[12]

The following documentation must be submitted by a father for children born out of wedlock:[13]

- the child's birth certificate indicating petitioner is natural father;

---

10. 8 C.F.R. § 204.2(c)(2)(i). *See supra* discussion at § 19.8, outlining the various immediate relative and family preference categories.

11. 8 C.F.R. § 204.2(c)(2)(iii).

12. Matter of Hernandez, 19 I & N Dec. 14 (BIA 1983).

13. 8 C.F.R. § 204.2(c)(2)(iii). *See* Pub. L.No. 104–51 (Nov. 15, 1995). The statute under INA § 101(b)(2), 8 U.S.C.A. § 1101(b)(2) was recently amended to change the definition of "child." It replaces the words "legitimate child" with the words "children born in wedlock" and replaces "illegitimate child" with the words "children born out of wedlock." Because of this statutory change, it will no longer be necessary to determine whether a child born out of wedlock is regarded as legitimate or illegitimate. However, where the natural (birth) father has ever had sole or joint custody of the child, it will still be necessary to determine whether the child has ever been legitimated under the laws of the child's or the father's residence or domicile. The subsequent marriage of the child's birth parents will legitimate a child born out of wedlock in most countries. Many countries have also established other procedures for legitimation. At this writing, INS regulations implementing this new statutory change have not yet been issued.

- where the birth certificate does not include father's name, or if the birth was not registered immediately after the child's birth, secondary evidence establishing paternity would need to be submitted, which may include an affidavit from the mother, and/or results of blood tests;
- proof that the petitioner had or has a *bona fide* parent-child relationship with the beneficiary (*i.e.* proof of joint residence, proof of financial support, or any other expression of parent concern);[14]
- proof of any change in the petitioner's or beneficiary's last name.

To establish a stepparent-stepchild relationship, the following are required:[15]

- the child's birth certificate evidencing names of natural parents;
- the petitioner's marriage certificate indicating that the petitioner married the child's natural parent prior to the child's 18th birthday. A stepmother may petition for her spouse's illegitimate child even though, her spouse as the natural father, may not be able to file his own petition;
- proof of termination of any and all previous marriages of the petitioner and spouse;
- proof of change, if any, in the beneficiary's last name.

Petitions for adopted children must include:[16]

- an adoption decree indicating child was adopted before his/her 16th birthday;
- proof that the child was in the legal custody of, and resided with the petitioner, for at least two years prior to the filing of a visa petition (*i.e.*, school or medical records and a copy of the court order granting custody of the child to petitioner);
- proof of parental control for the two years the child resided with the adoptive parent.[17]

The same type of documentation filed by parents on behalf of children is required by children filing a visa petition on behalf of their parents. Only a U.S. citizen who is 21 years of age or older may file a petition on behalf of a parent.[18]

In order to establish a sibling relationship, the petitioner must evidence that both the petitioner and beneficiary were the children of a common parent or adoptive parent. Where the petition is based upon a common natural mother, the relationship can be established by submit-

---

14. Matter of Pagnerre, 12 I & N Dec. 688 (BIA 1977).
15. 8 C.F.R. § 204.2(c)(2)(iv).
16. 8 C.F.R. § 204.2(c)(2)(vii).
17. Matter of Cuello, Int.Dec. 3117 (BIA 1989).
18. 8 C.F.R. § 204.2(e).

ting both the petitioner's and beneficiary's birth certificates, together with marriage certificates or other proof of evidence to show a change in either the petitioner's or beneficiary's surname. Where a petition is based upon a common father, stepparent or adoptive parent, all of the documents described above in each category in addition to birth certificates and proof of change of name would be required.[19]

§ 19.11 Family-Based Immigration—Qualifying as a Relation—"Child" and "Parent" Issues

The Immigration and Nationality Act defines the terms "child," "parent," "mother" and "father." Case law, however, must be consulted for interpretation of the definitions of these terms.

The INA defines the term "child" in six separate categories for purposes of immigration:

a) Legitimate Child

To qualify as a legitimate child, the child must be legitimate under the laws of the country of birth at the time of birth.[1] This includes children born in wedlock, who are considered legitimate for immigration purposes even where the parent's marriage will not be recognized because of public policy.[2] This category will also encompass children born out of wedlock if they were born in a country which does not distinguish between children born in and out of wedlock and accords children the same rights and status whether born in or out of wedlock.[3]

b) Legitimated Child

The INS requires that the act of legitimation take place before the child turns 18.[4] Legitimation must be valid under the law of either the child or the father's residence or domicile either in or out of the U.S., and must take place before the child reaches the age of 18. The child must be in the legal custody of the legitimating parents at the time of legitimation. Unless local law provides otherwise, however, biological fathers and mothers are deemed to have a natural right to custody.[5] Acknowledgment is not recognized as legitimation unless it confers upon the child the rights of a legitimate child, including inheritance rights.[6] Changes in the law of a particular country removing distinctions be-

---

19. 8 C.F.R. § 204.2(f)(2)(i), (ii).

§ 19.11

1. INA § 101(b); 8 U.S.C.A. § 1101(b). See Pub.L.No. 104–51 (Nov. 15, 1995) which changes the definition of illegitimate and illegitimate child, discussed, *supra*, at § 19.10, note 13.

2. Matter of Mahal, 12 I & N Dec. 409 (BIA 1967).

3. Matter of Clarke, 18 I & N Dec. 369 (BIA 1983).

4. Matter of Cortez, 16 I & N Dec. 289 (BIA 1977).

5. Matter of Rivers, 17 I & N Dec. 419 (BIA 1980); INA § 101(b)(1)(C); 8 U.S.C.A. § 1101(b)(1)(C).

6. De Los Santos v. INS, 690 F.2d 56 (2d Cir.1982).

tween children born in and out of wedlock will be recognized as having legitimated the child on the date the law took effect.[7]

c) Stepchild

A child may be classified as a stepchild provided the child was under the age of 18 when the marriage creating the relationship occurred, whether or not the child was born in or out of wedlock.[8] The step relationship can also outlast the marriage that created it.[9] Where parental interest continued despite divorce, the stepparent was able to successfully petition for the stepchild. As well, when the natural parent had died after marriage to the stepparent, the stepparent can still petition for the stepchild.[10] Where the stepchild relationship is based on a marriage which is deemed a sham marriage, however, no stepchild relationship is considered to exist despite the existence of a family relationship.[11]

d) Illegitimate Child (child born out of wedlock)[12]

A father may petition for an illegitimate child, provided the father has or had a *bona fide* parent-child relationship with the person. Benefits of this provision even apply to children who turned 21 before November 6, 1986, the effective date of this provision.[13]

e) Adopted Child

A child must be adopted while under the age of 16, and must have been in the legal custody of, and resided with, either or both of the adopting parents for at least two years to qualify as a "child" under the Act.[14] Residence may take place either before or after the adoption.[15] The adoption must be valid in the country where it took place.[16] Where customary adoption is recognized by a foreign country, it will be accepted for immigration purposes.[17] It is to be noted that the natural parent of a child who gained immigration benefits through adoption cannot receive any immigration benefits through the adopted child. This restriction does not extend to brothers and sisters or other natural relatives.[18]

f) Orphan Child

7. Matter of Clahar, 18 I & N Dec. 1 (BIA 1981).

8. INA § 101(b)(1)(B); 8 U.S.C.A. § 1101(b)(1)(B).

9. Matter of Mowrer, 17 I & N Dec. 613 (BIA 1981).

10. Matter of Pagnerre, 13 I & N Dec. 668 (BIA 1971).

11. Matter of Awwal, 19 I & N Dec. 617 (BIA 1988).

12. *See* Pub.L.No. 104–51 (Nov. 15, 1995) which updates the statutory definition of "child," "parent" and "father" and replaces the words "legitimate child" with the worlds "child born in wedlock" and replaces "illegitimate child" with the words "child born out of wedlock." *See supra,* § 19.10, note 13.

13. Pub.L.No. 99–601, 100 Stat. 3359, Nov. 6, 1986; Matter of Atembe, 19 I & N Dec. 427 (BIA 1986).

14. INA § 101(b)(1)(E); 8 U.S.C.A. § 1101(b)(1)(E).

15. Matter of M, I & N Dec. 118 (BIA 1959).

16. Matter of Garcia–Rodriguez, 16 I & N Dec. 438 (BIA 1978).

17. Matter of Kwok, 14 I & N Dec. 127 (BIA 1972).

18. Matter of Fuji, 12 I & N Dec. 495 (Dist.Dir.1967). This citation predates the current format utilized by the Interim Deci-

§ 19.11   IMMIGRATION AND NATIONALITY LAW   Ch. 19

A child is considered an orphan because of the death or disappearance of, abandonment or desertion by, or separation or loss from, both parents, or if the sole surviving parent is incapable of providing the proper care and irrevocably releases the child for emigration and adoption. The child must be under 16 at the time the petition is filed on his or her behalf to classify the child as an immediate relative. The orphan provision only applies to a petition by a U.S. citizen on behalf of a minor unmarried child. Special provisions related to orphan requirements and processing are discussed, *infra*, at Section 19.15.

For immigration purposes, the relationship of "parent" is recognized only if it exists or was created through one of the six child categories.[19]

Some of the most difficult issues to determine relate to the distinction between the child who is "legitimate," "legitimated," or "illegitimate" in cases relating to children born out of wedlock. Where a step relationship cannot be established in order to accord an immigration benefit, the question of legitimacy must be addressed.

The Immigration Reform and Control Act of 1986 modifies the definition of "child" to permit the conferral of immigration benefits based on a relationship between an illegitimate child and its natural father.[20] Provisions of the Act require that immigration benefits will accrue to the child "if the father has or had a *bona fide* parent-child relationship with the person." The constitutionality of the Act's distinction between natural mothers and natural fathers of illegitimate children had been upheld by the U.S. Supreme Court.[21] Congressional amendment was therefore required to equalize the treatment of such relationships.

Establishment of a *bona fide* relationship may include proof of financial support, as well as other documented actions reflecting the existence of such a relationship. Cohabitation of the parents is considered persuasive, but is not a requirement for a favorable adjudication of a petition filed on behalf of an illegitimate child by the natural father.

In addition to establishing that a *bona fide* relationship exists, the blood relationship may be established between father and child. Evidence may include a blood test if other evidence, such as the father's name on a birth certificate, or a judicial determination of paternity, is not available.

This amended provision of law regarding illegitimate children and natural fathers, while requiring additional documentation beyond what is required in the "stepchild provision," is obviously a useful addition in cases in which a stepchild relationship cannot be established. It is also useful that a parent-child relationship for purposes of conferring an immigration benefit can be established if the child has been legitimated

---

sions, where the BIA acts as decider in all decisions.

19. INA § 101(b)(2); 8 U.S.C.A. § 1101(b)(2).

20. INA § 101(b)(1)(D); 8 U.S.C.A. § 1101(b)(1)(D).

21. Fiallo v. Bell, 430 U.S. 787, 97 S.Ct. 1473, 52 L.Ed.2d 50 (1977).

by the age of 18 under the laws of the child's domicile or under the laws of the father's domicile, if the child is in the legal custody of the father at the time of legitimation.[22] A detailed study of the laws of the domiciles of the two parties would be required to determine the laws with regard to legitimation in the domicile, and whether "custody" requirements have been met.

The amended provision establishing a relationship between an illegitimate child with his or her father is a simpler provision with which to comply. The Board of Immigration Appeals[23] recently held that the provision should be flexible and applied generously so that fathers of children over 21 at the time the amendment took effect in 1986 may submit a visa petition on behalf of the child so long as the parent-child relationship was established when the child was under 21.[24]

While a legitimate child is included within the definition of "child" under § 101(b)(1)(A) of the Act (8 U.S.C.A. § 1101(b)(1)(A)), the term "legitimate" is not specifically defined. The Board has held that the term "legitimate" normally refers to a child born in wedlock, but that a child born out of wedlock will nonetheless be regarded as legitimate if the applicable laws of the foreign country have effectively eliminated all distinctions between legitimate and illegitimate children.[25]

In such cases, the test applied by the Board is equality of filial rights when compared to children born in wedlock. The Board has held that the laws of Haiti, Honduras, Jamaica, Guatemala, Colombia and the Republic of Cape Verde have effectively abolished the concept of illegitimacy so that all children born in those countries were deemed legitimate under Section 101(b)(1)(A) of the Act (8 U.S.C.A. § 1101(b)(1)(A)). Where applicable law abolishes all distinctions between children born in and out of wedlock after the child's birth, the child is deemed legitimated from the time the law changes, but not from the time of birth.[26]

§ 19.12 Family–Based Immigration—Qualifying as a Relation—"Marriage" Issues

In order for a person to qualify for immigration benefits as the spouse of a U.S. citizen or lawful permanent resident, it is essential that

---

22. INA § 101(b)(1)(C); 8 U.S.C.A. § 1101(b)(1)(C).

23. The Board of Immigration Appeals ("BIA") has been in existence under various names and with varying responsibilities since 1922. Since 1940, it has been known as the Board of Immigration Appeals and from 1983 to date has been placed in the Department of Justice in the Executive Office for Immigration Review ("EOIR"). The BIA acts as the delegate of the Attorney General in hearing and determining appeals from certain types of decisions of the INS and immigration judges. The appellate jurisdiction of the BIA as set forth in 8 C.F.R. § 3.1(b) includes appeals of district directors on visa petitions based on family relationships, administrative fines, and rescission of adjustment of status, among other appellate review functions.

24. Matter of Vizcaino, 19 Int.Dec. 3061 (BIA 1988).

25. Matter of Hernandez, 17 I & N Dec. 7 (BIA 1979); Matter of Pavlovic, 17 I & N Dec. 407 (BIA 1980); Matter of Sanchez, 16 I & N Dec. 671 (BIA 1979).

26. Matter of J & Y, 3 I & N Dec. 657 (BIA 1949).

§ 19.12   IMMIGRATION AND NATIONALITY LAW   Ch. 19

the alien and the U.S. citizen or resident be parties to a legally valid marriage.[1]

A key element to obtaining immigration benefits as a "spouse" includes the existence of a valid and subsisting marriage between the parties. A marriage void because of a legal impediment or failure to observe a legal requirement cannot be utilized to obtain immigration benefits. In general, the validity of a marriage will be judged by the law of the place where it is celebrated.[2] Further, there is a strong presumption in favor of the legality of the marriage.[3] The burden is on the person claiming immigration benefits on the basis of a marriage to establish the validity of the marriage. Marital relationships contracted in foreign countries will be generally acknowledged for immigration purposes, particularly if there has been a marriage ceremony, when the parties have held themselves out as husband and wife, have lived together, and considered themselves married, and where children have been born to them. In assessing the validity of marriages occurring in foreign countries, administrative agencies frequently turn to the Library of Congress for information concerning the relevant laws of that country.[4]

Additionally, relevant to the concept that a marriage occurred must be the fact that the marriage must continue to subsist and exist. Benefits are not bestowed upon terminated marriages. However, a humanitarian exception, introduced by the Immigration Act of 1990, permits the granting of immediate relative status on behalf of an alien who was the spouse of a U.S. citizen for at least two years at the time of his death and not then legally separated, provided the alien spouse files a visa petition as an immediate relative within two years and has not remarried.[5] Where parties are still married, but not living together, it was the previous administrative view that benefits for immediate relative status would be unavailable because immigration benefits are designed to promote the unity of families, and since the parties are no longer living together, they are not entitled to immediate relative status. The view that a marriage, although *bona fide*, must be "viable" to support continued immigration benefits has been rejected by several courts.[6] It is now the administrative position that immigration benefits based upon marriage may be granted, even if the parties are separated, although the

§ 19.12

1. The validity of the marriage can also have bearing on whether an alien can qualify as an unmarried son or daughter of a U.S. citizen or permanent resident, or as a child, defined at Section 101(b) of the Act, 8 U.S.C.A. § 1101(b), discussed *supra* at § 19.11.

2. Matter of Faruque, 10 I & N Dec. 561 (BIA 1964); Matter of Freeman, 11 I & N Dec. 482 (BIA 1966); Matter of Garcia, 16 I & N Dec. 623 (BIA 1978).

3. Matter of McKee, 17 I & N Dec. 332 (BIA 1980).

4. Matter of Hassan, 16 I & N Dec. 16 (BIA 1976).

5. INA § 201(b)(2)(A)(i); 8 U.S.C.A. § 1151 (b)(2)(A)(i), as amended by Section 101, Immigration Act of 1990, Pub.L.No. 101–649, 104 Stat. 4978.

6. Chan v. Bell, 464 F.Supp. 125 (D.D.C. 1978); Whetstone v. INS, 561 F.2d 1303 (9th Cir.1977); Bark v. INS, 511 F.2d 1200 (9th Cir.1975).

separation may be considered in determining whether the marriage was *bona fide*.[7]

Other factors affecting the legality of the marriage must be considered. Impediments to remarriage can be removed by retroactive annulment, legalizing second marriages from their inception.[8] Generally, the INS will not question the validity of a divorce, whether granted in the U.S. or in a foreign country, where one of the parties was physically present within the court's jurisdiction. Collateral attack on such divorces is beyond the ambit of normal administration and is precluded by principles of comity and, in the case of state divorces, by the Full Faith and Credit clause of the U.S. Constitution.

On occasion, even where a marriage is valid at its place of origin, it may, in some extraordinary manner, be inadequate to support preferred status. Marriages which are repugnant to public health or morals, including polygamous or incestuous marriages, are not recognized by the INS. Marriages between uncles and nieces, or marriages between first cousins are sanctioned in some countries and religious groups and recognized as valid by the INS.[9] Proxy marriages are generally not recognized by the INS, even in cases where they may be regarded as valid where performed.[10]

When marriages are entered into and have been discovered to be a sham; that is, entered into by the parties for the sole purpose of obtaining immigration benefits and without any intent to live together as husband and wife, a visa petition will be denied by the INS.[11] Conduct of the parties after marriage is considered relevant in ascertaining their intent at the time of marriage. In assessing such intent, the INS will often request documentation to support the claim of the continued existence and subsistence of the marriage, including evidence that the couple is living together. Common documentation requested includes tax returns, joint bank accounts, testimony regarding the courtship, wedding ceremony and marriage, and other documents supporting the claim that the couple is residing together.

Where marriage is terminated by the death of a spouse, a visa petition filed by the deceased petitioner may be denied.[12] Discretionary humanitarian relief is available to the surviving alien spouse of a U.S. citizen.[13]

---

7. Matter of Hann, 18 I & N Dec. 196 (BIA 1982).

8. *See* Gim, *Divorce—Alien Style and Other Family Problems*, 52 Int.Rel. 205 (1975).

9. Matter of Da Silva, 15 I & N Dec. 778 (BIA 1976); Matter of T-, 8 I & N Dec. 529 (BIA 1960).

10. In the Matter of W, 4 I & N Dec. 209 (BIA 1955); *cf.* Matter of H.H., 6 I & N Dec. 278 (BIA 1954).

11. Matter of A.E. (TX), 4 I & N Dec. 405 (BIA 1951).

12. Matter of Varela, 13 I & N Dec. 453 (BIA 1970).

13. 8 C.F.R. § 204.2(b)(1).

§ 19.13 Family-Based Immigration—Petitioning Procedures and Documentation

In order for an individual to apply for an immigrant visa based upon his or her family ties, the Immigration and Naturalization Service must first approve an alien relative petition confirming that the necessary family relationship exists for immediate relative or preference classification. The Form I-130 serves as a petition for all types of relative cases, including spouses, parents, children and siblings.

Form I-360 is utilized where petitions are filed by Amerasians, widows or widowers. Form I-600 is utilized for advance processing of Orphan petitions.

§ 19.14 Family-Based Immigration—Petitioning Procedure and Documentation—I-130 Petition

Once eligibility for a family preference or immediate relative classification has been determined, the procedure for either type of classification is substantially the same.

The I-130 petition is the preliminary step in obtaining permanent residence. Its approval by the INS certifies that the alien is eligible under one of the preferences or as an immediate relative for permanent residence. Actual conferral of such status requires another step after the approval of the petition: completion of an application for permanent residence (adjustment of status) at a local INS office in the U.S. or filing for an immigrant visa at a U.S. Embassy or Consulate abroad.

A separate petition for each beneficiary, together with a filing fee, must be submitted on Form I-130, Petition for Alien Relative. While no separate petition is necessary for the spouse and child of a principal beneficiary in one of the preference categories, if the spouse or child is accompanying or following to join the principal, spouses and children of immediate relatives cannot be included on the same Form I-130.[1]

The usual place for filing the petition is with the INS Service Center having jurisdiction over the place of residence of the petitioner.[2] Four Service Centers are designated for filing of I-130 petitions nationwide. They are located in California, Texas, Nebraska and Vermont. Each Service Center jurisdiction covers several states, and petitions may be filed by mail. When an application for adjustment of status is filed with the petition, as is permitted for certain immediate relatives,[3] the petition and the application must be filed in the INS District Office with jurisdiction over the place of residence of the beneficiary.

§ 19.14
1. 8 C.F.R. § 204.2(c)(1). See supra, § 19.8.
2. 8 C.F.R. § 204.1(e)(1).
3. See infra, § 19.62.

If the petitioner is resident abroad, the petition must be filed with a foreign office of the INS that is located in the country in which the petitioner resides, provided such an office exists.[4] When a petitioner and beneficiary physically present themselves at a U.S. Consulate with jurisdiction to process immigrant visa applications, the consular officer at that consulate is empowered to approve the petition, provided an INS foreign office does not have jurisdiction over the petition.[5] The INS has listed two examples of petitions which may be accepted by consular districts or overseas INS offices for humanitarian reasons, waiving the residency requirements: (1) when the beneficiary is a very young child or very old parent who needs the petitioner's care; and (2) when the qualifying marriage takes place abroad, so that it makes no sense to return to the U.S. to file the petition.[6]

Special procedures are applicable to obtain immediate relative classification for widows and widowers[7] A widow or widower may be classified as an immediate relative if (1) he or she has been married for at least two years to a U.S. citizen at the time of the citizen's death; (2) the petition is filed within two years of the citizen spouse's death, or before November 29, 1992 if the citizen spouse died before November 29, 1990; (3) the alien petitioner and citizen spouse were not legally separated at the time of death; and (4) the alien spouse has not remarried.[8]

A petition submitted by a widow or widower must be accompanied by evidence of the deceased spouse's citizenship and primary evidence of the relationship in the form of a marriage certificate issued by civil authorities, proof of termination of any prior marriages and the U.S. citizen's death certificate issued by civil authorities.[9]

A widow or widower must file Form I–360 to petition for classification as an immediate relative.[10] A separate Form I–360 must be filed by such children of the widow or widower, and should meet the eligibility requirements listed above unless the petition is filed with the widow or widower's I–360 petition. The child's petition must also be accompanied by evidence of the relationship between the child and widow/widower. An I–360 petition will not be approved for a child if the widow/widower is deceased or if the widow/widower has not filed an I–360 petition. The approved I–360 petition is forwarded to the National Visa Center, which now handles processing of the petition and determines the appropriate consulate abroad to which the petition may be forwarded for overseas processing. Should the petitioner be physically in the U.S. and eligible to apply for permanent residence under the adjustment of status provisions, he or she may do so, and INS will retain the petition.

4. 8 C.F.R. § 204.1(e)(2).
5. 8 C.F.R. § 204.1(e)(3).
6. Id.
7. 8 C.F.R. § 204.2(b).
8. 8 C.F.R. § 204.2(b)(1).
9. 8 C.F.R. § 204.2(b)(2).
10. 8 C.F.R. § 204.1(a).

§ 19.14   IMMIGRATION AND NATIONALITY LAW   Ch. 19

The INS follows a number of procedures aimed at screening out those petitions filed on behalf of beneficiaries who have previously been involved in fraud or otherwise have a history with the INS. Every I-130 that is properly filed is reported to the INS Central Office, where information is checked against a fraudulent petition index maintained by that office. When the Central Office does not report back to the district office regarding an indication of probable fraud within ten days of the date of mailing the report of the I-130, the INS Operations Instructions direct that the index be considered to have been checked, with negative results.[11] Further, all visa petitions must be checked against the Service Lookout Book, which keeps track of persons with a previous INS history. The Service Lookout Book is consulted for the name of the principal beneficiary, as well as the spouse and children who may derive preference status through the principal.

The INS investigation may include other elements such as an investigation regarding the authenticity of documents submitted in support of the I-130 petition.

The most frequent INS investigatory technique with regard to relative petitions is the infamous "Stokes" interview, established in New York, in which the *bona fides* of a questionable marriage are explored by INS officers through the questioning of the parties to the marriage.[12] This investigatory process was developed through litigation brought in the Southern District of New York which challenged previous Service policy in conducting investigation in cases of suspected fraudulent marriages.[13] If, in an initial interview, the Immigration Examiner doubted that the marriage was *bona fide*, a second hearing would be scheduled by INS to investigate, in further detail, the *bona fides* of the marriage. At such a hearing, the couple was separated and questioned in detail concerning all aspects of their marriage. Questions might include inquiries as to how the couple met, familiarity with each other's families and knowledge concerning each other's occupation and work habits. The questioner might even inquire as to what the color of each other's toothbrushes are, or how the couple traveled to the immigration interview that day. The INS officer would compare the answers of the couple to determine consistency and provide an opportunity to explain differences, and ultimately render a decision as to the *bona fides* of the marriage.

Pursuant to a consent decree in the *Stokes* decision, the government agreed to desist from conducting body searches or personal property searches of the petitioner or beneficiary, absent a lawful arrest, and further agreed not to request fingerprints or photographs from a U.S. citizen petitioner absent a *bona fide* question as to identity. The govern-

11. O.I. 204.1(b).
12. Stokes v. United States, 393 F.Supp. 24 (S.D.N.Y.1975).
13. *Id.*

ment also agreed to avoid posing questions regarding intimate details of the marital relationship. However, an Immigration official may still question the parties regarding whether or not the marriage has been consummated. The government also agreed not to encourage withdrawals of I-130 spouse visa petitions, and to advise persons prior to the withdrawal of a petition that they have the right to an adjudication pursuant to procedures set out in the consent decree. The interview is recorded and parties have a right to review the transcript for purposes of appeal of a denial.[14]

Should the I-130 petition be denied, the petitioner has a right to appeal the decision by filing a Notice of Appeal to the Board of Immigration Appeals at the INS district office where the decision was made. The Notice of Appeal must be filed within 15 days from the date of mailing of the Notification of Decision.[15] The consent decree further directs that, pending final adjudication of an I-130 spouse petition, the district director will not move to deport an alien beneficiary eligible to file for adjustment of status under Section 245 of the INA[16] or eligible for extended voluntary departure.

While the "*Stokes*" procedures apply only to the New York district, the INS Examinations Handbook contains carefully designed procedures for suspect marriage cases patterned after that decision. Such factors as an appreciable age difference between the parties to a marriage, the fact that the marriage took place shortly after the beneficiary's arrival in the U.S. with no prior acquaintanceship, and vast cultural or ethnic differences between the two parties are to be considered by the INS officer in adjudicating an I-130 petition.[17]

The struggle for full due process rights in I-130 spouse interviews is ongoing. In *Ali v. INS*,[18] a lawsuit filed in Massachusetts, the court recognized the important liberty interest involved in the marriage petition process, and acknowledged that:

> The marriage petition process judges a marriage's viability, and so intrudes government into a constitutionally protected zone of basic privacy and autonomy.... While that does not trigger the full panoply of procedural safeguards involved in criminal prosecution, it does mean that the private interest involved is high, and consequently the risk of an erroneous INS decision more damaging.[19]

§ 19.15 Family-Based Immigration—Orphans and Amerasians

Americans have increasingly looked to foreign babies as a source to

---

14. Stokes v. United States, 393 F.Supp. 24 (S.D.N.Y.1975).

15. 8 C.F.R. § 3.3.

16. 8 U.S.C.A. § 1255.

17. INS Examinations Handbook p. III-13. The Handbook is an internal manual issued to Immigration Service examiners.

18. 661 F.Supp. 1234 (D.Mass.1986).

19. *Id* at 1250.

meet their need to provide a loving and caring home in the U.S.[1] Prospective adoptive parents may identify a foreign orphan for adoption only to discover that the child's country of citizenship does not allow foreign adoptions, or that the child does not meet the strict immigration rules established by the U.S. The INS does provide, however, special eligibility provisions for orphans that mitigate the restrictive rules normally applicable to adopted children.[2]

In order to be considered an eligible orphan, a child must meet certain definitional requirements. The orphan child must be under the age of 16 at the time a visa petition is filed on its behalf. An eligible orphan has been defined as a child who "is an orphan because of the death or disappearance of, abandonment or desertion by, or separation or loss from, both parents."[3] Where one parent remains, that parent must be incapable of providing proper care for the child and must have, in writing, irrevocably released the child for emigration and adoption. When the child has been adopted abroad, the requirement of irrevocable release is considered to have been met if the adoption decree clearly sets forth that the adoptive petitioner resides in the U.S. and the child's only parent has agreed to release of the child for adoption.[4]

The child is considered to be an orphan for immigration purposes where the child has no parents due to the death or disappearance of, abandonment or desertion by, or separation or loss from both parents. Abandonment by both parents means that the parents have willfully forsaken all parental rights, obligations, and claims to the child as well as control and possession of the child without intending to transfer or without transferring those rights to any specific person. Relinquishment or release of the child by the parents to a prospective adoptive parent does not constitute abandonment. Further, the release of the child by parents to a third party for custodial care in anticipation of, or in preparation for, adoption, does not constitute abandonment unless a third party (i.e. a governmental agency, court, adoption agency or orphanage) is authorized under the child welfare laws of the foreign-sending country to act in such a capacity.[5]

A child who has been unconditionally "abandoned" to an orphanage is deemed to have no parents. A child is not unconditionally abandoned to an orphanage if the child has been placed temporarily in the orphanage and the parents intend to retrieve the child, the parent or parents are contributing or are attempting to contribute to the child's support, or the parent or parents otherwise exhibit that they have not terminated

---

§ 19.15

1. *See generally* Chapter 20 "Adoptions," *infra*.

2. INA § 101(b)(1)(F); 8 U.S.C.A. § 1101(b)(1)(F).
3. *Id.*
4. 8 C.F.R. § 204.3(d)(1)(v)(B)(2).
5. 8 C.F.R. § 204.3(d)(1)(iv)(B)(2).

their parental obligation to the child.[6]

Desertion by both parents means that both parents have unaccountably passed out of the child's life, their whereabouts are unknown and there is no reasonable hope of their reappearance, and any reasonable efforts to locate them, as determined by a competent authority in accordance with the law of the foreign-sending country, have been unsuccessful.[7]

A child is considered as having only a "surviving parent" if one parent has died and a step-relationship has not been formed (i.e., the surviving parent has not remarried).[8] A child is considered as having a "sole maternal parent" where it is established that the child is illegitimate, the father has disappeared, abandoned, or deserted the child, and the child has not acquired a step-parent.[9] Where the child has a maternal parent and has been legitimated by the father, or the country of birth makes no distinction between legitimate and illegitimate children, the child cannot be considered as having one parent, if both parents are alive.[10]

In all cases, a sole or surviving parent must be "incapable of providing proper care" for the child.[11] The parent would, by definition, be unable to provide for the child's basic needs, consistent with local standards of the foreign country. As indicated, an irrevocable release for the child's adoption and emigration must be obtained from the sole or surviving parent.

Only a U.S. citizen may file a petition to seek immediate relative status for an eligible orphan. Where a petitioner is married, the petitioner must file the petition jointly with his or her spouse. Unmarried petitioners must be at least 25 years of age to file orphan petitions and must be at least 24 years of age to file an application for advanced processing on Form I–600A, utilized to establish the prospective parent's eligibility to file for an orphan prior to the identification of an orphan for adoption.

In addition to the above requirements, the statute requires that the child either have been adopted abroad or be coming to the U.S. for adoption. Where adoption of a child occurs abroad, the adoptive parents

---

6. Matter of (Name Not Provided), A26–652–396 (AAU Feb. 28, 1988). (Abandonment not found where natural father arranged to have married brother adopt child.).

7. 8 C.F.R. § 204.3(b).

8. Matter of D., 8 I & N Dec. 628 (Reg'l Comm'r 1960).

9. 8 C.F.R. § 204.3(b). Recent statutory changes no longer require that a determination be made to assess whether a child born out of wedlock is regarded as legitimate or illegitimate under the laws of the foreign-sending country. However, where the natural (birth) father has ever had sole or joint legal custody of the child, it will still be necessary to determine whether the child may have been legitimated under the laws of the child's or the father's residence or domicile. See Pub.L.No. 104–51 (Nov. 15, 1995).

10. Matter of Del Conte, 10 I & N Dec. 761 (Dist.Dir.1964).

11. 8 C.F.R. § 204.3(b).

must have personally seen and observed the child prior to or during the adoption proceedings. Therefore, proxy adoptions are not recognized. Where the child is coming to the U.S. for adoption, the petitioner must establish that he has complied with the pre-adoption requirements, if any, of the state of the child's proposed residence.[12]

The Attorney General must also be satisfied that proper care will be provided to the child if he is admitted to the U.S. INS regulations provide that an evaluation of the petitioner's suitability as a parent must be made prior to according a child orphan status. Evaluations must be submitted in home study reports prepared by authorized individuals or entities, and home studies are required to ensure that proper care will be furnished to assure that orphans will not be placed in homes which would imperil their physical or mental health. It should be noted further that, as in the case of adopted children, the statute precludes the natural or prior adoptive parents of an eligible orphan from thereafter obtaining any immigration benefits by virtue of such parentage. Further, orphan status cannot be accorded to a child where a person or entity working on behalf of the prospective adoptive parents has given or will give money or other consideration directly or indirectly to the child's parents, agents or other individuals as payment for the child, or as inducement for the release of the child.

In order to succeed in processing an orphan petition, two separate determinations must be made in accordance with INS regulations. First, to be determined by the filing and approval of an advanced processing application, is the ability of the prospective adoptive parent or parents to provide a proper home environment and their suitability as parents. This determination will be based largely upon a home study report and fingerprint checks. In addition it must be determined whether or not the child is in fact an "orphan" as that term is defined pursuant to the Immigration and Nationality Act. Prospective adoptive parents may submit the documentation necessary for each of these determinations separately or simultaneously, depending upon whether an orphan has been identified. An orphan petition cannot be approved unless and until a preliminary favorable adjudication is obtained on the advance processing application. A favorable determination on the advance processing application, however, does not guarantee that the orphan petition will be approved.

There are essentially two ways that a child may be brought to the U.S. for the purpose of adoption or as the adopted child of a U.S. citizen or permanent resident. The first is the use of the I-130 petition to bring the child in as a relative of adoptive parents. The petition may be filed by either a U.S. citizen or a lawful permanent resident; but in the case of the latter, the beneficiary orphan would be subject to second preference visa number availability. Further, the petition may not be approved

---

12. 8 C.F.R. 204.3(d)(1)(iv)(B)(3); INA § 101(b)(1)(F); 8 U.S.C.A. § 1101(b)(1)(F).

unless the petitioner proves that he or she has resided with the child for two years and has had legal custody of the child for two years. These two requirement make this type of immigration of adopted children nearly impossible except for adoptive parents who adopt while living abroad. However, this procedure is also available for adopted children who enter the U.S. as non-immigrants, or who are in the U.S. illegally.

Prospective adoptive parents must submit Form I–600A with the district office of the Immigration and Naturalization Service nearest to their residence to file for advance processing to assure their eligibility for adoption. In addition, the application must be accompanied by proof of U.S. citizenship of at least one of the prospective adoptive parents, evidence of a legal marriage, evidence of legal termination of all previous marriages, fingerprints of the petitioners, and evidence that the petitioners have met any state requirements for adoption, such as a home study. The petitioners must also submit fingerprints for all adult members of the adoptive household.[13] The I–600A is adjudicated by the local District Office of the Immigration and Naturalization Service and is valid for a period of 18 months.

A final orphan petition (Form I–600) may be filed with the INS office having jurisdiction over the petitioner's place of residence, or with an overseas INS office or a consular officer. Evidence, such as proof of the approval of the Form I–600A (where applicable) and birth certificate of the child, must also accompany the petition. A consular officer may only approve an orphan petition when the advance processing application has already been approved by the Immigration and Naturalization Service, and when the petitioner has traveled abroad to a country which does not have an INS office. Where a consular official has questions about the approvability of a petition, it will be forwarded to an INS office having jurisdiction over that particular country. In an orphan case, a petition may be approved and immigrant visa issued for an orphan who is being adopted abroad, or for an orphan who is being brought to the U.S. for the purpose of adoption.

Pub.L.No. 97–359, 96 Stat. 1716, enacted in 1982, provides that children fathered by U.S. servicemen in Vietnam, Laos, Cambodia, Korea and Thailand between 1950 and the date of enactment are eligible for more favorable consideration as immediate relatives or in preference categories for permanent residence status if certain conditions are met.

Evidence not generally considered acceptable by the INS can be utilized to establish that children are, in fact, offspring of U.S. citizen fathers. Illegitimacy is not a consideration.[14] If it is established by the evidence cited that the child was fathered by a U.S. citizen, the natural father need not petition for the child. The petition can be filed by a responsible adult or by the child. Additionally, the child must have a sponsor who can guarantee legal custody under the laws of the state

---

13. 8 C.F.R. § 204.3(c)(1)(vi).   **14.** 8 C.F.R. § 204.4(a).

§ 19.15   IMMIGRATION AND NATIONALITY LAW   Ch. 19

where the child will reside until he or she is 18 years of age.[15] Financial guarantees for the support of a child are enforceable by the government. The natural mother must also release the child for immigration purposes. Depending upon their age and marital status, these children will qualify as immediate relatives of U.S. citizens or, in the first or fourth preference categories, as the unmarried or married adult sons or daughters of U.S. citizens.

§ 19.16   Family–Based Immigration—Abused Spouse and Children

This new provision of the Immigration and Nationality Act provides that the abused spouse or child of a lawful permanent resident or a U.S. citizen, or the parent of an abused child, may file a family preference petition on his or her own behalf without the participation of the abusive spouse or parent.[1] The self-petitioner must show that he or she has "good moral character"; entered into the marriage in good faith (if the petitioner is the spouse of either a U.S. citizen or permanent resident); is the victim of abuse or the parent of a victim of abuse; and would suffer extreme hardship if deported. A non-abused parent of a child abused by a lawful permanent resident or citizen may also self-petition.

Additionally, the abused spouse or child of a lawful permanent resident or U.S. citizen or the parent of an abused child, may apply for a special form of cancellation of removal and qualify for residence in the U.S.[2] In this instance, they need evidence of only three years of continuous physical presence in the U.S., rather than the usual seven years (or at times ten years), prior to filing the application for suspension of deportation. They must also evidence "good moral character" and extreme hardship if deported.[3]

An existing provision of the Immigration and Nationality Act allows a conditional resident spouse to waive the requirement to file a joint petition (with her U.S. citizen or lawful permanent resident spouse) to remove the condition on her residence if she can show that she entered into the marriage in good faith, and that either she or her child have been the victim of physical or emotional violence by her spouse.[4]

The Immigration and Naturalization Service has implemented interim rules activating these two new provisions of the Immigration and Nationality Act.[5]

Additionally, on January 1, 1995 an INS cable implementing provisions of the Anti–Crime Bill was issued regarding the filing of an I–360

---

15. 8 C.F.R. § 204.4(f)(1)(ii)(C).

§ 19.16

1. 8 U.S.C.A. § 1154(a)(1)(A)(iii)(I), (II).

2. *See infra,* § 19.48 for a discussion of obtaining permanent residence status through "cancellation of removal" proceedings.

3. INA § 240A(b)(2).

4. INA § 216(c)(4)(C); 8 U.S.C.A. § 1186a(c)(4)(C).

5. Pub.L. No. 103–322, 108 Stat. 1902 to 1955 (8 U.S.C.A. § 1151, § 1154, § 1186a note, § 1254, § 2245). *See also,* 61 Fed. Reg. 13061–79 (March 26, 1996).

Petition by an abused spouse or child.[6] The cable was designed to be an interim measure, anticipating the issuance of final regulations by the INS.

Requirements to self-petition for resident status include the provision of evidence of abuse by the victim, who may be in status, or on a non-immigrant visa, or out of status. Evidence, in addition to proof of citizenship status of the U.S. citizen spouse, may include a civil protection order, police records and reports, court records, complaints, arrest records, medical records, evidence of broken furniture, affidavit from the abused detailing his or her relationship with the abuser, and affidavits from witnesses, friends or relatives corroborating statements of the abused.

The marriage between the self-petitioner and the abuser must have been entered into in good faith.[7] Under current INS proposed regulations, the victim of domestic abuse or the parent of a child victim must be married to the abuser until the INS has approved the self-petition, although this is a major point of contention. Therefore, if a spouse receives a final divorce while the self-petition is pending, he or she would no longer be eligible for this form of relief according to current INS instructions. It is yet unclear whether divorce will bar the new provisions for suspension of deportation.

In addition, the self-petitioner must prove "good moral character". Good moral character is a term without precise meaning but which has been analyzed at length.[8] Additionally, the self-petitioner must have resided with the abuser at one time, but need not be residing with him at the time of the filing of the petition. The self-petitioner must also be currently residing in the U.S. at the time of filing of the petition.

It is problematic that the INS takes the position that divorce itself will not be cause to deny a self-petition, but does not elaborate regarding other factors which might merit the favorable adjudication of a self petition. Further, the definition of extreme hardship in this context has not yet been defined. Advocates are urging that INS adopt a definition tailored specifically to abused women.

At present, without final regulations, the procedure for denials and appeals of self-petition and suspension applications in this context remains unresolved.

§ 19.17 Employment–Based Immigration

The immigration selection system provides 140,000 visas annually for "employment-based" immigrants, described in Section 203(b) of the Act, 8 U.S.C.A. § 1153(b). Five preference groups of immigrants are

---

6. File HQ204–P, January 20, 1995 to all Field Offices.

7. INA § 204(a)(1)(A)(iii)(I); 8 U.S.C.A. § 1154(a)(1)(A)(iii)(I).

8. Sloan v. United States, 31 F.2d 902 (8th Cir.1929); United States. v. Cunha, 209 F.2d 326 (1st Cir.1954).

enumerated. The first three preferences are based upon an alien undertaking employment in his or her field in the U.S. An offer of permanent employment in the U.S. is a requirement for most such aliens, but those designated as "extraordinary" or "exceptional" ability aliens may be admitted as permanent residents without a job offer under certain circumstances. Most must obtain from the Department of Labor a certification that qualified U.S. workers are unable to fill an offered position and that the employment of an alien will not adversely affect the wages or working conditions of similarly employed U.S. workers.

The last two employment-based preferences do not involve standard employment situations. The fourth preference in the employment-based portion of the system covers aliens qualified for immigration as "Special Immigrants,"[1] most notably, religious workers. The fifth employment-based preference is set aside for aliens who invest a specific minimum amount of capital in a new commercial enterprise and who create employment for a specific number of U.S. workers. Detailed below in Section 19.42 are the provisions for the alien investor.

§ 19.18 Employment–Based Immigration—First Employment Preference Applicants (Priority Workers)

High priority is placed by Congress on the immigration of the three subcategories in the priority worker "first preference" category: that is, the extraordinary ability alien, the outstanding professor and researcher and the executive/managerial intracompany transferee. Individuals in this preference are exempt from the labor certification requirement.[1] With no shortage of visas available and lack of a labor certification requirement, therefore, immigration for the three subcategories included in the first preference could occur expeditiously, requiring only the time necessary for the INS to adjudicate a preference petition, followed by the time necessary to process a visa at a U.S. Consulate or through adjudication of an adjustment of status application in the U.S. The prerequisites for each of these subcategories of the first preference are discussed below.

Library References:
West's Key No. Digests, Aliens ⟲51.5.

§ 19.19 Employment–Based Immigration—First Employment Preference Applicants (Priority Workers)—Extraordinary Ability Aliens

The term "extraordinary ability" is defined by the INS regulations as a level of expertise indicating that the individual is one of those few

§ 19.17
1. INA § 101(a)(27)(C)—(J); 8 U.S.C.A. § 1101(a)(27)(C)—(J).

§ 19.18
1. INA § 203(b)(1); 8 U.S.C.A. § 1153(b)(1).

who have risen to the top of his or her field of endeavor.[1] INS rules permit an alien to establish extraordinary ability by evidence of receipt of a major, internationally recognized award, such as a Nobel Prize or an Academy Award.[2] In the absence of such an award, an alien must include at least three out of ten types of evidence listed in the regulations, which include:

- documentation of receipt of lesser nationally or internationally recognized prizes or awards for excellence in his or her field of endeavor;
- documentation of membership in associations in his or her field of endeavor which require outstanding achievements of their members, as judged by recognized international experts in their field;
- published materials in professional or major trade publications or major newspapers about the alien and relating to the alien's work in his or her field of endeavor (published materials must include title, date, author and be translated if necessary);
- evidence of participation, on a panel or individually, as a judge of the work of others in the same or an allied field of specialization;
- evidence of original scientific, scholarly or artistic contributions of major significance in his or her field of endeavor;
- evidence of the authorship of scholarly articles in his or her field, in professional journals or other major media;
- evidence of the display of his or her work in his or her field at artistic exhibitions;
- evidence that the alien has performed in a lead, starring or critical role for organizations or establishments that have a distinguished reputation;
- evidence of having commanded a high salary or other significantly high remuneration for services in relation to others in the field; or
- evidence of commercial successes in the performing arts, as shown by box office receipts or record, cassette, compact disk or video sales.[3]

Where the alien's occupation does not readily apply to the above-listed categories, the INS rule permits the submission of "comparable evidence" to establish the alien's eligibility for extraordinary worker status.[4]

§ 19.19
1. 8 C.F.R. § 204.5(h)(2).
2. 8 C.F.R. § 204.5(h)(3).
3. 8 C.F.R. § 204.5(h)(3).
4. 8 C.F.R. § 204.5(h)(4).

The Administrative Appeals Unit[5] has made it clear that merely submitting documentation from the categories listed in the regulations as indicated above is insufficient. The evidence submitted must establish that the beneficiary is an alien of extraordinary ability. The mere citation of an award of a prize or the publishing of a scholarly article, for instance, would be insufficient without further evidence establishing the significance of the prize or article in the field. To respond to the standard set forth by the INS, it might be appropriate to present credentials on behalf of the alien which would provide a basis of comparison between the alien and those persons who are merely average or typical in the field.[6] The INS has issued guidelines concerning the quality of evidence to be submitted by petitioners.[7] Items of little value might include publication of an alien's book by a "vanity press;" a footnoted reference to the alien's work without evaluation; a simple listing in a subject matter index or a neutral review. Items which would carry great weight would include peer-reviewed presentations at symposia; peer-reviewed articles in scholarly journals; testimonials from scholars describing the alien's contribution to an academic field; entries in a citation index citing the alien's work as authoritative; or participation as a reviewer for peer-reviewed scholarly journals and thesis direction.

In *Grimson v. INS*,[8] the federal court reviewed the type of evidence which might distinguish a hockey player as a top, rather than an average, player. Consideration was given to specific factors, including evidence of the player's average playing time as compared to a typical National Hockey League ("NHL") player; statistics regarding his starting or backup status; evidence regarding average and top NHL salaries and selection as an All-Star Game player. While the INS, which had preliminarily denied the petition, attempted to downplay comparison to other approved cases in the same field of endeavor, the court noted that the INS themselves made comparisons with others in the field and established the controlling standards for awarding extraordinary worker classification.[9]

---

5. The Administrative Appeals Unit ("AAU") hears appeals from denials of employment-based visa petitions, and is the appellate body which considers cases under the appellate jurisdiction of the Associate Commissioner, Examinations (8 C.F.R. § 103.1(f)). Consisting of 12 appellate examiners, including a Director and Deputy Director, rules governing the AAU were published in the Federal Register at 55 Fed.Reg. 20767–71 (May 21, 1990) and currently located at 8 C.F.R. § 103.1(f)(3)(E)(iii).

6. PRACTICE POINTER: In preparing the "Extraordinary Worker" petition, presenting documentation in the form of the alien's own credentials as well as others in his or her field who are familiar with the alien's work, and can attest to the nature of its importance would be helpful. Articles written about the alien, or providing citations to the alien's work, are also helpful.

7. *See* Memo from INS Acting Assistant Commissioner for Adjudications dated July 30, 1992.

8. No. 93 Civ. 3354 (N.D.Ill. Sept. 9, 1993).

9. *Id.*

§ 19.20 Employment–Based Immigration—First Employment Preference Applicants (Priority Workers)—Outstanding Professors and Researchers

Section 203(b)(1)(B) of the Act (8 U.S.C.A. § 1153) encompasses individuals who have been offered employment in order to obtain permanent residence as outstanding researchers or professors. An employer must file a preference petition with the INS on behalf of the alien.[1] The labor certification requirement is waived.

To qualify as an outstanding professor or researcher, the alien must be internationally recognized as outstanding in a specific academic field, possess a minimum of three years experience teaching or researching in that field and be entering the U.S. in a tenure or tenure-track teaching or comparable research position at a university or other institution of higher education.[2]

The position offered must be "permanent," which is defined as tenured, tenure-track, or for an indefinite or unlimited duration with the expectation of continued employment unless there is good cause for termination.[3] Where an offer of employment is of indefinite duration, but is terminable at will, this will likely satisfy the requirement of "permanent" employment.

Alternatively, an employer will qualify as a private company if it employs at least three full-time research employees and has documented accomplishments in the academic field in which the position is offered. While one might normally expect that an outstanding researcher or professor would be in possession of a Ph.D. degree, nothing in the statute or regulations requires the possession of a doctorate.

In order to qualify as "outstanding" in a specific academic field, an alien must demonstrate at least two of the following types of evidence:

- receipt of major prizes or awards;
- membership in associations which require outstanding achievement;
- published material in professional journals written by others about the alien's work;
- evidence that the alien participates as a judge of the work of others;
- original scientific or scholarly research contributions to the field; or

---

§ 19.20
1. 8 C.F.R. § 204.5(c), (i)(1).
2. INA § 203(b)(1)(B); 8 U.S.C.A. § 1153(b)(1)(B).
3. 8 C.F.R. § 204.5(i)(2).

- authorship of scholarly books or articles in journals with international circulation in the field.[4]

§ 19.21 Employment–Based Immigration—First Employment Preference Applicants (Priority Workers)—Managerial or Executive Intracompany Transferees

The third subcategory in the first employment–based preference for priority workers encompasses sponsorship for permanent residence by a multinational corporation for its executive or managerial employees.[1] A multinational manager or executive is eligible for priority worker status in this classification if he or she has been employed outside the U.S. in a managerial or executive capacity for at least one of the three years immediately preceding the filing of a petition, or, in the case of an alien presently in the U.S., one of the three years preceding entry to the U.S. as a nonimmigrant.[2] The regulations further require that the past employment outside the U.S. conform to the definition of "managerial" or "executive" capacity.[3] The past employment abroad must have been with the same employer, an affiliate, or a subsidiary of the employer and the alien must be entering the U.S. to work in an executive or managerial capacity. While an offer of employment is required under this classification from a U.S. employer, the labor certification requirement is waived.

The petitioner must be a U.S. employer which is a parent, affiliate, subsidiary or the same employer as the firm, corporation or other legal entity which employed the alien abroad. The U.S. petitioner must have been doing business for at least one year. An "affiliate" is defined as one of two subsidiaries which are owned or controlled by the same parent or individual, or by a group of individuals so long as each individual owns and controls approximately the same share or percentage of each entity.[4] Subsidiaries include direct or indirect ownership of at least half of another entity, ownership of 50% of a 50/50 joint venture, or ownership of less than 50% of an entity when one entity controls another.[5] The definitions of "affiliate" and "subsidiary" in the regulations are comparable to those found in the L–1 nonimmigrant intracompany transferee regulations.[6]

---

4. 8 C.F.R. § 204.5(i)(3)(i).

§ 19.21

1. INA § 203(b)(1)(C); 8 U.S.C.A. § 1153(b)(1)(C).

2. 8 C.F.R. § 204.5(j)(3)(i), as amended, 56 Fed.Reg. 60897, 60907 (Nov. 19, 1991); Karmali v. INS, 707 F.2d 408, 411 (9th Cir.1983); Matter of Continental Grain, 14 I & N Dec. 140 (D.D.1972). See letter of Edward H. Skerrett, Chief, Immigrant Branch, INS Adjudications, File HQ 204.23–C (May 24, 1994), discussed and reproduced in 71 Int.Rel. 792, 809 (June 13, 1994).

3. 8 C.F.R. § 204.5(j)(4).

4. 8 C.F.R. § 214.2(*l*)(1)(ii)(K),(L).

5. 8 C.F.R. § 204.5(j)(2), as amended, 56 Fed.Reg. 60897, 60907 (Nov. 29, 1991).

6. 8 C.F.R. § 214.2(*l*)(1)(ii)(K),(L).

Additionally, the beneficiary must be coming to the U.S. to assume managerial or executive duties. Managerial and executive duties have been specifically defined in the regulations.[7] In sum, the term "managerial" is applied to an assignment in the U.S. in which the employee will oversee the management in the organization or a department, subdivision, function or component of an organization; supervise and control the work of other supervisory, professional or managerial employees or manage an essential function within the organization, department or subdivision of the organization. Where other employees are directly supervised, the manager would be required to possess authority to hire and fire as well as perform other managerial personnel actions, or, if no other employee is directly supervised, function at a senior level within the organizational hierarchy or with respect to the function managed and exercise authority over day-to-day operations of the activity or function for which the employee has authority.

An executive assignment has been termed to include an assignment within an organization in which the employee (a) primarily directs the management of the organization or a major component or function of the organization; (b) establishes the goals and policies of the organization, component or function; (c) exercises wide latitude in discretionary decision-making; and (d) receives only general supervision or direction from high level executives, the Board of Directors or stockholders of the organization.[8]

The beneficiary's ownership of the U.S. employer is not an impediment to approval of a petition for a multi-national executive or manager.[9]

INS regulations also require that the international petitioning organization be doing business in at least the U.S. and one other country.[10] It defines "doing business" to mean the regular, systematic and continuous provision of goods or services; it does not include the mere presence of an agent or office.[11]

§ 19.22 Employment–Based Immigration—Second Employment Preference Applicants

The second employment-based preference encompasses aliens with advanced degrees in professional fields and aliens of exceptional ability in the sciences, arts, or business.[1] Job offers from U.S. employers are generally required; however, the requirement of a job offer may be waived for exceptional ability aliens and advanced-degree professionals if

---

7. 8 C.F.R. § 204.5(j)(2).

8. 8 C.F.R. § 214.2(*l*)(1)(ii)(C).

9. *See* Matter of (no name given), EAC 92 047 50484 (AAU Aug. 7, 1992).

10. 8 C.F.R. § 214.2(*l*)(1)(ii)(G)(2).

11. 8 C.F.R. §§ 204.5(j)(2), 214.2(*l*)(1)(ii)(G), (H).

§ 19.22

1. INA § 203(b)(2)(A); 8 U.S.C.A. § 1153(b)(2)(A).

to do so would be in the national interest.[2] Where a job offer is waived by the INS in the national interest, an alien will not be subject to the labor certification requirement normally applicable to second preference aliens.

Library References:
West's Key No. Digests, Aliens ⚖51.5.

§ 19.23 Employment–Based Immigration—Second Employment Preference Applicants—Exceptional Ability Aliens

To qualify as an exceptional ability alien, one must possess a degree of expertise above that ordinarily encountered in his or her field. Specifically, a degree, diploma, certificate or similar award from a college, university, school or other institution may not be considered by itself to be sufficient to establish eligibility for exceptional ability consideration; nor may a license or certificate to practice a profession or occupation be considered sufficient.

In order to merit classification as an alien of exceptional ability, an individual must possess and be prepared to submit to the INS at least three of the following types of evidence:

- an official academic record evidencing that the alien possesses a degree, diploma, certificate or similar award from a college, university, school or other institution of learning relating to the area of exceptional ability;
- evidence in the form of letters from current or former employers evidencing that the alien possesses at least ten years of full-time experience in the occupation for which he or she is being sought;
- a license to practice the profession or certification for a particular profession or occupation;
- evidence that the alien has commanded a salary or other remuneration for services, demonstrating exceptional ability;
- evidence of membership in professional associations;
- evidence of recognition for achievement and significant contributions to the industry or field by peers, governmental entities, or professional or business associations.[1]

To establish eligibility for this category, not only must the alien possess exceptional ability, but the job offered must require an individual of exceptional ability to perform it.[2] Additionally, the exceptional ability

---

2. INA § 203(b)(2)(B); 8 U.S.C.A. § 1153(b)(2)(B).

2. 8 C.F.R. § 204.5(k)(4).

§ 19.23
1. 8 C.F.R. § 204.5(k)(3)(ii).

alien must "substantially benefit prospectively the national economy, cultural or educational interests or welfare of the United States."[3]

The alien's exceptional ability must be in the sciences, arts or business. While these terms are not defined by statute or regulations, the INS has defined "fine arts" to include painting, sculpture, poetry, drawing, music, architecture, dancing and dramatic art.[4] The term "art" has also been established to encompass as broad a range of activities as "weaving or painting, arithmetic or navigation."[5] The term "business" has been interpreted to cover virtually every aspect of commercial affairs, including industry, communications, marketing, finance, entertainment and other activities.

§ 19.24 Employment–Based Immigration—Second Employment Preference Applicants—Advanced Degree Professionals

The second group in the second employment–based preference consists of members of the professions holding advanced degrees. The INS has defined a "profession" to be an occupation for which a U.S. baccalaureate degree (or its foreign equivalent) is the minimum requirement for entry into the field.[1] Only alien professionals possessing an advanced degree may qualify in the second employment–based preference. Alien professionals with only bachelor's degrees may qualify in the third employment–based preference, discussed *infra* at Sections 19.26 and 19.27.

An advanced degree is defined to mean any U.S. academic or professional degree (or foreign equivalent) that would be above a bachelor's degree level. A bachelor's degree plus at least five years of progressive experience in the specialty is considered to be the equivalent of a master's degree. The alien must, however, possess at least a bachelor's degree, as INS rules in this category do not allow for the evaluation of education and experience to determine whether the alien possesses the equivalent of a bachelor's degree.[2]

§ 19.25 Employment–Based Immigration—Second Employment Preference Applicants—The Role of "National Interest"

An alien may self-petition in the second employment–based category provided that he can establish that through the grant of lawful perma-

---

3. *See* Matter of (no name provided), A71 933 626 (AAU Apr. 13, 1993), citing 56 Fed.Reg. 60897, 60900 (Nov. 29, 1991).

4. Matter of Tagawa, 13 I & N Dec. 13 (D.D.1967).

5. *Id.* at 14.

§ 19.24

1. INA § 101(a)(32); 8 U.S.C.A. § 1101(a)(32); *See* O.I. 204.4(f); Essex Cryogenics Industries Inc., 14 I & N Dec. 196, 197 (Dep. Assoc. Comm. 1972).

2. *See* Matter of (no name provided), A70 208 505 (AAU Dec. 31, 1992).

nent resident status, he or she will "substantially benefit prospectively the national economy, cultural or educational interests, or the welfare of the United States."[1] This provision permits the waiver of the job offer—or labor certification—requirement. In this instance, the waiver is available not only in the case of persons of exceptional ability, but to professionals with an advanced degree as well. The term "national interest" is not defined in the statute and the INS has declined to define it in regulations, preferring instead to adjudicate applications on a case-by-case basis. Considerably more evidence must therefore be presented to prove a substantial prospective benefit to the welfare of the U.S. by granting permanent residence to the alien.[2]

The INS has provided some direction as to the "national interest" factor in a series of non-precedent decisions and has developed a non-exclusive test of national interest for aliens of exceptional ability in business, listing seven relevant factors.[3] Specifically, the improvement of the U.S. economy, wages and working conditions of U.S. workers; improvement of education and training programs for U.S. children and under-qualified workers; improvement of health care; provision of more affordable housing; improving the environment; making more productive use of natural resources; or a request from an interested U.S. government agency, will generally merit consideration for a "national interest" waiver.[4]

In order to request exemption from the labor certification requirement, an I-140 petition should be submitted, along with documentation to establish that the alien qualifies for the national interest waiver.[5]

§ 19.26 Employment–Based Immigration—Third Employment Preference Applicants

This classification is utilized for three subcategories of workers: those capable of performing skilled labor not of a temporary or seasonal nature requiring at least two years of training or experience;[1] profession-

---

§ 19.25

1. INA § 203(b)(2)(B); 8 U.S.C.A. § 1153(b)(2)(B), as enacted by IA90 § 121(a) as amended by § 302(b)(2)(D), Miscellaneous and Technical Immigration and Naturalization Service Amendments of 1991 (MTINA), Pub.L.No. 102–232, 105 Stat. 1733, effectively extending to professionals the waiver provision that IA90 had confined to persons of exceptional ability.

2. See INS Commentary on Regulations, 56 Fed.Reg. 60897, 60900 (Nov. 29, 1991).

PRACTICE POINTER: It would also be advisable for the attorney seeking information on such decisions to check the American Immigration Lawyers Association monthly publication for unpublished decisions, or to consult with colleagues in assessing what might constitute a meritorious "national interest" case.

3. See Matter of (no name provided), (NSC), A71 940 352 (AAU Nov. 30, 1992); Matter of (no name provided), (NSC), A70 537 406 (AAU Dec. 1, 1992).

4. 70 Int.Rel. 773 (June 14, 1993).

5. See infra, § 19.30 for an I-140 checklist.

§ 19.26

1. INA § 203(b)(3)(A); 8 U.S.C.A. § 1153(b)(3)(A), as amended by IA90 § 121(a).

als holding at least a baccalaureate degree; and "other workers" capable of performing unskilled labor requiring less than two years' training or experience.[2] In all subcategories of the third employment–based category, a labor certification is mandatory.[3]

The third group, "unskilled workers," is limited to only 10,000 of the 40,000 or more visas available in this preference category on an annual basis. While visas have been available on a current basis for most skilled workers and professionals, a substantial waiting list has developed for aliens classified as unskilled workers, stretching from 10–15 years. This waiting list encompasses household workers and other work classifications not requiring extensive training or experience to qualify.

Library References:
West's Key No. Digests, Aliens ⚖︎51.5.

§ 19.27 Employment–Based Immigration—Third Employment Preference Applicants—Professional and Skilled Workers

The first group in the third employment–based preference consists of aliens who possess bachelor's degrees and are members of the professions. This category is limited exclusively to professionals with actual U.S. bachelor's degrees or a foreign equivalent degree. Under the INS rules, an alien may not establish that he or she possesses a combination of education and experience that is equivalent to a bachelor's degree.[1] The INS has rejected as contrary to statute the notion that experience may be substituted for a degree.[2]

The second group in the third employment–based preference is comprised of aliens capable of performing skilled labor. A skilled labor position, as defined by the INA, is one requiring two years of training or experience to perform.[3] Further, it is important to note that the position offered must require two years of training or experience. The fact that an alien possesses at least two years of training or experience in an occupation does not necessarily qualify the alien as a skilled worker if an occupation does not require two years of training or experience.

The Department of Labor, through approval of a labor certification, must accept that two years of experience is in fact the minimum requirement for the position. For this reason, the minimum requirements, as delineated on the labor certification application by the employ-

---

2. *Id.*

3. INA § 212(a)(5)(C); 8 U.S.C.A. § 1182(a)(5)(C).

§ 19.27

1. 8 C.F.R. § 204.5(*l*)(2), as amended, 56 Fed.Reg. 60897, 60908 (Nov. 29, 1991).

2. *See* Commentary, 56 Fed.Reg. 60897, at 60900. However, demonstrating that the employment requires at least two years of experience also qualifies an applicant for this classification.

3. 8 C.F.R. § 204.5(*l*)(2).

er, assumes increasing importance under the preference system.[4] Failure to indicate the two-year minimum experience requirement, or the failure of the INS to recognize that the position is "skilled," might relegate the position to the unskilled worker category and thus to the greater wait under this category. Any professional who is not classified in a professional category because he/she cannot prove possession of a bachelor's degree should be able to qualify as a skilled worker and for all intents and purposes, qualify under the same visa category for purposes of visa issuance as the professional with a bachelor's degree if the requisite two years of experience can be established.[5]

§ 19.28 Employment–Based Immigration—Third Employment Preference Applicants—Unskilled Workers

The third group in the third employment–based preference consists of aliens who are capable of performing unskilled labor. Unskilled labor is defined as labor requiring less than two years of training or experience to perform.[1] The unskilled worker category covers individuals in the domestic household category, and other lesser-skilled occupations. In view of the fact that the quota is so heavily oversubscribed in this category, it would be appropriate for the practitioner to carefully weigh and analyze the client's experience and background to ascertain whether the alien might qualify under one of the more preferred employment-based categories.

§ 19.29 Employment–Based Immigration—I–140 Petition, Procedures and Documentation

The first three employment-based preferences require the filing of an I–140, Immigrant Petition for Alien Worker, with one of the INS Regional Service Centers. In February 1992, the INS issued a final revised version of Form I–140, which should be utilized for the first, second and third employment–based preferences. The petition seeks to solicit information from the petitioning organization regarding its ability to support and pay the potential immigrant.

The I–140 form is filed with one of the four INS Regional Service Centers having jurisdiction over the 50 U.S. states and U.S. territories including Guam, Puerto Rico and the Virgin Islands. They are located in California, Nebraska, Texas and Vermont.[1]

---

4. See infra, § 19.30.

5. 8 C.F.R. § 204.5(*l*)(4).

§ 19.28

1. INA § 203(b)(3)(B); 8 U.S.C.A. § 1153(b)(3).

§ 19.29

1. *Eastern Region*
Vermont Service Center
75 Lower Welden Street
St. Albans, VT 05479–0001
Tel: (802) 527-3160
States Falling Within Jurisdiction:

Library References:

West's Key No. Digests, Aliens ⚷44, 51.5.

Connecticut
Delaware
District of Columbia
Maine
Massachusetts
New Hampshire
New Jersey
New York
Pennsylvania
Puerto Rico
Rhode Island
Vermont
Virginia
Virgin Islands
West Virginia

Northern Region

Mail: Nebraska Service Center

    P.O. Box 82521

    Lincoln, NE 68501–2521

Overnight Delivery:

  Nebraska Service Center
  Fed. Bldg. & U.S. Courthouse
  100 Centennial Mall North
  Rm. B–26
  Lincoln, NE 68508–3898
  (402) 437–5218

States Falling Within Jurisdiction:

Idaho
Illinois
Indiana
Iowa
Kansas
Michigan
Minnesota
Missouri
Montana
Nebraska
North Dakota
Ohio
Oregon
South Dakota
Utah
Washington State
Wisconsin
Wyoming

Southern Region

Mail: Southern Service Center

    P.O. Box 152122, Dept. A

    Irving, TX 75015–2122

Overnight Delivery:

  Southern Service Center
  7701 N. Stemmons Freeway
  Dallas, TX 75257
  (214) 767–7769/7773
  Fax: (214) 767–7404

States Falling Within Jurisdiction:

Alabama
Arkansas
Florida
Georgia
Kentucky
Louisiana
Mississippi
New Mexico
North Carolina
Oklahoma
South Carolina
Tennessee
Texas

CAVEAT: Employment-based petitions are filed with the Vermont Service Center

Western Region

Mail: Western Service Center

    P.O. Box 30111

    Laguna Niguel, CA 92677–8011

Overnight delivery:

  Western Service Center
  2400 Avila Road
  2nd Floor, Room 2304
  Laguna Niguel, CA 92677
  Attn: Incoming Mail
  Phone:
  Fax: (714) 643–6120

States Falling Within Jurisdiction:

Arizona

California

Guam

Hawaii

Nevada

§ 19.30 Employment–Based Immigration—I–140 Petition, Procedures and Documentation—Checklist

The first three employment-based preferences require the submission of the I–140 petition. The petition itself is supported with evidence that constitutes the specific request for classification within one of the three categories.

For an employment-based petition in one of the first three preferences, the alien's U.S. employer, or the alien himself (if self-petitioning), must file with the appropriate INS Service Center the following documentation:

1. INS Form I–140, Immigrant Petition for Alien Worker;
2. where labor certification is applicable in the second and third employment–based preferences, original labor certifications, certified by the Department of Labor;
3. the petitioner's letter supporting the petition and offer of full-time employment;
4. supporting documentation establishing petitioner's ability to pay the proffered wage;
5. when requesting a national interest exemption, an explanation as to the reason for exemption and proof of the alien's contribution to the national interest of the U.S. and general welfare;
6. supporting documentation evidencing that the alien himself meets the job requirements as indicated on the application for alien labor certification (if requesting second or third employment–based preference category under the labor certification requirement). Such documentation might include evidence of the alien's employment experience, education, and special requirements, such as licensing, special computer hardware or software, etc.; and
7. an appropriate filing fee.

The I–140 petition submitted to the INS must prove each element as enumerated above and be in compliance with the requirements of each employment-based category. Specific circumstances may necessitate provision of additional documentation as appropriate and relevant.

§ 19.31 Employment–Based Immigration—Labor Certification

As indicated previously, applicants in the priority worker (first employment–based preference classification) are specifically exempt by statute from the labor certification requirement and are not required to present the generally prerequisite labor certification or clearance from the Department of Labor in order to be qualified to file a petition with the INS.

Second employment–based preference classification employees will generally be required to undergo the labor certification procedure; however, the Attorney General is authorized under limited circumstances, generally where approving the petition would be deemed in the national interest of the U.S., to exempt an applicant from the labor certification process.

All third preference aliens are required to obtain labor certification in support of their permanent residence applications.

The labor certification process, one of the more arduous and unpredictable requisite procedures to be undergone by an alien and his or her employer, was first introduced in 1965, and is premised on the theory that the entry of certain immigrants into the U.S. to perform labor will not be permitted unless the Secretary of Labor certifies that there is a shortage of workers to perform such labor and the employment of aliens would not adversely affect wages and working conditions.[1]

One should not undertake to submit such an application without careful preparation. Useful reference works for the review and preparation of labor certifications include the Department of Labor's *Dictionary of Occupational Titles*, which lists the basic descriptions of thousands of jobs and classifies them according to occupational categories. The *Occupational Outlook Handbook* describes the appropriate duties and specialties for various job descriptions within a profession and identifies entry-level and advanced qualifications. A supplement to the *Dictionary of Occupational Titles*, *Specific Vocational Preparation* (the so-called "SVP") codifies for each employment position identified in the *Dictionary of Occupational Titles* criteria as to what constitutes minimum "preparation" for that position.

Additionally, the *BALCA Deskbook* (published by BALCA itself) is an excellent resource material in understanding the intricacies of the labor certification process.[2]

Library References:

West's Key No. Digests, Aliens ⚿44.

§ 19.32 Employment–Based Immigration—Labor Certification—Procedures

The application for alien labor certification is filed by an employer on behalf of an alien with the local state (not federal) Employment

§ 19.31

1. INA § 212(a)(5)(A); 8 U.S.C.A. § 1182(a)(5)(A), formerly, INA § 212(a)(14).

2. BALCA Deskbook (1992 Edition), U.S. Department of Labor, Board of Alien Labor Certification Appeals compiled by Todd R. Smyth, Secretary to BALCA, bimonthly updates reprinted by American Immigration Lawyers Association.

Service ("Job Service") office of the Department of Labor in the area of intended employment for initial processing.[1] Ultimately it is referred to the regional office of the Employment and Training Administration ("ETA") of the federal Department of Labor.[2]

The application must include the statement of qualifications of the alien (Part B of Form ETA-750), a description of the job offer and of the employer's requirements for the position (Part A of Form ETA-750). On Part A, the employer must set forth his requirements with respect to the education, training, experience, special requirements and description of duties to be assumed in the proposed position.

The Department of Labor reviews the reasonableness of the required experience in view of current employment practices and will guide the employer in the recruitment process required to test the availability of U.S. workers for the position offered. The Job Service calculates prevailing wage, in conformance with established criteria, and further provides the employer with an opportunity to increase its wage offer if it is below prevailing wage. The employer thereafter, in accordance with instructions, advertises the position in a newspaper of general circulation or in a professional journal or trade publication. The advertisement must include the labor employment office identification number, its address and telephone number, but must not identify the employer. The advertisement must further describe the position, compensation and working conditions, and the employer's minimum requirements and training opportunities, if any.[3] Where multiple openings are available, an advertisement should specify the number of positions available.

In addition, with the exception of household workers, an employer must also post notice of the job opportunity at the place of business for at least ten consecutive business days, directing any applicants interested in the position to report to the employer and not to the Job Service.[4]

Upon completion of recruitment and reporting by the employer to the Job Service, the application is forwarded by the state office, together with the prevailing wage finding and any other appropriate information, including market data and recruitment results, to the regional certifying officer of the federal Department of Labor.[5]

State employment service offices do not possess authority to grant or deny labor certifications. Their role is merely to receive and process applications, aid in recruitment efforts, assemble facts regarding prevailing wage and availability of U.S. workers, and to forward applications with appropriate comment to the regional office of the Employment and

---

§ 19.32

1. In New York, all labor certification applications are filed with: State of New York, Department of Labor, Alien Labor Certification, 345 Hudson St., New York, N.Y. 10014-0703.

2. 20 C.F.R. § 656.21(a).

3. Matter of International Bridge, 90-INA-100 (BALCA Sept. 5, 1991).

4. 20 C.F.R. § 656.20(g).

5. 20 C.F.R. § 656.21(j)(2).

Training Administration. The state office further assigns a date of acceptance of processing to the application, which is later considered to be the alien's "priority date" for immigrant visa issuance purposes.[6]

The regional certifying officer possesses the authority to certify the labor certification, which then facilitates the filing of an employment-based petition on behalf of an alien by the employer with the INS. Alternatively, the certifying officer may deny the labor certification.[7]

§ 19.33 Employment–Based Immigration—Labor Certification—Legal Issues

The labor certification process is fraught with pitfalls and issues of concern, including the attorney's representation of both the employer and employee; the employer's good faith effort in recruiting; and how to deal with an alien beneficiary with ownership interest in the employer. In addition, the Department of Labor may contend that the labor certification contains unduly restrictive requirements, or may demand justification of business necessity for specific requirements, and it may challenge the sufficiency of the employer's recruitment efforts and *bona fides* of such efforts.

An area of considerable difficulty involves the employer sponsoring an alien applicant who possesses a direct ownership interest in the employing entity. The Board of Alien Labor Certification Appeals[1] will, in theory, grant such cases if, after considering the "totality of the circumstances," it appears that the job is clearly open to a U.S. worker even given the alien employee's ownership interest in the employing entity.[2] However, such cases rarely are granted.

Further, in view of the fact that employers do not necessarily match their requirements point-by-point with the generalized standard of the *Dictionary of Occupational Titles*, the minimum requirements of the employer often do not conform specifically to the Department of Labor determination as to what would normally be required for a position. When this occurs, a labor certification may be denied because the Department of Labor will claim that the requirement is unduly restric-

---

6. See supra, § 19.6 regarding priority dates.

7. See infra, § 19.31.

§ 19.33

1. Effective May 8, 1987, a Board of Alien Labor Certification Appeals ("BALCA") was created by the Department of Labor to adjudicate appeals from denials of labor certifications. BALCA may sit en banc, but normally sits in panels of three members. The intent to create one adjudicating body for appeals nationwide was to assure consistency and uniformity in the decision-making process. 52 Fed.Reg. 11217, April 8, 1987.

2. Modular Container Systems, 89–INA–228; Bulk Farms, Inc. v. Martin, 963 F.2d 1286 (9th Cir.1992), has held that self-employed aliens are excluded from being considered both the employer and employee. The court in this case noted that the new immigrant investor section of the INA should cover problems relating to the employer/owner sponsoring himself. *See infra*, § 19.42.

tive. In general, the employer must either justify the requirement or eliminate it in order to obtain the granting of the labor certification.

Another issue often arises with regard to the Department of Labor's examination of the alien's qualifications for the position offered as compared with the employer's stated requirements. The comparison is made to determine whether the alien was hired with less experience than what the employer requires. This scrutiny of the alien's background is permitted to assist the Department of Labor in determining whether the employer has stated his "actual minimum requirements" for the position as required by the regulations.[3] The Department of Labor does not assess whether a specific alien is qualified for the position offered; that falls within the jurisdiction of the INS.[4]

The practitioner should also be aware of ethical considerations[5] involved in properly representing the employer and employee simultaneously in the labor certification process. The attorney, whether hired by the employer or by the alien applicant, will generally ultimately represent both parties in the matter, since they are joint participants in the process. There are situations where the interests of the employer and employee may conflict, and the practitioner is left to determine the appropriate course of action. Such circumstances may include the desire of the employer to lengthen the labor certification process to assure continued services of the alien, which may conflict with the alien applicant's desire to have the process accelerated in order that he may obtain permanent residence in an expeditious manner, and perhaps leave the employer once permanent residence is granted; or the alien applicant may be considered excludable from the U.S. unbeknownst to the employer due to a past criminal conviction or visa fraud.

In drafting the labor certification for submission to the Department of Labor, the practitioner would be well advised to review in detail the alien's immigration history and the expectations of the alien and employer. Counsel should seek assurance that the job requirements as stated in the application for alien labor certification are *bona fide*, realistic and justifiable within the context of Department of Labor case law and precedent decisions.

§ 19.34 Employment–Based Immigration—Labor Certification—Job Description

When preparing the application for alien labor certification forms, the attorney must be sensitive to identifying exact job duties and critical

---

3. 20 C.F.R. § 656.21(b)(5).

4. London Typographers,, Inc. v. Sava, 628 F.Supp. 570 (S.D.N.Y.1986); Madany v. Smith, 696 F.2d 1008 (D.C.Cir.1983); Stewart Infra–Red Commissary v. Coomey, 661 F.2d 1 (1st Cir.1981).

5. **CAVEAT:** The practitioner must continually be alert to conflicts that may be encountered in all areas of immigration law practice, as many alien clients from foreign cultures are not familiar with U.S. law. Aliens in illegal status, fearful and unfamiliar with U.S. law, can be easy prey for the unscrupulous practitioner.

requirements for the position, and to assuring that the position does not contain any unduly restrictive requirements. The attorney must be keenly aware that the Department of Labor's role throughout this process is to assure that the American labor market is not adversely affected by the hiring of a particular alien. It is extremely difficult to be objective in these circumstances. The alien applicant will encourage the employer to be as restrictive as possible in identifying the necessary prerequisites for the position, so that when recruitment efforts are undertaken, it is less likely that an American would be qualified for the position. The Department of Labor, on the other hand, will attempt to broaden and standardize the requirements as much as possible, so that it is difficult to exclude a potential American worker.

In preparing the job description for Form ETA–750A—Application for Alien Labor Certification—Offer of Employment—the employer and alien generally review the educational requirements, training necessary for the position, if applicable, experience requirements, general job description and compensation to be offered for the position. As well, there may be a related occupation under which the alien and/or others may qualify for the position offered.[1] In *Matter of Delitizer Corporation of Newton*[2], the "sufficiently dissimilar test" was used to compare the job offered with the job in which experience was gained according to the job duties, supervisory responsibilities, position of the job within the employer's hierarchy, whether and by whom the job was previously filled, whether the position was newly created, prior employment practices of the employer regarding filled positions, the amount or percentage of time spent performing each duty in each job and salaries offered. In general, the Department of Labor has taken the position that particular skills and additional educational credentials acquired while the beneficiary of a labor certification is in the employ of an employer filing for certification may be required by the employer where the occupation for which certification is sought is a distinct occupation and if the expenses incident to obtaining additional skills, educational credentials or qualifications were borne by the alien and not by the employer.[3]

The meticulous preparation of the job description is crucial to the successful completion of the labor certification process. The requirements noted in the job description on Form ETA–750A (Application for Alien Employment Certification) will further require substantiation

§ 19.34

1. Matter of Tesseraet Corp., 90–INA–285; Matter of Valmet Automation, 90–INA–204; Matter of Deloitte–Touche; 90–INA–493 (BALCA, Feb. 7, 1992).

PRACTICE POINTER: In many instances an employer may wish to file an alien labor certification application on behalf of an alien who has gained experience "on the job." Experience gained with the same employer can generally be utilized where prior experience is considered to be more junior level, and substantially different from duties of the job offered in the application for alien labor certification.

2. 88–INA–482 (BALCA 1990) (en banc).

3. USDOL–AILA Liaison Minutes, January 17, 1990, Washington, D.C. Reprinted in 67 Int.Rel. 851 (July 30, 1990).

§ 19.34 IMMIGRATION AND NATIONALITY LAW Ch. 19

when submitting an immigrant visa petition (Form I–140) to the INS. For example, should the labor certification require a license or a degree and specific experience, the alien must furnish the INS with such documentation to establish eligibility and to assure favorable adjudication of the immigrant visa petition.

§ 19.35 Employment–Based Immigration—Labor Certification—Business Necessity

Briefly discussed above at § 19.33 was the issue of "business necessity" and the requirement that the employer justify business necessity for specific requirements in the application for alien labor certification.

Not unlikely to arise as an issue relating to business necessity would be a specific language requirement included in the application for alien labor certification, special knowledge and skills relating to occupations which might include technical, computer, or other skills, and how these requirements relate to the actual minimum requirements for the position offered.

It appears that BALCA has liberalized its requirements and in many cases upheld the language requirement where at least 30% of the employer's business involves utilizing a foreign language.[1] Business necessity for a foreign language may also be based on a desire to expand one's business. In *Remington Products*,[2] BALCA held that "the Act was not designed to preempt American employers from expanding their business to foreign markets ... [t]he question is whether or not the person hired for the job, who is going to travel and operate overseas in the performance of his duties, needs the specific foreign language capacity to do so." Further, where an employer requires fluency in a foreign language because it has expansion plans, the employer must establish definite and concrete plans requiring such language and understand that strict scrutiny will be applied to documentation presented in these cases.[3]

A uniform test for "business necessity" has been established by the Board of Alien Labor Certification Appeals. In *Matter of Information Industries*[4], BALCA set forth a new standard to establish the sufficiency of a justification based on business necessity for any position which would otherwise be deemed unduly restrictive. The job requirement in question must, according to BALCA, bear a reasonable relationship to the occupation in the context of the employer's business and be essential to perform, in a reasonable manner, the job duties as described by the

§ 19.35
1. Matter of Isak Sakai, 90–INA–330 (BALCA Oct. 31, 1991); Matter of Futures Travels, Inc., 90–INA–234 (BALCA July 30, 1991).
2. 89–INA–173 (BALCA Jan. 9, 1991).
3. Advanced Digital Corporation, 90–INA–137, 8 Immig.Rptr. B3–298 (BALCA May 21, 1991).
4. 88–INA–82, 6 Immig.Rptr. B3–182 (BALCA Feb. 9, 1989).

employer.[5] This general test is applied to requirements of the position which would not normally be required in the U.S. and might exceed the SVP requirement of the *Dictionary of Occupational Titles*. The test of "business necessity" might also arise in other contexts including the live-in requirement for a housekeeper and the justification for an unusual combination of duties for the position offered.[6] When preparing the labor certification application forms, the practitioner should be extremely careful in assuring that the employer can justify any special requirements, including language requirements, specific computer skills and knowledge, and should be able to provide documentation to back up his or her requirements.

§ 19.36 Employment–Based Immigration—Labor Certification—Recruitment

Once the state office of the Department of Labor has completed its review of the application and the requirements proposed, the employer will be instructed by the Job Service to advertise for the position in a newspaper of general circulation, trade journal, or ethnic publication to assess whether U.S. workers qualified for the position offered are available. Upon the receipt of resumes, the employer will generally review them, contact applicants, interview them and assess each applicant's qualifications for the position offered. Employers have been permitted to reject U.S. workers where they do not meet the true minimum requirements for the position, even without having interviewed workers, if it is clear from the resume. In *Matter of Bronx Medical and Dental Associates*,[1] the certifying officer concluded that a worker qualified for the position offered on the basis of a combination of qualifications she deemed to be equivalent to those specified by the employer. BALCA held that there was no justification for the certifying officer to substitute her own judgment for the employer's job requirements after the fact, and as long as the job requirements went unchallenged by the certifying officer, the employer could reject an applicant without granting an interview if such applicant failed to meet those specific requirements. Where the applicant's resume evidences that he or she meets the broad range of experience, education and training for the required job, raising the possibility that he or she might meet the employer's qualifications, BALCA has held that the employer must inquire further into the qualifications of the applicant.[2]

---

5. 88–INA–82, 6 Immig.Rptr. B3–182 (BALCA Feb. 9, 1989).

6. 20 C.F.R. § 656.21(b)(2)(ii), (iii).

§ 19.36

1. 90–INA–479 (BALCA Oct. 30, 1992) (en banc).

2. Gorchev & Gorchev Graphic Design, 89–INA–118, 8 Immig.Rptr. B3–197 (BALCA Nov. 29, 1990) (en banc); Anonymous Management, 87–INA–672, 6 Immig.Rptr. B3–57 (BALCA Sept. 8, 1988).

It is the employer who bears the burden of evidencing that a U.S. applicant is unqualified for the position offered. Additionally, an employer may not reject a U.S. worker because he or she is overqualified, or if it is believed that the U.S. worker will not stay on the job, or where the U.S. worker has problems documenting experience, or where the applicant's resume fails to show clearly whether the applicant is qualified for the position.[3] An employer is also not permitted to reject a worker for subjective reasons unless he or she can document how the reasons were arrived at and how they relate to the job duties.[4]

Another frequently litigated issue arises when an employer attempts to deal with an improper rejection of an applicant by recontacting such applicant at a later date. BALCA has consistently held that later contact cannot cure the initial improper rejection of the applicant.[5] The certifying officer is instructed to evaluate any factors in its determination of whether recruitment efforts were performed in good faith considering the following factors:

- the detailed and comprehensive nature of the U.S. applicant's resume;
- whether the employer's report was detailed and comprehensive or merely unresponsive;
- how contemporaneous and timely was the preparation of documentary evidence with the events in question; and
- how evidence was submitted (*i.e.* telephone bills, certified mailing receipts, etc.).[6]

Generally, letters from employers stating their reasons, sources and bases for rejecting U.S. workers, where sufficiently detailed, will suffice to establish good faith.

§ 19.37 Employment–Based Immigration—Labor Certification—Approvals

When an application for alien labor certification is approved, it is stamped with an official labor certification stamp and the approved labor certification and accompanying documents are returned to the employer or to the designated agent or attorney of the employer.[1] The granting of a labor certification is an important step in the alien's effort to enter the

---

3. Southpoint Seafood Market, 87–INA–614, 6 Immig.Rptr. B3–129 (BALCA Jan. 20, 1988); World Bazaar, 88–INA–54, 6 Immig.Rptr. B3–264 (BALCA June 14, 1989); Matter of Norman Industries, 88–INA–202, 6 Immig.Rptr. B3–70 (BALCA July 29, 1988).

4. Matter of American Fence Co., 93–INA–55, 12 Immig.Rptr. B3–132 (BALCA Dec. 27, 1993).

5. Matter of Mike's Refrigeration, 90–INA–258, 9 Immig.Rptr. B3–86 (BALCA July 30, 1991).

6. *Id.*

§ 19.37

1. 20 C.F.R. §§ 656.25(b), 656.28.

U.S. as an immigrant. Upon certification (approval) of the labor certification by the Department of Labor, the employer and alien are in a position to file the I–140 immigrant visa petition with the INS. The INS will assess the qualifications of the alien for the position offered, the employer's ability to employ the alien and the *bona fides* of a permanent, full-time job offer.[2]

§ 19.38 Employment–Based Immigration—Labor Certification—Notices of Findings

Certifying officers who propose to deny labor certification applications must issue to the employer a Notice of Findings, outlining the specific reasons for the decision and providing the employer and the alien with an opportunity to submit rebutting documentary evidence.[1] If rebuttal evidence is submitted, the certifying officer may then "certify" the labor certification. The Notice of Findings is generally based upon either the employer's failure to comply with regulations, or on findings regarding the availability of qualified U.S. workers, the adverse affect upon wages and working conditions of U.S. workers, or on more than one of these specific grounds. Additional Notices of Findings are permitted where an employer's rebuttal raises new issues not contained in the original Notice.[2]

Where labor certification is granted, the employer is in a position to file a petition with the INS. Where the application is denied, the certifying officer notifies parties of reasons for such denial and of their rights to an administrative appeal within 35 days.[3] Where a labor certification is denied, a Final Determination must evidence that all rebuttal materials were considered and the reasons that materials were deficient must be provided. Certifying officers are also instructed never to issue Final Determinations for a reason not previously explained in a prior Notice of Findings.[4] A labor certification denial becomes final where no appeal is filed, and since a failure to appeal is considered a failure to exhaust administrative remedies, it is a bar to judicial review.[5] A certifying officer may, however, choose to reconsider a final denial if such request is made by the employer, or jointly by the alien and employer, within 35 days after the issuance of a Final Determination, and new evidence considered by the certifying officer after accepting a request for a reconsideration becomes part of the record to be considered

---

2. *See supra*, § 19.29.

§ 19.38

1. 20 C.F.R. §§ 656.25(c), (d). The employer is given 35 days to submit rebuttal evidence. If no rebuttal is submitted, the Notice of Findings becomes the Final Determination denying the application.

2. TAG (DOL) p. 83.

3. 20 C.F.R. §§ 656.25(g), 656.26(a).

4. Phototake, 87–INA–667, 6 Immig.Rptr. B3–24 (BALCA July 20, 1988); The Little Mermaid Restaurant, 87–INA–675, 5 Immig.Rptr. B3–215 (BALCA March 9, 1988).

5. 20 C.F.R. § 656.25(c)(3).

in any later appeal to BALCA.[6] The failure of a certifying officer to rule on a timely motion for reconsideration will normally result in a remand of the case.[7]

§ 19.39 Employment–Based Immigration—Labor Certification—Denials and Administrative Appeal

When an application for alien labor certification is denied, a written request for review must be sent within 35 calendar days after the date of denial to the certifying officer who made the decision. The review request, statements and briefs, must set forth particular grounds for the request and must include all documents which accompanied the notice of denial.[1] When the appeal is assigned to a panel of judges at BALCA, the Board will provide parties 21 days to submit briefs and will make one of the following dispositions:

- affirm the denial of the labor certification;
- reverse the denial and direct the certifying officer to grant certification;
- remand the case to the certifying officer for further consideration or fact-finding and determination; or
- direct that a hearing be held.[2]

Generally, BALCA has decided reviews on the records and briefs submitted and evidentiary hearings have seldom been held. The Board will generally prepare a written decision and order and except when a case is remanded, the Board's decision is the final decision of the Secretary of Labor. Motions for reconsideration must be filed within ten days following the issuance of a decision and order by BALCA, and such motion for reconsideration must be made by the employer as well as the alien.[3] BALCA generally believes that it has no duty to grant a motion for reconsideration absent evidence of clear abuse of discretion. It is most likely to exercise its discretion favorably to petitioners who can bring to BALCA's attention that an important fact in the case has been overlooked, or a severe injustice has been perpetrated by the Board in reaching its final decision.

Appeal to the federal court will follow, should a petitioner/employer wish to challenge BALCA's decision, as all administrative remedies have been exhausted at this point.

6. Construction and Investment Corp. d/b/a Efficient Air, 88–INA–55, 6 Immig.Rptr. B3–231 (BALCA April 24, 1989).

7. HM Carpet, 90–INA–398 (BALCA Aug. 14, 1990).

§ 19.39
1. 20 C.F.R. § 656.26(b).

2. 20 C.F.R. § 656.27(c).

3. K Super KQ–254 A.M., 88–INA–397, 6 Immig.Rptr. B3–224 (BALCA May 31, 1989).

§ 19.40 Employment–Based Immigration—Fourth Employment Preference Applicants

The fourth employment–based preference classification is available to any alien who, for at least two years immediately preceding application for admission, has been a member of a religious denomination having a *bona fide* non-profit religious organization in the U.S. and has carried out duties in the vocation of minister or other religious worker of the religious denomination for the two year period.[1]

Others included in the fourth employment–based preference category are certain employees or retired employees of the U.S. government who have served abroad; certain employees under the Panama Canal Act of 1979; certain foreign medical graduates who entered the U.S. in H or J status[2] before January 10, 1978; certain officers and employees of international organizations who resided in the U.S. for requisite periods, and widows, widowers and unmarried sons or daughters of such officers and employees; certain persons declared dependent on a U.S. juvenile court or placed in state custody; and certain immigrants who have served in the U.S. Armed Forces.[3] Generally, the accompanying spouses and children of those described above are also fourth preference special immigrants.

The great bulk of visas issued in this preference are for religious workers. The others are relatively rare.

Library References:

West's Key No. Digests, Aliens ⬅51.5.

§ 19.41 Employment–Based Immigration—Fourth Employment Preference Applicants—Religious Workers and Ministers

Ministers and other religious workers must, for the two years immediately preceding their application for employment-based preference status, be members of a *bona fide* non-profit religious organization in the U.S. and perform duties within the organization for a period of two years in the vocation, professional work or other work that they will similarly be pursuing in the U.S. One class of religious workers may be entering the U.S. in the religious vocation or occupation in a professional capacity, others may simply be coming to work in the non-professional U.S. in a religious vocation or occupation on behalf of their employing

---

§ 19.40

1. INA § 203(b)(4); 8 U.S.C.A. § 1153(b)(4), as amended by IA90 § 121(a).

2. The "H" and "J" visas are just two of the nonimmigrant visa categories which cover the temporary stays of aliens in the U.S.

3. Pub.L.No. 96–70, § 3201(a), (c), 93

religious organization or tax-exempt affiliate.[1] Immigrants qualifying in the non-professional capacity would include individuals such as nuns or monks, religious instructors, counselors, cantors and catechists, workers in religious hospitals or religious health care facilities, missionaries, religious translators, or broadcasters. The provisions specifically exclude janitors, maintenance workers, fund-raisers and clerks.[2]

To qualify for this preference classification, one must file Form I-360 with the INS Service Center. In order to succeed with a petition for a "special immigrant" classification on behalf of a religious worker, the residence must be granted on or before September 30, 1997. The 1990 statute had a sunset provision which was extended by legislation to October 1, 1997. All INS forms and supporting documentation must be submitted before September 30, 1997.[3]

The petition must provide evidence indicating that the organization qualifies as a nonprofit organization in the form of either:

- documentation showing that it is exempt from taxation in accordance with § 501(c)(3) of the Internal Revenue Code of 1986;[4] or

- such documentation as is required by the Internal Revenue Service to establish eligibility for exemption under § 501(c)(3) of the Internal Revenue Code of 1986.[5]

Additionally, the petition must be accompanied by documentation from an authorized official of the religious organization in the U.S. which establishes that:

- the alien possesses at least two years of experience in the religious vocation, professional religious work, or other religious work immediately prior to the filing of the petition;[6]

- if the alien is a minister, he or she is authorized to conduct religious worship and to perform other duties usually performed by authorized members of the clergy, including a detailed description of such authorized duties;[7] or

- if the alien is a religious professional, he or she has at least a U.S. baccalaureate or its foreign equivalent required for entry into the

Stat. 496.

§ 19.41

1. **PRACTICE POINTER:** As with the principal *bona fide* non-profit organization, the affiliate must also be tax-exempt under IRC § 501(c)(3) and must be clearly associated with the religious denomination. Interestingly enough, a two year stint as an R-1 nonimmigrant (the nonimmigrant counterpart to this immigrant provision) within the U.S. would qualify a minister or other worker for residence as a special immigrant, as prior employment for the denomination need not have been abroad. 8 C.F.R. § 204.5(m)(1).

2. 8 C.F.R. § 204.5(m)(2).

3. Immigration and Nationality Technical Corrections Act of 1994, Pub.L.No. 103-416, § 214, 108 Stat. 4308; 8 C.F.R. § 204.5(m)(1).

4. 8 C.F.R. § 204.5(m)(3)(i)(A).

5. 8 C.F.R. § 204.5(m)(3)(i)(B).

6. 8 C.F.R. § 204.5(m)(3)(ii)(A).

7. 8 C.F.R. § 204.5(m)(3)(ii)(B).

religious profession;[8] and

- the organization petitioning must indicate how the alien will be paid or remunerated. The documentation should clearly indicate that the alien will not be dependent on supplemental employment or solicitation of funds for support.[9]

§ 19.42 Employment–Based Immigrants—Fifth Employment Preference Applicants (Immigrant Investors)

Fifth preference classification is available to immigrants seeking to enter the U.S. to engage in a new commercial enterprise which would benefit the U.S. economy and create at least ten full-time jobs.[1] Jobs offered must be for U.S. citizens, lawful permanent residents or other immigrants authorized to work, other than the applicant or his or her immediate family.

An applicant under this program must establish his or her business and have invested or be in the process of investing the required amount after November 29, 1990, the effective date of the Act. This provision of law, requiring investment after November 1990, was clearly constructed to ensure that the infusion of capital is fresh.[2]

Library References:

West's Key No. Digests, Aliens ⚛51.5.

§ 19.43 Employment–Based Immigrants—Fifth Employment Preference Applicants (Immigrant Investors)—Petition Procedures and Requirements

To qualify for an investor visa (formally known as the "Employment Creation" visa, due to the purpose of permitting immigrant investors to enhance employment opportunities in the U.S.), the alien must invest or be actively in the process of investing at least $1 million in the enterprise. Flexibility is granted to the INS to raise the $1 million figure as high as $3 million for "high employment areas," and to lower the figure as low as $500,000 for "targeted employment areas."[1]

The INS has ruled that the term "invest" within the meaning of this provision regarding the investor visa means the contribution of

---

8. 8 C.F.R. § 204.5(m)(3)(ii)(C).
9. 8 C.F.R. § 204.5(m)(4).

§ 19.42
1. INA § 203(b)(5); 8 U.S.C.A. § 1153(b)(5).
2. Matter of (name not provided), EAC 91 184 50136 (ESC, STA), Aug. 12, 1993 (investment made prior to November 29, 1990 and evidence of alien's expanded business operations after that date deemed insufficient).

§ 19.43
1. INA § 203(b)(5); 8 U.S.C.A. § 1153(b)(5); INA § 216A, 8 U.S.C.A. § 1186b.

capital in the form of equity or long-term debt financing. However, a debt financing arrangement between an alien and the new enterprise in which the alien is acting solely as creditor does not constitute a contribution of capital.[2] Capital as defined by INS regulations includes cash, cash equivalents including certificates of deposit, treasury bonds or other instruments that can be converted readily into cash, equipment, inventory, other tangible property and indebtedness secured by assets owned by the alien. Capital will be valued at fair market value in U.S. dollars.[3]

Congress was most concerned in assuring that an alien would not qualify under this provision as an immigrant investor if he would function as a "passive" investor. It must be evidenced that the alien will be engaged in a management role, exercising day-to-day managerial control or as a policymaker.[4]

To deter fraud, the residence obtained by the immigrant investor and any spouse or children on the basis of this classification is made conditional for two years.[5] Procedures developed for the immigrant investor are similar to those established under the Immigration Marriage Fraud Act for those who have obtained residence through marriage to a U.S. citizen or lawful permanent resident.[6] Based upon the investor's petition to remove the conditions to residence at the end of the two year period, the alien's petition is reviewed by the Service Center having jurisdiction over the location of the alien's enterprise and would necessarily be accompanied by evidence that the commercial enterprise proposed by the alien two years earlier was established, that the alien has invested or was in the process of investing the required capital and that the alien created or could be expected to create ten full-time positions. The alien must also evidence that he or she has "sustained actions required for removal of conditions" during his or her residence in the U.S., has met the capital investment requirement, and continuously maintained the investment during the conditional period.[7]

Initially, the petition to establish qualification as an immigrant investor is filed on Form I–526 with the required documentation to the INS Service Center having jurisdiction over the area where the new enterprise has or will have its headquarters and may be filed by the alien on his or her own behalf.[8]

Library References:

West's Key No. Digests, Aliens ⚖︎44, 51.5.

2. 8 C.F.R. § 204.6(j)(1), (2).
3. 8 C.F.R. § 204.6(e).
4. 8 C.F.R. § 204.6(j)(5).
5. INA § 216A, 8 U.S.C.A. § 1186b. See infra, § 19.73.
6. INA § 216; 8 U.S.C.A. § 1186a. See infra, § 19.72.
7. 8 C.F.R. § 216.6(a)(4).
8. 8 C.F.R. § 204.6(a), (b), (c).

§ 19.44 Employment–Based Immigrants—Fifth Employment Preference Applicants (Immigrant Investors)—Special Immigrant Investor Programs

In 1992, Congress enacted a five-year investor pilot program, to begin in October 1993 ("Pilot Program"), which was designated to create jobs indirectly by promoting exports, regional productivity and capacity investments.[1] This pilot program assigns 300 immigrant visas annually for five years to aliens making qualifying investments in a commercial enterprise located within a "regional center," defined as "any economic unit, public or private, which is involved with the promotion of economic growth, including increased export sales, improved regional productivity, job creation, and increased domestic capital investment."[2] To qualify, an alien must make the qualifying investment (the amount required under the basic program) within an approved regional center. The requirement of creating ten new jobs, however, is met by showing that, as a result of the new investment, such jobs will be created directly or indirectly through revenues generated from increased profits.

When an INS Regional Service Center adjudicates a Form I–526 petition for an immigrant investor filed by the individual investor under the Pilot Program, the petitioner is required to include a copy of the appropriate regional center designation by the Assistant Commissioner for Adjudications. New commercial enterprises must be located within an area specified in the regional center designation to be considered eligible under the Pilot Program.

As with the standard immigrant investor, residence granted is "conditional," with the filing of a petition to remove conditional status two years after the initial grant of conditional residence.

§ 19.45 Special Categories

There are several programs Congress has created to permit the admission of aliens as permanent residents which do not fit within the traditional immigration framework. Congress has legislated an amnesty program for aliens who were long-time illegal residents in the U.S., as well as adjustment of status programs for nurses and Soviet Scientists. Other special refugee groups are also eligible for resident status under special provisions. Discussed below at Sections 19.46 through 19.50 are current provisions which offer significant benefits to a wider group of aliens, including the Diversity (Lottery) Program, the Registry Program, and provisions regarding cancellation of removal, asylum and refugee status.

---

§ 19.44

1. *See* Depts. of Commerce, Justice & State, The Judiciary and Related Agencies Appropriations Act of 1993, Pub.L.No. 102–35, § 610; S.Rep.No. 918, 102d Cong., 2d Sess. (1992).

2. 8 C.F.R. § 204.6(e).

§ 19.46 Special Categories—The Diversity (Lottery) Program

Congress adopted its first Diversity Program in 1986, and extended it in 1988. The Diversity Program creates a third stream of immigration and enables individuals not eligible under the family or employment-based preferences an opportunity to immigrate to the U.S. Because of the success of the program, Congress enacted a permanent Diversity Program as part of the 1990 Act.[1] The Diversity Program allows aliens to immigrate to the U.S. even where they have no qualified family members or an employer to sponsor them. 55,000 visas per year are available to diversity applicants and their families. The Diversity Program is essentially a lottery, whereby applicants from designated countries may submit a request for registration. Should the alien be selected (by random drawing), he or she would be required to fulfill minimum eligibility requirements.[2]

To qualify as a diversity immigrant, the alien must come from a designated "low-admission" country, as determined by the Attorney General, and must possess at least a high school education or its equivalent or at least two years of work experience in an occupation requiring at least two years of training or experience, gained within five years of the date of application for a diversity visa. The two year requirement coincides with the definition of "skilled worker" for the third employment–based preference category.[3]

Library References:

West's Key No. Digests, Aliens ⊕51.5.

§ 19.47 Special Categories—Registry

As amended in 1958, 1965, 1986 and 1990, the INA authorizes the Attorney General, in his or her discretion, to create a record of lawful admission for permanent residence for long time residents of the U.S.[1]

Section 249 of the Immigration Act of 1990 (8 U.S.C.A. § 1259) grants aliens whose entry to the U.S. occurred prior to January 1, 1972 "registration" as lawful permanent residents of the U.S. The alien must establish entry prior to the designated date, continuous residence in the

---

§ 19.46

1. INA § 203(c); 8 U.S.C.A. § 1153(c).

2. PRACTICE POINTER: On a yearly basis the State Department announces the procedure for diversity lottery issuance. It is usually announced in the first quarter of each year. Diversity lottery number availability is distributed thereafter in the Visa Bulletin on a monthly basis by the State Department.

3. INA § 203(c)(2); 8 U.S.C.A. § 1153(c)(2).

§ 19.47

1. Nationality Act of 1940, § 328(b), 54 Stat. 1152.

U.S. since entry, and good moral character. Applicants must establish that they are not excludable under those grounds relating to "criminals, procurers and other immoral persons, subversives, violators of narcotics laws, smugglers of aliens and ineligibility to citizenship."[2]

While residence must be continuous from January 1, 1972 to the date of formal residence application, actual physical presence in the U.S. is not required during the entire period. Temporary absences, without abandonment of residence in the U.S., will not preclude the establishment of required continuous residence.[3] However, an enforced departure order or order of exclusion or deportation[4] will be considered to break the continuity of residence in the U.S.[5]

Relief will be granted under the registry provision even for those aliens who are deportable for entry without proper inspection or who have overstayed or violated terms of their temporary entry or for those who would be excludable on medical grounds.[6]

Registry is a useful tool for those attorneys confronted with a client who can prove his or her long-term residence in the U.S., and yet may not readily qualify under any of the other family or employment-based categories. Admittedly, it is rare that such an individual would present himself. Most such persons would likely by now have families who might sponsor them, job offers in the U.S. or alternate methods of establishing eligibility for residence.

Where it is determined post hoc that an applicant granted registry did not in fact qualify for residence status under the registry provisions, the status may be rescinded by the Attorney General.[7] Where an applicant for registry has naturalized during this period, a suit for denaturalization can be brought following rescission of residence status.[8]

---

2. *See* Matter of R-E-, 9 I & N Dec. 103 (Asst.Comm.1960).

3. Rodriguez–Barajas v. INS, 992 F.2d 94 (7th Cir.1993); Matter of Outin, 14 I & N Dec. 6 (BIA 1972); Matter of Ting, 11 I & N Dec. 849 (BIA 1966).

4. Mrvica v. Esperdy, 376 U.S. 560, 84 S.Ct. 833, 11 L.Ed.2d 911 (1964).

5. Matter of Contreras–Sotelo, 12 I & N Dec. 596 (BIA 1967); Matter of Young, 11 I & N Dec. 38 (BIA 1965). In addition to disqualifying applicants for registry who may be considered excludable or deportable, an administrative directive seeks to add two further disqualifications to those specifically enumerated in the statute, declaring that exchange visitors (J–1 nonimmigrants) subject to the two-year foreign residence requirement are absolutely barred from registry and that the excludability of foreign medical graduates should be considered as a "serious negative factor [and] . . . should be given great weight in a discretionary decision under Section 249." (Memorandum to all Regional Commissioners, File CO 249P (May 19, 1987).) The directive states that any decision proposing to grant registry to a foreign doctor is to be certified to the Associate Commissioner, Examinations. The directive also declares that persons excludable as Nazi persecutors are to be barred from registry as lacking good moral character. This is administrative dicta, and not codified at this time in the statute.

6. *See* Sana Love, *Health-Related Issues in Immigration Practice*, 91–6 Immigr. 18 Briefings (June 1991, Federal Publications).

7. INA § 246(a); 8 U.S.C.A. § 1256(a); Matter of Locicero, 11 I & N Dec. 805 (BIA 1966).

8. INA § 246(b); 8 U.S.C.A. § 1256(b).

§ 19.48 Special Categories—Cancellation of Removal

For individuals who have been living in the U.S. for a number of years without authorization, and face the prospect of being deported, an application for cancellation of removal may be granted, conferring permanent resident status on the alien. The statute requires that an alien who has not committed an aggravated felony offense[1] would be required to continuously be present in the U.S. for ten years, be a person of good moral character, and must evidence that deportation would impose extremely unusual hardship on a spouse, parent or child who is a U.S. citizen or lawful permanent resident.[2] Prior to April 1, 1997 this provision was known as "suspension of deportation" and had more liberal qualifying criteria.[3]

Issues relating to qualification under this ameliorative provision of the law include the definition of the alien's "continuous physical presence," the "meaningfully interruptive standard" as applied in the suspension of deportation context, the "extreme hardship" requirement, and the definition of "good moral character."[4]

When an immigration judge grants cancellation of removal, the case is forwarded to the appropriate INS district office with jurisdiction over the alien's residence in the U.S. Should the district director decide not to appeal the grant of cancellation, deportation proceedings will be deemed canceled and the case terminated. The district director will then create a record of admission of permanent residence for the alien. Denial of a request for cancellation of removal may be appealed to the Board of Immigration Appeals but not to a federal court.[5]

Library References:

West's Key No. Digests, Aliens ⇌40, 53.10(1).

§ 19.48

1. INA § 101(a)(43); 8 U.S.C.A. § 1101(a)(43) defines the term "aggravated felony" to include a broad array of crimes. The Immigration and Nationality Technical Corrections Act of 1994 (Pub.L.No. 103–416, 108 Stat. 4311, Oct. 25, 1994) adds new aggravated felonies including money laundering, child pornography, prostitution and trafficking in fraudulent documents. The Illegal Immigration Reform and Immigrant Responsibility Act ("IIRAIRA") of 1996 (Pub.L.No. 104–208, 110 Stat. 3009, Sept. 30, 1996) further expanded the category.

2. INA § 240A(b); 8 U.S.C.A. § 1250A(b).

3. INA § 244(a); 8 U.S.C.A. § 1254(a).

4. *See* INS v. Rios–Pineda, 471 U.S. 444, 105 S.Ct. 2098, 85 L.Ed.2d 452 (1985), Maldonado De Vasquez v. Ilchert, 614 F.Supp. 538 (N.D.Cal.1985); Chan v. INS, 610 F.2d 651 (9th Cir.1979); Phinpathya v. INS, 673 F.2d 1013 (9th Cir.1981)1 INS v. Wang, 450 U.S. 139, 101 S.Ct. 1027, 67 L.Ed.2d 123 (1981); Chiaramonte v. INS, 626 F.2d 1093 (2d Cir.1980); Matter of Anderson, 16 I & N Dec. 596 (BIA 1978); Gagliano v. INS, 353 F.2d 922 (2d Cir.1965).

5. INA § 242(a)(2)(B); 8 U.S.C.A. § 1252(a)(2)(B).

§ 19.49 Special Categories—Legislatively Created Programs

The majority of applications for lawful permanent resident status are dependent upon the availability of an immigrant visa under one of the prescribed immigrant visa categories as described above at Sections 19.8 to 19.44. There are also discretionary remedies yielding lawful permanent resident status, *i.e.,* through registry or cancellation of removal as described above at Sections 19.47 and 19.48. Applicants for residence may, however, be exempt from numerical restrictions through the implementation of legislatively created programs that are generally afforded as a one-time opportunity. One such program, recently terminated, was enacted in 1992 to grant benefits to certain scientists in the independent countries formerly part of the Soviet Union and Baltic states.[1] The purpose of this statute was to prevent such scientists from using their skills in aggressive, unstable or enemy countries around the world, and to encourage them instead to immigrate to the U.S.

Other special legislative programs have been enacted by Congress in the past, and are likely to continue to be enacted. The immigration practitioner would be well-advised to continually monitor special programs, and assess applicability of any new legislation to the background, qualifications or particular country conditions of particular clients.

Library References:

West's Key No. Digests, Aliens ⚖40, 51.5.

§ 19.50 Special Categories—Asylum and Refugee Status

Treatises, books and lengthy articles have been written on U.S. immigration policy as it relates to asylum and refugee status and eligibility of aliens to establish their claims and benefits to merit the conferral of such status. Only a brief and cursory study of this issue is called for in this chapter solely for the purpose of making the practitioner aware of this option for any client who may qualify for such a benefit.[1]

The Refugee Act of 1980 established a permanent and systematic procedure for the admission of refugees to the U.S. and for their resettlement and absorption.[2] It also no longer precluded the executive

---

§ 19.49

1. The Soviet Scientists Immigration Act of 1992, Pub.L.No. 101–509.

§ 19.50

1. An excellent resource for an understanding of INS policy and procedure can be found in The Basic Law Manual: U.S. Law and INS Asylum/Refugee Adjudications (1994), INS Publication.

2. Act of March 17, 1980, Pub.L.No. 96–212, 94 Stat. 102. Awareness by the U.S. to recognize the need to provide legislation for refugees and asylum applicants arose after World War II, which produced vast refugee problems. The U.S., in passing the Displaced Persons Act of 1948 (Act of June 25, 1948, 62 Stat. 1009, as amended June 16, 1950, 64 Stat. 219 and June 28, 1951, 65 Stat. 96), facilitated the entry of over 400,-

§ 19.50 IMMIGRATION AND NATIONALITY LAW Ch. 19

branch from granting protection to refugees fleeing from non-communist countries, or countries outside of the Middle East alone. Further, it established uniform standards for the three categories of persons seeking to enter or remain in the U.S. because of persecution.[3]

An alien present in the U.S., whether lawfully or unlawfully, or seeking admission at a U.S. port of entry is eligible to apply for asylum under INA § 208 (8 U.S.C.A. § 1158). The alien must establish that he or she is a "refugee" as defined at INA § 101(a)(42)(A) (8 U.S.C.A. § 1101(a)(42)(A)), and further that he or she has been "persecuted" in the country of nationality or has an "anticipated fear of persecution" if returned there on account of race, religion, nationality, membership in a particular social group or political opinion. The Supreme Court has ruled that an alien must establish a "well-founded fear of persecution" based upon one of the five categories above-mentioned to satisfy this standard.[4]

The INA directs the Attorney General to establish a procedure for asylum applicants. However, the statute specifies that an alien may be granted asylum in the discretion of the Attorney General.[5] Asylum applicants may therefore establish a well-founded fear on one of the statutory grounds, and yet their applications may still be denied in the discretion of the Attorney General.[6]

The granting of asylum to a principal applicant will facilitate issuance of asylum status to the spouse or child of such applicant if they accompany or follow-to-join the principal applicant.[7]

Library References:

West's Key No. Digests, Aliens ⇌53.10(3).

§ 19.51 Applying for Permanent Residence

One who qualifies for permanent residence through family reunification or one of the employment categories described *supra* must actually go through the process of applying for permanent residence in the U.S. in order to actually obtain the status of permanent resident and the

000 refugees during a four-year period. Limited recognition of worldwide refugee problems resulted in legislation in 1950, culminating in the Refugee Relief Act of 1953 (Act of August 7, 1953, 67 Stat. 400), which permitted the admission of 214,000 refugees within a three-year period.

3. "Refugees"—those individuals applying for status from outside the U.S.—are governed by INA § 207, 8 U.S.C.A. § 1157. "Asylees"—individuals applying for refugee protection while they are in the U.S. or at its borders—are governed by INA § 208, 8 U.S.C.A. § 1158. "Withholders"—individuals who request a determination from an asylum officer or judge not to return them to a specific country or countries—are governed by the Illegal Immigration Reform and Immigrant Responsibility Act ("IIRAIRA") of 1996 (Pub.L.No. 104–208, 110 Stat. 3009, Sept. 30, 1996), § 305(b).

4. INA v. Cardoza–Fonseca, 480 U.S. 421, 107 S.Ct. 1207, 94 L.Ed.2d 434, 4 Immig.Rptr. A1–1 (1987).

5. INA § 208(a); 8 U.S.C.A. § 1158(a). *See* Matter of Shirdel, 19 I & N Dec. 33, 1 Immig.Rptr. B1–12 (BIA 1984)

6. Matter of McMullen, 19 I & N Dec. 90 (BIA 1984).

7. O.I. § 208.15.

Ch. 19   EXCLUSIONARY GROUNDS   **§ 19.52**

coveted "green card." The Immigration Act initially contemplated and still provides that one may apply for permanent residence by obtaining an immigrant visa at a U.S. Consulate abroad, followed by an admission to the U.S. with that immigrant visa, thus becoming a permanent resident.[1]

The law also provides as an alternative method of becoming a permanent resident an adjustment of status procedure which takes place while the individual is physically present in the U.S.[2]

The "privilege" of applying while physically present in the U.S. was generally restricted to individuals who entered the U.S. legally and properly maintained their status or were the immediate relatives of U.S. citizens.[3] A provision enacted in 1994 expanded availability of adjustment of status even to individuals who were out of status in the U.S., provided that they paid a penalty fee.[4] As this book was going to press certain individuals may still be eligible to benefit from this provision.

In order to apply either for an immigrant visa at a U.S. Embassy or for adjustment of status at a local INS office while in the U.S., the applicant, in addition to having an approved preliminary petition which establishes that he or she qualifies in a particular visa category, must also show that he or she is not barred from the U.S. under one of the exclusionary grounds.

Thus, as an example, if an individual has an approved I–130 petition based upon the petition of his permanent resident spouse, but has committed the aggravated felony of murder, he would be barred from the U.S. and from adjusting his status or obtaining an immigrant visa, under one of the exclusionary grounds.[5]

§ 19.52 Applying for Permanent Residence—Exclusionary Grounds

An alien who is within one of the grounds for exclusion may not qualify for an immigrant visa or for adjustment of status. Nine classifications are enumerated.

Health-related grounds for exclusion are applicable to individuals who have a communicable disease of public health significance or who have a physical or mental disorder or behavior that may pose a threat to property, safety or welfare of the alien or others.[1] Waivers for this

---

§ 19.51

1. INA § 211(a); 8 U.S.C.A. § 1181(a).
2. INA § 245; 8 U.S.C.A. § 1255.
3. INA § 245(c); 8 U.S.C.A. § 1255(c).
4. INA § 245(i); 8 U.S.C.A. § 1255(i). This section was added to INA by Public Law No. 103–317 (Aug. 26, 1994). See infra, § 19.55.
5. INA § 212(a)(2); 8 U.S.C.A. § 1182(a)(2).

§ 19.52

1. INA § 212(a)(1); 8 U.S.C.A. § 1182(a)(1).

ground of excludability are available for an alien who has certain U.S. citizen or permanent resident relatives.[2]

Criminal activity also results in exclusion where the crime involves moral turpitude or is in violation of any law or regulation relating to a controlled substance.[3] Multiple convictions may result in exclusion even if the crimes do not involve moral turpitude.[4]

There is an exception for a single conviction committed under the age of 18, committed more than five years before the date of the application for a visa and for certain misdemeanor petty offenses.[5]

There are also special provisions for exclusion for controlled substance traffickers, those involved in prostitution, and for those involved in criminal activity who have asserted immunity from prosecution.[6]

Waivers of some of these grounds of exclusion are available to certain relatives of U.S. citizens and permanent residents.[7]

Security considerations and terrorist activities are grounds for exclusion.[8] In addition, one may be excluded if in the opinion of the Secretary of State the entry or proposed activities would have potentially serious adverse foreign policy consequences for the U.S.[9] Included as well in this category are those potential immigrants who are members of a totalitarian party, with the exception of those who have been members involuntarily.[10] Participants in Nazi persecution or genocide are also excludable.[11]

Aliens, who in the opinion of a consular officer at the time of the application for the visa or of the Attorney General (the INS) at the time of application for adjustment, are likely to become public charges are excludable from the U.S.[12] Thus, as part of each application for permanent residence, proof of ability to support oneself is an essential component.

Individuals, such as those described in Sections 19.22 and 19.26, *supra,* who require labor certification and do not have such labor certification, or medical doctors who do not have the appropriate medical

2. See INA § 212(g); 8 U.S.C.A. § 1182(g).
3. INA § 212(a)(2); 8 U.S.C.A. § 1182(a)(2).
4. See INA § 212(a)(2)(B); 8 U.S.C.A. § 1182(a)(2)(B).
5. See INA § 212(a)(2)(A)(ii); 8 U.S.C.A. § 1182(a)(2)(A)(ii).
6. See INA § 212(a)(2)(C), (D), (E); 8 U.S.C.A. § 1182(a)(2)(C), (D), (E).
7. See INA § 212(h); 8 U.S.C.A. § 1182(h).
8. INA § 212(a)(3)(A), (B); 8 U.S.C.A. § 1182(a)(3)(A), (B).
9. See INA § 212(a)(3)(C); 8 U.S.C.A. § 1182(a)(3)(C).
10. INA § 212(a)(3)(D); 8 U.S.C.A. § 1182(a)(3)(D).
11. INA § 212(a)(3)(E); 8 U.S.C.A. § 1182(a)(3)(E).
12. INA § 212(a)(4); 8 U.S.C.A. § 1182(a)(4).

qualifications, are also deemed excludable when they present themselves for admission as permanent residents without such documentation.[13]

Certain aliens who have previously been deported from the U.S., or were in the United States illegally on a previous stay, or who have made fraudulent misrepresentations in order to procure a visa or other documentation, as well as stowaways and smugglers, are excludable from the U.S.[14] Immigrants who present themselves without a valid immigrant visa or re-entry permit or other appropriate U.S. document are excludable from the U.S.[15]

Those immigrants who are permanently ineligible for U.S. citizenship and certain draft evaders are excludable from the U.S.[16] In addition, practicing polygamists, and those involved in international child abduction, are excludable.[17]

Individuals in the U.S. are subject to deportation if they were excludable at the time of their entry into the U.S.[18] Grounds of deportation are enumerated at Section 237(a) of the INA (8 U.S.C.A. § 1251(a)(1)).

It is essential before proceeding with an application for adjustment of status or for an immigrant visa to review the background of the alien applicant to assure that a potential ground for exclusion and deportation does not exist, or if it does exist, that a waiver or other remedy is applicable. Otherwise, proceeding with the application might not only result in a failure to obtain permanent residence, but the institution of deportation proceedings against the applicant alien.[19]

Library References:
West's Key No. Digests, Aliens ⚌45.

§ 19.53 Applying for Permanent Residence—Immigrant Visa Processing

For those individuals seeking permanent residence in the U.S. who are outside of the U.S., and even for many applicants who during the application procedure, are physically within the U.S., the application process takes place at an appropriate U.S. Embassy or Consulate.[1] Approved petitions for applicants are initially forwarded to the National

---

13. INA § 212(a)(5); 8 U.S.C.A. § 1182(a)(5).

14. INA § 212(a)(6); 8 U.S.C.A. § 1182(a)(6). *See also*, INA § 212(a)(9); 8 U.S.C.A. § 1182(a)(9).

15. INA § 212(a)(7); 8 U.S.C.A. § 1182(a)(7).

16. INA § 212(a)(8); 8 U.S.C.A. § 1182(a)(8).

17. INA § 212(a)(9); 8 U.S.C.A. § 1182(a)(9).

18. INA § 241(a)(1)(A); 8 U.S.C.A. § 1251(a)(1)(A).

19. *See* INA §§ 238, 239 (8 U.S.C.A. § 1252) for a description of the procedures and authority to arrest and deport aliens from the U.S.

§ 19.53

1. INA § 221; 8 U.S.C.A. § 1201.

Visa Center, currently located in Portsmouth, New Hampshire, which is responsible for distributing the approved petitions to the appropriate American Embassies or Consulates, after communicating with the applicant and determining jurisdiction and readiness to proceed.[2]

Generally, the responsible consular office will be the one that has jurisdiction over the alien's place of residence.[3] A consular office may also accept jurisdiction if the alien is physically present in that area and can establish that he or she will be able to remain in the area for the period required to process the application. Consulates may also, in their discretion or at the direction of the Department of State, accept visa applications for individuals who are not resident or physically present in that area.[4]

Consulates rarely, given their budget restrictions and workloads, accept cases on a discretionary basis, but may be directed to do so under policy guidelines for so-called "orphan" cases, involving individuals from jurisdictions that do not have a U.S. Embassy or Consulate operating.[5]

In addition, "hardship" cases will be accepted where compelling evidence is presented.[6]

Library References:

West's Key No. Digests, Aliens ⇒51.5.

§ 19.54 Applying for Permanent Residence—Immigrant Visa Processing—Framework of the Immigrant Visa Processing System

The National Visa Center located in Portsmouth, New Hampshire, handles the distribution of approved petitions and coordinates processing of the final application for permanent residence in its initial stages at Embassies and Consulates. If the applicant is not eligible for adjustment of status, or if the individual indicates on the petition that he or she desires to apply for permanent residence at a U.S. Embassy or Consulate, the INS will forward the approved petition to the National Visa Center.

If there is a quota backlog and an immigrant visa is not available for the applicant at the time the petition is received by the National Visa Center,[1] Packet IIIA,[2] which consists of a letter of explanation, is forwarded.

2. *See infra,* § 19.70.
3. 22 C.F.R. § 42.61.
4. *Id.*
5. *See* 59 Fed.Reg. 39952 (Aug. 5, 1994).
6. *See* 9 F.A.M. 42.61, Note 2.3–4.

§ 19.54
1. Visa availability is determined by the applicant's priority date. *See supra,* § 19.6.
2. The State Department formulated a series of Packets, numbered from I to IV, which provided information and instructions through the various stages of applying for permanent residence through immi-

Ch. 19 FRAMEWORK OF THE PROCESSING SYSTEM § 19.54

If the quota is current at the time that the National Visa Center receives the petition, Packet III is forwarded to the applicant, providing appropriate instructions as to what documentation must be collected in anticipation of an immigrant visa interview and forms to be completed to allow the American Embassy or Consulate to make a preliminary determination that the applicant is fully qualified to apply for an immigrant visa. The Packet will generally consist of the following items:

- letter from the National Visa Center confirming that immigrant visa processing has begun and confirming further which American Embassy or Consulate will be processing the case;

- Form OF–169, which consists of an instruction sheet to the applicant and a checklist of documents which the applicant must have available at the time of the interview. This form is to be signed and returned to the U.S. Embassy or Consulate processing the application when the applicant has all the documents indicated;

- Form OF–230 Part I, which is a biographic data sheet requiring the applicant to list where he or she has lived and worked since the age of 16, and outlining visa and criminal background information.

The Packet will generally also include information sheets giving advice on how to obtain appropriate police certificates and notary records; what documentation should be provided to establish that the applicant will not become a public charge; and other current relevant legal information, relating to the visa process.

The applicant returns Form OF–230 Part I to the American Embassy or Consulate, and returns Form OF–169 when, having collected all the appropriate documents, the applicant is ready for his or her immigrant visa interview. The supporting documents are not presented with the return of the forms; rather, the applicant is expected to bring them and present them at the time of the actual immigrant visa interview.[3]

When the consular post receives Form OF–169 with the applicant's confirmation that all documents are available, the post goes through a

grant visa processing at U.S. Embassies and Consulates. Packets I and II are strictly informational, relating to the preliminary stages of application for permanent residence and are not part of the actual process of applying. Although Packet IIIA (or Packet III) is usually the first documentation relating to consular processing that the applicant ever sees, and Packet IV includes the documentation to complete the case and is the second set of documentation that the applicant will usually see, the jargon has remained part of the INS and State Department culture, and these stages of the case continue to be referred to as "Packet III" and "Packet IV" processing.

3. On occasion, the State Department will issue instructions that will vary somewhat from this procedure. Some Consulates or Embassies will require additional forms or documents to accommodate local concerns. For certain programs, such as the Diversity (lottery) visa program, the National Visa Center was collecting copies of supporting documents in advance of forwarding the petitions to the U.S. Embassy or Consulates for processing.

§ 19.54   IMMIGRATION AND NATIONALITY LAW   Ch. 19

clearance procedure and requests an immigrant visa number from the Visa Office in Washington for those cases subject to quota limitations.

Upon receipt of the visa number from the Visa Office, which is a confirmation that there is availability under that quota, Packet IV is forwarded to the applicant. This Packet includes an actual appointment letter to appear for an immigrant visa interview, Form OF–230 Part II for each member of the family applying and instructions for a medical examination.[4]

Each applicant must personally appear at the immigrant visa interview, although the consular post has the discretion to waive appearances for children under the age of 14.[5]

At the interview, the consular officer must verify the *bona fides* of the application, that the individual in fact qualifies for visa issuance under the particular category,[6] and that none of the grounds of inadmissibility are applicable to the particular applicant.[7]

Consular officers tend to review with special care the visa history of the applicant to determine whether there was ever a fraudulent representation made to issue a visa to enter the U.S. and to assure that credentials presented to qualify are in fact *bona fide*.[8] If the consular officer has any doubt as to the admissibility of the applicant to the U.S., he or she may request an advisory opinion from the State Department.[9] Immigrant visas are generally issued for a period of six months, during which time the applicant is expected to present him or herself for admission to the U.S., at which time he or she is formally granted permanent resident status in the U.S.[10] There is no formal appeal of a denial of an immigrant visa. A denial notice will inform the applicant of the relevant provision of law or regulation and notify the applicant of any available administrative relief.[11] Regulations do provide that the senior consular officer at the post must review every denial of a visa

---

4. Medical examinations are required for all applicants. See INA § 221(d); 8 U.S.C.A. § 1201(d); 22 C.F.R. § 42.66. The medical examination takes place in the consular district and may require an appearance several days prior to the scheduled immigrant visa interview. Note the requirement to present documentation to establish an adequate vaccination history. INA § 212(a)(1)(A)(ii); 8 U.S.C.A. § 1182(a)(1)(A)(ii) newly instituted on Sept. 30, 1996.

5. 22 C.F.R. § 42.62.

6. See 9 F.A.M. § 42.42 Note 1.3.

7. The Consular Officer will generally refer to Volume 9 of the Foreign Affairs Manual for guidance, specifically at §§ 40.7(a)(1)—(a)(33).

8. **PRACTICE POINTER:** In preparing a client for an immigrant visa interview, it is especially important to review the nonimmigrant visa history of the applicant to assure that there is no ground for the consular officer to find fraud. If an individual previously entered the U.S. on a non-immigrant visa, e.g., visitor's visa, and remained in the U.S. thereafter, it could be inferred that he lied and always intended to enter the U.S. to remain permanently if he commenced employment in the U.S. within 30 days of his or her entry. Furthermore, if it becomes apparent that the applicant sold his property and quit his job abroad prior to applying for a visitor's visa, an inference can be made that fraud was committed in those circumstances as well.

9. See 9 F.A.M. § 42.41, Note 2.4 and § 40.6, Note 1.1.

10. 22 C.F.R. § 42.72(a).

11. 22 C.F.R. § 42.81(b).

application.[12] The consular officer may consult the State Department for an advisory opinion, and the applicant or his or her representative may contact the State Department as well. However, the review will only result in an advisory opinion, and only rulings concerning an interpretation of law are binding on the consular officer, not any application of the law to the facts.[13] In addition, no judicial review is available regarding the processing or adjudication of an immigrant visa application.[14]

§ 19.55 Applying for Permanent Residence—Immigrant Visa Processing—Special Requirements, Public Law No. 103–317

Pursuant to Public Law No. 103–317, enacted in August 1994, applicants who are physically present in the U.S. and not in lawful visa status and want to apply for an immigrant visa at the Embassy or Consulate must remain outside the U.S. for at least 90 days before the Consulate can complete the processing of a visa.[1] Accordingly, an applicant who has been physically present in the U.S. must document at the visa interview that he or she has been outside the U.S. for 90 days since departure, or alternatively that he or she is exempt from this requirement by virtue of having been in lawful nonimmigrant status at the time of departure from the U.S.[2]

§ 19.56 Applying for Permanent Residence—Immigrant Visa Processing—Checklist of Required Documents

The applicant must be prepared to answer questions at the time of his or her interview as to eligibility for the visa, and must establish that he or she is not otherwise inadmissible to the U.S. The bulk of the preparation, however, is to assure that the appropriate documents are ready for review by the consular officer. Packet III provides a list of instructions as to what documents must be presented and requires submission of a set of forms providing information as to the applicant's background and confirming that the applicant has collected the necessary documents.

---

12. 22 C.F.R. § 42.81(c).

13. 22 C.F.R. § 42.81(d).

14. *See* Kleindienst v. Mandel, 408 U.S. 753, 92 S.Ct. 2576, 33 L.Ed.2d 683 (1972).

§ 19.55

1. INA § 212(*o*); 8 U.S.C.A. § 1182(*o*). Individuals who have been unlawfully present in the U.S. after April 1, 1997 for more than 180 days are barred from reentry for three years, or for ten years if unlawful for more than a year. *See* INA § 212(a)(2)(B); 8 U.S.C.A. § 1182(a)(2)(B) enacted September 30, 1996. Pub.L. 104–208, 110 Stat. 3009.

2. 22 C.F.R. § 40.104. Certain spouses or children of aliens legalized under the special legalization program which took place in the 1980's (the "Family Unity" program) are also exempt from this 90 day requirement. The program covers spouses and unmarried minor children of aliens legalized under one of the three legalization programs established by the Immigration Reform and Control Act of 1986.

Packet IV confirms these instructions, schedules the appointment, and serves as the final warning to the applicant to appear with everything necessary to show that he or she is "documentarily qualified."

The following checklist, culled from Packets III and IV and other supplemental material, illustrates what the applicant should assemble and be prepared to submit to the U.S. Embassy at the time of his or her interview:

1. Passport(s)—for all applicants (husband/wife and children under 16 may be included in a single passport). A child, sixteen years of age or older who is included in his parent's passport but whose photograph does not appear in such passport, must have his own separate passport.

2. One copy—"Application for Immigrant Visa and Alien Registration" (Form OF–230) fully completed for each applicant.

3. One original (and one copy)—Birth Certificate—for each applicant. The certificate, which must show the parents' names, is called the "long form" certificate. (A "short form" birth certificate will not be accepted.) Original long form birth certificates are required for all unmarried children under 21 years of age even if they do not intend to immigrate at the time.

4. Unobtainable birth certificate: in rare cases, it may be impossible to obtain a birth certificate because records have been destroyed or the government will not issue one. In such cases, you should obtain a statement to that effect from the civil registrar's office and proceed to obtain secondary evidence of birth. A baptismal certificate may be submitted for consideration provided it contains the date and place of the applicant's birth and information concerning parentage, and provided the baptism took place shortly after birth. Should a baptismal certificate be unobtainable, a close relative, preferably the applicant's mother, should prepare a notarized statement giving the place and date of the applicant's birth, the names of both parents, and the maiden name of the mother. The statement must be executed before an official authorized to administer oaths or affirmations. In such cases, any other secondary evidence that might be available concerning the applicant's birth should also be brought.

5. One original (and one copy)—Adoption Certificate—for any applicant who has been adopted.

6. One original (and one copy)—Deed Poll—if the applicant has changed his or her name (except by marriage).

7. One original (and one copy)—Marriage Certificate.

8. One original (and one copy)—Divorce Decree or Death Certificate—for all marriages ended by death, divorce or annulment.

Ch. 19   CHECKLIST OF REQUIRED DOCUMENTS   § 19.56

9. One original (and one copy)—Military Service Record and Discharge Certificate—covering any period of military service in the Armed Services of any country.

10. One original (and one copy)—Police Certificate(s)—for each visa applicant aged sixteen years or over from the police authorities of each locality of the country of the applicant's nationality or current residence where he/she has resided for at least six months since reaching the age of sixteen. Police certificates are also required from all other countries where the applicant has resided for at least one year after the age of 16.

11. One original (and one copy)—Court Records—covering every conviction for any crime.

12. Two (2) separate photographs for each visa applicant, including infants, regardless of age. The photograph must be in color with a white background, on thin paper, glossy, unretouched and not mounted. The dimension of facial image should be about 1 inch from chin to top of hair, the subject should be shown in 3/4 frontal view showing right side of face with the right ear visible, except when prohibited by the applicant's religious practices. No earrings or eyeglasses should be worn.

13. Evidence of Support: An applicant for an immigrant visa may generally satisfy this requirement of the law by the presentation of documentary evidence establishing that:

- the applicant has, or will have, in the U.S. personal funds sufficient to provide support for the applicant and dependent family members, or sufficient to provide support until suitable employment is located;
- the applicant has arranged employment in the U.S. that will provide an adequate income for the applicant and dependent family members;
- relatives or friends in the U.S. will assure the applicant's support; or
- a combination of the above circumstances exists.

APPLICANT'S OWN FUNDS: An applicant who expects to be able to meet the public charge provisions of the law through personal financial resources may submit to the consular officer evidence of funds or income from one or more of the following sources:

- statement from a senior officer of a bank showing present balance of applicant's account, date account was opened, the number and amount of deposits and withdrawals during the past 12 months, and the average balance during the year (if there have been recent unusually large deposits, an explanation therefor should be given);
- proof of ownership of property or real estate, in the form of a title, deed or the equivalent, and a letter from a lawyer,

§ 19.56   IMMIGRATION AND NATIONALITY LAW   Ch. 19

    banker or responsible real estate agent showing its present valuation (any mortgages or loans against the property must be stated);

- letter or letters verifying ownership of stocks and bonds, with present market value or expected earnings indicated;
- statement from insurance company showing policies held and present cash surrender value;
- proof of income from business investments or other sources.

If the financial resources are derived from a source outside the U.S., a statement as to how the funds or income are to be transferred to the U.S. must be provided.

EMPLOYMENT: An applicant relying on an offer of prearranged employment to meet the public charge provisions of the law should have the prospective employer submit a notarized letter of employment on the letterhead stationery of the employing business. The letter should:

- contain a definite offer of employment;
- give a description of the job offered to the alien and an explanation of skills which qualify the alien for the position;
- state the rate of compensation to be paid and, if pertinent, additional information detailing other benefits to be included in lieu of cash payment;
- specify the location, type and duration (whether seasonal, temporary or indefinite) of the employment offered; and
- state whether the employment will be immediately available upon the applicant's arrival in the U.S.

14. Translations: all documents not in English must be accompanied by certified translations into English. Translations must be certified by a qualified independent translator and sworn to before a Notary Public or Commissioner of Oaths.

15. Fee—$200 or local equivalent, in cash, per visa.

16. Results of medical examination.

17. Although not specifically required, it is always advisable to bring additional documentation in support of the application, as follows:

    a. Copies of U.S. tax returns (if individual lived and worked in the U.S.);

    b. Copies of educational documents and letters of reference used in support of immigrant visa petition, if applicable;

    c. Previous passports if they contain U.S. visas and proof of past entries into the U.S.

There is no such thing as being overly prepared for an immigrant visa interview.

§ 19.57 Applying for Permanent Residence—Adjustment of Status

Individuals who are already present in the U.S., legally or illegally, often prefer to complete the process of applying for permanent residence locally, within the U.S. In a number of situations such individuals would be permitted to apply for adjustment of status.[1]

Applicants who qualify to apply need not travel overseas to a U.S. Embassy or Consulate, but may submit an application directly with the local INS office having jurisdiction over the applicant's place of residence in the U.S.

The adjustment of status procedure is quite attractive, particularly for those applicants who have concerns about eligibility, since applicants do have accessibility to administrative review in the context of deportation proceedings[2] and furthermore have some access though limited to federal courts upon the denial of an application in that context.[3]

The privilege of applying for adjustment of status has historically been restricted to individuals who entered the U.S. legally and remained legally in status, with a few limited exceptions.[4] Public Law No. 103–317, enacted on August 26, 1994, provided, on an experimental basis, for an expansion of eligibility for adjustment of status.[5]

Library References:

West's Key No. Digests, Aliens ⚖=53.10(2).

§ 19.58 Applying for Permanent Residence—Adjustment of Status—General Requirements

An individual is eligible for adjustment of status if he or she was inspected and admitted or paroled into the U.S., and an immigrant visa is immediately available (in other words, there is no quota backlog).[1]

The statute further restricts availability of adjustment of status with reference to individuals who are not immediate relatives of U.S. citizens as defined in § 201(b) (8 U.S.C.A. § 1151).[2] Not generally eligible are:

- individuals who accepted unauthorized employment;

---

§ 19.57

1. INA § 245; 8 U.S.C.A. § 1255.
2. 8 C.F.R. § 242.17.
3. Prior to deportation proceedings, *see* INA § 279; 8 U.S.C.A. § 1329. In deportation proceedings, *see* INA § 106(a); 8 U.S.C.A. § 1105a(a). *See also* Ruginski v. INS, 942 F.2d 13 (1st Cir.1991). *But see* INA § 242(a)(2)(B) added by Pub.L. 104–208, 110 Stat. 3009, Sept. 30, 1996.
4. INA § 245(c); 8 U.S.C.A. § 1255(c).
5. INA § 245(i); 8 U.S.C.A. § 1255(i) and Pub.L. No. 103–317 § 506(b).

§ 19.58

1. INA § 245(a); 8 U.S.C.A. § 1255(a).
2. *See supra,* § 19.8 for a full discussion of those individuals properly classifiable as immediate relatives of U.S. citizens (spouses, children under the age of 21 and parents).

§ 19.58   IMMIGRATION AND NATIONALITY LAW   Ch. 19

- those not in legal status or who failed to maintain continuously lawful status since entry into the U.S.;
- aliens admitted in transit without a visa;
- aliens who were admitted as nonimmigrant visitors under the Visa Waiver Pilot Program;[3] and
- individuals who entered the U.S. as alien crewmen.[4]

Also generally ineligible are individuals admitted as fiancés or fiancées under the "K" visa category[5] and certain applicants who are applying based upon marriage who are either already conditional residents of the U.S.[6] or who are in deportation proceedings.[7]

One may apply for adjustment of status even while in deportation proceedings, as long as the applicant is otherwise qualified to apply.[8]

§ 19.59 Applying for Permanent Residence—Adjustment of Status—Special Provisions of Section 245(i)

Some of those applicants who are generally ineligible for adjustment of status have been permitted the privilege of applying pursuant to Section 245(i) of the INA (8 U.S.C.A. § 155(i)); provided that they pay an additional fee of one thousand dollars. As this book was going to press it may be that certain individuals with preliminary petitions or applications filed will still be able to avail themselves of this provision. Children under the age of 17 and certain family members of individuals who benefitted from the amnesty programs held during the 1980s are exempt from this penalty fee.[1] Those classes of individuals now included in eligibility for adjustment of status are:

- aliens who entered without inspection (EWI);
- aliens who overstayed a valid period of nonimmigrant stay or failed to maintain their lawful status in the U.S.;
- aliens who have engaged in unauthorized employment;
- alien crew members;
- aliens admitted in transit without visas; and

3. Visitors who do not enter with visas. See 8 C.F.R. Pt. 217.
4. INA § 245(c); 8 U.S.C.A. § 1255(c).
5. INA § 245(d); 8 U.S.C.A. § 1255(d).
6. See infra,§ 19.72.
7. INA § 245(e); 8 U.S.C.A. § 1255(e).
8. 8 C.F.R. § 242.17.

§ 19.59
1. The Family Unity program, established by Section 301 of the Immigration Act of 1990, includes the spouses and unmarried children of aliens legalized under the legalization (amnesty) programs established by the Immigration Reform and Control Act of 1986. This program provided authorization for family members of these individuals to remain in the U.S. for extended periods of time until they too qualified for permanent residence in the U.S. by virtue of their relationship to the principal applicants for amnesty.

- aliens who entered the U.S. under the Visa Waiver Pilot Program.[2]

Stowaways, aliens admitted as "K" nonimmigrants and individuals otherwise excludable under the exclusionary provisions[3] still remain ineligible for adjustment of status under this provision.

§ 19.60 Applying for Permanent Residence—Adjustment of Status—Discretionary Factors

It is important to remember that granting an adjustment of status is "discretionary" in nature.[1] In the absence of adverse factors, however, approval of an adjustment of status is generally granted, and it is relatively rare that an individual who is statutorily eligible for adjustment of status will have an application denied as a matter of discretion. When adverse factors are present, the alien applicant may be required to show "unusual or even outstanding equities",[2] and in fact a balancing of the equities versus the adverse factors takes place.[3]

§ 19.61 Applying for Permanent Residence—Adjustment of Status—Application Process

The procedure and required forms will vary from district to district, and accordingly a slightly different list of forms might be required to submit an application for adjustment of status in New York City as compared to Buffalo, Rochester, or any of the other districts nationwide. Some offices provide for the submission of the application in person; others sanction "mail" submissions.[1]

The basic application consists of Form I–485, Application to Register Permanent Residence or Adjust Status, with supporting forms and documents.[2] As in the immigrant visa processing procedure at U.S. Embassies and Consulates, a medical examination is required, and in

2. INA § 245(i); 8 U.S.C.A. § 1255(i). However entrants without inspection may be ineligible. See INA § 212(a)(6)(A); 8 U.S.C.A. § 1181(a)(6)(A).

3. See INA § 212; 8 U.S.C.A. § 1182.

§ 19.60

1. INA § 245; 8 U.S.C.A. § 1255; see Elkins v. Moreno, 435 U.S. 647, 98 S.Ct. 1338, 55 L.Ed.2d 614 (1978).

2. Matter of Arai, 13 I & N Dec. 494, 496 (BIA 1970).

3. **PRACTICE POINTER:** Immigration officers, like consular officers, often are concerned with the intent of the applicant who has entered the U.S. in a nonimmigrant visa category. If an individual enters on a visitor's visa and very shortly thereafter applies for adjustment of status, the immigration examiner might try to infer that the individual had a preconceived intent of entering the U.S. permanently and had therefore either committed fraud or was at the very least in bad faith. It is prudent to avoid filing an application, if at all possible, within the 30 day period immediately after a last entry into the U.S.

§ 19.61

1. The INS contemplates a nationwide "mail-in" filing system where regional offices will receive the applications, set up the files and schedule the appointments at local district offices. Implementation of this program was announced, at least for cases based upon I–140, I–360 and I–526 petitions at 61 Fed.Reg. 56060 (Oct. 30, 1996).

2. See infra, § 19.65 a checklist for an adjustment of status application.

§ 19.61   IMMIGRATION AND NATIONALITY LAW   Ch. 19

lieu of police clearances, fingerprints are submitted with the application, which the INS forwards to the FBI for clearance.

Since it must be established that the individual qualifies in an appropriate visa category and that an immigrant visa is immediately available,[3] proof that a preliminary visa petition has been approved (usually the approval notice on Form I-797) must be submitted with the application.

Family members who are qualifying as derivatives of the principal applicant must, of course, submit documentation to prove relationship to the principal applicant.

The application must be filed with the INS office having jurisdiction over the place of residence of the applicant,[4] and generally a personal interview will be required, but can be waived for family members under the age of 14.

Some district offices, including New York City, have implemented a policy of waiving adjustment of status interviews in certain designated cases. Those include:

- cases based on an employment-based preference petition where the alien will continue employment with the same individual or firm for whom he or she is lawfully employed as a nonimmigrant;
- cases filed for the derivative spouse or child of an alien eligible for an employment-based interview waiver;
- cases involving the unmarried child of a U.S. citizen;
- cases involving the parent of a U.S. citizen; and
- cases clearly deniable without the need to verify information by interview.[5]

§ 19.62   Applying for Permanent Residence—Adjustment of Status—Concurrent Filing of Petition and Adjustment of Status

Generally, one may not file an application for adjustment of status unless an immigrant visa petition[1] has been filed and approved and a visa is immediately available.[2]

However, concurrent filing of the adjustment application and petition is authorized for immediate relatives of U.S. citizens (where there is no issue of visa availability) and for aliens eligible in one of the family-sponsored preference categories if there is no quota backlog and an

---

3. INA § 245(a); 8 U.S.C.A. § 1255(a).
4. 8 C.F.R. § 245.2(a)(1).
5. 8 C.F.R. § 245.6. Employment-based cases are now filed with Regional Service Centers. 61 Fed.Reg. 56060 (Oct. 30, 1996).

§ 19.62
1. Form I-140, Form I-130, Form I-360 or Form I-526.
2. 8 C.F.R. § 245.2(a)(2).

immigrant visa is immediately available.[3] This, in effect, reduces the processing time and eliminates one step in the overall procedure for qualifying for permanent residence in the U.S.

§ 19.63 Applying for Permanent Residence—adjustment of Status—Completion of the Process

In those cases where interviews are waived, the applicant, after filing the application, simply awaits notice from the INS of completion of the adjudication process. Generally, the applicant will then be called in to the INS to provide a fingerprint and signature to facilitate the manufacturing of the "green card" itself (Form I–551).

If an interview is scheduled, the applicant and designated family members will be requested to appear in person, normally presenting the applicant's passport, proof of entry into the U.S., all original documents used as part of the application process, current verification of employment and support, and documentation confirming the *bona fides* of the petition itself.[1]

The results of a medical examination taken at a designated facility must also be presented.[2]

During the course of the interview, the immigration examiner will review the *bona fides* of the application itself, review supporting documents, review grounds of excludability and the full background of the applicant and family members to confirm that the individual is eligible for permanent residence in the U.S. and is also eligible for adjustment of status under Section 245 of the INA (8 U.S.C.A. § 1255).

If it is determined that the individual is entitled to the classification, the immigration examiner will request a visa number from Washington, will grant adjustment of status to the applicant, and stamp the passport of the applicant with temporary evidence of his status as a permanent resident and "green card" holder.[3]

---

3. *See supra,* § 19.6. Note that there are, in fact, quota backlogs in most of the relative preference categories. Accordingly, concurrent filing will generally not be available except for immediate relatives of U.S. citizens.

§ 19.63

1. In the case of marriage situations, extensive documentation to establish the *bona fides* of the marriage is often requested. *See infra,* § 19.65.

2. INA § 234; 8 U.S.C.A. § 1224 provides that the examination must be made by medical officers of the U.S. Public Health Service or by other civil surgeons designated by the Attorney General. In fact, a list of such designated surgeons is provided by each local district office of the INS.

3. The actual "green card" itself is manufactured in a facility in Texas and mailed to the individuals directly at their home addresses some time after completion of the process.

PRACTICE POINTER: Often there are problems with the manufacture of the cards. In up to 25% of the cases, the applicant must be contacted again to provided new photographs or fingerprints. It is therefore important for applicants to follow-up after resident status is granted and for representatives to maintain contact with applicants until such time as it has been verified that the cards have been received.

§ 19.63   IMMIGRATION AND NATIONALITY LAW   Ch. 19

Departure from the U.S. during the pendency of an application for adjustment of status "abandons" that application.[4] However, an individual may apply for permission to travel during this process, requesting authorization known as "advance parole" by filing a formal application for such permission on Form I–131.[5] This permission will be granted when a *bona fide* business or personal reason for traveling arises. Different INS offices have varying standards as to what constitutes a sufficient business or personal necessity. Some are fairly liberal while others require that a true emergency exist.

§ 19.64 Applying for Permanent Residence—Adjustment of Status—Administrative and Judicial Review

In contrast to the process at U.S. Embassies and Consulates, decisions denying applications for adjustment of status are subject to extensive review.

Although no administrative appeal can be taken directly from a denial of an application for adjustment of status,[1] an applicant may submit a Motion to Reopen and Reconsider based upon additional legal arguments or additional facts or information not previously available.[2] In addition, if the INS institutes deportation proceedings against the applicant after denial of the application for adjustment of status, the applicant may renew his application for adjustment of status before the immigration judge.[3] Should the immigration judge deny the application for adjustment of status, a right of appeal exists to the Board of Immigration Appeals.[4] Denials by the Board of Immigration Appeals in deportation proceedings, however, can no longer be appealed to the U.S. Court of Appeals.[5]

§ 19.65 Applying for Permanent Residence—Adjustment of Status—Checklist

Although documentary requirements may vary slightly from district to district within New York, and within the U.S. generally, one will usually satisfy all local requirements by assembling the list of items indicated here:

1. *Application—Form I–485:*[1] Application to Register Permanent Residence or Adjust Status. This is the basic application form to apply for

---

4. 8 C.F.R. § 245.2(a)(4)(ii).
5. *See* O.I. 212.5(c).

5. INA § 242(a)(2)(B) added by Pub.L. 104–208, 110 Stat. 3009, Sept. 30, 1996.

§ 19.64
1. 8 C.F.R. § 245.2(a)(5).
2. 8 C.F.R. § 103.5.
3. 8 C.F.R. § 245.2(a)(1).
4. 8 C.F.R. § 3.1(b)(2).

§ 19.65
1. This application and other official forms can be obtained from the Government Printing Office or from local district offices of the INS. The forms are also available by calling a special government Form

Ch. 19   ADJUSTMENT OF STATUS—CHECKLIST   § 19.65

adjustment of status. One must be prepared and submitted for each family member applying.

2. *Form G–325A*: This government "Biographic Information" form elicits personal background information about each applicant. This form must be submitted on behalf of each applicant over the age of 14.

3. *Fingerprint Chart (Form FD–258)*: A fingerprint chart must be completed and submitted on behalf of each applicant over the age of 14.[2]

4. *Medical Examination (Form I–693)*: A report as to the results of a medical examination is prepared by the doctor on Form I–693. The exam must be made by a medical officer of the U.S. Public Health Service or by other civil surgeons designated by the Attorney General.[3]

5. *Photographs*: Photographs must be in color on a white background, 1 3/16" from the hair to just below the chin and 1" from left cheek to right ear, must show the entire face of the person in a 3/4 view showing the right ear and left eye.[4]

6. *Evidence of Financial Support*: A number of items can alternatively be produced to show financial support, depending on the circumstances of the case, including job letter on proper letterhead of the employer, pay statements for the immediately past two months prior to the filing of the application, current and previous W–2s and bank letters on bank stationery for all accounts showing the title of the account, date opened and current balance.

   - If the individual is supported by someone else, Form I–134, Affidavit of Support, must be executed and notarized and submitted with appropriate supporting documents. A new, contractually binding Affidavit of Support will be required mid–1997.

7. *Personal Documents*: Relevant personal documents must be submitted[5] such as a birth certificate for all applicants, and where a relative

---

Number: 1–800–870–3676. In addition, there are a number of computer software programs on the market that produce forms acceptable to the INS.

2. Fingerprints must be taken, effective March 1, 1997 at a Designated Fingerprint Service ("DFS"). 51 Fed.Reg. 57583 (Nov. 7, 1996). Lists of such agencies are available at local official and Regional Service Centers of the Immigration Service.

3. INA § 234; 8 U.S.C.A. § 1224. The INS district offices will provide a listing of designated civil surgeons authorized by the Attorney General in their area of jurisdiction.

4. PRACTICE POINTER: The INS is very particular with regard to the photographs. Although any photographer can be used, it is often a good idea to obtain the photographs from a studio that is proximate to the local district office. These businesses tend to have much greater experience in producing photographs that comply with the very particular specifications.

5. Under current regulations, photocopies of personal documents may be submitted provided that the applicant signs a

is the petitioner, birth certificate of the petitioner as well. Also to be submitted where relevant are the marriage certificate(s) of the party or parties and proof of termination of previous marriages.

8. *Petition Approval Notice*: To establish that the individual is eligible to apply for adjustment of status and that an immigrant visa is immediately available, a copy of the approval notice of the qualifying petition, Form I-797, should be submitted.[6]

9. *Income Tax Returns*: Copies of federal, state and city income tax returns, signed, dated and authenticated by the agency that accepted them are requested in many INS cases, particularly in spouse cases.[7]

10. *Marriage Cases*: In the so-called spouse or marriage cases, additional supplemental documents are requested, such as a wedding picture of the petitioner and beneficiary, any snapshots taken of the petitioner and beneficiary together since their marriage, financial documents showing that the two are financially interdependent, such as leases on apartments, rent receipts, hospital cards, union books, insurance policies, pay vouchers, bank books, charge cards showing the names of the petitioner and beneficiary and Social Security cards if available for the petitioner and beneficiary. In addition, it has been requested in such cases that letters from the employer of the petitioner and beneficiary are provided which indicate the marital status of the parties and any dependents claimed.

11. *Concurrent Filings*: In those cases where it is permitted to file the petition concurrently with the application for adjustment of status,[8] Form I-130, executed by the petitioner must be submitted with photographs of the petitioner and a Form G-325A executed on behalf of the petitioner as well.

12. *Proof of Entry and Status*: Each applicant should submit his or her passport and Form I-94,[9] if available. Copies of immigration documents to establish maintenance of status, such as approval notices of nonimmigrant visa petitions and previously issued Form I-94s, should be made available as well.

§ 19.66 Applying for Permanent Residence—Tactical Considerations

It is not sufficient to know the procedures for applying for an immigrant visa and for adjustment of status in the U.S. For those

---

statement assuring that the originals are available and would be provided upon request. 8 C.F.R. § 204.5(g)(1).

6. Approvals of I-130, I-140, I-360 and I-526 petitions are issued by the Regional Service Centers on Form I-797.

7. PRACTICE POINTER: Although official instructions indicate that tax returns must be "authenticated," normally most district offices will accept simple photocopies if there are no indicators of fraud or misrepresentation.

8. *See supra*, § 19.62.

9. Form I-94 is the arrival record issued to each nonimmigrant who enters the U.S. in a nonimmigrant visa status.

individuals residing outside the U.S., the only option is to apply for an immigrant visa, unless the individual in the interim makes an entry into the country. For those individuals who are already in the U.S., either legally in status in one of the various nonimmigrant visa categories or out of status, a number of factors must be considered before deciding whether to complete the process at a U.S. Embassy or Consulate or at a local district office of the INS.

§ 19.67 Applying for Permanent Residence—Tactical Considerations—Nonimmigrant Status as a Factor

Most individuals who enter the U.S. as nonimmigrants do so as visitors under the B–2 visitor for pleasure or B–1 visitor for business visa categories.[1] However, a number of individuals enter under nonimmigrant visa categories which authorize them to remain in the U.S. for very extended periods of time, such as students,[2] professional workers,[3] and intracompany transferees.[4]

Such individuals may qualify for permanent residence in the U.S. and must consider the advantages and disadvantages of applying at a local INS district office or through overseas processing at a U.S. Embassy or Consulate.

The first consideration is whether applying for permanent residence is necessary at all. Students are generally permitted to remain in the U.S. for the length of their academic program and often are entitled to an additional period of one year of practical training in the U.S. before they are required to return to their home countries.[5] Professional workers are generally authorized to remain in the U.S. for a period up to six years,[6] and intracompany transferees in some instances for as long as seven years.[7]

It is also important to note that nonimmigrants who desire to extend their stay in the U.S. or to renew their visas while they have already commenced the process of applying for permanent residence may discover the authorities to be uncooperative, since in most instances a prerequisite to qualifying in a nonimmigrant category is establishing that the applicant's intent is to remain in the U.S. on a temporary basis without intent to remain here permanently. One seeking entry into the U.S. may be excluded when presenting a nonimmigrant visa if it is

§ 19.67
1. INA § 101(a)(15)(B); 8 U.S.C.A. § 1101(a)(15)(B).
2. INA § 101(a)(15)(F); 8 U.S.C.A. § 1101(a)(15)(F).
3. INA § 101(a)(15)(H); 8 U.S.C.A. § 1101(a)(15)(H).
4. INA § 101(a)(15)(L); 8 U.S.C.A. § 1101(a)(15)(L).
5. 8 C.F.R. §§ 214.2(f)(5), (10).
6. 8 C.F.R. § 214.2(h)(13)(iii).
7. 8 C.F.R. § 214.2(*l*)(12)(i).

determined that he or she is in fact an immigrant not in possession of a proper immigrant visa![8]

This became such a serious problem, particularly with multinational companies employing personnel on a temporary basis who then decided that they required the individuals in the U.S. on a permanent basis, that a limited exception to the rule that a nonimmigrant may not have "immigrant intent" was established professional workers and intracompany transferees.[9]

But for most other visa holders, this exception does not apply. Thus, if a permanent resident alien of the U.S. were to marry a foreign national and file a preference petition for the spouse under the second family preference category,[10] he might not be able to bring his spouse into the U.S. until after the petition is approved and the quota in that category becomes current,[11] which could be a period of several years! Any attempt to get a visitor's visa or a student visa for the spouse would fail, because the spouse would not be able to establish that she has nonimmigrant intent with regard to her entry into the U.S., since she is married to a permanent resident of this country![12]

Another very significant factor in determining whether it is appropriate or necessary to apply for permanent residence would be the employment circumstances of a spouse. Often an individual is in the U.S. on a work visa for a company, but his or her spouse is not granted employment authorization based on the status of the principal. If the spouse on his or her own does not qualify for a nonimmigrant work visa, the only alternative might be to apply for permanent residence, so that both the principal applicant and the spouse are authorized to work. Applicants for adjustment of status are usually authorized to work during the pendency of the application, and of course continue such authorization after they are actually granted permanent residence in the U.S.[13]

§ 19.68 Applying for Permanent Residence—Tactical Considerations—Immigrant Visa Processing Versus Adjustment of Status

A number of factors must be considered in determining whether it is preferable to apply for adjustment of status or immigrant visa processing

---

8. INA § 214(b); 8 U.S.C.A. § 1184(b).

9. Id.

10. See supra, § 19.9.

11. See supra, § 19.6.

12. PRACTICE POINTER: If the spouse-to-be were to take the initiative and apply for a student visa or other such long-term nonimmigrant visa prior to becoming engaged and/or married, she might then be able to apply for entry into the U.S. and remain in the U.S. on an interim basis with her spouse after marriage, while the process of applying for permanent residence proceeds.

13. Most district offices will grant employment authorization to both the principal and the applicant at the time of the filing of the adjustment of status application or shortly thereafter. A formal application for such employment authorization is filed on Form I–765.

for an individual who is currently in the U.S. Some individuals simply may not qualify for adjustment of status in the U.S. and must apply for processing at a U.S. Embassy or Consulate.[1] Other individuals might be eligible for either adjustment of status or immigrant visa processing, but would be required to remain out of the country for a minimum of 90 days after departure if they were to choose immigrant visa processing,[2] making this option far less desirable.

Many individuals, however, have a real option of choosing either to apply for adjustment of status at a district office of the INS or to have their immigrant visa processed at an American Embassy or U.S. Consulate.[3]

Listed below are some of the more significant factors that must be considered in making this determination:

- **Processing Time**: An obvious consideration is processing time. How long is the local district office taking to complete the process of applying for adjustment of status as compared to the U.S. Embassy or Consulate that would have jurisdiction over this applicant?

- **Documentary Concerns**: There are some differences in documentary requirements. The most common consideration is with reference to "police clearances." When processing at a U.S. Embassy or Consulate, "police clearances" are required from each country where the applicant (or adult family member) has lived for at least one year.[4] For well-traveled individuals, the burden of obtaining such police clearances might be quite significant. Applicants for adjustment of status in the U.S. need not obtain police clearances, but simply must present fingerprint charts for clearance through the FBI.[5]

- **Travel Limitations**: Applicants for adjustment of status in the U.S. are not permitted to travel outside the U.S. without formally applying for permission to do so. Permission is usually limited to personal or business emergencies. The process of applying for and obtaining such permission may be quite inconvenient and/or difficult depending upon the particular policy of the local district office of the INS. Individuals applying for immigrant visa processing at a U.S. Consulate or Embassy may continue to travel without restriction if they are already in possession of a nonimmigrant visa which authorizes them to do so.

§ 19.68

1. See supra, § 19.58. Where Section 245(i) (8 U.S.C.A. 1255) is applicable, most individuals, even those who are illegally in the U.S., may qualify to adjust status here. Certain individuals, however, remain statutorily ineligible, *e.g.*, stowaways.

2. See supra, § 19.55.
3. Id.
4. 22 C.F.R. § 42.65(c).
5. O.I. 245.2(d).

§ 19.68   IMMIGRATION AND NATIONALITY LAW   Ch. 19

- **Employment Authorization**: An applicant for adjustment of status in the U.S. may normally obtain employment authorization for self, spouse and children during the pendency of the application. Applicants for immigrant visa processing will not obtain employment authorization until the process is completed and the applicants return to the U.S. as immigrants and are granted permanent resident status in the U.S.

- **Convenience and Expense**: Immigrant visa processing requires that the applicants physically travel to the U.S. Embassy or Consulate for the immigrant visa interview. Generally, all family members applying must appear personally for the medical examination and interview. Although Embassies and Consulates endeavor to give reasonable notice when scheduling such interviews, often notice is limited to a period of several weeks or less during which time an applicant must arrange to travel with his or her entire family to the appropriate U.S. Embassy or Consulate, however large the distance, to apply and then return to the U.S. This of course may present considerable practical difficulties.

- **Location of Family Members**: If the principal applicant is in the U.S. but other immediate family members are not, e.g., a teenage child in boarding school overseas, as a practical matter immigrant visa processing may be the only realistic option. The separated family member would not be able to apply to adjust status in the U.S. at a district office of the INS, since only individuals who are actually physically present in the U.S. may so apply. Accordingly, the principal applicant may choose to apply at a U.S. Embassy or Consulate so that the entire family can appear together and obtain permanent residence at the same time.[6]

- **Legal Considerations**: If there are potential legal problems or other eligibility problems or issues in the case, the jurisdiction chosen may be a significant factor. Applicants for immigrant visa processing who run into delays might find themselves forced to remain outside of this country while the matter is being resolved. Furthermore, rights of appeal are considerably more limited at a U.S. Embassy or Consulate as compared to a district office of the INS.[7] Even if there are no identifiable legal problems in a case,

---

6. PRACTICE POINTER: If for other reasons it is not practical to apply at a U.S. Embassy or Consulate on behalf of the principal applicant, he or she could adjust status in the U.S. and then, after permanent residence is granted to the principal applicant, the family member may apply separately for immigrant visa processing at the U.S. Embassy "following to join" the principal pursuant to INA § 203(d); 8 U.S.C.A. § 1153(d).

CAVEAT: Special attention must be paid to the age of children who are accompanying or following to join a parent. Such children are only eligible to follow to join while they are under 21 years of age and, accordingly, the process of obtaining permanent residence must be completed for such children before their 21st birthday. See INA § 101(b)(1); 8 U.S.C.A. § 1101(b)(1).

7. See supra, §§ 19.54, 19.64.

many applicants will choose to apply at a district office of the INS rather than at a U.S. Embassy or Consulate that has developed a reputation for being difficult or adversarial in its treatment of immigrant visa applicants.

It should be obvious to the practitioner that there are a number of factors and subtleties that go into the decision of where to apply and that such a decision must necessarily be made on a case-by-case basis. It is also important to note that circumstances and considerations can change during the pendency of an application and it might be appropriate under certain circumstances to change jurisdiction while the proceeding is ongoing.[8]

It is therefore extremely important to monitor the case on an ongoing basis and at each stage to determine whether the approach decided upon is still appropriate and correct.

Library References:

West's Key No. Digests, Aliens ⟲53.10(2).

---

8. A typical example of a case requiring changed jurisdiction would involve an employee of a multinational corporation who is applying for adjustment of status in the U.S., and during the pendency of that application is temporarily transferred overseas for a short interim assignment. In that circumstance, the individual would change tactics from applying for adjustment of status at the local district office in the U.S. to applying for completion of the process through immigrant visa processing at the U.S. Embassy or Consulate in the country where he or she is now temporarily residing.

§ 19.69 Applying for Permanent Residence—Tactical Considerations—Flowchart

Applying for Permanent Residence

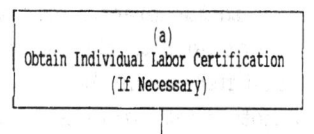

(a) Obtain Individual Labor Certification (If Necessary)

(b) File appropriate petition with Regional Service Center. (Immediate Relatives of U.S. citizens who are applying for adjustment of status may avoid this step.) If the applicant will be applying for immigrant visa processing at a U.S. Embassy or Consulate, he/she should direct the Regional Service Center to forward the approved petition to the National Visa Center for further processing.

(c) File Application for Adjustment of Status at the District Office of Immigration Service having jurisdiction (in conjunction with I-130 petition and supporting documents in the case of an Immediate Relative of U.S. Citizen). Those subject to Section 245(i) pay the special penalty fee. Upon Granting of Application, Individual is a Permanent Resident of the United States

(d) Applications for employment authorization and/or permission to travel for personal or business emergencies may be filed during the pendency of this application

(e) Adjustment of status is granted upon completion of an interview, or in cases where an interview is waived, upon completion of review of application.

(c) Forward completed Biographic Forms (received from the National Visa Center in Portsmouth, New Hampshire) to the United States Embassy or Consulate

(d) Collect necessary documents as instructed by the National Visa Center and upon receipt, submit form to the U.S. Embassy/Consulate reporting ready for final interview (in diversity [lottery] cases, biographic forms and report are forwarded to the National Visa Center, not to the Embassy or Consulate)

(e) Appear at the United States Embassy or Consulate when scheduled with completed interview forms and medical procedures as instructed by Embassy/Consulate, for completion of interview and receipt of immigrant visa.

(f) Permanent residence granted to the alien applicant (by the Immigration officer) upon his/her entry into the United States at the port of entry, upon the alien's presentation of an immigrant visa

§ 19.70 The Green Card and Its Limitations

Obtaining permanent residence in the U.S. does allow the individual to live in the U.S. permanently and obtain almost all kinds of employment with protection against discrimination.[1] However, it is not an absolute right of residence and abode. Permanent residents are subject to deportation[2] and can be excluded from the U.S.[3] on substantive grounds or for abandoning their residence in this country.[4] Others, as will be discussed below at Sections 19.72 to 19.73, are granted residence on an interim or "conditional" basis subject to subsequent conditions.

The ultimate goal of many permanent residents in the U.S. is to obtain U.S. citizenship through naturalization,[5] but permanent residents are not required to apply for U.S. citizenship if they choose not to.

Library References:
West's Key No. Digests, Aliens ⚖=44, 51.5.

§ 19.71 The Green Card and Its Limitations—Conditional Residence

Permanent resident status, while generally considered to be of indefinite duration, is limited in certain circumstances. The limitation is imposed initially for purposes of assuring the *bona fides* of the application, and subsequently to assure the continued viability of eligibility to maintain such status. Specifically, conditional resident status is granted to certain aliens who become permanent residents based upon marriage to a U.S. citizen or permanent resident alien.[1] Conditional resident status is also imposed upon employment creation fifth preference visa holders, with the intent to deter fraud by investors who do not intend to maintain an ongoing, employment-creating enterprise once they have become permanent residents.[2] Outlined below are some of the more significant features of this status, and the special requirements applied by U.S. immigration laws to conditional residence obtained through marriage and the fifth employment–based preference category.[3]

§ 19.70

1. INA § 274B; 8 U.S.C.A. § 1324b.

2. *See* INA § 241; 8 U.S.C.A. § 1251.

3. INA § 212; 8 U.S.C.A. § 1182.

4. INA § 212(a)(7); 8 U.S.C.A. 1182(a)(7). *See* 8 C.F.R. § 211.1.

5. INA §§ 310—322; 8 U.S.C.A. §§ 1421—1433.

§ 19.71

1. INA § 216; 8 U.S.C.A. § 1186a, added by Sec. 2(a), Act of Nov. 10, 1986, Pub. L.No. 99–639, 100 Stat. 3537.

2. INA § 216A; 8 U.S.C.A. § 1186b.

3. Other programs in the past have provided for a "temporary" green card. Specifically, the legalization program under Section 245A of INA, 8 U.S.C.A. § 1255a, provides for adjustment of status to permanent residence for aliens continuously residing illegally in the U.S. prior to January 1, 1982. Adjustment to permanent residence was granted in two stages. Under the first stage, undocumented aliens eligible for the program could obtain temporary residence for a period of 18 months and, after the 18 month period, could convert their status to permanent residence.

Another program utilizing conditional resident status involved granting temporary resident status to special agricultural workers. In order to qualify, aliens were required to evidence that they possessed the requisite number of days in seasonal agricultural work to merit temporary resident status. INA § 210; 8 U.S.C.A. § 1160.

§ 19.72 The Green Card and Its Limitations—Conditional Residence—Marriage Cases, Removal of Condition

The purpose of the Immigration Marriage Fraud Amendment ("IMFA") of 1986 (Marriage Fraud Act)[1] is to assure that marriages entered into by aliens and U.S. citizens or permanent residents were *bona fide* at the time of creation of the marriage and were not solely entered into for immigration purposes. Conditional resident status is granted only to those aliens married for a period of less than two years at the time permanent resident status is conferred.[2] The conditional basis of this status can be removed either by filing a joint petition during the 90 day period preceding the two-year anniversary of the alien's attaining conditional residence, or by waiver if the joint petition cannot be filed. This petition process provides the INS with a second opportunity to examine the *bona fides* of the marriage.[3]

Aliens becoming permanent residents based on marriage to a U.S. citizen are complete permanent residents in most respects in that they are entitled to work in the U.S. without limitation, permitted to travel freely in and out of the country with their Alien Registration Receipt Cards, and the time they spend as "conditional" permanent residents counts towards the residence and physical presence requirements for naturalization purposes as U.S. citizens.[4] The IMFA limits the permanent residence of these aliens only with respect to the fact that their residence is subject to termination if certain events occur within two years of the grant of residence, and they are required to petition to remove the conditional aspect of their resident status after a two-year conditional period.[5]

The conditional status provisions of the Marriage Fraud Act also cover children from a prior marriage of an alien spouse who is married to a permanent resident. These children are eligible to immigrate as "derivative" immigrants of the sponsoring spouse.[6] Alien children from prior marriages cannot become permanent residents derivatively through the marriage of their parent to a U.S. citizen, since no derivative status is provided under the Act for immediate relatives of citizens.[7]

A conditional resident alien married to a U.S. citizen may petition for unmarried sons or daughters who would be eligible to immigrate as second preference beneficiaries of a conditional resident spouse. As

§ 19.72
1. INA § 216; 8 U.S.C.A. § 1186a.
2. INA § 216(g)(1)(C); 8 U.S.C.A. § 1186a(g)(1)(C).
3. 8 C.F.R. § 216.2(b).
4. INA § 216(e); 8 U.S.C.A. § 1186a(e).
5. 8 C.F.R. § 216.3(a).
6. 8 C.F.R. § 216.4(a)(2).
7. *Id.*

second preference beneficiaries, these children will probably avoid conditional status altogether because of the considerable waiting periods to obtain an immigrant visa in the second preference category. By the time they are ready to apply for an immigrant visa or adjustment of status, the parent's conditional resident status will have been removed and therefore conditional status will not be imposed on the children.

The date for determining whether an alien spouse is a conditional resident is not the date on which the petition and supporting documentation are filed with the INS or consular office abroad, but the date on which the alien is actually accorded permanent resident status. On the date that permanent resident status is granted, the alien will only be subject to conditional resident status if the alien's marriage occurred within two years prior to the date of grant of residence.[8]

The law also requires that the Attorney General notify the conditional immigrant that his status remains conditional for a two-year period and that he will lose resident status unless he applies for removal of the condition within 90 days before the termination of the two-year conditional period.[9] The INS officer or consular official who interviews the alien granted conditional resident status will notify the alien at the time of the interview and in writing that his or her resident status is "conditional."

Further, the Attorney General is authorized to terminate conditional resident status within the two-year period if he determines that the qualifying marriage was entered into for the purpose of procuring the alien's entry as an immigrant;[10] or that the qualifying marriage has been annulled or terminated, other than through death of a spouse;[11] or that a fee or other consideration was given for the filing of the petition (other than an attorney's fee for assistance in preparing it).[12]

While the statute does not prescribe specific procedures for termination of conditional residence, it does state that the Attorney General must notify the parties involved of his or her decision to terminate conditional resident status.[13] This procedure is described in detail in the INS regulations. Termination is accomplished through a formal written notice to a conditional entrant. Prior to issuing a "Notice of Termination," the INS Director must provide the alien with an opportunity to

8. PRACTICE POINTER: The day upon which permanent residence will actually be granted will be one of two dates: the date on which an alien is admitted to the U.S. upon receipt of an immigrant visa issued at a U.S. Consulate outside of the country, or the date on which an adjustment of status application is approved at an INS office in the U.S.

9. INA § 216(d)(2)(A); 8 U.S.C.A. § 1186a(d)(2)(A), added by Sec. 2(a) of the 1986 Act, note 1, 8 C.F.R. § 216.2.

10. INA § 216(b)(1)(A)(i); 8 U.S.C.A. § 1186a(b)(1)(A)(i).

11. INA § 216(b)(1)(A)(ii); 8 U.S.C.A. § 1186a(b)(1)(A)(ii).

12. INA § 216(b)(1)(B); 8 U.S.C.A. § 1186a(b)(1)(B).

13. INA § 216(b)(1); 8 U.S.C.A. § 1186a(b)(1).

review and rebut evidence upon which his proposed decision is based.[14] Termination of such status, also terminates all rights and privileges of the conditional resident status including the authorization to accept and continue employment in the U.S.[15]

Individuals granted conditional resident status are required to jointly submit a petition to the Attorney General within 90 days prior to the end of the 24-month period attesting to the fact that they have remained married.[16] Where the parties to a good faith marriage are divorced or separated, Congress permits an alien spouse to file, within the two-year period, an application for removal of conditions to resident status through waiver of the application for a joint petition.[17] Failure to file a petition or waiver application or to appear (without good cause) for any required personal interview as mandated by the INS may result in the termination of the permanent resident's status as of the date of the second anniversary of the alien's lawful admission for permanent residence.[18] Late filings of the petition or waiver application will only be accepted when the alien establishes good cause and extenuating circumstances for the delinquency.[19] A timely filing of a joint petition or waiver application, however, will extend the conditional residence until the joint petition or the waiver application is finally approved.[20]

Where a joint petition is not filed because parties are separated or contemplating divorce, they may file a joint petition if they later become reconciled and request that the late filing be forgiven as a reasonable excuse.[21] However, no bar is imposed on the filing of a joint petition by parties who are separated.[22]

When a petition for removal of conditional resident status is properly filed and parties appear for any required interview that the Attorney General may schedule, he is required to make a decision within 90 days of the date of the interview either granting removal of the condition,[23] effective as of the day of the second anniversary of the conditional approval of lawful permanent residence, or where negative information is elicited during the interview process, the INS examiner must offer the

---

14. 8 C.F.R. § 216.3(a).
15. Id.
16. INA § 216(c)(1); 8 U.S.C.A. § 1186a(c)(1); 8 C.F.R. §§ 216.4, 216.5.
17. Note that the joint petition may be filed at any time prior to the expiration of the two-year period to apply for removal of the condition where a waiver is being requested due to the changed circumstance of the marriage. For example, when a citizen spouse dies before a joint petition can be submitted, an alien spouse may file a waiver application immediately thereafter.
18. INA § 216(c)(2); 8 U.S.C.A. § 1186a(c)(2); 8 C.F.R. § 216.4(a)(6).
19. INA § 216(d)(2); 8 U.S.C.A. § 1186a(d)(2).
20. See 66 Int.Rel. 925 (1989), describing procedures to be followed where parties have reconciled after a waiver application is filed.
21. Id.
22. See 67 Int.Rel. 430 (1990) (citizen spouse in jail on criminal charges; joint petition for removal may be submitted by an alien spouse).
23. INA § 216(c)(3)(B); 8 U.S.C.A. § 1186a(c)(3)(B).

parties an opportunity to rebut such information and the Director may deny the petition, providing reasons for denial and issuing an Order to Show Cause in Deportation Proceedings.[24]

In certain cases, Congress has provided for removal of the conditional resident status through discretionary waivers of the requirement for a joint petition where an alien can demonstrate that extreme hardship will result if the alien is deported, or the qualifying marriage was entered into in good faith by the alien spouse but the qualifying marriage has been terminated (other than through death of the spouse) and the alien is not at fault in failing to meet the requirements of filing a joint petition.[25] Waivers are also granted in cases where it is determined that the qualifying marriage was entered into in good faith by the alien spouse and during the marriage, the spouse or child was battered by or was the subject of extreme cruelty perpetrated by his or her spouse or citizen or permanent resident parent and the alien was not at fault in failing to meet the requirements of filing a joint petition.[26] In such cases, the Attorney General is required to consider factors provided by the alien spouse in granting removal of conditional residence based upon the request for waiver considering the above factors. Where a waiver is sought on the basis of extreme hardship, the alien is required to submit documentation in support of his or her request, and an interview may be held to determine the *bona fides* of the application filed by the resident alien.[27]

When a joint petition or waiver of the joint filing of a petition filed by a conditional resident is approved by the INS, the INS will notify the alien of its decision and will require the alien to report to a local district INS office for the processing of a new Alien Registration Receipt Card (Green Card), at which time the alien will surrender the old green card noted with the original termination date.[28]

When a petition is denied by the INS, an alien will receive notice of the decision and of the reasons for denial. The alien may request review of the INS decision in deportation proceedings.[29] In such proceedings, the burden of proof will be on the INS to establish, "by a preponderance of the evidence," that the petition was correctly denied.[30] Further, penalties may be assessed against U.S. citizens and aliens for violations of the Marriage Fraud Act. Individuals who knowingly enter into a marriage to evade provisions of the immigration laws may be imprisoned for up to five years and fined up to $250,000.[31] In addition, an immigrant visa petition may not be subsequently approved on behalf of an alien who has attempted or conspired to enter into a marriage for purposes of evading

24. 8 C.F.R. § 216.4(c), 216.4(d)(2).
25. 8 C.F.R. § 216.5.
26. 8 C.F.R. § 216.5(e)(3).
27. 8 C.F.R. § 216.5(d).
28. 8 C.F.R. §§ 216.4(d)(1), 216.5(f).
29. 8 C.F.R. §§ 216.4(d)(2), 216.5(f).
30. 8 C.F.R. § 216.4(d)(2); INA § 216(b)(2); 8 U.S.C.A. § 1186a(b)(2).
31. INA § 275(b); 8 U.S.C.A. § 1325(b).

immigration laws, regardless of whether the alien received a benefit from the attempt or conspiracy.[32]

There are other provisions under the Marriage Fraud Act designed to combat sham marriages. The INS cannot approve spousal second preference petitions of permanent residents who have been accorded their status based on a prior marriage unless a period of five years has elapsed after the petitioning alien acquired permanent resident status.[33] The alien, however, may establish through "clear and convincing evidence" that the prior marriage was not entered into for the purpose of evading immigration laws; or the prior marriage was terminated through the death of the petitioner's spouse.[34] This provision of law is designed to prevent an alien from utilizing his or her resident status to file spousal Second Preference petitions when the petitioning alien's status is based on a marriage entered into to evade the immigration laws. The burden of proof is on the petitioning alien to establish that a prior marriage was entered into in "good faith."

The INS is also required to reject a marriage-based petition and adjustment of status petition filed by a U.S. citizen or permanent resident on behalf of an alien spouse where a marriage occurred after November 10, 1986 and while the alien was either in deportation or exclusion proceedings or in judicial proceedings relating to the review of a deportation or exclusion order.[35]

Sons and daughters granted conditional residence must follow the same steps for removal of the conditions as their alien parent. Sons or daughters may be included in the application of the parent if the son or daughter was admitted to permanent resident classification concurrently with the alien spouse. The son or daughter is considered to have obtained residence concurrently if he or she obtained it on the same day or within 90 days of the alien spouse. Where a son or daughter was not admitted to permanent residence concurrently, then he or she must file an application for a waiver of the requirement to file a joint petition.[36] That application will be approved routinely as long as the alien spouse's joint petition or waiver application is approved by the INS.

Joint petitions filed by alien spouse and U.S. citizen petitioners are filed with one of the Regional Service Centers of the INS in California, Vermont, Nebraska or Texas.[37] The joint petition to remove the conditional basis of the alien's permanent resident status (Form I–751) is submitted to the Service Center with supporting documentation evidencing maintenance of marital status and the appropriate filing fee.

32. 8 C.F.R. § 204.2(a)(1)(ii).
33. 8 C.F.R. § 204.2(a)(1)(i).
34. 8 C.F.R. § 204.2(a)(1)(i)(A)(2).
35. INA § 204(h); 8 U.S.C.A. § 1154(h), added by Sec. 5(d) of 1986 Act.
36. 8 C.F.R. § 216.4(a)(2).
37. *See supra*, § 19.29, note 1, for addresses of all Regional Service Centers.

§ 19.73 The Green Card and Its Limitations—Conditional Residence—Immigrant Investors, Removal of Condition

In order to deter fraud by investors who do not intend to maintain an ongoing, employment-creating enterprise once they have become permanent residents, the INA has imposed the status of conditional resident upon such investors. Similar to the spouse of citizens and residents granted resident status subject to conditional provisions, the immigrant investor is required to file, within 90 days prior to the two-year anniversary date of receiving initial conditional resident status, a petition to remove such conditional resident status.[1]

In the petition, the alien investor must establish that he or she has complied with conditions of the investor program. Petitions should be filed with the INS Service Center having jurisdiction over the commercial enterprise.[2] The alien investor must provide evidence and documentation proving that the commercial enterprise was actually established by the alien; the alien invested or was actively in the process of investing the required capital; the alien sustained the enterprise and his investment in it throughout the period of conditional permanent resident status; the alien created or can be expected to create within a reasonable time ten full-time jobs for U.S. citizens, permanent residents or other immigrants lawfully authorized to work in the U.S.; and the commercial enterprise maintained the number of employees at no less than the pre-investment levels in the case of an alien who invested in a troubled business.[3] The petition, Form I-829, is filed by the investor with one of the four Regional Service Centers located throughout the country.[4]

The INS may request that the alien investor be interviewed within 90 days after the filing of a petition, but an interview requirement may be waived at the discretion of the INS.[5]

To petition to remove conditional resident status, an application is filed by the investor within 90 days prior to the two-year anniversary of the grant of residence.[6] Accompanying the petition form INS Form I-829, are the alien registration receipt cards of the investor and family members and supporting documentation as enumerated above as well as the appropriate filing fee.

Residence may be terminated if the INS determines during the two-year conditional period that:

§ 19.73

1. INA § 216A(a)(1); 8 U.S.C.A. § 1186b(a)(1).
2. 8 C.F.R. § 216.6(a)(2).
3. 8 C.F.R. § 216.6(a)(4).
4. 8 C.F.R. § 216.6(b)(1). See supra, § 19.29, note 1, for addresses of all Regional Service Centers.
5. INA § 216A(d)(3); 8 U.S.C.A. § 1186b(d)(3).
6. INA § 216A(c)(1); 8 U.S.C.A. § 1186(c)(1).

§ 19.73   IMMIGRATION AND NATIONALITY LAW   Ch. 19

- the new commercial enterprise was established for the sole purpose of evading U.S. immigration laws;
- the new commercial enterprise in fact was not established;
- the alien did not invest or was not in the process of investing the prescribed capital; or
- the alien was not sustaining the new commercial enterprise or the investment of capital as required.[7]

In addition, the INS may terminate conditional resident status where an alien investor fails to file the required petition for removal of conditional status within the 90 day period, as enumerated above.[8]

When the INS determines that it would be appropriate to interview an alien investor to assure his continued qualification for permanent resident status, the immigrant investor would be well advised to be armed with documentation establishing his eligibility for permanent resident status and the continued viability of his commercial enterprise. Upon granting of permanent resident status, within 90 days of the date of the filing or within 90 days of the date of a required interview,[9] the alien investor and family members included in the petition will be advised by the INS to report to a district office for processing of a new green card. Where derogatory information is uncovered during the interview process, the alien investor will be afforded an opportunity to rebut information prior to a final decision by the INS on the petition.[10] Where the alien investor fails to adequately rebut the information, the INS will deny the petition, terminate the alien's resident status and conditional resident status of family members and issue an Order to Show Cause commencing deportation proceedings. A review of the denial may be brought in deportation proceedings.[11]

§ 19.74   The Green Card and Its Limitations—Unconditional Permanent Residence

A permanent resident of the U.S. who is not subject to special conditions and limitations may still lose status as a permanent resident if he or she does not live here permanently. Simply having a "green card" in one's possession does not entitle an individual to maintain status as a permanent resident. An individual who lives outside of the U.S. and briefly reenters on a yearly basis will lose that status.[1]

The rights and obligations of an individual granted permanent residence in the U.S. described below are applicable as long as one

7. 8 C.F.R. § 216.3(a).
8. 8 C.F.R. § 216.6(a)(5).
9. 8 C.F.R. § 216.6(c)(1).
10. 8 C.F.R. § 216.6(c)(2).
11. 8 C.F.R. § 216.3.

§ 19.74

1. See Alvarez v. INS, 539 F.2d 1220 (9th Cir.1976).

Ch. 19 UNCONDITIONAL PERMANENT RESIDENCE § 19.74

maintains "an unrelinquished lawful permanent residence in the United States."[2]

A permanent resident of the United States is presumed to be a "resident" for purposes of tax classification and is required to file a 1040 Resident Return.[3] This does not preclude the possibility of claiming the "non-resident" deduction for overseas employment, which schedule is submitted in conjunction with a resident 1040 return.[4]

A permanent resident is required to keep in his possession at all times Form I–551 (the so-called "green card").[5] The card is considered a valid document for purposes of re-entry into the United States if it is used within one year of the last departure and the applicant is returning from "a temporary absence abroad" to "an unrelinquished lawful permanent residence in the United States."[6] The Immigration Examiner may inquire of the applicant and examine the documentation to determine if these are in fact the circumstances.

A permanent resident alien who reaches 14 years of age must within 30 days of his or her 14th birthday apply for a new green card, making application at the INS local office with jurisdiction over the alien's place of residence.[7]

In accordance with Section 211(a)(7) of the Immigration and Nationality Act (8 U.S.C.A. 1181(a)), an immigrant seeking admission to the United States will be excluded if he is not in possession of a valid immigrant visa or other valid entry document. In accordance with Section 211(b) of the Act, those documentary requirements may be waived for one who can qualify as a "returning resident immigrant," who is defined as an immigrant lawfully admitted for permanent residence who is returning from a temporary visit abroad.

If the request for entry into the United States is made within the year, the applicant need present only his passport and "green card" (unless he is returning from Canada or Mexico, in which case a green card alone is sufficient). In addition, he must establish that he is in fact a "returning" resident who has not abandoned such residence. Factors considered are:

- duration of absence from the United States;
- purpose of absence from the United States;
- location of family ties;
- location of property holdings, employment, etc.; and

2. 8 C.F.R. § 211.1; See INA § 101(a)(33); 8 U.S.C.A. § 1101(a)(33).

3. 26 U.S.C.A. § 7701(b). See IRS Publication 519 (Rev. 1995); see also Chapter 35 "Income Tax," infra.

4. 26 U.S.C.A. § 911.

5. INA § 264(e); 8 U.S.C.A. § 1304(e).

6. 8 C.F.R. § 211.1(b).

7. 8 C.F.R. § 264.1(g).

- the actual intention of the alien with respect to both location of his actual home and the anticipated length of his excursion.

The key factor in militating against an inference that an alien's lawful permanent residence status has been abandoned is a showing that the alien has a definite reason for proceeding abroad, that the visit abroad was expected to end within a relatively short period, fixed by some early event, and that the alien has held a continuing intention to return to the United States as a place of employment or business or as an actual home.[8]

When one anticipates being outside of the United States continuously for longer than a year, it is appropriate to obtain a Re–Entry Permit for presentation upon seeking entry into the United States, which will be permitted within the two year validity period of the Re–Entry Permit.[9]

Whether the returning resident presents a green card within one year or a Re–Entry Permit within two years, the Immigration Examiner at the port of entry has a right to question the applicant and determine whether the applicant does in fact qualify as a returning resident.

The rules, regulations and procedures leading to obtaining permanent residence in the U.S. are complex. It comes as a surprise to many person that the rules governing preservation and maintenance of permanent residence can be equally complex. The practitioner's responsibility to the client, which begins on the day the client enters his or her office seeking advice on becoming a permanent resident, continues throughout the process and continues even beyond the date when permanent residence is granted and the coveted "green card" is issued.

§ 19.75 Forms

There are literally dozens upon dozens of forms in use which are applicable to immigration practice. Relevant lists of forms in use can be found in the regulations[1] and a number of private publications provide a collection of relevant forms for information and use.[2]

Following are the so-called "work horses" of immigration practice:

- *Form I–130*, used for immediate relative and family preference petitions discussed, *supra*, in Sections 19.10 through 19.13 and specifically analyzed in Section 19.14;

- *Form I–140*, used for most employment preference petitions, which are discussed, *supra*, in Sections 19.17 through 19.28 and specifically referenced in Section 19.29;

---

8. Matter of Kane, 15 I & N Dec. 258 (BIA 1975).

9. INA § 223; 8 U.S.C.A. § 1203. *See also* 8 C.F.R. § 223.1.

§ 19.75

1. 8 C.F.R. § 299.1.

2. INS Forms Book, 3rd Ed., AILA Publications 1995.

- *Form I–485*, the application for adjustment of status, which topic is discussed, *supra*, in Sections 19.57 through 19.62; and

- *Form OF–230*, used in the process of applying for an immigrant visa, which topic is discussed, *supra*, in Sections 19.53 through 19.56.

Library References:

West's Key No. Digests, Aliens ⊚=44.

§ 19.76 Forms—Form I-130

U.S. Department of Justice
Immigration and Naturalization Service (INS)

Petition for Alien Relative

Instructions

Read the instructions carefully. If you do not follow the instructions, we may have to return your petition, which may delay final action. If more space is needed to complete an answer continue on separate sheet of paper.

1. **Who can file?**
   A citizen or lawful permanent resident of the United States can file this form to establish the relationship of certain alien relatives who may wish to immigrate to the United States. You must file a separate form for each eligible relative.

2. **For whom can you file?**
   A. If you are a citizen, you may file this form for:
      1) your husband, wife, or unmarried child under 21 years old
      2) your unmarried child over 21, or married child of any age
      3) your brother or sister if you are at least 21 years old
      4) your parent if you are at least 21 years old.
   B. If you are a lawful permanent resident you may file this form for:
      1) your husband or wife
      2) your unmarried child

   Note: If your relative qualifies under instruction A(2) or A(3) above, separate petitions are not required for his or her husband or wife or unmarried children under 21 years old. If your relative qualifies under instruction B(2) above, separate petitions are not required for his or her unmarried children under 21 years old. These persons will be able to apply for the same type of immigrant visa as your relative.

3. **For whom can you not file?**
   Your cannot file for people in the following categories:
   A. An adoptive parent or adopted child, if the adoption took place after the child became 16 years old, or if the child has not been in the legal custody and living with the parent(s) for at least two years.
   B. A natural parent if the United States citizen son or daughter gained permanent residence through adoption.
   C. A stepparent or stepchild, if the marriage that created this relationship took place after the child became 18 years old.
   D. A husband or wife, if your were not both physically present at the marriage ceremony, and the marriage was not consummated.
   E. A husband or wife if you gained lawful permanent resident status by virtue of a prior marriage to a United States citizen or lawful permanent resident unless:
      1) a period of five years has elapsed since you became a lawful permanent resident; OR
      2) you can establish by clear and convincing evidence that the prior marriage (through which you gained your immigrant status) was not entered into for the purpose of evading any provision of the immigration laws; OR
      3) your prior marriage (through which you gained your immigrant status) was terminated by the death of your former spouse.
   F. A husband or wife if he or she was in exclusion, deportation, rescission, or judicial proceedings regarding his or her right to remain in the United States when the marriage took place, unless such spouse has resided outside the United States for a two-year period after the date of the marriage.
   G. A husband or wife if the Attorney General has determined that such alien has attempted or conspired to enter into a marriage for the purpose of evading the immigration laws.
   H. A grandparent, grandchild, nephew, niece, uncle, aunt, cousin, or in-law.

4. **What documents do your need?**
   You must give INS certain documents with this form to prove you are eligible to file. You must also give the INS certain documents to prove the family relationship between you and your relative.
   A. For each document needed, give INS the original and one copy. However, because it is against the law to copy a Certificate of Naturalization, a Certificate of Citizenship or an Alien Registration Receipt Card (Form I-151 or I-551) give INS the original only. **Originals will be returned to you.**
   B. If you do not wish to give INS the original document, you may give INS a copy. The copy must be certified by:
      1) an INS or U.S. consular officer, or
      2) an attorney admitted to practice law in the United States, or
      3) an INS accredited representative (INS may still require originals).
   C. Documents in a foreign language must be accompanied by a complete English translation. The translator must certify that the translation is accurate and that he or she is competent to translate.

5. **What documents do you need to show you are a United States citizen?**
   A. If you were born in the United States, give INS your birth certificate.
   B. If you were naturalized, give INS your original Certificate of Naturalization.
   C. If you were born outside the United States, and you are a U.S. citizen through your parents, give INS:
      1) your original Certificate of Citizenship, or
      2) your Form FS-240 (Report of Birth Abroad of a United States Citizen).
   D. In place of any of the above, you may give INS your valid unexpired U.S. passport that was initially issued for at least 5 years.
   E. If you do not have any of the above and were born in the United States, see instruction under 8 below. *"What if a document is not available?"*

6. **What documents do you need to show you are a permanent resident?**
   You must give INS your alien registration receipt card (Form I-151 or Form I-551). Do not give INS a photocopy of the card.

7. **What documents do you need to prove family relationship?**
   You have to prove that there is a family relationship between your relative and yourself.

   In any case where a marriage certificate is required, if either the husband or wife was married before, you must give INS documents to show that all previous marriages were legally ended. In cases where the names shown on the supporting documents have changed, give INS legal documents to show how the name change occurred (for example a marriage certificate, adoption decree, court order, etc.)

   Find the paragraph in the following list that applies to the relative for whom you are filing.

Form I-130 (Rev. 4/11 '91) Y

FORMS—FORM I-130 § 19.76

If you are filing for your:

A. **husband or wife**, give INS
   1) your marriage certificate
   2) a color photo of you and one of your husband or wife, taken within 30 days of the date of this petition. These photos must have a white background. They must be glossy, unretouched, and not mounted. The dimension of the facial image should be about 1 inch from chin to top of hair in 3/4 frontal view, showing the right side of the face with the right ear visible. Using pencil or felt pen, lightly print name (and Alien Registration Number, if known) on the back of each photograph.
   3) a completed and signed G-325A (Biographic Information) for you and one for your husband or wife. Except for name and signature, you do not have to repeat on the G-325A the information given on your I-130 petition.

B. **child** and you are the **mother**, give the child's birth certificate showing your name and the name of your child.

C. **child** and you are the **father or stepparent**, give the child's birth certificate showing both parents' names and your marriage certificate. **Child** born out of wedlock and you are the **father**, give proof that a parent/child relationship exists or existed. For example, the child's birth certificate showing your name and evidence that you have financially supported the child. (A blood test may be necessary).

D. **brother or sister**, your birth certificate and the birth certificate of your brother or sister showing both parents' names. If you do not have the same mother, you must also give the marriage certificates of your father to both mothers.

E. **mother**, give your birth certificate showing your name and the name of your mother.

F. **father**, give your birth certificate showing the names of both parents and your parents' marriage certificate.

G. **stepparent**, give your birth certificate showing the names of both natural parents and the marriage certificate of your parent to your stepparent.

H. **adoptive parent or adopted child**, give a certified copy of the adoption decree, the legal custody decree if you obtained custody of the child before adoption, and a statement showing the dates and places you have lived together with the child.

8. **What if a document is not available?**
If the documents needed above are not available, you can give INS the following instead. (INS may require a statement from the appropriate civil authority certifying that the needed document is not available.)

   A. Church record: A certificate under the seal of the church where the baptism, dedication, or comparable rite occurred within two months after birth, showing the date and place of child's birth, date of the religious ceremony, and the names of the child's parents.

   B. School record: A letter from the authorities of the school attended (preferably the first school), showing the date of admission to the school, child's date and place of birth, and the names and places of birth parents, if shown in the school records.

   C. Census record: State or federal census record showing the names, place of birth, and date of birth or the age of the person listed.

   D. Affidavits: Written statements sworn to or affirmed by two persons who were living at the time and who have personal knowledge of the event you are trying to prove; for example, the date and place of birth, marriage, or death. The persons making the affidavits need not be citizens of the United States. Each affidavit should contain the following information regarding the person making the affidavit: his or her full name, address, date and place of birth, and his or her relationship to you, if any; full information concerning the event; and complete details concerning how the person acquired knowledge of the event.

9. **How should you prepare this form?**
   A. Type or print legibly in ink.
   B. If you need extra space to complete any item, attach a continuation sheet, indicate the item number, and date and sign each sheet.
   C. Answer all questions fully and accurately. If any item does not apply, please write "N/A".

10. **Where should you file this form?**
    A. If you live in the United States, send or take the form to the INS office that has jurisdiction over where you live.
    B. If you live outside the United States, contact the nearest American Consulate to find out where to send or take the completed form.

11. **What is the fee?**
You must pay seventy five dollars ($75.00) to file this form. **The fee will not be refunded, whether the petition is approved or not.** DO NOT MAIL CASH. All checks or money orders, whether U.S. or foreign, must be payable in U.S. currency at a financial institution in the United States. When a check is drawn on the account of a person other than yourself, write your name on the face of the check. If the check is not honored, INS will charge you $5.00.

Pay by check or money order in the exact amount. Make the check or money order payable to "Immigration and Naturalization Service". However,

   A. if you live in Guam. Make the check or money order payable to "Treasurer, Guam", or
   B. if you live in the U.S. Virgin Islands. Make the check or money order payable to "Commissioner of Finance of the Virgin Islands".

12. **When will a visa become available?**
When a petition is approved for the husband, wife, parent, or unmarried minor child of a United States citizen, these relatives do not have to wait for a visa number, as they are not subject to the immigrant visa limit. However, for a child to qualify for this category, all processing must be completed and the child must enter the United States before his or her 21st birthday.

For all other alien relatives there are only a limited number of immigrant visas each year. The visas are given out in the order in which INS receives properly filed petitions. To be considered properly filed, a petition must be completed accurately and signed, the required documents must be attached, and the fee must be paid.

For a monthly update on the dates for which immigrant visas are available, you may call (202) 647-0508.

13. **What are the penalties for committing marriage fraud or submitting false information or both?**
Title 8, United States Code, Section 1325 states that any individual who knowingly enters into a marriage contract for the purpose of evading any provision of the immigration laws shall be imprisoned for not more than five years, or fined not more than $250,000.00 or both.

Title 18, United States Code, Section 1001 states that whoever willfully and knowingly falsifies a material fact, makes a false statement, or makes use of a false document will be fined up to $10,000 or imprisoned up to five years, or both.

14. **What is our authority for collecting this information?**
We request the information on the form to carry out the immigration laws contained in Title 8, United States Code, Section 1154(a). We need this information to determine whether a person is eligible for immigration benefits. The information you provide may also be disclosed to other federal, state, local, and foreign law enforcement and regulatory agencies during the course of the investigation required by this Service. You do not have to give this information. However, if you refuse to give some or all of it, your petition may be denied.

15. **Reporting Burden.**
Public reporting burden for this collection of information is estimated to average 30 minutes per response, including the time for reviewing instructions, searching existing data sources, gathering and maintaining the data needed, and completing and reviewing the collection of information. Send comments regarding this burden estimate or any other aspect of this collection of information, including suggestions for reducing this burden, to: U.S. Department of Justice, Immigration and Naturalization Service (Room 5304), Washington, D.C. 20536, and to the Office of Management and Budget, Paperwork Reduction Project, **OMB No. 1115-0054**, Washington, D.C. 20503.

It is not possible to cover all the conditions for **eligibility** or to give **instructions** for **every** situation. If you have carefully read all the instructions and still have questions, **please contact your nearest INS** office.

§ 19.76 IMMIGRATION AND NATIONALITY LAW Ch. 19

U.S. Department of Justice
Immigration and Naturalization Service (INS)

OMB #1115-0054
Petition for Alien Relative

DO NOT WRITE IN THIS BLOCK - FOR EXAMINING OFFICE ONLY

Case ID#

A#

G-28 or Volag #

Section of Law
- ☐ 201 (b) spouse   ☐ 203 (a)(1)
- ☐ 201 (b) child   ☐ 203 (a)(2)
- ☐ 201 (b) parent   ☐ 203 (a)(4)
- ☐ 203 (a)(5)

AM CON:

Action Stamp

Fee Stamp

Petition was filed on: _____ (priority date)
- ☐ Personal Interview   ☐ Previously Forwarded
- ☐ Pet ☐ Ben. "A" File Reviewed ☐ Stateside Criteria
- ☐ Field Investigations   ☐ I-485 Simultaneously
- ☐ 204 (a)(2)(A) Resolved   ☐ 204 (h) Resolved

Remarks:

A. Relationship

1. The alien relative is my
   ☐ Husband/Wife ☐ Parent ☐ Brother/Sister ☐ Child
2. Are you related by adoption? ☐ Yes ☐ No
3. Did you gain permanent residence through adoption? ☐ Yes ☐ No

B. Information about you

1. Name (Family name in CAPS) (First) (Middle)
2. Address (Number and Street) (Apartment Number)
   (Town or City) (State/Country) (ZIP/Postal Code)
3. Place of Birth (Town or City) (State/Country)
4. Date of Birth (Mo/Day/Yr)
5. Sex ☐ Male ☐ Female
6. Marital Status ☐ Married ☐ Single ☐ Widowed ☐ Divorced
7. Other Names Used (including maiden name)
8. Date and Place of Present Marriage (if married)
9. Social Security Number
10. Alien Registration Number (if any)
11. Names of Prior Husbands/Wives
12. Date(s) Marriages(s) Ended

13. If you are a U.S. citizen, complete the following:
    My citizenship was acquired through (check one)
    ☐ Birth in the U.S.
    ☐ Naturalization (Give number of certificate, date and place it was issued)
    ☐ Parents
    Have you obtained a certificate of citizenship in your own name?
    ☐ Yes ☐ No
    If "Yes", give number of certificate, date and place it was issued

14a. If you are a lawful permanent resident alien, complete the following:
    Date and place of admission for, or adjustment to, lawful permanent residence, and class of admission

14b. Did you gain permanent resident status through marriage to a United States citizen or lawful permanent resident? ☐ Yes ☐ No

C. Information about your alien relative

1. Name (Family name in CAPS) (First) (Middle)
2. Address (Number and Street) (Apartment Number)
   (Town or City) (State/Country) (ZIP/Postal Code)
3. Place of Birth (Town or City) (State/Country)
4. Date of Birth (Mo/Day/Yr)
5. Sex ☐ Male ☐ Female
6. Marital Status ☐ Married ☐ Single ☐ Widowed ☐ Divorced
7. Other Names Used (including maiden name)
8. Date and Place of Present Marriage (if married)
9. Social Security Number
10. Alien Registration Number (if any)
11. Names of Prior Husbands/Wives
12. Date(s) Marriages(s) Ended

13. Has your relative ever been in the U.S.? ☐ Yes ☐ No
14. If your relative is currently in the U.S., complete the following. He or she last arrived as a (visitor, student, stowaway, without inspection, etc.)
    Arrival/Departure Record (I-94) Number   Date arrived (Month/Day/Year)
    Date authorized stay expired, or will expire, as shown on Form I-94 or I-95

15. Name and address of present employer (if any)
    Date this employment began (Month/Day/Year)

16. Has your relative ever been under immigration proceedings?
    ☐ Yes ☐ No Where _____ When _____
    ☐ Exclusion ☐ Deportation ☐ Recission ☐ Judicial Proceedings

INITIAL RECEIPT	RESUBMITTED	RELOCATED		COMPLETED			
		Rec'd	Sent	Approved	Denied	Returned	

Form I-130 (Rev. 4/11/91) Y

840

C. (continued) Information about your alien relative

16. List husband/wife and all children of your relative (if your relative is your husband/wife, list only his or her children).

(Name)	(Relationship)	(Date of Birth)	(Country of Birth)

17. Address in the United States where your relative intends to live
(Number and Street)   (Town or City)   (State)

18. Your relative's address abroad
(Number and Street)   (Town or City)   (Province)   (Country)   (Phone Number)

19. If your relative's native alphabet is other than Roman letters, write his or her name and address abroad in the native alphabet:
(Name)   (Number and Street)   (Town or City)   (Province)   (Country)

20. If filing for your husband/wife, give last address at which you both lived together:
(Name) (Number and Street) (Town or City) (Province) (Country)   From (Month) (Year)   To (Month) (Year)

21. Check the appropriate box below and give the information required for the box you checked:

☐ Your relative will apply for a visa abroad at the American Consulate in _____ (City) _____ (Country)

☐ Your relative is in the United States and will apply for adjustment of status to that of a lawful permanent resident in the office of the Immigration and Naturalization Service at _____ (City) _____ (State) _____. If your relative is not eligible for adjustment of status, he or she will apply for a visa abroad at the American Consulate in _____ (City) _____ (Country)

(Designation of a consulate outside the country of your relative's last residence does not guarantee acceptance for processing by that consulate. Acceptance is at the discretion of the designated consulate.)

D. Other Information

1. If separate petitions are also being submitted for other relatives, give names of each and relationship.

2. Have you ever filed a petition for this or any other alien before? ☐ Yes ☐ No
If "Yes," give name, place and date of filing, and result.

Warning: The INS investigates claimed relationships and verifies the validity of documents. The INS seeks criminal prosecutions when family relationships are falsified to obtain visas.

Penalties: You may, by law be imprisoned for not more than five years, or fined $250,000, or both, for entering into a marriage contract for the purpose of evading any provision of the immigration laws and you may be fined up to $10,000 or imprisoned up to five years or both, for knowingly and willfully falsifying or concealing a material fact or using any false document in submitting this petition.

Your Certification: I certify, under penalty of perjury under the laws of the United States of America, that the foregoing is true and correct. Furthermore, I authorize the release of any information from my records which the Immigration and Naturalization Service needs to determine eligibility for the benefit that I am seeking.

Signature _____ Date _____ Phone Number _____

Signature of Person Preparing Form if Other than Above

I declare that I prepared this document at the request of the person above and that it is based on all information of which I have any knowledge

Print Name _____ (Address) _____ (Signature) _____ (Date) _____

G-28 ID Number _____

Volag Number _____

§ 19.76   IMMIGRATION AND NATIONALITY LAW   Ch. 19

NOTICE TO PERSONS FILING FOR SPOUSES IF MARRIED LESS THAN TWO YEARS

Pursuant to section 216 of the Immigration and Nationality Act, your alien spouse may be granted conditional permanent resident status in the United States as of the date he or she is admitted or adjusted to conditional status by an officer of the Immigration and Naturalization Service. Both you and your conditional permanent resident spouse are required to file a petition, Form I-751, Joint Petition to Remove Conditional Basis of Alien's Permanent Resident Status, during the ninety day period immediately before the second anniversary of the date your alien spouse was granted conditional permanent residence.

Otherwise, the rights, privileges, responsibilities and duties which apply to all other permanent residents apply equally to a conditional permanent resident. A conditional permanent resident is not limited to the right to apply for naturalization, to file petitions in behalf of qualifying relatives, or to reside permanently in the United States as an immigrant in accordance with the immigration laws.

Failure to file Form I-751, Joint Petition to Remove the Conditional Basis of Alien's Permanent Resident Status, will result in termination of permanent residence status and initiation of deportation proceedings.

NOTE: You must complete items 1 through 6 to assure that petition approval is recorded. Do not write in the section below item 6.

1. Name of relative (Family name in CAPS)   (First)   (Middle)
2. Other names used by relative (including maiden name)
3. Country of relative's birth   4. Date of relative's birth (Month/Day/Year)
5. Your name (Last name in CAPS) (First) (Middle)   6. Your phone number

Action Stamp

SECTION
☐ 201 (b)(spouse)
☐ 201 (b)(child)
☐ 201 (b)(parent)
☐ 203 (a)(1)
☐ 203 (a)(2)
☐ 203 (a)(4)
☐ 203 (a)(5)

DATE PETITION FILED

☐ STATESIDE CRITERIA GRANTED

SENT TO CONSUL AT:

CHECKLIST

Have you answered each question?
Have you signed the petition?
Have you enclosed:

☐ The filing fee for each petition?
☐ Proof of your citizenship or lawful permanent residence?
☐ All required supporting documents for each petition?

If you are filing for your husband or wife have you included:

☐ Your picture?
☐ His or her picture?
☐ Your G-325A?
☐ His or her G-325A?

Relative Petition Card
Form I-130A (Rev. 4/11/91) Y

§ 19.77 Forms—Form I-140

U.S. Department of Justice
Immigration and Naturalization Service

OMB No. 1115-0061
Immigrant Petition for Alien Worker

Purpose Of This Form.
This form is used to petition for an immigrant based on employment.

Who May File.
Any person may file this petition in behalf of an alien who:
- has extraordinary ability in the sciences, arts, education, business, or athletics, demonstrated by sustained national or international acclaim, whose achievements have been recognized in the field; or
- is claiming exceptional ability in the sciences, arts, or business, and is seeking an exemption of the requirement of a job offer in the national interest.

A U.S. employer may file this petition who wishes to employ:
- an outstanding professor or researcher, with at least 3 years of experience in teaching or research in the academic area, who is recognized internationally as outstanding;
  - in a tenured or tenure-track position at a university or institution of higher education to teach in the academic area,
  - in a comparable position at a university or institution of higher education to conduct research in the area, or
  - in a comparable position to conduct research for a private employer who employs at least 3 persons in full-time research activities and has achieved documented accomplishments in an academic field;
- an alien who, in the 3 years preceding the filing of this petition, has been employed for at least 1 year by a firm or corporation or other legal entity and who seeks to enter the U.S. to continue to render services to the same employer or to a subsidiary or affiliate in a capacity that is managerial or executive;
- a member of the professions holding an advanced degree or an alien with exceptional ability in the sciences, arts, or business who will substantially benefit the national economy, cultural or educational interests, or welfare of the U.S.;
- a skilled worker (requiring at least 2 years of specialized training or experience in the skill) to perform labor for which qualified workers are not available in the U.S.;
- a member of the professions with a baccalaureate degree; or
- an unskilled worker to perform labor for which qualified workers are not available in the U.S.

General Filing Instructions.
Please answer all questions by typing or clearly printing in black ink. Indicate that an item is not applicable with "N/A". If an answer to a question is "none," write "none". If you need extra space to answer any item, attach a sheet of paper with your name and your A#, if any, and indicate the number of the item to which the answer refers. You must file your petition with the required Initial Evidence. Your petition must be properly signed and filed with the correct fee.

Initial Evidence.
If you are filing for an alien of extraordinary ability in the sciences, arts, education, business, or athletics, you must file your petition with:
- evidence of a one-time achievement (i.e., a major, internationally-recognized award); or
- at least three of the following:
  - receipt of lesser nationally or internationally recognized prizes or awards for excellence in the field of endeavor;
  - membership in associations in the field which require outstanding achievements as judged by recognized national or international experts;
  - published material about the alien in professional or major trade publications or other major media;
  - participation on a panel or individually as a judge of the work of others in the field or an allied field;
  - original scientific, scholarly, artistic, athletic, or business-related contributions of major significance in the field;
  - authorship of scholarly articles in the field, in professional or major trade publications or other major media;
  - display of the alien's work at artistic exhibitions or showcases;
  - evidence that the alien has performed in a leading or critical role for organizations or establishments that have a distinguished reputation;
  - evidence that the alien has commanded a high salary or other high remuneration for services, or
  - evidence of commercial successes in the performing arts, as shown by box office receipts or record, casette, compact disk, or video sales.
- If the above standards do not readily apply to the alien's occupation, you may submit comparable evidence to establish the alien's eligibility.

A U.S. employer filing for an outstanding professor or researcher must file the petition with:
- evidence of at least 2 of the following:
  - receipt of major prizes or awards for outstanding achievement in the academic field,
  - membership in associations in the academic field, which require outstanding achievements of their members,
  - published material in professional publications written by others about the alien's work in the academic field,
  - participation on a panel, or individually, as the judge of the work of others in the same or an allied academic field,
  - original scientific or scholarly research contributions to the academic field, or
  - authorship of scholarly books or articles, in scholarly journals with international circulation, in the academic field;
- evidence the beneficiary has at least 3 years of experience in teaching and/or research in the academic field; and
- if you are a university or other institution of higher education, a letter indicating that you intend to employ the beneficiary in a tenured or tenure-track position as a teacher or in a permanent position as a researcher in the academic field, or
- if you are a private employer, a letter indicating that you intend to employ the beneficiary in a permanent research position in the academic field, and evidence that you employ at least 3 full-time researchers and have achieved documented accomplishments in the field.

A U.S. employer filing for a multinational executive or manager must file the petition with a statement which demonstrates that:
- if the alien is outside the U.S., he/she has been employed outside the U.S. for at least 1 year in the past 3 years in a managerial or executive capacity by a firm or corporation or other legal entity, or by its affiliate or subsidiary; or
- if the alien is already in the U.S. working for the same employer, or a subsidiary or affiliate of the firm or corporation or other legal entity, by which the alien was employed abroad, he/she was employed by the entity abroad in a managerial or executive capacity for at least one year in the 3 years preceding his/her entry as a nonimmigrant;
  - the prospective employer in the U.S. is the same employer or a subsidiary or affiliate of the firm or corporation or other legal entity by which the alien was employed abroad;
  - the prospective U.S. employer has been doing business for at least one year; and
  - the alien is to be employed in the U.S. in a managerial or executive capacity and describing the duties to be performed.

A U.S. employer filing for a member of the professions with an advanced degree or a person with exceptional ability in the sciences, arts, or business must file the petition with:
- a labor certification (see GENERAL EVIDENCE) and either:
  - an official academic record showing that the alien has a U.S. advanced degree or an equivalent foreign degree, or an official academic record showing that the alien has a U.S. baccalaureate degree or an equivalent foreign degree and letters from current or former employers showing that the alien has at least 5 years of progressive post-baccalaureate experience in the specialty; or
  - at least 3 of the following:
    - an official academic record showing that the alien has a degree, diploma, certificate, or similar award from an institution of learning relating to the area of exceptional ability;
    - letters from current or former employers showing that the alien has at least 10 years of full-time experience in the occupation for which he/she is being sought;
    - a license to practice the profession or certification for a particular profession or occupation;
    - evidence that the alien has commanded a salary, or other remuneration for services, which demonstrates exceptional ability;
    - evidence of membership in professional associations; or
    - evidence of recognition for achievements and significant contributions to the industry or field by peers, governmental entities, or professional or business organizations.
- If the above standards do not readily apply to the alien's occupation, you may submit comparable evidence to establish the alien's eligibility.

A U.S. employer filing for a skilled worker must file the petition with:
- a labor certification (see GENERAL EVIDENCE); and requirement is 2 years of training or experience).
- evidence that the alien meets the educational, training, or experience and any other requirements of the labor certification (the minimum requirement is 2 years of training or experience).

Form I-140 (Rev. 12 02 91)

For sale by the U.S. Government Printing Office
Superintendent of Documents, Mail Stop: SSOP, Washington, DC 20402-9328

A U.S. employer filing for a professional must file the petition with:
- a labor certification (see GENERAL EVIDENCE);
- evidence that the alien holds a U.S. baccalaureate degree or equivalent foreign degree; and
- evidence that a baccalaureate degree is required for entry into the occupation.

A U.S. employer filing for its employees in Hong Kong must file its petition with a statement that demonstrates that:
- the company is owned and organized in the United States
- the employee is a resident of Hong Kong;
- the company, or its subsidiary or affiliate, is employing the person in Hong Kong, and has been employing him or her there for the past 12 months, or the company, or its subsidiary or affiliate, is employing him or her outside of Hong Kong during a temporary absence (i.e., of limited duration) and he or she had been employed in Hong Kong for 12 consecutive months prior to such absence(s), and that such employment is, and for that period has been, as an officer or supervisor, or in a capacity that is executive, managerial or involves specialized knowledge;
- the company employs at least 100 employees in the U.S. and at least 50 employees outside the U.S. and has a gross annual income of at least $50,000,000; and
- the company intends to employ the person in the United States as an officer or supervisor, or in a capacity that is executive, managerial or involves specialized knowledge, with salary and benefits comparable to others with similar responsibilities and experience within the company. A specific job description is required for immediate immigration; a commitment to a qualifying job is required for deferred immigration.

A U.S. employer filing for an unskilled worker must file the petition with:
- a labor certification (see GENERAL EVIDENCE); and
- evidence that the beneficiary meets any education, training, or experience requirements required in the labor certification.

General Evidence.
Labor certification. Petitions for certain classifications must be filed with a certification from the Department of Labor or with documentation to establish that the alien qualifies for one of the shortage occupations in the Department of Labor's Labor Market Information Pilot Program or for an occupation in Group I or II of the Department of Labor's Schedule A. A certification establishes that there are not sufficient workers who are able, willing, qualified, and available at the time and place where the alien is to be employed and that employment of the alien if qualified, will not adversely affect the wages and working conditions of similarly employed U.S. workers. Application for certification is made on Form ETA-750 and is filed at the local office of the State Employment Service. If the alien is in a shortage occupation, or for a Schedule A/Group I or II occupation, you may file a fully completed, uncertified Form ETA-750 in duplicate with your petition for determination by INS that the alien belongs to the shortage occupation.

Translations. Any foreign language document must be accompanied by a full English translation which the translator has certified as complete and correct, and by the translator's certification that he or she is competent to translate from the foreign language into English.

Copies. If these instructions state that a copy of a document may be filed with this petition, and you choose to send us the original, we may keep that original for our records.

Where To File.
File this petition at the INS Service Center with jurisdiction over the place where the alien will be employed.

If the employment will be in Alabama, Connecticut, Delaware, District of Columbia, Florida, Georgia, Maine, Maryland, Massachusetts, New Hampshire, New Jersey, New York, North Carolina, Pennsylvania, Puerto Rico, Rhode Island, South Carolina, Vermont, the Virgin Islands, Virginia, or West Virginia, mail your petition to: USINS Eastern Service Center, 75 Lower Welden Street, St. Albans, VT 05479-0001.

If the employment will be in Arizona, California, Guam, Hawaii, or Nevada, mail your petition to: USINS Western Service Center, P.O. Box 30040, Laguna Niguel, CA 92607-0040.

If the employment will be elsewhere in the U.S., mail your petition to: USINS Northern Service Center, 100 Centennial Mall North, Room, B-26, Lincoln, NE 68508.

Fee.
The fee for this petition is $70.00. The fee must be submitted in the exact amount. It cannot be refunded. DO NOT MAIL CASH. All checks and money orders must be drawn on a bank or other institution located in the United States and must be payable in United States currency. The check or money order should be made payable to the Immigration and Naturalization Service, except that:
- If you live in Guam, and are filing this application in Guam, make your check or money order payable to the "Treasurer, Guam."
- If you live in the Virgin Islands, and are filing this application in the Virgin Islands, make your check or money order payable to the "Commissioner of Finance of the Virgin Islands."

Checks are accepted subject to collection. An uncollected check will render the application and any document issued invalid. A charge of $5.00 will be imposed if a check in payment of a fee is not honored by the bank on which it is drawn.

Processing Information.
Acceptance. Any petition that is not signed or is not accompanied by the correct fee will be rejected with a notice that it is deficient. You may correct the deficiency and resubmit the petition. However, a petition is not considered properly filed until accepted by the Service. A priority date will not be assigned until the petition is properly filed.

Initial processing. Once the petition has been accepted, it will be checked for completeness, including submission of the required initial evidence. If you do not completely fill out the form, or file it without required initial evidence, you will not establish a basis for eligibility, and we may deny your petition.

Requests for more information or interview. We may request more information or evidence or we may request that you appear at an INS office for an interview. We may also request that you submit the originals of any copy. We will return these originals when they are no longer required.

Decision. If you have established eligibility for the benefit requested, your petition will be approved. If you have not established eligibility, your petition will be denied. You will be notified in writing of the decision on your petition.

Meaning of petition approval.
Approval of a petition means you have established that the person you are filing for is eligible for the requested classification. This is the first step towards permanent residence. However, this does not in itself grant permanent residence or employment authorization. You will be given information about the requirements for the person to receive an immigrant visa, or to adjust status, after your petition is approved.

Penalties.
If you knowingly and willfully falsify or conceal a material fact or submit a false document with this request, we will deny the benefit you are filing for, and may deny any other immigration benefit. In addition, you will face severe penalties provided by law, and may be subject to criminal prosecution.

Privacy Act Notice.
We ask for the information on this form, and associated evidence, to determine if you have established eligibility for the immigration benefit you are filing for. Our legal right to ask for this information is in 8 USC 11854. We may provide this information to other government agencies. Failure to provide this information, and any requested evidence, may delay a final decision or result in denial of your request.

Paperwork Reduction Act Notice.
We try to create forms and instructions that are accurate, can be easily understood, and which impose the least possible burden on you to provide us with information. Often this is difficult because some immigration laws are very complex. The estimated average time to complete and file this application is as follows: (1) 20 minutes to learn about the law and form; (2) 15 minutes to complete the form; and (3) 45 minutes to assemble and file the petition; for a total estimated average of 1 hour and 20 minutes per petition. If you have comments regarding the accuracy of this estimate, or suggestions for making this form simpler, you can write to the Immigration and Naturalization Service, 425 I Street, N.W., Room 5304, Washington, D.C. 20536; and the Office of Management and Budget, Paperwork Reduction Project, OMB No. 1115-0061, Washington, D.C. 20503.

Form I-140 (Rev. 12-2-91)

Ch. 19   FORMS—FORM I-140   § 19.77

U.S. Department of Justice
Immigration and Naturalization Service

OMB #1115-0061
Immigrant Petition for Alien Worker

START HERE - Please Type or Print

Part 1. Information about the person or organization filing this petition.

If an individual is filing, use the top Name line. Organizations should use the second line.

Family Name	Given Name	Middle Initial

Company or Organization

Address - Attn:

Street Number and Name		Room #
City	State or Province	
Country	ZIP/Postal Code	
IRS Tax #	Social Security #	

Part 2. Petition Type. This petition is being filed for: (check one)

a. ☐ An alien of extraordinary ability
b. ☐ An outstanding professor or researcher
c. ☐ A multinational executive or manager
d. ☐ A member of the professions holding an advanced degree or an alien of exceptional ability
e. ☐ A skilled worker (requiring at least two years of specialized training or experience) or professional
f. ☐ An employee of a U.S. business operating in Hong Kong
g. ☐ Any other worker (requiring less than two years training or experience)

Part 3. Information about the person you are filing for.

Family Name	Given Name	Middle Initial

Address - C/O

Street # and Name		Apt. #
City	State or Province	
Country	Zip or Postal Code	
Date of Birth (month/day/year)	Country of Birth	
Social Security # (if any)	A # (if any)	

If in the U.S.
Date of Arrival (month/day/year)	I-94 #
Current Nonimmigrant Status	Expires on (month/day/year)

Part 4. Processing Information.

Below give the U.S. Consulate you want notified if this petition is approved and if any requested adjustment of status cannot be granted.

U.S Consulate: City _____ Country _____

Form I-140 (Rev. 12-2-91)   *Continued on back.*

FOR INS USE ONLY

Returned | Receipt

Resubmitted

Reloc Sent

Reloc Rec'd

☐ Petitioner Interviewed
☐ Beneficiary Interviewed

Classification
☐ 203(b)(1)(A) Alien Of Extraordinary Ability
☐ 203(b)(1)(B) Outstanding Professor or Researcher
☐ 203(b)(1)(C) Multi-national executive or manager
☐ 203(b)(2) Member of professions w/adv degree or of exceptional ability
☐ 203(b)(3) (A) (i) Skilled worker
☐ 203(b)(3) (A) (ii) Professional
☐ 203(b)(3) (A) (iii) Other worker
☐ Sec. 124 IMMACT-Employee of U S business in Hong Kong

Priority Date	Consulate

Remarks

Action Block

To Be Completed by Attorney or Representative, if any
☐ Fill in box if G-28 is attached to represent the petitioner
VOLAG #
ATTY State License #

845

§ 19.77   IMMIGRATION AND NATIONALITY LAW   Ch. 19

Part 4. Processing Information. *(continued)*

If you gave a U.S. address in Part 3, print the person's foreign address below. If his/her native alphabet does not use Roman letters, print his/her name and foreign address in the native alphabet.

Name   Address

Are you filing any other petitions or applications with this one?   ☐ No   ☐ yes attach an explanation
Is the person you are filing for in exclusion or deportation proceedings?   ☐ No   ☐ yes attach an explanation
Has an immigrant visa petition ever been filed by or in behalf of this person?   ☐ No   ☐ yes attach an explanation

Part 5. Additional information about the employer.

Type of petitioner (check one): ☐ Self   ☐ Individual U.S. Citizen   ☐ Company or organization
☐ Permanent Resident   ☐ Other explain _____

If a company, give the following:
Type of business
Date Established   Current # of employees   Gross Annual Income   Net Annual Income

If an individual, give the following:
Occupation   Annual Income

Part 6. Basic information about the proposed employment.

Job Title   Nontechnical description of job

Address where the person will work if different from address in Part 1.

Is this a full-time position?   ☐ yes   ☐ No (hours per week _____)   Wages per week

Is this a permanent position?:   ☐ yes   ☐ No   Is this a new position? ☐ yes ☐ No

Part 7. Information on spouse and all children of the person you are filing for.

Provide an attachment listing the family members of the person you are filing for. Be sure to include their full name, relationship, date and country of birth, and present address.

Part 8. Signature. *Read the information on penalties in the instructions before completing this section.*

I certify under penalty of perjury under the laws of the United States of America that this petition, and the evidence submitted with it, is all true and correct. I authorize the release of any information from my records which the Immigration and Naturalization Service needs to determine eligibility for the benefit I am seeking.

Signature   Date

Please Note: *If you do not completely fill out this form, or fail to submit required documents listed in the instructions, you cannot be found eligible for the requested document and this application may to be denied.*

Part 9. Signature of person preparing form if other than above. *(Sign below)*

I declare that I prepared this application at the request of the above person and it is based on all information of which I have knowledge.

Signature   Print Your Name   Date

Firm Name and Address

*U.S. Government Printing Office: 1992 — 312-328/64898

Form I-140 (Rev. 12-2-91)

§ 19.78 Forms—Form I-485

U.S. Department of Justice
Immigration and Naturalization Service

OMB No. 1115-0053
Application to Register Permanent Residence or Adjust Status

Purpose of this Form.
This form is for a person who is in the United States to apply to adjust to permanent resident status or register for permanent residence while in the U.S. It may also be used by certain Cuban nationals to request a change in the date their permanent residence began.

Who May File.
Based on an immigrant petition. You may apply to adjust your status if:

- an immigrant visa number is immediately available to you based on an approved immigrant petition; or
- you are filing this application with a complete relative, special immigrant juvenile, or special immigrant military petition which if approved, would make an immigrant visa number immediately available to you.

Based on being the spouse or child of another adjustment applicant or of a person granted permanent residence. You may apply to adjust status if you are the spouse or child of another adjustment applicant, or of a lawful permanent resident, if the relationship existed when that person was admitted as a permanent resident in an immigrant category which allows derivative status for spouses and children.

Based on admission as the fiance(e) of a U.S. citizen and subsequent marriage to that citizen. You may apply to adjust status if you were admitted to the U.S. as the K-1 fiance(e) of a U.S. citizen and married that citizen within 90 days of your entry. If you were admitted as the K-2 child of such a fiance(e), you may apply based on your parent's adjustment application.

Based on asylum status. You may apply to adjust status if you have been granted asylum in the U.S. and are eligible for asylum adjustment. [Note: In most cases you become eligible after being physically present in the U.S. for one year after the grant of asylum if you still qualify as a refugee or as the spouse or child of refugee.]

Based on Cuban citizenship or nationality. You may apply to adjust status if:

- you are a native or citizen of Cuba, were admitted or paroled into the U.S. after January 1, 1959, and thereafter have been physically present in the U.S. for at least one year; or
- you are the spouse or unmarried child of a Cuban described above, and you were admitted or paroled after January 1, 1959, and thereafter have been physically present in the U.S. for at least one year.

Based on continuous residence since before January 1, 1972. You may apply for permanent residence if you have continuously resided in the U.S. since before January 1, 1972.

Other basis of eligibility. If you are not included in the above categories, but believe you may be eligible for adjustment or creation of record of permanent residence, contact your local INS office.

Applying to change the date your permanent residence began. If you were granted permanent residence in the U.S. prior to November 6, 1966, and are a native or citizen of Cuba, his or her spouse or unmarried minor child, you may ask to change the date your lawful permanent residence began to your date of arrival in the U.S. or May 2, 1964, whichever is later.

Persons Who Are Ineligible.
Unless you are applying for creation of record based on continuous residence since before 1/1/72, or adjustment of status under a category in which special rules apply (such as asylum adjustment, Cuban adjustment, special immigrant juvenile adjustment, or special immigrant military personnel adjustment), **you are not eligible for adjustment of status if any of the following apply to you:**

- you entered the U.S. in transit without a visa;
- you entered the U.S. as a nonimmigrant crewman;
- you were not admitted or paroled following inspection by an immigration officer;
- your authorized stay expired before you filed this application, you were employed in the U.S., prior to filing this application, without INS authorization, or you otherwise failed to maintain your nonimmigrant status, other than through no fault of your own or for technical reasons; unless you are applying because you are an immediate relative of a U.S. citizen (parent, spouse, widow, widower, or unmarried child under 21 years old), a K-1 fiance(e) or K-2 fiance(e) dependent who married the U.S. petitioner within 90 days of admission, or an "H" or "I" special immigrant (foreign medical graduates, international organization employees or their derivative family members);
- you are or were a J-1 or J-2 exchange visitor, are subject to the two-year foreign residence requirement, and have not complied with or been granted a waiver of the requirement;
- you have A, E or G nonimmigrant status, or have an occupation which would allow you to have this status, unless you complete Form I-508 (I-508F for French nationals) to waive diplomatic rights, privileges and immunities, and if you are an A or G nonimmigrant, unless you submit a completed Form I-566;
- you were admitted to Guam as a visitor under the Guam visa waiver program;
- you were admitted to the U.S. as a visitor under the Visa Waiver Pilot Program, unless you are applying because you are an immediate relative of a U.S. citizen (parent, spouse, widow, widower, or unmarried child under 21 years old);
- you are already a conditional permanent resident;
- you were admitted as a K-1 fiance(e) but did not marry the U.S. citizen who filed the petition for you, or were admitted as the K-2 child of a fiance(e) and your parent did not marry the U.S. citizen who filed the petition.

General Filing Instructions.
Please answer all questions by typing or clearly printing in black ink. Indicate that an item is not applicable with "N/A". If the answer is "none", write "none". If you need extra space to answer any item, attach a sheet of paper with your name and your alien registration number (A#), if any, and indicate the number of the item to which the answer refers. You must file your application with the required **Initial Evidence**. Your application must be properly signed and filed with the correct fee. If you are under 14 years of age, your parent or guardian may sign your application.

Translations. Any foreign language document must be accompanied by a full English translation which the translator has certified as complete and correct, and by the translator's certification that he or she is competent to translate from the foreign language into English.

Copies. If these instructions state that a copy of a document may be filed with this application, and you choose to send us the original, we may keep the original for our records.

Initial Evidence.
You must file your application with following evidence:

- **Birth certificate.** Submit a copy of your birth certificate or other record of your birth.
- **Photos.** Submit two (2) identical natural color photographs of yourself, taken within 30 days of this application. [Photos must have a white background, be unmounted, printed on thin paper, and be glossy and unretouched. They must show a three-quarter frontal profile showing the right side of your face, with your right ear visible and with your head bare. You may wear a headdress if required by a religious order of which you are a member. The photos must be no larger than 2 X 2 inches, with the distance from the top of the head to just below the chin about 1 and 1/4 inches. Lightly print your A# (or your name if you have no A#) on the back of each photo, using a pencil.]
- **Fingerprints.** Submit a complete set of fingerprints on Form FD-258 if you are between the ages of 14 and 75 [Do not bend, fold, or crease the fingerprint chart. You should complete the information on the top of the chart and write your A# (if any) in the space marked "Your no. OCA" or "Miscellaneous no MNU". You should not sign the chart until you have been fingerprinted, or are told to sign by the person who takes your fingerprints. The person who takes your fingerprints must also sign the chart and write his/her title and the date you are fingerprinted in the space provided on the chart. You may be fingerprinted by police, sheriff, or INS officials or other reputable person or organization. You should call the police, sheriff, organization, or INS office before you go there, since some offices do not take fingerprints or may take fingerprints only at certain times.].

Form I-485 (Rev. 09-09-92)N

- **Medical Examination.** Submit a medical examination report on the form you have obtained from INS [Not required if you are applying for creation of record based on continuous residence since before 1/1/72, or if you are a K-1 fiance(e) or K-2 dependent of a fiance(e) who had a medical examination within the past year as required for the nonimmigrant fiance(e) visa.].
- **Form G-325A,** Biographic Information Sheet. You must submit a completed G-325A if you are between 14 and 79 years of age.
- **Evidence of status.** Submit a copy of your Form I-94, Nonimmigrant Arrival/Departure Record, showing your admission to the U.S. and current status, or other evidence of your status.
- **Employment letter/Affidavit of Support.** Submit a letter showing you are employed in a job that is not temporary, an affidavit of support from a responsible person in the U.S., or other evidence that shows that you are not likely to become a public charge [Not required if you are applying for creation of record based on continuous residence since before 1/1/72, asylum adjustment, or a Cuban or a spouse or unmarried child of a Cuban who was admitted after 1/1/59].
- **Evidence of eligibility.**
  - **Based on an immigrant petition.** Attach a copy of the approval notice for an immigrant petition which makes a visa number immediately available to you, or submit a complete relative, special immigrant juvenile, or special immigrant military petition which, if approved, will make a visa number immediately available to you.
  - **Based on admission as the K-1 fiance(e) of a U.S. citizen and subsequent marriage to that citizen.** Attach a copy of the fiance(e) petition approval notice and a copy of your marriage certificate.
  - **Based on asylum status.** Attach a copy of the letter or Form I-94 which shows the date you were granted asylum.
  - **Based on continuous residence in the U.S. since before 1/1/72.** Attach copies of evidence that shows continuous residence since before 1/1/72.
  - **Based on Cuban citizenship or nationality.** Attach evidence of your citizenship or nationality, such as a copy of your passport, birth certificate or travel document.
  - **Based on you being the spouse or child of another adjustment applicant or person granted permanent residence based on issuance of an immigrant visa.** File your application with the application of that other applicant, or with evidence it is pending with the Service or has been approved, or evidence your spouse or parent has been granted permanent residence based on an immigrant visa and:
    - If you are applying as the spouse of that person, also attach a copy of your marriage certificate and copies of documents showing the legal termination of all other marriages by you and your spouse; or
    - If you are applying as the child of that person, also attach a copy of your birth certificate, and, if the other person is not your natural mother, copies of evidence, (such as a marriage certificate and documents showing the legal termination of all other marriages, and an adoption decree), to demonstrate that you qualify as his or her child.
  - **Other basis for eligibility.** Attach copies of documents proving that you are eligible for the classification.

Where To File.
File this application at the local INS office having jurisdiction over your place of residence.

Fee. The fee for this application is $120, except that it is $95 if you are less than 14 years old. The fee must be submitted in the exact amount. It cannot be refunded. **DO NOT MAIL CASH.** All checks and money orders must be drawn on a bank or other institution located in the United States and must be payable in United States currency. The check or money order should be made payable to the Immigration and Naturalization Service, except that:
- If you live in Guam, and are filing this application in Guam, make your check or money order payable to the "Treasurer, Guam."
- If you live in the Virgin Islands, and are filing this application in the Virgin Islands, make your check or money order payable to the "Commissioner of Finance of the Virgin Islands."

Checks are accepted subject to collection. An uncollected check will render the application and any document issued invalid. A charge of $5.00 will be imposed if a check in payment of a fee is not honored by the bank on which it is drawn.

Processing Information.

Acceptance. Any application that is not signed, or is not accompanied by the correct fee, will be rejected with a notice that the application is deficient. You may correct the deficiency and resubmit the application. An application is not considered properly filed until accepted by the Service.

Initial processing. Once an application has been accepted, it will be checked for completeness, including submission of the required initial evidence. If you do not completely fill out the form, or file it without required initial evidence, you will not establish a basis for eligibility, and we may deny your application.

Requests for more information. We may request more information or evidence. We may also request that you submit the originals of any copy. We will return these originals when they are no longer required.

Interview. After you file your application you will be notified to appear at an INS office to answer questions about the application. You will be required to answer these questions under oath or affirmation. You must bring your Arrival-Departure Record (Form I-94) and any passport to the interview.

Decision. You will be notified in writing of the decision on your application.

Travel Outside the U.S. If you plan to leave the U.S. to go to any other country, including Canada or Mexico, before a decision is made on your application, contact the INS office processing your application before you leave. In many cases, leaving the U.S. without advance written permission will result in automatic termination of your application. Also, you may experience difficulty upon returning to the U.S. if you do not have written permission to reenter.

Penalties.
If you knowingly and willfully falsify or conceal a material fact or submit a false document with this request, we will deny the benefit you are filing for, and may deny any other immigration benefit. In addition, you will face severe penalties provided by law, and may be subject to criminal prosecution.

Privacy Act Notice.
We ask for the information on this form, and associated evidence, to determine if you have established eligibility for the immigration benefit you are filing for. Our legal right to ask for this information is in 8 USC 1255 and 1259. We may provide this information to other government agencies. Failure to provide this information, and any requested evidence, may delay a final decision or result in denial of your request.

Paperwork Reduction Act Notice.
We try to create forms and instructions that are accurate, can be easily understood, and which impose the least possible burden on you to provide us with information. Often this is difficult because some immigration laws are very complex. The estimated average time to complete and file this application is computed as follows: (1) **20** minutes to learn about the law and form; (2) **25** minutes to complete the form; and (3) **270** minutes to assemble and file the application, including the required interview and travel time; for a total estimated average of **5 hours and 15 minutes** per application. If you have comments regarding the accuracy of this estimate, or suggestions for making this form simpler, you can write to both the Immigration and Naturalization Service, 425 I Street, N.W., Room 5304, Washington, D.C. 20536, and the Office of Management and Budget, Paperwork Reduction Project, OMB No. 1115-0053, Washington, D.C. 20503

Form I-485 (09-09-92)N G.P.O. : 1995 163-659

Ch. 19   FORMS—FORM I-485   § 19.78

U.S. Department of Justice
Immigration and Naturalization Service

OMB No. 1115-0053

Application to Register Permanent Residence or Adjust Status

START HERE - Please Type or Print

Part 1. Information about you.

Family Name	Given Name	Middle Initial

Address - C/O

Street Number and Name	Apt. #

City

State	Zip Code

Date of Birth (month/day/year)	Country of Birth

Social Security #	A # (if any)

Date of Last Arrival (month/day/year)	I-94 #

Current INS Status	Expires on (month/day/year)

Part 2. Application Type. *(check one)*

I am applying for adjustment to permanent resident status because:

a. ☐ an immigrant petition giving me an immediately available immigrant visa number has been approved (attach a copy of the approval notice), or a relative, special immigrant juvenile, or special immigrant military visa petition filed with this application will give me an immediately available visa number if approved.

b. ☐ My spouse or parent applied for adjustment of status or was granted lawful permanent residence in an immigrant visa category which allows derivative status for spouses and children.

c. ☐ I entered as a K-1 fiance(e) of a U.S. citizen whom I married within 90 days of entry, or I am the K-2 child of such a fiance(e) (attach a copy of the fiance(e) petition approval notice and the marriage certificate).

d. ☐ I was granted asylum or derivative asylum status as the spouse or child of a person granted asylum and am eligible for adjustment.

e. ☐ I am a native or citizen of Cuba admitted or paroled into the U.S. after January 1, 1959, and thereafter have been physically present in the U.S. for at least 1 year.

f. ☐ I am the husband, wife, or minor unmarried child of a Cuban described in (e) and am residing with that person, and was admitted or paroled into the U.S. after January 1, 1959, and thereafter have been physically present in the U.S. for at least 1 year.

g. ☐ I have continuously resided in the U.S. since before January 1, 1972.

h. ☐ Other-explain _____

I am already a permanent resident and am applying to have the date I was granted permanent residence adjusted to the date I originally arrived in the U.S. as a nonimmigrant or parolee, or as of May 2, 1964, whichever is later, and: *(Check one)*

i. ☐ I am a native or citizen of Cuba and meet the description in (e), above.

j. ☐ I am the husband, wife or minor unmarried child of a Cuban, and meet the description in (f), above

Form I-485 (09-09-92)N   *Continued on back.*

FOR INS USE ONLY

Returned	Receipt
Resubmitted	
Reloc Sent	
Reloc Rec'd	

☐ Applicant Interviewed

Section of Law
☐ Sec. 209(b), INA
☐ Sec. 13, Act of 9/11/57
☐ Sec. 245, INA
☐ Sec. 249, INA
☐ Sec. 1 Act of 11/2/66
☐ Sec. 2 Act of 11/2/66
☐ Other _____

Country Chargeable

Eligibility Under Sec. 245
☐ Approved Visa Petition
☐ Dependent of Principal Alien
☐ Special Immigrant
☐ Other _____

Preference

Action Block

To Be Completed by Attorney or Representative, if any
☐ Fill in box if G-28 is attached to represent the applicant
VOLAG#
ATTY State License #

§ 19.78 IMMIGRATION AND NATIONALITY LAW Ch. 19

Part 3. Processing Information.

A	City/Town/Village of birth	Current occupation
	Your mother's first name	Your father's first name

Give your name exactly how it appears on your Arrival/Departure Record (Form I-94):

Place of last entry into the U.S (City/State)	In what status did you last enter? *(Visitor, Student, exchange alien, crewman, temporary worker, without inspection, etc.)*
Were you inspected by a U.S. Immigration Officer? ☐ Yes ☐ No	
Nonimmigrant Visa Number	Consulate where Visa was issued
Date Visa was Issued (month/day/year)	Sex: ☐ Male ☐ Female	Marital Status: ☐ Married ☐ Single ☐ Divorced ☐ Widowed

Have you ever before applied for permanent resident status in the U.S? ☐ No ☐ Yes (give date and place of filing and final disposition):

B. List your present husband/wife, all of your sons and daughters (if you have none, write "none". If additional space is needed, use separate paper)

Family Name	Given Name	Middle Initial	Date of Birth (month/day/year)
Country of birth	Relationship	A #	Applying with you? ☐ Yes ☐ No
Family Name	Given Name	Middle Initial	Date of Birth (month/day/year)
Country of birth	Relationship	A #	Applying with you? ☐ Yes ☐ No
Family Name	Given Name	Middle Initial	Date of Birth (month/day/year)
Country of birth	Relationship	A #	Applying with you? ☐ Yes ☐ No
Family Name	Given Name	Middle Initial	Date of Birth (month/day/year)
Country of birth	Relationship	A #	Applying with you? ☐ Yes ☐ No
Family Name	Given Name	Middle Initial	Date of Birth (month/day/year)
Country of birth	Relationship	A #	Applying with you? ☐ Yes ☐ No

C. List your present and past membership in or affiliation with every political organization, association, fund, foundation, party, club, society, or similar group in the United States or in any other place since your 16th birthday. Include any foreign military service in this part. If none, write "none". Include the name of organization, location, dates of membership from and to, and the nature of the organization. If additional space is needed, use separate paper.

_____
_____
_____
_____
_____
_____

Form I-485 (Rev 09-09-92) N   Continued On Next Page

Part 3. Processing Information. *(Continued)*

Please answer the following questions. (If your answer is **"Yes"** on any one of these questions, explain on a separate piece of paper. Answering **"Yes"** does not necessarily mean that you are not entitled to register for permanent residence or adjust status).

1. Have you ever, in or outside the U. S.:
   a. knowingly committed any crime of moral turpitude or a drug-related offense for which you have not been arrested?
   b. been arrested, cited, charged, indicted, fined, or imprisoned for breaking or violating any law or ordinance, excluding traffic violations?
   c. been the beneficiary of a pardon, amnesty, rehabilitation decree, other act of clemency or similar action?
   d. exercised diplomatic immunity to avoid prosecution for a criminal offense in the U. S.?   ☐ Yes ☐ No

2. Have you received public assistance in the U.S. from any source, including the U.S. government or any state, county, city, or municipality (other than emergency medical treatment) , or are you likely to receive public assistance in the future?   ☐ Yes ☐ No

3. Have you ever:
   a. within the past 10 years been a prostitute or procured anyone for prostitution, or intend to engage in such activities in the future?
   b. engaged in any unlawful commercialized vice, including, but not limited to, illegal gambling?
   c. knowingly encouraged, induced, assisted, abetted or aided any alien to try to enter the U.S. illegally?
   d. illicitly trafficked in any controlled substance, or knowingly assisted, abetted or colluded in the illicit trafficking of any controlled substance?   ☐ Yes ☐ No

4. Have you ever engaged in, conspired to engage in, or do you intend to engage in, or have you ever solicited membership or funds for, or have you through any means ever assisted or provided any type of material support to, any person or organization that has ever engaged or conspired to engage, in sabotage, kidnapping, political assassination, hijacking, or any other form of terrorist activity?   ☐ Yes ☐ No

5. Do you intend to engage in the U.S. in:
   a. espionage?
   b. any activity a purpose of which is opposition to, or the control or overthrow of, the Government of the United States, by force, violence or other unlawful means?
   c. any activity to violate or evade any law prohibiting the export from the United States of goods, technology or sensitive information?   ☐ Yes ☐ No

6. Have you ever been a member of, or in any way affiliated with, the Communist Party or any other totalitarian party?   ☐ Yes ☐ No

7. Did you, during the period March 23, 1933 to May 8, 1945, in association with either the Nazi Government of Germany or any organization or government associated or allied with the Nazi Government of Germany, ever order, incite, assist or otherwise participate in the persecution of any person because of race, religion, national origin or political opinion?   ☐ Yes ☐ No

8. Have you ever engaged in genocide, or otherwise ordered, incited, assisted or otherwise participated in the killing of any person because of race, religion, nationality, ethnic origin, or political opinion?   ☐ Yes ☐ No

9. Have you ever been deported from the U.S., or removed from the U.S. at government expense, excluded within the past year, or are you now in exclusion or deportation proceedings?   ☐ Yes ☐ No

10. Are you under a final order of civil penalty for violating section 274C of the Immigration Act for use of fraudulent documents, or have you, by fraud or willful misrepresentation of a material fact, ever sought to procure, or procured, a visa, other documentation, entry into the U.S., or any other immigration benefit?   ☐ Yes ☐ No

11. Have you ever left the U.S. to avoid being drafted into the U.S. Armed Forces?   ☐ Yes ☐ No

12. Have you ever been a J nonimmigrant exchange visitor who was subject to the 2 year foreign residence requirement and not yet complied with that requirement or obtained a waiver?   ☐ Yes ☐ No

13. Are you now withholding custody of a U.S. Citizen child outside the U.S. from a person granted custody of the child?   ☐ Yes ☐ No

14. Do you plan to practice polygamy in the U.S.?   ☐ Yes ☐ No

Form I-485 (Rev. 09-09-92)N   Continued on back

Part 4. Signature. *(Read the information on penalties in the instructions before completing this section. You must file this application while in the United States.)*

I certify under penalty of perjury under the laws of the United States of America that this application, and the evidence submitted with it, is all true and correct. I authorize the release of any information from my records which the Immigration and Naturalization Service needs to determine eligibility for the benefit I am seeking.

| Signature | Print Your Name | Date | Daytime Phone Number |

Please Note: *If you do not completely fill out this form, or fail to submit required documents listed in the instructions, you may not be found eligible for the requested document and this application may be denied.*

Part 5. Signature of person preparing form if other than above. *(Sign Below)*

I declare that I prepared this application at the request of the above person and it is based on all information of which I have knowledge.

| Signature | Print Your Name | Date | Day time Phone Number |

Firm Name
and Address

Form I-485 (Rev. 09-09-92)N

§ 19.79 Forms—Form OF-230

OMB APPROVAL NO. 1405-0015
EXPIRES: 8-31-92
* ESTIMATED BURDEN: 1 HOUR

APPLICATION FOR IMMIGRANT VISA AND ALIEN REGISTRATION

PART I – BIOGRAPHIC DATA

INSTRUCTIONS: Complete one copy of this form for yourself and each member of your family, regardless of age, who will immigrate with you. Please print or type your answer to all questions. Questions that are **Not Applicable** should be so marked. If there is insufficient room on the form, answer on a separate sheet using the same numbers as appear on the form. Attach the sheet to this form.

WARNING: Any false statement or concealment of a material fact may result in your permanent expulsion from the United States.

This form (OF-230 PART I) is Part I of two parts which, together with Optional Form OF-230 PART II, constitute the complete Application for Immigrant Visa and Alien Registration.

1. FAMILY NAME   FIRST NAME   MIDDLE NAME

2. OTHER NAMES USED OR BY WHICH KNOWN *(If married woman, give maiden name)*

3. FULL NAME IN NATIVE ALPHABET *(If Roman letters not used)*

4. DATE OF BIRTH *(Day) (Month) (Year)*
5. AGE
6. PLACE OF BIRTH *(City or town) (Province) (Country)*

7. NATIONALITY *(If dual national, give both)*
8. SEX ☐ Male ☐ Female
9. MARITAL STATUS ☐ Single (Never married) ☐ Married ☐ Widowed ☐ Divorced ☐ Separated
Including my present marriage, I have been married _____ times.

10. PERSONAL DESCRIPTION
   a. Color of hair _____ c. Height _____
   b. Color of eyes _____ d. Complexion _____

11. OCCUPATION

12. MARKS OF IDENTIFICATION

13. PRESENT ADDRESS

Telephone number: Home _____ Office _____

14. NAME OF SPOUSE *(Maiden or family name)* *(First name)* *(Middle name)*

Date and place of birth of spouse:

Address of spouse *(If different from your own)*:

15. LIST NAME, DATE AND PLACE OF BIRTH, AND ADDRESSES OF ALL CHILDREN

NAME	DATE AND PLACE OF BIRTH	ADDRESS (If different from your own)

THIS FORM MAY BE OBTAINED GRATIS AT CONSULAR OFFICES OF THE UNITED STATES OF AMERICA

NSN 7540-00-130-8317
50230(1)-101
Previous editions obsolete

OPTIONAL FORM 230 Part I (ENGLISH)
REVISED 4-91
DEPT. OF STATE

§ 19.79   IMMIGRATION AND NATIONALITY LAW   Ch. 19

PAGE 2

16. PERSON(S) NAMED IN 14 AND 15 WHO WILL ACCOMPANY OR FOLLOW ME TO THE UNITED STATES.

17. NAME OF FATHER, DATE AND PLACE OF BIRTH, AND ADDRESS *(If deceased, so state, giving year of death)*

18. MAIDEN NAME OF MOTHER, DATE AND PLACE OF BIRTH, AND ADDRESS *(If deceased, so state, giving year of death)*

19. IF NEITHER PARENT IS LIVING PROVIDE NAME AND ADDRESS OF NEXT OF KIN *(nearest relative)* IN YOUR HOME COUNTRY

20. LIST ALL LANGUAGES YOU CAN SPEAK, READ, AND WRITE

LANGUAGE	SPEAK	READ	WRITE

21. LIST BELOW ALL PLACES YOU HAVE LIVED FOR SIX MONTHS OR LONGER SINCE REACHING THE AGE OF 16. BEGIN WITH YOUR PRESENT RESIDENCE.

CITY OR TOWN	PROVINCE	COUNTRY	OCCUPATION	DATES (FROM/TO)

22. LIST ANY POLITICAL, PROFESSIONAL, OR SOCIAL ORGANIZATIONS AFFILIATED WITH COMMUNIST, TOTALITARIAN, TERRORIST OR NAZI ORGANIZATIONS WHICH YOU ARE NOW OR HAVE BEEN A MEMBER OF OR AFFILIATED WITH SINCE YOUR 16TH BIRTHDAY.

NAME AND ADDRESS	FROM/TO	TYPE OF MEMBERSHIP

23. LIST DATES OF ALL PREVIOUS RESIDENCE IN OR VISITS TO THE UNITED STATES. *(If never, so state)* GIVE TYPE OF VISA STATUS IF ANY. GIVE I.N.S. "A" NUMBER IF ANY.

LOCATION	FROM/TO	VISA	I.N.S. FILE NO *(If known)*

SIGNATURE OF APPLICANT   DATE

NOTE: Return this completed form immediately to the consular office address on the covering letter. This form will become part of your immigrant visa and your visa application cannot be processed until this form is complete.

*Public reporting burden for this collection of information is estimated to average 24 hours per response, including time required for searching existing data sources, gathering the necessary data, providing the information required, and reviewing the final collection. Send comments on the accuracy of this estimate of the burden and recommendations for reducing it to: Department of State (OIS/RA/DR) Washington, D.C. 20520-0264, and to the Office of Information and Regulatory Affairs, Office of Management and Budget, Paperwork Reduction Project (1405-0015), Washington, D.C. 20503.

*U.S. Government Printing Office: 1992 — 312-071/50088

Ch. 19 FORMS—FORM OF-230 § 19.79

EXPIRES 8-31-92
* ESTIMATED BURDEN: 23 HOURS

APPLICATION FOR IMMIGRANT VISA AND ALIEN REGISTRATION

PART II – SWORN STATEMENT

INSTRUCTIONS: Complete one copy of this form for yourself and each member of your family, regardless of age, who will immigrate with you. Please print or type your answer to all questions. Questions that are Not Applicable should be so marked. If there is insufficient room on the form, answer on a separate sheet using the same numbers as appear on the form. Attach the sheet to this form. DO NOT SIGN this form until instructed to do so by the consular officer. The fee for filing this application is listed under tariff item No. 20. The fee should be paid in United States dollars or local currency equivalent, or by bank draft, when you appear before the consular officer.

WARNING: Any false statement or concealment of a material fact may result in your permanent exclusion from the United States. Even though you should be admitted to the United States, a fraudulent entry could be grounds for your prosecution and/or deportation.

This form (OF-230 Part II) is a continuation of Form OF-230 PART I, which together, constitute the complete Application for Immigrant Visa and Alien Registration.

24. FAMILY NAME	FIRST NAME	MIDDLE NAME

25. ADDRESS (Local)	26. FINAL ADDRESS TO WHICH YOU WILL TRAVEL IN THE UNITED STATES (Street address including ZIP code)
Telephone No.	Telephone No.

27. PERSON YOU INTEND TO JOIN (Name, address, and relationship)	28. NAME AND ADDRESS OF SPONSORING PERSON OR EMPLOYER

29. PURPOSE IN GOING TO THE UNITED STATES	30. LENGTH OF INTENDED STAY (If permanently, so state)

31. INTENDED PORT OF ENTRY	32. DO YOU HAVE A TICKET TO FINAL DESTINATION? ☐ Yes ☐ No

33. United States laws governing the issuance of visas require each applicant to state whether or not he or she is a member of any class of individuals excluded from admission into the United States. The excludable classes are described below in general terms. You should read carefully the following list and answer YES or NO to each category. The answers you give will assist the consular officer to reach a decision on your eligibility to receive a visa.

EXCEPT AS OTHERWISE PROVIDED BY LAW, ALIENS WITHIN THE FOLLOWING CLASSIFICATIONS ARE INELIGIBLE TO RECEIVE A VISA. DO ANY OF THE FOLLOWING CLASSES APPLY TO YOU?

a. An alien who has a communicable disease of public health significance, or has or has had a physical or mental disorder that poses, or is likely to pose a threat to the safety or welfare of the alien or others; an alien who is a drug abuser or addict. [212(a)(1)] YES ☐ NO ☐

b. An alien convicted of, or who admits committing a crime involving moral turpitude, or violation of any law relating to a controlled substance; an alien convicted of 2 or more offenses for which the aggregate sentences were 5 years or more; an alien coming to the United States to engage in prostitution or commercialized vice, or who has engaged in prostitution or procuring within the past 10 years; an alien who is or has been an illicit trafficker in any controlled substance; an alien who has committed a serious criminal offense in the United States and who has asserted immunity from prosecution. [212(a)(2)] YES ☐ NO ☐

c. Alien who seeks to enter the United States to engage in espionage, sabotage, export control violations, overthrow of the Government of the United States, or other unlawful activity; an alien who seeks to enter the United States to engage in terrorist activities; an alien who has been a member of or affiliated with the Communist or any other totalitarian party; an alien under the direction of the Nazi government of Germany, or any area occupied by, or allied with the Nazi Government of Germany, ordered, incited, assisted, or otherwise participated in the persecution of any person because of race, religion, national origin, or political opinion; an alien who has engaged in genocide. [212(a)(3)] YES ☐ NO ☐

d. An alien who is likely to become a public charge. [212(a)(4)] YES ☐ NO ☐

e. An alien who seeks to enter for the purpose of performing skilled or unskilled labor who has not been certified by the Secretary of Labor; an alien graduate of a foreign medical school seeking to perform medical services who has not passed the NBME exam or its equivalent. [212(a)(5)] YES ☐ NO ☐ Not Applicable ☐

f. An alien previously deported within one year, or arrested and deported within 5 years; an alien who seeks or has sought a visa, entry into the United States, or any U.S. immigration benefit by fraud or misrepresentation; an alien who knowingly assisted any other alien to enter or try to enter the United States in violation of the law; an alien who is in violation of Section 274C of the Immigration Act. [212(a)(6)] YES ☐ NO ☐

Previous editions obsolete

NSN 7540-00-149-0919
50230-106

*Public reporting burden for this collection of information is estimated to average 24 hours per response, including time required for searching existing data sources, gathering the necessary data, providing the information required, and reviewing the final collection. Send comments on the accuracy of this estimate of the burden and recommendations for reducing it to Department of State (O/S/RA/DR) Washington, D.C. 20520-0264 and to the Office of Information and Regulatory Affairs, Office of Management and Budget, Paperwork Reduction Project (1405-0015), Washington, D.C. 20503.

OPTIONAL FORM 230 Part II (English)
REVISED 4-91
DEPT. OF STATE

§ 19.79   IMMIGRATION AND NATIONALITY LAW   Ch. 19

PAGE 2

g. An alien who is permanently ineligible to U.S. citizenship; a person who has departed the United States to evade military service in time of war. [212(a)(8)] YES ☐ NO ☐

h. An alien who is coming to the United States to practice polygamy; an alien who is a guardian required to accompany an excluded alien; an alien who withholds custody of a child outside the United States from a United States citizen granted legal custody. [212(a)(9)] YES ☐ NO ☐

i. An alien who is a former exchange visitor who has not fulfilled the 2-year foreign residence requirement. [212(e)] YES ☐ NO ☐

If the answer to any of the foregoing questions is YES or if unsure, explain in the following space or on a separate sheet of paper.

---

34. Have you ever been arrested, convicted or ever been in a prison or almshouse; have you ever been the beneficiary of a pardon or an amnesty; have you ever been treated in an institution or hospital or other place for insanity or other mental disease. [222(a)] YES ☐ NO ☐

35. I am unlikely to become a public charge because of the following:
☐ Personal financial resources *(describe)*   ☐ Employment *(attach)*   ☐ Affidavit of Support *(attach)*

36. Have you ever applied for a visa to enter the United States? YES ☐ NO ☐
(If answer is Yes, state where and when, whether you applied for a nonimmigrant or an immigrant visa, and whether the visa was issued or refused.)

37. Have you been refused admission to the United States? YES ☐ NO ☐
(If answer is Yes, explain)

38. Were you assisted in completing this application? YES ☐ NO ☐
(If answer is Yes, give name and address of person assisting you, indicating whether relative, friend, travel agent, attorney, or other)
NAME   ADDRESS   RELATIONSHIP

39. The following documents are submitted in support of this application:
☐ Passport   ☐ Military record   ☐ Evidence of own assets
☐ Birth certificate ☐ Police certificate   ☐ Affidavit of support
☐ Marriage certificate ☐ Medical records   ☐ Offer of employment
☐ Death certificate ☐ Photographs   ☐ Other *(describe)*
☐ Divorce decree   ☐ Birth certificates of all children who will not be immigrating at this time. (List those for whom birth certificates are not available.)

DO NOT WRITE BELOW THE FOLLOWING LINE
The consular officer will assist you in answering items 40 and 41.

40. I claim to be exempt from ineligibility to receive a visa and exclusion under item _____ in Part 33 for the following reasons:
212(a)(5)   Beneficiary of a Waiver under:
☐ Not Applicable   ☐ 212(a)(3)(D)(ii)   ☐ 212(h)
☐ Not Required   ☐ 212(a)(3)(D)(iii)   ☐ 212(e)   ☐ 212(i)
☐ Attached   ☐ 212(a)(3)(D)(iv)   ☐ 212(g)(1)
                                          ☐ 212(g)(2)

41. I claim to be: I am subject to the following:
☐ A Family-Sponsored Immigrant   ☐ I derive foreign state chargeability   ☐ Preference: _____
☐ An Employment Based-Immigrant   under Sec. 202(b) through my _____   ☐ Numerical limitation: _____
☐ A Diversity Immigrant   (foreign state)
☐ A Special Category *(Specify)* _____
   (Returning resident, Hong Kong, Tibetan, Private Legislation, etc.)

I understand that I am required to surrender my visa to the United States Immigration Officer at the place where I apply to enter the United States, and that the possession of a visa does not entitle me to enter the United States if at that time I am found to be inadmissible under the immigration laws.
I understand that any willfully false or misleading statement or willfull concealment of a material fact made by me herein may subject me to permanent exclusion from the United States and, if I am admitted to the United States, may subject me to criminal prosecution and/or deportation.
I, the undersigned applicant for a United States immigrant visa, do solemnly swear (or affirm) that all statements which appear in this application, consisting of Optional Forms 230 PART I and 230 PART II combined, have been made by me, including the answers to items 1 through 41 inclusive, and that they are true and complete to the best of my knowledge and belief. I do further swear (or affirm) that, if admitted into the United States, I will not engage in activities which would be prejudicial to the public interest, or endanger the welfare, safety, or security of the United States; in activities which would be prohibited by the laws of the United States relating to espionage, sabotage, public disorder, or in other activities subversive to the national security; in any activity a purpose of which is the opposition to or the control, or overthrow of, the Government of the United States, by force, violence, or other unconstitutional means.
I understand all the foregoing statements, having asked for and obtained an explanation on every point which was not clear to me.

The relationship claimed in items 14 and 15 verified by   _____
documentation submitted to consular officer except as noted: (Signature of Applicant)

Subscribed and sworn to before me this ____ day of _____, 19___ at: _____

TARIFF ITEM NO. 20   _____
                                                                           (Consular Officer)

* U.S. Government Printing Office 1992-312-071/50073

Chapter 20

ADOPTIONS

by
Joseph R. Carrieri

Table of Sections

20.1	Scope Note.
20.2	Strategy.
20.3	___ Checklist: Pre-adoption—Counsel for Parents.
20.4	___ Checklist: Interview With Birth Mother.
20.5	Adoptions—Generally.
20.6	___ Defined.
20.7	___ Rationale.
20.8	___ Judicial Construction of Statutes.
20.9	___ Concurrent Jurisdiction.
20.10	___ ___ Where to File Adoption Proceedings.
20.11	___ Choice of Venue.
20.12	___ Types.
20.13	___ Effect of Adoption.
20.14	___ Who May Adopt—Statutory Mandates.
20.15	___ ___ Separated Persons.
20.16	___ ___ Foster Parents: Preference to Adopt.
20.17	___ ___ Second Parent Adoptions.
20.18	___ ___ Unwed Putative Fathers.
20.19	___ ___ Citizens and Aliens.
20.20	___ ___ Age as a Factor.
20.21	___ ___ Extended Family as Factor.
20.22	___ ___ Adult Unmarried Person.
20.23	___ Who May Be Adopted—In General.
20.24	___ ___ Adult Adoptions.
20.25	___ ___ Aliens.
20.26	___ ___ Non-marital Children.
20.27	___ ___ Interracial Adoptions.
20.28	___ ___ Religion as a Factor.
20.29	___ Consents Required—Statutory Mandate.
20.30	___ ___ Rights of Unwed Fathers.
20.31	___ ___ When Consent Not Required.
20.32	___ ___ Notice of a Proposed Adoption.
20.33	___ ___ Checklist of Fathers to Receive Notice of Adoption.
20.34	___ Persons Excluded from Notice.
20.35	___ Purpose of Notice.
20.36	___ Procedure.

ADOPTIONS Ch. 20

20.37	Private Placement Adoptions—In General.
20.38	___ Terminating Parental Rights Based Upon Abandonment.
20.39	___ Terminating Parental Rights Based Upon Mental Retardation.
20.40	___ Dual Representation Prohibited.
20.41	___ Independent Counsel.
20.42	___ Permissible Dual Representation.
20.43	___ Independent Representation of the Child.
20.44	___ The Attorney's Fee.
20.45	___ Locating an Infant for Adoption—The Attorney's Responsibility.
20.46	___ Illegal Sale of Babies.
20.47	___ Advertisement.
20.48	___ Foreign Infants.
20.49	___ Readoption of Foreign Infants.
20.50	___ Native American Children.
20.51	___ Residency Requirements.
20.52	___ Permissible Payments by Adoptive Parents.
20.53	___ Interstate Compact on the Placement of Children.
20.54	___ Pre-certification of Adoptive Parents—In General.
20.55	___ ___ Requirement of Pre-certification.
20.56	___ ___ Procedure.
20.57	___ ___ Checklist of Documents Needed for Certification.
20.58	___ Hospital Procedures—Physical Transfer of Custody of the Infant to the Adoptive Parents.
20.59	___ ___ Certification Procedures.
20.60	___ Petition for Temporary Guardianship—Legislative Background.
20.61	___ ___ Impact of Pre-placement Certification.
20.62	___ Procedure Upon Filing Petition for Temporary Guardianship.
20.63	___ Consent of Birth Parents.
20.64	___ ___ Extra-Judicial Consent.
20.65	___ ___ Judicial Consents.
20.66	___ ___ Personal Appearances Required.
20.67	___ ___ Step-Parent Adoptions.
20.68	___ Foreign Born Children.
20.69	___ Petition for Adoption.
20.70	___ The Agreement of Adoption.
20.71	___ Affidavit of Attorney Representing Adoptive Parents.
20.72	___ Confidential Affidavit.
20.73	___ Attorney's Affidavit of Financial Disclosure.
20.74	___ Notification of Order of Adoption; Report of Adoption.
20.75	___ Order of Adoption.
20.76	___ Birth Mother's Affidavit Regarding Putative Father.
20.77	___ Affidavit of Intermediary.
20.78	___ Attorney's Affidavit Regarding Legal Fees.
20.79	___ Affidavit of Explanation of Criminal Activity.
20.80	___ Investigation by Disinterested Person.
20.81	___ The Hearing.
20.82	___ Certificate of Adoption.
20.83	___ The New Birth Certificate.
20.84	___ Checklist of Documents Required for Private Placement Adoption.
20.85	Agency Adoptions—Defined.
20.86	___ Definition of "Authorized Agency."

Ch. 20   **ADOPTIONS**

20.87   ____ Venue.
20.88   ____ Child's Entry into the System.
20.89   ____ ____ Voluntary Transfer of Legal Custody of Children to the Authorized Agency.
20.90   ____ ____ Judicial Surrender.
20.91   ____ ____ Extra-Judicial Surrender.
20.92   ____ ____ Court Approval of Extra-Judicial Surrender.
20.93   ____ ____ Assigned Counsel.
20.94   ____ ____ Required Notice of Application.
20.95   ____ ____ Notification to Court.
20.96   ____ ____ Court Order.
20.97   ____ ____ Conditional Surrender.
20.98   ____ ____ Recording a Surrender.
20.99   ____ ____ Revocation of Surrender.
20.100   ____ ____ Proceedings Subsequent to Execution of Extra-Judicial Surrender.
20.101   ____ ____ Court Ordered Transfer of Children to Authorized Agency.
20.102   ____ Procedures.
20.103   ____ The Petition.
20.104   ____ The Agreement of Adoption.
20.105   ____ Verified Schedule.
20.106   ____ Affidavit of Financial Disclosure.
20.107   ____ Confidential Affidavit.
20.108   ____ Marital Affidavit.
20.109   ____ Child's Medical History.
20.110   ____ Supplemental Affidavit.
20.111   ____ Notification of Order of Adoption; Report of Adoption.
20.112   ____ Doctor's Certificate of Health.
20.113   ____ Authorization and Approval for Subsidized Adoption.
20.114   ____ Adoption Homestudy.
20.115   ____ Affidavit Identifying Party.
20.116   ____ Order of Adoption.
20.117   ____ Certificate of Adoption.
20.118   ____ Abuse Clearance Form.
20.119   ____ Unavailability of Abuse Clearance Form and Criminal Conviction Check.
20.120   ____ Attorney's Affidavit of Legal Fees.
20.121   ____ Checklist of Other Required Supporting Documentation.
20.122   ____ The Adoption Hearing.
20.123   Post-adoption Issues—The Open Adoption.
20.124   ____ Visitation With Siblings.
20.125   ____ Sealing Adoption Records.
20.126   ____ ____ Constitutionality of Laws Relating to Sealing Records.
20.127   ____ ____ Good Cause for Unsealing Records.
20.128   ____ ____ ____ Criminal Investigation and Probation Department.
20.129   ____ ____ ____ Requirement of Medical Information.
20.130   ____ ____ ____ Religion.
20.131   ____ Abrogation of Order.
20.132   Checklist of Facts and Allegations to be Included in the Petition for a Private Placement Adoption.

§ 20.1   ADOPTIONS   Ch. 20

20.133 Forms—Private Placement Adoptions—Petition for Certification as a Qualified Adoptive Parent.
20.134 _____ _____ Petition for Temporary Guardianship.
20.135 _____ _____ Judicial Consent of Natural Parent.
20.136 _____ _____ Extra-Judicial Consent of Natural Parent.
20.137 _____ _____ Petition for Adoption.
20.138 _____ _____ Order of Adoption (Private Placement).
20.139 _____ Agency Adoptions—Petition for Adoption.
20.140 _____ _____ Verified Schedule.
20.141 _____ _____ Marital Affidavit.
20.142 _____ _____ Marital Affidavit Dispensing With Consent of Spouse After Three Year Separation.
20.143 _____ _____ Confidential Affidavit.
20.144 _____ _____ Affidavit Pursuant to Section 111–a of the Domestic Relations Law.
20.145 _____ _____ Agreement of Adoption and Consent.
20.146 _____ _____ Affidavit Identifying Party.
20.147 _____ _____ Affidavit of Financial Disclosure by Parents.
20.148 _____ _____ Order of Adoption.

WESTLAW Electronic Research

See WESTLAW Electronic Research Guide preceding the Summary of Contents.

§ 20.1 Scope Note

This chapter is divided into six parts: (1) adoptions in general; (2) private adoptions; (3) agency adoptions; (4) post-adoption issues; (5) checklists; and (6) forms.[1] It outlines, and discusses, the substantive and procedural aspects of adoptions in the State of New York. The early sections discuss adoption law generally, such as the definition and purpose of adoptions. There are two types of adoptions within New York State, *i.e.*, agency adoptions and private adoptions. Germane to both types of adoption are the issues of who may adopt,[2] who may be adopted,[3] the consents required from the parents of the infant,[4] and a general discussion of the types of consents required of the biological mother,[5] the presumed father and the putative father.[6] Newly acquired rights of unwed fathers are fully discussed at Section 20.30. Just as important as the required consents, are those which are not required; this leads to a discussion of the concepts and issues of abandonment, permanent neglect, mental illness or mental retardation of the parents, surrender by

---

§ 20.1

1. For additional discussion of adoption, see Sobie, et al., *New York Family Court Practice* (West 1996) Ch. 5 "Adoptions."
2. DRL § 110; *see infra*, § 20.14.
3. DRL § 110; *see infra*, § 20.23.
4. DRL § 115–b; *see infra*, § 20.29.
5. *Id.*
6. Social Services Law § 384(c); *see infra*, § 20.30.

860

the parents and denial of paternity by the putative father.[7]

The next major topic is the adoption proceeding. The procedural aspects of the adoption proceeding involve the drafting and filing of numerous and detailed documents.[8]

The practitioner who encounters an adoption proceeding must know, and this chapter therefore details, the substantive and procedural aspects of private adoptions, pointing out the pitfalls that the practitioner may face such as with regard to dual representation,[9] the need for independent counsel,[10] the attorney's fee,[11] and the attorney's obligation not to place the child in violation of law.

As a direct result of the Lisa Steinberg case, the Legislature mandated the court's involvement at the inception of the adoption proceeding; hence, the requirement for pre-certification of adoptive parents which assures, to the extent possible, that the adoptive parents are certified as capable of receiving and caring for an infant.[12]

Once a prospective adoptive parent qualifies by certification and receives a child, the practitioner should be ready to file the petition for adoption and the other supporting documents which are identified and explained in this chapter. Also included are discussions of the agreements of adoption,[13] the attorney's affidavit,[14] the confidential affidavit,[15] the affidavit of financial disclosure, the report of adoption, the order of adoption and other documentation that may be required by the various surrogate's and family courts.[16]

The acceptable method of locating infants,[17] residency and venue issues,[18] and the Interstate Compact on the Placement of Children[19] are all discussed. Also addressed are step-parent adoptions[20] and foreign adoptions.[21] Additionally, checklists of the numerous documents required by the various courts are provided.[22]

7. Social Services Law § 384(b); see infra, § 20.31.

8. DRL § 115; Uniform Rules of the New York State Trial Courts, 22 NYCRR §§ 205.53–205.55, §§ 207.54–207.58; see infra, §§ 20.36, 20.84, 20.103.

9. Social Services Law § 374(6); see infra, § 20.42.

10. Social Services Law § 374(6); see infra, § 20.43.

11. In re Adoption of E.W.C., 89 Misc.2d 64, 389 N.Y.S.2d 743 (Surr.Ct., Nassau County, 1976); see infra, § 20.44.

12. DRL § 115–d; see infra, § 20.55.

13. See infra, § 20.70.

14. Uniform Rules—Family Court, 22 NYCRR § 205.53; see infra, § 20.71.

15. Uniform Rules—Family Court, 22 NYCRR § 205.53; see infra, § 20.72.

16. Uniform Rules—Family Court, 22 NYCRR § 205.53; see infra, §§ 20.73–20.75.

17. Social Services Law §§ 374, 389; see infra, § 20.45.

18. DRL § 115(2); Social Services Law § 384(b); see also, Matter of E.W.C., 89 Misc.2d 64, 389 N.Y.S.2d 743 (Surr.Ct., Nassau County, 1976); see infra, § 20.11.

19. Social Services Law § 374–a; see infra, § 20.53.

20. DRL § 110; see infra, § 20.67.

21. DRL § 115–a; see infra, § 20.48.

22. Uniform Rules—Family Court, 22 NYCRR § 205.53; see infra, § 20.121

§ 20.1

The later sections of the chapter deal with agency adoptions which differ from private adoptions in that one of the consenting parties is an authorized agency such as a Department of Social Services of a municipality.[23] Discussed in Sections 20.88 and 20.98 are the ways that the child enters into the foster care system, and the various ways in which a child becomes freed for adoption, such as a judicial surrender executed by the birth parents or a court ordered termination of parental rights. The surrender, "judicial and extra-judicial," is discussed in detail at Sections 20.90, 20.91 and 20.92, along with the proceedings subsequent to the execution of an extra-judicial surrender. Thereafter, a detailed analysis of the agency adoption procedures is outlined in Sections 20.102 to 20.109. The various documents required to complete the adoption are not only listed but are explained in detail in Sections 20.110 to 20.120. Near the end of the chapter a checklist of all other supporting documentation required by the adoption clerk in agency adoptions is set forth.[24] The chapter concludes with a discussion of the open adoption,[25] the sealing of adoption records,[26] the unsealing of adoption records[27] and, lastly, the abrogation of adoption.[28]

Throughout the chapter, the practitioner is given practical tips on the required documents to be filed with the various adoption clerks and the pitfalls to avoid, not only to prevent the rejection of the adoption but also to prevent the attorney from acting as an illegal intermediary, which is not only inappropriate, but criminal.[29]

§ 20.2 Strategy

When a prospective client is interviewed by an attorney, the practitioner must be mindful that the prospective adoptive parents are emotionally vulnerable in that they probably have tried unsuccessfully to have biological children of their own. They probably have also attempted to seek medical intervention. Thus, when prospective adoptive parents come to an attorney, they sometimes require immediate reassurance that the adoption process is a rational, logical alternative to having a biological child, and that an adoptive child may eventually be located. The strategy will differ depending on whether the adoption is through private placement or through an adoption agency.

Private Placement Adoptions. In a private placement, the adoption is between the birth parent and the adoptive parent, whereas in an agency adoption, the agreement of adoption is between the agency and the adoptive parent. In the agency adoption, dual representation is not a problem. In the private placement adoption, the attorney cannot repre-

---

23. DRL § 113; *see infra*, § 20.85.

24. Uniform Rules—Family Court, 22 NYCRR § 205.53; *see infra*, § 20.121.

25. Social Services Law § 383–c; *see infra*, § 20.123.

26. DRL § 114; *see infra*, § 20.125.

27. DRL § 114; *see infra*, § 20.127.

28. DRL § 114; *see infra*, § 20.131.

29. Social Services Law § 374(6); *see infra*, §§ 20.45–20.46.

sent both parties and must be extremely careful not to be the procurer of the infant, which is not only inappropriate, but criminal. Therefore, counsel should advise the prospective adoptive parents that it is they who must obtain the child, not the attorney. It is important to explain to the prospective adoptive parents at the initial interview that the proven methods of advertising can, and in many cases will, result in obtaining an infant for adoption.

Obtaining an Infant for Adoption. Counsel should explain to the prospective adoptive parents that they should prepare resumés and distribute the same to doctors, nurses, psychiatrists and anyone else who comes in contact with young women who may wish to give their children up for adoption. Clients should be counseled to advertise in the local newspapers that they want to adopt. Some attorneys recommend that a separate telephone line be installed so that every time the phone rings it is presumably a prospective birth mother hoping to find a good home for her infant. Those who persevere will usually adopt an infant within a year or two. The clients must be counseled that they may not present the biological mother with any money and that the safer procedure is to give a certain sum of money to the attorney to be held in escrow. When there are necessary expenses incidental to the birth of the child, the attorney representing the adoptive parents will disburse the money directly from the escrow account and will account to the court for such expenditures. Not everybody can afford to adopt and, therefore, it is imperative for the attorney to inform the client that most likely the client will be responsible to pay all medical bills and incidental expenses.[1]

Counsel for the Biological Mother. Once the adoptive parents make contact with a biological mother who is ready, willing and able to have her child adopted, the attorney representing the adoptive parents must make sure that he or she does not in any way represent the biological mother; nor may the attorney give the biological mother any advice. If the biological mother does not have her own attorney, the attorney for the adoptive parents may, in some counties, contact the adoption clerk of the family court or the surrogate's court who has a panel of attorneys versed in the adoption field who will render services to the biological mother without charging her a fee. It is the adoptive parents who must pay the fee to the attorney representing the biological mother. The attorney's fees, both for the adoptive parents and biological mother, may not be exorbitant and should not be more than $3,500, except in extraordinary cases and in those cases the court will require an affidavit of services.

The attorney for the biological mother must counsel her with respect to the legal ramifications of executing such initial documents as the extra-judicial consent, usually signed three or four days after the child is born, and which may be revoked by the biological mother within

§ 20.2
1. DRL § 115(8).

45 days, and the judicial consent executed before the court and which is immediately irrevocable. The attorney for the biological mother must also be sensitive to any emotional instability and, where appropriate, should recommend counseling as part of the adoption process. The fees for counseling would be legitimate fees to be paid by the adoptive parents.

Jurisdiction and Venue. The attorney for the biological mother must choose the court with the proper jurisdiction and appropriate venue.[2] In a private adoption, the proper jurisdiction would be in the family court or surrogate's court where the adoptive parents reside or, if the adoptive parents reside outside of New York, then where the infant resides. The attorneys for both parties must be mindful that if the child is born out of New York State, the Interstate Compact procedures must be followed and complied with.[3]

After the biological mother signs the extra-judicial consent, usually in the attorney's office (or if she signs a judicial consent before the court), the focus is on the attorney for the adoptive parents who must prepare the petition and agreement of adoption and all other supporting papers.

Where the adoptive parents have been certified by the court as qualified pre-adoptive parents, the petition for adoption and supporting papers must be filed with the appropriate court within ten days after the

[2] **PRACTICE POINTER:** The old adage, "why work, call the clerk," is never more true than in the choice of court and venue. While the term judge shopping has a negative connotation, in the field of adoption, it would be unwise for the practitioner not to choose the court and venue wisely. For example, in some counties the surrogate's court is avoided because a particular surrogate may be ultra-conservative and make it extremely difficult for an adoption to be finalized. For example, one surrogate requires that the rights of an unknown father "John Doe" be terminated by giving notice to this John Doe by publication. This practice is wasteful, unnecessary and costly and is not mandated by adoption statutes. It would therefore not be in the best interests of the client to file the adoption papers in that particular surrogate's court. Instead, knowledgeable practitioners in that particular jurisdiction would file in the family court. It is therefore essential that the practitioner know or become knowledgeable with respect to which courts are "pro-adoption" and are helpful to the practitioner. Sometimes a simple phone call or, better yet, a visit to the adoption clerk, will prevent needless delays and, perhaps, an aborted adoption. The adoption clerk will supply the practitioner with a full set of appropriate adoption forms with an instruction sheet so that up front the attorney knows what documents are needed in this particular court. For example, some courts require adoptive parents to be fingerprinted while other courts do not. In some jurisdictions, an adoption can take place within three weeks of filing the completed set of document forms where in another jurisdiction the wait can be as long as nine months.

[3] **CAVEAT:** If the child is born outside of New York State and the child is being placed in New York for adoption, the attorneys handling the adoption must comply with the requirements of the Interstate Compact as promulgated in Social Services Law § 374–a. Non-compliance with the Interstate Compact could result in the adoption petition being dismissed. In re Adoption of Jon K., 141 Misc.2d 949, 535 N.Y.S.2d 660 (Fam.Ct., Kings County, 1988). Non-compliance could also result in a reduction of the attorney's fees. In re Adoption of Calynn M.G., 137 Misc.2d 1005, 523 N.Y.S.2d 729 (Surr.Ct., Nassau County, 1987). Violation of adoption laws could also result in attorneys being disciplined. In re Adoption of Male Infant A., 150 Misc.2d

birth of the child. Assuming that the abuse clearance form and the fingerprint check prove negative, and after a three month wait from the time the child has been placed with the adoptive parents, the case is ready for the calendar. Because all of the important detail work has been thoroughly analyzed and completed, the adoption hearing is largely ceremonial.

Agency Adoptions. The focus is somewhat different with respect to agency adoptions. When the prospective adoptive parents first interview with the attorney, the child will ordinarily have been in a foster home for several years. Therefore, in an agency adoption, the focus is not on finding the child, but upon making sure that the child is adopted with all of the benefits to which the child is entitled. In the State of New York, the majority of foster children are adopted with a subsidy.[4] It is the attorney's obligation to make sure that the subsidy is in place prior to the adoption. In most subsidy adoptions, the usual stipend is approximately $400 per month until the child becomes twenty-one years of age. However, if the child has special needs, the attorney must assure that the special rates are in place which could be as much as $1,200 per month, plus medical and clothing allowances until the child reaches the age of 21. To permit an adoption without a subsidy in place could result in the forfeiture or denial of the subsidy. As a consequence, an attorney might become liable for damages in a malpractice action.[5]

An agency adoption is a shared responsibility. The attorney for the agency must prepare the verified schedule and affidavit of no appeal and file them along with the certified birth certificate, the abuse clearance form and any other forms required of the agency by the various adoption clerks. The attorney for the adoptive parents must file the petition for adoption, agreement for adoption, the order of adoption, supporting affidavits and other documents required by the various adoption clerks.

An essential element of the strategy of the attorney is to make certain that the prospective adoptive parents understand the importance of openly acknowledging any past criminal activity. Prospective adoptive parents may hold back information about their past criminal convictions even though all past criminal activity will be discovered due to the court rules requirement of a fingerprint check. It is therefore essential that the attorney know in advance if the prospective adoptive parents have

---

893, 578 N.Y.S.2d 988 (Fam.Ct., N.Y. County, 1991).

4. A subsidy adoption is one in which the adoptive parents are given a monthly stipend of approximately $400 by the state until the child reaches the age of 21. Social Services Law §§ 450–458.

5. PRACTICE POINTER: The best and easiest way for the attorney representing the adoptive parents to make sure that the subsidy is in place is to discuss this issue with the adoption caseworker or adoption supervisor employed by the authorized agency. It is the obligation of the agency to make sure that the subsidy is in place prior to the adoption. However, the ultimate responsibility lies with the attorney for the adoptive parents and until and unless the attorney sees the actual subsidy written approval, the adoption should not be finalized because the state, in most cases, will not give or increase the subsidy stipend once the adoption has been finalized.

been convicted of crimes. The attorney for the adoptive parents must advise them that criminal convictions will not necessarily prevent the adoption.[6] In practice, it rarely does. An explanatory affidavit setting forth the facts and circumstances surrounding the incident must be prepared and filed with the adoption clerk for review by the court. At the same time, the adoption agency must either amend the home study or file an addendum to the home study detailing the incident, the fact that they have knowledge of the incident and, despite the same and based upon all of the facts and circumstances surrounding the adoption, including the character, personality and integrity of the adoptive parents, that it is the recommendation of the authorized agency that the child be adopted by the adoptive parents. Lastly, if all the work has been completed in the appropriate matter, the adoption hearing, as with the private adoption, is mainly ceremonial and should be a pleasant experience.

§ 20.3 Strategy—Checklist: Pre-adoption—Counsel for Parents

Some of the pre-adoptive pitfalls that the practitioner must avoid in order not to compromise the adoption or face disciplinary action are:

1. With respect to locating an infant for adoption, the practitioner must be mindful that it is illegal to procure an infant for the prospective adoptive parent. Only the birth parent or an authorized agency may place an infant for adoption with the prospective adoptive parents.

2. It is impermissible to represent both the birth parent and the adoptive parent.[1]

3. The attorney's fee must be commensurate with the work involved and must be reasonable. A reasonable fee for private adoption is within the range of $2,000 to $3,500. If the fee paid to the attorney is extremely high the court may inquire as to whether the practitioner was actually receiving a procurement fee which, of course, is illegal.[2]

---

6. *See* the case of In re Alison V.V., 211 A.D.2d 988, 621 N.Y.S.2d 739 (3d Dep't 1995), wherein the appellate division held that the adoptive mother's conviction for disorderly conduct and hindering prosecution when she was seventeen years of age, should not have precluded her from being considered as an adoptive parent where at the time of the adoption proceeding she was thirty-four years of age, she had not engaged in any additional criminal activity, and at the time had been steadily employed and had been certified as a foster parent and had foster children in her home.

See however, 11 NYCRR § 421.16(p)(1) provides that if the adoptive parent was convicted of a crime involving the death of a infant under Titles H and O of the New York Penal Law, the adoption application must be denied. By way of illustration, if an adoptive parent pleads guilty to or is convicted of criminally negligent homicide involving the death of an infant, the adoption application of that person must be denied.

§ 20.3

1. Social Services Law § 374(6).
2. Social Services Law § 374(6).

4. Only reasonable and necessary payments on behalf of the birth parent by the adoptive parents are permissible. Either prior to or subsequent to the payments, all payments must be approved by the court. The practitioner must be aware that allowable expenses include medical and other expenses incidental to the pregnancy and birth of the child.[3]

5. The practitioner must be mindful that there must be full compliance with the Interstate Compact Act. If a child is born outside of the State of New York and is placed for adoption within the State, the Interstate Compact Act must be complied with. This Act has been codified in Social Services Law § 374–a.

6. Some practitioners concentrate so much on the birth mother that the putative father is ignored. The practitioner must be mindful that the consent of the father of a child born out of wedlock is required if he meets the standard established by the Court of Appeals in the case of Matter of Raquel Marie X.[4]

7. The practitioner must be mindful that it is no longer permissible for adoptive parents to receive a child physically for adoption unless the pre-certification procedures have been complied with. Typically persons seeking to commence a private placement adoption must, prior to any transfer of physical custody of any adoptive child, be certified as qualified adoptive parents by a court of competent jurisdiction. It is the attorney's obligation to make sure that the adoptive parents are properly certified as qualified adoptive parents before physically taking possession of the infant.

§ 20.4 Strategy—Checklist: Interview With Birth Mother[1]

When the attorney representing the birth mother first interviews her, the following background information should be obtained:

(1) Name

(2) Also known as

(3) Address

(4) Home telephone number

(5) Work telephone number

(6) Social security number

(7) Place of employment

---

3. DRL § 115(8).
4. 76 N.Y.2d 387, 559 N.Y.S.2d 855, 559 N.E.2d 418 (1990), cert. denied 498 U.S. 984, 111 S.Ct. 517, 112 L.Ed.2d 528 (1990).

§ 20.4
1. This information should be obtained in both private and agency adoptions.

§ 20.4 ADOPTIONS Ch. 20

(8) Emergency contact (name, address and telephone number)

(9) Maiden name (if married)

(10) Name of spouse

(11) Address of spouse

(12) Spouse's home telephone number

(13) Spouse work telephone number

(14) Spouse's social security number

(15) Spouse's place of employment

(16) Has a copy of the adoptive parents' homestudy been reviewed. If so, are they satisfied with the contents and, if not, would they like to review a copy of the homestudy

(17) Birth mother's religion; whether or not practicing

(18) Birth mother's racial background

(19) Birth's mother's nationality background

(20) If birth mother is a Native American, her tribal affiliation, where enrolled and degree of blood

(21) Birth mother's primary language

(22) Birth mother's second language

(23) Birth mother's height

(24) Birth mother's average pre-pregnancy weight

(25) Birth mother's eye color

(26) Birth mother's complexion

(27) Birth mother's natural hair color and texture

(28) Other distinguishing characteristics of birth mother

(29) Birth mother's build

(30) Birth mother's date of birth

(31) Birth mother's place of birth

(32) Birth mother's present general health

(33) Birth mother's blood type

(34) Is birth mother left handed or right handed

(35) Does birth mother where glasses or contact lenses and, if so, for what condition

(36) Birth mother's age at onset of menstruation

(37) Has birth mother had any major surgery and, if yes, for what and when

(38) Date birth mother was first seen by a doctor for this pregnancy

Ch. 20　　INTERVIEW WITH BIRTH MOTHER　　§ 20.4

(39) Weight gained during this pregnancy

(40) Due date for this pregnancy

(41) Birth mother's RH factor

(42) Doctor's name and address

(43) Name and address of hospital where delivery will take place

(44) Birth mother's medical insurance coverage including plan name, name of company, type and policy number

(45) Any medications, drugs or alcohol used before this pregnancy and during this pregnancy

(46) Does the birth mother smoke and, if yes, number of packs a day

(47) Did the birth mother have any complications or accidents during this pregnancy and, if yes, please describe.

(48) Number of previous pregnancies

(49) Number of previous deliveries

(50) Type of delivery (vaginal or caesarian)

(51) Was prior delivery full term or pre-term; if pre-term, number of weeks

(52) Congenital defects of birth mother

(53) Did birth mother have any surgery during this pregnancy and, if yes, please describe

(54) Last grade of school completed by birth mother

(55) Average grade in school

(56) Birth mother's favorite subjects

(57) Birth mother's difficult subjects

(58) Any extracurricular activities participated in

(59) Name of last school attended

(60) Any additional vocational training

(61) Plans for future schooling

(62) Is the birth mother's family aware of the pregnancy

(63) Is the birth mother's family aware of the adoption plans and, if so, how do they feel about the plans

(64) Birth mother's reasons for choosing adoption for the child

(65) Would the birth mother like to have contact with the child in the future

(66) Is the birth mother aware of the New York State Adoption Information Registry in Albany

§ 20.4 ADOPTIONS Ch. 20

(67) Has the birth mother had any psychological counseling related to this pregnancy and the adoption plans. If so, was she happy with the counseling and if not, would she like to receive additional counseling

(68) Was anyone in the birth mother's family adopted.

(69) Has anyone in the birth mother's family placed a child for adoption

(70) Does the birth mother have any memories or events of her childhood that were important to her or which had a significant effect on her

(71) Birth mother's description of her personality

(72) Birth mother's hobbies, special skills, talents and interest

(73) Birth mother's relationship with parents

(74) Birth mother's relationship with siblings

(75) Birth mother's plans for the future

(76) Birth mother's marital status

(77) Date of birth of spouse

(78) Place of birth of spouse

(79) Date of marriage

(80) Place of marriage

(81) Date of divorce

(82) Place of divorce

(83) Is the birth mother living with anyone

(84) Number of children

(85) Date of birth of any children

(86) Sex of any children

(87) Health and physical condition of any children

(88) Any developmental problems of any children

(89) Current whereabouts of any children.

(90) Has the birth father sired any prior children

(91) The following should be ascertained regarding the birth mother's mother: height, weight, race, eye color, hair color and texture, date of birth, place of birth, is mother living, if not, age and cause of death

(92) The following should be ascertained regarding the birth mother's father: height, weight, race, eye color, hair color and

texture, date of birth, place of birth, is mother living, if not, age and cause of death

(93) Has anyone in the birth mother's family given birth to twins, triplets, etc.

(94) Birth mother's current occupation

(95) Length of time employed at current job

(96) Any previous occupations of birth mother

(97) Is birth mother in the military and, if so, branch of service

(98) Does the birth mother have medical insurance or Medicaid. If yes, type of insurance, plan name and identification number.

§ 20.5 Adoptions—Generally

Adoptions have occurred for centuries and were practiced by the Athenians, the Spartans and the Romans. Adoptions were incorporated into French and Spanish law, but were unknown to the common law of England. Therefore, adoptions are authorized in both England and America solely by statute.[1] Adoptions laws, which were enacted by the State of New York in 1873, provided for the voluntary adoption of children upon the consent of the parents. Early adoption statutes regarded the adoption proceeding to be non-judicial, and as being an agreement between the parties to seek court approval of the adoption.[2] The current law of adoptions is found in Article 7 of the DRL §§ 109 through 117.[3] The Uniform Rules regarding adoption proceedings in the surrogate's court are found in 22 NYCRR §§ 207.54, *et seq*. The family court Uniform Rules regarding adoption proceedings are found in 22 NYCRR §§ 205.52, *et seq*.

Library References:

West's Key No. Digests, Adoption ⚭1.

§ 20.6 Adoptions—Defined

Domestic Relations Law § 110 defines adoption as the legal proceeding whereby one person takes another person into the relationship of child and thereby acquires the rights, and incurs the responsibilities, of a

---

§ 20.5

1. The Court of Appeals in the case of Matter of Adoption of Malpica–Orsini, 36 N.Y.2d 568, 370 N.Y.S.2d 511, 331 N.E.2d 486 (1975), appeal dismissed 423 U.S. 1042, 96 S.Ct. 765, 46 L.Ed.2d 631 (1976), noted the right to adoption of children and strangers to the blood was unknown to common law and exists only by statute.

2. Stevens v. Halstead, 181 App.Div. 198, 168 N.Y.S. 142 (2d Dep't 1917).

3. PRACTICE POINTER: Although adoption law is statutory, the practitioner should read the latest cases interpreting the statute. Family law practitioners are now ever mindful with the recent Court of Appeals case of In re Dana and In re Jacob, 86 N.Y.2d 651, 636 N.Y.S.2d 716, 660 N.E.2d 397 (1995), that the courts have liberally interpreted the meaning of the statutory language.

§ 20.6　　　　　　　　ADOPTIONS　　　　　　　　Ch. 20

parent in relation to such other person.[1] No person may be adopted except in accordance with Article 7 of the Domestic Relations Law. Adoption proceedings are judicial in nature and an Order of Adoption has the force and effect of, and is entitled to all of the presumptions that attach to, a judgment rendered by a court of general jurisdiction in a common law proceeding.

Library References:
West's Key No. Digests, Adoption ⬅1.

§ 20.7　Adoptions—Rationale

The courts have held that the primary purpose of an adoption is to promote the welfare of the child by establishing a parent-child relationship.[1] In *Matter of Adoption of E.W.C.*,[2] the court ruled in favor of the adoption and refused to magnify every defect in order to declare the adoption invalid. Judge Paula J. Hepner, in a well reasoned decision of first impression, wrote that the primary function of an adoption is to provide for the child's financial and emotional security and that the goal of adoption is to give legal effect to the parent-child relationship.[3]

Library References:
West's Key No. Digests, Adoption ⬅1.

§ 20.8　Adoptions—Judicial Construction of Statutes

Since adoptions were unknown in common law and exist solely as a creature of statute, statutes relating to adoptions are in derogation of the common law. In the past, the courts have held, therefore, that adoption statutes must be strictly construed.[1] In *Adams v. Nadel*,[2] the court stated that because adoption was not known to common law, adoption statutes must be strictly construed and what is not found in the statute is for the Legislature to supply and not the courts.

The principle that adoption statutes must be strictly construed, which was the law for hundreds of years, was diluted by a closely divided Court of Appeals which ruled that a person who is a *de facto* partner of a child's biological parent and is participating in the raising of the child,

---

§ 20.6

1. In Domestic Relations Law § 110 the term "person" relates to any human being, whether a relative by blood, or a stranger, regardless of age. In re Anonymous, 177 Misc. 683, 31 N.Y.S.2d 595 (Surr.Ct., Monroe County, 1941).

§ 20.7

1. *See* Matter of Adoption of Robert Paul P., 63 N.Y.2d 233, 481 N.Y.S.2d 652, 471 N.E.2d 424 (1984).

2. 89 Misc.2d 64, 389 N.Y.S.2d 743 (Surr.Ct., Nassau County, 1976).

3. In re Camilla, 163 Misc.2d 272, 620 N.Y.S.2d 897 (Fam.Ct., Kings County, 1994).

§ 20.8

1. *See* Matter of Adoption of Robert Paul P., 63 N.Y.2d 233, 481 N.Y.S.2d 652, 471 N.E.2d 424 (1984).

2. 124 N.Y.S.2d 427 (Sup.Ct., Kings County, 1953).

may adopt the infant. In the jointly decided cases of *In re Jacob* and *In re Dana*,[3] the court held that it made no difference whether the unmarried partner was heterosexual or homosexual. In *In re Jacob*, the court permitted the adoption by the mother's live-in male companion. In *In re Dana*, the Court of Appeals permitted the adoption by the longtime lesbian companion of the mother who bore the infant by artificial insemination.

Prior to these decisions, the plain language of Secton 110 of the Domestic Relations Law permitted only an adult unmarried person or an adult husband and his adult wife the ability to adopt another person. Many family law practitioners and observers favor these decisions as accommodating society's changing concept of the extended family. However, permitting an unmarried partner of the child's biological mother to adopt the child clearly is a liberal interpretation of Domestic Relations Law § 110, and it can no longer be said that in the State of New York adoption statutes must be strictly construed. Besides Section 110 of the Domestic Relations Law, Section 117 was also liberally construed to permit a "second parent" adoption without terminating the rights of the biological parent.

Library References:

West's Key No. Digests, Adoption ⚖=1.

§ 20.9 Adoptions—Concurrent Jurisdiction

The surrogate's court and the family court have concurrent jurisdiction over adoption;[1] hence, adoption proceedings may be commenced in either court.[2] Once an adoption proceeding has been commenced in the surrogate's court, it may not transfer the proceeding to the family court for final disposition.[3] It should be noted that the supreme court shares concurrent jurisdiction over adoption proceedings with the surrogate's court and the family court.[4] While this is so, the supreme court rarely entertains an adoption petition. A practitioner attempting to file an adoption proceeding in the supreme court would promptly be referred to the family court or surrogate's court.

Library References:

West's Key No. Digests, Adoption ⚖=10.

---

3. 86 N.Y.2d 651, 636 N.Y.S.2d 716, 660 N.E.2d 397 (1995).

§ 20.9

1. *See* Family Court Act § 641 and DRL § 111–b.

2. The rules relating to adoptions in the family court are contained in 22 NYCRR §§ 205.53 through 205.55 and the adoption rules with respect to the surrogate's court are contained in 22 NYCRR §§ 207.54 through 207.58 of the Uniform Rules of the New York State Trial Courts.

3. Matter of Adoption of Earl B. and Willie A., 119 Misc.2d 515, 463 N.Y.S.2d 724 (Fam.Ct., N.Y. County, 1983).

4. Kaplan v. Meskin, 108 A.D.2d 787, 485 N.Y.S.2d 117 (2d Dep't 1985).

§ 20.10 Adoptions—Concurrent Jurisdiction—Where to File Adoption Proceedings

Although the adoption proceeding may be filed in either the family court or the surrogate's court, the determination of where to file depends upon many factors.[1] The family court has jurisdiction over juvenile delinquency proceedings, persons in need of supervision proceedings and family disputes. The surrogate's court deals with infants, estates, accountings and guardianships. Hence, some attorneys prefer the surrogate's court because of the more serene atmosphere. The attorney representing the adoptive parents should choose the court which is more favorable to adoptions and whose staff will process the adoption more expeditiously.

Where the adoption is contested, and psychological and psychiatric evaluations of the parties are required, it may be determined that complicated issues of custody should be transferred to the family court, which has support personnel such as in the probation department and psychiatrists and psychologists available to make professional evaluations, diagnoses, and recommendations to the judge of the family court.[2] In *Matter of F.D.*, the court permitted the birth mother to withdraw her consent to the adoption and dismissed the petition. The court, after taking testimony for eighteen days concerning the validity of the mother's consent, declined to decide the issue of custody. The surrogate determined that the family court had the requisite support personnel in its probation department and could better determine issues of physical custody and the best interests of the child.[3]

Library References:

West's Key No. Digests, Adoption ⟐10.

§ 20.10

1. **PRACTICE POINTER:** Because the practitioner has a choice as to where to file the adoption proceeding, this initial decision may be crucial to the successful finalization of the adoption itself. Adoption practitioners who practice on a daily basis know which courts and which judges are friendly to adoptions and which judges and courts place barriers to adoption finalization. There is nothing wrong *per se* in forum shopping and judge shopping if the law permits such an option. The adoption attorney, although the proceedings may not be contested, is still an advocate for his clients' desire to adopt and, therefore, should make discreet inquiries as to which courts will provide a favorable atmosphere for adoptions. If it is known that a surrogate's court in one county requires the petitioner to terminate parental rights of a John Doe, it makes sense to file in the family court in the same county where it is well known that such termination of a John Doe is not required. Once it is determined in which court the petition will be filed, the practitioner should make a personal appearance at the court and visit with the adoption clerk. Most adoption clerks are friendly and helpful. At the very least, the adoption clerk will supply the requisite official forms and an instruction sheet so that it is clear which documents are required, including any special affidavits that are peculiar to that particular court. For example, some courts require supplemental affidavits, fingerprinting and affidavits of no appeal, while other courts may not.

2. *See* Matter of F.D., 105 Misc.2d 866, 433 N.Y.S.2d 318 (Surr.Ct., Nassau County, 1980).

3. *Id.*

§ 20.11 Adoptions—Choice of Venue

Domestic Relations Law § 115(2) relating to private adoptions provides that an adoption proceeding be instituted in the county where the adoptive parents reside or, if they reside outside New York State, in the county where the adoptive child resides. In an agency adoption, the Social Services Law provides that the adoption proceeding may be filed in the court which terminated parental rights or in the court which approved the surrender.[1]

The requirement to commence an adoption proceeding in a county in which the adoptive parents or adoptive child resides relates to venue. Generally, the selection of an improper venue is a waivable defect. In *Matter of Adoption of E.W.C.*,[2] the adoptive parents had residences in both Suffolk County, where they resided most of the year, and in Nassau County, where they maintained a summer and weekend residence. The court held that the adoption proceeding could be maintained in Nassau County and any improper venue would not be treated as a jurisdictional defect.

Library References:
West's Key No. Digests, Adoption ⟐10.

§ 20.12 Adoptions—Types

Whether the adoption takes place in the family court or the surrogate's court, there are basically two types of adoption: private placement adoptions and agency adoptions.

Private placement adoptions, which are sometimes called independent adoptions, involve the consent of the birth parents to an adoption directly with the adoptive parents.

Agency adoptions, on the other hand, involve an agreement between the agency and the adoptive parent.

Library References:
West's Key No. Digests, Adoption ⟐10.

§ 20.13 Adoptions—Effect of Adoption

The order of adoption has the effect of severing all legal rights between the adoptive infant and the biological parents.[1]

Once a child has been adopted, he or she is treated as the natural child of the adoptive parent. The adoptive parent and child acquire all of the rights, obligations and responsibilities of a natural parent and child.

§ 20.11
1. Social Services Law § 384(b).
2. 89 Misc.2d 64, 389 N.Y.S.2d 743 (Surr.Ct., Nassau County, 1976).

§ 20.13
1. Doe v. Roe, 37 A.D.2d 433, 326 N.Y.S.2d 421 (2d Dep't 1971).

The adoptive parents have full rights of legal custody over that child as if that child were born to them. Further, if the adoptive parents die without a will, the adoptive child will inherit as if the child were a natural child of the deceased adoptive parent.[2]

Library References:

West's Key No. Digests, Adoption ⚖20.

§ 20.14 Adoptions—Who May Adopt—Statutory Mandates

Domestic Relations Law § 110 specifies those persons who may adopt: (1) an adult, unmarried person or an adult husband and his adult wife, together, may adopt another person; (2) an adult married person who is living separate and apart from his or her spouse pursuant to a decree or judgment of separation or pursuant to a written agreement of separation; (3) an adult married person who has been living separate and apart from his or her spouse for at least three years prior to commencing adoption proceedings; (4) an adult or minor husband and his adult or minor wife, together, may adopt a child of either of them born in or out of wedlock; and (5) an adult or minor husband or an adult or minor wife may adopt such a child of the other spouse.[1]

Library References:

West's Key No. Digests, Adoption ⚖4.

§ 20.15 Adoptions—Who May Adopt—Separated Persons

An adult married person who has a legally enforceable separation agreement or is party to a marriage in which there is a valid decree of separation or has been living separate and apart from his or her spouse for at least three years prior to the commencement of an adoption proceeding and has become custodian of a child pursuant to court ordered foster care, may apply to the authorized agency for placement of the child for the purpose of adoption.[1] In 1991, the statute was amended to allow an adult married person, who had been living apart from his or her spouse for at least three years prior to commencing the adoption proceeding, to adopt even though the separation was not legally sanctioned.[2] As a result, some foster parents who, for economic or religious

---

2. *See* DRL § 117; Matter of Adoption of Robert Paul P., 63 N.Y.2d 233, 481 N.Y.S.2d 652, 471 N.E.2d 424 (1984).

§ 20.14

1. DRL § 110.

§ 20.15

1. DRL § 110.

2. Scheinkman, *Practice Commentaries*, DRL § 110, C:110:3, p. 401. *See also*, Sobie, et al., *New York Family Court Practice* (West 1996) § 5.4.

reasons, did not obtain a judicial divorce or separation, may now be able to adopt a child.[3]

Library References:

West's Key No. Digests, Adoption ⟐4.

§ 20.16 Adoptions—Who May Adopt—Foster Parents: Preference to Adopt

Social Services Law § 383(3) relates to foster parents who have cared for a foster child continuously for a period of twelve months or more. Such foster parents who wish to adopt the child, if the child is eligible for adoption, have a first preference and first consideration over all of the applicants to adopt that child.

Library References:

West's Key No. Digests, Adoption ⟐4.

§ 20.17 Adoptions—Who May Adopt—Second Parent Adoptions

Second parent adoptions refer to parents who are not married to each other but nonetheless adopt a child together.

While Domestic Relations Law § 110 permits adoption by unmarried persons individually, case law was split on the issue of whether unmarried couples may adopt a child. In *In re Hope*,[1] the court refused to allow an unmarried man to adopt the children of the woman with whom he was involved. The court reasoned that Domestic Relations Law § 110 did not authorize such an adoption and that, under Domestic Relations Law § 117, the effect of the adoption would be to terminate their mother's parental rights.

However, a different result was reached in *In re Adoption of Evan*,[2] in which the woman partner of a child's biological mother was permitted to adopt the child. The women had lived together in a long term relationship, and together had planned the birth of the child, who was conceived with a male friend's donated sperm.

The Court of Appeals in the jointly decided cases of *In re Jacob* and

---

3. PRACTICE POINTER: Because the attorney for the adoptive parents cannot file a divorce decree or separation decree where the parties are still married but living separate and apart, the attorney must prepare and have the adoptive parents sign a marital affidavit. Among other things, a marital affidavit must allege that the adoptive mother or father has lived separate and apart from his or her spouse for at least three years and request the court to permit a single parent adoption.

§ 20.17

1. 150 Misc.2d 319, 571 N.Y.S.2d 182 (Fam.Ct., Westchester County, 1991).

2. 153 Misc.2d 844, 583 N.Y.S.2d 997 (Surr.Ct., N.Y. County, 1992).

In re Dana,[3] made it clear that the law of the State of New York permits second parent adoptions. Many observers of adoption law and certainly the dissenters in the Court of Appeals are of the opinion that this case ended the strict interpretation of adoption statutes. The plain language of Domestic Relations Law §§ 110 and 117 permits two adult persons to adopt only if they are married to each other. In the case of *In re Dana*,[4] the Court of Appeals allowed a lesbian to adopt her life partner's child.[5] In the case of *In re Jacob*,[6] the Court of Appeals permitted unmarried heterosexual partners to adopt the child of one of them. In so holding, the Court of Appeals eroded the principle of strict construction of the statute by reasoning that, although the statute must be strictly construed, what also must be strictly construed and applied rigorously is legislative purpose as well as legislative language. The Court emphasized purpose in order to carry out what was in the best interests of the child. In both cases, the Court of Appeals determined that the infants were with loving, caring, nurturing parents and, therefore, their best interests dictated that the adoptions be permitted, although a somewhat novel concept.[7]

Library References:

West's Key No. Digests, Adoption ⚖4.

§ 20.18 Adoptions—Who May Adopt—Unwed Putative Fathers

Domestic Relations Law § 110 permits an adult unmarried person to adopt another person. Hence a biological parent is allowed to adopt his or her own child. In one case, when the biological mother, who was not married to the biological father, consented to the adoption and was allowed to preserve her parental rights and obligations, the biological father was allowed to adopt his own child.[1]

Library References:

West's Key No. Digests, Adoption ⚖4.

---

3. 86 N.Y.2d 651, 636 N.Y.S.2d 716, 660 N.E.2d 397 (1995).

4. *Id.*

5. In the case of In re Camilla, 163 Misc.2d 272, 620 N.Y.S.2d 897 (Fam.Ct., Kings County, 1994), the court held that the step-parent exemption from placement certification requirements for adoptive parents apply to all second parent adoptions, including adoption by lesbian partner of the biological mother.

6. 86 N.Y.2d 651, 636 N.Y.S.2d 716, 660 N.E.2d 397 (1995).

7. The court in defending criticism from the dissent noted that Massachusetts permitted second parent adoptions, Vermont permitted second parent adoptions and so did the State of Wisconsin. *See* 18 NYCRR § 421.16(h)(2) of the rules and regulations of the State of New York which provide that sexual orientation alone may not be determinative in an adoption proceeding. For a well reasoned opinion analyzing the cases discussing a parent's sexual orientation in relation to the adoption, *see* In re Caitlin, 163 Misc.2d 999, 622 N.Y.S.2d 835 (Fam.Ct., Monroe County, 1994).

§ 20.18

1. In re A.J.J., 108 Misc.2d 657, 438 N.Y.S.2d 444 (Surr.Ct., N.Y. County, 1981).

§ 20.19 Adoptions—Who May Adopt—Citizens and Aliens

New York statutes do not prohibit a person from adopting another person who is not a resident of the State of New York. In fact, Domestic Relations Law §§ 113 and 115 recognize that a person may adopt another who is not a resident of the State of New York. In one case, a court had approved the adoption of a resident child by foster parents who were aliens (Canadians).[1] However, the adoption of an alien minor by an American citizen does not confer American citizenship on the adopted person.[2]

Library References:

West's Key No. Digests, Adoption ⊜4.

§ 20.20 Adoptions—Who May Adopt—Age as a Factor

Domestic Relations Law § 110 permits an adult unmarried person, or an adult husband and his adult wife together, the right to adopt another person. While the section mandates that the person adopting be at least eighteen years of age, the statute is silent as to what age is too old to adopt. One judge of the Family Court, New York County, in the case of *In re Andres R.*,[1] held that a foster mother, sixty-seven years of age, was too old to adopt and he refused to approve the adoption. On appeal, the appellate division, while affirming the termination of parental rights, modified the order insofar as the judge had directed a younger person to be the adoptive parent. In modifying, the appellate division noted that the record below showed that the foster mother had provided an environment in which the child had lived and thrived and the family court was in error in refusing to approve an adoption by the foster mother based solely on her age of sixty-seven.[2]

Library References:

West's Key No. Digests, Adoption ⊜4.

§ 20.19

1. In re Adoption of Minor, 130 Misc. 793, 226 N.Y.S. 445 (Surr.Ct., Monroe County, 1927).
2. 1923, Op. Atty. Gen. 386.

§ 20.20

1. 216 A.D.2d 145, 629 N.Y.S.2d 7 (1st Dep't 1995).
2. **PRACTICE POINTER:** While the court may not dismiss the adoption petition based solely on the age of the adoptive parent or parents, in practice, where the adoptive parent or parents are elderly, the adoption clerks require an affidavit of back up resource. In practice, therefore, when an adoptive parent is in his or her sixties, usually a back up resource might be a daughter or niece who would sign an affidavit attesting to the fact that if the adoptive parent died or became infirm, that he or she would take over the care and custody of the child so that the child would not become a ward of the state.

§ 20.21 Adoptions—Who May Adopt—Extended Family as Factor

There is no question that when a child comes into foster care, extended family or next of kin, by statute, must be looked upon as the first resource, either as a custodian or as a foster parent.[1] However, once a child is in foster care the preference or presumption may no longer apply. Hence, the appellate division, in the case of *In re Maria Elizabeth A.*,[2] held that where a child has been in foster care with foster parents, no presumption favors the child's aunt or any other member of the "natural extended family" for dispositional purposes in a termination proceeding.[3]

Library References:

West's Key No. Digests, Adoption ⚖4.

§ 20.22 Adoptions—Who May Adopt—Adult Unmarried Person

Section 110 specifically provides for the adoption of a person by an adult unmarried person. Over the years, such adoptions were discriminated against. Such discrimination, however, is no longer permitted, for the courts have held that an adult unmarried person is not required to demonstrate exceptional circumstances before being allowed to adopt a child.[1]

Library References:

West's Key No. Digests, Adoption ⚖4.

§ 20.23 Adoptions—Who May Be Adopted—In General

Pursuant to Domestic Relations Law § 110, any person may be adopted. The term "person" has been defined as being synonymous with a human being, whether related by blood or a stranger, and regardless of

---

§ 20.21

1. Family Court Act §§ 1017, 1055; the concept of family has evolved to include the formation of parent-child relationships between grandparents who adopt their grandchildren, aunts and uncles who adopt their nieces and nephews, and between adult siblings who adopt their minor siblings. *See* In re Camilla, 163 Misc.2d 272, 620 N.Y.S.2d 897 (Fam.Ct., Kings County, 1994).

2. 219 A.D.2d 503, 631 N.Y.S.2d 334 (1st Dep't 1995); *see also*, Matter of Netfa P., 115 A.D.2d 390, 496 N.Y.S.2d 21 (1st Dep't 1985).

3. **PRACTICE POINTER:** If the attorney represents the extended family, the better practice would be not to wait for the dispositional hearing where there is no presumption in favor of any of the parties. The practitioner representing the aunt and uncle or grandparent should petition the court for custody. If the extended family member petitions for outright custody, some judges would favor such an arrangement over continued foster care with the possibility of an adoption.

§ 20.22

1. In re Alison V.V., 211 A.D.2d 988, 621 N.Y.S.2d 739 (3d Dep't 1995).

whether the person adopted is a minor or an adult.[1]

Library References:

West's Key No. Digests, Adoption ⚷5.

§ 20.24 Adoptions—Who May Be Adopted—Adult Adoptions

An adult adoption is one in which the adoptee has reached his majority, which in New York and most other jurisdictions, is eighteen years of age. Domestic Relations Law § 110 contemplates that the adopted person, whether adult or infant, becomes the child of the adoptive parents. Domestic Relations Law § 111(4) provides that consents required under subsection 1 of Section 111 shall not be required where the adoptive child is over the age of eighteen years.[1] Adult adoptions often legalize some type of long-standing relationship between the person being adopted and the adoptive parent. In *Matter of Adoption of Robert Paul P.*,[2] the Court of Appeals held that the adoption statutes may not be used as a quasi-marriage between, in this case, two men. In this case, the adoption was applied for on the grounds of social, economic and psychological reasons, including the disposition of the respective estates of the two males. The Court of Appeals, in denying the adoption, reinforced the traditional reason for adoption, *i.e.*, the legal proceeding whereby one person takes another person into the relationship of child and thereby acquires the rights and responsibilities of a parent. The Court of Appeals in so holding overruled the case of *In re Adult Anonymous II*,[3] which held that the adoption of one homosexual partner by another was legally permissible. The court, however, in *Matter of Adoption of Robert Paul P.*,[4] did not limit the ability of one adult to adopt another adult where the purpose is to create a parent-child relationship.

Library References:

West's Key No. Digests, Adoption ⚷5.

§ 20.25 Adoption—Who May Be Adopted—Aliens

Both the Social Services Law and the Domestic Relations Law provide for the adoption of alien orphans.[1] Domestic Relations Law § 115–a outlines the pre-adoption procedures that must be complied with before a child may arrive in the United States. These pre-adoption

§ 20.23

1. In re Matter of Anonymous, 177 Misc. 683, 31 N.Y.S.2d 595 (Surr.Ct., Monroe County, 1941).

§ 20.24

1. DRL § 111(4).
2. 63 N.Y.2d 233, 481 N.Y.S.2d 652, 471 N.E.2d 424 (1984).

3. 88 A.D.2d 30, 452 N.Y.S.2d 198 (1st Dep't 1982).

4. 63 N.Y.2d 233, 481 N.Y.S.2d 652, 471 N.E.2d 424 (1984).

§ 20.25

1. *See* Social Services Law § 371(10)(c) (agency adoptions) and DRL § 115–a(1) (private placement adoptions).

requirements apply only to private placement adoptions and not agency adoptions. The purpose of the pre-adoption procedures is to assure that the child does not come to the United States only to have the court reject the adoption.[2]

Library References:

West's Key No. Digests, Adoption ⚖5.

§ 20.26 Adoptions—Who May Be Adopted—Non-marital Children

A non-marital child (also referred to as "illegitimate" or "born out of wedlock") may be adopted by the child's natural father, even though the father has no intention of marrying the child's mother.[1] In *Matter of A.J.J.*, the natural father was permitted to adopt an infant conceived and born out of wedlock where the natural mother consented to the adoption. The parents had a long term relationship but did not intend to marry. In approving the adoption, the court also ruled, as requested by the parties, that the natural mother would not be relieved of her parental obligations and that the mother and child would retain their legal parent-child relationship, including all rights of inheritance.

Library References:

West's Key No. Digests, Adoption ⚖5.

§ 20.27 Adoptions—Who May Be Adopted—Interracial Adoptions

There is no law in the State of New York prohibiting interracial adoptions. On the contrary, an adoption may not be prohibited solely on the basis of race.[1] Today, interracial adoptions take place frequently and in the State of New York it is rare that anyone raises any objection to such interracial adoptions.

Library References:

West's Key No. Digests, Adoption ⚖5.

§ 20.28 Adoptions—Who May Be Adopted—Religion as a Factor

The Constitution of the State of New York and statutes adopted in conformity therewith require that a child be placed with persons of the

---

2. In re Adoption of Pyung B., 83 Misc.2d 794, 371 N.Y.S.2d 993 (Fam.Ct., Onondaga County, 1975).

§ 20.26

1. DRL § 110; see Matter of A.J.J., 108 Misc.2d 657, 438 N.Y.S.2d 444 (Surr.Ct., N.Y. County, 1981).

§ 20.27

1. Rockefeller v. Nickerson, 36 Misc.2d 869, 233 N.Y.S.2d 314 (Sup.Ct., N.Y. County, 1962).

same religious beliefs as the child "when practicable" and "consistent with the best interests of the child."[1] Such provisions are not unconstitutional. In *Dickens v. Ernesto*,[2] the Court of Appeals upheld the constitutionality of the statutory preferences for placing children with persons of the same religion. In *In re Adoption of Maxwell*,[3] the Court of Appeals held that the term in Domestic Relations Law § 113 "when practicable" allows the court discretion to approve an adoption by persons of a different religious faith from the child where extraordinary circumstances exist.[4]

After the Court of Appeals decision in *Maxwell*, the statutes which required religious conformity of child and adoptive parents "when practicable" were broadened,[5] to provide that such religious "matching" in foster care and adoption proceedings be "consistent with the best interests of the child."[6]

In re Elianne M.,[7] the court affirmed the family court's directive to transfer a Jewish child in foster care from a non-Jewish home to a Jewish home in order to safeguard the child's religion. The court concluded that the child's faith was not being preserved and protected in the non-Jewish home.

Library References:

West's Key No. Digests, Adoption ⚖=5.

§ 20.29 Adoptions — Consents Required — Statutory Mandate

Domestic Relations Law § 111 sets forth the classes of persons whose consent is required to an adoption as follows:

(a) the adoptive child, if over fourteen years of age, unless the judge or surrogate in his or her discretion dispenses with such consent.

(b) the parents or surviving parent, whether adult or infant, of a child conceived or born in wedlock.

§ 20.28

1. New York State Constitution, Art. VI, § 32; DRL § 113.

2. 30 N.Y.2d 61, 330 N.Y.S.2d 346, 281 N.E.2d 153 (1972).

3. 4 N.Y.2d 429, 176 N.Y.S.2d 281, 151 N.E.2d 848 (1958).

4. **PRACTICE POINTER:** Neither the parties nor the practitioner of family and adoption law should be discouraged by the statutory language or the case law because in reality the adoption judge rarely goes into the issue of religion. By the time the case reaches the court, the child would have been with the foster parents or adoptive parents for at least a year and in some cases four years and an adoption judge would hardly prohibit the adoption based upon differences in religion.

5. Family Court Act § 116(g); Social Services Law § 373(7); *see also*, DRL § 113.

6. L.1970, Ch.494.

7. 184 A.D.2d 98, 592 N.Y.S.2d 296 (1st Dep't 1992).

(c) the mother, whether adult or infant, of a child born out of wedlock.

(d) the father, whether adult or infant, of a child born out of wedlock and placed with the adoptive parents more than six months after birth, but only if such father shall have maintained substantial and continuous or repeated contact with the child as manifested by: (i) payment by the father toward the support of the child of a fair and reasonable sum, according to the father's means, and either (ii) the father's visiting the child at least monthly when physically and financially able to do so and not prevented from doing so by the person or authorized agency having lawful custody of the child, or (iii) the father's regular communication with the child or with the person or agency having care or custody of the child, when physically or financially unable to visit the child or prevented from doing so by the person or authorized agency having lawful custody of the child.

(e) the father, whether adult or infant, of a child born out of wedlock who is under the age of six months at the time he is placed for adoption, but only if: (i) such father openly lived with the child or the child's mother for a continuous period of six months immediately preceding the placement of the child for adoption; and (ii) such father openly held himself out to be the father of such child during such period; and (ii) such father paid a fair and reasonable sum, in accordance with his means, for the medical, hospital and nursing expenses incurred in connection with the mother's pregnancy or with the birth of the child;[1] and

(f) of any person or authorized agency having lawful custody of the adoptive child.

Library References:

West's Key No. Digests, Adoption ⟳7.2(1)–7.2(3).

§ 20.30 Adoptions—Consents Required—Rights of Unwed Fathers

Prior to the United States Supreme Court's decision in *Stanley v. Illinois*,[1] an unwed father had no rights with respect to the adoption of his child; he had no right to receive notice, his consent was not needed and he was generally treated as a non-entity with regard to the adoption proceeding.

§ 20.29

1. DRL § 111(1)(e) was declared unconstitutional in Matter of Raquel Marie X., 76 N.Y.2d 387, 559 N.Y.S.2d 855, 559 N.E.2d 418 (1990), cert. denied 498 U.S. 984, 111 S.Ct. 517, 112 L.Ed.2d 528 (1990).

§ 20.30

1. 405 U.S. 645, 92 S.Ct. 1208, 31 L.Ed.2d 551 (1972).

In *Stanley v. Illinois*, the United States Supreme Court held that an unwed father who had a relationship with his children, had a right to participate in a hearing regarding the best interests of the children prior to having his parental rights terminated. *Stanley*, however, was not interpreted as giving the unwed father a veto of an adoption where the biological mother had consented to the adoption. In *Caban v. Mohammed*,[2] the United States Supreme Court held that an unwed father has rights akin to those of the biological mother.

Domestic Relations Law § 111(1)(e), which attempted to define the rights of putative fathers, was declared unconstitutional by the New York State Court of Appeals in *Matter of Raquel Marie X*.[3] On remand from the Court of Appeals, the Appellate Division, Second Department, found that the biological father demonstrated a lack of fitness and an unwillingness to accept parental responsibility in light of the standards set forth by the Court of Appeals and, therefore, his interest in Raquel Marie was not entitled to constitutional protection and his consent to the adoption was not required.[4]

The Court of Appeals ruled that the six months "living together" requirement of Domestic Relations Law § 111(1)(e)(i) rendered the statute unconstitutional as there was an insufficient relationship between the requirement and a valid state interest.

The Court of Appeals established the following criteria to be applied in determining whether the consent of a father of a non-marital child is required:

(1) An assertion of custody;

(2) Prompt manifestation of parental responsibility;

(3) Public acknowledgment of paternity;

(4) Payment of pregnancy and birth expenses;

(5) Steps taken to establish legal responsibility for the child;

(6) Demonstration of a willingness to openly hold himself out to be the father of the child; and

(7) Registration with the appropriate authorities, such as the putative father registry or filing an intent to claim paternity either before the birth of the child or immediately following the birth of the child.[5]

---

2. 441 U.S. 380, 99 S.Ct. 1760, 60 L.Ed.2d 297 (1979).

3. 76 N.Y.2d 387, 559 N.Y.S.2d 855, 559 N.E.2d 418 (1990), cert. denied 498 U.S. 984, 111 S.Ct. 517, 112 L.Ed.2d 528 (1990).

4. *See* Matter of Raquel Marie X, 173 A.D.2d 709, 570 N.Y.S.2d 604 (2d Dep't 1991).

5. One case interpreting the Court of Appeals the decision in Matter of Raquel Marie X., was In re Baby Girl, 206 A.D.2d 932, 615 N.Y.S.2d 800 (4th Dep't 1994), wherein the appellate division held that the unwed father's consent was not required to finalize the adoption where the father knew or should have known that the mother was pregnant and the father failed to do all that

§ 20.31 Adoptions—Consents Required—When Consent Not Required

Domestic Relations Law § 111(2) provides that consent shall not be required of a parent or other person having custody of the child:

(1) who evinces an intent to forego his or her parental or custodial rights and obligations as manifested by his or her failure for a period of six months to visit the child and communicate with the child or person having legal custody of the child, although able to do so; or

(2) who has surrendered the child to an authorized agency under the provisions of Social Services Law § 383–c or § 384; or

(3) for whose child a guardian has been appointed under the provisions of Social Services Law § 384–b; or

(4) who, by reason of mental illness or mental retardation as defined in Social Services Law § 384–b(6), is presently and for the foreseeable future unable to provide proper care for the child. The determination as to whether a parent is mentally ill or mentally retarded shall be made in accordance with the criteria and procedures set forth in Social Services Law § 384–b(6); or

(5) who has executed an instrument, which shall be irrevocable, denying the paternity of the child or consenting to the other parent's surrender of the child or consenting to the child's adoption, such instrument having been executed after conception and acknowledged in the manner required to permit the recording of a deed.

Consequently, there are five situations where the consent of a parent or other person is not required:

(a) Abandonment;[1]

(b) Surrender;[2]

---

he could do to establish the parental relationship within six months immediately preceding the child's placement for adoption. The court went on to hold that timeliness or promptness is measured in terms of the baby's life and not in terms of the onset of the putative father's awareness of the child's existence.

§ 20.31
1. Matter of Stephan Joseph S., 158 A.D.2d 524, 551 N.Y.S.2d 289 (2d Dep't 1990); Matter of Devorah Leah B., 152 A.D.2d 566, 543 N.Y.S.2d 495 (2d Dep't 1989).

2. Matter of X., 84 Misc.2d 770, 376 N.Y.S.2d 825 (Surr.Ct., Cattaraugus County, 1975).

(c) Permanent neglect;[3]

(d) Mental illness or mental retardation;[4] or

(e) Denial of paternity.[5]

Library References:
West's Key No. Digests, Adoption ⚖7.3, 7.4(1)–7.4(6).

§ 20.32 Adoptions—Consents Required—Notice of a Proposed Adoption

Notice of the proposed adoption must be given to a person whose consent to the adoption is required, and such notice must be given by personal service; *i.e.*, the notice must be personally served upon the person whose consent to the adoption is required.[1]

Notice and an opportunity to be heard upon the proposed adoption may be afforded to a parent whose consent to adoption may not be required if the judge or surrogate so orders. Such notice in the family court may take the form of a summons. In the surrogate's court the notice takes the form of a citation. It should be noted that the notice required under Domestic Relations Law § 111 shall be given in such manner as the judge or surrogate may direct.[2]

Library References:
West's Key No. Digests, Adoption ⚖12.

§ 20.33 Adoptions—Consents Required—Checklist of Fathers to Receive Notice of Adoption

Domestic Relations Law § 111–a provides that notice of adoption proceedings shall be given to certain fathers of non-marital children. Those persons entitled to notice may be categorized as follows:

(1) Any person adjudicated by a court of the State of New York to be the father of the child;

(2) Any person adjudicated by a court of another State of the United States to be the father of the child;

(3) Any person who has timely filed an unrevoked notice of intent to claim paternity of the child;

(4) Any person who is recorded on the child's birth certificate as the child's father;

---

3. Matter of Adoption of Mark L. Jr., 172 A.D.2d 158, 567 N.Y.S.2d 697 (1st Dep't 1991).

4. Social Services Law §§ 384–b, (6–a), (6–b).

5. DRL § 111(2)(e).

§ 20.32

1. DRL § 111–a.

2. Some courts direct that the notice of the adoption be personally served upon the putative fathers where other courts permit service by ordinary mail.

(5) Any person who is openly living with the child and the child's mother at the time the adoption proceeding is initiated and who is also holding himself out to be the child's father;

(6) Any person who has been identified as the child's father by the mother in a written sworn statement;

(7) Any person who has married the child's mother within six months subsequent to the birth of the child and prior to the execution of a surrender instrument or the initiation of a proceeding to terminate parental rights pursuant to Social Services Law § 384–b; and

(8) Any person who has filed with the putative father registry (established pursuant to Social Services Law § 372–c) an instrument acknowledging paternity of the child pursuant to Estates, Powers and Trusts Law ("EPTL") § 4–1.2.

Library References:

West's Key No. Digests, Adoption ⚖12.

§ 20.34 Adoptions—Persons Excluded From Notice

Domestic Relations Law § 111–a excludes from the list of persons entitled to notice "any person who has been convicted of rape in the first degree involving forcible compulsion, under subdivision one of section 130.35 of the penal law, when the child who is the subject of the proceeding was conceived as a result of such rape."

Library References:

West's Key No. Digests, Adoption ⚖12.

§ 20.35 Adoptions—Purpose of Notice

The sole purpose of notice to the unwed father under Domestic Relations Law § 111–a is to enable the unwed father to present evidence to the court relevant to the best interests of the child.[1] However, the persons entitled to notice pursuant to Domestic Relations Law § 111–a, in contrast to the provisions of Domestic Relations Law § 111, are not entitled to veto the proposed adoption by withholding consent.[2]

The constitutionality of Domestic Relations Law § 111–a has been upheld by the United States Supreme Court and the New York State Court of Appeals.[3] Domestic Relations Law § 111–a permits unwed fathers to participate in the adoption proceeding to offer evidence as to

---

§ 20.35
1. DRL § 111–a(3).
2. Matter of Raquel Marie X., 76 N.Y.2d 387, 559 N.Y.S.2d 855, 559 N.E.2d 418 (1990), cert. denied 498 U.S. 984, 111 S.Ct. 517, 112 L.Ed.2d 528 (1990).

3. Lehr v. Robertson, 463 U.S. 248, 103 S.Ct. 2985, 77 L.Ed.2d 614 (1983) which affirmed the New York case of Matter of Adoption of Jessica XX, 54 N.Y.2d 417, 446 N.Y.S.2d 20, 430 N.E.2d 896 (1981).

what is in the best interests of the child, but does not permit them to veto the adoption because consent of the unwed father is not required in situations defined by Domestic Relations Law § 111–a.[4]

The notice required by Domestic Relations Law § 111–a shall be given at least 20 days prior to the adoption proceeding by delivering a copy of the notice to the unwed father.[5] The notice shall inform the unwed father of the time, date, place and purpose of the proceeding and shall advise him that his failure to appear shall constitute a denial of interest in the child which may result in the adoption of the child without further notice.[6]

If the terms of Domestic Relations Law § 111–a are not complied with, the unwed father may apply to the court to set aside the adoption order.[7]

It has been held that the birth mother has no obligation in an adoption proceeding to name the father.[8]

Library References:

West's Key No. Digests, Adoption ⚷12.

§ 20.36 Adoptions—Procedure

A proceeding to adopt a person is a judicial proceeding and the order of adoption shall have the force and effect of, and be entitled to, all of the presumptions attaching to a judgment rendered by a court of general jurisdiction.[1]

The proceeding is commenced by the filing of a petition.[2] An investigation must be made by the court and this is accomplished by a certified social worker in a private adoption and by an authorized agency in an agency adoption. The parties, including the birth parents, the adoptive parents and the infant, must also appear before the court.

---

4. In the case of Matter of Baby Girl S., 208 A.D.2d 930, 617 N.Y.S.2d 539 (2d Dep't 1994), the appellate division affirmed the family court holding that the natural father's consent to the adoption was not required where he was incarcerated and failed to submit any evidence of his willingness to promptly assume full custody of the infant upon his possible parole in one year and failed to submit any other person as a possible resource.

5. See DRL § 111–a(4).

6. See DRL § 111–a(6).

7. DRL § 111–a(7); cf., In re Matter of Cory Michael F., 124 A.D.2d 992, 508 N.Y.S.2d 798 (4th Dep't 1986).

8. Matter of Adoption of Jessica XX, 54 N.Y.2d 417, 446 N.Y.S.2d 20, 430 N.E.2d 896 (1981), aff'd sub nom. Lehr v. Robertson, 463 U.S. 248, 103 S.Ct. 2985, 77 L.Ed.2d 614 (1983).

§ 20.36

1. DRL § 110.

2. The rules of adoption in the family court are contained in Uniform Rules—Family Court, 22 NYCRR §§ 205.53 through 205.55 and are applicable to all agency and private placement adoptions. The rules of adoption in the surrogate's court are contained in Uniform Rules—Surrogate's Court, 22 NYCRR §§ 207.54 through 207.58.

§ 20.36   ADOPTIONS   Ch. 20

Because of prior abuses, the court requires detailed affidavits submitted by the attorneys who appear for an adoptive parent, a natural parent or an adoption agency. These affidavits are required to prevent fraud and illegal activity in the sale of babies in both agency and private placement adoptions. Each affidavit must be submitted prior to the entry of an adoption decree and filed with the Office of Court Administration of the State of New York and with the court in which the adoption proceeding has been initiated; courts will not schedule an adoption until the affidavit has been filed.

The adoption hearing is held before the court without a jury to preserve the privacy necessary to protect all parties involved in an adoption. In the case of *In re Sean B.W.*,[3] Surrogate Bennett held there is no constitutional right to a jury trial in an adoption proceeding.

The Surrogate's Court Procedure Act ("SCPA") provides for the appointment of a guardian *ad litem* to represent infants in contested adoption proceedings.[4]

Library References:
West's Key No. Digests, Adoption ⇌12.

§ 20.37   Private Placement Adoptions—In General

A private placement adoption involves an agreement between a birth parent or parents and an adoptive parent or parents,[1] *i.e.*, a consent signed by the birth parent or parents and an agreement to adopt executed by the adoptive parent or parents.[2]

Agency adoptions differ from private placement adoptions in that the agreement is between the adoptive parents and the authorized foster care agency.[3] In an agency adoption the parental rights over the child are presumed to have been terminated previously either by court action or by surrender.[4]

---

3. 86 Misc.2d 16, 381 N.Y.S.2d 656 (Surr.Ct., Nassau County, 1976).

4. SCPA § 403–a(1).

§ 20.37

1. CAVEAT: The practitioner must be mindful that any consents or agreement to adopt between the parties must be executed after the birth of the child. Any consents or agreements prior to the birth of the child are a nullity.

2. *See* DRL § 115 which contains the general provisions relating to private placement adoption.

3. CAVEAT: Social Services Law § 374(6) specifically prohibits an attorney or law firm to represent both the adoptive parents and the natural parents in a private placement adoption. No such law exists with respect to an agency adoption. However, the practitioner must be aware of the potential for conflict and when the conflict arises the attorney must withdraw from the adoption proceeding. For example, if an abuse clearance response shows that the adoptive parent was found to have abused a child in his or her care and the agency wishes to remove the adoptive children from the home, the attorney who represents the agency could not, under those circumstances, also represent the adoptive parents.

4. *See* DRL §§ 112, *et seq.*, which contain the provisions relating to adoptions from authorized agencies and permit the authorized agency to consent to the adop-

890

Ch. 20 TERMINATING PARENTAL RIGHTS § 20.39

Library References:
West's Key No. Digests, Adoption ⟐12.

§ 20.38 Private Placement Adoptions—Terminating Parental Rights Based Upon Abandonment

The Domestic Relations Law[1] provides that the consent of a parent may be dispensed with where the parent evinces an intent to forego his or her parental or custodial rights and obligations as manifested by his or her failure for a period of six months to visit the child and communicate with the child or person having legal custody of the child, although able to do so.[2] In the case of *In re Adoption of Randi Q.*,[3] the appellate division held that the biological mother had abandoned the child; thus her consent to the adoption was not required. In this case, the court also held that the mother's two isolated attempts at communication were not sufficient to defeat a finding of abandonment. In the case of *In re Kristin O.*,[4] the Appellate Division, Second Department, held that the father had abandoned the child by not having any communication with that child prior to the filing of the petition for approximately three and a half years.[5]

Library References:
West's Key No. Digests, Infants ⟐157.

§ 20.39 Private Placement Adoptions—Terminating Parental Rights Based Upon Mental Retardation

It has always been the practice in private adoptions that the adoptive parents may petition the court to dispense with the consent of the biological parent based upon the abandonment of the child by that parent. What was not clear until recently was whether or not a private individual could attempt to perfect the adoption, dispensing with the

tion of a child who is in the lawful custody of the foster care agency; In re Adoption of A. by K.S., 158 Misc.2d 760, 601 N.Y.S.2d 762 (Fam.Ct., N.Y. County, 1993).

§ 20.38

1. DRL § 111(2)(a).

2. **PRACTICE POINTER:** The practitioner who is knowledgeable in the field of adoptions would know that generally where there is to be a default by the birth parent or parents where there is abandonment alleged, the surrogate's court would make a finding of abandonment without the necessity of testimony. On the contrary, the family court usually will require testimony that the biological parent or parents did abandon the infant who is the subject of the adoption proceeding. Hence, under those circumstances, the practitioner may wish to file the adoption proceeding in the surrogate's court.

3. 214 A.D.2d 784, 624 N.Y.S.2d 474 (3d Dep't 1995).

4. 220 A.D.2d 670, 633 N.Y.S.2d 52 (2d Dep't 1995).

5. **CAVEAT:** The practitioner must note that abandonment is not failure to visit with the child for any six month period, but the critical time period is the six months immediately preceding the filing of the petition. In re Unido R., 109 Misc.2d 1031, 441 N.Y.S.2d 325 (Fam.Ct., N.Y. County,1981); In re Starr L.B., 130 Misc.2d 599, 497 N.Y.S.2d 597 (Fam.Ct., N.Y. County, 1985); In re Ricarte Angel C., 220 A.D.2d 514, 632 N.Y.S.2d 222 (2d Dep't 1995).

§ 20.39 ADOPTIONS Ch. 20

consent of the biological parent by alleging and proving that the parent was mentally retarded. Since the law with respect to mental retardation and terminating parental rights is found in Social Services Law §§ 384-b(6)(a) and (b), which deals with proceedings brought by an authorized agency. However, in the case of *In re Caroline*,[1] the Appellate Division was faced with the issue and held that private individuals may obtain private placement adoptions where parental consent is dispensed with on the ground of mental retardation and that in such a private placement adoption, the authorized agency does not have to be involved nor does the adoptive parents have to show that either they or an authorized agency used diligent efforts to try to reunite the child with the child's natural parent. In reaching this liberal interpretation of the Domestic Relations Law § 111(2)(d), the appellate division cited the recent Court of Appeals case of *In re Jacob*,[2] which permitted a second partner adoption. *In re Caroline* may be cited as an example of the court's new thinking that adoption laws need no longer be strictly construed, rather in following the recent Court of Appeals case of *In re Jacob*, the court may apply the principles of legislative purpose and the best interests of the child.[3]

Library References:
West's Key No. Digests, Infants ⚿158.

§ 20.40 Private Placement Adoptions—Dual Representation Prohibited

Until recently, an attorney would represent both the birth parents and the adoptive parents in an adoption proceeding or the attorney would only represent the adoptive parents and the biological mother was not represented. The attorney owed allegiance to the adoptive parents who had retained him and agreed to pay the attorney's fee. If the adoption did not take place, the attorney would either not get paid or would receive only a fraction of the expected fee. Under such circumstances, the birth mother could be pressured into completing the adoption even when she had serious doubts about giving up her child. Instead

---

§ 20.39

1. 218 A.D.2d 388, 638 N.Y.S.2d 997 (4th Dep't 1996).

2. 86 N.Y.2d 651, 636 N.Y.S.2d 716, 660 N.E.2d 397 (1995).

3. PRACTICE POINTER: Because the cause of action for termination of parental rights based upon mental retardation is rarely used in a private adoption proceeding and attorneys handling private adoptions may not be familiar with the presentment of such case, the practitioner should be fully familiar with Social Services Law § 384-b(4)(c). The practitioner should also be aware that it is not the mental retardation which is the basis for dispensing with the consent of the biological parent, but it is the finding of mental retardation which affects the ability of the biological parent to give adequate care to the infant. For cases relating to the cause of action for termination of parental rights based on mental retardation *see* In re Nereida S., 57 N.Y.2d 636, 454 N.Y.S.2d 61, 439 N.E.2d 870 (1982), rearg. denied 57 N.Y.2d 775, 454 N.Y.S.2d 1033, 440 N.E.2d 1343 (1982); *see also*, Matter of Strausberg, 92 Misc.2d 620, 400 N.Y.S.2d 1013 (Fam.Ct., Rockland County, 1978).

of receiving counseling, the biological mother was asked or possibly persuaded to sign the agreement of adoption.

In 1989, the adoption statutes were amended to prohibit attorneys from acting on behalf of both the natural and the adoptive parents.[1] Section 374(6) now provides that no attorney or law firm shall serve as the attorney for, or provide any legal services to both the natural parents and adoptive parents. In a private adoption, conflict may exist between the interests of the adoptive parents and the natural mother with respect to the determination of proper, reimbursable expenses to the natural mother, and her execution of affidavits and consent to the adoption.[2] Therefore, counsel for adoptive parents should avoid any actions which can be construed as joint representation of the adoptive parents and the natural mother.

§ 20.41 Private Placement Adoptions—Independent Counsel

To avoid a conflict of interest in private placement adoptions, the biological mother must be represented by independent counsel of her own selection; the attorney for the adoptive parents should not recommend an attorney to represent the birth mother. If she cannot afford an attorney, the birth mother should be referred to the adoption clerk of the court who will offer names of attorneys specializing in adoptions and who are on the panel of approved attorneys.[1] She may also be referred to a local bar association which will refer a qualified adoption attorney. Although the fee for the attorney for the natural parents is usually paid by the adoptive parents, the natural parents' attorney must represent the natural parents best interests only. The attorney for the adoptive parents may not make any special arrangements for the natural parents, such as medical, living or transportation expenses.

The dangers of an attorney representing both natural and adoptive parents is illustrated in the case of *Adoption of Samuel*,[2] where the

§ 20.40

1. Social Services Law § 374(6).

2. **CAVEAT:** It is not sufficient that counsel has advised the natural mother that he or she represented only the adoptive parents. If counsel for adoptive parents reviews the consent agreement or other legal documents with the natural mother, assists her in locating a place to live and obtains reimbursement of expenses and advises which expenses are reimbursable, a conflict exists. Such conduct is improper and illegal and must be avoided.

§ 20.41

1. **PRACTICE POINTER:** The attorney who is appointed to represent the birth mother should receive fair compensation. It is the practice of the courts to direct that the adoptive parents pay the attorney representing the indigent birth parent. Therefore, it is incumbent upon the attorney representing the birth parent to keep detailed time entries as it will be necessary to present an affidavit of services proving to the court the work that was done and the amount of time spent in processing the adoption.

2. 167 A.D.2d 909, 562 N.Y.S.2d 278 (4th Dep't 1990), aff'd 78 N.Y.2d 1047, 576 N.Y.S.2d 83, 581 N.E.2d 1338 (1991).

appellate division declared illegal the placement of the child with the adoptive parents by the attorney and restored custody of the child to the birth mother. The attorney not only represented both the birth mother and the adoptive parents, but, against the wishes of the birth mother, placed the child with the adoptive parents.

§ 20.42 Private Placement Adoptions—Permissible Dual Representation

The two categories of private adoptions commonly known as stepparent adoptions and adult adoptions present exceptions to the rule that all parties should have separate legal representation.

Step-parent adoptions generally occur in one of the following situations: (1) following the death of one of the biological parents, the surviving parent remarries and his or her spouse adopts; (2) the mother of a non-marital child subsequently marries and her spouse wishes to adopt the child; or (3) following the biological parents' divorce, the custodial spouse remarries and his or her spouse wishes to adopt.[1]

In the first situation, only two parties are involved: the surviving biological parent and the new spouse. New York law requires that the biological parent consent to the adoption by the new spouse.[2] The same attorney may represent the surviving biological parent and the new spouse because there is no conflict and no potential for conflict.

The second situation, involving a non-marital child, requires the participation of three parties: the mother, her new spouse or "life partner" and the biological father. There is no conflict if the same attorney represents the mother, whose consent to the adoption is necessary, and her new husband or "life partner," the prospective adoptive father. However, the biological father has substantial legal rights requiring separate, independent counsel. New York law classifies unwed fathers according to the nature of their involvement with the mother and child, and accords different rights to different classifications of fathers.[3] The biological father may be entitled only to notice of the proposed adoption, or his consent may be required, depending on the circumstances. If his consent is required, the father should not be represented by the same attorney who is representing the mother and her new husband.

In the third situation, where the biological parents of the child are divorced and the custodial parent's new spouse or "life partner" wishes to adopt, the same attorney may represent the custodial parent and his

§ 20.42

1. Matter of Adoption of Malpica–Orsini, 36 N.Y.2d 568, 370 N.Y.S.2d 511, 331 N.E.2d 486 (1975); Matter of Sean Y., 62 A.D.2d 426, 405 N.Y.S.2d 148 (3d Dep't 1978); Application of Garay, 136 Misc.2d 233, 518 N.Y.S.2d 723 (Surr.Ct., Kings County, 1987).

2. See DRL § 111(1)(b).

3. See DRL §§ 111(1)(d), (3), 111–a(2).

or her new spouse who wishes to adopt. However, the non-custodial biological parent, whose consent is required for the adoption, must have separate counsel. Even if the non-custodial parent initially consents to the adoption, he or she could revoke an extra-judicial consent or commence a proceeding to have it set aside on the basis of fraud, duress or coercion.[4]

If the non-custodial parent opposes adoption by the new spouse, the proceeding will become a contested adoption in which the custodial parent and spouse must prove that the non-custodial parent's consent is no longer required because of abandonment, failure to support the child, or some other cause set forth in the statute.[5]

§ 20.43 Private Placement Adoptions—Independent Representation of the Child

New York law provides that the consent of children 14 years of age or older is required for their adoption.[1] In an uncontested private adoption, independent counsel for the child is not required and appointment of an attorney or a guardian *ad litem* for the child is in the discretion of the court.[2]

The appointment of an attorney or guardian *ad litem* for the child is indicated when the proceeding becomes contested.[3] Contested adoption proceedings occur where there are allegations of fraud, duress or coercion in the execution or inducement of a biological parent's consent[4] or where the biological parent's consent has been revoked;[5] or where the adoptive parents allege that the non-custodial parent's consent is not required.[6]

In these circumstances, an attorney should be appointed for the child.[7] The attorney representing the child is expected to participate fully at any hearing, present evidence and elicit testimony that will enable the court to hear all of the facts relevant to the child's interest in a valid

---

4. *See* DRL § 115–b(7).
5. *See* DRL § 111(2)(a).

§ 20.43

1. *See* DRL § 111(1)(a).
2. *See* Family Court Act § 249.
3. *See* Matter of "Female" D., 83 A.D.2d 933, 442 N.Y.S.2d 575 (2d Dep't 1981); Matter of Adoption of Black, 57 Misc.2d 890, 293 N.Y.S.2d 797 (Surr.Ct., Oneida County, 1968).
4. DRL § 115–b(7).
5. DRL § 115–b(6).
6. *See* Corey L. v. Martin L., 45 N.Y.2d 383, 408 N.Y.S.2d 439, 380 N.E.2d 266 (1978); DRL § 111(2)(a); *see also*, Matter of Amanda, 197 A.D.2d 923, 602 N.Y.S.2d 461 (4th Dep't 1993), which held a proceeding to dispense with consent is not one in which a law guardian must be appointed for the infant.

7. The attorney appointed for the child must advocate for the child. It would be a mistake not to interview the child where the child is old enough to articulate his or her wishes. In some cases, this could be where the child is five years of age. Where the child is older, the attorney should inform the court of the child's wishes and advocate for those wishes unless it may not be in the best interests of the child. The recommendation of the attorney representing the child is given considerable weight by the court. *See* Matter of Wesley, 72 A.D.2d 137, 423 N.Y.S.2d 482 (1st Dep't 1980).

adoption, one that will survive legal challenge or appeal.[8] An attorney who represents a child in an adoption proceeding must advocate for the child and for the child's best interests.[9]

§ 20.44 Private Placement Adoptions—The Attorney's Fee

There is no set fee for handling an adoption proceeding. The attorneys representing the parties in an proceeding must have their fees approved by the court presiding over the adoption proceeding. Unless the adoption proceeding is contested, the attorney will receive a fee ranging between $2,000—$3,500. The fee will depend upon the number of hours spent, the complexity of the issues, and the experience and competency of the attorneys involved. The fee to the attorney for the adoptive parents and the fee to the attorney representing the birth parent or parents, are ordinarily paid by the adoptive parents.[1] If the fee to the attorney for the birth parent is extremely high, *i.e.*, over $5,000, the court may suspect that the practitioner is actually receiving a procurement fee. If such is the case, the attorney may be subject to sanctions and approval of the adoption may be denied. Social Services Law § 374(6) permits the adoptive parents to pay the "reasonable and actual legal fees charged for consultation and legal advice, preparation of papers and representation and other legal services rendered in connection with an adoption proceeding . . ." In *Matter of Male Infant B.*,[2] the court determined that a hearing was necessary to determine the reasonableness of the fees charged by the attorney in a private placement adoption.[3]

§ 20.45 Private Placement Adoptions—Locating an Infant for Adoption—The Attorney's Responsibility

It is illegal for an attorney to act as a procurer of children for prospective adoptive parents. Social Services Law § 374 permits only a

---

8. *See* Matter of Orlando F., 40 N.Y.S.2d 103, 386 N.Y.S.2d 64, 351 N.E.2d 711 (1976); Matter of Apel, 96 Misc.2d 839, 409 N.Y.S.2d 928 (Fam.Ct., Ulster County, 1978).

9. Id.

§ 20.44

1. PRACTICE POINTER: Not every adoption proceeding culminates in a finalized adoption. Many times the adoption is aborted. Therefore, it is not only fair but it is also appropriate for the attorneys representing the parties to obtain a retainer fee. It is not unusual for an attorney to do a substantial amount of work and to not get paid if the adoption is never finalized. The retainer fee will assure at least some modest payment. Of course, if the amount of work actually done does not cover the retainer fee, the unused portion must be returned.

2. 96 A.D.2d 1055, 466 N.Y.S.2d 482 (2d Dep't 1983).

3. The attorney representing the infant is usually appointed from a panel of attorneys commonly known as the 18(b) Panel. Article 18–B of the County Law provides that attorneys assigned to represent the child as a law guardian receive a sum of $25 an hour for out of court time and $40 an hour for court time.

biological parent, legal guardian or relative within the second degree, or an authorized agency to place children with prospective adoptive parents for adoption. It is a crime for an attorney or other person not a biological parent or legal guardian or relative within the second degree to place a child for adoption.[1]

Social Services Law § 374 explicitly states that no person may request, accept or receive any compensation or thing of value, directly or indirectly, in connection with the placing out or adoption of a child, or for assisting a parent, relative or guardian of a child in arranging for the placement of the child for the purpose of adoption. New York State limits who may arrange such private placements.[2] The statute anticipates that a private adoption is one in which the biological parent, guardian or a relative within the second degree places the child in an adoptive home of her own selection, without a paid intermediary selecting the adoptive parents.

The courts have referred violations by lawyers of Social Services Law § 374(2) and (6) to the criminal justice authorities and, in some cases, have dismissed the adoption petition.

In the case of *Matter of Adoption of Anonymous*,[3] the court dismissed the adoption petition, because the child was not "placed out" legally.[4] The lawyer was in communication with four or five doctors and one referred a family with whom the attorney subsequently placed the child.

In *Matter of the Adoption Proceeding of Jose L.*, the court denied an application for a "pre-adoption certificate," a prerequisite to bringing a child into the United States for the purpose of adoption.[5] The denial was based on the petitioning adoptive parents' failure to supply the court with detailed information concerning the adoptive father's payment of $10,000 to a Chilean social worker. This social worker was unable to prove that she disbursed the $10,000 to people permitted by New York's private placement adoption statutes to receive it. The court declined to allow the child to enter the country "only to have the adoption ultimately denied" because the circumstances gave rise to considerable concern that the child had been used for financial gain.[6] In *Adoption of Samuel*,[7] the adoption petition was dismissed and custody of the child was restored to the birth mother. The attorney, who had provided legal services to both the birth mother and the adoptive parents, had placed the child

§ 20.45

1. Social Services Law § 389.

2. **CAVEAT:** An attorney who places an infant for adoption in violation of Social Services Law § 374 commits a misdemeanor. A second violation is a felony. Social Services Law § 389.

3. 46 Misc.2d 928, 261 N.Y.S.2d 439 (Fam.Ct., Dutchess County, 1965).

4. Social Services Law §§ 371(10)(b), (12), 374(2).

5. 126 Misc.2d 612, 483 N.Y.S.2d 929 (Fam.Ct., Queens County, 1984).

6. 483 N.Y.S.2d at 931–932.

7. 167 A.D.2d 909, 562 N.Y.S.2d 278 (4th Dep't 1990).

with the adoptive parents against the wishes of the natural mother, in violation of Social Services Law § 374(6).

The courts do not always deny adoption petitions when the Social Services Law has been violated. In the case of *Matter of Adoption of E.W.C.*,[8] the birth mother attempted to revoke her consent following a private placement adoption proceeding. She alleged that the adoptive parents' attorney illegally "placed out" her child and received compensation for such activity. Although the court did not permit the birth mother to revoke her consent, the court disapproved of the placing out of the child by the attorney and disapproved the attorney's fee.

In the criminal proceeding of *People v. Michelman*,[9] the court stated that "the defendant's status as an 'intermediary' is tainted by the fees charged and the number of instances in which he was so involved."[10]

In *Matter of Baby Boy M.G.*,[11] the attorney for a New York couple hoping to adopt a child served as an "intermediary," putting the birth mother in contact with the adoptive parents. The birth mother retained counsel in Tennessee, where the child was born. The court opined that an adoptive couple's attorney does not violate the New York adoption statute when he merely counsels clients on how to legitimately locate an adoptable child and advises them on the legal hurdles involved in private adoption matters while not entering the gray area where he may be assuming the role of an authorized agency in violation of Social Services Law §§ 374 and 382.[12]

§ 20.46 Private Placement Adoptions—Illegal Sale of Babies

An adoptive couple will sometimes offer a birth parent a large amount of money—anywhere from $5,000 to $35,000—to insure the consent of the birth parent to the adoption of the child. Such payment is illegal and if the attorney is involved in or has knowledge of such a payment to procure the adoption, the attorney is subject to disciplinary action and the adoption may be disapproved by the court.[1] In *Matter of*

---

8. 89 Misc.2d 64, 389 N.Y.S.2d 743 (Surr.Ct., Nassau County, 1976).

9. 93 Misc.2d 297, 403 N.Y.S.2d 417 (Sup.Ct., Suffolk County, 1978).

10. 93 Misc.2d at 299, 403 N.Y.S.2d at 419; *See* People v. Scopas, 11 N.Y.2d 120, 227 N.Y.S.2d 5, 181 N.E.2d 754 (1962), Burke, J., dissenting; Matter of Slater, 8 A.D.2d 169, 186 N.Y.S.2d 558 (1st Dep't 1959); Anonymous v. Anonymous, 108 Misc.2d 1098, 439 N.Y.S.2d 255 (Sup.Ct., Queens County, 1981); Matter of Adoption of Anonymous, 46 Misc.2d 928, 261 N.Y.S.2d 439 (Fam.Ct., Dutchess County, 1965); *see also*, Matter of Adoption of Baby Boy, 147 Misc.2d 873, 556 N.Y.S.2d 463 (Surr.Ct., Rensselaer County, 1990).

11. 135 Misc.2d 252, 515 N.Y.S.2d 198 (Surr.Ct., Nassau County, 1987).

12. *Id.*

§ 20.46

1. Social Services Law § 374(2); Matter of Adoption of Samuel, 167 A.D.2d 909, 562 N.Y.S.2d 278 (4th Dep't 1990), aff'd 78 N.Y.2d 1047, 576 N.Y.S.2d 83, 581 N.E.2d 1338 (1991); Matter of Male Infant B., 96 A.D.2d 1055, 466 N.Y.S.2d 482 (2d Dep't 1983).

Adoption of Baby Boy M.G.,[2] Surrogate Radigan admonished physicians, lawyers or other individuals who may act in an unauthorized manner as intermediaries that they may be subject to criminal liability.[3]

Library References:

West's Key No. Digests, Adoption ⚖5, 6; Infants ⚖229.

§ 20.47 Private Placement Adoptions—Advertisement

Some attorneys advise the potential adoptive parents to advertise their desire to adopt. Advertisements are placed in local newspapers including "Pennysavers" and religious weeklies. Potential adoptive parents who use this method are also advised by their attorneys to have a separate telephone line with its own number installed for the sole purpose of receiving responses to the advertisements. Other potential adoptive parents prepare resumes outlining their educational and family backgrounds and distribute the resumes to doctors, nurses and attorneys hoping that someone will contact them if a baby is available for adoption. These methods are effective and legal. The court in *Matter of Adoption of Baby Boy M.G.*,[1] determined that the attorney did not violate adoption statutes when he counseled clients about how to locate adoptable children and how to avoid legal hurdles in private adoptions. It is essential, however that it is the potential adoptive parents who are advertising for a baby and not the attorney.

Library References:

West's Key No. Digests, Adoption ⚖5, 6; Infants ⚖229.

§ 20.48 Private Placement Adoption—Foreign Infants

Some attorneys specialize in foreign adoptions, *i.e.*, adoptions involv-

---

2. 135 Misc.2d 252, 515 N.Y.S.2d 198 (Surr.Ct., Nassau County, 1987).

3. *See also*, People v. Michelman, 93 Misc.2d 297, 403 N.Y.S.2d 417 (Sup.Ct., Suffolk County. 1978).

CAVEAT: Until the Legislature enacts procedures that the attorney must follow in adoption matters, the practitioner would do well to read Judge Radigan's decision in the case of Matter of Baby Boy M.G., 135 Misc.2d 252, 515 N.Y.S.2d 198 (Surr.Ct., Nassau County, 1987), wherein the court outlined the court's rules with respect to proper behavior in adoption proceedings: (1) the biological mother must have independent counsel from a court approved panel of attorneys familiar with adoption proceedings if she does not have an attorney of her own; (2) the attorney for the adoptive parents must not be involved in the placement of the child; (3) the use of independent search agencies involved in the procurement or placement of children are prohibited; (4) prior approval of expenditures involved in the pregnancy and birth of the child must be obtained from the court; and (5) consents by the biological parents to the proposed adoption must be made before the court or, if the parents are out of the state, before a court of similar jurisdiction in the state where the infant or parents reside.

§ 20.47

1. 135 Misc.2d 252, 515 N.Y.S.2d 198 (Surr.Ct., Nassau County, 1987).

ing children born in other countries.[1] Throughout the years, thousands of foreign children have been adopted by adoptive parents living in the State of New York.[2] Where the prospective adoptive couple does obtain an infant from a foreign country, it is usually necessary for the couple to go to the other country and take physical possession of the infant, but only after first obtaining an order from the appropriate court.[3]

Library References:

West's Key No. Digests, Adoption ⟾5, 6; Infants ⟾229.

§ 20.49 Private Placement Adoptions—Readoption of Foreign Infants

Persons who adopt an infant in a foreign country may petition the appropriate family court or surrogate's court for readoption pursuant to Domestic Relations Law § 115–a(8). The reason for the readoption is for the adoptive parents to obtain documentation from a court of the United States including, but not limited to, a new birth certificate and new order of adoption which will be given full faith and credit in every state in the United States. In the case of *Matter of Adoption of Dafina T.G.*,[1] the Surrogate's Court of Nassau County was faced with a readoption proceeding where the foreign adoption documents were not duly authenticated. The surrogate liberally construed § 115–a(8) and permitted the readoption even in the absence of authentication of the foreign documents where the court was satisfied as to the genuineness of the documents submitted. The court went on to say that even where the foreign adoption documents are not available or where the court is not

---

§ 20.48

1. **CAVEAT:** Before recommending that the potential adoptive couple actually go to a foreign country, the attorney should make inquiries into the environment in that foreign country. Adoption practitioners hear of stories where a potential adoptive mother would travel to a foreign country and literally get lost in the country and spend weeks or months struggling to leave the country, sometimes with a child and sometimes without.

2. **CAVEAT:** Where there is an agency adoption and the child is born out of the country and the adoptive parents live out of New York State, the adoptive parents still have the choice of doing the adoption in the county where the agency has its principal place of business. The attorney must be aware that in this circumstance, although the New York courts may and do finalize the adoption because jurisdiction and venue is proper, the fact of the matter is that the State of New York will not issue a new birth certificate. Hence, where a child was born out of the country and the adoptive parents lived in Michigan, but decided to finalize the adoption in New York State, in the County of Nassau, where the agency had its principal place of business, to their surprise and the surprise of the court, the State of New York would not issue a birth certificate because there was no nexus with the State of New York, *i.e.*, the child was born out of the country and the adoptive parents were residents of the State of Michigan. In this case, the only way to obtain a birth certificate is for the adoptive parents to have a readoption in the State of Michigan. If the attorney had been aware of this, he would have warned the adoptive parents and suggested that the adoption take place in the State of Michigan, where the adoptive parents resided, in order for them to have a birth certificate issued to them after the adoption was finalized.

3. DRL § 115–a.

§ 20.49

1. 161 Misc.2d 106, 613 N.Y.S.2d 329 (Surr.Ct., Nassau County, 1994).

satisfied as to their accuracy, the court will nevertheless consider permitting the matter to proceed to finalization where the child has resided with the adoptive couple for at least one year and where a home study is conducted and as a result approval of the adoption is recommended.

Library References:

West's Key No. Digests, Adoption ⚖=5, 6; Infants ⚖=229.

§ 20.50 Private Placement Adoptions—Native American Children

The Congress of the United States enacted 25 U.S.C.A. §§ 1901–1963, more commonly known as the Indian Child Welfare Act, because there were large numbers of Indian children who had been removed from their Native American families.[1] The adoption rate of Native American children was eight times that of non-Native American children and in the years 1971 and 1972, nearly one-fourth of the Native American children under the age of one had been placed for adoption.[2] By enacting the Indian Child Welfare Act, Congress made it more difficult to remove children from Native American parents or custodians and made it even more difficult for the courts to terminate parental rights of a Native American parent over a Native American child.[3] The law grants exclusive jurisdiction to tribal courts in child custody proceedings involving Native American children domiciled on a reservation.[4] Moreover, while the quantum of proof to terminate parental rights over a non-Native American child is clear and convincing proof,[5] to terminate parental rights over a Native American child, the state must prove its case beyond a reasonable doubt. The federal statute[6] provides that no termination of parental rights may be ordered in the absence of a

---

§ 20.50

1. PRACTICE POINTER: The practitioner, at the very first interview, should ascertain the heritage of the child to be adopted. If the child to be adopted is a Native American child, *i.e.*, Indian or Eskimo, then different rules of law will apply. For example, if a biological father's rights will have to be terminated, the quantum of proof is not clear and convincing which is the usual quantum of proof but where an Indian child is involved, the quantum of proof must be beyond a reasonable doubt. Further, the courts cannot, in the first instance, permit non-Native Americans to adopt a Native American child. First preference to adopt Native American children are relatives and Native Americans.

2. Mississippi Band of Choctaw Indians v. Holyfield, 490 U.S. 30, 109 S.Ct. 1597, 104 L.Ed.2d 29 (1989).

3. Because of the importance of the ramifications involved in an Indian child adoption, the State of New York promulgated 22 NYCRR § 205.51 of the Uniform Rules—Family Court which specifically provides that "in any proceeding in which the custody of a child is to be determined, the petition shall set forth whether the child is a Native American child subject to the Indian Child Welfare Act of 1978 (25 U.S.C.A. §§ 1901–1963), and the court shall proceed further, as appropriate, in accordance with the provisions of that act." Hence, the official form for the adoption petition must allege whether or not the child involved is a Native American child.

4. Mississippi Band of Choctaw Indians v. Holyfield, *supra*, note 2; *see also*, 25 U.S.C.A. § 1911(a).

5. *See* Social Services Law § 384-b(3)(g).

6. 25 U.S.C.A. § 1912(f).

determination supported by evidence beyond a reasonable doubt, including testimony of qualified expert witnesses, that the continued custody of the child by the Native American parent or Native American custodian is likely to result in serious emotional or physical damage to the child.

Where a Native American child is freed for adoption, the statute[7] provides that in any adoptive placement of a Native American child, a preference shall be given, in the absence of good cause to the contrary, to placement with (1) a member of the child's extended family; (2) other members of the Native American child's tribe; (3) other Native American families; or (4) an institution approved by a Native American tribe or operated by a Native American organization suitable to meet the Native American child's needs. The intention of the Indian Child Welfare Act, therefore, is to prevent the unnecessary removal of a child from a Native American home and if the child is removed, then custody should be given to Native American persons.

Library References:

West's Key No. Digests, Adoption ⚖=5, 6; Infants ⚖=229.

§ 20.51 Private Placement Adoption—Residency Requirements

Domestic Relations Law § 115, which contains the general provisions relating to private placement adoptions, does not require that the adoptive parents reside in the State of New York. The section provides that the venue of the private placement adoption proceeding shall be in the county where the adoptive parents reside or, if the adoptive parents are not residents of the State of New York, in the county where the adoptive child resides. The fact that an adoption proceeding is initiated in an unauthorized county may not constitute a jurisdictional defect.[1] In the case of *Matter of Adoption of E.W.C.*,[2] the court held that where the adoptive parents maintained one residence in Suffolk County, which was their home for most of the year, and another residence in Nassau County, which was their summer home and their home on weekends, the adoptive parents resided in Nassau County for the purpose of permitting the adoption petition to be brought in Nassau County. However, where the adoptive parents resided in New Jersey with the adoptive child and the adoptive parents sought an order approving the adoption in New York, the case was dismissed for lack of jurisdiction.[3]

---

7. 25 U.S.C.A. § 1915.

§ 20.51

1. Matter of Adoption of E.W.C., 89 Misc.2d 64, 389 N.Y.S.2d 743 (Surr.Ct., Nassau County, 1976).

2. *Id.*

3. Matter of Adoption of Danielle, 88 Misc.2d 78, 387 N.Y.S.2d 48 (Surr.Ct., Putnam County, 1976); *see also*, Estate of Gardiner, 144 Misc.2d 797, 545 N.Y.S.2d 466 (Surr.Ct., N.Y. County, 1989).

§ 20.52 Private Placement Adoptions—Permissible Payments by Adoptive Parents

The court must approve all payments to be made by the adoptive parents to or on behalf of the birth parents. The law provides[1] that the adoptive parents must present an affidavit describing all fees, compensation, other remuneration to be paid by the adoptive parents on account of or incidental to the birth or care of the child, the pregnancy or care of the adoptive child's mother or the placement or adoption of the child and on account of or incidental to assistance in arrangements for such placement or adoption.[2] The attorney representing the adoptive parents must also present an affidavit describing all fees, compensation and other remuneration received by him on account of or incidental to the placement or adoption of the child or assistance in arrangements for such placement or adoption. Expenses allowed by the court have included medical and other expenses incidental to the pregnancy and birth of the child and payments to a psychologist or certified social worker who counsels the birth parent on her decision whether to place the child for adoption. The allowance of such expenses is within the discretion of the court.[3] Wages lost as a result of the physical condition of the mother caused by the pregnancy have been held reimbursable expenses in a private placement adoption within the meaning of Domestic Relations Law § 115 and the Uniform Rules of the Court,[4] governing private placement adoptions.[5]

Library References:

West's Key No. Digests, Adoption ⛐5, 6; Infants ⛐229.

§ 20.53 Private Placement Adoptions—Interstate Compact on the Placement of Children

The Interstate Compact on the Placement of Children first became effective in 1960. Approximately 47 states have similar legislation.[1] It has been held that the purpose of the Interstate Compact on placement of children is to assure that the placement will be in the child's best

---

§ 20.52

1. DRL § 115(8).
2. See also, Social Services Law § 374(6).
3. Matter of Adoption of Anonymous, 131 Misc.2d 666, 501 N.Y.S.2d 240 (Surr. Ct., Westchester County, 1986).
4. 22 NYCRR § 207.55(b)(8)(vi).
5. Matter of Adoption of Baby Boy, 146 Misc.2d 896, 552 N.Y.S.2d 1005 (Fam.Ct., Rockland County, 1990).

§ 20.53

1. Social Services Law § 374–a "Historical and Statutory Notes."

§ 20.53 ADOPTIONS Ch. 20

interests and also to prevent states from exporting their foster care responsibilities to other states.[2]

When a child is born outside of the State of New York and is to be placed for adoption in New York, or the child is born in New York State and will be placed for adoption outside of New York, the requirements of the Interstate Compact on the Placement of Children must be observed.[3] In the case of *Matter of Adoption of Jon K.*,[4] the court declined to approve the adoption where the child had been brought into New York in violation of the Interstate Compact. However, in *Matter of Adoption of Baby Boy M.G.*,[5] the court granted the adoption despite the parties' failure to get approval of the Interstate Compact Administrator. In *Matter of Adoption of Calynn, M.G.*,[6] the court directed the parties to seek approval of placement from the Compact Administrator and to file an amended petition where they failed to allege compliance with the Interstate Compact. In *Matter of Adoption of Calynn, M.G.*,[7] the attorney's failure to obtain approval of the Interstate Compact Administrator resulted in the reduction of the attorney's fees. Compliance with the Interstate Compact includes contacting the Compact Administrator[8] for the sending state (the state where the child is born) before the birth of the child, to ascertain the state's requirements and restrictions, such as pre-placement home studies, consents, permissible payments on behalf of the natural parents and other matters incidental to the adoption of the child and obtain the appropriate approvals for the transport and adoption of the child. The application for approval pursuant to the Interstate Compact originates in the sending state. The Compact Administrator of the receiving state must also be notified of the proposed adoption and give approval of the placement. The child will not be permitted to leave the sending state until the sending state gives its approval.

The Compact Administrator will provide the approval forms that must be completed by the attorney for the birth parent. Proof of

2. Matter of H./M. Children, 217 A.D.2d 164, 634 N.Y.S.2d 675 (1st Dep't 1995).

3. **CAVEAT:** An interstate adoption is, by its very nature, filled with pitfalls. The attorney handling his or her first interstate adoption must be ever mindful that all of the requirements of the Interstate Compact must be observed or one of the effects of non-observance could be that the adoption may not be finalized. Section 374–a of the Social Services Law contains the entire law on the subject of the Interstate Compact on the Placement of Children. Although there are many aspects to the Interstate Compact, in sum, the attorney representing the adoptive parent must be certain that the child is not brought into New York until and unless approval is obtained not only from the sending state but also from New York State. The approval takes the form of a written Form ICPC–100(a). The adoption clerk will not give a finalization date until this form is filed with the adoption clerk. Form ICPC–100(a) is signed by both the sending state and the receiving state.

4. 141 Misc.2d 949, 535 N.Y.S.2d 660 (Fam.Ct., Kings County, 1988).

5. 135 Misc.2d 252, 515 N.Y.S.2d 198 (Surr.Ct., Nassau County, 1987).

6. 137 Misc.2d 1005, 523 N.Y.S.2d 729 (Surr.Ct., Nassau County, 1987).

7. Id.

8. New York's Compact Administrator is located in the Social Services Building, 40 North Pearl Street, Albany, New York 11213.

compliance with the provisions of the Interstate Compact must be filed with the court where the adoption is to be finalized.[9]

Library References:

West's Key No. Digests, Adoption ⚖5, 6; Infants ⚖229.

§ 20.54 Private Placement Adoptions—Pre-certification of Adoptive Parents—In General

Prior to 1989, it had been common practice for a birth mother to turn over her infant to the proposed adoptive parents at the time that the extra-judicial consent to adoption was executed. The extra-judicial consent was usually signed by the birth mother in the hospital on the second or third day after the birth of the child. This practice permitted prospective adoptive parents to take physical custody of an infant without any court involvement, awareness, or intervention. As such, the child was placed in the home of the prospective adoptive parents without any evaluation or home study of the prospective adoptive parents. In 1988, a number of publicized cases demonstrated that children were being placed by attorneys and baby brokers with inappropriate prospective adoptive parents who did not finalize the adoptions. In one case, where the infant was placed for adoption, but the adoption was never finalized, the infant was abused and died. No court was aware of this placement. Thousands of other placements were never made known to the courts of the State of New York. As a result of public outcry and the convening of the grand jury of New York County, new legislation was enacted. Safeguards were built into the adoption process so that the system would not lose track of children placed for adoption.[1]

Library References:

West's Key No. Digests, Adoption ⚖5, 6; Infants ⚖229.

§ 20.55 Private Placement Adoptions—Pre-certification of Adoptive Parents—Requirement of Pre-certification

Pursuant to Domestic Relations Law § 115–d, prior to taking physical custody of the adoptive child the prospective adoptive parents must complete and file a petition for certification as a qualified adoptive parent. In addition the adoptive parent must file an abuse clearance form (Form DSS–3937, a form supplied by the court); completed fingerprint cards; and an original and a copy of the proposed order certifying that the petitioners are qualified adoptive parents.

9. See DRL § 115–a; proof of compliance takes the form of a document entitled Form ICPC 100(a).

§ 20.54

1. DRL § 115(1)(b) (L.1989, Ch.700, effective November 1, 1989).

§ 20.55 ADOPTIONS Ch. 20

These papers are then filed with the adoption clerk. Domestic Relations Law § 115–d(2) requires that the court appoint a disinterested person to conduct a pre-placement investigation if the prospective adoptive parents do not intend to initiate such pre-placement investigation under Domestic Relations Law § 115–d(1)(d). The pre-placement investigation, or home study, is required because of the previous abuses in the adoption process. Under current law, the adoptive child may not be placed in the prospective adoptive home until the home study is completed and an order of certification is signed by the court. The report prepared by the disinterested person, usually a certified social worker, is then filed with the court. The adoption clerk will forward the abuse clearance request form to the New York Sate Department of Social Services in Albany for a determination as to whether any reports of child abuse, neglect or maltreatment have been filed against the prospective adoptive parents.[1] The adoption clerk will also arrange for the adoptive parents to have their fingerprints taken by the police department to determine if the adoptive parents have been convicted of any crimes. After all of the documentation has been received, the judge will then determine whether the prospective adoptive parents are appropriate and fit to receive the adoptive child.

Library References:
West's Key No. Digests, Adoption ⟐5, 6; Infants ⟐229.

§ 20.56 Private Placement Adoptions—Pre-certification of Adoptive Parents—Procedure

Under current law, a child may not be adopted without prior court intervention and approval. The process is begun by first obtaining certification from the court that the prospective adoptive parents are qualified for this responsibility.[1] In order for the prospective adoptive parents to be certified, a complete investigation of the home must be conducted and a written report filed with the court by a disinterested person selected, either by the prospective adoptive parents or the court. A proper "disinterested" person could be an individual certified social worker, or an organization such as the probation service of family court or an authorized agency designated by the court to conduct pre-placement investigations. The petition for certification, setting forth the information required by DRL § 115–d must be signed by the proposed adoptive parents, notarized and filed with the court. The court is also required to order a report from (1) the statewide register of child abuse and maltreatment setting forth whether the child and/or the proposed adoptive parents have been named in a report filed with the register, and

§ 20.55
1. For a definition of "child abuse," "neglect," and "maltreatment," see Social Services Law § 412.

§ 20.56
1. DRL § 115–d.

(2) from the New York State Division of Criminal Justice Services setting forth whether the proposed adoptive parents have been convicted of a crime. The court may waive the need for these reports.[2] Before the judge will issue an order of certification approving the prospective adoptive parents to receive the physical custody of the child, the judge must be satisfied that the prospective adoptive parents are not a subject of any report of abuse or maltreatment of a child or have not been convicted of a crime.[3] If the home study reveals a problem in the adoptive parents' background which may prevent certification and approval by the court, the judge may conduct a hearing to determine the nature and severity of the negative information revealed by the home study.[4]

A problem may arise where the adoptive parents reside out of state but wish to finalize the adoption in New York State. Such a problem arose in *Matter of Charnille*,[5] wherein the appellate division reversed the family court's order dismissing the adoption petition. In this case, the petitioner, a resident of New Jersey, requested a waiver of the requirements of a child abuse clearance. The petitioner presented the adoption judge with abuse clearance forms from New York State but the State of New Jersey refused to release reports from the New Jersey Central Register of Child Abuse and Maltreatment, and refused to release information regarding the criminal record of the petitioner. The court below also had the home study of the authorized agency recommending the adoption. The appellate division in reversing and reinstating the adoption petition, held that there was ample evidence in the record, including reports from the New York State Register of Child Abuse and Maltreatment and from the New York State Division of Criminal Justice Service, for the family court to make a determination in the best interests of the child, despite the absence of the New Jersey records.

If the court grants the application, the proposed adoptive parents may accept physical custody of the child for purposes of adoption, either prior to or contemporaneous with the filing of an adoption petition. The order approving the adoptive parents is effective for eighteen months and will be accepted by any other family or surrogate's court within the State of New York.[6] The certification may be extended when a petition for adoption is filed where less than a year remains upon original certification. The court may, on its own motion, or on the motion of the

2. *See* Uniform Rules for Surrogate's Court, 22 NYCRR § 207.61(c); Uniform Rules for the Family Court, 22 NYCRR § 205.58(c).

3. *Id.*

4. *See* In the Matter of Michael J.J., 200 A.D.2d 80, 613 N.Y.S.2d 715 (3d Dep't 1994), wherein the appellate division reversed the lower court's findings that the prospective adoptive father's history of alcohol abuse prevented him from becoming certified as a qualified adoptive parent. In this case, the family court, after becoming aware of the father's history of alcohol abuse, held a hearing to further explore the problem.

5. 206 A.D.2d 423, 613 N.Y.S.2d 946 (2d Dep't 1994).

6. *See* DRL § 115–d(6).

qualified parents, extend the certification for eighteen months from the time the adoption petition is filed. If the certification expired less than a year before the adoption proceeding was brought, the court may grant a similar extension, provided the qualified parents apply for such extension and set forth any change of circumstances since the last certification.[7]

Certification is not required where a step-parent seeks to adopt a step-child, and the child has resided with the birth parent and the step-parent for a continuous period of at least one year.[8]

The requirement of certification may be waived by a court on its own motion or upon the application of any party for good cause shown.[9]

Library References:

West's Key No. Digests, Adoption ⚖═5, 6; Infants ⚖═229.

§ 20.57 Private Placement Adoptions—Pre-certification of Adoptive Parents—Checklist of Documents Needed for Certification

In order to be certified as qualified adoptive parents, the following documentation must be filed with the court:

(1) petition for certification as qualified adoptive parents;

(2) affidavit and report of disinterested person for certification proceeding;

(3) order of certification as a qualified adoptive parent;

(4) Form DSS 3937, which is a request for information to determine whether the adoptive parents have ever been found to have abused or maltreated a child; and

(5) fingerprint cards which will then be sent through the Criminal Justice System to determine whether the potential adoptive parents have ever been convicted of any crime or crimes.

Library References:

West's Key No. Digests, Adoption ⚖═5, 6; Infants ⚖═229.

§ 20.58 Private Placement Adoptions—Hospital Procedure—Physical Transfer of Custody of the Infant to the Adoptive Parents

Prior to the birth of the child, the attorneys representing the birth mother and the adoptive parents should contact the social worker at the hospital where the baby is to be born to inquire as to the procedure in

---

7. *See, e.g.,* Matter of the Adoption of Doe, 161 Misc.2d 935, 615 N.Y.S.2d 823 (Fam.Ct., Ulster County, 1994).

8. DRL § 115–d(8).

9. DRL § 115(1)(b).

releasing the infant from the hospital. Some hospitals permit the adoptive parents to take the infant from the hospital as long as the birth mother signs the necessary consent forms provided by the hospital. The social worker connected with the hospital will arrange for the execution of the appropriate release forms permitting the release of the child to the adoptive parents. Some hospitals do not deal directly with the adoptive parents, but require an agent of the birth parent to take the child out of the hospital (*e.g.*, a grandmother, an aunt or the attorney representing the birth mother). Hospital procedure should be explained to the parties prior to the birth of the child in order to avoid unnecessary delay or confusion.

Library References:

West's Key No. Digests, Adoption ⇔5, 6; Infants ⇔229.

§ 20.59 Private Placement Adoptions—Hospital Procedure—Certification Procedures

Some hospitals require the order of certification to be filed with the hospital prior to releasing the infant. This procedure is preferable because the hospital authorities can be secure in the knowledge the adoptive parents have complied with the certification procedures mandated by law.[1]

Library References:

West's Key No. Digests, Adoption ⇔5, 6; Infants ⇔229.

§ 20.60 Private Placement Adoptions—Petition for Temporary Guardianship—Legislative Background

Biological parents sometimes relinquished physical custody of the child to the adoptive parents prior to court intervention. Instances of child abuse resulted because the prospective adoptive parents were not evaluated in order to determine whether they were suited for this responsibility. Although the commencement of an adoption proceeding resulted in an investigation pursuant to DRL § 116(2), it was possible for the child to be in the custody of adoptive parents for many months without the adoptive parents being evaluated. This was a source of concern for the New York State Legislature and, in 1988, legislation was passed providing for a mechanism to bring all private placement adoptions before the court as quickly as possible. The provisions for temporary guardianship were introduced with the passage of DRL § 115–c and Surrogate's Court Procedure Act § 1725.[1] *See also,* § 20.69, *infra.*

§ 20.59

1. DRL § 115.

§ 20.60

1. L.1988, Ch.577, eff. Oct. 1, 1988.

§ 20.60 ADOPTIONS Ch. 20

Library References:
West's Key No. Digests, Adoption ⚖=5, 6; Infants ⚖=229.

§ 20.61 Private Placement Adoptions—Petition for Temporary Guardianship—Impact of Preplacement Certification

As a consequence of an amendment to DRL § 115–c in 1988,[1] the certification proceedings found in DRL § 115–d have an impact upon a petition for temporary guardianship. An application for temporary guardianship must include an affidavit by the adoptive parents describing any change in circumstances affecting the adoption that have taken place since their certification as qualified adoptive parents. If the court has waived certification, an application for temporary guardianship, or a petition for the adoption of the child, must be filed with the court no later than five days after receiving physical custody of the child. The time period may be extended upon the motion of any person, or upon the court's own motion for good cause shown.

Library References:
West's Key No. Digests, Adoption ⚖=5, 6; Infants ⚖=229.

§ 20.62 Private Placement Adoptions—Procedure Upon Filing Petition for Temporary Guardianship

Upon the filing of a petition for temporary guardianship, or upon the filing of a petition for adoption where no previous application for temporary guardianship has been made,[1] the court is required to promptly determine whether to grant temporary guardianship.[2] Where the adoptive parents have been previously certified under DRL § 115–d, the petition for temporary guardianship must be brought within "10 court days"[3] of receiving physical custody of the child. Note that "10 court days" are longer than 10 calendar days since weekends and court holidays are excluded from the calculation. If the judge is satisfied that the prospective adoptive parents are qualified, the court will issue an order of temporary guardianship. An order or decree of temporary guardianship expires no later than nine months following its issuance, or upon the entry of a final order of adoption, whichever is sooner unless upon application, for good cause, the court extends the time.[4]

§ 20.61
1. L.1989, Ch.700, § 3, eff. Nov. 1, 1989.

§ 20.62
1. Pursuant to DRL § 115–c, the petition for adoption will also be deemed an application for temporary guardianship, where no prior application for temporary guardianship has been filed.

2. SCPA § 1725(1).
3. DRL § 115–c.
4. *See* SCPA § 1725(3)(c) (the decree may be extended up to three months); Uniform Rules for Surrogate's Court, 22 NYCRR § 207.58(2).

When an application for temporary guardianship has been filed, the petition for adoption must be filed within forty-five days after the natural parent's execute a consent to adoption.[5]

Library References:

West's Key No. Digests, Adoption ⇔5, 6; Infants ⇔229.

§ 20.63 Private Placement Adoptions—Consent of Birth Parents

There are two types of consents which may be executed by the birth parents in a private placement adoption:

(a) extra-judicial consent; and

(b) judicial consent.[1]

Library References:

West's Key No. Digests, Adoption ⇔7.1–7.7.

§ 20.64 Private Placement Adoptions—Consent of Birth Parents—Extra–Judicial Consent

An extra-judicial consent becomes irrevocable forty-five days after its execution unless written notice of revocation is received by the court, wherein the adoption proceeding is to be commenced, within the said 45 days.[1] Notwithstanding that the notice or revocation is received within 45 days, it will be given effect only if the adoptive parents fail to oppose the revocation or if they oppose it, the court determines that the best interests of the child will be served by enforcing the revocation. If the adoptive parents oppose the return of the child to the birth parent or parents, the child is not immediately returned to the natural parent, nor does the natural parent have any rights superior to the adoptive parent. At a hearing, the judge must determine the following:[2]

(a) whether the notice of revocation was timely and properly given;

(b) whether the best interests of the child would be served by:

(1) returning the child to the birth parent;

(2) continuing with the adoption proceeding;

(3) a disposition other than adoption by the adoptive parents;

---

5. See SCPA § 1725(5); Uniform Rules for Surrogate's Courts, 22 NYCRR § 207.58(1).

§ 20.63

1. DRL § 115–b. As the names imply, the extra-judicial consent is signed by the birth parent out of court and before a notary public. The judicial consent is signed in front of a judge or a surrogate.

§ 20.64

1. DRL § 115–b(3).
2. DRL § 115–b(3)(b)(iv).

§ 20.64 ADOPTIONS Ch. 20

(4) placing the child with an authorized agency.

DRL § 115–b(4)(a)(v) requires the court to advise the birth mother of her right to counsel of her own choosing. She is also entitled to supportive counseling and the appointment of an attorney pursuant to Family Court § 262, SCPA § 407, or Judiciary Law § 35.

DRL § 115–b was enacted in response to the "Baby Lenore" case. Baby Lenore was the infant in the case of *People ex rel. Scarpetta v. Spence-Chapin Adoption Service*,[3] wherein the New York Court of Appeals permitted the birth mother to revoke her consent to the adoption and, over the objections of the adoptive parents, returned the child to the birth mother and denied the foster parents the right to a hearing.

The Court of Appeals has made it clear that an extra-judicial consent will not be easily overturned. In the case of *Matter of Sarah K.*,[4] the court wrote that it was insufficient to show that the birth mother was simply mistaken as to the meaning of the consent form. Instead it was necessary to prove that the extra-judicial consent was signed under compulsion or threat, or against the birth parent's free will, or that the consent was secured by fraud.

Library References:

West's Key No. Digests, Adoption ⇔7.1–7.7.

§ 20.65 Private Placement Adoptions—Consent of Birth Parents—Judicial Consent

Domestic Relations Law § 115–b(2) outlines the procedure relating to a judicial consent. A judicial consent is signed in court before the judge.[1] Where the judicial consent is duly executed and acknowledged by the birth parent before the judge, no action or proceeding may be maintained by the consenting birth parent for the return or custody of the adoptive child. The judicial consent is irrevocable. One case has held that not only does a biological father relinquish all parental rights with respect to visitation after the adoption is finalized, he also relinquishes

---

3. 28 N.Y.2d 185, 321 N.Y.S.2d 65, 269 N.E.2d 787 (1971), cert. den'd 404 U.S. 805, 92 S.Ct. 54, 30 L.Ed.2d 38 (1971).

4. 66 N.Y.2d 223, 496 N.Y.S.2d 384, 487 N.E.2d 241 (1985), cert. den'd 475 U.S. 1108, 106 S.Ct. 1515, 89 L.Ed.2d 914 (1986).

§ 20.65

1. CAVEAT: The attorney for the birth parent must fully explain the meaning and impact of judicial consent to the client. The client must understand that once the consent is signed before the judge it is irrevocable and that there is no grace period that would permit a change of mind. The attorney should go over every word of the judicial consent, and in fact should read it to the birth mother, asking questions to make sure that she understands the ramifications of signing the judicial consent. This will help prevent an embarrassment when the court asks the birth mother whether she understands the document and whether it was explained to her. Nothing could be more embarrassing to an attorney then when, at the judicial signing of the consent, the mother confesses to the judge in response to his questions, that she does not know the meaning of the document she is signing.

all visitation rights with his children by executing the adoption consent.[2] In *Matter of Ricky A.A.*,[3] the court held that a judicial consent to an adoption is irrevocable absent fraud, duress or coercion.

The irrevocable nature of the judicial consent requires the judge to inform the birth parent of the consequences of signing the consent, that she has a right to be represented by legal counsel of her own choosing, that she is entitled to obtain supportive counseling, and that she has the right to the assignment of counsel free of charge pursuant to Judiciary Law § 35, the Family Court Act § 262 and the SCPA § 407, if she is financially unable to obtain such legal counsel.

Library References:

West's Key No. Digests, Adoption ⚖️7.1–7.7.

§ 20.66 Private Placement Adoptions—Consent of the Birth Parents—Personal Appearances Required

While the statute clearly authorizes the execution of extra-judicial consent (DRL § 115–b(3)), it is the policy of some courts to require the birth parents to appear before the court in order to ratify the consent. These courts appear not to recognize the validity of an extra-judicial consent and seem to ignore the fact that the statute does not require a personal appearance by the consenting natural parent. This policy was disavowed in *Matter of Adoption of Jarrett*.[1] Where, the appellate division refuted the family court's suggestion that it had the discretion not to honor an extra-judicial consent, and that it could require a judicial consent in all cases. *Jarrett* supports the proposition that adoptive parents may rely on properly executed extra-judicial consents. When offered to a court in a properly prepared manner, an extra-judicial consent is entitled to be accepted and, unless the natural parents register objection as provided by the statute, the consent should be enforced.

Library References:

West's Key No. Digests, Adoption ⚖️7.1–7.7.

2. Matter of Lisa W., 159 Misc.2d 359, 604 N.Y.S.2d 474 (Fam.Ct., Monroe County, 1993).

3. 146 A.D.2d 433, 541 N.Y.S.2d 264 (3d Dep't 1989), aff'd 75 N.Y.2d 885, 554 N.Y.S.2d 473, 553 N.E.2d 1021 (1990).

§ 20.66

1. 224 A.D.2d 1029, 637 N.Y.S.2d 912 (4th Dep't 1996). *See also,* Matter of De Filippis v. Kirchner, 217 A.D.2d 145, 636 N.Y.S.2d 134 (3d Dep't 1995) (failure of adoption consent to notify natural father in "18 point type" of his rights and obligations does not invalidate consent where he was fully informed).

§ 20.67 Private Placement Adoptions—Consent of the Birth Parents—Step-Parent Adoptions

A private placement adoption proceeding may be initiated by a step-parent wishing to adopt his or her spouse's child. For example, a husband who wants wish to adopt his wife's child requires the consent of the birth father. If, however, the birth father has abandoned his child, his consent is not required.

Abandonment is defined as an intent to forego parental rights by the failure to visit the child and communicate with the child or the person having legal custody of the child for a period of six (6) months.[1]

However, payment of a fair and reasonable sum of money towards the support of the child, according to the parent's means, is deemed to be a substantial communication by such parent with the child or person having legal custody of the child. Thus, an appropriate payment of support for the child should preclude the court from making a determination of abandonment.[2] In *Matter of Jennifer Lauren D.*,[3] the appellate division stated that a parent's failure to pay support was a significant factor in determining abandonment; however, such a finding could be avoided if the parent could set forth the reasons for the failure to pay support.

The court will not make a finding of abandonment where there has been interference with attempted parental contact. In *Matter of Shawn P.*,[4] the court refused to find abandonment where the evidence established that the mother interfered with and thwarted the natural father's attempts to visit with and communicate with the infant.[5]

A court also refused to find abandonment where the birth father filed a visitation petition, and obtained an order of visitation prior to the filing of the adoption petition by the mother and step-father. The court held that the actions of the birth father did not indicate a settled purpose to forego parental rights.[6] In *Matter of Michael Chad M.*, the court refused to find an abandonment by the birth father where the evidence established that the father's effort to maintain contact with his son were impeded by a protective order procured by the mother. The order had directed the father to refrain from any contact, oral or physical, with the child at any time or any place.[7] Additionally, where the

---

§ 20.67
1. DRL § 111(2)(a).
2. DRL § 111(6)(d).
3. 110 A.D.2d 699, 487 N.Y.S.2d 817 (2d Dep't 1985).
4. 187 A.D.2d 432, 589 N.Y.S.2d 565 (2d Dep't 1992).
5. *See also*, Matter of Edward Franz, 186 A.D.2d 256, 588 N.Y.S.2d 331 (2d Dep't 1992); Joseph Michael D., 138 A.D.2d 974, 526 N.Y.S.2d 305 (4th Dep't 1988).
6. *See* Matter of Adoption of Maria S., 145 Misc.2d 99, 545 N.Y.S.2d 676 (Fam.Ct., Queens County, 1989).
7. 143 A.D.2d 189, 531 N.Y.S.2d 637 (2d Dep't 1988).

child's whereabouts have been kept from the birth parent, the court will not make a finding of abandonment.[8]

The petitioner has the burden of proving that the natural parent abandoned the child without good reason,[9] and the proof offered must be "clear and convincing."[10]

Library References:

West's Key No. Digests, Adoption ⚖7.1–7.7.

§ 20.68 Private Placement Adoptions—Foreign Born Children

A shortage of adoptable children has led to an influx of children from foreign countries admitted into the United States as orphans to be adopted pursuant to federal statutes granting them non-quota immigrant status.[1] In such circumstances, DRL § 115–a requires that a pre-adoption investigation be made in order to determine whether the adoption is in the best interests of the child.

Children placed by certain international agencies which are supervised by, and comply with the regulation of, the Department of Social Services are treated as agency placements rather than private placements.[2] As such, a pre-adoption investigation is unnecessary. This procedure expedites the process of finding homes for orphans in New York State, shortens the time during which children are cared for in an institutional setting and assures the children some necessary protection.[3]

Library References:

West's Key No. Digests, Adoption ⚖7.1–7.7.

---

8. *See* Pavlovic v. Pavlovic, 124 A.D.2d 732, 508 N.Y.S.2d 234 (2d Dep't 1986).

9. Matter of Gross, 102 Misc.2d 1073, 425 N.Y.S.2d 220 (Fam.Ct., N.Y. County, 1980).

10. *See* Matter of Rose Marie M., 94 A.D.2d 734, 462 N.Y.S.2d 483 (2d Dep't 1983).

§ 20.68

1. *See* Chapter 19 "Immigration Law," *supra*.

2. Social Services Law § 371(10). Note that the procedures set forth in DRL § 115–a have no application to adoptions arising under Social Services Law § 371. *See* DRL § 115–a(7).

3. PRACTICE POINTER: The attorney representing the adoptive parents, upon learning the name of the agency involved, should call the Department of Social Services and request to speak to one of the staff attorneys to determine whether the agency placing the child is licensed to do business in the State of New York. Recently, a number of adoptions have been aborted because the agency placing the children with couples in New York State was either not licensed to do business in the State of New York or had its license to do business revoked. An example of why an agency's license was revoked occurred where the agency charged the adoptive couple approximately $28,000. When asked by the court for a detailed breakdown of expenses, the agency could not, or would not, provide the information. Since medical expenses are usually about $8,000 and other incidental expenses are approximately $6,000, the remaining monies could not be accounted for and presumably were exorbitant profits, thus creating the appearance of baby selling. *See* Matter of Adoption of A. by K.S., 158 Misc.2d 760, 601 N.Y.S.2d 762 (Fam. Ct., N.Y. County, 1993), in which the court discussed the difference between a private adoption and an agency adoption.

§ 20.69 Private Placement Adoptions—Petition for Adoption

The petition for adoption must be filed within ten days of taking physical custody of the child. Where, however, the court has waived the requirements for certification as a qualified adoptive parent, the petition for adoption must be filed within five days from obtaining physical custody of the child.[1] Where an application for temporary guardianship has been made, the petition must state that an adoption petition will be filed within forty-five days after the execution of the consent.[2] The petition for adoption is an official form and is supplied by the court. The petition must be signed by the adoptive parents, verified before a notary public and filed with the adoption clerk of the court in the county in which the adoptive parents reside.[3] If the adoptive parents do not live in New York State, the proceeding must be brought in the county where the child resides. While the petition for adoption must be filed within ten days of physically receiving the infant for adoption (or five days after receiving the infant if the court waived certification of the parents) it is not essential that all the other necessary documents be filed along with the petition. The filing of the petition will initiate the adoption proceedings.[4]

The official form for a private adoption was redrafted in November, 1991, and adopted by the Chief Administrator of the courts of the State of New York on January 6, 1992. One of the new provisions requires a statement whether the adoptive child is or is not a Native American child within the meaning of the Indian Child Welfare Act of 1978.[5] The judge must determine whether the provisions of the Act have been complied with. Specifically, a Native American child must first be offered for adoption to the extended family of the child such as grandparents, aunts, uncles or cousins, or, if none are found or willing to adopt, the child must be offered to Native American adoptive parents.[6]

Library References:

West's Key No. Digests, Adoption ⚖11.

§ 20.70 Private Placement Adoptions—The Agreement of Adoption

The agreement of adoption is an official form which the adoptive parents are required to sign. It is acknowledged twice, once before a notary public and again before the judge when the adoptive parents are

---

§ 20.69

1. DRL § 115–c. *See also,* SCPA § 1725(5) and Uniform Rules for Surrogate's Court, 22 NYCRR § 207.58.
2. SCPA § 1725(2)(d).
3. DRL § 115(2).
4. DRL § 116(2).
5. 25 U.S.C.A. §§ 1901–1963; Uniform Rules—Family Court, 22 NYCRR § 205.51.
6. 25 U.S.C.A. §§ 1901–1963. *See supra,* § 20.50.

present in court. It provides that the adoptive parents agree to adopt the infant and to treat the infant as their own lawful child; as a consequence, they acquire the rights and other responsibilities as the parents of the adoptive child.

Library References:
West's Key No. Digests, Adoption ⚖︎6.

§ 20.71 Private Placement Adoptions—Affidavit of Attorney Representing Adoptive Parents

This affidavit, prepared and executed by the attorney for the adoptive parents, identifies the adoptive parents for the judge.[1] In effect, the attorney for the adoptive parents is vouching for the identity of the petitioners. The attorney for the adoptive parents signs the affidavit before the judge on the day of the adoption and it is also signed by the judge.

Library References:
West's Key No. Digests, Adoption ⚖︎11.

§ 20.72 Private Placement Adoptions—Confidential Affidavit

The Confidential Affidavit is prepared by the attorney for the adoptive parents and is executed by them before a notary public. It includes the following information: their religious faith; marital status; educational status; health status; ownership of property; financial status and any record of a criminal conviction, involvement or finding of child abuse or neglect against the adoptive parents.

Library References:
West's Key No. Digests, Adoption ⚖︎11.

§ 20.73 Private Placement Adoptions—Attorney's Affidavit of Financial Disclosure

This affidavit[1] is an official form supplied by the Office of Court Administration ("OCA"); it was originally promulgated to monitor abuses of attorneys who were charging exorbitant fees. This form is completed by all attorneys in adoption proceedings, and an original and a copy are filed with the OCA. The OCA affidavit contains the name of the attorney, the amount of money that the attorney is charging for the adoption and a brief statement of the nature of the services rendered. The affidavit must also state how the attorney met and was retained by

§ 20.71
1. *See* Uniform Rules for Surrogate's Court, 22 NYCRR § 207.55(b)(2).

§ 20.73
1. *See* Uniform Rules for Surrogate's Court, 22 NYCRR § 207.55(b)(7).

the adoptive parents. The OCA will acknowledge receipt and return the copy to the attorney with the OCA's return receipt stamped on the copy. The receipted, stamped copy is then filed with the adoption clerk as proof that the filing requirements have been fulfilled.

Library References:

West's Key No. Digests, Adoption ⟜11.

§ 20.74 Private Placement Adoptions—Notification of Order of Adoption; Report of Adoption

If the infant to be adopted is born within the City of New York, the attorney for the adoptive parents must prepare a notification of order of adoption.[1] If the infant to be adopted was born outside of New York City, the attorney must prepare a New York State Report of Adoption.[2]

These are official forms supplied by the adoption clerk of the court. It contains identifying information about both the birth parent and the child. It is used by the appropriate public official to draft a new birth certificate for the adoptive parents, bearing the name of the adoptive parents and the new name of the adoptive child.

Library References:

West's Key No. Digests, Adoption ⟜14.

§ 20.75 Private Placement Adoptions—Order of Adoption

The attorney for the adoptive parents prepares the proposed order of adoption[1] and files an original and copy with the adoption clerk along with the other supporting papers prior to the adoption. When the adoption becomes final, the judge will sign the order of adoption.

The order of adoption states, *inter alia*, that the infant is to be regarded in all respects as the child of the adoptive parents. After the order is signed by the judge, a certified copy is delivered to the attorney for the adoptive parents.[2] Before the order of adoption is signed, the judge must be satisfied that the adoption is in the best interests of the child.[3] The signing of the order of adoption by the judge is not a mere ministerial act; it is necessary to complete the legal adoption of the child.

§ 20.74

1. PRACTICE POINTER: The clerk requires two certified copies of the original birth certificate.

2. PRACTICE POINTER: The clerk requires only one certified copy of the original birth certificate.

§ 20.75

1. *See* Uniform Rules for Surrogate's Court, 22 NYCRR § 207.55(b)(6).

2. DRL §§ 114, 116.

3. Matter of Stephan Joseph S., 158 A.D.2d 524, 551 N.Y.S.2d 289 (2d Dep't 1990).

Until such order has been signed, the adoption is not legally effective.[4]

Library References:

West's Key No. Digests, Adoption ⇐14.

§ 20.76 Private Placement Adoptions—Birth Mother's Affidavit Regarding Putative Father

If the mother of the child is not married, the adoption clerks require that the birth mother submit an affidavit concerning the identity of the putative father of the adoptive child. This affidavit is made pursuant to Domestic Relations Law § 111–a, and is known as the 111–a affidavit. A typical affidavit would include the following allegations:

(1) That no person has been adjudicated by a court of the State of New York, or of any other state to be the father of the child;

(2) That no person has filed an unrevoked notice of intent to claim paternity of the infant who is the subject of the adoption proceeding;

(3) That no person is recorded on the child's birth certificate as the child's father;

(4) That no person has been married to the mother within six months subsequent to the birth of the child and prior to the execution of a surrender instrument or the initiation of a proceeding pursuant to Social Services Law § 384–b;

(5) That no person has been identified as the child's father in a written sworn affidavit signed by the mother;

(6) That the mother was not married twelve months prior to the birth of the child;

(7) That the mother is not married presently;

(8) That the mother has not concealed her pregnancy from any person claiming to be or who may be the putative father of the child;

(9) That the mother has sole custody of the infant child and had voluntarily surrendered the infant to the proposed adoptive parents;

(10) That no person has come forth claiming to be the father and who has paid a fair and reasonable sum according to his means for the support of the child;

(11) That no person claiming to be the father openly lived with the child or the mother for a period of six months within a one year period immediately preceding the placement of the child for adop-

---

4. Matter of Estate of Mazzeo, 95 A.D.2d 91, 466 N.Y.S.2d 759 (3d Dep't 1983); see also, Estate of Conway, 74 Misc.2d 909, 346 N.Y.S.2d 682 (Surr.Ct., N.Y. County, 1973).

§ 20.76

tion and has openly held himself out to be the father of the child nor has any person claiming to be the father been prevented by the mother or anyone else from living with the mother;

(12) That no person claiming to be the father has inquired about the child's welfare, whereabouts or health;

(13) That no person claiming to be the father has communicated or visited with the child within the last six months prior to the filing of the petition for adoption;

(14) That no person claiming to be the father has sent any support, cards, gifts or letters to the child;

(15) That no person claiming to be the father has made efforts to support the mother of the child during her pregnancy or after the birth of the child;

(16) That no person claiming to be the father has evinced a willingness to assume the full parental responsibility (both financial and emotional) for the infant;

(17) That hospital, medical and nursing expenses incurred in connection with the mother's pregnancy or with the birth of the child have been paid by someone other than the putative father.

If it appears from the affidavit that a person has shown some indicia of fatherhood, *i.e.*, has supported the child, has visited the child or has filed an acknowledgment of paternity, the judge will require that the attorney representing the adoptive parents serve such putative father with a notice to show cause why the consent of that person to the adoption should not be dispensed with. The judge may hold a hearing and inquire into the facts and circumstances of the case and determine whether the person claiming to be the father is willing to assume the responsibilities of fatherhood and that it would be in the best interests of the child to be placed in his custody, or whether his consent to the adoption may be dispensed with. The best interests of the child is the primary consideration in such a hearing.[1]

Library References:

West's Key No. Digests, Adoption ⚖11.

§ 20.77 Private Placement Adoptions—Affidavit of Intermediary

Only an authorized agency, a parent, a legal guardian, or relative within the second degree is permitted to place out or board a child for

---

§ 20.76
1. DRL § 111–a; Matter of Raquel Marie X., 76 N.Y.2d 387, 559 N.Y.S.2d 855, 559 N.E.2d 418 (1990).

adoption.[1] When an intermediary has brought about the meeting of the adoptive parents and the birth parents, the court will require an Intermediary Affidavit which must explain the facts and circumstances surrounding the meeting between the birth parents and the adoptive parents. The purpose of the affidavit is to prevent baby brokers from involving themselves in the sale of babies for adoption. In *Adoption of Samuel*,[2] the court held that placement of an infant by an attorney was improper and restored custody of the infant to the birth mother. In *Matter of Adoption of Baby Boy M.G.*,[3] however, the court held that an attorney did not violate Social Services Law § 374 by merely having counseled clients on (1) how to legitimately locate an adoptable child and (2) by having given advice to the adoptive parents regarding the legal hurdles encountered in a private adoption proceeding.

Library References:

West's Key No. Digests, Adoption ⚖11.

§ 20.78 Private Placement Adoptions—Attorney's Affidavit Regarding Legal Fees

The court, in an adoption proceeding, may determine the reasonableness of the fees charged by the attorney. It is common practice, and permissible, for the adoptive parents to pay their own attorney's fees as well as the fees of the attorney representing the birth parent. Domestic Relations Law § 115(8) requires the attorney representing the adoptive parents to set forth, in an affidavit, all fees, compensation and other remuneration received for, or assisting in the arrangement of, the placement or adoption of the child.[1] In *Matter of Male Infant B.*,[2] the court recognized that the attorney representing the adoptive parents was entitled to reasonable and actual fees charged for consultation and legal services connected with the adoption proceedings. The attorney, however, may not receive compensation for the placing out or adoption of the child. In *Matter of Carballo by Tersigni*,[3] the court approved the adoption even though the attorney improperly sought a fee for acting as an intermediary and seeking an adoptive family for the infant. The court required the attorney to reimburse the petitioning adoptive parent for all

---

§ 20.77

1. Social Services Law § 374(2).
2. 167 A.D.2d 909, 562 N.Y.S.2d 278 (4th Dep't 1990), aff'd 78 N.Y.2d 1047, 576 N.Y.S.2d 83, 581 N.E.2d 1338 (1991).
3. 135 Misc.2d 252, 515 N.Y.S.2d 198 (Surr.Ct., Nassau County, 1987).

§ 20.78

1. DRL § 115(8) also requires the adoptive parents or parent to set forth, in an affidavit "all fees, compensation and other remunerations paid by such parent or parents on account of or incidental to the birth or care of the adopted child, the pregnancy or care of the adoptive child's mother ..."
2. 96 A.D.2d 1055, 466 N.Y.S.2d 482 (2d Dep't 1983).
3. 137 Misc.2d 553, 521 N.Y.S.2d 375 (Fam.Ct., Schenectady County, 1987).

§ 20.78 ADOPTIONS Ch. 20

fees and disbursements paid to him, and prohibited the attorney from rendering any legal bill for unpaid services and disbursements.

Each of the appellate divisions of the state have promulgated rules regarding the conduct of attorneys in adoption proceedings.[4] The rules require that an attorney must supply his or her name, address, telephone number, firm, affiliation, docket number of the adoption proceeding, the court where the proceeding is pending, fee arrangement, nature of the services rendered, names of attorneys or other persons, and agencies or corporations who will receive compensation in the manner in which the initial contract occurred between the attorney and the natural or adoptive parents.

The purpose of these rules, in conjunction with DRL § 115(8) is to prevent the sale of infants under the guise of adoption.

Library References:
West's Key No. Digests, Adoption ⚖11.

§ 20.79 Private Placement Adoptions—Affidavit of Explanation of Criminal Activity

If either the criminal clearance or the child abuse clearance reveals that the adoptive parent or parents were involved in criminal activity, convicted of a crime, or there was a finding of child abuse and neglect against them, the court will require an affidavit fully explaining the facts and circumstances surrounding the incident or incidents. The court may take such action as it deems appropriate, and if the criminal conviction is of a grievous nature, the adoption may be denied. If the crime involves the death of an infant, the petition for adoption must be denied. Convictions, however, may not always result in a negative determination. In the case of *In re Alison V.V.*,[1] the family court denied a potential adoptive mother certification to adopt on the ground that she was convicted of disorderly conduct and hindering prosecution when she was a teenager. The appellate division reversed, holding that the conviction should not have precluded her from being considered as an adoptive parent. In so deciding, the appellate division gave great weight to the affidavits submitted on her behalf.

Library References:
West's Key No. Digests, Adoption ⚖11.

§ 20.80 Private Placement Adoptions—Investigation by Disinterested Person

At the time of receiving the petition, agreement and consents, the court, upon finding that the provisions of Article 7 of the Domestic

---

4. *First Dep't*: 22 NYCRR § 603.23; *Second Dep't*: 22 NYCRR § 691.23; *Third Dep't*: 22 NYCRR § 806.14; *Fourth Dep't*: 22 NYCRR § 1022.33.

§ 20.79
1. 211 A.D.2d 988, 621 N.Y.S.2d 739 (3d Dep't 1995).

Relations Law have been complied with, and that the adoption is in the best interests of the child, issues an order of investigation. The order must direct that the investigation "shall not unnecessarily duplicate any previous investigations which have been made of the petitioner" pursuant to the pre-placement certification process set forth in DRL § 115–d.[1] The investigation is made by a disinterested person who the judge believes is qualified by training or experience, or by an agency designated by the judge.[2] DRL § 116(3)(a)-(f) sets forth the factors to be examined by the investigator. The list included, but is not limited to, the following:

(a) the marital and family status, and history, of the adoptive parents and the adoptive child;

(b) the physical and mental health of the adoptive parents and adoptive child;

(c) the property owned by and the income of the adoptive parents;

(d) the compensation paid and agreed upon with respect to the placement of the child for adoption;

(e) whether either adoptive parent has ever been a respondent in any proceeding concerning allegedly neglected, abandoned or delinquent children;

(f) any other facts relating to the familial, social, religious, emotional and financial circumstances of the adoptive parents which may be relevant to a determination of adoption.

The written report must be submitted to the judge within 30 days after the investigation was ordered, unless, for good cause shown, the time has been extended. The report must be filed before the final order of adoption is granted.

Upon receipt of the report, if the court finds apparent cause, it must require the petitioners to show cause why the child should not be removed from the home. The hearing is held upon notice to all persons whose consent is required for the adoption. The court has the discretion to require that the natural mother be given notice even if her consent was not needed. If the court is satisfied that the welfare of the child requires removal, it may direct that the child be removed from the home of the petitioners. The judge may return the child to a natural parent, or place the child with an authorized agency, or in the case of a surrogate, transfer the child to the family court.[3]

Library References:

West's Key No. Digests, Adoption ⚖13.

§ 20.80
1. DRL § 116(2).
2. DRL § 116(3).
3. DRL § 116(2).

§ 20.81 Private Placement Adoptions—The Hearing

Approximately two to six months after all papers have been filed, and after the court has received the investigator's report, the adoption hearing is scheduled. The adoptive parents, their attorney and the child are present in court to finalize the adoption. The hearing is more ceremonial than evidentiary, and lasts anywhere from two to ten minutes. Some judges have stenographers present taking the minutes of the hearing, while others do not. At the adoption hearing, the attorney for the adoptive parents acknowledges that the prospective adoptive parents are the same people who signed the petition for adoption, and all other supporting documents. The attorney identifies the persons before the judge as the adoptive parents. After the parties have been identified, the judge will inquire of the attorney and the prospective adoptive parents whether they have read all the affidavits, petitions, and consents. The judge will request the adoptive parents and the attorney to acknowledge that they have signed the documents and that the statements contained therein are their own and that they are true statements.

If the court finds that all of the statutory requirements have been complied with, and is satisfied that the best interests of the child will be promoted by the adoption, an order of adoption shall be signed and entered pursuant to DRL § 114.[1]

Library References:

West's Key No. Digests, Adoption ⇨13.

§ 20.82 Private Placement Adoptions—Certificate of Adoption

Upon finalization of the adoption, the adoption clerk will provide the attorney for the adoptive parents, either immediately after the adoption hearing, or by mail, with the order of adoption and a certificate of adoption. The latter document is evidence that the child has been adopted and recites the name of the court, the name of the judge and the date of the adoption. The certificate of adoption is valid and legal proof of the adoption and is accepted by schools, social security and other authorities as evidence of the adoption.

Library References:

West's Key No. Digests, Adoption ⇨14.

§ 20.83 Private Placement Adoptions—The New Birth Certificate

The order of adoption will direct that the name of the adoptive child be changed to the name stated in the agreement of adoption and that

§ 20.81
1. DRL § 116(4).

henceforth the child will be known by that name.[1] In approximately two to eighteen months, depending upon the municipality where the child was born, the attorney for the adoptive parents will receive a new birth certificate setting forth the child's new name, as well as showing that the adoptive parents are the parents of the child.[2]

§ 20.84 Private Placement Adoptions—Checklist of Documents Required for Private Placement Adoption

(1) Petition for Adoption

(2) Agreement of Adoption

(3) Affidavit of Attorney representing adoptive parents

(4) Confidential Affidavit

(5) Attorney's Affidavit of Financial Disclosure

(6) Notification of Order of Adoption

(7) Report of Adoption

(8) Order of Adoption

(9) Birth Mother's Affidavit regarding putative father (111–a Affidavit)

(10) Affidavit of Intermediary

(11) Attorney's Affidavit regarding legal fees

(12) Affidavit of explanation of criminal activity

(13) Certified copy of the birth certificate of the adoptive child which shall contain the information in Public Health Law § 4100–a(4)

(14) Certified marriage certificate where the adoptive parents are husband and wife or where the individual adoptive parent is a spouse of the natural parent

(15) Certified copy of a decree or judgment, where an adoptive parent's marriage has been terminated by decree or judgment

(16) Certified death certificate, where an adoptive or natural parent's marriage has been terminated by death or where it is alleged that consent and notice is not required because of death

(17) Affidavit of Financial Disclosure from the adoptive parent or parents, and from any person whose consent to the adoption is required by law.

The following documentation is also required to be filed with the adoption clerk in any private or independent adoption. The requirements for these documents may vary with the particular court and the adoption clerk should be consulted:

§ 20.83
1. DRL § 114(1).

2. Public Health Law § 4138(1)(c).

§ 20.84

(1) Medical certification as to the health of the adoptive parents;

(2) Medical certification as to the health of the adoptive child;

(3) Letters of reference concerning the adoptive parents' good character;

(4) Application for criminal clearance through New York State Division of Criminal Justice;

(5) Clearance application through New York State Child Abuse and Maltreatment Register.

§ 20.85 Agency Adoptions—Defined

Unlike private adoptions, however, where there are birth parents and adoptive parents involved in the agreement, agency adoptions involve the adoptive parents and an authorized agency.[1] The birth parents are not involved in agency adoptions because their parental rights have already been terminated by a court proceeding or by execution of a surrender terminating parental rights.[2]

§ 20.86 Agency Adoptions—Definition of "Authorized Agency"

An "authorized agency" is defined as any agency, association, corporation, institution, society or other organization incorporated or organized under the laws of the State of New York which is empowered by law to care for, to place out or to board out children, and which actually has its place of business in the State of New York and is approved, visited, inspected and supervised by the Department of Social Services.[1] There are basically two types of authorized agencies:

(1) A municipal Department of Social Services; and

(2) A voluntary child care agency or private child care agency.

§ 20.85

1. CAVEAT: The attorney representing the agency in an adoption must be mindful of a potential conflict of interest that may arise where the agency attorney also represents the adoptive parents. In practice, because foster care agency attorneys are familiar with the adoption procedures, they are often requested to represent the adoptive parents. Since the same attorney will be representing both parties, there is potential for a conflict of interest. In such circumstance, when it becomes clear that the attorney cannot represent the best interests of the adoptive parent, the attorney must inform the court and withdraw from the proceeding. While it is permissible for an attorney to represent both the authorized agency and the adoptive parents in an agency adoption, such is not the case in a private adoption. Section 374(6) of the Social Services Law specifically provides that no attorney or law firm may represent both the adoptive parents and the natural parents in an adoption proceeding.

2. *See* Matter of Adoption of A. by K.S., 158 Misc.2d 760, 601 N.Y.S.2d 762 (Fam. Ct., N.Y. County, 1993).

§ 20.86

1. Social Services Law 371(10). As to Indian affairs *see* Social Services Law §§ 39, 371(10)(b); regarding out of state agencies, *see* Social Services Law § 371(10)(c).

Ch. 20   CHILD'S ENTRY INTO THE SYSTEM   § 20.88

Library References:

West's Key No. Digests, Infants ⟜17.

§ 20.87 Agency Adoptions—Venue

The adoption proceeding must be instituted in the county where the adoptive parents reside or, if they do not reside in the State of New York, in the county where the authorized agency has its principal office.[1]

Foster parents have several options regarding the venue of an adoption proceeding. They may file a petition for adoption in the court where the termination of parental rights proceeding is pending.[2] This option is permissive, not mandatory, and the foster parents may apply to adopt the foster child in the county where they reside. Further, the foster parents may file the petition for adoption in the court where the birth parents have signed a surrender.[3] Thus, agency adoptions may take place (1) where the foster parents reside, (2) in the county where the court terminated parental rights, (3) in the county where the court took a surrender from the birth parents or (4) in the county where the agency has its principal office.[4]

Library References:

West's Key No. Digests, Adoption ⟜10.

§ 20.88 Agency Adoptions—Child's Entry into the System

There are basically two ways that an infant may be placed in the foster care system:

(1) voluntary commitment.[1]

(2) court intervention and court order finding either abuse or

---

§ 20.87

1. DRL § 113.
2. Social Services Law § 384–b.
3. Id.
4. **PRACTICE POINTER:** Where there are competing parties (e.g., aunt or grandmother of the foster child) the attorney for the adoptive parents may wish to direct adoption proceeding to the judge in the court more favorable to the adoptive parents. If the attorney representing the foster parents has reason to believe that the judge presiding at the termination proceeding favors the foster parents, then the attorney may file the petition for adoption with the clerk of the court where the termination proceeding is pending so that the same judge presiding over the termination proceeding will also preside over the adoption proceeding. On the other hand, if the attorney believes that the judge presiding over the termination proceeding favors a family member who may be seeking to adopt the child, then the attorney may file the adoption petition where the foster parents reside. In effect, Social Services Law § 384–b(10) gives the attorney for the foster parents the ability to seek the jurisdiction more favorable to his clients. This may be considered judge shopping, but the statute permits it. The attorney who does not take advantage of such a situation is doing his client a disservice.

§ 20.88

1. Social Services Law § 384.

§ 20.88   ADOPTIONS   Ch. 20

neglect by a parent.[2]

Library References:

West's Key No. Digests, Adoption ⊕4.

§ 20.89 Agency Adoptions—Child's Entry into the System—Voluntary Transfer of Legal Custody of Children to the Authorized Agency

Authorized agencies obtain legal custody over children in two ways:

(1) By written surrender;[1] and

(2) By court order.[2]

Library References:

West's Key No. Digests, Adoption ⊕1–7.7.

§ 20.90 Agency Adoptions—Child's Entry into the System—Judicial Surrender

When the birth parent is willing to sign a surrender terminating parental rights, thereby freeing the child for adoption, the caseworker employed by the authorized agency will contact the clerk of the court to make an appointment to appear before a judge of the family court in order to supervise the execution of the judicial surrender.[1]

---

2. *See, e.g.,* Family Court Act §§ 1052, 1055.

§ 20.89

1. Social Services Law § 383–c.
2. Social Services Law § 384–b.

§ 20.90

1. *See* Social Services Law § 383–c(3). The surrender may also be executed and acknowledged before a surrogate.

PRACTICE POINTER: The attorney for the agency who is to oversee the signing of the judicial surrender should prepare five copies of the judicial surrender and five copies of the application to execute the judicial surrender, which document is signed by the birth parent. The procedure in the family court is for the birth parent to execute the application and to have the signature notarized. At 9:00 a.m. the attorney representing the authorized agency should file the five applications to execute the surrender and five surrenders with the petition clerk. Thereafter, the petition clerk will prepare a new file, give it a docket number and the file will then be sent to the judge who has previously handled this case. Since all foster children come into care either through a court order or through a voluntary commitment which is subsequently approved by a judge, theoretically a judge would have already handled part of the case; the surrenders should be executed before that judge. Some time in late morning, the case will be called. If the birth parent is indigent, the judge will assign an attorney free of charge. Thereafter, the attorney for the birth parent will review the surrender documents with his client to make sure the birth parent understands the nature and effect of the document. The birth parent must understand that all parental rights are terminated by signing the judicial surrender before the court. Once the surrender is signed before the court, the surrender becomes irrevocable. The judge will examine the birth parent to make sure the birth parent understands the documents and understands the consequences of signing the judicial surrender. If the judge is satisfied that the birth parent fully understands what is going on and that the birth parent will lose all parental rights, the court will oversee the execution of the judicial surrender and will thereafter certify to the appropriate and proper execution by the birth parent. The surrender is then certified by

The judicial surrender must include, in plain language, and in conspicuous bold print on the first page of the written surrender that the parent:[2]

(1) has a right before signing the surrender to speak to an attorney of his or her own choosing or any other person she or he may wish to speak to;

(2) to have the lawyer or other person present with her or him at the time of the execution of the surrender;

(3) has the right to ask the court to appoint an attorney, free of charge, if the parent cannot afford to hire one; and

(4) has the right to supportive counseling.

The form shall also include that the child will be adopted without the parent's consent, without further notice to the parent and will be adopted by any person that the agency chooses unless the surrender document contains the name of the person or persons who will be adopting the child. This is considered a conditional surrender.[3]

The surrender shall include that the parent cannot be forced to sign it, and cannot be punished if he or she does not sign the instrument and would not be subject to any penalty for refusing to sign the surrender.

When the parent appears before the court, the judge or surrogate must inform the parent:[4]

---

the court clerk. It is the responsibility of the attorney for the foster care agency to record the surrender in the county clerk's office of the county where the surrender was taken. The book wherein the surrender is recorded is kept under seal and may be inspected pursuant to court order. *See* Social Services Law § 383–c(5)(e); *see also,* Social Services Law §§ 372(3), (4).

2. Social Services Law § 383–c(5).

3. CAVEAT: The attorney must be especially careful to explain to the birth parent, who is executing the surrender, that a condition placed in the surrender does not automatically give the birth parent the right to fulfillment of the condition. For example, if the condition of the surrender is visitation by the birth parent after the adoption, the birth parent must be made aware that there is no automatic entitlement to visitation. All the birth parent receives is standing to initiate a court proceeding to enforce visitation after the adoption. *See* Matter of Alexandra C., 157 Misc.2d 262, 596 N.Y.S.2d 958 (Fam.Ct., Queens County, 1993).

PRACTICE POINTER: If the birth parent executes a conditional surrender, usually the condition is that there will be visitation by the birth parent after the adoption and/or the person permitted to adopt the child is named. Usually the named person is a grandparent, relative or the present foster parent or parents. When a conditional surrender is entered into, there is usually another document executed called the "open adoption agreement." The open adoption agreement is usually prepared by the attorney for the foster parents and reserves to the birth parent the ability to visit with and keep in contact with the child after the adoption has been finalized. The birth parent, however, must be warned that such an open adoption agreement is not self-executing; it merely gives the birth parent standing to sue for visitation in the event that the adoptive parents refuse to abide by the terms of the open adoption agreement. The court, after a proceeding is brought by the birth parent, will decide whether visitation is appropriate and only grant it if it is in the best interests of the child. *See* Matter of Alexandra C., 157 Misc.2d 262, 596 N.Y.S.2d 958 (Fam.Ct., Queens County, 1993).

4. Social Services Law § 383–c(5).

§ 20.90

(1) Of the right to be represented by legal counsel;

(2) Of the right to obtain supportive counsel;

(3) Of the right to be assigned counsel, free of charge, if the parent cannot afford to hire one;

(4) Of the right to be informed of the consequences of signing the surrender; loss of the right to custody of the child, loss of visitation rights, and loss of the right to speak with, write to, or learn about the child, forever, unless the parties agree otherwise (open adoption); and

(5) That the surrender is final and irrevocable immediately upon its execution and acknowledgment.[5]

Once satisfied that the surrender is appropriate under the circumstances,[6] and that the birth parent executed the surrender knowingly, willingly and freely, the judge will sign the certification and acknowledgment, and the seal of the court will be affixed, together with the court clerk's certification.

Library References:

West's Key No. Digests, Adoption ⚖1–7.7.

§ 20.91 Agency Adoptions—Child's Entry into the System—Extra–Judicial Surrender

An extra-judicial surrender is signed by a birth parent outside of the court; usually in the office of the authorized agency.[1] It surrender must be executed and acknowledged by the parent in the presence of at least two witnesses and before a notary public. At least one witness must be an employee of an authorized agency who is trained, in accordance with the regulations of the Department of Social Services, to receive surrenders. At least one of the witnesses must be a person who is either a certified social worker, or an attorney who is not an employee, volunteer, consultant or agent of an attorney employed by the authorized agency to which the child is being surrendered.[2]

An extra-judicial surrender shall set forth, the following, in plain language, and in conspicuous bold print, on the first page of the instrument:[3]

---

5. *See* Social Services Law § 383–b(3)(b); *see also*, In the Matter of Female R., 202 A.D.2d 672, 609 N.Y.S.2d 295 (2d Dep't 1994), wherein the court held that the lower court was correct in denying, without a hearing, the mother's motion to revoke her judicial consent to surrender her daughter where the court determined that the mother received counseling and was represented by counsel and gave voluntary consent without fraud, duress or coercion.

6. In re Jerome E., 187 A.D.2d 85, 593 N.Y.S.2d 205 (1st Dep't 1993).

§ 20.91

1. *See* Social Services Law § 383–c(4).
2. *Id.*, § 383–c(4)(a).
3. *Id.*, § 383(5)(b).

Ch. 20   COURT APPROVAL OF SURRENDER   § 20.92

(1) The parent prior to signing the surrender has the right to speak to an attorney of his or her own choosing and to any other person the parent wishes to consult;

(2) At the signing of the surrender, the parent may have an attorney or any other person present;

(3) If the parent cannot afford to have an attorney, he or she has the right to ask the court to appoint one free of charge;

(4) The parent is entitled to have supportive counseling;

(5) The parent relinquishes all rights to have custody, visit with, speak with, write to or learn about the child, forever, unless the agreement sets forth different terms pursuant to Social Services Law § 383–c(2);[4]

(6) The child will be adopted without the parents consent and without further notice to the parent, and will be adopted by any person chosen by the agency, unless the surrender instrument contains the names of the adoptive parents;[5] and

(7) The parent cannot be compelled to execute the surrender instrument and cannot be punished for failing to sign the surrender.[6]

The extra-judicial surrender must also set forth the following:

(1) The name and address of the court wherein the application for approval of the extra-judicial surrender will be filed;

(2) That a revocation of the surrender will be effective if it is in writing and postmarked or received by the court named in the surrender within forty-five days of the signing of the surrender;

(3) That a revocation of the surrender made more than forty-five days after its signing will not be effective if the child has been placed in an adoptive home;

(4) The surrender shall be final and irrevocable, and the parent cannot revoke the surrender or bring a case in court to revoke the surrender or regain custody of the child; and

(5) That the agency will not notify the parent when the child is placed in an adoptive home, and the parent may lose all rights at the end of the forty-five day period without further notice.

Library References:

West's Key No. Digests, Adoption ⊖1–7.7.

§ 20.92   Agency Adoptions—Child's Entry into the System—Court Approval of Extra–Judicial Surrender

When the surrender is properly executed by the parent, the autho-

---

4. *See also*, Social Services Law § 383–c(5)(b)(ii).

5. *Id.*, § 383–c(5)(b)(iii).

6. *Id.*, § 383–c(5)(b)(iv).

rized agency must file an application for approval[1] of the extra-judicial surrender, within fifteen days of its execution, with the court in which the adoption proceeding is expected to be filed. If the court wherein the adoption proceeding is pending is unknown, the agency must file in the family court or the surrogate's court in the county where its principal office is located. The application must be accompanied by affidavits from all the witnesses before whom the surrender was executed and acknowledged.[2] These affidavits must include the following:

> (1) The day, time and place where the surrender was executed and acknowledged;
>
> (2) That the parent was provided with a copy of the surrender;
>
> (3) That the surrender was read in full to the parent in his or her principal language and the parent was given an opportunity to ask questions and obtain answers regarding the nature and consequence of the surrender; and
>
> (4) That the parent executed and acknowledged the surrender.

The authorized agency must also provide an affidavit executed by the employee responsible for providing or arranging supportive counseling. It must set forth:[3]

> (1) When supportive counseling was offered to the parent;
>
> (2) Whether the parent accepted the offer of supportive counseling;
>
> (3) If accepted, when supportive counseling was provided and the nature of such counseling.[4]

§ 20.92

1. Social Services Law § 383–c(4)(b).

2. *See supra*, § 20.91 regarding the witnesses to the surrender.

3. Social Services Law § 383–c(4)(c).

4. PRACTICE POINTER: As can be seen from the above recitation, the preparation of an extra-judicial surrender is laborious and, in practice, rarely utilized. Not only is it difficult to have all of the appropriate parties present at the execution of the extra-judicial surrender, but there are numerous conditions that must be fulfilled before the execution may be appropriately taken. For example, the agency must have a person trained in counseling the birth parent with respect to alternatives to the surrender and to the surrender itself. There must be a person at the authorized agency trained to oversee the preparation and execution of the surrender and these caseworkers must give affidavits attesting to the counseling and execution of the extra-judicial surrender. Besides, there must be present at the execution of the extra-judicial surrender a certified social worker or an attorney not associated with the authorized agency. This person is difficult to find and to have present at the execution of the surrender. Thereafter, once the surrender is taken before a notary public, the attorney for the agency now has fifteen days to bring on a petition with notice before the appropriate family court judge to have the surrender approved. The law requires that the judge direct notice to be given to the appropriate parties including all those whose rights would have to be terminated at a termination proceeding pursuant to Social Services Law § 384–b. Some judges require the parent who signed the surrender to also appear in court to be examined as to his or her comprehension of the implications of the surrender. Hence, no time will have been saved by utilizing an extra-judicial surrender. Thus, the practitioner would do well to avoid taking the extra-judicial surrender. It is the better practice to have the

A surrender for adoption executed by a parent whose child is in foster care must be executed before a judge.[5]

Library References:

West's Key No. Digests, Adoption ⬩1–7.7.

§ 20.93 Agency Adoptions—Child's Entry into the System—Assigned Counsel

Where the surrendering parent is indigent, counsel must be assigned to the parent.[1] Assigned counsel must counsel the parent and assist in the execution of the surrender.[2]

Library References:

West's Key No. Digests, Adoption ⬩1–7.7.

§ 20.94 Agency Adoptions—Child's Entry into the System—Required Notice of Application

Before approving the extra-judicial surrender, the judge must order notice to be given to the person who executed the surrender, to persons required to be given notice of the proceeding pursuant to Social Services Law § 384–c and to such other persons as the judge may require.[1]

Library References:

West's Key No. Digests, Adoption ⬩1–7.7.

§ 20.95 Agency Adoptions—Child's Entry into the System—Notification to Court

After the execution of the surrender and prior to the final order of adoption, if the agency receives any correspondence or communication from the parent or from someone acting for the parent that reasonably indicates the parents desire to revoke the surrender, the agency must promptly notify the court of the communication.[1]

Library References:

West's Key No. Digests, Adoption ⬩1–7.7.

parent appear and have the judicial surrender executed before the court.
5. Social Services Law § 383–c(7).

§ 20.93
1. Family Court Act § 262.
2. In re Jerome E., 187 A.D.2d 85, 593 N.Y.S.2d 205 (1st Dep't 1993).

§ 20.94
1. Social Services Law § 383–c(4)(d).

§ 20.95
1. Social Services Law § 383–c(4)(e).

§ 20.96 Agency Adoptions—Child's Entry into the System—Court Order

The court must enter an order approving or disapproving the surrender. If the judge disapproves the surrender, the surrender is deemed a nullity[1] and the child is returned to the authorized agency.[2] Where the court disapproves the surrender, it may require that any subsequent surrender be executed before the court, pursuant to Social Services Law § 383–c(3).[3]

Library References:

West's Key No. Digests, Adoption ⟜1–7.7.

§ 20.97 Agency Adoptions—Child's Entry into the System—Conditional Surrender

A conditional surrender is now permitted by law.[1] The Court of Appeals, in the jointly decided cases of in *In re Dana* and *In re Jacob*,[2] concluded that conditional surrenders are permitted pursuant to Social Services Law § 383–c. In *Matter of Alexandra C.*,[3] a lower court held that the parent signing a surrender could reserve the right to visitation with the child as a condition of consent to the adoption. However, the court cautioned, such reservation did not convey an automatic right to visitation, but rather gave the birth parent standing to initiate a court proceeding to enforce visitation.

Library References:

West's Key No. Digests, Adoption ⟜1–7.7.

§ 20.98 Agency Adoptions—Child's Entry into the System—Recording a Surrender

The surrender must be recorded in the county clerk's office where the surrender is executed, or where the principal office of such authorized agency is located. It is recorded in a book which the county clerk maintains under seal.[1] After the surrender is recorded, it is returned to the authorized agency or its attorney. There is a ten dollar fee for recording the surrender.

§ 20.96

1. Social Services Law § 383–c(4)(f).
2. *Id.* § 383–c(6).
3. *See supra*, note 1.

§ 20.97

1. Social Services Law § 383–c.
2. 86 N.Y.2d 651, 636 N.Y.S.2d 716, 660 N.E.2d 397 (1995).
3. 157 Misc.2d 262, 596 N.Y.S.2d 958 (Fam.Ct., Queens County, 1993).

§ 20.98

1. As to those individuals who may have access to the record, *see* Social Services Law §§ 372(3), (4).

§ 20.99 Agency Adoptions—Child's Entry into the System—Revocation of Surrender

If the court disapproves the surrender, or if a parent delivers or mails a revocation of an extra-judicial surrender to the court named therein within forty-five days of the execution of the surrender, it is deemed a nullity, and the child is returned to the custody of the authorized agency.[1]

If a parent delivers or mails a revocation of an extra-judicial surrender to the court named therein more than forty-five days after its execution, and the child has not been placed in an adoptive home, the surrender is deemed a nullity, and the child is returned to the custody of the authorized agency.[2]

Note, however, that adoptive parents having custody of a child through an authorized agency have the right, as an interested party, to intervene in any proceeding to set aside a surrender.[3]

Library References:

West's Key No. Digests, Adoption ⇔1–7.7.

§ 20.100 Agency Adoptions—Child's Entry into the System—Proceedings Subsequent to Execution of Extra-Judicial Surrender

The adoptive parents may commence the adoption proceeding in a court of competent jurisdiction, other than the court named in an extra-judicial surrender, provided that such commencement is initiated more than forty-five days after the surrender is executed.[1] Once an adoption has been finalized, the adoption is unassailable by the parent who executed a surrender.[2]

In any case in which the authorized agency determines that the person specified in the surrender will not adopt the child, the agency must promptly notify the parent, unless such notice is expressly waived by a statement written by the parent appended to or included in the instrument of surrender.[3]

§ 20.99
1. Social Services Law § 383–c(6)(a).
2. Id., § 383–c(6)(b).
3. Social Services Law § 383–c(9).

§ 20.100
1. Social Services Law § 383–c(8)(b).
2. See McGaffin v. Family and Children's Service of Albany, 6 Misc.2d 776, 164 N.Y.S.2d 444 (Sup.Ct., N.Y. County, 1957).
3. Social Services Law § 383–c(6)(c).

§ 20.100 ADOPTIONS Ch. 20

No child is considered to have been placed in the home of adoptive parents unless the fact of such placement, the date thereof, the date of the agreement, and the names and addresses of the adoptive parents are recorded in a bound volume maintained by the agency for the purposes of recording such information in chronological order.[4]

Library References:

West's Key No. Digests, Adoption ⊜1–7.7.

§ 20.101 Agency Adoptions—Child's Entry into the System—Court Ordered Transfer of Children to Authorized Agency

Where a birth parent has not executed a voluntary surrender, the authorized agency may obtain guardianship and custody over the child through court intervention.

A parent may lose parental rights to a child, thereby freeing the child for adoption through a court order, based upon one of the following grounds:

(1) Permanent neglect of the child;

(2) Mental illness, or mental retardation of the parent;

(3) Severe or repeated abuse of the child; or

(4) Abandonment.

The family court has exclusive jurisdiction to hear all these proceedings. The surrogate's court and the family court have concurrent jurisdiction where both parents are dead and no guardian has been appointed, or in abandonment proceedings.[1]

Library References:

West's Key No. Digests, Adoption ⊜1–7.7.

§ 20.102 Agency Adoptions—Procedures

Once parental rights have been terminated and the child freed for adoption, agency adoption proceedings may be brought either in the family court or the surrogate's court.

---

4. *Id.*, § 383–c(6)(b).

PRACTICE POINTER: The attorney representing the parent who signed a surrender should be aware that even though 45 days have expired since the signing of the surrender, the surrender still can be revoked if the authorized agency has not placed in a bound volume maintained by the agency the date when the child has been placed in the adoptive home, the names and addresses of the adoptive parents and the date of the agreement that the adoptive parents agreed to adopt the child. If such information is not contained in a bound volume listed in chronological order, the parent may still revoke the surrender.

§ 20.101

1. Social Services Law §§ 384–b(3)(d), (4); Family Court Act Article 6.

§ 20.103   Agency Adoptions—The Petition

In agency adoptions, the proceeding is initiated by the adoptive parents through the filing of the Petition and supporting documentation. The attorney for the adoptive parents will prepare a verified Petition which includes the following:

(1) The names and address of the petitioners, *i.e.*, the adoptive parents.

(2) Their age.

(3) Marital status.

(4) The first name and date and place of birth of the infant.

(5) A statement on information and belief that a Verified Schedule signed by the Executive Director to other official of the agency will be attached to the Petition.

(6) The religious faith of the adoptive parents.

(7) The religious faith of the adoptive child.

(8) The manner in which the adoptive parents obtained custody of the adoptive child.

(9) The time that the adoptive child resided with the adoptive parents.

(10) The occupation and income of the adoptive parents.

(11) The new name by which the adoptive child is to be known.

(12) An allegation that no previous application has been made to any court or judge for this adoption.

(13) A statement as to whether the adoptive child had been previous adopted.

(14) Compliance with the Interstate Compact for children brought into the state for adoption.[1]

(15) A statement that neither the adoptive parents nor the child was the subject of an indicated neglect or abuse report as filed with the Statewide Register of Child Abuse and Maltreatment.[2]

(16) The names and addresses of the biological parents, if known, and other characteristics of the biological parents such as (a) heritage; (b) education; (c) general physical appearance of parents at time of birth of adoptive child including height, weight, color of hair, eyes and skin; (d) occupation of parents at time of birth; (e) health

---

§ 20.103
1. DRL § 112.

2. DRL § 112(2).

and medical history of the adoptive child including all information setting forth conditions or diseases believed to be hereditary and any drugs or medication taken during pregnancy by the child's mother; and (f) any other information which may be a factor influencing the child's present or future health, talents, hobbies, and special interests of parents.[3]

Library References:

West's Key No. Digests, Adoption ⚖11.

§ 20.104 Agency Adoptions—The Agreement of Adoption

The agreement of adoption is a written instrument signed by the adoptive parents wherein they represent that they will in all respects treat the child as their own lawful child.[1] The agreement is also signed by an official of the agency, usually the executive director.[2] The child being adopted, if fourteen years or older, must also sign the agreement of adoption. All the signatures are acknowledged before a notary public. When the adoptive parents are before the court, their signatures are reacknowledged by the judge.

Library References:

West's Key No. Digests, Adoption ⚖6.

§ 20.105 Agency Adoptions—Verified Schedule

In every adoption, the agency must present to the court a Verified Schedule containing the following:

(1) The full name of the child;

(2) The manner in which the authorized agency obtained custody of the adoptive child (which is usually by surrender or court order);

(3) A statement why the consent of either or both of the parents of the adoptive child is unnecessary;

(4) A statement whether either parent has ever requested the agency to return the child within the required time of the execution and delivery of a surrender; and

(5) Information concerning the child's medical history.

Domestic Relations Law § 112(3) sets forth the requirements for the verified schedule prepared by the agency which contains information that is generally not known by the adoptive parents.

3. DRL § 112(2), (2–a).

2. DRL § 113.

§ 20.104
1. DRL § 112(2)(b).

§ 20.106 Agency Adoptions—Affidavit of Financial Disclosure

The Affidavit of Financial Disclosure[1] is signed by the adoptive parents and sets forth what, if any, money or anything of value was paid to any person or organization or agency in connection with the adoption.[2] Payment of any money beyond reasonable expenses associated with the adoption is prohibited.[3]

Library References:

West's Key No. Digests, Adoption ⚖11.

§ 20.107 Agency Adoptions—Confidential Affidavit

The Confidential Affidavit is executed by the adoptive parents and contains their pedigree and personal information. In addition it sets forth whether or not the adoptive parents were ever respondents in a proceeding relating to neglected, abandoned or delinquent children.[1] It also contains references from spiritual advisors, doctors and friends and is acknowledged before a notary public.

Library References:

West's Key No. Digests, Adoption ⚖11.

§ 20.108 Agency Adoptions—Marital Affidavit

The marital affidavit, required by the court, is signed by the adoptive parents and notarized. It must contain information regarding the marital history of the adoptive parents. The marital affidavit is utilized to finalize an adoption by one person where that person is still married. Under the old law a married person could not adopt a child without the spouse joining in the application. However, because of either lack of funds or religious conviction, some foster parents did not, or could not divorce and therefore could not adopt. Under the new law, a married foster parent can adopt by himself or herself where that foster parent has been living separate and apart from his or her spouse for at least three years. These allegations are made in the marital affidavit.[1]

§ 20.106

1. *See* Social Services Law § 374(6); 22 NYCRR 205.53(b)(8).
2. Matter of Juan P.H.C., 130 Misc.2d 387, 496 N.Y.S.2d 630 (Surr.Ct., N.Y. County, 1985).
3. *Id.*; *also see*, In the Matter of Jose L., 126 Misc.2d 612, 483 N.Y.S.2d 929 (Fam. Ct., Queens County, 1984).

§ 20.107

1. DRL § 112(2).

§ 20.108

1. 22 NYCRR § 207.55; DRL § 110.

§ 20.109 Agency Adoptions—Child's Medical History

The child's medical history is usually completed by the nurse in the Medical Department connected with the agency. It is a detailed four page report setting forth any illnesses the child may have had, a complete listing of immunizations, the prenatal history of the pregnancy and birth of the child, and the state of the current health or, where applicable, the cause of death of the natural parents and siblings of the adoptive child.[1] While it is contemplated that the medical history would be completed by the birth parents, this is usually not the case. The birth parents' rights have already been terminated, and usually the caseworkers for the authorized agency complete the adoptive child's medical history from agency medical records. The adoptive child's medical history form is given to the adoptive parents prior to the adoption. The adoptive parents are requested to sign a statement that the adoptive parents have received the child's medical history. The statement is then acknowledged before a notary public and filed with the adoption clerk.

Library References:
West's Key No. Digests, Adoption ⚖11.

§ 20.110 Agency Adoptions—Supplemental Affidavit

The Supplemental Affidavit verifies that the marital status and the place of residence are the same as at the time the Petition was filed, or that there have been no substantial changes since their certification as adoptive parents. The Supplemental Affidavit is signed by the adoptive parents and sworn before the judge. At the adoption hearing, the judge may inquire of the adoptive parents if there have been any major changes in their status such as a divorce, a conviction of any crime, loss of job, or if the adoptive parents have been named as a respondent in any abuse or neglect proceeding in the family court.

Library References:
West's Key No. Digests, Adoption ⚖11.

§ 20.111 Agency Adoptions—Notification of Order of Adoption; Report of Adoption

If the adoptive child was born in New York City, a Notification of Order of Adoption is prepared by the attorney for the adoptive parents and filed with the Commissioner of Health of the City of New York. It

§ 20.109
1. *See* DRL § 112(3), (5); Social Services Law § 373–a.

notifies the Commissioner that the child has been adopted and contains all the necessary pedigree information including the birth registration number, the original name of the infant at birth, and the infant's new name. This Notification of Order of Adoption is signed and sealed by the clerk of the court and forwarded directly to the Commissioner of Health of the City of New York.

If the adoptive child was born outside of New York City, a Report of Adoption is prepared. The Report of Adoption is sent to the New York State Commissioner of Health; it contains sufficient information for the Commissioner to issue a new birth certificate stating that the adoptive parents are the parents of the adoptive child.

The purpose of the Notification of Order of Adoption or Report of Adoption is to provide the appropriate official with sufficient information to issue a new birth certificate with the names of the adoptive parents appearing as the parents of the adoptive child. The adoptive child will now take on the name of the adoptive parents. There is no indication on the new birth certificate that the child has been adopted.

When the new birth certificate is issued, the old birth certificate, which names the birth parents, is sealed and may not be unsealed without a court order.

Library References:

West's Key No. Digests, Adoption ⇌14.

§ 20.112 Agency Adoptions—Doctor's Certificate of Health

The Doctor's Certificate of Health is a standard form on which the respective doctors provide certain information concerning the physical and mental health of the adoptive parents and the child. Any disabilities must be noted. The adoption clerk requires that the doctor's certificate be made no earlier than six months prior to the adoption date.

Library References:

West's Key No. Digests, Adoption ⇌11.

§ 20.113 Agency Adoptions—Authorization and Approval for Subsidized Adoption

Adoptions involving handicapped or hard to place children may be subsidized. In such cases adoptive parents receive approximately $400 monthly for a hard to place[1] child and up to $1,200 monthly for a child with special needs. In the City of New York, the authorization is prepared by the agency caseworker and is forwarded to the Adoption

§ 20.113

1. For a definition of a hard to place child, see Social Services Law § 451; as to maintenance subsidies, see Social Services Law § 453.

§ 20.113 ADOPTIONS Ch. 20

Documentation Unit, Division of Accountability, 80 Lafayette Street, New York, New York 10013. The authorization is signed by the appropriate caseworker for the agency. One court has held[2] that a family court judge could not direct the agency to grant adoptive parents a subsidy because such direction violated the agency's obligations to determine if the children were statutorily qualified for such subsidy.[3]

Library References:

West's Key No. Digests, Adoption ⚖11.

§ 20.114 Agency Adoptions—Adoption Homestudy

The Adoption Homestudy is a detailed notarized report prepared by the agency caseworkers and is executed by the Adoption Director or Executive Director.[1] The Adoption Homestudy provides the background information pertaining to the adoptive parents; it includes religious affiliation, marital status, and sets forth a detailed description of the home environment of the adoptive parents. It also includes financial information, the occupations of the petitioners, the names and history of the natural parents of the child, information concerning the child, and recommendations as to whether the adoption is in the best interests of the child.

Library References:

West's Key No. Digests, Adoption ⚖11.

§ 20.115 Agency Adoptions—Affidavit Identifying Party

This affidavit, signed by the attorney for the adoptive parents, identifies the adoptive parents to the court thereby confirming that the persons who physically appear before the court are the same as the adoptive parents selected by the agency to adopt the child.[1]

Library References:

West's Key No. Digests, Adoption ⚖11.

§ 20.116 Agency Adoptions—Order of Adoption

The signing of an adoption order is not considered a ministerial act.

2. In re Hasani B., 195 A.D.2d 404, 600 N.Y.S.2d 694 (1st Dep't 1993).

3. *See* Social Services Law § 450; *see also,* Social Services Law § 454 which relates to medical subsidies for handicapped children.

§ 20.114

1. DRL § 113(3). *See also,* DRL § 112(7).

§ 20.115

1. 22 NYCRR § 207.55(b)(2).

Thus, in the case of *Matter of Adoption of D.S.*[1], the surrogate declined to sign the order of adoption where the proposed adoptive father died after the petition was filed, but before an order could be signed by the court. The surrogate held that in order for an adoption to be effective, it must be signed prior to the death of the adoptive parent.

The order of adoption is prepared by the attorney for the adoptive parents and is signed by the judge. If the judge is satisfied that the adoption is in the best interests of the adoptive child, the court signs the order approving the adoption. The order legally changes the name of the infant to that of the adoptive parents. The child also acquires the status of a natural child, and inherits from the adoptive parents in the same manner.[2]

The order contains the full name, date and place of birth and reference to the schedule annexed to the petition. If there is no reasonable objection to the proposed name change, the order will direct that the name of the child be changed to the name stated in the agreement of adoption and that the child be known by that name.[3]

Library References:
West's Key No. Digests, Adoption ⚖11.

§ 20.117 Agency Adoptions—Certificate of Adoption

The Certificate of Adoption is signed by the clerk of the court and certifies the date the child was adopted, and that the judge has signed an Order of Adoption. The Certificate of Adoption has the same force and effect as a certified copy of the Order of Adoption. The adoptive parents do not receive a copy of the Order of Adoption but only the Certificate of Adoption.[1]

Library References:
West's Key No. Digests, Adoption ⚖11.

§ 20.118 Agency Adoptions—Abuse Clearance Form

The Abuse Clearance Form, which is provided by the State Central Register, certifies whether the adoptive parents and/or the adoptive child are the subject(s) of an indicated report of child abuse or maltreatment.[1] In an agency adoption, the adoptive parents must complete an abuse

§ 20.116
1. 160 Misc.2d 331, 609 N.Y.S.2d 139 (Surr.Ct., Ulster County, 1994).
2. *See* DRL § 117(1)(c); EPTL § 4–1.1(d); In re the Will of Upjohn, 304 N.Y. 366, 107 N.E.2d 492 (1952).
3. DRL § 114(1).

§ 20.117
1. DRL § 114(1).

§ 20.118
1. Social Services Law § 412(12) defines an "indicated report" to mean "a report made pursuant this title [Social Services Law] if an investigation determines that some credible evidence of the alleged abuse or maltreatment exists." *See also*, Social Services Law § 424–a.

clearance form which contains their names and places of residence for the past twelve years. The adoption clerk, after receiving the completed abuse clearance form sends it to the Department of Social Services in Albany, which checks to see if there has been any indication that the adoptive parents are or have been the subject of a case of child abuse or maltreatment. If there is an indication, the adoption clerk will require a detailed affidavit from the adoptive parents explaining the facts and circumstances surrounding the incident.

At anytime subsequent to the completion of the investigation, but in no event later than ninety days after the subject is notified that the report is indicated (*i.e.*, some credible evidence of abuse or maltreatment exists), the subject may request the Department of Social Services to amend or expunge the report. Upon receipt of such a request, the department first determines whether some credible evidence does, in fact, exist. If there is no such evidence, the report is expunged. If the request to expunge is denied, an administrative hearing is scheduled, and the investigating agency must prove by some credible evidence that the subject committed the acts of abuse or maltreatment indicated in the report.[2] If the hearing outcome is unfavorable, the subject may commence an Article 78 proceeding to review the administrative decision. The Court of Appeals in the case of *Matter of Lee TT. v. Dowling*,[3] held that the quantum of proof in order to make a finding of abuse and neglect, *i.e.*, some credible evidence that the subject committed the act or acts of abuse or maltreatment, was unconstitutional. In writing for the majority, Judge Simons stated that the Due Process Clause of the Federal Constitution required the Department of Social Services to substantiate reports of child abuse by a "fair preponderance of the evidence" before disseminating these reports to providers and licensing agencies as a screening device for future employment. Hence, the Department of Social Services must substantiate reports of abuse based on a fair preponderance of the evidence, and *not* on the lesser standard of some credible evidence, prior to disseminating reports.

While these reports of abuse are confidential, the information in the central register is available to law enforcement and child care agencies.[4]

Library References:
West's Key No. Digests, Adoption ⟐11.

§ 20.119 Agency Adoptions—Unavailability of Abuse Clearance Form and Criminal Conviction Check

Court rules require that the petitioner supply the adoption clerk with reports from the New York State Central Register of Child Abuse

---

2. Social Services Law § 422(8)(a). As to the hearing procedure, *see* Social Services Law § 422(8)(b).

3. 87 N.Y.2d 699, 642 N.Y.S.2d 181, 664 N.E.2d 1243 (1996).

4. Social Services Law § 422(4).

and Maltreatment, and the New York State Division of Criminal Justice Services, showing any indication that there was a finding of child abuse or a conviction of any crime. Many times foster parents will receive a child placed in their home in New York State and, before the adoption is finalized, move to another state. In these cases, the adoption clerks usually require reports from both New York State and the state of present residence. In one case, the adoptive parents supplied the requisite reports from New York State but could not supply the requisite reports from New Jersey. Because the New Jersey reports were not submitted, the family court dismissed the adoption petition. The appellate division, however, in *Matter of Antoine*,[1] reversed the order of the family court, reinstated the adoption petition, and observed that the reports were not submitted because the State of New Jersey refused to release the information to anyone except its own state agencies. The court would not hold New Jersey's refusal to release the reports against the adoptive parents and permitted the adoption.

Library References:

West's Key No. Digests, Adoption ⟐11.

§ 20.120 Agency Adoptions—Attorney's Affidavit of Legal Fees

The Attorney's Affidavit of Legal Fees must be filed with the Office of Court Administration. It is known as the OCA Affidavit. It must set forth a brief statement of the nature of services rendered, the names of persons, sharing in the legal fee, or receiving money, directly or indirectly, in connection with the proposed adoption. It must describe the circumstances of the initial contact between the attorney and the adoptive parents.[1]

In *Matter of Adoption of Vincent*,[2] Judge Marks of the Family Court held that the attorney for the agency sponsoring the adoption should not also represent the adoptive parent because of a potential conflict of interest. The judge relieved the "agency attorney" and appointed another attorney who was not connected with the agency sponsoring the adoption. This is the first reported case in which a judge of any court has held that an attorney who normally handles agency matters cannot also handle an adoption for a prospective adoptive parent whose adoption is being sponsored by that same agency. However, in *Matter of Dale P.*,[3] the court ordered the attorney representing the Commissioner of Social Services (authorized agency) to also represent the foster parent who

§ 20.119
1. 207 A.D.2d 829, 616 N.Y.S.2d 635 (2d Dep't 1994); *see also*, DRL § 112(2),(7).

§ 20.120
1. 22 NYCRR § 207.55.

2. 158 Misc.2d 942, 602 N.Y.S.2d 303 (Fam.Ct., N.Y. County, 1993).

3. 189 A.D.2d 325, 595 N.Y.S.2d 970 (2d Dep't 1993).

§ 20.120   ADOPTIONS   Ch. 20

wished to adopt the child. The Commissioner objected and appealed. The appellate division affirmed and allowed the attorney for the Commissioner (agency) to also represent the potential adoptive parent.

Library References:

West's Key No. Digests, Adoption ⚖︎11.

§ 20.121   Agency Adoptions—Checklist of Other Required Supporting Documentation

In addition to documents required by adoption clerks, the court rules require:

(1) Two original birth certificates for the child (City of New York, outside of the City of New York, only one birth certificate is required).

(2) Marriage certificate of adoptive parents.

(3) Divorce decree of an adoptive parent who has been divorced.

(4) Death certificate of a former spouse.

(5) Order of investigation.

(6) Putative Father Registry Form.

(7) Affidavit of No Appeal of the Order of Disposition.

(8) Child's entire medical record package from the time of placement to the present.[1]

Library References:

West's Key No. Digests, Adoption ⚖︎11.

§ 20.122   Agency Adoptions—The Adoption Hearing

After the adoption clerk has reviewed all of the documents submitted by the agency and by the attorney on behalf of the adoptive parents, the adoption clerk will schedule a date for the adoption hearing. If any problems arise, such as documents that are missing or require correction, or there is an indication that the adoptive parents were convicted of a crime or were found to have abused or neglected a child, the clerk will notify the attorney for the adoptive parents. The adoption clerk will require an affidavit from the adoptive parent or parents explaining the facts and circumstances of the incident. The adoption clerk will also request an affidavit from the authorized agency recommending that, despite the new circumstances, the adoption is still in the best interests of the child and should be finalized. If the affidavits provide a satisfactory explanation, the adoption may go forward.

§ 20.121

1. 22 NYCRR § 207.55.

At the adoption hearing, the adoptive parents appear before the court with their attorney and the infant to be adopted. It is not necessary for anyone from the agency to appear, as the appearance is dispensed with by court order. However, the usual practice is for the caseworker who worked on the case to appear at the adoption hearing in order to answer any questions asked by the court. The adoption hearing is brief. The judge reviews the papers which have been thoroughly reviewed by the Adoption Clerk. The judge will ask pertinent questions of the adoptive parents and have them re-swear to all of the affidavits previously submitted, and will also request the attorney identify the parties. The judge will then sign the adoption decree.[1]

The attorney for the adoptive parents will receive Certificates of Adoption within one to two weeks and will receive the amended birth certificate in eighteen months if the child was born in New York City, or sooner if the child was born outside of New York City.

Library References:

West's Key No. Digests, Adoption ⚖13.

§ 20.123 Post-adoption Issues—The Open Adoption

The court has the power not only to grant an adoption, but, if it is in the best interests of the child, grant the natural parent visitation rights after the adoption has been finalized.[1]

In the case of *Matter of Adoption of Raana Beth N.*,[2] the court, having determined that the natural father had abandoned the child, approved the adoption by the birth mother and her new husband. However, because all the parties were in agreement, the court granted visitation privileges to the natural father.

Although the court has the power to decree an open adoption, the appellate division has held that absent agreement and consent, the court could exercise this power only after a plenary hearing, taking into consideration the best interests of the child.[3]

Library References:

West's Key No. Digests, Adoption ⚖20.

§ 20.124 Post-adoption Issues—Visitation With Siblings

Social Services Law §§ 358–a(11) and 384–a(1–a) require that siblings and half siblings be placed together in foster care, when possible. If

§ 20.122
1. DRL §§ 113, 114.

§ 20.123
1. DRL § 111.

2. 78 Misc.2d 105, 355 N.Y.S.2d 956 (Surr.Ct., N.Y. County, 1974).

3. Matter of Abraham L., 53 A.D.2d 669, 385 N.Y.S.2d 103 (2d Dep't 1976).

this is not possible, provision for visitation or other forms of regular communication must be made. Placement together is presumed to be in the child's best interests, unless there is evidence that placement together or contact would be contrary to the child's health, safety or welfare.

Adoption orders that include a direction that the adoptive child have continued contact with siblings have been entered. In *Matter of Adoption of Anthony*,[1] the court directed visitation between an adoptive child and his siblings where the adoptive child knew the facts surrounding his adoption, had visited and maintained a relationship with his three siblings, and the adoptive parents and child's birth siblings knew each other.[2]

Library References:
West's Key No. Digests, Adoption ⚖20.

§ 20.125 Post-adoption Issues—Sealing Adoption Records

Domestic Relations Law § 114 contains provisions for the sealing of adoption records. No person is allowed access to the sealed record, order or any index thereof, except upon an order of a judge or surrogate of the court in which the order was made or of a justice of the Supreme Court. No order for disclosure or access and inspection shall be granted except on good cause shown and on due notice to the adoptive parents, and to such additional persons as they court may direct.

§ 20.126 Post-adoption Issues—Sealing Adoption Records—Constitutionality of Laws Relating to Sealing Records

The sealing requirements of Domestic Relations Law § 114 have been held to be constitutional, and not in violation of the Equal Protection Clause of the Fourteenth Amendment.[1]

§ 20.127 Post-adoption Issues—Sealing Adoption Records—Good Cause for Unsealing Records

Domestic Relations Law § 114 provides that adoption records may be unsealed for good cause. Good cause may be classified into three categories: (1) criminal, (2) psychological, and (3) medical.

§ 20.124

1. 113 Misc.2d 26, 448 N.Y.S.2d 377 (Fam.Ct., Bronx County, 1982).

2. *See also*, Matter of Patricia Ann W., 89 Misc.2d 368, 392 N.Y.S.2d 180 (Fam.Ct., Kings County, 1977); *c.f.*, Matter of Hatch, 199 A.D.2d 765, 605 N.Y.S.2d 428 (3d Dep't 1993), where the court denied visitation between siblings after the adoption because the siblings "never had the opportunity to develop any affectionate relations with each other."

§ 20.126

1. Alma Soc. Inc. v. Mellon, 601 F.2d 1225 (2d Cir.1979), cert. denied 444 U.S. 995, 100 S.Ct. 531, 62 L.Ed.2d 426 (1979). *See also*, Application of Romano, 109 Misc.2d 99, 438 N.Y.S.2d 967 (Surr.Ct., Kings County, 1989).

The desire to learn the identity of one's parents or to learn about one's ancestry, without more, does not constitute good cause pursuant to Domestic Relations Law § 114.[1]

§ 20.128 Post-adoption Issues—Sealing Adoption Records—Good Cause for Unsealing Records—Criminal Investigation and Probation Department

Domestic Relations Law § 114 has been ruled inapplicable to grand jury subpoenas. In *Matter of Grand Jury Subpoenas Duces Tecum*,[1] the appellate division held that a "Grand Jury is not a 'person' within the contemplation of Domestic Relations Law § 114" and, hence, the grand jury may subpoena confidential adoption records.

Library References:

West's Key No. Digests, Adoption ⚖5.

§ 20.129 Post-adoption Issues—Sealing Adoption Records—Good Cause for Unsealing Records—Requirement of Medical Information

In *Chattman v. Bennett*,[1] the appellate court directed the lower court to make available to petitioner her medical records and those of her natural parents, as well as any other material therein relating to possible genetic or hereditary conditions, while deleting therefrom any nonpertinent information, including the names of the natural parents.

Library References:

West's Key No. Digests, Adoption ⚖11.

§ 20.130 Post-adoption Issues—Sealing Adoption Records—Good Cause for Unsealing Records—Religion

A religious identity crisis may also provide good cause sufficient to allow unsealing of adoption records.[1]

§ 20.127

1. *See* Matter of Linda F.M., 52 N.Y.2d 236, 437 N.Y.S.2d 283, 418 N.E.2d 1302 (1981), dism'd 454 U.S. 806, 102 S.Ct. 79, 70 L.Ed.2d 76 (1981).

§ 20.128

1. 58 A.D.2d 1, 395 N.Y.S.2d 645 (1st Dep't 1977).

§ 20.129

1. 57 A.D.2d 618, 393 N.Y.S.2d 768 (2d Dep't 1977).

§ 20.130

1. *See* Alma Soc. Inc. v. Mellon, 601 F.2d 1225 (2d Cir.1979), cert. denied 444 U.S. 995, 100 S.Ct. 531, 62 L.Ed.2d 426 (1979).

§ 20.131 Post-adoption Issues—Abrogation of Order

Domestic Relations Law § 114 provides that a judge or surrogate of the court in which the order of adoption was made may open, vacate or set aside such order of adoption for fraud, newly discovered evidence or other sufficient cause.

In *Matter of Nina M.*,[1] the appellate division held that a former foster parent could not seek to abrogate the child's adoption. The court reiterated the principle that adoptions and the abrogation of adoptions were statutory and, as such, in derogation of the common law; as a consequence the statutes were to be strictly construed. In this case, there were no allegations of fraud, coercion or misrepresentation connected with the adoption. The petition alleged that the child's best interest required the abrogation of adoption. The appellate division held that a child's best interest was not one of the statutory grounds permitting the abrogation of an adoption.

Library References:

West's Key No. Digests, Adoption ⊕4, 5.

§ 20.132 Checklist—Facts and Allegations to Be Included in the Petition for a Private Placement Adoption

In drafting the petition for a private placement adoption, the following facts and allegation must be included:

1. The name and place of residence of the petitioning adoptive parents. (*See* § 20.51)

2. The full name, date and place of birth of the adoptive child. (*See* § 20.68)

3. The full name and last known address of the natural mother of the adoptive child. (*See* § 20.3)

4. The full name and last known address of the natural father of the adoptive child. (*See* §§ 20.29–20.33)

5. The religious faith of the adoptive child. (*See* § 20.28)

---

§ 20.131

1. 220 A.D.2d 869, 632 N.Y.S.2d 242 (3d Dep't, 1995); *see also*, In the Matter of Jenelle, 220 A.D.2d 853, 632 N.Y.S.2d 245 (3d Dep't 1995), wherein the appellate division refused to set aside the mother's extra-judicial consent to an adoption holding that allegations of lack of understanding the document or its consequences, or distress experienced by the birth mother, were insufficient to vitiate her consent as there was no duress or coercion.

6. Data concerning the natural parents of the adoptive child such as (a) heritage, (b) religious faith, (c) education, (d) general physical appearance, and (3) health and medical history. (*See* §§ 20.3, 20.27–28)

7. The manner in which the adoptive parent obtained custody of the child. (*See* §§ 20.3, 20.45)

8. The length of time the adoptive child resided with the adoptive parents. (*See* § 20.69)

9. Other persons living in the household. (*See* § 20.21)

10. The new name of the adoptive child.

11. The name and address of any persons having lawful custody of the adoptive child.

12. Information as to consents of the biological parents. (*See* §§ 20.63–20.67)

13. Whether the natural parents have requested the return of the adoptive child within 45 days of the execution of the extra-judicial consent. (*See* § 20.64)

14. Whether a guardian has been appointed for the infant. (*See* §§ 20.60–20.62)

15. All available information comprising the adoptive child's medical history.

16. A statement that the adoptive parents are not the subject of an indicated report as defined in Social Services Law § 412(12). (*See* § 20.56)

Library References:

West's Key No. Digests, Adoption ⚖11.

§ 20.133 Forms—Private Placement Adoptions—Petition for Certification as a Qualified Adoptive Parent[1]

DRL §§ 115, 115-d

_____ COURT OF THE STATE OF NEW YORK
COUNTY OF _____

In the Matter of the Adoption of
A Child Whose First Name Is

_____

by _____
Adoptive Parent(s)

(Docket)(File)No.
PETITION
(Certification
as a Qualified
Adoptive Parent)
(Private–Placement)

The Petitioner(s) respectfully alleges to this Court that:

1. (His)(Her)(Their) name(s) residential address and telephone number are: _____

2. (He)(She)(They) (is)(are) seeking certification by this court as (a) person(s) qualified to take custody of the adoptive child, _____, (prior to) (contemporaneous with) the filing of a private-placement adoption petition.

3. (He)(She)(They) have (not) been the subject of a pending child protective investigation or of an indicated report, as such terms are defined in section 412 of the Social Services Law, filed with the statewide register of child abuse and maltreatment pursuant to Title six of Article six of the Social Services Law.

4. A pre-placement investigation will be undertaken by a disinterested person, as such term is defined in Domestic Relations Law § 115-d(4), and a written report of such investigation will be furnished directly to the court by such disinterested person.

5. The marital, family status and history of the Petitioner(s) (is) (are): _____

6. The physical and mental health of the Petitioner(s) (is) (are): _____

§ 20.133
1. Form 22—Certification as Qualified Adoptive Parent (9/92).

7. Attached hereto and made a part hereof is a statement of all property owned by and income of the Petitioner(s).

8.(a) Petitioner(s) (has)(have)(not) ever been (a) respondent(s) in any proceeding in any court concerning alleged (abused) (neglected) (abandoned) (delinquent) children, (as follows:) _____

(b) *[Applicable only if petition seeks conditional certification pursuant of DRL § 115–d(6)]* (Petitioner(s) (has) (have) no prior criminal convictions or founded findings of child abuse or neglect.)

9. Petitioner(s) (has)(have)(not) made any prior application for certification as (a) qualified adoptive parent(s) (except: _____

and the disposition of such application was as follows:

_____
_____).

10. Petitioner(s) (do)(does) not intend to cause a pre-placement investigation to be undertaken and request(s) this court to appoint a disinterested person to conduct such pre-placement investigation.

WHEREFORE, Petitioner(s) pray(s) for an order (conditionally *[applicable only if petition seeks conditional certification under DRL § 115–d(6)]*) certifying Petitioner(s) as (a) qualified adoptive parent(s).

Dated: _____, 19__

_____
Adoptive Mother

_____
Adoptive Father

VERIFICATION

STATE OF NEW YORK)
) ss:
COUNTY OF _____)

_____, being duly sworn, says that (he)(she)(they) (is)(are) the Petitioner(s) in the above-named proceeding and that the foregoing petition is true to (his)(her)(their) own knowledge, except as to matters therein stated to be alleged on information and belief and as to those matters (he)(she)(they) believe(s) it to be true.

_____
(Adoptive mother)

_____
(Adoptive father)

§ 20.133 ADOPTIONS Ch. 20

Sworn to before me this
_____ day of _____, 19__

(Deputy) Clerk of the Court
Notary Public

Library References:

West's Key No. Digests, Adoption ⚖11.

§ 20.134 Forms—Private Placement Adoptions—Petition for Temporary Guardianship[1]

DRL § 115–c; SCPA § 1725

_____COURT OF THE STATE OF NEW YORK
COUNTY OF _____

In the Matter of the Temporary
Guardianship of A Child Whose   (Docket)(File)No.
First Name is _____
                                        PETITION FOR
                                        TEMPORARY
                                        GUARDIANSHIP

The Petitioner(s) respectfully allege(s) to the Court that:

1. Physical custody of *(first name) (last name)*, a child born on _____, was transferred to _____ and _____, for the purposes of adoption on the _____ day of _____, 19__, by _____, the child's (parent(s))(guardian(s)), (and requirements for certification of _____ and _____ as qualified adoptive parents herein was duly waived by order of the _____ Court, County of _____, dated _____)

2. The residence and telephone number of Petitioner(s) is _____

3. The full name(s) and address(es) of the natural parent(s) of the child are: _____

4. The anticipated name of the child subsequent to adoption will be _____

5. The anticipated residence of the child subsequent to adoption will be _____

---

§ 20.134
1. Form 21–A—Temporary Guardianship (9/89).

Ch. 20 TEMPORARY GUARDIANSHIP PETITION § 20.134

6. A consent to the adoption of the child was duly executed pursuant to Domestic Relations Law § 115–b on _____, 19__. A copy of the consent to the adoption is annexed hereto.

7. The child will be residing with Petitioner(s), and a petition for adoption of the child by Petitioner(s) will be filed in the _____. Court of the County of _____, State of New York, within 45 days of the execution of the consent to adoption of the child.

8. No previous petition has been filed or application made to any court of judge for the relief sought herein (except)

(include any proceeding(s) dismissed or withdrawn)

WHEREFORE, Petitioner(s) pray(s) for an order granting temporary guardianship of the child to Petitioner(s).

_____
Petitioner(s)

Dated: _____, 19__

VERIFICATION

STATE OF NEW YORK   )
) ss.:
COUNTY OF _____   )

_____, being duly sworn, says that (he) (she) (they) (is)(are) the Petitioner(s) in the above-named proceeding and that the foregoing petition is true to (his) (her) (their) own knowledge, except as to matters therein stated to be alleged on information and belief, and as to those matters (he)(she)(they) believe(s) it to be true.

_____
Petitioner(s)

Subscribed and sworn to before me this
_____ day of _____, 19__.

_____
(Deputy) Clerk of the Court
Notary Public

Library References:

West's Key No. Digests, Adoption ⚖11.

§ 20.135 Forms—Private Placement Adoptions—Judicial Consent of Natural Parent[1]

DRL §§ 115, 115-b

_____ COURT OF THE STATE OF NEW YORK
COUNTY OF _____

In the Matter of the Adoption of
A Child Whose First Name Is

_____

_____

(Docket) (File) No.

JUDICIAL CONSENT
(Natural Parent—
Private–Placement)

THIS CONSENT BECOMES IRREVOCABLE UPON EXECUTION OR ACKNOWLEDGMENT BEFORE ANY JUDGE OR SURROGATE IN NEW YORK STATE HAVING JURISDICTION OVER ADOPTION PROCEEDING(S). NO ACTION OR PROCEEDING FOR THE CUSTODY OF THE ADOPTIVE CHILD MAY BE MAINTAINED BY THE PARENT EXECUTING OR ACKNOWLEDGING THE WITHIN CONSENT.

    1. I, _____, residing at _____, natural (mother) (father) of _____, do hereby consent to the adoption of my (daughter) (son) , born on the _____ day of _____, 19__ *[optional]* by _____, adoptive parent(s)).

    2. I have been advised that this consent becomes irrevocable when executed or acknowledged before a judge or surrogate, and thereafter no action or proceeding may be maintained by me for the custody of the child. I also have been advised that before I acknowledge or execute this consent, I have a right to be represented by a lawyer of my own choosing and, if I am financially unable to obtain same, a lawyer will be assigned at public cost. I further have been advised that I have a right to obtain supportive counseling.

    [optional] 3. The full name and last known address of the other natural parent of the adoptive child is: _____.

Dated: _____, 19__.

_____
(Mother) (Father)

STATE OF _____)
) ss.:
COUNTY OF _____)

---

§ 20.135
1. Form 2–F—Judicial Consent–Natural Parent—Private Placement (1/93).

Ch. 20   CONSENT OF NATURAL PARENT   **§ 20.136**

On this _____ day of _____ 19__, before me personally came _____ the person described in and who executed the foregoing instrument, and (he) (she) acknowledged that (he) (she) executed the same. I have informed such person of the consequences of the act of execution and acknowledgment pursuant to the provisions of section 115–b of the Domestic Relations Law and have informed (him) (her) of the right to be represented by legal counsel of (his) (her) own choosing; of the right to obtain supportive counseling and of any rights to assigned counsel pursuant to section 262 of the Family Court Act, section 407 of the Surrogate's Court Procedure Act, or section 35 of the Judiciary Law. I have given (him) (her) a copy of this consent upon execution thereof.

                       Judge of the _____ Court
                       County of _____

(Seal of Court to be
affixed together
with Court Clerk's
certification)

Library References:

West's Key No. Digests, Adoption ⚖11.

§ 20.136 Forms—Private Placement Adoptions—Extrajudicial Consent of Natural Parent[1]

DRL §§ 115, 115–b

_____ COURT OF THE STATE OF NEW YORK
COUNTY OF _____

In the Matter of the Adoption of
A Child Whose First Name is
_____

(Docket) (File) No. _____

EXTRA–JUDICIAL CONSENT
(Natural Parent–Private–Placement)

THIS CONSENT MAY BE REVOKED WITHIN 45 DAYS OF THE EXECUTION OF THIS DOCUMENT. IF THE CONSENT IS NOT REVOKED WITHIN SAID 45 DAYS, NO PROCEEDING MAY BE MAINTAINED BY THE PARENT FOR THE RETURN OF THE CUSTODY OF THE CHILD. THE REVOCATION MUST BE IN WRITING AND RECEIVED BY THE COURT WHERE THE ADOPTION PRO-

---

§ 20.136

1. Form 2–G—Extrajudicial consent-Natural Parent–Private Placement (1/93).

§ 20.136   ADOPTIONS   Ch. 20

CEEDING IS TO BE COMMENCED WITHIN 45 DAYS OF THE EXECUTION OF THE CONSENT. THE NAME AND ADDRESS OF THE COURT IN WHICH THE ADOPTION PROCEEDING HAS BEEN OR IS TO BE COMMENCED IS

[DRL § 115–b provides that the consent shall state the name and address of the court in which the adoption proceeding has been, or will be, commenced]

IF THE ADOPTIVE PARENTS CONTEST THE REVOCATION, TIMELY NOTICE OF REVOCATION WILL NOT NECESSARILY RESULT IN THE RETURN OF THE CHILD TO THE PARENT, AND THE RIGHTS OF THE PARENT TO THE CUSTODY OF THE CHILD WILL NOT BE SUPERIOR TO THOSE OF THE ADOPTIVE PARENTS. A HEARING BEFORE A JUDGE WILL BE REQUIRED TO DETERMINE: (1) WHETHER THE NOTICE OF REVOCATION WAS TIMELY AND PROPERLY GIVEN; AND, IF NECESSARY, (2) WHETHER THE BEST INTERESTS OF THE CHILD WILL BE SERVED: (A) BY RETURNING CUSTODY OF THE CHILD TO THE PARENT; OR (B) BY CONTINUING THE ADOPTION PROCEEDING COMMENCED BY THE ADOPTIVE PARENTS; OR (C) BY DISPOSITION OTHER THAN ADOPTION BY THE ADOPTIVE PARENTS; OR (D) BY PLACEMENT OF THE CHILD WITH AN AUTHORIZED AGENCY. IF ANY SUCH DETERMINATION IS MADE, THE COURT WILL MAKE SUCH DISPOSITION OF THE CUSTODY OF THE CHILD AS WILL BEST SERVE THE INTERESTS OF THE CHILD.

THE PARENT HAS THE RIGHT TO LEGAL REPRESENTATION OF THE PARENT'S OWN CHOOSING, THE RIGHT TO SUPPORTIVE COUNSELING AND MAY HAVE THE RIGHT TO HAVE THE COURT APPOINT AN ATTORNEY PURSUANT TO SECTION 262 OF THE FAMILY COURT ACT, SECTION 407 OF THE SURROGATE'S COURT PROCEDURE ACT, OR SECTION 35 OF THE JUDICIARY LAW.

1. I _____, residing at _____, natural (mother)(father) of _____, do hereby consent to the adoption of my (daughter) (son) _____, born on _____, *[insertion of birth date is optional]* (by _____, adoptive parent(s)).

[optional] 2. The full name and last known address of the other natural parent of the adoptive child is _____.

3. I have (not) been represented by counsel. *[If represented, set forth counsel's name, address and telephone number]*

(Mother) (Father)

Date: _____, 19__

STATE OF _____)
) ss.:
COUNTY OF _____)

On this _____ day of _____, 19__, before me personally came _____, to me known and known to me to be the person described in and who executed the foregoing instrument and (he) (she) duly acknowledged to me that (he) (she) executed the same.

            Notary Public

Library References:

West's Key No. Digests, Adoption ⋘11.

§ 20.137 Forms—Private Placement Adoptions—Petition for Adoption

DRL §§ 111, 111–a, 112, 115;
SCPA § 1725(1)

_____ COURT OF THE STATE OF NEW YORK
COUNTY OF _____

In the Matter of the Adoption of
A Child Whose First Name is
_____

(Docket) (File) No. _____

PETITION FOR ADOPTION
(Private–Placement)

The Petitioner(s) respectfully allege(s) to this Court that:

1. *[Delete if inapplicable]* (a) The name and place of residence (include county) of the petitioning adoptive mother are: _____;

she is of (full age) (a minor), having been born on _____;

she is (*[Delete if inapplicable]* unmarried);

(*[Delete if inapplicable]* married to _____ and living together as husband and wife);

(*[Delete if inapplicable]* married to _____ and living separate and apart pursuant to a decree or judgment of separation or pursuant to a separation agreement subscribed by the parties thereto and acknowledged or proved in the form required to entitle a deed to be recorded);

(*[Omit if inapplicable]* married to _____ and living separate and apart for at least three years prior to commencement of the proceeding);

§ 20.137 ADOPTIONS Ch. 20

her religious faith is _____; her occupation is _____; her approximate annual income is $_____;

(b)*[Omit if inapplicable]* The name and place of residence (include county) of the petitioning adoptive father are: _____ _____;

he is of (full age) (a minor), having been born on _____;

he is (*[Omit if inapplicable]* unmarried);

(*[Omit if inapplicable]* married to _____ and living together as husband and wife);

(*[Omit if inapplicable]* married to _____ and living separate and apart pursuant to a decree or judgment of separation or pursuant to a separation agreement subscribed by the parties thereto and acknowledged or proved in the form required to entitle a deed to be recorded);

(*[Omit if inapplicable]* married to and living separate and apart for at least three years prior to commencement of the proceeding); his religious faith is _____; his occupation is _____; his approximate annual income is $_____.

2. The full name, date and place of birth of the adoptive child is

(attach certified copy of birth certificate)

3. (a) The full name and last known address of the natural mother of the adoptive child are: _____ _____

3. (b) The full name and last known address of the natural father of the adoptive child are: _____ _____

4. Upon information and belief the religious faith of the adoptive child is _____

5. Upon information and belief, the following is data as nearly as can be ascertained concerning the natural parents of the adoptive child:

(a) Age and date of birth

Father: _____

Mother: _____

(b) Heritage (nationality, ethnic background, race)

Father: _____

Mother: _____

(c) Religious faith

Father: _____

Mother: _____

Ch. 20 PETITION FOR ADOPTION § 20.137

(d) Education (number of years of school completed at time of birth of adoptive child)

Father: _____

Mother: _____

(e) General physical appearance at time of birth of adoptive child (height, weight, color of hair, eyes, skin)

Father: _____

Mother: _____

(f) Health and medical history at time of birth of adoptive child (including conditions or diseases believed to be hereditary, any drugs or medication taken during pregnancy by child's mother)

(Annex Form 1–E)

(g) Any other information which may be a factor influencing the adoptive child's present or future health, (including talents, hobbies and special interests of parents.) _____

6. The manner in which the adoptive parent(s) obtained custody of the adoptive child is as follows: _____

7. The adoptive child has resided with the adoptive parent(s) from

8. Other persons living in the household are: _____

9. The name by which the adoptive child is to be known is _____

10. Upon information and belief, the adoptive child has (not) been previously adopted.

11. The full name(s) and address(es) of any person having lawful custody of the adoptive child, (if known) are: _____

12. *[Omit if inapplicable]* (On information and belief, pursuant to Domestic Relations Law § 111,

(a) the consent of the natural mother of the adoptive child (is attached hereto) (is unnecessary because _____;)

(b) the consent of the natural father of the adoptive child (is attached hereto) (is unnecessary because _____;)

(c) the consent(s) of the above-named person(s) having lawful custody of the adoptive child (is attached hereto) (is unnecessary because _____;)

(d) the consent(s) of other person(s) (is attached hereto) (is unnecessary because _____;)

13. *[Omit if inapplicable]* (a) (The consent of the natural mother was executed pursuant to section 115–b(3) of the Domestic Relations Law on _____, 19__; the 45th day after execution of the consent is _____, 19__

13. *[Omit if inapplicable]* (b) (The consent of the natural father was executed pursuant to section 115–b(3) of the Domestic Relations Law on _____, 19__; the 45th day after execution of the consent is _____, 19__

[Omit if inapplicable] (14. That this court is not the court named in the consent(s) of the parent(s) of the adoptive child, attached hereto, as the court in which the adoption proceeding will be commenced, but that more than forty-five days have elapsed since the date of execution of said consent(s) and, on information and belief no written notice of revocation has been received by that court.)

[Omit if inapplicable] (15. That on information and belief said minor child has a (general) (testamentary) guardian.) (state nature, date and place of appointment)

16. To the best of the Petitioner(s)' information and belief, there are no persons other than those hereinbefore mentioned who are entitled (pursuant to Domestic Relations Law §§ 111(3), 111–a) to notice of this proceeding (except)

(set forth name, relationship and last known address)

17. Attached hereto and made a part hereof is a document setting forth all available information comprising the adoptive child's medical history.

18. The provisions of (section 374–a of the Social Services Law) (and) (section 382 of the Social Services Law) (have) (has) been complied with. The original approval signed by the Administrator of the Interstate Compact on the Placement of Children is attached hereto. *[See Domestic Relation Law § 115(12)]*

19. (a) That the adoptive parent(s) (has)(have) (no) knowledge that the child or an adoptive parent is the subject of an indicated report, or is another person named in an indicated report, as such terms are defined in section 412 of the Social Services Law, or has been the subject of or the respondent in a child protective proceeding which resulted in an order finding that the child is an abused or neglected child.

(b) The adoptive parent(s) (has) (have) (no) knowledge of any criminal record concerning themselves or any other adult residing in the

Ch. 20   PETITION FOR ADOPTION   § 20.137

household (except) _____

20. There is no prior or pending proceeding affecting the custody or status of the adoptive child (except) *[also include any proceedings dismissed or withdrawn]* _____

21. The adoptive child *[delete inapplicable provision]* (is) (is not) an Indian child within the meaning of the Indian Child Welfare Act of 1978 (25 U.S.C.A. §§ 1901–1963).

22. *[Insert any additional allegations]*

WHEREFORE, the Petitioner(s) pray(s) for an order granting temporary guardianship of the child to Petitioner(s) and approving the adoption of the adoptive child _____ by the Petitioner(s) and directing that the adoptive child shall be treated in all respects as the child of the Petitioner(s) and directing that the name of the adoptive child be changed and that (s)he shall henceforth be known by the name of _____ together with such other and further relief as may be just and proper.

Dated: _____, 19__

_____
Adoptive mother

_____
Adoptive father

_____
Adoptive child, if over age 18

Name of attorney: _____
Address: _____

Telephone No. _____

VERIFICATION

STATE OF NEW YORK)
) ss.:
COUNTY OF _____)

_____, being duly sworn, says that (he) (she) (they) (is) (are) the Petitioner(s) in the above-named proceeding and that the foregoing petition is true to (his) (her) (their) own knowledge, except as to matters therein stated to be alleged on information and belief and as to those matters (he) (she) (they) believe(s) it to be true.

_____
(Adoptive mother)

§ 20.137 ADOPTIONS Ch. 20

_____
(Adoptive father)

_____
(Adoptive child, if over age of 18)

Sworn to before me this
_____ day of _____, 19__

_____
(Deputy) Clerk of the Court
Notary Public

Resworn to before me this
_____ day of _____, 19__

Judge of the _____ Court

Library References:
West's Key No. Digests, Adoption ⚖11.

§ 20.138 Forms—Order of Adoption (Private Placement)

Secs. 111, 112, 114, 116 D.R.L.

Form 13–B
(Order of Adoption—
Private–Placement)

At a term of the _____ Court of the State of New York, held in and for the County of _____ at _____, New York, on _____, 19__.

PRESENT:
   Hon. _____
              Judge

In the Matter of the Adoption of
A Child Whose First Name Is
_____

(Docket/File) No. _____

ORDER OF ADOPTION
(Private–Placement)

    The petition of _____ (and _____), verified the day of _____, 19__, and filed in this court on the (_____) day of (_____), 19(__), having been duly presented to this Court, together with an agreement on the part of the petitioning adoptive parent(s) to adopt and treat the adoptive child as (his/her/their) own lawful child, whose birth day is

_____, 19__, and who was born at _____ as set forth in the petition for adoption herein, said petition having attached thereto and made a part thereof a document setting forth all available information comprising the adoptive child's medical history; together with the affidavit(s) of

and the consent(s) of

AND, although (his/her/their) consent(s) (is/are) not required, the Court having given notice of the proposed adoption to

(recite facts relative thereto)

AND the aforesaid petitioning adoptive parents and the adoptive child and all other persons whose consents are required as aforesaid having personally appeared before this Court for examination, except _

AND an investigation having been ordered and made and the written report of such investigation having been filed with the Court, as required by the Domestic Relations Law;

(AND the Court having (shortened/dispensed with) the (six-month) waiting period between its receiving the petition to adopt and this order of adoption, pursuant to section 116 of the Domestic Relations Law, because _____;)

(AND the adoptive child having resided with the petitioning adoptive parent(s) since _____ (and _____ the judge having dispensed with the (six-month) period of residency with the adoptive parent(s)), pursuant to sections 112 and 116 of the Domestic Relations Law because _____;)

(AND the Court having inquired of the statewide central register of child abuse and maltreatment and having been informed that (child/adoptive parent(s)) (is/are) (not) a subject of or another person named in an indicated report filed with such register as such terms are defined in section 412 of the Social Services Law, (AND there being available to this Court findings of a court inquiry made within the preceding twelve months of the statewide central register of child abuse and maltreatment that the (child/adoptive parent(s)) (is/are) (not) a subject of or another person named in an indicated report filed with such register as such terms are defined in section 412 of the Social Services Law) and the Court having given due consideration to any information contained therein)

§ 20.138   ADOPTIONS   Ch. 20

(AND this Court being satisfied that the best interests of the adoptive child will be promoted by the adoption and that there is no reasonable objection to the proposed change of the name of the adoptive child;)

NOW, on motion of _____, Attorney for the petitioners herein, and upon all the papers and proceedings herein, it is

ORDERED that the petition of _____ (and _____) for the adoption of _____, a person born on _____, 19__, at _____, be and the same hereby is allowed and approved; and it is further

ORDERED that the adoptive child shall henceforth be regarded and treated in all respects as the lawful child of the adoptive parent(s); and it is further

ORDERED that the name of the adoptive child be and the same hereby is changed to _____ and that the adoptive child shall hereafter be known by that name; and it is further

ORDERED that the Clerk prepare, certify and deliver to _____ a copy of this Order; and it is further

ORDERED that the child's medical history, heritage of the parents, which shall include nationality, ethnic background and race; education, which shall be the number of years of school completed by the parents at the time of the birth of the adoptive child; general physical appearance of the parents at the time of the birth of the adoptive child, including height, weight, color of hair, eyes, skin; occupation of the parents at the time of birth of the adoptive child; health and medical history of the parents at the time of birth of the adoptive child, including all available information setting forth conditions or diseases believed to be hereditary, any drugs or medication taken during pregnancy by the mother; any other information which may be a factor influencing the child's present or future health, talents, hobbies and special interests of the parents as contained in the petition shall be furnished to the adoptive parents; and it is

ORDERED that this order, together with all other papers pertaining to the adoption, shall be filed and kept as provided in the Domestic Relations Law and shall not be subject to access or inspections except as provided in said Law.

Dated: _____

ENTER

_____
(J.F.C.) (SURROGATE)

Library References:

West's Key No. Digests, Adoption ⚖11.

§ 20.139 Forms—Agency Adoptions—Petition for Adoption[1]

DRL §§ 111–a(1) and 112

_____ COURT OF THE STATE OF NEW YORK
COUNTY OF _____

In the Matter of the Adoption of
A Child Whose First Name is
_____

(Docket) (File) No. _____

PETITION FOR ADOPTION
(Agency)

The Petitioner(s) respectfully allege(s) to this Court that:

1. *[Omit if inapplicable]*(a) The name and place of residence of the petitioning adoptive mother is:*[include county]*

_____;

she is of full age, having been born on _____; she is

(*[Omit if inapplicable]* unmarried);

(*[Omit if inapplicable]* married to _____ and living together as husband and wife);

(*[Omit if inapplicable]* married to _____ and living separate and apart pursuant to a decree or judgment of separation or pursuant to a separation agreement subscribed by the parties thereto and acknowledged or proved in the form required to entitle a deed to be recorded);

(*[Omit if inapplicable]* married to _____ and living separate and apart for at least three years prior to commencement of the proceeding); her religious faith is _____; her occupation is _____; her approximate annual income is $ _____ (of which $ _____ is support and maintenance to be received from the Commissioner of Social Services on behalf of the adoptive child).

[Omit if inapplicable] (b) The name and place of residence of the petitioning adoptive father are: *[include county]* _____

_____;

he is of full age, having been born on _____; he is (*[Omit if inapplicable]* unmarried);

(*[Omit if inapplicable]* married to _____and living together as husband and wife);

(*[Omit if inapplicable]* married to _____ and living separate and apart pursuant to a decree or judgment of separation or pursuant to a

---

§ 20.139
1. Form 1–A—Petition–Agency (11/91).

§ 20.139 ADOPTIONS Ch. 20

separation agreement subscribed by the parties thereto and acknowledged or proved in the form required to entitle a deed to be recorded);

([Omit if inapplicable] married to _____ and living separate and apart for at least three years prior to commencement of the proceeding); his religious faith is _____; his occupation is _____; his approximate annual income is $ _____ (of which $ _____ is support and maintenance to be received from the Commissioner of Social Services on behalf of the adoptive child).

2. Upon information and belief, the adoptive child, whose first name is _____, was born on _____, 19__, at _____ and the religious faith of such child is _____

3. Upon information and belief, there will be annexed to this petition a schedule verified by a duly constituted official of _____, an authorized agency, as required by Domestic Relations Law § 112(3), concerning the adoptive child who is the subject of this proceeding.

4. Upon information and belief, the following are data as nearly as can be ascertained concerning the natural parents of the adoptive child:

(a) Age and date of birth

Father: _____

Mother: _____

(b) Heritage (nationality, ethnic background, race)

Father: _____

Mother: _____

(c) Religious faith

Father: _____

Mother: _____

(d) Education (number of years of school completed at time of birth of adoptive child)

Father: _____

Mother: _____

(e) General physical appearance at time of birth of adoptive child (height, weight, color of hair, eyes, skin)

Father: _____

Mother: _____

(f) Health and medical history at time of birth of adoptive child (including conditions or diseases believed to be hereditary, any drugs or medication taken during pregnancy by child's mother)

(Annex Form I–D)

(g) Any other information which may be a factor influencing the adoptive child's present or future health, (including talents, hobbies and special interests of parents.)

5. The adoptive child *[Omit if inapplicable alternative]* (is) (is not) an Indian child within the meaning of the Indian Child Welfare Act of 1978 (25 U.S.C.A. §§ 1901–1963).

6. The manner in which the adoptive parent(s) obtained the adoptive child is as follows: _____

[Omit if inapplicable](The placement is subject to the provisions of section 374–a of the Social Services Law and the provisions of such section have been complied with.)

7. The adoptive child has resided with the adoptive parent(s) from

7a. Other persons living in the household are: _____

8. The name by which the adoptive child is to be known is _____

9. Upon information and belief, the adoptive child has (not) been previously adopted.

10. To the best of Petitioner(s)' information and belief, there are no persons other than those mentioned herein or in the verified schedule annexed hereto who are entitled, pursuant to Sections 111(3) and 111–a of the Domestic Relations Law to notice of this proceeding *[Omit if inapplicable]* (except) (set forth name, relationship and last known address).

11. That the adoptive parent(s) (has)(have) (no) knowledge that the child or an adoptive parent is the subject of an indicated report, or is another person named in an indicated report, as such terms are defined in section 412 of the Social Services Law, or has been the subject of or the respondent in a child protective proceeding which resulted in an order finding that the child is an abused or neglected child.

12. There is no prior or pending proceeding affecting the custody or status of the adoptive child (except) (also include any proceeding(s) dismissed or withdrawn).

13. *[Insert any additional allegations.]*

WHEREFORE, the Petitioner(s) pray(s) for an order approving the adoption of the adoptive child by the Petitioner(s) and directing that the adoptive child shall be treated in all respects as the child of the Petitioner(s) and directing that the name of the adoptive child be changed and that (s)he shall henceforth be known by the name of

§ 20.139 ADOPTIONS Ch. 20

_____, together with such other and further relief as may be just and proper.

Dated: _____, 19__

_____
Adoptive mother

_____
Adoptive father

_____
Adoptive child, if over 18

VERIFICATION

STATE OF NEW YORK)
) ss.:
COUNTY OF _____)

_____, being duly sworn, says that (he) (she) (they) (is) (are) the Petitioner(s) in the above-named proceeding and that the foregoing petition is true to (his) (her) (their) own knowledge, except as to matters therein stated to be alleged on information and belief and as to those matters (he) (she) (they) believe(s) it to be true.

_____
Adoptive mother

_____
Adoptive father

_____
Adoptive child, if over 18

Sworn to before me this
___ day of ___, 19__

_____
(Deputy) Clerk of the Court
Notary Public

Resworn to before me this
___ day of ___, 19__

_____
Judge of the _____ Court

Library References:

West's Key No. Digests, Adoption ⚖=11.

Ch. 20   VERIFIED SCHEDULE   § 20.140

§ 20.140 Forms—Agency Adoptions—Verified Schedule[1]

DRL §§ 111-a, 112(3)
SSL § 384

_____ COURT OF THE STATE OF NEW YORK
COUNTY OF _____

In the Matter of the Adoption of
A Child Whose First Name is
_____

(Docket) (File) No. _____

VERIFIED SCHEDULE
(Agency)

TO THE _____ COURT:

1. I, _____, am a duly constituted official of _____, the authorized agency whose principal office is at _____, and who (has custody of) (is placing) the adoptive child named in the caption of this proceeding for adoption.

2. On information and belief, the full name, date and place of birth of the adoptive child are:

[Attach certified copy of birth certificate]

_____
_____
_____

3a. On information and belief, the full name and last known address of the natural mother of the adoptive child is: _____
_____

3b. On information and belief, the full name and last known address of the natural father of the adoptive child is: _____
_____

4. This agency obtained custody of the adoptive child in the following manner: _____
_____
_____

(*[See DRL § 112(3); delete if inapplicable]* and attached hereto is a copy of the document signed by the administrator of the interstate compact for the placement of children of the State of New York or his designee, that such placement complied with the provisions of the compact.)

§ 20.140   (12/90).
1. Form 1-B—Verified Schedule-Agency

§ 20.140 ADOPTIONS Ch. 20

5. *[Omit if inapplicable]* (a) The consent to this adoption by _____, natural mother of the adoptive child, (is attached hereto) (is unnecessary for the following reasons:) _____

_____

[Omit if inapplicable] (b) The consent to this adoption by _____, natural father of the adoptive child, (is attached hereto) (is unnecessary for the following reasons:)

_____

6. The natural parent(s) of the adoptive child (has) (have) not requested this agency to return the adoptive child to the natural parent(s) within thirty days of the execution and delivery of an instrument of surrender to an authorized agency (except) _____

7. Attached hereto and made a part hereof is a document setting forth all available information comprising the adoptive child's medical history.

Authorized Agency

By _____
Title

Dated: _____, 19__

VERIFICATION

STATE OF NEW YORK)
) ss.:
COUNTY OF _____)

_____, being duly sworn, deposes and says:

That (he) (she) is a duly constituted official of the above-named authorized agency, to wit, its _____;

That (he) (she) has read the foregoing Schedule and knows the contents thereof; that the same is true to (his) (her) own knowledge except as to matters therein stated to be alleged on information and belief and that as to those matters (he) (she) believes it to be true.

Agency Official

Sworn to before me this
_____ day of _____, 19__

(Deputy) Clerk of the Court
Notary Public

Library References:

West's Key No. Digests, Adoption ⚖11.

§ 20.141 Forms—Agency Adoptions—Marital Affidavit

_____ COURT OF THE STATE OF NEW YORK
COUNTY OF _____

In the Matter of the Adoption by
_____

(Docket) (File) No. _____

Of an adoptive child, having the first name of
_____

MARITAL AFFIDAVIT
(Agency)

Whose full name is contained in the Schedule Annexed to the Petition
_____

STATE OF NEW YORK)
) ss.:
COUNTY OF _____)

_____ (and) _____ being duly sworn, depose(s) and say(s):

1. We are the adoptive parent(s) in this proceeding, and we desire to adopt _____, and treat her as our child.

2. We have been advised by our attorney that it is necessary to inform the Court of our marital history.

3. We were married on the __ day of _____, 19__ in _____, New York, and neither of us were previously married.

_____
_____

Sworn to before me this
_____ day of _____, 19__

_____
NOTARY PUBLIC

Library References:

West's Key No. Digests, Adoption ⚖11.

§ 20.142 Forms—Agency Adoptions—Marital Affidavit Dispensing With Consent of Spouse After Three Year Separation

_____ COURT OF THE STATE OF NEW YORK
COUNTY OF _____

In the Matter of the Adoption by

_____

of an adoptive child, having the first name of

_____

Whose full name is contained in the Schedule Annexed to the Petition

(Docket) (File) No. _____

MARITAL AFFIDAVIT DISPENSING WITH CONSENT OF SPOUSE AFTER THREE YEAR SEPARATION

STATE OF NEW YORK)
) ss.:
COUNTY OF _____)

_____, being duly sworn, deposes and says:

1. I am the adoptive parent in this proceeding, and I am desire to adopt _____, and treat (him) (her) as my child.

2. I have been advised by my attorney that it is necessary to inform the Court of my marital history.

3. I married _____ on the ___ day of _____, 19__. We have been separated since _____, 19__.

WHEREFORE, your deponent respectfully requests that the adoption herein be finalized in accordance with Section 110 of the Domestic Relations Law which was amended on July 1, 1991.

_____

Sworn to before me this
_____ day of _____, 19__

_____
NOTARY PUBLIC

Library References:

West's Key No. Digests, Adoption ⚖=11.

§ 20.143 Forms—Agency Adoptions—Confidential Affidavit

_____ COURT OF THE STATE OF NEW YORK
COUNTY OF _____

In the Matter of the Adoption by

Of an adoptive child, having the first name of

Whose full name is contained in the Schedule Annexed to the Petition

(Docket) (File) No. _____

CONFIDENTIAL AFFIDAVIT for the _____ COUNTY _____ COURT

Attorney:

Address:

This confidential information must be submitted with all petitions for adoption.

All applicable questions must be answered by both foster parents.

STATE OF NEW YORK)
) ss.:
COUNTY OF _____)

[NAME OF ADOPTIVE PARENT(S)], being duly sworn, deposes and says that [THEY][SHE][HE] reside(s) in the County of and [ARE][IS] the foster [FATHER][MOTHER] of the child to be adopted:

CHILD:
    [NAME OF ADOPTIVE CHILD]

PROPOSED FOSTER FATHER:
    [NAME OF ADOPTIVE FATHER]   Age:
    [STREET ADDRESS]
    [CITY]   [TELEPHONE]

PROPOSED FOSTER MOTHER:
    [NAME OF ADOPTIVE MOTHER]   Age:
    [STREET ADDRESS]
    [CITY]   [TELEPHONE]

PREVIOUS MARRIAGE OF FOSTER FATHER (Proof of dissolution needed)
    N/A

PREVIOUS MARRIAGE OF FOSTER MOTHER
[NAME OF ADOPTIVE MOTHER] VS. [NAME OF EX–HUSBAND]

§ 20.143 ADOPTIONS

Married on [DATE] in [CITY AND STATE]
Divorce Decree signed on [DATE]
    Court,   County by Hon.

HEALTH REPORTS: Attach completed medical certificates for proposed foster mother, father and adoptive child.

Has either foster parent ever been a respondent in any proceeding concerning allegedly:

Neglected children: No
Abandoned children: No
Delinquent children: No

REFERENCES: Please fill in names and addresses:

Spiritual: _____
_____

Doctors: (Parents) _____
(Child) _____
_____

Friends: _____
_____
_____
_____

_____
[NAME OF ADOPTIVE PARENT(S)]

STATE OF NEW YORK)
) ss:
COUNTY OF _____)

On this _____ day of _____, 19__ before me personally came [NAME OF ADOPTIVE PARENT(S)], to me known and known to me to be the individual described in and who executed the foregoing instrument and she has read the contents thereof and that the same is true.

_____
NOTARY PUBLIC

Library References:

West's Key No. Digests, Adoption ⚖=11.

§ 20.144 Forms—Agency Adoptions—Affidavit Pursuant to Section 111-a of the Domestic Relations Law

_____ COURT OF THE STATE OF NEW YORK
COUNTY OF _____

In The Matter of

[NAME OF ADOPTIVE CHILD]

A dependent child under the age of 14 years, to the custody of

[NAME OF AGENCY],

an abandoned child, pursuant to Section 384-b of the Social Services Law.

Affidavit Pursuant To Section 111-a of The Domestic Relations Law

STATE OF NEW YORK)
) ss.:
COUNTY OF _____)

[NAME OF CASEWORKER], being duly sworn, deposes and says:

1. I am employed by [NAME OF AGENCY], an authorized agency, having the care and custody of the above-named child. I make this Affidavit with respect to this adoption proceeding pursuant to Section 111-a of the Domestic Relations Law with respect to the putative father of the infant.

2. The father of the infant is unknown, unidentified and unidentifiable.

3. No person is entitled to notice of this proceeding on the ground that:

   a) No person was adjudicated by a Court in this state to be the father of the child.

   b) No person was adjudicated by a Court of another state or territory in the United States to be the father of the child.

   c) No person has timely filed an unrevoked notice of intent to claim paternity of the child pursuant to Section 372-C of the Social Services Law.

   d) No person is recorded on the child's Birth Certificate as the child's father.

§ 20.144 ADOPTIONS Ch. 20

e) No person openly lived with the child or the child's mother at the time the proceeding was initiated and no person has held himself out to be the child's father.

f) No person has been identified as the child's father by the mother in a written sworn statement; and

g) No person has been married to the child's mother subsequent to the birth of the child.

WHEREFORE, your deponent respectfully requests that the adoption herein be finalized.

[NAME OF AGENCY]

By: _____
Title

Sworn to before me this
_____ day of _____, 19__

NOTARY PUBLIC

Library References:

West's Key No. Digests, Adoption ⚖11.

§ 20.145 Forms—Agency Adoptions—Agreement of Adoption and Consent[1]

DRL §§ 111(1)(f), 112(2)(b), 113

_____ COURT OF THE STATE OF NEW YORK
COUNTY OF _____

In the Matter of the Adoption of
A Child Whose First Name Is
_____
_____

(Docket) (File) No. _____

AGREEMENT OF ADOPTION
AND CONSENT
(Agency)

The undersigned petitioning adoptive parent(s) hereby agree(s) to adopt the above-named adoptive child and to treat said child in all respects as (his) (her) (their) own lawful child and to extend and assure to said child all the rights, benefits and privileges incident to such relationship, and to incur and fulfill all the responsibilities of (a) parent(s) with respect to said child.

§ 20.145
1. Form 2-A—Agreement of Adoption and Agency Consent (6/87).

Ch. 20   **AGREEMENT OF ADOPTION/CONSENT**   **§ 20.145**

Dated: _____, 19__

_____
(Adoptive mother)

_____
(Adoptive father)

The undersigned authorized agency hereby consents that the above-named adoptive child be adopted by the petitioning adoptive parent(s).

Name of Authorized Agency: _____

By: _____
                            Title

STATE OF NEW YORK)
) ss.:
COUNTY OF _____)

On this _____ day of _____, 19__, before me personally came _____, to me known and known to me to be the person(s) described in and who executed the foregoing instrument and _____ duly and severally acknowledged to me that _____ executed the same.

_____
Notary Public

STATE OF NEW YORK)
) ss.:
COUNTY OF _____)

On this _____ day of _____, 19__, before me personally came _____ to me known and who by me being duly sworn did depose and say: That he resides _____, County of _____ State of _____: that he is _____ of _____ (an authorized agency), the corporation described in and which executed the foregoing instrument, that he knows the seal of said corporation; that such seal affixed to said instrument is such corporate seal; that it was affixed to said instrument by order of the Board of _____ of such corporation in writing, and that he signed his name thereto by like order.

_____
Notary Public

STATE OF NEW YORK)
) ss.:
COUNTY OF _____)

§ 20.145 ADOPTIONS Ch. 20

On this _____ day of _____, 19__, before me personally came _____ proven to me by the oath of _____ an attorney admitted to practice in the State of New York to be the persons described in and who executed the foregoing instrument and _____ severally acknowledged that _____ executed the same.

                                    _____
                                    Judge of the _____ Court

Library References:

West's Key No. Digests, Adoption ⚿11.

§ 20.146 Forms—Agency Adoptions—Affidavit Identifying Party[1]

22 NYCRR 205.53(b)(2), 207.55

_____ COURT OF THE STATE OF NEW YORK
COUNTY OF _____

In the Matter of the Adoption of   (Docket) (File) No. _____
A Child Whose First Name Is
                                            AFFIDAVIT IDENTIFYING PARTY
_____   (Agency)

STATE OF NEW YORK)
) ss.:
COUNTY OF _____   )

_____, being duly sworn, deposes and says:

[Delete if inapplicable] (That (s)he is an attorney at law duly licensed to practice under the laws of the State of New York and has (his) (her) office at _____
_____;)

That (s)he knows _____ (and _____) and knows that s(he) (they) (is) (are) the same person(s) described in and who executed the annexed _____ (and _____ who (is) (are) now present before the Court).

                                    _____

Sworn to before me this
_____ day of _____, 19__

_____
Judge of the _____ Court

§ 20.146
1. Form 8–A—Affidavit Identifying Par-ty–Agency (1/87).

980

§ 20.147 Forms—Agency Adoptions—Affidavit of Financial Disclosure by Parents

SSL § 374(6); 22 NYCRR 205.53(b)(8)

_____ COURT OF THE STATE OF NEW YORK
COUNTY OF _____

In the Matter of the Adoption of
A Child Whose First Name Is
_____
_____

(Docket) (File) No. _____

AFFIDAVIT OF FINANCIAL
DISCLOSURE—PARENTS
(Agency)

STATE OF NEW YORK)
) ss.:
COUNTY OF _____)

_____ (and _____) being duly sworn, depose(s) and say(s):

That deponent(s) reside(s) at _____ and (is) (are) the (petitioning adoptive parent(s)) (natural parent(s)) of the above-named adoptive child;
and

That deponent(s) (has) (have) paid or given or caused to he paid or given or undertaken to pay or give the following expenses, contributions, compensation or things of value, either directly or indirectly, to any person, agency, association, corporation, institution, society or organization, in connection with the placing out of said adoptive child with deponent(s) or with the adoption of said child by deponent(s):

*[Specify recipient, amount, form and purpose
of each payment. If none, so state.]*

_____
_____
_____

That deponent(s) (has) (have) requested, received or accepted, either directly or indirectly, the following compensation or things of value from any person, agency, association, corporation, institution, society or other organization in connection with the placing out of said adoptive child with deponent(s) or with the adoption of said child by deponent(s).

*[Specify recipient, amount, form and purpose of each
payment requested or received. If none, so state.]*

_____
(Adoptive) (Natural) mother

§ 20.147 ADOPTIONS Ch. 20

(Adoptive) (Natural) father

Sworn to before me this
_____ day of _____, 19__

_____
Judge of the _____ Court

Library References:

West's Key No. Digests, Adoption ⚖14.

§ 20.148 Forms—Agency Adoptions—Order of Adoption[1]

DRL §§ 111, 112, 113, 114

At a Term of the _____ Court of the State of New York, held in and for the County of _____, at _____, New York, on the _____ day _____, 19_____.

PRESENT:

HON. _____
JUDGE

In the Matter of the Adoption of
A Child Whose First Name Is
_____

(Docket) (File) No. _____

ORDER OF ADOPTION
(Agency)

The petition of _____ (and _____), verified the _____ day of _____, 19__, having been duly presented to this Court, together with an agreement on the part of the petitioning adoptive parent(s) to adopt and treat as (his) (her) (their) own lawful child the adoptive child having the given first name of _____ and whose full name is _____, and whose birth day is _____, 19__, and who was born at _____ as set forth in the verified schedule annexed to the petition for adoption herein, said schedule having attached thereto and made a part thereof a document setting forth all available information comprising the adoptive child's medical history; together with the affidavit(s) of _____

§ 20.148

1. Form 13–A—Order of Adoption-Agency (9/89).

982

Ch. 20 ORDER OF ADOPTION § 20.148

and the consent(s) of _____

AND, although (his)(her)(their) consent(s) (is) (are) not required, the Court having given notice of the proposed adoption to

(recite facts relative thereto)

AND the aforesaid petitioning adoptive parents and the adoptive child and all other persons whose consents are required as aforesaid having personally appeared before this Court for examination, except _

AND an investigation having been ordered and made and the written report of such investigation having been filed with the Court, as required by the Domestic Relations Law;

(AND that the verified report of _____, the authorized agency, dated _____, is hereby accepted, pursuant to section 113 of the Domestic Relations Law, as the report of investigation required by section 112 of the Domestic Relations Law;)

AND the adoptive child having resided with the petitioning adoptive parent(s) since _____ (and the judge having dispensed with the six-month period of residency with the adoptive parent(s)), pursuant to section 112 of the Domestic Relations Law because _____

(AND the Court having inquired of the statewide central register of child abuse and maltreatment and having been informed that the (child) (adoptive parent(s) (is)(are) (not) a subject of or another person named in an indicated report filed with such register as such terms are defined in section 412 of the Social Services Law, (AND there being available to this Court findings of a court inquiry made within the preceding twelve months, of the statewide central register of child abuse and maltreatment that the (child) (adoptive parent(s) (is) (are) (not) a subject of or another person named in an indicated report filed with such register as such terms are defined in section 412 of the Social Services Law)) and the Court having given due consideration to any information contained therein;

AND this Court being satisfied that the best interests of the adoptive child will be promoted by the adoption and that there is no reasonable objection to the proposed change of the name of the adoptive child;

NOW, on motion of _____, Attorney for the petitioners herein, and upon all the papers and proceedings herein, it is

ORDERED that the petition of _____ (and _____) for the adoption of _____, a person born on _____, 19__, at _____, be and the same hereby is allowed and approved; and it is further

ORDERED that the said adoptive child shall henceforth be regarded and treated in all respects as the lawful child of the said adoptive parent(s); and it is further

ORDERED that the name of the said adoptive child be and the same hereby is changed to _____ and that the said adoptive child shall hereafter be known by that name; and it is further

(ORDERED that the Clerk prepare, certify and deliver to a copy of this order; and it is further)

ORDERED that the child's medical history, heritage of the parents, which shall include nationality, ethnic background and race; education, which shall be the number of years of school completed by the parents at the time of the birth of the adoptive child; general physical appearance of the parents at the time of the birth of the adoptive child, including height, weight, color of hair, eyes, skin; occupation of the parents at the time of birth of the adoptive child; health and medical history of the parents at the time of birth of the adoptive child, including all available information setting forth conditions or diseases believed to be hereditary, any drugs or medication taken during pregnancy by the mother; any other information which may be a factor influencing the child's present or future health, talents, hobbies and special interests of the parents as contained in the petition shall be furnished to the adoptive parents; and it is

ORDERED that this order, together with all other papers pertaining to the adoption, shall be filed and kept as provided in the Domestic Relations Law and shall not be subject to access or inspections except as provided in said Law.

Dated: _____, 19__

ENTER

_____

(J.F.C.) (SURROGATE)

GENERAL PRACTICE IN NEW YORK

Volume 22

By

ROBERT L. OSTERTAG
HON. JAMES D. BENSON

Sections 13.1 to 20.148

1999 Pocket Part

Insert this Pocket Part in back of Volume

ST. PAUL, MINN.
WEST GROUP
1999

GENERAL PRACTICE IN NEW YORK FORMS ON DISK™

The **Forms on Disk**™ which accompany these volumes provide instant access to WordPerfect 5.1/5.2 versions of the forms included in *General Practice in New York*. These electronic forms will save you hours of time drafting legal documents. The electronic forms can be loaded into your word processing software and formatted to match the document style of your law firm. These electronic forms become templates for you to use over and over without having to retype them each time.

The forms in Volumes 20, 21, 22, 23, 24 and 25 that are included on the accompanying disks are marked with the following disk icon for easy identification.

COPYRIGHT © 1999
By
WEST GROUP

This is the 1999 Pocket Part to Volume 22 of WEST'S NEW YORK PRACTICE SERIES

West's New York Practice Series

Vol. 1	Walker, et al., New York Limited Liability Companies and Partnerships: A Guide to Law and Practice
Vols. 2-4	Haig, et al., Commercial Litigation in New York State Courts
Vol. 5	Barker and Alexander, Evidence in New York State and Federal Courts
Vol. 6	Greenberg, Marcus, et al., New York Criminal Law
Vol. 7	Marks, et al., New York Pretrial Criminal Procedure
Vol. 8	Davies, Stecich, Gold, et al., New York Civil Appellate Practice
Vol. 9	Ginsberg, Weinberg, et al., Environmental Law and Regulation in New York
Vol. 10	Sobie, et al., New York Family Court Practice
Vols. 11-12	Scheinkman, et al., New York Law of Domestic Relation

Vol. 13	Taber, et al., Employment Litigation in New York
Vols. 14-16	Kreindler, Rodriguez, et al., New York Law of Torts
Vols. 17-19	Field, Moskin, et al., New York and Delaware Business Organizations: Choice, Formation, Operation, Financing and Acquisitions
Vols. 20-25	Ostertag, Benson, et al., General Practice in New York
Vol. 26	Borchers, Markell, et al., New York State Administrative Procedure and Practice
Vol. A	Borges, et al., Enforcing Judgments and Collecting Debts in New York
Vols. B-C	Bensel, Frank, McKeon, et al., Personal Injury Practice in New York
Vols. D-E	Preminger, et al., Trusts and Estates Practice in New York
Vols. F-G	Finkelstein and Ferrara, Landlord and Tenant Practice in New York

FOREWORD

Here is the first update to *General Practice in New York*, volume 22 of the New York Practice Series. The pocket part covers the significant changes in the applicable law from publication of the original volume until 1999. Many of the updates were prepared by one or more of the original chapter authors; others were editorially prepared in-house by West and are so indicated. With respect to chapters of the book not updated at all, West makes no representations with respect to the current status of ther material therein.

December 1999

COORDINATED RESEARCH IN NEW YORK FROM WEST

New York Practice 2d
David D. Siegel

Handling the DWI Case in New York
Peter Gerstenzang

New York Elder Law Practice
Vincent J. Russo and Marvin Rachlin

WEST'S McKINNEY'S FORMS

Civil Practice Law and Rules

Uniform Commercial Code

Business Corporation Law

Matrimonial and Family Law

Real Property Practice

Estates and Surrogate Practice

Criminal Procedure Law

Not-For-Profit Corporation Law

Tax Practice and Procedure

Local Government Forms

Selected Consolidated Law Forms

McKinney's Consolidated Laws of New York Annotated

West's New York Legal Update

New York Digest

New York Law Finder

PAMPHLETS

New York Civil Practice Law and Rules

New York Sentence Charts

Westlaw®

COORDINATED RESEARCH FROM WEST GROUP

WEST*Check*® and WESTMATE®

West CD–ROM Libraries™

To order any of these New York practice tools, call your West Group Representative or 1–800–328–9352.

NEED RESEARCH HELP?

If you have research questions concerning Westlaw or West Group Publications, call West Group's Reference Attorneys at 1–800–733–2889.

WESTLAW® ELECTRONIC RESEARCH GUIDE

Coordinating Legal Research with Westlaw

The *New York Practice Series* is an essential aid to legal research. Westlaw provides a vast, online library of over 8000 collections of documents and services that can supplement research begun in this publication, encompassing:

- Federal and state primary law (statutes, regulations, rules, and case law), including West's editorial enhancements, such as headnotes, Key Number classifications, annotations

- Secondary law resources (texts and treatises published by West Group and by other publishers, as well as law reviews)

- Legal news

- Directories of attorneys and experts

- Court records and filings

- Citators

Specialized topical subsets of these resources have been created for more than thirty areas of practice.

In addition to legal information, there are general news and reference databases and a broad array of specialized materials frequently useful in connection with legal matters, covering accounting, business, environment, ethics, finance, medicine, social and physical sciences.

This guide will focus on a few aspects of Westlaw use to supplement research begun in this publication, and will direct you to additional sources of assistance.

Databases

A database is a collection of documents with some features in common. It may contain statutes, court decisions, administrative materials, commentaries, news or other information. Each database has a unique identifier, used in many Westlaw commands to select a database of interest. For example, the database containing New York cases has the identifier NY-CS.

The Westlaw Directory is a comprehensive list of databases with information about each database, including the types of documents each contains. The first page of a standard or customized Westlaw Directory is displayed upon signing on to Westlaw, except when prior, saved re-

WESTLAW ELECTRONIC RESEARCH GUIDE

search is resumed. To access the Westlaw Directory at any time, enter DB.

Databases of potential interest in connection with your research include:

NY-AG	New York Attorney General Opinions
NYETH-EO	New York Ethics Opinions
NYETH-CS	Legal Ethics & Professional Responsibility - New York Cases
WLD-NY	West's Legal Directory - New York
LAWPRAC	The Legal Practice Database

For information as to currentness and search tips regarding any Westlaw database, enter the SCOPE command SC followed by the database identifier (e.g., SC NY-CS). It is not necessary to include the identifier to obtain scope information about the currently selected database.

Westlaw Highlights

Use of this publication may be supplemented through the Westlaw Bulletin (WLB), the Westlaw New York State Bulletin (WSB-NY) and various Topical Highlights. Highlights databases contain summaries of significant judicial, legislative and administrative developments and are updated daily; they are searchable both from an automatic list of recent documents and using general Westlaw search methods for documents accumulated over time. The full text of any judicial decision may be retrieved by entering FIND.

Consult the Westlaw Directory (enter DB) for a complete, current listing of highlights databases.

Retrieving a Specific Case

The FIND command can be used to quickly retrieve a case whose citation is known. For example:

FI 616 A.2d 1336

Updating Case Law Research

There are a variety of citator services on Westlaw for use in updating research.

KeyCite(SM) is an enhanced citator service that integrates all the case law on Westlaw. KeyCite provides direct and negative indirect history for any case within the scope of its coverage, citations to other decisions and secondary materials on Westlaw that have mentioned or discussed the cited case, and a complete integration with West Group's Key Number System so that you can track a legal issue explored in a case. KeyCite is as current as Westlaw and includes all cases on Westlaw, including unpublished opinions. To view the KeyCite history of a displayed

WESTLAW ELECTRONIC RESEARCH GUIDE

case, enter the command KC. To view the KeyCite information for a selected case, simply enter a command in the following form:

KC 113 SCT 2786

To see a complete list of publications covered by KeyCite, enter the command KC PUBS. To ascertain the scope of coverage, enter the command SC KC. For the complete list of commands available enter KC CMDS.

Retrieving Statutes, Court Rules and Regulations

Annotated and unannotated versions of the New York statutes are searchable on Westlaw (identifiers NY-ST-ANN and NY-ST), as are New York court rules (NY-RULES) and New York Administrative Code (NY-ADC).

The United States Code and United States Code - Annotated are searchable databases on Westlaw (identifiers USC and USCA, respectively), as are federal court rules (US-RULES) and regulations (CFR).

In addition, the FIND command may be used to retrieve specific provisions by citation, obviating the need for database selection or search. To FIND a desired document, enter FI, followed by the citation of the desired document, using the full name of the publication, or one of the abbreviated styles recognized by Westlaw.

If Westlaw does not recognize the style you enter, you may enter one of the following, using US, NY, or any other state code in place of XX:

FI XX-ST	Displays templates for codified statutes
FI XX-LEGIS	Displays templates for legislation
FI XX-RULES	Displays templates for rules
FI XX-ORDERS	Displays templates for court orders

Alternatively, entering FI followed by the publication's full name or an accepted abbreviation will normally display templates, useful jump possibilities, or helpful information necessary to complete the FIND process. For example:

FI USCA	Displays templates for United States Code - Annotated
FI FRAP	Displays templates for Federal Rules of Appellate Procedure
FI FRCP	Displays templates for Federal Rules of Civil Procedure
FI FRCRP	Displays templates for Federal Rules of Criminal Procedure
FI FRE	Displays templates for Federal Rules of Evidence
FI CFR	Displays templates for Code of Federal Regulations
FI FR	Displays templates for Federal Register

To view the complete list of FINDable documents and associated prescribed forms, enter FI PUBS.

WESTLAW ELECTRONIC RESEARCH GUIDE

Updating Research in re Statutes, Rules and Regulations

When viewing a statute, rule or regulation on Westlaw after a search or FIND command, it is easy to update your research. A message will appear on the screen if relevant amendments, repeals or other new material are available through the UPDATE feature. Entering the UPDATE command will display such material.

Documents used to update New York statutes are also searchable in New York Legislative Service (NY-LEGIS). Those used to update rules are searchable in New York Orders (NY-ORDERS).

Documents used to update federal statutes, rules, and regulations are searchable in the United States Public Laws (US-PL), Federal Orders (US-ORDERS) and Federal Register (FR) databases, respectively.

When documents citing a statute, rule or regulation are of interest, Shepard's Citations on Westlaw may be of assistance. That service covers federal constitutional provisions, statutes and administrative provisions, and corresponding materials from many states. The command SH PUBS displays a directory of publications which may be Shepardized on Westlaw. Consult the Westlaw manual for more information about citator services.

Using Westlaw as a Citator

For research beyond the coverage of any citator service, go directly to the databases (cases, for example) containing citing documents and use standard Westlaw search techniques to retrieve documents citing specific constitutional provisions, statutes, standard jury instructions or other authorities.

Fortunately, the specific portion of a citation is often reasonably distinctive, such as 22:636.1, 301.65, 401(k), 12-21-5, 12052. When it is, a search on that specific portion alone may retrieve applicable documents without any substantial number of inapplicable ones (unless the number happens to be coincidentally popular in another context).

Similarly, if the citation involves more than one number, such as 42 U.S.C.A. §1201, a search containing both numbers (e.g., 42 +5 1201) is likely to produce mostly desired information, even though the component numbers are common.

If necessary, the search may be limited in several ways:

A. Switch from a general database to one containing mostly cases within the subject area of the cite being researched;

WESTLAW ELECTRONIC RESEARCH GUIDE

B. Use a connector (&, /S, /P, etc.) to narrow the search to documents including terms which are highly likely to accompany the correct citation in the context of the issue being researched;

C. Include other citation information in the query. Because of the variety of citation formats used in documents, this option should be used primarily where other options prove insufficient. Below are illustrative queries for any database containing New York cases:

N.Y.Const.! Const.! Constitution /s 6 VI +3 3

will retrieve cases citing the New York State Constitution, Art. 6, §3; and

"Criminal Procedure Law" CPL /s 30.30

will retrieve cases citing Criminal Procedure Law §30.30.

Alternative Retrieval Methods

WIN® (Westlaw Is Natural™) allows you to frame your issue in plain English to retrieve documents:

Does new trial motion extend (toll) the time for filing (taking) appeal?

Alternatively, retrieval may be focused by use of the Terms and Connectors method:

TO(30) /P DI(NEW +1 TRIAL /P EXTEND!
EXTENSION TOLL! /P APPEAL)

In databases with Key Numbers, either of the above examples will identify Appeal and Error ⇐345.1 as a Key Number collecting headnotes relevant to this issue if there are pertinent cases.

Since the Key Numbers are affixed to points of law by trained specialists based on conceptual understanding of the case, relevant cases that were not retrieved by either of the language-dependent methods will often be found at a Key Number.

Similarly, citations in retrieved documents (to cases, statutes, rules, etc.) may suggest additional, fruitful research using other Westlaw databases (e.g., annotated statutes, rules) or services (e.g., citator services).

Key Number Search

Frequently, case law research rapidly converges on a few topics, headings and Key Numbers within West's Key Number System that are likely to contain relevant cases. These may be discovered from known, relevant reported cases from any jurisdiction; Library References in West publications; browsing in a digest; or browsing the Key Number System on Westlaw using the JUMP feature or the KEY command.

WESTLAW ELECTRONIC RESEARCH GUIDE

Once discovered, topics, subheadings or Key Numbers are useful as search terms (in databases containing reported cases) alone or with other search terms, to focus the search within a narrow range of potentially relevant material.

For example, to retrieve cases with at least one headnote classified to Appeal and Error ⇒345.1, sign on to a caselaw database and enter

>   30k345.1   [use with other search terms, if desired]

The topic name (Appeal and Error) is replaced by its numerical equivalent (30) and the ⇒ by the letter k. A list of topics and their numerical equivalents is in the Westlaw Reference Manual and is displayed in Westlaw when the KEY command is entered.

Using JUMP

Westlaw's JUMP feature allows you to move from one document to another or from one part of a document to another, then easily return to your original place, without losing your original result. Opportunities to move in this manner are marked in the text with a JUMP symbol (▶). Whenever you see the JUMP symbol, you may move to the place designated by the adjacent reference by using the Tab, arrow keys or mouse click to position the cursor on the JUMP symbol, then pressing Enter or clicking again with the mouse.

Within the text of a court opinion, JUMP arrows are adjacent to case cites and federal statute cites, and adjacent to parenthesized numbers marking discussions corresponding to headnotes.

On a screen containing the text of a headnote, the JUMP arrows allow movement to the corresponding discussion in the text of the opinion,

>   ▶ (3)

and allow browsing West's Key Number System beginning at various heading levels:

>   ▶ 30   APPEAL AND ERROR
>   ▶ 30VII   Transfer of Cause
>   ▶ 30VII(A)   Time of Taking Proceedings
>   ▶ 30k343   Commencement of Period of Limitation
>   ▶ 30k345.1 k.   Motion for new trial.

To return from a JUMP, enter GB (except for JUMPs between a headnote and the corresponding discussion in opinion, for which there is a matching number in parenthesis in both headnote and opinion). Returns from successive JUMPs (e.g., from case to cited case to case cited by cited case) without intervening returns may be accomplished by repeated entry of GB or by using the MAP command.

WESTLAW ELECTRONIC RESEARCH GUIDE

General Information

The information provided above illustrates some of the ways Westlaw can complement research using this publication. However, this brief overview illustrates only some of the power of Westlaw. The full range of Westlaw search techniques is available to support your research.

Please consult the Westlaw Reference Manual for additional information or assistance or call West's Reference Attorneys at 1-800-REF-ATTY (1-800-733-2889).

For information about subscribing to Westlaw, please call 1-800-328-9352.

SUMMARY OF CONTENTS

Volume 20

Page

Chapter
1. Business Organizations: Corporations — 2
2. Non-corporate Entities — 16
3. Municipal Law — 19
4. Municipal Law — 21
6. Buying and Selling a Small Business — 25

Volume 21

7. Consumer Law — 2
8. Enforcement of Money Judgments — 4
9. Bankruptcy — 5
11. Mortgage Foreclosure — 11
12. Purchase and Sale of Real Estate — 25

Volume 22

14. Eminent Domain — 2
15. Environmental Law — 5
16. Land Use Law — 8
17. Employment Law — 14
18. Civil Rights Law — 16
19. Immigration and Nationality Law Permanent Residence Applications — 39
20. Adoptions — 52

Volume 23

21. Domestic Relations — 2
22. Guardianship — 9
23. Elder Law — 21
24. Estate Planning — 30
25. Probate and Estate Administration — 37
26. Personal Injury — 51

Volume 24

28. Legal Malpractice — 2
29. Medical Malpractice — 20
30. Damages — 21

XVII

SUMMARY OF CONTENTS

Chapter | **Page**
31. Insurance 31
32. Workers' Compensation 34
33. Local Criminal Court Practice 39
34. Social Security Disability Cases 50
35. Income Tax 55
37. Civil Appellate Practice Before the Appellate Division and Other Intermediate Appellate Courts 58

Volume 25

38. Criminal Appellate Practice Before the Appellate Division and Other Intermediate Appellate Courts 2
39. Civil and Criminal Appeals to the Court of Appeals 4

Table of Statutes 5
Table of Rules and Regulations 15
Table of Cases 17
Index 31

WEST'S NEW YORK PRACTICE SERIES

General Practice
in New York

Volume 22

Chapter 14

EMINENT DOMAIN

by
Patricia Youngblood Reyhan

Table of Sections

14.32 Determination and Findings—Interplay with SEQRA
14.61 Acquisition of Property—Supreme Court Jurisdiction—Notice
14.78 Scope of Just Compensation—"Highest and Best Use"
14.88 Methods of Valuation to Determine Compensation—Cost Approach to Value

Westlaw Electronic Research
See Westlaw Electronic Research Guide preceding the Summary of Contents.

§ 14.32 Determination and Findings—Interplay with SEQRA

PAGE 135:

[*Add to note 2.*]

2. When an inverse condemnation (*see* § 14.14 *supra*) is determined to have occurred, the condemnor need not comply with SEQRA in all cases. Knapp v. County of Livingston, 175 Misc.2d 112, 667 N.Y.S.2d 662 (1997), *aff'd* 1999 WL 399425 (1999). The *Knapp* court noted that an inverse condemnation is less a physical permanent taking than "a procedural device, used by courts of equity, to award damages and resolve property disputes..." *Id.* at 117–118, 667 N.Y.S.2d at 666.

§ 14.61 Acquisition of Property—Supreme Court Jurisdiction—Notice

PAGE 152:

[*Add to end of section.*]

Village of Valley Falls v. Buchman, 179 Misc.2d 840, 686 N.Y.S.2d 693 (1999) illustrates how seriously the courts take the dual requirement of notice and publication. Petitioner, the Village, sought to acquire respondent's land to construct a sewer system and waste treatment plant and petitioned to file the required acquisition maps (§ 14.51 *supra*). Petitioner served respondent-owner by certified mail but did not publish. When respondent challenged this failure, petitioner argued that the court should waive the requirement in light of "the forgiving feature" of EDPL § 402(B)(2)(b). The final sentence of that section provides that "[t]he inadvertent failure to notify any condemnee, whether of record or not, will not invalidate any proceedings brought hereunder...." In rejecting petitioner's argument, the court noted that while failure to meet the strict requirement of notice might not invalidate the proceedings, this "forgiveness" does not relieve petitioners of a general obligation to meet the notice requirement prior to a final order. To hold otherwise "would, in effect, render meaningless the additional publication requirement." 179 Misc.2d at 842, 686 N.Y.S.2d at 694.

The "savings" clause in § 402(B)(2)(b) is triggered after the proceeding is concluded to shield the condemnor from post-proceeding attacks. It is not available before or during the proceeding, the periods to which the notice and publication requirements of the EDPL are specifically directed.

§ 14.78 Scope of Just Compensation—"Highest and Best Use"

PAGE 160:

[*Add to note 1.*]

1. In *Matter of* Acquisition of Real Property by the Village of Marathon, 174 Misc.2d 800, 666 N.Y.S.2d 365 (1997), the court noted four criteria generally used to determine a particular property's "highest and best use": legal permissibility, physical possibility, financial feasibility and maximum profitability.

§ 14.88 Methods of Valuation to Determine Compensation—Cost Approach to Value

PAGE 167:

[*Add to end of section.*]

In General Crushed Stone Company v. State, 93 N.Y.2d 23, 686 N.Y.S.2d 754, 709 N.E.2d 463 (1999), the Court of Appeals addressed the issue of the proper timing of an application for allowance under EDPL § 701. The dispute arose after the State condemned plaintiff's land and bituminous concrete plant in Rochester in order to facilitate improvements to Interstate 580. After the State made an offer, plaintiff filed an appropriation claim in the Court of Claims. Pre-trial proceedings over several years yielded a stipulation between the parties as to the value of the land ($100,000) and to the amount necessary to replace the plant "new" ($1,546,125). The sticking point arose because the appropriate appraisal methodology for "specialty" property (§ 14.89) was "replacement cost less depreciation" and the parties could not agree on the appropriate amount of depreciation. The Court of Claims agreed with claimant's depreciation figures and awarded claimant $1,741,992.31 plus interest.

The State determined not to appeal the judgment. Nearly six weeks after the judgment was entered claimant filed an application for allowance under § 701. The Court of Claims and the Appellate Division, relying on precedent, held claimant's application untimely.

§ 14.88   EMINENT DOMAIN   Ch. 14

In reversing, the Court of Appeals noted that § 701 itself contains no direction or limitation on timing. The purpose of the section suggests something about the timing of the application.

> The section assures that "a condemnee receives a fair recovery by providing an opportunity for condemnees whose property has been substantially undervalued to recover the costs of litigation establishing the inadequacy of the condemnor's offer" (Hakes v. State of New York, 81 N.Y.2d 392, 397, 599 N.Y.S.2d 498, 500, 615 N.E.2d 982). As the statute makes clear, the inadequacy of the condemnor's offer is shown by comparing it to the actual award valuing the property. For good reason, the court's determination of the property's value must be complete before the inquiry regarding allowances under the statute is possible. If an appeal is taken, the amount of the award could change, directly bearing on whether the award is "substantially in excess" of the State's offer.

Id. at ___.

The Court concluded that "[w]e would disrupt the important remedial purpose of section 701 if we were to hold that an application for allowable costs must be brought before, and incorporated into, the judgment determining the property's value." *Id.* Such application may be brought before or after the judgment on value or after any appeal therefrom. The fact that the State has actually paid the judgment amount will not affect this timing.

Chapter 15

ENVIRONMENTAL LAW

by
Steven Russo

Table of Sections

15.3   State Environmental Quality Review Act
15.4   ____ Determination of Significance
15.5   ____ The Environmental Impact Statement And Findings Statement
15.15 Wetlands Protection—The Federal Scheme
15.20 Air Pollution Control—The 1990 CAA Amendments
15.24 Regulation of Solid and Hazardous Waste—New York Hazardous Waste Regulation
15.30 ____ Lender Liability, Contribution and Indemnification Under CERCLA
15.32 Relevant Common Law Doctrines—Nuisance
15.33 ____ Trespass

Westlaw Electronic Research

See Westlaw Electronic Research Guide preceding the Summary of Contents.

§ 15.3 State Environmental Quality Review Act

PAGE 216:

3. *See also* Merson v. McNally, 90 N.Y.2d 742, 665 N.Y.S.2d 605, 688 N.E.2d 479 (1997) ("SEQRA's fundamental policy is to inject environmental considerations directly into governmental decision making.")

§ 15.4 State Environmental Quality Review Act—Determination of Significance

PAGE 220:

[*Insert at end of section.*]

A conditioned negative declaration is not permitted for a Type I action.[21] However, even in instances where a proposed project qualifies as a Type I action, an applicant may still voluntarily incorporate adjustments to the proposed project to mitigate concerns identified by the public and reviewing agencies *prior* to the issuance of a negative declaration, without transforming such negative declaration into a conditioned negative declaration.[22]

21. 6 NYCRR § 617.7(d).

22. Merson v. McNally, 90 N.Y.2d 742–43, 665 N.Y.S.2d 605, 610, 688 N.E.2d 479 (1997).

§ 15.5 State Environmental Quality Review Act—The Environmental Impact Statement And Findings Statement

PAGE 220:

1. *See* Merson v. McNally, 90 N.Y.2d 742, 751, 665 N.Y.S.2d 605, 609, 688 N.E.2d 479 (1997) ("[w]hile an EAF is used to determine significance or nonsignificance, the purpose of an EIS is to examine the potentially significant environmental impacts which may result from a project.")

§ 15.15 Wetlands Protection—The Federal Scheme

PAGE 239:

[*Insert text following note 8.*]

The Court of Appeals for the District of Columbia Circuit affirmed the District Court's decision in *American Mining Congress*, invalidating the ACE regulations providing that dredging activities that cause incidental "fallback" of dredged material constitutes the "discharge" of dredge or fill requiring a Section 404 permit.[8.1]

8.1 National Mining Association v. U.S. Army Corps of Engineers, 145 F.3d 1399 (D.C.Cir.1998).

[*Add to note 10.*]

10. On July 1, 1998, the ACE published proposed modifications to NWP 26 in the Federal Register. 63 Fed. Reg. 36040 (July 1, 1998). In October 1998 the ACE provided a revised schedule for issuance of amendments to its NWPs, including NWP 26, and delayed the expiration of the current NWP 26 until September 15, 1999.

§ 15.20 Air Pollution Control—The 1990 CAA Amendments

PAGE 246:

3. As of January 1999, New York has not yet requested a reclassification as a "maintenance area" that is in attainment of NAAQS for carbon monoxide. If EPA determines that the New York Metropolitan region has achieved NAAQS for carbon monoxide it will be reclassified as an area in attainment for this pollutant. Otherwise, EPA will have to reclassify the region as a serious nonattainment area, as altered in the main text.

§ 15.24 Regulation of Solid and Hazardous Waste— New York Hazardous Waste Regulation

PAGE 252:

[*Add to end of first paragraph.*]

One court has held that New York's extensive scheme for the regulation of hazardous waste disposal and cleanup shows an intent by the State to occupy the field and thus local laws that infringe on the legislature's broad grant of authority to the DEC in this area are preempted.[4.1]

4.1 Moreau v. New York State Department of Environmental Conservation, 178 Misc.2d 55, 678 N.Y.S.2d 241, 243 (Sup. Ct. Albany Co.1998.)

§ 15.30 Regulation of Inactive Hazardous Waste Sites—Lender Liability, Contribution and Indemnification Under CERCLA

PAGE 267:

[Re-write note 7 as follows.]

7. *Id.* **CAVEAT:** In the past, a contribution action was combined with a private cost recovery action under Section 107(a) against all other PRPs as a matter of course. However, while a split of authority still exists, every court of appeals that has addressed the issue has squarely held that a PRP may not commence a Section 107(a) action against other PRPs, but may only maintain an action for contribution. *E.g.*, Bedford Affiliates v. Sills, 156 F.3d 416 (2d Cir.1998); United Technologies Corp. v. Browning-Ferris, Inc., 33 F.3d 96, 103 (1st Cir.1994), *cert. denied* 513 U.S. 1183, 115 S.Ct. 1176, 130 L.Ed.2d 1128 (1995); Pneumo Abex Corp. v. High Point, Thomasville and Denton Railroad Co., 142 F.3d 769 (4th Cir.1998); Pinal Creek Group v. Newmont Mining Corp., 118 F.3d 1298, 1301 (9th Cir.1997); Akzo Coatings, Inc. v. Aigner Corp., 30 F.3d 761, 765 (7th Cir.1994), on remand 881 F.Supp. 1202 (D.Ind.1994); United States v. Colorado & Eastern Railroad Co., 50 F.3d 1530, 1536 (10th Cir.1995); Redwing Carriers, Inc. v. Saraland Apartments, 94 F.3d 1489 (11th Cir.1996). Nevertheless, a court may still allow a PRP to maintain a Section 107(a) action in cases where a PRP has neither admitted nor been adjudicated a PRP under CERCLA. Ninth Avenue Remedial Group v. Allis Chalmers Corp., 974 F.Supp. 684, 691 (N.D.Ind.1997). This is not merely a distinction without a difference, because in a contribution action a party is only liable for its equitable share of the damages, while liability under Section 107(a) is joint and several. *Restatement (Second) Torts,* § 886A(2) (1979). Thus, whether a PRP may maintain a private cost recovery action under Section 107(a) may determine who will be responsible for any orphan share of liability. In addition, a three year statute of limitations applies to contribution actions under Section 113(g) and a six year statute of limitations applies to Section 107(a) cost recovery actions. *See* United Technologies Corp. v. Browning-Ferris, Inc., 33 F.3d at 103.

§ 15.32 Relevant Common Law Doctrines—Nuisance

PAGE 272:

17. *See also* Chenango Inc. v. County of Chenango, 256 A.D.2d 793, 681 N.Y.S.2d 640 (3d Dep't 1998) (new "state of the art" landfill adjoining privately owned outdoor recreation area did not constitute a nuisance because the conditions upon which plaintiff's complaint is based "derive principally from the inherent attributes of the landfill rather than from any negligent operation of same.")

§ 15.33 Relevant Common Law Doctrines—Trespass

PAGE 274:

4. Prato v. Vigliotta, 253 A.D.2d 749, 677 N.Y.S.2d 380, 381 (2d Dep't 1998); *see also* Iglesias v. Dazi, 253 A.D.2d 515, 677 N.Y.S.2d 158 (2d Dep't 1998) (plaintiffs did not establish that defendants intentionally used pumps and sandbags or other artificial means to directly channel surface water so that the quantity and speed of the surface water flow was substantially increased, causing damage to plaintiffs' property).

Chapter 16

LAND USE LAW

by
John R. Nolon

Table of Sections

16.9	Local Land Use Law—Home Rule Authority—Floating Zone
16.12	Comprehensive Plan—Judicial Definition
16.18	Substantive Limits—Substantive Due Process
16.19	___ Procedural Due Process
16.22	___ Regulatory Takings
16.25	___ First Amendment
16.29	Local Process—Adoption
16.46	Judicial Review—Standards—Zoning Board of Appeals
16.48	___ Standing
16.85	Area Variance—Statutory Balancing Test—Balancing Factors
16.90	Special Use Permits
16.95	___ Summary
16.111	Particularized Actions—Spot Zoning—Challenge Dismissed
16.121	Special Regulations—Home Offices
16.125	___ Aesthetics

Westlaw Electronic Research

See Westlaw Electronic Research Guide preceding the Summary of Contents.

§ 16.9 Local Land Use Law—Home Rule Authority—Floating Zone

PAGE 309:

[*Re-write note 3 as follows.*]

3. 302 N.Y. at 120, 96 N.E.2d at 732.

[*Re-write note 10 as follows.*]

10. 302 N.Y. at 128, 96 N.E.2d at 737.

§ 16.12 Comprehensive Plan—Judicial Definition

PAGE 313:

[*Replace note 11 with the following.*]

11. For an early New York Case taking this view, see Harris v. Village of Dobbs Ferry, 208 App.Div. 853, 204 N.Y.S. 325 (2d Dep't 1924).

§ 16.18 Substantive Limits—Substantive Due Process
PAGE 323:

[*Insert right after carryover paragraph.*]

In *Countryman v. Schmitt*, 176 Misc.2d 736, 673 N.Y.S.2d 521 (Sup.Ct. Monroe County, 1998), a local regulation that created a preference system favoring, among other sites, those owned by the town or fire department was declared arbitrary and unreasonable and a violation of equal protection. The court noted that aesthetic concerns motivated the preference system and there was no rational basis for preferring town-owned land over privately owned land on aesthetic grounds.

§ 16.19 Substantive Limits—Procedural Due Process
PAGE 326:

[*Add to end of section.*]

"When a local land use decision that is to be referred to the county planning board under Section 239–m of the General Municipal Law is not referred as required, that failure amounts to a jurisdictional defect which renders the local action invalid." *Caruso v. Town of Oyster Bay*, 172 Misc.2d 93, 656 N.Y.S.2d 809 (Sup. Ct. Nassau County 1997), *aff'd* 250 A.D.2d 639, 672 N.Y.S.2d 418 (2d Dep't 1998). The town imposed a moratorium in response to a petition signed by plaintiff's neighbors expressing their concern regarding the division of plaintiff's property. The court stated that "a moratorium on building has been held a reasonable measure designed to temporarily halt development while the town considered comprehensive zoning changes and therefore a valid stopgap or interim zoning measure." The court concluded, however, that the moratorium was invalid for failure to follow the requirements for referral to the county. The court further held that the plaintiff's application "must be processed in the ordinary course of the Town's operations now that the moratorium is no longer in effect."

§ 16.22 Substantive Limits—Regulatory Takings
PAGE 330:

[*Add right after carryover paragraph.*]

A recreational zone created to implement the Town of Mamaroneck's Local Waterfront Revitalization Plan was sustained against a claim that it was unconstitutional as a taking without just compensation. *See Bonnie Briar Syndicate, Inc., v. Town of Mamaroneck*, 216 N.Y.L.J. 34 (1996) *aff'd* 242 A.D.2d 356, 661 N.Y.S.2d 1005 (2d Dep't 1997). In 1994, the Town Board adopted a new Recreation Zone that allowed only private recreational facilities as principal uses and did not permit any residential development. The purpose of the new law was to maintain open space, reduce the potential for substantial flood hazards and to maintain the suburban quality of the community, objectives that were

§ 16.22 LAND USE LAW Ch. 16

studied and established in the town's Local Waterfront Revitalization Plan. The plaintiff did not prove that the property could not yield a reasonable economic return under the regulation. The court refused to inquire whether less restrictive means were available to accomplish these objectives, deferring to the local legislature's judgment.

§ 16.25 Substantive Limits—First Amendment
PAGE 338:

[Add to end of section.]

The Court of Appeals upheld New York City's law that dispersed adult uses throughout the city in *Stringfellow's v. City of New York*, 91 N.Y.2d 382, 671 N.Y.S.2d 406, 694 N.E.2d 407 (1998). The court found New York City's law to be content-neutral because its predominant purpose was removing the negative secondary effects caused by adult uses, and not a "purposeful attempt to regulate speech." The Court's primary concern under constitutional analysis was whether the law struck the proper balance between "community needs and free expression." The court noted that a purposeful attempt at controlling the expressive content of adult businesses would fail constitutional scrutiny.

§ 16.29 Local Process—Adoption
PAGE 341:

[Replace note 7 with the following.]

7. Estabrook v. Chamberlain, 240 App. Div. 899, 267 N.Y.S. 425 (2d Dep't 1933), aff'd 240 App.Div. 1006, 268 N.Y.S. 1015 (1933).

§ 16.46 Judicial Review—Standards—Zoning Board of Appeals
PAGE 353:

[Add to end of section.]

Wilson v. Town of Mohawk, 246 A.D.2d 762, 668 N.Y.S.2d 62 (3d Dep't 1998), held that the Zoning Board of Appeals did not use the statutory factors in reaching its determination and therefore did not have substantial evidence to support its denial.

The Zoning Board of Appeals in *SV Space Development Corp. v. Town of Babylon Zoning Board of Appeals*, 256 A.D.2d 471, 682 N.Y.S.2d 95 (2d Dep't 1998) exceeded its authority by placing a two-year limit on a special use permit. The court found the time limit improper because "[t]he zoning ordinance does not provide for or contemplate durational limits in connection with the issuance of special use permits."

§ 16.48 Judicial Review—Standing
PAGE 355:

[Add after second paragraph in section.]

In *Williams v. Hertzwig*, 251 A.D.2d 655, 675 N.Y.S.2d 113 (2d Dep't 1998), the defendant purchased property and erected and maintained a dog kennel without obtaining the requisite special use permit. Plaintiff, who owned adjacent property, brought an action for an injunction, but failed to submit any evidence of injury or depreciation of its property due to the defendant's illegal use. The Appellate Division found that an "allegation of close proximity may give rise to an inference of injury enabling a nearby property owner to maintain an action without proof of actual injury." As it was undisputed that plaintiff's property was adjacent to defendant's property, the Court found that the plaintiff had standing. The plaintiff's preliminary injunction was granted, precluding the defendant from operating the kennel for the duration of the action.

§ 16.85   Area Variance—Statutory Balancing Test—Balancing Factors

PAGE 386:

[Add after second paragraph in section.]

In *Necker Pottick, Fox Run Woods Builders Corp. v. Duncan*, 251 A.D.2d 333, 673 N.Y.S.2d 740 (2d Dep't 1998), the Zoning Board of Appeals denied the plaintiff's application for a frontage variance. The court found that there was not substantial evidence because "the Zoning Board merely reiterated the ... balancing test without stating the specific facts or reasons that it relied upon in making its determination to deny the [plaintiff's] application." The court granted the application because "the only opposition presented in this case was the generalized grievances of a group of neighboring property owners.... [C]ivic opposition was not based on facts, but on the weight of numbers, i.e., how many neighboring property owners were in opposition."

§ 16.90   Special Use Permits

PAGE 393:

[Add to end of section.]

In *Sunrise Plaza Associates v. Town Board of the Town of Babylon*, 250 A.D.2d 690, 673 N.Y.S.2d 165 (2d Dep't 1998), the court held that the Town Board may issue a special use permit for the operation of a proposed restaurant, even though the landowner had previously obtained a parking variance from the Town zoning ordinance. The plaintiff claimed that the special use permit had been improperly granted because the landowner's proposed use was not in compliance with the requirements of the Town ordinance. The court rejected this argument, stating that "[t]he Town Board ... properly awarded [the] special use permit inasmuch as the proposed restaurant, operating with a parking variance, was found to be consistent with the surrounding area and would not pose a detriment thereto." The court further noted that "Town Law § 274–b(3) expressly provides for the issuance of a special use permit in conjunction with an area variance."

§ 16.95 Special Use Permits—Summary

PAGE 397:

[*Replace note 3 with the following.*]

3. 30 N.Y.2d at 372, 334 N.Y.S.2d at 147, 285 N.E.2d at 298.

§ 16.111 Particularized Actions—Spot Zoning—Challenge Dismissed

PAGE 418:

[*Add to end of section.*]

The court in *Rye Citizens Committee v. Board of Trustees for the Village of Port Chester*, 249 A.D.2d 478, 671 N.Y.S.2d 528 (2d Dep't 1998), rejected the plaintiff's claim that the construction of a retail facility constituted spot zoning and upheld the dismissal of the petition and proceeding. The court stated that the record showed approval for the project to be in accord with a comprehensive plan calculated to serve the general welfare of the community. The court based its conclusion partially on the fact that a SEQRA review established the land to be in a predominately commercial area and compatible with commercial and retail character of the area in which it is situated.

§ 16.121 Special Regulations—Home Offices

PAGE 429:

[*Add as fourth paragraph in section.*]

Plaintiff was served with a criminal summons for the operation of a fence construction business on his property in *Saglibene v. Baum*, 246 A.D.2d 599, 668 N.Y.S.2d 39 (2d Dep't 1998). Plaintiff had petitioned the Zoning Board of Appeals to declare the fence business a customary home occupation. The Board concluded that the business was not customary under the ordinance. The plaintiff challenged the board's determination but failed because it could not prove that its determination was arbitrary and capricious.

§ 16.125 Special Regulations—Aesthetics

PAGE 436:

[*Add after second paragraph in section.*]

In *Wal-Mart Stores, Inc. v. Planning Board of the Town of North Elba*, 238 A.D.2d 93, 668 N.Y.S.2d 774 (3d Dep't 1998), the court sustained the Planning Board's denial of a conditional use permit and site plan application for the development of a large retail store. The court held that it was appropriate for the Planning Board to place great weight on the visual effect of the development because it was located within an area designated a "Scenic Preservation Overlay," established to protect the view of a nearby mountain. The court stated that "despite all efforts to screen the store and parking area from the road, their presence would nevertheless bring about a noticeable change in the visual character of this critical area."

[Add after fourth paragraph in section.]

In *Countryman v. Schmitt*, 176 Misc.2d 736, 673 N.Y.S.2d 521 (Sup. Ct. Monroe County, 1998), a local regulation which created a preference system favoring, among other sites, those owned by the town or fire department was declared arbitrary and unreasonable and a violation of equal protection. The court noted that aesthetic concerns motivated the preference system and there was no rational basis for preferring town-owned land over privately owned land on aesthetic grounds.

Chapter 17

EMPLOYMENT LAW

by
Wayne N. Outten
and
Jack A. Raisner

Table of Sections

17.43 Statutory Causes of Action—Disability

Westlaw Electronic Research

See Westlaw Electronic Research Guide preceding the Summary of Contents.

§ 17.43 Statutory Causes of Action—Disability

PAGE 521:

[Replace last paragraph on page with the following.]

New York State Human Rights Law ("NYSHRL").[5] The NYSHRL defines "disability" more broadly than the ADA, by including any "physical mental or medical impairment" that "prevents the exercise of a normal bodily function" or is clinically demonstrable.[5.1] Like the ADA, the NYSHRL covers individuals who are regarded as, or have a record of being, impaired.[6] Prior to 1997, however, the NYSHRL excluded from its coverage disabled individuals who could not perform their jobs in "reasonable" manner, and did not impose an affirmative duty on employers to reasonably accommodate such individuals, thus its protections were quite narrow.[6.1] The NYSHRL was amended to impose on employers the duty to provide reasonable accommodations to individuals with known disabilities.[7] The employer is relieved of that duty, however, if it can demonstrate that providing the accommodation with impose an undue hardship on the operation of its business, or if the employee is physically unable to perform the job even with a reasonable accommodation.[7.1] Given the breadth of the NYSHRL's coverage and its ADA-like reasonable accommodation provision, the NYSHRL provides an alternative for employees who are unable to satisfy the ADA's stricter definition of disability, although it lacks an attorneys' fees provision.

[Insert new note 5.1.]

5.1 N.Y. Exec. L. § 292 (21).

[*Add to note 6.*]

6. *See also* Reeves v. Johnson Controls World Servs., Inc., 140 F.3d 144 (2d Cir. 1998), In Reeves, the Court noted the "controlling authority" of the New York Court of Appeals' decision in State Div. of Human Rights v. Xerox Corp., 65 N.Y.2d 213, 491 N.Y.S.2d 106, 480 N.E.2d 695 (1985), which explained that the term "disability" in NYSHRL includes conditions that do not "substantially limit a major life activity." Accordingly, the Reeves Court concluded that an "medically diagnosable impairment" is a disability under the NYSHRL. Reeves, 140 F.3d at 155.

[*Insert new note 6.1.*]

6.1 *See* Guzman v. ARC XVI Inwood, Inc., 1999 WL 178786 (S.D.N.Y.1999)(applying pre–1997 NYSHRL law to termination of plaintiff on leave for over one year due to pregnancy-related complications who was unable to return to work).

[*Replace current note 7 with the following.*]

7. N.Y. Exec. L. § 296(3)(a) provides "It shall be an unlawful discriminatory practice for an employer ... to refuse to provide reasonable accommodations to the known disabilities of an employee ..."

[*Add new note 7.1.*]

7.1 N.Y. Exec. Law § 296(3)(b), (3–a)(g).

Chapter 18

CIVIL RIGHTS LAW

by
Marilyn Trautfield Sugarman

Table of Sections

18.2	Strategy
18.5	Jurisdiction Over Civil Rights Actions
18.10	New York Bill of Rights—Search and Seizure—Civil Liability
18.12	___ Rights of Persons Accused of Crimes
18.13	___ ___ Public Trial/Closure of Courtroom
18.14	___ ___ Exclusion of Public or Press
18.15	___Rights of Jurors
18.18	General Federal Civil Rights Provisions—42 U.S.C.A. § 1983
18.19	___ Other Federal Civil Rights Provisions
18.21	Police and Prosecutorial Misconduct—Excessive Force
18.22	___ False Arrest
18.23	___ False Imprisonment
18.25	___ Malicious Prosecution
18.27	First Amendment—Freedom of Speech
18.28	___ Freedom of Religion
18.29	Rights of Prisoners
18.31	Defenses to Federal Actions—Absolute Immunity
18.32	___ Qualified Immunity
18.33	___ Eleventh Amendment
18.34	___ *Monell* and Its Progeny
18.35	___ *Respondeat Superior*
18.36	___ Abstention
18.37	___ *Res Judicata* and Collateral Estoppel
18.38	___ Statute of Limitations
18.45	Housing—Prohibition Against Discrimination in Private Housing—Owners and Lessors
18.46	___ ___ Real Estate Agents and Brokers
18.47	___ ___ Cooperatives
18.49	___ ___ Remedies for Discrimination—Administrative Proceedings
18.50	___ ___ Remedies for Discrimination—Actions in State and Federal Court
18.51	___ *Prima Facie* Case and Burden of Proof
18.52	___ Summary of Procedure for Filing an Administrative Claim and Challenging an SDHR Order
18.53	Education
18.54	Equal Rights in Places of Public Accommodation and Amusement
18.55	___ General Provisions
18.57	___ Persons With Disabilities Accompanied by a Guide Dog, Hearing Dog or Service Dog
18.60	Employment Discrimination Provisions Exclusive to the New York Civil Rights Law—In General

18.64	Right of Privacy—Generally
18.65	___ Police Officers, Corrections Officers and Firefighters
18.66	___ Victims of Sex Offenses
18.70	Changing One's Name—Procedure for Petition to Change Name—Special Procedures for Infants
18.74	Heart Balm Statute
18.76	___ Action for Return of Gifts Made in Contemplation of Marriage
18.80	Miscellaneous Rights and Immunities—Frivolous Litigation—Protection From SLAPP Suits
18.82	___ Libel and Slander—Defenses
18.83	___ Breast Feeding
18.84	___ Suspension of Rights Due to Imprisonment
18.85	___ Shield Law
18.86	___ Performing Abortion
18.86a	___ Confidentiality of Records of Genetic Tests

Westlaw Electronic Research

See Westlaw Electronic Research Guide preceding the Summary of Contents.

---

§ 18.2 Strategy

PAGE 614:

4. In City of Monterey v. Del Monte Dunes at Monterey, Ltd., ___ U.S. ___, 119 S.Ct. 1624, 143 L.Ed.2d 882 (1999), the Court held that § 1983 does not confer a right to a jury trial.

[Insert as text after note 4.]

Depending on where the action is commenced, and the nature of the claims asserted, a jury trial may not be available.[4.1]

4.1 Generally, claims under § 1983 are entitled to a jury trial, although the Seventh Amendment right to a jury trial does not apply to suits seeking only injunctive relief. City of Monterey v. Del Monte Dunes at Monterey, Ltd., ___ U.S. ___, 119 S.Ct. 1624, 143 L.Ed.2d 882 (1999).

§ 18.5 Jurisdiction Over Civil Rights Actions

PAGE 616:

3. Brown v. State of New York [main volume], appeal after remand, 250 A.D.2d 314, 681 N.Y.S.2d 170 (3d Dep't 1998). The Third Department held that the statute of limitations for a constitutional tort is three years.

§ 18.10 New York Bill of Rights—Search and Seizure—Civil Liability

PAGE 623:

12. The Supreme Court has held that police do not have the authority to search people and their cars without consent after ticketing them for routine traffic violations. Knowles v. Iowa, 525 U.S. 113, 119 S.Ct. 484, 142 L.Ed.2d 492 (1998).

§ 18.10

[*Insert as text at end of section.*]

A plaintiff in a federal civil rights action which is based on an illegal search may recover only nominal damages for invasion of privacy. The plaintiff is not entitled to compensation for the harm caused by a conviction or incarceration. Townes v. City of New York, 176 F.3d 138 (2d Cir.1999).

§ 18.12 New York Bill of Rights—Rights of Persons Accused of Crimes

PAGE 625:

2. *See also* People v. Davidson, 89 N.Y.2d 881, 653 N.Y.S.2d 254, 675 N.E.2d 1206 (1996) (defendant's exclusion from sidebar discussions of potential jurors requires reversal); People v. Maher, [People v. Ricks, People v. Mack], 89 N.Y.2d 318, 653 N.Y.S.2d 79, 675 N.E.2d 833 (1996)(same); *but see* People v. Camacho, 90 N.Y.2d 558, 664 N.Y.S.2d 578, 687 N.E.2d 396 (1997) (exclusion of defendant during preliminary screening of jurors did not require reversal). In People v. Hok Ming Chan, 230 A.D.2d 165, 656 N.Y.S.2d 22 (1st Dep't 1997), the First Department held that defendants' exclusion from a discussion concerning partial closure of the courtroom did not require reversal.

CAVEAT: In United States v. Rosario, 111 F.3d 293 (2d Cir.1997), *cert. denied* ___ U.S. ___, 118 S.Ct. 319, 139 L.Ed.2d 246 (1997) the court held that defendant waived his right to be present during post-verdict questioning of a juror by failing to make a contemporaneous objection.

§ 18.13 New York Bill of Rights—Rights of Persons Accused of Crimes—Public Trial/Closure of Courtroom

PAGE 625:

1. The decision in Ayala [Steven] v. Speckard, 89 F.3d 91 (2d Cir.1996) [main volume] was adhered to upon rehearing, 102 F.3d 649 (2d Cir.1996), but was then vacated upon rehearing en banc. See 131 F.3d 62, cert. denied ___ U.S. ___, 118 S.Ct. 2380, 141 L.Ed.2d 747 (1998).

The 1996 Ayala decision had spawned numerous decisions, many of which were highly critical of Ayala. The First Department declined to follow Ayala in People v. Pepe, 235 A.D.2d 221, 653 N.Y.S.2d 101 (1997). Similarly, in People v. Ramos [People v. Robert Ayala], 90 N.Y.2d 490, 662 N.Y.S.2d 739, 685 N.E.2d 492 (1997), which also involved the closure of the courtroom for testimony of undercover police officers in "buy and bust" drug arrests, the New York Court of Appeals rejected the stricter rules set forth in Ayala (*i.e.*, that the court has an affirmative duty to explicitly consider alternatives to closure, even sua sponte) and instead placed the burden on the defendant who opposes closure to suggest alternatives to closure. The court noted that while excluding the general public might be justified, it was error to exclude the defendant's family members.

Following the 1996 decision in Ayala, the Second Circuit decided Pearson v. James, 105 F.3d 828 (2d Cir.1997). Two of the judges in Pearson denounced the Ayala decision, but were constrained to find that the Ayala decision mandated a new trial for Pearson, since the trial judge had closed the courtroom during the undercover officer's testimony without considering alternatives to closure. Pearson was consolidated with Ayala and another case, Okonkwo v. Lacy, which were heard together en banc, since all three cases concern closure of the courtroom for testimony of undercover police officers in "buy and bust" drug arrests.

PAGE 626:

3. Cosentino v. Kelly [main volume], cert. denied 520 U.S. 1229, 117 S.Ct. 1821, 137 L.Ed.2d 1029 (1997).

Guzman v. Scully, 80 F.3d 772 (2d Cir. 1996) [main volume], appeal after new trial, 258 A.D.2d 263, 682 N.Y.S.2d 851 (1999).

Following the appeal, the defendant entered a plea of guilty.

[*Insert as text after note 3.*]

Upon rehearing en banc in *Ayala, supra*, the Second Circuit expressed its belief that open trials are strongly favored, and that the trial court should "require persuasive evidence of serious risk to an important interest in ordering any closure, and to realize that the more extensive is the closure requested, the greater must be the gravity of the required interest and the likelihood of risk to that interest."[3.1] The court declined to decide whether a sua sponte obligation to consider alternatives to complete closure exists, since in each of the three cases, the judge only closed the courtroom for the testimony of one witness. The court did note, however, that once a judge determines that limited closure is warranted as an alternative to complete closure, the judge need not sua sponte consider additional alternatives. Rather, the party objecting to the trial court's proposal must come forward with any other alternatives.[3.2]

3.1 *Supra*, Ayala, note 1, 131 F.3d at 70.
3.2 Id. at 71.

4. Peterson v. Williams, [main volume], *cert. denied* 519 U.S. 878, 117 S.Ct. 202, 136 L.Ed.2d 138 (1996).

§ 18.14 New York Bill of Rights—Rights of Persons Accused of Crimes—Exclusion of Public or Press

2. *See supra*, People v. Ayala and People v. Ramos, § 18.13, note 1 (noting that while excluding the general public might be justified when undercover police officers testify, it was error to exclude the defendant's family members); People v. Chan, *supra* § 18.12, note 2 (trial judge did not err by excluding group of men from a suppression hearing in a kidnapping case, since the victim, who was testifying, feared the men had come to kill him).

§ 18.15 New York Bill of Rights—Rights of Jurors

PAGE 627:

5. *See also* Tankleff v. Senkowski, 135 F.3d 235 (2d Cir.1998) (Trial court erred in rejecting defendant's Batson challenge to government's peremptory strikes of African-American jurors on ground that defendant was not African-American; defendant could object to race-based exclusion of jurors regardless of whether he and excluded jurors were of same race); Campbell v. Louisiana, 523 U.S. 392, 118 S.Ct. 1419, 140 L.Ed.2d 551 (1998) (Caucasian defendant has standing to raise equal protection challenge to discrimination against black persons in the selection of grand jurors).

7. *See also* United States v. Somerstein, 959 F.Supp. 592 (E.D.N.Y.1997) (Batson applies to prosecutor's alleged use of peremptory challenges to excuse Jewish venirepersons).

8. People v. Rambersed, [main volume] *aff'd* 254 A.D.2d 81, 680 N.Y.S.2d 205 (1st Dep't 1998), lv. denied, 93 N.Y.2d 856, 688 N.Y.S.2d 504, 710 N.E.2d 1103 (1999).

9. People v. Hameed, [main volume], *cert. denied* 519 U.S. 1065, 117 S.Ct. 704, 136 L.Ed.2d 625 (1997); *see also* People v. Pena, 251 A.D.2d 26, 675 N.Y.S.2d 330 (1st Dep't 1998) (denying defendant's *Batson* challenge to exclusion of two African-American women because prosecutor's reasons were not pretextual); People v. Wooley, 249 A.D.2d 46, 671 N.Y.S.2d 58 (1st Dep't 1998) (defense attorney's reasons for exclusion of the only three white female jurors was pretextual); People v. Dalhouse, 240 A.D.2d 420, 658 N.Y.S.2d 408 (2d Dep't 1997) (prosecutors reasons for exclusion of several Black potential jurors was pretextual).

§ 18.18 General Federal Civil Rights Provisions—42 U.S.C.A. § 1983

PAGE 630:

2. *See also* Monsky v. Moraghan, 127 F.3d 243 (2d Cir.1997), cert. denied ___ U.S. ___, 119 S.Ct. 66, 142 L.Ed.2d 52 (1998) (plaintiff sufficiently alleged that judge acted under color of state law, where judge was allowed to enter court's office with his dog, and remain there during alleged harassment of litigant, because he was a judge).

PAGE 631:

5. Singer v. Fulton County Sheriff [main volume], cert. denied 517 U.S. 1189, 116 S.Ct. 1676, 134 L.Ed.2d 779 (1996)

8. In the same vein, the Supreme Court held in Breard v. Greene, 523 U.S. 371, 118 S.Ct. 1352, 140 L.Ed.2d 529 (1998) that the country of Paraguay could not bring an action against a state, nor could the country or its Consul General bring an action under federal civil rights statutes to set aside a Paraguayan national's conviction, since the country is neither a "person" nor a person "within the jurisdiction" of the United States.

§ 18.19 General Federal Civil Rights Provisions—Other Federal Civil Rights Provisions

PAGE 632:

1. Graham v. Henderson, 89 F.3d 75, 82 (2d Cir.1996) (§ 1985(3)) does not include conspiracies based on economic or commercial views, status, or activities; mere assertion of racial motivation is insufficient to state conspiracy claim.

2. *See also* Thomas v. Roach, 165 F.3d 137 (2d Cir.1999).

[Insert as text at end of first full paragraph.]

In a civil rights action under 42 U.S.C.A. § 1985(3), the court has discretion to award reasonable attorneys' fees to "the prevailing party," as provided by 42 U.S.C.A. § 1988(b).[3.1]

3.1 LeBlanc–Sternberg v. Fletcher, 143 F.3d 765, 769 (2d Cir.1998).

4. Thomas, *supra*, note 2.

PAGE 633:

[Delete citation in first sentence of first full paragraph and replace with the following.]

42 U.S.C.A. §§ 12101, *et seq.*

7. On June 22, 1999, the Supreme Court decided a trio of cases under the ADA, each of which sets forth the standards for determining whether an individual is disabled under the ADA. *See* Sutton v. United Airlines, Inc., 527 U.S. ___, 119 S.Ct. 2139, ___ L.Ed.2d ___ (1999); Murphy v. United Parcel Service, Inc., 527 U.S. ___, 119 S.Ct. 2133, ___ L.Ed.2d ___ (1999); Albertsons, Inc. v. Kirkingburg, 527 U.S. ___, 119 S.Ct. 2162, ___ L.Ed.2d ___ (1999).

8. *[Insert after CAVEAT.]*

The importance of pleading under all applicable federal and state statutes is demonstrated by the Supreme Court's decision in Schenck v. Pro–Choice Network of Western New York, 519 U.S. 357, 117 S.Ct. 855, 137 L.Ed.2d 1 (1997), where the § 1985(3) claim was dismissed but the claim under Civil Rights Law § 40–c survived.

§ 18.21 Police and Prosecutorial Misconduct—Excessive Force

PAGE 634:

[Add to Practice Pointer in note 2.]

2. Claims against federal officers may be brought under the Federal Tort Claims Act. Tapia–Ortiz v. Doe, 171 F.3d 150 (2d Cir. 1999).

[Insert at end of note 2.]

PRACTICE POINTER: A claim of excessive force should be brought against the individual officers and, where appropriate, the Police Department and the municipality or other political subdivision. The practitioner needs to be aware of potential *Monell* problems (see § 18.34 in main volume). For example, in Board of County Commissioners of Bryan County, Oklahoma v. Brown, 520 U.S. 397, 117 S.Ct. 1382, 137 L.Ed.2d 626 (1997), *reh. denied*, 520 U.S. 1283, 117 S.Ct. 2472, 138 L.Ed.2d 227 (1997), the Supreme Court held that the county was not liable for the sheriff's isolated decision to hire a deputy without adequate screening, because plaintiff failed to demonstrate that the decision reflected a conscious disregard for a high risk that the deputy would use excessive force.

[Add note 2.1 at end of last sentence of paragraph.]

2.1 *See e.g.*, Passino v. State, ___ A.D.2d ___, 689 N.Y.S.2d 258 (3d Dep't 1999) (Police officer's use of pepper spray to effect control over arrestee was objectively reasonable under the circumstances, and did not constitute excessive force; arrestee had been lawfully arrested for driving while intoxicated, was agitated and exhibited belligerent behavior, and refused repeated requests to remove his hands from his pocket to be handcuffed, and the officer followed State Police policy governing the use of force by complying with levels one through three of the guidelines before employing the use of pepper spray).

PAGE 635:

3. Harvey v. Brandt, 254 A.D.2d 718, 677 N.Y.S.2d 867 (4th Dep't 1998) (plaintiff raised triable issue of fact as to whether is entitled to the defense of qualified immunity); *see also*, Thomas v. Roach, 165 F.3d 137 (2d Cir.1999) (summary judgment denied on qualified immunity defense, since there are material issues of fact as to whether officers' use of force was reasonable).

The Second Circuit has confined the time-frame of the qualified immunity inquiry to the officer's knowledge of circumstances immediately prior to and at the moment that he made the split-second decision to employ deadly force. Salim v. Proulx, 93 F.3d 86, 92 (2d Cir.1996). Since at the moment the officer employed deadly force it was objectively reasonable for him to believe that his actions did not violate decedent's constitutional rights, officer had qualified immunity from suit.

[Add to PRACTICE POINTER at end of note 3.]

For cases discussing damages in excessive force cases, see Amato v. City of Saratoga Springs, 170 F.3d 311 (2d Cir.1999) and Atkins v. New York City, 143 F.3d 100 (2d Cir.1998).

§ 18.22 Police and Prosecutorial Misconduct—False Arrest

PAGE 635:

2. *See also* Weyant v. Okst, 101 F.3d 845, 852 (2d Cir.1996), which reiterates that under New York law, "a plaintiff claiming false arrest must show, inter alia,

§ 18.22

that the defendant intentionally confined him without his consent and without justification." The court further noted that "[a] § 1983 claim for false arrest, resting on the Fourth Amendment right of an individual to be free from unreasonable seizures, including arrest without probable cause, is substantially the same as a claim for false arrest under New York law." *Id.* (citation omitted).

CAVEAT: Probable cause to arrest constitutes justification and is a complete defense to an action for false arrest, whether the action is brought under state law or under § 1983. *Weyant, supra.*

PAGE 636:

[*Insert as text at end of section.*]

The Statute of Limitations for a false arrest claim under § 1983 is three years. Federal law governs the issue of when a false arrest claim accrues, which is at the time of the arrest.[5]

5. Covington v. City of New York, 171 F.3d 117 (2d Cir.1999).

PAGE 636:

4. *See also* Posr v. Court Officer Shield #207, 180 F.3d 409, 416 (2d Cir.1999)("an officer is immune if it was reasonable for him to believe, reasonably, that the plaintiff was breaking the law."); Lowth v. Town of Cheektowaga, 82 F.3d 563 (2d Cir.1996) (since freedom from false arrest is a clearly established right, the question of qualified immunity turns on whether the officer' action were objectively reasonable under the circumstances). In Lowth, the court held that the officer was entitled to immunity since he had probable cause under New York law to arrest an individual for unlawful endangerment, where the individual had, without authorization, moved an unmarked police vehicle which was blocking her driveway. For an excellent analysis of the qualified immunity defense, *see* Ricciuti v. New York City Transit Authority, 124 F.3d 123 (2d Cir.1997). The Second Circuit found that with respect to one arrest that the officer had a reasonable basis for believing there was probable cause, and was entitled to qualified immunity. In a second arrest arising from the same incident, the court rejected the defense of qualified immunity.

§ 18.23 Police and Prosecutorial Misconduct—False Imprisonment

PAGE 637:

7. *See also* Hyatt v. United States, 968 F.Supp. 96 (E.D.N.Y.1997) (In action under Federal Tort Claims Act for false imprisonment, plaintiff, who had not lost any wages and had suffered no post-imprisonment stress, was awarded $297,000 in compensatory damages for the loss of liberty for 99 days).

§ 18.25 Police and Prosecutorial Misconduct—Malicious Prosecution

PAGE 638:

1. *See also* Ricciuti v. New York City Transit Authority, 124 F.3d 123 (2d Cir. 1997).

2. *See also* Posr v. Court Officer Shield #207, 180 F.3d 409, 417 (2d Cir.1999) (dismissal on speedy trial grounds qualified as favorable termination); Breen v. Garrison, 169 F.3d 152 (2d Cir.1999) (dismissal of charge for facial insufficiency is not a decision on the merits); MacFawn v. Kresler, 88 N.Y.2d 859, 644 N.Y.S.2d 486, 666 N.E.2d 1359 (1996)(criminal proceeding where information was dismissed on procedural grounds, where the court dismissed the charges because it concluded that the facts alleged by the People were insufficient to support the charge, did not terminate favorably to the accused since the final dis-

position was not on the merits and did not indicate the accused's innocence); DiBlasio v. City of New York, 102 F.3d 654, 657 (2d Cir.1996)(absence of a final determination in DiBlasio's favor is the fatal flaw in his claim of malicious prosecution); DiCecilia v. Early, 234 A.D.2d 335, 651 N.Y.S.2d 94 (2d Dep't 1996) (dismissal of criminal charges in the interest of justice, after complainant failed to appear to testify at trial, was not a judicial determination of accused's innocence on the merits, precluding cause of action for malicious prosecution).

In Ricciuti, *supra*, note 1, the Second Circuit held that where the reasons for a dismissal of the charges are in dispute, the matter should be submitted to a jury.

[*Insert at end of note 4.*]

4. **CAVEAT:** In Heck v. Humphrey, main volume § 18.23, *supra*, note 4, the Supreme Court stated that, if the criminal trial resulted in a conviction, the cause of action of the malicious prosecution plaintiff would not accrue until "the conviction or sentence is reversed, expunged, invalidated, or impugned by the grant of a writ of habeas corpus." 512 U.S. at 477, 114 S.Ct. at 2373. However, in DiBlasio, *supra*, note 2, the Second Circuit opined that the Supreme Court did not mean that the grant of a writ of habeas corpus which overturns a conviction does not constitute a determination in favor of the accused.

PAGE 639:

5. *See also* Kotler v. State, 255 A.D.2d 429, 680 N.Y.S.2d 586 (2d Dep't 1998) In Kotler, claimant brought action against State for unjust conviction and imprisonment in the Court of Claims. The Second Department held that claimant, who was incarcerated for ten years, eight months, and two days as a result of his conviction of two counts of rape was properly awarded $1,510,000 in damages.

[*Insert at end of Practice Pointer:*]

Velaire v. City of Schenectady, 235 A.D.2d 647, 651 N.Y.S.2d 735 (3d Dep't 1997).

[*Insert n.7 at end of last full sentence of text:*]

7. In Ricciuti v. New York City Transit Authority, 124 F.3d 123 (2d Cir.1997), the Second Circuit rejected the defense of qualified immunity, holding that the police had conspired to create false information and the officers had then conspired to have plaintiffs prosecuted on the false information; *see also* Lowth v. Town of Cheektowaga, 82 F.3d 563, 569 (2d Cir.1996) (since "it is not disputed that freedom from false arrest, from malicious prosecution, and from the use of excessive force are all clearly established rights, ... the question of qualified immunity in this case turns on whether the actions of [the officers] were objectively reasonable under the circumstances."

§ 18.27   First Amendment—Freedom of Speech

PAGE 641:

[*Add to text as second-to-last paragraph, after note 7.*]

Freedom of speech issues also arise with respect to challenges to zoning regulations.[7.1]

7.1 Stringfellow's of New York, Ltd. v. City of New York, 91 N.Y.2d 382, 671 N.Y.S.2d 406, 694 N.E.2d 407 (1998) (zoning ordinances that regulate adult entertainment establishments fulfilled legitimate governmental purpose of controlling negative secondary effects of adult uses and did not have impermissible goal of attempting to regulate content of expression).

§ 18.27　　　　　　　CIVIL RIGHTS LAW　　　　　　　Ch. 18

[*Insert as n. 7.2 at end of first sentence in last paragraph of section.*]

7.2 Children's Village v. Greenburgh Eleven Teachers' Union Federation of Teachers, Local 1532, 258 A.D.2d 610, 685 N.Y.S.2d 754 (2d Dep't 1999) (proposed injunctive relief to prohibit distribution of literature at school was a prior restraint on free speech in violation of First Amendment).

§ 18.28　First Amendment—Freedom of Religion

PAGE 641:

1. Williams v. Bright, [main volume] was remanded by the First Department for a new trial on damages, 230 A.D.2d 548, 557, 658 N.Y.S.2d 910, 916 (1st Dep't), appeal dismissed 90 N.Y.2d 935, 664 N.Y.S.2d 273, 686 N.E.2d 1368 (1997). The Appellate Division found that instruction on mitigation of damages, requiring jury to determine whether plaintiff acted reasonably as Jehovah's Witness in declining recommended surgeries following automobile accident, constituted endorsement of religion in violation of First Amendment.

PRACTICE POINTER: The court in *Williams* included a supplement to modify the jury instructions contained in New York's pattern jury instruction with respect to this issue.

2. In City of Boerne v. Flores, 521 U.S. 507, 117 S.Ct. 2157, 138 L.Ed.2d 624 (1997), the Supreme Court declared that RFRA [discussed in main volume] was unconstitutional, in that the statute's enactment exceeded Congress' power under § 5 of the Fourteenth Amendment.

3. Griffin v. Coughlin, 88 N.Y.2d 674, 649 N.Y.S.2d 903, 673 N.E.2d 98 (1996) [main volume], cert. denied 519 U.S. 1054, 117 S.Ct. 681, 136 L.Ed.2d 607 (1997).

PAGE 642:

7. Williams v. Bright was reversed and remanded by the First Department. *See supra* note 1.

PAGE 643:

[*Add to text at end of section.*]

In *Matter of Medvedev v. Wing*[11] and *Matter of Buchanan v. Wing*,[12] the courts rejected plaintiffs' claims that the computerized finger imaging procedure utilized by the Department of Social Services infringes upon the freedom of religion and upheld denial of benefits. Similarly, in *In re Miller*,[13] the court held that a law requiring an applicant for a pistol permit or license to submit a photograph with the application did not violate free exercise clause of First Amendment, nor did it violate the free exercise clause of the state constitution. Finally, in *Warner v. Orange County Dept. of Probation*,[14] the plaintiff commenced an action claiming that condition of probation requiring his attendance at Alcoholics Anonymous meetings violated the First Amendment establishment clause. Even though plaintiff failed to object to religious content of the meetings at his sentencing, the court held he did not waive his claim, but awarded only nominal damages of one dollar.

11. 249 A.D.2d 755, 671 N.Y.S.2d 806 (3d Dep't 1998).
12. 245 A.D.2d 634, 636, 664 N.Y.S.2d 865, 867 (3d Dep't 1997).
13. 252 A.D.2d 156, 684 N.Y.S.2d 368 (4th Dep't 1998).
14. 115 F.3d 1068 (2d Cir.1996), opinion following remand 968 F.Supp. 917 (S.D.N.Y.1997), *aff'd* 173 F.3d 120 (2d Cir. 1999).

§ 18.29 Rights of Prisoners

1. Griffin v. Coughlin, 88 N.Y.2d 674, 649 N.Y.S.2d 903, 673 N.E.2d 98 (1996) [main volume], cert. denied 519 U.S. 1054, 117 S.Ct. 681, 136 L.Ed.2d 607 (1997).

§ 18.31 Defenses to Federal Actions—Absolute Immunity

PAGE 644:

2. [*Insert at end of first paragraph of footnote:*]
See also Tucker v. Outwater, 118 F.3d 930 (2d Cir.1997) (judge entitled to absolute immunity even if she acted in excess of jurisdiction since, at most, her mistakes were "procedural errors" that did not deprive her of subject matter jurisdiction). In October 1996, Congress amended § 1983 to bar injunctive relief "in any action brought against a judicial officer for an act or omission taken in such officer's judicial capacity ... unless a declaratory decree was violated or declaratory relief was unavailable." 42 U.S.C.A. § 1983; Federal Courts Improvement Act of 1996, Pub.L. No. 104–317, § 309(c), 110 Stat. 3847, 3853.

CAVEAT: As the Second Circuit noted in Hili v. Sciarrotta, 140 F.3d 210, 215 (2d Cir.1998), "[t]he term "judicial officer" is not defined in the amendment, although the legislative history of the amendment refers parenthetically to 'judicial officers' as '(justices, judges and magistrates).' S.Rep. No. 104–366, at 37 (1996), reprinted in 1996 U.S.C.C.A.N. 4202, 4217. It is not clear from the language of the amendment or from ... the legislative history whether the new restriction on the granting of injunctive relief against 'judicial officers' was meant to extend to other officials whose entitlement to absolute immunity from damages had been recognized in light of their roles in judicial proceedings."

[*Insert at end of third paragraph of footnote:*]

See also Rodriguez v. Weprin, 116 F.3d 62 (2d Cir.1997) (judicial immunity extended to court clerks for actions taken arising from performance of their jobs).

PAGE 645:

3. Doe v. Phillips, 81 F.3d 1204 (2d Cir. 1996) [main volume], cert. denied D'Amelia v. Doe, 520 U.S. 1115, 117 S.Ct. 1244, 137 L.Ed.2d 326 (1997).

4. Bogan v. Scott-Harris, 523 U.S. 44, 118 S.Ct. 966, 140 L.Ed.2d 79 (1998) (local legislators).

5. Tulloch v. Coughlin, 50 F.3d 114 (2d Cir.1995)[main volume], on remand to 1995 WL 780970 (W.D.N.Y.1995), appeal dismissed 101 F.3d 1393 (2d Cir.1996); see also, Montero v. Travis, 171 F.3d 757 (2d Cir.1999) (parole board commissioner who presided over parole revocation hearing entitled to absolute immunity); Scotto v. Almenas, 143 F.3d 105 (2d Cir.1998) (no absolute immunity for parole officer who recommended warrant be issued for parolee's arrest, but absolute immunity for parole division supervisor who signed arrest based upon parole officer's recommendation).

§ 18.32 Defenses to Federal Actions—Qualified Immunity

PAGE 646:

1. [*Insert at end of CAVEAT.*] While not an issue in New York, the Supreme Court has ruled that private prison guards who are sued under § 1983 do not have qualified immunity from suit. Richardson v. McKnight, 521 U.S. 399, 117 S.Ct. 2100, 138 L.Ed.2d 540 (1997).

2. See also Brown v. City of Oneonta, 106 F.3d 1125 (2d Cir.1997) (college employees were entitled to qualified immunity for claim that they violated students privacy rights under the Family Educational Rights and Privacy Act, since no clearly established right was infringed).

§ 18.32 CIVIL RIGHTS LAW Ch. 18

PAGE 647:

3. *See also* Townes v. City of New York, 176 F.3d 138 (2d Cir.1999) (arrestee had clearly established right, in 1984, to be free from unreasonable seizure, at least as to warrantless, suspicionless seizure of the person, while he was taxicab passenger).

6. In County of Sacramento v. Lewis, 523 U.S. 833, __ n. 5, 118 S.Ct. 1708, 1714 n. 5, 140 L.Ed.2d 1043 (1998), the Supreme Court held that a federal court faced with a suit alleging the deprivation of a constitutional right under § 1983 should ordinarily decide whether the constitutional right alleged by the plaintiff actually exists, and, only if it does, then the court should decide whether defendants were entitled to qualified immunity because the right was not clearly established at the time of the alleged violation. *See also* Wilson, __ U.S. at __, 119 S.Ct. at 1697. But, in Horne v. Coughlin, 178 F.3d 603 (2d Cir.1999) the Second Circuit held that *Sacramento* does not require lower courts to express views on the constitutional question, and that it was preferable in this case not to express such views.

8. Hemphill v. Schott, 141 F.3d 412 (2d Cir.1998) (factual issue as to whether officer's conduct was objectively reasonable precludes summary judgment).

§ 18.33 Defenses to Federal Actions—Eleventh Amendment

PAGE 648:

1. Seminole Tribe of Florida v. Florida, 517 U.S. 44, 54, 116 S.Ct. 1114, 1122, 134 L.Ed.2d 252 (1996)[main volume]; *see also* Idaho v. Coeur d'Alene Tribe of Idaho, 521 U.S. 261, 117 S.Ct. 2028, 138 L.Ed.2d 438 (1997).

PAGE 649:

2. *See also* Jones v. New York State Division of Military and Naval Affairs, 166 F.3d 45 (2d Cir.1999); United States v. City of Yonkers, 96 F.3d 600 (2d Cir.1996) (New York State, New York Education Department, and New York Board of Regents, were not considered persons subject to suit under § 1983).

3. *See also* Spencer v. Doe, 139 F.3d 107 (2d Cir.1998)(dismissing claims against state agency officials, in their official capacities, where plaintiff sought monetary damages arising out of alleged sexual abuse of plaintiff while he was in custody of juvenile secure facility, as barred by the Eleventh Amendment).

[*Insert paragraph as text after note 5.*]

If an action has been commenced in state court against a state agency or its officials, defendants may remove the action to federal court and may then assert the Eleventh Amendment as a defense. The federal court would then be precluded from hearing the barred claim, but may proceed to hear the other claims.[5.1]

5.1 Wisconsin Dept. of Corrections v. Schacht, 524 U.S. 381, 118 S.Ct. 2047, 141 L.Ed.2d 364 (1998).

§ 18.34 Defenses to Federal Actions—*Monell* and Its Progeny

PAGE 649:

[*Insert after note 2.*]

2. **CAVEAT:** It can sometimes be difficult to determine which entity an individual is considered a policymaker for. In McMillian v. Monroe County, Alabama, 520 U.S. 781, 117 S.Ct. 1734, 138 L.Ed.2d 1 (1997), the parties agreed that the sheriff is a "poli-

cymaker" for § 1983 purposes, but they disagreed about whether he is a policymaker for Monroe County or for the State of Alabama. The court held that with respect to this particular area at issue, the sheriff represents the State of Alabama, rather than the county, and dismissed the claims against the County.

In Myers v. County of Orange, 157 F.3d 66 (2d Cir.1998), the Court held that the district attorney acted as policymaker for county, rather than for state, in implementing unconstitutional policy against entertaining of criminal cross-complaints, permitting county to be held liable.

PAGE 650:

3. In Board of County Commissioners of Bryan County, Oklahoma v. Brown, 520 U.S. 397, 117 S.Ct. 1382, 137 L.Ed.2d 626 (1997) the Court cautioned that it is not enough for a § 1983 plaintiff merely to identify conduct properly attributable to the municipality. Rather, a plaintiff must also demonstrate that, through its deliberate conduct, the municipality was the "moving force" behind the injury alleged. That is, a plaintiff must show that the municipal action was taken with the requisite degree of culpability and must demonstrate a direct causal link between the municipal action and the deprivation of federal rights. In *Brown*, the Court held that the County was not liable for sheriff's single decision to hire a deputy after an inadequate background check. 520 U.S. at 404, 117 S.Ct. at 1388.

CAVEAT: Brown was a 5–4 decision. Justice Breyer, in his dissenting opinion, notes that "[t]he original principle [behind *Monell*] has generated a body of interpretive law that is so complex that the law has become difficult to apply. Justice Breyer concluded that the Court should "focus upon the continued viability of *Monell* 's distinction between vicarious municipal liability and municipal liability based upon policy and custom." 520 U.S. at 431, 117 S.Ct. at 1401.

In Warner v. Orange County Dept. of Probation, 115 F.3d 1068 (2d Cir.1996), opinion following remand 968 F.Supp. 917 (S.D.N.Y.1997), aff'd 173 F.3d 120 (2d Cir. 1999), the Court held that the county probation department could be found liable for claim that certain conditions of probation violated the First Amendment.

4. Municipal liability under a failure to train theory, pursuant to § 1983, requires, in part, that municipal employees violate or are likely to violate a clearly established federal constitutional right. Townes v. City of New York, 176 F.3d 138 (2d Cir.1999). See also, Thomas v. Roach, 165 F.3d 137 (2d Cir.1999) (insufficient evidence to show that City of Bridgeport had a policy of deliberate indifference that led to plaintiff's injuries).

§ 18.35 Defenses to Federal Actions—*Respondeat Superior*

PAGE 651:

1. Municipality's § 1983 liability for unconstitutional acts of its employees cannot result from a theory of respondeat superior; rather, it can be imposed only if the acts in question were carried out in execution of a government's policy or custom. Thomas v. Roach, supra, § 18.34 note 4.

2. Scotto v. Almenas, 143 F.3d 105 (2d Cir.1998)(Parole division supervisor could not be subjected to § 1983 damages liability based on respondeat superior or on his failure to supervise parole officer adequately).

§ 18.36 Defenses to Federal Actions—Abstention

PAGE 652:

4. *See also* Schlagler v. Phillips, 166 F.3d 439 (2d Cir.1999) (trial court erred by not abstaining from interfering with state prosecution, in accordance with Younger abstention doctrine).

6. *See also* Quackenbush v. Allstate Insurance Co., 517 U.S. 706, 116 S.Ct. 1712, 135 L.Ed.2d 1 (1996) (district court's remand order was an unwarranted application of Burford doctrine); Hachamovitch v. DeBuono, 159 F.3d 687 (2d Cir.1998) (Burford abstention was not warranted).

8. *See also* Fleet Bank v. Burke, 160 F.3d 883 (2d Cir.1998).

§ 18.36   CIVIL RIGHTS LAW   Ch. 18

[Insert as text at end of section, after note 8.]

There is another category of abstention, that was not discussed in the main volume. In *Colorado River Water Conservation Dist. v. United States*,[9] the Supreme Court held that abstention may also be appropriate in cases that do not fit neatly within these traditional categories. Abstention under *Colorado River* applies where state and federal courts exercise concurrent jurisdiction simultaneously. The Supreme Court held that although a pending action in a state court does not generally bar proceedings involving the same matter in a federal court, a federal court may dismiss a federal suit for "reasons of wise judicial administration" where there are "exceptional" circumstances.[10] To determine whether abstention under *Colorado River* is appropriate, a district court is required to weigh six factors, with the balance heavily weighted in favor of the exercise of jurisdiction. The six factors include:

(1) the assumption of jurisdiction by either court over any res or property;

(2) the inconvenience of the federal forum;

(3) the avoidance of piecemeal litigation;

(4) the order in which jurisdiction was obtained;

(5) whether state or federal law supplies the rule of decision; and

(6) whether the state court proceeding will adequately protect the rights of the party seeking to invoke federal jurisdiction.[11]

No single factor is necessarily decisive and the test is not a mechanical checklist.[12]

Also not contained in main volume is a discussion of the *Rooker-Feldman* doctrine. The *Rooker-Feldman* doctrine provides that the lower federal courts lack subject matter jurisdiction over a case if the exercise of jurisdiction over that case would result in the reversal or modification of a state court judgment. Such jurisdiction is lacking because within the federal system, only the Supreme Court may review a state court judgment. The first case to identify this principle was *Rooker v. Fidelity Trust Co.*,[13] where plaintiff sought a declaration from the federal district court that a judgment of the Indiana state court was void because it violated the Contracts Clause. Plaintiff had petitioned the Supreme Court for direct review and been denied, so that the suit represented an end run around direct review. In holding that the district court lacked jurisdiction over the case, the Supreme Court stated that "[u]nder the legislation of Congress, no court of the United States other than this court could entertain a proceeding to reverse or modify the judgment for errors of that character."[14] In *District of Columbia Court of Appeals v. Feldman*,[15] plaintiffs brought separate actions challenging the validity of a rule of the District of Columbia that prevented them from sitting for the District's bar exam. The Supreme Court distinguished between a challenge to the rule governing bar admission and a challenge to a judgment of a state court applying that rule.

Because promulgation of a rule is a non-judicial act, a federal court would have jurisdiction over a general challenge to state bar rules. The court further noted that a federal court lacks jurisdiction over any claims that are inextricably intertwined with a state court's determinations in a judicial proceeding.[16]

On appeal, the Second Circuit reviews a district court's decision to abstain on an abuse of discretion standard.[17]

9. 424 U.S. 800, 817–18, 96 S.Ct. 1236, 1246, 1247, 47 L.Ed.2d 483 (1976).

10. Id.

11. Burnett v. Physician's Online, Inc., 99 F.3d 72, 76 (2d Cir.1996).

12. Id. at 77; see also Village of Westfield v. Welch's, 170 F.3d 116 (2d Cir.1999).

13. 263 U.S. 413, 44 S.Ct. 149, 68 L.Ed. 362 (1923).

14. Id. at 416, 44 S.Ct. at 150.

15. 460 U.S. 462, 103 S.Ct. 1303, 75 L.Ed.2d 206 (1983).

16. Id. at 482 n. 16, 103 S.Ct. at 1315 n. 16.

17. Burnett, supra, note 11.

§ 18.37 Defenses to Federal Actions—*Res Judicata* and Collateral Estoppel

PAGE 653:

1. Hemphill v. Schott, 141 F.3d 412, 416 (2d Cir.1998) (collateral estoppel applies to only those "distinctly put in issue and directly determined" in criminal prosecution.)

2. See also, Rivet v. Regions Bank of Louisiana, 522 U.S. 470, 118 S.Ct. 921, 925, 139 L.Ed.2d 912 (1998);

4. Johnson v. Watkins, 101 F.3d 792 (2d Cir.1996) (collateral estoppel does not preclude arrestee's cause of action for false arrest and malicious prosecution, since defendants do not have the opportunity to obtain review of facts determined in pretrial suppression hearing).

7. See also Matter of Juan C. v. Cortines, 89 N.Y.2d 659, 657 N.Y.S.2d 581, 679 N.E.2d 1061 (1997) (family court prosecution of minor is not entitled to preclusive effect in later proceeding suspending student from school for carrying a weapon due to a lack of identity of the parties).

PAGE 654:

8. Parker v. Blauvelt Volunteer Fire Company, Inc., 93 N.Y.2d 343, 690 N.Y.S.2d 478, 712 N.E.2d 647 (1999) (holding that a § 1983 claim was not prohibited by claim preclusion because the plaintiff could not have sought damages in his prior Article 78 proceeding arising out of the same facts); Hachamovitch v. DeBuono, 159 F.3d 687 (2d Cir.1998) (§ 1983 action is not barred where a plaintiff has previously brought an Article 78 proceeding to challenge administrative action).

§ 18.38 Defenses to Federal Actions—Statute of Limitations

PAGE 654:

1. See also Ormiston v. Nelson, 117 F.3d 69 (2d Cir.1997) (§ 1983 actions in New York are governed by New York's three-year statute of limitations for unspecified personal injury actions).

3. In Tapia–Ortiz v. Doe, 171 F.3d 150 (2d Cir.1999), the court held that plaintiff's failure, until two years after the statute of limitations expired, to name specifically in his complaint the officers who allegedly violated his rights was fatal to his claim.

§ 18.38   CIVIL RIGHTS LAW   Ch. 18

PAGE 655:

[Add note 3.1 to sentence after note 3.]

3.1 Covington v. City of New York, 171 F.3d 117 (2d Cir.1999).

5. In Black v. Coughlin, 76 F.3d 72, 75 (2d Cir.1996), the Second Circuit held that a cause of action under § 1983 for the denial of due process in a prison disciplinary hearing accrues at the time that a prisoner succeeds in having the disciplinary ruling reversed in state court. Similarly, in Heck v. Humphrey, 512 U.S. 477, 114 S.Ct. 2364, 129 L.Ed.2d 383 (1994), the Court held that a § 1983 cause of action for damages attributable to an unconstitutional conviction or sentence does not accrue until the conviction or sentence has been invalidated.

See also Ormiston v. Nelson, *supra* note 1 (when a § 1983 action is brought for involuntary medical or psychiatric confinement, the accrual date will depend upon the claimant's condition during confinement and whether patient was able to comprehend his loss of liberty).

[Insert as text at end of section.]

The Second Circuit has held that the equitable defense of laches does not bar a legal claim for damages under § 1983 that is otherwise timely filed.[9]

9. Ivani Contracting Corp. v. City of New York, 103 F.3d 257 (2d Cir.), cert. denied, 520 U.S. 1211, 117 S.Ct. 1695, 137 L.Ed.2d 821 (1997).

§ 18.45 Housing—Prohibition Against Discrimination in Private Housing—Owners and Lessors

PAGE 659:

4. See also Levin v. Yeshiva Univ., 180 Misc.2d 829, 691 N.Y.S.2d 280 (Sup.Ct., N.Y. County, 1999) (University's policy of restricting occupancy in university housing to students and their spouses and not to students and non-married partners did not discriminate against homosexuals).

[Add to text after note 4.]

It is unlawful for landlords to discriminate against someone solely because that individual has children.[4.1]

4.1 Filicore v. Jossel, 173 Misc.2d 42, 660 N.Y.S.2d 786 (Sup.Ct., N.Y. County, 1997) (upholding the constitutionality of Real Property Law § 236, which provides that a building owner or agent who either refuses to rent or later sets unfair conditions based on the fact that the tenant has a child or children is guilty of a misdemeanor and is subject to civil damages).

§ 18.46 Housing—Prohibition Against Discrimination in Private Housing—Real Estate Agents and Brokers

PAGE 661:

[Insert paragraph at end of section.]

Real estate brokers who are themselves the victims of discrimination may recover damages as well.[5.1]

5.1 See, e.g., Feggoudakis v. New York State Div. of Human Rights, 230 A.D.2d 739, 646 N.Y.S.2d 175 (2d Dep't 1996). In Feggoudakis, the owner of real property was found to have discriminated against a prospective purchaser, who is black, by refusing to sell to her. The realtor who represented the prospective purchaser, who is also black, was also found to be a victim of petitioner's discrimination, and upheld SDHR award of $5,000 in compensatory damages and $2,500 in punitive damages.

§ 18.47 Housing—Prohibition Against Discrimination in Private Housing—Cooperatives

PAGE 662:

[*Insert before first full paragraph.*]

Cooperatives are also liable for failure to approve a prospective subtenant for discriminatory reasons.[2.1]

2.1 Broome v. Biondi, 17 F.Supp.2d 211 (S.D.N.Y.1997).

3. *See also* § 18.50, n. 2.1.

§ 18.49 Housing—Prohibition Against Discrimination in Private Housing—Remedies for Discrimination—Administrative Proceedings

PAGE 663:

4. A 1997 amendment to § 297(3)(c) provides that the Division may, subject to judicial review, "dismiss the complaint on the grounds of untimeliness if the complaint is untimely or on the grounds that the election of remedies is annulled."

§ 18.50 Housing—Prohibition Against Discrimination in Private Housing—Remedies for Discrimination—Actions in State and Federal Court

PAGE 666:

2. *See also* Broome v. Biondi, 17 F.Supp.2d 211 (S.D.N.Y.1997). The Broomes, an interracial couple who were the proposed subtenants of a cooperative apartment, and the owner of the cooperative apartment, claimed the cooperative discriminated against the Broomes in denying their request to sublease. After a jury trial, the jury awarded the Broomes $230,000 in compensatory damages and $410,000 in punitive damages on their discrimination claims under the Federal Fair Housing Act and the New York Human Rights Law. The apartment owner was awarded $100,000 in compensatory damages (which was later reduced by the court to $25,310) and $57,000 in punitive damages on her Federal Fair Housing Act and New York Human Rights Law retaliation claims; $5,000 in compensatory damages on her breach of contract claim, $1,000 in compensatory damages and $5,000 in punitive damages on her breach of fiduciary claim; and $1,000 in compensatory damages and $5,000 in punitive damages on her claim for tortious interference with the performance of a contract.

[*Insert as text before first full paragraph.*]

It is now well established that landlords and owners must make reasonable accommodations for tenants with disabilities. Whether a requested accommodation is "reasonable" is fact specific, and must be determined on a case-by-case basis.[2.1]

2.1 In Hubbard v. Samson Management, 994 F.Supp. 187 (S.D.N.Y.1998), a disabled tenant commenced an action for damages and injunctive relief after her request for a free parking space was denied. The landlord had proposed to designate a fee-paid parking space for the tenant. The

§ 18.50   CIVIL RIGHTS LAW   Ch. 18

court held the landlord's proposal did not constitute reasonable accommodation. But, in Rodriguez v. 551 West 157th St. Owners Corp., 992 F.Supp. 385 (S.D.N.Y.1998), the court held that construction of wheelchair ramp or lift on existing building for four mobility-impaired tenants was not "reasonable accommodation" under federal Fair Housing Act, where installation would cost landlord $25,000 to $55,000, and landlord had incurred financial losses in operation of building over past three years.

§ 18.51 Housing—*Prima Facie* Case and Burden of Proof

PAGE 667:

[*Insert note 2.1 at end of sentence following note 2.*]

2.1 *See* Fine v. Berman, 238 A.D.2d 220, 657 N.Y.S.2d 6 (1st Dep't 1997) (Board of Directors had valid reasons for not approving plaintiff's application, including his admittedly untruthful answers on his application form, his persistent tardiness in paying rent to his present landlord and his lack of any apparent assets, which were legitimate, non-discriminatory reasons for the Board's determination and were not pretext for discrimination based on sexual orientation).

[*Insert after text in main volume.*]

    In stating a claim under the Federal Fair Housing Act, 42 U.S.C.A. § 3601, *et seq.*, plaintiff need allege only discriminatory effect and need not show that the decision complained of was made with discriminatory intent.

4. *See* Soules v. United States Department of Housing and Urban Development, 967 F.2d 817, 822 (2d Cir.1992).

§ 18.52 Housing—Summary of Procedure for Filing an Administrative Claim and Challenging an SDHR Order

PAGE 668:

4. A 1997 amendment to § 297(3)(c) provides that the Division may, subject to judicial review, "dismiss the complaint on the grounds of untimeliness if the complaint is untimely or on the grounds that the election of remedies is annulled."

§ 18.53 Education

PAGE 670:

5. *See also*, Mrs. B. v. Milford Board of Educ., 103 F.3d 1114 (2d Cir.1997)(State must fund student's placement in residential facility).

[*Add to text following note 6.*]

    Attorneys' fees are available to the prevailing party.[6.1]

6.1 *See* G.M. v. New Britain Board of Educ., 173 F.3d 77 (2d Cir.1999). The court in G.M. clarified the standards for determining when plaintiffs are prevailing parties under the IDEA, and held that plaintiffs are still entitled to attorneys' fees even if they settle a case and make concessions during the settlement process.

PAGE 671:

[*Add to text before first full paragraph.*]

In *Davis v. Monroe County Board of Education*,[7.1] the Supreme Court held that school districts may be held liable for sexual harassment of one student by another under Title IX. To hold the school district liable, students must show that a school official who had the authority to take corrective action knew about the alleged harassment and failed to take appropriate corrective action.

7.1 ___ U.S. ___, ___ S.Ct. ___, ___ L.Ed.2d ___ (1999).

8. The district court decision in Brzonkala was heard by the Fourth Circuit en banc. The Fourth Circuit declared the law unconstitutional in March 1999 in a 7–4 decision. 169 F.3d 820 (4th Cir.1999). In Ericson v. Syracuse Univ., 45 F.Supp.2d 344 (S.D.N.Y.1999), the court upheld the VAWA, rejecting the Fourth Circuit's conclusion in Brzonkala. It is expected that Brzonkala will be heard by the Supreme Court.

§ 18.54 Equal Rights in Places of Public Accommodation and Amusement

PAGE 672:

[*Insert at end of first paragraph of footnote.*]

4. See also D'Amico v. Commodities Exchange, Inc., 235 A.D.2d 313, 652 N.Y.S.2d 294 (1st Dep't 1997) (trading floor of commodities exchange was a "place of public accommodation" within meaning of Human Rights Law).

PAGE 673:

4. Cahill v. Rosa, 89 N.Y.2d 14, 651 N.Y.S.2d 344, 674 N.E.2d 274 (1996), discussed in the main volume, was decided together with Cahill v. Rosa [Lasser v. Rosa], 89 N.Y.2d 14, 651 N.Y.S.2d 344, 674 N.E.2d 274 (1996). On remand following the Court of Appeals' decision, the Second Department held in Cahill that the SDHR's finding of discrimination was supported by substantial evidence, and confirmed the award of $10,000 to the complainant. Cahill v. Rosa, 235 A.D.2d 534, 653 N.Y.S.2d 854 (2d Dep't), lv. denied 90 N.Y.2d 801, 660 N.Y.S.2d 554, 683 N.E.2d 19 (1997). In Lasser, the Second Department found that the administrative determination that the dentist had discriminated against patient based on HIV status was not supported by substantial evidence. Lasser v. Rosa, 237 A.D.2d 361, 654 N.Y.S.2d 822 (2d Dep't 1997).

§ 18.55 Equal Rights in Places of Public Accommodation and Amusement—General Provisions

PAGE 674:

[*Insert in "CAVEAT" before citation to Harvey*].

7. See also Whiting v. The Incorporated Village of Old Brookville, 8 F.Supp.2d 202 (S.D.N.Y.1998) (failure to notify Attorney General of Civil Rights Law § 40–c claim required dismissal of the claim)

§ 18.57 Equal Rights in Places of Public Accommodation and Amusement—Persons With Disabilities Accompanied by a Guide Dog, Hearing Dog or Service Dog

PAGE 675:

1. *See also* Albert v. Solimon, 252 A.D.2d 139, 684 N.Y.S.2d 375 (4th Dep't 1998) (examination room in medical office is not a "public facility" under Civil Rights Law § 47). In Albert, a 3–2 decision, the court upheld dismissal of plaintiff's claim of discrimination based on physician's conduct of ordering patient's service dog to leave the examination room. The court relied heavily on Perino, which it noted was the only other reported case involving this section of the Civil Rights Law.

The dissent in Albert would have reversed that part of the decision with respect to Civil Rights Law § 47, noting that the appropriate inquiry is whether the medical office is a public facility.

PRACTICE POINTER: The decision in Perino and the majority decision in Albert are instructive, in that both decisions recognize that the same building may have both a public and private facility under the same roof.

§ 18.60 Employment Discrimination Provisions Exclusive to the New York Civil Rights Law—In General

PAGE 677:

5. Section 44–a does not provide a private cause of action. Whiting v. The Incorporated Village of Old Brookville, 8 F.Supp.2d 202, 212 (S.D.N.Y.1998).

§ 18.64 Right of Privacy—Generally

PAGE 680:

1. A 1995 amendment substituted "name, portrait, picture or voice" for references to "name, portrait or picture." The amendment overrules Maxwell v. N.W. Ayer, Inc., 159 Misc.2d 454, 605 N.Y.S.2d 174 (Sup. Ct., N.Y. County, 1993).

PAGE 681:

10. *See also* Grodin v. Liberty Cable, 244 A.D.2d 153, 664 N.Y.S.2d 276 (1st Dep't 1997) (where defendant made no effort to obtain plaintiff's consent to the reuse of plaintiff's image and voice, plaintiff was not subject to provisions of Screen Actors Guild agreement waiving protections under §§ 50 and 51).

PAGE 682:

15. *See also* Abdelrazig v. Essence Communications, Inc., 225 A.D.2d 498, 639 N.Y.S.2d 811 (1st Dep't 1996) (claim that publication of article and plaintiff's photograph wearing traditional African garb was really an "advertisement in disguise" is too speculative to withstand summary judgment motion) . .

16. *See also* Grodin v. Liberty Cable, 244 A.D.2d 153, 664 N.Y.S.2d 276 (1st Dep't 1997) (question of fact as to whether reuse of plaintiff's likeness was too incidental to afford any viable breach of privacy claims).

§ 18.65 Right of Privacy—Police Officers, Corrections Officers and Firefighters

PAGE 683:

[Add to text after note 4.]

In Matter of Daily Gazette Co. v. City of Schenectady,[4.1] the Court of Appeals held that disclosure of records is not limited to requests made in the context of actual or potential litigation. Rather, the Court reiterated that "the decisive factor in determining whether an officer's personnel record was exempted from FOIL disclosure under Civil Rights Law § 50-a was the potential use of the information contained therein, not the specific purpose of the particular individual requesting access, nor whether the request was actually made in contemplation of litigation."[4.2]

4.1 93 N.Y.2d 145, 688 N.Y.S.2d 472, 710 N.E.2d 1072 (1999).

4.2 93 N.Y.2d at 156, 688 N.Y.S.2d at 477. After reviewing the factors, the Court held that the requested records were exempt from disclosure under § 50-a.

§ 18.66 Right of Privacy—Victims of Sex Offenses

PAGE 685:

[Add new paragraph after second paragraph of section.]

When a victim voluntarily discloses his or her identity, the victim waives his or her right to nondisclosure under § 50-b.[3.1]

3.1 Feeney v. City of New York, 255 A.D.2d 483, 680 N.Y.S.2d 646 (2d Dep't 1998).

§ 18.70 Changing One's Name—Procedure for Petition to Change Name—Special Procedures for Infants

PAGE 687:

4. See Matter of Mercado v. Townsend, 225 A.D.2d 555, 638 N.Y.S.2d 762 (2d Dep't 1996), where Second Department reversed the judgment granting the father of an infant born out-of-wedlock to change the child's surname to his. The court determined that the child's retention of his surname, which he shared with his mother and half-brother, "might minimize embarrassment, harassment, and confusion in school and social contacts." 225 A.D.2d at 556, 638 N.Y.S.2d at 763.

§ 18.74 Heart Balm Statute

PAGE 689:

1. See also Sahid v. Chambers, 237 A.D.2d 175, 655 N.Y.S.2d 20 (1st Dep't 1997). In Sahid, a father brought an action against his children's psychiatrists, alleging that defendants conspired with his ex-wife to "brainwash" the children against him so as to deprive him of his right to visitation. The court upheld dismissal of the complaint, noting that the pleading "alleges nothing more than alienation of affections, which is expressly prohibited by Civil Rights Law § 80-a."

§ 18.76 Heart Balm Statute—Action for Return of Gifts Made in Contemplation of Marriage

PAGE 690:

3. See also Raji v. Nejad, 256 A.D.2d 12, 680 N.Y.S.2d 520 (1st Dep't 1998). Mr. Raji was married at the time the gifts—a condominium, some jewelry, a luxury car, cash and furnishings—had been given to defendant. Although defendant ended the engagement, the First Department upheld dismissal of the action on the ground that plaintiff was married at the time the gifts were made. The lower court took judicial notice of the contents of its own files to determine that plaintiff's divorce judgment was not signed until after the gifts had been given.

5. See also Leshowitz v. Conklin, 245 A.D.2d 343, 665 N.Y.S.2d 593 (2d Dep't 1997) (affirming judgment of $17,095 for value of ring after termination of engagement).

§ 18.80 Miscellaneous Rights and Immunities—Frivolous Litigation—Protection From SLAPP Suits

PAGE 693:

2. See Ansonia Associates Limited Partnership v. Ansonia Tenants' Coalition, 253 A.D.2d 706, 677 N.Y.S.2d 575 (1st Dep't 1998). In Ansonia, the First Department held that defendants' conduct in disturbing visitors to a condominium project for the purpose of discourage sales or rentals of apartments was not protected speech and that plaintiffs' action was not a SLAPP suit.

§ 18.82 Miscellaneous Rights and Immunities—Libel and Slander—Defenses

PAGE 695:

1. See also Posner v. New York Law Publishing Co., 228 A.D.2d 318, 644 N.Y.S.2d 227 (1st Dep't) (cartoon was constitutionally protected comment on a subject of public commentary, and was constitutionally protected opinion), lv denied, 89 N.Y.2d 805, 653 N.Y.S.2d 917, 676 N.E.2d 499 (1996).

PAGE 696:

5. See also Foster v. Churchill, 87 N.Y.2d 744, 642 N.Y.S.2d 583, 665 N.E.2d 153 (1996) (common interest privilege).

§ 18.83 Miscellaneous Rights and Immunities—Breast Feeding

PAGE 697:

[add the following paragraph.]

Currently, there is no provision requiring employers to provide reasonable accommodation to women engaged in breastfeeding or breast pumping. No cause of action lies under either Title VII of the Civil Rights Act of 1964, as amended, or under the Americans with Disabilities Act for an employer's failure to accommodate a woman's need to breastfeed or use a breast pump.[2]

2. *See* Martinez v. N.B.C. Inc., 49 F.Supp.2d 305 (S.D.N.Y.1999). The court in *Martinez* noted that Minnesota law, unlike New York law, requires employers to reasonably accommodate breast pumping. Minn.St.Ann.§ 181.939 (West 1998).

§ 18.84 Miscellaneous Rights and Immunities—Suspension of Rights Due to Imprisonment

PAGE 698:

2. In Hillard v. Clark, 254 A.D.2d 756, 677 N.Y.S.2d 857 (4th Dep't 1998), the court held that §§ 79(2) and 79–a[2] does not bar inmates from making and seeking to enforce FOIL requests.

4. An inmate may validly enter into marriage up to imposition of sentence, or while on parole, or after discharge from parole. People v. Smith, 227 A.D.2d 655, 641 N.Y.S.2d 905 (3d Dep't 1996).

§ 18.85 Miscellaneous Rights and Immunities—Shield Law

PAGE 699:

9. For a case in which the privilege was overcome, *see* Matter of Grand Jury Subpoenas Served On National Broadcasting Co., 178 Misc.2d 1052, 683 N.Y.S.2d 708 (Sup. Ct., N.Y. County, 1998). The court held that prosecutors had met their burden of showing that outtakes were highly material and relevant, were critical to assertion of charges against demonstrators who had injured officers, and were not obtainable from any alternative source, so as to compel disclosure of outtakes.

§ 18.86 Miscellaneous Rights and Immunities—Performing Abortion

PAGE 700:

[*Add the following paragraph.*]

Section 79–i is a criminal statute, and does not provide a private right of action for retaliatory discharge by medical personnel who are fired for refusing to participate in an abortion.[1]

1. Larson v. Albany Medical Center, 252 A.D.2d 936, 676 N.Y.S.2d 293, 295 (3d Dep't 1998). The court did, however, allow plaintiffs to raise a claim of violation of Executive Law § 296(1)(a), forbidding termination due to religious beliefs, even thought the claim was not raised in the trial court.

[*Add the Following New Section in text.*]

§ 18.86a Miscellaneous Rights and Immunities—Confidentiality of Records of Genetic Tests

In 1996, the New York Legislature adopted a new section of the Civil Rights Law, § 79–*l*, which concerns the confidentiality of genetic tests. The statute was then amended the next year. The statute provides that written informed consent is necessary before a genetic test taken from an individual may be performed. All records, findings and results of any genetic test performed on a person are deemed confidential, and cannot be disclosed without the written informed consent of the person to whom such test relates. The penalties for violation of these provisions are a civil fine of not more than $1,000 or, for a willful

§ 18.86a

violation, a fine of not more than $5,000 or imprisonment of not more than ninety days, or both.

Chapter 19

IMMIGRATION AND NATIONALITY LAW PERMANENT RESIDENCE APPLICATIONS

by
David Grunblatt
and
Roxanne Levine

Table of Sections

19.4	Overview of the U.S. Immigration System
19.9	Family–Based Immigration—Family Preference Categories
19.10	____ Qualifying as a Relation
19.11	____ Qualifying as a Relation—"Child" and "Parent" Issues
19.12	____ Qualifying as a Relation—"Marriage" Issues
19.14	____ Petitioning Procedure and Documentation—I–130 Petition
19.16	____ Abused Spouse and Children
19.21	Employment–Based Immigration—First Employment Preference Applicants (Priority Workers)—Managerial or Executive Intracompany Transferees
19.25	____ Second Employment Preference Applicants—The Role of "National Interest"
19.29	____ I–140 Petition, Procedures and Documentation
19.32	____ Labor Certification—Procedures
19.41	____ Fourth Employment Preference Applicants—Religious Workers and Ministers
19.43	____ Fifth Employment Preference Applicants (Immigrant Investors)—Petition Procedures and Requirements
19.50	Special Categories—Asylum and Refugee Status
19.51	Applying for Permanent Residence
19.52	____ Grounds for Inadmissibility
19.55	Affidavits of Support
19.56	Applying for Permanent Residence—Immigrant Visa Processing—Checklist of Required Documents
19.59	____ Immigrant Visa Processing—Special Requirements of Section 245(i)
19.63	____ Adjustment of Status—Completion of the Process
19.65	____ Adjustment of Status—Checklist
19.79	Forms—Form OF–230

Westlaw Electronic Research

See Westlaw Electronic Research Guide preceding the Summary of Contents.

§ 19.4 IMMIGRATION AND NATIONALITY LAW Ch. 19

§ 19.4 Overview of the U.S. Immigration System

PAGE 741:

[*Re-write second sentence of section as follows.*]

Permanent residents of the U.S. are issued the so-called "green card," properly known as a permanent resident card.

[*Replace note 2 with the following.*]

2. 63 Fed.Reg. 70313 (Dec. 21, 1998).

§ 19.9 Family–Based Immigration—Family Preference Categories

PAGE 750:

[*Re-write last paragraph as follows.*]

In general, when status is sought on the basis of the petitioner's U.S. citizenship, or lawful permanent resident status, an unexpired U.S. passport, birth certificate establishing that the petitioner was born in the U.S., certificate of citizenship or certificate of naturalization, lawful permanent resident ("Green Card") forms I–151 or I–551, or other proof given by the INS that evidences the petitioner's lawful status is generally accepted to establish eligibility of a petitioner to qualify the beneficiary for immigration benefits.

§ 19.10 Family–Based Immigration—Qualifying as a Relation

PAGE 752:

[*Last full paragraph on page amended as follows.*]

Petitions involving children legitimated through the marriage of their parents must include proof that the marriage took place before the child turned 18. If legitimation was based on changes in the law, the change must have taken place before the child turned 18. If based upon the law in the father's place of residence, the INS position is that the father must have moved to that jurisdiction before the child turned 18.[12]

[*Add to end of note 13.*]

13. 8 C.F.R. § 204.2(d)(2)(i), (ii), (iii).

PAGE 753:

[*Add to end of note 14.*]

14. The BIA discusses the standard of proof required in Matter of Vizcaino, 19 I & N Dec. 644, 1988 WL 235455 (BIA 1988) and Matter of Pineda, Int. Dec. 3112 (BIA 1989). The Immigration Service has adopted these standards in their regulations at 8 C.F.R. § 204.2(d)(2)(iii).

§ 19.11 Family–Based Immigration—Qualifying as a Relation—"Child" and "Parent" Issues

PAGE 755:

[*Add to end of note 12.*]

12. An illegitimate child who has not been legitimated may be treated as a child for immigration purposes. The INA has been amended to substitute the term "child born out of wedlock" for "illegitimate child." INA § 101(b)(2); 8 U.S.C.A. § 1101(b)(2).

[*Add to end of note 13.*]

13. 8 C.F.R. § 204.2(f)(ii).

§ 19.12 Family–Based Immigration—Qualifying as a Relation—"Marriage" Issues

PAGE 759:

[*Replace last paragraph with the following.*].

Widows and widowers of U.S. citizens may file a petition and be classified as an immediate relative under section 201(b) of the Immigration and Nationality Act if:

(i) He or she has been married for at least two years to a United States citizen. (Note: the United States citizen is not required to have had the status of United States citizen for the entire two year period, but must have been a United States citizen at the time of death.)

(ii) The petition is filed within two years of the death of the citizen spouse or before November 29, 1992, if the citizen spouse died before November 29 1990;

(iii) The alien petitioner and the citizen spouse were not legally separated at the time of the citizen's death; and

(iv) The alien spouse has not remarried.

If a petition is submitted by the widow or widower of a deceased citizen, it must be accompanied by evidence of citizenship of the United States citizen and primary evidence, if available, of the relationship in the form of a marriage certificate issued by civil authorities, proof of the termination of all prior marriages of both husband and wife, and the United States citizen's death certificate issued by civil authorities. To determine the availability of primary documents, the Service will refer to the Department of State's Foreign Affairs Manual (FAM). When the FAM shows that primary documents are generally available in the country at issue but the petitioner claims that his or her document is unavailable, a letter from the appropriate registrar stating that the document is not available will be required before the Service will accept secondary evidence. Secondary evidence will be evaluated for its authenticity and credibility. Secondary evidence may include:

§ 19.12   IMMIGRATION AND NATIONALITY LAW   Ch. 19

(i) Such evidence of the marriage and termination of prior marriages as religious documents, tribal records, censure records, or affidavits; and

(ii) Such evidence of the United States citizen's death as religious documents, funeral service records, obituaries, or affidavits. Affidavits submitted as secondary evidence pursuant to paragraphs (b)(2)(i) and (b)(2)(ii) of this section must be sworn to or affirmed by people who have personal knowledge of the event to which they attest. Each affidavit should contain the full name and address, date and place of birth of the person making the affidavit and his or her relationship, if any, to the widow or widower. Any such affidavit must contain complete information and details explaining how knowledge of the event was acquired.

(4) *Derivative beneficiaries.* A child of an alien widow or widower classified as an immediate relative is eligible for derivative classification as an immediate relative. Such a child may be included in the principal alien's immediate relative visa petition, and may accompany or follow to join the principal alien to the United States. Derivative benefits do not extend to an unmarried or married son or daughter of an alien widow or widower.[12]

[*Replace note 12 with the following.*]

12. 8 C.F.R. § 204.2(b)

[*Delete note 13.*]

§ 19.14   Family–Based Immigration—Petitioning Procedure and Documentation—I–130 Petition

PAGE 760:

[*Replace note 1 with the following.*]

1. 8 C.F.R. § 204.2(d)(4)

§ 19.16   Family–Based Immigration—Abused Spouse and Children

PAGE 769:

[*Replace final paragraph of section with the following.*]

INS regulations outlining procedures for qualifying for favorable treatment and to obtain a positive adjudication of an abused spouse petition, as well as procedures for denial and appeal can be found at 8 C.F.R. § 204.2(c).

§ 19.21 Employment–Based Immigration—First Employment Preference Applicants (Priority Workers)—Managerial or Executive Intracompany Transferees

PAGE 775:

[Add to note 10.]

10. Where partnerships organized in the United States provide accounting services under an internationally recognized name pursuant to an agreement with a worldwide coordinating organization owned and controlled by member accounting firms, and a partnership or similar organization is organized outside the United States to provide accounting services, it must be considered an affiliate of the U.S. partnership if it markets its accounting services under the same internationally recognized name. P.L. 101-649, Title II, § 206(a), 104 Stat. 5022 (November 29, 1990).

§ 19.25 Employment Based Immigration—Second Employment Preference Applicants—The Role of "National Interest"

PAGE 777:

[Replace entire section.]

An alien may self-petition in the Second Employment–Based Category provided that he can establish that through the grant of lawful permanent resident status he or she will "substantially benefit prospectively the national economy, cultural or educational interests, or welfare of the United States."[1] This provision permits the waiver of the job offer—or labor certification—requirement. In this instance, the waiver is available not only in the case of persons of exceptional ability but to professionals with an advanced degree as well. The term "national interest" is not defined in the statute and the INS has declined to define it in regulations, preferring instead to adjudicate applications on a case-by-case basis. Considerably more evidence must therefore be presented to prove a substantial prospective benefit to the welfare of the U.S. by granting permanent residence to the alien.[2]

The INS has provided some direction as to the "national interest" factor in a series of non-precedent decision and has developed a non-exclusive test of national interest for aliens of exceptional ability in business, listing seven relevant factors.[3] Specifically, the improvement of the U.S. economy, wages and working conditions of U.S. workers; improvement of education and training programs for U.S. children and under-qualified workers; improvement of health care; provision of more affordable housing; improving the environment; making more productive use of natural resources; or a request from an interested U.S. government agency, will generally merit consideration for a "national interest" waiver.[4]

Most recently, the Administrative Appeals Unit ("A.A.U.") of the Immigration Service designated its first precedent decision governing petitions requesting national interest waivers of the labor certification requirement. In Re New York State Department of Transportation

§ 19.25 IMMIGRATION AND NATIONALITY LAW Ch. 19

(NYSDOT),[4.1] the A.A.U. developed a three-pronged test outlining eligibility for aliens to obtain national interest waivers:

- The beneficiary must seek to work in an area of "substantial intrinsic merit";
- The beneficiary's work must have a benefit which will be "national in scope";
- The beneficiary must "serve the national interest to a substantially greater degree than would an available U.S. worker have the same minimum qualifications."

The Immigration Service further states that in evaluating an individual's prospective benefit, it will also consider whether the alien's past record justifies projections of future benefits to the national interest and whether the alien will serve the national interest to a substantially greater degree than would an available U.S. worker possessing the same minimum qualifications.

This decision, given the difficulty for individuals to meet its high standards, has placed a chill on the national interest visa category. By default, it is forcing petitioning employers and aliens to file extraordinary worker petitions, and to fall back to the traditional labor certification process as a means by which aliens can qualify for permanent resident status. It remains to be seen whether the A.A.U. decision will be challenged in federal court or will be modified by future Immigration Service regulations, to date not issued.

In order to request exemption from the labor certification requirement, an I–140 petition would be submitted, along with documentation to establish that the alien qualifies for the national interest waiver.[5]

1. INA § 203(b)(2)(B), 8 U.S.C.A. § 1153(b)(2)(B), as enacted by IA90 § 121(a) as amended by § 302(b)(2)(D), Miscellaneous and Technical Immigration and Naturalization Service Amendments of 1991 (MTINA), Pub.L.No. 102–232, 105 Stat. 1733, effectively extending to professionals the waiver provision that IA90 had confined to persons of exceptional ability.

2. See INS Commentary on Regulations, 56 Fed.Reg. 60897, 60900 (Nov. 29, 1991).

PRACTICE POINTER: It would also be advisable for the attorney seeking information on such decisions to check the American Immigration Lawyers Association monthly publication, for unpublished decisions, or to consult with colleagues in assessing what might constitute a meritorious "national interest" case.

3. See Matter of (no name provided), (NSC), A71 940 352 (AAU Nov. 30, 1992); Matter of (no name provided), (NSC), A70 537 406 (AAU Dec. 1, 1992).

4. 70 Int.Rel. 773 (June 14, 1993).

4.1 Int. Dec. #3363. In re New York State Dept. of Transportation (Acting Associate Commissioner, Programs), August 7, 1998

5. See § 19.30 infra for an I–140 checklist.

§ 19.29 Employment–Based Immigration—I–140 Petition, Procedures and Documentation

PAGE 780:

[Replace note 1 with the following.]

1. Eastern Region
Vermont Service Center
75 Lower Welden Street

St. Albans, VT 05479–0001
Tel: (802) 527–3160

States Falling Within Jurisdiction:

Connecticut	Pennsylvania
Delaware	Puerto Rico
District of Columbia	Rhode Island
Maine	Vermont
Massachusetts	Virginia
New Hampshire	Virgin Islands
New Jersey	West Virginia
New York	

Northern Region

Mail: Nebraska Service Center
P.O. Box 82521
Lincoln, NE 68501–2521

Overnight Delivery:

United States Department of Justice
Immigration and Naturalization Service
Lincoln Service Center
850 "S" Street
Lincoln, NE 68508
(402) 437–5218

States Falling Within Jurisdiction

Idaho	Nebraska
Illinois	North Dakota
Indiana	Ohio
Iowa	Oregon
Kansas	South Dakota
Michigan	Utah
Minnesota	Washington State
Missouri	Wisconsin
Montana	Wyoming

Southern Region

Mail: Southern Service Center
P.O. Box 152122, Dept. A
Irving, TX 75015–2122

Overnight Delivery:
Southern Service Center
7701 N. Stemmons Freeway
Dallas, TX 75257
(214) 767–7769/7773
Fax: (214) 767–7404

States Falling Within Jurisdiction

Alabama	New Mexico
Arkansas	North Carolina
Florida	Oklahoma
Georgia	South Carolina
Kentucky	Tennessee
Louisiana	Texas
Mississippi	

Western Region

mail: Western Service Center
P.O. Box 30111
Laguna Niguel, CA 92677–8011

Overnight delivery:
Western Service Center
2400 Avila Road
2nd Floor, Room 2304
Laguna Niguel, CA 92677
Attn: Incoming Mail
Phone:
Fax: (714) 643–6120

States Falling Within Jurisdiction

Arizona	Hawaii
California	Nevada
Guam	

§ 19.32   Employment–Based Immigration—Labor Certification—Procedures

PAGE 784:

[Replace note 1 with the following]

1. In New York, all labor certification applications are filed with: State of New York, Department of Labor, Alien Labor Certification, P.O. Box 703, New York, NY 10014–0703. The Department of Labor, in October 1996, issued substantial revisions to the labor certification process under the terms of General Administrative Letter (GAL) 1–97. These changes generally involve an advance recruitment effort by the employer and a determination by the State Employment Security Agency ("SESA") as to the bona fides of the application in general, as outlined in § 19.33—19.36, infra. Should the SESA determine that the employer, prior to the filing of the labor certification, has made a bona fide effort to locate workers and failed to locate same, it will expedite the labor certification process. The employer, in these circumstances, would request a reduction in recruitment (known as "RIR") evidencing that it has, for a period of at least six months prior to filing, conducted recruitment in a pattern

§ 19.32 IMMIGRATION AND NATIONALITY LAW Ch. 19

conforming to, and meeting Department of Labor regulations. GAL 1–97 also contains provisions for a "limited review" of cases and will "fast track" such cases where the case is considered clearly approvable. Given the extensive delays experienced at State Labor Department offices nationwide, this process, known colloquially as "RIR," adds a new alternative for expediting the labor certification process and securing an approved labor certification on behalf of your client.

§ 19.41 Employment–Based Immigration—Fourth Employment Preference Applicants—Religious Workers and Ministers

PAGE 794:

[Add to end of first full paragraph, following note referent 3 in the text.]

The Religious Workers Act of 1997 (Pub.L.No. 105–54, 111 Stat 1175, Oct. 6, 1997) states that current legislation has extended the permanent religious worker provisions of the Immigration and Nationality Act to September 30, 2000.

§ 19.43 Employment–Based Immigrants—Fifth Employment Preference Applicants (Immigrant Investors)—Petition Procedures and Requirements

PAGE 796:

[Add to end of note 4.]

4. The Administrative Appeals Unit ("A.A.U.") has recently issued four precedent decisions involving immigrant investors which significantly tighten eligibility requirements for the immigrant investor and make it extremely difficult, if not financially infeasible to meet its more stringent requirements. Int. Dec. 3359, Matter of Soffici (Comm. June 30, 1998); Int. Dec. 3360, Matter of Immuzi (Comm. July 13, 1998), Int. Dec. 3361, Matter of Hsiung (Assoc. Comm. July 31, 1998); and Int. Dec. 3362, Matter of Ho (Assoc. Comm. July 31, 1998).

[Replace last paragraph with the following.]

Petitions to establish qualification as an immigrant investor are filed on Form I–526 with the required documentation to the Texas Service Center. Petitions by this Center will be accepted from clients filing nationwide.[8]

[Replace note 8 with the following.]

8. Notice, 63 Fed.Reg. 67135 (December 4, 1998).

§ 19.50 Special Categories—Asylum and Refugee Status

PAGE 802:

[Insert new paragraph after note referent 6 in the text.]

The Illegal Immigration Reform and Immigrant Responsibility Act of 1996 (IIRAIRA)[6.1] added significant changes to both procedural and substantive aspects of asylum applications and withholding of removal proceedings. The new statute makes it extremely difficult to achieve asylum. Asylum applicants arriving at a port of entry with fraudulent documents or lacking documents may be summarily excluded unless they can prove a credible fear of persecution.[6.2] Noncitizens who knowingly file fictitious claims for asylum will be barred from future immigration benefits. Asylum applicants are further mandated to file asylum claims within one year of arrival in the United States unless their home country conditions have changed or due to extraordinary circumstances.[6.3]

6.1 Illegal Immigration Reform and Immigrant Responsibility Act of 1996 (IIRAIRA) enacted as Division C of The Omnibus Consolidated Appropriations Act of 1996, Pub.L.No. 104–208, 110 Stat. 3009.

6.2 8 CFR § 208.30.

6.3 8 CFR § 208.4(a)(5).

§ 19.51 Applying for Permanent Residence

PAGE 803:

[In paragraph 4, replace "exclusionary grounds" in the last sentence to]

grounds of inadmissibility

[Re-write section title as follows.]

§ 19.52 Applying for Permanent Residence—Grounds for Inadmissibility

PAGE 803:

[Re-write entire section.]

An alien may not be within one of the grounds for inadmissibility to qualify for an immigrant visa or for adjustment of status. Nine classifications are enumerated.

Health-related grounds for inadmissibility are applicable to individuals who have a communicable disease of public health significance or who have a physical or mental disorder or behavior that may pose a threat to property, safety or welfare of the alien or others.[1] Waivers for this ground of excludability are available for an alien who has certain U.S. citizen or permanent resident relatives.[2]

Criminal activity also results in inadmissibility for any crime involving moral turpitude or in violation of any law or regulation relating to a controlled substance.[3] Multiple convictions may result in inadmissibility even if the crimes do not involve moral turpitude.[4]

There is an exception for a single conviction committed under the age of 18, committed more than five years before the date of the application for a visa.[5]

There are also special provisions for inadmissibility for controlled substance traffickers, those involved in prostitution and for those in-

§ 19.52 IMMIGRATION AND NATIONALITY LAW Ch. 19

volved in criminal activity who have asserted immunity from prosecution.[6]

Waivers of some of these grounds of inadmissibility are available to certain relatives of U.S. citizens and permanent residents.[7]

Security considerations and terrorist activities are grounds for inadmissibility.[8] In addition, one may be excluded if in the opinion of the Secretary of State the entry or proposed activities would have potentially serious adverse foreign policy consequences for the U.S.[9] Included as well in this category are those potential immigrants who are members of a totalitarian party, with the exception of those who have been members involuntarily.[10] Participants in Nazi persecution or genocide are also inadmissible.[11]

Aliens who are in the opinion of a consular officer at the time of the application for the visa or of the Attorney General (the INS) at the time of application for adjustment likely to become a public charge are inadmissible to the U.S.[12] Thus, as part of each application for permanent residence, proof of ability to support oneself is an essential component.

Individuals such as those described in §§ 19.22 and 19.26 *supra* who require labor certification and do not have such labor certification or medical doctors who do not have the appropriate medical qualifications are also deemed inadmissible when they present themselves for admission as permanent residents without such documentation.[13]

Certain aliens who have previously been removed from the U.S. or who have made fraudulent misrepresentations in order to procure a visa or other documentation, stowaways, and smugglers, are inadmissible to the U.S.[14] Immigrants who present themselves without a valid immigrant visa or re-entry permit or other appropriate U.S. document are inadmissible to the U.S.[15]

Those immigrants who are permanently ineligible for U.S. citizenship and certain draft evaders are inadmissible to the U.S.[16] In addition, practicing polygamists and those involved in international child abduction are inadmissible.[17]

Individuals in the U.S. are subject to removal if they were inadmissible at the time of their entry into the U.S.[18] Grounds of removal are enumerated at § 237 of the INA (8 U.S.C.A. § 1227).

It is essential before proceeding with an application for adjustment of status or for an immigrant visa to review the background of the alien applicant to assure that a potential ground for inadmissibility and removal does not exist or if it does exist, that a waiver or other remedy is applicable. Otherwise, proceeding with the application might not only result in a failure to obtain permanent residence, but the institution of removal proceedings against the applicant alien.[19]

PAGE 805:

[*Replace note 17 with the following.*]

17. INA § 212(a)(10), 8 U.S.C.A. § 1182(a)(10).

[*Replace note 19 with the following.*]

19. *See* INA §§ 228, 239 (8 U.S.C.A. §§ 1228, 1229) for a description of the procedures and authority to arrest and remove aliens from the U.S.

PAGE 809:

[*Entire section, including section title, replaced.*]

§ 19.55 Affidavits of Support

Certain applicants applying for adjustment of status in the United States or applying for an immigrant visa abroad after the effective date of December 19, 1997 must comply with the new, and somewhat onerous, regulations promulgated by the Attorney General concerning affidavits of support, Form I-864.

Affidavits of support may be executed by individuals who (1) are citizens or nationals of the United States, or aliens lawfully admitted to the United States for permanent residence; (2) are at least 18 years of age; (3) are domiciled in any of the several states of the United States, the District of Columbia, or any territory or possession of the United States; (4) are petitioning for the admission of an alien under section 204 of the Immigration and Nationality Act; and (5) demonstrate the means to maintain an annual income equal to at least 125 percent of the federal poverty guidelines.[1] Affidavits of support may also be submitted by individuals who cannot demonstrate the means to maintain an annual income equal to at least 125 percent of the federal poverty guidelines,[2] but who accept joint and several liability with an individual who, although not petitioning for admission of the alien applicant, accepts joint and several liability with the petitioning sponsor and demonstrates the means to maintain an annual income equal to at least 125 percent of the federal poverty guidelines.[3]

The new form of affidavit of support must be executed by all petitioners in family-related petitions filed after December 19, 1997. They need not be executed by principal beneficiaries of employment-based petitions on behalf of family members. The standard Affidavit of Support, Form I-134, is still considered an acceptable document for such applicants.

Accompanying the Form I-864, Affidavit of Support form, generally, would be the following documents:

1. Petitioner's I-864 with notarized signature
2. Copies of petitioner's federal tax return for the three most recent years

3. Evidence of petitioner's employment

4. Evidence of petitioner's assets (if used to qualify)

5. Any Form I–864A submitted by the petitioner's household member with all original signatures notarized, copies of household member's federal tax returns for the three most recent tax years, household member's evidence of employment, and evidence of assets

6. Documentation for dependents including, for each dependent, a photocopy of the signed and notarized Form I–864 and I–864A filed on behalf of the principal applicant

7. Documentation for any joint sponsor should follow subsequently in the same order as provided above for the petitioner.[4]

1. INA § 213A(f)(1); 8 U.S.C.A. § 1183(f)(1); 8 CFR § 213a.2(c), 62 Fed. Reg. 54346 (October 20, 1997), effective December 19, 1997.

2. 8 CFR § 213a.1, 62 Fed.Reg. 54346 (October 20, 1997), effective December 19, 1997.

3. INA § 214A(f)(2), (5), 8 U.S.C.A. § 1183a(f)(2), (5); 8 CFR 213a.2(c), 62 Fed. Reg. 54346 (October 20, 1997), effective December 29, 1997.

4. 63 Fed.Reg. 27193 (May 18, 1998).

§ 19.56 Applying for Permanent Residence—Immigrant Visa Processing—Checklist of Required Documents

PAGE 812:

[*Replace Item 15 with the following.*]

15. Fee—$345 or local equivalent, in cash, per visa.

PAGE 814:

[*Replace entire section, including section title.*]

§ 19.59 Applying for Permanent Residence—Immigrant Visa Processing—Special Requirements of Section 245(i)

Section 245 of the Immigration and Nationality Act allows applicants for permanent residence to apply for adjustment of status in the United States if certain conditions are met. Some of these requirements include the prerequisite inspection and admission or parole of the applicant, and evidence that he or she has not engaged in unauthorized employment. From October 1, 1994 to January 14, 1998 aliens wishing to pay an additional fee specified in section 245(i) who met all other provisions of law could adjust status under that section.[1]

In order to take advantage of section 245(i) after January 14, 1998, aliens are now required to be beneficiaries of immigrant visa petitions filed with the Attorney General on or before January 14, 1998, or an application for alien labor certification filed with the Secretary of Labor on or before that date.[2] Further guidance and INS regulations concern-

Ch. 19   IMMIGRATION AND NATIONALITY LAW   § 19.79

ing interpretation of section 245(i) have yet to be promulgated as of the date of this writing.

1. INA § 245(i); 8 U.S.C.A. § 1255(i).
2. *See* Memorandum of the Executive Associate Commissioner, Robert L. Bach, Office of Policy and Programs, INS Headquarters, April 14, 1999.

§ 19.63   Applying for Permanent Residence—Adjustment of Status—Completion of the Process

PAGE 817:

[*Add to note 3.*]

3. **PRACTICE POINTER:** Often there are problems with the manufacture of the cards. In up to 25% of the cases, the applicant must be contacted again to provided new photographs or fingerprints. It is therefore important for applicants to follow-up after resident status is granted and for representatives to maintain contact with applicants until such time as it has been verified that the cards have been received.

§ 19.65   Applying for Permanent Residence—Adjustment of Status—Checklist

PAGE 819:

[*Replace item 6 with the following.*]

6. *Evidence of Financial Support*: A number of items can alternatively be produced to show financial support, depending on the circumstances of the case, including job letter on proper letterhead of the employer, pay statements for the immediately past two months prior to the filing of the application, current and previous W–2s and bank letters on bank stationery for all accounts showing the title of the account, date opened and current balance. If the individual is supported by someone else, Form I–864, Affidavit of Support, must be executed and notarized and submitted with appropriate supporting documents (*see* § 19.55, *supra*).

§ 19.79   Forms—Form OF–230

PAGE 853:

[*This form has been updated.*]

Contact the State Department VISA office at 202–663–1225 for more information.

Chapter 20

ADOPTIONS

by
Joseph R. Carrieri

Table of Sections

20.2	Strategy
20.11	Adoptions—Choice of Venue
20.30	___ Consents Required—Rights of Unwed Fathers
20.101	Agency Adoptions—Child's Entry Into the System—Court Ordered Transfer of Children to Authorized Agency
20.133	Forms—Private Placement Adoptions—Petition for Certification as a Qualified Adoptive Parent 💾
20.134	___ ___ Petition for Temporary Guardianship 💾
20.136	___ ___ Extra-judicial Consent of Birth or Legal Parent 💾
20.137	___ ___ Petition for Adoption 💾
20.138	___ Order of Adoption (Private Placement) 💾
20.139	___ Agency Adoptions—Petition for Adoption 💾
20.140	___ ___ Verified Schedule 💾
20.145	___ ___ Agreement of Adoption and Consent 💾
20.146	___ ___ Affidavit Identifying Party 💾
20.147	___ ___ Affidavit of Financial Disclosure by Parents 💾

Forms on Disk

💾 Forms contained in this chapter (except preprinted forms) may be electronically retrieved from the companion disk.

Westlaw Electronic Research

See Westlaw Electronic Research Guide preceding the Summary of Contents.

---

§ 20.2 Strategy

PAGE 863:

[*Insert right before "Obtaining an Infant for Adoption" section.*]

Certification. It is important for the practitioner when representing adoptive parents to immediately focus on having the adoptive parents certified as qualified adoptive parents. Pursuant to DRL §§ 115 and 115(d), the petition certifying the clients as qualified adoptive parents, the order qualifying them as adoptive parents, and the affidavit of the disinterested person doing the home study must be drafted and filed with the family or surrogate's court in the proper venue. Along with the documents, the fingerprint cards must be completed and the abuse clearance form pursuant to DRL § 112 must also be completed and filed.

If the clients are serious about obtaining a child and proceeding with the adoption, these procedures are essential. The hospitals have become sophisticated to the need for certification of adoptive parents as qualified and the hospital will not release a baby from the hospital until the order qualifying them as certified to receive a child has been received. Therefore, if this procedure is not followed initially, if a baby becomes available it is likely that the opportunity to receive a child by the adoptive parents will be lost unless the order is already in place. If, however, prospective adoptive parents arrive at the attorney's office with a baby about to be born, the attorney should seek to obtain from the court a conditional certification as a qualified adoptive parent which may be issued by the court if the petition and supporting documents are filed immediately along with a home study by a qualified person, even before obtaining the abuse clearance results and the results of the fingerprints. If need be, this could literally be done in a few days.

PAGE 866:

[*Insert at end of section.*]

One of the most important pieces of legislation enacted in the last twenty years with respect to adoptions and foster care is the Adoption and Safe Families Act which was enacted by the Congress of the United States in 1997. On February 11, 1999, Governor Pataki signed into law Chapter 7 of the Laws of 1999 to bring New York State into compliance with the requirements of the Federal Adoption and State Families Act. Social Services Law § 378–a was amended in 1999 to provide that criminal record checks must be made of all prospective foster and adoptive parents and all persons in the household over eighteen years of age .. Prior to this enactment, it was not possible to fingerprint prospective foster parents, and many times foster parents received foster children when in fact those foster parents had been convicted of felonies, and in some cases murder. The voluntary agencies were unaware of the criminal records of foster parents until they became adoptive parents and had their fingerprints checked by the appropriate family or surrogate's court prior to the adoption. Then and only then did the agencies discover that many of the foster parents indeed had been convicted of violent crimes. This fingerprinting process includes all present foster parents and is to be done as part of the certification process or re-certification of foster parents. A person cannot foster a child or adopt a child if that person has a felony conviction for child abuse, neglect, spousal abuse, crime against a child, child pornography, felony conviction involving violence (including rape, sexual assault, or homicide, but not crimes of physical assault unless they occurred within the last five years). Lastly, a person cannot foster a child or be an adoptive parent if that person has a conviction for any drug-related offense within the last five years. If upon re-certification a foster parent or adoptive parent is determined to have one of the above convictions, the children must be removed from the home. Further, if a foster of adoptive parent has any criminal conviction, except those enumerated above, or anyone in the

§ 20.2 ADOPTIONS Ch. 20

household over the age of eighteen has any criminal conviction, it is left to the discretion of the agency whether or not that person can foster or adopt a child. However, a safety assessment evaluation must be done to determine the appropriateness of the certification of adoption. The law took effect immediately, i.e., February 11, 1999, and contained no "grandfathered" provisions. Therefore, the law pertains to present foster and adoptive parents.

§ 20.11 Adoptions—Choice of Venue
PAGE 875:

[*Delete last sentence of first paragraph and replace with the following.*]

In an agency adoption, the Social Services Law provides that an adoption may be filed in the court which terminated parental rights or in the court which approved the surrender executed by the biological parent, or in the county where the adoptive parents reside, or finally, if the adoptive parents reside outside of the state of New York, in the county where the agency has its principal place of business.

§ 20.30 Adoptions—Consents Required—Rights of Unwed Fathers
PAGE 885:

[*Add to end of section.*]

Practitioners have seen the shift in emphasis back and forth, focusing first on the parent, and now on the child. There is no question that the Adoption and Safe Families Act, which was signed into law in New York State on February 11, 1999, has focused on the well-being and best interests of the child. Implicit in this focus is the shift away from the paramount rights of the biological parents. Contingency planning, i.e., return the child, and if not possible, adoption, has given way to concurrent planning, i.e. the agency must work simultaneously towards reunification to the parent and, at the same time, plan for permanency of the child through adoption. Specifically, courts have refused to entertain a petition against a putative father who does not have the indicia of fatherhood, i.e., has supported the child, visited the child, or in some substantial way become part of the child's life. Some judges in the family courts have taken the position that the agency must show that the father had maintained substantial and continuous contact with the child as manifested by child support and visitation with the child. Lacking such, some judges would not permit the agency to terminate parental rights of such a respondent father, taking the position that he had no rights to be terminated and he was not a consent father. In the case of *Matter of Kasiem*, 230 A.D.2d 796, 646 N.Y.S.2d 541 (2d Dept, 1996), the higher court affirmed the family court judge's determination, after fact finding, that the putative father's consent to the adoption of the infant was not necessary because he had not maintained substantial and continuous or repeated contact with the child within the meaning of Domestic Relations Law § 111(1)(d). The appellate division held that the agency did not have to prove that the putative father abandoned the child and that the family court properly permitted the agency to withdraw its petition as against the putative father. This case is important for the proposition that not every father whose name appears in the progress notes or on the birth certificate or who is named by the mother is a consent father.

§ 20.101 Agency Adoptions—Child's Entry Into the System—Court Ordered Transfer of Children to Authorized Agency

PAGE 936:

[*Add to end of section.*]

The practitioner of foster care law must familiarize him or herself with the Federal Adoption and Safe Families Act which was signed into law by President Clinton on November 19, 1997. The Adoption and Safe Families Act, more commonly known as ASFA, was enacted by the Congress of the United States to enable the individual states to enact legislation to achieve the goals of safety, permanency, and child and family well-being. To that end, the New York State Legislature implemented the Federal Adoption and Safe Families Act, which became effective on February 11, 1999 in the State of New York. The statute became effective immediately and is retroactive to all children currently in foster care, including proceedings involving the termination of parental rights .. New York's Adoption and Safe Families Act has impacted on Social Services Law § 384-b, involving termination of parental rights, in several respects. First, the law is clear that the health and safety of the infant is to be of paramount concern. Termination of parental rights petitions by law must now be filed for any child in care fifteen out of the most recent twenty-two months and the time is to be calculated as starting at the time of the finding of abuse or neglect under Article 10 of the Family Court Act or sixty days after temporary placement in foster care, whichever date is sooner. Also, petitions to terminate parental rights must be filed where any child is determined by the court to be an abandoned child and where any child whose parents have been convicted of certain felony crimes as further described in the statute. The statute is mandatory that the petition to terminate parental rights must be filed, unless there are certain exceptions, such as the child is in the care of a relative or the agency documents in the most recent case plan give a compelling reason why it is not in the child's best interests to have a termination petition filed. Compelling reasons include (1) the child is in foster care based upon a PINS or juvenile delinquency proceeding, (2) the child has a permanency goal other than adoption, such as independent living, (3) the child is fourteen years of age and older and will not consent to adoption, (4) there are insufficient grounds to file a termination of parental rights proceeding, or (5) an Article 10 proceeding is still pending.

§ 20.133 Forms—Private Placement Adoptions—Petition for Certification as a Qualified Adoptive Parent

D.R.L. §§ 115, 115–d

Form 22
(Certification
As Qualified
Adoptive Parent)
12/97

SURROGATE'S COURT OF THE STATE OF NEW YORK
COUNTY OF
....

In the Matter of the Adoption of
A Child whose First Name is

by Adoptive Parent(s)

(Docket)(File) No.

PETITION
(Certification
as a Qualified
Adoptive Parent)
(Private–Placement)

....

The Petitioner(s) respectfully allege(s) to this Court that:

[Delete inapplicable provisions]:

1. (His)(Her)(Their) name(s), residential address and telephone number are: _____

_____

_____

Petitioner (specify name): _____

Petitioner (specify name): _____

2. (He)(She)(They) (is)(are) seeking certification by this court as (a) person(s) qualified to take custody of the adoptive child [specify first name]: , (prior to) (contemporaneous with) the filing of a private-placement adoption petition.

3. (He)(She)(They) (has) (have) (not) been the subject of a pending child protective investigation or of an indicated report, as such term is defined in section 412 of the Social Services Law, filed with the statewide register of child abuse and maltreatment pursuant to Title six of Article six of the Social Services Law.

4. A pre-placement investigation will be undertaken by a disinterested person, as such term is defined in section four of 115–d of the Domestic Relations Law, and a written report of such investigation will be furnished directly to the court by such disinterested person.

5. The marital, family status and history of the Petitioner(s) (is) (are): _____

_____

Petitioner (specify name): _____

Petitioner (specify name): _____

6. The physical and mental health of the Petitioner(s) (is)(are): __

Petitioner (specify name): _____

Petitioner (specify name): _____

    7. Attached hereto and made a part hereof is a statement of all property owned by and income of the Petitioner(s).

    8. Petitioner(s) (has) (have)(not ever been) (a) respondent(s) in any proceeding in a court concerning alleged (abused) (neglected) (abandoned) children, (except as follows): _____

Petitioner (specify name): _____

Petitioner (specify name): _____

    (b) (Petitioner(s) (have) no prior criminal convictions or founded findings of child abuse or neglect (except as follows): _____

Petitioner (specify name): _____

Petitioner (specify name): _____

    9. Petitioner(s) (has)(have) (not) made any prior application for certification as (a) qualified adoptive parent(s); if so, the disposition and disposition date of such application was as follows: _____

Petitioner (specify name): _____

Petitioner (specify name): _____

_____);

    10. Petitioner(s) (do)(does) (not) intend to cause a pre-placement investigation to be undertaken (and request(s) this court to appoint a disinterested person to conduct such pre-placement investigation;)

    WHEREFORE, Petitioner (s) pray(s) for an order (conditionally)[1] certifying Petitioner(s) as (a) qualified adoptive parent(s).

                      _____/_____
                        Petitioner: typed or printed name / signature

                        _____/_____
                        Petitioner: typed or printed name / signature

                        _____/_____
                        Attorney: typed or printed name/ signature

§ 20.133   ADOPTIONS   Ch. 20

                              Attorney's Address and Telephone
                              Number

              VERIFICATION

STATE OF NEW YORK   )
)   SS:
COUNTY   )

being duly sworn, says that (he)(she)(they) (is)(are) the Petitioner(s) in the above-named proceeding and that the foregoing petition is true to (his)(her)(their) own knowledge, except as to matters (he)(she)(they) believe(s) to be true.

                              _____/_____
                              Adoptive Parent: typed or printed name/ signature

                              _____/_____ Adoptive Parent: typed or printed name/ signature

Sworn to before me this
day of ____, 19__.

_____
(Deputy) Clerk of the Court
Notary Public

1. Applicable only if petition seeks conditional certification pursuant to D.R.L. Section 115–d(6).

§ 20.134 Forms—Private Placement Adoptions—Petition for Temporary Guardianship

D.R.L.§ 115–c; S.C.P.A.§ 1725   Form 21–A
                                        (Temporary
                                        Guardianship)
                                        12/97

SURROGATE'S COURT OF THE STATE OF NEW YORK
COUNTY OF
....

In the Matter of the Temporary
Guardianship of A Child Whose   (Docket)(File)No.
First Name is
                                        Petition for Temporary
                                        Guardianship

....

The Petitioner(s) respectfully allege(s) to the Court that:

1. Physical custody of (first name) (last name) , a child born on , was transferred to and for the purposes of adoption on the day of

58

_____, 19__, by _____, the child's (parent(s))(guardian(s)), (and requirements for certification of as, qualified adoptive parents herein was duly waived by order of the _____, Court, County of dated

2. The residence and telephone number of Petitioner(s) is _____

3. The full name(s) and addresse(s) of the natural parent(s) of the child are: _____

4. The anticipated name of the child subsequent to adoption will be _____

5. The anticipated residence of the child subsequent to adoption will be _____.

6. A consent to the adoption of the child was duly executed pursuant to section 115–b of the Domestic Relations Law on _____, 19__. A copy of the consent to the adoption is annexed hereto.

7. The child will be residing with Petitioner(s), and a petition for adoption of the child by Petitioner(s) will be filed in the Court of the County of _____, State of New York, within 45 days of the execution of the consent to adoption of the child.

8. No previous petition has been filed or application made to any court or judge for the relief sought herein (except)[include any proceedings dismissed or withdrawn]

WHEREFORE, Petitioner(s) pray(s) for an order granting temporary guardianship of the child to Petitioner(s).

_____
Petitioner(s)

_____
Applicant

_____
Print or type name

_____
Signature of Attorney, if any

_____
Attorney's Name (Print or Type)

_____
Attorney's Address and Telephone Number

Dated: _____ 19__

§ 20.134 ADOPTIONS Ch. 20

VERIFICATION

STATE OF NEW YORK)
) SS:
COUNTY OF   )

____, being duly sworn, says that (he) (she) (they) (is)(are) the Petitioner(s) in the above-named proceeding and that the foregoing petition is true to (his) (her) (their) own knowledge, except as to matters therein stated to be alleged on information and belief, and as to those matters (he)(she)(they) believe(s) it to be true.

_____
                                        Petitioner(s)

Subscribed and sworn to before me
this day of ____, 19___.

_____
                          (Deputy) Clerk of the Court
                          Notary Public

§ 20.136 Forms—Private Placement Adoptions—Extrajudicial Consent of Birth or Legal Parent 🗄

D.R.L. §§ 115, 115–b   Form 2–G
                                        (Extrajudicial Consent-
                                        Birth or Legal Parent—
                                        Private-placement)
                                        12/97

COURT OF THE STATE OF NEW YORK
COUNTY OF _____
_____
In the Matter of the Adoption of   (Docket)(File) No.
A Child whose First Name is

                                        EXTRAJUDICIAL CONSENT
                                        (Birth or Legal Parent—
                                        Private–Placement)
_____

THIS CONSENT MAY BE REVOKED WITHIN 45 DAYS OF THE EXECUTION OF THIS DOCUMENT. IF THE CONSENT IS NOT REVOKED WITHIN SAID 45 DAYS, NO PROCEEDING MAY BE MAINTAINED BY THE PARENT FOR THE RETURN OF THE CUSTODY OF THE CHILD. THE REVOCATION MUST BE IN WRITING AND RECEIVED BY THE COURT WHERE THE ADOPTION PROCEEDING IS TO BE COMMENCED WITHIN 45 DAYS OF THE EXECUTION OF THE CONSENT. THE NAME AND ADDRESS OF THE COURT IN WHICH THE ADOPTION PROCEEDING HAS BEEN OR IS TO BE COMMENCED IS

IF THE ADOPTIVE PARENTS CONTEST THE REVOCATION, TIMELY NOTICE OF REVOCATION WILL NOT NECESSARILY RESULT IN THE RETURN OF THE CHILD TO THE PARENT, AND THE RIGHT OF THE PARENT TO THE CUSTODY OF THE CHILD WILL NOT BE SUPERIOR TO THOSE OF THE ADOPTIVE PARENTS. A HEARING BEFORE A JUDGE WILL BE REQUIRED TO DETERMINE: (1) WHETHER THE NOTICE OF REVOCATION WAS TIMELY AND PROPERLY GIVEN; AND IF NECESSARY, (2) WHETHER THE BEST INTERESTS OF THE CHILD BE SERVED: (A) BY RETURNING CUSTODY OF THE CHILD TO THE PARENT; OR (B) BY CONTINUING THE ADOPTION PROCEEDING COMMENCED BY THE ADOPTIVE PARENTS; OR (C) BY DISPOSITION OTHER THAN ADOPTION BY THE ADOPTIVE PARENTS; OR (D) BY PLACEMENT OF THE CHILD WITH AN AUTHORIZED AGENCY. IF ANY SUCH DETERMINATION IS MADE, THE COURT WILL MAKE SUCH DISPOSITION OF THE CUSTODY OF THE CHILD AS WILL BEST SERVE THE INTERESTS OF THE CHILD.

THE PARENT HAS THE RIGHT TO LEGAL REPRESENTATION OF THE PARENT'S OWN CHOOSING, THE RIGHT TO SUPPORTIVE COUNSELING AND MAY HAVE THE RIGHT TO HAVE THE COURT APPOINT AN ATTORNEY PURSUANT TO SECTION 262 OF THE FAMILY COURT ACT, SECTION 407 OF THE SURROGATE'S COURT PROCEDURE ACT, OR SECTION 35 OF THE JUDICIARY LAW.

1. I _____, [specify name]: , residing at _____, (birth)(legal) parent of _____ [specify first name of child]: do hereby consent to the adoption of my (daughter)(son) who was , born on [specify date]: _____, (by [specify name]: _____, adoptive parent(s)).

2. The full name and last known address of the other (birth)(legal) parent of the adoptive child are: _____

_____

3. I have (not) been represented by counsel. (If represented, state counsel's name, address and telephone number: _____

_____.)

Date:

                                        _____

                                        (Birth)(Legal) parent: typed or printed name/ signature

                                        _____

                                        Adoptive Parent: typed or printed name/ signature

§ 20.136 ADOPTIONS Ch. 20

Adoptive Parent: typed or printed name / signature

Adoptive child if over 18: typed or printed name/ signature

Attorney if any: typed or printed name/signature

Attorney's Address and Telephone number

STATE OF NEW YORK)
) ss.:
COUNTY OF)

On this _____ day of _____, 19__, the person who executed the foregoing instrument, personally came before me and acknowledged that (he)(she) acknowledged that (he)(she) executed the same.

Notary Public

§ 20.137 Forms—Private Placement Adoptions—Petition for Adoption

D.R.L.§§ 111, 111–a, 112, 115
S.C.P.A. § 1725(1)

Form 1–C
(Petition–Private
-Placement)
12/97

SURROGATE'S COURT OF THE STATE OF NEW YORK
COUNTY OF ....

In the Matter of Adoption of
A Child Whose First Name Is

(Docket)(File) No.

PETITION FOR
ADOPTION
(Private–Placement)

....
The Petitioner(s) respectfully allege(s) to this Court that:

[Delete inapplicable provisions.]:
    1. Petitioning adoptive parent [specify name]: _____

        a. resides at [specify address, including county]: _____

        b. is of full age, having been born on [specify date of birth]:

Ch. 20   ADOPTIONS   § 20.137

    c. is (unmarried) _____ (married to [specify name]: _____ and living together (married to [specify name]: _____ and living separate and apart pursuant to a decree or judgment of separation or pursuant to a separation agreement subscribed by the parties thereto and acknowledged or proved in the form required to entitle a deed to be recorded); (married to [specify name]: _____ and living separate and apart for at least three years prior to commencement of the proceeding);

    d. is of the following religious faith, if any: _____

    e. is engaged in the following occupation [specify]: _____ and earns $ _____ (of which $ _____ is support and maintenance to be received from the Commissioner of Social Services on behalf of the adoptive child).

2. Petitioning adoptive parent [specify name]: _____

    a. resides at [specify address, including county]: _____

    b. is of full age, having been born on [specify date of birth]:

    c. is (unmarried) _____ (married to [specify name]: _____ and living together (married to [specify name]: _____ and living separate and apart pursuant to a decree or judgment of separation or pursuant to a separation agreement subscribed by the parties thereto and acknowledged or proved in the form required to entitle a deed to be recorded); (married to [specify name]: _____ and living separate and apart for at least three years prior to commencement of the proceeding);

    d. is of the following religious faith, if any: _____

    e. is engaged in the following occupation [specify]: _____ and earns $ _____ in approximate annual income (of which $ _____ is support and maintenance to be received from the Commissioner of Social Services on behalf of the adoptive child).

3. The full name, date and place of birth of the adoptive child is

[attach certified copy of birth certificate]

4. Upon information and belief, the religious faith of the adoptive child, if any, is _____.

§ 20.137   ADOPTIONS   Ch. 20

5. The following is information, as nearly as can be ascertained, concerning the birth or legal parents of the adoptive child:

    (a) Full name and last known address

Parent (specify full name and address, if known): _____

Parent (specify full name and address, if known): _____

    (b) Age and date of birth

Parent (specify name): _____

Parent (specify name): _____

    (c) Heritage (specify nationality, ethnic background, race)

Parent (specify name): _____

Parent (specify name): _____

    (d) Religious faith, if any

Parent (specify name): _____

Parent (specify name): _____

    (e) Education (specify number of years of school or degrees completed at time of birth of adoptive child)

Parent (specify name): _____

Parent (specify name): _____

    (f) General physical appearance at time of birth of adoptive child (height, weight, color of hair, eyes, skin)

Parent (specify name): _____

Ht: _____ Wt: _____

Hair Color: _____ Eye Color: _____

Skin Color: _____

Parent (specify name): _____

Ht: _____ Wt: _____

Hair Color: _____ Eye Color: _____

Skin Color: _____

    (g) Annex Form 1–D which provides health and medical history at time of birth of adoptive child, including conditions or diseases believed to be hereditary and any drugs or medication taken during pregnancy by child's mother.

    (h) Any other information which may be a factor influencing the adoptive child's present or future well-being, including talents, hobbies and special interests of parents: [attach separate sheet if necessary]

6. The manner in which the adoptive parent(s) obtained the adoptive child is as follows: _____

7. The adoptive child resided with the adoptive parent(s) from [indicate date]: _____.

8. Other persons living in the household are: [Specify names and dates of birth]: _____
_____.

9. The name by which the adoptive child is to be known is: ____.

10. Upon information and belief, the adoptive child (has) (has not) been previously adopted.

11. The full name(s) and address(es) of any person(s) having lawful custody of the adoptive child, if known (is)(are) _____
_____
_____

12. On information and belief, pursuant to Domestic Relations Law § 111,

    (a) the consent of the birth or legal parent of the adoptive child (is attached hereto) (is not required because _____
_____;)

    (b) the consent of the birth or legal parent of the adoptive child (is attached hereto) (is not required because _____
_____;)

    (c) the consent(s) of the above-named person(s) having lawful custody of the adoptive child (is attached hereto) (is not required because _____
_____;)

    (d) The consent(s) of other person(s)[specify name(s)]: _____ (is attached hereto) (is not required because _____
_____.)

13(a)(The consent of the birth or legal parent [specify name]: _____ was executed pursuant to section 115–b(3) of the Domestic Relations Law on _____, 19__; the 45th day after execution of the consent is _____, 19__.

(b) (The consent of the birth or legal parent [specify name]: _____ was executed pursuant to Section 115–b(3) of the Domestic Relations Law on _____, 19__; the 45th day after execution of the consent is _____, 19__.)

(14. This court is not the court named in the consent(s) of the parent(s) of the adoptive child, attached hereto, as the court in which the adoption proceeding will be commenced, but more than 45 days have elapsed since the date of execution of said consent(s) and, on information and belief, no written notice of revocation has been received by that court.)

(15. That on information and belief said minor child has a (general) (testamentary) guardian. [state nature, date and place of appointment]:

§ 20.137　　　　　　　　ADOPTIONS　　　　　　　　Ch. 20

16. To the best of the Petitioner(s)' information and belief, there are no persons other than those mentioned herein or in the verified scheduled annexed hereto who are entitled, pursuant to Domestic Relation Law § 111(3) and 111-a, to notice of this proceeding (except)

Name: _____ Relationship: _____

Last known address: _____.

Name _____ Relationship: _____

Last known address: _____.

Name Relationship: _____

Last known address: _____.

17. Attached hereto and made a part hereof is Form 1-D setting forth all available information comprising the adoptive child's medical history.

18. The placement is subject to the provisions of Social Services Law section(s) (374-a) (382) and the provisions of such section(s) have been complied with. The original approval signed by the Administrator of the Interstate Compact on the Placement of Children is attached hereto.

19. (a) The adoptive parent(s) (has)(have) (no) knowledge that the child or an adoptive parent is the subject of an indicated report or is another person named in an indicated report of child abuse or maltreatment, as such terms are defined in section 412 of the Social Services Law, or has been the subject of or the respondent in a child protective proceeding which resulted in an order finding that the child is an abused or neglected child.

(b) The adoptive parent(s) (has)(have) (no) knowledge of any criminal record concerning themselves or any other adult residing in the household (except) _____

_____

_____

20. There are no prior or pending proceedings affecting the custody or status of the adoptive child, including any proceedings dismissed or withdrawn, (except) [specify type of proceeding, court, disposition, if any, and date of disposition, if any]:

21. The adoptive child (is)(is not) an Indian child within the meaning of the Indian Child Welfare Act of 1978 (25 U.S.C. §§ 1901–1963).

22. [Insert any additional allegations.]

WHEREFORE, the Petitioner(s) prays(s) for an order approving granting temporary guardianship of the child to Petitioner(s) and the adoption of the adoptive child [specify first name]: _____ by the Petitioner(s) and directing that the adoptive child shall be treated in all respects as the child of the Petitioner(s) and directing that the name of the adoptive child be changed and that (s)he shall henceforth be known by the name of _____ together with such other and further relief as may be just and proper.

Dated: ____, 19__.

_____/_____
Adoptive Parent: typed or printed name/ signature

_____/_____
Adoptive Parent: typed or printed name / signature

_____/_____
Adoptive child if over 18: typed or printed name / signature

_____/_____
Attorney , if any: typed or printed name/ signature

_____
Attorney's Address and Telephone Number

VERIFICATION

STATE OF NEW YORK)
) SS:
COUNTY OF)

_____ being duly sworn, says that (he)(she) (they)(is)(are) the Petitioner(s) in the above-named proceeding and that the foregoing petition is true to (his)(her)(their) own knowledge, except as to matters where in stated to be alleged on information and belief and as to those matters (he)(she) (they) believe(s) it to be true.

_____/_____
Adoptive Parent: typed or printed name/ signature

_____/_____
Adoptive Parent: typed or printed name/ signature

_____/_____
Adoptive child if over 18: typed or printed name/ signature

Sworn to before me this
____ day of ____, 19__.

(Deputy)Clerk of the Court
Notary Public

Resworn to before me this
____ day of ____, 19__.

_____
Judge of the Court

§ 20.138 Forms—Order of Adoption (Private Placement) 💾

D.R.L. §§ 111, 112(2)(b), 113, 114

Form 13–B
(Order of Adoption
Private–Placement)
12/97

At a term of the Surrogate's Court of the State of New York, held in and for the County of _____ at _____, New York, on _____,

PRESENT:
    Hon. _____
                Judge

In the Matter of the Adoption of
A Child Whose First Name Is

_____

(Docket)(File) No.

ORDER OF ADOPTION
(Private–Placement)

The Petition of _____ (and _____), verified the day of _____, 19__, having been duly presented to this Court, together with an agreement on the part of the petitioning adoptive parent(s) to adopt and treat as (his)(her)(their) own lawful child and whose birth day is 19 , and who was born at _____ as set forth in the petition for adoption herein, said petition having been attached thereto and made a part thereof a document setting forth all available information comprising the adoptive child's medical history; together with the affidavit(s) of

_____;

and the consent(s) of

_____

AND, although (his)(her)(their) consent(s) (is)(are) not required, the Court having given notice of the proposed adoption to
    [recite facts relative thereto]

AND the aforesaid petitioning adoptive parents and the adoptive child and all other persons whose consents are required as aforesaid having personally appeared before this Court for examination, except _____;

AND an investigation having been ordered and made and the written report of such investigation having been filed with the Court, as required by the Domestic Relations Law;

(AND the Court having (shortened)(dispensed with) the six-month waiting period between its receiving the petition to adopt and this order of adoption, pursuant to section 116 of the Domestic Relations Law, because _____;)

AND the adoptive child having resided with the petitioning adoptive parent(s) since _____ (and _____ the judge having dispensed with the six-month period of residency with the adoptive parent(s), pursuant to section 112 and 116 of the Domestic Relations Law because _____

(AND the court having inquired of the statewide central register of child abuse and maltreatment and having been informed that the (child) (adoptive parent(s)) (is)(are)(not) a subject of or another person named in an indicated report filed with such register as such terms are defined in section 412 of the Social Services Law, (AND there being available to this Court findings of a court inquiry made within the preceding twelve months, of the statewide central register of child abuse and maltreatment that the (child) (adoptive parent(s)) (is)(are) (not) a subject of or another parson named in an indicated report filed with such register as such terms are defined in section 412 of the Social Services Law) and the Court having given due consideration to any information contained therein;

AND this Court being satisfied that the best interests of the adoptive child will be promoted by the adoption and that there is no reasonable objection to the proposed change of the name of the adoptive child;

NOW, on motion of _____ Attorney for the petitioners) herein, and upon all the papers and proceedings herein, it is

ORDERED that the petition of _____ (and _____) for the adoption of _____ a person born on _____, 19__, at _____, be and the same hereby is allowed and approved; and it is further

ORDERED that the said adoptive child shall henceforth be regarded and treated in all respects as the lawful child of the said adoptive parent(s); and it is further

§ 20.138   ADOPTIONS   Ch. 20

ORDERED that the name of the said adoptive child be and the same hereby is changed to _____ and that the said adoptive child shall hereafter be known by that name; and it is further

(ORDERED that the Clerk prepare, certify and deliver to _____ a copy of this order; and it is further)

ORDERED that the child's medical history, heritage of the parents, which shall include nationality, ethnic background and race; education, which shall be the number of years of school completed by the parents at the time of the birth of the adoptive child; general physical appearance of the parents at the time of the birth of the adoptive child, including height, weight, color of hair, eyes, skin; occupation of the parents at the time of birth of the adoptive child; health and medical history of the parents at the time of birth of the adoptive child, including all available information setting forth conditions or diseases believed to be hereditary, any drugs or medication taken during pregnancy by the mother; and other information which may be a factor influencing the child's present or future well-being, talents, hobbies and special interests of the parents as contained in the petition shall be furnished to the adoptive parents; and it is

ORDERED that this order, together with all other papers pertaining to the adoption, shall be filed and kept as provided in the Domestic Relations Law and shall not be subject to access or inspections except as provided in said Law.

ENTER

_____

Surrogate

Dated: ____, 19__.

§ 20.139   Forms—Agency Adoptions—Petition for Adoption 💾

D.R.L. §§ 111-a(1), 112

Form 1–A
(Adoption
Petition–Agency)
12/97

SURROGATE'S COURT OF THE STATE OF NEW YORK
COUNTY OF _____
....

In the Matter of the Adoption of
A Child Whose First Name is

(Docket)(File) No.

PETITION FOR
ADOPTION
(Agency)

....

The Petitioner(s) respectfully allege(s) to this Court that [Delete inapplicable provisions]:

1. Petitioning adoptive parent [specify name]: _____

_____

Ch. 20 ADOPTIONS § 20.139

    a. resides at [specify address, including county]: _____

    b. is of full age, having been born on [specify date of birth]: _____

    c. is (unmarried) _____ (married to [specify name]: _____ and living together; (married to [specify name]: _____ and living separate and apart pursuant to a decree or judgment of separation or pursuant to a separation agreement subscribed by the parties thereto and acknowledged or proved in the form required to entitle a deed to be recorded); (married to [specify name]: _____ and living separate and apart for at least three years prior to commencement of the proceeding);

    d. is of the following religious faith, if any: _____

    e. is engaged in the following occupation [specify]: _____ and earns $ _____ in approximate annual income (of which $ _____ is support and maintenance to be received from the Commissioner of Social Services on behalf of the adoptive child).

2. Petitioning adoptive parent [specify name]: _____

    a. resides at [specify address, including county]: _____

    b. is of full age, having been born on [specify date of birth]: _____

    c. is (unmarried) _____ (married to [specify name]: _____ and living together; (married to [specify name]: _____ and living separate and apart pursuant to a decree or judgment of separation or pursuant to a separation agreement subscribed by the parties thereto and acknowledged or proved in the form required to entitle a deed to be recorded); (married to [specify name]: _____ and living separate and apart for at least three years prior to commencement of the proceeding);

    d. is of the following religious faith: _____

    e. is engaged in the following occupation [specify]: _____ and earns $ _____ in approximate annual income (of which $ _____ is support and maintenance to be received from the Commissioner of Social Services on behalf of the adoptive child).

3. Upon information and belief, the adoptive child, whose first name is _____, was born on _____, 19 __, at and the religious faith of such child is _____.

4. Upon information and belief, there will be annexed to this petition a schedule verified by a duly constituted official of _____, an authorized agency, as required by section 112(3) of the Domestic Relations Law, concerning the adoptive child who is the subject of this proceeding.

5. The following is information, as nearly as can be ascertained, concerning the birth or legal parents of the adoptive child:

(a) Age and date of birth

Parent (specify name): _____

Parent (specify name): _____

(b) Heritage (specify nationality, ethnic background, race)

Parent (specify name): _____

Parent (specify name): _____

(c) Religious faith, if any

Parent (specify name): _____

Parent (specify name): _____

(d) Education (specify number of years of school or degrees completed at time of birth of adoptive child)

Parent (type name): _____

Parent (type name): _____

(e) General physical appearance at time of birth of adoptive child (height, weight, color of hair, eyes, skin)

Parent (type name): _____

Ht: _____ Wt: _____

Hair Color: _____ Eye Color: _____

Skin Color: _____

Parent (type name):

Ht: _____ Wt: _____

Hair Color: _____ Eye Color: _____

Skin Color: _____

(f) Annex Form 1-D which provides health and medical history of birth parents at time of birth of adoptive child, including conditions or diseases believed to be hereditary and any drugs or medication taken during pregnancy by child's mother.

(g) Any other information which may be a factor influencing the adoptive child's present or future well-being, including talents, hobbies and special interests of parents: [attach separate sheet if necessary]

6. The adoptive child (is)(is not) an Indian child within the meaning of the Indian Child Welfare Act of 1978 (25 U.S.C.A. §§ 1901–1963).

7. The manner in which the adoptive parent(s) obtained the adoptive child is as follows: _____

(8. The placement is subject to the provisions of section(s)(374-a) (382) of the Social Services Law and the provisions of such sections have been complied with. The original approval signed by the Administrator of the Interstate Compact on the placement of Children is attached hereto.)

9. The adoptive child resided with the adoptive parent(s) from [specify date]: _____.

10. Other persons living in the household are [specify names and dates of birth]: _____

11. The name by which the adoptive child is to be known is: ____.

12. Upon information and belief, the adoptive child (has)(has not) been previously adopted.

13. To the best of Petitioner(s)' information and belief, there are no persons other than those mentioned herein or in the verified schedule annexed hereto who are entitled, pursuant to Sections 111(3) and 111–a of the Domestic Relations Law, to notice of this proceeding (except):

    Name: _____ Relationship: _____

    Last known address: _____.

    Name: _____ Relationship: _____

    Last known address: _____.

    Name Relationship: _____

    Last known address: _____.

14(a). The adoptive parent(s) (has)(have) (no) knowledge that the child or an adoptive parent is the subject of an indicated report, or is another person named in an indicated report of child abuse or maltreatment, as such terms are defined in section 412 of the Social Services Law, or has been the subject of or the respondent in a child protective proceeding which resulted in an order finding that the child is an abused or neglected child.

(b). The adoptive parent(s) (has)(have) (no) knowledge of any criminal record concerning themselves or any other adult residing in the household (except) _____

15. There are no prior or pending proceedings affecting the custody or status of the adoptive child, including any proceeding[s] dismissed or withdrawn, *(except)[specify type of proceeding, court, disposition, if any, and date of disposition, if any]:

16. [Insert any additional allegations.]

§ 20.139 ADOPTIONS Ch. 20

WHEREFORE, the Petitioner(s) prays(s) for an order approving the adoption of the adoptive child [specify first name]: _____ by the Petitioner(s) and directing that the adoptive child shall be treated in all respects as the child of the Petitioner(s) and directing that the name of the adoptive child be changed and that (s)he shall henceforth be known by the name of _____, together with such other and further relief as may be just and proper.

Dated: _____, 19__.

_____/_____
Adoptive Parent: typed or printed name/ signature

_____/_____
Adoptive Parent: typed or printed name / signature

_____/_____
Adoptive child if over 18: typed or printed name/ signature

_____/_____
Attorney if any: typed or printed name/signature

_____
Attorney's Address and Telephone number

VERIFICATION

STATE OF NEW YORK)
) SS:
COUNTY OF)

_____ being duly sworn, says that (he)(she) (they)(is)(are) the Petitioner(s) in the above-named proceeding and that the foregoing petition is true to (his)(her)(their) own knowledge, except as to matters where in stated to be alleged on information and belief and as to those matters (he)(she) (they) believe(s) it to be true.

_____/_____
Adoptive Parent: typed or printed name/ signature

_____/_____
Adoptive Parent: typed or printed name/ signature

_____/_____
Adoptive child if over 18: typed or printed name/ signature

Sworn to before me this
____ day of ____, 19__.

_____
(Deputy)Clerk of the Court
Notary Public

Resworn to before me this
____ day of ____, 19__.

_____
Judge of the Court

§ 20.140 Forms—Agency Adoptions—Verified Schedule 💾

D.R.L.; §§ 111–a, 112(3)
S.S.L. § 384

Form 1–B
(Verified Schedule-Agency)
12/97

SURROGATE'S COURT OF THE STATE OF NEW YORK
COUNTY OF _____

In the Matter of the Adoption of
A Child Whose First Name is

(Docket) (File) No.

VERIFIED SCHEDULE (Agency)

TO THE COURT:

1. I, _____, am a duly constituted official of _____, the authorized agency whose principal office is at _____, and who (has custody of) (is placing) the adoptive child named in the caption of this proceeding for adoption.

2. On information and belief, the full name, date and place of birth of the adoptive child are:

[Attach certified copy of birth certificate]
_____
_____
_____

3a. On information and belief, the full name and last known address of the natural mother of the adoptive child are: _____

3b. On information and belief, the full name and last known address of the natural father of the adoptive child are: _____

4. This agency obtained custody of the adoptive child in the following manner:

§ 20.140　　　　　　　　ADOPTIONS　　　　　　　　Ch. 20

* (and attached hereto is a copy of the document signed by the administrator of the interstate compact for the placement of children of the State of New York or his designee, that such placement complied with the provisions of the compact.)

5. ** (a) The consent to this adoption by _____, natural mother of the adoptive child, (is attached hereto) (is unnecessary for the following reasons:) _____

**(b) The consent to this adoption be , natural father of the adoptive child, (is attached hereto) (is unnecessary for the following reasons:) ___

6. The natural parent(s) of the adoptive child (has) (have) not requested this agency to return the adoptive child to the natural parent(s) within thirty days of the execution and delivery of an instrument of surrender to an authorized agency (except) _____

7. Attached hereto and made a part hereof is a document setting forth all available information comprising the adoptive child's medical history.

Date:

_____
Authorized Agency
By _____

_____
Title

_____
Petitioner

_____
Print or type name

_____
Signature of Attorney, if any

_____
Attorney's Name (Print or Type)

* See D.R.L. Sec. 112(3); delete if inapplicable.
** Omit if inapplicable

Attorney's Address and Telephone Number

VERIFICATION

STATE OF NEW YORK   )
) SS:
COUNTY OF   )

_____ being duly sworn, deposes and says:

That (he) (she) is a duly constituted official of the above-named authorized agency, to wit, its _____;

That (he) (she) has read the foregoing Schedule and knows the contents thereof; that the same is true to (his) (her) own knowledge except as to matters therein stated to be alleged on information and belief and that as to those matters (he) (she) believes it to be true.

_____
Agency Official

Sworn to before me this
____ day of ____, 19__.

_____
(Deputy) Clerk of the Court
Notary Public

§ 20.145 Forms—Agency Adoptions—Agreement of Adoption and Consent

D.R.L.§ 111(1)(f), 112(2)(b), 113

Form 2–A
(Agreement of Adoption and Consent—Agency)
12/97

SURROGATE'S COURT OF THE STATE OF NEW YORK
COUNTY OF

In the Matter of the Adoption of
A Child Whose First Name Is

(Docket)(File) No.

AGREEMENT OF ADOPTION AND CONSENT (Agency)

The undersigned petitioning adoptive parent(s) hereby agree(s) to adopt the above-named adoptive child and to treat said child in all

§ 20.145   ADOPTIONS   Ch. 20

respects as (his) (her) (their) own lawful child and to extend and assure to said child all the rights, benefits and privileges incident to such relationship, and to incur and fulfill all the responsibilities of (a parent) (parents) with respect to said child.

Dated:

_____/_____
Adoptive Parent: typed or printed name/ signature

_____/_____
Adoptive Parent: typed or printed name / signature

_____/_____
Adoptive child if over 18: typed or printed name/ signature

_____/_____
Attorney if any: typed or printed name/signature

_____
Attorney's Address and Telephone number

The undersigned authorized agency hereby consents to the adoption of the above-named adoptive child by the petitioning adoptive parent(s).

Name of Authorized Agency:
_____

By: _____

Title

STATE OF NEW YORK   )
) SS:
COUNTY   )

On this day of _____, 19__, _____, the person who executed the foregoing instrument, personally came before me and acknowledged that (he)(she) executed the same.

_____
Notary Public

STATE OF NEW YORK   )
) SS:
COUNTY   )

78

On this day of _____, 19__, _____, the person who executed the foregoing instrument, personally came before me and acknowledged that (he)(she) executed the same.

_____
Notary Public

STATE OF NEW YORK   )
) SS:
COUNTY   )

On this day of _____, 19__, before me personally came _____, to me known and who by me being duly sworn did depose and say:

That he/she resides at

County of State of :
that he/she is [specify position]:
of [specify authorized agency]:

(an authorized agency), the corporation described in and which executed the foregoing instrument, that he/she knows the seal of said corporation; that such seal affixed to said instrument is such corporate seal; that it was affixed to said instrument by order of the Board of _____ of such corporation in writing, and that he/she signed his/her name thereto.

_____
Notary Public

State of New York   )
) SS:
County of   )

On this day of _____, 19__,

_____, proven to me by the oath of _____, an attorney admitted to practice in the State of New York, to be the person who executed the foregoing instrument, personally came before me and acknowledged that (he)(she) executed the same.

_____
Judge of the Court

§ 20.146 Forms—Agency Adoptions—Affidavit Identifying Party 💾

22 NYCRR 207.55(b)(2)

Form 8–A
(Affidavit
Identifying
Party–Agency)
12/97

SURROGATE'S COURT OF THE STATE OF NEW YORK
COUNTY OF

§ 20.146   ADOPTIONS   Ch. 20

....
In the Matter of Adoption of   (Docket)(File) No.
A Child Whose First Name Is

AFFIDAVIT
IDENTIFYING
PARTY
(Agency)
....

STATE OF NEW YORK   )
)   SS:
COUNTY OF   )

(That (s)he is an attorney at law duly licensed to practice under the laws of the State of New York and has (his) (her) office at _____;)[1]

That (s)he knows _____ (and _____) and knows that s(he)(they) (is)(are) the same person(s) described in and who executed the annexed (and who (is)(are) now present before the Court).

                             _____
                                     Affiant

Sworn to before me this
____ day of ____, 19__.

_____
Judge of the Court

1. Delete if inapplicable

§ 20.147 Forms—Agency Adoptions—Affidavit of Financial Disclosure by Parents

S.S.L. § 374(6);   Form 9–A
22 NYCRR 207.55(b)(8)   (Affidavit of Financial
                                                   Disclosure—Parents
                                                   -Agency)
                                                   12/97

SURROGATE'S COURT OF THE STATE OF NEW YORK
COUNTY OF _____

In the Matter of the Adoption of   (Docket)(File) No.
A Child whose First Name is

AFFIDAVIT OF
FINANCIAL
DISCLOSURE-
PARENTS
(Agency)

STATE OF NEW YORK   )
)   SS:
COUNTY   )

_____ (and _____) being duly sworn, depose(s) and say(s):

1. That deponent(s) reside(s) at _____ and (is)(are) the (petitioning adoptive parent(s) (birth or legal parent(s)) of the above-named adoptive child;

and

2. That deponent(s) (has)(have) paid or given or caused to be paid or given or undertaken to pay or give the following expenses, contributions, compensation or things of value, either directly or indirectly, to any person, agency, association, corporation, institution, society or organization, in connection with the placing out of said adoptive child with deponent(s) or with the adoption of said child by deponent(s):

[Specify recipient, amount, form, and purpose
of each payment. If none, so state.]

_____

_____

_____;

3. That deponent(s)(has)(have) requested, received or accepted, either directly or indirectly, the following compensation or things or value from any person, agency, association, corporation, institution, society or other organization in connection with the placing out of said adoptive child with deponent(s) or with the adoption of said child by deponent(s).

[Specify source, amount, form and purpose of each payment
requested or received. If none, so state.]

_____/_____
*(Adoptive) (Birth)(Legal) Parent: typed or printed name/ signature

_____/_____
*(Adoptive)(Birth) (Legal) Parent: typed or printed name/ signature

_____/_____
Adoptive child if over 18: typed or printed name/ signature

_____/_____
Attorney if any: typed or printed name/signature

_____
Attorney's Address and Telephone number

Sworn to before me this
____ day of ____, 19__.

_____
Judge of the Court

_____
*Delete inapplicable provisions